Human Resource Management

GAINING A COMPETITIVE ADVANTAGE **7e**

RAYMOND A. NOE
The Ohio State University

JOHN R. HOLLENBECK
Michigan State University

BARRY GERHART
University of Wisconsin–Madison

PATRICK M. WRIGHT
Cornell University

McGraw-Hill Irwin

McGraw-Hill
Irwin

HUMAN RESOURCE MANAGEMENT: GAINING A COMPETITIVE ADVANTAGE

Published by McGraw-Hill/Irwin, a business unit of The McGraw-Hill Companies, Inc., 1221 Avenue of the Americas, New York, NY, 10020. Copyright © 2010, 2008, 2006, 2003, 2000, 1997, 1994 by The McGraw-Hill Companies, Inc. All rights reserved. No part of this publication may be reproduced or distributed in any form or by any means, or stored in a database or retrieval system, without the prior written consent of The McGraw-Hill Companies, Inc., including, but not limited to, in any network or other electronic storage or transmission, or broadcast for distance learning.

Some ancillaries, including electronic and print components, may not be available to customers outside the United States.

This book is printed on acid-free paper.

4 5 6 7 8 9 0 DOW/DOW 1 0 9 8 7 6 5 4 3 2 1

ISBN 978-0-07-353047-5
MHID 0-07-353047-6

Vice president and editor-in-chief: *Brent Gordon*
Publisher: *Paul Ducham*
Executive editor: *John Weimeister*
Director of development: *Ann Torbert*
Developmental editor: *Sara Knox Hunter*
Editorial assistant: *Heather Darr*
Vice president and director of marketing: *Robin J. Zwettler*
Executive marketing manager: *Anke Braun Weekes*
Vice president of editing, design, and production: *Sesha Bolisetty*
Project manager: *Dana M. Pauley*
Senior production supervisor: *Debra R. Sylvester*
Interior designer: *Pam Verros*
Senior photo research coordinator: *Lori Kramer*
Photo researcher: *Ira C. Roberts*
Lead media project manager: *Brain Nacik*
Cover design: *Pam Verros*
Interior design: *Pam Verros*
Cover image: istockphoto.com
Typeface: *10.5/12 Goudy*
Compositor: *Laserwords Private Limited*
Printer: *R. R. Donnelley*

Library of Congress Cataloging-in-Publication Data

Human resource management : gaining a competitive advantage / Raymond A.
    Noe . . . [et al.].—7th ed.
      p. cm.
      Includes index.
      ISBN-13: 978-0-07-353047-5 (alk. paper)
      ISBN-10: 0-07-353047-6 (alk. paper)
      1. Personnel management—United States. I. Noe, Raymond A.
HF5549.2.U5H8 2010
   658.3—dc22   2009029687

www.mhhe.com

In tribute to the life and ways of
my parents
— R. A. N.

**To my parents, Harold and Elizabeth, my wife,
Patty, and my children, Jennifer, Marie, Timothy,
and Jeffrey
— J. R. H.**

To my parents, Robert and Shirley, my wife,
Heather, and my children, Chris and Annie
— B. G.

**To my parents, Patricia and Paul, my wife, Mary,
and my sons, Michael and Matthew
—P. M. W.**

ABOUT THE AUTHORS

RAYMOND A. NOE is the Robert and Anne Hoyt Designated Professor of Management at The Ohio State University. He was previously a professor in the Department of Management at Michigan State University and the Industrial Relations Center of the Carlson School of Management, University of Minnesota. He received his BS in psychology from The Ohio State University and his MA and PhD in psychology from Michigan State University. Professor Noe conducts research and teaches undergraduate as well as MBA and PhD students in human resource management, managerial skills, quantitative methods, human resource information systems, training, employee development, and organizational behavior. He has published articles in the *Academy of Management Journal, Academy of Management Review, Journal of Applied Psychology, Journal of Vocational Behavior,* and *Personnel Psychology.* Professor Noe is currently on the editorial boards of several journals including *Personnel Psychology, Journal of Applied Psychology,* and *Journal of Organizational Behavior.* Professor Noe has received awards for his teaching and research excellence, including the Herbert G. Heneman Distinguished Teaching Award in 1991 and the Ernest J. McCormick Award for Distinguished Early Career Contribution from the Society for Industrial and Organizational Psychology in 1993. He is also a fellow of the Society of Industrial and Organizational Psychology.

JOHN R. HOLLENBECK received his PhD in Management from New York University in 1984, and is currently the Eli Broad Professor of Management at the Eli Broad Graduate School of Business Administration at Michigan State University. Dr. Hollenbeck has published over 75 articles and book chapters on the topics of work motivation and group behavior with more than 45 of these appearing in the most highly cited refereed outlets. According to the Institute for Scientific Research, this body of work has been cited over 1,700 times by other researchers. He was the acting editor at *Organizational Behavior and Human Decision Processes* in 1995, the associate editor at *Decision Sciences* between 1998 and 2004, and the editor of *Personnel Psychology* from 1996 to 2002. He currently serves on the editorial board of the *Academy of Management Journal, Academy of Management Review, Journal of Applied Psychology, Personnel Psychology,* and *Organizational Behavior and Human Decision Processes.* Dr. Hollenbeck's teaching has been recognized with several awards, including the Michigan State University Teacher-Scholar Award in 1987 and the Michigan State University Distinguished Faculty Award in 2006. Dr. Hollenbeck is currently a Fellow of the Academy of Management, the American Psychological Association, and the Society of Industrial and Organizational Psychology.

BARRY GERHART is the Bruce R. Ellig Distinguished Chair in Pay and Organizational Effectiveness and Director of the Strategic Human Resources Program at the University of Wisconsin–Madison. He was previously the Frances Hampton Currey Chair in Organizational Studies at the Owen School of Management at Vanderbilt University and Associate Professor and Chairman of the Department of Human Resource Studies, School of Industrial and Labor Relations at Cornell University. He received his BS in psychology from Bowling Green State University in 1979 and his PhD in industrial relations from the University of Wisconsin–Madison in 1985. His research is in the areas of compensation/rewards, staffing, and employee attitudes. Professor Gerhart has worked with a variety of organizations, including TRW, Corning, and Bausch & Lomb. His work has appeared in the *Academy of Management Journal, Industrial Relations, Industrial and Labor Relations Review, Journal of Applied Psychology, Personnel Psychology,* and *Handbook of Industrial and Organizational Psychology,* and he has served on the editorial boards of the *Academy of Management Journal, Industrial and Labor Relations Review,* and the *Journal of Applied Psychology.* He was a co-recipient of the 1991 Scholarly Achievement Award, Human Resources Division, Academy of Management.

PATRICK M. WRIGHT is Professor of Human Resource Studies and Director of the Center for Advanced Human Resource Studies in the School of Industrial and Labor Relations at Cornell University. He was formerly Associate Professor of Management and Coordinator of the Master of Science in Human Resource Management program in the College of Business Administration and Graduate School of Business at Texas A&M University. He holds a BA in psychology from Wheaton College and an MBA and a PhD in organizational behavior/human resource management from Michigan State University. He teaches, conducts research, and consults in the areas of personnel selection, employee motivation, and strategic human resource management. His research articles have appeared in journals such as the *Academy of Management Journal, Journal of Applied Psychology, Organizational Behavior and Human Decision Processes, Journal of Management,* and *Human Resource Management Review.* He has served on the editorial boards of *Journal of Applied Psychology* and *Journal of Management* and also serves as an ad hoc reviewer for *Organizational Behavior and Human Decision Processes, Academy of Management Journal,* and *Academy of Management Review.* In addition, he has consulted for a number of organizations, including Whirlpool Corporation, Amoco Oil Company, and the North Carolina State government.

PREFACE

The U.S. economy—as well as the economies of most other countries across the globe—are experiencing job loss and a lack of consumer confidence due to a worldwide recession fueled by the subprime mortgage scandal and the collapse of the stock market. Many well-known companies in the financial sector and manufacturing sectors—including AIG, Freddie Mac and Fannie Mae, Lehman Brothers, WAMU, General Motors, and Chrysler—are undergoing massive restructuring, receiving bailout money resulting in increased government ownership, and have either declared or are operating under the threat of bankruptcy. The poor economy means more companies are downsizing their workforces, delaying plans for new operations and growth, and closely scrutinizing human resource budgets to cut unnecessary programs and costs. This is occurring even in companies such as NetApp, Google, Zappos.com, and Microsoft, who are known for gaining a competitive advantage through their human resource practices and are included on *Fortune* magazine's list of "The 100 Best Companies to Work For."

At the same time companies are taking steps to deal with the current economic conditions, they are also paying closer attention to how to engage in business practices that are economically sound but sustainable. That is, business practices that are ethical, protect the environment, and contribute to the communities from which the business draws financial, physical, and human resources needed to provide its product and services. Consumers are demanding accountability in business practices: making money for shareholders should not involve abandoning ethics, ruining the environment, or taking advantage of employees from developing countries!

Regardless of whether a company's strategic direction involves downsizing, restructuring, growth, or a merger or acquisition, how human resources are managed is crucial for providing "value" to customers, shareholders, employees, and the community in which they are located. Our definition of "value" includes not only profits but also employee growth and satisfaction, additional employment opportunities, stewardship of the environment, and contributions to community programs. If a company fails to effectively use its financial capital, physical capital, and human capital to create "value," it will not survive. The way a company treats its employees (including those who are forced to leave their jobs) will influence the company's public reputation and brand as a responsible business, especially in a poor economy. For example, companies such as McDonald's, Coca-Cola, Caterpillar, and Estee Lauder are sticking with their recruiting, training and development, and employee recognition plans but, at the same time, ensuring that all employees (including top-level managers) make shared sacrifices (such as salary freezes and pay cuts) needed to sustain their businesses.

We believe that all aspects of human resource management—including how companies interact with the environment; acquire, prepare, develop, and compensate employees; and design and evaluate work—can help companies meet their competitive challenges and create value. Meeting challenges is necessary to create value and to gain a competitive advantage.

The Competitive Challenges

The challenges that organizations face today can be grouped into three categories:

- **The sustainability challenge.** Sustainability refers to the ability of a company to survive and exceed in a dynamic competitive environment. Sustainability depends on how well a company meets the needs of those who have an interest in seeing that the company succeeds. Challenges to sustainability include the ability to deal with economic and social changes, engage in responsible and ethical business practices, efficiently use natural resources and protecting the environment, provide high-quality products and services, and develop methods and measures (also known as metrics) to determine if the company is meeting stakeholder needs. Companies in today's economy use mergers and acquisitions, growth, and downsizing to successfully compete. Companies rely on skilled workers to be productive, creative, and innovative and to provide high-quality customer service; their work is demanding and companies cannot guarantee job security. One issue is how to attract and retain a committed, productive workforce in turbulent economic conditions that offer opportunity for financial success, but can also turn sour, making every employee expendable. Forward-looking businesses are capitalizing on the strengths of a diverse workforce. The examples of Enron, WorldCom, and Health South Corporation provide a vivid example of how sustainability depends on ethical and responsible business practices, including the management of human resources. Another important issue is how to meet financial objectives through meeting both customer and employee needs. To meet the sustainability challenge companies must engage in human resource management practices that address short-term needs but help to ensure the long-term success of the firm. The development and choice of human resource management practices should support business goals and strategy.

- **The global challenge.** Companies must be prepared to compete with companies from around the world either in the United States or abroad. Companies must both defend their domestic markets from foreign competitors and broaden their scope to encompass global markets. Recent threats to and successes of U.S. businesses (consider the semiconductor and steel industries) have proven that globalization is a continuing challenge.

- **The technology challenge.** Using new technologies such as computer-aided manufacturing, virtual reality, expert systems, and the Internet can give companies an edge. New technologies can result in employees "working smarter" as well as providing higher-quality products and more efficient services to customers. Companies that have realized the greatest gains from new technology have human resource management practices that support the use of technology to create what is known as high-performance work systems. Work, training programs, and reward systems often need to be reconfigured to support employees' use of new technology. The three important aspects of high-performance work systems are (1) human resources and their capabilities, (2) new technology and its opportunities, and (3) efficient work structures and policies that allow employees and technology to interact. Companies are also using e-HRM (electronic HRM) applications to give employees more ownership of the employment relationship through the ability to enroll in and participate in training programs, change benefits, communicate with co-workers and customers online, and work "virtually" with peers in geographically different locations.

We believe that organizations must successfully deal with these challenges to create and maintain value, and the key to facing these challenges is a motivated, well-trained, and committed workforce.

The Changing Role of the Human Resource Management Function

The human resource management (HRM) profession and practices have undergone substantial change and redefinition. Many articles written in both the academic and practitioner literature have been critical of the traditional HRM function. Unfortunately, in many organizations HRM services are not providing value but instead are mired down in managing trivial administrative tasks. Where this is true, HRM departments can be replaced with new technology or outsourced to a vendor who can provide higher-quality services at a lower cost. Although this recommendation is indeed somewhat extreme (and threatening to both HRM practitioners and those who teach human resource management!), it does demonstrate that companies need to ensure that their HRM functions are creating value for the firm.

Technology should be used where appropriate to automate routine activities, and managers should concentrate on HRM activities that can add substantial value to the company. Consider employee benefits: Technology is available to automate the process by which employees enroll in benefits programs and to keep detailed records of benefits usage. This use of technology frees up time for the manager to focus on activities that can create value for the firm (such as how to control health care costs and reduce workers' compensation claims).

Although the importance of some HRM departments is being debated, everyone agrees on the need to successfully manage human resources for a company to maximize its competitiveness. Several themes emerge from our conversations with managers and our review of research on HRM practices. First, in today's organizations, managers themselves are becoming more responsible for HRM practices and most believe that people issues are critical to business success. Second, most managers believe that their HRM departments are not well respected because of a perceived lack of competence, business sense, and contact with operations. A study by Deloitte consulting and *The Economist* Intelligence Unit found that only 23 percent of business executives believe that HR currently plays a significant role in strategy and operational results. Third, many managers believe that for HRM practices to be effective they need to be related to the strategic direction of the business. This text emphasizes how HRM practices can and should contribute to business goals and help to improve product and service quality and effectiveness.

Our intent is to provide students with the background to be successful HRM professionals, to manage human resources effectively, and to be knowledgeable consumers of HRM products. Managers must be able to identify effective HRM practices to purchase these services from a consultant, to work with the HRM department, or to design and implement them personally. The text emphasizes how a manager can more effectively manage human resources and highlights important issues in current HRM practice.

We think this book represents a valuable approach to teaching human resource management for several reasons:

- The text draws from the diverse research, teaching, and consulting experiences of four authors who have taught human resource management to undergraduates, traditional day MBA students as a required and elective course, and more experienced managers and professional employees in weekend and evening MBA programs. The teamwork approach gives a depth and breadth to the coverage that is not found in other texts.

- Human resource management is viewed as critical to the success of a business. The text emphasizes how the HRM function, as well as the management of human resources, can help companies gain a competitive advantage.
- The book discusses current issues such as e-HRM, talent management, diversity, and employee engagement, all of which have a major impact on business and HRM practice.
- Strategic human resource management is introduced early in the book and integrated throughout the text.
- Examples of how new technologies are being used to improve the efficiency and effectiveness of HRM practices are provided throughout the text.
- We provide examples of how companies are evaluating HRM practices to determine their value.

Organization

Human Resource Management: Gaining a Competitive Advantage includes an introductory chapter (Chapter 1) and five parts.

Chapter 1 provides a detailed discussion of the global, new economy, stakeholder, and work system challenges that influence companies' abilities to successfully meet the needs of shareholders, customers, employees, and other stakeholders. We discuss how the management of human resources can help companies meet the competitive challenges.

Part 1 includes a discussion of the environmental forces that companies face in attempting to capitalize on their human resources as a means to gain competitive advantage. The environmental forces include the strategic direction of the business, the legal environment, and the type of work performed, and physical arrangement of the work.

A key focus of the strategic human resource management chapter is highlighting the role that staffing, performance management, training and development, and compensation play in different types of business strategies. A key focus of the legal chapter is enhancing managers' understanding of laws related to sexual harassment, affirmative action, and accommodations for disabled employees. The various types of discrimination and ways they have been interpreted by the courts are discussed. The chapter on analysis and design of work emphasizes how work systems can improve company competitiveness by alleviating job stress and by improving employees' motivation and satisfaction with their jobs.

Part 2 deals with the acquisition and preparation of human resources, including human resource planning and recruitment, selection, and training. The human resource planning chapter illustrates the process of developing a human resource plan. Also, the strengths and weaknesses of staffing options such as outsourcing, use of contingent workers, and downsizing are discussed. Strategies for recruiting talented employees are emphasized. The selection chapter emphasizes ways to minimize errors in employee selection and placement to improve the company's competitive position. Selection method standards such as validity and reliability are discussed in easily understandable terms without compromising the technical complexity of these issues.

The chapter discusses selection methods such as interviews and various types of tests (including personality, honesty, and drug tests) and compares them on measures of validity, reliability, utility, and legality.

We discuss the components of effective training systems and the manager's role in determining employees' readiness for training, creating a positive learning environment, and ensuring that training is used on the job. The advantages and disadvantages of different training methods are described, such as e-learning and mobile training.

Part 3 explores how companies can determine the value of employees and capitalize on their talents through retention and development strategies. The performance management chapter examines the strengths and weaknesses of performance management methods that use ratings, objectives, or behaviors. The employee development chapter introduces the student to how assessment, job experiences, formal courses, and mentoring relationships are used to develop employees. The chapter on retention and separation discusses how managers can maximize employee productivity and satisfaction to avoid absenteeism and turnover. The use of employee surveys to monitor job and organizational characteristics that affect satisfaction and subsequently retention is emphasized.

Part 4 covers rewarding and compensating human resources, including designing pay structures, recognizing individual contributions, and providing benefits. Here we explore how managers should decide the pay rate for different jobs, given the company's compensation strategy and the worth of jobs. The advantages and disadvantages of merit pay, gainsharing, and skill-based pay are discussed. The benefits chapter highlights the different types of employer-provided benefits and discusses how benefit costs can be contained. International comparisons of compensation and benefit practices are provided.

Part 5 covers special topics in human resource management, including labor–management relations, international HRM, and managing the HRM function. The collective bargaining and labor relations chapter focuses on traditional issues in labor–management relations, such as union structure and membership, the organizing process, and contract negotiations; it also discusses new union agendas and less adversarial approaches to labor–management relations. Social and political changes, such as introduction of the euro currency in the European Community, are discussed in the chapter on global human resource management. Selecting, preparing, and rewarding employees for foreign assignments are also discussed. The text concludes with a chapter that emphasizes how HRM practices should be aligned to help the company meet its business objectives. The chapter emphasizes that the HRM function needs to have a customer focus to be effective.

Acknowledgments

As this book enters its seventh edition, it is important to acknowledge those who started it all. The first edition of this book would not have been possible if not for the entrepreneurial spirit of two individuals. Bill Schoof, president of Austen Press, gave us the resources and had the confidence that four unproven textbook writers could provide a new perspective for teaching human resource management. John Weimeister, our editor, provided us with valuable marketing information, helped us in making major decisions regarding the book, and made writing this book an enjoyable process. We continue to enjoy John's friendship and hospitality at national meetings. We were fortunate to have the opportunity in the seventh edition to work with John again.

We also worked with an all-star development and project management team, including Sara Hunter, Kathryn Mikulic, Dana Pauley, and Heather Darr. Their suggestions, patience, gentle prodding, and careful oversight kept the author team focused on providing a high-quality revision while meeting publication deadline. Many thanks to Kathryn Mikulic and Dana Pauley, project managers, for their careful review of the revised manuscript.

We would also like to thank the professors who gave of their time to review the text to help craft this seventh edition. Their helpful comments and suggestions have greatly helped to enhance this edition:

Richard Arvey
National University of Singapore

Steve Ash
University of Akron

Carlson Austin
South Carolina State University

Alison Barber
Michigan State University

Kathleen Barnes
University of Wisconsin, Superior

James E. Bartlett, II
University of South Carolina–Columbia

Ron Beaulieu
Central Michigan University

Philip Benson
New Mexico State University

Nancy Bereman
Wichita State University

Chris Berger
Purdue University

Carol Bibly
Triton College

Wendy Boswell
Texas A&M University

Sarah Bowman
Idaho State University

Charles Braun
University of Kentucky

James Browne
University of Southern Colorado

Gerald Calvasina
Southern Utah University

Martin Carrigan
University of Findlay

Georgia Chao
Michigan State University

Walter Coleman
Florida Southern College

Mary Connerley
Virginia Tech University

Donna Cooke
Florida Atlantic University, Davis

Craig Cowles
Bridgewater State College

Michael Crant
University of Notre Dame

Shannon Davis
North Carolina State University

Roger Dean
Washington & Lee University

John Delery
University of Arkansas

Jennifer Dose
Messiah College

Tom Dougherty
University of Missouri

Berrin Erdogan
Portland State University

Angela Farrar
University of Nevada, Las Vegas

Dyanne Ferk
University of Illinois–Springfield

Robert Figler
University of Akron

Art Fischer
Pittsburgh State University

Barry Friedman
State University of New York at Oswego

Cynthia Fukami
University of Denver

Daniel J. Gallagher
University of Illinois–Springfield

Donald G. Gardner
University of Colorado at Colorado Springs

Bonnie Fox Garrity
D'Youville College

Sonia Goltz
Michigan Technological University

Bob Graham
Sacred Heart University

Terri Griffith
Washington University

Ken Gross
University of Oklahoma, Norman

John Hannon
SUNY—Buffalo

Bob Hatfield
Indiana University

Alan Heffner
James Monroe Center

Fred Heidrich
Black Hills State University

Rob Heneman
Ohio State University

Gary Hensel
McHenry County College

Kim Hester
Arkansas State University

Nancy Higgins
Montgomery College, Rockville

Wayne Hockwater
Florida State University

Denise Tanguay Hoyer
Eastern Michigan University

Fred Hughes
Faulkner University

Natalie J. Hunter
Portland State University

Sanford Jacoby
University of California, Los Angeles

Frank Jeffries
University of Alaska, Anchorage

Gwen Jones
Fairleigh Dickinson University

Marianne Koch
University of Oregon

Tom Kolenko
Kennesaw State College

Elias Konwufine
Keiser University

Ken Kovach
George Mason University

Vonda Laughlin
Carson-Newman College

Helen LaVan
DePaul University

Renee Lerche
University of Michigan

Nancy Boyd Lillie
University of North Texas

Larry Mainstone
Valparaiso University

Liz Malatestinic
Indiana University

Nicholas Mathys
DePaul University

Patricia Martina
University of Texas, San Antonio

Lisa McConnell
Oklahoma State University

Stuart Milne
Georgia Institute of Technology

Jim Morgan
California State University, Chico

Gary Murray
Rose State College

Cheri Ostroff
Teachers College Columbia

Teresa Palmer
Illinois State University

Robert Paul
Kansas State University

Sam Rabinowitz
Rutgers University

Katherine Ready
University of Wisconsin

Mike Ritchie
University of South Carolina

Gwen Rivkin
Cardinal Stritch University

Mark Roehling
Michigan State University

Mary Ellen Rosetti
Hudson Valley Community College

Miyako Schanely
Jefferson Community College

Robert Schappe
University of Michigan, Dearborn

Josh Schwarz
Miami University, Ohio

Christina Shalley
Georgia Tech

Richard Simpson
University of Utah

Mark Smith
Mississippi Gulf Coast Community College, Gulfport

Scott Snell
University of Virginia

Howard Stanger
Canisius College

Cynthia Sutton
Indiana University, South Bend

Peg Thomas
Pennsylvania State University–Behrend

Steven L. Thomas
Missouri State University

Tom Timmerman
Tennessee Technology University

George Tompson
University of Tampa

K. J. Tullis
University of Central Oklahoma

Dan Turban
University of Missouri, Columbia

Charles Vance
Loyola Marymount University

Kim Wade
Washington State University

Renee Warning
University of Central Oklahoma

George Whaley
San Jose State University

Daniel Yazak
Montana State University, Billings

Ryan D. Zimmerman
Texas A&M University

We would also like to thank the reviewers and focus group participants who made important suggestions for previous editions of this text. Their comments have helped to develop the book from edition to edition:

Joan Benek-Rivera
University of Pennsylvania, Bloomsburg

Angela Boston
The University of Texas at Arlington

Ronald Brownie
Purdue University, North Central

Jon Bryan
Bridgewater State College

LeAnne Coder
Western Kentucky University

Louis Firenze
Northwood University

Julie Indvik
California State University, Chico

Roy Johnson
Iowa State University

Gwendolyn Jones
University of Akron

Beth Koufteros
Texas A&M University

Chalmer Labig
Oklahoma State University

Patricia Lanier
University of Louisiana at Lafayette

Susan Madsen
Utah Valley University

Pat Setlik
Harper College

Sarah Sanders-Smith
Purdue University, North Central

Jack Schoenfelder
Ivy Tech Community College

Richard Shuey
Thomas More College

Kris Sperstad
Chippewa Valley Technical College

Linda Turner
Morrisville State College

Linda Urbanski
University of Toledo

William Van Lente
Alliant International University

Raymond A. Noe
John R. Hollenbeck
Barry Gerhart
Patrick M. Wright
June 2009

Guided Tour

The Seventh Edition of *Human Resource Management: Gaining a Competitive Advantage* was developed to teach students how to face and meet a variety of challenges within their organizations and how to gain a competitive advantage for their companies.

Throughout this text, the pedagogy focuses on HRM practices and strategies companies can employ to be competitive. These boxes, cases, and applications are found in every chapter and provide excellent real-business examples to underscore key concepts throughout the text.

Please take a moment to learn about this new edition and its exciting enhancements by paging through this visual guide outlining the text's features.

The popular boxes **"Competing through Sustainability," "Competing through Globalization,"** and **"Competing through Technology"** have been updated with all new references to recent companies and examples. Their practical relevance and timeliness to HR issues are essential for student learning in the classroom.

COMPETING THROUGH SUSTAINABILITY
Volunteerism and Going Green Are Reaping Dividends for Employees, Communities, and the Environment

A growing number of companies have made sustainability an important part of their business strategy. For example, at General Mills, volunteerism is one of the ways that the company lives its corporate values. The CEO and senior leaders serve on nonprofit boards and are involved in the community. Five years ago, following General Mills' acquisition of Pillsbury, company leaders in the Meals Division brought the newly merged team of employees to volunteer for the Perspectives Family Center, which helps families in transition. This resulted from the suggestion that volunteerism could be used to strengthen the new work team. Meals Division employees support projects such as painting child care center rooms, participating in school supply drives, and delivering Christmas trees. The employees' involvement was initiated from a business need, but now volunteerism is part of the business. General Mills' customer service center works with Catholic Charities USA, serving meals to homeless people and working at a shelter for homeless children—teaching them how to maintain a healthy diet, leading fitness activities, and helping with projects such as redecorating rooms in the shelter. Yoplait employees, partners with the Greater Minneapolis Crisis Nursery, help cook meals. Besides helping the community, Steve Sange

General Mills' company chairman, believes that employees are developing leadership and other skills.

Pharmaceutical company Novartis supports REPSSI, an African-based philanthropic organization that provides emotional and psychological support to children affected

resources and the environment. The Personal Sustainability Project (PSP) is a voluntary program that is focused on helping associates integrate sustainability into their own lives by making small changes to everyday habits. The goals relate to improving employees' own health and wellness as well as the health

COMPETING THROUGH GLOBALIZATION
Managing the New Class of Global Worker

As more and more companies move work to India, they are facing a number of challenges they never expected. In the information technology sector, where companies initially sought an 80 percent reduction in labor cost, they now face a war for talent and spiraling salaries. This stems from the newer, younger breed of Indian worker, who displays attitudes much more similar to developed Western countries such as the United States than those of their parents and grandparents.

Companies face competing challenges of addressing both the frustrations and the desires of this younger generation. For instance, they are likely to complain about the traditions

of arranged marriage and the caste system as well as their interactions with Westerners, who they feel sometimes treat them condescendingly. Many of the engineers are fascinated with the newest technologies, but their work for clients requires traditional tools and techniques. Finally, they are eager to get promotions and overseas assignments, yet there are practical limits to how quickly they can advance.

This requires companies to be innovative in how they seek to manage this new generation. For instance, Infosys seeks to learn from younger employees by setting up the "Voice of Youth Council." This consists of a dozen people under 30 who

sit on the executive committee that deals with business strategy and HR policies, and it was this group that was instrumental in creating a program for identifying and encouraging innovation. In addition, IBM has created an internal MBA program consisting of testing, on-the-job training, seminars, and e-mail quizzes about how to effectively deal with workplace problems. This program was specifically aimed at keeping ambitious recruits on board and providing them with the training they need to manage a growing staff.

SOURCE: S. Hamm, "Young and Impatient in India; Workers Raised in an Age of Economic Optimism Want It All, and They Want It Now," *BusinessWeek*, January 28, 2008, p. 45.

COMPETING THROUGH TECHNOLOGY
Protecting against Genetic Discrimination

The technology developments within the field of genetics, the decoding of the human genome, and advances in the field of genomic medicine have enabled researchers to identify genes that inform individuals whether they may be at risk for developing a certain disease or disorder. For instance, individuals with family members who have had colon cancer are more likely to develop it than those with no family history of such cancer. While useful for individuals to begin to take preventive measures to minimize the

chance of getting these disorders, there are potential harmful effects as well.

For instance, given the rapidly rising health insurance costs to companies, what if they began doing genetic screening to identify job candidates that might later develop costly diseases? This was the concern that prompted Congress to pass the Genetic Information Nondiscrimination Act (GINA) of 2008. GINA prohibits the use of genetic information in making decisions related to any terms, conditions, or privileges

of employment; prohibits covered entities from intentionally acquiring genetic information; requires confidentiality with respect to genetic information (with limited exceptions); and prohibits retaliation. Genetic information includes, for example, information about an individual's genetic tests, genetic tests of a family member, and family medical history.

SOURCE: http://www.shrm.org/ Advocacy/PublicPolicyStatusReports/ Courts-Regulations/CivilRights/ Documents/5.1.09%20GINA%20 Title%20II%20comments.pdf

78

However, age discrimination complaints make up a large percentage of the complaints filed with the Equal Employment Opportunity Commission, and the number of complaints continues to grow whenever the economy is slow. For example, as we see in Figure 3.1, the cases increased during the early 1990s when many firms were downsizing, but the number of cases decreased as the economy expanded. The number of charges increased again as the economy began slowing again in 2000. This often stems from firms seeking to lay off older (and thus higher paid) employees when they are downsizing. These cases can be costly; most cases are settled out of court, but such settlements run from $50,000 to $400,000 per employee.[8] In one recent case, Schering-Plough fired 35-year employee Fred Maiorino after he twice failed to accept an early retirement offer made to all sales representatives. After hearing testimony that Maiorino's boss had plastered his file with negative paperwork aimed at firing him, rather than trying to help him improve his performance, the jurors unanimously decided he had been discriminated against because of his age. They awarded him $435,000 in compensatory damages and $8 million in punitive damages.[9]

The Vocational Rehabilitation Act of 1973

This act covers executive agencies and contractors and subcontractors that receive more than $2,500 annually from the federal government. It requires them to engage in affirmative action for individuals with disabilities. Congress designed this act to encourage employers to actively recruit qualified individuals with disabilities and to make reasonable accommodations to allow them to become active members of the labor market. The Employment Standards Administration of the Department of Labor enforces this act.

112

Learning objectives at the beginning of each chapter inform students about the key concepts they should understand after reading through the chapter.

Throughout each chapter, a design element calls out where the learning for each learning objective begins in the text. This element will guide students in their comprehension of the chapter topics and provide a reminder of the learning objectives throughout the chapter.

"Evidence-Based HR" sections within the chapters highlight the growing trend to demonstrate how HR contributes to a company's competitive advantage. Two of the six new HR competencies of high-performing HR professionals (credible activist and strategic architect) emphasize the need to influence managers, share information, and develop people strategies that contribute to the business. Evidence-based HR shows how HR decisions are based on data and not just intuition. The company examples used show how HR practices influence the company's bottom line or key stakeholders including shareholders, employees, customers, or the community.

The **chapter-opening stories** are updated with new, relevant examples of real business problems or issues that provide background for the issues discussed in the chapter.

Enter the World of Business

Job Design: Back to the Future at Toyota

In 2007, Toyota Motor Corporation surpassed General Motors as the world's largest carmaker. This was the accomplishment of a long-term goal that could only be obtained by a strong focus on rapid growth and expansion. However, in the process of focusing on this goal, many insiders at Toyota believed that the organization was straying from some of its core values, especially as this related to the organization's structure and design of jobs. In fact, in 2009, Toyota reported its first annual operating loss since 1938, and due to the economic recession, the company had to lay off workers for the first time since 1950. As industry observer Tokai Gakuin, noted, "Toyota was so focused on becoming the world's largest automaker that it failed to cut production quickly enough in 2008, as the economic crisis struck the U.S., its largest market."

The steps that the company took to restore profitability provide a lesson in how to compete via organizational design and job design. First, with respect to manufacturing jobs, the fast-paced expansion of Toyota's plants both in Japan and the United States was, in some cases, purchased at the price of reduced quality standards. The number of recalls for manufacturing defects tripled in the last three years, and quality ratings slipped noticeably. In response to this, the company streamlined jobs, tightened job descriptions and enhanced training programs in a way that slowed production but increased quality. For example, quality control inspectors were required to put on a glove and massage the door of every Camry in a soft circular motion in search of tiny dents for roughly 15 minutes prior to sending the car further down the production line.

With respect to sales jobs, because of Toyota's ambitious quotas, sales personnel often used

high-pressure techniques to get customers to purchase cars more quickly, and then, after the sale was made, often handed over the cars without properly inspecting them. Thus, even when customers loved their cars, they often hated their car-buying experience. Toyota quickly responded to this problem by sending out five-person evaluation teams to sales units that were ranked low in customer satisfaction and reanalyzed all the jobs in those units—all the way from the top manager to the car washer. In each case, the team tried to create a personal link between each customer and each person who was responsible for their car, all of which resulted in slower sales, but happier customers.

Finally, with respect to managerial jobs, Toyota's middle-level managers made the case that in contrast to the organization's traditional, slow, consensus-based, decision-making process with a long-term focus, too many recent decisions were made single-handedly by the president, Katsuaki Watanabe. For example, middle-level managers noted how Watanabe quickly flip-flopped on where to build factories, first increasing production overseas when the Japanese yen was strong (and hence made production in Japan more expensive), and then quickly reverting production back within the United States when the yen lost value. Because currency exchange rates fluctuate a great deal over [...] short-term gain in profitabili[...] long-term inefficiencies ass[...] up and closing factories. W[...] ally replaced as president b[...] grandson of the organization[...] Toyoda, who promised to r[...] tion's traditional approach to [...] ture and job design.

Sources: D. Welch, "Staying Paranoid a[...] 2007, pp. 80-82; I. Rowley, "Even Toyo[...] January 11, 2007, pp. 33-36; N. Shiro[...] Amid Sales Slump," The Wall Street[...] pp. A1-A2; N. Shirouzu and J. Murphy,[...] the Basics," The Wall Street Journal, Fe[...]

Enhancing Recruiter Impact. Although research suggests that recruiters do not have much influence on job choice, this does not mean recruiters cannot have an impact. For example, in contexts where applicants already have high awareness of the organization because its products are well known, the impact of the recruiter is weaker than in contexts where the applicant has low product awareness.[105] Organizations can take several steps to increase the impact that recruiters have on those they recruit. First, recruiters can provide timely feedback. Applicants react very negatively to delays in feedback, often making unwarranted attributions for the delays (such as, the organization is uninterested in my application). Second, recruiting can be done in teams rather than by individuals. As we have seen, applicants tend to view line personnel (job incumbents and supervisors) as more credible than personnel specialists, so these kinds of recruiters should be part of any team. On the other hand, personnel specialists have knowledge that is not shared by line personnel (who may perceive recruiting as a small part of their "real" jobs), so they should be included as well.

A Look Back

Our chapter-opening story described how the failure to accurately forecast the supply and demand of labor leads to both long-term problems in terms of the organization's competitive position against foreign rivals and short-term problems associated with securing government bailout money. These problems, in turn, led to the termination of longtime CEO Rick Wagoner and sparked a debate about whether an insider or outsider ought to be recruited to take his place.

Questions

1. At the national level, do you think it is appropriate for the federal government to demand the resignation of a CEO like Rick Wagoner? Do you think it is appropriate for the federal government to have a say in who is recruited to be his successor?

2. If you were a le[...] not request a g[...] to directly sup[...] more self-suffic[...] to them rather [...]

The end-of-chapter segment, **"A Look Back,"** encourages students to recall the chapter's opening story and apply it to what they have just learned. New to this edition, a case icon will send you online for cases written by Alan Fazzari and Joseph Mosca that pertain to chapter material.

---

264   PART 2   Acquisition and Preparation of Human Resources

Experiences such as these are prompting other employers to slow down the hiring process so that they have a much better idea of exactly whom they are asking to join their organizational family. Some firms do not only background checks but also extensive psychological testing to ensure that a person is who he or she claims to be and also fits the culture of the organization. You never know what these kinds of investigations will uncover—unless, of course, you fail to perform them.

Questions

1. People applying for jobs are always motivated to display themselves in the best light, and as a result, this can sometimes lead to inaccurate portrayals of abilities, skills, experiences, and personality. Based upon what you have read in this chapter, how should you approach a job applicant's written application and résumé if your

goal is to make sure that they accurately reflect the person's past experiences and accomplishments?

2. In the face-to-face interview process, what steps can be taken to ensure that the applicant is being frank and honest with you, and what steps should you take if you feel that he or she is portraying an inaccurate picture of himself or herself?

3. Beyond the traditional approaches of going over the application and conducting face-to-face interviews, what other steps can you as an employer take to ensure that the person who is being hired for the job has the right abilities, skills, past experiences and personality?

SOURCES: G. David, "You Just Hired Him: Should You Have Known Better," *Fortune*, October 29, 2001, pp. 205–6; D. Foust, "When the CEO Is Too Good to Be True," *BusinessWeek*, July 16, 2001, pp. 62–63; C. Daniels, "Does This Man Need a Shrink?" *Fortune*, February 5, 2001.

● MANAGING PEOPLE: FROM THE PAGES OF *BUSINESSWEEK*

Bridging the Generation Gap

Employment agency Randstad teams newbies with older staff to great effect For a pair of colleagues born four decades apart, Penelope Burns and Rinath Benjamin spend a lot of time together. Burns, 68, and Benjamin, 29, are sales agents at the Manhattan office of employment agency Randstad USA. They sit inches apart, facing each other. They hear every call the other makes. They read every e-mail the other sends or receives. Sometimes they finish each other's sentences.

This may seem a little strange, but the unconventional pairing is all part of Randstad's effort to ensure that its twentysomething employees—the flighty, praise-seeking Generation Y that we hear so much about—fit in and, more to the point, stick around. The Dutch company, which has been expanding in the U.S., is hoping to win the hearts, minds, and loyalty of its young employees by teaming them up with older, more experienced hands. Every new sales agent is assigned a partner to work with until their business has grown to a certain size, which usually takes a few years. Then they both start over again with someone who has just joined the company. "This makes the corporate world more personal, approachable," says Randstad USA Chief Executive Stef Witteveen. "It's easier for the Gen Yers to identify with their jobs. They don't

calls, and the other is in the office interviewing potential workers and handling the paperwork. Then they switch.

Randstad brought its partnership program to the U.S. in the late 1990s. But it wasn't until two years ago, once Randstad had integrated the personnel from the various firms it had acquired, that it began recruiting new employees. Last year it hired about 600 people, 420 of whom are in their twenties. Knowing that these Gen Yers need lots of attention in the workplace, Randstad executives figured that if they shared a job with someone whose own success depended on theirs, they were certain to get all the nurturing they required. As Belle Rose Ragins, a professor of human resource management at the University of Wisconsin at Milwaukee, puts it: "Gen Y's psychological contract is with the relationships embedded within the organization, not the organization itself."

No Touchdowns Allowed Of course, Randstad doesn't simply put people together and hope it all works out. First it figures out who will play well with others. To assess that, the human resources department conducts extensive interviews and requires candidates to shadow a sales agent for half a day. "We have certain questions that we look for them to answer with 'we'

BusinessWeek **cases** look at incidents and real companies as reported by the nation's number one business weekly and encourage students to critically evaluate each problem and apply the chapter contents.

Page 1 (Chapter 7)

1. I try to learn as much as I can from the courses I take. 5 4 3 2 1
2. I believe I tend to learn more from my courses than other students do. 5 4 3 2 1
3. When I'm involved in courses and can't understand something, I get so frustrated I stop trying to learn. 5 4 3 2 1

EXERCISING STRATEGY

Zappos Knows How to Kick It

Zappos, based in Las Vegas, is an online retailer with the initial goal of trying to be the best Web site for buying shoes by offering a wide variety of brands, styles, colors, sizes, and widths. The zappos.com brand has grown to offer shoes, handbags, eyewear, watches and accessories for online purchase. Zappos' vision is that in the future, online sales will account for 30 percent of all retail sales in the United States and that Zappos will be the company with the best service and selection. As a result, Zappos believes it can become the online service leader, drawing customers and expanding into selling other products. Zappos CEO Tony Heish has shaped the company's culture, brand, and business strategy around 10 core values:

- Deliver WOW through service.
- Embrace and drive change.
- Create fun and a little weirdness.
- Be adventurous, creative, and open-minded.
- Pursue growth and learning.
- Build open and honest relationships with communication.
- Build a positive team and family spirit.
- Do more with less.
- Be passionate and determined.
- Be humble.

For example, "Deliver WOW through service" means that call center employees need to provide excellent customer service. Call center employees encourage callers to order more than one size or color because shipping and return shipping is free. They are also encouraged to use their imaginations to meet customer needs.

Most employees at Zappos are hourly. All new hires complete four weeks of training, including two weeks working the phones. New recruits are offered $2,000 to leave the company during training to weed out individuals who will not be happy working at the company. Due to a downturn in sales, Zappos was forced to cut costs, including laying off 124 employees. Heish handled the downsizing in a positive way. Laid-off employees with less than two years of service were paid through the end of the year. Everyone received six months of paid health coverage. Zappos also allowed laid-off employees to keep their 40 percent employee discount through Christmas.

Questions

1. How can training help Zappos meet the competitive challenges it is facing?
2. Which of Zappos' 10 core values do you believe that training can influence the most compared to selection, work design, or compensation. The least? Why?

SOURCES: Zappos Web site, www.zappos.com; J. O'Brien, "Zappos Knows How to Kick It," Fortune, February 2, 2009, pp. 55–66.

MANAGING PEOPLE: FROM THE PAGES OF *BUSINESSWEEK*

BusinessWeek   On-the-Job Video Gaming

Interactive training tools are captivating employees and saving companies money Laura Holshouser's favorite video game includes Halo, Tetris, and an online training game developed by her employer. A training game? That's right. The 24-year-old graduate student, who manages a Cold Stone Creamery ice-cream store in Riverside, Calif., stumbled across the game on the corporate Web site in October.

It teaches portion control and customer service in a cartoon-like simulation of a Cold Stone store. Players scoop cones against the clock and try to avoid serving too much ice cream. The company says more than 8,000 employees, or about 30 percent of the total, voluntarily downloaded the game in the first week. "It's so much fun," says Holshouser. "I e-mailed it to everyone at work."

The military has used video games as a training tool since the 1980s. Now the practice is catching on with companies, too, ranging from Cold Stone to Cisco Systems Inc. to Canon Inc. Corporate trainers are betting that games' interactivity and fun will hook young, media-savvy employees like Holshouser and help them grasp and retain sales, technical, and management skills. "Video games

Page 2 (Chapter 8)

DISCUSSION QUESTIONS

1. What are examples of administrative decisions that might be made in managing the performance of professors? Developmental decisions?
2. What would you consider the strategy of your university (e.g., research, undergraduate teaching, graduate teaching, a combination)? How might the performance management system for faculty members fulfill its strategic purpose of eliciting the types of behaviors and results required by this strategy?
3. If you were developing a performance measurement system for faculty members, what types of attributes would you seek to measure? Behaviors? Results?
4. What sources of performance information would you use to evaluate faculty members' performance?
5. The performance of students is usually evaluated with an overall results measure of grade point average. How is this measure contaminated? How is it deficient? What other measures might you use to more adequately evaluate student performance?
6. Think of the last time you had a conflict with another person, either at work or at school. Using

the guidelines for performance feedback, how would you provide effective performance feedback to that person?
7. Explain what fairness has to do with performance management.
8. Why might a manager intentionally distort appraisal results? What would you recommend to minimize this problem?
9. Can computer monitoring of performance ever be acceptable to employees? Explain.
10. A delivery driver contaminated a hospital's oxygen supply by refilling the hospital's main oxygen supply with trichloroethane, a mild anesthetic. Following detection of the contamination, all patients were switched to oxygen tanks and no patients were injured. How would you diagnose the cause of this performance problem? Explain.
11. One of the weaknesses of using customer evaluations of employee performance is their expense (postage, phone interviews, etc.). Can you think of other weaknesses? Strengths?

SELF-ASSESSMENT EXERCISE

How do you like getting feedback? To test your attitudes toward feedback, take the following quiz. Read each statement, and write A next to each statement you agree with. If you disagree with the statement, write D.

_____ 1. I like being told how well I am doing on a project.
_____ 2. Even though I may think I have done a good job, I feel a lot more confident when someone else tells me so.
_____ 3. Even when I think I could have done something better, I feel good when other people think well of me for what I have done.
_____ 4. It is important for me to know what people think of my work.
_____ 5. I think my instructor would think worse of me if I asked him or her for feedback.
_____ 6. I would be nervous about asking my instructor how she or he evaluates my behavior in class.
_____ 7. It is not a good idea to ask my fellow students for feedback; they might think I am incompetent.
_____ 8. It is embarrassing to ask other students for their impression of how I am doing in class.
_____ 9. It would bother me to ask the instructor for feedback.

_____ 10. It is not a good idea to ask the instructor for feedback because he or she might think I am incompetent.
_____ 11. It is embarrassing to ask the instructor for feedback.
_____ 12. It is better to try to figure out how I am doing on my own, rather than to ask other students for feedback.

For statements 1–4, add the total number of As: _____
For statements 5–12, add the total number of As: _____
For statements 1–4, the greater the number of As, the greater your preference and trust in feedback from others. For statements 5–12, the greater the number of As, the greater the risk you believe there is in asking for feedback.

How might this information be useful in understanding how you react to feedback in school or on the job?

SOURCES: Based on D. B. Fedor, R. B. Rensvold, and S. M. Adams, "An Investigation of Factors Expected to Affect Feedback Seeking: A Longitudinal Field Study," *Personnel Psychology* 45 (1992), pp. 779–805; S. J. Ashford, "Feedback Seeking in Individual Adaptation: A Resource Perspective," *Academy of Management Journal* 29 (1986), pp. 465–87.

Page 3 (Appendix)

APPENDIX

Human Resource Certification Institute PHR/SPHR Test Specifications

HRCI conducts two levels of certification testing, the Professional in Human Resources (PHR) and the Senior Professional in Human Resources (SPHR). Following is the body of knowledge that HRCI recommends studying in preparing to take the certification exam. This body of knowledge is divided into six categories or functional areas within HR: Strategic Management, Workforce Planning and Employment, Human Resource Development, Total Rewards, and Risk Management. After the heading for each functional area, the PHR and SPHR weighted percentages are given. The PHR exam deals more heavily with questions on an operational level, whereas the SPHR exam focuses more on strategy. Additionally, within each functional area, the information is split under the headings Responsibilities and Knowledge.

Your text is a helpful resource in mastering many of the concepts that are tested in the PHR/SPHR exam. Visit the text Web site at www.mhhe.com/noe7e for a complete listing of page references for each of the knowledge requirements in the HRCI body of knowledge.

01 STRATEGIC MANAGEMENT (12%, 29%)

Developing, contributing to, and supporting the organization's mission, vision, values, strategic goals, and objectives; formulating policies; guiding and leading the change process; and evaluating HR's contributions to organizational effectiveness.

Responsibilities:

01 Interpret information related to the organization's operations from internal sources, including financial/accounting, business development, marketing, sales, operations, and information technology, in order to contribute to the development of the organization's strategic plan.
02 Interpret information from external sources related to the general business environment, industry practices and developments, technological developments, economic environment, labor pool, and legal and regulatory environment, in order to contribute to the development of the organization's strategic plan.
03 Participate as a contributing partner in the organization's strategic planning process.
04 Establish strategic relationships with key individuals in the organization to influence organizational decision-making.

05 Establish relationships/alliances with key individuals and organizations in the community to assist in achieving the organization's strategic goals and objectives.
06 Develop and utilize metrics to evaluate HR's contributions to the achievement of the organization's strategic goals and objectives.
07 Develop and execute strategies for managing organizational change that balance the expectations and needs of the organization, its employees, and all other stakeholders.
08 Develop and align the organization's human capital management plan with its strategic plan.
09 Facilitate the development and communication of the organization's core values and ethical behaviors.
10 Reinforce the organization's core values and behavioral expectations through modeling, communication, and coaching.
11 Develop and manage the HR budget in a manner consistent with the organization's strategic goals, objectives, and values.
12 Provide information for the development and monitoring of the organization's overall budget.

SOURCE: The PHR/SPHR test specifications are defined and updated by the Human Resource Certification Institute (HRCI) every three to five years to reflect actual HR practice.

Explanatory captions

Exercising Strategy cases at the end of each chapter provide additional cases with discussion questions. These examples pose strategic questions based on real-life practices.

Self-Assessment Exercises at the end of chapters provide a brief exercise for students to complete and evaluate their own skills.

An **appendix** has been included to provide students with the information they need to study for the PHR or SPHR exam at their fingertips. Page references to the topics found in this text can be found on the text Web site at www.mhhe.com/noe7e.

Improved Online Content

Visit the text Web site at
www.mhhe.com/noe7e
for the following features:

- Self-grading quizzes
- Interactive exercises
- Relevant professional Web links
- Video cases and clips
- A guide to studying for the PHR/ SPHR exam using this text
- Manager's Hot Seat exercises

Supplements for Students and Instructors

INSTRUCTOR'S RESOURCE CD

This multimedia CD-ROM includes the instructor's manual, test bank, computerized test bank, and PowerPoint. These individual supplements are available in print-on-demand only.

INSTRUCTOR'S MANUAL

The Instructor's Manual contains a lecture outline and notes, answers to the discussion questions, additional questions and exercises, teaching suggestions, video case notes and answers, and answers to the end-of-chapter case questions.

TEST BANK

The test bank has been revised and updated to reflect the content of the 7th edition of the book. Each chapter includes multiple choice, true/false, and essay questions.

EZ TEST

McGraw-Hill's EZ Test is a flexible and easy-to-use electronic testing program. The program allows instructors to create tests from book-specific items. It accommodates a wide range of question types and instructors may add their own questions. Multiple versions of the test can be created and any test can be exported for use with course management systems such as WebCT, BlackBoard or PageOut. The program is available for Windows and Macintosh environments.

VIDEOS

Videos for each chapter on HRM issues are available with this edition. On the HRM video DVD, you'll find a new video produced by the SHRM Foundation, entitled "Seeing Forward: Succession Planning at 3M." Two new videos specifically address recession-related HR issues: "Some Workers Willing to Sacrifice to Avoid Layoffs" and "Stretched Small Business Owners Forced to Lay Off Employees." Other notable videos available for this edition include "Johnson & Johnson eUniversity" for the chapter on training and "Hollywood Labor Unions" for the chapter on collective bargaining and labor relations.

POWERPOINT

This presentation program features detailed slides for each chapter, which are also found on the OLC.

ONLINE LEARNING CENTER (www.mhhe.com/noe7e)

This text-specific Web site follows the text chapter by chapter. As students read the book, they can go online to take self-grading quizzes, review material, or work through interactive exercises. Also available on the OLC are video clips with discussion questions, relevant professional Web links, additional Internet activities, and current news with daily updates. Professors can also download the supplements here (these are password protected). OLCs can be delivered multiple ways—professors and students can access them directly through the textbook Web site, through PageOut, or within a course management system (i.e., WebCT, Blackboard, TopClass).

MANAGER'S HOT SEAT

This interactive video software is an optional package with the text. It includes 21 interactive segments with actors in situations with real-life managers—and the managers have to react live and unscripted. Segments include topics like interviewing, office romance, personal disclosure, and diversity. Six of these segments are new to this edition.

MANAGEMENT IN THE MOVIES

McGraw-Hill offers a *Management in the Movies* DVD loaded with scenes from major Hollywood movies and TV shows. Each movie has been clipped to highlight a specific scene (each is less than two and a half minutes) and linked to specific topics including groups, ethics, diversity, global management, and more. Along with the DVD, McGraw-Hill provides an instructor's manual with suggestions for use of the clip, clip summaries, and discussion questions to accompany each segment.

GUIDE TO USING NBC'S *THE OFFICE*

The *Instructor's Guide for Using Clips from NBC's The Office in Your HRM Classroom* includes teaching notes and discussion questions that tie specific chapter content into scenes from the popular NBC sitcom *The Office*. Instructors will need to obtain copies of the television show episodes.

BRIEF CONTENTS

CONTENTS

Human Resource Management

GAINING A COMPETITIVE ADVANTAGE

Human Resource Management: Gaining a Competitive Advantage

LO LEARNING OBJECTIVES

After reading this chapter, you should be able to:

Starbucks: Refocusing on the Brew Using HR Practices

Starbucks, the Seattle-based coffee store, has experienced incredible growth in the past several years by opening more than four stores and adding 200 employees each day. However, Starbucks has had to change its strategy and reposition its brand to cope with the recession that has caused consumers to save more and spend less. Because of its growth goals, the company made poor selection for new stores, cluttered the stores with merchandise, and lost its focus on coffee. Howard Schultz, who returned to the Starbucks chief executive officer (CEO) position in 2008, has supported refocusing the company on coffee by ordering a phaseout of breakfast sandwiches and cutting the number of new store openings. The company has had to change its human resource policies and emphasize certain practices more than others while still trying to preserve its value-and-treat-employees-right approach that is part of the company culture. One of the company's six guiding principles is "to provide a great work environment and treat each other with respect and dignity."

Starbucks has taken several drastic steps in its human resource practices to ensure that it can survive the sharp decline in its sales. CEO Howard Schultz and other top executives did not earn bonuses in 2008 as a result of the company's poor financial performance. Schultz asked the board of directors to reduce his $1.2 million in base pay to $1. The compensation committee agreed to cut his pay to less than $4 per month in salary, although he will still receive his stock compensation. The committee put the company's new corporate jet up for sale. Starbucks has had to close 300 underperforming stores and layoff 6,700 employees. Starbucks also announced that it would no longer match employees' contributions to their 401(k) retirement plans. However,

Starbucks continues to offers comprehensive health benefits that exceed those provided by other retailers. Although 85 percent of its employees are part-time, they are still eligible for full-time benefits if they work 240 hours a quarter. Less than 30 percent of part-time workers in the United States receive health care, paid sick leave, or eligibility for bonuses or stock options. Starbucks provides all employees and their same-sex or opposite-sex partners comprehensive health benefits that include medical, dental, and vision care as well as tuition reimbursement, stock options, vacation, and the 401(k) retirement plan.

To cope with the economic conditions, Starbucks' best customers are saving money by making fewer visits to Starbucks each month. To ensure that customers are delighted and coffee served meets high-quality standards, Starbucks went so far as to shut down operations of most of its stores in February 2008 for three and a half hours for a full-day training event. Training is integral for Starbucks to successfully compete in the weak economy in which customers are spending less. The training event, known as "Perfect the Art of Expresso," was designed to help baristas deliver high-quality expresso. One activity consisted of pulling an expresso shot and then evaluating the process and the product (Was it the right color? Did it take too long or too short a time?). Staff discussions about how the training would benefit customers were held at each store. Employees were told to greet regular customers by their first name and to not resteam milk that had been steamed once. To counter perceptions that Starbucks is the home of the $4 cup of coffee, the company is training baristas to tell customers that the average price of a Starbucks beverage is less than $3 and 90 percent of Starbucks drinks cost less than $4. Baristas are also encouraged to promote to customers its new discounted paring of coffee and breakfast for $3.95.

Schultz believes that one of Starbucks' most serious problems is that its successes have left the company too cautious. Part of this is because he is seen as the soul of the company, which causes employees to consider "What will Howard think?" before making decisions. He creates passion but also creates anxiety. Schultz is trying to change his image and at the same time make Starbucks more innovative. When one employee in a California store suggested that he could create better artwork than what was hanging on the walls, Schultz told him to put his pictures up saying, "Don't ask for permission, ask for forgiveness."

Sources: Based on G. Weber, "Preserving the Counter Culture," *Workforce Management*, February 2005, pp. 28–34; J. Adamy, "Schultz's Second Act Jolts Starbucks," *Wall Street Journal*, May 19, 2008, pp. A1, A11; M. Weinstein, "Fresh Cup of Training," *Training*, May 2008, p. 10; J. Adamy, "Starbucks Plays Common Joe," *The Wall Street Journal*, February 9, 2009, p. B3; J. Adamy, "Starbucks CEO, Top Officials Didn't Get Bonuses for 2008," *The Wall Street Journal*, January 23, 2009, B3; J. Adamy, "Starbucks Could Cut 410(k) Match," *The Wall Street Journal*, December 24, 2008, p. B3; J. Adamy, "At Starbucks, a Tall Order for New Cuts, Store Closures," *The Wall Street Journal*, January 29, 2009, pp. B2,B3; J. Adamy, "Starbucks Shift Focus to Value, Cost Cutting," *Wall Street Journal*, December 5, 2008, p. B1.

Introduction

Competitiveness
A company's ability to maintain and gain market share in its industry.

Starbucks illustrates the key role that human resource management (HRM) plays in determining the survival, effectiveness, and competitiveness of U.S. businesses. **Competitiveness** refers to a company's ability to maintain and gain market share in its industry. Starbucks' human resource management practices are helping support the company's business strategy and provide services the customer values. The value of a product or service is determined by its quality and how closely the product fits customer needs.

Competitiveness is related to company effectiveness, which is determined by whether the company satisfies the needs of stakeholders (groups affected by business practices). Important stakeholders include stockholders, who want a return on their investment; customers, who want a high-quality product or service; and employees, who desire interesting work and reasonable compensation for their services. The community, which wants the company to contribute to activities and projects and minimize pollution of the environment, is also an important stakeholder. Companies that do not meet stakeholders' needs are unlikely to have a competitive advantage over other firms in their industry.

Human Resource Management (HRM)
Policies, practices, and systems that influence employees' behavior, attitudes, and performance.

Human resource management (HRM) refers to the policies, practices, and systems that influence employees' behavior, attitudes, and performance. Many companies refer to HRM as involving "people practices." Figure 1.1 emphasizes that there are several important HRM practices. The strategy underlying these practices needs to be considered to maximize their influence on company performance. As the figure shows, HRM practices include analyzing and designing work, determining human resource needs (HR planning), attracting potential employees (recruiting), choosing employees (selection), teaching employees how to perform their jobs and preparing them for the future (training and development), rewarding employees (compensation), evaluating their performance (performance management), and creating a positive work environment (employee relations). The HRM practices discussed in this chapter's opening highlighted how effective HRM practices support business goals and objectives. That is, effective HRM practices are strategic! Effective HRM has been shown to enhance company performance by contributing to employee and customer satisfaction, innovation, productivity, and development of a favorable reputation in the firm's community.[1] The potential role of HRM in company performance has only recently been recognized.

figure 1.1

Human Resource Management Practices

We begin by discussing the roles and skills that a human resource management department and/or managers need for any company to be competitive. The second section of the chapter identifies the competitive challenges that U.S. companies currently face, which influence their ability to meet the needs of shareholders, customers, employees, and other stakeholders. We discuss how these competitive challenges are influencing HRM. The chapter concludes by highlighting the HRM practices covered in this book and the ways they help companies compete.

What Responsibilities and Roles Do HR Departments Perform?

Only recently have companies looked at HRM as a means to contribute to profitability, quality, and other business goals through enhancing and supporting business operations.

Table 1.1 shows the responsibilities of human resource departments. The average ratio of HR department staff to total number of employees has been 1.0 for every 93 employees served by the department.[2] The median HR department expenditure per employee was $1,409. Labor costs represent approximately 30 percent of company revenue.

The HR department is solely responsible for outplacement, labor law compliance, record keeping, testing, unemployment compensation, and some aspects of benefits administration. The HR department is most likely to collaborate with other company functions on employment interviewing, performance management and discipline, and efforts to improve quality and productivity. Large companies are more likely than small ones to employ HR specialists, with benefits specialists being the most prevalent. Other common specializations include recruitment, compensation, and training and development.[3]

Many different roles and responsibilities can be performed by the HR department depending on the size of the company, the characteristics of the workforce, the industry, and the value system of company management. The HR department may take full responsibility for human resource activities in some companies, whereas in others it may share the roles and responsibilities with managers of other departments such as

table 1.1

Responsibilities of
HR Departments

Employment and recruiting	Interviewing, recruiting, testing, temporary labor coordination
Training and development	Orientation, performance management skills training, productivity enhancement
Compensation	Wage and salary administration, job descriptions, executive compensation, incentive pay, job evaluation
Benefits	Insurance, vacation leave administration, retirement plans, profit sharing, stock plans
Employee services	Employee assistance programs, relocation services, outplacement services
Employee and community relations	Attitude surveys, labor relations, publications, labor law compliance, discipline
Personnel records	Information systems, records
Health and safety	Safety inspection, drug testing, health, wellness
Strategic planning	International human resources, forecasting, planning, mergers and acquisitions

SOURCE: Based on SHRM-BNA Survey No. 66, "Policy and Practice Forum: Human Resource Activities, Budgets, and Staffs, 2000–2001," Bulletin to Management, Bureau of National Affairs Policy and Practice Series, June 28, 2001. Washington, DC: Bureau of National Affairs.

finance, operations, or information technology. In some companies the HR department advises top-level management; in others the HR department may make decisions regarding staffing, training, and compensation after top managers have decided relevant business issues.

One way to think about the roles and responsibilities of HR departments is to consider HR as a business within the company with three product lines. Figure 1.2 shows the three product lines of HR. The first product line, administrative services and transactions, is the traditional product that HR has historically provided. The newer HR products—business partner services and the strategic partner role—are the HR functions that are being challenged by top managers to deliver. For example,

figure 1.2

HR as a Business with Three Product Lines

| **Administrative Services and Transactions:** Compensation, hiring and staffing
 • Emphasis: Resource efficiency and service quality | **Business Partner Services:** Developing effective HR systems and helping implement business plans, talent management
 • Emphasis: Knowing the business and exercising influence—problem solving, designing effective systems to ensure needed competencies | **Strategic Partner:** Contributing to business strategy based on considerations of human capital, business capabilities, readiness, and developing HR practices as strategic differentiators
 • Emphasis: Knowledge of HR and of the business, competition, the market, and business strategies |

SOURCE: Adapted from Figure 1, "HR Product Lines," in E. E. Lawler, "From Human Resource Management to Organizational Effectiveness," *Human Resource Management* 44 (2005), pp. 165–69.

consider the expectations and perceptions the CEOs of Hyperion, Revlon, and Air Products and Chemicals Inc. have for HR.[4] The Hyperion CEO wants his HR leaders to be able to question the CEO and executive team members and ensure the success of basic administrative functions, thus the HR team can elevate itself to a higher level of performance within the company culture and ensure that employees are able to perform at the highest level. At Revlon, the expectation is that HR can think strategically and innovatively, plan and execute, and have a very strong connection to the business. The CEO of Air Products and Chemicals believes the HR function is critical for the long-term success of the company because it can help get people excited about change, when most are by nature resistant to change.

HR at SYSCO Corporation, the number one food service marketer and distributor in North America, is successfully delivering business partner services and serving as a strategic partner.[5] The senior vice president and chief administrative officer is responsible for ensuring that HR strategy is aligned with the business strategy. SYSCO tries to differentiate itself from competitors in the marketplace by providing value in its products and customer service to the customer. HR at SYSCO focuses on ensuring that five processes are in place. These processes stress a common understanding of the company's mission values and goals, establishment of clear expectations between employees and managers using the performance management process, operating within laws, ensuring that employees are inspired to come to work, and giving every employee the skills and technology needed to contribute to the company. HR, a strategic partner in all of the processes, works together with senior management to develop programs and guidelines to support the processes. It then markets them to line managers, who execute and customize the programs for their specific business. To determine if these processes are working three key dimensions are measured: employee satisfaction, number of employees the company uses per 100,000 cases it sells, and employee retention data for each function in the company. Top executives meet four times each year to review the metrics to see if they are consistent with operating expenses and pretax earnings. For example, since the late 1990s SYSCO has moved the retention rate for its 10,000 marketing associates from 70 to 82 percent, resulting in more than $70 million dollars saved per year.

What Competencies Do HR Professionals Need?

HR professionals need to have the six competencies shown in Figure 1.3. These are the most recent competencies identified by the Human Resource Competency Study, which has identified HR competencies for more than 15 years. The competencies are shown as a three-tier pyramid with the Credible Activist Competency the most important for high performance as an HR professional and effective HR leader. Demonstrating these competencies can help HR professionals show managers that they are capable of helping the HR function create value, contribute to the business strategy, and shape the company culture. They also help the HR department effectively and efficiently provide the three HR products discussed earlier and shown in Figure 1.2. Although great emphasis is placed on the strategic role of HR, effective execution of the operational executor competency—necessary administrative services filling open jobs, paying employees, benefits enrollment, keeping employee records, and completing legally required paperwork (such as W-2 forms and EEO reports)—is still important! As we discuss later in the chapter, technological advances have made available e-HRM and human resource information systems,

figure 1.3

Six Competencies
for the HR
Profession

**Credible
Activist**

- Deliver results
  with integrity
- Share information
- Build trusting relationships
- Influencing others, providing
  candid observation, taking
  appropriate risks

**Cultural
Steward**

- Facilitates
  change
- Developing and
  valuing the culture
- Helping employees
  navigate the culture
  (find meaning in
  their work, manage
  work/life balance,
  encourage innovation)

**Talent
Manager/
Organizational
Designer**

- Develop talent
- Design reward
  systems
- Shape the
  organization

**Strategic
Architect**

- Recognize
  business trends
  and their impact
  on the business
- Evidence-based
  HR
- Develop people
  strategies that
  contribute to
  the business strategy

Business Ally

- Understanding how the business
  makes money
- Understand language of business

Operational Executor

- Implementing workplace policies
- Advancing HR technology
- Administer day-to-day work of
  managing people

SOURCE: Based on R. Grossman, "New Competencies for HR," *HR Magazine* (June 2007):
pp. 58–62; HR Competency Assessment Tools at www.shrm.org/competencies/benefits.asp

which make administration of services more efficient and effective and free up time for
HR to focus on strategic issues. Successful HR professionals must be able to share information, build relationships, and influence persons both inside and outside the company,
including managers, employees, community members, schools, customers, vendors, and
suppliers.

Sometimes helping employees can also involve crisis management activities such
as those HR professionals had to perform during and following Hurricane Katrina.
The Avis executive vice president of human resources was responsible for making
sure that employees in Katrina's path got to safety.[6] Employees were given 1-800
phone numbers to call if they got into trouble. Employees were given release time to

evacuate their families as the storm approached. When employees called in following the storm, they were asked if they needed housing, food, or medical care or if they had missing relatives. HR called emergency shelters to find missing employees and sent trucks with Avis signs throughout the stricken area trying to locate missing employees who had evacuated. Employees were paid their salaries even if they were unable to work, and copayments for medical care were waived.

How Is the HRM Function Changing?

The amount of time that the HRM function devotes to administrative tasks is decreasing, and its roles as a strategic business partner, change agent, and employee advocate are increasing.[7] HR managers face two important challenges: shifting their focus from current operations to strategies for the future[8] and preparing non-HR managers to develop and implement human resource practices (recall the role of HR in Starbucks' success from the chapter-opening story).

The role of HRM in administration is decreasing as technology is used for many administrative purposes, such as managing employee records and allowing employees to get information about and enroll in training, benefits, and other programs. Advances in technology such as the Internet have decreased the HRM role in maintaining records and providing self-service to employees.[9] **Self-service** refers to giving employees online access to information about HR issues such as training, benefits, compensation, and contracts; enrolling online in programs and services; and completing online attitude surveys. For example, General Motors' (GM) goal for its e-HR investment was to create an employee-friendly one-stop shop for employees to enroll in benefits, review their HR data, and get certificates for employee car discounts.[10] The portal, known as "mySocrates," is the place employees go for information about GM. Managers use the system for performance reviews. HR uses it for communications of benefits, training programs, and other programs, which saves time as well as printing and distribution costs. Annual benefits enrollment used to take several days. Now it takes a few minutes.

Outsourcing of the administrative role has also occurred. **Outsourcing** refers to the practice of having another company (a vendor, third-party provider, or consultant) provide services. One study suggests that 80 percent of companies now outsource at least one HR activity.[11] The HR responsibilities most likely to be outsourced completely include employee assistance and counseling, flexible spending account administration, and background and criminal background checks. Outsource providers such as ADP, Accenture HR Services, Convergys, and Hewitt provide payroll services as well as recruiting, training, record managements, and expatriation. The primary reasons for outsourcing are to save money and spend more time on strategic business issues. One study suggests that 91 percent of U.S. companies have taken steps to standardize their HR processes to prepare for outsourcing.[12]

Examples of strategic business issues that HR might help address include identifying new business opportunities; assessing possible merger, acquisition, or divestiture strategies; or working on recruiting and developing talent.[13] As a result, HR functions related to these areas such as employee development, performance management, communications plans and strategies, policy development and implementation and organizational development are outsourced least frequently. For example, outsourcing payroll and benefits administration is saving the American Stock Exchange in New York $2.8 million per year. When the Canadian Imperial Bank of Commerce

Self-Service
Giving employees online access to HR information.

Outsourcing
The practice of having another company provide services.

contracted with Electronic Data Systems (EDS) Corporation to take over payroll, benefits administration, and other HR processing for the Toronto-based bank, the bank had 30 incompatible HR systems and had not invested in e-HRM (use of the Web for HR operations).[14] EDS revised the bank's payroll, benefits, executive compensation, and human resources information technology systems, and it created my.HR, a Web portal used by managers and employees. Use of EDS has not required any additional costs over the bank's yearly HR budget. When the bank outsourced payroll it cut 200 jobs from its centralized HR staff, leaving the remaining HR staff to focus on strategic issues such as recruiting, training, and union contract negotiations. The centralized staff members moved over to EDS.

Cardinal Health, a provider of health care products, services, and technology, headquartered in Dublin, Ohio, signed a contract with ExcellerateHRO to provide administrative functions.[15] The goal of the outsourcing was to increase the contribution of human resources to strategy and increase the company's global human resource capabilities. Human resource professionals remaining at Cardinal will work in strategic areas such as talent management, organizational effectiveness, and total rewards. In addition, human resource "business partners" placed across the company will focus on strategic activities while establishing new HR operations in the field. Although the outsourcing of HR is expected to grow, many contracts have ended because of lack of understanding of the outsourcing provider's capabilities, failure to reach goals such as anticipated cost reductions, and poor delivery of services.[16] A key aspect of any outsourcing decision is an understanding of the company's vision for HR and an assessment of the costs of performing HR functions within the company compared with the potential savings through outsourcing.

Traditionally, the HRM department (also known as "Personnel" or "Employee Relations") was primarily an administrative expert and employee advocate. The department took care of employee problems, made sure employees were paid correctly, administered labor contracts, and avoided legal problems. The HRM department ensured that employee-related issues did not interfere with the manufacturing or sales of products or services. Human resource management was primarily reactive; that is, human resource issues were a concern only if they directly affected the business. Although that still remains the case in many companies that have yet to recognize the competitive value of human resource management, other companies believe that HRM is important for business success and therefore have expanded the role of HRM as a change agent and strategic partner.

Other roles such as practice development and strategic business partnering have increased. One of the most comprehensive studies ever conducted regarding HRM concluded that "human resources is being transformed from a specialized, standalone function to a broad corporate competency in which human resources and line managers build partnerships to gain competitive advantage and achieve overall business goals."[17] HR managers are increasingly included on high-level committees that are shaping the strategic direction of the company. These managers report directly to the CEO, president, or board of directors and propose solutions to business problems.

Consider the role of HR at Google and FedEx Corporation.[18] The Google vice president of HR is part of the company's 13-member management group. He reports to the CEO and works with the rest of the executives to help them achieve their objectives. The HR function is organized around three principles: the HR function wants to (1) be as innovative as the product side of the business, (2) minimize the infrastructure needed to keep the business running by emphasizing that managers and

table 1.2

Questions Used to
Determine If Human
Resources Are
Playing a Strategic
Role in the Business

1. What is HR doing to provide value-added services to internal clients?
2. What can the HR department add to the bottom line?
3. How are you measuring the effectiveness of HR?
4. How can we reinvest in employees?
5. What HR strategy will we use to get the business from point A to point B?
6. What makes an employee want to stay at our company?
7. How are we going to invest in HR so that we have a better HR department than our competitors?
8. From an HR perspective, what should we be doing to improve our marketplace position?
9. What's the best change we can make to prepare for the future?

SOURCES: Data from A. Halcrow, "Survey Shows HR in Transition," *Workforce*, June 1988, p. 74; P. Wright, *Human Resource Strategy: Adapting to the Age of Globalization* (Alexandria, VA: Society for Human Resource Management Foundation, 2008).

employees should work together rather than sending employees to HR, and (3) anticipate business needs and be prepared with a plan to meet those needs.

The corporate vice president for human resources at FedEx keeps HR focused on business objectives by setting HR objectives based on those set by the CEO. She oversees different task forces on HR issues to ensure that the operating companies are involved and that HR objectives are consistent across the company. She sits on the nine-member strategic management committee, which includes the CEO, the CEOs from the operating companies, the chief financial officer, and the head of marketing and communications. Also, she manages leadership development for the top 400 positions in the company and oversees a program for high-performing vice presidents that helps them develop a cross-functional perspective of the company. In the program, vice presidents learn about differences in the companies operating units and complete an international assignment in China to increase their understanding of different political environments. The FedEx HR function includes a team at each of four operating companies plus a corporate headquarters team that develops strategy and disseminates it to the operating units.

As part of its strategic role, one of the key contributions that HR can make is to engage in evidence-based HR. **Evidence-based HR** refers to demonstrating that human resources practices have a positive influence on the company's bottom line or key stakeholders (employees, customers, community, shareholders). This helps show that the money invested in HR programs is justified and that HR is contributing to the company's goals and objectives. Evidence-based HR requires collecting data on such metrics as productivity, turnover, accidents, employee attitudes and medical costs and showing their relationship with HR practices. This provides evidence that HR is as important to the business as finance, accounting, and marketing! HR decisions should be made on the basis of data and not just intuition. The chapter opener showed how Starbucks is using turnover and employee satisfaction data as metrics or indicators of the success of its HR programs. Throughout each chapter of the book, we provide examples of evidence-based HR.

Table 1.2 provides several questions that managers can use to determine if HRM is playing a strategic role in the business. If these questions have not been considered, it is highly unlikely that (1) the company is prepared to deal with competitive challenges or (2) human resources are being used to help a company gain a competitive

Evidence-Based HR
Demonstrating that human resource practices have a positive influence on the company's bottom line or key stakeholders (employees, customers, community, shareholders).

advantage. The bottom line for evaluating the relationship between human resource management and the business strategy is to consider this question: "What is HR doing to ensure that the right people with the right skills are doing the right things in the jobs that are important for the execution of the business strategy?"[19] We will discuss strategic human resource management in more detail in Chapter 2.

Why have HRM roles changed? Managers see HRM as the most important lever for companies to gain a competitive advantage over both domestic and foreign competitors. We believe this is because HRM practices are directly related to companies' success in meeting competitive challenges. These challenges and their implications for HRM are discussed later in the chapter.

The HRM Profession

There are many different types of jobs in the HRM profession. Table 1.3 shows various HRM positions and their salaries. A survey conducted by the Society of Human Resource Management to better understand what HR professionals do found that the primary activities of HR professionals are performing the HR generalist role (providing a wide range of HR services), with fewer involved in other activities such as the HR function at the executive level of the company, training and development, HR consulting, and administrative activities.[20]

HR salaries vary depending on education and experience as well as the type of industry. As you can see from Table 1.3, some positions involve work in specialized areas of HRM like recruiting, training, or labor and industrial relations. HR generalists usually make between $50,000 and $80,000 depending on their experience and education level. Generalists usually perform the full range of HRM activities, including recruiting, training, compensation, and employee relations. Most HR professionals chose HR as a career because they found HR appealing as a career, they wanted to work with people, or they were asked by chance to perform HR tasks and responsibilities.[21]

A college degree is held by the vast majority of HRM professionals, many of whom also have completed postgraduate work. Business typically is the field of study (human resources or industrial relations), although some HRM professionals have degrees in the social sciences (economics or psychology), the humanities, or law. Those who have completed graduate work have master's degrees in HR management, business management, or a similar field. This is important because to be successful in HR, you need to speak the same language as the other business functions. You have to have

table 1.3

Median Salaries for HRM Positions

POSITION	SALARY
Top HR executive	$164,500
Employee benefits manager	91,800
HR manager	84,500
Compensation analyst	64,000
Professional and technical staff recruiter	62,200
Employee training specialist	58,200
HR generalist	58,000

SOURCE: Based on J. Dooney and E. Esen, "HR Salaries Weaken with the Economy," *HR Magazine's 2009 HR Trendbook* (Alexandria, VA: Society for Human Resource Management, 2009), p. 14.

credibility as a business leader, which means being able to understand finance and build a business case for HR activities. Professional certification in HRM is less common than membership in professional associations. A well-rounded educational background will likely serve a person well in an HRM position. As one HR professional noted, "One of the biggest misconceptions is that it is all warm and fuzzy communications with the workers. Or that it is creative and involved in making a more congenial atmosphere for people at work. Actually it is both of those some of the time, but most of the time it is a big mountain of paperwork which calls on a myriad of skills besides the 'people' type. It is law, accounting, philosophy, and logic as well as psychology, spirituality, tolerance, and humility."[22]

Many top-level managers and HR professionals believe that the best way to develop the future effective professionals needed in HR is to take employees with a business point of view and train them. For example, United Parcel Services (UPS) wants its leaders to move up in the company with lifelong careers in many different functions.[23] The senior vice president for human resources at UPS started out loading trucks and became a delivery truck driver and delivery supervisor before he moved to several HR positions. He then joined the legal department and served as general counsel before he took the top HR position at UPS. At companies like General Electric, Citigroup, and Baxter Health Care, training programs are used to develop HR professionals' skills. Also, HR professionals often rotate through job assignments in non-HR functions to help them learn about the business and become more strategic business partners.[24] For example, just several years ago for the first time in company history at General Motors, an HR person reported directly to the company CEO.[25] Many of the transactional activities are being outsourced or performed with the use of technology. GM is trying to develop HR people so that they can take on the role of internal consultants. The company has a global HR curriculum that helps HR employees understand what the goals of HR are, what the changes in HR at GM mean to them, and what the plans are for the HR function. The courses focus on helping HR employees gain business knowledge such as finance, change management skills, and the ability to develop relationships across the company. GM hopes that in the near future HR employees will be able to work with business units to diagnose problems. At the same time HR employees are being trained, top HR managers are working with line managers to help them understand that HR is available to help them with strategy, not transactional work. Line managers are now taking responsibility for some HR activities. For example, GM recently introduced a new compensation plan for employees that was implemented by line managers without any help from HR.

The primary professional organization for HRM is the Society for Human Resource Management (SHRM). SHRM is the world's largest human resource management association with more than 210,000 professional and student members throughout the world. SHRM provides education and information services, conferences and seminars, government and media representation, and online services and publications (such as *HR Magazine*). You can visit SHRM's Web site to see their services at www.shrm.org.

Competitive Challenges Influencing Human Resource Management

Three competitive challenges that companies now face will increase the importance of human resource management practices: the challenge of sustainability, the global challenge, the technology challenge. These challenges are shown in Figure 1.4.

figure 1.4

Competitive
Challenges
Influencing U.S.
Companies

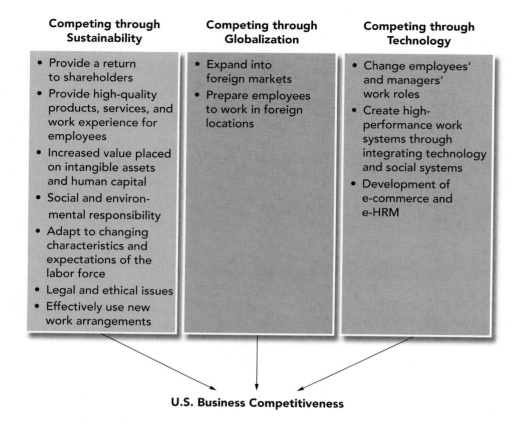

Competing through Sustainability
- Provide a return to shareholders
- Provide high-quality products, services, and work experience for employees
- Increased value placed on intangible assets and human capital
- Social and environmental responsibility
- Adapt to changing characteristics and expectations of the labor force
- Legal and ethical issues
- Effectively use new work arrangements

Competing through Globalization
- Expand into foreign markets
- Prepare employees to work in foreign locations

Competing through Technology
- Change employees' and managers' work roles
- Create high-performance work systems through integrating technology and social systems
- Development of e-commerce and e-HRM

U.S. Business Competitiveness

The Sustainability Challenge

Sustainability
The ability of a company to survive in a dynamic competitive environment. Based on an approach to organizational decision making that considers company's ability to make a profit without sacrificing the resources of its employees, the community, or the environment.

Traditionally, sustainability has been viewed as one aspect of corporate social responsibility related to the impact of the business on the environment.[26] However, we take a broader view of sustainability. **Sustainability** refers to a company's ability to make a profit without sacrificing the resources of its employees, the community, or the environment.[27] Company success is based on how well the company meets the needs of its stakeholders. **Stakeholders** refers to shareholders, the community, customers, employees, and all of the other parties that have an interest in seeing that the company succeeds. Sustainability includes the ability to deal with economic and social changes, practice environmental responsibility, engage in responsible and ethical business practices, provide high-quality products and services, and put in place methods to determine if the company is meeting stakeholders' needs.

Several changes in the economy have important implications for human resource management. Some key statistics about the economy and the workforce are shown in Table 1.4. These include the changing structure of the economy, the development of e-business, and more growth in professional and service occupations. Growth in these occupations means that skill demands for jobs have changed, with knowledge becoming more valuable. Not only have skill demands changed, but remaining competitive in a global economy requires demanding work hours and changes in traditional employment patterns. The creation of new jobs, aging employees leaving the workforce, slow population growth, and a lack of employees who have the skills needed to perform the jobs in greatest demand means that demand for employees will exceed

LO2
Discuss the implications of the economy, the makeup of the labor force, and ethics for company sustainability.

table 1.4

Summary of Key Labor Statistics Influencing HRM

- Total employment will increase from 150.6 million in 2006 to 166.2 million by 2016.
- Professional specialty and service occupations will grow the fastest and add the most jobs from 2006 to 2016.
- More job openings are expected from the need to replace workers (34 million) than from employment growth in the economy.
- The 77 million baby boomers (born between 1946 and 1964) will begin to leave the workforce between 2006 and 2016 as they become eligible for retirement.
- The projected median age of the labor force by 2016 is 42, the highest ever recorded.
- Immigrants will add 4 million persons to the population by 2016.

SOURCES: A. Dohn and L. Shniper, "Occupational Employment Projections to 2016," *Monthly Labor Review*, November 2007, pp. 86–125; M. Toossi, "Labor Force Projections to 2016: More Workers in Their Golden Years," *Monthly Labor Review*, November 2007, pp. 33–52; E. Figueroa and R. Woods, "Industry Employment Projections to 2016," *Monthly Labor Review*, November 2007, pp. 53–85.

supply. This has created a "war for talent" that has increased the attention companies pay to attracting and retaining human resources.

Economic Changes

The U.S. and global economy is currently in a recession. In the United States, the current economic downturn is the worst since the years following World War II. The economy lost 5 million jobs since the beginning of 2008 and the unemployment rate grew to more than 8 percent by March 2009.[28] Most consumers have seen their homes lose value, as well as experienced substantial declines in retirement savings and household wealth, due to collapse of the stock market. The recession has a number of probable causes, including the subprime lending scandals and collapse and failure of major financial institutions such as Bear Sterns, Lehman Brothers, and Merrill-Lynch.[29] All of the bad news has contributed to a lack of confidence in the economy, making it difficult for businesses and consumers to get credit and loans. Most industries have not escaped the crisis, especially retailers, automakers, manufacturing, and construction. Retailers reported record sales declines for the 2008 holiday season as consumers reduced their holiday spending. The Big Three automakers have received bailout money from the government but still face the risk of bankruptcy, which could cause hundreds of thousands of employees to lose their jobs. The highest unemployment rate at the end of 2008 was 15.3 percent in the construction sector as plans for new homes and office buildings are postponed or canceled. The economic slowdown is not limited to the United States. The economies of China and India have slowed, and Europe, Mexico, and Japan have slipped into recession. President Obama proposed—and Congress passed—an economic stimulus plan that is intended to create jobs and increase consumer and investor confidence, although its impact may not be realized for several years.

The implications of this economic period for human resource management are far-reaching. The poor economy means more companies are downsizing their workforces, delaying plans for new operations and growth, and revisiting human resource budgets to cut unnecessary programs and costs. For example, in January 2009 more than 655,000 jobs were lost, including cuts of employees from Pfizer, Texas Instruments, Home Depot, General Motors, Boeing, Alcoa, Andersen, and World Wrestling

Stakeholders
The various interest groups who have relationships with, and consequently, whose interests are tied to the organization (e.g., employees, suppliers, customers, shareholders, community).

Entertainment.[30] Employees are delaying retirement, and newly retired employees are returning to work out of necessity because of loss of value of their retirement assets (on March 5, 2009, the Dow Jones Industrial Average closed at its lowest point since April 1977). One estimate is that companies plan to cut their training budget more than 10 percent in response to the economic crises.[31] Morale and team-building activities were the most likely targets for budget cuts, followed by professional development, all-staff training, and recruitment.[32]

Despite the budget cuts, many HR departments are helping companies adapt to the poor economic times and prepare them to be well-positioned when business conditions improve. For example, Capital One asks its managers to determine current workloads and staffing needs.[33] HR projects changes in the workforce based on this information. This has allowed Capital One to forecast labor needs with more precision, helping the company to avoid hiring new employees only to have to lay them off. Nucor Corporation implemented a "Share the Pain" program. The program helps Nucor reduce labor costs without reducing productivity by using reduced hours or wages. Isis Pharmaceuticals capitalizes on downturns to recruit and hire top scientific talent at bargain salaries. Xilinx Inc. responded to the economic downturn with salary reductions, mandatory vacations, and a sabbatical program that paid employees a small salary if they went to school or worked for nonprofits. The strategy saved more than $35 million in labor costs.

Both Philips Electronics and Estee Lauder are continuing their talent management efforts.[34] Philips Electronics is cutting its training budget but will continue to offer its Inspire program for high-potential employees, emphasizing business strategy and personal leadership topics. Philips believes that investing in leadership development will help the company weather the recession and prepare for economic recovery. Estee Lauder Companies, the cosmetic maker, realized lower profit and sales, resulting in elimination of more than 2,000 jobs over the next two years. But Lauder is continuing its leadership development programs, which will emphasize innovation and managing change in turbulent business conditions.

The affects of the recession are also worsened by rising health care costs and the economic implications of increasing retiree benefit costs.[35] Companies are under pressure to increase employee productivity to alleviate higher costs such as health care. To control costs, companies have cut employee and retiree health care benefits and pension contributions, increased the employee contribution to pay for these benefits, and even hired and fired employees based on their smoking habits! For example, Scott's Miracle-Gro Company, the lawn care company, banned smoking and encourages employees to complete a health-risk assessment designed to identify employees who are at risk for heart, cancer, and other diseases.[36] Employees at risk are assigned a health coach, who draws up an action plan that may include recommendations such as exercise or change of diet. Employees who refuse the health assessment pay $40 per month more in health care premiums; at-risk employees who refuse to work with a health coach pay an additional $67 per month. We discuss what companies are doing to offset health care and pension costs in Chapter 13, Employee Benefits.

HR programs and the HR function are under pressure to relate to the business strategy and show a return on investment. Customer focus needs to be included in all HRM practices. New technology combined with economic uncertainty will mean that administrative and transactional HR activities will be delivered via technology, creating less need for HR professionals to provide these activities. The aging workforce combined with reduced immigration because of security concerns may lead employers to focus more on retraining employees or encouraging older, skilled workers to delay retirement or work part-time.[37]

Employment and Occupational Growth Projections and Skill Requirements. The competition for labor is affected by the growth and decline of industries, jobs, and occupations. Competition for labor is also influenced by the number and skills of persons available for full-time work. The labor force is projected to increase 13 million to 166.2 million in 2016. Most growth is expected within service-providing industries in which employment is projected to increase 15.8 million, rising to 130.2 million by 2016.[38] Employment in services is expected to account for 86 percent of all jobs. Examples of service-providing industries include educational services, health care, leisure and hospitality, transportation, government, utilities, and wholesale and retail trade. Jobs in goods-producing industries including mining, construction, and manufacturing, are projected to decrease, falling to 21.8 million in 2016.

Table 1.5 shows examples of the projected fastest growing occupations between 2006 and 2016. Professional and related occupations and the services occupational group are expected to add the most jobs and have the fastest growth rate between 2006 and 2016.[39] Health care practitioners and technical occupations are projected to add the most jobs (1.4 million), and computer and mathematical occupations are expected to grow the fastest (24.8 percent growth rate). In the services occupation group, by 2016 food preparation and related services are expected to generate the most new jobs, and health care support is expected to grow the fastest (27 percent).

table 1.5

Examples of the Fastest Growing Occupations

OCCUPATION	EMPLOYMENT CHANGE 2006–2016		MOST SIGNIFICANT EDUCATION OR TRAINING
	NUMBER (IN THOUSANDS)	PERCENT	
Network systems and data communications analysts	140	54	Bachelor's degree
Personal and home health care aids	389	51	Short-term on-the-job training
Home health care aides	384	49	Short-term on-the-job training
Computer software engineering applications	226	45	Bachelor's degree
Veterinary technologists and technicians	29	41	Associate degree
Personal financial advisors	72	41	Bachelor's degree
Makeup artists, theatrical and performance	1	40	Postsecondary vocational award
Medical assistants	148	35	Moderate-term on-the-job training
Veterinarians	22	35	First professional degree

SOURCE: Based on A. Dohm and L. Shniper, "Occupational Employment Projections to 2016," *Monthly Labor Review*, November 2007, pp. 86–125.

Medical and dental assistants, nurses, and home health aides are examples of health care support occupations. Fishery, forestry, and farming occupations and production occupations are expected to have declines in the number of jobs between 2006 and 2016. The aging of the population and the labor force means that jobs in health care and social assistance services are expected to have the fastest growth rate between 2006 and 2016, adding 4 million new jobs, or 27 percent of all new nonagricultural wage and salary jobs.

Occupations that require a bachelor's degree or higher for an entry-level position will grow faster than average for all occupations. Eighteen of the 30 of the fastest growing occupations are in professional and related occupations, and 10 are in service occupations. Fifteen of the 30 fastest growing occupations require a bachelor's degree or higher as their most significant source of education and training. Most of the 30 fastest growing occupations are considered professional and related occupations, which include health care, education, and science-related occupations.

The future U.S. labor market will be both a knowledge economy and a service economy.[40] There will be many high-education professional and managerial jobs and low-education service jobs. Boundaries between knowledge and service work are blurring, creating "technoservice" occupations that combine service technology and software application. Software application engineers, technical support, engineering, and scientific consulting jobs work directly with customers, and customers influence the product design process.

Table 1.6 shows the top 10 content and skill areas that corporate leaders surveyed considered most critical over the next five years. However, new entrants to the workplace lack these and other skills needed for companies to compete in the global economy. A study of American manufacturers conducted by the National Association of Manufacturing found that 36 percent indicated that employees had insufficient reading, writing, and communications skills.[41] Despite the need for high-level skills many job applicants lack the necessary skills. Surveys of employers found that over half reported that high school graduates are deficient in problem solving/critical thinking, written and oral communications, and professionalism/work ethic.[42] Employers are more positive about four-year college graduates, although approximately 25 percent reported they were deficient in written communication, English writing skills, and

table 1.6

Top 10 Knowledge and Skills Expected to Increase in Importance

RANK	BASIC KNOWLEDGE AND APPLIED SKILLS	PERCENTAGE
1	Critical thinking/problem solving	77.8%
2	Information technology application	77.4
3	Teamwork/collaboration	74.2
4	Creativity/innovation	73.6
5	Diversity	67.1
6	Leadership	66.9
7	Oral communications	65.9
8	Professionalism/work ethic	64.4
9	Ethics/social responsibility	64.3
10	Written communications	64.0

SOURCE: J. Casner-Lotto and L. Barrington, "Are They Really Ready to Work?" Research Report, The Conference Board, Corporate Voices for Working Families, Partnership for 21st Century Skills, and Society for Human Resource Management, October 2006.

leadership skills. Eighty percent of the manufacturers reported that they are facing a shortage of experienced workers, especially production workers, machinists, and craft workers. An online poll of members of the American Society for Training and Development found that 97 percent of respondents indicated a current skill gap in their companies.[43] Also, business leaders such as Bill Gates have expressed their concern at the comparatively low numbers of U.S. students in the science and engineering fields. China graduates about four times the number of engineers as the United States, although they are not all trained at the same level as U.S. engineers.[44] Japan graduates twice as many engineers and South Korea graduates nearly as many engineers as the United States. This has resulted in a shortage of engineering and other technical professionals.

Companies are involved in training current employees as well as establishing partnerships with schools to help improve the skills of the current and future U.S. workforce. For example, at Whirlpool, building a dishwasher requires that the sheet of steel used on the sides of the machine be the correct width.[45] Employees must be able to ensure that the steel meets specifications by calibrating equipment, which requires algebra-level math knowledge. Whirpool is finding that employees lack the math problem-solving skills needed to perform the job. As a result, Whirpool has developed training programs to improve workforce skills. About 25 percent of the programs focus on remedial skills. IBM, Hewlett-Packard, and Advanced Micro Devices are making efforts to increase the skills of the workforce by investing in local secondary schools.[46] IBM's Transition to Teaching program allows employees to take leaves of absences to student teach for three months. Eligible employees must meet certain requirements such as 10 years of service with IBM; a bachelor's degree in math or science, or a higher degree in a related field; and some experience teaching, tutoring, or volunteering in schools. IBM hopes that many of its experienced employees with math and engineering backgrounds will take advantage of the program, providing high-quality math and science teachers for public schools.

Another way to look at occupational growth is to consider the pay related to the occupation. That is, occupations that are fastest growing provide high pay (average earnings are in the top half of distribution of earnings of all occupations). Examples of these occupations include network systems and data communications analysts, database administrators, physician assistants, software engineers, graphic designers, and structural iron and steel workers.[47] It is important to notice that the fastest growing and highest paid occupations are not exclusively limited to health or computer-related occupations or occupations which require a college degree. However, employers have a preference for hiring individuals with skills associated with higher levels of education. This also translates into higher earnings for employees.

Increased Value Placed on Intangible Assets and Human Capital. Today more and more companies are interested in using intangible assets and human capital as a way to gain an advantage over competitors. A company's value includes three types of assets that are critical for the company to provide goods and services: financial assets (cash and securities), physical assets (property, plant, equipment), and intangible assets. Table 1.7 provides examples of intangible assets. **Intangible assets** include human capital, customer capital, social capital, and intellectual capital. Intangible assets are equally or even more valuable than financial and physical assets but they are difficult to duplicate or imitate.[48] By one estimate, up to 75 percent of the source of value in a company is in intangible assets.[49]

Intangible Assets
A type of company asset including human capital, customer capital, social capital, and intellectual capital.

table 1.7

Examples of
Intangible Assets

Human capital
- Tacit knowledge
- Education
- Work-related know-how
- Work-related competence

Customer capital
- Customer relationships
- Brands
- Customer loyalty
- Distribution channels

Social capital
- Corporate culture
- Management philosophy
- Management practices
- Informal networking systems
- Coaching/mentoring relationships

Intellectual capital
- Patents
- Copyrights
- Trade secrets
- Intellectual property

SOURCES: Based on L. Weatherly, *Human Capital: The Elusive Asset* (Alexandria, VA: 2003 SHRM Research Quarterly); E. Holton and S. Naquin, "New Metrics for Employee Development," *Performance Improvement Quarterly* 17 (2004), pp. 56–80; M. Huselid, B. Becker, and R. Beatty, *The Workforce Scorecard* (Boston: Harvard University Press, 2005).

Intangible assets have been shown to be responsible for a company's competitive advantage. Human resource management practices such as training, selection, performance management, and compensation have a direct influence on human and social capital through influencing customer service, work-related know-how and competence, and work relationships. For example, consider companies in the airline industry. Southwest Airlines consistently is profitable and highly ranked in on-time arrivals and other indicators of airline success.[50] One of the distinctions between Southwest Airlines and its competitors is how it treats its employees. For example, Southwest has a policy of no layoffs and was able to maintain this record even during the difficult time for airlines following 9/11. Southwest also emphasizes training and development to provide its employees with skills to perform multiple jobs. This allows Southwest airplanes to be quickly cleaned and serviced at airports because employees have multiple skill sets that can be applied to various aspects of getting an aircraft ready for departure. As a result of these human resource policies, Southwest employees are loyal, productive, and flexible (which contributes to the success of the airline). Other airlines may have similar or greater levels of financial assets and have physical assets that are comparable to Southwest's (e.g., same type of airplanes, similar gates), but what contributes to Southwest's success and gives the company a competitive advantage are its intangible assets in the form of human capital. American and United Airlines have similar (or greater!) financial and physical assets but have not been successful trying to compete with Southwest by offering flights on the same routes.

Recognizing the importance of human capital and social capital, John Chambers, Cisco Systems CEO, has transformed the company from one with one or two primary products with most important decisions made by the top 10 people in the company to one where networks of employee councils and boards and Web 2.0 applications encourage executives to work together.[51] Business unit leaders now share responsibilities for each other's success. Cisco's directory is designed to help anyone inside the company find answers to questions, a product demo, or the right person to speak to a customer in any language, anywhere in the world. As a result of this more face-to-face and electronic collaboration, Cisco Systems has been able to get products to market faster.

Intangible assets have been shown to be related to a company's bottom line. A study by the American Society for Training and Development of more than 500 publicly traded U.S.-based companies found that companies that invested the most in training and development had a shareholder return 86 percent higher than companies in the bottom half and 46 percent higher than the market average.[52]

One way companies try to increase intangible assets is through attracting, developing, and retaining knowledge workers. **Knowledge workers** are employees who contribute to the company not through manual labor, but through what they know about customers or a specialized body of knowledge. Employees cannot simply be ordered to perform tasks; they must share knowledge and collaborate on solutions. Knowledge workers contribute specialized knowledge that their managers may not have, such as information about customers. Managers depend on them to share information. Knowledge workers have many job opportunities. If they choose, they can leave a company and take their knowledge to a competitor. Knowledge workers are in demand because companies need their skills and jobs requiring them are growing (see Tables 1.5 and 1.6).

> **Knowledge Workers**
> Employees who own the intellectual means of producing a product or service.

To completely benefit from employees' knowledge requires a management style that focuses on developing and empowering employees. **Empowering** means giving employees responsibility and authority to make decisions regarding all aspects of product development or customer service.[53] Employees are then held accountable for products and services; in return, they share the rewards and losses of the results. For empowerment to be successful, managers must be trained to link employees to resources within and outside the company (people, Web sites, etc.), help employees interact with their fellow employees and managers throughout the company, and ensure that employees are updated on important issues and cooperate with each other. Employees must also be trained to understand how to use the Web, e-mail, and other tools for communicating, collecting, and sharing information.

> **Empowering**
> Giving employees responsibility and authority to make decisions.

As more companies become knowledge-based, it's important that they promote and capture learning at the employee, team, and company levels. At Nissan Motor's U.S. operations, 16 teams, each with 8 to 16 salaried employees from different departments, meet weekly to discuss issues such as quality, diversity, or supply chain management.[54] The team members, chosen by management, are considered to be high performers who have demonstrated that they are receptive to new ideas. The teams are used to challenge the organization and propose new initiatives to make the company more creative and innovative. For example, as a result of one team's discussion of how to save money, a proposal for working at home was developed. The team conducted an experiment to determine the benefits of working at home. A pilot study of working at home with 41 employees found that it resulted in reduced operating costs and improved morale, as well as productivity increases for employees who worked at home. As a result, a virtual office initiative is in place at Nissan's headquarters in Nashville, Tennessee. The company's employees who analyze market trends and identify concepts for Nissan will work from home in Los Angeles.

In addition to acquiring and retaining knowledge workers, companies need to be able to adapt to change. *Change* refers to the adoption of a new idea or behavior by a company. Technological advances, changes in the workforce or government regulations, globalization, and new competitors are among the many factors that require companies to change. Change is inevitable in companies as products, companies, and entire industries experience shorter life cycles.[55] For example, Chrysler announced a restructuring plan that will eliminate 11,000 production jobs and 2,000 white-collar jobs as the company sells businesses that do not fit with its car building mission and productivity improvements.[56]

A changing environment means that all employees must embrace a philosophy of learning. A **learning organization** embraces a culture of lifelong learning, enabling all employees to continually acquire and share knowledge. Improvements in product or service quality do not stop when formal training is completed.[57] Employees need to have the financial, time, and content resources (courses, experiences, development opportunities) available to increase their knowledge. Managers take an active role in identifying training needs and helping to ensure that employees use training in their work. Also, employees should be actively encouraged to share knowledge with colleagues and other work groups across the company using e-mail and the Internet.[58] For a learning organization to be successful requires that teams of employees collaborate to meet customer needs. Managers need to empower employees to share knowledge, identify problems, and make decisions. This allows the company to continuously experiment and improve.

Changes in Employment Expectations. The need for companies to make rapid changes as a result of new technologies, competitors, and customer demands has played a major role in reshaping the employment relationship.[59] New or emergent business strategies that result from these changes cause companies to merge, acquire new companies, grow, and in some cases downsize and restructure. This has resulted in changes in the employment relationship. The **psychological contract** describes what an employee expects to contribute and what the company will provide to the employee for these contributions.[60] Unlike a sales contract, a psychological contract is not written. Traditionally, companies expected employees to contribute time, effort, skills, abilities, and loyalty. In return, companies would provide job security and opportunities for promotion. However, in the new economy a new type of psychological contract is emerging.[61] The competitive business environment demands frequent changes in the quality, innovation, creativeness, and timeliness of employee contributions and the skills needed to provide them. This has led to company restructuring, mergers and acquisitions, layoffs, and longer hours for many employees. Companies demand excellent customer service and high productivity levels. Employees are expected to take more responsibility for their own careers, from seeking training to balancing work and family. In exchange for top performance and working longer hours without job security, employees want companies to provide flexible work schedules, comfortable working conditions, more autonomy in accomplishing work, training and development opportunities, and financial incentives based on how the company performs. Employees realize that companies cannot provide employment security, so they want employability—that is, they want their company to provide training and job experiences to help ensure that employees can find other employment opportunities. The human resource management challenge is how to build a committed, productive workforce in turbulent economic conditions that offer opportunity for financial success but can also quickly turn sour, making every employee expendable.

Learning Organization
Employees are continually trying to learn new things.

Psychological Contract
Expectations of employee contributions and what the company will provide in return.

Concerns with Employee Engagement. **Employee engagement** refers to the degree to which employees are fully involved in their work and the strength of their commitment to their job and the company.[62] Employees who are engaged in their work and committed to the company they work for give companies competitive advantage including higher productivity, better customer service, and lower turnover.[63] What is the state of employee engagement in U.S. companies? One survey of 50,000 employees across different companies showed that about 13 percent of employees are disengaged, poor performers who put in minimal effort on the job and are likely to leave the organization. Some 76 percent of employees exhibit moderate engagement; that is, they are marginally committed to the company and perform their jobs to the level expected by their manager. Only 11 percent of employees had high levels of engagement: they exhibited strong commitment to the company and were high performers who helped other employees with their work, volunteered for new responsibilities, and were constantly looking for ways to perform their jobs better.[64]

Perhaps the best way to understand engagement is to consider how companies measure employee engagement. Companies measure employees' engagement levels with attitude or opinion surveys (we discuss these in detail in Chapter 10). Although the types of questions asked on these surveys vary from company to company, research suggests the questions generally measure 10 common themes shown in Table 1.8. As you probably realize after reviewing the themes shown in Table 1.8, employees' engagement is influenced by how managers treat employees as well as human resource practices such as recruiting, selection, training and development, performance management, work design, and compensation. For example, companies should recruit and select employees who are able to perform the job, are willing to work toward achieving the company strategy, and will react favorably to the work environment. Performance management systems need to provide employees with opportunities to receive performance feedback and recognition for their accomplishments. Compensation including incentives, benefits, and nonfinancial perks such as on-site day care or travel discounts contribute to employee engagement. Training and development gives employees the opportunity for personal growth within the company. Work that is designed to be meaningful and allows employees to use a variety of their skills relates to several different aspects of engagement including satisfaction, intention to stay, pride, and opportunity to perform challenging work.

Employee Engagement
The degree to which employees are fully involved in their work and the strength of their job and company commitment.

Pride in employer
Satisfaction with employer
Satisfaction with the job
Opportunity to perform challenging work
Recognition and positive feedback from contributions
Personal support from manager
Effort above and beyond the minimum
Understanding the link between one's job and the company's mission
Prospects for future growth with the company
Intention to stay with the company

table 1.8
Common Themes of Employee Engagement

SOURCE: Based on R. Vance, *Employee Engagement and Commitment* (Alexandria, VA: Society for Human Resource Management, 2006).

EVIDENCE-BASED HR

Consider Fabick Caterpillar (CAT), a company that sells, rents, and repairs Caterpillar construction equipment.[65] The company serves construction businesses and contractors in Missouri and southern Illinois and pipeline contractors throughout the world. Fabick CAT has more than 600 employees in 12 locations, each considered a separate operation, with headquarters in Fenton, Missouri. The business that Doug Fabick inherited from his father in 1999 wasn't in the top 25 percent of CAT dealerships in the United States. Fabick tried to understand how some CAT dealerships around the country performed better than others by studying traditional financial indicators, but he could find no common trend. Fabick conducted several yearly assessments of employee engagement in 2003 and 2004 and the results were not good: only 16 percent of employees were engaged. One parts department had highly engaged employees and Fabick discovered that human resource practices were responsible for success. As a result, Fabick began investing in developing the talents and strengths of parts, service, and operations managers. Managers were trained in how to increase engagement, including how to best select managers and new employees who had the right skills and abilities to succeed in their jobs. The new human resource practices had a major impact on the company's "bottom line." When sales groups were divided by engagement level into top half and bottom half and compared, the top half increased their percentage of industry net sales by 24 percent compared to only 8 percent in the lower engagement group. Also, sales groups in the top half had overall customer engagement scores that were 8 percent higher compared to sales groups in the bottom half.

Talent Management
A systematic planned strategic effort by a company to attract, retain, develop, and motivate highly skilled employees and managers.

Talent Management. **Talent management** refers to a systematic planned strategic effort by companies to attracting, retaining, developing and motivating highly skilled employees and managers. Companies report that the most important talent management challenges they face are identifying employees with managerial talent and training and developing them for managerial positions.[66] Many companies do not have employees with the necessary competencies to manage in a global economy.[67] To successfully manage in a global economy, managers need to be self-aware and be able to build international teams, create global management and marketing practices, and interact and manage employees from different cultural backgrounds. Managers contribute to employee engagement by performing basic management functions (planning, organizing, controlling, leading) but also through the use of good communication skill, helping employees develop, and working collaboratively with employees.

For example, consider Schwan Foods and Yum! Brands.[68] Schwan Food company, makers of frozen pizzas and pies, is selecting employees with leadership talent to attend programs involving management classes and coaching sessions. These employees, considered "high-potential" managers, also receive challenging job assignments that require them to capitalize on their skill strengths and develop new skill sets (such as helping to launch a new joint venture in Mexico). Yum! Brands has more than 35,000 KFC, Pizza Hut, and Taco Bell restaurants worldwide. The company needs to develop a large number of managers to meet demands for new restaurants resulting from growth plans, such as to open two KFC restaurants a day in China. To support and sustain global growth in restaurant operations, Yum! is preparing new managers through identifying and assigning them job experiences that involve food innovation, marketing, and developing general management skills.

Surveys results suggest that opportunities for career growth, learning, and development and performing exciting and challenging work are some of the most important factors in determining employees' engagement and commitment to their current employer.[69] It is important to identify employees who want to develop their skills and seek promotions and keep them growing through new job experiences and training. For example, Liz Claiborne tries to avoid turnover of the company's best employees by creating jobs with growth potential.[70] These jobs involve new assignments that require employees to apply their skills in different ways or to learn new skills. Sales managers are encouraged to spend more time in operations, where they can learn about product flow, delivery, and other technical processes. This helps sales mangers become qualified for general manager jobs. Bristol-Meyers encourages employees in corporate staff positions to exchange jobs with another employee who works in the business units such as the pharmaceutical business.

● Yum! Brands plans to open two KFC's a day in China will require heavy reliance on talent management to develop successful managers for every store.

Use of Alternative Work Arrangements. **Alternative work arrangements** include independent contractors, on-call workers, temporary workers, and contract company workers. The Bureau of Labor Statistics estimates that alternative work arrangements make up 11 percent of total employment.[71] There are 10.3 million independent contractors, 2.5 million on-call workers, 1.2 million temporary help agency workers, and approximately 813,000 workers employed by contract firms. Since 2001 the proportion of total employed workers who were independent contractors has increased approximately 6 percent but the proportion is similar for the other alternative arrangements. Contingent workers, or workers who do not expect their jobs to last or who believe their jobs are temporary, account for approximately 2 to 4 percent of total employment.

Alternative Work Arrangements
Independent contractors, on-call workers, temporary workers, and contract company workers who are not employed full-time by the company.

More workers in alternative employment relationships are choosing these arrangements. Alternative work arrangements can benefit both individuals and employers. More and more individuals don't want to be attached to any one company. They want the flexibility to work when and where they choose. They may want to work fewer hours to effectively balance work and family responsibilities. Also, individuals who have been downsized may choose alternative work arrangements while they are seeking full-time employment. From the company perspective, it is easier to add temporary employees when they are needed and easier to terminate their employment when they are not needed. Part-time workers can be a valuable source of skills that current employees may not have and are needed for a specific project that has a set completion date. Nike uses 3,700 temporary employees each year as part of its global workforce of 28,000.[72] The temporary employees help Nike deal with cyclical labor needs during the business cycle and ongoing needs for specialized talent to meet strategic initiatives such as new-product development or retail store concepts. Companies like BMW are using contingent workers to help staff new production lines and also to take over old production lines while permanent employees train for and move to a new production process. Employees who may elect alternative work arrangements include those with a wide range and level of skills such as teachers, engineers, managers, administrative assistants, nurses, and bank tellers.

Demanding Work, but with More Flexibility. The globalization of the world economy and the development of e-commerce have made the notion of a 40-hour work week obsolete. As a result, companies need to be staffed 24 hours a day, seven days a week. Employees in manufacturing environments and service call centers are being asked to move from 8- to 12-hour days or to work afternoon or midnight shifts. Similarly, professional employees face long hours and and work demands that spill over into their personal lives. Personal digital assistants (PDAs), pagers, and cell phones bombard employees with information and work demands. In the car, on vacation, on planes, and even in the bathroom, employees can be interrupted by work demands. More demanding work results in greater employee stress, less satisfied employees, loss of productivity, and higher turnover—all of which are costly for companies.

Many companies are taking steps to provide more flexible work schedules, protect employees' free time, and more productively use employees' work time. Employees consider flexible schedules a valuable way to ease the pressures and conflicts of trying to balance work and nonwork activities. Employers are using flexible schedules to recruit and retain employees and to increase satisfaction and productivity.

Best Buy, the largest consumer electronics outlet in the United States, created a radical new workplace in response to concerns of headquarters' employees that their managers lacked trust that they would do their work without close supervision and that employee evaluations were being influenced by whether they looked busy and filled up their schedule with meetings that created the appearance of work.[73] The Results-Only Work Environment (ROWE) allows employees to decide how, when, and where they get the job done. Whether they choose to work in the office or somewhere else, salaried employees are required to put in as much time as it takes to do the work. The goal of the experiment is to reshape the workplace, achieve a greater degree of work/life balance, and redefine the nature of work. Physical attendance at meetings is optional. The only requirement is that employees meet productivity goals. When employee relations manager Steve Hance participates in a morning teleconference with co-workers or corporate clients he may be calling in using a cell phone from his fishing boat on a lake or from the woods where he hunts wild turkeys. He says, "No one at Best Buy really knows where I am. Nor do they really care." Surveys of employees who work in divisions that have converted to ROWE suggest they have improved relationships with family and friends and are more engaged at work. They feel more focused and energized about their work and are more committed to the company. The ROWE and its implications for employee retention are discussed in Chapter 10.

Dow Corning has a no-meetings week once a quarter which allows employees to reduce travel and work without interruptions.[74] The no-meeting weeks allow employees such as Laura Asiala, a global manager, a break from her normal workday, which starts as early as 5 AM and lasts as late as midnight. The no-meetings weeks give her the opportunity to spend evenings with her two sons, free from overseas calls. IBM has "ThinkFridays," free time on Friday afternoons, which IBM programmers spread across three continents can use to research new technologies or work on papers or patents, free from phone calls, e-mails, and instant messaging.

Meeting the Needs of Stakeholders, Shareholders, Customers, Employees, and Community

As we mentioned earlier, company effectiveness and competitiveness are determined by whether the company satisfies the needs of stakeholders. Stakeholders include stockholders (who want a return on their investment), customers (who want a high-quality product or service), and employees (who desire interesting work and reasonable compensation for their services). The community, which wants the company to contribute to activities and projects and minimize pollution of the environment, is also an important stakeholder.

Measuring Performance to Stakeholders: The Balanced Scorecard. The **balanced scorecard** gives managers an indication of the performance of a company based on the degree to which stakeholder needs are satisfied; it depicts the company from the perspective of internal and external customers, employees, and shareholders.[75] The balanced scorecard is important because it brings together most of the features that a company needs to focus on to be competitive. These include being customer-focused, improving quality, emphasizing teamwork, reducing new product and service development times, and managing for the long term.

The balanced scorecard differs from traditional measures of company performance by emphasizing that the critical indicators chosen are based on the company's business strategy and competitive demands. Companies need to customize their balanced scorecards based on different market situations, products, and competitive environments.

The balanced scorecard can be useful in managing human resources. Communicating the scorecard to employees gives them a framework that helps them see the goals and strategies of the company, how these goals and strategies are measured, and how they influence the critical indicators. For example, J.P. Morgan Chase used the balanced scorecard to change the behavior of customer service representatives.[76] Before the company implemented the scorecard, if a customer requested a change in a banking service, the representative would have simply met the customer's need. Based on knowledge of the scorecard, the customer service representative might now ask if the customer is interested in the bank's other services such as financial planning, mortgages, loans, or insurance.

The balanced scorecard should be used to (1) link human resource management activities to the company's business strategy and (2) evaluate the extent to which the HRM function is helping the company meet its strategic objectives. Measures of HRM practices primarily relate to productivity, people, and process.[77] Productivity measures involve determining output per employee (such as revenue per employee). Measuring people includes assessing employees' behavior, attitudes, or knowledge. Process measures focus on assessing employees' satisfaction with people systems within the company. People systems can include the performance management system, the compensation and benefits system, and the development system. To show that HRM activities contribute to a company's competitive advantage, managers need to consider the questions shown in Table 1.9 and be able to identify critical indicators or metrics related to human resources. As shown in the last column of Table 1.9, critical indicators of HR practices primarily relate to people, productivity, and processes.

For example, at Tellabs, a company that provides communication service products (such as optical networking) around the world, key results tracked on the balanced scorecard include revenue growth, customer satisfaction, time to market for new products, and employee satisfaction.[78] Every employee has a bonus plan; bonuses are tied to performance as measured by the scorecard. The performance appraisal process measures employee performance according to departmental objectives that support the scorecard. At quarterly meetings, how employee performance is evaluated according to the scorecard is shared with every employee, and the information is also available on the company intranet Web site.

Balanced Scorecard
A means of performance measurement that gives managers a chance to look at their company from the perspectives of internal and external customers, employees, and shareholders.

LO3
Discuss how human resource management affects a company's balanced scorecard.

table 1.9

The Balanced Scorecard

PERSPECTIVE	QUESTIONS ANSWERED	EXAMPLES OF CRITICAL BUSINESS INDICATORS	EXAMPLES OF CRITICAL HR INDICATORS
Customer	How do customers see us?	Time, quality, performance, service, cost	Employee satisfaction with HR department services Employee perceptions of the company as an employer
Internal	What must we excel at?	Processes that influence customer satisfaction, availability of information on service and/or manufacturing processes	Training costs per employee, turnover rates, time to fill open positions
Innovation and learning	Can we continue to improve and create value?	Improve operating efficiency, launch new products, continuous improvement, empowering of workforce, employee satisfaction	Employee/skills competency levels, engagement survey results, change management capability
Financial	How do we look to shareholders?	Profitability, growth, shareholder value	Compensation and benefits per employee, turnover costs, profits per employee, revenues per employee

SOURCE: Based on B. Becker, M. Huselid, and D. Ulrich, *The HR Scorecard: Linking People, Strategy, and Performance* (Boston: Harvard Business School Press, 2001).

Social Responsibility. Increasingly, companies are recognizing that social responsibility can help boost a company's image with customers, gain access to new markets, and help attract and retain talented employees. Companies thus try to meet shareholder and general public demands that they be more socially, ethically, and environmentally responsible. For example, Bill Gates, former chief executive officer and Microsoft Corporation founder, through personal involvement in a charitable foundation dedicated to bringing science and technology to improve lives around the world, has improved Microsoft's corporate reputation. Whole Foods has been praised as environmentally and socially responsible for its focus on high-quality organic products.[79] Other companies such as Halliburton and BP are viewed less positively due to perceptions that they are responsible for environmental damage or are using political connections to profit from the Iraq war.

Cell phone manufacturers such as Nokia, Motorola, and Palm are introducing phones that have fewer toxic materials and are easily recyclable. This helps these companies improve their image in the marketplace and helps them get better access to global markets in which new rules and laws restrict the amount of toxic substances (such as lead and mercury) in electronics.[80] Virgin Group's Chairman Richard Branson has pledged to use $3 billion of Virgin's profit in fighting climate change.

Danone, a company that makes yogurts (Dannon) and mineral waters (Evian), recently invested in a factory in Bangladesh to make a yogurt fortified to help stop malnutrition and priced at seven cents to be affordable.[81] This investment gives Danone access to a large market for its products, demonstrates the company is socially responsible, and at the same time helps alleviate local malnutrition as well as creating jobs.

COMPETING THROUGH SUSTAINABILITY
Volunteerism and Going Green Are Reaping Dividends for Employees, Communities, and the Environment

A growing number of companies have made sustainability an important part of their business strategy. For example, at General Mills, volunteerism is one of the ways that the company lives its corporate values. The CEO and senior leaders serve on nonprofit boards and are involved in the community. Five years ago, following General Mills' acquisition of Pillsbury, company leaders in the Meals Division brought the newly merged team of employees to volunteer for the Perspectives Family Center, which helps families in transition. This resulted from the suggestion that volunteerism could be used to strengthen the new work teams. Meals Division employees support projects such as painting child care center rooms, participating in school supply drives, and delivering Christmas trees. The employees' involvement was initiated from a business need, but now volunteerism is part of the business. General Mills' customer service center works with Catholic Charities USA, serving meals to homeless people and working at a shelter for homeless children—teaching them how to maintain a healthy diet, leading fitness activities, and helping with projects such as redecorating rooms in the shelter. Yoplait employees, partners with the Greater Minneapolis Crisis Nursery, help cook meals. Besides helping the community, Steve Sanger,

General Mills' company chairman, believes that employees are developing leadership and other skills.

Pharmaceutical company Novartis supports REPSSI, an African-based philanthropic organization that provides emotional and psychological support to children affected by the HIV/AIDS epidemic. The company's trainers provide REPSSI's employees with leadership development training. The charity wants to grow from serving 500,000 children to helping 5 million children by 2011. However, to meet this service goal, REPSSI managers need training in communication skills, providing feedback, intercultural skills, and project management. Novartis transformed its corporate training programs into a form useful for REPSSI. The training content is delivered through instructor-led courses and e-learning. Novartis and training vendor partners, including business schools, send speakers at their own expense to Africa. Instructors are also available for follow-up after each course is completed.

Wal-Mart, frequently criticized because of its labor practices, has been very active in sustainability initiatives. Wal-Mart's environmental goals are simple and straightforward: to be supplied 100 percent by renewable energy, to create zero waste, and to sell products that sustain our natural

resources and the environment. The Personal Sustainability Project (PSP) is a voluntary program that is focused on helping associates integrate sustainability into their own lives by making small changes to everyday habits. The goals relate to improving employees' own health and wellness as well as the health of the planet. According to figures posted on the company's Web site, employees have recycled 675,538 pounds of aluminum, 282,476 pounds of glass, 5,953,357 pounds of paper and cardboard, and 3,177,851 pounds of plastic. Also, employees walked, biked, and swam more than 1,109,421 total miles; cooked 368,779 healthy meals; and lost a total combined weight of 184,315 pounds. More than 19,000 employee report they've quit or reduced smoking. Beyond supporting associates in their efforts to integrate sustainability into their own lives, the program encourages them to work in teams to undertake projects in their communities. For instance, one store developed a used-tire recycling program; another helped their local community to clean up a wildlife area.

SOURCES: Based on M. Weinstein, "Charity Begins @ Work," *Training*, May 2008, pp. 56–58; M. Laff, "Triple Bottom Line," *T + D*, February 2009, pp. 34–39; www.walmartstores.com Web site for Wal-mart stores, Sustainability Progress Update, March 4, 2009.

HR professionals play an important role in developing sustainable business practices and programs at Vodaphone and Xcel Energy.[82] For example, at Vodaphone, a telecommunications company, HR helped design a travel reduction program requiring every employee to justify why meetings cannot be replaced with teleconferencing. As a result, each year more than 13,000 flights have been eliminated, resulting in a 5,500-ton reduction in carbon. At Xcel Energy, 33 percent of senior executives' incentive compensation is linked to environmental goals such as reducing emissions, improving energy efficiency, and developing innovative technologies. Xcel also offers its employees and customers a wind source program in Colorado, Minnesota, and New Mexico. HR professionals provide employees with training on environmental stewardship, including ways to be more energy efficient.

The "Competing through Sustainability" box highlights the sustainable business practices of several companies.

Customer Service and Quality Emphasis

Companies' customers judge quality and performance. As a result, customer excellence requires attention to product and service features as well as to interactions with customers. Customer-driven excellence includes understanding what the customer wants and anticipating future needs. Customer-driven excellence includes reducing defects and errors, meeting specifications, and reducing complaints. How the company recovers from defects and errors is also important for retaining and attracting customers.

Due to increased availability of knowledge and competition, consumers are very knowledgeable and expect excellent service. This presents a challenge for employees who interact with customers. The way in which clerks, sales staff, front-desk personnel, and service providers interact with customers influences a company's reputation and financial performance. Employees need product knowledge and service skills, and they need to be clear about the types of decisions they can make when dealing with customers.

To compete in today's economy, whether on a local or global level, companies need to provide a quality product or service. If companies do not adhere to quality standards, their ability to sell their product or service to vendors, suppliers, or customers will be restricted. Some countries even have quality standards that companies must meet to conduct business there. **Total quality management (TQM)** is a companywide effort to continuously improve the ways people, machines, and systems accomplish work.[83] Core values of TQM include the following:[84]

Total Quality Management (TQM)
A cooperative form of doing business that relies on the talents and capabilities of both labor and management to continually improve quality and productivity.

- Methods and processes are designed to meet the needs of internal and external customers.
- Every employee in the company receives training in quality.
- Quality is designed into a product or service so that errors are prevented from occurring rather than being detected and corrected.
- The company promotes cooperation with vendors, suppliers, and customers to improve quality and hold down costs.
- Managers measure progress with feedback based on data.

There is no universal definition of quality. The major differences in its various definitions relate to whether customer, product, or manufacturing process is emphasized. For example, quality expert W. Edwards Deming emphasized how well a product or service meets customer needs. Phillip Crosby's approach emphasizes how well the service or manufacturing process meets engineering standards.

The emphasis on quality is seen in the establishment of the **Malcolm Baldrige National Quality Award** and the **ISO 9000:2000** quality standards. The Baldrige award, created by public law, is the highest level of national recognition for quality that a U.S. company can receive. To become eligible for the Baldrige, a company must complete a detailed application that consists of basic information about the firm as well as an in-depth presentation of how it addresses specific criteria related to quality improvement. The categories and point values for the Baldrige award are found in Table 1.10. The award is not given for specific products or services. Three awards may be given annually in each of these categories: manufacturing, service, small business, education, and health care. All applicants for the Baldrige Award undergo a rigorous examination process that takes from 300 to 1,000 hours. Applications are reviewed by an independent board of about 400 examiners who come primarily from the private sector. One of the major benefits of applying for the Baldrige Award is the feedback report from the examining team noting the company's strengths and areas for improvement.[85]

The Baldrige award winners usually excel at human resources practices, including training and development. For example, consider two of the 2007 Baldrige award winners.[86] Sharp HealthCare is San Diego County's largest health care system, serving more than 785,000 people each year. Sharp is a not-for-profit organization that employs 14,000 staff members and 2,600 affiliated physicians; operates seven hospitals,

Malcolm Baldrige National Quality Award
An award established in 1987 to promote quality awareness, to recognize quality achievements of U.S. companies, and to publicize successful quality strategies.

ISO 9000:2000
Quality standards adopted worldwide.

table 1.10
Categories and Point Values for the Malcolm Baldrige National Quality Award Examination

Leadership The way senior executives create and sustain corporate citizenship, customer focus, clear values, and expectations and promote quality and performance excellence	120
Measurement, Analysis, and Knowledge Management The way the company selects, gathers, analyzes, manages, and improves its data, information, and knowledge assets	90
Strategic Planning The way the company sets strategic direction, how it determines plan requirements, and how plan requirements relate to performance management	85
Workforce Focus Company's efforts to develop and utilize the workforce and to maintain an environment conducive to full participation, continuous improvement, and personal and organizational growth	85
Process Management Process design and control, including customer-focused design, product and service delivery, support services, and supply management	85
Business Results Company's performance and improvement in key business areas (product, service, and supply quality; productivity; and operational effectiveness and related financial indicators)	450
Customer and Market Focus Company's knowledge of the customer, customer service systems, responsiveness to customer, customer satisfaction	85
Total Points	1,000

SOURCE: Based on 2008 Baldrige National Quality Program Criteria for Performance Excellence from the Web site for the National Institute of Standards and Technology, www.quality.nist.gov.

three medical groups, and 19 oupatient clinics; and manages its own health insurance plan. Sharp HealthCare meets and exceeds patients expectations by providing high-quality care and services that are accessible, convenient, and cost-effective. Sharp has made considerable investment in its employees—including use of yearly employee surveys to gauge the satisfaction and engagement of the workforce, action teams, performance improvement teams—and lean/Six Sigma teams encourage employee participation in creating change and increasing organizational effectiveness. Sharp's training expenditures per employee exceed those of the best-in-class companies (as identified by the American Society for Training and Development). Sharp University offers training programs for developing current and future leaders. It provides each employee with a $1,000 fund to take advantage of educational opportunities offered outside the organization. PRO-TEC Coating Company, located in rural Leipsic, Ohio, is an industry leader in developing high-strength steel that inhibits corrosion. High-strength steel is used mainly in manufacturing cars, trucks, and sport utility vehicles. From 2002–2006, the company produced an estimated 85 percent of the high-strength steel supply in the United States. PRO-TEC's 236 employees work in self-directed teams and are empowered to use continuous improvement processes to fix problems as they occur. All employees participate in a profit-sharing plan that provides an average annual payout of 15 percent of employees base pay. Surveys, meetings, and management "walkarounds" are some of the methods used to obtain employees feedback. PRO-TEC is committed to lifelong learning for its employees. Employees are given time off to attend classes and reimbursed for tuition and costs of books.

The ISO 9000:2000 standards were developed by the International Organization for Standardization (ISO) in Geneva, Switzerland.[87] ISO 9000 is the name of a family of standards (ISO 9000, 9001, 9004, and 10011) that include requirements for dealing with issues such as how to establish quality standards and document work processes to help companies understand quality system requirements. ISO 9000:2000 has been adopted as a quality standard in nearly 100 countries, including Austria, Switzerland, Norway, Australia, and Japan. The ISO 9000:2000 standards apply to companies in many different industries—for example, manufacturing, processing, servicing, printing, forestry, electronics, steel, computing, legal services, and financial services. ISO 9001 is the most comprehensive standard because it covers product or service design and development, manufacturing, installation, and customer service. It includes the actual specification for a quality management system. ISO 9004 provides a guide for companies that want to improve.

Why are standards useful? Customers may want to check that the product they ordered from a supplier meets the purpose for which it is required. One of the most efficient ways to do this is when the specifications of the product have been defined in an International Standard. That way, both supplier and customer are on the same wavelength, even if they are based in different countries, because they are both using the same references. Today, many products require testing for conformance with specifications or compliance with safety or other regulations before they can be put on many markets. Even simpler products may require supporting technical documentation that includes test data. With so much trade taking place across borders, it may just not be practical for these activities to be carried out by suppliers and customers, but rather by specialized third parties. In addition, national legislation may require such testing to be carried out by independent bodies, particularly when the products concerned have health or environmental implications. One example of an

ISO standard is on the back cover of this book and nearly every other book. On the back cover is something called an ISBN number. ISBN stands for International Standard Book Number. Publishers and booksellers are very familiar with ISBN numbers, because they are the method through which books are ordered and bought. Try buying a book on the Internet, and you will soon learn the value of the ISBN number—there is a unique number for the book you want! And it is based on an ISO standard.

In addition to competing for quality awards and seeking ISO certification, many companies are using the Six Sigma process and lean thinking. The **Six Sigma process** refers to a process of measuring, analyzing, improving, and then controlling processes once they have been brought within the narrow Six Sigma quality tolerances or standards. The objective of Six Sigma is to create a total business focus on serving the customer, that is, to deliver what customers really want when they want it. For example, at General Electric introducing the Six Sigma quality initiative meant going from approximately 35,000 defects per million operations—which is average for most companies, including GE—to fewer than 4 defects per million in every element of every process GE businesses perform—from manufacturing a locomotive part to servicing a credit card account to processing a mortgage application to answering a phone.[88] Training is an important component of the process. Six Sigma involves highly trained employees known as Champions, Master Black Belts, Black Belts, and Green Belts who lead and teach teams that are focusing on an ever-growing number of quality projects. The quality projects focus on improving efficiency and reducing errors in products and services. Today GE has over 100,000 employees trained in Six Sigma. Employees are working on more than 6,000 quality projects. Since 1996, when the Six Sigma quality initiative was started, it has produced more than $2 billion in benefits for GE. Training can help companies meet the quality challenge by teaching employees statistical process control and engaging in "lean" processes. Cardinal Fastener & Speciality Company, a Cleveland, Ohio, company, needed to shorten the lead time it required on orders or face losing business to global competition.[89] The company manufactures bolts used in construction, heavy equipment, wind turbine, and other industries. To help improve its competitiveness, Cardinal Fastener engaged in lean thinking, an approach to eliminate "waste." **Lean thinking** is a way to do more with less effort, time, equipment, and space, but still provide customers with what they need and want. Part of lean thinking includes training workers in new skills or how to apply old skills in new ways so they can quickly take over new responsibilities or use new skills to help fill customer orders. As a result of lean thinking, machines were moved so that operators could make a bolt or fastener complete from start to finish, resulting in a decrease in the time it takes to make a finished product. Quality is near perfect, and inventory has been reduced 54 percent.

In addition to developing products or providing services that meet customer needs, one of the most important ways to improve customer satisfaction is to improve the quality of employees' work experiences. Research shows that satisfied employees are more likely to provide high-quality customer service. Customers who receive high-quality service are more likely to be repeat customers. As Table 1.11 shows, companies that are recognized as providing elite customer service emphasize state-of-the-art human resource practices including rigorous employee selection, employee loyalty, training, and keeping employees satisfied by offering generous benefits.

Six Sigma Process
System of measuring, analyzing, improving, and controlling processes once they meet quality standards.

Lean Thinking
A process used to determine how to use less effort, time, equipment, and space but still meet customers' requirements.

table 1.11

Examples of HR Practices That Enhance Customer Service

Wegmans
Gives away $59 million in scholarships to 19,000 employees. Senior managers sit side-by-side with employees listening in on phones in the company's call center.

Ritz Carlton
Despite having 20 service standards, front-line employees have flexibility to make customers' experiences more personal, unusual, and memorable.

Four Seasons Hotels
No employee gets a job before passing four interviews. Each employee receives a free nights' stay for himself or herself and a guest, along with free dinner at employee orientation. The free stay helps employees, most of whom otherwise could not afford to stay at the hotel, understand what being a customer feels like. They grade the hotel services such as time for room service to arrive and number of times a phone rings when calling the front desk.

Cadillac
Performance of repair technicians is carefully monitored to ensure they are not repeating mistakes in repairs. Dealers who maintain good customer service ratings based on customer surveys receive cash rewards.

Starbucks
Entry-level baristas get 24 hours of training that prepares them to stay calm and courteous in busy times.

Publix Super Markets
Employees receive bonuses based on their unit's performance and share grants as part of their incentive plans.

Cabela
Job candidates must pass a difficult 150-question test that measures their outdoor sports expertise.

SOURCE: Based on J. McGregor, "Customer Service Champs," *BusinessWeek*, March 5, 2007, pp. 52–64.

Changing Demographics and Diversity of the Workforce

Company performance on the balanced scorecard is influenced by the characteristics of its labor force. The labor force of current employees is often referred to as the **internal labor force.** Employers identify and select new employees from the external labor market through recruiting and selection. The **external labor market** includes persons actively seeking employment. As a result, the skills and motivation of a company's internal labor force are influenced by the composition of the available labor market (the external labor market). The skills and motivation of a company's internal labor force determine the need for training and development practices and the effectiveness of the company's compensation and reward systems.

Three important changes in the demographics and diversity of the workforce are projected. First, the average age of the workforce will increase. Second, the workforce will become more diverse in terms of gender and racial composition, and immigration will continue to affect the size and diversity of the workforce.

Aging of the Workforce. The labor force will continue to age, and the size of the 16–24 youth labor force will decrease to its lowest level in 30 years. Figure 1.5 compares the projected distribution of the age of the workforce in 2006 and 2016. The 55 years and older workforce is expected to grow by approximately 47 percent between 2006 and 2016, more than five times the 8.5 percent growth projected for the entire workforce.[90] The labor force participation of those 55 years and older is expected to

Internal Labor Force
Labor force of current employees.

External Labor Market
Persons outside the firm who are actively seeking employment.

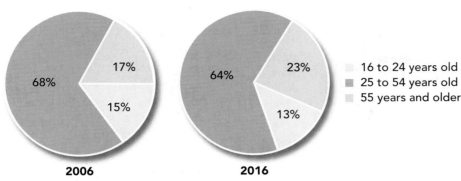

figure 1.5

Comparison of the
Age Distribution of
the 2006 and 2016
Labor Force

SOURCE: Based on M. Toossi, "Labor Force Projections to 2016: More Workers in Their Golden Years," *Monthly Labor Review*, November 2007, pp. 33–51.

grow because older individuals are leading healthier and longer lives than in the past, providing the opportunity to work more years; the high cost of health insurance and decrease in health benefits causes many employees to keep working to keep their employer-based insurance or to return to work after retirement to obtain health insurance through their employer; and the trend toward pension plans based on individuals' contributions to them rather than years of service provides an incentive for older employees to continue working. The aging labor force means companies are likely to employ a growing share of older workers—many in their second or third career. Older people want to work and many say they plan a working retirement. Despite myths to the contrary, worker performance and learning are not adversely affected by aging.[91] Older employees are willing and able to learn new technology. An emerging trend is for qualified older workers to ask to work part-time or for only a few months at a time as a means to transition to retirement. Employees and companies are redefining the meaning of retirement to include second careers as well as part-time and temporary work assignments. An aging workforce means that employers will increasingly face HRM issues such as career plateauing, retirement planning, and retraining older workers to avoid skill obsolescence. Companies will struggle with how to control the rising costs of benefits and health care. Companies face competing challenges with older workers. Companies will have to ensure that older workers are not discriminated against in hiring, training, and workforce reduction decisions. At the same time companies will want to encourage retirement and make it financially and psychologically acceptable.

Consider how Borders Group, the bookstore, is capitalizing on older workers through hiring and retention.[92] Because 50 percent of book purchases in the United States are made by customers over 45, Borders believes that older workers can relate better to its customers. To attract and retain older workers, Borders added medical and dental benefits for part-time workers. The company is planning to add a "passport" program, enabling employees to work half-time in one part of the country and half-time at a different store in another part of the country. This accommodates the needs of older employees who may live in warmer climates such as Florida during winter months but in other areas the rest of the year. Some 16 percent of Borders' employees are over the age of 50, better than 75 percent more than when the program started. Borders' investment is having a positive impact on retention. The turnover rate for workers over 50 is 10 times less than for those under 30 years old, and turnover has dropped 30 percent since the start of the program.

figure 1.6

The U.S. Workforce, 2016

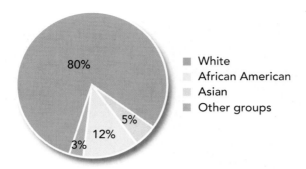

SOURCE: Based on M. Toossi, "Labor Force Projections to 2016: More Workers in Their Golden Years," *Monthly Labor Review*, November 2007, pp. 33–52.

As many older workers leave the workforce permanently or decide to work part-time, another challenge companies face is how to capture their unique knowledge and expertise so it can be used and shared with remaining employees. To ensure that the expertise of retiring engineers isn't lost, NASA is using phone interviews to capture their experiences.[93] The engineers have been designated as NASA Discipline Experts because each has been identified by NASA as an expert in a specific field of study such as propulsion or shuttle life support. The experiences captured on audiotape are turned into courses held at universities that offer graduate programs in aeronautics such as the University of Maryland. A similar approach is used at the federal Department of Housing and Urban Development, where many employees are now retirement-eligible.[94] Subject matter experts are identified and trained to conduct workshops or make presentations. The agency uses its own studios to videotape the presentations and broadcast the information to Housing and Urban Development sites across the United States. The video is made available on the company's internal Web site. When interviewers are used to "capture knowledge," it is important that they know what questions to ask and how to get the employee to talk about the knowledge. Many experienced employees may not recognize what is special about their personal knowledge and, as a result, have a difficult time speaking about it.

Increased Diversity of Workforce. As Figure 1.6 shows, by 2016 the workforce is expected to be 80 percent white, 12 percent African America, 5 percent Asian, and 3 percent other groups, which includes individuals of multiple racial origin, American Indian, Alaskan Native or Native Hawaiian, and other Pacific Islanders.[95] The diversity of the workforce is expected to increase from 2006 to 2016. African Americans, Hispanics, and Asians are projected to increase in the labor force at higher rates than white non-Hispanics. Asians are expected to be one of the fastest growing groups, with a 2.7 percent growth rate between 2006 and 2016. Due to immigration, Asians and Hispanics have been the fastest growing groups in the labor force since 1986, and this is expected to continue through 2016.

Influence of Immigration. Many U.S. industries, including meatpacking, construction, farming, and service, rely on immigrants from Mexico and other countries to perform short-term or labor-intensive jobs. Although determining exactly the number of illegal workers in the United States is difficult, estimates are that of the hotel industry's 1.5 million employees, 150,000 are illegal immigrants, in the roofing industry one in three workers are thought to be illegal immigrants, and one-third of restaurant workers are Hispanic. While the U.S. government is debating how to deal with illegal immigration, many companies would face a labor crisis if they were forced to terminate employment of illegal immigrants, many of whom have lived and worked in the United States for years but lack the work authorizations and visas needed to work legally in this country. For example, one landscape company owner employs 60 people, including 40 immigrants. Without their labor, he would be out of business.[96] Even if employers do check immigrants' documentation, they have no way of knowing if the documents are real and may not even have a legal obligation to validate work documents. For example, in the California agriculture industry, farmers are required to check only that workers have the necessary papers and then forward the information to the government before putting a worker on the job.[97]

Many employers argue that most of the immigrants are hard-working and loyal and deserve to be granted legal status and citizenship. Others argue that illegal immigrants should be jailed or immediately extradited to their home country. While the national debate over this issue continues it is important to note that many midsized to small companies in the hotel, building cleaning, roofing, poultry, and construction industries could face a severe labor shortage crippling their businesses if immigration reform requires illegal immigrants to quit their jobs or return to their home countries before applying for work permits.[98] U.S. immigration and customs officials are increasing efforts to stop illegal immigration. Three top executives of a national cleaning service were arrested for allegedly employing illegal immigrants as well as nearly 200 employees believed to be illegal immigrants.[99]

Besides women and minorities another source of diversity in the workforce is disabled workers. Disabled workers can also be a source of competitive advantage. Wiscraft Inc., a Milwaukee company, contracts with companies such as Briggs & Stratton Corporation and Harley-Davidson to do assembly, packaging, and machining work.[100] At least 75 percent of Wiscraft's employees are legally blind. But the company is not a charity. It competes with other companies for contracts. It receives no subsidies from local, state, or federal governments. Employees have to rely on public transportation or friends or relatives to get to work. Kathy Walters said she could have worked at another company but chose Wiscraft because of its supportive culture. Walters, who is legally blind, believes she would have had trouble finding a job that offered health benefits and paid as well as her job at Wiscraft. The company has received ISO 9001:2000 certification, evidence that it provides high-quality work and can compete internationally.

The heterogeneous composition of the workforce challenges companies to create HRM practices that ensure that the talents, skills, and values of all employees are fully utilized to help deliver high-quality products and services.

Because the workforce is predicted to become more diverse in terms of age, ethnicity, and racial background, it is unlikely that one set of values will characterize all employees. For example, the "Silent Generation," born between 1925 and 1945, tend to be uncomfortable challenging the status quo and authority. They value income and employment security. "Baby boomers," born between 1946 and 1964, value unexpected rewards for work accomplishments, opportunities to learn new things, praise, recognition, and time with the manager. "Millennials," born between 1978 and 1999, love the latest technology, are ambitious and goal-oriented, and seek meaningful work. They want to be noticed, respected, and involved. Millennials work to live while boomers live to work. Companies are being proactive to help employees and managers understand generational differences. A survey conducted at Ernst & Young LLC found that Generation Y employees (born after 1980) want and ask for more frequent and candid feedback than baby boomers (born between 1946 and 1964).[101] As a result, Ernst and Young developed an online "Feedback Zone" where employees can provide or ask for feedback at any time. Also, the company assigns every employee a mentor and offers training for managers on how to give effective feedback. To make sure employees understand generational differences and how to connect and communicate with employees from different generations, Aflac, the insurance provider, offers a training program called "Connecting Generations."[102] Aflac believes that employees in all age groups will be more effective if they understand how members of each generation approach their jobs. The program reviews the characteristics of each generation represented in the workplace. It also describes the effects of family and world events on each generation, analyzes their work styles and employment characteristics, and helps show connections to bridge generation gaps.

Most employees, however, value several aspects of work regardless of their background. Employees view work as a means to self-fulfillment—that is, a means to more fully use their skills and abilities, meet their interests, and allow them to live a desirable life-style.[103] One report indicated that employees who are given opportunities to fully use and develop their skills receive greater job responsibilities, believe the promotion system is fair, and have a trustworthy manager who represents the employees' best interests are more committed to their companies.[104] Fostering these values requires companies to develop HRM practices that provide more opportunity for individual contribution and entrepreneurship.[105] Because many employees place more value on the quality of nonwork activities and family life than on pay and production, employees will demand more flexible work policies that allow them to choose work hours and locations where work is performed.

The implications of the changing labor market for managing human resources are far-reaching. Because labor market growth will be primarily in female and minority populations, U.S. companies will have to ensure that employees and human resource management systems are free of bias to capitalize on the perspectives and values that women and minorities can contribute to improving product quality, customer service, product development, and market share. Managing cultural diversity involves many different activities, including creating an organizational culture that values diversity, ensuring that HRM systems are bias-free, facilitating higher career involvement of women, promoting knowledge and acceptance of cultural differences, ensuring involvement in education both within and outside the company, and dealing with employees' resistance to diversity.[106] Table 1.12 presents ways that managing cultural diversity can provide a competitive advantage. Traditionally, in many U.S. companies the costs of poorly managing cultural diversity were viewed mainly as increased legal fees associated with discrimination cases. However, as Table 1.12 illustrates, the implications of successfully managing a diverse workforce go beyond legal concerns. How diversity issues are managed has implications for creativity, problem solving, retaining good employees, and developing markets for the firm's products and services. To successfully manage a diverse workforce, managers must develop a new set of skills, including:

1. Communicating effectively with employees from a wide variety of cultural backgrounds.
2. Coaching and developing employees of different ages, educational backgrounds, ethnicity, physical ability, and race.
3. Providing performance feedback that is based on objective outcomes rather than values and stereotypes that work against women, minorities, and handicapped persons by prejudging these persons' abilities and talents.

4. Creating a work environment that makes it comfortable for employees of all backgrounds to be creative and innovative.
5. Recognizing and responding to generational issues.[107]

Diversity is important for tapping all employees' creative, cultural, and communication skills and using those skills to provide competitive advantage as shown in Table 1.12. For example, the Latino Employee Network at Frito-Lay played a key role during the development of Doritos Guacamole Flavored Tortilla Chips.[108] The chips generated more than $500 million in sales during their first year, making this one of the most successful product launches in the company's history. Network members provided feedback on the taste and packaging to ensure that the product would be seen as authentic in the Latino community. Texas Instruments (TI) was interested in hiring a talented engineer but she was reluctant to accept employment because she feared the Dallas location would not welcome an Indian woman.[109] Representatives of TI's Indian Diversity Initiative spoke with her and shared their experiences. The Indian-American employee network was key in making her decision to join the company.

The retail grocer Safeway's market share is being challenged by specialty grocers and big-box stores such as Wal-Mart and Target.[110] To beat the competition Safeway

		table 1.12
1. Cost argument	As organizations become more diverse, the cost of a poor job in integrating workers will increase. Those who handle this well will thus create cost advantages over those who don't.	How Managing Cultural Diversity Can Provide Competitive Advantage
2. Employee attraction and retention argument	Companies develop reputations on favorability as prospective employers for women and ethnic minorities. Those with the best reputations for managing diversity will win the competition for the best personnel. As the labor pool shrinks and changes composition, this edge will become increasingly important.	
3. Marketing argument	For multinational organizations, the insight and cultural sensitivity that members with roots in other countries bring to the marketing effort should improve these efforts in important ways. The same rationale applies to marketing to subpopulations within domestic operations.	
4. Creativity argument	Diversity of perspectives and less emphasis on conformity to norms of the past (which characterize the modern approach to management of diversity) should improve the level of creativity.	
5. Problem-solving argument	Heterogeneity in decisions and problem-solving groups potentially produces better decisions through a wider range of perspectives and more thorough critical analysis of issues.	
6. System flexibility argument	An implication of the multicultural model for managing diversity is that the system will become less determinate, less standardized, and therefore more fluid. The increased fluidity should create greater flexibility to react to environmental changes (i.e., reactions should be faster and cost less).	

SOURCES: *Academy of Management Executive*, by T. H. Cox and S. Blake. Copyright © 1991 by Academy of Management. Reproduced with permission of Academy of Management via Copyright Clearance Center; N. Lockwood, *Workplace Diversity: Leveraging the Power of Difference for Competitive Advantage* (Alexandria, VA: Society for Human Resource Management, 2005).

invested in programs to attract, develop, and retain its best talent and to position the company as an employer of choice. Because 70 percent of its customers are women, Safeway wanted to broaden the diversity of its workforce to better reflect its customers. Male leaders had been the norm in the retail grocery industry, but Safeway took initiatives to help women and women of color advance into management. The initiatives included the CEO speaking regularly with employees about diversity issues in live discussions and taped satellite broadcasts sent weekly to store managers. Employees have access to DVDs featuring interviews with successful employees who are women and people of color. The company ensures that all employees who qualify for its Retail Leadership Program (RLP), including women who work part-time and used flextime to coordinate work schedules with family responsibilities, have the same opportunities for coaching, development, and advancement as employees who work traditional hours. A women's leadership network sponsors development meetings between high-potential women and executives who suggest new job opportunities that can help them advance to the next level. Every Safeway manager is expected to mentor his or her own employees. The women's programs have been very successful. Since 2000, the number of women store managers has increased by 42 percent, including an increase of 31 percent of white women and 92 percent of women of color. The number of women who completed the RLP program increased by 37 percent. Safeway has won national recognition as a company that promotes the career advancement of women and minorities. Independent financial analysts have concluded that the advancement of women and minorities has increased the company's sales and earnings.

The bottom line is that to gain a competitive advantage, companies must harness the power of the diverse workforce. These practices are needed not only to meet employee needs but to reduce turnover costs and ensure that customers receive the best service possible. The implication of diversity for HRM practices will be highlighted throughout this book. For example, from a staffing perspective, it is important to ensure that tests used to select employees are not biased against minority groups. From a work design perspective, employees need flexible schedules that allow them to meet nonwork needs. From a training perspective, it is clear that all employees need to be made aware of the potential damaging effects of stereotypes. From a compensation perspective, new benefits such as elder care and day care need to be included in reward systems to accommodate the needs of a diverse workforce.

Legal and Ethical Issues

Five main areas of the legal environment have influenced human resource management over the past 25 years.[111] These areas are equal employment opportunity legislation, employee safety and health, employee pay and benefits, employee privacy, and job security. Attention is likely to continue to be paid to age, race, and religious discrimination, and discrimination against physically challenged employees.

There is also likely to be continued discussion about legislation to prohibit discrimination by employers and health insurers against employees based on their genetic makeup. Advances in medicine and genetics allow scientists to predict from DNA samples a person's likelihood of contracting certain diseases. To reduce health care costs, companies may want to use this information to screen out job candidates or reassign current employees who have a genetic predisposition to a disease that is triggered by exposure to certain working conditions. The Genetic Information Non-discrimination Act of 2008 is the first federal law prohibiting health insurers from denying coverage or charging higher premiums based on genetic information. It also prohibits companies from using genetic information to make hiring, firing, and other job placement decisions.

The number of court battles over company policies to reduce health care and other benefits costs is likely to increase. Many companies (such as IBM, Microsoft, and Harrah's Entertainment) are calculating the health care premiums that employees pay on the basis of their health and habits and participation in wellness programs (e.g., counseling, weight loss, smoking cessation, physical fitness). For example, Scott's Miracle-Gro has an antismoking policy designed to improve employee health and cut medical costs.[112] A two-week employee of Scott's Miracle-Grow who was fired when his drug test detected nicotine in his blood is suing the company, claiming that Scott's antismoking policy is discriminatory because the company fired him before he was eligible for health benefits and had the opportunity to take advantage of the company's wellness program.

Although women and minorities are advancing into top management ranks, "glass ceilings" are still keeping women and minorities from getting the experiences necessary to move to top management positions.[113] A survey showed that women held only 10 percent of all of the corporate officer positions in the *Fortune* top 50 companies.[114] We are likely to see more challenges to sex and race discrimination focusing on lack of access to training and development opportunities that are needed to be considered for top management positions.

An area of litigation that will continue to have a major influence on HRM practices involves job security. As companies are forced to close plants and lay off employees because of restructuring, technology changes, or financial crisis, cases dealing with the illegal discharge of employees have increased. The issue of what constitutes employment at will—that is, employment that can be terminated at any time without notice—will be debated. As the age of the workforce increases, the number of cases dealing with age discrimination in layoffs, promotions, and benefits will likely rise. Employers' work rules, recruitment practices, and performance evaluation systems will need to be revised to ensure that these systems do not falsely communicate employment agreements the company does not intend to honor (such as lifetime employment) or discriminate on the basis of age.

Recent court rulings in discrimination and privacy cases suggest that companies need to pay more attention to extant electronic records and voice mails, where they might be found, and what the information contained in the records is used for.[115] Courts are likely to react negatively to informal nonstandardized communications of performance evaluations, pay raises, and other decisions from managers to employees using e-mail and voice mails.

Many decisions related to managing human resources are characterized by uncertainty. Ethics can be considered the fundamental principles by which employees and companies interact.[116] These principles should be considered in making business decisions and interacting with clients and customers. As a result of corporate scandals at Enron, Arthur Andersen, Tyco International, and WorldCom Inc., current interests in ethics focus on transparency and honesty in accounting systems as well as criminal behavior.

Ethical, successful companies can be characterized by four principles.[117] First, in their relationships with customers, vendors, and clients, these companies emphasize mutual benefits. Second, employees assume responsibility for the actions of the company. Third, such companies have a sense of purpose or vision the employees value and use in their day-to-day work. Finally, they emphasize fairness; that is, another person's interests count as much as their own.

Sarbanes-Oxley Act of 2002
A congressional act passed in response to illegal and unethical behavior by managers and executives. The Act sets stricter rules for business especially accounting practices including requiring more open and consistent disclosure of financial data, CEOs' assurance that the data is completely accurate, and provisions that affect the employee–employer relationship (e.g., development of a code of conduct for senior financial officers).

Corporate scandals such as those at Enron and WorldCom have increased attention on preventing illegal and unethical behavior by managers and executives. The **Sarbanes-Oxley Act of 2002** sets strict rules for corporate behavior and sets heavy fines and prison terms for noncompliance: organizations are spending millions of dollars each year to comply with regulations under the Sarbanes-Oxley Act, which imposes criminal penalties for corporate governing and accounting lapses, including retaliation against whistle-blowers reporting violations of Security and Exchange Commission rules.[118] Due to Sarbanes-Oxley and new Security and Exchange Commission regulations that impose stricter standards for disclosing executive pay, corporate boards are paying more attention to executive pay as well as issues like leadership development and succession planning.[119] This has resulted in an increase in the number of HR executives and individuals with HR expertise who are being asked to serve on corporate boards to provide data and analysis. For example, a CEO or chief financial officer (CFO) who falsely represents company finances may be fined up to $1 million and/or imprisoned for up to 10 years. The penalty for willful violations is up to $5 million and/or 20 years imprisonment. The law requires CEOs and CFOs to certify corporate financial reports, prohibits personal loans to officers and directors, and prohibits insider trading during pension fund blackout periods.[120] A "blackout" is any period of more than three consecutive business days during which the company temporarily stops 50 percent or more of company plan participants or beneficiaries from acquiring, selling, or transferring an interest in any of the company's equity securities in the pension plan. The law also requires retention of all documents relevant to a government investigation.

The law also has a number of provisions that directly affect the employer–employee relationship.[121] For example, the act prohibits retaliation against whistle-blowers (individuals who have turned in the company or one of its officers for an illegal act) and government informants. To comply with the act, every employer will need to issue new policies. For example, the act requires all public companies to develop a code of ethics for senior financial officers. HR professionals will need to document the fact that employees have received these policies and have attended training to ensure their compliance with the act. Because of the potential liability for retaliation in the context of discrimination and harassment, policies should include assurances that an employee will not be retaliated against for making a complaint or for serving as a witness. Executive compensation programs will need to be reviewed and modified to ensure that the program is in compliance with the no personal loans and no sales of pension funds during blackout periods provisions.

One way for companies to cope with the responsibilities under Sarbanes-Oxley when a whistle-blowing complaint is made is through use of an ombudsman. British Petroleum America created an ombudsman position to make sure that concerns and complaints from employees, especially regarding safety, are heard.[122] The ombudsman is a former U.S. district court judge who is recognized for independence and integrity, so employees can be comfortable expressing their concerns. The ombudsman's job is to find the facts and resolve problems in as considerate, fair, thoughtful a way as possible. The position was developed in response to the lack of attention that managers paid to employees' complaints about pipeline corrosion and other problems at an oil field in Alaska that caused BP to shut down production, leading to a rise in oil prices.

Nationwide Insurance has a confidential employee "helpline."[123] Many of the calls require interaction between the company's three-person ethics staff and much larger HR staff. As is typical for most such help lines, about two-thirds of the calls concern issues squarely in HR's bailiwick—conflicts with co-workers, for example, or treatment by supervisors or sexual harassment. The reason, says Pat Hendey, director of associate relations, is that "a lot of times employees don't know who to call, but they always seem to be able to find the ethics hotline. What they like is that they can do it anonymously."

HR investigates many concerns, including employee allegations of internal conflicts of interest. The rest of the helpline cases are delegated to internal security, legal, and other departments for investigation. The ethics staff itself handles the legwork for only about 5 percent of the cases that come in via the helpline. HR relies on ethics officers to look into issues such as potential conflicts of interest. For example, the ethics officers have checked out employees who would like to run a business or who want to go out and teach a particular course with a competitor. What brings HR and ethics into even closer quarters at Nationwide than at other companies is that Nationwide has moved beyond a compliance-based stance on ethics toward a "value-based" approach where expectations and transmission of ethical behavior become integral to the company culture. To promote an ethical culture, HR and the ethics office collaborate on activities such as the ethics office's periodic communications blitzes.

Human resource managers must satisfy three basic standards for their practices to be considered ethical.[124] First, HRM practices must result in the greatest good for the largest number of people. Second, employment practices must respect basic human rights of privacy, due process, consent, and free speech. Third, managers must treat employees and customers equitably and fairly. Throughout the book we highlight ethical dilemmas in human resource management practices.

The Global Challenge

Companies are finding that to survive they must compete in international markets as well as fend off foreign corporations' attempts to gain ground in the United States. To meet these challenges, U.S. businesses must develop global markets, use their practices to improve global competitiveness, and better prepare employees for global assignments.

LO4
Discuss what companies should do to compete in the global marketplace.

Every business must be prepared to deal with the global economy. Global business expansion has been made easier by technology. The Internet allows data and information to be instantly accessible and sent around the world. The Internet, e-mail, and video conferencing enable business deals to be completed between companies thousands of miles apart.

Globalization is not limited to any particular sector of the economy, product market, or company size.[125] Companies without international operations may buy or use goods that have been produced overseas, hire employees with diverse backgrounds, or compete with foreign-owned companies operating within the United States.

Businesses around the world are attempting to increase their competitiveness and value by increasing their global presence, often through mergers and acquisitions. The "Competing through Globalization" box shows how Merck KGaA successfully completed its acquisition of Serono by focusing on creating a shared culture.

Entering International Markets

Many companies are entering international markets by exporting their products overseas, building manufacturing facilities or service centers in other countries, entering into alliances with foreign companies, and engaging in e-commerce. Developing nations such as Taiwan, Indonesia, and China may account for more than 60 percent of the world economy by 2020.[126] For example, Coca-Cola is trying to build a global juice business though deals in Latin America, Russia, and China.[127] Power Curbers Inc., a small North Carolina manufacturer, sells construction-related machinery to more than 70 countries, including Australia, China, Central America, and western Europe. Its equipment helped complete the Eurotunnel under the English Channel. Technical Materials, a 250-employee Rhode Island company, has been exporting high-technology materials systems to China. At Texas Instruments (TI) with approximately 30,000 employees worldwide, 80 percent of sales come from customers outside the United States. More than 50 percent of the wireless phones sold worldwide contain TI's digital signal processing.

Global companies are struggling both to find and retain talent employees, especially in emerging markets. Companies are moving into China, India, eastern Europe, the Middle East, Southeast Asia, and Latin American, but the demand for talented employees exceeds supply. Also, companies often place successful U.S. managers in charge of overseas operations, but these managers lack the cultural understanding necessary to attract, motivate, and retain talented employees. To cope with these problems, companies are taking actions to better prepare their managers and their families for overseas assignments and to ensure that training and development opportunities are available for global employees. Cross-cultural training prepares employees and their families to understand the culture and norms of the country they are being relocated to and to return to their home country after the assignment. Cross-cultural training is discussed in Chapter 10.

IBM obtains more than two-thirds of its revenue from outside the United States and is seeking to build team leadership in order to compete in emerging markets around the world. IBM's Corporate Service Program donates the time and service of about 600 employees for projects in countries such as Turkey, Romania, Ghana, Vietnam, the Phillipines, and Tanzania.[128] The goal of the program is to develop a leadership team that learns about the needs and culture of these countries, at the same time providing valuable community service. For example, eight IBM employees from five countries traveled to Timisoara, Romania. Each employee was assigned to help a different company or nonprofit organization. One software-development manager helped GreenForest, a manufacturer of office, hotel, school, and industrial furniture, reach its goal of cutting costs and becoming more efficient by recommending computer equipment and systems needed to increase production and exports to western Europe. Another employee worked with a nonprofit organization that offers services to disabled adults. Besides benefiting the companies, the employees have also found that the experience has helped them understand cultural differences, improve their communication and teamwork skills, and gain insights on global marketing and strategy.

AP Moller-Maersk Group is a world leader in shipping, transportation, and logistics.[129] AP Moller-Maersk has very selective hiring as well as extensive training and development practices. In its entry-level Maersk International Shipping Education program, one employee is hired for approximately 200 applicants. The new employees receive job assignments that help them understand the entire company and its global operations, not just one functional area. The company also provides extensive coaching and assessment of managerial potential and provides regular feedback to keep employees focused on the things they need to do to reach their career goals.

Many companies are involved in global acquisitions and mergers to gain market share. Many acquisitions and mergers fail to gain the synergies and the expected value because the merging of two different company cultures is difficult and often done ineffectively (e.g., consider the problems of the Chrysler and Mercedes-Benz merger). Merck KGaA of Germany had 11,000 employees working on producing cardiac and cancer-fighting drugs. Serono S.A., a Swiss-based biotechnology company with 5,000 employees, offered clinicians leading drugs for neurology, infertility, dermatology, and endocrinology. The two companies appeared to be compatible on the basis of their products, but their cultures and business models were very different. Merck KGaA's culture was characterized by family control, stability, and long-term growth, while Serono S.A.'s culture emphasized speed, agility, and an entrepreneurial spirit. Serono was organized by functions such as commercial, development, research, and technical operations. At Merck, a country head manager was in charge of all activities in the country.

In 2007 Merck completed its acquisition of Serono without losing talented scientific, managerial, sales, or manufacturing employees. The new company, Merck Serono International S.A., operates with a mix of functional and country models. By all measures, the acquisition and merger have been successful: the new company grew more than 7 percent in 2007 and 2008, faster than the overall pharmaceutical market. Employees are highly engaged. That is, employees satisfaction with pay and benefits, trust, information sharing, collaboration, and teamwork are 10 percent higher than survey results for employees at other merging or reorganizing companies. Eighteen months after the merger, no member of the new senior management team had left the company.

What caused this acquisition to be successful? When the deal was announced, Merck communicated that Serono's culture was not going to be suppressed by Merck's policies. A central integration office was established and top management team appointments were announced. As soon as the acquisition was finalized, an HR integration team with representatives from both companies started work. The motto of the integration became the "best of both." The top priorities of the team included fast, open, fair, and transparent postings and hiring of more than 2,000 management positions worldwide; frequent communications with employees using Webcasts, meetings, and newsletters; and creation of an interim compensation and benefits philosophy to redefine stock and incentive and retention plans, integrate two different performance management systems, and identify a common culture that linked the two companies' employees. Although surveys indicated that employees felt the two company's cultures were different, they identified commonalities such as a focus on quality, innovation, teamwork, customer service, and a common vocabulary. Change management workshops were used to help employees adjust to the merger and create personal action plans.

SOURCE: Based on N. Davis, "Merger Kept 'the Best of Both,'" *HR Magazine*, November 2008, pp. 54–56.

Offshoring

Offshoring refers to the exporting of jobs from developed countries, such as the United States, to countries where labor and other costs are lower. India, Canada, China, Russia, Ireland, Mexico, Brazil, and the Philippines are some of the destination countries for offshored jobs. Why are jobs offshored?[130] The main reason is labor costs. Workers in other countries earn a fraction of the wages of American workers performing the same job. For example, Indian computer programmers receive about

Offshoring
Exporting jobs from developed to less developed countries.

$10 an hour compared to $60 per hour earned by U.S. programmers. Other reasons include the availability of a highly skilled and motivated workforce. Both India and China have high numbers of engineering and science graduates. China graduated 325,000 engineers in 2004, five times as many as the United States. Each year, India graduates 2 million English-speaking students with strong technical and quantitative skills.[131] Finally, cheap global telecommunications costs allow companies with engineers 6,000 miles away to complete design work and interact with other engineers as if they were located in the office down the hall.

Initially, offshoring involved low-skilled manufacturing jobs with repeatable tasks and specific guidelines for how the work was to be completed. Offshoring now includes high-skilled manufacturing jobs and is also prevalent in the service and information technology sectors, for example, telephone call center, accounting bookkeeping and payroll, legal research, software engineers, architecture, and design.

For example, in contrast to computer and printer manufacturer Hewlett-Packard, which hired its first foreign workers 20 years after its founding in 1939, search engine Google employed people outside the United States just three years after its 1998 start.[132] OfficeTiger, which provides business services to banks, insurance companies, and other clients, has 200 employees in the United States and 2,000 in southern India. Whether its clients need typesetting or marketing research, Indian employees can submit their work over the Internet. Because Indian workers are generally paid only one-fifth U.S. earnings for comparable jobs, OfficeTiger offers attractive prices. The company is growing and expects that two-thirds of its future hires will be in India, Sri Lanka, and countries other than the United States.[133] Regardless of company size, talent comparable to that in the United States is available at lower costs overseas.[134] Gen3Partners, a Boston-based product innovation company, has a research and development lab in St. Petersburg, Russia, with 90 scientists and engineers, all with advanced degrees. Russia has a tradition of scientific excellence, and comparable talent costs less than in the United States. For small companies such as Cobalt Group, a Seattle, Washington, automotive online services company, labor costs for its 50 research and development engineers who work in a technology center in India are about one-third of the U.S. costs.

However, as a result of 9/11 and concerns that American employees should get the first chance at U.S. jobs, immigration rules have made it difficult for immigrants to seek employment. Also, visa limits have restricted the number of highly skilled professionals and technical employees who can work in the United States. A maximum of 65,000 H1B visas, which allow a U.S. company to employ a foreign worker for up to six years, are made available each year, and all are taken on the first day they are available.[135] For example, for fiscal year 2009 which began in October 2008, the U.S. Citizenship and Immigration Services received 163,000 applications for the 65,000 H1B visas.[136] The U.S. Senate is considering legislation that would impact immigrant employment.

Although companies may be attracted to offshoring because of potential lower labor costs, several other issues have emerged that are also important. First, can employees in the offshored locations provide a level of customer service the same as or higher than customers receive from U.S. operations? Second, would offshoring demoralize U.S. employees such that the gains from offshoring would be negated by lower motivation, lower satisfaction, and higher turnover? Third, are local managers adequately trained to motivate and retain offshore employees? Fourth, what is the potential effect, if any, of political unrest in the countries in which operations are offshored? Fifth, what effect would offshoring have on the public image of the company? Would customers or potential customers avoid purchasing products or services because they believe offshoring costs U.S. employees their jobs? Would offshoring have an adverse effect on recruiting new employees?

Because of the disadvantages of offshoring discussed above and the total costs of working with different languages, cultures, and time zones, many companies are **onshoring,** or moving jobs to rural America.[137] Onshoring may be most attractive to companies that have brands tied to the United States because they fear the political fallout related to offshoring. Dell opened a call center in Twins Falls, Idaho, after closing one in India because of customer complaints. US Bank considered opening a call center in India but decided against it because of the bad publicity that would have resulted. US Bank chose instead to put the call center in Coeur d'Alene, Idaho, where the 500 new jobs would reduce the area's unemployment rate and make a difference in the quality of life in the community.[138]

Onshoring
Exporting jobs to rural parts of the United States.

There is considerable debate whether offshoring results in loss of jobs for Americans or actually creates new jobs. Smaller entrepreneurial companies are finding that offshoring helps them expand their business. For example, Xpitax, a 50-employee company in Braintree, Massachusetts, helps small accounting firms transfer the work of preparing clients' tax forms to a team of accountants in India. Trained in U.S. tax law, the accountants are paid the same wages per day as an American accountant can earn in one hour. The returns are prepared in 12 to 24 hours.[139] Companies such as GE Medical Systems are hiring highly skilled Indian engineers at lower wages than U.S. engineers receive (a top engineering graduate from India earns about one-eighth of U.S. starting pay) enabling the company to create better research and development teams to speed up product launches and prototype development and to upgrade quality.[140] This will allow GE Medical Systems and other companies to cut research and development costs, introduce new products, and save or create new jobs in the United States.

The Technology Challenge

Technology has reshaped the way we play (e.g., games on the Internet), communicate (e.g., cell phones), plan our lives (e.g., electronic calendars that include Internet access), and where we work (e.g., small, powerful personal computers allow us to work at home, while we travel, and even while we lie on the beach!). The Internet has created a new business model—e-commerce, in which business transactions and relationships can be conducted electronically. The Internet is a global collection of computer networks that allows users to exchange data and information. Seventy-nine percent of adults, approximately 178 million, go online, spending an average of 11 hours a week on the Internet.[141] Seventy-two percent access the Internet from home, while 37 percent do so from work. For example, customers can now read *The Wall Street Journal* and many local newspapers online. They can send online greeting cards from Blue Mountain Arts. Through the Web you can purchase clothes, flowers, and airline tickets and even have someone pick up groceries for you. Companies can connect with job candidates across the world on www.monster.com, and employees can connect with friends, family, and co-workers using MySpace at www.myspace.com.

How and Where People Work

Advances in sophisticated technology along with reduced costs for the technology are changing many aspects of human resource management. Technological advances in electronics and communications software have made possible mobile technology

LO5
Identify the characteristics of the workforce and how they influence human resource management.

such as personal digital assistants (PDAs) and iPods as well as improving the Internet. The Internet and the Web allow employees to send and receive information as well as to locate and gather resources, including software, reports, photos, and videos. The Internet gives employees instant access to experts whom they can communicate with and to newsgroups, which are bulletin boards dedicated to specific areas of interest, where employees can read, post, and respond to messages and articles. Internet sites also have home pages—mailboxes that identify the person or company and contain text, images, sounds, and video.

For example, Willow CSN is a provider of home-based call center agents (Cyber-Agents).[142] Willow contracts with businesses such as Office Max, whose call centers need more employees at certain hours. The CyberAgents choose the shifts they want to work on a Web site. They work a variable number of hours ranging from 10 to 32 hours per week and are paid based on the number of calls they answer. They take calls at home using the same software and equipment as the agents at the client's call center. The agents are monitored and calls recorded just as though they were working in a traditional call center. They can get help from supervisors or co-workers in an online chat room.

Robotics, computer-assisted design, radio frequency identification, and nanotechnology are transforming manufacturing.[143] Technology has also made equipment easier to operate, helping companies cope with skill shortages and allowing older workers to postpone retirement. For example, consider working a grader construction vehicle (which is used to smooth and level dirt on roadways and other construction projects). Older vehicle models required operating as many as 15 levers in addition to a steering wheel and several foot pedals. As a result, working the grader usually left operators with sore backs and shoulders at the end of the day. Caterpillar's latest version of the grader includes redesigned controls that use only two joysticks and eliminate the physical demands of pushing pedals and turning a steering wheel. Besides reducing the physical demands, the redesign of the grader without a steering wheel resulted in operators having better visibility of the steel blade and switches for lights, windshield wipers, and the parking brake could be grouped together in one place in the cab.

Technology is pushing the boundaries of artificial intelligence, speech synthesis, wireless communications, and networked virtual reality.[144] Realistic graphics, dialogue, and sensory cues can now be stored onto tiny, inexpensive computer chips. These advances have the potential for freeing workers from going to a specific location to work and from traditional work schedules. For example, a recent survey found that 37 percent of employers offer telecommuting on a part-time basis and 23 percent on a full-time basis.[145] Telecommuting has the potential to increase employee productivity, encourage family-friendly work arrangements, and help reduce traffic and air pollution. But at the same time technologies may result in employees being on call hours a day, seven days a week. Many companies are taking steps to provide more flexible work schedules to protect employees' free time and to more productively use employees' work time. For example, employees at Sun Microsystems can work almost anywhere and anytime because their work and information are available online.[146] Under Sun's iWork program, which uses both flexible hours and flexible workspaces, employees can work in several different locations. They may use Sun's flexible offices located in 12 drop-in centers, as well as 115 other locations around the world. The locations of the drop-in centers help employees reduce the amount of time they spend commuting to a central location. This also helps employees set up flexible arrangements where they can go to and from work to pick up and drop off family members, perhaps finishing work at home. They may also receive approval to work at home.

Most employees are happy with the flexibility the program gives them including the convenience of choosing a location and the greater personal control over how to balance work and personal time. Sun is saving money by reducing office space and the expenses related to a traditional office arrangement.

High-Performance Work Systems

New technology causes changes in skill requirements and work roles and often results in redesigning work structures (e.g., using work teams).[147] **High-performance work systems** maximize the fit between the company's social system (employees) and its technical system.[148] For example, computer-integrated manufacturing uses robots and computers to automate the manufacturing process. The computer allows the production of different products simply by reprogramming the computer. As a result, laborer, material handler, operator/assembler, and maintenance jobs may be merged into one position. Computer-integrated manufacturing requires employees to monitor equipment and troubleshoot problems with sophisticated equipment, share information with other employees, and understand the relationships between all components of the manufacturing process.[149] Consider the changes Canon Inc., known for office imaging, computer peripherals, and cameras, has made to speed up the development and production process.[150] Canon is using a procedure called concurrent engineering, where production engineers work together with designers. This allows them to more easily exchange ideas to improve a product or make it easier to manufacture. Canon also now has production employees work in "cells," where they perform multiple tasks and can more easily improve the production process. Previously, employees worked in an assembly line controlled by a conveyor belt. The new cell system requires lower parts inventory and less space, cutting factory operating and real estate costs. Also, employees are more satisfied working in cells because they feel more responsibility for their work.

Working in Teams. Through technology, the information needed to improve customer service and product quality becomes more accessible to employees. This means that employees are expected to take more responsibility for satisfying the customer and determining how they perform their jobs. One of the most popular methods for increasing employee responsibility and control is work teams. *Work teams* involve employees with various skills who interact to assemble a product or provide a service. Work teams may assume many of the activities usually reserved for managers, including selecting new team members, scheduling work, and coordinating activities with customers and other units in the company. To give teams maximum flexibility, cross-training of team members occurs. *Cross-training* refers to training employees in a wide range of skills so they can fill any of the roles needed to be performed on the team.

Use of new technology and work designs such as work teams needs to be supported by specific human resource management practices. These practices include the following actions:

- Employees choose or select new employees or team members.
- Employees receive formal performance feedback and are involved in the performance improvement process.
- Ongoing training is emphasized and rewarded.
- Rewards and compensation are linked to company performance.
- Equipment and work processes encourage maximum flexibility and interaction between employees.

High-Performance Work Systems
Work systems that maximize the fit between the company's social system and technical system.

LO6
Discuss human resource management practices that support high-performance work systems.

- Employees participate in planning changes in equipment, layout, and work methods.
- Employees understand how their jobs contribute to the finished product or service.

Changes in Skill Requirements. High-performance work systems have implications for employee selection and training. Employees need job-specific knowledge and basic skills to work with the equipment created with the new technology. Because technology is often used as a means to achieve product diversification and customization, employees must have the ability to listen and communicate with customers. Interpersonal skills, such as negotiation and conflict management, and problem-solving skills are more important than physical strength, coordination, and fine-motor skills—previous job requirements for many manufacturing and service jobs. Although technological advances have made it possible for employees to improve products and services, managers must empower employees to make changes.

Working in Partnerships. Besides changing the way that products are built or services are provided within companies, technology has allowed companies to form partnerships with one or more other companies. **Virtual teams** refer to teams that are separated by time, geographic distance, culture, and/or organizational boundaries and that rely almost exclusively on technology (e-mail, Internet, videoconferencing) to interact and complete their projects. Virtual teams can be formed within one company whose facilities are scattered throughout the country or the world. A company may also use virtual teams in partnerships with suppliers or competitors to pull together the necessary talent to complete a project or speed the delivery of a product to the marketplace. PricewaterhouseCoopers's learning and education department has 190 employees who are located in 70 offices in different cities.[151] These employees work together on virtual teams that range in size from 5 to 50 people. Shared databases are used for background information and developing work, each office has videoconferencing, software is used to track calendars and connect employees via their personal computers to their virtual teams.

Software developers are positioning employees around the world with clusters of three or four facilities, six to eight hours apart, to keep projects moving 24 hours a day.[152] The intent is to increase productivity and reduce project completion time by allowing employees to focus continuously on projects through using highly talented engineers who can work in their own time zone and location without having to move to a different country or work inconvenient hours. Also, globally distributed projects can draw on employees from many different cultures, backgrounds, and perspectives helping to produce services and products that can better meet the needs of global customers. The challenges are how to organize work so that teams in different locations and different work shifts can share task with minimum interaction.

Employees must be trained in principles of employee selection, quality, and customer service. They need to understand financial data so they can see the link between their performance and company performance.

Changes in Company Structure and Reporting Relationships. The traditional design of U.S. companies emphasizes efficiency, decision making by managers, and dissemination of information from the top of the company to lower levels. However, this structure will not be effective in the current work environment, in which personal computers give employees immediate access to information needed to complete customer orders or modify product lines. In the adaptive organizational structure, employees are in a constant state of learning and performance improvement. Employees are free to move wherever they are needed in the company. The adaptive

Virtual Teams
Teams that are separated by time, geographic distance, culture and/or organizational boundaries and rely exclusively on technology for interaction between team members.

organization is characterized by a core set of values or a vital vision that drives all organizational efforts.[153] Previously established boundaries between managers and employees, employees and customers, employees and vendors, and the various functions within the company are abandoned. Employees, managers, vendors, customers, and suppliers work together to improve service and product quality and to create new products and services. Line employees are trained in multiple jobs, communicate directly with suppliers and customers, and interact frequently with engineers, quality experts, and employees from other functions.

Consider the case of Putnam Investments, where the company culture and organizational structure may have contributed to unethical behavior.[154] Putnam has taken several steps in response to a corporate scandal in which portfolio managers were violating company policies by rapidly trading funds and allowing certain clients to do the same. The company believed that the unethical and illegal behavior was a result of a rigid hierarchical organizational structure and a hypercompetitive business environment. To create a more relaxed culture better for collaboration and reduced focus on short-term gains the CEO prepared guiding principles for the company including personal integrity, mutual respect, and the highest professional standards. Putnam reduced its staff to flatten the organization and give employees more autonomy and independence in their jobs. The flatter structure has provided more opportunities for retail and institutional portfolio managers to cross-sell investment products. To create a more collegial environment, dress is now business casual. Also, to increase employee involvement when developing human resource policies and practices Putnam now has an employee advisory council, which meets four time a year with the CEO.

Increased Use and Availability of e-HRM and Human Resource Information Systems. **Electronic human resource management (e-HRM)** refers to the processing and transmission of digitized information used in HRM, including text, sound, and visual images from one computer or electronic device to another. New technologies and advances in software, including avatars, collaborative social networks, and mobile technologies such as personal digital assistants and iPods, are influencing training, development, work design, recruiting, and other aspects of HR. Table 1.13 shows the implications of e-HRM. For example, Capital One, a financial service company, uses an audio learning program that allows employees to learn through their iPods at their

Electronic Human Resource Management (e-HRM)
The processing and transmission of digitized information used in HRM.

table 1.13
Implications of e-HRM for HRM Practices

HRM PRACTICE	IMPLICATIONS OF e-HRM
Analysis and design of work	Employees in geographically dispersed locations can work together in virtual teams using video, e-mail, and the Internet.
Recruiting	Post job openings online; candidates can apply for jobs online.
Training	Online learning can bring training to employees anywhere, anytime.
Selection	Online simulations, including tests, videos, and e-mail, can measure job candidates' ability to deal with real-life business challenges.
Compensation and benefits	Employees can review salary and bonus information and seek information about and enroll in benefit plans.

own convenience.[155] The company has also developed a mobile audio learning channel. The channel supplements competency-based and leadership and management programs and other existing company training courses. It is also used to ensure that employees receive information when they need it. The Federal Aviation Administration (FAA) has 50,000 employees spread throughout the country.[156] Proposals that required input from employees spread throughout the country took years to complete. New software allows the FAA to create virtual shared workspaces for employees. FAA employees and industry experts can now interact in virtual "rooms" to debate ideas and work on shared documents. The virtual rooms have saved the FAA more than $3 million in travel costs and $2 million in employee time, and they have reduced the time needed for most proposals to become rules to one year. United Parcel Service (UPS) implemented a software system that each evening maps out the next day's schedule for its drivers.[157] The software designs each route to minimize the number of left turns, reducing the time and gas that drivers waste at traffic lights. Customers get their packages on time and drivers can make it home in the evening for dinner.

Human Resource Information System (HRIS)
A system used to acquire, store, manipulate, analyze, retrieve, and distribute HR information.

Companies continue to use human resource information systems to store large quantities of employee data including personal information, training records, skills, compensation rates, absence records, and benefits usages and costs. A **human resource information system (HRIS)** is a computer system used to acquire, store, retrieve, and distribute information related to a company's human resources.[158] An HRIS can support strategic decision making, help the company avoid lawsuits, provide data for evaluating policies and programs, and support day-to-day HR decisions. Florida Power & Light Company, based in Juno Beach, Florida, uses HRIS applications to provide information to employees and to support decision making by managers. More than 10,000 employees in 20 states can use the information system to learn about their benefits. Managers use the system to track employees' vacation and sick days and to make changes in staffing and pay. Using the HRIS, managers can request the HRIS system to automatically prepare a personnel report; they no longer have to contact the HR department to request one.[159] The "Competing through Technology" box shows how Aetna Corporation has used software to help in talent management.

The use of company intranets, a network that uses Internet tools but limits access to authorized users in the company, and Web portals designed to serve as gateways to the Internet that highlight links to relevant information are becoming common practice. As we mentioned earlier in the chapter (in the discussion of how HR's role in administration is decreasing), company intranets and Web portals allow employees and managers online access to information about HR issues, offer self-enrollment programs, and provide feedback through surveys (self-service). Employees can look up workplace policies and information about training programs and enroll online, choose benefits and change salary deductions, and review employment contracts. Self-service at Mapics, a software developer based in Atlanta, allows managers and employees to keep track of vacation time.[160] This helps with scheduling and enables managers to encourage employees to use their remaining vacation time. Mapics changed its vacation policy to require that employees take their vacation time or lose it at the end of the year. Before self-service, Mapics lacked reliable information on company vacation time, resulting in a liability of a million dollars worth of accrued, unused vacation time. Self-service improved management and employee satisfaction with HR services at the same time it cut costs.

More sophisticated systems extend management applications to decision making in areas such as compensation and performance management. Managers can

COMPETING THROUGH TECHNOLOGY
Talent Manager Helps Aetna Corporation Identify and Develop
Employees' Skills to Gain a Competitive Advantage

Aetna Corporation is one of the nation's leaders in health care; dental, pharmacy, group life, and disability insurance; and employee benefits. Aetna is dedicated to helping people achieve health and financial security by providing easy access to safe, cost-effective, high-quality health care and protecting their finances against health-related risks. Aetna's vision is to earn the distinction, financially and by reputation, of being the preferred benefits company in all aspects of our business.

An important part of Aetna's business strategy is to foster a culture of inclusion that grows a diverse talent pool and recognizes and rewards the contributions of each of the company's more than 35,000 employees while allowing them to do their best work. At Aetna Corporation, the CEO and the HR director work together to realize this aspect of the business strategy by creating a comprehensive talent management system that will help all employees reach their full potential. Ronald Williams, Aetna's chairman and CEO, spends about 30 percent of his time on people issues, focusing on turnover, succession, and loss of talent. Williams often seeks information about talent management from his HR director. He is interested in questions such as, "How do we know our managers are assessing and developing individuals?" As a result, Williams

asked his HR director to build a system that would help managers identify, train, and track talent throughout the company. William believes it is essential to manage the entire talent pool of the company, not just the top performers, to be competitive.

HR is loading data about Aetna's 34,000 employees into a talent management system accessible to both employees and managers. Information about every job and employee will soon be accessible with only a click of the mouse. Information in the talent management system comes from HR, managers, and employees. HR managers provide the information that connects individual employees to job descriptions and related skills and competencies. The job descriptions in the database identify the critical competencies and skills needed for each position. Employees provide their own background information, work history, and skills inventory and provide information on development plans and career goals. Managers rate their employees on skills and competencies. Employees will be able to see their manager's ratings and comments on their job performance and potential. Managers, employees, and HR professionals can all update information as job descriptions, employee skill sets, or performance ratings change.

The system, called Talent Manager, can provide reports

and analyses of employees at all levels. HR can identify solid performers, at-risk employees, and possible job–employee mismatches. Also, HR and managers can analyze talent needs and surpluses of each of Aetna's five job families: nursing, clinical, actuarial, operational, and underwriting. Managers and HR professionals can see all information related to each job within the organization, including up-to-date job descriptions, competencies required for success, and the pipeline or "bench" of candidates ready to move into a job. Also, Talent Manager can increase employees' awareness of job openings and allow managers to identify potential job candidates. Previously, employees learned of job opportunities from job postings. Using Talent Manager, they can express their interest in open positions and provide their qualifications to hiring managers. Talent Manager allows managers in any of Aetna's four companies to identify employees with specific skills or competencies who may be a good fit for a job opening by using key terms such as "speaks Portuguese" or "has worked in India" to searching the system.

SOURCES: Based on R. Grossman, "Steering a Business Turnaround," *HR Magazine*, April 2008, pp. 73–80; Aetna Corporation Web site at www.aetna.com; Authoria Talent Management Software at Web site for Authoria, Inc. at www.authoria.com.

HR Dashboard
HR metrics such as productivity, absenteeism that are accessible by employees and managers through the company intranet or human resource information system.

schedule job interviews or performance appraisals, guided by the system to provide the necessary information and follow every step called for by the procedure.[161] One of the most creative uses of Internet technology is the development of HR dashboards. An **HR dashboard** is a series of indicators or metrics that managers and employees have access to on the company intranet or human resource information system. For example, Cisco Systems views building talent as a priority so it has added to its dashboard of people measures a metric to track how many people move and the reasons why.[162] This allows Cisco to identify divisions that are developing new talent.

Competitiveness in High-Performance Work Systems. Unfortunately, many managers have tended to consider technological and structural innovations independent of each other. That is, because of immediate demands for productivity, service, and short-term profitability, many managers implement a new technology (such as a networked computer system) or a new work design (like service teams organized by product) without considering how a new technology might influence the efficiency or effectiveness of the way work is organized.[163] Without integrating technology and structure, a company cannot maximize production and service.

Human resource management practices that support high-performance work systems are shown in Table 1.14. The HRM practices involved include employee selection, performance management, training, work design, and compensation. These practices are designed to give employees skills, incentives, knowledge, and autonomy. Research studies suggest that high-performance work practices are usually associated with increases in productivity and long-term financial performance.[164] Research also suggests that it is more effective to improve HRM practices as a whole, rather than focus on one or two isolated practices (such as the pay system or selection system).[165] There may be a best HRM system, but whatever the company does, the practices must be aligned with each other and be consistent with the system if they are to positively affect company performance.[166] We will discuss this alignment in more detail in Chapters 2 and 16.

Consider how human resource management practices support the high-performance work system at the Global Engineering Manufacturing Alliance (GEMA) plant in Dundee, Michigan.[167] The plant is more automated and employs fewer workers than most engine plants, 275 compared with 600 to 2,000 employees at other engine plants. The goal of the plant is to be the most productive engine plant in the world. The UAW endorsed the high-performance workplace because it recognized that the company needs to be competitive to avoid losing jobs. The implications of this work system for labor relations is discussed in Chapter 14.

The plant's hourly employees rotate jobs and shifts, increasing the company's flexibility. The plant's culture emphasizes problem solving and that anyone can do anything, anytime, anywhere. Everyone has the same title: team member or team leader. By rotating jobs the plant wants to keep workers motivated in their work and avoid injuries. Team leaders and engineers don't stay in their offices; they are expected to work on the shop floor as part of six-person teams. Contractors are also seen as part of the team, working alongside assembly workers and engineers and wearing the same uniforms. Most auto plants have a day and night shift with senior workers usually choosing to work the day shift. At GEMA, employees rotate shifts in crews of three, working 10 hours per day, four days per week, alternating between days and nights. Every third week of their rotation they get five days off in addition to any vacation time. Counseling is available

table 1.14

How HRM Practices
Support High-
Performance Work
Systems

Staffing	• Employees participate in selecting new employees, e.g., peer interviews.
Work Design	• Employees understand how their jobs contribute to the finished product or service. • Employees participate in planning changes in equipment, layout, and work methods. • Work may be organized in teams. • Job rotation used to develop skills. • Equipment and work processes are structured and technology is used to encourage flexibility and interaction between employees. • Work design allows employees to use a variety of skills. • Decentralized decision making, reduced status distinctions, information sharing. • Increased safety.
Training	• Ongoing training emphasized and rewarded. • Training in finance and quality control methods.
Compensation	• Team-based performance pay. • Part of compensation may be based on company or division financial performance.
Performance Management	• Employees receive performance feedback and are actively involved in the performance improvement process.

SOURCES: Based on A. Zacharatos, J. Barling, and R. Iverson, "High Performance Work Systems and Occupational Safety," *Journal of Applied Psychology* 90 (2005), pp. 77–93; S. Way, "High Performance Work Systems and Intermediate Indicators of Performance within the U.S. Small Business Sector," *Journal of Management* 28 (2002), pp. 765–85; J. A. Neal and C. L. Tromley, "From Incremental Change to Retrofit: Creating High-Performance Work Systems," *Academy of Management Executive* 9 (1995), pp. 42–54; M. A. Huselid, "The Impact of Human Resource Management Practices on Turnover, Productivity, and Corporate Financial Performance," *Academy of Management Journal* 38 (1995), pp. 635–72.

to help employees adjust to the rotating work schedule. The work schedule allows the plant to be in operation 21 hours per day, 6 days per week, 294 days a year. But employees work only 196 days a year. The alternating shifts also help employees to know and work with each other and salaried employees, who work only during daytime.

To hire employees who could work in a team environment emphasizing problem solving and flexibility, GEMA recruited using local newspapers within 70 miles of Dundee. GEMA worked with local civil rights organizations to find diverse candidates. Nonexempt employees whose wages start at $21 and increase to $30 within five years must have a two-year technical degree, a skilled journeyman's card, or five years experience in advanced machining.

Job candidates have to make it through a difficult screening process that takes 12 hours. The process requires candidates to take tests, participate in team activities in which they confront challenges facing the plant (e.g., process in the plant is inefficient), and interviews with operations managers and team leaders. When the plant is ahead of its production schedule employees receive training in class and on the shop floor in topics such as how to assemble an engine to math skills.

GEMA gives employees access to technology that helps them monitor productivity. Large electronic screens hanging from the plant ceiling provide alerts of any machinery parts that are ending their lifespan and need to be replaced before they malfunction. A performance management system available on personal computers, as well as a display board, alerts employees to delays or breakdowns in productivity. This is different from most engine plants where only managers have access to this information. The technology empowers all employees to fix problems, not just managers or engineers. GEMA provides rewards and bonuses for employees who develop innovative problem solutions.

Meeting Competitive Challenges through HRM Practices

LO7
Provide a brief description of human resource management practices.

We have discussed the global, stakeholder, new economy, and high-performance work system challenges U.S. companies are facing. We have emphasized that management of human resources plays a critical role in determining companies' success in meeting these challenges. HRM practices have not traditionally been seen as providing economic value to the company. Economic value is usually associated with equipment, technology, and facilities. However, HRM practices have been shown to be valuable. Compensation, staffing, training and development, performance management, and other HRM practices are investments that directly affect employees' motivation and ability to provide products and services that are valued by customers. Research has shown that companies that attempt to increase their competitiveness by investing in new technology and becoming involved in the quality movement also invest in state-of-the-art staffing, training, and compensation practices.[168] Figure 1.7 shows examples of human resource management practices that help companies deal with the three challenges. For example, to meet the sustainability challenge, companies need to identify through their selection processes whether prospective employees value customer relations and have the levels of interpersonal skills necessary to work with fellow employees in teams. To meet all three challenges, companies need to capitalize on the diversity of values, abilities, and perspectives that employees bring to the workplace.

HRM practices that help companies deal with the competitive challenges can be grouped into the four dimensions shown in Figure 1.8. These dimensions include the human resource environment, acquiring and preparing human resources, assessment and development of human resources, and compensating human resources. In addition, some companies have special issues related to labor–management relations, international human resource management, and managing the human resource function.

Managing the Human Resource Environment

Managing internal and external environmental factors allows employees to make the greatest possible contribution to company productivity and competitiveness. Creating a positive environment for human resources involves

- Linking HRM practices to the company's business objectives—that is, strategic human resource management.
- Ensuring that HRM practices comply with federal, state, and local laws.
- Designing work that motivates and satisfies the employee as well as maximizes customer service, quality, and productivity.

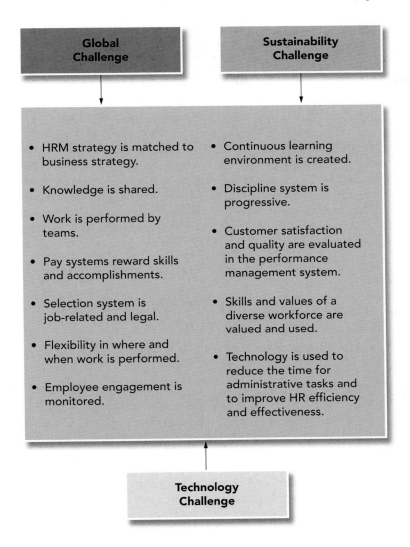

Global Challenge

Sustainability Challenge

- HRM strategy is matched to business strategy.

- Knowledge is shared.

- Work is performed by teams.

- Pay systems reward skills and accomplishments.

- Selection system is job-related and legal.

- Flexibility in where and when work is performed.

- Employee engagement is monitored.

- Continuous learning environment is created.

- Discipline system is progressive.

- Customer satisfaction and quality are evaluated in the performance management system.

- Skills and values of a diverse workforce are valued and used.

- Technology is used to reduce the time for administrative tasks and to improve HR efficiency and effectiveness.

Technology Challenge

Dimensions of HRM Practices

Managing the human resource environment	Acquiring and preparing human resources	Assessment and development of human resources	Compensating human resources

Competitiveness

Acquiring and Preparing Human Resources

Customer needs for new products or services influence the number and type of employees businesses need to be successful. Terminations, promotions, and retirements also influence human resource requirements. Managers need to predict the number and type of employees who are needed to meet customer demands for products and services.

Managers must also identify current or potential employees who can successfully deliver products and services. This area of human resource management deals with

- Identifying human resource requirements—that is, human resource planning, recruiting employees, and selecting employees.
- Training employees to have the skills needed to perform their jobs.

Assessment and Development of Human Resources

Managers need to ensure that employees have the necessary skills to perform current and future jobs. As we discussed earlier, because of new technology and the quality movement, many companies are redesigning work so that it is performed by teams. As a result, managers and employees may need to develop new skills to succeed in a team environment. Companies need to create a work environment that supports employees' work and nonwork activities. This area of human resource management addresses

- Measuring employees' performance.
- Preparing employees for future work roles and identifying employees' work interests, goals, values, and other career issues.
- Creating an employment relationship and work environment that benefits both the company and the employee.

Compensating Human Resources

Besides interesting work, pay and benefits are the most important incentives that companies can offer employees in exchange for contributing to productivity, quality, and customer service. Also, pay and benefits are used to reward employees' membership in the company and attract new employees. The positive influence of new work designs, new technology, and the quality movement on productivity can be damaged if employees are not satisfied with the level of pay and benefits or believe pay and benefits are unfairly distributed. This area of human resource management includes

- Creating pay systems.
- Rewarding employee contributions.
- Providing employees with benefits.

Special Issues

In some companies, employees are represented by a labor union. Managing human resources in a union environment requires knowledge of specific laws, contract administration, and the collective bargaining process.

Many companies are globally expanding their business through joint ventures, mergers, acquisitions, and establishing new operations. Successful global expansion depends on the extent to which HRM practices are aligned with cultural factors as well as management of employees sent to work in another country. Human resource management practices must contribute to organizational effectiveness.

Human resource management practices of both managers and the human resource function must be aligned and contribute to the company's strategic goals. The final chapter of the book explains how to effectively integrate human resource management practices.

table 1.15

Topics Covered in
This Book

Organization of This Book

The topics in this book are organized according to the four areas of human resource management and special issues. Table 1.15 lists the chapters covered in the book.

The content of each chapter is based on academic research and examples of effective company practices. Each chapter includes examples of how the human resource management practice covered in the chapter helps a company gain a competitive advantage by addressing sustainability, global, and technological challenges. Also, each chapter includes an example of a company that demonstrates how HR practices add value (evidence-based HR).

A LOOK BACK

Starbucks is trying to retain customers in a recessionary economic period.

Questions

1. What HR practices do you believe are most critical for Starbucks to maintain the coffee experience and customer service it's known for?
2. Do you think the culture and HR practices Starbucks is using during the recession would also help the bottom line at companies in other industries such as health care, manufacturing, or research and development? Explain why or why not.
3. Could Starbucks be as successful without its current HR practices? Explain.

    Please see the Video Case and Case Study that correspond to this chapter online at www.mhhe.com/noe7e.

SUMMARY

This chapter introduced the roles and activities of a company's human resource management function and emphasized that effective management of human resources can contribute to a company's business strategy and competitive advantage. HR can be viewed as having three product lines: administrative services, business partner services, and strategic services. To successfully manage human resources, individuals need personal credibility, business knowledge, understanding of the business strategy, technology knowledge, and the ability to deliver HR services. Human resource management practices should be evidence-based, that is, based on data showing the relationship between the practice and business outcomes related to key company stakeholders (customers, shareholders, employees, community). In addition to contributing to a company's business strategy, human resource practices are important for helping companies deal with sustainability, globalization, and technology challenges. The sustainability challenges are related to the economy, the characteristics and expectations of the labor force, how and where work is done, the value placed on intangible assets and human capital, and meeting stakeholder needs (ethical practices, high-quality products and services, return to shareholders, and social responsibility). Global challenges include entering international markets, immigration, and offshoring. Technology challenges include using new technologies to support flexible and virtual work arrangements, high-performance work systems, and developing effective e-HRM practices and human resource information systems.

The chapter concludes by showing how the book is organized. The book includes four topical areas: the human resource environment (strategic HRM, legal, analysis and design of work), acquisition and preparation of human resources (HR planning and recruitment, selection, training), assessment and development of human resources (performance management, development, training), compensation of human resources (pay structures, recognizing employee contributions with pay, benefits), and special topics (collective bargaining and labor relations, managing human resources globally, and strategically managing the HR function). All of the topical areas are important for companies to deal with the competitive challenges and contribute to business strategy.

KEY TERMS

Competitiveness, 4
Human resource management
    (HRM), 4
Self-service, 9
Outsourcing, 9
Evidence-based HR, 11
Sustainability, 14
Stakeholders, 14
Intangible assets, 19
Knowledge workers, 21
Empowering, 21
Learning organization, 22

Psychological contract, 22
Employee engagement, 23
Talent management, 24
Alternative work arrangements, 25
Balanced scorecard, 27
Total quality management
    (TQM), 30
Malcolm Baldrige National Quality
    Award, 31
ISO 9000:2000, 31
Six Sigma process, 33
Lean thinking, 33

Internal labor force, 34
External labor market, 34
Sarbanes-Oxley Act of 2002, 42
Offshoring, 45
Onshoring, 47
High-performance work systems, 49
Virtual teams, 50
Electronic human resource
    management (e-HRM), 51
Human resource information system
    (HRIS), 52
HR dashboard, 54

DISCUSSION QUESTIONS

1. Traditionally, human resource management practices were developed and administered by the company's human resource department. Line managers are now playing a major role in developing and implementing HRM practices. Why do you think non-HR managers are becoming more involved in developing and implementing HRM practices?

2. Staffing, training, compensation, and performance management are important HRM functions. How can each of these functions help companies succeed in meeting the global challenge, the challenge of using new technology, and the sustainability challenge?

3. What are intangible assets? How are they influenced by human resource management practices?

4. What is "evidence-based HR"? Why might an HR department resist becoming evidence-based?

5. Do you agree with the statement "Employee engagement is something companies should be concerned about only if they are making money"? Explain.

6. This book covers four human resource management practice areas: managing the human resource environment, acquiring and preparing human resources, assessment and development of human resources, and compensating human resources. Which area do you believe contributes most to helping a company gain a competitive advantage? Which area do you believe contributes the least? Why?

7. What is the balanced scorecard? Identify the four perspectives included in the balanced scorecard. How can HRM practices influence the four perspectives?

8. Is HRM becoming more strategic? Explain your answer.

9. What is sustainability? How can HR practices help a company become more socially and environmentally conscious?

10. Explain the implications of each of the following labor force trends for HRM: (1) aging workforce, (2) diverse workforce, (3) skill deficiencies.

11. What role do HRM practices play in a business decision to expand internationally?

12. What might a quality goal and high-performance work systems have in common in terms of HRM practices?

13. What disadvantages might result from outsourcing HRM practices? From employee self-service? From increased line manager involvement in designing and using HR practices?

14. What factors should a company consider before offshoring? What are the advantages and disadvantages of offshoring?

SELF-ASSESSMENT EXERCISE: DO YOU HAVE WHAT IT TAKES TO WORK IN HR?

Instructions: Read each statement and circle *yes* or *no*.

Yes No 1. I have leadership and management skills I have developed through prior job experiences, extracurricular activities, community service, or other noncourse activities.

Yes No 2. I have excellent communications, dispute resolution, and interpersonal skills.

Yes No 3. I can demonstrate an understanding of the fundamentals of running a business and making a profit.

Yes No 4. I can use spreadsheets and the World Wide Web, and I am familiar with information systems technology.

Yes No 5. I can work effectively with people of different cultural backgrounds.

Yes No 6. I have expertise in more than one area of human resource management.

Scoring: The greater the number of yes answers, the better prepared you are to work in an HR department. For questions you answered *no,* you should seek courses and experiences to change your answer to *yes*—and better prepare yourself for a career in HR!

SOURCE: Based on B. E. Kaufman, "What Companies Want from HR Graduates," *HR Magazine*, September 1994.

EXERCISING STRATEGY: ZAPPOS FACES COMPETITIVE CHALLENGES

Zappos, based in Las Vegas, is an online retailer with the initial goal of trying to be the best Web site for buying shoes by offering a wide variety of brands, styles, colors, sizes, and widths. The zappos.com brand has grown to offer shoes, handbags, eyewear, watches, and accessories for online purchase. Zappos' vision is that in the future, online sales will account for 30 percent of all retail sales in the United States, and Zappos will be the company with the best service and selection. As a result, Zappos believes it can become the online service leader, drawing customers and expanding into selling other products. Zappos

believes that the speed at which a customer receives an online purchase plays a critical role in how that customer thinks about shopping online again in the future, so they are focusing on making sure the items get delivered to our customers as quickly as possible.

Zappos CEO Tony Heish has shaped the company's culture, brand, and business strategy around 10 core values. They are:

Deliver WOW through service.

Embrace and drive change.

Create fun and a little weirdness.

Be adventurous, creative, and open-minded.

Pursue growth and learning.

Build open and honest relationships with communication.

Build a positive team and family spirit.

Do more with less.

Be passionate and determined.

Be humble.

Deliver WOW through Service means that call center employees need to provide excellent customer service. Call center employees encourage callers to order more than one size or color because shipping and return shipping is free. They are also encouraged to use their imaginations to meet customer needs.

Zappos' employment practices help perpetuate its company culture. For example, the HR team uses unusual interview questions—such as, How weird are you? and What's your theme song?—to find employees who are creative and have strong individuality. Zappos provides free lunch in the cafeteria (cold cuts) and a full-time life coach (employees have to sit on a red velvet throne to complain), managers are encouraged to spend time with employees outside of the office, and any employee can reward another employee a $50 dollar bonus for good performance. Most employees at Zappos are hourly. All new

hires complete four weeks of training, including two weeks working the phones. New recruits are offered $2,000 to leave the company during training to weed out individuals who will not be happy working at the company.

Due to a downturn in sales, Zappos was forced to cut costs, including laying off 124 employees. Heish handled the downsizing in a positive way. Laid-off employees with less than two years of service were paid through the end of the year. Everyone received six months of paid health coverage. Zappos also allowed laid-off employees to keep their 40 percent employee discount through Christmas.

SOURCES: Based on Web site for Zappos, www.zappos.com; J. O'Brien, "Zappos Knows How to Kick It," *Fortune*, February 2, 2009, pp. 55–66.

Questions

1. What challenges is Zappos facing that may derail its attempt to be the best online retailer? How can human resource management practices help Zappos meet these challenges?
2. Do you think that employees of Zappos have high levels of engagement? Why?
3. Which of Zappos' 10 core values do you believe that human resource practices can influence the most? The least? Why? For each of the core values, identify the HR practices that are related to it. Explain how each of the HR practice(s) you identified is related to the core values.

MANAGING PEOPLE FROM THE PAGES OF *BUSINESSWEEK*

BusinessWeek ## Cutting Work Hours without Cutting Staff

It's cheaper to trim hours or pay than to slash staff—which is why companies are getting creative with alternatives like furloughs and unpaid leave.

Instead of jettisoning workers during the Great Depression, Iowa-based window maker Pella had its employees wash and rewash the windows it could not sell. These days, companies such as FedEx, Dell, and Motorola are adopting their own tactics to hold on to jobs, from hiring freezes to companywide unpaid vacations. (All have had to resort to layoffs as well.) And some are doing more than chopping pay or perks.

Vermont's Rhino Foods, which makes the cookie dough for Ben & Jerry's ice cream, recently sent 15 factory workers to nearby lip balm manufacturer Autumn Harp for a week to help it handle a holiday rush. The employees were paid by Rhino, which then invoiced its neighbor for the hours worked. President Ted Castle is looking to adopt a similar approach with salaried managers, too. "It's a lot easier to just do the layoff," says Castle. "But in the long term, it's not easier for the business."

Across the U.S., some 37% of human resources managers say they're now spending more time devising alternatives to layoffs vs. six months ago, according to a recent survey by the Society for Human Resource Management. Peter Cappelli, director of the Center for Human Resources at the Wharton School of Business, notes that a 5% salary cut costs less than a 5% layoff because there are no severance payments. Some state governments even make the decision easier with a program called WorkShare, which allows companies to reduce employees' work hours and make up the difference through unemployment benefits. "We would have had to take more draconian measures, such as more layoffs, were it not for this program," says Mel White, a vice-president at Portland (Ore.)-based Classic Exhibits, which makes displays for trade shows.

Training existing staff to do more A typical move amid hiring freezes: training existing staff to do more. Luxury Retreats, a villa rental agency in Montreal, shuffled 8 of its 75 employees from areas such as product development to sales. CEO Joe Poulin even moved his personal assistant to the accounting department. "You have to be really efficient with your resources in times like these," says Poulin. Steelmaker Nucor, meanwhile, has cut factory time for many of its 22,000 hourly employees. On the days they're not making steel joists, though, workers are paid their base salary to perform maintenance or take classes.

In China, accounting giant Ernst & Young offered its 9,000 mainland and Hong Kong employees a chance to take one month of unpaid leave during the first half of this year. About 90% of the firm's auditors have opted in. Bin Wolfe, head of human resources for the region, says the move will slash EY's payroll costs by 17%.

Some try to motivate staff even while trimming their pay. Matt Cooper, vice-president of Larkspur (Calif.) recruiting firm Accolo, asked employees to take five days of unpaid leave this quarter but won't dock paychecks

until March. If big deals come through, he'll lift the pay cut. And he shaved costs by sleeping on his brother-in-law's couch during a recent business trip to New York. Instead of paying $1,500 for a week in a hotel room, Cooper spent 10% of that on dinner for the two of them and a nice bottle of wine.

Questions

1. Besides being cheaper, for what other reasons might companies try to avoid cutting their staffs and laying off employees during an economic downturn?
2. What evidence would you collect or look for to demonstrate that furloughs, unpaid leave, and salary or wage freezes are reducing costs and not negatively affecting the business?
3. Some companies have a "no layoff policy" regardless of economic conditions. Do you think this is a good idea? Why or why not?

NOTES

1. A. S. Tsui and L. R. Gomez-Mejia, "Evaluating Human Resource Effectiveness," in *Human Resource Management: Evolving Rules and Responsibilities*, ed. L. Dyer (Washington, DC: BNA Books, 1988), pp. 1187–227; M. A. Hitt, B. W. Keats, and S. M. DeMarie, "Navigating in the New Competitive Landscape: Building Strategic Flexibility and Competitive Advantage in the 21st Century," *Academy of Management Executive* 12, no. 4 (1998), pp. 22–42; J. T. Delaney and M. A. Huselid, "The Impact of Human Resource Management Practices on Perceptions of Organizational Performance," *Academy of Management Journal* 39 (1996), pp. 949–69.
2. F. Hansen, "2006 Data Bank Annual," *Workforce Management*, December 11, 2006, p. 48.
3. SHRM-BNA Survey No. 66, "Policy and Practice Forum: Human Resources Activities, Budgets, and Staffs: 2000–2001," Bulletin to Management, Bureau of National Affairs Policy and Practice Series, June 28, 2001 (Washington, DC: Bureau of National Affairs).
4. R. Stolz, "CEOs Who Get It," *Human Resource Executive*, March 16, 2006, pp. 1, 18–25.
5. W. Cascio, "From Business Partner to Driving Business Success: The Next Step in the Evolution of HR Management," *Human Resource Management* 44 (2005), pp. 159–63.
6. C. Cornell, "Riding Out the Storm," *Human Resource Executive*, April 2006, pp. 44, 46.
7. A. Halcrow, "Survey Shows HRM in Transition," *Workforce*, June 1998, pp. 73–80: J. Laabs, "Why HR Can't Win Today," *Workforce*, May 1998, pp. 62–74; C. Cole, "Kodak Snapshots," *Workforce*, June 2000, pp. 65–72; W. Ruona and S. Gibson, "The Making of Twenty-First Century HR: An Analysis of the Convergence of HRM, HRD, and OD," *Human Resource Management* 43 (2004), pp. 49–66.
8. Towers Perrin, *Priorities for Competitive Advantage: An IBM Study Conducted by Towers Perrin*, 1992.
9. S. Greengard, "Building a Self-Service Culture That Works," *Workforce*, July 1998, pp. 60–64.
10. G. Yohe, "Building Your Case," *Human Resource Executive*, March 2, 2003, pp. 22–26.
11. S. Caudron, "HR Is Dead Long Live HR," *Workforce*, January 2003, pp. 26–29; Society for Human Resource Management, *HR's Evolving Role in Organizations and Its Impact on Business Strategy* (Alexandria, VA: Society for Human Resource Management, 2008); "The Buying Services Game" *HR Magazine*, November 2008, pp. 77–82.
12. P. Ketter, "HR Outsourcing Accelerates," *T + D*, February 2007, pp. 12–13.
13. P. Babcock, "A Crowded Space," *HR Magazine*, March 2006, pp. 68–74.
14. M. Rafter, "Promise Fulfilled," *Workforce Management*, September 2005, pp. 51–54.
15. M. Schoeff Jr., "Cardinal Health HR to Take More Strategic Role," *Workforce Management*, April 24, 2006, p. 7.
16. T. Starner, "Managing the Handoff," *Human Resource Executive*, March 2, 2005, pp. 1, 18–25; S. Westcott, "Should It Stay or Go?" *Human Resource Executive*, May 16, 2005, pp. 30–33.
17. Towers Perrin, *Priorities for Competitive Advantage.*
18. F. Hansen, "Top of the Class," *Workforce Management*, June 23, 2008, pp. 1, 32.
19. P. Wright, *Human Resource Strategy: Adapting to the Age of Globalization* (Alexandria, VA: Society for Human Resource Management Foundation, 2008).
20. L. Claus and J. Collison, *The Maturing Profession of Human Resources: Worldwide and Regional View* (Alexandria, VA: Society for Human Resource Management, 2005).
21. Ibid.
22. J. Wiscombe, "Your Wonderful, Terrible HR Life," *Workforce*, June 2001, pp. 32–38.
23. Hansen, "Top of the Class."
24. R. Grossman, "Putting HR in Rotation," *HR Magazine*, March 2003, pp. 50–57.
25. Caudron, "HR Is Dead Long Live HR"; S. Bates, "Business Partners," *HR Magazine*, September 2003, pp. 45–49.

26. A. Jones, "Evolutionary Science, Work/Life Integration, and Corporate Responsibility," *Organizational Dynamics* 32 (2002), pp. 17–31.

27. A. Fox, "Get in the Business of Being Green," *HR Magazine*, June 2008, p. 45.

28. K. Evans and K. Maher, "Yearly Job Loss Worst Since 1945," *The Wall Street Journal*, January 10–11, 2009, pp. A1-2; S. Reddy, R. Smith, and K. Maher, "Job Losses Are Worst Since '74," *The Wall Street Journal*, December 6–7, 2008, pp. A1 & A8; D. DePass, "Factories Can't Stop the Bleeding," *Columbus Dispatch*, December 21, 2008, p. D3; "US Unemployment Rate Jumps to 8.1%," www.dispatch.com, March 6, 2009.

29. R. Curran, "Dow Jones Industrials Lost 18% in Their Worst Week Ever," *The Wall Street Journal*, October 11–12, 2008, p. B3; T. Lauricella, "Dow Fall 281.40, Now Down 25% for the Year,' *The Wall Street Journal*, March 6, 2009, p. C1.

30. E. White and S. Thurm, "Layoffs Continue in the New Year," *The Wall Street Journal*, January 10–11, 2009, p. A2; S. Wartenberg, "44,400 Jobs Gone," *Columbus Dispatch*, January 27, 2009, pp. A1, A4. S. Reddy, "Jobless Rate Hits 8.5%," *The Wall Street Journal*, April 4–5, 2009, p. A1.

31. J. McGregor, "Keeping Talent in the Fold," *BusinessWeek*, November 3, 2008, pp. 51–52.

32. R. Zeidner, "Strategies for Savings in a Down Economy," *HR Magazine*, February 2009, pp. 26–33.

33. S. Wells, "Managing a Downturn," *HR Magazine*, May 2008, pp. 48–52.

34. D. Mattioli, "Despite Cutbacks, Firms Invest in Developing Leaders," *The Wall Street Journal*, February 9, 2009, p. B4.

35. Society for Human Resource Management, "HR Insight into the Economy," *Workplace Visions* 4 (2008), p. 4; Society for Human Resource Management, "Workplace Trends: An Overview of the Findings of the Latest SHRM Workplace Forecast," *Workplace Visions* 3 (2008), pp. 1–6.

36. M. Conlin, "Get Healthy or Else," *BusinessWeek*, February 26, 2007, pp. 58–69.

37. "Workplace Visions," *Society for Human Resource Management* 4 (2002).

38. E. Figueroa and R. Woods, "Industry Output and Employment Projections to 2016," *Monthly Labor Review*, November 2007, pp. 53–85.

39. A. Dohm and L. Shniper, "Occupational Employment Projections to 2016," *Monthly Labor Review*, November 2007, pp. 86–125.

40. M. Hilton, "Skills for Work in the 21st Century: What Does the Research Tell Us?" *Academy of Management Executive*, November 2008, pp. 63–78; "Manufacturing: Engine of US Innovation," *National Association of Manufacturing* (October 4, 2006), available at www.nam.org (accessed January 21, 2009).

41. J. Rossi, "The 'Future' of U.S. Manufacturing," *TD*, March 2006, pp. 12–13.

42. Society for Human Resource Management, Conference Board, Partnership for 21st Century Skills, Corporate Voices for Working Families, *Are They Ready to Work?* (New York: Conference Board, 2006).

43. R. Davenport, "Eliminate the Skills Gap," *TD*, February 2006, pp. 26–34.

44. National Science Board, *Science and Engineering Indicators*, vol. 1, (Arlington, VA: National Science Foundation, 2006).

45. M. Schoeff, "Amid Calls to Bolster U.S. Innovation, Experts Lament Paucity of Basic Math Skills," *Workforce Management*, March 2006, pp. 46–49.

46. J. Barbian, "Get 'em While They're Young," *Training*, January 2004, pp. 44–46; E. Frauenheim, "IBM Urged to Take Tech Skills to Classrooms," *Workforce Management*, October 24, 2005, pp. 8–9; K. Maher, "Skills Shortage Gives Training Programs New Life," *The Wall Street Journal*, June 3, 2005, p. A2.

47. M. Horrigan, "Employment Projections to 2012: Concepts and Context," *Monthly Labor Review* 127 (2004), pp. 3–22.

48. J. Barney, *Gaining and Sustaining a Competitive Advantage* (Upper Saddle River, NJ: Prentice Hall, 2002).

49. L. Weatherly, *Human Capital: The Elusive Asset* (Alexandria, VA: 2003 SHRM Research Quarterly).

50. W. Zeller, "Southwest: After Kelleher, More Blue Skies," *BusinessWeek*, April 2, 2001, p. 45; S. McCartney, "Southwest Sets Standards on Costs," *The Wall Street Journal*, October 10, 2002, p. A2; S. Warren and M. Trottman, "Southwest's Dallas Duel," *The Wall Street Journal*, May 10, 2005, pp. B1, B4.

51. E. McGirt, "Revolution in San Jose," *Fast Company*, January 2009, pp. 89–94, 134–136.

52. L. Bassi, J. Ludwig, D. McMurrer, and M. Van Buren, *Profiting from Learning: Do Firms' Investments in Education and Training Pay Off?* (Alexandria, VA: American Society for Training and Development, September 2000).

53. T. J. Atchison, "The Employment Relationship: Untied or Re-Tied," *Academy of Management Executive* 5 (1991), pp. 52–62.

54. J. Marquez, "Driving Ideas Forward at Nissan," *Workforce Management*, July 17, 2006, p. 28.

55. P. Drucker, *Management Challenges for the 21st Century* (New York: HarperBusiness, 1999); Howard N. Fullerton Jr., "Labor Force Projections to 2008: Steady Growth and Changing Composition," *Monthly Labor Review*, November 1999, pp. 19–32.

56. J. Stoll, "Chrysler Details Program to Cut White-Collar Jobs," *The Wall Street Journal*, February 24–25, 2007, p. A3.

57. D. Senge, "The Learning Organization Made Plain and Simple," *Training and Development Journal*, October 1991, pp. 37–44.

58. L. Thornburg, "Accounting for Knowledge," *HR Magazine*, October 1994, pp. 51–56.

59. J. O'Toole and E. Lawler III, *The New American Workplace* (New York: Palgrave McMillan, 2006).

60. D. M. Rousseau, "Psychological and Implied Contracts in Organizations," *Employee Rights and Responsibilities Journal* 2 (1989), pp. 121–29.

61. D. Rousseau, "Changing the Deal While Keeping the People," *Academy of Management Executive* 11 (1996), pp. 50–61; M. A. Cavanaugh and R. Noe, "Antecedents and Consequences of the New Psychological Contract," *Journal of Organizational Behavior* 20 (1999), pp. 323–40.

62. R. Vance, *Employee Engagement and Commitment* (Alexandria, VA: Society for Human Resource Management, 2006).

63. For examples see M. Huselid, "The Impact of Human Resource Management Practices on Turnover, Productivity, and Corporate Financial Performance," *Academy of Management Journal* 38 (1995), pp. 635–72; S. Payne and S. Webber, "Effects of Service Provider Attitudes and Employment Status on Citizenship Behaviors and Customers' Attitudes and Loyalty Behavior," *Journal of Applied Psychology* 91 (2006), pp. 365–68; J. Hartner, F. Schmidt, and T. Hayes, "Business-Unit Level Relationship between Employee Satisfaction, Employee Engagement, and Business Outcomes: A Meta-analysis," *Journal of Applied Psychology* 87 (2002), pp. 268–79; I. Fulmer, B. Gerhart, and K. Scott, "Are the 100 Best Better? An Empirical Investigation of the Relationship between Being a 'Great Place to Work' and Firm Performance," *Personnel Psychology* 56 (2003), pp. 965–93; "Working Today: Understanding What Drives Employee Engagement," *Towers Perrin Talent Report* (2003).

64. Corporate Leadership Council, *Driving Performance and Retention through Employee Engagement* (Washington, DC: Corporate Executive Board, 2004).

65. J. Robinson, "A Caterpillar Dealer Unearths Employee Engagement" (October 12, 2006), at http://gmj.gallup.com/content/24874/1/A-Caterpillar-Dealer-Unearths-Employee-Engagement.aspx.

66. *Talent Management: The State of the Art* (Stamford, CT: Towers-Perrin, 2005).

67. Society for Human Resource Management, *Workplace Visions* 5 (2000), pp. 3–4.

68. E. White, "Manager Shortage Spurs Small Firms to Grow Their Own," *The Wall Street Journal*, February 5, 2007, pp. B1, B4; P. Galagan, "Talent Management: What Is It, Who Owns It, and Why Should You Care?" *T+D*, May 2008, pp. 40–44.

69. P. Cappelli, "Talent Management for the Twenty-First Century," *Harvard Business Review*, March 2008, pp. 74–81.

70. C. Hymowitz, "Best Way to Save: Analyze Why Talent Is Going Out the Door," *The Wall Street Journal*, September 24, 2007, p. B1; C. Hymowitz, "They Ponder Layoffs, but Executives Still Face Gaps in Talent," *The Wall Street Journal*, January 28, 2008, p. B1.

71. Bureau of Labor Statistics, "Contingent and Alternative Employment Arrangements, February 2005" from www.bls.gov (accessed January 21, 2009).

72. F. Hansen, "A Permanent Strategy for Temporary Hires," *Workforce Management*, February 26, 2007, pp. 25–30.

73. P. Kiger, "Flexibility to the Fullest," *Workforce Management*, September 25, 2006, pp. 1, 16–23.

74. S. Shellenbarger, "Time-Zoned: Working around the Round-the-Clock Workday," *The Wall Street Journal*, February 15, 2007, p. D1.

75. R. S. Kaplan and D. P. Norton, "The Balanced Scorecard—Measures That Drive Performance," *Harvard Business Review*, January–February 1992, pp. 71–79; R. S. Kaplan and D. P. Norton, "Putting the Balanced Scorecard to Work," *Harvard Business Review*, September–October 1993, pp. 134–47.

76. M. Gendron, "Using the Balanced Scorecard," *Harvard Business Review*, October 1997, pp. 3–5.

77. S. Bates, "The Metrics Maze," *HR Magazine*, December 2003, pp. 50–55; D. Ulrich, "Measuring Human Resources: An Overview of Practice and a Prescription for Results," *Human Resource Management* 36 (1997), pp. 303–20.

78. E. Raimy, "A Plan for All Seasons," *Human Resource Executive*, April 2001, pp. 34–38.

79. R. Alsop, "How Boss's Deeds Buff a Firm's Reputation," *The Wall Street Journal*, January 31, 2007, pp. B1, B2; S. Zadek, "Separating Smart from Great," *Fortune*, October 23, 2006. From CNNMoney.com.

80. M. Lev-Ram, "Cell-Phone Makers See Green by Going Green," *Business 2.0 Magazine*, August 11, 2006. From CNNMoney.com.

81. S. Prasso, "Saving the World One Cup of Yogurt at a Time," *Fortune*, February 19, 2007, pp. 96–102.

82. A. Fox, "Get in the Business of Being Green," *HR Magazine*, June 2008, p. 45

83. J. R. Jablonski, *Implementing Total Quality Management: An Overview* (San Diego: Pfeiffer, 1991).

84. R. Hodgetts, F. Luthans, and S. Lee, "New Paradigm Organizations: From Total Quality to Learning World-Class," *Organizational Dynamics*, Winter 1994, pp. 5–19.

85. A. Pomeroy, "Winners and Learners," *HR Magazine*, April 2006, pp. 62–67.

86. "Malcolm Baldrige 2007 Award Recipient: PRO-TECH Coating Company" available at 2007 Baldrige Award recipients 2007 profiles at www.nist.gov; "Malcolm Baldrige 2007 Award Recipient, "Sharp HealthCare" available at 2007 Baldrige Award recipients 2007 profiles at www.nist.gov.

87. S. L. Jackson, "What You Should Know about ISO 9000," *Training*, May 1992, pp. 48–52; Bureau of Best Practices, *Profile of ISO 9000* (Boston: Allyn and Bacon, 1992); "ISO 9000 International Standards for Quality Assurance," *Design Matters*, July 1995, http://www.best.com/ISO 9000/att/ISONet.html/. See www.iso9000y2k.com, a Web site containing ISO 9000:2000 documentation.

88. General Electric 1999 Annual Report, www.ge.com/annual99.

89. D. Arnold, "Cardinal Fastener Soars with Lean Thinking," from www.cardinalfastener.com (accessed January 19, 2008).

90. Toosi, "Labor Force Projections to 2016."

91. N. Lockwood, *The Aging Workforce* (Alexandria, VA: Society for Human Resource Management, 2003).

92. J. Marquez, "Novel Ideas at Borders Lure Older Workers," *Workforce Management*, May 2005, pp. 28, 30.

93. M. Weinstein, "NASA Training Program Blasts Off," *Training*, December 2005, pp. 8–9; J. Salopek, "The New Brain Drain," *TD*, June 2005, pp. 23–25; P. Harris, "Beware of the Boomer Brain Drain!" *TD*, January 2006, pp. 30–33; M. McGraw, "Bye-Bye Boomers," *Human Resource Executive*, March 2, 2006, pp. 34–37.

94. P. Harden, "The Federal Exodus," *Human Resource Executive*, November 2005, pp. 70–73.

95. M. Toossi, "Labor Force Projections to 2016! More Workers in the Golden Years," *Monthly Labor Review*, November 2007, pp. 33–52; J. Franklin, "An Overview of BLS Projections to 2016, *Monthly Labor Review*, November 2007, pp. 3–12.

96. B. Newman, "Employers Have a Lot to Lose," *The Wall Street Journal*, April 11, 2006, pp. B1, B4.

97. M. Jordan, J. Kronholz, and B. Newman, "Off the Job, onto the Streets," *The Wall Street Journal*, April 11, 2006, pp. B1, B4; I. Speizer, "Roots of the Immigration Debate," *Workforce Management*, August 14, 2006, pp. 1, 18–26.

98. Ibid.

99. R. Block, "Homeland Security Strategy Hits Executives, Illegal Workers," *The Wall Street Journal*, February 23, 2007, p. A5.

100. M. Johnson, "Blind Workers Find Fulfillment at Wiscraft Inc.," *Columbus Dispatch*, February 18, 2006, p. F2.

101. B. Hite, "Employers Rethink How They Give Feedback," *The Wall Street Journal*, October 13, 2008, p. B5; E. White, "Age Is as Age Does: Making the Generation Gap Work for You," *The Wall Street Journal*, June 30, 2008, p. B3; P. Harris, "The Work War," *TD*, May 2005, pp. 45–48; C. Hirshman, "Here They Come," *HR Executive*, July 2006, pp. 1, 22–26.

102. M. Rowh, "Older and Wiser," *Human Resource Executive*, August 2008, pp. 35–37.

103. B. Wooldridge and J. Wester, "The Turbulent Environment of Public Personnel Administration: Responding to the Challenge of the Changing Workplace of the Twenty-First Century," *Public Personnel Management* 20 (1991), pp. 207–24; J. Laabs, "The New Loyalty: Grasp It. Earn It. Keep It," *Workforce*, November 1998, pp. 34–39.

104. "Employee Dissatisfaction on Rise in Last 10 Years, New Report Says," *Employee Relations Weekly* (Washington, DC: Bureau of National Affairs, 1986).

105. D. T. Hall and J. Richter, "Career Gridlock: Baby Boomers Hit the Wall," *The Executive* 4 (1990), pp. 7–22.

106. T. H. Cox and S. Blake, "Managing Cultural Diversity: Implications for Organizational Competitiveness," *The Executive* 5 (1991), pp. 45–56.

107. M. Loden and J. B. Rosener, *Workforce America!* (Homewood, IL: Business One Irwin, 1991); N. Lockwood, *Workplace Diversity: Leveraging the Power of Difference for Competitive Advantage* (Alexandria: VA: Society for Human Resource Management, 2005).

108. R. Rodriguez, "Diversity Finds Its Place," *HR Magazine*, August 2006, pp. 56–61.

109. J. Taylor Arnold, "Employee Networks," *HR Magazine*, June 2006, pp. 145–52.

110. A. Pomeroy, "Cultivating Female Leaders," *HR Magazine*, February 2007, pp. 44–50.

111. J. Ledvinka and V. G. Scarpello, *Federal Regulation of Personnel and Human Resource Management*, 2nd ed. (Boston: PWS-Kent, 1991).

112. D. White, "The New Frontier," *Human Resource Executive*, October 16, 2005, pp. 32–34.

113. N. Lockwood, *The Glass Ceiling: Domestic and International Perspectives* (Alexandria, VA: Society for Human Resource Management, 2004).

114. *Women in U.S. Corporate Leadership: 2003* (New York: Catalyst, 2003).

115. J. Zhang, "Genetic-Discrimination Ban Nears Congressional Approval," *The Wall Street Journal*, February 15, 2007, p. A11.

116. M. Pastin, *The Hard Problems of Management: Gaining the Ethics Edge* (San Francisco: Jossey-Bass, 1986); T. Thomas, J. Schermerhorn, Jr., and J. Dienhart, "Strategic Leadership of Ethical Behavior in Business," *Academy of Management Executive* 18 (2004), pp. 56–66.

117. Ibid.

118. K. Gurchiek, "Sarbanes-Oxley Compliance Costs Rising," *HR Magazine*, January 2005, pp. 29, 33.

119. R. Grossman, "HR and the Board," *HR Magazine*, January 2007, pp. 52–58.

120. J. Segal, "The 'Joy' of Uncooking," *HR Magazine* 47 (11) (2002).

121. D. Buss, "Corporate Compasses," *HR Magazine* 49 (6) (2004), pp. 126–32.

122. C. Cornell, "Someone Who Will Listen," *Human Resource Executive*, February 2007, p. 16.

123. D. Buss, "Working It Out," *HRMagazine online*, www.shrm.org/hrmagazine/04June.

124. G. F. Cavanaugh, D. Moberg, and M. Velasquez, "The Ethics of Organizational Politics," *Academy of Management Review* 6 (1981), pp. 363–74.

125. "Manufacturing: Engine of US Innovation," *National Association of Manufacturing* (October 4, 2006), available at www.nam.org (accessed January 21, 2009).

126. C. Hill, *International Business* (Burr Ridge, IL: Irwin/McGraw-Hill, 1997).

127. B. McKay, "Coke Bets on Russia for Sales Even as Economy Falls Flat," *The Wall Street Journal*, January 28, 2009, pp. A1, A12.

128. C. Hymowitz, "IBM Combines Volunteer Service, Teamwork to Cultivate Emerging Markets," *The Wall Street Journal*, August 4, 2008, p. B6.

129. D. Ready and J. Conger, "How to Fill the Talent Gap," *The Wall Street Journal*, September 15–16, 2007, pp. R4, R5.

130. J. Schramm, "Offshoring," *Workplace Visions* 2 (Alexandria, VA: Society for Human Resource Management, 2004); P. Babcock, "America's Newest Export: White Collar Jobs," *HR Magazine* 49 (4) 2004, pp. 50–57.

131. F. Hansen, "U.S. Firms Going Wherever the Knowledge Workers Are," *Workforce Management*, October 2005, pp. 43–44.

132. Jim Hopkins, "To Start Up Here, Companies Hire Over There," *USA Today*, February 10, 2005, downloaded at www.usatoday.com.

133. Ibid.

134. Hansen, "U.S. Firms Going Where the Knowledge Workers Are."

135. R. Grossman, "The Truth about the Coming Labor Shortage," *HR Magazine*, March 2005, pp. 47–53; S. Ladika, "The Brain Race," *HR Magazine*, April 2006, pp. 69–74.

136. M. Schoeff Jr., "The Immigration Squeeze," *Workforce Management*, May 19, 2008, pp. 23–27.

137. J. Marquez, "Going Rural: A U.S. Alternative to Offshoring," *Workforce Management*, September 2005, pp. 16–17.

138. R. Chittum, "Call Centers Phone Home," *The Wall Street Journal*, June 9, 2004, pp. B1, B8.

139. J. Kahn, "Small Firms Find That Outsourcing Cuts Both Ways," *Fortune*, April 28, 2004, at www.fortune.com.

140. M. Kripalani and P. Engardio, "The Rise of India," *BusinessWeek*, December 8, 2003, pp. 66–76.

141. S. Ho, "Poll Finds Nearly 80 Percent of U.S. Adults Go Online," (November 5, 2007), www.reuters.com (accessed March 2, 2009).

142. H. Dolezalek, "Virtual Agent Nation," *Training*, June 2004, p. 12.

143. I. Brat, "A Joy(stick) to Behold," *The Wall Street Journal*, June 23, 2008, p. R5.

144. A. Weintraub, "High Tech's Future Is in the Toy Chest," *BusinessWeek*, August 26, 2002, pp. 124–26.

145. *2002 Benefits Survey* (Alexandria, VA: Society of Human Resource Management Foundation, 2002).

146. S. Greengard, "Sun's Shining Example," *Workforce Management*, March 2005, pp. 48–49.

147. P. Choate and P. Linger, *The High-Flex Society* (New York: Knopf, 1986); P. B. Doeringer, *Turbulence in the American Workplace* (New York: Oxford University Press, 1991).

148. J. A. Neal and C. L. Tromley, "From Incremental Change to Retrofit: Creating High-Performance Work Systems," *Academy of Management Executive* 9 (1995), pp. 42–54.

149. K. A. Miller, *Retraining the American Workforce* (Reading, MA: Addison-Wesley, 1989).

150. S. Moffett, "Separation Anxiety," *The Wall Street Journal*, September 27, 2004, p. R11.

151. J. Gordon, "Do Your Virtual Teams Deliver Only Virtual Performance?" *Training*, June 2005, pp. 20–25.

152. A. Gupta, "Expanding the 24-Hour Workplace," *The Wall Street Journal*, September 15–16, 2007, pp. R9, R11.

153. T. Peters, "Restoring American Competitiveness: Looking for New Models of Organizations," *The Executive* 2 (1988), pp. 103–10.

154. J. Marquez, "Taking a Longer View," *Workforce Management*, May 22, 2006, pp. 18–22.

155. "Outstanding Training Initiatives: Capital One: Audio Learning in Stereo," *Training*, March 2006, p. 64.

156. J. Marquez, "Firms Tap Virtual Work Spaces to Ease Collaboration, Debate among Scattered Employees," *Workforce Management*, May 22, 2006, pp. 38–39.

157. D. Foust, "How Technology Delivers for UPS," *BusinessWeek*, March 5, 2007, p. 60.

158. M. J. Kavanaugh, H. G. Guetal, and S. I. Tannenbaum, *Human Resource Information Systems: Development and Application* (Boston: PWS-Kent, 1990).

159. Bill Roberts, "Empowerment or Imposition?" *HR Magazine*, June 2004, downloaded from Infotrac at http://web7.infotrac. galegroup.com.

160. Ibid.

161. L. Weatherly, "HR Technology: Leveraging the Shift to Self-Service," *HR Magazine*, March 2005.

162. N. Lockwood, *Maximizing Human Capital: Demonstrating HR Value with Key Performance Indicators* (Alexandria, VA: SHRM Research Quarterly, 2006).

163. R. N. Ashkenas, "Beyond the Fads: How Leaders Drive Change with Results," *Human Resource Planning* 17 (1994), pp. 25–44.

164. M. A. Huselid, "The Impact of Human Resource Management Practices on Turnover, Productivity, and Corporate Financial Performance," *Academy of Management Journal* 38 (1995), pp. 635–72; U.S. Dept. of Labor, *High-Performance Work Practices and Firm Performance* (Washington, DC: U.S. Government Printing Office, 1993); J. Combs, Y. Liu, A. Hall, and D. Ketchen, "How Much Do High-Performance Work Practices Matter? A Meta-analysis of Their Effects on Organizational Performance," *Personnel Psychology* 59 (2006), pp. 501–28.

165. B. Becker and M. A. Huselid, "High-Performance Work Systems and Firm Performance: A Synthesis of Research and Managerial Implications," in *Research in Personnel and Human Resource Management* 16, ed. G. R. Ferris (Stamford, CT: JAI Press, 1998), pp. 53–101; A. Zacharatos, J. Barling, and R. Iverson, "High Performance Work Systems and Occupational Safety," *Journal of Applied Psychology* 90 (2005), pp. 77–93.

166. B. Becker and B. Gerhart, "The Impact of Human Resource Management on Organizational Performance: Progress and Prospects," *Academy of Management Journal* 39 (1996), pp. 779–801.

167. J. Marquez, "Engine of Change," *Workforce Management*, July 17, 2006, pp. 20–30.

168. S. A. Snell and J. W. Dean, "Integrated Manufacturing and Human Resource Management: A Human Capital Perspective," *Academy of Management Journal* 35 (1992), pp. 467–504; M. A. Youndt, S. Snell, J. W. Dean Jr., and D. P. Lepak, "Human Resource Management, Manufacturing Strategy, and Firm Performance," *Academy of Management Journal* 39 (1996), pp. 836–66.

PART

1

The Human Resource Environment

Strategic Human Resource Management

LO LEARNING OBJECTIVES

After reading this chapter, you should be able to:

LO1   Describe the differences between strategy formulation and strategy implementation. *page 74*

LO2   List the components of the strategic management process. *page 75*

LO3   Discuss the role of the HRM function in strategy formulation. *page 78*

LO4   Describe the linkages between HRM and strategy formulation. *page 79*

LO5   Discuss the more popular typologies of generic strategies and the various HRM practices associated with each. *page 83*

LO6   Describe the different HRM issues and practices associated with various directional strategies. *page 91*

GM's Attempt to Survive

The auto industry currently faces a financial crisis, to the point that General Motors, the once-great, world-leading automobile manufacturer, may have to declare bankruptcy without almost $30 billion in government aid. However, the aid is only a stopgap—something to get GM through the next few years while they try to restructure the company in a way that will make them viable for the long term. What kind of restructuring is required? In essence, GM needs to create a new business model that will enable them to sell enough cars at a high enough price to cover their costs, and it is the costs that are killing them.

Critics of GM talk about the fact that GM has higher labor costs than their foreign competitors. This is true, but misleading. GM's average hourly wage for their existing workforce is reasonably competitive. However, the two aspects that make GM uncompetitive are their benefit costs (in particular, health care) and, most importantly, the cost of their legacy workforce.

A legacy workforce describes the former workers (i.e., those no longer working for the company) to whom the firm still owes financial obligations. GM and the United Auto Workers (UAW) union have negotiated contracts over the years that provide substantial retirement benefits for former GM workers. In particular, retired GM workers have defined benefit plans that guarantee a certain percentage of their final (pre-retirement) salary as a pension payment as long as they live as well as having the company pay for their health insurance. In addition, the contract specifies that workers are entitled to retire at full pension after 30 years of service. So, someone who started at age 18 can retire at age 48 and, according to actuarial tables, potentially get 30 more years of payments and health insurance for the 30 years they worked.

This might have seemed sustainable when the projections were that GM would continue growing

its sales and margins. However, since the 1970s, foreign competitors have been eating away at GM's market share to the extent that GM's former 50 percent of the market has shrunk to closer to 20 percent. In addition, with the current economic crisis, the market itself has been shrinking, leaving GM with a decreasing percentage of a decreasing market. For instance, in December 2005, GM sold 26 percent of the cars in the global market of almost 1.5 million, but by December 2008, that market had shrunk to just under 900,000, and GM's share had gone to 25 percent. In January 2009, the market had shrunk to 656,000, and GM was down to 20 percent of those sales. Thus, in addition to the legacy workforce, they have a significant number of plants with thousands of employees who are completely unnecessary, given the volume of cars GM can produce and sell.

So, the crisis facing GM consists of falling revenues and stable, or even increasing fixed costs (the existing workforce as well as the legacy workforce). What can GM do to change its business model?

Sources: P. Ingrassia "GM's Plan: Susidize Our 48-Year Old Retirees," *The Wall Street Journal*, February 19, 2009, http://online.wsj.com/article/SB123500874299418721.html; S. Terlep and N. King, "Bondholders Say GM's Plan Fails to Tackle Issues," *The Wall Street Journal*, February 19, 2009, http://online.wsj.com/article/SB123500467245718075.html?mod=testMod.

Introduction

As the General Motors example just illustrated, business organizations exist in an environment of competition. They can use a number of resources to compete with other companies. These resources are physical (such as plant, equipment, technology, and geographic location), organizational (the structure, planning, controlling, and coordinating systems, and group relations), and human (the experience, skill, and intelligence of employees). It is these resources under the control of the company that provide competitive advantage.[1]

The goal of strategic management in an organization is to deploy and allocate resources in a way that gives it a competitive advantage. As you can see, two of the three classes of resources (organizational and human) are directly tied to the human resource management function. As Chapter 1 pointed out, the role of human resource management is to ensure that a company's human resources provide a competitive advantage. Chapter 1 also pointed out some of the major competitive challenges that companies face today. These challenges require companies to take a proactive, strategic approach in the marketplace.

To be maximally effective, the HRM function must be integrally involved in the company's strategic management process.[2] This means that human resource managers should (1) have input into the strategic plan, both in terms of people-related issues and in terms of the ability of the human resource pool to implement particular strategic alternatives; (2) have specific knowledge of the organization's strategic goals; (3) know what types of employee skills, behaviors, and attitudes are needed to support the strategic plan; and (4) develop programs to ensure that employees have those skills, behaviors, and attitudes.

We begin this chapter by discussing the concepts of business models and strategy and by depicting the strategic management process. Then, we discuss the levels of integration between the HRM function and the strategic management process in strategy formulation. Next, we review some of the more common strategic models and, within the context of these models, discuss the various types of employee skills, behaviors, and attitudes, and the ways HRM practices aid in implementing the strategic plan. Finally, we discuss the role of HR in creating competitive advantage.

What Is a Business Model?

A business model is a story of how the firm will create value for customers and, more important, how it will do so profitably. We often hear or read of companies that have "transformed their business model" in one way or another, but what that means is not always clear. To understand this, we need to grasp a few basic accounting concepts.

First, fixed costs are generally considered the costs that are incurred regardless of the number of units produced. For instance, if you are producing widgets in a factory, you have the rent you pay for the factory, depreciation of the machines, the utilities, the property taxes, and so on. In addition, you generally have a set number of employees who work a set number of hours with a specified level of benefits, and while you might be able to vary these over time, on a regular basis you pay the same total labor costs whether your factory runs at 70 percent capacity or 95 percent capacity.

Second, you have a number of variable costs, which are those costs that vary directly with the units produced. For instance, all of the materials that go into the widget might cost a total of $10, which means that you have to charge at least $10 per widget, or you cannot even cover the variable costs of production.

Third is the concept of "contribution margins," or margins. Margins are the difference between what you charge for your product and the variable costs of that product. They are called contribution margins because they are what contributes to your ability to cover your fixed costs. So, for instance, if you charged $15 for each widget, your contribution margin would be $5 ($15 price − $10 variable cost).

Fourth, the gross margin is the total amount of margin you made and is calculated as the number of units sold times the contribution margin. If you sold 1,000,000 units, your gross margin would then be $5,000,000. Did you make a profit? That depends. Profit refers to what is left after you have paid your variable costs and your fixed costs. If your gross margin was $5,000,000, and your fixed costs were $6,000,000, then you lost $1,000,000.

So, returning to the GM case that began this chapter, what does it mean to redesign the GM business model for long-term competitiveness? If you look at Figure 2.1, you'll see that the solid lines represent the old GM business model, which was based on projections that GM would be able to sell 4 million units at a reasonably high margin, and thus completely cover its fixed costs to make a strong profit. However, the reality was that its products didn't sell at the higher prices, so to try to sell 4 million vehicles, GM offered discounts, which cut into its margins. When GM ended up selling only 3.5 million vehicles, and those were sold at a lower margin, the company could not cover its fixed costs, resulting in a $9 billion loss in 2008 (this is illustrated by the dotted blue line in the figure). So, when GM refers to the "redesigned business model," what it is referring to is a significant reduction in fixed costs (through closing plants and cutting workers) to get the fixed-cost base low enough (the dotted red line) to be able to still be profitable selling fewer cars at lower margins (again, the dotted blue line).

One can easily see how, given the large component that labor costs are to most companies, reference to business models almost inevitably leads to discussions of labor costs. These can be the high cost associated with current unionized employees in developed countries within North America or Europe or, in some cases, the high costs associated with a legacy workforce. For instance, the Big Three automakers have huge numbers of retired or laid-off workers for whom they still have the liability of paying pensions and health care benefits. This is a significant component of their fixed-cost base, which makes it difficult for them to compete with other automakers that either have fewer

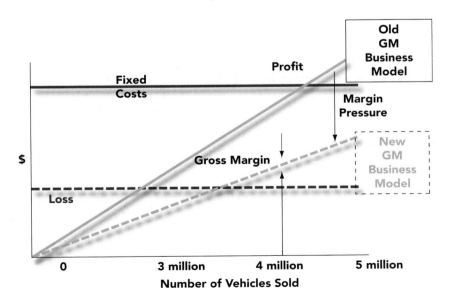

figure 2.1

An Illustration of a Business Model for GM

As the economic turmoil continues to force companies to better manage their labor costs, retailers are finding that information technology can enable them to schedule their workforce in ways that maximize customer service while minimizing labor costs. Retailers around the world from every industry segment—including Wal-Mart, GameStop, IKEA, Payless, and PUMA—use "scheduling optimization software" solutions to drive store productivity, control labor costs, and minimize compliance risk. Such systems integrate data such as the number of customers at different hours of the day, the time needed to sell certain products, and/or the time needed to unload a truck to help predict how many workers a store needs at any given hour. This enables the stores to cut costs by having fewer unnecessary paid employees being paid during slow times. Nikki Baird of Forrester Research Inc. says, "There's been a new push for labor optimization. You want to have the flexibility to more closely match . . . shifts to when the demand is there." For instance, Wal-Mart, in a test of 39 stores, found that 70 percent of customers said the checkout experience had improved. Wal-Mart spokeswoman Sarah Clark states, "The advantages are simple. We will benefit by improving the shopping experience by having the right number of associates to meet our customers' needs when they shop our stores."

And far from being a solution that exploits workers, the advanced schedule optimization in fact creates the best-fit employee schedules based on employee skills, availabilities, and work/life preferences. It also helps retailers to effectively comply with federal, state, and corporate work rules covering employee scheduling, shifts, meals, breaks, union requirements, and the use of minor age employees.

Research by Kronos found that 71 percent of the respondents found that such workforce management technology helps them control their labor costs, but more interestingly, 88 percent said that their store associates have reacted positively to the scheduling technology.

SOURCE: "Kronos® for Retail Schedules 1.5 Million Associates," *Computer Technology Journal*, January 29, 2009, p. 275.

retirees to cover or have no comparable costs because their home governments provide pensions and health care. The "Competing through Technology" box describes how a number of retailers are using technology to effectively match employee schedules to customer traffic in order to effectively serve their customers in an efficient manner.

What Is Strategic Management?

LO1
Describe the differences between strategy formulation and strategy implementation.

Many authors have noted that in today's competitive market, organizations must engage in strategic planning to survive and prosper. Strategy comes from the Greek word *strategos*, which has its roots in military language. It refers to a general's grand design behind a war or battle. In fact, *Webster's New American Dictionary* defines strategy as the "skillful employment and coordination of tactics" and as "artful planning and management."

Strategic management is a process, an approach to addressing the competitive challenges an organization faces. It can be thought of as managing the "pattern or plan that integrates an organization's major goals, policies, and action sequences into a cohesive whole."[3] These strategies can be either the generic approach to competing or the specific adjustments and actions taken to deal with a particular situation.

First, business organizations engage in generic strategies that often fit into some strategic type. One example is "cost, differentiation, or focus."[4] Another is "defender, analyzer, prospector, or reactor."[5] Different organizations within the same industry often have different generic strategies. These generic strategy types describe the consistent way the company attempts to position itself relative to competitors.

However, a generic strategy is only a small part of strategic management. The second aspect of strategic management is the process of developing strategies for achieving the company's goals in light of its current environment. Thus, business organizations engage in generic strategies, but they also make choices about such things as how to scare off competitors, how to keep competitors weaker, how to react to and influence pending legislation, how to deal with various stakeholders and special interest groups, how to lower production costs, how to raise revenues, what technology to implement, and how many and what types of people to employ. Each of these decisions may present competitive challenges that have to be considered.

Strategic management is more than a collection of strategic types. It is a process for analyzing a company's competitive situation, developing the company's strategic goals, and devising a plan of action and allocation of resources (human, organizational, and physical) that will increase the likelihood of achieving those goals. This kind of strategic approach should be emphasized in human resource management. HR managers should be trained to identify the competitive issues the company faces with regard to human resources and think strategically about how to respond.

Strategic human resource management (SHRM) can be thought of as "the pattern of planned human resource deployments and activities intended to enable an organization to achieve its goals."[6] For example, many firms have developed integrated manufacturing systems such as advanced manufacturing technology, just-in-time inventory control, and total quality management in an effort to increase their competitive position. However, these systems must be run by people. SHRM in these cases entails assessing the employee skills required to run these systems and engaging in HRM practices, such as selection and training, that develop these skills in employees.[7] To take a strategic approach to HRM, we must first understand the role of HRM in the strategic management process.

Components of the Strategic Management Process

The strategic management process has two distinct yet interdependent phases: strategy formulation and strategy implementation. During **strategy formulation** the strategic planning groups decide on a strategic direction by defining the company's mission and goals, its external opportunities and threats, and its internal strengths and weaknesses. They then generate various strategic alternatives and compare those alternatives' ability to achieve the company's mission and goals. During **strategy implementation,** the organization follows through on the chosen strategy. This consists of structuring the organization, allocating resources, ensuring that the firm has skilled employees in place, and developing reward systems that align employee behavior with the organization's strategic goals. Both of these strategic management phases must be performed effectively. It is important to note that this process does not happen sequentially. As we will discuss later with regard to emergent strategies, this process entails a constant cycling of information and decision making. Figure 2.2 presents the strategic management process.

In recent years organizations have recognized that the success of the strategic management process depends largely on the extent to which the HRM function is involved.[8]

Strategic Human Resource Management (SHRM)
A pattern of planned human resource deployments and activities intended to enable an organization to achieve its goals.

Strategy Formulation
The process of deciding on a strategic direction by defining a company's mission and goals, its external opportunities and threats, and its internal strengths and weaknesses.

LO2
List the components of the strategic management process.

Strategy Implementation
The process of devising structures and allocating resources to enact the strategy a company has chosen.

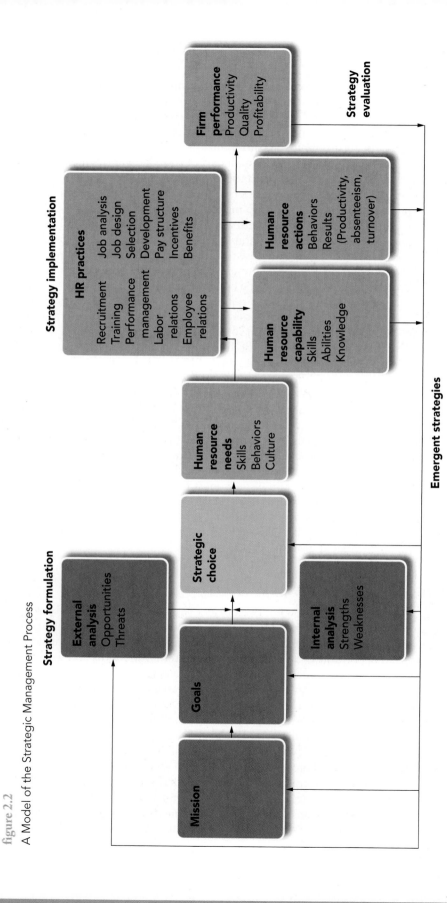

figure 2.2
A Model of the Strategic Management Process

Linkage between HRM and the Strategic Management Process

The strategic choice really consists of answering questions about competition—that is, how the firm will compete to achieve its missions and goals. These decisions consist of addressing the issues of where to compete, how to compete, and with what to compete, which are described in Figure 2.3.

Although these decisions are all important, strategic decision makers often pay less attention to the "with what will we compete" issue, resulting in poor strategic decisions. For example, PepsiCo in the 1980s acquired the fast-food chains of Kentucky Fried Chicken, Taco Bell, and Pizza Hut ("where to compete" decisions) in an effort to increase its customer base. However, it failed to adequately recognize the differences between its existing workforce (mostly professionals) and that of the fast-food industry (lower skilled people and high schoolers) as well as its ability to manage such a workforce. This was one reason that PepsiCo, in 1998, spun off the fast-food chains. In essence, it had made a decision about where to compete without fully understanding what resources would be needed to compete in that market.

Boeing illustrates how failing to address the "with what" issue resulted in problems in its "how to compete" decisions. When the aerospace firm's consumer products division entered into a price war with Airbus Industrie, it was forced to move away from its traditional customer service strategy toward emphasizing cost reduction.[9] The strategy was a success on the sales end as Boeing received large numbers of orders for aircraft from firms such as Delta, Continental, Southwest, and Singapore Airlines. However, it had recently gone through a large workforce reduction (thus, it didn't have enough people to fill the orders) and did not have the production technology to enable the necessary increase in productivity. The result of this failure to address "with what will we compete" in making a decision about how to compete resulted in the firm's inability to meet delivery deadlines and the ensuing penalties it had to pay to its customers. The end result is that after all the travails, for the first time in the history of the industry, Airbus sold more planes than Boeing in 2003. Luckily, Boeing was able to overcome this stumble, in large part because of a number of stumbles on the part of its chief rival, Airbus. Boeing's 787 Dreamliner has generated a number of orders, while Airbus's behemoth A380 has been beset by a number of production delays, enabling Boeing to regain its market lead. The "Competing through Globalization" box describes the challenges firms face in competing for talent in a global labor market.

figure 2.3

Strategy—Decisions about Competition

1. Where to compete?
    In what market or markets (industries, products, etc.) will we compete?
2. How to compete?
    On what criterion or differentiating characteristic(s) will we compete? Cost? Quality? Reliability? Delivery?
3. With what will we compete?
    What resources will allow us to beat our competition?
    How will we acquire, develop, and deploy those resources to compete?

As more and more companies move work to India, they are facing a number of challenges they never expected. In the information technology sector, where companies initially sought an 80 percent reduction in labor cost, they now face a war for talent and spiraling salaries. This stems from the newer, younger breed of Indian worker, who displays attitudes much more similar to developed Western countries such as the United States than those of their parents and grandparents.

Companies face competing challenges of addressing both the frustrations and the desires of this younger generation. For instance, they are likely to complain about the traditions of arranged marriage and the caste system as well as their interactions with Westerners, who they feel sometimes treat them condescendingly. Many of the engineers are fascinated with the newest technologies, but their work for clients requires traditional tools and techniques. Finally, they are eager to get promotions and overseas assignments, yet there are practical limits to how quickly they can advance.

This requires companies to be innovative in how they seek to manage this new generation. For instance, Infosys seeks to learn from younger employees by setting up the "Voice of Youth Council." This consists of a dozen people under 30 who sit on the executive committee that deals with business strategy and HR policies, and it was this group that was instrumental in creating a program for identifying and encouraging innovation. In addition, IBM has created an internal MBA program consisting of testing, on-the-job training, seminars, and e-mail quizzes about how to effectively deal with workplace problems. This program was specifically aimed at keeping ambitious recruits on board and providing them with the training they need to manage a growing staff.

SOURCE: S. Hamm, "Young and Impatient in India; Workers Raised in an Age of Economic Optimism Want It All, and They Want It Now," *BusinessWeek*, January 28, 2008, p. 45.

Role of HRM in Strategy Formulation

LO3
Discuss the role of the HRM function in strategy formulation.

As the preceding examples illustrate, often the "with what will we compete" questions present ideal avenues for HRM to influence the strategic management process. This might be through either limiting strategic options or forcing thoughtfulness among the executive team regarding how and at what cost the firm might gain or develop the human resources (people) necessary for such a strategy to be successful. For example, HRM executives at PepsiCo could have noted that the firm had no expertise in managing the workforce of fast-food restaurants. The limiting role would have been for these executives to argue against the acquisition because of this lack of resources. On the other hand, they might have influenced the decision by educating top executives as to the costs (of hiring, training, and so on) associated with gaining people who had the right skills to manage such a workforce.

A firm's strategic management decision-making process usually takes place at its top levels, with a strategic planning group consisting of the chief executive officer, the chief financial officer, the president, and various vice presidents. However, each component of the process involves people-related business issues. Therefore, the HRM function needs to be involved in each of those components. One recent study of 115 strategic business units within *Fortune* 500 corporations found that between 49 and 69 percent of the companies had some link between HRM and the strategic planning process.[10] However, the level of linkage varied, and it is important to understand these different levels.

figure 2.4

Linkages of Strategic Planning and HRM

SOURCE: Adapted from K. Golden and V. Ramanujam, "Between a Dream and a Nightmare: On the Integration of the Human Resource Function and the Strategic Business Planning Process," *Human Resource Management* 24 (1985), pp. 429–51.

Four levels of integration seem to exist between the HRM function and the strategic management function: administrative linkage, one-way linkage, two-way linkage, and integrative linkage.[11] These levels of linkage will be discussed in relation to the different components of strategic management. The linkages are illustrated in Figure 2.4.

Administrative Linkage

In administrative linkage (the lowest level of integration), the HRM function's attention is focused on day-to-day activities. The HRM executive has no time or opportunity to take a strategic outlook toward HRM issues. The company's strategic business planning function exists without any input from the HRM department. Thus, in this level of integration, the HRM department is completely divorced from any component of the strategic management process in both strategy formulation and strategy implementation. The department simply engages in administrative work unrelated to the company's core business needs.

LO4
Describe the linkages between HRM and strategy formulation.

One-Way Linkage

In one-way linkage, the firm's strategic business planning function develops the strategic plan and then informs the HRM function of the plan. Many believe this level of integration constitutes strategic HRM—that is, the role of the HRM function is to design systems and/or programs that implement the strategic plan. Although one-way linkage does recognize the importance of human resources in implementing the strategic plan, it precludes the company from considering human resource issues while formulating the strategic plan. This level of integration often leads to strategic plans that the company cannot successfully implement.

Two-Way Linkage

Two-way linkage allows for consideration of human resource issues during the strategy formulation process. This integration occurs in three sequential steps. First, the strategic planning team informs the HRM function of the various strategies the company is considering. Then HRM executives analyze the human resource implications of the various strategies, presenting the results of this analysis to the strategic planning team. Finally, after the strategic decision has been made, the strategic plan is passed on to the HRM executive, who develops programs to implement it. The strategic planning function and the HRM function are interdependent in two-way linkage.

Integrative Linkage

Integrative linkage is dynamic and multifaceted, based on continuing rather than sequential interaction. In most cases the HRM executive is an integral member of the senior management team. Rather than an iterative process of information exchange, companies with integrative linkage have their HRM functions built right into the strategy formulation and implementation processes. It is this role that we will discuss throughout the rest of this chapter.

Thus, in strategic HRM, the HRM function is involved in both strategy formulation and strategy implementation. The HRM executive gives strategic planners information about the company's human resource capabilities, and these capabilities are usually a direct function of the HRM practices.[12] This information about human resource capabilities helps top managers choose the best strategy because they can consider how well each strategic alternative would be implemented. Once the strategic choice has been determined, the role of HRM changes to the development and alignment of HRM practices that will give the company employees having the necessary skills to implement the strategy.[13] In addition, HRM practices must be designed to elicit actions from employees in the company.[14] In the next two sections of this chapter we show how HRM can provide a competitive advantage in the strategic management process.

Strategy Formulation

Five major components of the strategic management process are relevant to strategy formulation.[15] These components are depicted in Figure 2.5. The first component is the organization's mission. The mission is a statement of the organization's reason for being; it usually specifies the customers served, the needs satisfied and/or the values received by the customers, and the technology used. The mission statement is often accompanied by a statement of a company's vision and/or values. For example, Table 2.1 illustrates the mission and values of Merck & Co., Inc.

An organization's **goals** are what it hopes to achieve in the medium- to long-term future; they reflect how the mission will be operationalized. The overarching goal of most profit-making companies in the United States is to maximize stockholder wealth. But companies have to set other long-term goals in order to maximize stockholder wealth.

External analysis consists of examining the organization's operating environment to identify the strategic opportunities and threats. Examples of opportunities are customer markets that are not being served, technological advances that can aid the company, and labor pools that have not been tapped. Threats include potential labor shortages, new competitors entering the market, pending legislation that might adversely affect the company, and competitors' technological innovations.

Internal analysis attempts to identify the organization's strengths and weaknesses. It focuses on the quantity and quality of resources available to the organization—financial,

Goals
What an organization hopes to achieve in the medium- to long-term future.

External Analysis
Examining the organization's operating environment to identify strategic opportunities and threats.

figure 2.5
Strategy Formulation

HR input

SOURCE: Adapted from K. Golden and V. Ramanujam, "Between a Dream and a Nightmare," *Human Resource Management* 24 (1985), pp. 429–51.

capital, technological, and human resources. Organizations have to honestly and accurately assess each resource to decide whether it is a strength or a weakness.

External analysis and internal analysis combined constitute what has come to be called the SWOT (strengths, weaknesses, opportunities, threats) analysis. After going through the SWOT analysis, the strategic planning team has all the information it needs to generate a number of strategic alternatives. The strategic managers compare these alternatives' ability to attain the organization's strategic goals; then they make their **strategic choice.** The strategic choice is the organization's strategy; it describes the ways the organization will attempt to fulfill its mission and achieve its long-term goals.

Many of the opportunities and threats in the external environment are people-related. With fewer and fewer highly qualified individuals entering the labor market, organizations compete not just for customers but for employees. It is HRM's role to keep close tabs on the external environment for human resource–related opportunities and threats, especially those directly related to the HRM function: potential labor shortages, competitor wage rates, government regulations affecting employment, and so on. For example, as discussed in Chapter 1, U.S. companies are finding that more and more high school graduates lack the basic skills needed to work, which is one source of the "human capital shortage."[16] However, not recognizing this environmental threat, many companies have encouraged the exit of older, more skilled workers while hiring less skilled younger workers who require basic skills training.[17]

Internal Analysis
The process of examining an organization's strengths and weaknesses.

Strategic Choice
The organization's strategy; the ways an organization will attempt to fulfill its mission and achieve its long-term goals.

MISSION STATEMENT

Merck & Co., Inc. is a leading research-driven pharmaceutical products and services company. Merck discovers, develops, manufactures and markets a broad range of innovative products to improve human and animal health. The Merck-Medco Managed Care Division manages pharmacy benefits for more than 40 million Americans, encouraging the appropriate use of medicines and providing disease management programs.

Our Mission

The mission of Merck is to provide society with superior products and services—innovations and solutions that improve the quality of life and satisfy customer needs—to provide employees with meaningful work and advancement opportunities and investors with a superior rate of return.

Our Values

1. **Our business is preserving and improving human life.** All of our actions must be measured by our success in achieving this goal. We value above all our ability to serve everyone who can benefit from the appropriate use of our products and services, thereby providing lasting consumer satisfaction.

2. **We are committed to the highest standards of ethics and integrity.** We are responsible to our customers, to Merck employees and their families, to the environments we inhabit, and to the societies we serve worldwide. In discharging our responsibilities, we do not take professional or ethical shortcuts. Our interactions with all segments of society must reflect the high standards we profess.

3. **We are dedicated to the highest level of scientific excellence and commit our research to improving human and animal health and the quality of life.** We strive to identify the most critical needs of consumers and customers; we devote our resources to meeting those needs.

4. **We expect profits, but only from work that satisfies customer needs and benefits humanity.** Our ability to meet our responsibilities depends on maintaining a financial position that invites investment in leading-edge research and that makes possible effective delivery of research results.

5. **We recognize that the ability to excel—to most competitively meet society's and customers' needs—depends on the integrity, knowledge, imagination, skill, diversity, and teamwork of employees, and we value these qualities most highly.** To this end, we strive to create an environment of mutual respect, encouragement, and teamwork—a working environment that rewards commitment and performance and is responsive to the needs of employees and their families.

SOURCE: www.merck.com/about/mission.html.

An analysis of a company's internal strengths and weaknesses also requires input from the HRM function. Today companies are increasingly realizing that their human resources are one of their most important assets. In fact, one estimate is that over one-third of the total growth in U.S. gross national product (GNP) between 1943 and 1990 was the result of increases in human capital. A company's failure to consider the strengths and weaknesses of its workforce may result in its choosing strategies it is not capable of pursuing.[18] However, some research has demonstrated that few companies have achieved this level of linkage.[19] For example, one company chose a strategy of cost reduction through technological improvements. It built a plant designed around a computer-integrated manufacturing system with statistical process controls.

Although this choice may seem like a good one, the company soon learned otherwise. It discovered that its employees could not operate the new equipment because 25 percent of the workforce was functionally illiterate.[20]

Thus, with an integrative linkage, strategic planners consider all the people-related business issues before making a strategic choice. These issues are identified with regard to the mission, goals, opportunities, threats, strengths, and weaknesses, leading the strategic planning team to make a more intelligent strategic choice. Although this process does not guarantee success, companies that address these issues are more likely to make choices that will ultimately succeed.

Recent research has supported the need to have HRM executives integrally involved in strategy formulation. One study of U.S. petrochemical refineries found that the level of HRM involvement was positively related to the refinery manager's evaluation of the effectiveness of the HRM function.[21] A second study of manufacturing firms found that HRM involvement was highest when top managers viewed employees as a strategic asset and associated with reduced turnover.[22] However, both studies found that HRM involvement was unrelated to operating unit financial performance.

Research has indicated that few companies have fully integrated HRM into the strategy formulation process.[23] As we've mentioned before, companies are beginning to recognize that in an intensely competitive environment, managing human resources strategically can provide a competitive advantage. Thus, companies at the administrative linkage level will either become more integrated or face extinction. In addition, companies will move toward becoming integratively linked in an effort to manage human resources strategically.

It is of utmost importance that all people-related business issues be considered during strategy formulation. These issues are identified in the HRM function. Mechanisms or structures for integrating the HRM function into strategy formulation may help the strategic planning team make the most effective strategic choice. Once that strategic choice is determined, HRM must take an active role in implementing it. This role will be discussed in the next section.

Strategy Implementation

After an organization has chosen its strategy, it has to execute that strategy—make it come to life in its day-to-day workings. The strategy a company pursues dictates certain HR needs. For a company to have a good strategy foundation, certain tasks must be accomplished in pursuit of the company's goals, individuals must possess certain skills to perform those tasks, and these individuals must be motivated to perform their skills effectively.

LO5
Discuss the more popular typologies of generic strategies and the various HRM practices associated with each.

The basic premise behind strategy implementation is that "an organization has a variety of structural forms and organizational processes to choose from when implementing a given strategy," and these choices make an economic difference.[24] Five important variables determine success in strategy implementation: organizational structure; task design; the selection, training, and development of people; reward systems; and types of information and information systems.

As we see in Figure 2.6, HRM has primary responsibility for three of these five implementation variables: task, people, and reward systems. In addition, HRM can directly affect the two remaining variables: structure and information and decision processes. First, for the strategy to be successfully implemented, the tasks must be designed and grouped into jobs in a way that is efficient and effective.[25] In Chapter 4

figure 2.6

Variables to
Be Considered
in Strategy
Implementation

we will examine how this can be done through the processes of job analysis and job design. Second, the HRM function must ensure that the organization is staffed with people who have the necessary knowledge, skill, and ability to perform their part in implementing the strategy. This goal is achieved primarily through recruitment, selection and placement, training, development, and career management—topics covered in Chapters 5, 6, 7, and 9. In addition, the HRM function must develop performance management and reward systems that lead employees to work for and support the strategic plan. The specific types of performance management systems are covered in Chapter 8, and the many issues involved in developing reward systems are discussed in Chapters 11 through 13. In other words, the role of the HRM function becomes one of (1) ensuring that the company has the proper number of employees with the levels and types of skills required by the strategic plan[26] and (2) developing "control" systems that ensure that those employees are acting in ways that promote the achievement of the goals specified in the strategic plan.[27]

In essence, this is what has been referred to as the "vertical alignment" of HR with strategy. Vertical alignment means that the HR practices and processes are aimed at addressing the strategic needs of the business. But the link between strategy and HR practices is primarily through people. For instance, as IBM moved from being a manufacturer of personal computers to being a fully integrated service provider, the types of people it needed changed significantly. Instead of employing thousands of workers in manufacturing or assembly plants, IBM increasingly needed software engineers to help write new "middleware" programs, and an army of consultants who could help their corporate customers to implement these systems. In addition, as IBM increasingly differentiated itself as being the "integrated solutions" provider (meaning it could sell the hardware, software, consulting, and service for a company's entire information technology needs), employees needed a new mindset which emphasized cooperating across different business divisions rather than running independently. Thus, the change in strategy required different kinds of skills, different kinds of employees, and different kinds of behaviors. The "Competing through Sustainability" box illustrates how IBM is aiding society while developing its future leaders.

COMPETING THROUGH SUSTAINABILITY
IBM Integrates Leadership Development and Corporate Social Responsibility

In a global environment, employees of large multinational companies such as IBM need to be able to work with strangers in strange lands, and often on unfamiliar projects. While the usual process for building such skills is through expensive expatriate assignments, IBM has created the Service Corps as a way to build these skills while helping society.

One hundred IBM employees from 33 countries will form 12 teams deployed to projects in Romania, Turkey, Vietnam, the Philippines, Ghana and Tanzania. IBM said it would select another 100 in the first year of the program and have a total of 600 participants over the next three years. The projects are being coordinated through nonprofit organizations and have all the trappings of corporate philanthropy. But that is not why they were created, or how they are being used.

"This is a management development exercise for high-potential people at IBM," said Randy MacDonald, senior vice president for human resources.

Clearly, the Service Corps concept sits well with the IBM employees. More than 5,500 of them, from more than 50 countries, applied for the program. IBM narrowed the pool to those who had been designated as fast-trackers, who had familiarity with volunteerism, and who submitted the best short essays on how participation would help them develop as leaders. The applications of those who passed that first cut were sent to the heads of IBM's eight geographic regions, who chose which of their employees to send.

After their four-week trips, the participants will go through two months of intensive debriefing to discuss what they learned about leadership—and about the countries they visited.

"It feels good to help in a developing country, even as you enhance your career," said Julie T. Lockwood, 31, a supply chain manager at IBM in Boulder, Colorado, who will be on the Ghana team. "This will help my internal résumé more than an assignment in a developed country."

SOURCE: S. Deutsch, "Volunteering Abroad to Climb at IBM," *New York Times*, March 26, 2008, Sect. C, p. 4.

How does the HRM function implement strategy? As Figure 2.7 shows, it is through administering HRM practices: job analysis/design, recruitment, selection systems, training and development programs, performance management systems, reward systems, and labor relations programs. The details of each of these HRM practices are the focus of the rest of this book. However, at this point it is important to present a general overview of the HRM practices and their role in strategy implementation. We then discuss the various strategies companies pursue and the types of HRM systems congruent with those strategies. First we focus on how the strategic types are implemented; then we discuss the HRM practices associated with various directional strategies.

HRM Practices

The HRM function can be thought of as having six menus of HRM practices, from which companies can choose the ones most appropriate for implementing their strategy. Each of these menus refers to a particular functional area of HRM: job analysis/design, recruitment/selection, training and development, performance management, pay structure/incentives/benefits, and labor–employee relations.[28] These menus are presented in Table 2.2.

figure 2.7
Strategy Implementation

Job Analysis and Design

Companies produce a given product or service (or set of products or services), and the manufacture of these products requires that a number of tasks be performed. These tasks are grouped together to form jobs. **Job analysis** is the process of getting detailed information about jobs. **Job design** addresses what tasks should be grouped into a particular job. The way that jobs are designed should have an important tie to the strategy of an organization because the strategy requires either new and different tasks or different ways of performing the same tasks. In addition, because many strategies entail the introduction of new technologies, this affects the way that work is performed.[29]

In general, jobs can vary from having a narrow range of tasks (most of which are simplified and require a limited range of skills) to having a broad array of complex tasks requiring multiple skills. In the past, the narrow design of jobs has been used to increase efficiency, while the broad design of jobs has been associated with efforts to increase innovation. However, with the advent of total quality management methods and a variety of employee involvement programs such as quality circles, many jobs are moving toward the broader end of the spectrum.[30]

Employee Recruitment and Selection

Recruitment is the process through which the organization seeks applicants for potential employment. **Selection** refers to the process by which it attempts to identify applicants with the necessary knowledge, skills, abilities, and other characteristics

Job Analysis
The process of getting detailed information about jobs.

Job Design
The process of defining the way work will be performed and the tasks that will be required in a given job.

Recruitment
The process of seeking applicants for potential employment.

table 2.2

Menu of HRM
Practice Options

Job Analysis and Design

Few tasks	↔	Many tasks
Simple tasks	↔	Complex tasks
Few skills required	↔	Many skills required
Specific job descriptions	↔	General job descriptions

Recruitment and Selection

External sources	↔	Internal sources
Limited socialization	↔	Extensive socialization
Assessment of specific skills	↔	Assessment of general skills
Narrow career paths	↔	Broad career paths

Training and Development

Focus on current job skills	↔	Focus on future job skills
Individual orientation	↔	Group orientation
Train few employees	↔	Train all employees
Spontaneous, unplanned	↔	Planned, systematic

Performance Management

Behavioral criteria	↔	Results criteria
Developmental orientation	↔	Administrative orientation
Short-term criteria	↔	Long-term criteria
Individual orientation	↔	Group orientation

Pay Structure, Incentives, and Benefits

Pay weighted toward salary and benefits	↔	Pay weighted toward incentives
Short-term incentives	↔	Long-term incentives
Emphasis on internal equity	↔	Emphasis on external equity
Individual incentives	↔	Group incentives

Labor and Employee Relations

Collective bargaining	↔	Individual bargaining
Top-down decision making	↔	Participation in decision making
Formal due process	↔	No due process
View employees as expense	↔	View employees as assets

SOURCES: Adapted from R. S. Schuler and S. F. Jackson, "Linking Competitive Strategies with Human Resource Management Practices," *Academy of Management Executive* 1 (1987), pp. 207–19; and C. Fisher, L. Schoenfeldt, and B. Shaw, *Human Resource Management*, 2nd ed. (Boston: Houghton Mifflin, 1992).

that will help the company achieve its goals. Companies engaging in different strategies need different types and numbers of employees. Thus, the strategy a company is pursuing will have a direct impact on the types of employees that it seeks to recruit and select.[31]

Employee Training and Development

A number of skills are instilled in employees through training and development. **Training** refers to a planned effort to facilitate the learning of job-related knowledge, skills, and behavior by employees. **Development** involves acquiring knowledge, skills, and behavior that improve employees' ability to meet the challenges of a variety of existing jobs or jobs that do not yet exist. Changes in strategies often require changes

Selection
The process by which an organization attempts to identify applicants with the necessary knowledge, skills, abilities, and other characteristics that will help it achieve its goals.

Training
A planned effort to facilitate the learning of job-related knowledge, skills, and behavior by employees.

Development
The acquisition of knowledge, skills, and behaviors that improve an employee's ability to meet changes in job requirements and in client and customer demands.

Performance Management
The means through which managers ensure that employees' activities and outputs are congruent with the organization's goals.

in the types, levels, and mixes of skills. Thus, the acquisition of strategy-related skills is an essential element of the implementation of strategy. For example, many companies have recently emphasized quality in their products, engaging in total quality management programs. These programs require extensive training of all employees in the TQM philosophy, methods, and often other skills that ensure quality.[32]

Through recruitment, selection, training, and development, companies can obtain a pool of human resources capable of implementing a given strategy.[33]

Performance Management

Performance management is used to ensure that employees' activities and outcomes are congruent with the organization's objectives. It entails specifying those activities and outcomes that will result in the firm's successfully implementing the strategy. For example, companies that are "steady state" (not diversified) tend to have evaluation systems that call for subjective performance assessments of managers. This stems from the fact that those above the first-level managers in the hierarchy have extensive knowledge about how the work should be performed. On the other hand, diversified companies are more likely to use quantitative measures of performance to evaluate managers because top managers have less knowledge about how work should be performed by those below them in the hierarchy.[34]

Similarly, executives who have extensive knowledge of the behaviors that lead to effective performance use performance management systems that focus on the behaviors of their subordinate managers. However, when executives are unclear about the specific behaviors that lead to effective performance, they tend to focus on evaluating the objective performance results of their subordinate managers.[35]

An example of how performance management can be aligned with strategy is provided in Figure 2.8. This comes from a firm in the health care industry whose strategy consisted of five "strategic imperatives," or things that the company was trying to accomplish. In this company all individuals set performance objectives each year, and each of their objectives have to be tied to at least one of the strategic imperatives. The senior VP of HR used the firm's technology system to examine the extent to which each business unit or function was focused on each of the imperatives. The figure illustrates the percentage of objectives that were tied to each imperative across the different units. It allows the company to determine if the mix of objectives is right enterprisewide as well as within each business unit or function.

figure 2.8

Percentage of Objectives Identified in Individual Performance Plans That Are Tied to Each Strategic Imperative

Strategic Imperative	Business A	Business B	International	Investment	Finance	Legal	IT	HR&S	Enterprise
Achieve superior medical performance	10.5%	12.5%	2.7%	7.6%	3.1%	2.7%	11.4%	2.1%	10.0%
Effectively serve our customers	24.7%	27.2%	36.7%	12.2%	10.3%	27.2%	18.9%	19.5%	23.7%
Create great products and services	5.6%	6.1%	10.1%	9.8%	5.0%	10.1%	15.3%	8.9%	6.9%
Create a winning environment	27.7%	29.7%	30.1%	29.9%	30.3%	33.7%	22.4%	39.4%	27.7%
Establish a cost advantage	31.5%	24.5%	20.5%	40.5%	51.3%	26.3%	32%	30.0%	31.7%
Total	100%	100%	100%	100%	100%	100%	100%	100%	100%

Pay Structure, Incentives, and Benefits

The pay system has an important role in implementing strategies. First, a high level of pay and/or benefits relative to that of competitors can ensure that the company attracts and retains high-quality employees, but this might have a negative impact on the company's overall labor costs.[36] Second, by tying pay to performance, the company can elicit specific activities and levels of performance from employees.

In a study of how compensation practices are tied to strategies, researchers examined 33 high-tech and 72 traditional companies. They classified them by whether they were in a growth stage (greater than 20 percent inflation-adjusted increases in annual sales) or a maturity stage. They found that high-tech companies in the growth stage used compensation systems that were highly geared toward incentive pay, with a lower percentage of total pay devoted to salary and benefits. On the other hand, compensation systems among mature companies (both high-tech and traditional) devoted a lower percentage of total pay to incentives and a high percentage to benefits.[37]

Labor and Employee Relations

Whether companies are unionized or not, the general approach to relations with employees can strongly affect their potential for gaining competitive advantage. In the late 1970s Chrysler Corporation was faced with bankruptcy. Lee Iacocca, the new president of Chrysler, asked the union for wage and work-rule concessions in an effort to turn the company around. The union agreed to the concessions, in return receiving profit sharing and a representative on the board. Within only a few years, the relationship with and support from the union allowed Chrysler to pull itself out of bankruptcy and into record profitability.[38]

However, as the opening case illustrates, General Motors has already gone to its unions to ask for givebacks that would help them reduce their costs.

Companies can choose to treat employees as an asset that requires investment of resources or as an expense to be minimized.[39] They have to make choices about how much employees can and should participate in decision making, what rights employees have, and what the company's responsibility is to them. The approach a company takes in making these decisions can result in it either successfully achieving its short- and long-term goals or ceasing to exist.

Recent research has begun to examine how companies develop sets of HRM practices that maximize performance and productivity. For example, one study of automobile assembly plants around the world found that plants that exhibited both high productivity and high quality used "HRM best practices," such as heavy emphasis on recruitment and hiring, compensation tied to performance, low levels of status differentiation, high levels of training for both new and experienced employees, and employee participation through structures such as work teams and problem-solving groups.[40] Another study found that HRM systems composed of selection testing, training, contingent pay, performance appraisal, attitude surveys, employee participation, and information sharing resulted in higher levels of productivity and corporate financial performance, as well as lower employee turnover.[41] Finally, a recent study found that companies identified as some of the "best places to work" had higher financial performances than a set of matched companies that did not make the list.[42] Similar results have also been observed in a number of other studies.[43]

In addition to the relationship between HR practices and performance in general, in today's fast-changing environment, businesses have to change quickly, requiring changes in employees' skills and behaviors. In one study the researchers found that the flexibility of HR practices, employee skills, and employee behaviors were all positively related to firm financial performance, but only the skill flexibility was related to cost efficiency.[44] While these relationships are promising, the causal direction has not yet been proven. For instance, while effective HR practices should help firms perform better, it is also true that highly profitable firms can invest more in HR practices.[45] The research seems to indicate that while the relationship between practices and performance is consistently positive, we should not go too far out on a limb arguing that increasing the use of HRM practices will automatically result in increased profitability.[46]

Strategic Types

As we previously discussed, companies can be classified by the generic strategies they pursue. It is important to note that these generic "strategies" are not what we mean by a strategic plan. They are merely similarities in the ways companies seek to compete in their industries. Various typologies have been offered, but we focus on the two generic strategies proposed by Porter: cost and differentiation.[47]

According to Michael Porter of Harvard, competitive advantage stems from a company's being able to create value in its production process. Value can be created in one of two ways. First, value can be created by reducing costs. Second, value can be created by differentiating a product or service in such a way that it allows the company to charge a premium price relative to its competitors. This leads to two basic strategies. According to Porter, the "overall cost leadership" strategy focuses on becoming the lowest cost producer in an industry. This strategy is achieved by constructing efficient large-scale facilities, by reducing costs through capitalizing on the experience curve, and by controlling overhead costs and costs in such areas as research and development, service, sales force, and advertising. This strategy provides above-average returns within an industry, and it tends to bar other firms' entry into the industry because the firm can lower its prices below competitors' costs.

The "differentiation" strategy, according to Porter, attempts to create the impression that the company's product or service is different from that of others in the industry. The perceived differentiation can come from creating a brand image, from technology, from offering unique features, or from unique customer service. If a company succeeds in differentiating its product, it will achieve above-average returns, and the differentiation may protect it from price sensitivity. For instance, Dell Computer Company built its reputation on providing the lowest cost computers through leveraging its supply chain and direct selling model. However, recently they have seen their share eroding as the consumer market grows and HP has offered more differentiated, stylish-looking computers sold through retail outlets where customers can touch and feel them. In addition, Apple has differentiated itself through its own operating system that integrates well with peripheral devices such as the iPod and iPhone. In both cases, these companies can charge a premium (albeit higher for Apple) over Dell's pricing.[48]

HRM Needs in Strategic Types

While all of the strategic types require competent people in a generic sense, each of the strategies also requires different types of employees with different types of behaviors and attitudes. As we noted earlier, different strategies require employees with specific skills and also require these employees to exhibit different "role behaviors."[49] **Role behaviors** are the behaviors required of an individual in his or her role as a jobholder in a social work environment. These role behaviors vary on a number of dimensions. Additionally, different role behaviors are required by the different strategies. For example, companies engaged in a cost strategy require employees to have a high concern for quantity and a short-term focus, to be comfortable with stability, and to be risk averse. These employees are expected to exhibit role behaviors that are relatively repetitive and performed independently or autonomously.

Thus, companies engaged in cost strategies, because of the focus on efficient production, tend to specifically define the skills they require and invest in training employees in these skill areas. They also rely on behavioral performance management systems with a large performance-based compensation component. These companies promote internally and develop internally consistent pay systems with high pay differentials between superiors and subordinates. They seek efficiency through worker participation, soliciting employees' ideas on how to achieve more efficient production.

On the other hand, employees in companies with a differentiation strategy need to be highly creative and cooperative; to have only a moderate concern for quantity, a long-term focus, and a tolerance for ambiguity; and to be risk takers. Employees in these companies are expected to exhibit role behaviors that include cooperating with others, developing new ideas, and taking a balanced approach to process and results.

Thus differentiation companies will seek to generate more creativity through broadly defined jobs with general job descriptions. They may recruit more from outside, engage in limited socialization of newcomers, and provide broader career paths. Training and development activities focus on cooperation. The compensation system is geared toward external equity, as it is heavily driven by recruiting needs. These companies develop results-based performance management system and divisional–corporate performance evaluations to encourage risk taking on the part of managers.[50]

> **Role Behaviors**
> Behaviors that are required of an individual in his or her role as a jobholder in a social work environment.

EVIDENCE-BASED HR

A study of HRM among steel minimills in the United States found that mills pursuing different strategies used different systems of HRM. Mills seeking cost leadership tended to use control-oriented HRM systems that were characterized by high centralization, low participation, low training, low wages, low benefits, and highly contingent pay, whereas differentiator mills used "commitment" HRM systems, characterized as the opposite on each of those dimensions. A later study from the same sample revealed that the mills with the commitment systems had higher productivity, lower scrap rates, and lower employee turnover than those with the control systems.

SOURCE: J. Arthur, "The Link between Business Strategy and Industrial Relations Systems in American Steel Mini-Mills," *Industrial and Labor Relations Review* 45 (1992), pp. 488–506.

Directional Strategies

As discussed earlier in this chapter, strategic typologies are useful for classifying the ways different organizations seek to compete within an industry. However, it is also necessary to understand how increasing size (growth) or decreasing it (downsizing)

> **LO6**
> Describe the different HRM issues and practices associated with various directional strategies.

affects the HRM function. For example, the top management team might decide that they need to invest more in product development or to diversify as a means for growth. With these types of strategies, it is more useful for the HRM function to aid in evaluating the feasibility of the various alternatives and to develop programs that support the strategic choice.

Companies have used five possible categories of directional strategies to meet objectives.[51] Strategies emphasizing market share or operating costs are considered "concentration" strategies. With this type of strategy, a company attempts to focus on what it does best within its established markets and can be thought of as "sticking to its knitting." Strategies focusing on market development, product development, innovation, or joint ventures make up the "internal growth" strategy. Companies with an internal growth strategy channel their resources toward building on existing strengths. Those attempting to integrate vertically or horizontally or to diversify are exhibiting an **"external growth" strategy,** usually through mergers or acquisitions. This strategy attempts to expand a company's resources or to strengthen its market position through acquiring or creating new businesses. Finally, a "divestment," or downsizing, strategy is one made up of retrenchment, divestitures, or liquidation. These strategies are observed among companies facing serious economic difficulties and seeking to pare down their operations. The human resource implications of each of these strategies are quite different.

Concentration Strategies

Concentration strategies require that the company maintain the current skills that exist in the organization. This requires that training programs provide a means of keeping those skills sharp among people in the organization and that compensation programs focus on retaining people who have those skills. Appraisals in this strategy tend to be more behavioral because the environment is more certain, and the behaviors necessary for effective performance tend to be established through extensive experience.

Internal Growth Strategies

Internal growth strategies present unique staffing problems. Growth requires that a company constantly hire, transfer, and promote individuals, and expansion into different markets may change the necessary skills that prospective employees must have. In addition, appraisals often consist of a combination of behaviors and results. The behavioral appraisal emphasis stems from the knowledge of effective behaviors in a particular product market, and the results appraisals focus on achieving growth goals. Compensation packages are heavily weighted toward incentives for achieving growth goals. Training needs differ depending on the way the company attempts to grow internally. For example, if the organization seeks to expand its markets, training will focus on knowledge of each market, particularly when the company is expanding into international markets. On the other hand, when the company is seeking innovation or product development, training will be of a more technical nature, as well as focusing on interpersonal skills such as team building. Joint ventures require extensive training in conflict resolution techniques because of the problems associated with combining people from two distinct organizational cultures.

External Growth Strategy
An emphasis on acquiring vendors and suppliers or buying businesses that allow a company to expand into new markets.

Concentration Strategy
A strategy focusing on increasing market share, reducing costs, or creating and maintaining a market niche for products and services.

Internal Growth Strategy
A focus on new market and product development, innovation, and joint ventures.

Mergers and Acquisitions

Increasingly we see both consolidation within industries and mergers across industries. For example, British Petroleum's recent agreement to acquire Amoco Oil represents a consolidation, or reduction in number of firms within the industry. On the other hand, Citicorp's merger with Traveller's Group to form Citigroup represents firms from different industries (pure financial services and insurance) combining to change the dynamics within both. Whatever the type, one thing is for sure—mergers and acquisitions are on the increase, and HRM needs to be involved.[52] In addition, these mergers more frequently consist of global megamergers, in spite of some warnings that these might not be effective.

According to a report by the Conference Board, "people issues" may be one of the major reasons that mergers do not always live up to expectations. Some companies now heavily weigh firm cultures before embarking on a merger or acquisition. For example, prior to acquiring ValueRx, executives at Express Scripts Inc. interviewed senior executives and middle managers at the potential target firm in order to get a sense of its culture.[53] In spite of this, fewer than one-third of the HRM executives surveyed said that they had a major influence in how mergers are planned, yet 80 percent of them said that people issues have a significant impact after the deals are finalized.[54]

In addition to the desirability of HRM playing a role in evaluating a merger opportunity, HRM certainly has a role in the actual implementation of a merger or acquisition. Training in conflict resolution is also necessary when companies engage in an external growth strategy. All the options for external growth consist of acquiring or developing new businesses, and these businesses often have distinct cultures. Thus many HRM programs face problems in integrating and standardizing practices across the company's businesses. The relative value of standardizing practices across businesses must be weighed against the unique environmental requirements of each business and the extent of desired integration of the two firms. For example, with regard to pay practices, a company may desire a consistent internal wage structure to maintain employee perceptions of equity in the larger organization. In a recent new business developed by IBM, the employees pressured the company to maintain the same wage structure as IBM's main operation. However, some businesses may function in environments where pay practices are driven heavily by market forces. Requiring these businesses to adhere to pay practices in other environments may result in an ineffective wage structure.

Downsizing

Of increasing importance to organizations in today's competitive environment is HRM's role in **downsizing** or "rightsizing." The number of organizations undergoing downsizing has increased significantly. In fact, from the third to the fourth quarter of 2008, mass layoffs almost doubled.[55]

One would have great difficulty ignoring the massive "war for talent" that went on during the late 1990s, particularly with the notable dot-com craze. Firms during this time sought to become "employers of choice," to establish "employment brands," and to develop "employee value propositions" as ways to ensure that they would be able to attract and retain talented employees.

Downsizing
The planned elimination of large numbers of personnel, designed to enhance organizational effectiveness.

Layoffs over the past 4 years

r = revised   p = preliminary

Source: http://www.bls.gov/news.release/mslo.nr0.htm.

The current economic crisis means that one important question facing firms is, How can we develop a reputation as an employer of choice, and engage employees to the goals of the firm, while laying off a significant portion of our workforce? How firms answer this question will determine how they can compete by meeting the stakeholder needs of their employees.

In spite of the increasing frequency of downsizing, research reveals that it is far from universally successful for achieving the goals of increased productivity and increased profitability. For example, Table 2.3 illustrates the results of a survey conducted by the American Management Association indicating that only about one-third of the companies that went through downsizings actually achieved their goal of increased productivity. Another survey by the AMA found that over two-thirds of the companies that downsize repeat the effort a year later.[56] Also, research by the consulting firm Mitchell & Company found that companies that downsized during the 1980s lagged the industry average stock price in 1991.[57] Thus it is important to understand the best ways of managing downsizings, particularly from the standpoint of HRM.

Downsizing presents a number of challenges and opportunities for HRM.[58] In terms of challenges, the HRM function must "surgically" reduce the workforce by cutting only the workers who are less valuable in their performance. Achieving this is difficult because the best workers are most able (and often willing) to find alternative employment and may leave voluntarily prior to any layoff. For example, in 1992 General Motors and the United Auto Workers agreed to an early retirement program for individuals between the ages of 51 and 65 who have been employed for 10 or more

DESIRED OUTCOME	PERCENTAGE THAT ACHIEVED DESIRED RESULT
Reduced expenses	46%
Increased profits	32
Improved cash flow	24
Increased productivity	22
Increased return on investment	21
Increased competitive advantage	19
Reduced bureaucracy	17
Improved decision making	14
Increased customer satisfaction	14
Increased sales	13
Increased market share	12
Improved product quality	9
Technological advances	9
Increased innovation	7
Avoidance of a takeover	6

table 2.3

Effects of Downsizing on Desired Outcomes

SOURCE: From *The Wall Street Journal*, Eastern Edition June 6, 1991. Copyright © 1991 by Dow Jones & Co. Inc. Reproduced with permission of Dow Jones & Co., Inc. via Copyright Clearance Center.

years. The program provided those who agreed to retire their full pension benefits, even if they obtained employment elsewhere, and as much as $13,000 toward the purchase of a GM car.[59] As mentioned in the opening case, this is part of GM's labor cost problem.

Early retirement programs, although humane, essentially reduce the workforce with a "grenade" approach. This type of reduction does not distinguish between good and poor performers but rather eliminates an entire group of employees. In fact, recent research indicates that when companies downsize by offering early retirement programs, they usually end up rehiring to replace essential talent within a year. Often the company does not achieve its cost-cutting goals because it spends 50 to 150 percent of the departing employee's salary in hiring and retraining new workers.[60]

Another HRM challenge is to boost the morale of employees who remain after the reduction; this is discussed in greater detail in Chapter 5. Survivors may feel guilt over keeping their jobs when their friends have been laid off, or they may envy their friends who have retired with attractive severance and pension benefits. Their reduced satisfaction with and commitment to the organization may interfere with work performance. Thus the HRM function must maintain open communication with remaining employees to build their trust and commitment rather than withholding information.[61] All employees should be informed of the purpose of the downsizing, the costs to be cut, the duration of the downsizing, and the strategies to be pursued. In addition, companies going through downsizing often develop compensation programs that tie the individual's compensation to the company's success. Employee ownership programs often result from downsizing, and gainsharing plans such as the Scanlon plan (discussed in Chapter 12) originated in companies facing economic difficulties.

In spite of these challenges, downsizing provides opportunities for HRM. First, it often allows the company to "get rid of dead wood" and make way for fresh ideas.

In addition, downsizing is often a unique opportunity to change an organization's culture. In firms characterized by antagonistic labor–management relations, downsizing can force the parties to cooperate and to develop new, positive relationships.[62] Finally, downsizing can demonstrate to top-management decision makers the value of the company's human resources to its ultimate success. The role of HRM is to effectively manage the process in a way that makes this value undeniable. We discuss the implications of downsizing as a labor force management strategy in Chapter 5.

Strategy Evaluation and Control

A final component to the strategic management process is that of strategy evaluation and control. Thus far we have focused on the planning and implementation of strategy. However, it is extremely important for the firm to constantly monitor the effectiveness of both the strategy and the implementation process. This monitoring makes it possible for the company to identify problem areas and either revise existing structures and strategies or devise new ones. In this process we see emergent strategies appear as well as the critical nature of human resources in competitive advantage.

The Role of Human Resources in Providing Strategic Competitive Advantage

Thus far we have presented the strategic management process as including a step-by-step procedure by which HRM issues are raised prior to deciding on a strategy and then HRM practices are developed to implement that strategy. However, we must note that human resources can provide a strategic competitive advantage in two additional ways: through emergent strategies and through enhancing competitiveness.

Emergent Strategies

Having discussed the process of strategic management, we also must distinguish between intended strategies and emergent strategies. Most people think of strategies as being proactive, rational decisions aimed toward some predetermined goal. The view of strategy we have presented thus far in the chapter focuses on intended strategies. Intended strategies are the result of the rational decision-making process used by top managers as they develop a strategic plan. This is consistent with the definition of strategy as "the pattern or plan that integrates an organization's major goals, policies, and action sequences into a cohesive whole."[63] The idea of emergent strategies is evidenced by the feedback loop in Figure 2.2.

Most strategies that companies espouse are intended strategies. For example, when Howard Schultz founded Starbucks, he had the idea of creating a third place (between work and home) where people could enjoy traditional Italian-style coffee. He knew that the smell of the coffee and the deeper, darker, stronger taste would attract a new set of customers to enjoy coffee the way he thought it should be enjoyed. This worked, but as Starbucks grew, customers began asking if they could have nonfat milk in their lattes, or if they could get flavor shots in their coffees. Schultz swore that such things would essentially pollute the coffee and refused to offer them. Finally, after repeated requests from his store managers who kept hearing customers demanding such things, Schultz finally relented.[64]

Emergent strategies, on the other hand, consist of the strategies that evolve from the grassroots of the organization and can be thought of as what organizations actually do, as opposed to what they intend to do. Strategy can also be thought of as "a pattern in a stream of decisions or actions."[65] For example, when Honda Motor Company first entered the U.S. market with its 250-cc and 350-cc motorcycles in 1959, it believed that no market existed for its smaller 50-cc bike. However, the sales on the larger motorcycles were sluggish, and Japanese executives running errands around Los Angeles on Honda 50's attracted a lot of attention, including that of a buyer with Sears, Roebuck. Honda found a previously undiscovered market as well as a new distribution outlet (general retailers) that it had not planned on. This emergent strategy gave Honda a 50 percent market share by 1964.[66]

The distinction between intended and emergent strategies has important implications for human resource management.[67] The new focus on strategic HRM has tended to focus primarily on intended strategies. Thus HRM's role has been seen as identifying for top management the people-related business issues relevant to strategy formulation and then developing HRM systems that aid in the implementation of the strategic plan.

However, most emergent strategies are identified by those lower in the organizational hierarchy. It is often the rank-and-file employees who provide ideas for new markets, new products, and new strategies. HRM plays an important role in facilitating communication throughout the organization, and it is this communication that allows for effective emergent strategies to make their way up to top management. For example, Starbucks' Frappucino was a drink invented by one of the store employees in California; Starbucks leaders (including Schultz) thought it was a terrible idea. They fought it in a number of meetings, but the employee kept getting more and more information supporting her case for how much customers seemed to like it. The leaders finally gave the go-ahead to begin producing it, and it has become a $1 billion a year product, and one that has contributed to the Starbucks brand.[68]

Enhancing Firm Competitiveness

A related way in which human resources can be a source of competitive advantage is through developing a human capital pool that gives the company the unique ability to adapt to an ever-changing environment. Recently managers have become interested in the idea of a "learning organization," in which people continually expand their capacity to achieve the results they desire.[69] This requires the company to be in a constant state of learning through monitoring the environment, assimilating information, making decisions, and flexibly restructuring to compete in that environment. Companies that develop such learning capability have a competitive advantage. Although certain organizational information-processing systems can be an aid, ultimately the people (human capital) who make up the company provide the raw materials in a learning organization.[70]

Thus, the role of human resources in competitive advantage should continue to increase because of the fast-paced change characterizing today's business environment. It is becoming increasingly clear that even as U.S. automakers have improved the quality of their cars to compete with the Japanese, these competitors have developed such flexible and adaptable manufacturing systems that they can respond to customer needs more quickly.[71] This flexibility of the manufacturing process allows the emergent strategy to come directly from the marketplace by determining and responding to the exact mix of customer desires. It requires, however, that the company have people in place who have the skills to similarly adapt quickly.[72] As Howard Schultz, the founder and chairman of Starbucks, says, "If people relate to the company they work for, if they form an emotional tie to it and buy into its dreams, they will pour their heart into making it better. When employees have self-esteem and self-respect they can contribute so much more; to their company, to their family, to the world."[73] This statement exemplifies the increasing importance of human resources in developing and maintaining competitive advantage.[74]

A LOOK BACK

TRANSFORMING GM

So, what does GM's current plan for changing its business model look like? They have suggested the need to layoff 47,000 employees worldwide, close five additional plants in North America, and eliminating four of the company's eight brands. In addition, they are in talks with the UAW to restructure $20 billion in obligations to retired hourly workers. UAW President Ron Gettelfinger is hopeful that the government will take responsibility for some of GM's $47 billion in retiree health obligations.

In spite of this, the bondholders of GM feel that the company is not going far enough. They want to see even greater cuts in the commitments to the legacy workforce, without which they do not believe GM can survive over the long term. In addition, critics of GM suggest that its best hope is to declare bankruptcy. Under a bankruptcy filing, GM could void its contracts with suppliers and its unions and start negotiating from scratch. They believe that this is the only way that GM can get its costs down to a level that would make it a sustainable enterprise.

Questions

1. Which do you think is a more effective option: working with the unions to get some givebacks or declaring bankruptcy and forcing the union to renegotiate?
2. How might GM change the way it manages its workforce as part of its transformation?
3. Notice that little of the discussion dealt with GM's products. What would a few extremely successful products do for GM's business model? What would a line of mediocre or poor products do to this transformation process?

SOURCE: S. Terlep and N. King, "Bondholders Say GM's Plan Fails to Tackle Issues," *The Wall Street Journal*, February 19, 2009, http://online.wsj.com/article/SB123500467245718075.html?mod=testMod

  Please see the Video Case and Case Study that correspond to this chapter online at www.mhhe.com/noe7e.

SUMMARY

A strategic approach to human resource management seeks to proactively provide a competitive advantage through the company's most important asset: its human resources. While human resources are the most important asset, they are also usually the single largest controllable cost within the firm's business model. The HRM function needs to be integrally involved in the formulation of strategy to identify the people-related business issues the company faces. Once the strategy has been determined, HRM has a profound impact on the implementation of the plan by developing and aligning HRM practices that ensure that the company has motivated employees with the necessary skills. Finally, the emerging strategic role of the HRM function requires that HR professionals in the future develop business, professional–technical, change management, and integration competencies. As you will see more clearly in later chapters, this strategic approach requires more than simply developing a valid selection procedure or state-of-the-art performance management systems. Only through these competencies can the HR professional take a strategic approach to human resource management.

KEY TERMS

Strategic human resource
   management (SHRM), 75
Strategy formulation, 75
Strategy implementation, 75
Goals, 80
External analysis, 80
Internal analysis, 81

Strategic choice, 81
Job analysis, 86
Job design, 86
Recruitment, 86
Selection, 87
Training, 88
Development, 88

Performance management, 88
Role behaviors, 91
External growth strategy, 92
Concentration strategy, 92
Internal growth strategy, 92
Downsizing, 93

DISCUSSION QUESTIONS

1. Pick one of your university's major sports teams (like football or basketball). How would you characterize that team's generic strategy? How does the composition of the team members (in terms of size, speed, ability, and so on) relate to that strategy? What are the strengths and weaknesses of the team? How do they dictate the team's generic strategy and its approach to a particular game?

2. Do you think that it is easier to tie human resources to the strategic management process in large or in small organizations? Why?

3. Consider one of the organizations you have been affiliated with. What are some examples of human resource practices that were consistent with that organization's strategy? What are examples of practices that were inconsistent with its strategy?

4. How can strategic management within the HRM department ensure that HRM plays an effective role in the company's strategic management process?

5. What types of specific skills (such as knowledge of financial accounting methods) do you think HR professionals will need to have the business, professional-technical, change management, and integrative competencies necessary in the future? Where can you develop each of these skills?

6. What are some of the key environmental variables that you see changing in the business world today? What impact will those changes have on the HRM function in organizations?

SELF-ASSESSMENT EXERCISE

Think of a company you have worked for, or find an annual report for a company you are interested in working for. (Many companies post their annual reports online at their Web site.) Then answer the following questions.

Questions

1. How has the company been affected by the trends discussed in this chapter?

2. Does the company use the HR practices recommended in this chapter?

3. What else should the company do to deal with the challenges posed by the trends discussed in this chapter?

EXERCISING STRATEGY: STRATEGY AND HRM AT DELTA AIRLINES

In 1994 top executives at Delta Air Lines faced a crucial strategic decision. Delta, which had established an unrivaled reputation within the industry for having highly committed employees who delivered the highest quality customer service, had lost more than $10 per share for two straight years. A large portion of its financial trouble was due to the $491 million acquisition of Pan Am in 1991, which was followed by the Gulf War (driving up fuel costs) and the early 1990s recession (causing people to fly less). Its cost per available seat mile (the cost to fly one passenger one mile) was 9.26 cents, among the highest in the industry. In addition, it was threatened by new discount competitors with significantly lower costs—in particular, Valujet, which flew out of Delta's Atlanta hub. How could Delta survive and thrive in such an environment? Determining the strategy for doing so was the top executives' challenge.

Chairman and chief executive officer Ron Allen embarked upon the "Leadership 7.5" strategy, whose goal was to reduce the cost per available seat mile to 7.5 cents, comparable with Southwest Airlines. Implementing this strategy required a significant downsizing over the following three years, trimming 11,458 people from its 69,555-employee workforce (the latter number representing an 8 percent reduction from two years earlier). Many experienced customer service representatives were laid off and replaced with lower paid, inexperienced, part-time workers. Cleaning service of planes as well as baggage handling were outsourced, resulting in layoffs of long-term Delta employees. The numbers of maintenance workers and flight attendants were reduced substantially.

The results of the strategy were mixed as financial performance improved but operational performance plummeted. Since it began its cost cutting, its stock price more than doubled in just over two years and its debt was upgraded. On the other hand, customer complaints about dirty airplanes rose from 219 in 1993 to 358 in 1994 and 634 in 1995. On-time performance was so bad that passengers joked that Delta stands for "Doesn't Ever Leave The

Airport." Delta slipped from fourth to seventh among the top 10 carriers in baggage handling. Employee morale hit an all-time low, and unions were beginning to make headway toward organizing some of Delta's employee groups. In 1996 CEO Allen was quoted as saying, "This has tested our people. There have been some morale problems. But so be it. You go back to the question of survival, and it makes the decision very easy."

Shortly after, employees began donning cynical "so be it" buttons. Delta's board saw union organizers stirring blue-collar discontent, employee morale destroyed, the customer service reputation in near shambles, and senior managers exiting the company in droves. Less than one year later, Allen was fired despite Delta's financial turnaround. His firing was "not because the company was going broke, but because its spirit was broken."

Delta's Leadership 7.5 strategy destroyed the firm's core competence of a highly experienced, highly skilled, and highly committed workforce that delivered the highest quality customer service in the industry. HRM might have affected the strategy by pointing out the negative impact that this strategy would have on the firm. Given the strategy and competitive environment, Delta might have sought to implement the cost cutting differently to reduce the cost structure but preserve its source of differentiation.

The present state of Delta provides further support to these conclusions. With the family atmosphere dissolved and the bond between management and rank-and-file employees broken, employees have begun to seek other ways to gain voice and security. By fall 2001 Delta had two union organizing drives under way with both the flight attendants and the mechanics. In addition, labor costs have been driven up as a result of the union activity. The pilots signed a lucrative five-year contract that will place them at the highest pay in the industry. In an effort to head off the organizing drive, the mechanics were recently given raises to similarly put them at the industry top. Now the flight attendants are seeking industry-leading pay regardless of but certainly encouraged by the union drive.[75]

The Delta Air Lines story provides a perfect example of the perils that can await firms that fail to adequately address human resource issues in the formulation and implementation of strategy.

SOURCE: M. Brannigan and E. De Lisser, "Cost Cutting at Delta Raises the Stock Price but Lowers the Service," *The Wall Street Journal*, June 20, 1996, pp. A1, A8; M. Brannigan and J. White, "So Be It: Why Delta Air Lines Decided It Was Time for CEO to Take Off," *The Wall Street Journal*, May 30, 1997, p. A1.

Questions

1. How does the experience of Delta Air Lines illustrate the interdependence between strategic decisions of "how to compete" and "with what to compete"? Consider this with regard to both strategy formulation and strategy implementation.
2. If you were in charge of HRM for Delta Air Lines now, what would be your major priorities?

● MANAGING PEOPLE: FROM THE PAGES OF *BUSINESSWEEK*

BusinessWeek   ## Is Dell Too Big for Michael Dell?

He's back in charge—and he may have the toughest job in the computer business Welcome back, Michael. Don't get too comfortable.

By returning to the top job at Dell Inc., replacing departing chief executive Kevin Rollins, founder Michael S. Dell takes on perhaps the toughest job in the computer industry. Since mid-2005 the PC maker has battled problems with customer service, quality, and the effectiveness of its direct-sales model. Lately, rivals Hewlett-Packard Co. and Apple Inc. have been gaining in sales and market share. On January 31, the day Rollins's departure was announced, the Round Rock (Texas) company disclosed that its fourth-quarter earnings and sales would fall short of analyst estimates. It's also under scrutiny by the Securities & Exchange Commission and a U.S. attorney for accounting irregularities.

As recently as last November, Dell insisted to *Business-Week* that Rollins's job was safe. Now, in an interview, he insists the decision to push Rollins out started with him. "I recommended to our board that I become the CEO," Dell says. For years, Dell and Rollins were held up as a prime example of the company's "two-in-a-box" management structure, in which two leaders worked together in lockstep. When Rollins was president, Michael Dell was CEO; when Rollins was promoted to CEO in 2004, Michael remained chairman. But financial performance has been deteriorating for a while now, and Michael Dell apparently ran out of patience in light of the latest disappointment. "People are looking forward to a change," said an analyst at one of Dell's largest institutional shareholders. Indeed, the company's share price jumped 3.6 percent in the couple of hours after the shift was announced.

But does Michael Dell have what it takes to turn the company around? It's been years since he shouldered day-to-day operational responsibility on his own. Since the early 1990s, Dell has always had a strong No. 2; back then, the company had less than $3 billion in yearly sales. Today

it is a $60 billion company. But Dell says he has a clear plan. He believes the company's supply chain and manufacturing can be improved. "I think you're going to see a more streamlined organization, with a much clearer strategy."

But none of the paths to improve performance will be easy. Dell doesn't have the innovation DNA of an Apple or even an HP, should it want to overhaul its utilitarian products and services. Any effort to crank up R&D would crimp margins. Trying to win over more consumers, the fastest-growing part of the market, may well require a move away from its direct-sales model into retail. That could prove costly as well. Dell himself says he doesn't anticipate leaving the direct-sales model behind: "It's a significant strength of the company." Nor does a big acquisition seem to be an option, given that Dell has never done one in the past.

Slots to fill But standing in place also looks hazardous, since Dell may now be slipping in its core corporate business, too. According to a January 30 study done by Goldman, Sachs & Co., Dell is losing share in business spending for PCs. (Hewlett-Packard is also losing share of spending, while Lenovo and Apple are gaining.) "Dell's troubles seem to be bleeding into its corporate business, which, up until now, had been a stronghold," the report said. Dell has also lost the top spot in the worldwide PC market-share rankings. In the fourth quarter, Hewlett-Packard's worldwide market share grew to 18.1 percent, while Dell's share dropped to 14.7 percent, according to market researcher IDC.

Dell also has several slots to fill in the executive suite; Rollins is only the latest departure among key managers. But for the first time in years, the tough choices will be solely in the lap of the man who started the company in his University of Texas dorm room back in 1984. "I'm not hiring a COO or a CEO," Dell says, "I'm going to be the CEO for the next several years." He adds: "We're going to fix this business."

Questions

1. How does the case describe Dell's transformed strategy over the years in terms of where to compete, how to compete, and with what to compete?
2. What are the major people issues that exist as Michael Dell retakes the reins at Dell?

3. How would HR help in addressing the issues that Dell faces?

SOURCE: L. Lee and P. Burrows, "Is Dell Too Big for Michael Dell?" Reprinted from the April 4, 2007, issue of *BusinessWeek* by special permission. Copyright © 2007 by The McGraw-Hill Companies, Inc.

● NOTES

1. J. Barney, "Firm Resources and Sustained Competitive Advantage," *Journal of Management* 17 (1991), pp. 99–120.
2. L. Dyer, "Strategic Human Resource Management and Planning," in *Research in Personnel and Human Resources Management*, ed. K. Rowland and G. Ferris (Greenwich, CT: JAI Press, 1985), pp. 1–30.
3. J. Quinn, *Strategies for Change: Logical Incrementalism* (Homewood, IL: Richard D. Irwin, 1980).
4. M. Porter, *Competitive Strategy: Techniques for Analyzing Industries and Competitors* (New York: Free Press, 1980).
5. R. Miles and C. Snow, *Organizational Strategy, Structure, and Process* (New York: McGraw-Hill, 1978).
6. P. Wright and G. McMahan, "Theoretical Perspectives for Strategic Human Resource Management," *Journal of Management* 18 (1992), pp. 295–320.
7. D. Guest, "Human Resource Management, Corporate Performance and Employee Well-Being: Building the Worker into HRM," *Journal of Industrial Relations* 44 (2002), pp. 335–58; B. Becker, M. Huselid, P. Pinckus, and M. Spratt, "HR as a Source of Shareholder Value: Research and Recommendations," *Human Resource Management* 36 (1997), pp. 39–47.
8. P. Boxall and J. Purcell, *Strategy and Human Resource Management* (Basingstoke, Hants, U.K.: Palgrave MacMillan, 2003).
9. F. Biddle and J. Helyar, "Behind Boeing's Woes: Chunky Assembly Line, Price War with Airbus," *The Wall Street Journal*, April 24, 1998, pp. A1, A16.
10. K. Martell and S. Carroll, "How Strategic Is HRM?" *Human Resource Management* 34 (1995), pp. 253–67.
11. K. Golden and V. Ramanujam, "Between a Dream and a Nightmare: On the Integration of the Human Resource Function and the Strategic Business Planning Process," *Human Resource Management* 24 (1985), pp. 429–51.
12. P. Wright, B. Dunford, and S. Snell, "Contributions of the Resource-Based View of the Firm to the Field of Strategic HRM: Convergence of Two Fields," *Journal of Management* 27 (2001), pp. 701–21.
13. J. Purcell, N. Kinnie, S. Hutchinson, B. Rayton, and J. Swart, *Understanding the People and Performance Link: Unlocking the Black Box* (London: CIPD, 2003).
14. P. M. Wright, T. Gardner, and L. Moynihan, "The Impact of Human Resource Practices on Business Unit Operating and Financial Performance," *Human Resource Management Journal* 13 no. 3, (2003), pp. 21–36.
15. C. Hill and G. Jones, *Strategic Management Theory: An Integrated Approach* (Boston: Houghton Mifflin, 1989).
16. W. Johnston and A. Packer, *Workforce 2000: Work and Workers for the Twenty-First Century* (Indianapolis, IN: Hudson Institute, 1987).
17. "Labor Letter," *The Wall Street Journal*, December 15, 1992, p. A1.
18. P. Wright, G. McMahan, and A. McWilliams, "Human Resources and Sustained Competitive Advantage: A Resource-Based Perspective," *International Journal of Human Resource Management* 5 (1994), pp. 301–26.
19. P. Buller, "Successful Partnerships: HR and Strategic Planning at Eight Top Firms," *Organizational Dynamics* 17 (1988), pp. 27–42.
20. M. Hitt, R. Hoskisson, and J. Harrison, "Strategic Competitiveness in the 1990s: Challenges and Opportunities for U.S. Executives," *The Executive* 5 (May 1991), pp. 7–22.
21. P. Wright, G. McMahan, B. McCormick, and S. Sherman, "Strategy, Core Competence, and HR Involvement as Determinants of HR Effectiveness and Refinery Performance." Paper presented at the 1996 International Federation of Scholarly Associations in Management, Paris, France.
22. N. Bennett, D. Ketchen, and E. Schultz, "Antecedents and Consequences of Human Resource Integration with Strategic Decision Making." Paper presented at the 1995 Academy of Management Meeting, Vancouver, BC, Canada.
23. Golden and Ramanujam, "Between a Dream and a Nightmare."
24. J. Galbraith and R. Kazanjian, *Strategy Implementation: Structure, Systems, and Process* (St. Paul, MN: West, 1986).
25. B. Schneider and A. Konz, "Strategic Job Analysis," *Human Resource Management* 27 (1989), pp. 51–64.
26. P. Wright and S. Snell, "Toward an Integrative View of Strategic Human Resource Management," *Human Resource Management Review* 1 (1991), pp. 203–25.
27. S. Snell, "Control Theory in Strategic Human Resource Management: The Mediating Effect of Administrative Information," *Academy of Management Journal* 35 (1992), pp. 292–327.
28. R. Schuler, "Personnel and Human Resource Management Choices and Organizational Strategy," in *Readings in Personnel and Human Resource Management*, 3rd ed., ed. R. Schuler, S. Youngblood, and V. Huber (St. Paul, MN: West, 1988).
29. J. Dean and S. Snell, "Integrated Manufacturing and Job Design: Moderating Effects of Organizational Inertia," *Academy of Management Journal* 34 (1991), pp. 776–804.
30. E. Lawler, *The Ultimate Advantage: Creating the High Involvement Organization* (San Francisco: Jossey-Bass, 1992).
31. J. Olian and S. Rynes, "Organizational Staffing: Integrating Practice with Strategy," *Industrial Relations* 23 (1984), pp. 170–83.
32. G. Smith, "Quality: Small and Midsize Companies Seize the Challenge—Not a Moment Too Soon," *BusinessWeek*, November 30, 1992, pp. 66–75.
33. J. Kerr and E. Jackofsky, "Aligning Managers with Strategies: Management Development versus Selection," *Strategic Management Journal* 10 (1989), pp. 157–70.
34. J. Kerr, "Strategic Control through Performance Appraisal and Rewards," *Human Resource Planning* 11 (1988), pp. 215–23.

35. Snell, "Control Theory in Strategic Human Resource Management."
36. B. Gerhart and G. Milkovich, "Employee Compensation: Research and Practice," in *Handbook of Industrial and Organizational Psychology*, 2nd ed., ed. M. Dunnette and L. Hough (Palo Alto, CA: Consulting Psychologists Press, 1992), pp. 481–569.
37. D. Balkin and L. Gomez-Mejia, "Toward a Contingency Theory of Compensation Strategy," *Strategic Management Journal* 8 (1987), pp. 169–82.
38. A. Taylor, "U.S. Cars Come Back," *Fortune*, November 16, 1992, pp. 52, 85.
39. S. Cronshaw and R. Alexander, "One Answer to the Demand for Accountability: Selection Utility as an Investment Decision," *Organizational Behavior and Human Decision Processes* 35 (1986), pp. 102–18.
40. P. MacDuffie, "Human Resource Bundles and Manufacturing Performance: Organizational Logic and Flexible Production Systems in the World Auto Industry," *Industrial and Labor Relations Review* 48 (1995), pp. 197–221; P. McGraw, "A Hard Drive to the Top," *U.S. News & World Report* 118 (1995), pp. 43–44.
41. M. Huselid, "The Impact of Human Resource Management Practices on Turnover, Productivity, and Corporate Financial Performance," *Academy of Management Journal* 38 (1995), pp. 635–72.
42. B. Fulmer, B. Gerhart, and K. Scott, "Are the 100 Best Better? An Empirical Investigation of the Relationship between Being a 'Great Place to Work' and Firm Performance," *Personnel Psychology* 56 (2003), pp. 965–93.
43. J. E. Delery and D. H. Doty, "Modes of Theorizing in Strategic Human Resource Management: Tests of Universalistic, Contingency and Configurational Performance Predictions," *Academy of Management Journal* 39 (1996), pp. 802–83; D. Guest, J. Michie, N. Conway, and M. Sheehan, "Human Resource Management and Corporate Performance in the UK," *British Journal of Industrial Relations* 41 (2003), pp. 291–314; J. Guthrie, "High Involvement Work Practices, Turnover, and Productivity: Evidence from New Zealand," *Academy of Management Journal* 44 (2001), pp. 180–192; J. Harter, F. Schmidt, and T. Hayes, "Business-Unit-Level Relationship between Employee Satisfaction, Employee Engagement, and Business Outcomes: A Meta-analysis," *Journal of Applied Psychology* 87 (2002), pp. 268–79; Watson Wyatt, Worldwide, "Human Capital Index®: Human Capital as a Lead Indicator of Shareholder Value" (2002).
44. M. Bhattacharya, D. Gibson, and H. Doty, "The Effects of Flexibility in Employee Skills, Employee Behaviors, and Human Resource Practices on Firm Performance," *Journal of Management* 31 (2005), pp. 622–40.
45. D. Guest, J. Michie, N. Conway, and M. Sheehan, "Human Resource Management and Corporate Performance in the UK," *British Journal of Industrial Relations* 41 (2003), pp. 291–314; P. Wright, T. Gardner, L. Moynihan, and M. Allen, "The HR-Performance Relationship: Examining Causal Direction," *Personnel Psychology* 58 (2005), pp. 409–76.
46. P. Wright, *No Strategy: Adaptive to the Age of Globalization* (Arlington, VA: SHRM Foundation, 2008).
47. M. Porter, *Competitive Advantage* (New York: Free Press, 1985).
48. C. Lawton, "How HP Reclaimed Its PC Lead over Dell," June 2007; "Can Dell's Turnaround Strategy Keep HP at Bay?" September 2007, *Knowledge@Wharton*, http://knowledge.wharton.upenn.edu/article.cfm?articleid=1799.
49. R. Schuler and S. Jackson, "Linking Competitive Strategies with Human Resource Management Practices," *Academy of Management Executive* 1 (1987), pp. 207–19.
50. R. Miles and C. Snow, "Designing Strategic Human Resource Management Systems," *Organizational Dynamics* 13, no. 1 (1984), pp. 36–52.
51. A. Thompson and A. Strickland, *Strategy Formulation and Implementation: Tasks of the General Manager*, 3rd ed. (Plano, TX: BPI, 1986).
52. J. Schmidt, *Making Mergers Work: The Strategic Importance of People* (Arlington, VA: SHRM Foundation, 2003).
53. G. Fairclough, "Business Bulletin," *The Wall Street Journal*, March 5, 1998, p. A1.
54. P. Sebastian, "Business Bulletin," *The Wall Street Journal*, October 2, 1997, p. A1.
55. www.bls.gov/news.release/mslo.nro.gov.
56. S. Pearlstein, "Corporate Cutback Yet to Pay Off," *Washington Post*, January 4, 1994, p. B6.
57. K. Cameron, "Guest Editor's Note: Investigating Organizational Downsizing—Fundamental Issues," *Human Resource Management* 33 (1994), pp. 183–88.
58. W. Cascio, *Responsible Restructuring: Creative and Profitable Alternatives to Layoffs* (San Francisco: Berrett-Koehler, 2002).
59. N. Templin, "UAW to Unveil Pact on Slashing GM's Payroll," *The Wall Street Journal*, December 15, 1992, p. A3.
60. J. Lopez, "Managing: Early-Retirement Offers Lead to Renewed Hiring," *The Wall Street Journal*, January 26, 1993, p. B1.
61. A. Church, "Organizational Downsizing: What Is the Role of the Practitioner?" *Industrial–Organizational Psychologist* 33, no. 1 (1995), pp. 63–74.
62. N. Templin, "A Decisive Response to Crisis Brought Ford Enhanced Productivity," *The Wall Street Journal*, December 15, 1992, p. A1.
63. Quinn, *Strategies for Change*.
64. H. Schultz and D. Yang, *Pour Your Heart Into It* (New York: Hyperion, 1987).
65. R. Pascale, "Perspectives on Strategy: The Real Story behind Honda's Success," *California Management Review* 26 (1984), pp. 47–72.
66. Templin, "A Decisive Response to Crisis."
67. P. Wright and S. Snell, "Toward a Unifying Framework for Exploring Fit and Flexibility in Strategic Human Resource Management," *Academy of Management Review* 23, no. 4 (1998), pp. 756–72.
68. H. Behar, *It's Not about the Coffee: Lessons for Putting People First from a Life at Starbucks* (New York, NY: Penguin Group, 2007).
69. T. Stewart, "Brace for Japan's Hot New Strategy," *Fortune*, September 21, 1992, pp. 62–76.
70. B. Dunford, P. Wright, and S. Snell, "Contributions of the Resource-Based View of the Firm to the Field of Strategic HRM: Convergence of Two Fields," *Journal of Management* 27 (2001), pp. 701–21.
71. C. Snow and S. Snell, *Staffing as Strategy*, vol. 4 of *Personnel Selection* (San Francisco: Jossey-Bass, 1992).
72. T. Batten, "Education Key to Prosperity—Report," *Houston Chronicle*, September 7, 1992, p. 1B.
73. Schultz and Yang, *Pour Your Heart Into It*.
74. G. McMahan, University of Texas at Arlington, personal communications.
75. M. Brannigan, "Delta Lifts Mechanics' Pay to Top of Industry Amid Push by Union," *The Wall Street Journal Interactive*, August 16, 2001; M. Adams, "Delta May See Second Big Union," *USA Today*, August 27, 2001, p. 1B.

CHAPTER

3

The Legal Environment: Equal Employment Opportunity and Safety

LO LEARNING OBJECTIVES

After reading this chapter, you should be able to:

LOI Identify the three branches of government and the role each plays in influencing the legal environment of human resource management. *page 106*

LO2 List the major federal laws that require equal employment opportunity and the protections provided by each of these laws. *page 108*

LO3 Discuss the roles, responsibilities, and requirements of the federal agencies responsible for enforcing equal employment opportunity laws. *page 116*

LO4 Identify the four theories of discrimination under Title VII of the Civil Rights Act, and apply these theories to different discrimination situations. *page 119*

LO5 Discuss the legal issues involved with preferential treatment programs. *page 131*

LO6 Identify behavior that constitutes sexual harassment, and list things that an organization can do to eliminate or minimize it. *page 132*

LO7 Identify the major provisions of the Occupational Safety and Health Act (1970) and the rights of employees that are guaranteed by this act. *page 136*

ENTER THE WORLD OF BUSINESS

Wal-Mart's Legal Problems

Wal-Mart has become one of the largest, most admired, and ironically, most detested companies in the world. Its "Always Low Prices, Always" motto and business model have enabled it to become the world's largest private employer with retail outlets all over the world. This success has led to its frequent inclusion on *Fortune*'s Most Admired Companies list. However, its positive reputation has taken serious blows over the past few years, at least in part because of its practices for managing people.

Union leaders criticize Wal-Mart for its low pay and modest health insurance. Wal-Mart defends itself by noting that it pays competitively with similar organizations. However, what undeniably has hurt Wal-Mart's image is the large number of discrimination suits that it has faced over the past 10 years. For instance, it recently settled a class-action race discrimination suit regarding its hiring of drivers, agreeing to a $17.5 million settlement while denying that it had engaged in any pattern or practice of discrimination. The most important one is a class-action suit brought on behalf of 2 million former female Wal-Mart employees. The suit, known as *Dukes v. Wal-Mart*, alleges that Wal-Mart discouraged the promotion of women store employees to managerial positions and that it paid them less than men across all jobs. The plaintiff's lawyers argued that women made up 63.4 percent of Wal-Mart's nonmanagerial workers, but only 33.6 percent of the store's salaried managers. They also suggest that the 33.6 percent is far below the 56.5 percent of female managers at Wal-Mart's top 20 competitors.

An earlier analysis of liability in the lawsuit by the Goldman Sachs Group Inc., based on a potential plaintiff group of 1.6 million workers, estimated potential damages at $1.5 billion to $3.5 billion if Wal-Mart loses. Punitive damages potentially push the figure to a range of $13.5 billion to $31.5 billion, the analysis said. Did Wal-Mart really discriminate against 2 million of its former employees, and if so, how would you know?

Sources: Bloomberg News, "Wal-Mart to Settle Bias Lawsuit," *Los Angeles Times*, February 21, 2009, p. C3; R. Parloff and S. Kaufman, "The War Over Unconscious Bias," *Fortune*, October 15, 2007, p. 90.

Introduction

In the opening chapter, we discussed the environment of the HRM function, and we noted that several environmental factors affect an organization's HRM function. One is the legal environment, particularly the laws affecting the management of people. As the troubles at Wal-Mart indicate, legal issues can cause serious problems for a company's success and survival. In this chapter, we first present an overview of the U.S. legal system, noting the different legislative bodies, regulatory agencies, and judicial bodies that determine the legality of certain HRM practices. We then discuss the major laws and executive orders that govern these practices.

One point to make clear at the outset is that managers often want a list of "dos and don'ts" that will keep them out of legal trouble. They rely on rules such as "Don't ever ask a female applicant if she is married" without understanding the "why" behind these rules. Clearly, certain practices are illegal or inadvisable, and this chapter will provide some valuable tips for avoiding discrimination lawsuits. However, such lists are not compatible with a strategic approach to HRM and are certainly not the route to developing a competitive advantage. They are simply mechanical reactions to the situations. Our goal is to provide an understanding of how the legislative, regulatory, and judicial systems work to define equal employment opportunity law. Armed with this understanding, a manager is better prepared to manage people within the limits imposed by the legal system. Doing so effectively is a source of competitive advantage. Doing so ineffectively results in competitive disadvantage. Rather than viewing the legal system as a constraint, firms that embrace the concept of diversity can often find that they are able to leverage the differences among people as a tremendous competitive tool.

 The Legal System in the United States

LO1
Identify the three branches of government and the role each plays in influencing the legal environment of human resource management.

The foundation for the U.S. legal system is set forth in the U.S. Constitution, which affects HRM in two ways. First, it delineates a citizen's constitutional rights, on which the government cannot impinge.[1] Most individuals are aware of the Bill of Rights, the first 10 amendments to the Constitution; but other amendments, such as the Fourteenth Amendment, also influence HRM practices. The Fourteenth Amendment, called the equal protection clause, states that all individuals are entitled to equal protection under the law.

Second, the Constitution established three major governing bodies: the legislative, executive, and judicial branches. The Constitution explicitly defines the roles and responsibilities of each of these branches. Each branch has its own areas of authority, but these areas have often overlapped, and the borders between the branches are often blurred.

Legislative Branch

The legislative branch of the federal government consists of the House of Representatives and the Senate. These bodies develop laws that govern many HRM activities. Most of the laws stem from a perceived societal need. For example, during the civil rights movement of the early 1960s, the legislative branch moved to ensure that various minority groups received equal opportunities in many areas of life. One of these areas was employment, and thus Congress enacted Title VII of the Civil Rights Act. Similar perceived societal needs have brought about labor laws such as the Occupational Safety and Health Act, the Employee Retirement Income Security Act, the Age Discrimination in Employment Act, and, more recently, the Americans with Disabilities Act of 1990 and the Civil Rights Act of 1991.

Executive Branch

The executive branch consists of the president of the United States and the many regulatory agencies the president oversees. Although the legislative branch passes the laws, the executive branch affects these laws in many ways. First, the president can propose bills to Congress that, if passed, would become laws. Second, the president has the power to veto any law passed by Congress, thus ensuring that few laws are passed without presidential approval—which allows the president to influence how laws are written.

Third, the regulatory agencies, under the authority of the president, have responsibility for enforcing the laws. Thus, a president can influence what types of violations are pursued. For example, many laws affecting employment discrimination are enforced by the Equal Employment Opportunity Commission under the Department of Justice. During President Jimmy Carter's administration, the Department of Justice brought a lawsuit against Birmingham, Alabama's, fire department for not having enough black firefighters. This suit resulted in a consent decree that required blacks to receive preferential treatment in hiring and promotion decisions. Two years later, during Ronald Reagan's administration, the Department of Justice sided with white firefighters in a lawsuit against the city of Birmingham, alleging that the preferential treatment required by the consent decree discriminated against white firefighters.[2]

Fourth, the president can issue executive orders, which sometimes regulate the activities of organizations that have contracts with the federal government. For example, Executive Order 11246, signed by President Lyndon Johnson, required all federal contractors and subcontractors to engage in affirmative action programs designed to hire and promote women and minorities within their organizations. Fifth, the president can influence the Supreme Court to interpret laws in certain ways. When particularly sensitive cases come before the Court, the attorney general, representing the executive branch, argues for certain preferred outcomes. For example, one court case involved a white female schoolteacher who was laid off from her job in favor of retaining a black schoolteacher with equal seniority and performance with the reason given as "diversity." The white woman filed a lawsuit in federal court and the (first) Bush administration filed a brief on her behalf, arguing that diversity was not a legitimate reason to use race in decision making. She won in federal court, and the school district appealed. The Clinton administration, having been elected in the meantime, filed a brief on behalf of the school district, arguing that diversity was a legitimate defense.

Finally, the president appoints all the judges in the federal judicial system, subject to approval from the legislative branch. This affects the interpretation of many laws.

Judicial Branch

The judicial branch consists of the federal court system, which is made up of three levels. The first level consists of the U.S. District Courts and quasi-judicial administrative agencies. The district courts hear cases involving alleged violations of federal laws. The quasi-judicial agencies, such as the National Labor Relations Board (or NLRB, which is actually an arm of the executive branch, but serves a judicial function), hear cases regarding their particular jurisdictions (in the NLRB's case, disputes between unions and management). If neither party to a suit is satisfied with the decision of the court at this level, the parties can appeal the decision to the U.S. Courts of Appeals. These courts were originally set up to ease the Supreme Court's caseload, so appeals generally go from the federal trial level to one of the 13 appellate courts before they can be heard by the highest level, the Supreme Court. The Supreme Court must grant certiorari before hearing an appealed case. However, this is not usually granted unless two appellate courts have come to differing decisions on the same point of law or if the case deals with an important interpretation of constitutional law.

The Supreme Court serves as the court of final appeal. Decisions made by the Supreme Court are binding; they can be overturned only through legislation. For example, Congress, dissatisfied with the Supreme Court's decisions in certain cases such as *Wards Cove Packing v. Atonio*, overturned those decisions through the Civil Rights Act of 1991.[3]

Having described the legal system that affects the management of HR, we now explore some laws that regulate HRM activities, particularly equal employment opportunity laws. We first discuss the major laws that mandate equal employment opportunity in the United States. Then we examine the agencies involved in enforcing these laws. This leads us into an examination of the four theories of discrimination, with a discussion of some relevant court cases. Finally, we explore some equal employment opportunity issues facing today's managers.

LO2
List the major federal laws that require equal employment opportunity and the protections provided by each of these laws.

Equal Employment Opportunity (EEO)
The government's attempt to ensure that all individuals have an equal opportunity for employment, regardless of race, color, religion, sex, age, disability, or national origin.

Equal Employment Opportunity

Equal employment opportunity (EEO) refers to the government's attempt to ensure that all individuals have an equal chance for employment, regardless of race, color, religion, sex, age, disability, or national origin. To accomplish this, the federal government has used constitutional amendments, legislation, and executive orders, as well as the court decisions that interpret these laws. (However, equal employment laws are not the same in all countries.) The major EEO laws we discuss are summarized in Table 3.1.

Constitutional Amendments

Thirteenth Amendment

The Thirteenth Amendment of the Constitution abolished slavery in the United States. Though one might be hard-pressed to cite an example of race-based slavery in the United States today, the Thirteenth Amendment has been applied in cases where the discrimination involved the "badges" (symbols) and "incidents" of slavery.

table 3.1

Summary of Major EEO Laws and Regulations

ACT	REQUIREMENTS	COVERS	ENFORCEMENT AGENCY
Thirteenth Amendment	Abolished slavery	All individuals	Court system
Fourteenth Amendment	Provides equal protection for all citizens and requires due process in state action	State actions (e.g., decisions of government organizations)	Court system
Civil Rights Acts (CRAs) of 1866 and 1871 (as amended)	Grants all citizens the right to make, perform, modify, and terminate contracts and enjoy all benefits, terms, and conditions of the contractual relationship	All individuals	Court system
Equal Pay Act of 1963	Requires that men and women performing equal jobs receive equal pay	Employers engaged in interstate commerce	EEOC
Title VII of CRA	Forbids discrimination based on race, color, religion, sex, or national origin	Employers with 15 or more employees working 20 or more weeks per year; labor unions; and employment agencies	EEOC
Age Discrimination in Employment Act of 1967	Prohibits discrimination in employment against individuals 40 years of age and older	Employers with 15 or more employees working 20 or more weeks per year; labor unions; employment agencies; federal government	EEOC
Rehabilitation Act of 1973	Requires affirmative action in the employment of individuals with disabilities	Government agencies; federal contractors and subcontractors with contracts greater than $2,500	OFCCP
Americans with Disabilities Act of 1990	Prohibits discrimination against individuals with disabilities	Employers with more than 15 employees	EEOC
Pregnancy Discrimination Act	Prohibits discrimination on the basis of pregnancy, childbirth, or related medical conditions	Employers with more than 15 employees	EEOC
Executive Order 11246	Requires affirmative action in hiring women and minorities	Federal contractors and subcontractors with contracts greater than $10,000	OFCCP
Civil Rights Act of 1991	Prohibits discrimination (same as Title VII)	Same as Title VII, plus applies Section 1981 to employment discrimination cases	EEOC

Fourteenth Amendment

The Fourteenth Amendment forbids the states from taking life, liberty, or property without due process of law and prevents the states from denying equal protection of the laws. Passed immediately after the Civil War, this amendment originally applied only to discrimination against blacks. It was soon broadened to protect other groups such as aliens and Asian-Americans, and more recently it has been applied to the protection of whites in allegations of reverse discrimination. In *Bakke v. California Board of Regents,* Alan Bakke alleged that he had been discriminated against in the selection of entrants to the University of California at Davis medical school.[4] The university had set aside 16 of the available 100 places for "disadvantaged" applicants who were members of racial minority groups. Under this quota system, Bakke was able to compete for only 84 positions, whereas a minority applicant was able to compete for all 100. The court ruled in favor of Bakke, noting that this quota system had violated white individuals' right to equal protection under the law.

One important point regarding the Fourteenth Amendment is that it is applicable only to "state actions." This means that only the decisions or actions of the government or of private groups whose activities are deemed state actions can be construed as violations of the Fourteenth Amendment. Thus, one could file a claim under the Fourteenth Amendment if one were fired from a state university (a government organization) but not if one were fired by a private employer.

Congressional Legislation

The Reconstruction Civil Rights Acts (1866 and 1871)

The Thirteenth Amendment eradicated slavery in the United States, and the Reconstruction Civil Rights Acts were attempts to further this goal. The Civil Rights Act passed in 1866 was later broken into two statutes. Section 1982 granted all persons the same property rights as white citizens. Section 1981 granted other rights, including the right to enter into and enforce contracts. Courts have interpreted Section 1981 as granting individuals the right to make and enforce employment contracts. The Civil Rights Act of 1871 granted all citizens the right to sue in federal court if they felt they had been deprived of some civil right. Although these laws might seem outdated, they are still used because they allow the plaintiff to recover both compensatory and punitive damages.

In fact, these laws came to the forefront in a Supreme Court case: *Patterson v. McClean Credit Union.*[5] The plaintiff had filed a discrimination complaint under Section 1981 for racial harassment. After being hired by McClean Credit Union, Patterson failed to receive any promotions or pay raises while she was employed there. She was also told that "blacks work slower than whites." Thus, she had grounds to prove discrimination and filed suit under Section 1981, arguing that she had been discriminated against in the making and enforcement of an employment contract. The Supreme Court ruled that this situation did not fall under Section 1981 because it did not involve the making and enforcement of contracts. However, the Civil Rights Act of 1991 amended this act to include the making, performance, modification, and termination of contracts, as well as all benefits, privileges, terms, and conditions of the contractual relationship.

The Equal Pay Act of 1963

The Equal Pay Act, an amendment to the Fair Labor Standards Act, requires that men and women in the same organization who are doing equal work must be paid equally. The act defines equal in terms of skill, effort, responsibility, and working conditions. However, the act allows for reasons why men and women performing the same job might be paid differently. If the pay differences are the result of differences in seniority, merit, quantity or quality of production, or any factor other than sex (such as shift differentials or training programs), then differences are legally allowable.

Title VII of the Civil Rights Act of 1964

This is the major legislation regulating equal employment opportunity in the United States. It was a direct result of the civil rights movement of the early 1960s, led by such individuals as Dr. Martin Luther King Jr. It was Dr. King's philosophy that people should "not be judged by the color of their skin but by the content of their character." To ensure that employment opportunities would be based on character or ability rather than on race, Congress wrote and passed Title VII, which President Lyndon Johnson signed into law.

Title VII states that it is illegal for an employer to "(1) fail or refuse to hire or discharge any individual, or otherwise discriminate against any individual with respect to his compensation, terms, conditions, or privileges of employment because of such individual's race, color, religion, sex, or national origin, or (2) to limit, segregate, or classify his employees or applicants for employment in any way that would deprive or tend to deprive any individual of employment opportunities or otherwise adversely affect his status as an employee because of such individual's race, color, religion, sex, or national origin." The act applies to organizations with 15 or more employees working 20 or more weeks a year that are involved in interstate commerce, as well as state and local governments, employment agencies, and labor organizations.

The "Competing through Technology" box describes how advances in genomic medicine have prompted Congress to provide protections against using it for employment decisions.

Age Discrimination in Employment Act (ADEA)

Passed in 1967 and amended in 1986, this act prohibits discrimination against employees over the age of 40. The act almost exactly mirrors Title VII in terms of its substantive provisions and the procedures to be followed in pursuing a case.[6] As with Title VII, the EEOC is responsible for enforcing this act.

The ADEA was designed to protect older employees when a firm reduces its workforce through layoffs. By targeting older employees, who tend to have higher pay, a firm can substantially cut labor costs. Recently, firms have often offered early retirement incentives, a possible violation of the act because of the focus on older employees. Early retirement incentives require employees to sign an agreement waiving their rights to sue under the ADEA. Courts have tended to uphold the use of early retirement incentives and waivers as long as the individuals were not coerced into signing the agreements, the agreements were presented in a way that the employees could understand, and the employees were given enough time to make a decision.[7]

COMPETING THROUGH TECHNOLOGY
Protecting against Genetic Discrimination

The technology developments within the field of genetics, the decoding of the human genome, and advances in the field of genomic medicine have enabled researchers to identify genes that inform individuals whether they may be at risk for developing a certain disease or disorder. For instance, individuals with family members who have had colon cancer are more likely to develop it than those with no family history of such cancer. While useful for individuals to begin to take preventive measures to minimize the chance of getting these disorders, there are potential harmful effects as well.

For instance, given the rapidly rising health insurance costs to companies, what if they began doing genetic screening to identify job candidates that might later develop costly diseases? This was the concern that prompted Congress to pass the Genetic Information Nondiscrimination Act (GINA) of 2008. GINA prohibits the use of genetic information in making decisions related to any terms, conditions, or privileges of employment; prohibits covered entities from intentionally acquiring genetic information; requires confidentiality with respect to genetic information (with limited exceptions); and prohibits retaliation. Genetic information includes, for example, information about an individual's genetic tests, genetic tests of a family member, and family medical history.

SOURCE: http//www.shrm.org/ Advocacy/PublicPolicyStatusReports/ Courts-Regulations/CivilRights/ Documents/5.1.09%20GINA%20 Title%20II%20comments.pdf

However, age discrimination complaints make up a large percentage of the complaints filed with the Equal Employment Opportunity Commission, and the number of complaints continues to grow whenever the economy is slow. For example, as we see in Figure 3.1, the cases increased during the early 1990s when many firms were downsizing, but the number of cases decreased as the economy expanded. The number of charges increased again as the economy began slowing again in 2000. This often stems from firms seeking to lay off older (and thus higher paid) employees when they are downsizing. These cases can be costly; most cases are settled out of court, but such settlements run from $50,000 to $400,000 per employee.[8] In one recent case, Schering-Plough fired 35-year employee Fred Maiorino after he twice failed to accept an early retirement offer made to all sales representatives. After hearing testimony that Maiorino's boss had plastered his file with negative paperwork aimed at firing him, rather than trying to help him improve his performance, the jurors unanimously decided he had been discriminated against because of his age. They awarded him $435,000 in compensatory damages and $8 million in punitive damages.[9]

The Vocational Rehabilitation Act of 1973

This act covers executive agencies and contractors and subcontractors that receive more than $2,500 annually from the federal government. It requires them to engage in affirmative action for individuals with disabilities. Congress designed this act to encourage employers to actively recruit qualified individuals with disabilities and to make reasonable accommodations to allow them to become active members of the labor market. The Employment Standards Administration of the Department of Labor enforces this act.

figure 3.1

Age Discrimination Complaints, 1991–2007

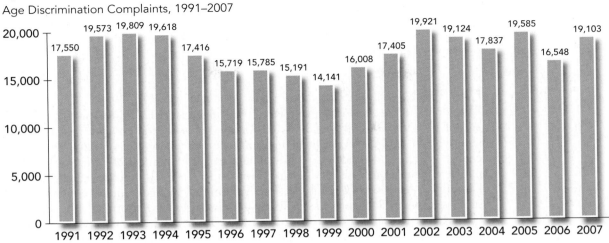

SOURCE: Equal Employment Opportunity Commission, at http://eeoc.gov/stats/adea.html.

Vietnam Era Veteran's Readjustment Act of 1974

Similar to the Rehabilitation Act, this act requires federal contractors and subcontractors to take affirmative action toward employing Vietnam veterans (those serving between August 5, 1964, and May 7, 1975). The Office of Federal Contract Compliance Programs (OFCCP), discussed later in this chapter, has authority to enforce this act.

Pregnancy Discrimination Act

The Pregnancy Discrimination Act is an amendment to Title VII of the Civil Rights Act. It makes illegal discrimination on the basis of pregnancy, childbirth, or related medical conditions as a form of unlawful sex discrimination. An employer cannot refuse to hire a pregnant woman because of her pregnancy, a pregnancy-related condition, or the prejudices of co-workers, clients, or customers. For instance, in a recent court case, the retail store Motherhood Maternity, a Philadelphia-based maternity clothes retailer, settled a pregnancy discrimination and retaliation lawsuit brought by the Equal Employment Opportunity Commission (EEOC). The EEOC had charged that the company refused to hire qualified female applicants because they were pregnant. As a result of the settlement, Motherhood Maternity agreed to a three-year consent decree requiring them to pay plaintiffs $375,000, adopt and distribute an antidiscrimination policy specifically prohibiting discrimination on the basis of pregnancy, train its Florida employees on the new policy, post a notice of resolution of the lawsuit, and provide twice a year reports to the EEOC on any pregnancy discrimination complaints.[10]

In addition, regarding pregnancy and maternity leave, employers may not single out pregnancy-related conditions for special procedures to determine an employee's ability to work, and if an employee is temporarily unable to perform during her pregnancy, the employer must treat her the same as any temporarily disabled employees. The act also requires that any health insurance must cover expenses for pregnancy-related conditions on the same basis as costs for other medical conditions. Finally, pregnancy-related benefits cannot be limited to married employees, and if an employer provides any benefits to workers on leave, they must also provide the same benefits for those on leave for pregnancy-related conditions.

Civil Rights Act of 1991

The Civil Rights Act of 1991 (CRA 1991) amends Title VII of the Civil Rights Act of 1964, Section 1981 of the Civil Rights Act of 1866, the Americans with Disabilities Act, and the Age Discrimination in Employment Act of 1967. One major change in EEO law under CRA 1991 has been the addition of compensatory and punitive damages in cases of discrimination under Title VII and the Americans with Disabilities Act. Before CRA 1991, Title VII limited damage claims to equitable relief such as back pay, lost benefits, front pay in some cases, and attorneys' fees and costs. CRA 1991 allows compensatory and punitive damages when intentional or reckless discrimination is proven. Compensatory damages include such things as future pecuniary loss, emotional pain, suffering, and loss of enjoyment of life. Punitive damages are meant to discourage employers from discriminating by providing for payments to the plaintiff beyond the actual damages suffered.

Recognizing that one or a few discrimination cases could put an organization out of business, thus adversely affecting many innocent employees, Congress has put limits on the amount of punitive damages. Table 3.2 depicts these limits. As can be seen, damages range from $50,000 to $300,000 per violation, depending on the size of the organization. Punitive damages are available only if the employer intentionally discriminated against the plaintiff(s) or if the employer discriminated with malice or reckless indifference to the employee's federally protected rights. These damages are excluded for an employment practice held to be unlawful because of its disparate impact.[11]

The addition of damages to CRA 1991 has had two immediate effects. First, by increasing the potential payoff for a successful discrimination suit, it has increased the number of suits filed against businesses. Second, organizations are now more likely to grant all employees an equal opportunity for employment, regardless of their race, sex, religion, or national origin. Many organizations have felt the need to make the composition of their workforce mirror the general population to avoid costly lawsuits. This act adds a financial incentive for doing so.

Americans with Disabilities Act (ADA) of 1990

Americans with Disabilities Act (ADA) of 1990
A 1990 act prohibiting individuals with disabilities from being discriminated against in the workplace.

One of the most far-reaching acts concerning the management of human resources is the **Americans with Disabilities Act.** This act protects individuals with disabilities from being discriminated against in the workplace. It prohibits discrimination based

table 3.2

Maximum Punitive Damages Allowed under the Civil Rights Act of 1991

EMPLOYER SIZE	DAMAGE LIMIT
14 to 100 employees	$ 50,000
101 to 200 employees	100,000
201 to 500 employees	200,000
More than 500 employees	300,000

on disability in all employment practices such as job application procedures, hiring, firing, promotions, compensation, and training—in addition to other employment activities such as advertising, recruitment, tenure, layoff, leave, and fringe benefits. Because this act is so new, we will cover its various stipulations individually.

The ADA defines a disability as a physical or mental impairment that substantially limits one or more major life activities, a record of having such an impairment, or being regarded as having such an impairment. The first part of the definition refers to individuals who have serious disabilities—such as epilepsy, blindness, deafness, or paralysis—that affect their ability to perform major life activities such as walking, seeing, performing manual tasks, learning, caring for oneself, and working. The second part refers to individuals who have a history of disability, such as someone who has had cancer but is currently in remission, someone with a history of mental illness, and someone with a history of heart disease. The third part of the definition, "being regarded as having a disability," refers, for example, to an individual who is severely disfigured and is denied employment because an employer fears negative reactions from others.[12]

Thus the ADA covers specific physiological disabilities such as cosmetic disfigurement and anatomical loss affecting the neurological, musculoskeletal, sensory, respiratory, cardiovascular, reproductive, digestive, genitourinary, hemic, or lymphatic systems. In addition, it covers mental and psychological disorders such as mental retardation, organic brain syndrome, emotional or mental illness, and learning disabilities. However, conditions such as obesity, substance abuse, eye and hair color, and lefthandedness are not covered.[13]

In addition, the Americans with Disabilities Act Amendments Act (ADAAA), effective January 1, 2009, broadened the scope of who is considered to be an individual with a disability. It states that the definition of disability should be broadly construed and that the "question of whether an individual's impairment is a disability under the ADA should not demand extensive analysis." The Supreme Court had interpreted the term "substantially limited" in a major life activity to require the individual to be "significantly restricted," but the ADAAA states that this is too high a standard and directs the EEOC to revise its regulations to set a lower standard. Also, regarding the term "regarded as disabled," previously employers could avoid liability by showing that the impairment did not substantially limit a major life activity. However, the ADAAA states that an employee can prove he or she was subjected to an illegal act "because of an actual or perceived physical or mental impairment whether or not the impairment limits or is perceived to limit a major life activity."

Executive Orders

Executive orders are directives issued and amended unilaterally by the president. These orders do not require congressional approval, yet they have the force of law. Two executive orders directly affect HRM.

Executive Order 11246

President Johnson issued this executive order, which prohibits discrimination based on race, color, religion, sex, and national origin. Unlike Title VII, this order applies only to federal contractors and subcontractors. Employers receiving more than

$10,000 from the federal government must take affirmative action to ensure against discrimination, and those with contracts greater than $50,000 must develop a written affirmative action plan for each of their establishments within 120 days of the beginning of the contract. The Office of Federal Contract Compliance Procedures enforces this executive order.

Executive Order 11478

President Richard M. Nixon issued this order, which requires the federal government to base all its employment policies on merit and fitness, and specifies that race, color, sex, religion, and national origin should not be considered. (The U.S. Office of Personnel Management is in charge of this.) The order also extends to all contractors and subcontractors doing $10,000 worth of business with the federal government. (The relevant government agencies have the responsibility to ensure that the contractors and subcontractors comply with the order.)

Enforcement of Equal Employment Opportunity

LO3
Discuss the roles, responsibilities, and requirements of the federal agencies responsible for enforcing equal employment opportunity laws.

As discussed previously, the executive branch of the federal government bears most of the responsibility for enforcing all EEO laws passed by the legislative branch. In addition, the executive branch must enforce the executive orders issued by the president. The two agencies responsible for the enforcement of these laws and executive orders are the Equal Employment Opportunity Commission and the Office of Federal Contract Compliance Programs, respectively.

Equal Employment Opportunity Commission (EEOC)
The government commission to ensure that all individuals have an equal opportunity for employment, regardless of race, color, religion, sex, age, disability, or national origin.

Equal Employment Opportunity Commission (EEOC)

An independent federal agency, the EEOC is responsible for enforcing most of the EEO laws, such as Title VII, the Equal Pay Act, and the Americans with Disabilities Act. The EEOC has three major responsibilities: investigating and resolving discrimination complaints, gathering information, and issuing guidelines.

Investigation and Resolution

Individuals who feel they have been discriminated against must file a complaint with the EEOC or a similar state agency within 180 days of the incident. Failure to file a complaint within the 180 days results in the case's being dismissed immediately, with certain exceptions, such as the enactment of a seniority system that has an intentionally discriminatory purpose. For instance, the recent Lilly Ledbetter Fair Pay Act signed by President Obama was crafted in direct response to the 180-day window. Ledbetter had been an area manager at the Goodyear Tire and Rubber plant in Alabama from 1979 to 1998, during which time she received lower raises than the males. The differences were such that by the end of her career she was making $6,700 less per year than her male counterparts, and because pension payments were related to the salary at the time of retirement, she received smaller pension payments. When she filed the lawsuit, the Supreme Court ruled that the illegal acts were the pay raise decisions themselves (which fell far outside the 180-day window); Ledbetter wanted to argue that every time she received a pension check lower than her peers it served as an act of discrimination. Thus, Congress passed the act specifying that an "illegal act" occurs when (1) a discriminatory compensation decision is adopted; (2) an employee becomes subject to the decision; or (3) an employee is affected by it application, including each time compensation is paid.

Once the complaint is filed, the EEOC takes responsibility for investigating the claim of discrimination. The complainant must give the EEOC 60 days to investigate the complaint. If the EEOC either does not believe the complaint to be valid or fails to complete the investigation, the complainant may sue in federal court. If the EEOC determines that discrimination has taken place, its representatives will attempt to provide a reconciliation between the two parties without burdening the court system with a lawsuit. Sometimes the EEOC enters into a consent decree with the discriminating organization. This decree is an agreement between the agency and the organization that the organization will cease certain discriminatory practices and possibly institute additional affirmative action practices to rectify its history of discrimination.

If the EEOC cannot come to an agreement with the organization, it has two options. First, it can issue a "right to sue" letter to the alleged victim, which certifies that the agency has investigated and found validity in the victim's allegations. Second, although less likely, the agency may aid the alleged victim in bringing suit in federal court.

Information Gathering

The EEOC also plays a role in monitoring the hiring practices of organizations. Each year organizations with 100 or more employees must file a report (EEO-1) with the EEOC that provides the number of women and minorities employed in nine different job categories. The EEOC computer analyzes these reports to identify patterns of discrimination that can then be attacked through class-action suits.

Issuance of Guidelines

A third responsibility of the EEOC is to issue guidelines that help employers determine when their decisions are violations of the laws enforced by the EEOC. These guidelines are not laws themselves, but the courts give great deference to them when hearing employment discrimination cases.

For example, the *Uniform Guidelines on Employee Selection Procedures* is a set of guidelines issued by the EEOC, the Department of Labor, the Department of Justice, and the U.S. Civil Service Commission.[14] This document provides guidance on the ways an organization should develop and administer selection systems so as not to violate Title VII. The courts often refer to the *Uniform Guidelines* to determine whether a company has engaged in discriminatory conduct or to determine the validity of the procedures it used to validate a selection system. Another example: Since the passage of the ADA, employers have been somewhat confused about the act's implications for their hiring procedures. Therefore, the EEOC issued guidelines in the *Federal Register* that provided more detailed information regarding what the agency will consider legal and illegal employment practices concerning disabled individuals. Although companies are well advised to follow these guidelines, it is possible that courts will interpret the ADA differently from the EEOC. Thus, through the issuance of guidelines the EEOC gives employers directions for making employment decisions that do not conflict with existing laws.

Office of Federal Contract Compliance Programs (OFCCP)

The OFCCP is the agency responsible for enforcing the executive orders that cover companies doing business with the federal government. Businesses with contracts for more than $50,000 cannot discriminate in employment based on race, color, religion, national origin, or sex, and they must have a written affirmative action plan on file.

These plans have three basic components.[15] First, the **utilization analysis** compares the race, sex, and ethnic composition of the employer's workforce with that of the available labor supply. For each job group, the employer must identify the percentage of its workforce with that characteristic (e.g., female) and identify the percentage of workers in the relevant labor market with that characteristic. If the percentage in the employer's workforce is much less than the percentage in the comparison group, then that minority group is considered to be "underutilized."

Second, the employer must develop specific **goals and timetables** for achieving balance in the workforce concerning these characteristics (particularly where underutilization exists). Goals and timetables specify the percentage of women and minorities that the employer seeks to have in each job group and the date by which that percentage is to be attained. These are not to be viewed as quotas, which entail setting aside a specific number of positions to be filled only by members of the protected class. Goals and timetables are much more flexible, requiring only that the employer have specific goals and take steps to achieve those goals. In fact, one study that examined companies with the goal of increasing black employment found that only 10 percent of them actually achieved their goals. Although this may sound discouragingly low, it is important to note that these companies increased their black employment more than companies that set no such goals.[16]

Third, employers with federal contracts must develop a list of **action steps** they will take toward attaining their goals to reduce underutilization. The company's CEO must make it clear to the entire organization that the company is committed to reducing underutilization, and all management levels must be involved in the planning process. For example, organizations can communicate job openings to women and minorities through publishing the company's affirmative action policy, recruiting at predominantly female or minority schools, participating in programs designed to increase employment opportunities for underemployed groups, and removing unnecessary barriers to employment. Organizations must also take affirmative steps toward hiring Vietnam veterans and individuals with disabilities.

The OFCCP annually audits government contractors to ensure that they actively pursue the goals in their plans. These audits consist of (1) examining the company's affirmative action plan and (2) conducting on-site visits to examine how individual employees perceive the company's affirmative action policies. If the OFCCP finds that the contractors or subcontractors are not complying with the executive order, then its representatives may notify the EEOC (if there is evidence that Title VII has been violated), advise the Department of Justice to institute criminal proceedings, request that the Secretary of Labor cancel or suspend any current contracts, and forbid the firm from bidding on future contracts. This last penalty, called debarment, is the OFCCP's most potent weapon.

Having discussed the major laws defining equal employment opportunity and the agencies that enforce these laws, we now address the various types of discrimination and the ways these forms of discrimination have been interpreted by the courts in a number of cases.

Utilization Analysis
A comparison of the race, sex, and ethnic composition of an employer's workforce with that of the available labor supply.

Goals and Timetables
The part of a written affirmative action plan that specifies the percentage of women and minorities that an employer seeks to have in each job group and the date by which that percentage is to be attained.

Action Steps
The written affirmative plan that specifies what an employer plans to do to reduce underutilization of protected groups.

Types of Discrimination

How would you know if you had been discriminated against? Assume that you have applied for a job and were not hired. How do you know if the organization decided not to hire you because you are unqualified, because you are less qualified than the individual ultimately hired, or simply because the person in charge of the hiring decision "didn't like your type"? Discrimination is a multifaceted issue. It is often not easy to determine the extent to which unfair discrimination affects an employer's decisions.

Legal scholars have identified three theories of discrimination: disparate treatment, disparate impact, and reasonable accommodation. In addition, there is protection for those participating in discrimination cases or opposing discriminatory actions. In the act, these theories are stated in very general terms. However, the court system has defined and delineated these theories through the cases brought before it. A comparison of the theories of discrimination is given in Table 3.3.

Disparate Treatment

Disparate treatment exists when individuals in similar situations are treated differently and the different treatment is based on the individual's race, color, religion, sex, national origin, age, or disability status. If two people with the same qualifications

LO4
Identify the four theories of discrimination under Title VII of the Civil Rights Act and apply these theories to different discrimination situations.

Disparate Treatment
A theory of discrimination based on different treatments given to individuals because of their race, color, religion, sex, national origin, age, or disability status.

table 3.3

Comparison of Discrimination Theories

TYPES OF DISCRIMINATION	DISPARATE TREATMENT	DISPARATE IMPACT	REASONABLE ACCOMMODATION
Show intent?	Yes	No	Yes
Prima facie case	Individual is member of a protected group, was qualified for the job, and was turned down for the job, and the job remained open	Statistical disparity in the effects of a facially neutral employment practice	Individual has a belief or disability, provided the employer with notice (request to accommodate), and was adversely affected by a failure to be accommodated
Employer's defense	Produce a legitimate, nondiscriminatory reason for the employment decision or show bona fide occupational qualification (BFOQ)	Prove that the employment practice bears a manifest relationship with job performance	Job-relatedness and business necessity, undue hardship, or direct threat to health or safety
Plaintiff's rebuttal	Reason offered was merely a "pretext" for discrimination	Alternative procedures exist that meet the employer's goal without having disparate impact	
Monetary damages	Compensatory and punitive damages	Equitable relief (e.g., back pay)	Compensatory and punitive damages (if discrimination was intentional or employer failed to show good faith efforts to accommodate)

apply for a job and the employer decides whom to hire based on one individual's race, the individual not hired is a victim of disparate treatment. In the disparate treatment case the plaintiff must prove that there was a discriminatory motive—that is, that the employer intended to discriminate.

Whenever individuals are treated differently because of their race, sex, or the like, there is disparate treatment. For example, if a company fails to hire women with school-age children (claiming the women will be frequently absent) but hires men with school-age children, the applicants are being treated differently based on sex. Another example would be an employer who checks the references and investigates the conviction records of minority applicants but does not do so for white applicants. Why are managers advised not to ask about marital status? Because in most cases, a manager will either ask only the female applicants or, if the manager asks both males and females, he or she will make different assumptions about females (such as "She will have to move if her husband gets a job elsewhere") and males (such as "He's very stable"). In all these examples, notice that (1) people are being treated differently and (2) there is an actual intent to treat them differently.[17]

The nearby "Competing through Globalization" box illustrates how people can be subtly treated differently in France.

To understand how disparate treatment is applied in the law, let's look at how an actual court case, filed under disparate treatment, would proceed.

The Plaintiff's Burden

As in any legal case, the plaintiff has the burden of proving that the defendant has committed an illegal act. This is the idea of a "prima facie" case. In a disparate treatment case, the plaintiff meets the prima facie burden by showing four things:

1. The plaintiff belongs to a protected group.
2. The plaintiff applied for and was qualified for the job.
3. Despite possessing the qualifications, the plaintiff was rejected.
4. After the plaintiff was rejected, the position remained open and the employer continued to seek applicants with similar qualifications, or the position was filled by someone with similar qualifications.

Although these four elements may seem easy to prove, it is important to note that what the court is trying to do is rule out the most obvious reasons for rejecting the plaintiff's claim (for example, the plaintiff did not apply or was not qualified, or the position was already filled or had been eliminated). If these alternative explanations are ruled out, the court assumes that the hiring decision was based on a discriminatory motive.

The Defendant's Rebuttal

Once the plaintiff has made the prima facie case for discrimination, the burden shifts to the defendant. The burden is different depending on whether the prima facie case presents only circumstantial evidence (there is no direct evidence of discrimination such as a formal policy to discriminate, but rather discriminatory intent must be inferred) or direct evidence (a formal policy of discrimination for some perceived legitimate reason). In cases of circumstantial evidence, the defendant simply must

The year 2006 saw a string of violent protests and riots in and around Paris as poor ethnic (mostly North African) residents sought to express their dissatisfaction with their current state. Now a number of companies and the government are working together to try to effectively manage the diverse workforce and potentially reduce the economic disparities that exist in this "egalitarian" society.

The basic problem stems from what appears to be widespread discrimination in employment among French companies. According to research conducted by Jean-Francois Amadieu, a professor of sociology at the University of Paris, job candidates with North African–sounding names have one-third the chance of getting an interview compared to those with French-sounding names. He concludes that a significant number of French firms could be rightfully sued for discrimination.

As an example, Manuella Arulnayagam graduated from engineering school in 2003 and spent a year sending out her résumé. The daughter of Sri Lankan immigrants, she did not receive a single interview. In fact, at one job fair, a recruiter took one glance at her résumé and dropped it in the garbage can. She states, "Throughout my whole life and studies I never wanted to believe that my name or my address could be a problem."

One of the potential obstacles to better managing diversity in France actually stems from the legal system. In the interest of ensuring equality, French law precludes collecting information on race, ethnicity, religion, and other characteristics. However, this makes it difficult for French employers to proactively recruit or target particular minority groups.

One solution has been to go straight to the so-called *banlieues,* or poor immigrant neighborhoods, to attempt to recruit minority workers. Firms such as the cosmetic maker L'Oreal send managers to poor-area high schools to coach students in writing résumés and proper behavior in job interviews.

In addition, more progressive HR departments in companies like insurer AXA or carmaker Peugeot automatically strip personal data that might imply racial or ethnic status from résumés before forwarding them to recruiters. If those making the decisions to offer interviews do not know the ethnicity of the applicant, they cannot discriminate on that basis.

SOURCE: M. Valla, "France Seeks Path to Workplace Diversity," *The Wall Street Journal,* January 3, 2007, p. A2.

---

produce a legitimate, nondiscriminatory reason, such as that, although the plaintiff was qualified, the individual hired was more qualified.

However, in cases where direct evidence exists, such as a formal policy of hiring only women for waitress jobs because the business is aimed at catering to male customers, then the defendant is more likely to offer a different defense. This defense argues that for this job, a factor such as race, sex, or religion was a **bona fide occupational qualification (BFOQ).** For example, if one were hiring an individual to hand out towels in a women's locker room, being a woman might be a BFOQ. However, there are very few cases in which race or sex qualifies as a BFOQ, and in these cases it must be a necessary, rather than simply a preferred characteristic of the job.

UAW v. Johnson Controls, Inc., illustrates the difficulty in using a BFOQ as a defense.[18] Johnson Controls, a manufacturer of car batteries, had instituted a "fetal protection" policy that excluded women of childbearing age from a number of jobs in which they would be exposed to lead, which can cause birth defects in children. The

Bona Fide Occupational Qualification (BFOQ)
A job qualification based on race, sex, religion, and so on, that an employer asserts is a necessary qualification for the job.

company argued that sex was a BFOQ essential to maintaining a safe workplace. The Supreme Court did not uphold the company's policy, arguing that BFOQs are limited to policies that are directly related to a worker's ability to do the job.

The Plaintiff's Rebuttal

If the defendant provides a legitimate, nondiscriminatory reason for its employment decision, the burden shifts back to the plaintiff. The plaintiff must now show that the reason offered by the defendant was not in fact the reason for its decision but merely a "pretext" or excuse for its actual discriminatory decision. This could entail providing evidence that white applicants with very similar qualifications to the plaintiff have often been hired while black applicants with very similar qualifications were all rejected. To illustrate disparate treatment, let's look at the first major case dealing with disparate treatment, *McDonnell Douglas Corp. v. Green.*

McDonnell Douglas Corp. v. Green.   This Supreme Court case was the first to delineate the four criteria for a prima facie case of discrimination. From 1956 to 1964, Green had been an employee at McDonnell Douglas, a manufacturing plant in St. Louis, Missouri, that employed about 30,000 people. In 1964 he was laid off during a general workforce reduction. While unemployed, he participated in some activities that the company undoubtedly frowned upon: a "lock-in," where he and others placed a chain and padlock on the front door of a building to prevent the employees from leaving; and a "stall-in," where a group of employees stalled their cars at the gates of the plant so that no one could enter or leave the parking lot. About three weeks after the lock-in, McDonnell Douglas advertised for qualified mechanics, Green's trade, and he reapplied. When the company rejected his application, he sued, arguing that the company didn't hire him because of his race and because of his persistent involvement in the civil rights movement.

In making his prima facie case, Green had no problem showing that he was a member of a protected group, that he had applied for and was qualified for the job (having already worked in the job), that he was rejected, and that the company continued to advertise the position. The company's defense was that the plaintiff was not hired because he participated in the lock-in and the stall-in. In other words, the company was merely refusing to hire a troublemaker.

The plaintiff responded that the company's stated reason for not hiring him was a pretext for discrimination. He pointed out that white employees who had participated in the same activities (the lock-in and stall-in) were rehired, whereas he was not. The court found in favor of the plaintiff.

This case illustrates how similarly situated individuals (white and black) can be treated differently (whites were hired back whereas blacks were not) with the differences in treatment based on race. As we discuss later, most plaintiffs bring cases of sexual harassment under this theory of discrimination, sexual harassment being a situation where individuals are treated differently because of their sex.

Mixed-Motive Cases

In a mixed-motive case, the defendant acknowledges that some discriminatory motive existed but argues that the same hiring decision would have been reached even without the discriminatory motive. In *Hopkins v. Price Waterhouse,* Ann Hopkins was an accountant who had applied for partnership in her firm. Although she had brought in a large amount of business and had received high praise from her clients, she was turned down for a partnership on two separate occasions. In her performance reviews, she had been told to adopt more feminine dress and speech and received many other comments that suggested gender-based stereotypes. In court, the company admitted that a sex-based stereotype existed but argued that it would have come to the same decision (not promoted Hopkins) even if the stereotype had not existed.

One of the main questions that came out of this case was, Who has the burden of proof? Does the plaintiff have to prove that a different decision would have been made (that Hopkins would have been promoted) in the absence of the discriminatory motive? Or does the defendant have to prove that the same decision would have been made?

According to CRA 1991, if the plaintiff demonstrates that race, sex, color, religion, or national origin was a motivating factor for any employment practice, the prima facie burden has been met, and the burden of proof is on the employer to demonstrate that the same decision would have been made even if the discriminatory motive had not been present. If the employer can do this, the plaintiff cannot collect compensatory or punitive damages. However, the court may order the employer to quit using the discriminatory motive in its future employment decisions.

Disparate Impact

The second type of discrimination is called **disparate impact.** It occurs when a facially neutral employment practice disproportionately excludes a protected group from employment opportunities. A facially neutral employment practice is one that lacks obvious discriminatory content yet affects one group to a greater extent than other groups, such as an employment test. Although the Supreme Court inferred disparate impact from Title VII in the *Griggs v. Duke Power* case, it has since been codified into the Civil Rights Act of 1991.

Disparate Impact
A theory of discrimination based on facially neutral employment practices that disproportionately exclude a protected group from employment opportunities.

There is an important distinction between disparate impact and disparate treatment discrimination. For there to be discrimination under disparate treatment, there has to be intentional discrimination. Under disparate impact, intent is irrelevant. The important criterion is that the consequences of the employment practice are discriminatory.

For example, if, for some practical reason, you hired individuals based on their height, you may not have intended to discriminate against anyone, and yet using height would have a disproportionate impact on certain protected groups. Women tend to be shorter than men, so fewer women will be hired. Certain ethnic groups, such as those of Asian ancestry, also tend to be shorter than those of European ancestry. Thus, your facially neutral employment practice will have a disparate impact on certain protected groups.

This is not to imply that simply because a selection practice has disparate impact, it is necessarily illegal. Some characteristics (such as height) are not equally distributed across race and gender groups; however, the important question is whether the characteristic is related to successful performance on the job. To help you understand how disparate impact works, let's look at a court proceeding involving a disparate impact claim.

The Plaintiff's Burden

In a disparate impact case, the plaintiff must make the prima facie case by showing that the employment practice in question disproportionately affects a protected group relative to the majority group. To illustrate this theory, let's assume that you are a manager who has 60 positions to fill. Your applicant pool has 80 white and 40 black applicants. You use a test that selects 48 of the white and 12 of the black applicants. Is this a disparate impact? Two alternative quantitative analyses are often used to determine whether a test has adverse impact.

The **four-fifths rule** states that a test has disparate impact if the hiring rate for the minority group is less than four-fifths (or 80 percent) of the hiring rate for the majority group. Applying this analysis to the preceding example, we would first calculate the hiring rates for each group:

$$\text{Whites} = 48/80 = 60\%$$
$$\text{Blacks} = 12/40 = 30\%$$

Then we would compare the hiring rate of the minority group (30%) with that of the majority group (60%). Using the four-fifths rule, we would determine that the test has adverse impact if the hiring rate of the minority group is less than 80 percent of the hiring rate of the majority group. Because it is less (i.e., 30%/60% = 50%, which is less than 80%), we would conclude that the test has adverse impact. The four-fifths rule is used as a rule of thumb by the EEOC in determining adverse impact.

The **standard deviation rule** uses actual probability distributions to determine adverse impact. This analysis uses the difference between the expected representation (or hiring rates) for minority groups and the actual representation (or hiring rate) to determine whether the difference between these two values is greater than would occur by chance. Thus, in our example, 33 percent (40 of 120) of the applicants were blacks, so one would expect 33 percent (20 of 60) of those hired to be black. However, only 12 black applicants were hired. To determine if the difference between the expected representation and the actual representation is greater than we would expect by chance, we calculate the standard deviation (which, you might remember from your statistics class, is the standard deviation in a binomial distribution):

$$\sqrt{\text{Number hired} \times \frac{\text{Number of minority applicants}}{\text{Number of total applicants}} \times \frac{\text{Number of nonminority applicants}}{\text{Number of total applicants}}}$$

or in this case:

$$\sqrt{60 \times \frac{40}{120} \times \frac{80}{120}} = 3.6$$

If the difference between the actual representation and the expected representation (20 − 12 = 8 in this case) of blacks is greater than 2 standard deviations (2 × 3.6 = 7.2 in this case), we would conclude that the test had adverse impact against blacks, because we would expect this result less than 1 time in 20 if the test were equally difficult for both whites and blacks.

The *Wards Cove Packing Co. v. Atonio* case involved an interesting use of statistics. The plaintiffs showed that the jobs in the cannery (lower paying jobs) were filled primarily with minority applicants (in this case, American Eskimos). However, only a small percentage of the noncannery jobs (those with higher pay) were filled by non-minorities.

Four-Fifths Rule A rule that states that an employment test has disparate impact if the hiring rate for a minority group is less than four-fifths, or 80 percent, of the hiring rate for the majority group.

Standard Deviation Rule A rule used to analyze employment tests to determine disparate impact; it uses the difference between the expected representation for minority groups and the actual representation to determine whether the difference between the two is greater than would occur by chance.

The plaintiffs argued that this statistical disparity in the racial makeup of the cannery and noncannery jobs was proof of discrimination. The federal district, appellate, and Supreme Courts all found for the defendant, stating that this disparity was not proof of discrimination.

Once the plaintiff has demonstrated adverse impact, he or she has met the burden of a prima facie case of discrimination.[19]

Defendant's Rebuttal

According to CRA 1991, once the plaintiff has made a prima facie case, the burden of proof shifts to the defendant, who must show that the employment practice is a "business necessity." This is accomplished by showing that the practice bears a relationship with some legitimate employer goal. With respect to job selection, this relationship is demonstrated by showing the job relatedness of the test, usually by reporting a validity study of some type, to be discussed in Chapter 6. For now, suffice it to say that the employer shows that the test scores are significantly correlated with measures of job performance.

Measures of job performance used in validation studies can include such things as objective measures of output, supervisor ratings of job performance, and success in training.[20] Normally, performance appraisal ratings are used, but these ratings must be valid for the court to accept the validation results. For example, in *Albermarle Paper v. Moody*, the employer demonstrated that the selection battery predicted performance (measured with supervisors' overall rankings of employees) in only some of the 13 occupational groups in which it was used. In this case, the court was especially critical of the supervisory ratings used as the measure of job performance. The court stated, "There is no way of knowing precisely what criteria of job performance the supervisors were considering."[21]

Plaintiff's Rebuttal

If the employer shows that the employment practice is the result of some business necessity, the plaintiff's last resort is to argue that other employment practices could sufficiently meet the employer's goal without adverse impact. Thus, if a plaintiff can demonstrate that selection tests other than the one used by the employer exist, do not have adverse impact, and correlate with job performance as highly as the employer's test, then the defendant can be found guilty of discrimination. Many cases deal with standardized tests of cognitive ability, so it is important to examine alternatives to these tests that have less adverse impact while still meeting the employer's goal. At least two separate studies reviewing alternative selection devices such as interviews, biographical data, assessment centers, and work sample tests have concluded that none of them met both criteria.[22] It seems that when the employment practice in question is a standardized test of cognitive ability, plaintiffs will have a difficult time rebutting the defendant's rebuttal.

Griggs v. Duke Power.   To illustrate how this process works, let's look at the *Griggs v. Duke Power* case.[23] Following the passage of Title VII, Duke Power instituted a new system for making selection and promotion decisions. The system required either a high school diploma or a passing score on two professionally developed tests (the Wonderlic Personnel Test and the Bennett Mechanical Comprehension Test). A passing score was set so that it would be equal to the national median for high school graduates who had taken the tests.

The plaintiffs met their prima facie burden showing that both the high school diploma requirement and the test battery had adverse impacts on blacks. According to the 1960 census, 34 percent of white males had high school diplomas, compared with only 12 percent of black males. Similarly, 58 percent of white males passed the test battery, whereas only 6 percent of blacks passed.

Duke Power was unable to defend its use of these employment practices. A company vice president testified that the company had not studied the relationship between these employment practices and the employees' ability to perform the job. In addition, employees already on the job who did not have high school diplomas and had never taken the tests were performing satisfactorily. Thus, Duke Power lost the case.

It is interesting to note that the court recognized that the company had not intended to discriminate, mentioning that the company was making special efforts to help undereducated employees through financing two-thirds of the cost of tuition for high school training. This illustrates the importance of the consequences, as opposed to the motivation, in determining discrimination under the disparate impact theory.

Pattern and Practice

In showing class action pattern and practice lawsuits, the plaintiffs attempt to show three things. First, they show some statistical disparities between the composition of some group within the company compared to some other relevant group. For instance, the opening case described how the plaintiff's lawyers pointed to two comparative statistics as evidence of discrimination. First, they compared the female representation in the non-managerial (63.4%) vs the managerial (33.6%) employee groups. They also compared the female representation in the managerial group (again, 33.6%) with that in their top 20 competitors (56.5%). They also calculated that hourly female workers were paid, on average, $1,100 less than men and salaried women received 14,500 less. However, Wal-Mart disputes the list of comparison companies, arguing that if a broader group is used reflecting Wal-Mart's wide geographic footprint and variety of products offered, it does not differ from that group. It also claims that if it had claimed its highest-level hourly-wage supervisors as "managers" on its EEO-1 forms, as many of the comparison companies do, the entire disparity disappears. They also note that of the applicants for managerial positions, only 15% are female, and that of those promoted, 18% are female. Finally, regarding pay, Wal-Mart's experts suggested that the plaintiff's pay comparisons did not account for crucial factors such as the number of hours worked or whether the work was night-shift work which pays more. Their analyses suggested that when pay was compared at the department level, where pay decisions are determined, 92.8% of all stores showed no statistically significant pay disparities, and that of the remainder, 5.2% showed disparities favoring men while 2.0% showed disparities favoring women.

Second, the plaintiff tries to show that there are individual acts of intentional discrimination that suggest that the statistical disparity is a function of the larger culture. In the Dukes case, the plaintiffs argued that at Monday morning meetings of high-level Sam's Club executives, female store employees were referred to as "Janie Q's," and that this continued even after a woman executive complained that she found the term demeaning. While Wal-Mart executives might find the term endearing, the case will be heard by a San Francisco jury which may find the term offensive and condescending.

Finally, the plaintiff usually tries to make the case that the promotion and/or pay procedures leave too much discretion to managers, providing the avenue through which their unconscious biases can play a part. In the Dukes case the plaintiffs brought in expert witnesses to argue that the performance management processes were extremely subjective, and that male managers have subconscious tendencies to favor male over female employees.

Reasonable Accommodation

Reasonable accommodation presents a relatively new theory of discrimination. It began with regard to religious discrimination, but has recently been both expanded and popularized with the passage of the ADA. Reasonable accommodation differs from these two theories in that rather than simply requiring an employer to refrain from some action, reasonable accommodation places a special obligation on an employer to affirmatively do something to accommodate an individual's disability or religion. This theory is violated when an employer fails to make reasonable accommodation, where that is required, to a qualified person with a disability or to a person's religious observation and/or practices.

Reasonable Accommodation
Making facilities readily accessible to and usable by individuals with disabilities.

Religion and Accommodation

Often individuals with strong religious beliefs find that some observations and practices of their religion come into direct conflict with their work duties. For example, some religions forbid individuals from working on the sabbath day when the employer schedules them for work. Others might have beliefs that preclude them from shaving, which might conflict with a company's dress code. Although Title VII forbids discrimination on the basis of religion just like race or sex, religion also receives special treatment requiring employers to exercise an affirmative duty to accommodate individuals' religious beliefs and practices. As Figure 3.2 shows, the number of religious discrimination charges has consistently increased over the past few years, jumping significantly in 2002.

In cases of religious discrimination, an employee's burden is to demonstrate that he or she has a legitimate religious belief and provided the employer with notice of the need to accommodate the religious practice, and that adverse consequences occurred due to the employer's failure to accommodate. In such cases, the employer's major defense is to assert that to accommodate the employee would require an undue hardship.

Examples of reasonably accommodating a person's religious obligations might include redesigning work schedules (most often accommodating those who cannot work on their sabbath), providing alternative testing dates for applicants, not requiring union membership and/or allowing payment of "charitable contributions" in lieu of union dues, or altering certain dress or grooming requirements. Note that although an employer is required to make a reasonable accommodation, it need not be the one that is offered by the employee.[24]

In one case, Wal-Mart agreed to settle with a former employee who alleged that he was forced to quit in 1993 after refusing to work on Sunday. Wal-Mart agreed to pay the former employee unspecified damages, to instruct managers on employees' rights to have their religious beliefs accommodated, and to prepare a computer-based manual describing employees' rights and religious harassment.[25]

figure 3.2

Religious Discrimination Complaints, 1991–2007

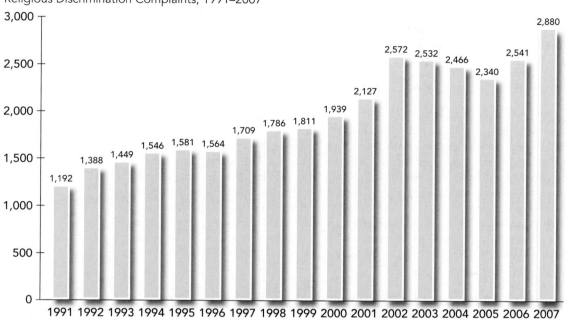

SOURCE: www.eeoc.gov/stats/religion.html.

Following the attack of 9/11, a number of cases sprang up with regard to discrimination against Muslims, partly accounting for the significant increase in religious discrimination complaints in 2002. In one case, the EEOC and Electrolux Group settled a religious accommodation case brought by Muslim workers from Somalia. The Islamic faith requires Muslims to offer five prayers a day, with two of these prayers offered within restricted time periods (early morning and sunset). Muslim employees alleged that they were disciplined for using an unscheduled break traditionally offered to line employees on an as-needed basis to observe their sunset prayer. Electrolux worked with the EEOC to respect the needs of its Muslim workers without creating a business hardship by affording them with an opportunity to observe their sunset prayer.[26]

Religion and accommodation also bring up the question as to what to do when different rights collide. For instance, John Nemecek had been a respected business professor at Spring Arbor University for 15 years. Spring Arbor is an evangelical college in Michigan which began to take issue with some of his behavior. After he began wearing earrings and makeup and asking friends to call him "Julie" he found himself demoted and fired because his womanly appearance violated "Christian behavior." In 2004 a doctor diagnosed Prof. Nemecek with a "gender-identity disorder," in which one's sexual identity differs from one's body. Soon after, the school began taking away some of his responsibilities, and then issued him a contract revoking his dean's post, reassigning him to a non-tenure-track role in which he would work from home, teaching online. It also required him to not wear any makeup or female clothing or to display any outward signs of femininity when visiting campus. Gayle Beebe, the university's president, said "We felt through a job reassignment we could give him the space to work on this issue." Prof. Nemecek signed the contract but then violated

COMPETING THROUGH SUSTAINABILITY
Wal-Mart Goes Green

This chapter has focused on the numerous legal problems Wal-Mart has faced over the past few years. However, as part of the transformation of Wal-Mart, CEO Lee Scott has pushed the company into pro-actively promoting sustainability through its products and business practices. Wal-Mart faced increasing data that customers were fleeing Wal-Mart because of its bad publicity. In fact, a confidential 2004 report found that between 2 and 8 percent of its customers stopped shopping there because of all the negative press they had heard—a concept that came to be known as "headline risk." Critics complained that Wal-Mart paid too little, did not offer adequate health insurance, and was a polluter. This got Scott's attention.

Scott publicly stated that Wal-Mart was embracing sustainability, laying out ambitious long-term goals for the company: running its operations solely on renewable energy, creating zero waste, and selling products that sustain the earth's resources and environment.

Wal-Mart's suppliers had little choice but to follow its lead. Now the approximately 200 million Wal-Mart customers buy fluorescent light bulbs that use up to 75 percent less electricity than incandescent bulbs, concentrated laundry detergent that uses 50 percent less water, and prescription drugs that contain 50 percent less packaging.

For instance, Wal-Mart says that by selling only concentrated liquid laundry detergent, its customers will save more than 400 million gallons of water, 95 million pounds of plastic resin, 125 million pounds of cardboard, and 520,000 gallons of diesel fuel over three years. A. G. Lafley, CEO of Procter & Gamble, gives the credit to Scott. "Lee pushed me," he said. "We totally, totally changed the way we manufacture liquid laundry detergents in the U.S. and, now, around the world."

The transformation helps the environment and Wal-Mart's image, but it also has a direct impact on the bottom line. Wal-Mart saves $3.5 million a year by recycling loose plastic and selling it to processors. After redesigning its trucks and the processes for loading them, its fleet had a 25 percent improvement in fuel efficiency.

"As businesses, we have a responsibility to society," Scott said in his last public speech as Wal-Mart chief. "Let me be clear about this point. There is no conflict between delivering value to shareholders, and helping solve bigger societal problems."

SOURCE: J. Marquez, "Wal-Mart Puts on a New Face," *Workforce Management*, August 14, 2006, p. 29.

---

it by showing up on campus with earrings and makeup on four separate occasions. The professor filed his complaint with the EEOC and the university then declined to renew his contract. Prof. Nemecek, whose Baptist church also asked him to leave the congregation, says of the university, "Essentially, they're saying they can define who is a Christian. I don't agree that our biology determines our gender."[27]

Disability and Accommodation

As previously discussed, the ADA made discrimination against individuals with disabilities illegal. However, the act itself states that the employer is obligated not just to refrain from discriminating, but to take affirmative steps to accommodate individuals who are protected under the act.

Under disability claims, the plaintiff must show that she or he is a qualified applicant with a disability and that adverse action was taken by a covered entity. The employer's defense then depends on whether the decision was made without regard to the disability or in light of the disability. For example, if the employer argues that the plaintiff is not qualified, then it has met the burden, and the question of reasonable accommodation becomes irrelevant.

If, however, the decision was made "in light of" the disability, then the question becomes one of whether the person could perform adequately with a reasonable accommodation. This leads to three potential defenses. First, the employer could allege job-relatedness or business necessity through demonstrating, for example, that it is using a test that assesses ability to perform essential job functions. However, then the question arises of whether the applicant could perform the essential job functions with a reasonable accommodation. Second, the employer could claim an undue hardship to accommodate the individual. In essence, this argues that the accommodation necessary is an action requiring significant difficulty or expense. Finally, the employer could argue that the individual with the disability might pose a direct threat to his own or others' health or safety in the workplace. This requires examining the duration of the risk, the nature and severity of potential harm, the probability of the harm occurring, and the imminence of the potential harm. For instance, Wal-Mart was sued by one of its employees who was a fitting room attendant with cerebral palsy and confined to a wheelchair. The employee requested to use a grabber and a shopping cart to help her pick up and hold clothes. However, she was prevented from using both by the manager, who then implemented progressive discipline ending in the attendant's termination. While the case it still pending, it illustrates the kinds of actions that employers should consider in making accommodations.[28]

What are some examples of reasonable accommodation with regard to disabilities? First is providing readily accessible facilities such as ramps and/or elevators for disabled individuals to enter the workplace. Second, job restructuring might include eliminating marginal tasks, shifting these tasks to other employees, redesigning job procedures, or altering work schedules. Third, an employer might reassign a disabled employee to a job with essential job functions he or she could perform. Fourth, an employer might accommodate applicants for employment who must take tests through providing alternative testing formats, providing readers, or providing additional time for taking the test. Fifth, readers, interpreters, or technology to offer reading assistance might be given to a disabled employee. Sixth, an employer could allow employees to provide their own accommodation such as bringing a guide dog to work.[29] Note that most accommodations are inexpensive. A study by Sears Roebuck & Co. found that 69 percent of all accommodations cost nothing, 29 percent cost less than $1,000, and only 3 percent cost more than $1,000.[30]

EVIDENCE-BASED HR

As information technology becomes more and more ubiquitous in the workplace, some have begun to explore the implications for people with disabilities. Researchers at the Employment and Disability Institute at Cornell University recently reviewed the accessibility of 10 job boards and 31 corporate e-recruiting Web sites using Bobby 3.2, a software program designed to check for errors that cause accessibility concerns. They found that none of the job boards and only a small minority of the e-recruiting sites met the Bobby standards.

In phase 2 of the study, they surveyed 813 HR professionals who were members of the Society for Human Resource Management (SHRM). Between 16 and 46 percent of the HR professionals were familiar with six of the most common assistive technologies to adapt computers for disabled individuals (screen magnifiers, speech recognitions software, video captioning, Braille readers/displays, screen readers, guidelines for Web design). In addition, only 1 in 10 said they knew that their firm had evaluated the Web sites for accessibility to people with disabilities.

This study indicates that while firms may not have any intention of discriminating against people with disabilities, the rapid expansion of information technology combined with an inattention to and/or lack of education regarding accessibility issues may accidentally lead them to do so.

SOURCE: S. Bruyere, S. Erickson, and S. VanLooy, "Information Technology and the Workplace: Implications for Persons with Disabilities," *Disability Studies Quarterly* 25, no. 2 (Spring 2005), at www.dsq-sds.org.

Retaliation for Participation and Opposition

Suppose you overhear a supervisor in your workplace telling someone that he refuses to hire women because he knows they are just not cut out for the job. Believing this to be illegal discrimination, you face a dilemma. Should you come forward and report this statement? Or if someone else files a lawsuit for gender discrimination, should you testify on behalf of the plaintiff? What happens if your employer threatens to fire you if you do anything?

Title VII of the Civil Rights Act of 1964 protects you. It states that employers cannot retaliate against employees for either "opposing" a perceived illegal employment practice or "participating in a proceeding" related to an alleged illegal employment practice. Opposition refers to expressing to someone through proper channels that you believe that an illegal employment act has taken place or is taking place. Participation refers to actually testifying in an investigation, hearing, or court proceeding regarding an illegal employment act. Clearly, the purpose of this provision is to protect employees from employers' threats and other forms of intimidation aimed at discouraging the employees from bringing to light acts they believe to be illegal.

These cases can be extremely costly for companies because they are alleging acts of intentional discrimination, and therefore plaintiffs are entitled to punitive damages. For example, a 41-year-old former Allstate employee who claimed that a company official told her that the company wanted a "younger and cuter" image was awarded $2.8 million in damages by an Oregon jury. The jury concluded that the employee was forced out of the company for opposing age discrimination against other employees.[31]

In a recent case, Target Corporation agreed to pay $775,000 to a group of black workers who charged that at one store, the company condoned a racially hostile work environment exemplified by inappropriate comments and verbal berating based on race. When one of the black employees objected to this treatment, he was allegedly retaliated against, forcing him to resign.[32]

This does not mean that employees have an unlimited right to talk about how racist or sexist their employers are. The courts tend to frown on employees whose activities result in a poor public image for the company unless those employees had attempted to use the organization's internal channels—approaching one's manager, raising the issue with the HRM department, and so on—before going public.

LO5
Discuss the legal issues involved with preferential treatment programs.

Current Issues Regarding Diversity and Equal Employment Opportunity

LO6
Identify behavior that constitutes sexual harassment, and list things that an organization can do to eliminate or minimize it.

Because of recent changes in the labor market, most organizations' demographic compositions are becoming increasingly diverse. A study by the Hudson Institute projected that 85 percent of the new entrants into the U.S. labor force over the next decade will be females and minorities.[33] Integrating these groups into organizations made up predominantly of able-bodied white males will bring attention to important issues like sexual harassment, affirmative action, and the "reasonable accommodation" of employees with disabilities.

Sexual Harassment

Clarence Thomas's Supreme Court confirmation hearings in 1991 brought the issue of sexual harassment into increased prominence. Anita Hill, one of Thomas's former employees, alleged that he had sexually harassed her while she was working under his supervision at the Department of Education and the Equal Employment Opportunity Commission. Although the allegations were never substantiated, the hearing made many people more aware of how often employees are sexually harassed in the workplace and, combined with other events, resulted in a tremendous increase in the number of sexual harassment complaints being filed with the EEOC, as we see in Figure 3.3. In addition, after President Clinton took office and faced a sexual harassment lawsuit by Paula Corbin Jones for his alleged proposition to her in a Little Rock hotel room, the number of sexual harassment complaints took another jump from

figure 3.3
Sexual Harassment Charges, 1991–2007

Number of charges
% filed by men

SOURCE: www.eeoc.gov/stats/harass.html.

1993 to 1994—again, potentially due to the tremendous amount of publicity regarding sexual harassment. However, the number of cases filed has actually decreased substantially since 2000.

Sexual harassment refers to unwelcome sexual advances (see Table 3.4). It can take place in two basic ways. "Quid pro quo" harassment occurs when some kind of benefit (or punishment) is made contingent on the employee's submitting (or not submitting) to sexual advances. For example, a male manager tells his female secretary that if she has sex with him, he will help her get promoted, or he threatens to fire her if she fails to do so; these are clearly cases of quid pro quo sexual harassment.

The *Bundy v. Jackson* case illustrates quid pro quo sexual harassment.[34] Sandra Bundy was a personnel clerk with the District of Columbia Department of Corrections. She received repeated sexual propositions from Delbert Jackson, who was at the time a fellow employee (although he later became the director of the agency). She later began to receive propositions from two of her supervisors: Arthur Burton and James Gainey. When she raised the issue to their supervisor, Lawrence Swain, he dismissed her complaints, telling her that "any man in his right mind would want to rape you," and asked her to begin a sexual relationship with him. When Bundy became eligible for a promotion, she was passed over because of her "inadequate work performance," although she had never been told that her work performance was unsatisfactory. The U.S. Court of Appeals found that Bundy had been discriminated against because of her sex, thereby extending the idea of discrimination to sexual harassment.

A more subtle, and possibly more pervasive, form of sexual harassment is "hostile working environment." This occurs when someone's behavior in the workplace creates an environment that makes it difficult for someone of a particular sex to work. Many plaintiffs in sexual harassment lawsuits have alleged that men ran their fingers through the plaintiffs' hair, made suggestive remarks, and physically assaulted them by touching their intimate body parts. Other examples include having pictures of naked women posted in the workplace, using offensive sexually explicit language, or using sex-related jokes or innuendoes in conversations.[35]

Note that these types of behaviors are actionable under Title VII because they treat individuals differently based on their sex. In addition, although most harassment cases involve male-on-female harassment, any individual can be harassed. For example, male employees at Jenny Craig alleged that they were sexually harassed, and a federal jury found that a male employee had been sexually harassed by his male boss.[36]

table 3.4

EEOC Definition of Sexual Harassment

Unwelcome sexual advances, requests for sexual favors, and other verbal or physical contact of a sexual nature constitute sexual harassment when
1. Submission to such conduct is made either explicitly or implicitly a term or condition of an individual's employment,
2. Submission to or rejection of such conduct by an individual is used as the basis for employment decisions affecting such individual, or
3. Such conduct has the purpose or effect of unreasonably interfering with an individual's work performance or creating an intimidating, hostile, or offensive working environment.

SOURCE: EEOC guideline based on the Civil Rights Act of 1964, Title VII.

In addition, Ron Clark Ford of Amarillo, Texas, recently agreed to pay $140,000 to six male plaintiffs who alleged that they and others were subjected to a sexually hostile work environment and different treatment because of their gender by male managers. Evidence gathered showed that the men were subjected to lewd, inappropriate comments of a sexual nature, and had their genitals and buttocks grabbed against their will by their male managers. The defendants argued that the conduct was "harmless horseplay."[37]

Finally, Babies 'R' Us agreed to pay $205,000 to resolve a same-sex suit. The lawsuit alleged that Andres Vasquez was subjected to a sexually hostile working environment and was the target of unwelcome and derogatory comments as well as behavior that mocked him because he did not conform to societal stereotypes of how a male should appear or behave.

Sexual harassment charge filings with the EEOC by men have increased to 15 percent of all filings in 2002 from 10 percent of filings in 1994. While the commission does not track same-sex, male-on-male charges, anecdotal evidence shows that most harassment allegations by men are against other men.[38]

There are three critical issues in these cases. First, the plaintiff cannot have "invited or incited" the advances. Often the plaintiff's sexual history, whether she or he wears provocative clothing, and whether she or he engages in sexually explicit conversations are used to prove or disprove that the advance was unwelcome. However, in the absence of substantial evidence that the plaintiff invited the behavior, courts usually lean toward assuming that sexual advances do not belong in the workplace and thus are unwelcome. In *Meritor Savings Bank v. Vinson*, Michelle Vinson claimed that during the four years she worked at a bank she was continually harassed by the bank's vice president, who repeatedly asked her to have sex with him (she eventually agreed) and sexually assaulted her.[39] The Supreme Court ruled that the victim's voluntary participation in sexual relations was not the major issue, saying that the focus of the case was on whether the vice president's advances were unwelcome.

A second critical issue is that the harassment must have been severe enough to alter the terms, conditions, and privileges of employment. Although it has not yet been consistently applied, many courts have used the "reasonable woman" standard in determining the severity or pervasiveness of the harassment. This consists of assessing whether a reasonable woman, faced with the same situation, would have reacted similarly. The reasonable woman standard recognizes that behavior that might be considered appropriate by a man (like off-color jokes) might not be considered appropriate by a woman.

The third issue is that the courts must determine whether the organization is liable for the actions of its employees. In doing so, the court usually examines two things. First, did the employer know about, or should he or she have known about, the harassment? Second, did the employer act to stop the behavior? If the employer knew about it and the behavior did not stop, the court usually decides that the employer did not act appropriately to stop it.

To ensure a workplace free from sexual harassment, organizations can follow some important steps. First, the organization can develop a policy statement that makes it very clear that sexual harassment will not be tolerated in the workplace. Second, all employees, new and old, can be trained to identify inappropriate workplace behavior. Third, the organization can develop a mechanism for reporting sexual harassment that encourages people to speak out. Fourth, management can prepare to take prompt disciplinary action against those who commit sexual harassment as well as appropriate action to protect the victims of sexual harassment.[40]

Affirmative Action and Reverse Discrimination

Few would disagree that having a diverse workforce in terms of race and gender is a desirable goal, if all individuals have the necessary qualifications. In fact, many organizations today are concerned with developing and managing diversity. To eliminate discrimination in the workplace, many organizations have affirmative action programs to increase minority representation. Affirmative action was originally conceived as a way of taking extra effort to attract and retain minority employees. This was normally done by extensively recruiting minorities on college campuses, advertising in minority-oriented publications, and providing educational and training opportunities to minorities.[41] However, over the years, many organizations have resorted to quotalike hiring to ensure that their workforce composition mirrors that of the labor market. Sometimes these organizations act voluntarily; in other cases, the quotas are imposed by the courts or by the EEOC. Whatever the impetus for these hiring practices, many white and/or male individuals have fought against them, alleging what is called reverse discrimination.

An example of an imposed quota program is found at the fire department in Birmingham, Alabama. Having admitted a history of discriminating against blacks, the department entered into a consent decree with the EEOC to hold 50 percent of positions at all levels in the fire department open for minorities even though minorities made up only 28 percent of the relevant labor market. The result was that some white applicants were denied employment or promotion in favor of black applicants who scored lower on a selection battery. The federal court found that the city's use of the inflexible hiring formula violated federal civil rights law and the constitutional guarantee of equal protection. The appellate court agreed, and the Supreme Court refused to hear the case, thus making the decision final.

Ricci v. DeStefano represents another recent case that has been appealed to the Supreme Court regarding the potential for reverse discrimination based on a situation in New Haven, Connecticut. In this case a professional consulting firm developed a firefighter test specifically eliminating questions that had adverse impact against minority members (based on pilot study testing). However, when the test was given, no blacks made the promotion list, so the city simply ignored the test and promoted no one. White and hispanic firefighters who would have been on the promotion list sued, stating that the failure to use the test results discriminated against them because of their race. The district and appellate courts ruled that because no blacks were promoted either (becase there were no promotions), there had been no discrimination.

The entire issue of affirmative action should evoke considerable attention and debate over the next few years. Although most individuals support the idea of diversity, few argue for the kinds of quotas that have to some extent resulted from the present legal climate. In fact, one recent survey revealed that only 16 percent of the respondents favored affirmative action with quotas, 46 percent favored it without quotas, and 28 percent opposed all affirmative action programs. One study found that people favor affirmative action when it is operationalized as recruitment, training, and attention to applicant qualifications but oppose it when it consists of discrimination, quotas, and preferential treatment.[42]

Outcomes of the Americans with Disabilities Act

The ADA was passed with the laudable goals of providing employment opportunities for the truly disabled who, in the absence of legislation, were unable to find employment. Certainly, some individuals with disabilities have found employment as a result of its passage. However, as often occurs with legislation, the impact is not necessarily what was intended. First, there has been increased litigation. The EEOC reports that more than 200,000 complaints have been filed since passage of the act. Approximately 50 percent of the complaints filed have been found to be without reasonable cause. For example, in July 1992 GTE Data Services fired an employee for stealing from other employees and bringing a loaded gun to work. The fired employee sued for reinstatement under the ADA, claiming that he was the victim of a mental illness and thus should be considered disabled.[43]

A second problem is that the kinds of cases being filed are not what Congress intended to protect. Although the act was passed because of the belief that discrimination against individuals with disabilities occurred in the failure to hire them, 52.2 percent of the claims deal with firings, 28.9 percent with failure to make reasonable accommodation, and 12.5 percent with harassment. Only 9.4 percent of the complaints allege a failure to hire or rehire.[44] In addition, although the act was passed to protect people with major disabilities such as blindness, deafness, lost limbs, or paralysis, these disabilities combined account for a small minority of the disabilities claimed. As we see in Table 3.5, the biggest disability category is "other," meaning that the plaintiff claims a disability that is not one of the 35 types of impairment listed in the EEOC charge data system. The second largest category is "being regarded as disabled" accounting for 17.7 percent of all charges, followed by "back impairment" claims at 8.3 percent. As an example, recently a fired employee sued IBM asking for $5 million in damages for violation of the Americans with Disabilities Act. The employee had been fired for spending hours at work visiting adult chat rooms on his computer. He alleged that his addiction to sex and the Internet stemmed from trauma experienced by seeing a friend killed in 1969 during an Army patrol in Vietnam.[45]

Finally, the act does not appear to have had its anticipated impact on the employment of Americans with disabilities. According to the National Organization on Disability, 22 million of the 54 million disabled Americans are unemployed.[46]

For these reasons, Congress has explored the possibility of amending the act to more narrowly define the term disability.[47] The debate continues regarding the effectiveness of the ADA.

Employee Safety

LO7
Identify the major provisions of the Occupational Safety and Health Act (1970) and the rights of employees that are guaranteed by this act.

In March 2005, officials at the BP refinery in Texas City, Texas, were aware of the fact that some repairs needed to be done on some of the equipment in an octane-boosting processing unit. On March 23, knowing that some of the key alarms were not working, managers authorized a start-up of the unit. The start-up resulted in the deadliest petrochemical accident in 15 years, killing 15 people and injuring an additional 170.[48]

Like equal employment opportunity, employee safety is regulated by both the federal and state governments. However, to fully maximize the safety and health of

table 3.5

Sample of Complaints Filed under the ADA

	1997	1998	1999	2000	2001	2002	2003	2004	2005	2006	2007
Number of complaints	18,108	17,806	17,007	15,864	16,470	15,964	15,377	15,576	14,893	15,575	17,734
% dealing with *											
Asthma	1.5%	1.9%	1.8%	2.0%	1.6%	1.6%	1.6%	1.5%	1.6%	1.7%	1.0%
Back impairment	14.9	12.9	12.2	10.2	9.3	9.5	8.6	8.0	8.4	8.1	8.3
Cancer	2.5	2.6	2.3	2.7	2.8	2.9	2.9	2.8	2.7	3.2	3.3
Diabetes	3.7	3.7	4.0	4.1	4.3	4.7	4.8	4.7	4.5	4.8	5.1
Hearing	2.8	2.9	2.9	3.1	2.9	3.2	3.1	3.4	3.2	3.3	3.0
Vision	2.4	2.4	2.5	2.3	2.3	2.6	2.6	2.5	2.3	2.3	2.5
Heart	3.7	3.8	3.8	3.3	3.6	4.0	3.7	3.5	3.3	3.4	3.7
Regarded as disabled	11.4	11.1	11.6	13.7	12.8	13.7	16.8	18.2	17.4	17.2	17.7
Drug addiction	0.8	0.7	0.5	0.6	0.5	0.6	0.6	0.5	0.3	0.5	0.5
Other	27.7	27.8	28.7	30.0	31.7	30.1	26.3	19.0	21.4	21.8	26.6

*Not all complaints are listed.

SOURCE: EEOC, http://www.eeoc.gov/stats/ada-receipts.html.

workers, employers need to go well beyond the letter of the law and embrace its spirit. With this in mind, we first spell out the specific protections guaranteed by federal legislation and then discuss various kinds of safety awareness programs that attempt to reinforce these standards.

The Occupational Safety and Health Act (OSHA)

Occupational Safety and Health Act (OSHA)
The law that authorizes the federal government to establish and enforce occupational safety and health standards for all places of employment engaging in interstate commerce.

Although concern for worker safety would seem to be a universal societal goal, the **Occupational Safety and Health Act of 1970 (OSHA)**—the most comprehensive legislation regarding worker safety—did not emerge in this country until the early 1970s. At that time, there were roughly 15,000 work-related fatalities every year.

OSHA authorized the federal government to establish and enforce occupational safety and health standards for all places of employment engaging in interstate commerce. The responsibility for inspecting employers, applying the standards, and levying fines was assigned to the Department of Labor. The Department of Health was assigned responsibility for conducting research to determine the criteria for specific operations or occupations and for training employers to comply with the act. Much of this research is conducted by the National Institute for Occupational Safety and Health (NIOSH).

Employee Rights under OSHA

General Duty Clause
The provision of the Occupational Health and Safety Act that states that an employer has an overall obligation to furnish employees with a place of employment free from recognized hazards.

The main provision of OSHA states that each employer has a general duty to furnish each employee a place of employment free from recognized hazards that cause or are likely to cause death or serious physical harm. This is referred to as the **general duty clause.** Some specific rights granted to workers under this act are listed in Table 3.6. The Department of Labor recognizes many specific types of hazards, and employers are required to comply with all the occupational safety and health standards published by NIOSH.

A recent example is the development of OSHA standards for occupational exposure to blood-borne pathogens such as the AIDS virus. These standards identify 24 affected industrial sectors, encompassing 500,000 establishments and 5.6 million workers. Among other features, these standards require employers to develop an exposure control plan (ECP). An ECP must include a list of jobs whose incumbents might be exposed to blood, methods for implementing precautions in these jobs, postexposure follow-up plans, and procedures for evaluating incidents in which workers are accidentally infected.

table 3.6
Rights Granted to Workers under the Occupational Safety and Health Act

Employees have the right to
1. Request an inspection.
2. Have a representative present at an inspection.
3. Have dangerous substances identified.
4. Be promptly informed about exposure to hazards and be given access to accurate records regarding exposures.
5. Have employer violations posted at the work site.

Although NIOSH publishes numerous standards, regulators clearly cannot anticipate all possible hazards that could occur in the workplace. Thus, the general duty clause requires employers to be constantly alert for potential sources of harm in the workplace (as defined by the standards of a reasonably prudent person) and to correct them. For example, managers at Amoco's Joliet, Illinois, plant realized that over the years some employees had created undocumented shortcuts and built them into their process for handling flammable materials. These changes appeared to be labor saving but created a problem: workers did not have uniform procedures for dealing with flammable products. This became an urgent issue because many of the experienced workers were reaching retirement age, and the plant was in danger of losing critical technical expertise. To solve this problem, the plant adopted a training program that met all the standards required by OSHA. That is, it conducted a needs analysis highlighting each task new employees had to learn and then documented these processes in written guidelines. New employees were given hands-on training with the new procedures and were then certified in writing by their supervisor. A computer tracking system was installed to monitor who was handling flammable materials, and this system immediately identified anyone who was not certified. The plant met requirements for both ISO 9000 standards and OSHA regulations and continues to use the same model for safety training in other areas of the plant.[49]

● OSHA is responsible for inspecting businesses, applying safety and health standards, and levying fines for violations. OSHA regulations prohibit notifying employers of inspections in advance.

OSHA Inspections

OSHA inspections are conducted by specially trained agents of the Department of Labor called compliance officers. These inspections usually follow a tight "script." Typically, the compliance officer shows up unannounced. For obvious reasons, OSHA's regulations prohibit advance notice of inspections. The officer, after presenting credentials, tells the employer the reasons for the inspection and describes, in a general way, the procedures necessary to conduct the investigation.

An OSHA inspection has four major components. First, the compliance officer reviews the employer's records of deaths, injuries, and illnesses. OSHA requires this kind of record keeping from all firms with 11 or more full- or part-time employees. Second, the officer, typically accompanied by a representative of the employer (and perhaps by a representative of the employees), conducts a "walkaround" tour of the employer's premises. On this tour, the officer notes any conditions that may violate specific published standards or the less specific general duty clause. The third component of the inspection, employee interviews, may take place during the tour. At this time, any person who is aware of a violation can bring it to the attention of the officer. Finally, in a closing conference the compliance officer discusses the findings with the employer, noting any violations. The employer is given a reasonable time frame in which to correct these violations. If any violation represents imminent danger (that is, could cause serious injury or death before being eliminated through the normal enforcement procedures), the officer may, through the Department of Labor, seek a restraining order from a U.S. district court. Such an order compels the employer to correct the problem immediately.

Citations and Penalties

If a compliance officer believes that a violation has occurred, he or she issues a citation to the employer that specifies the exact practice or situation that violates the act. The employer is required to post this citation in a prominent place near the location of the violation—even if the employer intends to contest it. Nonserious violations may be assessed up to $1,000 for each incident, but this may be adjusted downward if the employer has no prior history of violations or if the employer has made a good-faith effort to comply with the act. Serious violations of the act or willful, repeated violations may be fined up to $10,000 per incident. Fines for safety violations are never levied against the employees themselves. The assumption is that safety is primarily the responsibility of the employer, who needs to work with employees to ensure that they use safe working procedures.

In addition to these civil penalties, criminal penalties may also be assessed for willful violations that kill an employee. Fines can go as high as $20,000, and the employer or agents of the employer can be imprisoned. Criminal charges can also be brought against anyone who falsifies records that are subject to OSHA inspection or anyone who gives advance notice of an OSHA inspection without permission from the Department of Labor.

The Effect of OSHA

OSHA has been unquestionably successful in raising the level of awareness of occupational safety. Table 3.7 presents recent data on occupational injuries and illnesses. Yet legislation alone cannot solve all the problems of work site safety.[50] Many industrial accidents are a product of unsafe behaviors, not unsafe working conditions. Because the act does not directly regulate employee behavior, little behavior change

table 3.7

Some of the Most Recent Statistics Provided by the Bureau of Labor Statistics Regarding Workplace Illnesses and Injuries

NONFATAL INJURIES AND ILLNESSES, PRIVATE INDUSTRY	FATAL WORK-RELATED INJURIES
Total recordable cases: 4,002,700 in 2007	Total fatalities (all sectors): 5,488(p) in 2007
Cases involving days away from work: 1,158,900 in 2007	Total fatalities (private industry): 4,956(p) in 2007
Cases involving sprains, strains, tears: 444,510 in 2007	Highway incidents (private industry): 1,157(p) in 2007
Cases involving injuries to the back: 235,960 in 2007	Falls (private industry): 803(p) in 2007
Cases involving falls: 253,410 in 2007	Homicides (private industry): 524(p) in 2007

p-Preliminary
SOURCE: www.bls.gov

can be expected unless employees are convinced of the standards' importance.[51] This has been recognized by labor leaders. For example, Lynn Williams, president of the United Steelworkers of America, noted, "We can't count on government. We can't count on employers. We must rely on ourselves to bring about the safety and health of our workers."[52]

Because conforming to the statute alone does not necessarily guarantee safety, many employers go beyond the letter of the law. In the next section we examine various kinds of employer-initiated safety awareness programs that comply with OSHA requirements and, in some cases, exceed them.

Safety Awareness Programs

Safety awareness programs go beyond compliance with OSHA and attempt to instill symbolic and substantive changes in the organization's emphasis on safety. These programs typically focus either on specific jobs and job elements or on specific types of injuries or disabilities. A safety awareness program has three primary components: identifying and communicating hazards, reinforcing safe practices, and promoting safety internationally.

> **Safety Awareness Programs**
> Employer programs that attempt to instill symbolic and substantive changes in the organization's emphasis on safety.

Identifying and Communicating Job Hazards

Employees, supervisors, and other knowledgeable sources need to sit down and discuss potential problems related to safety. The **job hazard analysis technique** is one means of accomplishing this.[53] With this technique, each job is broken down into basic elements, and each of these is rated for its potential for harm or injury. If there is consensus that some job element has high hazard potential, this element is isolated and potential technological or behavioral changes are considered.

Another means of isolating unsafe job elements is to study past accidents. The **technic of operations review (TOR)** is an analysis methodology that helps managers determine which specific element of a job led to a past accident.[54] The first step in a TOR analysis is to establish the facts surrounding the incident. To accomplish this, all members of the work group involved in the accident give their initial impressions of what happened. The group must then, through group discussion, reach a consensus on the single, systematic failure that most contributed to the incident as well as two or three major secondary factors that contributed to it.

> **Job Hazard Analysis Technique**
> A breakdown of each job into basic elements, each of which is rated for its potential for harm or injury.

> **Technic of Operations Review (TOR)**
> Method of determining safety problems via an analysis of past accidents.

An analysis of jobs at Burger King, for example, revealed that certain jobs required employees to walk across wet or slippery surfaces, which led to many falls. Specific corrective action was taken based on analysis of where people were falling and what conditions led to these falls. Now Burger King provides mats at critical locations and has generally upgraded its floor maintenance. The company also makes slip-resistant shoes available to employees in certain job categories.[55]

Communication of an employee's risk should take advantage of several media. Direct verbal supervisory contact is important for its saliency and immediacy. Written memos are important because they help establish a "paper trail" that can later document a history of concern regarding the job hazard. Posters, especially those placed near the hazard, serve as a constant reminder, reinforcing other messages.

In communicating risk, it is important to recognize two distinct audiences. Sometimes relatively young or inexperienced workers need special attention. Research by the National Safety Council indicates that 40 percent of all accidents happen to individuals in the 20-to-29 age group and that 48 percent of all accidents happen to workers during their first year on the job.[56] The employer's primary concern with respect to this group is to inform them. However, the employer must not overlook experienced workers. Here the key concern is to remind them. Research indicates that long-term exposure to and familiarity with a specific threat lead to complacency.[57] Experienced employees need retraining to jar them from complacency about the real dangers associated with their work. This is especially the case if the hazard in question poses a greater threat to older employees. For example, falling off a ladder is a greater threat to older workers than to younger ones. More than 20 percent of such falls lead to a fatality for workers in the 55-to-65 age group, compared with just 10 percent for all other workers.[58]

Reinforcing Safe Practices

One common technique for reinforcing safe practices is implementing a safety incentive program to reward workers for their support and commitment to safety goals. Initially, programs are set up to focus on improving short-term monthly or quarterly goals or to encourage safety suggestions. These short-term goals are later expanded to include more wide-ranging, long-term goals. Prizes are typically distributed in highly public forums (like annual meetings or events). These prizes usually consist of merchandise rather than cash because merchandise represents a lasting symbol of achievement. A good deal of evidence suggests that such programs are effective in reducing injuries and their cost.[59]

Whereas the safety awareness programs just described focus primarily on the job, other programs focus on specific injuries or disabilities. Lower back disability (LBD), for example, is a major problem that afflicts many employees. LBD accounts for approximately 25 percent of all workdays lost, costing firms nearly $30 billion a year.[60] Human resource managers can take many steps to prevent LBD and rehabilitate those who are already afflicted. Eye injuries are another target of safety awareness programs. The National Society to Prevent Blindness estimates that 1,000 eye injuries occur every day in occupational settings.[61] A 10-step program to reduce eye injuries is outlined in Table 3.8. Similar guidelines can be found for everything from chemical burns to electrocution to injuries caused by boiler explosions.[62]

table 3.8

A 10-Step Program for Reducing Eye-Related Injuries

1. Conduct an eye hazard job analysis.
2. Test all employees' vision to establish a baseline.
3. Select protective eyewear designed for specific operations.
4. Establish a 100 percent behavioral compliance program for eyewear.
5. Ensure that eyewear is properly fitted.
6. Train employees in emergency procedures.
7. Conduct ongoing education programs regarding eye care.
8. Continually review accident prevention strategies.
9. Provide management support.
10. Establish written policies detailing sanctions and rewards for specific results.

SOURCE: T. W. Turrif, "NSPB Suggests 10-Step Program to Prevent Eye Injury," *Occupational Health and Safety* 60 (1991), pp. 62–66.

How do you manage a global supply chain consisting of thousands of independent vendors scattered across the globe in a way that ensures they provide safe workplaces that respect human rights?

In 2003 The Gap Inc. was the first retailer to release a social responsibility report, offering a comprehensive overview of its approach to social responsibility with a particular focus on the workplace practices of vendors in its global supply chain. The report was broadly lauded for its openness and honesty about both the successes and failures in this arena. In fact, this report won *Business Ethics* magazine's Social Reporting Award for "unprecedented honesty in reporting on factory conditions."

The Gap's 2004 Social Responsibility Report continued that discussion and provided new information on the company's progress, challenges, and new initiatives. Eva Sage-Gavin is the executive vice president of Human Resources and Corporate Communications at Gap, and here's how she describes its CSR efforts.

"There are really four key areas, and we think of corporate social responsibility across Gap, Inc., in these four strategic ways. The first one is this whole idea of sustainable solutions in our supply chain. This consists of working on a four-part strategy to improve working conditions, monitor factories, integrate labor standards into our business practices, and the whole idea of collaborating with outside partners to drive industry-wide change. So that's the first big centerpiece of how we think about CSR. The second is with our employees and making Gap, Inc., a place where people can really flourish and build their careers in a positive work environment. The third is community involvement, including everything from our foundation to our volunteerism. And the fourth key area in corporate social responsibility for us is environment, health, and safety. This is everything from the average store energy consumption to the safety of our stores for customers and employees to a high-level environmental impact assessment for all of our business operations.

"We think that this is critical to our long-term growth and the sustainability of our business. We see there are three elements to the benefits. First is the idea of our employee attraction and retention. Our employees tell us they want to work for a company that's socially responsible and they tell us through a variety of channels that they love working for a company that they believe is doing what's right. The second piece for us is a better supply chain. We know that better factory working conditions lead to better factories, and better factories make better products. The sourcing team can also select and make better buying decisions. We also introduced an integrated scorecard into the retail industry that gives factories feedback and scores on criteria such as quality, innovation, speed to market, and cost, and it considers the manufacturers' compliance history. Finally, our focus on sustainability creates win-win scenarios for everyone involved in our environmental impact. When we reduce our energy usage we also reduce cost. Obviously that's a win-win all the way around.

"I can say confidently that it's a critical part of our long-term growth and sustainability of our business. We know that our success depends on our employees and it depends on creating value for our shareholders, but ultimately it's about the customer experience and their desire to purchase great products. We know that we won't do that without employees who are engaged, satisfied, proud to work here—employees that want to exceed our customers' expectations. It's a very competitive global environment. We also know that improved factory working conditions lead to better factories, and that leads to a better supply chain."

SOURCE: E. Sage-Gavin, and P. Wright, "Corporate Social Responsibility at Gap, Inc.: An Interview with Eva Sage-Gavin," *Human Resource Planning*, vol. 30.1 (2007), pp. 45–48.

Promoting Safety Internationally

Given the increasing focus on international management, organizations also need to consider how to best ensure the safety of people regardless of the nation in which they operate. Cultural differences may make this more difficult than it seems. For example, a recent study examined the impact of one standardized corporationwide safety policy on employees in three different countries: the United States, France, and Argentina. The results of this study indicated that the same policy was interpreted differently because of cultural differences. The individualistic, control-oriented culture of the United States stressed the role of top management in ensuring safety in a top-down fashion. However, this policy failed to work in Argentina, where the collectivist culture made employees feel that safety was everyone's joint concern; therefore, programs needed to be defined from the bottom up.[63]

At the beginning of this section we discussed a horrific accident at BP's Texas City refinery. After examining the causes of the explosion, the U.S. Chemical Safety and Hazard Investigation Board asked BP to set up an independent panel that would focus on overseeing radical changes in BP's safety procedures. This panel was tasked with investigating the safety culture at BP along with the procedures for inspecting equipment and reporting near-miss accidents. The panel's charter is not just to oversee the Texas City refinery, but also to look at the safety practices in refineries that BP has acquired over the years.[64]

The "Competing through Globalization" box illustrates how The Gap has strategically managed a measurement and reporting system with regard to its suppliers to ensure that it is being socially responsible. This reporting system reveals The Gap's concern with human rights and safety in the workplace, usually the workplaces of their suppliers, scattered all across the globe.

A LOOK BACK:

WAL-MART'S DISCRIMINATION?

At the opening and throughout this chapter, we have referred to the *Dukes v. Wal-Mart* case because it will be a watershed case for deciding the future of class-action discrimination suits. After reading about how pattern and practice discrimination suits proceed, do you think Wal-Mart has discriminated against 2 million female former employees?

Regardless of the merits of this particular suit, Wal-Mart has heard the message that it has problems—and has responded accordingly. For instance, in 2006 the company began hiring 300 human resource managers to work in the field, in addition to the 100 executives in its Bentonville, Arkansas, headquarters. Now their HR field structure contains five divisional heads, 27 regional HR directors, and 342 field HR managers. By placing more HR professionals side-by-side with store managers, they hope to provide more discipline to workforce decisions to ensure better compliance with the legal requirements.

Questions

1. Based on what you read, do you think that Wal-Mart will win or lose the class-action discrimination case brought against it?
2. Assume that you have taken over the HR function at Wal-Mart and want to make sure that your pay system is fair, so you commission a salary study that

reveals pay differences between men and women. If you publicize the data and try to fix the problem, you open the company up to liability for past discrimination. What will you do?

Sources: J. Marquez, "Wal-Mart Puts on a New Face," *Workforce Management*, August 14, 2006, p. 29; R. Parloff and S. Kaufman, "The War Over Unconscious Bias," *Fortune*, October 15, 2007, p. 90.

  Please see the Video Case and Case Study that correspond to this chapter online at www.mhhe.com/noe7e.

SUMMARY

Viewing employees as a source of competitive advantage results in dealing with them in ways that are ethical and legal as well as providing a safe workplace. An organization's legal environment—especially the laws regarding equal employment opportunity and safety—has a particularly strong effect on its HRM function. HRM is concerned with the management of people, and government is concerned with protecting individuals. One of HRM's major challenges, therefore, is to perform its function within the legal constraints imposed by the government. Given the multimillion-dollar settlements resulting from violations of EEO laws (and the moral requirement to treat people fairly regardless of their sex or race) as well as the penalties for violating OSHA, HR and line managers need a good understanding of the legal requirements and prohibitions in order to manage their businesses in ways that are sound, both financially and ethically. Organizations that do so effectively will definitely have a competitive advantage.

KEY TERMS

Equal employment opportunity (EEO), 108
Americans with Disabilities Act (ADA) of 1990, 114
Equal Employment Opportunity Commission (EEOC), 116
Utilization analysis, 118
Goals and timetables, 118

Action steps, 118
Disparate treatment, 119
Bona fide occupational qualification (BFOQ), 121
Disparate impact, 123
Four-fifths rule, 124
Standard deviation rule, 124
Reasonable accommodation, 127

Occupational Safety and Health Act (OSHA), 138
General duty clause, 138
Safety awareness programs, 141
Job hazard analysis technique, 141
Technic of operations review (TOR), 141

DISCUSSION QUESTIONS

1. Disparate impact theory was originally created by the court in the *Griggs* case before finally being codified by Congress 20 years later in the Civil Rights Act of 1991. Given the system of law in the United States, from what branch of government should theories of discrimination develop?

2. Disparate impact analysis (the four-fifths rule, standard deviation analysis) is used in employment discrimination cases. The National Assessment of Education Progress conducted by the U.S. Department of Education found that among 21- to 25-year-olds (a) 60 percent of whites, 40 percent of Hispanics, and 25 percent of blacks could locate information in a news article or almanac; (b) 25 percent of whites, 7 percent of Hispanics, and 3 percent of blacks could decipher a bus schedule; and (c) 44 percent of whites, 20 percent of Hispanics, and 8 percent of blacks could correctly determine the change they were due from the purchase of a two-item restaurant meal. Do these tasks (locating information in a news article, deciphering a bus schedule, and determining correct change) have adverse impact? What are the implications?

3. Many companies have dress codes that require men to wear suits and women to wear dresses. Is this discriminatory according to disparate treatment theory? Why?

4. Cognitive ability tests seem to be the most valid selection devices available for hiring employees, yet they also have adverse impact against blacks and Hispanics. Given the validity and adverse impact, and considering that race norming is illegal under CRA 1991, what would you say in response to a recommendation that such tests be used for hiring?

5. How might the ADA's reasonable accommodation requirement affect workers such as law enforcement officers and firefighters?

6. The reasonable woman standard recognizes that women have different ideas than men of what constitutes appropriate behavior. What are the implications of this distinction? Do you think it is a good or bad idea to make this distinction?

7. Employers' major complaint about the ADA is that the costs of making reasonable accommodations will reduce their ability to compete with businesses (especially foreign ones) that do not face these requirements. Is this a legitimate concern? How should employers and society weigh the costs and benefits of the ADA?

8. Many have suggested that OSHA penalties are too weak and misdirected (aimed at employers rather than employees) to have any significant impact on employee safety. Do you think that OSHA-related sanctions need to be strengthened, or are existing penalties sufficient? Defend your answer.

SELF-ASSESSMENT EXERCISE

Take the following self-assessment quiz. For each statement, circle T if the statement is true or F if the statement is false.

What do you know about sexual harassment?

1. A man cannot be the victim of sexual harassment. T F
2. The harasser can only be the victim's manager or a manager in another work area. T F
3. Sexual harassment charges can be filed only by the person who directly experiences the harassment. T F
4. The best way to discourage sexual harassment is to have a policy that discourages employees from dating each other. T F
5. Sexual harassment is not a form of sex discrimination. T F
6. After receiving a sexual harassment complaint, the employer should let the situation cool off before investigating the complaint. T F
7. Sexual harassment is illegal only if it results in the victim being laid off or receiving lower pay. T F

EXERCISING STRATEGY: HOME DEPOT'S BUMPY ROAD TO EQUALITY

Home Depot is the largest home products firm selling home repair products and equipment for the "do-it-yourselfer." Founded 20 years ago, it now boasts 100,000 employees and more than 900 warehouse stores nationwide. The company's strategy for growth has focused mostly on one task: build more stores. In fact, an unwritten goal of Home Depot executives was to position a store within 30 minutes of every customer in the United States. They've almost made it. In addition, Home Depot has tried hard to implement a strategy of providing superior service to its customers. The company has prided itself on hiring people who are knowledgeable about home repair and who can teach customers how to do home repairs on their own. This strategy, along with blanketing the country with stores, has led to the firm's substantial advantage over competitors, including the now-defunct Home Quarters (HQ) and still-standing Lowe's.

But Home Depot has run into some legal problems. During the company's growth, a statistical anomaly has emerged. About 70 percent of the merchandise employees (those directly involved in selling lumber, electrical supplies, hardware, and so forth) are men, whereas about 70 percent of operations employees (cashiers, accountants, back office staff, and so forth) are women. Because of this difference, several years ago a lawsuit was filed on behalf of 17,000 current and former employees as well as up to 200,000 rejected applicants. Home Depot explained the disparity by noting that most female job applicants have experience as cashiers, so they are placed in cashier positions; most male applicants express an interest in or aptitude for home repair work such as carpentry or plumbing. However, attorneys argued that Home Depot was reinforcing gender stereotyping by hiring in this manner.

More recently, five former Home Depot employees sued the company, charging that it had discriminated against African American workers at two stores in southeast Florida. The five alleged that they were paid less than white workers, passed over for promotion, and given critical performance reviews based on race. "The company takes exception to the charges and believes they are without merit," said Home Depot spokesman Jerry Shields. The company has faced other racial discrimination suits as well, including one filed by the Michigan Department of Civil Rights.

To avoid such lawsuits in the future, Home Depot could resort to hiring and promoting by quota, ensuring an equal distribution of employees across all job categories—something that the company has wanted to avoid because it believes such action would undermine its competitive advantage. However, the company has taken steps to broaden and strengthen its own nondiscrimination policy by adding sexual orientation to the written policy. In addition, company president and CEO Bob Nardelli announced in the fall of 2001 that Home Depot would take special steps to protect benefits for its more than 500 employees who serve in the Army reserves and had been activated. "We will make up any difference between their Home Depot pay and their military pay if it's lower," said Nardelli. "When they come home [from duty], their jobs and their orange aprons are waiting for them."

In settling the gender discrimination suit the company agreed to pay $65 million to women who had been steered to cashiers' jobs and had been denied promotions. In addition, the company promised that every applicant would get a "fair shot." Home Depot's solution to this has been to leverage technology to make better hiring decisions that ensure the company is able to maximize diversity.

Home Depot instituted its Job Preference Program, an automated hiring and promotion system, across its 900 stores at a cost of $10 million. It has set up kiosks where potential applicants can log on to a computer, complete an application, and undergo a set of prescreening tests. This process weeds out unqualified applicants. Then the system prints out test scores along with structured interview questions and examples of good and bad answers for the managers interviewing those who make it through the prescreening. In addition, the Home Depot system is used

for promotions. Employees are asked to constantly update their skills and career aspirations so they can be considered for promotions at nearby stores.

The system has been an unarguable success. Managers love it because they are able to get high-quality applicants without having to sift through mounds of résumés. In addition, the system seems to have accomplished its main purpose. The number of female managers has increased 30 percent and the number of minority managers by 28 percent since the introduction of the system. In fact, David Borgen, the co-counsel for the plaintiffs in the original lawsuit, states, "No one can say it can't be done anymore, because Home Depot is doing it bigger and better than anyone I know."

SOURCES: "Home Depot Says Thanks to America's Military; Extends Associates/Reservists' Benefits, Announces Military Discount," company press release, October 9, 2001; S. Jaffe, "New Tricks in Home Depot's Toolbox?" *BusinessWeek* Online, June 5, 2001, at www.businessweek.com; "HRC Lauds Home Depot for Adding Sexual Orientation to Its Non-discrimination Policy," Human Rights Campaign, May 14, 2001, at www.hrc.org; "Former Home Depot Employees File Racial Discrimination Lawsuit," Diversity at Work, June 2000, at www.diversityatwork.com; "Michigan Officials File Discrimination Suit against Home Depot," Diversity at Work, February 2000, at www.diversityatwork.com; M. Boot, "For Plaintiffs' Lawyers, There's No Place Like Home Depot," *The Wall Street Journal*, interactive edition, February 12, 1997.

Questions

1. If Home Depot was correct in that it was not discriminating, but simply filling positions consistent with those who applied for them (and very few women were applying for customer service positions), given your reading of this chapter, was the firm guilty of discrimination? If so, under what theory?
2. How does this case illustrate the application of new technology to solving issues that have never been tied to technology? Can you think of other ways technology might be used to address diversity/EEO/affirmative action issues?

● MANAGING PEOPLE: FROM THE PAGES OF *BUSINESSWEEK*

BusinessWeek *Brown v. Board of Education:* A Bittersweet Birthday

Decades of progress on integration have been followed by disturbing slippage

May 17 marks the 50th anniversary of *Brown v. Board of Education*, the landmark Supreme Court ruling that declared racially segregated "separate but equal" schools unconstitutional. The case is widely regarded as one of the court's most important decisions of the 20th century, but the birthday celebration will be something of a bittersweet occasion. There's no question that African Americans have made major strides since—economically, socially, and educationally. But starting in the late 1980s, political backlash

brought racial progress to a halt. Since then, schools have slowly been resegregating, and the achievement gap between white and minority schoolchildren has been widening again. Can the United States ever achieve the great promise of integration? Some key questions follow.

What did the Court strike down in 1954? Throughout the South and in border states such as Delaware, black and white children were officially assigned to separate schools. In Topeka, Kansas, the lead city in the famous case, there were 18 elementary schools for whites and just 4 for blacks, forcing many African American children to travel a long way to school. The idea that black schools were "equal" to those for whites was a cruel fiction, condemning most black kids to a grossly inferior education.

Surely we've come a long way since then?   Yes, though change took a long time. Over 99 percent of Southern black children were still in segregated schools in 1963. The 1960s civil rights movement eventually brought aggressive federal policies such as busing and court orders that forced extensive integration, especially in the South. So by 1988, 44 percent of Southern black children were attending schools where a majority of students were white, up from 2 percent in 1964. "We cut school desegregation almost in half between 1968 and 1990," says John Logan, director of the Lewis Mumford Center for Comparative Urban and Regional Research at State University of New York at Albany.

What's the picture today?   There have been some real gains. The share of blacks graduating from high school has nearly quadrupled since *Brown*, to 88 percent today, while the share of those ages 25 to 29 with a college degree has increased more than sixfold, to 18 percent.

Another important trend is in housing, which in turn helps determine the characteristics of school districts. Residential integration is improving, albeit at a glacial pace. There's still high housing segregation in major metropolitan areas, but it has fallen four percentage points, to 65 percent, on an index developed by the Mumford Center. Some of the gains are happening in fast-growing new suburbs where race lines aren't so fixed. A few big cities have improved, too. In Dallas, for example, black–white residential segregation fell from 78 percent in 1980 to 59 percent in 2000.

Why haven't schools continued to desegregate, too?   The increased racial mixing in housing hasn't been nearly large enough to offset the sheer increase in the ranks of minority schoolchildren. While the number of white elementary school kids remained flat, at 15.3 million, between 1990 and 2000, the number of black children climbed by 800,000, to 4.6 million, while Hispanic kids jumped by 1.7 million, to 4.3 million. The result: Minorities now comprise 40 percent of public school kids, vs. 32 percent in 1990. And as the nonwhite population has expanded, so have minority neighborhoods—and schools.

So minorities have lost ground?   Yes, in some respects. By age 17, black students are still more than three years behind their white counterparts in reading and math. And whites are twice as likely to graduate from college. Taken as a whole, U.S. schools have been resegregating for 15 years or so, according to studies by the Harvard University Civil Rights Project. "We're celebrating [Brown] at a time when schools in all regions are becoming increasingly segregated," says project co-director Gary Orfield.

What role has the political backlash against integration played?   The courts and politicians have been pulling back from integration goals for quite a while. In 1974, the Supreme Court ruled that heavily black Detroit didn't have to integrate its schools with the surrounding white suburbs. Then, in the 1980s, the growing backlash against busing and race-based school assignment led politicians and the courts to all but give up on those remedies, too.

So what are the goals now?   The approach has shifted dramatically. Instead of trying to force integration, the United States has moved toward equalizing education. In a growing number of states, the courts have been siding with lawsuits that seek equal or "adequate" funding for minority and low-income schools.

The No Child Left Behind Act goes even further. It says that all children will receive a "highly qualified" teacher by 2006 and will achieve proficiency in math and reading by 2014. It specifically requires schools to meet these goals for racial subgroups. Paradoxically, it sounds like separate but equal again. Both the equal-funding suits and No Child Left Behind aim to improve all schools, whatever their racial composition. Integration is no longer the explicit goal.

Can schools equalize without integrating?   It's possible in some cases, but probably not for the United States as a whole. The Education Trust, a nonprofit group in Washington, D.C., has identified a number of nearly all-black, low-income schools that have achieved exceptional test results. But such success requires outstanding leadership, good teachers, and a fervent commitment to high standards.

These qualities are far more difficult to achieve in large urban schools with many poor kids—the kind most black and Hispanic students attend. The average minority student goes to a school in which two-thirds of the students are low-income. By contrast, whites attend schools that are just 30 percent low-income.

So are black–white achievement gaps as much about poverty as race?   Yes, which is why closing them is difficult with or without racial integration. Studies show that middle-class students tend to have higher expectations, more engaged parents, and better teachers. Poor children, by contrast, often come to school with far more personal problems. Yet poor schools are more likely to get inferior teachers, such as those who didn't major in the subject they teach. Many poor schools also lose as many as 20 percent of their teachers each year, while most middle-class suburban schools have more stable teaching staffs. "Research suggests that when low-income students attend middle-class schools, they do substantially better," says Richard Kahlenberg, senior fellow at the Century Foundation, a public policy think tank in New York City.

Is it possible to achieve more economic integration?   There are a few shining examples, but they take enormous political commitment. One example that education-system reformers love to highlight is Wake County,

N.C., whose 110,000-student school district includes Raleigh. In 2000, it adopted a plan to ensure that low-income students make up no more than 40 percent of any student body. It also capped those achieving under grade level at 25 percent. Moreover, it used magnet schools offering specialized programs, such as one for gifted children, to help attract middle-income children to low-income areas.

Already, 91 percent of the county's third- to eighth-graders work at grade level in math and reading, up from 84 percent in 1999. More impressive, 75 percent of low-income kids are reading at grade level, up from just 56 percent in 1999, as are 78 percent of black children, up from 61 percent. "The academic payoff has been pretty incredible," says Walter C. Sherlin, a 28-year Wake County schools veteran and interim director of the nonprofit Wake Education Partnership.

Could this serve as a national model? For that to happen in many cities, school districts would have to merge with the surrounding suburbs. Wake County did this, but that was back in the 1970s and part of a long-term plan to bring about racial integration. In the metro Boston area, by contrast, students are balkanized into dozens of tiny districts, many of which are economically homogeneous. The result: Some 70 percent of white students attend schools that are over 90 percent white and overwhelmingly middle-class. Meanwhile, 97 percent of the schools that are over 90 percent minority are also high-poverty. Similar patterns exist in most major cities, but most affluent white suburbs aren't likely to swallow a move like Wake County's.

How important is funding equality within states? It's critical, especially if segregation by income and race persists. Massachusetts, for instance, has nearly tripled state aid to schools since 1993, with over 90 percent of the money going to the poorest towns. That has helped make Massachusetts a national leader in raising academic achievement.

Nationally, though, there are still huge inequities in school spending, with the poorest districts receiving less money than the richest—even though low-income children are more expensive to educate. Fixing these imbalances would be costly. Even in Massachusetts, a lower court judge ruled on April 26 that the system still shortchanges students in the poorest towns. Nationally, it would cost more than $50 billion a year in extra funding to correct inequities enough to meet the goals of No Child, figures Anthony P. Carnevale, a vice president at Educational Testing Service.

If, somehow, the United States could achieve more economic integration, would racial integration still be necessary? Proficiency on tests isn't the only aim. As the Supreme Court said last year in a landmark decision on affirmative action in higher education: "Effective participation by members of all racial and ethnic groups in the civic life of our nation is essential if the dream of one nation, indivisible, is to be realized." It's hard to see how students attending largely segregated schools, no matter how proficient, could be adequately prepared for life in an increasingly diverse country. In this sense, integrating America's educational system remains an essential, though still elusive, goal.

Questions

1. While segregation of public schools has been outlawed, the article notes that schools are not necessarily "desegregating" (i.e., there are still predominantly minority and predominantly nonminority schools). If students are to work in increasingly diverse workforces, is the current system failing them? Why or why not?
2. The black–white gap continues to exist with regard to reading, math, and graduation rates. What are the implications of this on organizations' selection systems (i.e., disparate impact)?
3. Given the lack of a "diverse" educational experience for a large percentage of black children, and the gap between them and their white counterparts, what must organizations do to leverage diversity as a source of competitive advantage?

SOURCE: W. Symonds, "A Bittersweet Birthday," *BusinessWeek*, May 17, 2004, pp. 66–62.

● NOTES

1. J. Ledvinka, *Federal Regulation of Personnel and Human Resource Management* (Boston: Kent, 1982).
2. *Martin v. Wilks*, 49 FEP Cases 1641 (1989).
3. *Wards Cove Packing Co. v. Atonio*, FEPC 1519 (1989).
4. *Bakke v. Regents of the University of California*, 17 FEPC 1000 (1978).
5. *Patterson v. McLean Credit Union*, 49 FEPC 1814 (1987).
6. J. Friedman and G. Strickler, *The Law of Employment Discrimination: Cases and Materials*, 2nd ed. (Mineola, NY: Foundation Press, 1987).
7. "Labor Letter," *The Wall Street Journal*, August 25, 1987, p. 1.
8. J. Woo, "Ex-Workers Hit Back with Age-Bias Suits," *The Wall Street Journal*, December 8, 1992, p. B1.
9. W. Carley, "Salesman's Treatment Raises Bias Questions at Schering-Plough," *The Wall Street Journal*, May 31, 1995, p. A1.
10. http://www.eeoc.gov/press/1-8-07.html.
11. Special feature issue: "The New Civil Rights Act of 1991 and What It Means to Employers," *Employment Law Update* 6 (December 1991), pp. 1–12.
12. "ADA: The Final Regulations (Title I): A Lawyer's Dream/An Employer's Nightmare," *Employment Law Update* 16, no. 9 (1991), p. 1.

13. "ADA Supervisor Training Program: A Must for Any Supervisor Conducting a Legal Job Interview," *Employment Law Update* 7, no. 6 (1992), pp. 1–6.
14. Equal Employment Opportunity Commission, "Uniform Guidelines on Employee Selection Procedures," *Federal Register* 43 (1978), pp. 38290–315.
15. Ledvinka, *Federal Regulation*.
16. R. Pear, "The Cabinet Searches for Consensus on Affirmative Action," *The New York Times*, October 27, 1985, p. E5.
17. *McDonnell Douglas v. Green*, 411 U.S. 972 (1973).
18. *UAW v. Johnson Controls, Inc.* (1991).
19. Special feature issue: "The New Civil Rights Act of 1991," pp. 1–6.
20. *Washington v. Davis*, 12 FEP 1415 (1976).
21. *Albermarle Paper Company v. Moody*, 10 FEP 1181 (1975).
22. R. Reilly and G. Chao, "Validity and Fairness of Some Alternative Employee Selection Procedures," *Personnel Psychology* 35 (1982), pp. 1–63; J. Hunter and R. Hunter, "Validity and Utility of Alternative Predictors of Job Performance," *Psychological Bulletin* 96 (1984), pp. 72–98.
23. *Griggs v. Duke Power Company*, 401 U.S. 424 (1971).
24. B. Lindeman and P. Grossman, *Employment Discrimination Law* (Washington, DC: BNA Books, 1996).
25. M. Jacobs, "Workers' Religious Beliefs May Get New Attention," *The Wall Street Journal*, August 22, 1995, pp. B1, B8.
26. EEOC, "EEOC and Electrolux Reach Voluntary Resolution in Class Religious Accommodation Case," at www.eeoc.gov/press/9-24-03.
27. S. Sataline, "Who's Wrong when Rights Collide?" *The Wall Street Journal*, March 6, 2007, p. B1.
28. "Manager's Failure to Accommodate Creates Liability for Store," *Disability Compliance Bulletin*, January 15, 2009.
29. Lindeman and Grossman, *Employment Discrimination Law*.
30. J. Reno and D. Thornburgh, "ADA—Not a Disabling Mandate," *The Wall Street Journal*, July 26, 1995, p. A12.
31. Woo, "Ex-Workers Hit Back."
32. EEOC, "Target Corp. to Pay $775,000 for Racial Harassment: EEC Settles Suit for Class of African American Employees; Remedial Relief Included," at www.eeoc.gov/press/1-26-07.html.
33. W. Johnston and A. Packer, *Workforce 2000* (Indianapolis, IN: Hudson Institute, 1987).
34. *Bundy v. Jackson*, 641 F.2d 934, 24 FEP 1155 (D.C. Cir., 1981).
35. L. A. Graf and M. Hemmasi, "Risqué Humor: How It Really Affects the Workplace," *HR Magazine*, November 1995, pp. 64–69.
36. B. Carton, "At Jenny Craig, Men Are Ones Who Claim Sex Discrimination," *The Wall Street Journal*, November 29, 1995, p. A1; "Male-on-Male Harassment Suit Won," *Houston Chronicle*, August 12, 1995, p. 21A.
37. EEOC, "Texas Car Dealership to Pay $140,000 to Settle Same-Sex Harassment Suit by EEOC," at www.eeoc.gov/press/10-28-02.
38. EEOC, "Babies 'R' Us to Pay $205,000, Implement Training Due to Same-Sex Harassment of Male Employee," at www.eeoc.gov/press/1-15-03.
39. *Meritor Savings Bank v. Vinson* (1986).
40. R. Paetzold and A. O'Leary-Kelly, "The Implications of U.S. Supreme Court and Circuit Court Decisions for Hostile Environment Sexual Harassment Cases," in *Sexual Harassment: Perspectives, Frontiers, and Strategies*, ed. M. Stockdale (Beverly Hills, CA: Sage); R. B. McAfee and D. L. Deadrick, "Teach Employees to Just Say 'No'!" *HR Magazine*, February 1996, pp. 586–89.
41. C. Murray, "The Legacy of the 60's," *Commentary*, July 1992, pp. 23–30.
42. D. Kravitz and J. Platania, "Attitudes and Beliefs about Affirmative Action: Effects of Target and of Respondent Sex and Ethnicity," *Journal of Applied Psychology* 78 (1993), pp. 928–38.
43. J. Mathews, "Rash of Unintended Lawsuits Follows Passage of Disabilities Act," *Houston Chronicle*, May 16, 1995, p. 15A.
44. C. Bell, "What the First ADA Cases Tell Us," *SHRM Legal Report* (Winter 1995), pp. 4–7.
45. J. Fitzgerald, "Chatty IBMer Booted," *New York Post*, February 18, 2007.
46. National Organization on Disability 2006 Annual Report at www.nod.org.
47. K. Mills, "Disabilities Act: A Help, or a Needless Hassle," *B/CS Eagle*, August 23, 1995, p. A7.
48. C. Cummins and T. Herrick, "Investigators Fault BP for More Lapses in Refinery Safety," *The Wall Street Journal*, August 18, 2005, p. A3.
49. V. F. Estrada, "Are Your Factory Workers Know-It-All?" *Personnel Journal*, September 1995, pp. 128–34.
50. R. L. Simison, "Safety Last," *The Wall Street Journal*, March 18, 1986, p. 1.
51. J. Roughton, "Managing a Safety Program through Job Hazard Analysis," *Professional Safety* 37 (1992), pp. 28–31.
52. M. A. Verespec, "OSHA Reform Fails Again," *Industry Week*, November 2, 1992, p. 36.
53. R. G. Hallock and D. A. Weaver, "Controlling Losses and Enhancing Management Systems with TOR Analysis," *Professional Safety* 35 (1990), pp. 24–26.
54. H. Herbstman, "Controlling Losses the Burger King Way," *Risk Management* 37 (1990), pp. 22–30.
55. L. Bryan, "An Ounce of Prevention for Workplace Accidents," *Training and Development Journal* 44 (1990), pp. 101–2.
56. J. F. Mangan, "Hazard Communications: Safety in Knowledge," *Best's Review* 92 (1991), pp. 84–88.
57. T. Markus, "How to Set Up a Safety Awareness Program," *Supervision* 51 (1990), pp. 14–16.
58. J. Agnew and A. J. Saruda, "Age and Fatal Work-Related Falls," *Human Factors* 35 (1994), pp. 731–36.
59. R. King, "Active Safety Programs, Education Can Help Prevent Back Injuries," *Occupational Health and Safety* 60 (1991), pp. 49–52.
60. J. R. Hollenbeck, D. R. Ilgen, and S. M. Crampton, "Lower Back Disability in Occupational Settings: A Review of the Literature from a Human Resource Management View," *Personnel Psychology* 45 (1992), pp. 247–78.
61. T. W. Turriff, "NSPB Suggests 10-Step Program to Prevent Eye Injury," *Occupational Health and Safety* 60 (1991), pp. 62–66.
62. D. Hanson, "Chemical Plant Safety: OSHA Rule Addresses Industry Concerns," *Chemical and Engineering News* 70 (1992), pp. 4–5; K. Broscheit and K. Sawyer, "Safety Exhibit Teaches Customers and Employees about Electricity," *Transmission and Distribution* 43 (1992), pp. 174–79; R. Schuch, "Good Training Is Key to Avoiding Boiler Explosions," *National Underwriter* 95 (1992), pp. 21–22.
63. M. Janssens, J. M. Brett, and F. J. Smith, "Confirmatory Cross-Cultural Research: Testing the Viability of a Corporation-wide Safety Policy," *Academy of Management Journal* 38 (1995), pp. 364–82.
64. Cummins and Herrick, "Investigators Fault BP."

The Analysis and Design of Work

 LEARNING OBJECTIVES

After reading this chapter, you should be able to:

LO1 Analyze an organization's structure and work-flow process, identifying the output, activities, and inputs in the production of a product or service. *page 155*

LO2 Understand the importance of job analysis in strategic human resource management. *page 168*

LO3 Choose the right job analysis technique for a variety of human resource activities. *page 171*

LO4 Identify the tasks performed and the skills required in a given job. *page 173*

LO5 Understand the different approaches to job design. *page 174*

LO6 Comprehend the trade-offs among the various approaches to designing jobs. *page 181*

ENTER THE WORLD OF BUSINESS

Job Design: Back to the Future at Toyota

In 2007, Toyota Motor Corporation surpassed General Motors as the world's largest carmaker. This was the accomplishment of a long-term goal that could only be obtained by a strong focus on rapid growth and expansion. However, in the process of focusing on this goal, many insiders at Toyota believed that the organization was straying from some of its core values, especially as this related to the organization's structure and design of jobs. In fact, in 2009, Toyota reported its first annual operating loss since 1938, and due to the economic recession, the company had so much extra capacity that they had to lay off workers for the first time since 1950. As industry observer Tokai Gakuin, noted, "Toyota was so focused on becoming the world's largest automaker that it failed to cut production quickly enough in 2008, as the economic crisis struck the U.S., its largest market."

The steps that the company took to restore profitability provide a lesson in how to compete via organizational design and job design. First, with respect to manufacturing jobs, the fast-paced expansion of Toyota's plants both in Japan and the United States was, in some cases, purchased at the price of reduced quality standards. The number of recalls for manufacturing defects tripled in the last three years, and quality ratings by analysts such as J.D. Powers and Associates slipped noticeably. In response to this, the company streamlined jobs, tightened job descriptions and enhanced training programs in a way that slowed production but increased quality. For example, quality control inspectors were required to put on a glove and massage the door of every Camry in a soft circular motion in search of tiny dents for roughly 15 minutes prior to sending the car further down the production line.

With respect to sales jobs, because of Toyota's ambitious quotas, sales personnel often used high-pressure techniques to get customers to purchase cars more quickly, and then, after the sale was made, often handed over the cars without properly inspecting them. Thus, even when customers loved their cars, they often hated their car-buying experience. Toyota quickly responded to this problem by sending out five-person evaluation teams to sales units that were ranked low in customer satisfaction and reanalyzed all the jobs in those units—all the way from the top manager to the car washer. In each case, the team tried to create a personal link between each customer and each person who was responsible for their car, all of which resulted in slower sales, but happier customers.

Finally, with respect to managerial jobs, Toyota's middle-level managers made the case that in contrast to the organization's traditional, slow, consensus-based, decision-making process with a long-term focus, too many recent decisions were made single-handedly by the president, Katsuaki Watanabe. For example, middle-level managers noted how Watanabe quickly flip-flopped on where to build factories, first increasing production overseas when the Japanese yen was strong (and hence made production in Japan more expensive), and then quickly reverting production back within the United States when the yen lost value. Because currency exchange rates fluctuate a great deal over short time periods, the short-term gain in profitability often resulted in long-term inefficiencies associated with starting up and closing factories. Watanabe was eventually replaced as president by Akio Toyoda, the grandson of the organization's founder, Kiichiro Toyoda, who promised to restore the organization's traditional approach to organizational structure and job design.

Sources: D. Welch, "Staying Paranoid at Toyota," *BusinessWeek*, July 2, 2007, pp. 80–82; I. Rowley, "Even Toyota Isn't Perfect," *BusinessWeek*, January 11, 2007, pp. 33–36; N. Shirouzu, "Toyota to Change Leader Amid Sales Slump," *The Wall Street Journal*, December 28, 2008, pp. A1–A2; N. Shirouzu and J. Murphy, "A Scion Drives Toyota Back to the Basics," *The Wall Street Journal*, February, 24, 2009, pp. B1–B3.

Introduction

In Chapter 2 we discussed the processes of strategy formulation and strategy implementation. Strategy formulation is the process by which a company decides how it will compete in the marketplace; this is often the energizing and guiding force for everything it does. Strategy implementation is the way the strategic plan gets carried out in activities of organizational members. We noted five important components in the strategy implementation process, three of which are directly related to the human resource management function and one of which we will discuss in this chapter: the task or job.

Many central aspects of strategy formulation address how the work gets done, in terms of individual job design as well as the design of organizational structures that link individual jobs to each other and the organization as a whole. The way a firm competes can have a profound impact on the ways jobs are designed and how they are linked via organizational structure. In turn, the fit between the company's structure and environment can have a major impact on the firm's competitive success.

For example, if a company like Toyota wants to compete by producing and selling the largest *quantity* of automobiles, then the organization and jobs are structured one way. However, if the company wants to be the top producer in terms of *quality* and customer satisfaction, the organization and jobs may need to be designed in a different way. Throughout this chapter, we provide examples of the kinds of decisions that need to be made with regard to how organizations should be structured and to the jobs that exist within these organizations, so you can learn how these choices affect a number of outcomes. This includes not just quantity and quality of production, but also outcomes like coordination; innovation; and worker attraction, motivation, and retention. In many cases, there are trade-offs associated with the choices, and the more you know about these trade-offs, the better decisions you can make in terms of making your team or organization more competitive.

Thus, it should be clear from the outset of this chapter that there is no "one best way" to design jobs and structure organizations. The organization needs to create a fit between its environment, competitive strategy, and philosophy on the one hand, with its jobs and organizational design on the other. Thus, in our opening story, we saw how Toyota became number 1 in sales volume by following one approach, but then changed this approach when it decided to put more emphasis on quality and customer satisfaction. Failing to design effective organizations and jobs has important implications for competitiveness. Many years ago, some believed that the difference between U.S. auto producers and their foreign competitors could be traced to American workers; however, when companies like Toyota and Honda came into the United States and demonstrated clearly that they could run profitable car companies with American workers, the focus shifted to processes and organization. It is now clear that the success of many of these non-U.S. firms was attributable to how they structured the work and designed their organizations. For example, Toyota's new plant in San Antonio, Texas differs in many ways from the General Motors plant in Arlington, Texas, but the nature of the workforce is not one of them.[1]

This chapter discusses the analysis and design of work and, in doing so, lays out some considerations that go into making informed decisions about how to create and link jobs. The chapter is divided into three sections, the first of which deals with "big-picture" issues related to work-flow analysis and organizational structure. The remaining two sections deal with more specific, lower-level issues related to job analysis and job design.

The fields of job analysis and job design have extensive overlap, yet in the past they have been treated differently.[2] Job analysis has focused on analyzing existing jobs to gather information for other human resource management practices such as selection, training, performance appraisal, and compensation. Job design, on the other hand, has focused on redesigning existing jobs to make them more efficient or more motivating to jobholders.[3] Thus job design has had a more proactive orientation toward changing the job, whereas job analysis has had a passive, information-gathering orientation. However, as we will show in this chapter, these two approaches are interrelated.

Work-Flow Analysis and Organization Structure

In the past, HR professionals and line managers have tended to analyze or design a particular job in isolation from the larger organizational context. *Work-flow design* is the process of analyzing the tasks necessary for the production of a product or service, prior to allocating and assigning these tasks to a particular job category or person. Only after we thoroughly understand work-flow design can we make informed decisions regarding how to initially bundle various tasks into discrete jobs that can be executed by a single person.

Organization structure refers to the relatively stable and formal network of vertical and horizontal interconnections among jobs that constitute the organization. Only after we understand how one job relates to those above (supervisors), below (subordinates), and at the same level in different functional areas (marketing versus production) can we make informed decisions about how to redesign or improve jobs to benefit the entire organization.

Finally, work-flow design and organization structure have to be understood in the context of how an organization has decided to compete. Both work-flow design and organization structure can be leveraged to gain competitive advantage for the firm, but how one does this depends on the firm's strategy and its competitive environment.

LOI
Analyze an organization's structure and work-flow process, identifying the output, activities, and inputs in the production of a product or service.

Work-Flow Analysis

A theme common to nearly all organizations is the need to identify clearly the outputs of work, to specify the quality and quantity standards for those outputs, and to analyze the processes and inputs necessary for producing outputs that meet the quality standards.[4] This conception of the work-flow process is useful because it provides a means for the manager to understand all the tasks required to produce a number of high-quality products as well as the skills necessary to perform those tasks. This work-flow process is depicted in Figure 4.1. In this section we present an approach for analyzing the work process of a department as a means of examining jobs in the context of an organization.

Analyzing Work Outputs

Every work unit—whether a department, team, or individual—seeks to produce some output that others can use. An output is the product of a work unit and is often an identifiable thing, such as a completed purchase order, an employment test, or a hot, juicy hamburger. However, an output can also be a service, such as the services provided by an airline that transports you to some destination, a housecleaning service that maintains your house, or a baby-sitter who watches over your children.

figure 4.1

Developing a
Work-Unit Activity
Analysis

We often picture an organization only in terms of the product that it produces, and then we focus on that product as the output. So, for example, in our opening story, the product for Toyota is an automobile. Merely identifying an output or set of outputs is not sufficient. Once these outputs have been identified, it is necessary to specify standards for the quantity or quality of these outputs. For example, a productivity improvement technique known as ProMES (productivity measurement and evaluation system) focuses attention on both identifying work-unit outputs and specifying the levels of required performance for different levels of effectiveness.[5] With ProMES, the members of a work unit identify each of the products (outputs) of the work unit for the various customers. They then evaluate the effectiveness of each level of products in the eyes of their customers. A recent large-scale review of more than 80 studies of firms that have applied the ProMES system suggests that the use of this system for improving work flow results in large improvements in productivity that can last for many years.

Analyzing Work Processes

Once the outputs of the work unit have been identified, it is possible to examine the work processes used to generate the output. The work processes are the activities that members of a work unit engage in to produce a given output. Every process consists of operating procedures that specify how things should be done at each stage of the development of the product. These procedures include all the tasks that must be performed in the production of the output. The tasks are usually broken down into those performed by each person in the work unit. Of course, in many situations where the work that needs to be done is highly complex, no single individual is likely to have all the required skills. In these situations, the work may be assigned to a team, and team-based job design is becoming increasingly popular in contemporary organizations.[6] In addition to providing a wider set of skills, team members can back each other up, share work when any member becomes overloaded, and catch each other's errors.

Teams are not a panacea, however, and for teams to be effective, it is essential that the level of task interdependence (how much they have to cooperate) matches the level of outcome interdependence (how much they share the reward for task accomplishment).[7] That is, if work is organized around teams, team bonuses rather than individual pay raises need to play a major role in terms of defining rewards. Teams also have to be given the autonomy to make their own decisions in order to maximize the flexible use of their skill and time and thus promote problem solving.[8] In addition, some members of teams may lean too much on the other team members and fail to develop their own skills or take responsibility for their own tasks, and so even in teams it is critical to establish individual accountability of behavior.[9]

For example, Louis Vuitton, the maker of top-of-the-line bags and purses, used to design work processes centered on individuals. In this old system, each Vuitton worker did a highly specialized tasks (cutting leather and canvas, stitching seams, attaching the handle, and so on), and then, when each person was finished, he or she would sequentially send the bag to the next person in line. A typical line would be staffed by 20 to 30 people. In 2006, the company switched to a team-based design where teams of six to nine people all work together simultaneously to assemble the bags. Workers are cross-trained in multiple tasks and can flexibly change roles and shift production from one bag to another if any one bag becomes a "hit" and another becomes a "dud." The length of time it took to produce the same bags dropped from eight days to one day, and Vuitton customers, who had often had to be placed on waiting lists for their most popular products, were able to get their hands on the product much more quickly. This speed to market is critical given the emotional nature of this purchase—after all, if one is ready to spend $700 on a tote bag, it is best not to have to delay that decision.[10]

Again, to design work systems that are maximally efficient, a manager needs to understand the processes required in the development of the products for that work unit. Often, as workloads increase within a work group, the group will grow by adding positions to meet these new requirements. However, when the workload lightens, members may take on tasks that do not relate to the work unit's product in an effort to appear busy. Without a clear understanding of the tasks necessary to the production of an output, it is difficult to determine whether the work unit has become overstaffed. Understanding the tasks required allows the manager to specify which tasks are to be carried out by which individuals and eliminate tasks that are not necessary for the desired end. This ensures that the work group maintains a high level of productivity.

The notion of "lean production" was pioneered by Toyota, the company in our opening vignette, but this idea has spread to many other companies that performed intense studies of their own work processes to find and eliminate waste, redundancies, and inefficiencies. For example, IBM shed 14,000 jobs between 2003 and 2006 in an effort to thin management ranks at its bureaucratic European operations. Much of the work of these former "managers" was pushed down to individual consultants who were given greater autonomy to make their own decisions. In addition to shedding layers of management, IBM shut down and sold corporate office space and workers were told to work at home, at the clients location, or at smaller satellite offices distributed throughout the world.[11] Indeed, as the "Competing through Technology"

This job may look tedious or possibly even uninteresting. Considering how to engage employees in seeing the benefits of their work outside of the lab is an important way to motivate them through their day.

box illustrates, lean production not only increases current efficiency, it also helps buffer workers from layoffs when economic conditions worsen.

IBM is not the only company focused on eliminating midlevel managers. For example, at Unifi Inc., a textile producer, factory equipment is connected via high-speed data lines so that shop floor data can be relayed in real time to analysts at corporate headquarters, eliminating the need for local supervisors.[12] This kind of remote monitoring is becoming especially popular in multinational corporations as a means of standardizing work outputs. Although not all employees respond positively to technological changes in the nature of work, such changes are becoming increasingly critical in competing in the contemporary business environment.[13]

Analyzing Work Inputs

The final stage in work-flow analysis is to identify the inputs used in the development of the work unit's product. As shown in Figure 4.1, these inputs can be broken down into the raw materials, equipment, and human skills needed to perform the tasks. *Raw materials* consist of the materials that will be converted into the work unit's product. *Equipment* refers to the technology and machinery necessary to transform the raw materials into the product. The final inputs in the work-flow process are the *human skills* and efforts necessary to perform the tasks. Obviously, the human skills consist of the workers available to the company, but increasingly organizations are recruiting the inputs of customers as a critical input or designing processes and products. For example, at Xerox, the organization was developing a two-engine model of a copier, with one engine driving standard black-and-white printing tasks, and the second one driving color tasks. One of the customers noted that what would be better was a two-engine model, where the second engine could drive both tasks in emergency cases when the first engine shut down. All of the customers on the design team loved this idea, which had never really crossed the minds of the engineering team. The result was the new Nuvera 288 Digital Perfecting System, that became one of Xerox's top-selling models. As team leader Steve Hoover noted, "the team had a certain idea of what customers wanted, but actually talking to them really changed that."[14]

To compete successfully, organizations often have to scour the world for the best raw materials, the best equipment, and the people with the best skills, and then try to integrate all of this seamlessly in the work processes that merge all these factors. As we have seen, IBM has been on the forefront of incorporating new technological equipment in the processes, in order to eliminate office space and reduce middle layers of management. This company has also searched high and wide for people with the best sets of skills as well. For example, symbolically, IBM's 2006 Annual Investors Meeting was held in Bangalore, India.

India is central to IBM's future because it is a source of high-skilled, low-cost talent, especially in the area of software development. Indeed, the size of IBM's staff in India

Any amount of job loss in a large economy results in a great deal of human suffering—and this includes the losses experienced during the recent recession of 2008–2009. However, among those who closely study the relationship between the general health of the economy and employment levels, a paradox of the most recent recession is how small many of the layoffs in the manufacturing sector of the economy were, given the huge drop in production levels. For example, 14 months into the recession of 2000, manufacturers cut 9.5 percent of their employees in response to a 2 percent cut in production. In contrast, 14 months into the most recent recession, the same 9.5 percent of employees were laid off in response to a 12 percent cut in production. If the same ratio of job cuts to production cuts from the year 2000 held in the year 2009, this would have resulted in an astounding layoff rate of more than 50 percent of manufacturing employees.

Many have attributed the lower job cut–to–production cut ratio experienced in the most recent recession to the use of job redesign initiatives that emphasize lean production over more traditional approaches. *Lean production* refers to processes developed in Japan, but then adopted worldwide, emphasizing manufacturing goods with a minimum amount of time, materials, money—and most importantly—people. Lean production tries to leverage technology, along with small numbers of flexible, well-trained, and skilled personnel in order to produce more custom-based products at less cost. This can be contrasted with more traditional "batch work" methods, where large groups of low-skilled employees churn out long runs of identical mass products that are stored in inventories for later sale. In lean production systems, there are fewer employees to begin with, and the skill levels of those employees are so high that the opportunity to cut costs by laying off employees is simply less viable.

For example, at Parker Hannifan Corporation's plastics manufacturing plant in South Carolina, lean production techniques have cut the number of people required to run the plant to such a small number that permanently pulling one highly trained person off the line saves very little money, and yet makes it impossible to sustain production at all. In addition, the work has been restructured to create smaller production runs that result in reduced inventories, so that when a downturn hits, it is noticed more quickly and can be responded to more gradually. In the past, by the time a recession was detected, inventories had bulged to such a level that more employees had to be laid off more quickly and for longer time periods.

Indeed, in some cases, inventories are being abandoned altogether, and companies at the edge of the lean production process do not even manufacture any products until customers actually place an order for them. For example, surgical device maker Conmed used to forecast demand for its products one to two months ahead, and when those forecasts turned out to be inaccurate, it would either lose sales or stockpile inventories. Today, because the length of time it takes to produce its devices has decreased from six weeks to 48 hours, they do not even manufacture any products that are not already sold. The impact of this can be seen at Conmed's plant in Utica, New York, where a $93,000 inventory that used to take up 3,300 square feet on the factory floor has been all but eliminated. This allowed the company to take back lost sales from Chinese competitors that, despite their lower labor costs, face the costs of long lead times, inventory pileups, and quality problems and transportation costs. As David Johnson, vice president for global operations at Conmed notes, "If more U.S. companies deploy these job design methods we can compete with anybody and still provide security to our workforce."

SOURCES: T. Aeppel and J. Lahart, "Lean Factories Find It Hard to Cut Jobs Even in a Slump," *The Wall Street Journal,* March 9, 2009, pp. B2–B3; A. Taylor, "Lean Times: What Caterpillar Can Learn," *Fortune,* January 29, 2009, pp. 35–37; P. Engardio, "Lean and Mean Gets Extreme," *BusinessWeek,* March 23, 2009, pp. 60–62.

surged from 9,000 to 43,000 between 2003 and 2006. However, this is just one part of the puzzle. Some of IBM operations require high-skill employees who have to work on-site with hardware issues in close proximity to U.S. customers, and hence IBM also opened a new center in Boulder, Colorado. IBM also needs the very narrow skills of people with doctorates in the hard sciences, and thus it opened a research lab in Yorktown Heights, New York. Some low-skill jobs that IBM needs are done by workers from China, Brazil, or eastern Europe, depending on where the call originates and the language spoken by the customer. The key to this strategy is not just going where one can get cheap labor, but, instead, going where one can get just the exact kind of labor needed at the best price. As noted by Robert Moffat, IBM's senior vice president, "Some people think the world is centered in India and that's it. Globalization is more than that. Our customers need the right skills, in the right place at the right time."[15]

Indeed research consistently shows that creating a good fit between the skills and values of workers and the tasks and missions they are assigned is a powerful determinant of organizational success that cannot be taken lightly.[16] As the "Competing through Globalization" box shows, new technologies such as "innovation portals" can help promote the speed with which global teams can be created, coordinated, and monitored to enhance organizational effectiveness.

Organization Structure

Whereas work-flow design provides a longitudinal overview of the dynamic relationships by which inputs are converted into outputs, organization structure provides a cross-sectional overview of the static relationships between individuals and units that create the outputs. Organization structure is typically displayed via organizational charts that convey both vertical reporting relationships and horizontal functional responsibilities.

Dimensions of Structure

Centralization
Degree to which decision-making authority resides at the top of the organizational chart.

Departmentalization
Degree to which work units are grouped based on functional similarity or similarity of work flow.

Two of the most critical dimensions of organization structure are centralization and departmentalization. **Centralization** refers to the degree to which decision-making authority resides at the top of the organizational chart as opposed to being distributed throughout lower levels (in which case authority is *decentralized*). **Departmentalization** refers to the degree to which work units are grouped based on functional similarity or similarity of work flow.

For example, a school of business could be organized around functional similarity so that there would be a marketing department, a finance department, and an accounting department, and faculty within these specialized departments would each teach their area of expertise to all kinds of students. Alternatively, one could organize the same school around work-flow similarity, so that there would be an undergraduate unit, a graduate unit, and an executive development unit. Each of these units would have its own marketing, finance, and accounting professors who taught only their own respective students and not those of the other units.

Structural Configurations

Although there are an infinite number of ways to combine centralization and departmentalization, two common configurations of organization structure tend to emerge in organizations. The first type, referred to as a *functional structure*, is shown in Figure 4.2. A functional structure, as the name implies, employs a functional departmentalization scheme with relatively high levels of centralization. High levels of

Due to the increased complexity of work, as well as the increased demand to compete based upon speed, most organizations have changed the job design process from one focused on individual, stand-alone jobs toward jobs that were designed for teams. Increasingly, however, the globalization of product and labor markets has created additional pressure for quick collaboration within global teams. One response to this demand has been the creation of "innovation portals," that is, technology that helps individual employees with a problem or innovative idea to tap into the global network of talent within the organization or even outside its own boundaries.

For example, at IBM, innovation portals take the form of specially designated "chat rooms," where any employee with a new idea or project can recruit team members, line up resources, and tap into market research or engineering skills available anywhere within this large and sprawling multinational firm. An entrepreneurial IBM employee can often create a virtual global team with cross-functional skills to tackle some problem in as little as two hours. For example, in one case, when a client needed to launch a new service that would allow video streaming for cell phones, an IBM project leader was able to organize a 20-person team that included staff from 10 different countries in just two weeks. The entire project was completed within two months. On average, IBM's own internal research suggests that the use of such portals has decreased the length of time it takes to get projects up and running from six months to 30 days. In the last three years alone, IBM has employed more than 90,000 workers in such global teams, and these groups have been responsible for leading 70 new businesses and creating 10 new products.

Because of its size and global scope, IBM tends to use its portals to create teams where all the members are IBM employees. This is often not an option for smaller firms that are not international in their scope. Hence, many smaller firms use innovation portals to link specialists within their own companies to independent contractors or specialists in other companies. There are many different models for such global collaboration, but the key dimensions by which most differ deal with how well structured the problem is and how dominant any one member of the team is in terms of command and control. For example, the "Orchestra Model" of global teams is one where there is a well-structured problem and one dominant member of the team who controls the process. For example, the Boeing 787 project used a portal owned by Boeing to recruit partners from their own list of suppliers but also included independent contractors to help develop components for Boeing's new airplane. Boeing was clearly in control of this well-scripted and planned project, but it was able to reach far outside its own local talent base to create global teams for accomplishing complex tasks.

Alternatively, some portals follow a "Jam Session Model" of global teaming, where the problem is unstructured and there are no dominant members. For example, the Tropical Disease Initiative was an innovation portal project where many different academics and scientists concerned about fighting global diseases came together to take on diseases that were not widespread enough to create a strong profit potential for commercial pharmaceutical teams. This democratically led community of scientists tended to focus not on well-structured problems (e.g., curing malaria), but instead focused on emergent opportunities, where some new finding in the scientific literature was studied for its potential to provide assistance in treating any of a large number of diseases off a fixed list of "unprofitable diseases."

Regardless of what model is employed, innovation portals create opportunities to create global teams that can accomplish tasks that are well beyond the scope of any one of its members.

SOURCES: P. Engardio, "Managing a Global Workforce," *BusinessWeek,* August 20, 2007, pp. 48–51; J. Marquez, "Connecting a Virtual Workforce," *Workforce Management,* September 22, 2008, pp. 18–28; S. Nambison and M. Sawhney, *The Global Brain,* (Philadelphia, PA: Wharton School Publishing, 2008).

figure 4.2

The Functional Structure

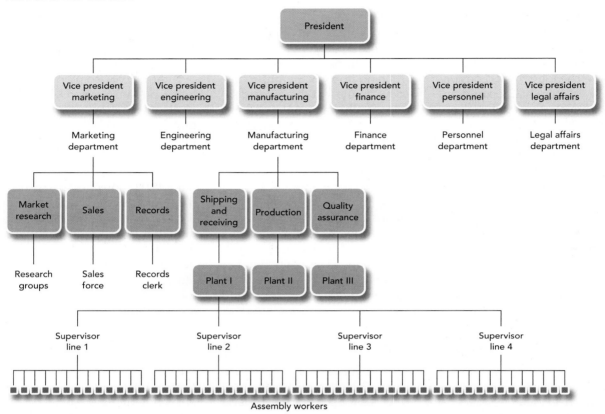

SOURCE: Adapted from J. A. Wagner and J. R. Hollenbeck, *Organizational Behavior: Securing Competitive Advantage*, 3rd ed. (New York: Prentice Hall, 1998).

centralization tend to go naturally with functional departmentalization because individual units in the structures are so specialized that members of the unit may have a weak conceptualization of the overall organization mission. Thus, they tend to identify with their department and cannot always be relied on to make decisions that are in the best interests of the organization as a whole.

Alternatively, a second common configuration is a *divisional structure*, three examples of which are shown in Figures 4.3, 4.4, and 4.5. Divisional structures combine a divisional departmentalization scheme with relatively low levels of centralization. Units in these structures act almost like separate, self-sufficient, semi-autonomous organizations. The organization shown in Figure 4.3 is divisionally organized around different products; the organization shown in Figure 4.4 is divisionally organized around geographic regions; and the organization shown in Figure 4.5 is divisionally organized around different clients.

Because of their work-flow focus, their semi-autonomous nature, and their proximity to a homogeneous consumer base, divisional structures tend to be more flexible and innovative. They can detect and exploit opportunities in their respective consumer base faster than the more centralized functionally structured organizations. The perceived autonomy that goes along with this kind of structure also means that most

figure 4.3

Divisional Structure: Product Structure

SOURCE: Adapted from J. A. Wagner and J. R. Hollenbeck, *Organizational Behavior: Securing Competitive Advantage*, 3rd ed. (New York: Prentice Hall, 1998).

figure 4.4

Divisional Structure: Geographic Structure

SOURCE: Adapted from J. A. Wagner and J. R. Hollenbeck, *Organizational Behavior: Securing Competitive Advantage*, 3rd ed. (New York: Prentice Hall, 1998).

employees prefer it and feel they are more fairly treated than when they are subject to centralized decision-making structures.[17] An example of this structure can be seen at Microsoft, which converted from a functional structure to a divisional structure. Throughout the 1990s, revenue growth at Microsoft averaged more than 30 percent per year, making it one of the most successful business organizations in the world. However, with success comes new challenges, and both external and internal pressures created problems that have cut into Microsoft's dominance. Internally, as the organization increased in size and scope, the decision-making process at Microsoft was slowing to a crawl, and Microsoft experienced turnover among key personnel, many of whom became millionaires as the company grew, but whose intrinsic motivation was low because they did not feel that they had enough autonomy in their jobs. As one manager noted, "In the past, the system was optimized for people to get stuff done. Now, everybody is always preparing for a meeting."[18]

figure 4.5

Divisional Structure: Client Structure

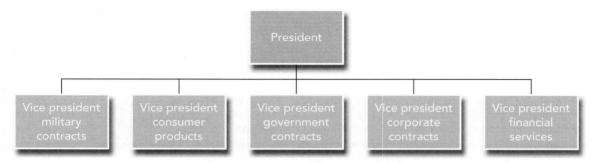

SOURCE: Adapted from J. A. Wagner and J. R. Hollenbeck, *Organizational Behavior: Securing Competitive Advantage,* 3rd ed. (New York: Prentice Hall, 1998).

To turn this situation around, CEO Steve Ballmer took unprecedented steps in strategically restructuring the organization to respond to these new competitive pressures. The question guiding this reorganization was how best to divvy up the 55,000 Microsoft employees and define their jobs so that innovation and productivity could be maximized, while turnover and bureaucratic impediments could be minimized. Turning first to the organization's structure, it was clear that Microsoft was too centralized given its current size.

Ballmer wanted to decentralize the organization and create a large number of semiautonomous business divisions (e.g., a Personal Computer Division, a Server Division, a Gaming Division) that had responsibility for their own profit and loss figures. Some leaders at Microsoft initially resisted this move, however, because they felt that all Microsoft products had to work seamlessly together, and independent divisions would not provide for effective coordination and collaboration across units. Ballmer realized, "We'd have to come up with a structure unlike anything out there, to simultaneously give divisions enough autonomy to manage themselves, yet make it easier for them to cooperate and integrate the technology."[19]

The solution was a structure that relied on seven autonomous divisions that were supported by a new concept in workflow design that formalized how product development would both proceed within divisions and then be transferred across divisions. The seven divisions divided the work up into separate units for operating systems (Windows Client), desktop applications (Information Worker), business services, (Business Solutions), servers systems (Server and Tools), mobile devices (Mobile and Embedded Devices), Internet services (MSN), and X-Box and other gaming applications (Home Entertainment). Within each unit, a new product development process called the Software Engineering Strategy laid out a universally applied procedure that dictated how a project moved from the "incubator phase" to the "definer phase" to the "owner phase," stipulating where the "participants," "reviewers," and "coaches" should provide input into the process."[20]

On the one hand, one of the immediate results of the new structure was that it clearly revealed how much money was being lost in certain divisions such as MSN and the Home Entertainment Divisions relative to the tried-and-true Windows Client Division. Although disheartening in some cases, this at least provided a benchmark from which to measure improvement as the divisions moved forward. More critically, however, these structural changes at the organization level spilled down to individual jobs, both clarifying who was supposed to do what and motivating individuals to sink or swim in their new, more autonomous roles. This helped reduce the turnover rates among the key players by increasing their intrinsic motivation. As one of Microsoft's new division leaders noted, all the new divisional managers "sense a chance to do one last great thing in their working lives," and this is the type of attitude that may help propel Microsoft back to the lofty rates of growth that it once enjoyed.

However, on the downside, divisional structures are not very efficient because of the redundancy associated with each group carrying its own functional specialists. Also, divisional structures can "self-cannibalize" if the gains achieved in one unit come at the expense of another unit. For example, Kinko's stores are structured divisionally with highly decentralized control. Each manager can set his or her own price and has autonomy to make his or her own decisions. But the drawback to this is lack of coordination in the sense that "every Kinko's store considers every other Kinko's store a competitor; they vie against each other for work, they bid against each other competing on price."[21] The exact same problem has been cited at Whole Foods Markets, which operates 189 stores throughout the United States. Whole Foods' stores emphasize organic produce, and individual store managers are encouraged to be entrepreneurial, with little guidance from central headquarters. Same-store sales growth at Whole Foods was averaging 15 percent in 2004 but was down to 6 percent in 2006, largely because of competition between one Whole Foods store and another.[22]

Lack of coordination caused by decentralized and divisional structures can be especially problematic with new and emerging organizations that do not have a great deal of history or firmly established culture. Higher levels of centralization and more functional design of work make it easier in this context to keep everyone on the same page while the business builds experience.[23] Decentralized and divisional structures can also create problems if the stand-alone divisions start making decisions that are overly risky or out of line with the organization's larger goals. For example, many analysts felt that many of the problems associated with the near bankruptcy of Citibank in 2009 were caused by excessive risk taking in several autonomous divisions that were not being closely monitored by any centralized authority. This was especially the case with the division that managed collateralized debt obligations (CDOs). Many conservative banking analysts warned that CDOs and other similar derivatives spread risk and uncertainty throughout the economy more widely and did little to reduce risk through diversification. This belief was validated in the 2008 recession, when the housing market crashed and thousands of people defaulted on their mortgages.[24]

Alternatively, functional structures are very efficient, with little redundancy across units, and provide little opportunity for self-cannibalization or for rogue units running wild. Also, although the higher level of oversight in centralized structures tends to reduce the number of errors made by lower level workers, when errors do occur in overly centralized systems, they tend to cascade through the system as a whole more quickly and can, therefore, be more debilitating. For example, when there was a blackout throughout a large part of the East and Midwest in the summer of 2003, many felt that the overly centralized nature of the nation's power grid was a major source of this crisis.[25] Moreover, these structures tend to be inflexible and insensitive to subtle differences across products, regions, or clients.

Functional structures are most appropriate in stable, predictable environments, where demand for resources can be well anticipated and coordination requirements between jobs can be refined and standardized over consistent repetitions of activity. This type of structure also helps support organizations that compete on cost, because efficiency is central to make this strategy work. Divisional structures are most appropriate in unstable, unpredictable environments, where it is difficult to anticipate demands for resources, and coordination requirements between jobs are not consistent over time. This type of structure also helps support organizations that compete on differentiation or innovation, because flexible responsiveness is central to making this strategy work. To increase their flexibility, many contemporary organizations are changing in the direction away from functional structures to more divisional structures, but this is often more difficult than it seems.[26] In many cases, norms and habits that are often created by the original structure persist even after the boxes on the organization chart have been rearranged, and the cultural influences can be as important as structural influences when it comes to determining outcomes of such transitions.[27]

Structure and the Nature of Jobs

Finally, moving from big-picture issues to lower-level specifics, the type of organization structure also has implications for the design of jobs. Jobs in functional structures need to be narrow and highly specialized. Workers in these structures (even middle managers) tend to have little decision-making authority or responsibility for managing coordination between themselves and others. For example, at Nucor Steel, production at its 30 minimill plants has doubled almost every two years and profit margins have pushed beyond 10 percent largely because of its flat, divisional structure. At Nucor, individual plant managers have wide autonomy in how to design work at their own mills. Nucor plants sometimes compete against each other, but the CEO makes sure that the competition is healthy, and that best practices are distributed throughout the organization as fast as possible, preventing any long-term sustainable advantage to any one plant. Moreover, the profit-sharing plan that makes up the largest part of people's pay operates at the organizational level, which also promotes collaboration among managers who want to make sure that every plant is successful. Thus, after taking over a new mill for the first time, one new plant manager got a call or visit from every other manager, offering advice and assistance. As the new manager noted, "It wasn't idle politeness. I took them up on it. My performance impacted their paycheck."[28]

Nucor employs just four levels of management and operates a headquarters of just 66 people, compared to one of its competitors, U.S. Steel, which has over 20 levels and 1,200 people at its headquarters. This gives Nucor a long-term sustainable competitive advantage, which it has held for close to 15 years. Sales at Nucor grew from $4.5 billion in 2000 to over $13 billion in 2006. During the same period, U.S. Steel's volume decreased by 6 percent. This has translated into success for both investors (roughly 400 percent return on investment in the last five years) and workers, whose wages average $100,000 a year, compared to $70,000 a year at U.S. Steel. As one industry analyst notes, "In terms of a business model, Nucor has won this part of the world," and much of that victory can be explained by their superior structure and process for managing work.[29]

The choice of structure also has implications for people who would assume the jobs created in functional versus divisional structures. For example, managers of divisional structures often need to be more experienced or high in cognitive ability relative to managers of functional structures.[30] The relatively smaller scope and routine nature of jobs created in centralized and functional structures make them less sensitive to individual differences between workers. The nature of the structure also has implications for relationships, in the sense that in centralized and functional structures people tend to think of fairness in terms or rules and procedures, whereas in decentralized and divisional structures, they tend to think of fairness in terms of outcomes and how they are treated interpersonally.[31] For example, Netflix, the online video rental service, is widely recognized as an employer that tends to give a wide degree of autonomy to managers. CEO Reed Hastings tends to pay managers very well and gives them unlimited vacation time. They are also free to structure their own compensation package (cash versus stock) as well as the way they do their own work. In return, Hastings expects extremely high performance and accountability. Indeed, as marketing manager Heather McIlhany notes, "Netflix has a tough but fulfilling culture that will only work with fully formed adults who are not looking for a place to hide or pass the buck." This combination of freedom and responsibility among its workers has helped Netflix fight off many competitors, including Wal-Mart, who briefly ventured into the online video rental business. Many thought that Wal-Mart would put an end to Netflix, but after several years of failing to make inroads into this market, Wal-Mart pulled out in 2007 and referred all of its former customers to Netflix.[32]

Finally, flatter structures also have implications for organizational culture in terms of ethics and accountability. For example, in 2004, in a highly public scandal, Putnam Investments was fined $110 million for engaging in "market timing," that is, jumping quickly in and out of funds in order to take advantage of momentary market inefficiencies. This is considered an unethical practice within the industry because it increases fund expenses which, in turn, harms long-term investors. Many long-term investors left the organization, some of whom had more than $800 million being managed by Putnam.

According to Putnam insiders, the organization's tall and narrow organizational structure created a situation in which too many people were managing other people and telling them what they had to do to get promoted. Because the only way to earn more money at Putnam was to climb the corporate ladder, too much pressure was put on managers and employees alike to boost short-term results in order to attract the attention of those high above. The culture was one where people tended to ask "What is the fine for this?" instead of "What does this do to help my clients?" When new CEO Ed Haldeman was brought in to repair the damage, one of his first steps was to remove hundreds of salespeople, and then flatten the structure. The goal was to attract a different kind of employee, who would be less interested in short-term gains and hierarchical promotions handed out by others and more interested in establishing personal long-term relationships with customers and more collaborative relationships with colleagues. In Haldeman's words, "To retain and attract the best people, it's necessary to provide them with autonomy and independence to make their own decisions."[33]

In our next section, we cover specific approaches for analyzing and designing jobs. Although all of these approaches are viable, each focuses on a single, isolated job. These approaches do not necessarily consider how that single job fits into the overall work flow or structure of the organization. Thus, to use these techniques effectively, we have to understand the organization as a whole. Without this big-picture appreciation, we might redesign a job in a way that might be good for that one job but out of line with the work flow, structure, or strategy of the organization. In an effectively structured organization, people not only know how their job fits into the bigger picture, they know how everyone else fits as well. Thus, when one of Microsoft's managers says, "I'm not confused about who to go to in order to get something done—there's greater clarity now," this is a sign that the new structure may be meeting the internal needs of the organization's members.[34]

Job Analysis

Job Analysis
The process of getting detailed information about jobs.

Job analysis refers to the process of getting detailed information about jobs. Job analysis has deep historical roots. For example, in his description of the "just" state, Socrates argued that society needed to recognize three things. First, there are individual differences in aptitudes for work, meaning that individuals differ in their abilities. Second, unique aptitude requirements exist for different occupations. Third, to achieve high-quality performance, society must attempt to place people in occupations that best suit their aptitudes. In other words, for society (or an organization) to succeed, it must have detailed information about the requirements of jobs (through job analysis) and it must ensure that a match exists between the job requirements and individuals' aptitudes (through selection).[35]

Whereas Socrates was concerned with the larger society, it is even more important for organizations to understand and match job requirements and people to achieve high-quality performance. This is particularly true in today's competitive marketplace. Thus the information gained through job analysis is of utmost importance; it has great value to both human resource and line managers.

LO2
Understand the importance of job analysis in strategic human resource management.

The Importance of Job Analysis

Job analysis is such an important activity to HR managers that it has been called the building block of everything that personnel does.[36] This statement refers to the fact that almost every human resource management program requires some type of information that is gleaned from job analysis: selection, performance appraisal, training and development, job evaluation, career planning, work redesign, and human resource planning.

Work Redesign. As previously discussed, job analysis and job design are interrelated. Often a firm will seek to redesign work to make it more efficient or effective. To redesign the work, detailed information about the existing job(s) must be available. In addition, redesigning a job will, in fact, be similar to analyzing a job that does not yet exist.

Human Resource Planning. In human resource planning, planners analyze an organization's human resource needs in a dynamic environment and develop activities that enable a firm to adapt to change. This planning process requires accurate information about the levels of skill required in various jobs to ensure that enough individuals are available in the organization to meet the human resource needs of the strategic plan.[37]

Selection. Human resource selection identifies the most qualified applicants for employment. To identify which applicants are most qualified, it is first necessary to determine the tasks that will be performed by the individual hired and the knowledge, skills, and abilities the individual must have to perform the job effectively. This information is gained through job analysis.[38]

Training. Almost every employee hired by an organization will require training. Some training programs may be more extensive than others, but all require the trainer to have identified the tasks performed in the job to ensure that the training will prepare individuals to perform their jobs effectively.[39]

Performance Appraisal. Performance appraisal deals with getting information about how well each employee is performing in order to reward those who are effective, improve the performance of those who are ineffective, or provide a written justification for why the poor performer should be disciplined. Through job analysis, the organization can identify the behaviors and results that distinguish effective performance from ineffective performance.[40]

Career Planning. Career planning entails matching an individual's skills and aspirations with opportunities that are or may become available in the organization. This matching process requires that those in charge of career planning know the skill requirements of the various jobs. This allows them to guide individuals into jobs in which they will succeed and be satisfied.

Job Evaluation. The process of job evaluation involves assessing the relative dollar value of each job to the organization to set up internally equitable pay structures. If pay structures are not equitable, employees will be dissatisfied and quit, or they will not see the benefits of striving for promotions. To put dollar values on jobs, it is necessary to get information about different jobs to determine which jobs deserve higher pay than others.[41]

The Importance of Job Analysis to Line Managers

Job analysis is clearly important to the HR department's various activities, but why it is important to line managers may not be as clear. There are many reasons. First, managers must have detailed information about all the jobs in their work group to understand the work-flow process. Second, managers need to understand the job requirements to make intelligent hiring decisions. Very seldom do employees get hired by the human resource department without a manager's input. Managers will often interview prospective applicants and recommend who should receive a job offer. Third, a manager is responsible for ensuring that each individual is performing satisfactorily (or better). This requires the manager to evaluate how well each person is performing and to provide feedback to those whose performance needs improvement. Again, this requires that the manager clearly understand the tasks required in every job. Finally, it is also the manager's responsibility to ensure that the work is being done safely, knowing where potential hazards might manifest themselves and creating a climate where people feel free to interrupt the production process if dangerous conditions exist.[42]

Job Analysis Information

Nature of Information

Two types of information are most useful in job analysis: job descriptions and job specifications. A **job description** is a list of the tasks, duties, and responsibilities (TDRs) that a job entails. TDRs are observable actions. For example, a clerical job requires the jobholder to type. If you were to observe someone in that position for a day, you would certainly see some typing. When a manager attempts to evaluate job performance, it is most important to have detailed information about the work performed in the job (that is, the TDRs). This makes it possible to determine how well an individual is meeting each job requirement. Table 4.1 shows a sample job description.

A **job specification** is a list of the knowledge, skills, abilities, and other characteristics (KSAOs) that an individual must have to perform the job. *Knowledge* refers to factual or procedural information that is necessary for successfully performing a

Job Description
A list of the tasks, duties, and responsibilities that a job entails.

Job Specification
A list of the knowledge, skills, abilities, and other characteristics (KSAOs) that an individual must have to perform a job.

table 4.1

A Sample Job
Description

> **Job Title:** Maintenance Mechanic
> **General Description of Job:** General maintenance and repair of all equipment used in the operations of a particular district. Includes the servicing of company vehicles, shop equipment, and machinery used on job sites.
>
> 1. *Essential Duty (40%): Maintenance of Equipment*
>   Tasks: Keep a log of all maintenance performed on equipment. Replace parts and fluids according to maintenance schedule. Regularly check gauges and loads for deviances that may indicate problems with equipment. Perform nonroutine maintenance as required. May involve limited supervision and training of operators performing maintenance.
>
> 2. *Essential Duty (40%): Repair of Equipment*
>   Tasks: Requires inspection of equipment and a recommendation that a piece be scrapped or repaired. If equipment is to be repaired, mechanic will take whatever steps are necessary to return the piece to working order. This may include a partial or total rebuilding of the piece using various hand tools and equipment. Will primarily involve the overhaul and troubleshooting of diesel engines and hydraulic equipment.
>
> 3. *Essential Duty (10%): Testing and Approval*
>   Tasks: Ensure that all required maintenance and repair has been performed and that it was performed according to manufacturer specifications. Approve or reject equipment as being ready for use on a job.
>
> 4. *Essential Duty (10%): Maintain Stock*
>   Tasks: Maintain inventory of parts needed for the maintenance and repair of equipment. Responsible for ordering satisfactory parts and supplies at the lowest possible cost.
>
> *Nonessential Functions*
> Other duties as assigned.

task. A *skill* is an individual's level of proficiency at performing a particular task. *Ability* refers to a more general enduring capability that an individual possesses. Finally, *other characteristics* might be personality traits such as one's achievement motivation or persistence. Thus KSAOs are characteristics about people that are not directly observable; they are observable only when individuals are carrying out the TDRs of the job. If someone applied for the clerical job discussed, you could not simply look at the individual to determine whether he or she possessed typing skills. However, if you were to observe that individual typing something, you could assess the level of typing skill. When a manager is attempting to fill a position, it is important to have accurate information about the characteristics a successful jobholder must have. This requires focusing on the KSAOs of each applicant.

Sources of Job Analysis Information

In performing the job analysis, one question that often arises is, Who should make up the group of incumbents that are responsible for providing the job analysis information? Whatever job analysis method you choose, the process of job analysis entails obtaining information from people familiar with the job. We refer to these people as *subject-matter experts* because they are experts in their knowledge of the job.

In general, it will be useful to go to the job incumbent to get the most accurate information about what is actually done on the job. This is especially the case when it is difficult to monitor the person who does the job. However, particularly when the job analysis will be used for compensation purposes, incumbents might have an incentive to exaggerate their duties. Thus, you will also want to ask others familiar with the job, such as supervisors, to look over the information generated by the job incumbent. This serves as a check to determine whether what is being done is congruent with what is supposed to be done in the job. One conclusion that can be drawn from this research is that incumbents may provide the most accurate estimates of the actual time spent performing job tasks. However, supervisors may be a more accurate source of information about the importance of job duties. Incumbents also seem more accurate in terms of assessing safety-related risk factors associated with various aspects of work, and in general the further one moves up the organizational hierarchy, the less accurate the risk assessments.[43] Although job incumbents and supervisors are the most obvious and frequently used sources of job analysis information, other sources, such as customers, can be helpful, particularly for service jobs. Finally, when it comes to analyzing skill levels, external job analysts who have more experience rating a wide range of jobs may be the best source.[44]

Job Analysis Methods

There are various methods for analyzing jobs and no "one best way." In this section, we discuss two methods for analyzing jobs: the position analysis questionnaire and the Occupational Information Network (O*NET). Although most managers may not have time to use each of these techniques in the exact manner suggested, the three provide some anchors for thinking about broad approaches, task-focused approaches, and person-oriented approaches to conducting job analysis.

LO3
Choose the right job analysis technique for a variety of human resource activities.

Position Analysis Questionnaire (PAQ)

We lead this section off with the PAQ because this is one of the broadest and most well-researched instruments for analyzing jobs. Moreover, its emphasis on inputs, processes, relationships, and outputs is consistent with the work-flow analysis approach that we used in leading off this chapter (Figure 4.1).

The PAQ is a standardized job analysis questionnaire containing 194 items.[45] These items represent work behaviors, work conditions, and job characteristics that can be generalized across a wide variety of jobs. They are organized into six sections:

1. *Information input*—Where and how a worker gets information needed to perform the job.
2. *Mental processes*—The reasoning, decision making, planning, and information processing activities that are involved in performing the job.
3. *Work output*—The physical activities, tools, and devices used by the worker to perform the job.
4. *Relationships with other persons*—The relationships with other people required in performing the job.
5. *Job context*—The physical and social contexts where the work is performed.
6. *Other characteristics*—The activities, conditions, and characteristics other than those previously described that are relevant to the job.

The job analyst is asked to determine whether each item applies to the job being analyzed. The analyst then rates the item on six scales: extent of use, amount of time, importance to the job, possibility of occurrence, applicability, and special code

table 4.2

Overall Dimensions
of the Position
Analysis
Questionnaire

Decision/communication/general responsibilities
Clerical/related activities
Technical/related activities
Service/related activities
Regular day schedule versus other work schedules
Routine/repetitive work activities
Environmental awareness
General physical activities
Supervising/coordinating other personnel
Public/customer/related contact activities
Unpleasant/hazardous/demanding environment
Nontypical work schedules

(special rating scales used with a particular item). These ratings are submitted to the PAQ headquarters, where a computer program generates a report regarding the job's scores on the job dimensions.

Research has indicated that the PAQ measures 32 dimensions and 13 overall dimensions of jobs (listed in Table 4.2) and that a given job's scores on these dimensions can be very useful. The significant database has linked scores on certain dimensions to scores on subtests of the General Aptitude Test Battery (GATB). Thus, knowing the dimension scores provides some guidance regarding the types of abilities that are necessary to perform the job. Obviously, this technique provides information about the work performed in a format that allows for comparisons across jobs, whether those jobs are similar or dissimilar. Another advantage of the PAQ is that it covers the work context as well as inputs, outputs, and processes.

In spite of its widespread use, the PAQ is not without problems. One problem is that to fill out the test, an employee needs the reading level of a college graduate; this disqualifies some job incumbents from the PAQ. In fact, it is recommended that only job analysts trained in how to use the PAQ should complete the questionnaire, rather than job incumbents or supervisors. Indeed, the ratings of job incumbents tend to be lower in reliability relative to ratings from supervisors or trained job analysts.[46] A second problem associated with the PAQ is that its general, standardized format leads to rather abstract characterizations of jobs. Thus it does not lend itself well to describing the specific, concrete task activities that comprise the actual job, and it is not ideal for developing job descriptions or redesigning jobs. Methods that do focus on this aspect of the work are needed if this is the goal.

The Occupational Information Network (O*NET)

The *Dictionary of Occupational Titles* (DOT) was born during the 1930s and served as a vehicle for helping the new public employment system link the demand for skills and the supply of skills in the U.S. workforce. Although this system served the country well for more than 60 years, it became clear to officials at the U.S. Department of Labor that jobs in the new economy were so qualitatively different from jobs in the old economy, that the DOT no longer served its purpose. Technological changes in the nature of work, global competition, and a shift from stable, fixed manufacturing jobs to a more flexible, dynamic, service-based economy were quickly making the system obsolete.[47]

For all these reasons, the Department of Labor abandoned the DOT in 1998 and developed an entirely new system for classifying jobs referred to as the Occupational Information Network, or O*NET. Instead of relying on fixed job titles and narrow task descriptions, the O*NET uses a common language that generalizes across jobs to describe the abilities, work styles, work activities, and work context required for various occupations that are more broadly defined (e.g., instead of the 12,000 jobs in the DOT, the O*NET describes only 1,000 occupations).[48] Although it was developed to analyze jobs in the U.S. economy, research suggests that the ratings tend to be transportable across countries. That is, if one holds the job title constant (e.g., first-line supervisor, office clerk, computer programmer), the ratings of the job tend to be the same even if the job is located in a different country.[49]

The O*NET is being used by many employers and employment agencies. For example, after closing its Seattle-based headquarters, Boeing used the O*NET system to help find new jobs for the workers who were laid off because of the impending move.[50] The State of Texas has used the O*NET to identify emerging occupations within the state whose requisite knowledge, skills, and abilities are underrepresented in the current occupational system. This information will be used to help train Texas residents to be prepared for the jobs of the future. Finally, educational organizations like the Boys and Girls Clubs of America have used the O*NET to help design activities for children from disadvantaged backgrounds that would improve their standing on skills that are likely to be needed by future employers.[51]

Although these examples show its value for employers, the O*NET was also designed to help job seekers. For example, the O*NET seems particularly well suited to describing the literacy requirements associated with alternative jobs. Thus, individuals who want to improve their ability to find employment can obtain relatively accurate information about what jobs they are qualified for given their current literacy level from the O*NET. They can also see how much their literacy skills would have to improve if they wanted to apply for higher-level jobs characterized by higher levels of complexity.[52] To see if you think this new system meets the goal of promoting "the effective education, training, counseling, and employment needs of the American workforce," visit its Web site yourself at http://online.onetcenter.org/ and see if the skills it lists for your current job or your "dream job" match what you know from your own experiences and expectations.

Dynamic Elements of Job Analysis

Although we tend to view jobs as static and stable, in fact, jobs tend to change and evolve over time. Those who occupy or manage the jobs often make minor, cumulative adjustments to the job that try to match either changing conditions in the environment or personal preferences for how to conduct the work.[53] Indeed, although there are numerous sources for error in the job analysis process,[54] most inaccuracy is likely to result from job descriptions simply being outdated. For this reason, in addition to statically defining the job, the job analysis process must also detect changes in the nature of jobs.

For example, in today's world of rapidly changing products and markets, some people have begun to question whether the concept of "the job" is simply a social artifact that has outlived its usefulness. Indeed, many researchers and practitioners are pointing to a trend referred to as "dejobbing" in organizations. This trend consists of viewing organizations as a field of work needing to be done rather than a set of discrete jobs held by specific individuals. For example, at Amazon.com, HR director

LO4
Identify the tasks performed and the skills required in a given job.

Scott Pitasky notes, "Here, a person might be in the same 'job,' but three months later be doing completely different work."[55] This means Amazon.com puts more emphasis on broad worker specifications ("entrepreneurial and customer-focused") than on detailed job descriptions ("C++ programming") that may not be descriptive one year down the road.

Also, jobs tend to change with changes in the economy in the sense that economic downturns tend to be associated with organizational downsizing efforts. Research suggests that successful downsizing efforts almost always entail some changes in the nature, and not just the number, of jobs.[56] In fact, in the most recent recession of 2008, for example, the new job requirements for the reduced set of jobs left over after downsizing efforts tend to be broader in scope and come with less close supervision relative to the jobs prior to the economic downturn.[57] Failure to take into consideration the nature of the new jobs created after downsizing events is critical because, without support from HR, survivors of downsizing events tend to be less committed to the organization and have higher rates of subsequent turnover when the economy returns to normal.[58]

Job Design

LO5
Understand the different approaches to job design.

So far we have approached the issue of managing work in a passive way, focusing only on understanding what gets done, how it gets done, and the skills required to get it done. Although this is necessary, it is a very static view of jobs, in that jobs must already exist and that they are already assumed to be structured in the one best way. However, a manager may often be faced with a situation in which the work unit does not yet exist, requiring jobs within the work unit to be designed from scratch. Sometimes work loads within an existing work unit are increased, or work group size is decreased while the same work load is required. Finally, sometimes the work is not being performed in the most efficient manner. In these cases, a manager may decide to change the way that work is done in order for the work unit to perform more effectively and efficiently. This requires redesigning the existing jobs.

EVIDENCE-BASED HR

The biggest trend in job analysis today is a move to broaden job descriptions and minimize job classifications in order to support adaptability and flexibility. For example, consultants brought in to study Volkswagen AG found evidence that proved it took twice as long to build a car relative to Toyota. Much of this was attributable to highly detailed job classification systems that limited the work that different people could do. Thus, an engineer who was focused on axles could focus only on axles, which stifled communication across departments and made it difficult to trace the source of complex problems that resulted from interactions between departments. This and other problems associated with Volkswagen's work process contributed to a 60 percent loss in profits between 2001 and 2006. New CEO Wolfgang Bernhard was brought in to rectify this situation, and one of his first steps was to tear up existing narrow job descriptions and replace them with a more flexible cross-functional team arrangement.

A similar story can be found at Spirit AeroSystems. In 2005, as part of an effort to shed weak assets and underperforming units, Boeing sold its Wichita plant to Spirit.

The Wichita plant was Boeing's biggest internal supplier of fuselages and nosecones, but it was consistently uncompetitive relative to other external suppliers that Boeing did not own. Based on the evidence collected by Boeing, it was cheaper for Boeing to get rid of this internal supplier than try to fix it; thus the Wichita plant and all of its employees became expendable. Spirit AeroSystems came in to purchase the plant, and the first step management took was to reduce the 160 job classifications and job descriptions down to 13. It also worked alongside the union to rewrite many inflexible work rules that created inefficiencies and redundancies throughout the work process. Within 18 months, the Wichita plant was turning a profit of over $250 million a year (much of it from Boeing) and raised $1.4 billion as part of an IPO in 2007. Each unionized employee at that point received a check for more than $60,000 as part of a profit-sharing arrangement. As one of the company's union workers noted, "This is what we are going to have to do to be globally competitive."

SOURCES: S. Power, "Top Volkswagen Executive Tries U.S.-Styled Turnaround Tactics," *The Wall Street Journal*, July 17, 2006, pp. A1, A11; S. Holmes, "Soaring Where Boeing Struggled," *BusinessWeek*, February 19, 2007, pp. 72.

Job design is the process of defining how work will be performed and the tasks that will be required in a given job. **Job redesign** refers to changing the tasks or the way work is performed in an existing job. To effectively design jobs, one must thoroughly understand the job as it exists (through job analysis) and its place in the larger work unit's work-flow process (work-flow analysis). Having a detailed knowledge of the tasks performed in the work unit and in the job, a manager then has many alternative ways to design a job. This can be done most effectively through understanding the trade-offs between certain design approaches.

Research has identified four basic approaches that have been used among the various disciplines (such as psychology, management, engineering, and ergonomics) that have dealt with job design issues.[59] Although these four approaches comprehensively capture the historical approaches to this topic, one still needs to go below the category level to get a full appreciation of the exact nature of jobs and how they can be changed.[60] All jobs can be characterized in terms of how they fare according to each approach; thus a manager needs to understand the trade-offs of emphasizing one approach over another. In the next section we discuss each of these approaches and examine the implications of each for the design of jobs. Table 4.3 displays how jobs are characterized along each of these dimensions, and the Work Design Questionnaire (WDQ), a specific instrument that reliably measures these and other job design characteristics is available for use by companies wishing to comprehensively assess their jobs on these dimensions.[61]

Job Design
The process of defining the way work will be performed and the tasks that will be required in a given job.

Job Redesign
The process of changing the tasks or the way work is performed in an existing job.

Mechanistic Approach

The mechanistic approach has roots in classical industrial engineering. The focus of the mechanistic approach is identifying the simplest way to structure work that maximizes efficiency. This most often entails reducing the complexity of the work to provide more human resource efficiency—that is, making the work so simple that anyone can be trained quickly and easily to perform it. This approach focuses on designing jobs around the concepts of task specialization, skill simplification, and repetition.

table 4.3

Major Elements of Various Approaches to Job Design

The mechanistic approach
   Specialization
   Skill variety
   Work methods autonomy
The motivational approach
   Decision-making autonomy
   Task significance
   Interdependence
The biological approach
   Physical demands
   Ergonomics
   Work conditions
The perceptual approach
   Job complexity
   Information processing
   Equipment use

SOURCE: From Michael A. Campion and Paul W. Thayer, "Job Design: Approaches, Outcomes, and Trade-Offs," *Organizational Dynamics*, Winter 1987, Volume 15, No. 3. Copyright © 1987, with permission from Elsevier.

Scientific management was one of the earliest and best-known statements of the mechanistic approach.[62] According to this approach, productivity could be maximized by taking a scientific approach to the process of designing jobs. Scientific management first sought to identify the "one best way" to perform the job. This entailed performing time-and-motion studies to identify the most efficient movements for workers to make. Once the best way to perform the work is identified, workers should be selected based on their ability to do the job, they should be trained in the standard "one best way" to perform the job, and they should be offered monetary incentives to motivate them to work at their highest capacity.

The scientific management approach was built upon in later years, resulting in a mechanistic approach that calls for jobs to be designed so that they are very simple and lack any significant meaningfulness. By designing jobs in this way, the organization reduces its need for high-ability individuals and thus becomes less dependent on individual workers. Individuals are easily replaceable—that is, a new employee can be trained to perform the job quickly and inexpensively.

Many jobs structured this way are performed in developing countries where low-skilled and inexpensive labor is abundant. As one might expect, this includes a host of "low-tech" manufacturing and assembly jobs, but increasingly this also involves "digital factory jobs." For example, *ProQuest Historical Newspaper* provides a service where subscribers can access the contents of any article ever published by one of nine major U.S. newspapers simply by entering an author name, keyword, or image. You might wonder how all of this historical, nondigital information and text is entered into this digital database, and the answer would be found in Madras, Spain. Here workers take this material and enters the headline, author, major key words, and first paragraph of the work by hand into the database, and then run a program to attach a visual file to the rest of the article. This menial work is conducted by 850 workers, who comprise three 8-hour shifts that work 24 hours a day, 7 days a week.[63] It would be difficult, if not impossible to find workers in the United States willing to put up with work this boring. In some cases, jobs designed via mechanistic practices result in work that is so simple that a child could do it, and this is exactly what can happen in some undeveloped countries. This can lead to a backlash against companies that benefit from this unethical practice, and increasingly, organizations are taking the lead in preventing these kinds of practices. For example, when it learned that Uzbekistan cotton growers were using child labor to pick their crops, Wal-Mart used its power to force them to abandon this practice. Working with other large U.S. retailers, Wal-Mart took the lead to create the first system for tracking where cotton came from and organized a boycott against Uzbekistan, which quickly acquiesced to the corporate giant's pressure, freeing the children to return to school.[64] At the time, almost everyone else perceived that Wal-Mart was a corporate villain and bully, assaulting workers, the environment, and consumers. Over the course of his tenure as the Wal-Mart CEO, H. Lee Scott dramatically reversed this perception, and now Wal-Mart is routinely listed as one of the most sustainable and corporately responsible organizations in the United States.[65]

Motivational Approach

The motivational approach to job design has roots in organizational psychology and management literature and, in many ways, emerged as a reaction to mechanistic approaches to job design. It focuses on the job characteristics that affect psychological meaning and motivational potential, and it views attitudinal variables (such as satisfaction, intrinsic motivation, job involvement, and behavioral variables such as attendance and performance) as the most important outcomes of job design. The prescriptions of the motivational approach focus on increasing the meaningfulness of jobs through such interventions as job enlargement, job enrichment, and the construction of jobs around sociotechnical systems.[66]

A model of how job design affects employee reactions is the "Job Characteristics Model."[67] According to this model, jobs can be described in terms of five characteristics. *Skill variety* is the extent to which the job requires a variety of skills to carry out the tasks. *Task identity* is the degree to which a job requires completing a "whole" piece of work from beginning to end. *Autonomy* is the degree to which the job allows an individual to make decisions about the way the work will be carried out. *Feedback* is the extent to which a person receives clear information about performance effectiveness from the work itself. *Task significance* is the extent to which the job has an important impact on the lives of other people. Although all five characteristics are important, the belief that the task is significant because performing it well leads to outcomes one values may be the most critical motivational aspect of work.[68] This can often be enhanced by making it clear to the worker how his or her job affects other people, whether they be customers, co-workers or society in general.[69] Increasingly, as the "Competing through Sustainability" box illustrates, the meaningfulness or work can also be increased by showing how it enhances eco-friendly outcomes on the environment.

These five job characteristics determine the motivating potential of a job by affecting the three critical psychological states of "experienced meaningfulness," "responsibility," and "knowledge of results." According to the model, when the core job characteristics (and thus the critical psychological states) are high, individuals will have a high level of internal work motivation. This is expected to result in higher quantity and quality of work as well as higher levels of job satisfaction.[70] Of the three critical psychological states, research suggest that "experienced meaningfulness may be the most important when it comes to managing work-related stress."[71]

In the story that opened this chapter, we noted how Toyota became the largest automaker in 2007 and how its approach to designing work had to be adjusted when it confronted the challenges associated with the recession that began in 2008. Toyota was not the most profitable car company in 2007, however. That distinction belonged to BMW, a company whose approach to organizational design and job design is so unique that it is often referred to as the "anti-Toyota." The reason for this is that whereas Toyota does all it can to simplify and standardize work procedures and decision making, BMW embraces complexity and stresses creativity. This difference can be traced to BMW business strategy, where CEO Helmut Planke notes, "I cannot recall having seen clear and convincing correlation between size and success. Our own goal is clear: to be the leader in every premium segment of the international automotive industry."

This strategy to be the top producer in a niche category—and not the largest producer overall—leads BMW to take a different approach to how it structures work relative to Toyota, especially in the fact of a crisis like the recession. On the one hand, because it is a premium brand with largely affluent customers, BMW fared better than most carmakers during the most recent recession, but its challenges for the long-term future are different. In particular, the company needs to be at the forefront of what it means to be "premium," and recently, this has much less to do with power and performance of an automobile and much more with sustainability. BMW recognizes that its traditional customer base is aging, and that if it wants to compete in the future, it needs to attract, young, well-educated, affluent customers, most of whom live in urban areas and are sensitive to environmental issues.

To reinvent the company in a greener form, a new project team was designed to examine every aspect of the automobile production process, as well as the performance characteristics of the car, to create a more environmentally friendly experience for both the buyer and the seller. The task, referred to as Project i, was led by veteran engineer Ulrich Kranz, who created a cross-functional team of 80 to 100 specialists who were given wide latitude and autonomy to question every current practice and policy at the Bavarian automaker. Rather than emphasizing standardization and efficiency of work practices (like one would see at Toyota), this resulted in a much more free-wielding, experimental, and risk-seeking approach to how the work gets done. In fact, some of the models being toyed with run on just two or three wheels. The goal is to bring speed and style to the otherwise well-intentioned but dull eco-car niche.

The BMW MINI E, introduced in 2009, was one of the first products created by this team. The MINI E, powered by 600 pounds of lithium batteries and a 200-horsepower electric motor, can go from 0 to 60 mph in 8 seconds and has a top speed of 100 mph. And, most importantly for any BMW aficionado, according to test drivers, the MINI E hugs corners at top speeds like it's riding on a rail. As one BMW insider noted, "The focus on sheer driving pleasure will not work anymore. You have to be socially acceptable as well." Time will only tell if BMW's approach to design, where the emphasis is on experimentation instead of efficiency, will be able to redefine what "high performance" means in the years ahead.

SOURCES: A. Taylor, "Bavaria's Next Top Model," *BusinessWeek*, March 30, 2009, pp. 100–105; J. Ewing, "BMW's Push into Electric Cars," *BusinessWeek*, March 12, 2009, pp. 21–22; A. Aston and M. Vella, "BMW Takes an Electric Mini for a Spin," *BusinessWeek*, March 24, 2009, p. 33.

Job design interventions emphasizing the motivational approach tend to focus on increasing the meaningfulness of jobs. Much of the work on job enlargement (broadening the types of tasks performed), job enrichment (empowering workers by adding more decision-making authority to jobs), and self-managing work teams has its roots in the motivational approach to job design. In enriched jobs, leadership is not the sole prerogative of one person, but rather is distributed throughout the team, and research shows that this can enhance group performance—especially in service jobs where these is a great deal of direct interpersonal interaction between team members and clients.[72] Not all workers respond positively to enriched jobs like these because it requires some degree of flexibility and responsiveness to other people, but with the right workers, interventions such as these have been found to have dramatic effects on employee motivation.[73]

In some cases, even work that may not be that interesting can be made significant by clarifying the link between what workers do and the outcomes of their work, perhaps far down the chain. For example, in medicine, a stent is an expandable wire form or perforated tube that is inserted into an artery to help promote blood flow after a heart operation. The actual work that goes into stent production is an assembly line process where each worker does a very small and, some might argue, boring task. To help increase the meaningfulness of this work, however, the company sponsors a party each year where line workers get to meet people whose lives were saved by the stents that were produced on that line. This is often a moving emotional experience for both parties and helps the employees see the impact of their work in a context where this would not naturally happen.[74] Thus, although at some point it might be necessary to pay workers in order to motivate them, it is even more important to show job incumbents why their jobs are important. Indeed, one of the secrets behind effective transformational leaders is their ability to help workers see the larger meaning in what they are doing on a day-to-day basis.[75]

Biological Approach

The biological approach to job design comes primarily from the sciences of biomechanics (i.e., the study of body movements), work physiology, and occupational medicine, and it is usually referred to as *ergonomics*. **Ergonomics** is concerned with examining the interface between individuals' physiological characteristics and the physical work environment. The goal of this approach is to minimize physical strain on the worker by structuring the physical work environment around the way the human body works. It therefore focuses on outcomes such as physical fatigue, aches and pains, and health complaints. Research in this tradition looks a bit more on the context in which it takes place rather than the work itself, and hence issues like lighting, space, and hours worked become more salient from this perspective.[76]

Ergonomics
The interface between individuals' physiological characteristics and the physical work environment.

The biological approach has been applied in redesigning equipment used in jobs that are physically demanding. Such redesign is often aimed at reducing the physical demands of certain jobs so that anyone can perform them. In addition, many biological interventions focus on redesigning machines and technology, such as adjusting the height of the computer keyboard to minimize occupational illnesses (like carpal tunnel syndrome). The design of chairs and desks to fit posture requirements is very important in many office jobs and is another example of the biological approach to job design. In addition to the direct effects of these kinds of interventions on worker well-being, these types of programs also have a positive psychological effect on workers by emphasizing an organizational climate that values safety and health.[77]

Often redesigning work to make it more worker-friendly also leads to increased efficiencies. For example, at International Truck and Engine Corporation, one of the most difficult aspects of truck production was pinning the axles to the truck frame. Traditionally, the frame was lowered onto the axle and a crew of six people, armed with oversized hammers and crowbars, forced the frame onto the axle. Because the workers could not see the bolts they had to tighten under the frame, the bolts were often not fastened properly, and many workers injured themselves in the process. After a brainstorming session, the workers and engineers figured that it would be better to flip the frame upside down and attach the axles from above instead of below. The result was a job that could be done twice as fast by half as many workers, who were much less likely to make mistakes or get injured.[78]

Perceptual–Motor Approach

The perceptual–motor approach to job design has roots in human-factors literature. Whereas the biological approach focuses on physical capabilities and limitations, the perceptual–motor approach focuses on human mental capabilities and limitations. The goal is to design jobs in a way that ensures they do not exceed people's mental capabilities and limitations. This approach generally tries to improve reliability, safety, and user reactions by designing jobs to reduce their information-processing requirements. In designing jobs, one looks at the least capable worker and then constructs job requirements that an individual of that ability level could meet. Similar to the mechanistic approach, this approach generally decreases the job's cognitive demands.

Recent changes in technological capacities hold the promise of helping to reduce job demands and errors, but in some cases, these developments have actually made the problem worse. The term "absence presence" has been coined to refer to the reduced attentive state that one might experience when simultaneously interacting with multiple media. For example, someone might be talking on a cell phone while driving a car, or surfing the net while attending a business meeting, or checking e-mail while preparing a presentation. In all these cases, the new technology serves as a source of distraction from the primary task, reducing performance and increasing the opportunities for errors.[79] Indeed, research shows that on complex tasks, even very short interruptions can break one's train of thought and derail performance. Thus, e-mail servers that have a feature that signals the arrival of each incoming message might best be turned off if the job incumbent cannot resist the temptation this creates to interrupt ongoing activity.[80]

In addition to external disruptions, information processing errors are also increased in any context that requires a "handoff" of information from one person to another. Indeed, problems with handoffs have become a major concern in the field of medicine. As Mike Leonard, physician leader for patient safety at Kaiser Colorado Hospital, notes, "In almost all serious avoidable episodes of patient harm, communication failures play a central role." This would include information that fails to get handed off from nurses, doctors, and medical technicians to one another (e.g., the results of the most recent test that was handed to the attending doctor does not get handed to the attending nurse) or information that fails to get handed off from one work shift to another (e.g., a patient who has already received medication from one shift gets it again from the next shift). Problems between shifts are especially likely due to fatigue and burnout, which may be present at the end of a shift for workers in stressful jobs.[81]

Increasingly, hospitals are borrowing the "SBAR" method, originally developed in commercial and military aviation as a means to hand off an airplane moving through different people's airspace, to standardize communication protocols at the handoff point in medical contexts. SBAR stands for situation, background, assessment, and recommendation, which constitute the four components of every successful handoff. That is, in a few seconds, the person handing off the patient needs to get control of the situation by demanding the listener's attention (situation), then relay enough information to establish the context or the problem (background), then give an overall evaluation of the condition (assessment), and finally make a specific suggestion about the next best course of action (recommendation). At one hospital that introduced this procedure, the rate of adverse events (i.e., unexpected medical problems that cause harm) was reduced by more than half, from 90 to 40 for every 1,000 patients treated.[82]

Trade-Offs among Different Approaches to Job Design

LO6
Comprehend the trade-offs among the various approaches to designing jobs.

A great deal of research has aimed at understanding the trade-offs and implications of these different job design strategies.[83] Many authors have called for redesigning jobs according to the motivational approach so that the work becomes more psychologically meaningful. However, one study examined how the various approaches to job design are related to a variety of work outcomes. For example, in this study, job incumbents expressed higher satisfaction with jobs scoring high on the motivational approach. Also, jobs scoring high on the biological approach were ones for which incumbents expressed lower physical requirements. Finally, the motivational and mechanistic approaches were negatively related to each other, suggesting that designing jobs to maximize efficiency very likely results in a lower motivational component to those jobs.

Although the motivational and mechanistic approaches to job design do work against one another somewhat, at the same time there is not a tight, one-on-one correspondence between the two. Thus, not all efficiency-producing changes result in dissatisfying work, and not all changes that promote satisfaction create inevitable inefficiencies. By carefully and simultaneously attending to both efficiency and satisfaction aspects of job redesign, managers can sometimes achieve the best of both worlds.[84] For example, at the new Indiana Heart Hospital in Indianapolis, much of the work was digitized in order to create a paperless organization. There are more than 600 computer terminals placed throughout the facility, and the doctors and staff directly enter or access information from these terminals as needed. This has eliminated the need for nurses' stations, chart racks, medical records departments, file storage rooms, and copiers and has cut down paperwork, resulting in an increase in efficiency, but also increased job satisfaction by eliminating bureaucracy, allowing the staff more immediate access to needed information. This has affected the bottom line by reducing the length of time a patient stays in the hospital from an average of five days at other hospitals to three days at Indiana Heart Hospital. This allows the hospital to process more patients per bed relative to the competition, giving them a direct source of competitive advantage.[85]

A LOOK BACK

This chapter opened with a vignette that illustrated the trade-offs associated with alternative methods for organizational design and job design. We showed how one type of design was associated with larger production quantity at Toyota, but that an alternative type of design was better suited for maximizing production quality. Throughout the chapter we also illustrated how other decisions regarding job design affected a whole host of different outcomes.

Questions

1. Based on this chapter, what do you consider to be the three most important decisions to make with respect to organizational design? If you were the CEO of a company that was going to compete against Toyota, how would you design your organization?

2. In the story that opened this chapter, we saw how Toyota was switching from a design that emphasized quantity to one that emphasized quality. One could imagine a different company that felt compelled to change in the opposite direction. Do you thing changing designs in different directions creates unique problems, and if so, what directional shifts might be easier to execute?

3. Toyota's business has both a production aspect related to building cars, and a customer service aspect associated with selling cars. How tightly integrated are these two aspects of the organization, and what can be done to create a tighter structural link between these two substructures or between the manufacturing jobs and the customer service jobs?

 Please see the Video Case that corresponds to this chapter online at www.mhhe .com/noe7e.

SUMMARY

The analysis and design of work is one of the most important components to developing and maintaining a competitive advantage. Strategy implementation is virtually impossible without thorough attention devoted to work-flow analysis, job analysis, and job design. Managers need to understand the entire work-flow process in their work unit to ensure that the process maximizes efficiency and effectiveness. To understand this process, managers also must have clear, detailed information about the jobs that exist in the work unit, and the way to gain this information is through job analysis. Equipped with an understanding of the work-flow process and the existing job, managers can redesign jobs to ensure that the work unit is able to achieve its goals while individuals within the unit benefit on the various work outcome dimensions such as motivation, satisfaction, safety, health, and achievement. This is one key to competitive advantage.

KEY TERMS

Centralization, 160
Departmentalization, 160
Job analysis, 168

Job description, 169
Job specification, 169
Job design, 175

Job redesign, 175
Ergonomics, 179

DISCUSSION QUESTIONS

1. Assume you are the manager of a fast-food restaurant. What are the outputs of your work unit? What are the activities required to produce those outputs? What are the inputs?
2. Based on Question 1, consider the cashier's job. What are the outputs, activities, and inputs for that job?
3. Consider the "job" of college student. Perform a job analysis on this job. What are the tasks required in the job? What are the knowledge, skills, and abilities necessary to perform those tasks? What environmental trends or shocks (like computers) might change the job, and how would that change the skill requirements?
4. Discuss how the following trends are changing the skill requirements for managerial jobs in the United States: (a) increasing use of computers, (b) increasing international competition, (c) increasing work–family conflicts.
5. Why is it important for a manager to be able to conduct a job analysis? What are the negative outcomes that would result from not understanding the jobs of those reporting to the manager?
6. What are the trade-offs between the different approaches to job design? Which approach do you think should be weighted most heavily when designing jobs?
7. For the cashier job in Question 2, which approach to job design was most influential in designing that job? In the context of the total work-flow process of the restaurant, how would you redesign the job to more heavily emphasize each of the other approaches?

SELF-ASSESSMENT EXERCISE

The chapter described how the Department of Labor's Occupational Information Network (O*NET) can help employers. The system was also designed to help job seekers. To see if you think this new system meets the goal of promoting "the effective education, training, counseling, and employment needs of the American workforce," visit O*NET's Web site at http://online. onetcenter.org/.

Look up the listing for your current job or dream job. List the skills identified for that job. For each skill, evaluate how well your own experiences and abilities enable you to match the job requirements.

EXERCISING STRATEGY: FROM BIG BLUE TO EFFICIENT BLUE

IBM was long known as "Big Blue" because of its size, in terms of both the number of employees and the amount of revenue and costs associated with its operations. However, as the old saying goes, "the bigger they are, the harder they fall." In 1993 IBM racked up over $8 billion in losses when it was blindsided by the switch in consumer preferences from mainframe computers to smaller, networked personal computers.

The new incoming CEO, Lou Gerstner, needed to engineer one of the greatest turnarounds in modern business; he started with a new vision of what the company would become, as well as a strategy for getting where the company needed to be. The strategy had both an external aspect, focused on changing from an old-fashioned manufacturing company to a modern service provider, and an internal aspect of restructuring operations to reduce costs and promote efficiencies.

Nowhere was this internal strategy change felt more strongly than in the human resource division. In 1993, the HRM function at IBM was large, decentralized, and regionally based, with branch offices all over the world employing over 3,500 people. By the year 2000 there was only one single, centralized unit located in Raleigh, North Carolina, and this unit employed fewer than 1,000 people.

The key to the successful downsizing effort was its emphasis on matching size changes with changes in structure and the substitution of technology for labor. Instead of interacting face-to-face with the local human resources office, all communication would be technologically mediated and directed to the central Raleigh facility via telephone, e-mail, or fax. Moreover, user-friendly software was developed to help employees answer their questions without any other human involvement.

The sprawling, geographically dispersed units were replaced with an efficient three-tier system. The first tier was composed of broadly trained human resource generalists who received telephone calls from any of IBM's 700,000 HRM "customers" (employees) and tried to respond to any queries that could not be handled via the automated system. The second tier, a smaller number of highly trained specialists (such as in 401k plans, OSHA requirements, or selection standards), took any calls that exceeded the knowledge level of the generalists. Finally, the third tier consisted of even a smaller number of top executives charged with keeping the HRM practices in line with the overall corporate strategy being developed by Gerstner.

Amazingly, despite the radical downsizing of this unit, employee satisfaction with service actually increased to over 90 percent, and Gerstner singled out the reengineering of this department as a success story that should serve as a benchmark to the rest of the company's divisions. Moreover, the restructuring and redesign of these IBM jobs have formed a "blue"-print for many other HRM departments in other organizations.

Questions

1. In terms of our discussion of organizational structure, in what ways did the structure at IBM change under Lou Gerstner and what impact did this have on individual jobs?

2. Compare and contrast the direction of structural change at IBM with the direction of change we saw in the structural realignment at Microsoft (that was also discussed in the text).

3. Since both IBM and Microsoft achieved their goals by changing their structures and job design in opposite directions, what does this say about the relationship between organization structure and job design on the one hand and organizational performance and job satisfaction on the other?

SOURCES: S. N. Mehta, "What Lucent Can Learn from IBM," *Fortune*, June 25, 2001, p. 40; G. Flynn, "Out of the Red, Into the Blue," *Workforce*, March 2000, pp. 50–52; P. Gilster, "Making Online Self-Service Work," *Workforce*, January 2001, pp. 54–61; J. Hutchins, "The U.S. Postal Service Delivers an Innovative HR Strategy," *Workforce*, October 2000, pp. 116–18.

● MANAGING PEOPLE: FROM THE PAGES OF *BUSINESSWEEK*

BusinessWeek ## Lessons from Saturn's Fall

GM's "Different Kind of Car Company" was a great marketing idea, but low margins and confused branding doomed the experiment Nineteen years after emerging as a "Different Kind of Car Company," Saturn is headed for oblivion. A moment of silence, please, because Saturn once represented a new beginning for General Motors (GM), which hoped the brand would catch the ascendant Japanese. The experiment fizzled and instead became an object lesson in what happens when a company fails to back up bold thinking with bold execution.

Saturn was a stroke of marketing brilliance. Not only had GM created a standalone company with its own factory and dealer network, it had torn up the rules of auto retailing. Saturn's original S-Series compact had one fixed price, a revelation for buyers who hated haggling with salespeople. The debut car sold for less than $11,000 and was a bona fide hit.

But the newborn Saturn had sibling rivals inside GM. In 1990, just a year before launching its first car, Saturn lost its patron when then-CEO Roger B. Smith retired. Soon it was battling for money and attention with GM's other brands, especially Oldsmobile. That partly explains why it took GM eight years to come up with a larger car, the doomed L-Series sedan, and almost a decade to replace the S-Series.

By the time GM started giving Saturn decent cars earlier this decade, the parent no longer knew who its offspring was. Pretty soon, Saturn began lurching from one brand message to the next. In 2001 it became a "forward-thinking company." Before long it was all about the customer again. When that didn't work, Saturn emphasized its cars—hawking new models with the slogan "Like Always, Like Never Before."

In 2007, GM nudged Saturn upscale and began selling the Aura family sedan, which boasted Lexus-level style and comfort. Suddenly, a brand that had started out selling affordable cars was charging up to $29,000 for a family sedan. That might have worked had GM spent several years reaching out to affluent buyers. But it didn't.

By then, GM's research was showing that the Saturn brand was badly damaged. When the automaker showed buyers the Aura with the nameplate removed, the car scored a respectable 3.4 out of 4. With the Saturn badge affixed to the hood, the same car scored a measly 2.0. Saturn, in a way, tells a larger story about GM. The automaker is making better cars, but most of its brands are so diminished that few buyers believe it.

Questions

1. In terms of organizational design, would you describe the structure at General Motors, with its emphasis on separate Oldsmobile, Pontiac, Chevrolet, and Cadillac products, a functional or divisional design? What were some of the drawbacks with that specific type of organizational design, and how did those figure into Saturn's demise?

2. In terms of organizational design, would you describe the structure at General Motors, where all the budgets are authorized by the CEO (and not the managers of Oldsmobile, Pontiac, Chevrolet, and Cadillac products) centralized or decentralized? What are some of

the drawbacks with that specific type of structure, and how did these figure into Saturn's demise?

3. In what way does a choice of structural "departmentation" (i.e., divisional versus functional) tend to "fit" best with a specific corresponding choice with respect to decision-making structure (i.e., centralization versus decentralization)? In what way did GM's choice with respect to departmentation not fit with its choice with respect to centralization, and how did this figure into Saturn's demise?

4. General Motors struggled to compete effectively against companies like Toyota and BMW for years, but because many people believed the company "was too big to fail," it received large amounts of government bailout money in the early days of the Barack Obama administration. Some have suggested that if a company is too big to fail, then it is simply too big. Based on what you learned in this chapter, what are two alternative structural methods for making General Motors smaller and more competitive?

● NOTES

1. L. Hawkins and N. Shirouzo, "A Tale of Two Auto Plants," *The Wall Street Journal,* May 24, 2006, pp. B1–B2.
2. D. Ilgen and J. Hollenbeck, "The Structure of Work: Job Design and Roles," in *Handbook of Industrial & Organizational Psychology,* 2nd ed., ed. M. Dunnette and L. Hough (Palo Alto, CA: Consulting Psychologists Press, 1991), pp. 165–208.
3. R. Griffin, *Task Design: An Integrative Approach* (Glenview, IL: Scott Foresman, 1982).
4. B. Brocka and M. S. Brocka, *Quality Management: Implementing the Best Ideas of the Masters* (Homewood, IL: Business One Irwin, 1992).
5. R. D. Pritchard, M. M. Harrell, D. Diaz Granados, and M. J. Guzman, "The Productivity Measurement and Enhancement System: A Meta-analysis," *Journal of Applied Psychology* 93 (2008), pp. 540–67.
6. G. L. Stewart and M. R. Barrick, "Team Structure and Performance: Assessing the Mediating Role of Intrateam Process and the Moderating Role of Task Type," *Academy of Management Journal* 43 (2000), pp. 135–48.
7. G. S. Van der Vegt, B. J. M. Emans, and E. Van de Vliert, "Patterns of Interdependence in Work Teams: A Two-Level Investigation of the Relations with Job and Team Satisfaction," *Personnel Psychology* 54 (2001), pp. 51–70.
8. F. P. Morgeson, M. D. Johnson, M. A. Campion, G. J. Medsker, and T. V. Mumford, "Understanding Reactions to Job Redesign: A Quasi-Experimental Investigation of the Moderating Effects of Organizational Context on Perceptions of Performance and Behavior," *Personnel Psychology* 59 (2006), pp. 333–63.
9. C. M. Barnes, J. R. Hollenbeck, D. T. Wagner, D. S. DeRue, J. D. Nahrgang, and K. M. Schwind, "Harmful Help: The Costs of Backing-up Behaviors in Teams," *Journal of Applied Psychology* 93 (2008), pp. 529–39.
10. C. Passariello, "Louis Vuitton Tries Modern Methods on Factory Line," *The Wall Street Journal,* October 9, 2006, pp. A1, A15.
11. P. Glader, "It's Not Easy Being Lean," *The Wall Street Journal,* June 19, 2006, pp. B1, B3.
12. D. Little, "Even the Supervisor Is Expendable: The Internet Allows Factories to Be Managed from Anywhere," *BusinessWeek,* July 23, 2001, p. 78.
13. M. G. Morris and V. Venkatesh, "Age Differences in Technology Adoption Decisions: Implications for a Changing Workforce," *Personnel Psychology* 53 (2000), pp. 375–403.
14. N. Byrnes, "Xerox' New Design Team: Customers," *BusinessWeek,* May, 7, 2007, p. 72.
15. S. Hamm, "Big Blue Shift," *BusinessWeek,* June 5, 2006, pp. 108–10.

16. A. L. Kristof-Brown, B. D. Zimmerman, and E. C. Johnson, "Consequences of Individuals' Fit at Work: A Meta-analysis of Person–Job, Person–Organization, Person–Group, and Person–Supervisor Fit," *Personnel Psychology* 58 (2005), pp. 281–342.
17. M. Schminke, M. L. Ambrose, and R. S. Cropanzano, "The Effect of Organizational Structure on Perceptions of Procedural Fairness," *Journal of Applied Psychology* 85 (2000), pp. 294–304.
18. J. Greene, "Microsoft's Midlife Crisis," *BusinessWeek,* April 19, 2004, pp. 88–98.
19. J. Kerstetter, "Gates and Ballmer on Making the Transition," *BusinessWeek,* April 19, 2004, pp. 96–97.
20. G. B. Schlender, "Ballmer Unbound: How Do You Impose Order on a Giant Runaway Mensa Meeting?" *Fortune,* January 26, 2004, pp. 117–24.
21. T. Neff and J. Citrin, "You're in Charge: Now What?" *Fortune,* January 24, 2005, pp. 109–20.
22. S. Gray, "Natural Competitor," *The Wall Street Journal,* December 4, 2006, pp. B1, B3.
23. W. D. Sine, H. Mitsuhashi, and D. A. Kirsch, "Revisiting Burns and Stalker: Formal Structure and New Venture Performance in Emerging Economic Sectors," *Academy of Management Journal* 49 (2006), pp. 121–32.
24. J. Marquez, "Banking on a New Culture at Citibank," *Workforce Management,* May 19, 2008, pp. 1–3.
25. B. Nussaum, "Technology, Just Make It Simpler," *BusinessWeek,* September 8, 2003, p. 38.
26. H. Moon, J. R. Hollenbeck, S. E. Humphrey, D. R. Ilgen, B. West, A. Ellis, and C.O.L.H. Porter, "Asymmetrical Adaptability: Dynamic Structures as One-Way Streets," *Academy of Management Journal* 47 (2006), pp. 681–96.
27. M. D. Johnson, J. R. Hollenbeck, D. R. Ilgen, S.E. Humphrey, C. J. Meyer, and D. K. Jundt, "Cutthroat Cooperation: Asymmetrical Adaptation of Team Reward Structures," *Academy of Management Journal* 49 (2006), pp. 103–20.
28. P. Glader, "It's Not Easy Being Lean," *The Wall Street Journal,* June 19, 2006, pp. B1, B3.
29. N. Byrnes, "The Art of Motivation," *BusinessWeek,* May 1, 2006, pp. 57–62.
30. J. R. Hollenbeck, H. Moon, A. Ellis, B. West, D. R. Ilgen, L. Sheppard, C. O. Porter, and J. A. Wagner, "Structural Contingency Theory and Individual Differences: Examination of External and Internal Person–Team Fit," *Journal of Applied Psychology* 87 (2002), pp. 599–606.
31. M. L. Ambrose and M. Schminke, "Organization Structure as a Moderator of the Relationship between Procedural Justice, Interactional Justice, Perceived Organizational Support, and

Supervisory Trust," *Journal of Applied Psychology* 88 (2003), pp. 295–305.

32. M. Conlin, "Netflix: Flex to the Max," *BusinessWeek*, September 24, 2007, pp. 72–74.

33. J. A. Marquez, "Taking a Longer View," *Workforce Management*, May 21, 2006, pp. 18–22.

34. B. Schlender, "Ballmer Unbound: How Do You Impose Order on a Giant Runaway Mensa Meeting?" *Fortune*, January 26, 2004, p. 123.

35. E. Primoff and S. Fine, "A History of Job Analysis," in *The Job Analysis Handbook for Business, Industry, and Government*, ed. S. Gael (New York: Wiley, 1988), pp. 14–29.

36. W. Cascio, *Applied Psychology in Personnel Management*, 4th ed. (Englewood Cliffs, NJ: Prentice Hall, 1991).

37. J. Walker, *Human Resource Strategy* (New York: McGraw-Hill, 1992).

38. R. Gatewood and H. Feild, *Human Resource Selection*, 2nd ed. (Hinsdale, IL: Dryden, 1990).

39. I. Goldstein, *Training in Organizations*, 3rd ed. (Pacific Grove, CA: Brooks/Cole, 1993).

40. K. Murphy and J. Cleveland, *Performance Appraisal: An Organizational Perspective* (Boston: Allyn & Bacon, 1991).

41. R. Harvey, L. Friedman, M. Hakel, and E. Cornelius, "Dimensionality of the Job Element Inventory (JEI): A Simplified Worker-Oriented Job-Analysis Questionnaire," *Journal of Applied Psychology* 73 (1988), pp. 639–46.

42. D. A. Hofmann, F. P. Morgeson, and S. J. Gerras, "Climate as a Moderator of the Relationship between Leader–Member Exchange and Content-Specific Citizenship: Safety Climate as an Exemplar," *Journal of Applied Psychology* 88 (2003), pp. 170–78.

43. A. K. Weyman, "Investigating the Influence of Organizational Role on Perceptions of Risk in Deep Coal Mines," *Journal of Applied Psychology* 88 (2003), pp. 404–12.

44. L. E. Baranowski and L. E. Anderson, "Examining Rater Source Variation in Work Behavior to KSA Linkages," *Personnel Psychology* 58 (2005), pp. 1041–54.

45. E. McCormick and R. Jeanneret, "The Position Analysis Questionnaire," in *The Job Analysis Handbook for Business, Industry, and Government*, pp. 880–901.

46. E. C. Dierdorff and M. A. Wilson, "A Meta-analysis of Job Analysis Reliability," *Journal of Applied Psychology* 88 (2003), pp. 635–46.

47. N. G. Peterson, M. D. Mumford, W. C. Borman, P. R. Jeanneret, and E. A. Fleishman, *An Occupational Information System for the 21st Century: The Development of O*NET* (Washington, DC: American Psychological Association, 1999).

48. N. G. Peterson, M. D. Mumford, W. C. Borman, P. R. Jeanneret, E. A. Fleishman, K. Y. Levin, M. A. Campion, M. S. Mayfield, F. P. Morgenson, K. Pearlman, M. K. Gowing, A. R. Lancaster, M. B. Silver, and D. M. Dye, "Understanding Work Using the Occupational Information Network (O*NET): Implications for Practice and Research," *Personnel Psychology* 54 (2001), pp. 451–92.

49. P. J. Taylor, W. D. Li, K. Shi, and W. C. Borman, "The Transportability of Job Information Across Countries," *Personnel Psychology* 61 (2008), pp. 69–111.

50. S. Holmes, "Lots of Green Left in the Emerald City," *BusinessWeek Online* (March 28, 2000).

51. D. Dyer, "O*NET in Action," O*NET Web site, http://online.onetcenter.org/.

52. C. C. Lapolice, G. W. Carter, and J. W. Johnson, "Linking O*NET Descriptors to Occupational Literacy Requirements Using Job Component Validation," *Personnel Psychology* 61 (2008), pp. 405–441.

53. M. K. Lindell, C. S. Clause, C. J. Brandt, and R. S. Landis, "Relationship between Organizational Context and Job Analysis Ratings," *Journal of Applied Psychology* 83 (1998), pp. 769–76.

54. F. P. Morgeson and M. A. Campion, "Social and Cognitive Sources of Potential Inaccuracy in Job Analysis," *Journal of Applied Psychology* 82 (1997), pp. 627–55.

55. S. Caudron, "Jobs Disappear When Work Becomes More Important," *Workforce*, January 2000, pp. 30–32.

56. D. S. DeRue, J. R. Hollenbeck, M. D. Johnson, D. R. Ilgen, and D. K. Jundt, "How Different Team Downsizing Approaches Influence Team-level Adaptation and Performance," *Academy of Management Journal* 51 (2008), pp. 182–96.

57. F. Hanson, "A Leg Up in Down Times," *Workforce Management*, January 19, 2009, p. 14.

58. C. O. Trevor and A. J. Nyberg, "Keeping Your Headcount When All About You Are Losing Theirs: Downsizing, Voluntary Turnover Rates, and the Moderating Role of HR Practices," *Academy of Management Journal* 51 (2008), pp. 259–76.

59. M. Campion and P. Thayer, "Development and Field Evaluation of an Interdisciplinary Measure of Job Design," *Journal of Applied Psychology* 70 (1985), pp. 29–34.

60. J. R. Edwards, J. A. Scully, and M. D. Brtek, "The Measurement of Work: Hierarchical Representation of the Multimethod Job Design Questionnaire," *Personnel Psychology* 52 (1999), pp. 305–24.

61. F. P. Morgeson and S. E. Humphrey, "The Work Design Questionnaire (WDQ): Developing and Validating a Comprehensive Measure for Assessing Job Design and the Nature of Work," *Journal of Applied Psychology* 91 (2006), pp. 1312–39.

62. F. Taylor, *The Principles of Scientific Management* (New York: W. W. Norton, 1967) (originally published in 1911 by Harper & Brothers).

63. B. Helm, "Life on the Web's Factory Floor," *BusinessWeek*, May 22, 2006, pp. 70–71.

64. M. Gunther, "Wal-Mart: A Bully Benefactor," CNNMoney.com, December 5, 2008, p. 1.

65. L. Delevevigne, "Surprising Corporate Do-gooders," CNN.Money.com, January 20, 2009, p. 1.

66. R. Griffin and G. McMahan, "Motivation through Job Design," in *OB: The State of the Science*, ed. J. Greenberg (Hillsdale, NJ: Lawrence Erlbaum Associates, 1993).

67. R. Hackman and G. Oldham, *Work Redesign* (Boston: Addison-Wesley, 1980).

68. A. M. Grant, "The Significance of Task Significance," *Journal of Applied Psychology* 93 (2007), pp. 108–24.

69. A. M. Grant, E. M. Campbell, G. Chen, K. Cottone, D. Lapedia, and K. Lee, "Impact and Art of Motivation Maintenance: The Effects of Contact with Beneficiaries on Persistence Behavior," *Organizational Behavior and Human Decision Processes* 103 (2007), pp. 53–67.

70. M. Schrage, "More Power to Whom?" *Fortune* (July 23, 2001), p. 270.

71. A. A. Grandey, G. M. Fisk, and D. D. Steiner, "Must 'Service with a Smile' Be Stressful?" *Journal of Applied Psychology* 90, (2005), pp. 893–904.

72. J. B. Carson, P. E. Tesluk, and J. A. Marrone, "Shared Leadership in Teams: An Investigation of Antecedent Conditions and Performance." *Academy of Management Journal* 50 (2007), pp. 1217–34.

73. F. W. Bond, P. E. Flaxman, and D. Bunce, "The Influence of Psychological Flexibility on Work Redesign: Mediated Moderation of a Work Reorganization Intervention," *Journal of Applied Psychology* 93 (2008), pp. 645–54.

74. W. E. Byrnes, "Making the Job Meaningful All the Way Down the Line," *BusinessWeek*, May 1, 2006, p. 60.

75. J. A. Colquitt and R. F. Piccalo, "Transformational Leadership and Job Behaviors: The Mediating Role of Core Job Characteristics," *Academy of Management Journal* 49 (2006), pp. 327–40.

76. S. Sonnentag and F. R. H. Zijistra, "Job Characteristics and Off-the-Job Activities as Predictors of Need for Recovery, Well-Being, and Fatigue," *Journal of Applied Psychology* 91 (2006), pp. 330–50.

77. S. Mewman, M. A. Griffen, and C. Mason, "Safety in Work Vehicles: A Multilevel Study Linking Safety Values and Individual Predictors to Work-related Driving Crashes," *Journal of Applied Psychology* 93 (2008), pp. 632–44.

78. S. F. Brown, "International's Better Way to Build Trucks," *Fortune*, February 19, 2001, pp. 210k–210v.

79. D. K. Berman, "Technology Has Us So Plugged into Data, We Have Turned Off," *The Wall Street Journal*, November 10, 2003, pp. A1–A2.

80. J. Baker, "From Open Doors to Gated Communities," *BusinessWeek*, September 8, 2003, p. 36.

81. L. E. LaBlanc, J. J. Hox, W. B. Schaufell, T. W. Taris, and M.C.W. Peters, "Take Care! The Evaluation of a Team-Based Burnout Intervention Program for Oncology Health Care Providers," *Journal of Applied Psychology* 92 (2007), pp. 213–27.

82. L. Landro, "Hospitals Combat Errors at the 'Hand-Off,'" *The Wall Street Journal*, June 28, 2006, pp. D1, D2.

83. J. R. Edwards, J. A. Scully, and M. D. Brteck, "The Nature and Outcomes of Work: A Replication and Extension of Interdisciplinary Work-Design Research," *Journal of Applied Psychology* 85 (2000), pp. 860–68.

84. F. P. Morgeson and M. A. Campion, "Minimizing Trade-Offs When Redesigning Work: Evidence from a Longitudinal Quasi-Experiment," *Personnel Psychology* 55 (2002), pp. 589–612.

85. E. Florian, "IT Takes on the ER," *Fortune*, November 24, 2003, pp. 193–200.

Acquisition and Preparation of Human Resources

CHAPTER

5

Human Resource Planning and Recruitment

LO LEARNING OBJECTIVES

After reading this chapter, you should be able to:

LO1   Discuss how to align a company's strategic direction with its human resource planning. *page 193*

LO2   Determine the labor demand for workers in various job categories. *page 194*

LO3   Discuss the advantages and disadvantages of various ways of eliminating a labor surplus and avoiding a labor shortage. *page 197*

LO4   Describe the various recruitment policies that organizations adopt to make job vacancies more attractive. *page 211*

LO5   List the various sources from which job applicants can be drawn, their relative advantages and disadvantages, and the methods for evaluating them. *page 214*

LO6   Explain the recruiter's role in the recruitment process, the limits the recruiter faces, and the opportunities available. *page 221*

The Forecast Calls for Change

As we saw in the opener of Chapter 2, which focused on GM's "legacy workforce," after racking up more than $80 billion in losses in the four-year period between 2004 and 2008, in 2009, General Motors was on the brink of bankruptcy. As one of the nation's largest employers, as well as an American manufacturing icon, this development had major financial as well as symbolic implications for the United States. Many believed that GM was "too big to fail" and even some of the company's major competitors—including Toyota, Honda, and Ford—were in favor of government support to help bolster the failing giant. These competitors realized that failure at GM was likely to spill over and create bankruptcy among key auto parts suppliers that all the companies relied on. Hence, failure at GM would actually harm its competitors more than it might help them by ravaging their own supplier base.

After $13 billion in bailout money from the Bush administration failed to help turn around this situation, GM went back to the government looking for another round of bailouts. However, after studying GM's forecasts and plans for the future, President Obama's Automotive Task Force rejected their request and gave the troubled automaker 60 days to come up with new forecasts and plans. At the heart of this rebuke was the criticism that the company's forecasts were unrealistic and far too rosy, given the objective statistics. The task force also noted that GM's future plans were too cautious and incremental relative to the revolutionary changes that the situation seemed to demand.

Specifically, the task force was heavily critical of the company's forecasts regarding demand for GM cars relative to the cars of foreign producers, as well as its forecasts that predicted a rebound in the sales of trucks and large SUVs, a major GM staple. According to the task force, GM had a history of making poor forecasts, which was one of the major reasons behind the organization's current predicament. As we saw in the opening to Chapter 2, the task force cited how GM failed to accurately forecast how increased life spans would affect the generous pension plans that it was contractually obligated to pay. This was only part of the forecasting problem, however. In addition to this, the task force cited how the company failed to accurately forecast how the rise in health care costs that it was contractually obligated to pay would affect future profitability and failed to accurately forecast how rising oil prices and environmental concerns would effect the demand for gas-guzzling trucks, SUVs, and Hummers. Due to the lack of realism in these forecasts, the task force concluded that GM would wind up having a much larger surplus of labor relative to what it projected. Moreover, the company's plan for what to do with this excess amount of labor was also criticized because it essentially would dump these workers into the infamous JOBS bank that paid laid-off workers for not working at all.

The task force concluded that GM was going to have to make more painful cuts and layoffs relative to what were reflected in its forecasts and plans, and at the very least, the task force demanded at least one layoff—that of the CEO Rick Wagoner. The task force noted that since Wagoner became CEO in 2000, the company's market share dropped from 28 percent to 22 percent and that the stock price dropped from $70 to $3 a share. He also was criticized by members of the U.S. Congress, who noted that when he flew to Washington to beg for taxpayer money, he took a private jet. Many outsiders demanded that the task force recruit an outsider to replace Wagoner because, as one industry analyst noted, "the plain fact is that GM leadership is far too inbred to bring about radical change." However, an insider, Fritz Henderson, was chosen, because the task force felt that only an insider would have the depth of knowledge to revise the forecasts and plans given the short time frame required for the turnaround. Although some felt that the task force was overly harsh on Wagoner, it is worth noting that he had a relatively soft landing, receiving a $20 million severance package for his efforts.

Sources: M. Dolan, "Task Force Says GM Can Bounce Back with Changes," *The Wall Street Journal*, March 30, 2009, p. A1; J. D. Stoll, "Wagoner, With Knack for Survival, Finally Hits a Dead End," *The Wall Street Journal*, March 30, 2009, p. A3; P. Ingrassia, "Wagoner Had to Go," *The Wall Street Journal*, April 1, 2009, pp. B1–B2; M. Krantz and D. Jones, "GM CEO Rick Wagoner's Pension Plan Valued at $20 million," *USA Today*, April 1, 2009, p. C1.

Introduction

As the opening vignette illustrates, employers and human resource managers do not exist in a vacuum. In many cases, global movements, political pressures, cultural preferences, and product market developments all simultaneously influence the supply and demand for labor. On the one hand, this dynamic nature of managing human resources makes the field challenging and difficult. On the other hand, however, this complexity provides a great opportunity to carve out unique and sustainable sources of competitive advantage if you or your human resource department can find a better way of doing business relative to your competitors. Firms that win out in this competition grow and prosper, while those that fail to forecast the future and plan accordingly run the risk of going out of business, just like General Motors.

The purpose of this chapter is to examine factors that influence the supply and demand for labor, and, in particular, focus on what human resources managers can do in terms of planning and executing human resource policies that give their firms competitive advantage in a dynamic environment.

Two of the major ways that societal trends and events affect employers are through (1) consumer markets, which affect the demand for goods and services, and (2) labor markets, which affect the supply of people to produce goods and services. In some cases, as we saw in the opening story, the market might be characterized by a labor surplus. In other cases, the market may be characterized by a shortage of labor. Reconciling the difference between the supply and demand for labor presents a challenge for organizations, and how they address this will affect their overall competitiveness.

There are three keys to effectively utilizing labor markets to one's competitive advantage. First, companies must have a clear idea of their current configuration of human resources. In particular, they need to know the strengths and weaknesses of their present stock of employees. Second, organizations must know where they are going in the future and be aware of how their present configuration of human resources relates to the configuration that will be needed. Third, where there are discrepancies between the present configuration and the configuration required for the future, organizations need programs that will address these discrepancies. Under conditions of a labor surplus, this may mean creating an effective downsizing intervention. Under conditions of a labor shortage, this may mean waging an effective recruitment campaign.

This chapter looks at tools and technologies that can help an organization develop and implement effective strategies for leveraging labor market "threats" into opportunities to gain competitive advantage. In the first half of the chapter, we lay out the actual steps that go into developing and implementing a human resource plan. Through each section, we focus especially on recent trends and practices (like downsizing, employing temporary workers, and outsourcing) that can have a major impact on the firm's bottom line and overall reputation. In the second half of the chapter, we familiarize you with the process by which individuals find and choose jobs and the role of personnel recruitment in reaching these individuals and shaping their choices.

The Human Resource Planning Process

An overview of human resource planning is depicted in Figure 5.1. The process consists of forecasting, goal setting and strategic planning, and program implementation and evaluation. We discuss each of these stages in the next sections of this chapter.

LO1
Discuss how to align a company's strategic direction with its human resource planning.

Forecasting

The first step in the planning process is **forecasting,** as shown in the top portion of Figure 5.1. In personnel forecasting, the HR manager attempts to ascertain the supply of and demand for various types of human resources. The primary goal is to predict areas within the organization where there will be future labor shortages or surpluses.

Forecasting, on both the supply and demand sides, can use either statistical methods or judgmental methods. Statistical methods are excellent for capturing historic trends in a company's demand for labor, and under the right conditions they give predictions that are much more precise than those that could be achieved through subjective judgments of a human forecaster. For example, changes in price are often a good indicator of capacity-related problems, which in turn are a good predictor of demand for labor. Thus, when prices for many manufactured good fell more than 5 percent in early 2007, this was an indicator that retailers had too many products piling up in inventories, and this was predictive of the recession in 2008. In contrast,

Forecasting
The attempts to determine the supply of and demand for various types of human resources to predict areas within the organization where there will be future labor shortages or surpluses.

figure 5.1

Overview of the Human Resource Planning Process

to the manufacturing sector, however, prices in the service sector of the economy that year actually went up by 3 percent, suggesting there was less of an overcapacity problem in that sector. Human resource professionals need to recognize how prices for their product predict future demand for labor so they can react quickly to oversupply problems.[1]

On the other hand, many important events that occur in the labor market have no historical precedent; hence, statistical methods that work from historical trends are of little use in such cases. For example, the depth and scope of the recession in 2008 was larger than anyone had experienced since the Great Depression in 1930; hence, making predictions about how big General Motors needed to be and what kinds of products it should be selling led to a contentious debate between business and political leaders. With no historical precedent, one must rely on the pooled subjective judgments of experts, and their "best guesses" might be the only source from which to make inferences about the future. Typically, because of the complementary strengths and weaknesses of the two methods, companies that engage in human resource planning use a balanced approach that includes both statistical and judgmental components.

Determining Labor Demand

LO2
Determine the labor demand for workers in various job categories.

Typically, demand forecasts are developed around specific job categories or skill areas relevant to the organization's current and future state. Once the job categories or skills are identified, the planner needs to seek information that will help predict whether the need for people with those skills or in that job category will increase or decrease in the future. Organizations differ in the sophistication with which such forecasts are derived.

At the most sophisticated level, an organization might have statistical models that predict labor demand for the next year given relatively objective statistics on leading indicators from the previous year. A **leading indicator** is an objective measure that accurately predicts future labor demand. For example, a manufacturer of automobile parts that sells its product primarily to the Big Three automakers would use several objective statistics on the Big Three automakers for one time period to predict how much demand there would be for the company's product at a later time period. Inventory levels, sales levels, employment levels, and price levels at the Big Three in one year might predict the demand for labor in the production assembler job category in the next year.

Leading Indicator
An objective measure that accurately predicts future labor demand.

For example, using historical records, one might use multiple regression techniques to assess the best predictive model for estimating demand for production assemblers from information on sales levels, inventory levels, employment levels, and price levels at the Big Three. This is not a statistics book, so a detailed explanation of regression techniques is beyond our scope. Rather, we simply note here that this technique will convert information of four or more leading indicators into a single predicted value for demand for production assemblers that is optimal—at least according to the historical data. For example, the demand for nurses in a community can historically be predicted very well by knowing the average age of the community members. Thus, if the average age of American citizens is going up, which it is, then one can expect an increase in the need for nurses. Studies based on these historical trends suggest that by the year 2014, our economy will need 1.2 million more nurses relative to what is available today.[2]

EVIDENCE-BASED HR

Historical data are useful not only for making long-term predictions of labor demand in broad categories like nursing but also for more day-to-day specific predictions within a specific organization. For example, Wal-Mart has introduced a worker scheduling system that is based on extremely reliable predictions regarding how many customers are going to be in specific stores on specific days at specific times. That is, based on historical evidence, specific stores can predict the volume of traffic and schedule workers based on this evidence. Thus, rather than simply scheduling workers in straight eight-hour shifts, the stores can schedule people to work when they are most needed based on historical evidence. Other retailers like Radio Shack and Payless Shoes have developed similar software, which, according to HR director Larry Liebach, "optimizes our schedules to better anticipate when customers will be in our stores so that we can better engage them."

SOURCE: K. Maher, "Wal-Mart Seeks New Flexibility in Worker Shifts," *The Wall Street Journal*, January 3, 2007, p. A1.

Statistical planning models are useful when there is a long, stable history that can be used to reliably detect relationships among variables. However, these models almost always have to be complemented by subjective judgments of people who have expertise in the area. There are simply too many "once-in-a-lifetime" changes that have to be considered and that cannot be accurately captured in statistical models. For example, terrorism and instability in the Middle East, combined with an unprecedented demand for oil in emerging economies like China and India, have resulted in increasingly high and unpredictable energy prices. This in turn has led to a resurgence of interest in nuclear power in the United States, and more than 20 new nuclear plants are in the process of being built. Past concerns about the safety of nuclear power plants may resurface, however, and thus it is difficult to predict strictly from historical trends whether the demand for workers trained in nuclear power technology is going to increase.[3]

Determining Labor Supply

Once a company has projected labor demand, it needs to get an indicator of the firm's labor supply. Determining the internal labor supply calls for a detailed analysis of how many people are currently in various job categories (or who have specific skills) within the company. This analysis is then modified to reflect changes in the near future caused by retirements, promotions, transfers, voluntary turnover, and terminations.

As in the case of labor demand, projections for labor supply can be derived either from historical statistical models or through judgmental techniques. One type of statistical procedure that can be employed for this purpose involves transitional matrices. **Transitional matrices** show the proportion (or number) of employees in different job categories at different times. Typically these matrices show how people move in one year from one state (outside the organization) or job category to another state or job category.[4]

Table 5.1 shows a hypothetical transitional matrix for our parts manufacturer, focusing on seven job categories. Although these matrices look imposing at first, you will see that they are easy to read and use in determining the internal labor supply.

Transitional Matrix
Matrix showing the proportion (or number) of employees in different job categories at different times.

table 5.1

A Hypothetical
Transitional Matrix
for an Auto Parts
Manufacturer

2007	2010							
	(1)	(2)	(3)	(4)	(5)	(6)	(7)	(8)
(1) Sales manager	.95							.05
(2) Sales representative	.05	.60						.35
(3) Sales apprentice		.20	.50					.30
(4) Assistant plant manager				.90	.05			.05
(5) Production manager				.10	.75			.15
(6) Production assembler					.10	.80		.10
(7) Clerical							.70	.30
(8) Not in organization	.00	.20	.50	.00	.10	.20	.30	

A matrix like the one in this table can be read in two ways. First, we can read the rows to answer the question "Where did people in this job category in 2007 go by 2010?" For example, 70 percent of those in the clerical job category (row 7) in 2007 were still in this job category in 2010, and the remaining 30 percent had left the organization. For the production assembler job category (row 6), 80 percent of those in this position in 2007 were still there in 2010. Of the remaining 20 percent, half (10 percent) were promoted to the production manager job category, and the other half (10 percent) left the organization. Finally, 75 percent of those in the production manager job category in 2007 were still there in 2010, while 10 percent were promoted to assistant plant manager and 15 percent left the organization.

Reading these kinds of matrices across rows makes it clear that there is a career progression within this firm from production assembler to production manager to assistant plant manager. Although we have not discussed rows 1 through 3, it might also be noted that there is a similar career progression from sales apprentice to sales representative to sales manager. In this organization, the clerical category is not part of any career progression. That is, this job category does not feed any other job categories listed in Table 5.1.

A transitional matrix can also be read from top to bottom (in the columns) to answer the question "Where did the people in this job category in 2010 come from (Where were they in 2007)?" Again, starting with the clerical job (column 7), 70 percent of the 2010 clerical positions were filled by people who were also in this position in 2007, and the remaining 30 percent were external hires (they were not part of the organization in 2007). In the production assembler job category (column 6), 80 percent of those occupying this job in 2010 occupied the same job in 2007, and the other 20 percent were external hires. The most diversely staffed job category seems to be that of production manager (column 5): 75 percent of those in this position in 2010 held the same position in 2007; however, 10 percent were former production assemblers who were promoted, 5 percent were former assistant plant managers who were demoted, and 10 percent were external hires who were not with the company in 2007.

Matrices such as these are extremely useful for charting historical trends in the company's supply of labor. More important, if conditions remain somewhat constant, they can also be used to plan for the future. For example, if we believe that we are going to have a surplus of labor in the production assembler job category in the next three years, we note that by simply initiating a freeze on external hires, the ranks of this position will be depleted by 20 percent on their own. Similarly, if we believe that we will have a labor shortage in the area of sales representatives, the matrix informs us that we may want to (1) decrease the amount of voluntary turnover in this position, since 35 percent of those in this category leave every three years, (2) speed the training of those in the sales apprentice job category so that they can be promoted more quickly than in the past, and/or (3) expand external recruitment of individuals for this job category, since the usual 20 percent of job incumbents drawn from this source may not be sufficient to meet future needs. As with labor demand, historical precedents for labor supply may not always be reliable indicators of future trends. Thus, statistical forecasts of labor supply also need to be complemented with judgmental methods.

Determining Labor Surplus or Shortage

Once forecasts for labor demand and supply are known, the planner can compare the figures to ascertain whether there will be a labor shortage or labor surplus for the respective job categories. When this is determined, the organization can determine what it is going to do about these potential problems. For example, we previously noted that it is relatively easy to predict from historical data that in the future, the United States is likely to experience a shortage of nurses and, perhaps, a shortage of workers with knowledge of nuclear power. In contrast, as we saw in our chapter-opening vignette, overcapacity problems related to automobile production would suggest that there will be a labor surplus of autoworkers in the future. Similarly, the most recent data on overcapacity problems in the semiconductor industry point to the fact that there is likely to be a surplus of workers in that industry as well.[5]

LO3
Discuss the advantages and disadvantages of various ways of eliminating a labor surplus and avoiding a labor shortage.

Goal Setting and Strategic Planning

The second step in human resource planning is goal setting and strategic planning, as shown in the middle of Figure 5.1. The purpose of setting specific quantitative goals is to focus attention on the problem and provide a benchmark for determining the relative success of any programs aimed at redressing a pending labor shortage or surplus. The goals should come directly from the analysis of labor supply and demand and should include a specific figure for what should happen with the job category or skill area and a specific timetable for when results should be achieved.

The auto parts manufacturer, for instance, might set a goal to reduce the number of individuals in the production assembler job category by 50 percent over the next three years. Similarly, the firm might set a goal to increase the number of individuals in the sales representative job category by 25 percent over the next three years.

Once these goals are established, the firm needs to choose from the many different strategies available for redressing labor shortages and surpluses. Table 5.2 shows some of the options for a human resource planner seeking to reduce a labor surplus. Table 5.3 shows some options available to the same planner intent on avoiding a labor shortage.

This stage is critical because the many options available to the planner differ widely in their expense, speed, effectiveness, amount of human suffering, and revocability (how easily the change can be undone). For example, if the organization can anticipate a labor surplus far enough in advance, it may be able to freeze hiring and then just let natural attrition adjust the size of the labor force. If successful, an organization may be able to avoid layoffs altogether, so that no one has to lose a job.

table 5.2

Options for Reducing an Expected Labor Surplus

OPTION	SPEED	HUMAN SUFFERING
1. Downsizing	Fast	High
2. Pay reductions	Fast	High
3. Demotions	Fast	High
4. Transfers	Fast	Moderate
5. Work sharing	Fast	Moderate
6. Hiring freeze	Slow	Low
7. Natural attrition	Slow	Low
8. Early retirement	Slow	Low
9. Retraining	Slow	Low

table 5.3

Options for Avoiding an Expected Labor Shortage

OPTION	SPEED	REVOCABILITY
1. Overtime	Fast	High
2. Temporary employees	Fast	High
3. Outsourcing	Fast	High
4. Retrained transfers	Slow	High
5. Turnover reductions	Slow	Moderate
6. New external hires	Slow	Low
7. Technological innovation	Slow	Low

One of the difficulties that General Motors experienced (the company in the opening story of this chapter), was that when faced with a surplus of labor, they were contractually obligated to send workers to the JOBS bank program, where they got paid for not working. In contrast, Toyota (the company in our opening vignette in our previous chapter) sent all of their surplus workers to training programs where they upgraded their skills. Toyota workers took classes in a host of areas including safety procedures, productivity improvement workshops, materials handling, as well as decision making and ethics.[6]

Unfortunately for many workers, in the past decade the typical organizational response to a surplus of labor has been downsizing, which is fast but high in human suffering. The widespread use of downsizing is a contributing factor in the largest number of personal bankruptcies ever recorded in the United States. Beyond this economic impact, the psychological impact spills over and affects families, increasing the rates of divorce, child abuse, and drug and alcohol addiction.[7] The typical organizational response to a labor shortage has been either hiring temporary employees or outsourcing, responses that are fast and high in revocability. Given the pervasiveness of these choices, we will devote special subsections of this chapter to each of these options.

Downsizing

The planned elimination of large numbers of personnel designed to enhance organizational effectiveness.

Downsizing

We define **downsizing** as the planned elimination of large numbers of personnel designed to enhance organizational effectiveness. Although one tends to think of downsizing as something that a company turns to in times of recession like we saw in 2008 and 2009, if fact, many organizations engaged in downsizing in the 2002–2007 time period. During that period, in more than 80 percent of the cases where downsizing took place, the organizations initiating the cutbacks were making a profit at the time.

Surveys indicate four major reasons that organizations engaged in downsizing. First, many organizations are looking to reduce costs, and because labor costs represent a big part of a company's total costs, this is an attractive place to start. For example, when the financial industry collapsed in 2008, firms in that industry were forced to slash payrolls. Many of these firms eventually received bailout money from the government that helped them dip back into the labor pool, but as the "Competing through Globalization" box shows, some were surprised that these firms were looking to use taxpayer money to replace U.S. workers with workers holding H-1B visas.

Second, in some organizations, closing outdated plants or introducing technological changes to old plants reduced the need for labor. For example, Eastman Machine is a Buffalo, New York–based manufacturer of equipment that is used for cutting fabric. In order to stave off low-priced competition from Chinese rivals, Eastman expanded heavily into the market for highly automated, computer-driven cutting machines that are not currently available in Asia. This eliminated much of the manual work that was formerly performed at the plant, and now, the same amount of product and revenue that was once generated by a 120-person workforce can be produced with a staff of 80, requiring a downsizing of one-third of the workforce.[8]

A third reason for downsizing was that, for economic reasons, many firms changed the location of where they did business. Some of this shift was from one region of the United States to another—in particular, many organizations moved from the Northeast, the Midwest, and California to the South and the mountain regions of the West. In some cases, technology is employed to move work that one might think was not that mobile. For example, the McDonald's restaurant chain experimented with drive-up windows in Michigan that were staffed with lower-wage workers located in Fargo, North Dakota. What looked like a standard drive-up squawk box was actually a long-distance connection, where Michigan orders were taken down by a worker in North Dakota who then relayed the order information back to the Michigan staff.[9] Some of this shift was also due to jobs moving out of the United States altogether. For example, close to 300,000 white-collar jobs were transferred from the United States to India in 2003 alone.[10]

Although downsizing has an immediate effect on costs, much of the evidence suggests that it has negative effects on long-term organizational effectiveness, especially for some types of firms. For example, in firms that are high in research and development intensity, downsizing has been linked to lower long-term organizational profits.[11] Also, the negative effects of downsizing seem to be exacerbated in service industry's characterized by high levels of customer contact.[12] In addition, when downsizing efforts are not complemented by changes in the nature of work roles, then performance also tends to suffer.[13] The negative effect of downsizing on performance was especially high among firms that engaged in high-involvement work practices, such as employing teams and pay-for-performance incentives. Thus, the more a firm attempts to compete through its human resources, the more devastating the impact of layoffs is on productivity.[14]

Still, many employers engage in this tactic and hence it is important to understand what goes into an effective versus ineffective downsizing campaign. There seem to be a number of reasons for the failure of most downsizing efforts to live up to expectations in terms of enhancing firm performance. First, although the initial cost savings are a short-term plus, the long-term effects of an improperly managed downsizing effort can be negative. Downsizing not only leads to a loss of talent, but in many cases it disrupts the social networks needed to promote creativity and flexibility.[15] Second,

Due to the near total collapse of the financial industry in the United States in 2008, the United States government provided more than $200 billion in bailout money to more than 400 banks, 25 percent of which went to Citigroup and Bank of America, two of the countries largest financial institutions. Given the level of support the U.S. taxpayer was providing these organizations, many were shocked to learn that at the same time these companies were laying off U.S. workers, they were also taking steps to increase hiring levels of foreign workers. As one outraged U.S. senator noted, "What has been the response of Wall Street to the loss of 100,000 of their own workers? What these banks have announced is that they are requesting to hire 21,000 foreign workers over the next six years through the H-1B Visa Program to fill these jobs."

The H-1B Visa Program was originally designed to let U.S. companies fill high-skill positions for which no local workers were available. Employers seeking the visas apply to the Department of Labor for each potential hire; once the applications are approved, the employers can petition U.S. Citizenship and Immigration Services for the visa, which lasts for three years and can be extended to six. Most of these visas are generally granted, until the cap of 65,000 is reached. Typically, this limit is reached within a few days of the April 1 application deadline, and many employers in specific industries have lobbied hard to get the cap raised.

For example, Microsoft led the nation in 2008 for H-1B visas, and HR executives at Microsoft have argued that each H-1B visa issued in the technology sector of the economy creates five new jobs for U.S. workers. As an extreme example, they cite the case of Sergey Brin, the Russian-born co-founder of Google, who first entered the U.S. on an H-1B visa. In other industries, like farming, lobbyists argue that U.S. workers simply refuse to work in that industry regardless of the nature of the economy. For example, despite double-digit unemployment rates in the state of Michigan, the lack of sufficient numbers of immigrant workers led to a substantial percentage of crops rotting in the fields in 2008. Finally, in industries like nursing and computer programming, there is a chronic shortage of trained personnel, and this means that firms have to scour the world for suitable talent in these areas.

At the same time many employers are lobbying for raising the limit on H-1B visas, however, many politicians have argued for a reduction in the number of visas in order to protect U.S. jobs during the most recent recession. Some have suggested that many of these shortages are really illusory. For example, the American Nursing Association notes that there are 500,000 registered nurses who do not work in health care because of the low pay and poor working conditions. Similarly, low pay and adverse working conditions have been argued to lie at the root of the shortage of programmers and farm workers, and that "fixing" the jobs in these industries would eliminate the shortages and wind up reducing the overall level of unemployment in the United States. In the end, the argument hinges on the availability of U.S. workers, and Senator Charles Grassley promised to put the pressure on employers, noting that "I want to make sure that every employer searches to make sure there is no American available to do the job."

SOURCES: C. Bailik, "Work-Visa Numbers Get Squishy—and Get Played," *The Wall Street Journal*, March 31, 2009, pp. C1–C2; M. Herbst, "Immigration: One Reform at a Time," *BusinessWeek*, February 2, 2009, p. 50; V. Wadhwa, "America's Immigrant Brain Drain," *BusinessWeek*, March 16, 2009, p. 68; M. Herbst, "A Narrowing Window for Foreign Workers?" *BusinessWeek*, March 16, 2009, p. 65.

many downsizing campaigns let go of people who turn out to be irreplaceable assets. In fact, one survey indicated that in 80 percent of the cases, firms wind up replacing some of the very people who were let go. Indeed, the practice of hiring back formerly laid-off workers has become so routine that many organizations are increasingly using software formerly used for tracking job applicants to track their laid-off employees.[16]

A third reason downsizing efforts often fail is that employees who survive the purges often become narrow-minded, self-absorbed, and risk-averse. Motivation levels drop off because any hope of future promotions—or even a future—with the company dies out. Many employees also start looking for alternative employment opportunities.[17] The negative publicity associated with a downsizing campaign can also hurt the company's image in the labor market, making it more difficult to recruit employees later. Especially in an age of blogs and text messaging, the once-private practice of laying off employees is becoming increasingly transparent, and any organizational mistake that gets made in the process is likely to become highly public.[18] The key to avoiding this kind of reputation damage is to ensure that the need for the layoff is well explained and that procedures for implementing the layoff are fair.[19] Although this may seem like common sense, many employers execute layoffs in ways that make matters worse. For example, in September 2006, Radio Shack human resource managers decided to inform 400 people that they were laid off by e-mail.[20] This makes a dehumanizing event even more dehumanizing, and the negative publicity that attended this decision will surely hurt the company's future recruitment efforts if business turns around. This also increases the likelihood that disgruntled employees are likely to sue for loss of wages. Angry ex-employees often bring suit based upon the Worker Adjustment and Retraining Notification Act. This act requires that employers give workers 60 days warning regarding layoffs, as well as severance pay. Many employers seem to be unaware of this act, and because of the recession, there was spike in lawsuits in 2009 based upon this act.[21]

The key to a successful downsizing effort is to avoid indiscriminant across-the-board cuts, and instead perform surgical strategic cuts that not only reduce costs, but also improve the firm's competitive position. For example, Raven Industries, a Sioux Falls manufacturer of a wide variety of plastic products, had to cut its workforce, but went about the process in a manner that would help make the company "China proof." They went from having 10 different divisions to 4, eliminating manufacturing of certain low-margin products that could be produced cheaper in China (e.g., generic plastic covers for pickup trucks) and pouring more resources into more profitable custom-made covers for widely different agricultural machines. In the process, the organization decreased in size almost by half (from 1,500 workers to 750), but revenue was off by less than 20 percent. Two years after this strategic downsizing effort, the company's share price increased from $4.50 to over $30.[22]

Early Retirement Programs and Buyouts

Another popular means of reducing a labor surplus is to offer an early retirement program. As shown in Figure 5.2, the average age of the U.S. workforce is increasing. But although many baby boomers are approaching traditional retirement age, early indications are that this group has no intention of retiring any time soon.[23] Several forces fuel the drawing out of older workers' careers. First, the improved health of older people in general, in combination with the decreased physical labor in many jobs, has made working longer a viable option. Second, this option is attractive for many workers because they fear Social Security will be cut, and many have skimpy employer-sponsored pensions that may not be able to cover their expenses. Third, age

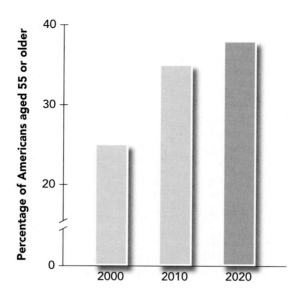

figure 5.2

Aging of the U.S. Population, 2000–2020

discrimination legislation and the outlawing of mandatory retirement ages have created constraints on organizations' ability to unilaterally deal with an aging workforce. Finally, many employers are increasingly concerned about losing the wealth of experience that older workers bring to their companies, and as the "Competing through Sustainability" box shows, many are doing whatever it takes to retain more senior members of their organization.

Although an older workforce has some clear advantages for employers in terms of experience and stability, it also poses problems. First, older workers are sometimes more costly than younger workers because of their higher seniority, higher medical costs, and higher pension contributions. When the value of the experience offsets these costs, then employers are fine; but if it does not, it becomes difficult to pass these costs to consumers. Second, because older workers typically occupy the best-paid jobs, they sometimes prevent the hiring or block the advancement of younger workers. This is frustrating for the younger workers and leaves the organization in a perilous position whenever the older workers decide to retire.

In the face of such demographic pressures, many employers try to induce voluntary attrition among their older workers through early retirement incentive programs. These programs come in an infinite variety. Depending on how lucrative they are, they meet with varied success. Although some research suggests that these programs do induce attrition among lower-performing older workers, to a large extent, such programs' success is contingent upon accurate forecasting. For example, at FedEx, the company had to scramble to find workers for the busy holiday season in 2003, when more people opted to take early retirement packages than anticipated. In contrast, at Electronic Data Systems, only one-third of the number of anticipated people opted to accept buyouts in a 2004 program that had to be reapplied in 2005 with a more lucrative set of enticements. Although mistakes in either direction can be costly, an under-enrolled program creates an additional set of problems if employees start to think that they should wait it out and hope for an even better package further down the line. This makes the process of calculating one's future labor supply much more complex. As one HR manager notes, "It's a very dicey issue. You have to encourage people to leave and tell them this is the best offer you are going to get."[24]

Despite the fact that most employers were cutting payrolls during the most recent recession, the data revealed that most of the attrition was among younger workers and that employment levels for workers over 55 years of age actually increased during that time period. Indeed, pay-level data reflected a similar trend. Whereas inflation-adjusted wages for workers in the "25–55 age group" dropped on average more than 2 percent in the most recent data, employees in the 55 and older age category experienced wage gains of more than 4 percent. Several specific industries seemed to be particularly protective of their older workers, and this can be traced to some of their past practices with respect to managing previous labor surpluses.

For example, in 2009, Boeing cut 10,000 jobs, but almost none of these cuts included their most senior employees. Part of this can be attributed to Boeing's experience in the 1990s, when similar cuts were obtained by supplying the workforce with voluntary buyout plans. Left to decide on their own, workers with the most experience— and hence best alternative employment opportunities— accepted the buyouts. When the recession ended, however, and the company tried to expand, it was hurt by labor shortages in the jobs that required the most experience.

Richard Hartnett, Boeing's chief of global staffing, noted in 2009 that "We don't ever want to get ourselves stuck in that situation again," and this time around, when it came to reducing the size of the labor force, few of the cuts were voluntary. Instead, this time Boeing is picking and choosing who stays and who leaves, and more often than not, workers with the higher levels of experience are being kept on.

In the oil industry, past labor surpluses were met with "attrition-related" adjustments. Rather than directly laying workers off, most employers in the industry simply did not hire new workers when older ones retired. The lack of hiring meant that many younger people gave up on that industry as a viable career alternative, and enrollments in undergraduate programs related to the oil industry dropped 85 percent from 1982 to 2003. With more than 40 percent of their workforce now over the age of 50 and no replacements in sight, employers like Conoco are struggling to keep their most senior employees from retiring with higher pay and more lucrative benefits. As Michael, Killalea, Vice President of the International Association of Drilling Contractors, notes, "We skipped an entire generation of workers, and we cannot make the transition fast enough without extending the service of our most senior employees."

Finally, another example of this can be seen at the Federal Aviation Authority, the group that oversees airline safety. The majority of Air Traffic Controllers who currently work for this agency were hired in the mid-1980s after then-President Ronald Reagan fired more than 10,000 controllers who were illegally striking. Now, 25 years later, most of these controllers are nearing the age of retirement, and the FAA is desperately trying to retain these workers for as long as possible in order to help ease the transition to a younger, less experienced workforce. The problem, however, is that strained labor–management relations have created a situation where job dissatisfaction among current controllers is very high, and a mass exodus is taking place. As one departing controller noted, "It is only a matter of time before an accident occurs, and the pervasive feeling among experienced controllers is that I don't want to be there when it happens." This kind of quote strikes fear into the hearts of would-be flyers and dramatizes the generic need in the economy for all sorts of employers to hold on to their most senior and experienced members.

SOURCES: P. Coy, "Golden Paychecks," *BusinessWeek*, July 2, 2007, p. 13; J. Weber, "This Time, Old Hands Keep Their Jobs," *BusinessWeek*, February 9, 2009, p. 50; M. Herbst, "Big Oil's Talent Hunt," *BusinessWeek*, December 24, 2007, pp. 62–63; J. Marquez, "Taking Flight," *Workforce Management*, June 9, 2009, pp. 1–21.

For this and other reasons, many early retirement programs are simply converted into buyouts for specific workers that have nothing to do with age. For example, in 2006, Ford reduced the size of its unionized workforce by close to 50 percent using across-the-board buyouts of workers. Depending on the length of service, some employees received as little as $35,000 to leave, whereas those with the longest tenure receive as much as $145,000.[25]

In contrast to Ford, one part of the plan at General Motors (discussed in our opening story) was to reduce the surplus of labor by buying out the contracts of long tenured workers. In this most recent buyout plan at GM, 22,000 of its 62,000 unionized workers were offered $20,000 plus a $25,000 voucher toward the purchase of a GM car if they were willing to retire. This offer was much less lucrative relative to previous buyouts announced at the company, and for that reason, many outsiders thought that this part of their plan was also unrealistic in terms of generating its hoped for benefits.[26] A similar program at the *Washington Post* offered workers roughly a year and a half in salary, and this offer seemed to be more in line with what it generally takes to get people to leave voluntarily. Interestingly, while the *Post* was cutting the number of employees, the *New York Times* decided to reduce pay levels by roughly 3 percent and not layoff or buyout any employees. Rather than seeing size as a liability, Executive Editor Bill Keller saw it as a source of unique competitive advantage for the *Times* (in fact, the largest newsroom in the country), describing his current stock of employees as "the engine of our long term success."[27]

Employing Temporary Workers

Whereas downsizing has been a popular method for reducing a labor surplus, hiring temporary workers and outsourcing has been the most widespread means of eliminating a labor shortage. Temporary employment affords firms the flexibility needed to operate efficiently in the face of swings in the demand for goods and services. In fact, a surge in temporary employment often precedes a jump in permanent hiring, and is often a leading indicator that the economy is expanding. For example, the number of temporary workers grew from 215 million to 230 million between 2003 and 2004, signaling to many the end of the 2001 recession.[28] In addition to flexibility, hiring temporary workers offers several other advantages:

- The use of temporary workers frees the firm from many administrative tasks and financial burdens associated with being the "employer of record."
- Small companies that cannot afford their own testing programs often get employees who have been tested by a temporary agency.
- Many temporary agencies train employees before sending them to employers, which reduces training costs and eases the transition for both the temporary worker and the company.
- Because the temporary worker has little experience in the host firm, she brings an objective perspective to the organization's problems and procedures that is sometimes valuable. Also, since the temporary worker may have a great deal of experience in other firms, she can sometimes identify solutions to the host organization's problems that were confronted at a different firm. Thus temporary employees can sometimes help employers to benchmark and improve their practices.

Certain disadvantages to employing temporary workers need to be overcome to effectively use this source of labor. For example, in the service sector of the economy, low levels of commitment to the organization and its customers on the part of temporary employees, often spills over and reduces the level of customer loyalty.[29] Instead of replacing long-term employees with temporary employees, many organizations try to buffer their "core employees" from wild swings in demand by supplementing their core staff with a small set of temporary workers who act more like assistants to the core staff than potential replacements.[30] In addition, there is often tension between a firm's temporary employees and its full-time employees. Surveys indicate that 33 percent of full-time employees perceive the temporary help as a threat to their own job security. This can lead to low levels of cooperation and, in some cases, outright sabotage if not managed properly. Firms are more likely to derive the performance benefits from temporary employees when the current set of workers perceive their job security is high relative to when they feel threatened.[31]

There are several keys to managing this problem. First, the organization needs to have bottomed out in terms of any downsizing effort before it starts bringing in temporaries. A downsizing effort is almost like a death in the family for employees who survive, and a decent time interval needs to exist before new temporary workers are introduced into this context. Without this time delay, there will be a perceived association between the downsizing effort (which was a threat) and the new temporary employees (who may be perceived by some as outsiders who have been hired to replace old friends). Any upswing in demand for labor after a downsizing effort should probably first be met by an expansion of overtime granted to core full-time employees. If this demand persists over time, one can be more sure that the upswing is not temporary and that there will be no need for future layoffs. The extended stretches of overtime will eventually tax the full-time employees, who will then be more receptive to the prospect of hiring temporary employees to help lessen their load.

Second, if the organization is concerned about the reactions of full-time workers to the temporaries, it may want to go out of its way to hire "nonthreatening" temporaries. For example, although most temporary workers want their temporary assignments to turn into full-time work (75 percent of those surveyed expressed this hope), not all do. Some prefer the freedom of temporary arrangements. These workers are the ideal temporaries for a firm with fearful full-time workers.[32] In many cases, temporary staffing firms have access to this type of employee, and this explains the massive growth rate for firms in that industry. For example, Manpower Inc., one of the larger temporary employment agencies, has seen an increase in stock price of more than 35 percent between 2005 and 2007.[33]

Of course, in attempting to convince full-time employees that they are valued and not about to be replaced by temporary workers, the organization must not create the perception that temporary workers are second-class organizational citizens. HR staff can also prevent feelings of a two-tiered society by ensuring that the temporary agency provides benefits to the temporaries that are at least minimally comparable to those enjoyed by the full-time workers with whom they interact. This not only reduces the benefit gap between the full-time and part-time workers but also helps attract the best part-time workers in the first place.

Outsourcing and Offshoring

Whereas a temporary employee can be brought in to manage a single job, in other cases a firm may be interested in getting a much broader set of services performed by an outside organization; this is called **outsourcing.** Outsourcing is a logical choice when a firm simply does not have certain expertise and is not willing to invest time and effort into developing it. For example, ironically, companies increasingly outsource

Outsourcing
An organization's use of an outside organization for a broad set of services.

many of their human resource management tasks to outside vendors who specialize in efficiently performing many of the more routine administrative tasks associated with this function. Figure 5.3 shows a forecast for growth rates in the human resource outsourcing (HRO) industry. Cost savings in this area are easily obtained because rather than purchase and maintain their own specialized hardware and software, as well as specialized staff to support such systems, companies can time-share the facilities and expertise of a firm that focuses on this technology.

Thus, a moderate-size company that might otherwise need to have a 15- to 30-person HR staff can get by with just 5 to 7 people devoted to HR because they share services with outside firms like Accenture,[34] thus benefiting from economies of scale. In addition to managing the size of the HR unit, the hope is also that this frees up HR managers to focus on more strategic issues. As Samuel Borgese, VP of HR for Catalina Restaurant Group, notes, "This allows us to keep strategic tasks in-house with tactical support form the outsourcing vendor. It's very difficult for a VP of HR to be a strategic player if he or she is managing the HR infrastructure."[35]

In other cases, outsourcing is aimed at simply reducing costs by hiring less expensive labor to do the work, and, more often than not, this means moving the work outside the country. **Offshoring** is a special case of outsourcing where the jobs that move actually leave one country and go to another. This kind of job migration has always taken place; however, rapid technological changes have made the current trends in this area historically unprecedented. Offshoring is controversial because close to 800,000 white-collar jobs have moved from the United States to India, eastern Europe, Southeast Asia, and

Offshoring
A special case of outsourcing where the jobs that move actually leave one country and go to another.

figure 5.3
U.S. Multiprocess HR Outsourcing Forecast

NelsonHall puts the market for multiprocess HRO at $1.475 billion by 2010 for the midmarket, which it defines as companies with 1,000–10,000 employees. NelsonHall defines multiprocess HRO as two or more major HR tasks outsourced to a single vendor, so this market is broader than the market for comprehensive HRO.

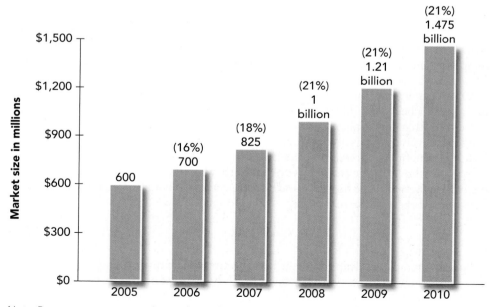

Note: Percentage = compound annual growth rate.
SOURCE: NelsonHall, "Multiple HR Outsourcing in the U.S.: Market Assessment," June 2006.

China in the last eight years. In addition to restricting job growth in the United States this has also affected wages, in the sense that while the average rate of salary growth during an economic recovery is usually around 6–8 percent, because of offshoring, salary growth in the most recent recovery was actually negative (−1 percent)

Although initially many jobs that were outsourced were low scope and simple jobs, increasingly, higher skilled work is being done overseas. For example, in 2006, DuPont moved legal services associated with its $100 million asbestos case litigation to a team of lawyers working in the Philippines. Some of this work reflects the sort of tedious copying of documents (more than 2 million pages) that is associated with a typical offshoring project, but much of the work requires actual legal judgments (e.g., determining the relevance of the document to the case or its need for confidentiality) that normally would be performed by U.S. lawyers. Paralegal work by U.S. firms can run up to $150 an hour versus $30 in the Philippines, and lawyers' salaries in the Philippines are one-fifth of their counterparts' in the United States.[36]

Indeed, the stereotype that "call center" staffing is the only type of work being offshored is increasingly invalid, as countries like China, India, and those in eastern Europe try to climb the skill ladder of available work. In India alone, whereas 85 percent of the work offshored there in 2000 reflected call center work, by 2006 this was reduced to 35 percent. The growth in India is now in higher-paying contracts dealing with business process improvement, processing mortgages, handling insurance claims, overseeing payrolls, and reading X-rays and other medical tests.[37] Many of the simple call center jobs that moved to India are either moving deeper into the rural Indian villages[38] or, ironically, moving back to the United States. Indeed, call center jobs are increasingly being performed by U.S. workers who are now operating out of their own homes instead of massive call centers like those run overseas. One recent survey indicated that 25 percent of call center employees are based in their own homes, and some have estimated that this will grow by another 25 percent between 2006 and 2010.[39]

Although this may seem problematic for U.S. employers, in fact, if effectively managed, firms that offshore certain aspects of work gain an undeniable competitive advantage over their rivals. Ignoring this source of advantage is self-defeating, and akin to putting one's head in the sand. For example, Levi-Strauss tried for years to compete against other low-cost jeans manufacturers who offshored their labor. However, after years of one plant shutdown after another, in 2003 the firm finally gave up and closed down all of its U.S. manufacturing plants. The move, which many saw as inevitable, was long overdue and had it been made earlier, the company might have been able to avoid losing over $20 million.

When making the decision to offshore some product or service, organizations should consider several critical factors. Many who failed to look before they leaped onto the offshoring bandwagon have been disappointed by their results. Quality control problems, security violations, and poor customer service experiences have in many cases wiped out all the cost savings attributed to lower wages and more. There are several steps a company should take to ensure the success of this strategy. First, when choosing an outsourcing vendor, it is usually the bigger and older the better. Small overseas upstarts often promise more than they can deliver and take risks that one is not likely to see in larger, more established contractors.[40] Second, do not offshore any work that is proprietary or requires tight security. One software developer that hired an Indian firm to debug its programs later found that the firm copied the software and sold it under its own brand name.[41] In general, the work that is outsourced needs to be "modular" in the sense that the work is self-contained and does not require the outsourcing firm to provide any information that is best kept secret for

Employees at Pella Windows agreed to a four-day workweek to avoid massive layoffs in the midst of a labor surplus.

competitive reasons.[42] Third, it is generally a good idea to start small and then monitor the work very closely, especially in the beginning. Typically, if problems are going to develop, they manifest themselves quickly to those who are paying close attention.[43]

Finally, rather than treating offsourced work as just a cost-containment strategy, firms are increasingly looking for "transformational offshoring," which promotes growth and opens up avenues of new revenue. That is, the increased sophistication of outsourcing firms means that they are better able to partner with companies on an equal basis in developing innovative and unique ways to do business. This development has prompted one CEO to note that "I think we will end up with companies that deliver products faster, at lower cost, and are better able to compete against anyone in the world."[44]

Altering Pay and Hours

Companies facing a shortage of labor may be reluctant to hire new full-time or part-time employees. Under some conditions, these firms may have the option of trying to garner more hours out of the existing labor force. Despite having to pay workers time-and-a-half for overtime production, employers see this as preferable to hiring and training new employees—especially if they are afraid that current demand for products or services may not extend to the future. Also, for a short time at least, many workers enjoy the added compensation. However, over extended periods, employees experience stress and frustration from being overworked in this manner. At some point, most employers in the U.S. will have to respond to a labor shortage with an increase in wages, which then has to be passed on to consumers in terms of an increase in price.

In the face of a labor surplus, organizations can sometimes avoid layoffs if they can get their employees to take pay cuts. For example, when DiamondCluster Inc., a Chicago-based technology consulting firm, experienced a downturn in demand for its services, rather than reduce the workforce, it instead convinced the workers to take an across-the-board 20 percent pay cut. Although painful, the workers eventually accepted the need for this move and perceived that it was better than a series of layoffs.[45] Alternatively, one can avoid layoffs and hold the pay rate constant but reduce the number of hours of all the workers. For example, during the recent recession, Pella Windows shifted from a five-day workweek to a four-day workweek, but kept each and every worker on the payroll. Although most of Pella's employees would prefer to work the full week, most also agreed that this was a more humane way to reduce the surplus of labor relative to laying off 20 percent of the workforce altogether. Moreover, Pella believed that the recession was going to be short and that government bailout money aimed at improving the nation's infrastructure would eventually translate into increased sales of their windows. By not laying off workers, the company would be able to ramp up more quickly and take advantage of a forecasted spike in demand shortly down the road. Similar goals can be accomplished by asking employees to take unpaid vacations. For example, 90 percent of the accountants at the Hong Kong office of Ernst & Young agreed to take a month off without pay in the spring of 2009, reducing payroll costs by just under 20 percent.[46]

While these kinds of swings in labor supply and demand are not historically uncommon in the manufacturing industry, one unique aspect of the recession of 2008–2009 was the degree to which similar methods were aimed at professional workers. A "furlough" is a short-term elimination of paid workdays applied to salaried workers, as opposed to "hourly workers." For example, at Arizona State University and the University of Maryland, professional workers were furloughed for between 9 to 15 days, saving the institutions roughly $25 million.[47]

Furloughs are controversial because, unlike most hourly workers who go home after the assembly line stops running, the work of most white-collar professionals simply piles up when they leave the office for extended periods of time. Indeed, at Arizona State and Maryland, most of the professional workers came to work anyway, meaning that the furloughs were actually pay cuts, not reductions in hours. Also furloughs are controversial because they hit higher-paid employees harder than lower-paid employees, and if these pay differences were a result of some type of pay-for-performance system, this means that the best employees take the biggest hit. On the other hand, some argue that this aspect of furloughs is actually desirable in the sense that those at the bottom of the pay grade are more likely to need the money to meet basic needs like food and rent relative to those at the top of the pay system.

Program Implementation and Evaluation

The programs developed in the strategic-choice stage of the process are put into practice in the program-implementation stage, shown at the bottom of Figure 5.1. A critical aspect of program implementation is to make sure that some individual is held accountable for achieving the stated goals and has the necessary authority and resources to accomplish this goal. It is also important to have regular progress reports on the implementation to be sure that all programs are in place by specified times and that the early returns from these programs are in line with projections.

The final step in the planning process is to evaluate the results. Of course, the most obvious evaluation involves checking whether the company has successfully avoided any potential labor shortages or surpluses. Although this bottom-line evaluation is critical, it is also important to go beyond it to see which specific parts of the planning process contributed to success or failure.

The Special Case of Affirmative Action Planning

We have argued that human resource planning is an important function that should be applied to an organization's entire labor force. It is also important to plan for various subgroups within the labor force. For example, affirmative action plans forecast and monitor the proportion of various protected group members, such as women and minorities, that are in various job categories and career tracks. The proportion of workers in these subgroups can then be compared with the proportion that each subgroup represents in the relevant labor market. This type of comparison is called a **workforce utilization review.** This process can be used to determine whether there is any subgroup whose proportion in the relevant labor market is substantially different from the proportion in the job category.

If such an analysis indicates that some group—for example, African Americans—makes up 35 percent of the relevant labor market for a job category but that this same group constitutes only 5 percent of the actual incumbents in that job category in that organization, then this is evidence of underutilization. Underutilization could come about because of problems in selection or from problems in internal movement, and this could be seen via the transitional matrices discussed earlier in this chapter.

Workforce Utilization Review
A comparison of the proportion of workers in protected subgroups with the proportion that each subgroup represents in the relevant labor market.

This kind of review is critical for many different reasons. First, many firms adopt "voluntary affirmative action programs" to make sure underutilization does not occur and to promote diversity. Second, companies might also engage in utilization reviews because they are legally required to do so. For example, Executive Order 11246 requires that government contractors and subcontractors maintain affirmative action programs. Third, affirmative action programs can be mandated by the courts as part of the settlement of discrimination complaints.

These kinds of affirmative programs are often controversial because they are seen as unfair by many nonminorities.[48] Indeed, even some minorities feel that these kinds of programs unfairly stigmatize the most highly qualified minority applicants because of perceptions that their hiring was based on something other than their skills and abilities.[49] However, when the evidence provided from a workforce utilization review makes it clear that a specific minority group has been historically underrepresented because of past discrimination, and that increasing the level of representation will benefit workforce diversity and competitiveness, then these kinds of programs are easier to justify to all involved.[50] Organizations need to realize, however, that affirmative action plans need to be complemented with communication programs that clearly spell out the needs and benefits that these programs bring to the organization and the larger society.[51]

The Human Resource Recruitment Process

As the first half of this chapter shows, it is difficult to always anticipate exactly how many (if any) new employees will have to be hired in a given year in a given job category. The role of human resource recruitment is to build a supply of potential new hires that the organization can draw on if the need arises. Thus, **human resource recruitment** is defined as any practice or activity carried on by the organization with the primary purpose of identifying and attracting potential employees. It thus creates a buffer between planning and actual selection of new employees, which is the topic of our next chapter.

Recruitment activities are designed to affect (1) the number of people who apply for vacancies, (2) the type of people who apply for them, and/or (3) the likelihood that those applying for vacancies will accept positions if offered. The goal of an organizational recruitment program is to ensure that the organization has a number of reasonably qualified applicants (who would find the job acceptable) to choose from when a vacancy occurs.

The goal of the recruiting is not simply to generate large numbers of applicants. If the process generates a sea of unqualified applicants, the organization will incur great expense in personnel selection (as discussed more fully in the next chapter), but few vacancies will actually be filled. This problem of generating too many applicants is often promulgated by the use of wide-reaching technologies like the Internet to reach people. For example, when Trend Micro was trying to fill a management position, it posted an advertisement on several online job boards, which resulted in a flood of nearly 1,000 resumes.[52]

The goal of personnel recruitment is not to finely discriminate among reasonably qualified applicants either. Recruiting new personnel and selecting new personnel are both complex processes. Each task is hard enough to accomplish successfully, even when one is well focused. Organizations explicitly trying to do both at the same time will probably not do either well. For example, research suggests that recruiters provide

Human Resource Recruitment
The practice or activity carried on by the organization with the primary purpose of identifying and attracting potential employees.

Job Choice

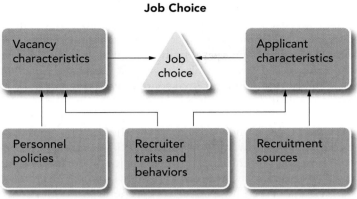

Recruitment Influences

figure 5.4

Overview of
the Individual
Job Choice—
Organizational
Recruitment Process

less information about the company when conducting dual-purpose interviews (interviews focused on both recruiting and selecting applicants).[53] Also, applicants apparently remember less information about the recruiting organization after dual-purpose interviews.[54] Finally, applicants respond less positively to highly structured interviews, and yet this is precisely the type of interview that has the highest validity in terms of making effective screening decisions.[55]

Because of strategic differences among companies (see Chapter 2), the importance assigned to recruitment may differ. In general, however, as shown in Figure 5.4, all companies have to make decisions in three areas of recruiting: (1) personnel policies, which affect the kinds of jobs the company has to offer; (2) recruitment sources used to solicit applicants, which affect the kinds of people who apply; and (3) the characteristics and behaviors of the recruiter. These, in turn, influence both the nature of the vacancies and the nature of the people applying for jobs in a way that shapes job choice decisions.[56]

Personnel Policies

Personnel policies is a generic term we use to refer to organizational decisions that affect the nature of the vacancies for which people are recruited. If the research on recruitment makes one thing clear, it is that characteristics of the vacancy are more important than recruiters or recruiting sources when it comes to predicting job choice.

LO4
Describe the various
recruitment policies that
organizations adopt to
make job vacancies more
attractive.

Internal versus External Recruiting: Job Security

One desirable feature of a vacancy is that it provides ample opportunity for advancement and promotion. One organizational policy that affects this is the degree to which the company "promotes from within"—that is, recruits for upper-level vacancies internally rather than externally. Indeed, a 2001 survey of MBA students found that this was their top consideration when evaluating a company.[57]

We discuss internal versus external recruiting both here and in the section "Recruitment Sources" later in this chapter because this policy affects the nature of both the job and the individuals who apply. For now, we focus on the effects that promote-from-within policies have on job characteristics, noting that such policies make it clear to applicants that there are opportunities for advancement within the company.

These opportunities spring not just from the first vacancy but from the vacancy created when a person in the company fills that vacancy. Similarly, during downtimes, organizations with strong internal recruiting orientations typically have developed information systems that support reassigning potentially dislocated workers to different jobs in the company.

A good example of the power of tapping internal sources of recruits is provided by Edwards Lifesciences, a medical device maker that has grown an average of 7 percent a year for the last 10 years. Edwards Lifesciences workforce planning model begins with the identification of the 75 most critical jobs in the company and then identifies two or three individuals that would serve as potential excellent replacements or successors for the person currently occupying that job. Identifying these internal candidates early allows the firm to invest in them slowly, but surely, providing them with extra training both in technical areas and general leadership skills. This give the company a deep "bench" from which to draw talent, and indeed more than 70 percent of its most critical jobs are staffed from this bench.[58] The potential for extra training and the hope of upward advancement is a highly motivating element of the culture and helps keep attrition and turnover to some of the lowest rates in the industry.

In addition to employing promote from within and internal recruiting sources, perceptions of job security and long-term commitment to the organization are also promoted by "due process policies." **Employment-at-will policies** state that either party in the employment relationship can terminate that relationship at any time, regardless of cause. Companies that do not have employment-at-will provisions typically have extensive due process policies. **Due process policies** formally lay out the steps an employee can take to appeal a termination decision. Organizational recruiting materials that emphasize due process, rights of appeal, and grievance mechanisms send a message that job security is high; employment-at-will policies suggest the opposite. Research indicates that job applicants find companies with due process policies more attractive than companies with employment-at-will policies.[59]

Extrinsic and Intrinsic Rewards

Because pay is an important job characteristic for almost all applicants, companies that take a "lead-the-market" approach to pay—that is, a policy of paying higher-than-current-market wages—have a distinct advantage in recruiting. Pay can also make up for a job's less desirable features—for example, paying higher wages to employees who have to work midnight shifts. These kinds of specific shift differentials and other forms of more generic compensating differentials will be discussed in more detail in later chapters that focus on compensation strategies. We merely note here that "lead" policies make any given vacancy more attractive to applicants.

Increasingly, organizations that compete for applicants based on pay do so using pay forms other than wages and salary. In the 1990s many employers attempted to recruit employees with promises of stock option plans. However, the 2001 recession saw stock values drop sharply, thus reducing the attractiveness of this specific inducement. In addition, many people became aware of restrictions on stock option plans in the wake of the Enron bankruptcy in December 2001. Some low-level and midlevel Enron employees held stock options worth more than $1 million. When Enron stock started to slide, the company prevented its employees from cashing out their options, leaving many to helplessly watch their stock become worthless. Other Enron employees whose 401(k) plans were entirely based on Enron stock (which they too could not

---

Employment-at-Will Policies
Policies which state that either an employer or an employee can terminate the employment relationship at any time, regardless of cause.

Due Process Policies
Policies by which a company formally lays out the steps an employee can take to appeal a termination decision.

sell) also suffered. It only made matters worse when the U.S. Securities and Exchange Commission suggested that Enron's top executives illegally made more than $1 billion off stock sales just prior to the bankruptcy announcement.

There are limits to what can be done in terms of using pay to attract people to certain jobs, however. For example, the U.S. Army, because of the ongoing wars in Iraq and Afghanistan, struggled and failed to meet its 2005 recruiting goals for new soldiers, despite offering a $20,000 signing bonus and a $400 a month raise in base pay for infantry positions. As General Michael Rochelle, head of Army recruiting, notes, "We can't get started down a slippery slope where we are depending on money to lure people in. The reality is that while we have to remain at least competitive, we're never going to be able to pay as much as the private sector." To offset this disadvantage in extrinsic financial rewards, the Army has to rely on more intrinsic rewards related to patriotism and personal growth opportunities that people associate with military service. For example, Rochelle suggests that "the idea that being a soldier strengthens you for today and for tomorrow, for whatever you go on to do in life, that clearly resonates with them," and thus this serves as an alternative means of appealing to recruits.[60] The Army's Partnership for Youth Success Program uses this idea to match recruits with private-sector employers who are interested in hiring former soldiers who have received the skills and experiences that the Army provides.

The Army also uses partnerships to help retain current soldiers, and one of these focuses on spouses. Because of the short-term nature of military deployments, spouses in the military have often struggled to find stable employment, and because marital discord is a primary negative influence on reenlistment, helping the spouses of soldiers can in turn promote retention. The Army partners with firms like Home Depot, Sprint, CVS, Sears, and Dell because these employers have many branches in different parts of the country. Thus, if the soldier is forced to redeploy from one base to another, the private company may well have openings that would allow the spouse to simply transfer from one branch to another. Partnerships like this help support soldiers but do not necessarily result in direct competition on pay with respect to private employers.[61]

Home Depot has this same type of recruiting partnership with other organizations such as the American Association of Retired Persons (AARP). The AARP signs up interested members as part of a database and then works with Home Depot to find suitable jobs for its members. Because many AARP members have outside income from pensions or Social Security, competition on wages is not as significant a factor for this segment of the labor force as it is for younger workers who are raising families. Moreover, Home Depot's own research makes it clear that the turnover and absenteeism rates are lower for older workers than for their younger colleagues. As Home Depot's CEO notes, "When you look at the knowledge and career experience, and the passion of the members of the AARP, this is a gold mine of resources to draw upon, and this helps us gain competitive advantage."[62]

Image Advertising

Organizations often advertise specific vacancies (discussed next in the section "Recruitment Sources"). Sometimes, however, organizations advertise just to promote themselves as a good place to work in general.[63] Image advertising is particularly important for companies in highly competitive labor markets that perceive themselves as having a bad image. Indeed, research evidence suggests that the impact of company image on applicant reactions ranks second only to the nature of the work itself.[64]

Even though it does not provide any information about any specific job, image advertising is often effective because job applicants develop ideas about the general reputation of the firm (i.e., its brand image) and then this spills over to influence their expectations about the nature of specific jobs or careers at the organization.[65] Although someone once said that there is no such thing as bad publicity, this is not always true when it comes to recruiting. Although familiarity is better than lack of familiarity in general, applicants seem to be especially sensitive to bad publicity, and thus advertising campaigns are often used to try to send a positive message about the organization.[66] Although a firm can try to create an image using television advertisements or Web pages, research suggests that face-to-face contact (such as that provided by job fairs) is a much stronger avenue to enhance one's image.[67]

Research suggests that the language associated with the organization's brand image is often similar to personality trait descriptions that one might more commonly use to describe another person (such as innovative or competent or sincere).[68] These perceptions then influence the degree to which the person feels attracted to the organization, especially if there appears to be a good fit between the traits of the applicant and the traits that describe the organization.[69] Applicants seem particularly sensitive to issues of diversity and inclusion in these types of advertisements, and hence organizations that advertise their image need to go out of their way to ensure that the actors in their advertisements reflect the broad nature of the labor market constituencies that they are trying to appeal to in terms of race, gender, and culture.[70]

Recruitment Sources

LO5

List the various sources from which job applicants can be drawn, their relative advantages and disadvantages, and the methods for evaluating them.

The sources from which a company recruits potential employees are a critical aspect of its overall recruitment strategy. The total labor market is expansive; any single organization needs to draw from only a fraction of that total. The size and nature of the fraction that applies for an organization's vacancies will be affected by how (and to whom) the organization communicates its vacancies. The type of person who is likely to respond to a job advertised on the Internet may be different from the type of person who responds to an ad in the classified section of a local newspaper. In this section we examine the different sources from which recruits can be drawn, highlighting the advantages and disadvantages of each.

Internal versus External Sources

We discussed internal versus external sources of recruits earlier in this chapter and focused on the positive effects that internal recruiting can have on recruits' perceptions of job characteristics. We will now discuss this issue again, but with a focus on how using internal sources affects the kinds of people who are recruited.

In general, relying on internal sources offers a company several advantages. First, it generates a sample of applicants who are well known to the firm. Second, these applicants are relatively knowledgeable about the company's vacancies, which minimizes the possibility of inflated expectations about the job. Third, it is generally cheaper and faster to fill vacancies internally. A good example of this can be seen in our chapter-opening vignette regarding GM. Even though most people felt that GM needed to bring in an outsider to instill more change in the conservative company, the speed and technical nature of the work that had to be done dictated that an insider be selected to replace Rick Wagoner. The company had only 60 days to come up with a revised plan, and no outsider could have been expected to both learn the business and come up with a technically viable plan in such a short time period.

A good example of the value of an internal recruitment system can be seen in the experience of Sun Trust. In 2000, Sun Trust, a large and diversified banking institution with close to 30,000 employees, was organized into 28 separate regional centers, each with its own Human Resource Department. Each department operated independently, and thus they all had different technologies, different services, and different forms and procedures for all sorts of HR activities including recruiting. This precluded any form of coordinated activity across regions and also created huge redundancies and inefficiencies. In 2002, the organization restructured its Human Resource Department and went from being a decentralized and divisional structure to a more centralized and functional structure (see Chapter 4 for a discussion of these different dimensions of structure). Job descriptions and recruiting practices were standardized, and all existing employees' skill sets were entered into a central database to promote internal movement within the organization. One year later, the time it took to fill a vacancy went from 30 days to 20 days, and the cost per hire dropped from $1,100 to $900. Much of this was attributed to the more efficient utilization of internal applicants.[71]

With all these advantages, you might ask why any organization would ever employ external recruiting methods. There are several good reasons why organizations might decide to recruit externally. First, for entry-level positions and perhaps even for some specialized upper-level positions, there may not be any internal recruits from which to draw. Second, bringing in outsiders may expose the organization to new ideas or new ways of doing business. Using only internal recruitment can result in a workforce whose members all think alike and who therefore may be poorly suited to innovation.[72] For example, for most of its 100-year history, retailer JCPenney followed a practice of strictly promoting from within. This led to a very strong culture that in many ways was still closely related to the one first established by JCPenney himself in the late 1800s. The company's image was very conservative, and the behavior and attire of the employees was very formal. This culture made it difficult to attract and retain younger workers, however, and the accounting department estimated that turnover was costing the company $400 million a year. To stem the tide, JCPenney brought in an outsider, Mike Ullman, as the new CEO in 2006, and his first steps in redirecting the company were to loosen up the culture and hire more outsiders into key management positions. This was central to the CEO's new competitive strategy, in the sense that, in Ullman's own words, "In retailing today, you have to realize there is too much property and too much merchandise—what there isn't enough of is talent. If I had a choice to honor the past and lose, or move forward and win, I pick winning."[73]

Finally, recruiting from outside sources is a good way to strengthen one's own company and weaken one's competitors at the same time. This strategy seems to be particularly effective during bad economic times, where "counter cyclical hiring" policies create once-in-a-lifetime opportunities for acquiring talent.[74] For example, during the most recent recession, many firms that were top performers—and hence able to weather the storm better than their lower-performing competitors—viewed this as an excellent opportunity to poach the highest-performing individuals within struggling companies.[75] Thus, for many organizations, times of crisis and turbulence are actually the best time for them to shine by leveraging their current talent and success to bring in more talent and achieve even greater success over the long term.[76]

Direct Applicants and Referrals

Direct Applicants
People who apply for a job vacancy without prompting from the organization.

Referrals
People who are prompted to apply for a job by someone within the organization.

Direct applicants are people who apply for a vacancy without prompting from the organization. **Referrals** are people who are prompted to apply by someone within the organization. These two sources of recruits share some characteristics that make them excellent sources from which to draw.

First, many direct applicants are to some extent already "sold" on the organization. Most of them have done some homework and concluded that there is enough fit between themselves and the vacancy to warrant their submitting an application. This process is called *self-selection*. A form of aided self-selection occurs with referrals. Many job seekers look to friends, relatives, and acquaintances to help find employment, and evoking these social networks can greatly aid the job search process for both the job seeker and the organization.[77] Current employees (who are knowledgeable of both the vacancy and the person they are referring) do their homework and conclude that there is a fit between the person and the vacancy; they then sell the person on the job. Indeed, research shows that new hires that used at least one informal source reported having greater prehire knowledge of the organization than those who relied exclusively on formal recruitment sources. These kinds of "word-of mouth" endorsements from credible sources seem to have a particularly strong effect early in the recruitment process when people are still unfocused in their search process.[78] Ironically, as more and more recruiting is accomplished via impersonal sources like the Internet, the ability to draw on personal sources of information on recruits is becoming even more valuable. At companies like Sprint, the percentage of new hires from this source has gone from 8 percent to 34 percent in the last three years alone.[79]

When one figures into these results the low costs of such sources, they clearly stand out as one of the best sources of new hires, and some employers even offer financial incentives to current employees for referring applicants who are accepted and perform acceptably on the job (stay 180 days, for example).[80] Other companies play off their good reputations in the labor market to generate direct applications. In the war for talent, some employers who try to entice one new employee from a competitor will often try to leverage that one person to try to entice even more people away. The term "liftout" has been coined for this practice of trying to recruit a whole team of people. For example, when Mike Mertz was recruited as the new chief executive at Optimus, a computer servicing outfit, within hours of leaving his former employer, he in turn recruited seven other former colleagues to join Optimus. Liftouts are seen as valuable because in recruiting a whole intact group, as Mertz notes, "You get the dynamics of a functioning team without having to create that yourself."[81] Indeed, the team chemistry and coordination that often takes years to build is already in place after a liftout, and this kind of speed provides competitive advantage. Of course, having a whole team lifted out of your organization is devastating, because customers are frequently next to leave, following the talent rather than standing pat, and hence firms have to work hard to make sure that they can retain their critical teams.

Advertisements in Newspapers and Periodicals

Advertisements to recruit personnel are ubiquitous, even though they typically generate less desirable recruits than direct applications or referrals—and do so at greater expense. However, because few employers can fill all their vacancies with direct applications and referrals, some form of advertising is usually needed. Moreover, an employer can take many steps to increase the effectiveness of this recruitment method.

The two most important questions to ask in designing a job advertisement are, What do we need to say? and To whom do we need to say it? With respect to the first question, many organizations fail to adequately communicate the specifics of the vacancy. Ideally, persons reading an ad should get enough information to evaluate the job and its requirements, allowing them to make a well-informed judgment regarding their qualifications. This could mean running long advertisements, which costs more. However, these additional costs should be evaluated against the costs of processing a huge number of applicants who are not reasonably qualified or who would not find the job acceptable once they learn more about it.

Perhaps the biggest problem with most advertisements is that they are often written to be overdemanding in terms of the actual skill requirements that are needed for the work, decreasing the number of legitimate applicants more than necessary. Some have estimated that roughly half of the labor shortage in certain engineering fields can be traced to this problem. For example, as one recruiter of software engineers noted with respect to his company's search policy, "I say smart people can learn sister applications, but there is a reluctance among hiring managers to see that. If they use a SAP database system, they won't even look at someone with experience with PeopleSoft."[82]

In terms of whom to reach with this message, the organization placing the advertisement has to decide which medium it will use. The classified section of local newspapers is the most common medium. It is a relatively inexpensive means of reaching many people within a specified geographic area who are currently looking for work (or at least interested enough to be reading the classifieds). On the downside, this medium does not allow an organization to target skill levels very well. Typically, classified ads are read by many people who are either over- or underqualified for the position. Moreover, people who are not looking for work rarely read the classifieds, and thus this is not the right medium for luring people away from their current employers. Specially targeted journals and periodicals may be better than general newspapers at reaching a specific part of the overall labor market. In addition, employers are increasingly using television—particularly cable television—as a reasonably priced way of reaching people.

Electronic Recruiting

The growth of the information superhighway has opened up new vistas for organizations trying to recruit talent. There are many ways to employ the Internet, and increasingly organizations are refining their use of this medium. In fact, a recent survey of HR executives indicated that electronic job boards were the most effective source of recruits for 36 percent of the respondents, well ahead of local newspapers (21 percent), job fairs (4 percent), and walk-ins and referrals (1 percent).[83]

Obviously, one of the easiest ways to get into "e-cruiting" is to simply use the organization's own Web page to solicit applications. By using their own Web page, organizations can highly tune their recruitment message and focus in on specific people. For example, the interactive nature of this medium allows individuals to fill out surveys that describe what they are looking for and what they have to offer the organizations. These surveys can be "graded" immediately and recruits can be given direct feedback about how well they are matched for the organization. Research shows that this type of immediate feedback regarding their fit is helpful both to recruits and to the organization, by quickly and cheaply eliminating misfits for either side.[84] Indeed, customizing e-recruiting sites to maximize their targeted potential for helping people effectively match their own values with the organization's values, and their skills with the demands of the job is probably their best feature.[85] As the "Competing through Technology" box shows, the Obama administration is trying to leverage this technology to overhaul the way the federal government recruits future employees in an era of expanded government hiring.

Of course, smaller and less well-known organizations may not attract any attention to their own Web sites, and thus for them this is not a good option. A second way for organizations to use the Web is to interact with the large, well-known job sites such as Monster.com, HotJobs.com, or CareerBuilder.com. These sites attract a vast array of applicants, who submit standardized résumés that can be electronically searched using key terms. Applicants can also search for companies in a similar fashion; the hope, of course, is that there may be a match between the employer and the applicant. The biggest downside to these large sites, however, is their sheer size and lack of differentiation. Because of this limitation of the large sites, smaller, more tailored Web sites called "niche boards" focus on certain industries, occupations, or geographic areas. For example, Telecommcareers.net is a site devoted to, as the name implies, the telecommunications industry. CIO.com, a companion site to *CIO Magazine*, is an occupational board that specializes in openings for chief information officers.

The increased familiarity of Web devotees with Web logs or "blogs" has created other opportunities for recruiters to reach out and have public or semi-public conversations with recruits. Microsoft's senior recruiter for marketing, Heather Hamilton, manages a blog that describes what it is like to work at a marketing career at Microsoft. Interested candidates can read what she posts, and then ask questions or provide their own information. This allows many other "passive" applicants to see the answers to previous questions or what other people who are applying to the organization are like. In one week alone, this blog was viewed by over 25,000 people, and as Hamilton notes, "the big thing for me is reach. . . . as a recruiter, I could be on the phone all day every day and not be able to reach that many people."[86]

The growing use of iPods has also opened up a new and rich avenue to get information from employer to applicant via podcasts. A podcast is an audio or audio/visual program that can be placed on the Web by an employer and then downloaded onto a computer or an iPod for subsequent viewing. Podcast are like e-mails in the sense that they can be used to reach out to a large number of people; however, the rich nature of the media—which employs color, sound, and video—is much more powerful than a simple text-only e-mail. "Podcasts really make the job description comes alive," notes Dan Finnigan, a general manager at HotJobs.com, and the ability to describe the organization's culture is so much more emotionally charged with this media relative to mere words on a page.[87]

Social networking sites such as Facebook and MySpace.com are yet another avenue for employers to reach out to younger workers in their own environments. Neither Facebook nor MySpace allow employers to create pages as members, but it does allow them to purchase pages in order to create what is called a "sponsored group." Ernst & Young's sponsored group page has been joined by more than 5,000 Facebook users, who can access information about Ernst & Young and chat with recruiters from the company in a blog-like manner.[88] Unlike more formal media, the conversations held here are very informal and serve as an easy first step for potential recruits to take in their relationship with the company.

As with any new and developing technology, all of these approaches present some unique challenges. From an employer's perspective, the interactive, dynamic, and unpredictable nature of blogs and social networking sites means that sometimes,

COMPETING THROUGH TECHNOLOGY
Web-Based Recruiting: The Portal to Federal Jobs

In the 10 years between 1999 and 2008, much of the work that was once done by the federal government was outsourced to the private sector. Indeed, during this time period, the number of federal contractors grew by more than 50 percent as part of a major privatization program. When Barack Obama became president, however, he vowed to reverse this trend. In fact, there were roughly 2 million federal workers prior to the 2008 election, and President Obama had argued on the campaign trail that he was looking to add another 500,000 people to the federal rolls. One reason for this was the general public perception that private contractors were not up to some of the challenges that they faced (e.g., the Hurricane Katrina crisis). In addition, however, the sheer amount of money that Obama was committed to spending, plus his promise to create more transparency in how government money was being spent, dictated a higher degree of in-sourcing. The ability to monitor how outside firms spend their money is very low, and the administration knew that the opportunity for misuse of funds, corruption, or just being surprised at how money was being spent was very high.

The questions then became, of course, was the talent level within the federal government ready for this new expanded role, and if not, was the government going to be able to recruit the talent it needed to offset any shortages? In the opinion of many observers, the answer to both questions was uncertain.

For example, with respect to the current talent base, many of the labor shortages faced by the federal government laid in middle-level management positions that had been gutted over the past 20 years. In that time period, the government only provided across-the-board cost-of-living adjustments that failed to distinguish top performers from mediocre performers. Because of this, many of the best workers left for private sectors jobs after having developed experience and working their way to middle-level ranks. As John Hamre, CEO of the Center for Strategic and International Studies, noted, "We have not brought in talent in systematic ways for the past 15 years. Government is enfeebled precisely at a time when we need a stronger, more capable and sophisticated government."

Changing this situation was not going to be easy. For example, anyone who has ever tried to apply for a job with the federal government knows the process is onerous. There are a whole host of confusing forms to fill out, and the lag between actually applying for a job and receiving a confirmation of this could take months, let alone the time it takes to actually receive an offer. As Scott Cameron, the director of a major public sector consulting firm, noted, "It is a nightmare to apply for a federal service job. If any American company recruited people the same way the federal government does, then that company would be out of business."

Perhaps because Barack Obama's presidential campaign was unprecedented in the success it achieved using the Internet as a means of recruiting support and supporters, it is not all that surprising that he would try to leverage the same technology to recruit a more talented workforce. The first attempt at this was a Web site called www.change.gov. This was a single, one-stop Web portal for applicants set up during the Obama transition. Although a noble effort, this site was troubled from the beginning. One of the problems with the site was that it did not identify specific openings and failed to provide substantive job descriptions. In addition, the site turned out to be mostly just a portal for collecting résumés and did little to screen unqualified workers or identify needed talent. Most of the decisions about applicants recruited from this site had to be made the old-fashioned way—reading and arriving at subjective judgments. When the Obama team took office, the www.change.gov site was replaced with the www.whitehouse.gov site, which corrected some of the deficiencies associated with the original www.change.gov site. You can see for yourself whether this new site is new and improved by going specifically to http://www.whitehouse.gov/blog_post/apply_for_a_job/.

SOURCES: M. Schoeff, "A Renaissance for Government Work?" *Workforce Management,* February 16, 2009, pp. 32–33; L. Lavell, "The Hunt: Lost in Job Search Limbo," *Business,* March 29, 2009, p. 21; D. Jones, "Hundreds Apply for Custom's Jobs," *BusinessWeek,* March 22, 2009, p. 33.

people who have negative things to say about the organization join in on the conversations, and this can be difficult to control. The biggest liability from the applicant's perspective is the need to protect his or her identity, because this medium has also been a haven for identity thieves, who post false openings in the hope of getting some applicant to provide personal information.[89] In general, an applicant interacting with these types of sites should never provide Social Security numbers or set up bank accounts or submit to security checks until they have visited the employer and met them in person. These sites help employers and applicants take the first step toward building a relationship, and these other steps should not be taken until much, much later.

Public and Private Employment Agencies

The Social Security Act of 1935 requires that everyone receiving unemployment compensation be registered with a local state employment office. These state employment offices work with the U.S. Employment Service (USES) to try to ensure that unemployed individuals eventually get off state aid and back on employer payrolls. To accomplish this, agencies collect information from the unemployed about their skills and experiences.

Employers can register their job vacancies with their local state employment office, and the agency will attempt to find someone suitable using its computerized inventory of local unemployed individuals. The agency makes referrals to the organization at no charge, and these individuals can be interviewed or tested by the employer for potential vacancies. Because of certain legislative mandates, state unemployment offices often have specialized "desks" for minorities, handicapped individuals, and Vietnam-era veterans. Thus, this is an excellent source for employers who feel they are currently underutilizing any of these subgroups.

Public employment agencies serve primarily the blue-collar labor market; private employment agencies perform much the same service for the white-collar labor market. Unlike public agencies, however, private employment agencies charge the organization for the referrals. Another difference between private and public employment agencies is that one doesn't have to be unemployed to use a private employment agency.

One special type of private employment agency is the so-called executive search firm (ESF). These agencies are often referred to as *headhunters* because, unlike the other sources we have examined, they operate almost exclusively with people who are currently employed. Dealing with executive search firms is sometimes a sensitive process because executives may not want to advertise their availability for fear of their current employer's reaction. Thus, ESFs serve as an important confidentiality buffer between the employer and the recruit. Along with newspapers and classified advertisements, ESFs may have suffered the most damage in recent years due to the combination of reduced employment levels because of the recent recession on the one hand and increased use of low cost electronic search vehicles on the other. Many have questioned whether the ESFs have a viable business model, given the recent changes in the economy and in technology.[90]

Colleges and Universities

Most colleges and universities have placement services that seek to help their graduates obtain employment. Indeed, on-campus interviewing is the most important source of recruits for entry-level professional and managerial vacancies.[91] Organizations tend to focus especially on colleges that have strong reputations in areas for which they have critical needs (chemical engineering, public accounting, or the like).[92]

Many employers have found that to effectively compete for the best students, they need to do more than just sign prospective graduates up for interview slots. One of the best ways to establish a stronger presence on a campus is with a college internship program. For example, Dun & Bradstreet funds a summer intern program for minority MBA students and often hires these interns for full-time positions when they graduate.[93] These kinds of programs allow an organization to get early access to potential applicants and to assess their capacities directly. Another way of increasing one's presence on campus is to participate in university job fairs. In general, a job fair is a place where many employers gather for a short time to meet large numbers of potential job applicants. Although job fairs can be held anywhere (such as at a hotel or convention center), campuses are ideal locations because of the many well-educated, yet unemployed, individuals who live there. Job fairs are a rather inexpensive means of generating an on-campus presence and can even provide one-on-one dialogue with potential recruits—dialogue that could not be achieved through less interactive media like newspaper ads. Finally, as more organizations attempt to compete on a global level, the ability to recruit individuals who will be successful both at home and abroad is a growing concern. Many organizations feel that college campuses are one of the best places to search for this type of transportable talent.

Evaluating the Quality of a Source

Because there are few rules about the quality of a given source for a given vacancy, it is generally a good idea for employers to monitor the quality of all their recruitment sources. One means of accomplishing this is to develop and compare yield ratios for each source.[94] Yield ratios express the percentage of applicants who successfully move from one stage of the recruitment and selection process to the next. Comparing yield ratios for different sources helps determine which is best or most efficient for the type of vacancy being investigated. Data on cost per hire are also useful in establishing the efficiency of a given source.[95]

Table 5.4 shows hypothetical yield ratios and cost-per-hire data for five recruitment sources. For the job vacancies generated by this company, the best two sources of recruits are local universities and employee referral programs. Newspaper ads generate the largest number of recruits, but relatively few of these are qualified for the position. Recruiting at nationally renowned universities generates highly qualified applicants, but relatively few of them ultimately accept positions. Finally, executive search firms generate a small list of highly qualified, interested applicants, but this is an expensive source compared with other alternatives.

Recruiters

The last part of the model presented in Figure 5.4 that we will discuss is the recruiter. We consider the recruiter this late in the chapter to reinforce our earlier observation that the recruiter often gets involved late in the process. In many cases, by the time a recruiter meets some applicants, they have already made up their minds about what they desire in a job, what the current job has to offer, and their likelihood of receiving a job offer.[96]

Moreover, many applicants approach the recruiter with some degree of skepticism. Knowing that it is the recruiter's job to sell them on a vacancy, some applicants may

LO6
Explain the recruiter's role in the recruitment process, the limits the recruiter faces, and the opportunities available.

table 5.4

Hypothetical Yield Ratios for Five Recruitment Sources

	RECRUITING SOURCE				
	LOCAL UNIVERSITY	RENOWNED UNIVERSITY	EMPLOYEE REFERRALS	NEWSPAPER AD	EXECUTIVE SEARCH FIRMS
Résumés generated	200	400	50	500	20
Interview offers accepted	175	100	45	400	20
Yield ratio	87%	25%	90%	80%	100%
Applicants judged acceptable	100	95	40	50	19
Yield ratio	57%	95%	89%	12%	95%
Accept employment offers	90	10	35	25	15
Yield ratio	90%	11%	88%	50%	79%
Cumulative yield ratio	90/200 45%	10/400 3%	35/50 70%	25/500 5%	15/20 75%
Cost	$30,000	$50,000	$15,000	$20,000	$90,000
Cost per hire	$333	$5,000	$428	$800	$6,000

discount what the recruiter says relative to what they have heard from other sources (like friends, magazine articles, and professors). For these and other reasons, recruiters' characteristics and behaviors seem to have less impact on applicants' job choices than we might expect.

Recruiter's Functional Area. Most organizations must choose whether their recruiters are specialists in human resources or experts at particular jobs (supervisors or job incumbents). Some studies indicate that applicants find a job less attractive and the recruiter less credible when he is a personnel specialist.[97] This does not completely discount personnel specialists' role in recruiting, but it does indicate that such specialists need to take extra steps to ensure that applicants perceive them as knowledgeable and credible.

Recruiter's Traits. Two traits stand out when applicants' reactions to recruiters are examined. The first, which could be called "warmth," reflects the degree to which the recruiter seems to care about the applicant and is enthusiastic about her potential to contribute to the company. The second characteristic could be called "informativeness." In general, applicants respond more positively to recruiters who are perceived as warm and informative. These characteristics seem more important than such demographic characteristics as age, sex, or race, which have complex and inconsistent effects on applicant responses.[98]

Recruiter's Realism. Perhaps the most well-researched aspect of recruiting deals with the level of realism that the recruiter incorporates into his message. Because the recruiter's job is to attract candidates, there is some pressure to exaggerate the positive features of the vacancy while downplaying the negative features. Applicants are highly sensitive to negative information. On the other hand, if the recruiter goes too far in a positive direction, the candidate can be misled and lured into taking the job under false pretenses.[99] This can lead to a serious case of unmet expectations and a high turnover rate.[100] In fact, unrealistic descriptions of a job may even lead new job incumbents to believe that the employer is deceitful.[101]

Many studies have looked at the capacity of "realistic job previews" to circumvent this problem and help minimize early job turnover. On the whole, the research indicates that realistic job previews do lower expectations and can help reduce future turnover in the workforce.[102] Certainly, the idea that one can go overboard in selling a vacancy to a recruit has merit. However, the belief that informing people about the negative characteristics of the job will totally "inoculate" them to such characteristics seems unwarranted, based on the research conducted to date.[103] Thus we return to the conclusion that an organization's decisions about personnel policies that directly affect the job's attributes (pay, security, advancement opportunities, and so on) will probably be more important than recruiter traits and behaviors in affecting job choice. Indeed, research indicates that structured interventions that help applicants simply make good decisions about which jobs are best for them may work out best for both employers and applicants. That is, helping applicants better understand their own needs and qualifications and then linking this to the current openings may be best in the long run for all concerned, even if it does not result in an immediate hire.[104]

Enhancing Recruiter Impact. Although research suggests that recruiters do not have much influence on job choice, this does not mean recruiters cannot have an impact. For example, in contexts where applicants already have high awareness of the organization because its products are well known, the impact of the recruiter is weaker than in contexts where the applicant has low product awareness.[105] Organizations can take several steps to increase the impact that recruiters have on those they recruit. First, recruiters can provide timely feedback. Applicants react very negatively to delays in feedback, often making unwarranted attributions for the delays (such as, the organization is uninterested in my application). Second, recruiting can be done in teams rather than by individuals. As we have seen, applicants tend to view line personnel (job incumbents and supervisors) as more credible than personnel specialists, so these kinds of recruiters should be part of any team. On the other hand, personnel specialists have knowledge that is not shared by line personnel (who may perceive recruiting as a small part of their "real" jobs), so they should be included as well.

A LOOK BACK

Our chapter-opening story described how the failure to accurately forecast the supply and demand of labor leads to both long-term problems in terms of the organization's competitive position against foreign rivals and short-term problems associated with securing government bailout money. These problems, in turn, led to the termination of longtime CEO Rick Wagoner and sparked a debate about whether an insider or outsider ought to be recruited to take his place.

Questions

1. At the national level, do you think it is appropriate for the federal government to demand the resignation of a CEO like Rick Wagoner? Do you think it is appropriate for the federal government to have a say in who is recruited to be his successor?
2. If you were a leader at a U.S. auto company like Ford, who paid taxes but did not request a government bailout, do you think it is fair for the government to directly support one of your competitors with taxpayer money? If Ford was more self-sufficient than General Motors, would it be better to direct support to them rather than General Motors?

3. If you were a leader at a foreign competitor of General Motors, would you consider that federal government's bailout a form of "protectionism"? If the Japanese government was not giving money to its own firms, would it be fair for them to apply a protective tariff on General Motors cars entering Japan to offset the direct aid General Motors is getting from the government?

4. In what way did the business represented by General Motors fail in the competitive marketplace, and would the organization, the country, and the world be better or worse off it the organization simply went into bankruptcy? If an organization is "too big to fail," what does this say about large size as a source of competitive advantage?

 Please see the Video Case that corresponds to this chapter online at www.mhhe .com/noe7e.

SUMMARY

Human resource planning uses labor supply and demand forecasts to anticipate labor shortages and surpluses. It also entails programs that can be utilized to reduce a labor surplus (such as downsizing and early retirement programs) and eliminate a labor shortage (like bringing in temporary workers or expanding overtime). When done well, human resource planning can enhance the success of the organization while minimizing the human suffering resulting from poorly anticipated labor surpluses or shortages. Human resource recruiting is a buffer activity that creates an applicant pool that the organization can draw from in the event of a labor shortage that is to be filled with new hires. Organizational recruitment programs affect applications through personnel policies (such as promote-from-within policies or due process provisions) that affect the attributes of the vacancies themselves. They can also impact the nature of people who apply for positions by using different recruitment sources (like recruiting from universities versus advertising in newspapers). Finally, organizations can use recruiters to influence individuals' perceptions of jobs (eliminating misconceptions, clarifying uncertainties) or perceptions of themselves (changing their valences for various work outcomes).

KEY TERMS

Forecasting, 193
Leading indicator, 194
Transitional matrix, 195
Downsizing, 198

Outsourcing, 205
Offshoring, 206
Workforce utilization review, 209
Human resource recruitment, 210

Employment-at-will policies, 212
Due process policies, 212
Direct applicants, 216
Referrals, 216

DISCUSSION QUESTIONS

1. Discuss the effects that an impending labor shortage might have on the following three subfunctions of human resource management: selection and placement, training and career development, and compensation and benefits. Which subfunction might be most heavily impacted? In what ways might these groups develop joint cooperative programs to avert a labor shortage?

2. Discuss the costs and benefits associated with statistical versus judgmental forecasts for labor demand and labor supply. Under what conditions might either of these techniques be infeasible? Under what conditions might both be feasible, but one more desirable than the other?

3. Some companies have detailed affirmative action plans, complete with goals and timetables, for women

and minorities, and yet have no formal human resource plan for the organization as a whole. Why might this be the case? If you were a human resource specialist interviewing with this company for an open position, what would this practice imply for the role of the human resource manager in that company?

4. Recruiting people for jobs that entail international assignments is increasingly important for many companies. Where might one go to look for individuals interested in these types of assignments? How might recruiting practices aimed at these people differ from those one might apply to the "average" recruit?

5. Discuss the relative merits of internal versus external recruitment. What types of business strategies might best be supported by recruiting externally, and what types might call for internal recruitment? What factors might lead a firm to decide to switch from internal to external recruitment or vice versa?

SELF-ASSESSMENT EXERCISE

Most employers have to evaluate hundreds of résumés each week. If you want your résumé to have a good chance of being read by prospective employers, you must invest time and energy not only in its content, but also in its look. Review your résumé and answer yes or no to each of the following questions.

1. Does it avoid typos and grammatical errors?
2. Does it avoid using personal pronouns (such as I and me)?
3. Does it clearly identify what you have done and accomplished?
4. Does it highlight your accomplishments rather than your duties?
5. Does it exceed two pages in length?
6. Does it have correct contact information?
7. Does it have an employment objective that is specific and focuses on the employer's needs as well as your own?
8. Does it have at least one-inch margins?
9. Does it use a maximum of two typefaces or fonts?
10. Does it use bullet points to emphasize your skills and accomplishments?
11. Does it avoid use of underlining?
12. Is the presentation consistent? (Example: If you use all caps for the name of your most recent workplace, do you do that for previous workplaces as well?)

The more "yes" answers you gave, the more likely your résumé will attract an employer's attention and get you a job interview!

EXERCISING STRATEGY: SOUTHWEST AIRLINES: FOCUSED ON TAKE-OFFS, NOT LAYOFFS

In the summer of 2001, the airline industry was facing severe problems due to slumping business travel and vacationer demand. In fact, Northwest Airlines announced draconian cuts in both schedules and service; Midway Airlines declared bankruptcy in August of that year, citing a "calamitous" decline in air traffic. However, as bad as things were, they soon got worse.

The September 11, 2001, terrorist attacks on New York and Washington, DC, devastated the whole nation, but few segments of the economy felt the impact as dramatically as the already struggling airline industry. Even after reducing scheduled flights by more than 20 percent, most planes were taking off with fewer than half their seats filled, and airline shares lost a third of their value on the stock exchange. Most airlines needed to cut costs drastically in order to make ends meet, and over 100,000 employees were eventually laid off from American Airlines, United Airlines, US Airways, Continental Airlines, and America West.

Southwest Airlines bucked this trend, however. Indeed, despite the regular ups and downs of the airline industry, in its 30 years of operation, Southwest had never laid off employees; remarkably, it was able to maintain this record even during the difficult fall 2001 period. Southwest's no-layoff policy is one of the core values that underlie its human resource strategy, and insiders stress that it is one of the main reasons why the Southwest workforce is so fiercely loyal, productive, and flexible.

The high productivity of these workers helps keep labor costs low, and these savings are passed on to consumers in the form of lower prices that are sometimes half those offered by competitors. High levels of job security also promote a willingness on the part of Southwest employees to be innovative on the job without fearing that they will be punished for any mistakes. Southwest also finds that satisfied employees help create satisfied customers and can even help in recruiting new employees when economic conditions are conducive to growth.

In order to keep this perfect no-layoff record in 2001, Southwest executives assembled into an emergency command and control center in Dallas and brainstormed methods other than layoffs that could reduce costs. Decisions were made to delay the planned purchase of new planes, as well as to scrap ongoing plans to renovate the company's headquarters. The company, which had no debt and over a billion dollars in cash, also leaned heavily on this "rainy-day" fund to help get through tough times. It was a difficult and painful process, but as CEO Jim Parker noted, "We are willing to suffer some damage, even to our stock price, to protect the jobs of our people."

Questions

1. In this chapter, we explored several alternatives to layoffs as a means of reducing a labor surplus. Compare and contrast the list we generated with what was done at Southwest in the wake of the 9/11 attacks. How did the response at Southwest differ from the other airlines?

2. Southwest Airlines' "no-layoff policy" is an important component of its overall culture and strategy. In what ways does this no-layoff policy, which clearly hurts the airline in the short term, give Southwest a competitive advantage over other airlines in the long term?

3. In this chapter, we looked at the increased use of offshoring, where jobs are moved from the United States to other countries where labor rates are cheaper. In what ways is offshoring similar and different from a simple layoff? If there are some long-term benefits from avoiding layoffs, what might be the long-term advantages of trying to avoid offshoring?

SOURCES: M. Arndt, "Suddenly, Carriers Can't Get off the Ground," *BusinessWeek*, September 3, 2001, pp. 36–37; M. Arndt, "What Kind of Rescue?" *BusinessWeek*, October 1, 2001, pp. 36–37; W. Zeller, "Southwest: After Kelleher, More Blue Skies," *BusinessWeek*, April 2, 2001, p. 45; M. Conlin, "Where Layoffs Are a Last Resort," *BusinessWeek*, October 8, 2001, p. 42.

● MANAGING PEOPLE: FROM THE PAGES OF *BUSINESSWEEK*

BusinessWeek   Hang the Recession, Let's Bulk Up

The housing collapse let Sonnenschein Nath & Rosenthal follow its growth plan by gobbling up more than half the attorneys at a failed rival   While many rivals retreat and retrench, the corporate law firm Sonnenschein Nath & Rosenthal sees the downturn as a chance to gain market share. Its success will turn in large part on Sonnenschein's skill at exploiting the weakness of a fellow firm that entered the recession without a viable strategy.

For many high-end lawyers, as for the companies and banks they represent, these are times to eat or be eaten. In December, Sonnenschein, a well-established second-tier firm based in Chicago, cannibalized Thatcher Proffitt & Wood, an old New York partnership. Thatcher had grown fat on mortgage-backed securities work but stumbled when the housing market collapsed and no one wanted to buy bonds confected from home loans.

Sonnenschein gobbled up 100 Thatcher attorneys, swelling its ranks to 800 lawyers in 15 offices. After providing legal counsel for 160 years, Thatcher dissolved, leaving its remaining 70 lawyers to find other homes.

With profits down at most corporate law firms, attorneys are scrambling. "All the strong firms are working hard to pull good people or groups out of firms that are not performing as well," says law firm management consultant Peter Zeughauser. When San Francisco-based Heller Ehrman collapsed last year, former partners fled to such rivals as Washington-based Covington & Burling.

An Unlikely Expansion

The consolidation in the law business resembles, on a smaller scale, what's happening in banking. Professional services firms confront both extreme peril—and potential opportunity—as their reeling clients question every bill from high-priced outside advisers. Executive search firms such as Chicago-based Heidrick & Struggles International are redefining their mission as companies shed rather than hire top-echelon employees.

Sonnenschein's expansion at first glance appears to border on the reckless. The bulk of the lawyers it hoisted from Thatcher's sinking ship work in securitization and real estate finance, specialties that are moribund.

But Joseph J. Andrew, a member of Sonnenschein's management committee, says the firm plans to pair Thatcher's financial-services lawyers with Sonnenschein's large regulatory and lobbying practices in Washington. Because of the enormous federal bailout of so many banks and Wall Street firms, he says, "there is now a nexus between the capital markets and the U.S. government in a way that there never has been in history before."

Sonnenschein client Sopris Capital Advisors applauds its law firm's maneuvering. Neil Subin, an investment director for the New York-based hedge fund, who invests in distressed businesses, says that the ex-Thatcher attorneys could help him find value in beaten down structured-finance assets: "That is a huge opportunity."

Plus, says Sonnenschein's Andrew, "We're not bringing on a capital markets practice at the height. We're bringing them in at the bottom." In other words, former Thatcher partners can expect pay cuts. Sonnenschein associates face a salary freeze for 2009, the firm said in an internal memo in December.

Meanwhile, Sonnenschein's growth doesn't appear to have alienated its lucrative lobbying customers. Clients of the firm's Washington office last year included American International Group, Boeing, and MillerCoors, according to federal records analyzed by the Center for Responsive Politics, a nonprofit research group.

The Chicago-based firm's determination to expand dates back to a plan it instituted in 2006, before the start of the current economywide debacle. The strategy called for opening new offices around the country and taking on additional lawyers in a range of areas.

Determining that breadth and scale are vital to its success, Sonnenschein aimed for revenue of about $900 million within five years, which would place it among the top 25 firms nationwide. The recession might make that goal difficult to achieve. Even with its enlarged ranks, Sonnenschein expects revenue of only $550 million in 2009.

Most of Sonnenschein's growth has come by recruiting "laterals"—lawyers with established practices—rather than by hiring newly minted attorneys. Elliott I. Portnoy, its Washington-based chairman, who came over from another firm in 2002, says that building a cohesive culture is a core consideration.

Still, the bonds are only so tight. Even as it has grown, the firm has periodically let go attorneys and staff from areas in which business declined. Last year, Sonnenschein laid off about 60 attorneys in real estate and other practices hit by the souring economy.

Questions

1. What were some of the decisions and problems that caused Thatcher Proffitt & Wood to struggle in 2008, and how did this relate to the general problems facing the economy at that time? What were some of the likely lessons that were learned by Thatcher Proffitt & Wood attorneys based on this experience, and in what way might these attorneys be better at their jobs now than they were before?

2. How did the salaries of the ex-Thatcher Proffitt & Wood attorneys who went to work for Sonnenschein, Nath and Rosenthal compare with their old salaries? What were the areas of expertise that the lawyers at Thatcher Proffitt & Wood specialized in, and in what way was there a surplus of labor for people with these skills in 2008?

3. Why did Sonnenschein, Nath and Rosenthal feel that there was going to be an increase in demand for people with the skills of former Thatcher Proffitt & Wood attorneys, in the years ahead? In what ways does this type of "countercyclical" hiring create competitive advantage for firms?

4. What was the eventual long-term outcome for Thatcher Proffitt & Wood, and what happened to the 70 attorneys who were not able to jump ship in a timely fashion? How does the notion of "first-mover advantage" and fear and insecurity play into the hands of recruiters who prey on struggling firms?

SOURCE: M. Orey, "Hang the Recession, Let's Bulk Up," *BusinessWeek*, January 26, 2009, pp. 80–81.

NOTES

1. P. Coy, "What Falling Prices Tell Us," *BusinessWeek*, February 9, 2009, pp. 24–26.
2. K. Doheny, "Nursing Is in Critical Condition," *Workforce Management*, October 9, 2006, pp. 39–41.
3. A. Aston, "Who Will Run the Plants?" *BusinessWeek*, January 22, 2007, p. 78.
4. D. W. Jarrell, *Human Resource Planning: A Business Planning Approach* (Englewood Cliffs, NJ: Prentice Hall, 1993).
5. P. Coy, "Global Overcapacity," *BusinessWeek*, February 16, 2009, p. 26.
6. L. Chappel, "Toyota Plants Idling, But Workers Aren't," *Workforce Management*, September 8, 2008, pp. 22–24.
7. M. Conlin, "Savaged by the Slowdown," *BusinessWeek*, September 17, 2001, pp. 74–77.
8. N. D. Schwartz, "Will 'Made in the USA' Fade Away?" *Fortune*, November 24, 2003, pp. 98–110.
9. J. Schneider, "I'll Take a Big Mac, Fires and Hey How's the Weather in Fargo? *Lansing State Journal*, January 15, 2009, p. B1.
10. J. E. Hilsenrath, "Behind the Outsourcing Debate: Surprisingly, Few Hard Numbers," *The Wall Street Journal*, April 22, 2004, pp. A1–A3.
11. J. P. Guthrie, "Dumb and Dumber: The Impact of Downsizing on Firm Performance as Moderated by Industry Conditions," *Organization Science* 19 (2008), pp. 108–23.
12. J. McGregor, A. McConnon, and D. Kiley, "Customer Service in a Shrinking Economy," *BusinessWeek*, February 19, 2009, pp. 34–35.
13. D. S. DeRue, J. R. Hollenbeck, M. D. Johnson, D. R. Ilgen, and D. K. Jundt, "How Different Team Downsizing Approaches Influence Team-level Adaptation and Performance," *Academy of Management Journal* 51 (2008), pp. 182–96.
14. C. D. Zatzick and R. D. Iverson, "High-Involvement Management and Workforce Reduction: Competitive Advantage or Disadvantage?" *Academy of Management Journal* 49 (2006), pp. 999–1015.
15. P. P. Shaw, "Network Destruction: The Structural Implications of Downsizing," *Academy of Management Journal* 43 (2000), pp. 101–12.
16. J. Schu, "Internet Helps Keep Goodwill of Downsized Employees," *Workforce*, July 2001, p. 15.
17. C. O. Trevor, and A. J. Nyberg, "Keeping Your Headcount When All About You Are Losing Theirs: Downsizing, Voluntary

Turnover Rates, and the Moderating Role of HR Practices," *Academy of Management Journal* 51 (2008), pp. 259–76.

18. E. Frauenheim, "Technology Forcing Firms to Shed More Light on Layoffs," *Workforce Management*, January 19, 2009, pp. 7–8.

19. D. Skarlicki, J. H. Ellard, and B. R. C. Kellin, "Third Party Perceptions of a Layoff: Procedural, Derogation, and Retributive Aspects of Justice," *Journal of Applied Psychology* 83 (1998), pp. 119–27.

20. J. Holton, "You've Been Deleted," *Workforce Management*, September 11, 2006, p. 42.

21. E. Thronton, "The Hidden Perils of Layoffs," *BusinessWeek*, March 2, 2009, pp. 52–53.

22. J. E. Hilsenrath, "Adventures in Cost Cutting," *The Wall Street Journal*, May 10, 2004, pp. A1–A3.

23. J. Marquez, "The Would-be Retirees," *Workforce Management*, November 3, 2008, pp. 24–28.

24. J. S. Lublin and S. Thurm, "How Companies Calculate Odds in Buyout Offers," *The Wall Street Journal*, March 27, 2006, pp. B1–B2.

25. S. Gustafson, "38,000 Took Buyouts, Ford Says," *Columbus (Ohio) Dispatch*, November 2006, pp. E1–E2.

26. J. Bennett and J. D. Stoll, "GM Logs 7,500 Buyouts; Chrysler Extends Deadline," *The Wall Street Journal*, March 26, 2009, pp. C1–C2.

27. R. Adams, "New York Times Will Cut Salaries; Washington Post to Offer Buyouts," *The Wall Street Journal*, March 26, 2009, p. C1.

28. J. Weber, "Not Just a Temporary Lift," *BusinessWeek*, January 19, 2004.

29. S. A. Johnson and B. E. Ashforth, "Externalization of Employment in a Service Environment: The Role of Organizational and Customer Identification," *Journal of Organizational Behavior* 29 (2008), pp. 287–309.

30. M. Vidal and L.M. Tigges, "Temporary Employment and Strategic Staffing in the Manufacturing Sector," *Industrial Relations* 48 (2009), pp. 55–72.

31. M. L. Kraimer, S. J. Wayne, R. C. Liden, and R. T. Sparrowe, "The Role of Job Security in Understanding the Relationship between Employees' Perceptions of Temporary Workers and Employees' Performance," *Journal of Applied Psychology* 90 (2005), pp. 389–398.

32. J. Feife, R. Schook, B. Schyns, and B. Six, "Does the Form of Employment Make a Difference? Commitment of Traditional, Temporary, and Self-employed Workers," *Journal of Vocational Behavior* 72 (2008), pp. 81–94.

33. C. Hajim, "Bodies in Motion," *Fortune*, February 19, 2007, p. 114.

34. J. Marquez, "Inside Job," *Workforce Management*, February 12, 2006, pp. 19–21.

35. F. Hanson, "Special Report: Mid-market Outsourcing," *Workforce Management*, February 12, 2007, pp. 23–26.

36. P. Engardio, "Let's Offshore the Lawyers," *BusinessWeek*, September 18, 2006, pp. 42–43.

37. M. Kripalani, "Call Center? That's so 2004," *BusinessWeek*, August 7, 2006, pp. 40–41.

38. S. Hamm, "Outsourcing Heads to the Outskirts," *BusinessWeek*, January 22, 2007, p. 56.

39. S. Shellenbarger, "Outsourcing Jobs to the Den," *The Wall Street Journal*, January 2, 2006, p. D1.

40. W. Zellner, "Lessons from a Faded Levi-Strauss," *BusinessWeek*, December 15, 2003, p. 44.

41. A. Meisler, "Think Globally, Act Rationally," *Workforce*, January 2004, pp. 40–45.

42. A. Tiwana, "Does Firm Modularity Complement Ignorance? A Field Study of Software Outsourcing Alliances," *Strategic Management Journal* 29 (2008), pp. 1241–52.

43. S. E. Ante, "Shifting Work Offshore? Outsourcer Beware," *BusinessWeek*, January 12, 2004, pp. 36–37.

44. P. Engardio, "The Future of Outsourcing," *BusinessWeek*, January 30, 2006, pp. 50–58.

45. D. Foust, "A Smarter Squeeze?" *BusinessWeek*, December 31, 2001, pp. 42–44.

46. O. Kharif, "Chopping Hours, Not Heads," *BusinessWeek*, January 5, 2009, p. 85; M. Boyle, "Cutting Costs without Cutting Jobs," *BusinessWeek*, March 9, p. 55.

47. D. Mattioli and S. Murray, "Employers Hit Salaried Staff with Furloughs," *The Wall Street Journal*, February 24, 2009, pp. C1–C3.

48. K. Aquino, M. M. Steward, and A. Reed, "How Social Dominance Orientation and Job Status Influence Perceptions of African-American Affirmative Action Beneficiaries," *Personnel Psychology* 58 (2005), pp. 703–744.

49. R. Cropanzano, J. E. Slaughter, and P. D. Bachiochi, "Organizational Justice and Black Applicants Reactions to Affirmative Action," *Journal of Applied Psychology* 90 (2005), pp. 1168–84.

50. D. A. Harrison, D. A. Kravitz, D. M. Mayer, L. M. Leslie, and D. Lev-Arey, "Understanding Attitudes toward Affirmative Action Programs in Employment: Summary and Meta-analysis of 35 Years of Research," *Journal of Applied Psychology* 91 (2006), pp. 1013–36.

51. F. A. White, M. A. Charles, and J. K Nelson, "The Role of Persuasive Arguments in Changing Affirmative Action Attitudes and Expressed Behavior in Higher Education," *Journal of Applied Psychology* 93 (2008), pp. 1271–86.

52. M. Totty, "New Tools for Frazzled Recruiters," *The Wall Street Journal*, October 23, 2006, p. C11.

53. C. K. Stevens, "Antecedents of Interview Interactions, Interviewers' Ratings, and Applicants' Reactions," *Personnel Psychology* 51 (1998), pp. 55–85.

54. A. E. Barber, J. R. Hollenbeck, S. L. Tower, and J. M. Phillips, "The Effects of Interview Focus on Recruitment Effectiveness: A Field Experiment," *Journal of Applied Psychology* 79 (1994), pp. 886–96.

55. D. S. Chapman and D. I. Zweig, "Developing a Nomological Network for Interview Structure: Antecedents and Consequences of the Structured Selection Interview," *Personnel Psychology* 58, (2005), pp. 673–702.

56. R. Kanfer, C. R. Wanberg, and T. M. Kantrowitz, "Job Search and Employment: A Personality–Motivational Analysis and Meta-Analytic Review," *Journal of Applied Psychology* 86 (2001), pp. 837–55.

57. S. J. Marks, "After School," *Human Resources Executive*, June 15, 2001, pp. 49–51.

58. G. Ruiz, "Cardiovascular Device Maker Pinpoints and Tracks Mission Critical Jobs," *Workforce Management*, March 26, 2007, p. 24.

59. M. Magnus, "Recruitment Ads at Work," *Personnel Journal* 64 (1985), pp. 42–63.

60. P. J. Kiker, "Recruitment Battles," *Workforce Management*, October 24, 2005, pp. 20–31.

61. S. Shellenbarger, "Military Recruits: Companies Make New Effort to Hire Spouses of Soldiers," *The Wall Street Journal*, December 15, 2005, p. D1.

62. K. Greene, "AARP Is to Recruit Older Workers for Home Depot," *The Wall Street Journal*, February 6, 2004, p. B5.

63. S. L. Rynes and A. E. Barber, "Applicant Attraction Strategies: An Organizational Perspective," *Academy of Management Review* 15 (1990), pp. 286–310.

64. D. S. Chapman, K. L. Uggerslev, S. A. Carroll, K. A. Piasentin, and D. A. Jones, "Applicant Attraction to Organizations and Job Choice: A Meta-analytic Review of the Correlates of Recruiting Outcomes," *Journal of Applied Psychology* 90 (2005), pp. 928–44.

65. C. Collins and C. K. Stevens, "The Relationship between Early Recruitment-Related Activities and the Application Decisions of New Labor Market Entrants: A Brand Equity Approach to Recruitment," *Journal of Applied Psychology* 87 (2002), pp. 1121–33.

66. M. E. Brooks, S. Highhouse, S. S. Russell, and D. C. Mohr, "Familiarity, Ambivalence, and Firm Reputation: Is Corporate Fame a Double-Edged Sword?" *Journal of Applied Psychology* 88 (2003), pp. 904–14.

67. D. N. Cable and K. Y. Yu, "Managing Job Seekers' Organizational Image Beliefs: The Role of Media Richness and Media Credibility," *Journal of Applied Psychology* 91 (2006), pp. 828–40.

68. F. Lievens and S. Highhouse, "The Relation of Instrumental and Symbolic Attributes to a Company's Attractiveness as an Employer," *Personnel Psychology* 56 (2003), pp. 75–102.

69. J. E. Slaughter, M. J. Zickar, S. Highhouse, and D. C. Mohr, "Personality Trait Inferences about Organizations: Development of a Measure and Assessment of Construct Validity," *Journal of Applied Psychology* 89 (2004), pp. 85–103.

70. D. R. Avery, "Reactions to Diversity in Recruitment Advertising—Are Differences Black and White?" *Journal of Applied Psychology* 88 (2003), pp. 672–79.

71. M. Hammers, "One Out of Many," *Workforce*, November 2003, pp. 59–60.

72. R. S. Schuler and S. E. Jackson, "Linking Competitive Strategies with Human Resource Management Practices," *Academy of Management Executive* 1 (1987), pp. 207–19.

73. E. Byron, "Call Me Mike," *The Wall Street Journal*, March 27, 2006, pp. B1, B4.

74. G. Colvin, "How to Manage Your Business in a Recession," *Fortune*, January 19, 2009, pp. 88–93.

75. M. Orey, "Hang the Recession, Let's Bulk Up," *BusinessWeek*, February 2, 2009, pp. 80–81.

76. J. Collins, "How Great Companies Turn Crisis Into Opportunity," *Fortune*, February 2, 2009, pp. 49.

77. C. R. Wanberg, R. Kanfer, and J.T. Banas, "Predictors and Outcomes of Networking Intensity among Job Seekers," *Journal of Applied Psychology* 85 (2000), pp. 491–503.

78. G. Van Hoye and F. Lievens, "Tapping the Grapevine: A Closer Look at Word-of-Mouth as a Recruitment Source," *Journal of Applied Psychology* 94 (2009), pp. 341–52.

79. J. Mintz, "Large Firms Increasingly Rely on Employee Job Referrals," *The Wall Street Journal*, March 1, 2005, p. B4.

80. A. Halcrow, "Employers Are Your Best Recruiters," *Personnel Journal* 67 (1988), pp. 42–49.

81. J. McGregor, "I Can't Believe They Took the Whole Team," *BusinessWeek*, December 18, 2006, pp. 120–22.

82. S. Begley, "Behind 'Shortage' of Engineers: Employers Grow More Choosy," *The Wall Street Journal*, November 16, 2005, pp. A1, A12.

83. J. Smith, "Is Online Recruiting Getting Easier?" *Workforce*, September 2, 2001, p. 25.

84. B. R. Dineen, S. R. Ash, and R. A. Noe, "A Web of Applicant Attraction: Person–Organization Fit in the Context of Web-Based Recruitment," *Journal of Applied Psychology* 87(2002), pp. 723–34.

85. B. Dineen and R. A. Noe, "Effects of Customization on Applicant Decisions and Applicant Pool Characteristics in a Web-based Recruiting Context," *Journal of Applied Psychology* 94 (2009), pp. 224–34.

86. K. Maher, "Blogs Catch on as Recruiting Tool," *The Wall Street Journal*, September 28, 2004, p. B10.

87. A. Singh, "Podcasts Extend Recruiters Reach," *The Wall Street Journal*, April 24, 2006, p. B3.

88. E. White, "Ernst & Young Reaches Out to Recruits on Facebook," *The Wall Street Journal*, January 8, 2007, p. B5

89. D. Mattioli, "Who's Reading On-Line Resumes? Identity Crooks," *The Wall Street Journal*, October 17, 2006, p B9.

90. A. McConnon, "A Headhunter Searches for a Second Life," *BusinessWeek*, January 26, 2009, pp. 80–81.

91. P. Smith, "Sources Used by Employers When Hiring College Grads," *Personnel Journal*, February 1995, p. 25.

92. J. W. Boudreau and S. L. Rynes, "Role of Recruitment in Staffing Utility Analysis," *Journal of Applied Psychology* 70 (1985), pp. 354–66.

93. L. Winter, "Employers Go to School on Minority Recruiting," *The Wall Street Journal*, December 15, 1992, p. B1.

94. R. Hawk, *The Recruitment Function* (New York: American Management Association, 1967).

95. K. D. Carlson, M. L. Connerly, and R. L. Mecham, "Recruitment Evaluation: The Case for Assessing the Quality of Applicants Attracted," *Personnel Psychology* 55 (2002), pp. 461–94.

96. C. K. Stevens, "Effects of Preinterview Beliefs on Applicants' Reactions to Campus Interviews," *Academy of Management Journal* 40 (1997), pp. 947–66.

97. M. S. Taylor and T. J. Bergman, "Organizational Recruitment Activities and Applicants' Reactions at Different Stages of the Recruitment Process," *Personnel Psychology* 40 (1984), pp. 261–85.

98. L. M. Graves and G. N. Powell, "The Effect of Sex Similarity on Recruiters' Evaluations of Actual Applicants: A Test of the Similarity–Attraction Paradigm," *Personnel Psychology* 48 (1995), pp. 85–98.

99. A. Meisler, "Little White Lies," *Workforce*, November 2003, pp. 88–89.

100. J. P. Wanous, *Organizational Entry: Recruitment, Selection and Socialization of Newcomers* (Reading, MA: Addison-Wesley, 1980).

101. P. Hom, R. W. Griffeth, L. E. Palich, and J. S. Bracker, "An Exploratory Investigation into Theoretical Mechanisms Underlying Realistic Job Previews," *Personnel Psychology* 51 (1998), pp. 421–51.

102. J. M. Phillips, "The Effects of Realistic Job Previews on Multiple Organizational Outcomes: A Meta-analysis," *Academy of Management Journal* 41 (1998), pp. 673–90.

103. P. G. Irving and J. P. Meyer, "Reexamination of the Met-Expectations Hypothesis: A Longitudinal Analysis," *Journal of Applied Psychology* 79 (1995), pp. 937–49.

104. Y. Ganzach, A. Pazy, Y. Hohayun, "Social Exchange and Organizational Commitment: Decision-Making Training for Job Choice as an Alternative to the Realistic Job Preview," *Personnel Psychology* 55 (2002), pp. 613–37.

105. C. Collins, "The Interactive Effects of Recruitment Practices and Product Awareness on Job Seekers' Employer Knowledge and Application Behaviors," *Journal of Applied Psychology* 92 (2007), pp. 180–90.

CHAPTER

6

Selection and Placement

Who Is Screening the Screeners?

In May 2006, after an extensive legal proceeding following the typical procedures for rules of evidence, an administrative law judge for the U.S. Department of Labor concluded that Theron Carter, a 61-year-old unemployed truck driver from Michigan, was a hero. Carter was a whistle-blower, bringing to light safety violations at his place of employment that could have cost the lives of many innocent drivers. Despite being told by his supervisor to ignore a series of violations, Carter persisted in his objections, up to the point that he was eventually fired. The judge concluded that Carter's termination was illegal and ordered the firm to pay him damages and back pay. The only problem is that Carter is still unable to obtain work, because, despite eliminating the discharge from his record, the background checking industry still has him listed as "a chronic complainer" based on his former supervisor's report.

One can understand why, in an age when employers are constantly seeing and reading stories in the press regarding workplace violence, theft, and fraud, some would feel the need to closely vet each and every employee. This is especially the case because many employers are held legally responsible for the illegal acts of people they hire. Under U.S. law, lawsuits claiming negligent hiring are "uncapped," and hence there is no limit to the liability that employers face if found guilty. For this and other reasons, over the past 10 years, the number of employers who conduct routine background checks has gone from 51 to 96 percent. In fact, demand for this information is so strong that we are seeing unprecedented growth in the employee background checking industry. Among the major players in this industry, in the period

between 2007 and 2008, revenue is up more than 20 percent and profits up more than 50 percent. This has attracted a number of new entrants to the industry, and, as one would expect, this type of growth in an essentially unregulated industry has led to a number of problems.

Perhaps the biggest problem within this industry over the past 10 years has been the expanding scope of background investigations. In the early days of the industry, screening companies merely searched for objective information related to past criminal history and, perhaps, credit history. Increasingly, however, firms are going well beyond this and assembling "digital dossiers" based on telephone interviews with friends, co-workers, and former bosses. Untrained call center employees inquire about work habits, personal character, drug and alcohol consumption practices, and just about anything else the source wants to talk about. Unlike past criminal convictions, however, that are typically handed out only after passing some due process criterion, almost all of these charges are just gossip and hearsay. Thus, in Theron Carter's case, the background screening firm removed his termination from the record because it was court ordered but still maintained that he was a chronic complainer, a charge they assert was not specifically addressed by the judge.

Lester Rosen, president of the Employment Screening Resources, notes that "essentially this is the Wild, Wild West—an unregulated industry with easy money and, ironically, not a huge emphasis hiring quality people to do the screening." Most companies compete on speed and price, and not accuracy, which is more difficult to assess. For this reason, Rosen's firm still sticks strictly to criminal record and credit history checks as their service provided and leaves the collection of all information regarding skills and personalities to more qualified and trained HR specialists. Because organizations are now increasingly being sued for discrimination claims based on faulty background checks, this might be a good policy for all organizations. At the very least, as a potential job applicant, you might want to check the accuracy of what these companies are saying about you. Most of these firms will share the information they have about you and correct it for a fee. It is again ironic that the less accurate you suspect the company is, the more you would probably be willing to pay for that service.

Sources: C. Terhune, "The Trouble with Background Checks," *Business-Week,* June 9, 2009, pp. 58; F. Hanson and G. Hernandez, "Caution Amid the Credit Crunch," *Workforce Management,* February 16, 2009, pp. 35–36; A. Hedger, "Three Ways to Improve Your Employee Screening," *Workforce Management,* March 16, 2009, pp. 26–30.

Introduction

Any organization that intends to compete through people must take the utmost care with how it chooses organizational members. These decisions have a critical impact on the organization's ability to compete, as well as each and every job applicant's life. These decisions are too important to be left to the whim of untrained individuals, and as you can see from the opening story, handing this critical task over to some outsourcing firm may not be the best solution to this problem. This is not only unfair to applicants who are wrongly denied jobs, but it is also a questionable business practice because it hurts the firm's ability to compete. Jack Welch, the legendary former CEO at General Electric says it best:

> What could possibly be more important than who gets hired? Business is a game, and as with all games, the team that puts the best people on the field and gets them playing together wins. It's that simple.[1]

Thus the idea of taking this most important decision and outsourcing it to another firm is hard to defend both legally and economically.

This is as true at the level of individual firms, as it is with respect to competition between nations. The United States has always been a magnet for talent from other nations, and this country grew economically powerful through the contributions of many different people who emigrated here from other countries. Some have suggested the United States is losing its edge in this regard, however, and that "this is America's most serious long-term threat."[2] That is, social and economic inequality, racial and ethnic bias, growing political intolerance, and a failing educational system are contributing to a state of reverse migration, where highly trained professionals who came to this country are now leaving the United States in larger percentages than those coming in. When the country is in a recession, and jobs are hard to find for U.S. workers, some might think this is fine, but in reality, it is the people with high skills who are most likely to pull the United States out of a recession.[3] Innovation and economic growth are fueled by people, and the firms or countries that bring in the best people will be the ones that compete most successfully.

The purpose of this chapter is to familiarize you with ways to minimize errors in employee selection and placement and, in doing so, improve your company's competitive position. The chapter first focuses on five standards that should be met by any selection method. The chapter then evaluates several common selection methods according to those standards.

Selection Method Standards

Personnel selection is the process by which companies decide who will or will not be allowed into organizations. Several generic standards should be met in any selection process. We focus on five: (1) reliability, (2) validity, (3) generalizability, (4) utility, and (5) legality. The first four build off each other in the sense that the preceding standard is often necessary but not sufficient for the one that follows. This is less the case with legal standards. However, a thorough understanding of the first four standards helps us understand the rationale underlying many legal standards.

Reliability

Much of the work in personnel selection involves measuring characteristics of people to determine who will be accepted for job openings. For example, we might be interested in applicants' physical characteristics (like strength or endurance), their cognitive abilities (such as mathematical ability or verbal reasoning capacity), or aspects of their personality (like their initiative or integrity). Whatever the specific focus, in the end we need to quantify people on these dimensions (assign numbers to them) so we can order them from high to low on the characteristic of interest. Once people are ordered in this way, we can decide whom to hire and whom to reject.

One key standard for any measuring device is its reliability. We define **reliability** as the degree to which a measure is free from random error. If a measure of some supposedly stable characteristic such as intelligence is reliable, then the score a person receives based on that measure will be consistent over time and in different contexts.

Estimating the Reliability of Measurement

Most measurement in personnel selection deals with complex characteristics like intelligence, integrity, and leadership ability. However, to appreciate some of the complexities in measuring people, we will consider something concrete in discussing these concepts: the measurement of height. For example, if we were measuring an applicant's height, we might start by using a 12-inch ruler. Let's say the first person we measure turns out to be 6 feet 1 and 4/16 inches tall. It would not be surprising to find out that someone else measuring the same person a second time, perhaps an hour later, found this applicant's height to be 6 feet and 12/16 inches. The same applicant, measured a third time, maybe the next day, might be measured at 6 feet 1 and 8/16 inches tall.

As this example makes clear, even though the person's height is a stable characteristic, we get slightly different results each time he is assessed. This means that each time the person is assessed, we must be making slight errors. If a measurement device were perfectly reliable, there would be no errors of measurement. If we used a measure of height that was not as reliable as a ruler—for example, guessing someone's height after seeing her walk across the room—we might see an even greater amount of unreliability in the measure. Thus *reliability* refers to the measuring instrument (a ruler versus a visual guess) rather than to the characteristic itself.

We can estimate reliability in several different ways, however; and because most of these rely on computing a correlation coefficient, we will briefly describe and illustrate this statistic. The *correlation coefficient* is a measure of the degree to which two sets of numbers are related. The correlation coefficient expresses the strength of the relationship in numerical form. A perfect positive relationship (as one set of numbers

LOI
Establish the basic scientific properties of personnel selection methods, including reliability, validity, and generalizability.

Reliability
The consistency of a performance measure; the degree to which a performance measure is free from random error.

goes up, so does the other) equals $+1.0$; a perfect negative relationship (as one goes up, the other goes down) equals -1.0. When there is no relationship between the sets of numbers, the correlation equals .00. Although the actual calculation of this statistic goes beyond the scope of this book (see any introductory statistics book or spreadsheet program), it will be useful for us to conceptually examine the nature of the correlation coefficient and what this means in personnel selection contexts.

When assessing the reliability of a measure, for example, we might be interested in knowing how scores on the measure at one time relate to scores on the same measure at another time. Obviously, if the characteristic we are measuring is supposedly stable (like intelligence or integrity) and the time lapse is short, this relationship should be strong. If it were weak, then the measure would be inconsistent—hence unreliable. This is called assessing *test–retest reliability*.

Plotting the two sets of numbers on a two-dimensional graph often helps us to appreciate the meaning of various levels of the correlation coefficient. Figure 6.1, for example, examines the relationship between student scholastic aptitude in one's junior and senior years in high school, where aptitude for college is measured in three ways: (1) via the scores on the Scholastic Aptitude Test (SAT), (2) via ratings from a high school counselor on a 1-to-100 scale, and (3) via tossing dice. In this plot, each number on the graphs represents a person whose scholastic aptitude is assessed twice (in the junior and senior years), so in Figure 6.1a, 1_1 represents a person who scored 1580 on the SAT in the junior year and 1500 in the senior year; 20_{20} represents a person who scored 480 in the junior year and 620 in the senior year.

Figure 6.1a shows a very strong relationship between SAT scores across the two years. This relationship is not perfect in that the scores changed slightly from one year to the next, but not a great deal. Indeed, if there were a perfect 1.0 correlation, the plot would show a straight line at a 45-degree angle. The correlation coefficient for this set of data is in the .90 range. In this case, .90 is considered the test–retest estimate of reliability.

Turning to Figure 6.1b, we see that the relationship between the high school counselors' ratings across the two years, while still positive, is not as strong. That is, the counselors' ratings of individual students' aptitudes for college are less consistent over the two years than their test scores. The correlation, and hence test–retest reliability, of this measure of aptitude is in the .50 range.

Finally, Figure 6.1c shows a worst-case scenario, where the students' aptitudes are assessed by tossing two six-sided dice. As you would expect, the random nature of the dice means that there is virtually no relationship between scores taken in one year and scores taken the next. Hence, in this instance, the correlation and test–retest estimate of reliability are .00. Although no one would seriously consider tossing dice to be a measure of aptitude, it is worth noting that research shows that the correlation of overall ratings of job applicants' suitability for jobs based on unstructured interviews is very close to .00. Thus, one cannot assume a measure is reliable without actually checking this directly. Novices in measurement are often surprised at exactly how unreliable many human judgments turn out to be.

Standards for Reliability

Regardless of what characteristic we are measuring, we want highly reliable measures. Thus, in the previous example, when it comes to measuring students' aptitudes for college, the SAT is more reliable than counselor ratings, which in turn are more reliable than tossing dice. But in an absolute sense, how high is high enough—.50, .70, .90? This

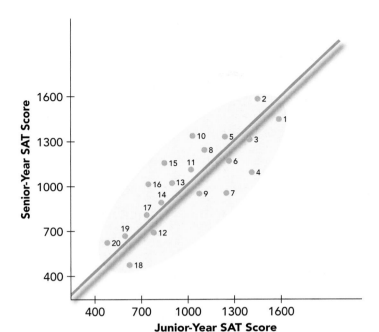

figure 6.1a

figure 6.1a

Measurements of a
Student's Aptitude

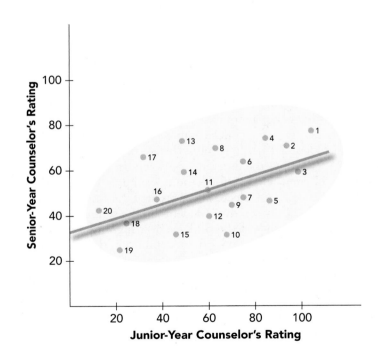

figure 6.1b

is a difficult question to answer specifically because the required reliability depends in part on the nature of the decision being made about the people being measured.

For example, let's assume some college admissions officer was considering several students depicted in Figures 6.1a and 6.1b. Turning first to Figure 6.1b, assume the admissions officer was deciding between Student 1 (1_1) and Student 20 (20_{20}). For

figure 6.1c

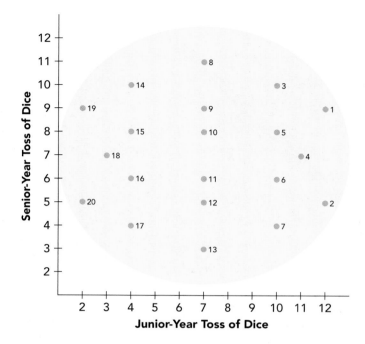

this decision, the .50 reliability of the ratings is high enough because the difference between the two students is so large that one would make the same decision for admission regardless of the year in which the rating was taken. That is, Student 1 (with scores of 100 and 80 in the junior and senior year, respectively) is always admitted and Student 20 (with scores of 12 and 42 for junior and senior years, respectively) is always rejected. Thus, although the ratings in this case are not all that reliable in an absolute sense, their reliability is high enough for this decision.

On the other hand, let's assume the same college admissions officer was deciding between Student 1 (1_1) and Student 2 (2_2). Looking at Figure 6.1a, it is clear that even with the highly reliable SAT scores, the difference between these students is so small that one would make a different admission decision depending on what year one obtained the score. Student 1 would be selected over Student 2 if the junior-year score was used, but Student 2 would be chosen over Student 1 if the senior-year score was used. Thus, even though the reliability of the SAT exam is high in an absolute sense, it is not high enough for this decision. Under these conditions, the admissions officer needs to find some other basis for making the decision regarding these two students (like high school GPA or rank in graduating class).

Although these two scenarios clearly show that no specific value of reliability is always acceptable, they also demonstrate why, all else being equal, the more reliable a measure is, the better. For example, turning again to Figures 6.1a and 6.1b, consider Student 9 (9_9) and Student 14 (14_{14}). One would not be able to make a decision between these two students based on scholastic aptitude scores if assessed via counselor ratings, because the unreliability in the ratings is so large that scores across the two years conflict. On the other hand, one would be able to base the decision on scholastic aptitude scores if assessed via the SAT, because the reliability of the SAT scores is so high that scores across the two years point to the same conclusion. Moreover, if there are differences between scores the first time someone takes a test and the second time, research evidence suggests that the second score is usually more predictive of future outcomes.[4]

There are many ways to increase the reliability of a test, including writing clear and unambiguous items and increasing the length of the test. In addition, new technologies that allow for the development of computer adaptive testing can generate highly reliable tests by tailoring the item sequencing and selection process differently for each individual. That is, with computer adaptive testing, there is no standard set of questions that everyone takes; instead, there is a massive pool of items, and the one that pops up on the test taker's screen depends partially on how that person did with past items. The program first sends some items of average difficulty, and if the respondent answers these correctly, the computer sends a set of more difficult items. If these are answered correctly, then a different set of even more difficult items is sent. If these are missed, then the program ratchets downs and sends easier items. The program continues iteratively until the exact level of difficulty is achieved where the respondent can get the items right about half the time. Although this process is incredibly efficient in terms of establishing the exact level of the person's ability, in the end, each test taker does not receive the exact same test, and some may feel this is unfair.[5]

Validity

We define **validity** as the extent to which performance on the measure is related to performance on the job. A measure must be reliable if it is to have any validity. On the other hand, we can reliably measure many characteristics (like height) that may have no relationship to whether someone can perform a job. For this reason, reliability is a necessary but insufficient condition for validity.

Criterion-Related Validation

One way of establishing the validity of a selection method is to show that there is an empirical association between scores on the selection measure and scores for job performance. If there is a substantial correlation between test scores and job-performance scores, **criterion-related validity** has been established.[6] For example, Figure 6.2 shows the relationship between 2009 scores on the Scholastic Aptitude Test (SAT) and 2010 freshman grade point average (GPA). In this example, there is roughly a .50 correlation between the SAT and GPA. This .50 is referred to as a *validity coefficient*. Note that we have used the correlation coefficient to assess both reliability and validity, which may seem somewhat confusing. The key distinction is that the correlation reflects a reliability estimate when we are attempting to assess the same characteristic twice (such as SAT scores in the junior and senior years), but the correlation coefficient reflects a validity coefficient when we are attempting to relate one characteristic (SAT) to performance on some task (GPA).

Criterion-related validity studies come in two varieties. **Predictive validation** seeks to establish an empirical relationship between test scores taken *prior* to being hired and eventual performance on the job. Because of the time and effort required to conduct a predictive validation study, many employers are tempted to use a different design. **Concurrent validation** assesses the validity of a test by administering it to people already on the job and then correlating test scores with existing measures of each person's performance. The logic behind this strategy is that if the best performers currently on the

---

Validity
The extent to which a performance measure assesses all the relevant—and only the relevant—aspects of job performance.

Criterion-Related Validity
A method of establishing the validity of a personnel selection method by showing a substantial correlation between test scores and job-performance scores.

Predictive Validation
A criterion-related validity study that seeks to establish an empirical relationship between applicants' test scores and their eventual performance on the job.

Concurrent Validation
A criterion-related validity study in which a test is administered to all the people currently in a job and then incumbents' scores are correlated with existing measures of their performance on the job.

figure 6.2

Relationship
between 2009 SAT
Scores and 2010
Freshman GPA

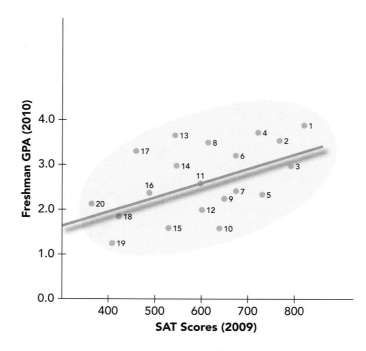

job perform better on the test than those who are currently struggling on the job, the test has validity. (Figure 6.3 compares the two types of validation study.)

Despite the extra effort and time needed for predictive validation, it is superior to concurrent validation for a number of reasons, First, job applicants (because they are seeking work) are typically more motivated to perform well on the tests than are current employees (who already have jobs). Second, current employees have learned many things on the job that job applicants have not yet learned. Therefore, the correlation between test scores and job performance for current employees may not be the same as the correlation between test scores and job performance for less knowledgeable job applicants. Third, current employees tend to be homogeneous—that is, similar to each other on many characteristics. Thus, on many of the characteristics needed for success on the job, most current employees will show restriction in range. This restricted range makes it hard to detect a relationship between test scores and job-performance scores because few of the current employees will be very low on the characteristic you are trying to validate. For example, if emotional stability is required for a nursing career, it is quite likely that most nurses who have amassed five or six years' experience will score high on this characteristic. Yet to validate a test, you need both high test scorers (who should subsequently perform well on the job) and low test scorers (who should perform poorly on the job). Thus, although concurrent studies can sometimes help one anticipate the results of predictive studies, they do not serve as substitutes.

Obviously, we would like our measures to be high in validity; but as with the reliability standard, we must also ask, how high is high enough? When trying to determine how much validity is enough, one typically has to turn to tests of statistical significance. A test of statistical significance answers the question, "How likely is it that a correlation of this size could have come about through luck or chance?"

Table 6.1 shows how big a correlation between a selection measure and a measure of job performance needs to be to achieve statistical significance at a level of .05 (that is, there is only a 5 out of 100 chance that one could get a correlation this big by chance

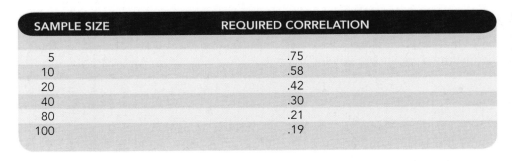

figure 6.3

Graphic Depiction of Concurrent and Predictive Validation Designs

Concurrent Validation

Measure all current job incumbents on attribute

Measure all current job incumbents' performance

Obtain correlation between these two sets of numbers

Predictive Validation

Measure all job applicants on attribute

Hire some applicants and reject others

Wait for some time period

Measure all newly hired job incumbents' performance

Obtain correlation between these two sets of numbers

table 6.1

Required Level of Correlation to Reach Statistical Significance as a Function of Sample Size

SAMPLE SIZE	REQUIRED CORRELATION
5	.75
10	.58
20	.42
40	.30
80	.21
100	.19

alone). Although it is generally true that bigger correlations are better, the size of the sample on which the correlation is based plays a large role as well. Because many of the selection methods we examine in the second half of this chapter generate correlations in the .20s and .30s, we often need samples of 80 to 90 people.[7] A validation study with a small sample (such as 20 people) is almost doomed to failure from the start.

Content Validation

Content Validation
A test-validation strategy performed by demonstrating that the items, questions, or problems posed by a test are a representative sample of the kinds of situations or problems that occur on the job.

When sample sizes are small, an alternative test validation strategy, content validation, can be used. **Content validation** is performed by demonstrating that the items, questions, or problems posed by the test are a representative sample of the kinds of situations or problems that occur on the job. A test that is content valid exposes the job applicant to situations that are likely to occur on the job, and then tests whether the applicant currently has sufficient knowledge, skill, or ability to handle such situations.

For example, one general contracting firm that constructed tract housing needed to hire one construction superintendent.[8] This job involved organizing, supervising, and inspecting the work of many subcontractors involved in the construction process. The tests developed for this position attempted to mirror the job. One test was a scrambled subcontractor test, where the applicant had to take a random list of subcontractors (roofing, plumbing, electrical, fencing, concrete, and so on) and put them in the correct order that each should appear on the site. A second test measured construction error recognition. In this test, the applicant went into a shed that was specially constructed to have 25 common and expensive errors (like faulty wiring and upside-down windows) and recorded whatever problems she could detect.

Many of the new simulations that organizations are using are essentially computer-based role-playing games, where applicants play the role of the job incumbent, confronting the exact types of people and problems real-live job incumbents would face. The simulations are just like traditional role-playing games (e.g., Dungeons and Dragons), and the applicant's reactions and behaviors are scored to see how well they match with what one would expect from the ideal employee.[9] Because the content of these tests so closely parallels the content of the job, one can safely make inferences from one to the other. Although criterion-related validity is established by empirical means, content validity is achieved primarily through a process of expert judgment.

The ability to use content validation in small sample settings makes it generally more applicable than criterion-related validation. However, content validation has two limitations. First, one assumption behind content validation is that the person who is to be hired must have the knowledge, skills, or abilities at the time she is hired. Second, because subjective judgment plays such a large role in content validation, it is critical to minimize the amount of inference involved on the part of judges. Thus the judges' ratings need to be made with respect to relatively concrete and observable behaviors (for example, "applicant detects common construction errors" or "arranges optimal subcontractor schedules").

Generalizability

Generalizability
The degree to which the validity of a selection method established in one context extends to other contexts.

Generalizability is defined as the degree to which the validity of a selection method established in one context extends to other contexts. Thus, the SAT may be a valid predictor of someone's performance (e.g., as a measure of someone's GPA in an undergraduate program), but, does this same test predict performance in graduate programs? If the test does not predict success in this other situation, then it does not "generalize" to this other context. Thus, rather than rely on the SAT for all types of programs, separate tests like the GMAT, LSAT, MCAT, and GRE may be needed for particular types of graduate schools.

There are three primary "contexts" over which we might like to generalize: different situations (jobs or organizations), different samples of people, and different time periods. Just as reliability is necessary but not sufficient for validity, validity is necessary but not sufficient for generalizability.

It was once believed, for example, that validity coefficients were situationally specific—that is, the level of correlation between test and performance varied as one went from one organization to another, even though the jobs studied seemed to be identical. Subsequent research has indicated that this is largely false. Rather, tests tend to show similar levels of correlation even across jobs that are only somewhat similar (at least for tests of intelligence and cognitive ability). Correlations with these kinds of tests change as one goes across widely different kinds of jobs, however. Specifically, the more complex the job, the higher the validity of many tests.

It was also believed that tests showed differential subgroup validity, which meant that the validity coefficient for any test–job performance pair was different for people of different races or genders. This belief was also refuted by subsequent research, and, in general, one finds very similar levels of correlations across different groups of people.[10]

Because the evidence suggests that test validity often extends across situations and subgroups, *validity generalization* stands as an alternative for validating selection methods for companies that cannot employ criterion-related or content validation. Validity generalization is a three-step process. First, the company provides evidence from previous criterion-related validity studies conducted in other situations that shows that a specific test (such as a test of emotional stability) is a valid predictor for a specific job (like nurse at a large hospital). Second, the company provides evidence from job analysis to document that the job it is trying to fill (nurse at a small hospital) is similar in all major respects to the job validated elsewhere (nurse at a large hospital). Finally, if the company can show that it uses a test that is the same as or similar to that used in the validated setting, then one can "generalize" the validity from the first context (large hospital) to the new context (small hospital).

Utility

Utility is the degree to which the information provided by selection methods enhances the bottom-line effectiveness of the organization. Strategic approaches to human resource management place a great deal of importance in determining the financial worth of their human capital, and, as you can see from the "Competing through Technology" box, great strides have been made in assessing this value.[11] In general, the more reliable, valid, and generalizable the selection method is, the more utility it will have. On the other hand, many characteristics of particular selection contexts enhance or detract from the usefulness of given selection methods, even when reliability, validity, and generalizability are held constant.

Figures 6.4a and 6.4b, for example, show two different scenarios where the correlation between a measure of extroversion and the amount of sales revenue generated by a sample of sales representatives is the same for two different companies: Company A and Company B. Although the correlation between the measure of extroversion and sales is the same, Company B derives much more utility or practical benefit from the measure. That is, as indicated by the arrows proceeding out of the boxes (which indicate the people selected), the average sales revenue of the three people selected by Company B (Figure 6.4b) is $850,000 compared to $780,000 from the three people selected by Company A (Figure 6.4a).

Utility
The degree to which the information provided by selection methods enhances the effectiveness of selecting personnel in real organizations.

LO2
Discuss how the particular characteristics of a job, organization, or applicant affect the utility of any test.

Traditional approaches to validating employment tests and methods have relied on subjective appraisals from supervisors as the primary criterion. A test was valid if it predicted what future supervisors are likely to say about that person after having worked with them for a short time. As you might imagine, and as we will see in much more detail in Chapter 8, the perceptions of these supervisors are often biased, unreliable, and based on incomplete information. Therefore, one might question what the ability to predict this actually implies, and the need for finding some alternative, more reliable, valid and less biased criterion has been an ongoing concern in the area of human resources.

Increasingly, the combination of social networking software—and the technology to analyze data that can be collected by this software—is ushering in a new age of methods to determine employee value. *Data mining*, that is, the process of electronically going through massive amounts of data generated by networked computers, has proven valuable in many areas of business. In the area of operations, it has been used to streamline supply chains. In marketing, it has been used to more effectively target audiences. Now, in the area of human resource management, it is being used to identify who are the most important and valuable employees within the firm.

For example, at Microsoft, they have software that allows them to code who talks to whom, how often, and about what content. This allows them to see who tends to originate ideas (sparkplugs), who seems to build on them and pass them on (super-connectors), and who seems to hold them up (bottlenecks). Deciding who should get credit for a great idea has always been a contentious and controversial process in organizations that rely on subjective appraisals; however, with this new "process tracing technology," once the market identifies an idea as a winner, the organization can really go back and objectively determine its source and trajectory.

In addition to tracing specific ideas, this software also, over the longer haul, can be used to help identify who is at the center and who is at the periphery of the organization's social network. For example, at IBM, someone who is routinely copied on ideas from a large number of people, from a large number of different departments, and from many different sources (supervisors, peers, subordinates, and clients) is identified as someone who must be playing a major leadership role in the organization. Once identified, these people are fast-tracked for future leadership roles and shielded from downsizing efforts such as those that marked the 2008 recession. Although, as is the case with any objective indicator, one might be able to game this system in different ways, in general, this shows the desire that some companies have to go beyond the single subjective impression of a supervisor when it comes to determining the value of each and every employee.

SOURCES: S. Baker, "How Much Is That Worker Worth," *BusinessWeek*, March 23, 2009, pp. 46–48; S. Baker, "Putting a Price on Social Networks," *BusinessWeek*, April 8, 2009, pp. 45–47; S. Baker, "Reading the Body Language of Leadership," *BusinessWeek*, March 30, 2009, p. 48.

The major difference between these two companies is that Company B generated twice as many applicants as Company A. This means that the selection ratio (the percentage of people selected relative to the total number of people tested) is quite low for Company B (3/20) relative to Company A (3/10). Thus, the people selected by Company B have higher amounts of extroversion than those selected by Company A; therefore, Company B takes better advantage of the relationship between extroversion and sales. Thus, the utility of any test generally increases as the selection ratio gets lower, so long as the additional costs of recruiting and testing are not excessive.

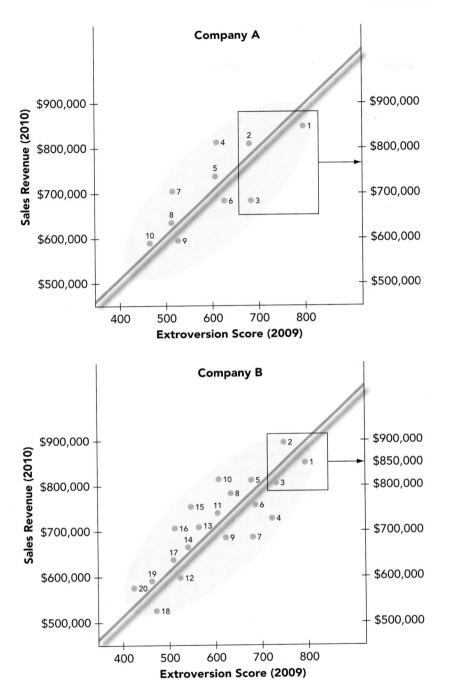

figure 6.4a

Utility of Selecting
on Extroversion
Scores when
Selection Ratio
Is High

figure 6.4b

Utility of Selecting
on Extroversion
Scores when
Selection Ratio
Is Low

This means that when the economy is in a recession, and there are more people look-ing for work than there are jobs, the utility of valid selection techniques is especially high. This is another reason countercyclical hiring, a notion we mentioned in our last chapter, can be especially effective in terms of establishing long-term competitive advantage. Figure 6.5 shows how the recession of 2008 powerfully affected selection ratios and why this was actually a very good time to be hiring employees.[12]

figure 6.5

The Effects of an
Economic Recession
on Selection Ratios

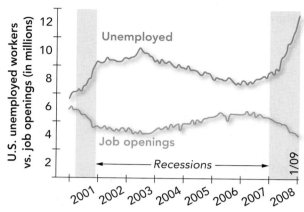

SOURCE: Bureau of Labor Statistics, 2009.

Many other factors relate to the utility of a test. For example, the value of the product or service produced by the job incumbent plays a role: the more valuable the product or service, the more value there is in selecting the top performers. The cost of the test, of course, also plays a role. More expensive tests will on average have less utility unless they produce more valid predictions. A good recent example of this can be seen in the drug testing industry. Although few would dispute the reliability and validity of a properly conducted drug test, these can be relatively expensive, and employers are increasingly unwilling to pay the cost for these tests given the yield. Most drug tests yield few hard core drug abusers, and one study showed that given the hit rate of one test used in one department of the federal government, it cost the agency $77,000 per detected drug addict. Thus, although roughly 70 percent of companies were employing drug tests in 1996, that same figure is closer to 60 percent in 2003, due largely to cost/benefit questions such as this.[13]

Legality

LO3
Describe the government's
role in personnel selection
decisions, particularly in
the areas of constitutional
law, federal laws, executive
orders, and judicial
precedent.

The final standard that any selection method should adhere to is *legality*. All selection methods should conform to existing laws and existing legal precedents. Many issues related to selecting employees safely under U.S. law were discussed generically in Chapter 3. Our treatment there was broad and dealt with legal aspects in all areas of human resource management. In this chapter we focus more narrowly on issues that relate directly to personnel selection, bypassing constitutional amendments and focusing more squarely on federal legislation and executive orders.

Federal Legislation

Three primary federal laws form the basis for a majority of the suits filed by job applicants. First, the Civil Rights Act of 1991 (discussed in Chapter 3), an extension of the Civil Rights Act of 1964, protects individuals from discrimination based on race, color, sex, religion, and national origin with respect to hiring as well as compensation and working conditions. The 1991 act differs from the 1964 act in three important areas.

First, it defines employers' explicit obligation to establish the business necessity of any neutral-appearing selection method that has had adverse impact on groups specified by the law. This is typically done by showing that the test has significant criterion-related or content validity. If the employer cannot show such a difference, which the research suggests will be difficult, then the process may be ruled illegal. It should also be noted that "customer preference" or "brand image" is not a legally defensible means of justifying a process that has adverse impact.

For example, recently the retailer Abercrombie & Fitch was sued because it systematically screened out nonwhite applicants. Testimony in the trial suggested that one corporate representative visited a store, pointed to a blond-haired, blue-eyed model, and said, "This is the A&F look." She then told the manager that "she had better make the store look more like this."[14] This is not a legal defense, nor is the defense that "our customers prefer to buy from people of this or that race." For example, Walgreens was targeted for a class action suit by the Equal Employment Opportunity Commission for a documented statistical tendency to place African American managers in stores that served largely African American populations. Because managerial salaries at Walgreens are based partially on sales, and sales in these largely urban communities are smaller than more affluent suburban communities and malls, this had the effect of lowering salaries for all African American managers.[15]

Second, the 1991 act allows the individual filing the complaint to have a jury decide whether he or she may recover punitive damages (in addition to lost wages and benefits) for emotional injuries caused by the discrimination. This can generate large financial settlements as well as poor public relations that can hinder the organization's ability to compete.

Finally, the 1991 act explicitly prohibits the granting of preferential treatment to minority groups. Preferential treatment is often attractive because many of the most valid methods for screening people, especially cognitive ability tests and work sample tests, often are high in adverse impact.[16] Thus, there is somewhat of a trade-off in terms of selecting the highest scorers on validated tests on the one hand and creating diversity in the workforce on the other hand.[17] One potential way to "have your cake and eat it too" is to simply rank the scores of different races or gender groups within their own groups, and then taking perhaps the top 10 percent of scorers from each group, instead of the top 10 percent that would be obtained if one ignored race or gender. Many feel that this practice is justified because it levels the playing field in a context where, as the "Competing through Sustainability" box shows, unconscious bias works against African Americans. However, the 1991 act specifically outlaws this practice (sometimes referred to as *race norming*). The reason for this is that adjusting scores in this way has been found to have a number of negative effects, not only on the attitudes of white males who claim it causes reverse discrimination,[18] but on the proposed beneficiaries of such preferential treatment. Research shows that when selection decisions are perceived as being based partially on group membership, it undermines the confidence and hurts the job performance of the women or minority group members the program was designed to help.[19]

Rather than employing race norming, employers can partially achieve both goals of maximizing predicted future performance and diversity in three ways. First, aggressive recruiting of members of protected groups allows an employer to generate a larger pool of protected group members, and, by being highly selective within this larger group, the scores of admitted applicants will more closely match those of all the other groups.[20] Second, as we see later in this chapter, different selection methods have different degrees of adverse impact, and multistage selection batteries that use different methods at different stages can also help.[21] The key is to use methods that have low adverse impact early in the process and only employ the methods that

One might think that with the election of the first African American president, the United States may have turned the corner on racism and prejudicial attitudes. Think again. A series of recent headline stories and research studies seem to suggest that racism in this country, while changing, has not necessarily disappeared. Whereas racist behavior was once overt and intentional, many have argued that contemporary racism has become more private and unconscious. Indeed, the notion of unconscious bias has changed the way employment discrimination has been treated by both managers and the legal system that monitors their behavior.

For example, in April 2009, an advocacy group for workers showed evidence that in the fine dining industry in New York City, two trained actors with identical résumés applied for jobs at randomly chosen venues. The only difference between the two applicants was that one was an African American and the other a caucasian. Videotaped evidence, as well as formal correspondence with the restaurants, confirmed that the caucasian applicant was much more likely to be offered a formal interview, and then secure the job, relative to the African American applicant. This

is a tried-and-true procedure for testing for discrimination in hiring, and, in many ways, the findings reported are disappointing but not new.

What is new, however, is the increasing belief that the type of bias can be traced to unconscious thought processes rather than overt prejudice and discrimination. Unlike the traditional "blind taste tester" methodology described in the New York City restaurant episode, increasingly research is using functional magnetic resonance imaging (fMRI) methodologies to see exactly how the human brain reacts to people of alternative races. This research makes it clear that when confronted with pictures of people of alternative races, almost instantaneous chemical reactions occur that are associated with perceived threat. The speeds with which these reactions took place made it impossible for there to be actual cognitive processing of the information, and hence this bias had to be unconscious.

Originally, researchers believed that this was triggered by perceptions of novelty, perhaps, because caucasians were less likely to encounter African Americans; however, testing with African Americans revealed the exact same tendency. As one of the scientists noted,

"What we are seeing is something very subtle that may be learned as a function of being a member of this society, where there are negative portrayals of African Americans in the media." Most of the participants in this research strongly denied any overt prejudiced beliefs, but the experience opened their eyes to potential unconscious beliefs that may be affecting their judgment. It also demonstrated the need for having formal checks in the system to prevent these kinds of problems. As the lead investigator for the New York City restaurant investigation noted, "The more informal the human resources practices, the more likely bias gets to operate in things like hiring decisions and wages. The restaurant industry, which has traditionally flown by the seat of its pants, is exactly the kind of circumstance where unconscious stereotypes tend to govern decisions."

SOURCES: R. Parloff, "The War over Unconscious Bias," *Fortune*, October 15, 2007, pp. 90–98; D. Hajela, "Report Finds Job Segregation in NYC Restaraunts," *USA Today*, April 1, 2009, p. B1; M. D. Lieberman, "Gut Feelings," in *Oxford Companion to Emotion and the Affective Sciences*, eds. D. Sandar and K. Scherer (Oxford, UK: Oxford University Press, 2009), pp. 200–1; E. Stannard, "Unconscious Bias Can Inhibit Reaction to Racism," *The New Haven Register*, January 9, 2009, p. C.2.

have high adverse impact later. Third, by directly showing the degree to which past unfair practices and unconscious bias has resulted in adverse impact in the past, the nonbeneficiaries of affirmative action programs are much more likely to view them as acceptable as a form of short-term remedy.[22]

The Age Discrimination in Employment Act of 1967 is also widely used in personnel selection. Court interpretations of this act also mirror those of the Civil Rights Act, in the sense that if any neutral-appearing practice happens to have adverse impact on those over 40, the burden of proof shifts to the employer, who must show business necessity to avoid a guilty verdict.[23] The act does not protect younger workers (thus there is never a case for "reverse discrimination" here), and like the most recent civil rights act, it allows for jury trials and punitive damages. This act outlaws almost all "mandatory retirement" programs (company policies that dictate that everyone who reaches a set age must retire).

Litigation brought forward under this act surged in recent years. Two trends have combined to generate this increase: the general aging of the workforce and recent attempts by organizations to downsize. Together these trends have displaced many older workers, who have brought age discrimination suits against their former employers. The long list of companies sued under this act includes CBS Inc., McDonnell Douglas, Northwest Airlines, Disney, and Martin Marietta.[24]

Finally, the Americans with Disabilities Act (ADA) of 1991 protects individuals with physical and mental disabilities (or with a history of the same). It extends the Vocational Rehabilitation Act of 1973, requiring employers to make "reasonable accommodation" to disabled individuals whose handicaps may prevent them from performing essential functions of the job as currently designed. "Reasonable accommodation" could include restructuring jobs, modifying work schedules, making facilities accessible, providing readers, or modifying equipment. The ADA does not require an organization to hire someone whose disability prevents him or her from performing either critical or routine aspects of the job nor does it require accommodations that would cause "undue hardship."[25] However, technological advancements in the area of accommodations, along with the general shift in jobs from those that are physically demanding to those that are more mentally challenging, is increasing the percentage of jobs that disabled workers can hold.[26] Unfortunately, when there is a downturn in the economy, nondisabled workers start to compete for the same very jobs, which places the disabled at a disadvantage. For example, the percentage of disabled workers in the workforce rose in the period between 2001 and 2006 but sharply fell off in 2007 and 2008 due to the economic recession.[27]

Executive Orders

As noted in Chapter 3, the executive branch of the government also regulates hiring decisions through the use of executive orders. Executive Order 11246 parallels the protections provided by the Civil Rights Act of 1964 but goes beyond the 1964 act in two important ways. First, not only do the executive orders prohibit discrimination, they actually mandate that employers take affirmative action to hire qualified minority applicants. Although many organizations attempt to promote diversity through training programs, the fact is that training programs are not very effective at creating a more integrated workforce. The best predictor of whether an organization becomes diverse is simply whether or not there is a person whose job it is to monitor and change hiring numbers (e.g., a diversity officer), and who is held strictly accountable for achieving quantifiable results in this regard.[28]

Executive orders also allow the government to suspend all business with a contractor while an investigation is being conducted (rather than waiting for an actual finding), which puts a great deal of pressure on employers to comply with these orders. Executive orders are monitored by the Office of Federal Contract Compliance Programs (OFCCP), which issues guidelines (like the Affirmative Action Program Guidelines published by the Bureau of National Affairs in 1983) to help companies comply.

Types of Selection Methods

LO4
List the common methods used in selecting human resources.

The first half of this chapter laid out the five standards by which we can judge selection measures. In the second half of this chapter, we examine the common selection methods used in various organizations and discuss their advantages and disadvantages in terms of these standards.

Interviews

LO5
Describe the degree to which each of the common methods used in selecting human resources meets the demands of reliability, validity, generalizability, utility, and legality.

A selection interview has been defined as "a dialogue initiated by one or more persons to gather information and evaluate the qualifications of an applicant for employment." The selection interview is the most widespread selection method employed in organizations, and there have been literally hundreds of studies examining their effectiveness.[29]

Unfortunately, the long history of research on the employment interview suggests that, without proper care, it can be unreliable, low in validity, and biased against a number of different groups.[30] Moreover, interviews are relatively costly because they require at least one person to interview another person, and these persons have to be brought to the same geographic location. Finally, in terms of legality, the subjectivity embodied in the process, as well as the opportunity for unconscious bias effects, often makes applicants upset, particularly if they fail to get a job after being asked apparently irrelevant questions. Employers can also get into trouble in interview contexts when they do not pose the exact same questions to all applicants, since bias might be revealed in the nature of questions asked.[31] In the end, subjective selection methods like the interview must be validated by traditional criterion-related or content-validation procedures if they show any degree of adverse impact.

Fortunately, more recent research has pointed to a number of concrete steps that one can employ to increase the utility of the personnel selection interview.[32] First, HR staff should keep the interview structured, standardized, and focused on accomplishing a small number of goals. That is, they should plan to come out of each interview with quantitative ratings on a small number of dimensions that are observable (like interpersonal style or ability to express oneself) and avoid ratings of abilities that may be better measured by tests (like intelligence). In addition to coming out of the interview with quantitative ratings, interviewers should also have a structured note-taking system that will aid recall when it comes to justifying the ratings.[33]

Second, ask questions dealing with specific situations that are likely to arise on the job, and use these to determine what the person is likely to do in that situation. These types of **situational interview** items have been shown to have quite high predictive validity.[34] Situational judgment items come in two varieties, as shown in Table 6.2. Some items are "experience-based" and require the applicant to reveal an actual experience he or she had in the past when confronting the situation. Other items are "future-oriented" and ask what the person is likely to do when confronting a certain hypothetical situation in the future. Research suggests that these types of items can both show validity but that experience-based items often outperform future-oriented items. Experience-based items also appear to reduce some forms of impression management such as ingratiation better than future-oriented items.[35] Regardless of the past or future frame, an additional benefit of situational interview items is that their standardization and the concrete behavioral nature of the information that is collected mean that they can be effectively employed, even by those who have little training in psychological assessment.[36]

Situational Interview
An interview procedure where applicants are confronted with specific issues, questions, or problems that are likely to arise on the job.

table 6.2

Examples of
Experience-Based
and Future-Oriented
Situational Interview
Items

Experience-based

Motivating employees:	"Think about an instance when you had to motivate an employee to perform a task that he or she disliked but that you needed to have done. How did you handle that situation?"
Resolving conflict:	"What was the biggest difference of opinion you ever had with a co-worker? How did you resolve that situation?"
Overcoming resistance to change:	"What was the hardest change you ever had to bring about in a past job, and what did you do to get the people around you to change their thoughts or behaviors?"

Future-oriented

Motivating employees:	"Suppose you were working with an employee who you knew greatly disliked performing a particular task. You needed to get this task completed, however, and this person was the only one available to do it. What would you do to motivate that person?"
Resolving conflict:	"Imagine that you and a co-worker disagree about the best way to handle an absenteeism problem with another member of your team. How would you resolve that situation?"
Overcoming resistance to change:	"Suppose you had an idea for change in work procedures that would enhance quality, but some members of your work group were hesitant to make the change. What would you do in that situation?"

Situational interviews can be particularly effective when assessing sensitive issues dealing with the honesty and integrity of candidates. Clearly, simply asking people directly whether they have integrity will not produce much in the way of useful information. However, questions that pose ethical dilemmas and ask respondents to discuss how they dealt with such situations in the past are often revealing in terms of how different people deal with common dilemmas. For example, by stating "We have all observed someone stretching the rules at work, so give me two examples of situations in which you faced this dilemma and how you dealt with it," the interviewer forces the applicant to reveal how he or she deals with ethical dilemmas as an observer. Since the person is an observer and not the perpetrator in this case, he or she will be less defensive in terms of revealing how he or she deals with ethical issues. When assessing sensitive characteristics like this, research suggests that it is often best to wait until later in the interview to pose such questions, after some degree of rapport has been established and the candidate is less self-conscious.[37]

It is also important to use multiple interviewers who are trained to avoid many of the subjective errors that can result when one human being is asked to rate another.

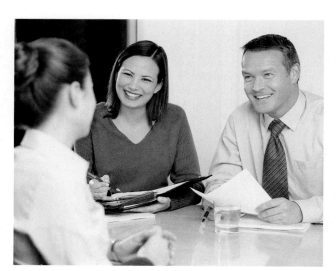

When more than one person is able to interview a candidate for a position, there is significant advantage in removing any errors or biases that a single individual might make in choosing the correct person for the job. In today's technological world, it is becoming easier for multiple people to give their input in an interview by watching a video tape or listening via conference call if they cannot be there in person.

Many employers are now videotaping interviews and then sending the tapes (rather than the applicants) around from place to place. This is seen by some as a cost-effective means of allowing numerous raters to evaluate the candidate under standard conditions.[38]

Limiting the subjectivity of the process is central to much of this training, and research suggests that it is best to ask interviewers to be "witnesses" of facts that can later be integrated via objective formulas, as opposed to being "judges" allowed to idiosyncratically weigh how various facts should be combined to form the final recommendation.[39] In addition to being a witness, the interviewer sometimes has to be the prosecuting attorney, because in some cases the interviewees may be motivated to try to present an overly positive, if not outright false, picture of their qualifications. People seem to be particularly prone to present false information when the competition for jobs is high, and data on résumé fraud indicated a spike in detected fraud during the recent recession of 2007. Part of this spike was attributable to the behavior of applicants, but part of it was also due to the ease with which employers can access basic information on applicants from sources like Google.[40] The data from a 2006 survey of executive recruiters bears this out and reveals that it is common practice for employers to search the Web for information on applicants. In fact, 35 percent of those respondents stated that they eliminated candidates based upon what they learned from Web searches—up from 25 percent the year before.[41] Some of this is attributable directly to content placed on blogs or social networking sites, where the person may have disclosed information that a previous employer may have wanted to keep confidential (product launches, production problems, personnel matters, and so on). In other cases, the content of the person's digital identity may be at odds with the image or corporate culture that is being promoted by the organization. For example, a former Delta Airlines flight attendant, Ellen Simonetti, was fired because she posted suggestive pictures in her work uniform on her personal Web site. In the case of Delta, the company had previously been charged with sexism in the content of their marketing and was trying to move away from that image when Simonetti posed in her uniform.[42]

The important point to take away from these lessons is that one needs to manage his or her digital identity the same way one manages his or her résumé. For example, the first step, of course, is to know exactly what pops up on you if your name is searched. If your search turns up something potentially unflattering or embarrassing, remember it may not be enough just to remove it from your page. The Internet does not come with an eraser, and others may have picked up and forwarded information, so that information may still be out there. If possible, posting a correction may be a better approach because you can always point to that if some particular content becomes an issue. Because some information about you may have been posted by someone else, if this is inaccurate, it needs to be challenged, and a record of your challenge should be kept in hand so it, too, can be pointed to in the future. Finally, you may be able to manage what information pops up for you (and in what order) by hiring a search-engine optimization firm that will create both sites and hits for sites that will drive the incriminating information far, far down the list that is generated for you using various search algorithms.[43]

If your digital record seems clear, then the next steps are much easier. First, try to minimize your digital footprint as much as possible, especially when it comes to information that is private. Second, make sure you do not post anything new that might portray you in a negative light. Although this may seem like common sense, for many people, blogging or managing their personal Web site is therapeutic, if not addictive, and thus, this advice is hard to take. Although it is possible to register with an online profile manager like LinkedIn, it is almost never safe to assume that you will be anonymous, and so the general rule should be that if you cannot say anything nice, don't say anything at all.[44]

Interviewers need to be critical and look for inconsistencies or gaps in stories or experiences in those who are providing information. Increasingly, interviewers are seeking training that helps them detect nonverbal signs that someone is trying to be deceptive, such as hand tremors, darting eyes, mumbled speech, and failing to maintain eye contact that may be a cause for concern and increased scrutiny.[45] In fact, one such trained observer in the U.S. Customs Department was credited with thwarting a terrorist mission aimed at disrupting the nation's Millennium Celebrations in Los Angeles. The officer spotted several behavioral manifestations of deceptiveness, then pulled the driver over for a detailed search that uncovered a substantial amount of bombmaking materials.[46]

References, Biographical Data, and Application Blanks

Just as few employers would think of hiring someone without an interview, nearly all employers also use some method for getting background information on applicants before an interview. This information can be solicited from the people who know the candidate through reference checks.

The evidence on the reliability and validity of reference checks suggests that these are, at best, weak predictors of future success on the job. The main reason for this low validity is that the evaluations supplied in most reference letters are so positive that it is hard to differentiate applicants. This problem with reference letters has two causes. First, the applicant usually gets to choose who writes the letter and can thus choose only those writers who think the highest of her abilities. Second, because letter writers can never be sure who will read the letters, they may fear that supplying damaging information about someone could come back to haunt them. This fear is well placed. For example, in 2003, a jury awarded $283,000 to a truck driver whose past employer told a would-be employer that he "was late most of the time, regularly missed two days a week, had a problem with authority and a poor work ethic."[47] In fact, there are even companies that provide a reference checking service for people who feel that they may be getting a damaging reference from an employer. For roughly $90, BadReferences.com will call and document what information past employers are providing for individuals who have such concerns. Applicants who are armed with this kind of evidence are in a strong legal position, and Michael Rankin, chief services officer at BadReferences, notes that "We haven't lost a case in twenty years."[48] Thus, it is clearly not in the past employers' interest to reveal too much information beyond job title and years of service. In general, the validity of reference checks increases when the employer goes beyond the list provided by the applicant, and employers who rely heavily on this source tend to seek a large number of references (10 to 12) and contact those people directly by phone for a more interactive and, possibly, open and anonymous exchange of information.[49]

The evidence on the utility of biographical information collected directly from job applicants is much more positive, especially for certain outcomes like turnover.[50] The low cost of obtaining such information significantly enhances its utility, especially when the information is used in conjunction with a well-designed, follow-up interview that complements, rather than duplicates, the biographical information bank.

Again, as with the interview, the biggest concern with the use of biographical data, as we saw in our chapter-opening vignette, is that applicants who supply the information may be motivated to misrepresent themselves. Background checks can help on this score, but as we saw in the vignette that opened this chapter, many firms that provide background checks are unreliable themselves. Because of this, as you can see in the "Competing through Globalization" box, in some countries, this is not even a viable option.

In addition, background checks offer no guarantee, because of the increased sophistication of those in the dishonesty business. For example, there are now Web sites that will not only provide fake degrees, but also staffed telephone numbers that will provide further bogus information to callers. Some universities and state prison systems have even been hacked into by companies that try to insert or delete their clients' names from databases.[51] Even the U.S. Transportation Safety Administration, the organization in charge of national security at airports, struggles with this problem. In the ramp-up of hiring that followed the 9/11 attacks, the agency hired more than 1,200 people for sensitive security jobs who later turned out to have criminal records.[52]

Although it is not a panacea, to some extent forcing applicants to elaborate on their responses to biodata questions can sometimes be helpful.[53] A good elaboration forces applicants to support their answers with evidence that includes names of other people involved, dates, locations, and objective evidence that would support a thorough cross-checking. Thus, rather than just asking someone if they have ever led a sales team, an elaborated item would force the applicant to name all members of the team, where and when the team was together, and what sales they accomplished citing specific products, figures, and customers. The evidence suggests that forced elaboration reduces the traditional measures of faking behavior.[54]

Physical Ability Tests

Although automation and other advances in technology have eliminated or modified many physically demanding occupational tasks, many jobs still require certain physical abilities or psychomotor abilities. In these cases, tests of physical abilities may be relevant not only to predicting performance but to predicting occupational injuries and disabilities as well.[55] There are seven classes of tests in this area: ones that evaluate (1) muscular tension, (2) muscular power, (3) muscular endurance, (4) cardiovascular endurance, (5) flexibility, (6) balance, and (7) coordination.[56]

The criterion-related validities for these kinds of tests for certain jobs are quite strong.[57] Unfortunately, these tests, particularly the strength tests, are likely to have an adverse impact on some applicants with disabilities and many female applicants. For example, roughly two-thirds of all males score higher than the highest-scoring female on muscular tension tests.[58]

Because of this there are two key questions to ask in deciding whether to use these kinds of tests. First, is the physical ability essential to performing the job and is it mentioned prominently enough in the job description? Neither the Civil Rights Act

Applicant background checks are increasingly important when screening for jobs in the United States. We saw how aggressively the industry that performs this service has expanded in this country and how issues related to the inaccuracy of information collected from these sources has led to problems. One sees much less of this kind of problem outside the United States, however. In Europe, criminal background checks are limited, credit screening is rare, and call center interviews with former co-workers and bosses is unheard of. There are several reasons for these differences between Europe and the United States.

First, in terms of values and culture, in Europe, the applicant's right to privacy trumps the organization's right to know. As noted by Andrew Boling, partner at Baker and McKenzie, a Chicago-based HR outsourcing firm, "outside the United States, individual privacy rights enjoy the same protections that we give to our First Amendment—in Europe what's private, stays private." Thus, a U.S. firm that seeks an employee's consent to do a background check is likely to be denied in Europe, and performing the check without consent would be illegal in many countries.

Second, relative to the United States, there are far fewer incidences of workplace violence in Europe, and the rates of theft and fraud, are also much lower. Similarly, unlike Americans, Europeans tend to carry less debt, and hence background checks for credit problems rarely turn up applicants whose financial situation is so dire that one might be afraid of trusting them around money. At the height of the U.S. financial crisis in 2007, for example, more than 40 percent of people who were screened on credit card balances would have been rejected as viable hires given most standards adopted by companies that do background checks. The percentage of similarly situated bad risks in Europe is simply much lower.

Third, although the greater deference to individual privacy would seem to put the employer at a disadvantage, on the other side of the equation, the legal concept of negligent hiring is also largely unheard of in Europe. This reduces the need for employers to show copious amounts of due diligence in order to protect themselves legally. As in any country, individual employees in Europe may run afoul of the law or commit egregious acts; however, this is an issue between the offender and the law, and a person's employing organization is rarely held legally responsible for his or her actions.

Finally, if the legal motivation to perform due diligence and avoid negligent hiring suits is taken out of the picture, the decision to do a background check lies solely on its perceived value in screening out future problems. However, as we saw in our opening vignette, much of the information collected by firms doing background checks is inaccurate, and the objective evidence regarding the effectiveness of these firms in preventing future problems is weak. For example, most fraud is committed by long-term employees who know the firm well, not repeat offenders who move from place to place. Thus, only 7 percent of convicted fraud perpetrators had any criminal record whatsoever prior to the offense they were convicted for, and hence they would not be caught in any screen. Moreover, in roughly half the cases where a fraud conviction was upheld by a U.S. court, the companies that were harmed *did perform a background check*. Thus, for a whole host of reasons, the use of background checks is likely to stay a uniquely American tradition.

SOURCES: F. Hanson, "Worker Screening Limited Overseas," *Workforce Management,* February 16, 2009, p. 37; F. Hanson and G. Hernandez, "Caution Amid the Credit Crunch," *Workforce Management,* February 16, 2009, pp. 35–36; C. Terhune, "The Trouble with Background Checks," *BusinessWeek,* June 9, 2009, p. 58.

nor the ADA requires employers to hire individuals who cannot perform essential job functions, and both accept a written job description as evidence of the essential functions of the job. Second, is there a probability that failure to adequately perform the job would result in some risk to the safety or health of the applicant, co-workers, or clients? The "direct threat" clause of the ADA makes it clear that adverse impact against those with disabilities is warranted under such conditions.

Cognitive Ability Tests

Cognitive Ability Tests
Tests that include three dimensions: verbal comprehension, quantitative ability and reasoning ability.

Verbal Comprehension
Refers to a person's capacity to understand and use written and spoken language.

Quantitative Ability
Concerns the speed and accuracy with which one can solve arithmetic problems of all kinds.

Reasoning Ability
Refers to a person's capacity to invent solutions to many diverse problems.

Cognitive ability tests differentiate individuals based on their mental rather than physical capacities. Cognitive ability has many different facets, although we will focus only on three dominant ones. **Verbal comprehension** refers to a person's capacity to understand and use written and spoken language. **Quantitative ability** concerns the speed and accuracy with which one can solve arithmetic problems of all kinds. **Reasoning ability,** a broader concept, refers to a person's capacity to invent solutions to many diverse problems.

Some jobs require only one or two of these facets of cognitive ability. Under these conditions, maintaining the separation among the facets is appropriate. For example, the verbal requirements associated with many jobs in the U.S. economy has increased over the years, but this has occurred a time when we have actually witnessed decreases in scores on standardized tests measuring these skills.[59] For example, a survey of more than 400 large firms suggested that as many as 30 percent of the applicants for entry-level positions have such poor reading and writing scores that it would be impossible to put them on the job without remedial training.[60] If this is the only cognitive ability that is related to the job, then this would be the only one that should be used to make decisions. However, many jobs that are high in complexity require most, if not all, of the facets, and hence one general test is often as good as many tests of separate facets.[61] Highly reliable commercial tests measuring these kinds of abilities are widely available, and they are generally valid predictors of job performance in many different kinds of contexts, including widely different countries.[62] The validity of these kinds of tests is related to the complexity of the job, however, in that one sees higher criterion-related validation for complex jobs than for simple jobs. The predictive validity for these tests is also higher in jobs that are dynamic and changing over time and thus require adaptability on the part of the job incumbent.[63]

For example, the jobs of top-level executives could be fairly characterized as complex and dynamic, and analytic problem solving has consistently been shown to be a major predictor of success in this occupation.[64] Despite this, many of the top executive MBA programs, including 13 of the top 25 as ranked by *BusinessWeek*, have dropped the use of the GMAT in recent years.[65] The schools traditionally explain eliminating this screen in terms of placing more emphasis on diversity and experience relative to sheer brain power. However, due to the lucrative nature of these programs in terms of generating revenue for the schools, some have suggested that this is primarily a ploy to reduce barriers to entry, admit more students, and generate more revenue. This strategy may backfire, however, if the students who are eventually brought into these programs become a burden to their classmates or a liability to future employers. Indeed, there is some evidence that the ability to screen on general cognitive ability is the single greatest virtue associated with the most selective schools, and that controlling for this, the MBA degree itself is not a valid predictor for long-term executive success.[66]

One of the major drawbacks to these tests is that they typically have adverse impact on some minority groups. Indeed, the size of the differences is so large that some have advocated abandoning these types of tests for making decisions regarding who will be accepted for certain schools or jobs.[67] The notion of race norming, alluded to earlier, was born of the desire to use these high-utility tests in a manner that avoided adverse impact. Although race norming was made illegal by the recent amendments to the Civil Rights Act, some have advocated the use of banding to both achieve the benefits of testing and minimize its adverse impact. The concept of *banding* suggests that similar groups of people whose scores differ by only a small amount all be treated as having the same score. Then, within any band, preferential treatment is given to minorities. Most observers feel preferential treatment of minorities is acceptable when scores are tied, and banding simply broadens the definition of what constitutes a tied score.[68]

For example, in many classes a score of 90–100 percent may constitute a 4.0 for the course. This means that even though someone scoring 99 outperformed someone with a score of 91, each gets the same grade (a 4.0). Banding uses the same logic for all kinds of tests. Thus, if one was going to use the grade in the class as a selection standard, this would mean that the person with the 91 is equal to the person with the 99 (i.e., they both score a 4.0), and if their scores are tied, preference should be given to the minority. Like race norming, banding is very controversial, especially if the bands are set too wide.[69]

Personality Inventories

While ability tests attempt to categorize individuals relative to what they can do, personality measures tend to categorize individuals by what they are like. Research suggests that there are five major dimensions of personality, known as "the Big Five": (1) extroversion, (2) adjustment, (3) agreeableness, (4) conscientiousness, and (5) inquisitiveness. Table 6.3 lists each of these with a corresponding list of adjectives that fit each dimension.

Although it is possible to find reliable, commercially available measures of each of these traits, the evidence for their validity and generalizability is mixed at best.[70] For example, conscientiousness, which captures the concepts of self-regulation and self-motivation, is one of the few factors that displays any validity across a number of different job categories, and many real-world managers rate this as one of the most important characteristics they look for in employees. People high in conscientiousness show more stamina at work, which is helpful in many occupations. Despite this, the use of personality traits in selection contexts has risen over the years, and a 2006

1. Extroversion	Sociable, gregarious, assertive, talkative, expressive
2. Adjustment	Emotionally stable, nondepressed, secure, content
3. Agreeableness	Courteous, trusting, good-natured, tolerant, cooperative, forgiving
4. Conscientiousness	Dependable, organized, persevering, thorough, achievement-oriented
5. Inquisitiveness	Curious, imaginative, artistically sensitive, broad-minded, playful

table 6.3

The Five Major Dimensions of Personality Inventories

study indicates that 35 percent of U.S. organizations employ these kinds of tests when selecting personnel.[71] Part of this is attributable to the wider use of team-based structures that put more emphasis on collaboration at work. In contexts where task interdependence between individuals is stressed, personality conflicts become more salient and disruptive relative to situations where individuals are working alone.[72] Team contexts require that people create and maintain roles and relationships, and several traits like agreeableness and conscientiousness seem to promote effective role taking.[73] On the other hand, people who are high in disagreeableness and low in conscientiousness are more prone to engage in counterproductive behavior in group contexts.[74] One important element of staffing in team-based structures, however, relates to how the selection of one team member influences the requirements associated with other team members.[75] In some cases, organizations might try to select people who have very similar values and personality traits in order to create a strong team culture. When there is a strong team culture, everyone shares the same views and traits, promoting harmony and cohesiveness.[76]

In other cases, people putting together a team go out of their way to make sure that the people on the team have different values and personalities. The hope here is that a diversity of opinion that promotes internal debate and creativity.[77] For example, when assembling his leadership team in 2009, President Barack Obama took a "Team of Rivals" approach where, like Abraham Lincoln, he selected people who had previously been critical of him, including his vice president Joe Biden and his secretary of state, Hillary Clinton.[78] Lincoln, Obama had once said, "was confident enough to be willing to have these dissenting voices and confident enough to listen to the American people and to push them outside of their comfort zone."[79] Many considered this move on Obama's part to be a very risky move. On the one hand, by surrounding himself with a team of strong-minded, independent thinkers who would not necessarily act as simple "yes men," he assured himself that he would get a great deal of unbiased and unique thoughts on every conceivable challenge to his administration. On the other hand, could he really count on these individuals to faithfully execute the decisions that he made, especially when one of those decisions was, perhaps, inconsistent with the advice that he was offered?

If one does take this approach to staffing a team, it is critical that ones also takes steps to make sure that there are not strong "fault lines" within the group that create strong and opposing subgroups. Diversity can be built into a team, and subgrouping problems avoided with judicious selection. For example, imagine a four-person group comprised of two men and two women, two marketing experts and two engineers, and two people from the United States and two people from France. One way this diversity could configure itself is such that the two males were also both engineers and both from the United States, and the two women were both marketing experts from France. In this configuration, the group has a strong fault line because all three dimensions of diversity converge, and it is easy to predict how this group might break apart into two subgroups. In contrast, the same level of diversity could be configured in a group where one of the men was an engineer, but one of the women was an engineer also. Similarly, one of the marketing experts was a man and one was woman. Finally, one of the men was from France and one was from the United States. In this second configuration, there is no strong fault line, and it is harder to see how the group is likely to fall apart.[80]

Strong fault lines such as this have been found to negatively affect group performance and viability. Training group members to value diversity can often offset these negative effects; however, it is still better if we can "cross-categorize people and avoid strong fault lines. One way to achieve this is through reward structures that place people who differ on other dimensions into "subteams" that have a common goal and all obtain the same reward for meeting that goal. This type of cooperative goal creates a new dimension of diversity where two people who differ on one dimension (gender) are the same when it comes to rewards.[81]

The concept of "emotional intelligence" is also important in team contexts and has been used to describe people who are especially effective in fluid and socially intensive contexts. Emotional intelligence is traditionally conceived of having five aspects: (1) self-awareness (knowledge of one's strengths and weaknesses), (2) self-regulation (the ability to keep disruptive emotions in check), (3) self-motivation (how to motivate oneself and persevere in the face of obstacles), (4) empathy (the ability to sense and read emotions in others), and (5) social skills (the ability to manage the emotions of other people). Danial Goleman, one of the primary proponents of this construct, noted that "in the new workplace, with its emphasis on flexibility, teams and a strong customer orientation, this crucial set of emotional competencies is becoming increasingly essential for excellence in every job in every part of the world."[82] Although there is not a great deal of direct empirical research on emotional intelligence, there is a great deal of overlap between many of its dimensions and aspects of the Big Five, and there is a large body of evidence regarding these.

In addition to the development of team-based structures, the use of personality measures as screening devices has also increased because of the increased use of multinational structures and the increase in the number of jobs that require that people work in foreign locales. The number of people that are asked to work outside their own country has increased steadily over time, and more often than not, the decision of whom to send where is based primarily on technical skills. However, in one large study of expatriates working in Hong Kong, Japan, and Korea, high levels of emotional stability and openness to experience were two of the strongest predictors of adjustment and performance, and these tended to trump technical expertise when it came to predicting who would succeed and fail. In this study, the cost of an adjustment failure (i.e., someone who has to come home prior to finishing his or her assignment) was estimated at over $150,000 per person, and hence the stakes are high in this context.[83]

Finally, the validity for almost all of the Big Five factors in terms of predicting job performance also seems to be higher when the scores are not obtained from the applicant but are instead taken from other people.[84] The lower validity associated with self-reports of personality can be traced to three factors. First, people sometimes lack insight into what their own personalities are actually like (or how they are perceived by others), so their scores are inaccurate or unreliable. Second, people's personalities sometimes vary across different contexts. Thus, someone may be very conscientious when it comes to social activities such as planning a family wedding or a fraternity party, but less conscientious when it comes to doing a paid job. Someone else may work hard at the office, and then not lift a finger to do household chores. Third, unlike intelligence tests, people are much better at "faking" their responses to personality items.[85] Research suggests that when people fill out these inventories when applying for a job, their scores on conscientiousness and emotional stability are much higher relative to when they are just filling out the same questionnaires anonymously for research purposes.[86]

Several steps can be used to try to reduce faking. For example, if employers simply warn applicants that they are going to cross-check the applicants' self-ratings with other people, this seems to reduce faking.[87] Also, the degree to which people can fake various personality traits is enhanced with questionnaires, and one sees much less faking of traits when interviewers are assessing the characteristics.[88]

All of this reinforces the idea that it is better to obtain this information from people other than the job applicant, and that it is better to use this information to reject low scorers but not necessarily hire all higher scores on the basis of self-reports alone.[89]

EVIDENCE-BASED HR

It is essential to collect empirical evidence and validate personality tests in specific contexts rather than assuming that they will work because you were told that by a commercial developer of such tests. For example, one context where measures of personality have been validated with empirical evidence is in the context of franchise operations. A franchise operation is usually part of a national chain (e.g., Burger King, Kentucky Fried Chicken, World Gyms) but is run locally in an entrepreneurial fashion by a single individual. Evidence within this industry indicates that the amount of revenue each franchise generates varies widely, despite the similarity of product, advertising, and size across the corporation. To learn why this was the case, one franchise operator distributed a set of personality items to all current franchisees and identified each item that distinguished those generating revenue in the top 80th percentile from those whose revenue generation placed them in the bottom 20th percentile. The distinguishing items were then used to select future franchisees who tended to resemble the current high performers and not the current low performers (note this is what was referred to earlier as a concurrent design), resulting in an increase in annual royalties per franchise from $6,500 a month to $52,000.

SOURCE: J. Bennett, "Do You Have What It Takes?" *The Wall Street Journal*, September 19, 2006, p. R11.

Work Samples

Work-sample tests attempt to simulate the job in a prehiring context to observe how the applicant performs in the simulated job. The degree of fidelity in work samples can vary greatly. In some cases, applicants respond to a set of standardized hypothetical case studies and role play how they would react to certain situations.[90] Often these standardized role plays employ interactive video technology to create "virtual job auditions."[91] In other cases, the job applicants are brought to the employers' location and actually perform the job for a short time period as part of a "job tryout."[92] Finally, although not generally considered a test, the practice whereby employers hire someone on a temporary basis and then, after a rather long trial (six months to a year), hire that person permanently is in essence an extended work-sample test.[93]

In some cases, employers will sponsor competitions where contestants (who at this point are not even considered job applicants) vie for attention by going head-to-head in solving certain job-related problems. These sorts of competitions have been common in some industries like architecture and fashion design, but their use is spreading across many other business contexts. These competitions tend to be cost effective in generating a lot of interest, and some have attracted as many as 1,000 contestants who bring their talents to bear on specific problems faced by the employing organization.[94] Competitions are particularly well-suited for assessing and "discovering" young people who may not have extended track records or portfolios to evaluate.

As part of its own fight in the war for talent, Google sponsors an event called "Google Code Jam," which attracts more than 10,000 contestants a year from all over the world. This one-day competition requires contestants work to solve some very difficult programming problems under relatively high levels of time pressure. For example, finalists have to develop software that would perform unique and difficult searches employing a minimum number of "clicks" or develop a complex interactive war game from scratch in under two hours. The winner of the contest receives $7,000 and a guaranteed job at Google's prestigious Research and Development Center, but, in fact, Google usually winds up hiring more than half of the 50 finalists each year (but that is not guaranteed). The finalists in this contest represent the best of the best in terms of world's top programmers, and as Robert Hughes, director of the Code Jam, notes, "Wherever the best talent is, Google wants them."[95]

With all these advantages of work-sample tests come two drawbacks. First, by their very nature the tests are job-specific, so generalizability is low. Second, partly because a new test has to be developed for each job and partly because of their nonstandardized formats, these tests are relatively expensive to develop. It is much more cost-effective to purchase a commercially available cognitive ability test that can be used for a number of different job categories within the company than to develop a test for each job. For this reason, some have rated the utility of cognitive ability tests higher than work-sample tests, despite the latter's higher criterion-related validity.

In the area of managerial selection, work-sample tests are typically the cornerstone in assessment centers. Generically, the term **assessment center** is used to describe a wide variety of specific selection programs that employ multiple selection methods to rate either applicants or job incumbents on their managerial potential. Someone attending an assessment center would typically experience work-sample tests such as an in-basket test and several tests of more general abilities and personality. Because assessment centers employ multiple selection methods, their criterion-related validity tends to be quite high. Assessment centers seem to tap a number of different characteristics, but "problem-solving ability" stands out as probably the most important skill tapped via this method.[96] The idiosyncratic and unique nature of the different exercises, however, has led some to suggest that the exercises themselves should be scored for winners and losers without making any reference to higher order characteristics like skills, abilities, or traits.[97] Research indicates that one of the best combinations of selection methods includes work-sample tests with a highly structured interview and a measure of general cognitive ability. The validity coefficient expected from such a combined battery often exceeds .60.[98]

Assessment Center
A process in which multiple raters evaluate employees' performance on a number of exercises.

Honesty Tests and Drug Tests

Many problems that confront society also exist within organizations, which has led to two new kinds of tests: honesty tests and drug-use tests. Many companies formerly employed polygraph tests, or lie detectors, to evaluate job applicants, but this changed with the passage of the Polygraph Act in 1988. This act banned the use of polygraphs in employment screening for most organizations. However, it did not eliminate the problem of theft by employees. As a result, the paper-and-pencil honesty testing industry was born.

Paper-and-pencil honesty tests come in a number of different forms. Some directly emphasize questions dealing with past theft admissions or associations with people who stole from employers. Other items are less direct and tap more basic traits such as social conformity, conscientiousness, or emotional stability.[99] Some sample items are shown in Table 6.4. A large-scale independent review of validity studies suggests they can predict both theft and other disruptive behaviors. Another positive feature

table 6.4

Sample Items from a
Typical Integrity Test

1. It's OK to take something from a company that is making too much profit.
2. Stealing is just a way of getting your fair share.
3. When a store overcharges its customers, it's OK to change price tags on merchandise.
4. If you could get into a movie without paying and not get caught, would you do it?
5. Is it OK to go around the law if you don't actually break it?

SOURCE: From *Inc.: The Magazine for Growing Companies.* Copyright © 1992 by Mansueto Ventures LLC. Reproduced with permission of Mansueto Ventures LLC. via Copyright Clearance Center.

of these tests is that one does not see large differences attributable to race or sex, so they are not likely to have adverse impact on these demographic groups.[100]

As is the case with measures of personality, some people are concerned that people confronting an honesty test can fake their way to a passing score. The evidence suggests that people instructed to fake their way to a high score (indicating honesty) can do so. However, it is not clear that this affects the validity of the predictions made using such tests. That is, it seems that despite this built-in bias, scores on the test still predict future theft. Thus, the effect of the faking bias is not large enough to detract from the test's validity.[101]

As with theft, there is a growing perception of the problems caused by drug use among employees. The major controversies surrounding drug tests involve not their reliability and validity but whether they represent an invasion of privacy, an unreasonable search and seizure, or a violation of due process. Urinalysis and blood tests are invasive procedures, and accusing someone of drug use is a serious matter. Employers considering the use of drug tests would be well advised to make sure that their drug-testing programs conform to some general rules. First, these tests should be administered systematically to all applicants for the same job. Second, testing seems more defensible for jobs that involve safety hazards associated with failure to perform.[102] Test results should be reported back to the applicant, who should be allowed an avenue of appeal (and perhaps retesting). Tests should be conducted in an environment that is as unintrusive as possible, and results from those tests should be held in strict confidence. Finally, when testing current employees, the program should be part of a wider organizational program that provides rehabilitation counseling.[103]

A LOOK BACK

In the vignette that opened this chapter, we saw how the lives of job applicants and the viability of organizations are strongly affected by decisions regarding who is accepted and rejected for positions. These are some of the most important decisions an organization is likely to make. Thus, the idea that one might just hand this major responsibility over to an outsourcing firm whose own selection criteria for its call center workers is unknown has to be viewed as questionable. Thankfully, there are numerous alternatives to this for making such decisions, many of which have been validated and supported by years of research, and these were highlighted in this chapter.

Questions

1. Based on this chapter, what are the best methods of obtaining information about job applicants?
2. What are the best characteristics to look for in applicants, and how does this depend on the nature of the job?
3. If you could use only two of the methods described in this chapter and could assess only two of the characteristics discussed, which would you choose, and why?

 Please see the Video Case that corresponds to this chapter online at www.mhhe.com/noe7e.

SUMMARY

In this chapter we examined the five critical standards with which all personnel selection methods should conform: reliability, validity, generalizability, utility, and legality. We also looked at nine different selection methods currently used in organizations and evaluated each with respect to these five standards. Table 6.5 summarizes these selection methods and can be used as a guide in deciding which test to use for a specific purpose. Although we discussed each type of test individually, it is important to note in closing that there is no need to use only one type of test for any one job. Indeed, managerial assessment centers use many different forms of tests over a two- or three-day period to learn as much as possible about candidates for important executive positions. As a result, highly accurate predictions are often made, and the validity associated with the judicious use of multiple tests is higher than for tests used in isolation.

KEY TERMS

Reliability, 233
Validity, 237
Criterion-related validity, 237
Prediction validation, 237
Concurrent validation, 237

Content validation, 240
Generalizability, 240
Utility, 241
Situational interview, 248
Cognitive ability tests, 254

Verbal comprehension, 254
Quantitative ability, 254
Reasoning ability, 254
Assessment center, 259

DISCUSSION QUESTIONS

1. We examined nine different types of selection methods in this chapter. Assume that you were just rejected for a job based on one of these methods. Obviously, you might be disappointed and angry regardless of what method was used to make this decision, but can you think of two or three methods that might leave you most distressed? In general, why might the acceptability of the test to applicants be an important standard to add to the five we discussed in this chapter?
2. Videotaping applicants in interviews is becoming an increasingly popular means of getting multiple assessments of that individual from different perspectives.

Can you think of some reasons why videotaping interviews might also be useful in evaluating the interviewer? What would you look for in an interviewer if you were evaluating one on videotape?
3. Distinguish between concurrent and predictive validation designs, discussing why the latter is preferred over the former. Examine each of the nine selection methods discussed in this chapter and determine which of these would have their validity most and least affected by the type of validation design employed.
4. Some have speculated that in addition to increasing the validity of decisions, employing rigorous selection

table 6.5

A Summary of Personnel Selection Methods

METHOD	RELIABILITY	VALIDITY	GENERALIZABILITY	UTILITY	LEGALITY
Interviews	Low when unstructured and when assessing nonobservable traits	Low if unstructured and nonbehavioral	Low	Low, especially because of expense	Low because of subjectivity and potential interviewer bias; also, lack of validity makes job-relatedness low
Reference checks	Low, especially when obtained from letters	Low because of lack of range in evaluations	Low	Low, although not expensive to obtain	Those writing letters may be concerned with charges of libel
Biographical information	High test–retest, especially for verifiable information	High criterion-related validity; low in content validity	Usually job-specific, but have been successfully developed for many job types	High; inexpensive way to collect vast amounts of potentially relevant data	May have adverse impact; thus often develop separate scoring keys based on sex or race
Physical ability tests	High	Moderate criterion-related validity; high content validity for some jobs	Low; pertain only to physically demanding jobs	Moderate for some physical jobs; may prevent expensive injuries and disability	Often have adverse impact on women and people with disabilities; need to establish job-relatedness
Cognitive ability tests	High	Moderate criterion-related validity; content validation inappropriate	High; predictive for most jobs, although best for complex jobs	High; low cost and wide application across diverse jobs in companies	Often have adverse impact on race, especially for African Americans, though decreasing over time
Personality inventories	High	Low to moderate criterion-related validity for most traits; content validation inappropriate	Low; few traits predictive for many jobs, except conscientiousness	Low, although inexpensive for jobs where specific traits are relevant	Low because of cultural and sex differences on most traits, and low job-relatedness in general
Work-sample tests	High	High criterion and content validity	Usually job-specific, but have been successfully developed for many job types	High, despite the relatively high cost to develop	High because of low adverse impact and high job-relatedness
Honesty tests	Insufficient independent evidence	Insufficient independent evidence	Insufficient independent evidence	Insufficient independent evidence	Insufficient history of litigation, but will undergo scrutiny
Drug tests	High	High	High	Expensive, but may yield high payoffs for health-related costs	May be challenged on invasion-of-privacy grounds

methods has symbolic value for organizations. What message is sent to applicants about the organization through hiring practices, and how might this message be reinforced by recruitment programs that occur before selection and training programs that occur after selection?

SELF-ASSESSMENT EXERCISE

Reviews of research about personality have identified five common aspects of personality, referred to as the Big Five personality traits. Find out which are your most prominent traits. Read each of the following statements, marking "Yes" if it describes you and "No" if it does not.

1. In conversations I tend to do most of the talking.
2. Often people look to me to make decisions.
3. I am a very active person.
4. I usually seem to be in a hurry.
5. I am dominant, forceful, and assertive.
6. I have a very active imagination.
7. I have an active fantasy life.
8. How I feel about things is important to me.
9. I find it easy to feel myself what others are feeling.
10. I think it's interesting to learn and develop new hobbies.
11. My first reaction is to trust people.
12. I believe that most persons are basically well intentioned.
13. I'm not crafty or shy.
14. I'd rather not talk about myself and my accomplishments.
15. I'd rather praise others than be praised myself.
16. I come into situations being fully prepared.
17. I pride myself on my sound judgment.
18. I have a lot of self-discipline.
19. I try to do jobs carefully so they don't have to be done again.
20. I like to keep everything in place so I know where it is.
21. I enjoy performing under pressure.
22. I am seldom sad or depressed.
23. I'm an even-tempered person.
24. I am levelheaded in emergencies.
25. I feel I am capable of coping with most of my problems.

The statements are grouped into categories. Statements 1–5 describe extroversion, 6–10 openness to experience, 11–15 agreeableness, 16–20 conscientiousness, and 21–25 emotional stability. The more times you wrote "Yes" for the statements in a category, the more likely you are to have the associated trait.

EXERCISING STRATEGY: NEVER HAVING TO SAY "YOU NEVER KNOW"

Seymour Schlager had an impressive résumé. He had both MD and JD degrees, as well as a PhD in microbiology. He had experience as a director of established AIDS research at Abbott Laboratories and as an entrepreneur in a small, upstart pharmaceutical company. He seemed like a perfect fit for the medical director job open at Becton Dickinson, a large medical device company, and was hired on the spot.

One fact about Schlager that did not come out of the application process was that he was convicted of attempted murder in 1991 and had spent several years in prison as a result of this crime. While any reader of this book could type Schlager's name into almost any Internet search engine and uncover at least one of the 24 articles written about his case—some of which were front-page material in the *Chicago Tribune*—apparently no one at Becton Dickinson felt this was necessary.

Although this is an extreme case, the practice of stretching, shading, spinning, and outright lying on one's résumé is hardly uncommon, and when one is in the business of hiring complete strangers, it pays to "be afraid—be very afraid." Although many firms fail to perform routine background checks on their hires, organizations that provide such checks can point to some startling statistics. For example, Kroll Associates, one of the leading investigative agencies for top-level executives, notes that of the 70 background checks it did in the year 2000, 39 percent turned up problems such as fraud, bankruptcy, and SEC violations that were serious enough to nix the employment offers being considered.

One reason for the lack of "due diligence" on the part of employers is that in a labor shortage, too many are in a rush to secure top talent. For example, when the firm Christian and Timbers narrowed the search for the new CEO of Pinpoint Networks Inc. down to six candidates, rather than let the firm finish its work, the young founders of this company were so infatuated with the résumé of one applicant that they immediately took over and closed the search. Unfortunately, when it became clear 13 weeks later that the new CEO, Anthony J. Blake, was not who he claimed to be, it was too late. Without a seasoned CEO, Pinpoint blew the opportunity to attract venture capital when it was still available. When the technology sector tanked later that year, Pinpoint was forced to lay off more than a third of its workforce.

Experiences such as these are prompting other employers to slow down the hiring process so that they have a much better idea of exactly whom they are asking to join their organizational family. Some firms do not only background checks but also extensive psychological testing to ensure that a person is who he or she claims to be and also fits the culture of the organization. You never know what these kinds of investigations will uncover—unless, of course, you fail to perform them.

Questions

1. People applying for jobs are always motivated to display themselves in the best light, and as a result, this can sometimes lead to inaccurate portrayals of abilities, skills, experiences, and personality. Based upon what you have read in this chapter, how should you approach a job applicant's written application and résumé if your goal is to make sure that they accurately reflect the person's past experiences and accomplishments?
2. In the face-to-face interview process, what steps can be taken to ensure that the applicant is being frank and honest with you, and what steps should you take if you feel that he or she is portraying an inaccurate picture of himself or herself?
3. Beyond the traditional approaches of going over the application and conducting face-to-face interviews, what other steps can you as an employer take to ensure that the person who is being hired for the job has the right abilities, skills, past experiences and personality?

SOURCES: G. David, "You Just Hired Him: Should You Have Known Better," *Fortune*, October 29, 2001, pp. 205–6; D. Foust, "When the CEO Is Too Good to Be True," *BusinessWeek*, July 16, 2001, pp. 62–63; C. Daniels, "Does This Man Need a Shrink?" *Fortune*, February 5, 2001.

● MANAGING PEOPLE: FROM THE PAGES OF *BUSINESSWEEK*

BusinessWeek   ## Bridging the Generation Gap

Employment agency Randstad teams newbies with older staff to great effect For a pair of colleagues born four decades apart, Penelope Burns and Rinath Benjamin spend a lot of time together. Burns, 68, and Benjamin, 29, are sales agents at the Manhattan office of employment agency Randstad USA. They sit inches apart, facing each other. They hear every call the other makes. They read every e-mail the other sends or receives. Sometimes they finish each other's sentences.

This may seem a little strange, but the unconventional pairing is all part of Randstad's effort to ensure that its twentysomething employees—the flighty, praise-seeking Generation Y that we have read so much about—fit in and, more to the point, stick around. The Dutch company, which has been expanding in the U.S., is hoping to win the hearts, minds, and loyalty of its young employees by teaming them up with older, more experienced hands. Every new sales agent is assigned a partner to work with until their business has grown to a certain size, which usually takes a few years. Then they both start over again with someone who has just joined the company. "This makes the corporate world more personal, approachable," says Randstad USA Chief Executive Stef Witteveen. "It's easier for the Gen Yers to identify with their jobs. They don't drown in their cubicles."

Randstad has been pairing people up almost since it opened for business four decades ago. The founder's motto was "Nobody should be alone." The original aim was to boost productivity by having sales agents share one job and trade off responsibilities. The system has been refined over the years and now each week one person is out making sales calls, and the other is in the office interviewing potential workers and handling the paperwork. Then they switch.

Randstad brought its partnership program to the U.S. in the late 1990s. But it wasn't until two years ago, once Randstad had integrated the personnel from the various firms it had acquired, that it began recruiting new employees. Last year it hired about 600 people, 420 of whom are in their twenties. Knowing that these Gen Yers need lots of attention in the workplace, Randstad executives figured that if they shared a job with someone whose own success depended on theirs, they were certain to get all the nurturing they required. As Belle Rose Ragins, a professor of human resource management at the University of Wisconsin at Milwaukee, puts it: "Gen Y's psychological contract is with the relationships embedded within the organization, not the organization itself."

No Touchdowns Allowed

Of course, Randstad doesn't simply put people together and hope it all works out. First it figures out who will play well with other people. To assess that, the human resources department conducts extensive interviews and requires candidates to shadow a sales agent for half a day. "We have certain questions that we look for them to answer with 'we' instead of 'I'," says HR chief Genia Spencer. "Somebody who needs to be recognized as the star, who needs personal achievement and doesn't like to share that, won't work in a unit. Partners cannot compete with each other." One question Randstad asks is: What's your most memorable moment while being on a team? "If they answer: 'When I scored the winning touchdown,' that's a deal killer," says

Spencer. "Everything about our organization is based on the team and group."

Before joining Randstad in January, 2006, Benjamin had worked for six years as a sales agent at Verizon. When she first heard about Randstad's partnering program she was a little apprehensive. "It was completely different. I was used to being responsible for everything," she says. "Here you are forced to be open, to tell everything." But Burns knew they could work together. "I tested her during the interview to see if she had a sense of humor, if I could tease her a little bit and she would know it was to relieve the tension." The older woman is feisty and competitive. She is distinguished by a big, raspy voice; in another era, she would have been called brassy. Burns has been an agent at Randstad since 1998 and in all, she has been in the business for some two decades. Benjamin is quick, direct, confident. She's big on e-mail, texting, and her BlackBerry.

One of the most compelling features of Randstad's partnering program is that neither person is "the boss." And both are expected to teach the other.

> Burns: "People think I run the works. I don't. She trains me as much as I train her."
>
> Benjamin: "We have a great rapport. She's like my grandmother."
>
> Burns: "You can get cynical when you've been in the business as long as I have. She doesn't let me get that way."
>
> Benjamin: "During our training, we learn that we are each other's boss. The biggest shock was to have someone asking what I'm doing all the time. Now I'm over that."

Soon after Benjamin started, she suggested they begin to use the electronic payroll system Randstad offers to save time and reduce their paperwork. Burns hesitated: She had been filling out time sheets for the talent (as the temporary employees are called) and wasn't sure how they would take to the new task. But Benjamin persuaded her it would ultimately be simpler for everyone. "You don't have to drag me into the future, just give me a little push," says Burns. Now, when someone hasn't logged on in time, Burns calls and says: "Rinath says you have to get your time sheet in."

Burns, who has had a couple of other partners, says the younger agents are often too impatient. "They want to tell clients about problems before we have a solution. Sometimes new people don't realize that's not a good idea." She says Benjamin wants to act quickly, but hasn't made that mistake. "She tells me to take a breath," says Benjamin.

These are relationships like any other, full of promise yet always vulnerable to dysfunction. And even the best ones require a lot of maintenance. As Lucille Santos, a 61-year-old senior agent in North Haven, Conn., says, "My antennae are always up." Her partner, Allison

Kaplan, is 28, and this is her first office job. "We need to be sure that we're asking the right questions and saying the right things to the clients and talent," says Santos. "In the beginning, Allison might have been a little timid about telling applicants they weren't dressed appropriately. I gave her some explicit suggestions, and she learned from watching me."

Gaining Perspective

Santos says Kaplan has taught her to relax a little bit more at work. "I'm from the old school," she says. "It's important that people take lunch, and I don't always look upon that type of thing so well. She put that into perspective for me."

Randstad encourages people to solve problems with their partners and breaks up teams only when the situation is fairly dire—when, say, one person is sabotaging the other or when productivity suffers because of constant bickering. In those cases, which the company says are rare, the uncooperative partner usually ends up leaving the company.

Even so, Randstad's ability to keep its employees has improved. The company used to have a retention rate of 50%, which is the industry standard. In the past year, its rate has increased to 60%. "We have determined a clear connection between being in a unit and feeling more successful and productive," says Spencer.

CEO Witteveen, who is 44, acknowledges that some managers resist having to accommodate the idiosyncrasies of Gen Y. "It's natural to think: Why should I do all these kinds of things for them? No one did that for me. You have to get over that. You have to think beyond your own feelings of fairness. It's about improving the relationship with the employee." He says he, too, had to learn to appreciate the concerns of the younger generation even though he gets practice at home. "I have two Gen Y kids, and they come with all the features," he says.

Questions

1. Personnel selection decisions typically are based on the fit for one person for one job. In what way does Randstad's use of partnership teams alter the typical way one might think about selection decisions?

2. What are some personal characteristics that might be viewed positively when staffing a single job, but that might actually be viewed negatively when staffing partnership teams?

3. Randstad deliberately creates variance in age when forming partnership teams. In what ways might younger workers and older workers be in a position to uniquely support each other when working in sales teams?

4. Other than age, what other types of traits or abilities might one want to see when creating variance in partnership teams?

SOURCE: Susan Berfield, "Bridging the Generation Gap," *BusinessWeek*, September 1, 2007, pp. 60–61.

NOTES

1. J. Welch and S. Welch, "So Many CEO's Get This Wrong," *BusinessWeek*, July 17, 2006, p. 92.
2. A. Bernstein, "Talent: Will America Lose Out," *BusinessWeek*, May 16, 2005, p. 16.
3. V. Wadhwa, "America's Immigrant Brain Drain," *BusinessWeek*, March 16, 2009, p. 68.
4. F. Lievens, T. Buyse, and P. R. Sackett, "Retest Effects in Operational Selection Settings: Development and Test of a Framework," *Personnel Psychology* 58 (2005), pp. 981–1007.
5. D. Weichmann and A.M. Ryan, "Reactions to Computerized Testing in Selection Contexts," *International Journal of Selection and Assessment*, June 2003, pp. 215–29.
6. C. H. Van Iddekinge and R. E. Ployhart, "Developments in the Criterion-Related Validation of Selection Procedures: A Critical Review and Recommendations for Practice," *Personnel Psychology* 61 (2008), pp. 871–925.
7. J. Cohen, *Statistical Power Analysis for the Behavioral Sciences* (New York: Academic Press, 1977).
8. D. D. Robinson, "Content-Oriented Personnel Selection in a Small Business Setting," *Personnel Psychology* 34 (1981), pp. 77–87.
9. M. V. Rafter, "Assessment Providers Scoring Well," *Workforce Management*, January 19, 2009, pp. 24–25.
10. F. Schmidt, H. Le, I. S. Oh, and J. Shaffer, "General Mental Ability, Job Performance, and Red Herrings: Responses to Osterman, Hauser, and Schmitt," *Academy of Management Perspectives* 21 (2007), pp. 64–76.
11. E. Zimmerman, "What Are Employees Worth?" *Workforce*, February 2001, p. 36.
12. A. Eccles, "How to Get a Job," *Fortune*, April 13, 2009, pp. 49–56.
13. A. Meisler, "Negative Results," *Workforce*, October 2003, pp. 35–40.
14. A. Meisler, "When Bad Things Happen to Hot Brands," *Workforce*, July 2003, pp. 20–21.
15. M. Schoeff, "Walgreen Suit Reflects EEOC's Latest Strategy," *Workforce Management*, March 16, 2007, p. 8.
16. P. Roth, P. Bobko, L. McFarland, and M. Buster, "Work Sample Tests in Personnel Selection: A Meta-analysis of Black-White Differences in Overall Exercise Scores," *Personnel Psychology* 61 (2008), pp. 637–61.
17. R. E. Ployhart and B. C. Holtz, "The Diversity-Validity Dilemma: Strategies for Reducing Racioethnic and Sex Group Differences and Adverse Impact in Selection," *Personnel Psychology* 61 (2008), pp. 153–72.
18. G. Flynn, "The Reverse Discrimination Trap," *Workforce*, June 2003, pp. 106–7.
19. M. E. Heilman, W. S. Battle, C. E. Keller, and R. A. Lee, "Type of Affirmative Action Policy: A Determinant of Reactions to Sex-Based Preferential Selection," *Journal of Applied Psychology* 83 (1998), pp. 190–205.
20. D. A. Newman and J. S. Lyon, "Recruitment Efforts to Reduce Adverse Impact: Targeted Recruiting for Personality, Cognitive Ability and Diversity," *Journal of Applied Psychology* 94 (2009), pp. 298–317.
21. D. M. Finch, B. D. Edwards, and J. C. Wallace, "Multistage Selection Strategies: Simulating the Effects of Adverse Impact and Expected Performance for Various Predictor Combinations," *Journal of Applied Psychology* 94 (2009), pp. 318–340.
22. A. S. Levi and Y. Fried, "Differences between African Americans and Whites in Reactions to Affirmative Action Programs in Training, Promotion, and Layoffs," *Journal of Applied Psychology* 93 (2008), pp. 1118–29.
23. A. Gutman, "Smith versus City of Jackson: Adverse Impact in the ADEA (Well Sort Of)," *Industrial Psychologist*, July 2005, pp. 31–32.
24. R. Ableson, "Fighting Discrimination Takes Will and Cash," *Taipei Times*, July 2, 2001, pp. 21–22.
25. S. Sonnenberg, "Unreasonable Accommodations," *Workforce*, August 2003, pp. 16–17.
26. J. Mullich, "Hiring without Limits," *Workforce*, June 2002, pp. 53–58.
27. M. C. Nazario, "Non-disabled Job Seekers Taking Jobs of Disabled," CNN.com, March 18, 2009.
28. L. T. Cullen, "The Diversity Delusion," *Time*, May 7, 2007, p. 45.
29. R. A. Posthuma, F. R. Morgeson, and M. A. Campion, "Beyond Employment Interview Validity: A Comprehensive Narrative Review of Recent Research and Trends over Time," *Personnel Psychology* 55 (2002), pp. 1–81.
30. R. Pingitore, B. L. Dugoni, R. S. Tindale, and B. Spring, "Bias against Overweight Job Applicants in a Simulated Interview," *Journal of Applied Psychology* 79 (1994), pp. 909–17.
31. F. Hanson, "Keeping Interviews on Point to Stay Out of Legal Hot Water," *Workforce Management*, August 14, 2006, pp. 44–45.
32. M. A. McDaniel, D. L. Whetzel, F. L. Schmidt, and S. D.Maurer, "The Validity of Employment Interviews: A Comprehensive Review and Meta-Analysis," *Journal of Applied Psychology* 79 (1994), pp. 599–616; A. I. Huffcutt and W. A. Arthur, "Hunter and Hunter (1984) Revisited: Interview Validity for Entry-Level Jobs," *Journal of Applied Psychology* 79 (1994), pp. 184–90.
33. C. H. Middendorf and T. H. Macan, "Note-Taking in the Interview: Effects on Recall and Judgments," *Journal of Applied Psychology* 87 (2002), pp. 293–303.
34. M. A. McDaniel, F. P. Morgeson, E. B. Finnegan, M. A. Campion, and E. P. Braverman, "Use of Situational Judgment Tests to Predict Job Performance: A Clarification of the Literature," *Journal of Applied Psychology* 86 (2001), pp. 730–40.
35. A. P. J. Ellis, B. J. West, A. M. Ryan, and R. P. DeShon, "The Use of Impression Management Tactics in Structured Interviews: A Function of Question Type?" *Journal of Applied Psychology* 87 (2002), pp. 1200–8.
36. S. Maurer, "A Practitioner-Based Analysis of Interviewer Job Expertise and Scale Format as Contextual Factors in Situational Interviews," *Personnel Psychology* 55 (2002), pp. 307–27.
37. W. C. Byham, "Can You Interview for Integrity?" *Across the Board*, March 2004, pp. 34–38.
38. T. Libby, "Surviving the Group Interview," *Forbes*, March 24, 1986, p. 190; Dipboye, *Selection Interviews: Process Perspectives* (Cincinnati, OH: South-Western, 1991) p. 210.
39. Y. Ganzach, A. N. Kluger, and N. Klayman, "Making Decisions from an Interview: Expert Measurement and Mechanical Combination," *Personnel Psychology* 53 (2000), pp. 1–21.
40. C. Tuna, "How to Spot Resume Fraud," *The Wall Street Journal*, November 13, 2008, p. C1.
41. J. Twist, "Pitfalls of Work Blogs," *BBC News*, May 15, 2006, p. 1.
42. M. Conlin, "You Are What You Post," *BusinessWeek*, March 27, 2006, pp. 52–53.

43. D. Stead, "Just a Click Away," *BusinessWeek*, June 26, 2006, p. 9.

44. O. Kharif, "Big Brother Is Reading Your Blog," *BusinessWeek*, February 28, 2006, p. 32.

45. S. F. Dingfelder, "To Tell the Truth," *Monitor on Psychology*, March 2004, pp. 22–23.

46. A. Davis, J. Pereira, and W. M. Bulkeley, "Security Concerns Bring Focus on Translating Body Language," *The Wall Street Journal*, August 15, 2002, pp. A1–A3.

47. D. D. Hatch, "Bad Reference for Ex-Employee Judged Defamatory," *Workforce*, December 2003, p. 20.

48. E. Zimmerman, "A Subtle Reference Trap for Unwary Employers," *Workforce*, April 2003, p. 22.

49. J. S. Lublin, "Bulletproofing Your References in the Hunt for a New Job," *The Wall Street Journal*, April 7, 2009, p. C1.

50. M. R. Barrick and R. D. Zimmerman, "Reducing Voluntary Turnover through Selection," *Journal of Applied Psychology* 90 (2005), pp. 159–66.

51. S. Pustizzi, "Résumé Fraud Gets Slicker and Easier," CNN.com, March 11, 2004, p. 1.

52. K. Gordon, "Big, Fast and Easily Bungled," *Workforce*, August 2003, pp. 47–49.

53. N. Schmitt, F. L. Oswald, B. H. Kim, M. A. Gillespie, L. J. Ramsey, and T. Y. Yoo, "The Impact of Elaboration on Socially Desirable Responding and the Validity of Biodata Measures," *Journal of Applied Psychology* 88 (2003), pp. 979–88.

54. N. Schmitt and C. Kunce, "The Effects of Required Elaboration of Answers to Biodata Questions," *Personnel Psychology* 55 (2002), pp. 569–87.

55. M. Barnekow-Bergkvist, U. Aasa, K. A. Angquist, and H. Johansson, "Prediction of Development of Fatigue during a Simulated Ambulance Work Task from Physical Performance Tests," *Ergonomics* 47 (2004), pp. 1238–50.

56. J. Hogan, "Structure of Physical Performance in Occupational Tasks," *Journal of Applied Psychology* 76 (1991), pp. 495–507.

57. N. D. Henderson, M. W. Berry, and T. Matic, "Field Measures of Strength and Fitness Predict Firefighter Performance on Physically Demanding Tasks," *Personnel Psychology* 60 (2007), pp. 431–73.

58. J. Hogan, "Physical Abilities," in *Handbook of Industrial & Organizational Psychology*, 2nd ed., ed. M. D. Dunnette and L. M. Hough (Palo Alto, CA: Consulting Psychologists Press, 1991).

59. M. Schoeff, "Skill Levels of U.S. Grads Leave Employers Cold," *Workforce Management*, April 7, 2007, p. 14.

60. J. Smerd, "New Workers Sorely Lacking Literacy Skills," *Workforce Management*, December 10, 2007, pp. 6.

61. M. J. Ree, J. A. Earles, and M. S. Teachout, "Predicting Job Performance: Not Much More Than g," *Journal of Applied Psychology* 79 (1994), pp. 518–24.

62. J. F. Salagado, N. Anderson, S. Moscoso, C. Bertua, and F. De Fruyt, "International Validity Generalization of GMA and Cognitive Abilities: A European Community Meta-Analysis," *Personnel Psychology* 56 (2003), pp. 573–605.

63. J. A. LePine, J. A. Colquitt, and A. Erez, "Adaptability to Changing Task Contexts: Effects of General Cognitive Ability, Conscientiousness, and Openness to Experience," *Personnel Psychology* 53 (2000), pp. 563–93.

64. D. Foust, "How to Pick a Business Brain," *BusinessWeek*, February 20, 2006, p. 104.

65. G. Gloeckler, "Sidestepping the GMAT," *BusinessWeek*, August 8, 2005, pp. 71–72.

66. L. Lavelle, "Is the MBA Overrated?" *BusinessWeek*, March 20, 2006, pp. 78–79.

67. R. J. Barro, "Why Colleges Shouldn't Dump the SAT," *BusinessWeek*, April 9, 2001, p. 20.

68. D. A. Kravitz and S. L. Klineberg, "Reactions to Versions of Affirmative Action among Whites, Blacks, and Hispanics," *Journal of Applied Psychology* (2000), pp. 597–611.

69. M. A. Campion, J. L. Outtz, S. Zedeck, F. S. Schmidt, J. E. Kehoe, K. R. Murphy, and R. M. Guion, "The Controversy over Score Banding in Personnel Selection: Answers to 10 Key Questions," *Personnel Psychology* 54 (2001), pp. 149–85.

70. F. P. Morgeson, M. A. Campion, R. L. Dipboye, J. R. Hollenbeck, K. R. Murphy, and N. Schmitt, "Reconsidering the Use of Personality Tests in Personnel Selection Contexts," *Personnel Psychology* 60 (2007), pp. 683–729.

71. E. Freudenheim, "Personality Testing Controversial, but Poised to Take Off," *Workforce Management*, August 14, 2006, p. 38.

72. V. Knight, "Personality Tests as Hiring Tools," *The Wall Street Journal*, March 15, 2006, p. B1.

73. G. L. Steward, I. S. Fulmer, and M. R. Barrick, "An Exploration of Member Roles as a Multilevel Linking Mechanism for Individual Traits and Team Outcomes," *Personnel Psychology* 58 (2005), pp. 343–65.

74. M. Mount, R. Ilies, and E. Johnson, "Relationship of Personality Traits and Counterproductive Work Behaviors: The Mediation Effects of Job Satisfaction," *Personnel Psychology* 59 (2006), pp. 591–622.

75. S. E. Humphrey, J. R. Hollenbeck, C. J. Meyer, and D. R. Ilgen, "Trait Configurations in Self-managed Teams: A Conceptual Examination of the Use of Seeding for Maximizing and Minimizing Trait Variance in Teams," *Journal of Applied Psychology* 92 (2007), pp. 885–92.

76. A. Hedger, "Employee Screening: Common Challenges, Smart Solutions," *Workforce Management*, March 17, 2008, pp. 39–46.

77. J. Welch and S. Welch, "Team Building: Right and Wrong," *BusinessWeek*, November 24, 2008, p. 130.

78. Y. J. Dreazen and S. Gorman, "Obama National Security Team Set," *The Wall Street Journal*, December 1, 2008, p. A1.

79. J. Williams, "Will Lincoln's 'Team of Rivals' Play Today?" *The Boston Globe*, November 21, 2008, p. A1.

80. A. C. Homan, D. van Knippenberg, G. A. van Kleff, and C. K. W. De Dreu, "Bridging Faultlines by Valuing Diversity: Diversity Beliefs, Information Elaboration, and Performance in Diverse Work Groups," *Journal of Applied Psychology* 92 (2007), pp. 1189–99.

81. A. C. Homan, J. R. Hollenbeck, S. E. Humphrey, D. Van Knippenberg, D. R. Ilgen, and G. Van Kleef, "Facing Differences with an Open Mind: Openness to Experience, Salience of Intragroup Differences, and Performance of Diverse Work Groups," *Academy of Management Journal* 51 (2008), pp. 1204–22.

82. D. Goleman, "Sometimes, EQ Is More Important than IQ," CNN.com, January 14, 2005, p. 1.

83. M. A. Shaffer, D. A. Harrison, H. Gregersen, J. S. Black, L. A. Ferzandi, "You Can Take It With You: Individual Differences and Expatriate Effectiveness," *Journal of Applied Psychology* 91 (2006), pp. 109–25.

84. J. M. Hunthausen, D. M. Truxillo, T. N. Bauer, and L. B. Hammer, "A Field Study of Frame of Reference Effects on Personality Test Validity," *Journal of Applied Psychology* 88 (2003), pp. 545–51.

85. N. Schmitt and F. L. Oswald, "The Impact of Corrections for Faking on the Validity of Non-cognitive Measures in Selection Contexts," *Journal of Applied Psychology*, 2006, pp. 613–21.

86. S. A. Birkland, T. M. Manson, J. L. Kisamore, M. T. Brannick, and M. A. Smith, "Faking on Personality Measures,"

International Journal of Selection and Assessment 14 (December 2006), pp. 317–35.

87. N. L Vasilopoulos, J. M. Cucina, and J. M. McElreath, "Do Warnings of Response Verification Moderate the Relationship between Personality and Cognitive Ability?" *Journal of Applied Psychology* 90 (2005), pp. 306–22.

88. C. H. Van Iddekinge, P. H. Raymark, and P. L. Roth, "Assessing Personality with a Structured Employment Interview: Construct-Related Validity and Susceptibility to Response Inflation," *Journal of Applied Psychology* 90 (2005), pp. 536–52.

89. R. Mueller-Hanson, E. D., Heggestad, and G. C. Thornton, "Faking and Selection: Considering the Use of Personality from Select-In and Select-Out Perspectives," *Journal of Applied Psychology* 88 (2003), pp. 348–55.

90. C. Palmeri, "Putting Managers to the Test," *BusinessWeek*, November 20, 2006, p. 82.

91. C. Winkler, "Job Tryouts Go Virtual: Online Job Simulations Provide Sophisticated Candidate Assessments," *HR Magazine*, September 2006, pp. 10–15.

92. E. White, "Walk a Mile in My Shoes," *The Wall Street Journal*, January 16, 2006, B3.

93. A. Hedger, "Six Ways to Strengthen Staffing," *Workforce Management*, January 15, 2007.

94. K. Maher, "Win in a Competition, Land on Square that Offers Job," *The Wall Street Journal*, June 1, 2004, p. B10.

95. J. Puliyenthuruthel, "How Google Searches—For Talent," *BusinessWeek*, April 11, 2005, pp. 32–34.

96. W. Arthur, E. A. Day, T. L. McNelly and P. S. Edens, "Meta-Analysis of the Criterion-Related Validity of Assessment Center Dimensions," *Personnel Psychology* 56 (2003), pp. 125–54.

97. C. E. Lance, T. A. Lambert, A. G. Gewin, F. Lievens, and J. M. Conway, "Revised Estimates of Dimension and Exercise Variance Components in Assessment Center Postexercise Dimension Ratings," *Journal of Applied Psychology* 89 (2004), pp. 377–85.

98. F. L. Schmidt and J. E. Hunter, "The Validity and Utility of Selection Methods in Personnel Psychology: Practical and Theoretical Implications of 85 Years of Research Findings," *Psychological Bulletin* 124 (1998), pp. 262–74.

99. J. E. Wanek, P. R. Sackett, and D. S. Ones, "Toward an Understanding of Integrity Test Similarities and Differences: An Item-Level Analysis of Seven Tests," *Personnel Psychology* 56 (2003), pp. 873–94.

100. D. S. Ones and C. Viswesvaran, "Gender, Age, and Race Differences on Overt Integrity Tests: Results across Four Large-Scale Job Applicant Data Sets," *Journal of Applied Psychology* 83 (1998), pp. 35–42.

101. M. R. Cunningham, D. T. Wong, and A. P. Barbee, "Self-Presentation Dynamics on Overt Integrity Tests: Experimental Studies of the Reid Report," *Journal of Applied Psychology* 79 (1994), pp. 643–58.

102. M. E. Paronto, D. M. Truxillo, T. N. Bauer, and M. C. Leo, "Drug Testing, Drug Treatment, and Marijuana Use: A Fairness Perspective," *Journal of Applied Psychology* 87 (2002), pp. 1159–66.

103. K. R. Murphy, G. C. Thornton, and D. H. Reynolds, "College Students' Attitudes toward Drug Testing Programs, *Personnel Psychology* 43 (1990), pp. 615–31.

Training

LO LEARNING OBJECTIVES

After reading this chapter, you should be able to:

Learning Isn't Perishable at Wegmans Food Markets

At Wegmans Food Markets, learning is how the company differentiates itself from other supermarkets. Learning is not part of the competitive strategy: it *is* the competitive strategy.

Wegmans Food Markets is known as much for carrying 700 different types of cheeses as it is for being one of the best companies to work for. In 2008 Wegmans was named to *Fortune* magazine's list of the "100 Best Companies to Work For," ranked number 5. This marks the 11th consecutive year Wegmans has appeared on the annual list and its 5th year ranked among the top 10. Wegmans makes a considerable investment in training. The company recently branched out of its traditional locations in New York, Pennsylvania, and New Jersey to open two stores in Virginia. The company spent more than $1 million training staff.

Because the level of service is as important as is product knowledge, Wegmans offers classroom training as well as hands-on training. Because Wegmans is a food business, learning with the five senses is very important. Employees are put through rigorous courses in areas such as operations, product knowledge, and cooking. But employees first receive training about the products they are selling, what makes them good, and how to prepare them. Wegmans believes that with knowledge, employees can provide real value to customers. Part of the company's strategy is to help customers understand the products so they will buy a new product. Wegmans mails *Menu* magazine to about 1 million addresses four times a year. It has recipes, cooking techniques, and product advice. Customers come to the stores looking for products needed for the recipes and tips on how to prepare them. As a result, cooking coaches and sales staff go through a session each week on how to make a meal of the week. This training increases their product knowledge and makes them comfortable selling products.

Wegmans wants to teach people the company values. The values include caring and trust. Wegmans tries to find people who will care about the customers and care about their Wegmans teammates. High food safety standards are also important and are emphasized in technical training.

Wegmans also has special programs for teenagers who work in the stores. For example, the company has an apprenticeship program with about 250 people in it each year. The apprentices take on a team project on some aspect of the department they are working in. After studying for five months, the teams give presentations. The company also offers work-study programs. The three-year work-study program offers more than 1,500 hours of paid, school-supervised work experience, supported by related instruction at school. Students may receive high school credits for this experience. With the support of a mentor, students complete structured rotations through a variety of departments—bakery, produce, seafood, and other departments—based on career interests. The students learn and enhance their customer service, teamwork, product knowledge, food safety, and technical skills. Students in their last rotation during their senior year in high school focus on gaining new experiences in merchandising, product preparation, selling skills, and department sales concepts and finish off the program by completing a senior research project. Students who successfully finish the program receive either a full-time employment opportunity or, if attending college, a Scholarship Award and an opportunity to compete for the Store Operations Summer Internship program immediately after high school graduation. The Wegmans Scholarship Program encourages all employees to pursue educational goals. Wegmans has awarded more than $67 million in scholarships to more than 21,000 employees since the beginning of the Scholarship Program. Why does Wegmans invest time and money in training students? Wegmans has a lot of young adults working in the stores and they are responsible for making a difference to customers by providing excellent service. Also, Wegmans believes that the success of all of its learning programs helps contribute to the company reputation as the employer of first choice, builds community goodwill, and helps retain employees who are committed to continuous improvement.

How does Wegmans Food Markets measure the return on its investment in training? CEO Danny Wegman says, "People are continuing to learn and have more confidence. We don't have a formula for measuring that, but we ask ourselves 'Are we being successful as a company? Are we getting good feedback from our people on the various courses we are offering? Do they feel they [the courses] are relevant to their success as individuals and part of the company?' "

Source: Based on www.wegmans.com Web site for Wegmans Food Markets, and T. Bingham and P. Galagan, "A Higher Level of Learning," *TD*, September 2005, pp. 32–36.

 # Introduction

As the chapter-opening story shows, learning is an important part of Wegmans Food Markets' business strategy. Training helps employees at Wegmans develop specific skills that enable them to succeed in their current job and develop for the future. Wegmans also recognizes that learning involves not just formal training courses but also job experiences and interactions between employees. From Wegmans perspective, training leads to better customer service and product sales. Wegmans recognizes that its industry is becoming competitive—success will require smart, motivated employees who can delight customers and help sell products.

Why is the emphasis on strategic training important? Companies are in business to make money, and every business function is under pressure to show how it contributes to business success or face spending cuts and even outsourcing. To contribute to a company's success, training activities should help the company achieve its business strategy.

There is both a direct and an indirect link between training and business strategy and goals. Training can help employees develop skills needed to perform their jobs, which directly affects the business. Giving employees opportunities to learn and develop creates a positive work environment, which supports the business strategy by attracting talented employees as well as motivating and retaining current employees.

Why do Wegmans and many other companies believe that an investment in training can help them gain a competitive advantage? Training can

- Increase employees' knowledge of foreign competitors and cultures, which is critical for success in foreign markets.
- Help ensure that employees have the basic skills to work with new technology, such as robots and computer-assisted manufacturing processes.
- Help employees understand how to work effectively in teams to contribute to product and service quality.
- Ensure that the company's culture emphasizes innovation, creativity, and learning.
- Ensure employment security by providing new ways for employees to contribute to the company when their jobs change, their interests change, or their skills become obsolete.
- Prepare employees to accept and work more effectively with each other, particularly with minorities and women.[1]

In this chapter, we emphasize the conditions through which training practices can help companies gain competitive advantage and how managers can contribute to a high-leverage training effort and create a learning organization. The chapter begins by discussing a systematic and effective approach to training design. Next we review training methods and training evaluation. The chapter concludes with a discussion of training issues including cross-cultural preparation, managing diversity, and socializing employees.

High-Leverage Training Strategy: A Systematic Approach

In general, **training** refers to a planned effort by a company to facilitate employees' learning of job-related competencies. These competencies include knowledge, skills, or behaviors that are critical for successful job performance. The goal of training is for employees to master the knowledge, skill, and behaviors emphasized in training programs and to apply them to their day-to-day activities. Recently it has been acknowledged that to offer a competitive advantage, training has to involve more than just basic skill development.[2] Training is moving from a primary focus on teaching employees specific skills to a broader focus of creating and sharing knowledge.[3] That is, to use training to gain a competitive advantage, a firm should view training broadly as a way to create intellectual capital. Intellectual capital includes basic skills (skills needed to perform one's job), advanced skills (such as how to use technology to share information with other employees), an understanding of the customer or manufacturing system, and self-motivated creativity.

Traditionally most of the emphasis on training has been at the basic and advanced skill levels. But some estimate that 85 percent of the jobs in the United States and Europe require extensive use of knowledge. This requires employees to share knowledge and creatively use it to modify a product or serve the customer, as well as to understand the service or product development system.

Many companies have adopted this broader perspective, which is known as high-leverage training. **High-leverage training** is linked to strategic business goals and objectives, uses an instructional design process to ensure that training is effective, and compares or benchmarks the company's training programs against training programs in other companies.[4]

High-leverage training practices also help to create working conditions that encourage continuous learning. **Continuous learning** requires employees to understand the entire work system including the relationships among their jobs, their work units, and the company. (Continuous learning is similar to the idea of system understanding mentioned earlier.)[5] Employees are expected to acquire new skills and knowledge, apply them on the job, and share this information with other employees. Managers identify training needs and help to ensure that employees use training in their work. To facilitate the sharing of knowledge, managers may use informational maps that show where knowledge lies within the company (e.g., directories that list what a person does as well as the specialized knowledge she possesses) and use technology such as groupware or the Internet that allows employees in various business units to work simultaneously on problems and share information.[6]

The emphasis on high-leverage training has been accompanied by a movement to link training to performance improvement or business strategy.[7] Companies have lost money on training because it is poorly designed, because it is not linked to a

LO1
Discuss how training can contribute to companies' business strategy.

Training
A planned effort to facilitate the learning of job-related knowledge, skills, and behavior by employees.

High-Leverage Training
Training practice that links training to strategic business goals, has top management support, relies on an instructional design model, and is benchmarked to programs in other organizations.

Continuous Learning
A learning system that requires employees to understand the entire work process and expects them to acquire new skills, apply them on the job, and share what they have learned with other employees.

performance problem or business strategy, or because its outcomes are not properly evaluated.[8] That is, companies have been investing money into training simply because of beliefs that it is a good thing to do. The perspective that the training function exists to deliver programs to employees without a compelling business reason for doing so is being abandoned. Today, training is being evaluated not on the basis of the number of programs offered and training activity in the company but on how training addresses business needs related to learning, behavior change, and performance improvement. In fact, training is becoming more performance-focused. That is, training is used to improve employee performance, which leads to improved business results. Training is seen as one of several possible solutions to improve performance. Other solutions can include such actions as changing the job or increasing employee motivation through pay and incentives. Today, there is a greater emphasis on[9]

- Providing educational opportunities for all employees. These educational opportunities may include training programs, but they also include support for taking courses offered outside the company, self-study, and learning through job rotation.
- An ongoing process of performance improvement that is directly measurable rather than organizing one-time training events.
- The need to demonstrate to executives, managers, and trainees the benefits of training.
- Learning as a lifelong event in which senior management, trainer managers, and employees have ownership.
- Training being used to help attain strategic business objectives, which help companies gain a competitive advantage.

Figure 7.1 shows the strategic training and development process with examples of strategic initiatives, training activities, and metrics. The strategic training and development process involves identifying strategic training and development initiatives that will help achieve the business strategy. Employees participate in specific training and development activities that support these initiatives. The final step of the process involves collecting measures or metrics. The metrics are used to determine if training helped contribute to goals related to the business strategy.

PricewaterhouseCoopers is a good example of a company that uses high-leverage training.[10] Its learning and education (L&E) team was restructured to better link it to

figure 7.1

The Strategic Training and Development Process

the business goals related to value and impact. L&E works with the business to understand what it wants education to be. It ensures ongoing innovation in training delivery and instructional methods by evaluating emerging technologies and using them in small pilot projects. The chief learning officer in charge of L&E is a member of the company's leadership team, giving him the opportunity to discuss ideas regarding training methods, delivery, and content with other top-level managers. L&E sponsors traditional and virtual classroom courses, self-study, team-based learning, action learning projects, coaching and mentoring, and conferences. L&E has served more than 150,000 users each year with more than 6,000 courses, 12,000 classroom-based training sessions, and 19,000 Web-based training session. PricewaterhouseCoopers uses a learning management system to create a single access point for training activities. To help employees learn on an as-needed basis, the company's e-learning includes video and audio conferencing, a virtual classroom, and webcasting. To evaluate the success of training, L&E considers its influence on outcomes such as retention of top people. Also, focus groups are used to determine if trainees and managers are satisfied with the training. A program on sustainability was designed to help partners understand how to provide solutions for their clients. The company's investment in the program has paid off. The company believes it has achieved a return on investment of more than 1,000 percent in new business sold and reputation gains in the marketplace. L&E plans in the future to further strengthen the relationship among training, development, and the business by focusing in on how they can make learning even more accessible and close to the point where employees need it on their jobs. L&E wants to integrate learning and knowledge to speed employees' development and improve their competencies.

This discussion is not meant to underestimate the importance of "traditional training" (a focus on acquisition of knowledge, skills, and abilities), but it should alert you that for many companies, training is evolving from a focus on skills to an emphasis on learning and creating and sharing knowledge.

Designing Effective Training Activities

A key characteristic of training activities that contribute to competitiveness is that they are designed according to the instructional design process.[11] **Training design process** refers to a systematic approach for developing training programs. Instructional System Design (ISD) and the ADDIE model (analysis, design, development, implementation, evaluation) are two specific types of training design processes you may know. Table 7.1 presents the six steps of this process, which emphasizes that effective training practices involve more than just choosing the most popular or colorful training method.

Step 1 is to assess needs to determine if training is needed. Step 2 involves ensuring that employees have the motivation and basic skills to master training content. Step 3 addresses whether the training session (or the learning environment) has the factors necessary for learning to occur. Step 4 is to ensure that trainees apply the content of training to their jobs. This requires support from managers and peers for the use of training content on the job as well as getting the employee to understand how to take personal responsibility for skill improvement. Step 5 involves choosing a training method. As we shall see in this chapter, a variety of training methods are available ranging from traditional on-the-job training to newer technologies such as the Internet. The key is to choose a training method that will provide the appropriate

LO2
Explain the role of the manager in identifying training needs and supporting training on the Job.

Training Design Process
A systematic approach for developing training programs.

table 7.1

The Training Process

1. Needs assessment
   - Organizational analysis
   - Person analysis
   - Task analysis
2. Ensuring employees' readiness for training
   - Attitudes and motivation
   - Basic skills
3. Creating a learning environment
   - Identification of learning objectives and training outcomes
   - Meaningful material
   - Practice
   - Feedback
   - Observation of others
   - Administering and coordinating program
4. Ensuring transfer of training
   - Self-management strategies
   - Peer and manager support
5. Selecting training methods
   - Presentational methods
   - Hands-on methods
   - Group methods
6. Evaluating training programs
   - Identification of training outcomes and evaluation design
   - Cost–benefit analysis

learning environment to achieve the training objectives. Step 6 is evaluation—that is, determining whether training achieved the desired learning outcomes and/or financial objectives.

The training design process should be systematic yet flexible enough to adapt to business needs. Different steps may be completed simultaneously. Keep in mind that designing training unsystematically will reduce the benefits that can be realized. For example, choosing a training method before determining training needs or ensuring employees' readiness for training increases the risk that the method chosen will not be the most effective one for meeting training needs. Also, training may not even be necessary and may result in a waste of time and money! Employees may have the knowledge, skills, or behavior they need but simply not be motivated to use them. Next we will discuss important aspects of the training design process.

Needs Assessment

LO3
Conduct a needs assessment.

Needs Assessment
The process used to determine if training is necessary.

The first step in the instructional design process, **needs assessment,** refers to the process used to determine if training is necessary. Figure 7.2 shows the causes and outcomes resulting from needs assessment. As we see, many different "pressure points" suggest that training is necessary. These pressure points include performance problems, new technology, internal or external customer requests for training, job redesign, new legislation, changes in customer preferences, new products, or employees' lack of basic skills as well as support for the company's business strategy (e.g., growth, global business expansion). Note that these pressure points do not guarantee that training is the correct solution. Consider, for example, a delivery truck driver whose

figure 7.2

The Needs Assessment Process

Reasons or "pressure points"

- Legislation
- Lack of basic skills
- Poor performance
- New technology
- Customer requests
- New products
- Higher performance standards
- New jobs
- Business growth or contraction
- Global business expansion

What is the context?

Organization analysis

Task analysis

Person analysis

In what do they need training?

Who needs training?

Outcomes

- What trainees need to learn
- Who receives training
- Type of training
- Frequency of training
- Buy-versus-build training decision
- Training versus other HR options such as selection or job redesign
- How training should be evaluated

job is to deliver anesthetic gases to medical facilities. The driver mistakenly hooks up the supply line of a mild anesthetic to the supply line of a hospital's oxygen system, contaminating the hospital's oxygen supply. Why did the driver make this mistake, which is clearly a performance problem? The driver may have done this because of a lack of knowledge about the appropriate line hookup for the anesthetic, anger over a requested salary increase that his manager recently denied, or mislabeled valves for connecting the gas supply. Only the lack of knowledge can be addressed by training. The other pressure points require addressing issues related to the consequence of good performance (pay system) or the design of the work environment.

Needs assessment typically involves organizational analysis, person analysis, and task analysis.[12] Organizational analysis considers the context in which training will occur. That is, **organizational analysis** involves determining the business appropriateness of training, given the company's business strategy, its resources available for training, and support by managers and peers for training activities.

Person analysis helps identify who needs training. **Person analysis** involves (1) determining whether performance deficiencies result from a lack of knowledge, skill, or ability (a training issue) or from a motivational or work-design problem; (2) identifying who needs training; and (3) determining employees' readiness for training. **Task analysis** includes identifying the important tasks and knowledge, skill, and behaviors that need to be emphasized in training for employees to complete their tasks.

In practice, organizational analysis, person analysis, and task analysis are usually not conducted in any specific order. However, because organizational analysis is concerned with identifying whether training fits with the company's strategic objectives and whether the company wants to devote time and money to training, it is usually conducted first. Person analysis and task analysis are often conducted at the same time because it is often difficult to determine whether performance deficiencies are a training problem without understanding the tasks and the work environment.

What outcomes result from a needs assessment? As shown in Figure 7.2, needs assessment shows who needs training and what trainees need to learn, including the tasks in which they need to be trained plus knowledge, skill, behavior, or other job requirements. Needs assessment helps determine whether the company will purchase training from a vendor or consultant or develop training using internal resources.

Organizational Analysis
A process for determining the business appropriateness of training.

Person Analysis
A process for determining whether employees need training, who needs training, and whether employees are ready for training.

Task Analysis
The process of identifying the tasks, knowledge, skills, and behaviors that need to be emphasized in training.

Steelcase spends considerable time and energy on needs assessment.[13] Course designers are responsible for ensuring that all of Steelcase University's training and development capabilities help drive business performance and lead strategic change for the company. The university helps to identify how behaviors need to change to align with new performance standards and future directions. The university tries to understand and provide solutions for critical business needs. Learning consultants serve as team members in key functional groups across the company. The learning consultant becomes aware of business challenges the function is facing and identifies the required business results. This helps identify a learning solution that can overcome behavior gaps. Consultants look for solutions that balance skill and knowledge development, management commitment, and demands of the work environment. If any of the three are missing, performance will not improve. The consultants serve as liaisons between the business unit and a team of project managers, instructional designers, and tech developers to communicate learning needs. The team may provide an already available course that meets the need or create a learning solution specific to the needs of the employees within the function.

Organizational Analysis

Managers need to consider three factors before choosing training as the solution to any pressure point: the company's strategic direction, the training resources available, and support of managers and peers for training activities.

Support of Managers and Peers

Various studies have found that peer and manager support for training is critical. The key factors to success are a positive attitude among peers and managers about participation in training activities; managers' and peers' willingness to tell trainees how they can more effectively use knowledge, skills, or behaviors learned in training on the job; and the availability of opportunities for the trainees to use training content in their jobs.[14] If peers' and managers' attitudes and behaviors are not supportive, employees are not likely to apply training content to their jobs.

Company Strategy

Strategic Training and Development Initiatives
Learning-related actions that a company takes to achieve its business strategy.

In Chapter 2 we discussed the importance of business strategy for a company to gain a competitive advantage. Several types of strategies were discussed, including growth and disinvestment. As Figure 7.1 highlights, training should help companies achieve the business strategy. Table 7.2 shows possible strategic training and development initiatives and their implications for training practices. **Strategic training and development initiatives** are learning-related actions that a company should take to help achieve its business strategy.[15] The initiatives are based on the business environment, an understanding of the company's goals and resources, and insight into potential training and development options. They provide the company with a road map to guide specific training and development activities. They also show how training will help the company reach its goals and add value. The plan or goal the company chooses to achieve strategic objectives has a major impact on whether resources (money, trainers' time, program development) should be devoted to addressing a training pressure point.

table 7.2

Strategic Training and Development Initiatives and Their Implications

STRATEGIC TRAINING AND DEVELOPMENT INITIATIVES	IMPLICATIONS
Diversify the learning portfolio	• Use new technology such as the Internet for training • Facilitate informal learning • Provide more personalized learning opportunities
Expand who is trained	• Train customers, suppliers, and employees • Offer more learning opportunities to nonmanagerial employees
Accelerate the pace of employee learning	• Quickly identify needs and provide a high-quality learning solution • Reduce the time to develop training programs • Facilitate access to learning resources on an as-needed basis
Improve customer service	• Ensure that employees have product and service knowledge • Ensure that employees have skills needed to interact with customers • Ensure that employees understand their roles and decision-making authority
Provide development opportunities and communicate to employees	• Ensure that employees have opportunities to develop • Ensure that employees understand career opportunities and personal growth opportunities • Ensure that training and development addresses employees' needs in current job as well as growth opportunities
Capture and share knowledge	• Capture insight and information from knowledgeable employees • Logically organize and store information • Provide methods to make information available (e.g., resource guides, Web sites)
Align training and development with the company's strategic direction	• Identify needed knowledge, skills, abilities, or competencies • Ensure that current training and development programs support the company's strategic needs
Ensure that the work environment supports learning and transfer of training	• Remove constraints to learning, such as lack of time, resources, and equipment • Dedicate physical space to encourage teamwork, collaboration, creativity, and knowledge sharing • Ensure that employees understand the importance of learning • Ensure that managers and peers are supportive of training, development, and learning

SOURCE: Based on S. Tannenbaum, "A Strategic View of Organizational Training and Learning," in *Creating, Implementing and Managing Effective Training and Development,* ed. K. Kraiger (San Francisco: Jossey-Bass, 2002), pp. 10–52.

It is important to identify the prevailing business strategy to ensure that the company allocates enough of its budget to training, that employees receive training on relevant topics, and that employees get the right amount of training.[16] For example, consider how globalization has affected the training practices of KLA-Tencor, a manufacturer of equipment and systems for semiconductor manufacturers.[17] KLA-Tencor has factories in China, Taiwan, Singapore, and India in order to better serve its customers, such as Intel, who also have global locations. KLA-Tencor needs to train employees in installing and servicing machine tools in its global operations. Employees also need to know how to adjust the machines to maximize productivity so they can educate customers on how to use it more effectively. Technology training is provided regionally because trainees needs hands-on experience with the machines. KLA-Tencor finds local instructors who are qualified to teach in the local language. The local instructors are trained in how to deliver the technical training and use the machines. Before teaching courses on their own, the local instructors co-teach a class with another trainer to ensure they are comfortable and proficient in delivering training.

EMC's products helps companies store, protect, and organize employee, customer, and product information.[18] In five years, EMC grew from offering 200 to 300 products to more than 4,000 products based on a business strategy that included acquiring 40 companies whose products complemented EMC's product line. The acquisition strategy meant that a necessary strategic training initiative for EMC was to develop and expand its professional certification program (Proven Professionals). The certification program is critical for the company's technical employees and its customers to understand the value of its products and how to install and support them. The program includes 10 technologies with certification available, and within each certification area, employees and customers can attain associate, specialist, and expert levels.

Despite the recession, instead of cutting worker hours or downsizing, Toyota Motor Corporation is keeping employees at the plants, spending their time in training programs designed to improve their job skills and find more efficient and effective methods for assembling vehicles.[19] At GM, Ford, and Chrysler, based on their union contracts, employees are paid for not working when their assembly lines are shut down. If a plant is shut down temporarily, employees receive most of their pay but don't have to show up for work. At its Princeton plant, Toyota uses downtime to improve employees' quality control and productivity skills, keeping good on its pledge to never lay off any of its full-time, nonunion employees. The training has already resulted in continuous improvements (also known as *kaizen*). One example was a Teflon ring designed by an assembly-line employee that helps prevent paint damage when an electrical switch is installed on the edge of a vehicle's door.

Training Resources

It is necessary to identify whether the company has the budget, time, and expertise for training. For example, if the company is installing computer-based manufacturing equipment in one of its plants, it has three possible strategies to have computer-literate employees. First, the company can use internal consultants to train all affected employees. Second, the company may decide that it is more cost-effective to identify computer-literate employees by using tests and work samples. Employees who fail the test or perform below standards on the work sample can be reassigned to other jobs. Choosing this strategy suggests that the company has decided to devote resources to selection and placement rather than training. Third, if it lacks time or expertise, the company may decide to purchase training from a consultant.

Many companies identify vendors and consultants who can provide training services by using requests for proposals.[20] A **request for proposal (RFP)** is a document that outlines for potential vendors and consultants the type of service the company is seeking, the type and number of references needed, the number of employees who need to be trained, funding for the project, the follow-up process used to determine level of satisfaction and service, the expected completion date of the project, and the date when proposals must be received by the company. The request for proposal may be mailed to potential consultants and vendors or posted on the company's Web site. The request for proposal is valuable because it provides a standard set of criteria against which all consultants will be evaluated. The RFP also helps eliminate the need to evaluate outside vendors who cannot provide the needed services.

Request for Proposal (RFP)
A document that outlines for potential vendors and consultants the type of service the company is seeking, references needed, number of employees who should be trained, project funding, the follow-up process, expected completion date, and the date when proposals must be received by the company.

table 7.3

Questions to
Ask Vendors and
Consultants

How do your products and services fit our needs?

How much and what type of experience does your company have in designing and delivering training?

What are the qualifications and experiences of your staff?

Can you provide demonstrations or examples of training programs you have developed?

Would you provide references of clients for whom you worked?

What evidence do you have that your programs work?

Will the training program be customized to meet the company's needs?

How long will it take to develop the training program?

How much will your services cost?

What instructional design methods do you use?

SOURCES: Adapted from R. Zemke and J. Armstrong, "Evaluating Multimedia Developers," *Training Magazine,* November 1996, pp. 33–38; B. Chapman, "How to Create the Ideal RFP," *Training,* January 2004, pp. 40–43.

Usually the RFP helps identify several vendors who meet the criteria. The next step is to choose the preferred provider. Table 7.3 provides examples of questions to ask vendors.

Person Analysis

Person analysis helps the manager identify whether training is appropriate and which employees need training. In certain situations, such as the introduction of a new technology or service, all employees may need training. However, when managers, customers, or employees identify a problem (usually as a result of a performance deficiency), it is often unclear whether training is the solution.

A major pressure point for training is poor or substandard performance—that is, a gap between employees' current performance and their expected performance. Poor performance is indicated by customer complaints, low performance ratings, or on-the-job accidents or unsafe behavior. Another potential indicator of the need for training is if the job changes so current performance levels need improvement or employees must complete new tasks.

Figure 7.3 shows the factors that influence employees' performance and learning. These factors are person characteristics, input, output, consequences, and feedback.[21] **Person characteristics** refer to the employees' knowledge, skill, ability, and attitudes. **Input** relates to the instructions that tell employees what, how, and when to perform. Input also refers to the support given to employees to help them perform. This support includes resources such as equipment, time, or budget. Support also includes feedback and reinforcement from managers and peers. **Output** refers to the job's performance standards. **Consequences** are the incentives employees receive for performing well. **Feedback** is the information employees receive while they are performing.

From a manager's perspective, to determine if training is needed, for any performance problem you need to analyze characteristics of the performer, input, output, consequences, and feedback. How might this be done? Based on the model in Figure 7.3, you should ask several questions to determine if training is the likely solution to a performance problem.[22]

Person Characteristics An employee's knowledge, skills, abilities, and attitudes.

Input Instructions that tell employees what, how, and when to perform; also the support they are given to help them to perform.

Output A job's performance standards.

Consequences The incentives that employees receive for performing well.

Feedback Information that employees receive while they are performing concerning how well they are meeting objectives.

figure 7.3

Factors That
Influence Employee
Performance and
Learning

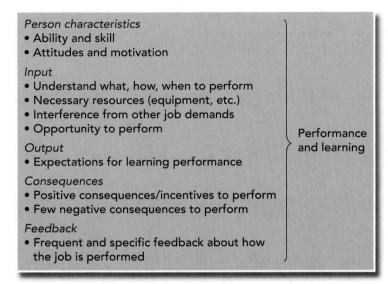

Person characteristics
- Ability and skill
- Attitudes and motivation

Input
- Understand what, how, when to perform
- Necessary resources (equipment, etc.)
- Interference from other job demands
- Opportunity to perform

Output
- Expectations for learning performance

Consequences
- Positive consequences/incentives to perform
- Few negative consequences to perform

Feedback
- Frequent and specific feedback about how the job is performed

Performance
and learning

SOURCES: G. Rummler, "In Search of the Holy Performance Grail," *Training and Development*, April 1996, pp. 26–31; C. Reinhart, "How to Leap over Barriers to Performance," *Training and Development*, January 2000, pp. 20–24; G. Rummler and K. Morrill, "The Results Chain," *TD*, February 2005, pp. 27–35.

Assess whether

1. The performance problem is important and has the potential to cost the company a significant amount of money from lost productivity or customers.
2. Employees do not know how to perform effectively. Perhaps they received little or no previous training or the training was ineffective. (This problem is a characteristic of the person.)
3. Employees cannot demonstrate the correct knowledge or behavior. Perhaps they were trained but they infrequently or never used the training content (knowledge, skills, etc.) on the job. (This is an input problem.)
4. Performance expectations are clear (input) and there are no obstacles to performance such as faulty tools or equipment.
5. There are positive consequences for good performance, whereas poor performance is not rewarded. For example, if employees are dissatisfied with their compensation, their peers or a union may encourage them to slow down their pace of work. (This involves consequences.)
6. Employees receive timely, relevant, accurate, constructive, and specific feedback about their performance (a feedback issue).
7. Other solutions such as job redesign or transferring employees to other jobs are too expensive or unrealistic.

If employees lack the knowledge and skill to perform and the other factors are satisfactory, training is needed. If employees have the knowledge and skill to perform, but input, output, consequences, or feedback are inadequate, training may not be the best solution. For example, if poor performance results from faulty equipment, training cannot solve this problem, but repairing the equipment will! If poor performance results from lack of feedback, then employees may not need training, but their managers may need training on how to give performance feedback.

Task Analysis

A task analysis, defined on page 277, identifies the conditions in which tasks are performed. The conditions include identifying equipment and the environment the employee works in, time constraints (deadlines), safety considerations, or performance standards. Task analysis results in a description of work activities, including tasks performed by the employee and the knowledge, skills, and abilities required to successfully complete the tasks. A *job* is a specific position requiring the completion of specific tasks. A *task* is a statement of an employee's work activity in a specific job. There are four steps in task analysis:

1. Select the job(s) to be analyzed.
2. Develop a preliminary list of tasks performed on the job by interviewing and observing expert employees and their managers and talking with others who have performed a task analysis.
3. Validate or confirm the preliminary list of tasks. This involves having a group of subject matter experts (job incumbents, managers, and so on) answer in a meeting or on a written survey several questions regarding the tasks. The types of questions that may be asked include the following: How frequently is the task performed? How much time is spent performing each task? How important or critical is the task for successful performance of the job? How difficult is the task to learn? Is performance of the task expected of entry-level employees?[23]

   Table 7.4 presents a sample task analysis questionnaire. This information is used to determine which tasks will be focused on in the training program. The person or committee conducting the needs assessment must decide the level of ratings across dimensions that will determine that a task should be included in the training program. Tasks that are important, frequently performed, and of moderate-to-high levels of difficulty should be trained. Tasks that are not important and are infrequently performed will not be trained. It is difficult for managers and trainers to decide if tasks that are important, are performed infrequently, and require minimal difficulty should be included in training. Managers and trainers must determine whether important tasks—regardless of how frequently they are performed or their level of difficulty—will be included in training.

4. Identify the knowledge, skills, or abilities necessary to successfully perform each task. This information can be collected using interviews and questionnaires. Information concerning basic skill and cognitive ability requirements is critical for determining if certain levels of knowledge, skills, and abilities will be prerequisites for entrance to the training program (or job) or if supplementary training in underlying skills is needed. For training purposes, information concerning how difficult it is to learn the knowledge, skill, or ability is important—as is whether the knowledge, skill, or ability is expected to be acquired by the employee before taking the job.[24]

Example of a Task Analysis

Each of the four steps of a task analysis can be seen in this example from a utility company. Trainers were given the job of developing a training system in six months.[25] The purpose of the program was to identify tasks and knowledge, skills, abilities, and other considerations that would serve as the basis for training program objectives and lesson plans.

table 7.4

Sample Task Statement Questionnaire

Name	Date
Position	

Please rate each of the task statements according to three factors: the *importance* of the task for effective performance, how *frequently* the task is performed, and the degree of *difficulty* required to become effective in the task. Use the following scales in making your ratings.

Importance	*Frequency*
4 = Task is critical for effective performance.	4 = Task is performed once a day.
3 = Task is important but not critical for effective performance.	3 = Task is performed once a week.
2 = Task is of some importance for effective performance.	2 = Task is performed once every few months.
1 = Task is of no importance for effective performance.	1 = Task is performed once or twice a year.
0 = Task is not performed.	0 = Task is not performed.

Difficulty
4 = Effective performance of the task requires extensive prior experience and/or training (12–18 months or longer).
3 = Effective performance of the task requires minimal prior experience and training (6–12 months).
2 = Effective performance of the task requires a brief period of prior training and experience (1–6 months).
1 = Effective performance of the task does not require specific prior training and/or experience.
0 = This task is not performed.

Task	*Importance*	*Frequency*	*Difficulty*
1. Ensuring maintenance on equipment, tools, and safety controls			
2. Monitoring employee performance			
3. Scheduling employees			
4. Using statistical software on the computer			
5. Monitoring changes made in processes using statistical methods			

The first phase of the project involved identifying potential tasks for each job in the utility's electrical maintenance area. Procedures, equipment lists, and information provided by subject matter experts (SMEs) were used to generate the tasks. SMEs included managers, instructors, and senior technicians. The tasks were incorporated into a questionnaire administered to all technicians in the electrical maintenance department. The questionnaire included 550 tasks. Figure 7.4 shows sample items from the questionnaire for the electrical maintenance job. Technicians were asked to rate each task on importance, difficulty, and frequency of performance. The rating scale for frequency included zero. A zero rating indicated that the technician rating the task had never performed the task. Technicians who rated a task zero were asked not to evaluate the task's difficulty and importance.

Customized software was used to analyze the ratings collected via the questionnaire. The primary requirement used to determine whether a task required training was its importance rating. A task rated "very important" was identified as one requiring training regardless of its frequency or difficulty. If a task was rated moderately important but difficult, it also was designated for training. Tasks rated unimportant, not difficult, and done infrequently were not designated for training.

The list of tasks designated for training was reviewed by the SMEs to determine if it accurately described job tasks. The result was a list of 487 tasks. For each of the 487

figure 7.4

Sample Items from Task Analysis Questionnaires for an Electrical Maintenance Job

Job: Electrical Maintenance Worker

Task Performance Ratings

Task #s	Task Description	Frequency of Performance	Importance	Difficulty
199-264	Replace a light bulb	0 1 2 3 4 5	0 1 2 3 4 5	0 1 2 3 4 5
199-265	Replace an electrical outlet	0 1 2 3 4 5	0 1 2 3 4 5	0 1 2 3 4 5
199-266	Install a light fixture	0 1 2 3 4 5	0 1 2 3 4 5	0 1 2 3 4 5
199-267	Replace a light switch	0 1 2 3 4 5	0 1 2 3 4 5	0 1 2 3 4 5
199-268	Install a new circuit breaker	0 1 2 3 4 5	0 1 2 3 4 5	0 1 2 3 4 5

Frequency of Performance	Importance	Difficulty
0=never 5=often	1=negligible 5=extremely high	1=easiest 5=most difficult

SOURCE: E. F. Holton III and C. Bailey, "Top-to-Bottom Curriculum Redesign," *Training and Development*, March 1995, pp. 40–44. Reprinted with permission of *Training & Development*.

tasks, two SMEs identified the necessary knowledge, skills, abilities, and other factors required for performance. This included information on working conditions, cues that initiate the task's start and end, performance standards, safety considerations, and necessary tools and equipment. All data were reviewed by plant technicians and members of the training department. More than 14,000 knowledge, skill, ability, and other considerations were clustered into common areas. An identification code was assigned to each group that linked groups to task and knowledge, skill, ability, and other factors. These groups were then combined into clusters that represented qualification areas. That is, the task clusters related to linked tasks that the employees must be certified in to perform the job. The clusters were used to identify training lesson plans and course objectives; trainers also reviewed the clusters to identify prerequisite skills.

Ensuring Employees' Readiness for Training

The second step in the training design process is to evaluate whether employees are ready to learn. *Readiness for training* refers to whether (1) employees have the personal characteristics (ability, attitudes, beliefs, and motivation) necessary to learn program content and apply it on the job and (2) the work environment will facilitate learning and not interfere with performance.

Although managers are not often trainers, they play an important role in influencing employees' readiness for training. **Motivation to learn** is the desire of the trainee to learn the content of the training program.[26] Various research studies have shown that motivation is related to knowledge gain, behavior change, or skill acquisition in

LO4
Evaluate employees' readiness for training.

Motivation to Learn
The desire of the trainee to learn the content of a training program.

training programs.[27] Managers need to ensure that employees' motivation to learn is as high as possible. They can do this by ensuring employees' self-efficacy; understanding the benefits of training; being aware of training needs, career interests, and goals; understanding work environment characteristics; and ensuring employees' basic skill levels. Managers should also consider input, output, consequences, and feedback because these factors influence motivation to learn.

Self-Efficacy

Self-efficacy is the employees' belief that they can successfully learn the content of the training program. The training environment is potentially threatening to many employees who may not have extensive educational experience or who have little experience in the particular area emphasized by the training program. For example, training employees to use equipment for computer-based manufacturing represents a potential threat, especially if employees are intimidated by new technologies and do not have confidence in their ability to master the skills needed to use the technology. Research has demonstrated that self-efficacy is related to performance in training programs.[28] Managers can increase employees' self-efficacy level by

1. Letting employees know that the purpose of training is to try to improve performance rather than to identify areas in which employees are incompetent.
2. Providing as much information as possible about the training program and purpose of training prior to the actual training.
3. Showing employees the training success of their peers who are now in similar jobs.
4. Providing employees with feedback that learning is under their control and they have the ability and the responsibility to overcome any learning difficulties they experience in the program.

Understanding the Benefits or Consequences of Training

Employees' motivation to learn can be enhanced by communicating to them the potential job-related, personal, and career benefits they may receive as a result of attending the training program. These benefits may include learning a more efficient way to perform a process or procedure, establishing contacts with other employees in the firm (networking), or increasing opportunities to pursue different career paths. The communication from the manager about potential benefits should be realistic. Unmet expectations about training programs have been shown to adversely affect motivation to learn.[29]

Awareness of Training Needs, Career Interests, and Goals

To be motivated to learn in training programs, employees must be aware of their skill strengths and weaknesses and of the link between the training program and improvement of their weaknesses.[30] Managers should make sure that employees understand why they are asked to attend training programs, and they should communicate the link between training and improvement of skill weaknesses or knowledge deficiencies. This can be accomplished by sharing performance appraisal information with employees, holding career development discussions, or having employees complete self-evaluations of their skill strengths and weaknesses and career interests and goals.

If possible, employees need to choose programs to attend and must perceive how actual training assignments are made to maximize motivation to learn. Several studies have suggested that giving trainees a choice regarding which programs to attend and then honoring those choices maximizes motivation to learn. Giving employees choices but not necessarily honoring them can reduce motivation to learn.[31]

Work Environment Characteristics

Employees' perceptions of two characteristics of the work environment—situational constraints and social support—are critical determinants of motivation to learn. *Situational constraints* include lack of proper tools and equipment, materials and supplies, budgetary support, and time. *Social support* refers to managers' and peers' willingness to provide feedback and reinforcement.[32]

To ensure that the work environment enhances trainees' motivation to learn, managers need to

1. Provide materials, time, job-related information, and other work aids necessary for employees to use new skills or behavior before participating in training programs.
2. Speak positively about the company's training programs to employees.
3. Let employees know they are doing a good job when they use training content in their work.
4. Encourage work group members to involve each other in trying to use new skills on the job by soliciting feedback and sharing training experiences and situations in which training content was helpful.
5. Give employees time and opportunities to practice and apply new skills or behaviors to their work.

Basic Skills

Employees' motivation to learn in training activities can also be influenced by the degree to which they have **basic skills**—cognitive ability and reading and writing skills needed to understand the content of training programs. Recent forecasts of the skill levels of the U.S. workforce indicate that managers will likely have to work with employees who lack those skills.[33]

Managers need to conduct a literacy audit to determine employees' basic skill levels. Table 7.5 shows the activities involved in a literacy audit.

Cognitive Ability. **Cognitive ability** includes verbal comprehension (understand and use written and spoken language), quantitative ability (speed and accuracy in solving math problems), and reasoning ability (logic in solving problems).[34] Research shows that cognitive ability is related to successful performance in all jobs.[35] The importance of cognitive ability for job success increases as the job becomes more complex.

Cognitive ability influences job performance and ability to learn in training programs. If trainees lack the cognitive ability level necessary to perform job tasks, they will not perform well. Also, trainees' level of cognitive ability can influence whether they can learn in training programs.[36] Trainees with low levels of cognitive ability are more likely to fail to complete training or (at the end of training) receive low grades on tests to measure how much they have learned.

Basic Skills
Reading, writing, and communication skills needed to understand the content of a training program.

Cognitive Ability
Includes three dimensions: verbal comprehension, quantitative ability, and reasoning ability.

table 7.5

Performing a
Literacy Audit

Step 1.	Observe employees to determine the basic skills they need to succeed in their jobs. Note the materials employees use on the job, the tasks performed, and the reading, writing, and computations completed by employees.
Step 2.	Collect all materials that are written and read on the job and identify computations that must be performed to determine the necessary level of basic skill proficiency. Materials include bills, memos, and forms such as inventory lists and requisition sheets.
Step 3.	Interview employees to determine the basic skills they believe are needed to do the job. Consider the basic-skill requirements of the job yourself.
Step 4.	Determine whether employees have the basic skills needed to successfully perform their jobs. Combine the information gathered by observing and interviewing employees and evaluating materials they use on their jobs. Write a description of each job in terms of reading, writing, and computation skills needed to perform successfully.
Step 5.	Develop or buy tests that ask questions relating specifically to the employees' jobs. Ask employees to complete the tests.
Step 6.	Compare test results with the description of the basic skills required for the job (from step 5). If the level of employees' reading, writing, and computation skills does not match the basic skills required by the job, then a basic skills problem exists.

SOURCE: U.S. Department of Education, U.S. Department of Labor. *The Bottom Line: Basic Skills in the Workplace* (Washington, DC: 1988), pp. 14–15.

As discussed in Chapter 6, to identify employees without the cognitive ability to succeed on the job or in training programs, companies use paper-and-pencil cognitive ability tests. Determining a job's cognitive ability requirement is part of the task analysis process discussed earlier in this chapter.

Reading Ability. Lack of the appropriate reading level can impede performance and learning in training programs. Material used in training should be evaluated to ensure that its reading level does not exceed that required by the job. **Readability** refers to the difficulty level of written materials.[37] A readability assessment usually involves analysis of sentence length and word difficulty.

Readability
The difficulty level of
written materials.

If trainees' reading level does not match the level needed for the training materials, four options are available. First, determine whether it is feasible to use video or on-the-job training, which involves learning by watching and practicing rather than by reading. Second, employees without the necessary reading level could be identified through reading tests and reassigned to other positions more congruent with their skill levels. Third, again using reading tests, identify employees who lack the necessary reading skills and provide them with remedial training. Fourth, determine whether the job can be redesigned to accommodate employees' reading levels. The fourth option is certainly most costly and least practical. Therefore, alternative training methods need to be considered, or you can elect a nontraining option. Nontraining options include selecting employees for jobs and training opportunities on the basis of reading, computation, writing, and other basic skill requirements.

The "Competing through Sustainability" box shows how companies are partnering with nonprofit groups to develop worker skills and in return get a motivated and committed workforce.

COMPETING THROUGH SUSTAINABILITY
Capitalizing on Local Talent

Many companies rely on welfare-to-work programs and nonprofit community groups to provide employment and training to the unemployed or hard-to-employ. The relationship is beneficial for the employees, the company, and the local community. Employees receive wage-paying jobs, companies get a committed and motivated workforce, and living and working standards are raised in the communities where the companies are located.

Mark Goldsmith, a former Revlon executive, started his own nonprofit organization called Getting Out and Staying Out (GOSO). GOSO is working with more than 200 inmates serving prison sentences in New York. GOSO works with young prisoners who are attending school and have been in prison only a short time period. It provides individual job and education counseling and interview preparation, maintains a job bank of openings from employers willing to hire former inmates, provides educational scholarships, and holds seminars. One seminar taught by a retired construction company executive focused on the skills required to become a successful tradesperson. GOSO has been successful. Fewer than 10 percent of the 400 released inmates GOSO has worked with have been arrested again, compared with two-thirds of prisoners nationwide who have been rearrested. Seventy-five percent of the former prisoners in GOSO are employed or attending school. Former inmates stop by to share good news about a job, discuss problems they are having at home or work, or return for counseling if they lose or don't get a job, want to change jobs, or decide to go back to school.

The primary mission of Greater Chicago Food Depository, a nonprofit food bank, has been to feed the hungry. The food bank, and others around the country affiliated with America's Second Harvest, have been offering 30 chef training classes to about 1,000 students. These programs teach low-income students the basic of cooking such as slicing, dicing, sizing, and fricasseeing, as well as advanced skills, with the goal of getting each student a job. Also, the program teaches the students life skills such as punctuality, responsibility, teamwork, and commitment. As one of the executive chef instructors told her 17 students on the first day of class, "When you're out there working and you're fifteen minutes late, I'm already calling someone to do your job." Seventy percent of program graduates find jobs within one month, and more than 65 percent retain their first job for at least six months. For students who succeed, the program helps them escape from the cycle of poverty.

Standard Aero San Antonio, a jet engine repair and overhaul company that provides services to the U.S. Navy and Air Force, needed new technicians to overhaul and repair jet engines but found few qualified employees. As a result, the company partnered with a local community college and a community-based organization that helps unemployed and underemployed people in the San Antonio, Texas, community. A local community college developed a five-month customized training program to help meet the company's need for technicians. Each student receives full wages and benefits from the beginning of training. The community organization provides child care and transportation to help the trainees finish the program. Out of 42 students, 37 completed the training program and were hired by Standard Aero. Standard Aero estimates a saving of $105,000 for the first class of employees, with a retention rate of 95 percent. The program provides benefits to the community by developing taxpaying workers and the company receives the advantage of access to trained, qualified workers.

SOURCE: Based on G. Johnson, "Grab Your Partner," *Training*, June 2004, pp. 32–38; C. Hymowitz, "Executives Teach Inmates How to Be Employees," *The Wall Street Journal*, March 17, 2008, pp. B1, B3; R. Thurow, "To Tackle Hunger, a Food Bank Tries Training Chefs," *The Wall Street Journal*, November 28, 2006, pp. A1, A13.

Creating a Learning Environment

Learning permanently changes behavior. For employees to acquire knowledge and skills in the training program and apply this information in their jobs, the training program must include specific learning principles. Educational and industrial psychologists and instructional design specialists have identified several conditions under which employees learn best.[38] Table 7.6 shows the events that should take place for learning to occur in the training program and their implications for instruction.

Consider how several companies are creating a positive learning environment.[39] At Toshiba America Business Solutions in Irvine, California, a mobile flexible training program was developed to train new dealers with no experience with the company's products. Training to Go is a blended learning approach with work-based and classroom learning sessions. Delivering the information in multiple ways engages the learners and aids in retention. Colorado Springs Utilities, a community-owned utility,

table 7.6

Conditions for Learning and Their Importance

CONDITIONS FOR LEARNING	IMPORTANCE AND APPLICATION TO TRAINING
Need to know why they should learn	Employees need to understand the purpose or objectives of the training program to help them understand why they need training and what they are expected to accomplish.
Meaningful training content	Motivation to learn is enhanced when training is related to helping learner (such as related to current job tasks, problems, enhancing skills, or dealing with jobs or company changes). The training context should be similar to the work environment.
Opportunities for practice	Trainees need to demonstrate what is learned (knowledge, skill, behavior) to become more comfortable using it and to commit it to memory. Let trainees choose their practice strategy.
Feedback	Feedback helps learner modify behavior, skill, or use knowledge to meet objectives. Videotape, other trainees, and the trainer are useful feedback sources.
Observe experience, and interact with others	Adults learn best by doing. Gain new perspectives and insights by working with others. Can learn by observing the actions of models or sharing experiences with each other in communities of practice.
Good program coordination and administration	Eliminate distractions that could interfere with learning, such as cell-phone calls. Make sure the room is properly organized, comfortable, and appropriate for the training method (e.g., movable seating for team exercises). Trainees should receive announcements of the purpose of training, place, hour, and any pretraining materials such as cases or readings.
Commit training content to memory	Facilitate recall of training content after training. Examples include using concept maps showing relationships among ideas, using multiple types of review (writing, drawing, role-plays), teaching key words, or providing a visual image. Limit instruction to manageable units that don't exceed memory limits; review and practice over multiple days (overlearning).

SOURCES: Based on R. M. Gagne, "Learning Processes and Instruction," *Training Research Journal* 1 (1995/1996), pp. 17–28; M. Knowles, *The Adult Learner,* 4th ed. (Houston: Gulf, 1990); A. Bandura, *Social Foundations of Thought and Action* (Englewood Cliffs, NJ: Prentice Hall, 1986); E. A. Locke and G. D. Latham, *A Theory of Goal Setting and Task Performance* (Englewood Cliffs, NJ: Prentice Hall, 1990); B. Mager, *Preparing Instructional Objectives,* 2nd ed. (Belmont, CA: Lake, 1984); B.J. Smith and B. L. Delahaye, *How to Be an Effective Trainer,* 2nd ed. (New York: John Wiley and Sons, 1987); K. A. Smith-Jentsch, F. G. Jentsch, S. C. Payne, and E. Salas, "Can Pretraining Experience Explain Individual Differences in Learning?" *Journal of Applied Psychology* 81 (1996), pp. 110–16.

provides natural gas, water, and electric services to more than 600,000 customers. All of the company executives issue public statements in support of learning, participate in learning events as instructors or speakers, and include learning objectives as part of their performance goals. Every training program begins with a brainstorming session to identify themes and activities that engage trainees, helping them enjoy training more and retain more of what they have learned. In a safety training class, students experience a simulated emergency and have to respond using skills they have learned along with their knowledge of an evacuation plan. The trainees perform different roles and activities in response to a power shutdown. The trainer then critiques their performance and trainees discuss what they have learned (or still need to learn). Trainees complete a written exam and review to ensure knowledge retention. The training offered to truck technicians at ArvinMeritor was revised to get the learners more involved. Technicians complete online prework that helps them learn about rear-drive axle components, operations, and preventive maintenance. Next, live, in-person class time is used for hands-on work such as disassembling and reassembling drive axle parts and making adjustments to drive axles. After training, learners complete post-work, which reviews the concepts covered in the hands-on sessions. Every four to six months, learners are asked to go online to practice using simulation technology that allows them to select tools from their tool box to measure or adjust or otherwise work with drive axle components using their computer mouse.

Companies can facilitate both face-to-face and electronic communities of practice. **Communities of practice** are groups of employees who work together, learn from each other, and develop a common understanding of how to get work accomplished.[40] For example, at Siemens Power Transmission in Wendell, North Carolina, managers were wondering how to stop employees from gathering in the cafeteria for informal discussions during work time.[41] However, managers discovered that employees were developing problem-solving strategies, sharing product and procedural information, and providing career counseling to each other. As a result, they placed pads of paper and over-head projectors in the cafeteria as aides for informal meetings. Both Nokia and Intel have online communities of practice. Nokia Corporation, the mobile phone maker, takes advantage of local innovations around the world by setting up Web sites and Wikis to encourage employees to share what they know.[42] Researchers are invited to record their findings in blogs and collaborate with universities, design firms, and telecommunications industry partners. The technical know-how and broader understanding of the way different cultures address mobility has helped Nokia remain competitive in the world's mobile phone market. At Intel, a community of practice is used to connect trainers and training developers from the company's more than 90 groups of training employees so they can share resources, be introduced to new technology, and gain access to professional development opportunities.[43]

Communities of Practice
Groups of employees who work together, learn from each other, and develop a common understanding of how to get work accomplished.

Ensuring Transfer of Training

Transfer of training refers to on-the-job use of knowledge, skills, and behaviors learned in training. As Figure 7.5 shows, transfer of training is influenced by the climate for transfer, manager support, peer support, opportunity to use learned capabilities, technology support, and self-management skills. As we discussed earlier, learning is influenced by the learning environment (such as meaningfulness of the material and opportunities for practice and feedback) and employees' readiness for training (for example, their self-efficacy and basic skill level). If no learning occurs in the training program, transfer is unlikely.

Transfer of Training
The use of knowledge, skills, and behaviors learned in training on the job.

figure 7.5

Work Environment
Characteristics
Influencing Transfer
of Training

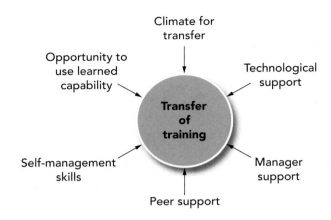

figure 7.5

Work Environment
Characteristics
Influencing Transfer
of Training

Climate for Transfer

One way to think about the work environment's influence on transfer of training is to consider the overall climate for transfer. **Climate for transfer** refers to trainees' perceptions about a wide variety of characteristics of the work environment that facilitate or inhibit use of trained skills or behavior. These characteristics include manager and peer support, opportunity to use skills, and the consequences for using learned capabilities.[44] Research has shown that transfer of training climate is significantly related to positive changes in behaviors following training.

Climate for Transfer
Trainees' perceptions of characteristics of the work environment (social support and situational constraints) that can either facilitate or inhibit use of trained skills or behavior.

Manager Support

Manager support refers to the degree to which trainees' managers (1) emphasize the importance of attending training programs and (2) stress the application of training content to the job. Table 7.7 shows what managers should do to support training. For example, at Men's Wearhouse, managers are expected to spend part of their budget on training. A series of meetings are held with managers to explain the purpose of training and the manager's role in helping employees learn and use skills in the stores.[45] Managers can communicate expectations to trainees, provide encouragement and resources needed to

table 7.7

What Managers
Should Do to
Support Training

Understand the content of the training.
Know how training relates to what you need employees to do.
In performance appraisals, evaluate employees on how they apply training to their jobs.
Support employees' use of training when they return to work.
Ensure that employees have the equipment and technology needed to use training.
Prior to training, discuss with employees how they plan to use training.
Recognize newly trained employees who use training content.
Give employees release time from their work to attend training.
Explain to employees why they have been asked to attend training.
Give employees feedback related to skills or behavior they are trying to develop.
If possible, be a trainer.

SOURCE: Based on A. Rossett, "That Was a Great Class, but . . ." *Training and Development,* July 1997, p. 21.

apply training on the job. One company asked trainees and their bosses to prepare and send memos to each other. The memos described what the other person should "start to do," "continue to do," "do less," or "stop doing" to help learning transfer.[46]

At Ingersoll Rand, to ensure that top managers understand and support the role that training and development can play in the company, a "ladder of engagement" model was created.[47] Top managers are engaged in training and development in many different ways, including providing input into learning program development, serving as trainers or co-trainers, visiting courses as an executive speaker, or serving as advisory council members for Ingersoll Rand's corporate university.

The greater the level of manager support, the more likely that transfer of training will occur.[48] The basic level of support that a manager should provide is acceptance, that is, allowing trainees to attend training. The highest level of support is to participate in training as an instructor (teaching in the program). Managers who serve as instructors are more likely to provide lower-level support functions such as reinforcing use of newly learned capabilities, discussing progress with trainees, and providing opportunities to practice. Managers can also facilitate transfer through use of action plans. An **action plan** is a written document that includes the steps that the trainee and manager will take to ensure that training transfers to the job. The action plan includes (1) a goal identifying what training content will be used and how it will be used (project, problem); (2) strategies for reaching the goal, including resources needed; (3) strategies for getting feedback (such as meetings with the manager); and (4) expected outcome (what will be different?). The action plan includes a schedule of specific dates and times when the manager and trainee agree to meet to discuss the progress being made in using learned capabilities on the job.

At a minimum, special sessions should be scheduled with managers to explain the purpose of the training and set expectations that they will encourage attendance at the training session, provide practice opportunities, reinforce use of training, and follow up with employees to determine the progress in using newly acquired capabilities.

Action Plan
Document summarizing what the trainee and manager will do to ensure that training transfers to the job.

Peer Support

Transfer of training can also be enhanced by creating a support network among the trainees.[49] A **support network** is a group of two or more trainees who agree to meet and discuss their progress in using learned capabilities on the job. This could involve face-to-face meetings or communications via e-mail. Trainees can share successful experiences in using training content on the job; they can also discuss how they obtained resources needed to use training content or how they coped with a work environment that interfered with use of training content.

Web sites or newsletters might be used to show how trainees are dealing with transfer of training issues. Available to all trainees, the newsletter or Web site might feature interviews with trainees who were successful in using new skills or provide tips for using new skills. Managers may also provide trainees with a mentor—a more experienced employee who previously attended the same training program. The mentor, who may be a peer, can provide advice and support related to transfer of training issues (such as how to find opportunities to use the learned capabilities).

Support Network
Trainees who meet to discuss their progress in using learned capabilities on the job.

Opportunity to Use Learned Capabilities

Opportunity to use learned capabilities (**opportunity to perform**) refers to the extent to which the trainee is provided with or actively seeks experience with newly learned knowledge, skill, and behaviors from the training program.[50] Opportunity to perform

Opportunity to Perform
Trainee is provided with or actively seeks experience using newly learned knowledge, skills, or behavior.

is influenced by both the work environment and trainee motivation. One way trainees can use learned capabilities is through assigned work experiences (problems or tasks) that require their use. The trainees' manager usually plays a key role in determining work assignments. Opportunity to perform is also influenced by the degree to which trainees take personal responsibility to actively seek out assignments that allow them to use newly acquired capabilities. Trainees given many opportunities to use training content on the job are more likely to maintain learned capabilities than trainees given few opportunities.[51]

Technological Support: EPSS and Knowledge Management Systems

Electronic
Performance
Support Systems
(EPSS)
Computer
applications that
can provide (as
requested) skills
training, information
access, and expert
advice.

Electronic performance support systems (EPSS) are computer applications that can provide, as requested, skills training, information access, and expert advice.[52] EPSSs may be used to enhance transfer of training by giving trainees an electronic information source that they can refer to as needed as they attempt to apply learned capabilities on the job.

At Reuters, the news and financial information company, employees who deal with orders for financial systems information and data needed a way to get their questions answered on an as-needed basis because they did not have the time to attend training sessions.[53] Typical questions included how to register financial traders to access Reuters' information and systems and how to coordinate installation of Reuters' technology on the trading floor. Reuters purchased an EPSS that provides employees with help tabs on their computer screens as they perform tasks. The help tabs provide answers to questions about the steps employees need to complete different processes (such as user registration).

Knowledge
Management
Process of
enhancing com-
pany performance
by designing and
using tools, systems,
and cultures to
improve creation,
sharing, and use of
knowledge.

Knowledge management refers to the process of enhancing company performance by designing and implementing tools, processes, systems, structures, and cultures to improve the creation, sharing, and use of knowledge.[54] Consider several examples of the methods companies use to share and create knowledge. At MWH Global, an engineering and environmental consulting company, a software program was used to analyze the data that employees provided about which colleagues they most frequently interacted with and whom they turned to for expertise.[55] The program plotted a web of interconnecting nodes and lines representing people and relationships. The web provides a corporate map of how work gets done, lists the well-connected technical experts, and helps identify informal connections between people that are missing on a traditional organizational chart.

Caterpillar Inc. has moved toward becoming a learning organization with the help of knowledge management.[56] Thirty years ago Caterpillar Inc., a manufacturer of construction and mining equipment, engines, and gas turbines, had most of its value in plant and physical equipment. Today, intangible assets such as intellectual capital account for most of the company's value. Caterpillar's knowledge sharing system, a Web-based system known as Knowledge Network, has 3,000 communities of practice. They range in size from small teams to hundreds of employees from across the world. The communities of practice are used to distribute information, post questions, provide space for reference materials, and have links to standards and regulations relevant to the community. One community of practice focuses on bolted joints and fasteners. The community of practice gives specialized engineers who generally work alone in manufacturing facilities the ability to ask other engineers questions or get second opinions on designs and problems.

Caterpillar also has external communities of practice made up of dealers, suppliers, and customers.

Caterpillar's communities of practice using the Knowledge Network have resulted in improved decision making, increased collaboration and teamwork, improved work quality, and better product design and development. For example, members of the Bolted Joints and Fasteners community and the Dealer Service Training community saved more than $1.5 million from online discussions. The company also tracks participation using metrics such as number of discussions and number of people logged into the system, with the goal of increasing the amount of discussion and activity in the system.

Self-Management Skills

Training programs should prepare employees to self-manage their use of new skills and behaviors on the job.[57] Specifically, within the training program, trainees should set goals for using skills or behaviors on the job, identify conditions under which they might fail to use them, identify the positive and negative consequences of using them, and monitor their use of them. Also, trainees need to understand that it is natural to encounter difficulty in trying to use skills on the job; relapses into old behavior and skill patterns do not indicate that trainees should give up. Finally, because peers and supervisors on the job may be unable to reward trainees using new behaviors or to provide feedback automatically, trainees need to create their own reward system and ask peers and managers for feedback.

Consider how Vanderbilt University Medical Center (VUMC) emphasizes transfer of training.[58] To improve patient safety and quality, VUMC initiated a team training program. The program teaches participants about patient safety mistakes and how to avoid them, team building, cross-checking and communications, decision making, and performance feedback. Participants are provided classroom training that shows how concepts from aviation flight crew training can be applied to patient safety and quality care by talking about how to create an effective team (crew), how to communicate effectively (briefings), how to recognize potential problems and what to do about them, how to make informed decisions, and how to critique performance (debrief). For example, the module on crew resource management focuses on how crew resource management is applied to health care and how it improves patient safety and quality of care.

Several steps are taken to make sure transfer of training occurs, that is, what is learned in the program is used and supported at work. Before the training starts, VUMC leaders are prepared to help the training succeed. Senior administrators, medical directors, and nursing staff attend a boot camp, which highlights the team training program. A safety climate survey is conducted to determine how each department perceives the VUMC attitudes toward safety practices and patient safety issues. Then, each department is reviewed to find built-in errors that are system problems and to evaluate how the team communicates and deals with conflict. After this, training, observation, coaching, and feedback are provided by medical supervisors. Checklists are provided for certain procedures such as patient handoffs, medication administration, and briefing and debriefing sessions to help participants use the strategies emphasized in training to improve safety and the quality of patient care. Patients also help ensure safety. They are asked to watch a video created by VUMC when they are admitted to the hospital. The video emphasizes the importance of asking questions about medications and medical procedures.

LO5
Discuss the strengths
and weaknesses of
presentation, hands-on, and
group training methods.

Selecting Training Methods

A number of different methods can help employees acquire new knowledge, skills, and behaviors. Figure 7.6 provides an overview of the frequency of use of training methods. Instructor-led classroom still remains the most frequently used training method.

Regardless of whether the training method is traditional or technology based, for training to be effective it needs to be based on the training design model shown in Table 7.1. Needs assessment, a positive learning environment, and transfer of training are critical for training program effectiveness.

Presentation Methods

Presentation Methods
Training methods in
which trainees are
passive recipients of
information.

Presentation methods refer to methods in which trainees are passive recipients of information. Presentation methods include traditional classroom instruction, distance learning, audiovisual techniques, and mobile technology such as iPods and PDAs. These are ideal for presenting new facts, information, different philosophies, and alternative problem-solving solutions or processes.

Instructor-Led Classroom Instruction. Classroom instruction typically involves having the trainer lecture a group. In many cases the lecture is supplemented with question-and-answer periods, discussion, or case studies. Classroom instruction remains a popular training method despite new technologies such as interactive video and computer-assisted instruction. Traditional classroom instruction is one of the least expensive, least time-consuming ways to present information on a specific topic to many trainees. The more active participation, job-related examples, and exercises that the instructor can build into traditional classroom instruction, the more likely trainees will learn and use the information presented on the job.

Teleconferencing
Synchronous
exchange of audio,
video, or text
between individuals
or groups at two or
more locations.

Distance learning is used by geographically dispersed companies to provide information about new products, policies, or procedures as well as skills training and expert lectures to field locations.[59] Distance learning features two-way communications between people. Distance learning currently involves two types of technology.[60] First, it includes teleconferencing. **Teleconferencing** refers to synchronous exchange of audio, video, and/or text between two or more individuals or groups at two or more locations. Trainees attend training programs in training facilities in which they can

figure 7.6

Overview of Use of
Training Methods

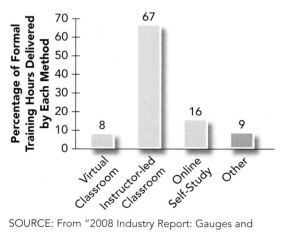

SOURCE: From "2008 Industry Report: Gauges and Drivers," *Training*, November/December 2008, p. 24.

communicate with trainers (who are at another location) and other trainees using the telephone or personal computer. A second type of distance learning also includes individualized, personal-computer–based training.[61] Employees participate in training anywhere they have access to a personal computer. This type of distance learning may involve multimedia training methods such as Web-based training. Course material and assignments can be distributed using the company's intranet, video, or CD-ROM. Trainers and trainees interact using e-mail, bulletin boards, and conferencing systems. Both types of distance learning can also allow trainees to respond to questions posed during the training program using a keypad.

Teleconferencing usually includes a telephone link so that trainees viewing the presentation can call in questions and comments to the trainer. Also, satellite networks allow companies to link up with industry-specific and educational courses for which employees receive college credit and job certification. IBM, Digital Equipment, and Eastman Kodak are among the many firms that subscribe to the National Technological University, which broadcasts courses throughout the United States that technical employees need to obtain advanced degrees in engineering.[62]

An advantage of distance learning is that the company can save on travel costs. It also allows employees in geographically dispersed sites to receive training from experts who would not otherwise be available to visit each location. Intuit finds that a traditional classroom environment is good for introducing software and providing trainees with the opportunity to network. Virtual classroom training is used for courses on special software features, demonstrations, and troubleshooting using application-sharing features. For example, JCPenney, which produces more than 200 different interactive distance learning (IDL) programs each year uses distance learning to reach every associate.[63] Each store has a training room, where up to 12 employees sign on to the program and watch on a large television screen. Each employee has his or her own keypad to interact. Employees are able to watch the satellite broadcast live or later view a tape of the program. Regardless of whether watching the program live or via tape, employees can answer questions such as, "How many square feet does your store have for lingerie?"; at the end of the program, managers and trainers can access a report on how every store answered. Evaluations of the interactive distance learning satellite have been positive. IDL has allowed JCPenney's to deliver training to every employee in the company. Eight-six percent of employees report that they use the training to effectively perform their jobs.

Online learning also has disadvantages. FileNeT Corporation was concerned with how its sales force was going to keep up with new software and software updates.[64] FileNeT tried self-paced online learning but discovered that salespeople did not like to read a lot of material about new products on the Web. Enrollment in online courses dwindled, and salespeople flooded the company's training department with requests for one-on-one assistance. To solve the training problem, the company decided to use webcasting. **Webcasting** involves classroom instructions that are provided online through live broadcasts. Webcasting helped spread the sales force training throughout the year rather than cramming it into twice-a-year sales meetings. Webcasting also helped ensure that the salespeople all received the same information. The salespeople liked the webcasts because of the timely information that helped them have conversations with customers. The live sessions were also popular because participants could ask questions. Webcasting has not replaced face-to-face training at FileNeT; classroom training is still about 80 percent of training, but that percentage has decreased by 10 percent. Webcasting has also resulted in savings of $500,000 annually (one of the twice-yearly sales meetings was canceled).

Webcasting
Classroom instruction provided online via live broadcasts.

The major disadvantage of distance learning is the potential for lack of interaction between the trainer and the audience. A high degree of interaction between trainees and the trainer is a positive learning feature that is missing from distance learning programs that merely use technology to broadcast a lecture to geographically dispersed employees. All that is done in this case is repurposing a traditional lecture (with its limitations for learning and transfer of training) for a new training technology! That's why establishing a communications link between employees and the trainer is important. Also, on-site instructors or facilitators should be available to answer questions and moderate question-and-answer sessions.

Audiovisual Techniques. *Audiovisual instruction* includes overheads, slides, and video. It has been used for improving communications skills, interviewing skills, and customer-service skills and for illustrating how procedures (such as welding) should be followed. Video is, however, rarely used alone. It is usually used in conjunction with lectures to show trainees real-life experiences and examples. Video is also a major component of behavior modeling and, naturally, interactive video instruction. Morse Bros., located in Tangent, Oregon, is one of only a few ready-mix firms in the Northwest that provide regular training for their drivers. Drivers play a key role in determining the success of the business. Excessive idling at construction sites, avoiding rollovers at construction sites, and product training can reduce costs and raise customer satisfaction. Morse Bros. produces training videos, which are presented by mentor-drivers. The mentor-driver's job is to select the weekly video, schedule viewing sessions, keep attendance records, and guide a wrap-up discussion following each video. The mentor-drivers are trained to call attention to key learning points covered in the video and relate the topics to issues the drivers deal with on the job. Because training sessions are scheduled early in the morning at the beginning of the drivers' shift, time is limited. Videos seldom run more than 10 minutes. For example, one called *Another Pair of Eyes* trains drivers to observe test procedures used by testing agencies at job sites. Samples are tested several times a month. A sample that fails can leave the company liable for demolition and removal of the concrete structure. Morse Bros. provides training on test procedures because samples often fail a test due to contamination (such as dirt) that gets into the test cylinder. At each training session, drivers answer several questions related to the content of the program. At the end of a session, drivers and the mentor-driver discuss anything that might be interfering with the quality of the product or timeliness of delivery. Mentor-drivers then share this information with company managers.[65]

The use of video in training has a number of advantages. First, the trainer can review, slow down, or speed up the lesson, which permits flexibility in customizing the session depending on trainees' expertise. Second, trainees can be exposed to equipment, problems, and events that cannot be easily demonstrated, such as equipment malfunctions, angry customers, or emergencies. Third, trainees get consistent instruction; program content is not affected by the interests and goals of a particular trainer. Fourth, videotaping trainees allows them to see and hear their own performance without the interpretation of the trainer. As a result, trainees cannot attribute poor performance to the bias of external evaluators such as the trainer or peers.

Most problems in video result from the creative approach used.[66] These problems include too much content for the trainee to learn, poor dialogue between the actors (which hinders the credibility and clarity of the message), overuse of humor or music, and drama that makes it confusing for the trainee to understand the important learning points emphasized in the video.

Mobile Technologies: iPods and PDAs. Mobile technologies such as iPods and PDAs allow training and learning to occur naturally throughout the workday or at home, allow employees to be connected to communities of learning, and give employees the ability to learn at their own pace by reviewing material or skipping over content they know.[67] The typical users for mobile learning include employees who are part of a workforce that spends most of its time traveling, visiting customers, clients, or various company locations (such as sales, security officers, executives, or inspectors) and has limited time available to spend in traditional training activities or e-learning. At Tyco International Ltd., a safety products producer, service technicians' PDAs are used to manage service orders, conduct inspections, and generate quotes for customers.[68] Tyco is using the PDAs to deliver a short course teaching sales technicians how to program and set a burglar alarm. The course includes a simulation of an alarm panel. The ability to use their PDAs for learning is perfect for the sales technicians, who are constantly traveling responding to service requests—meaning they have little time for traditional training or online learning.

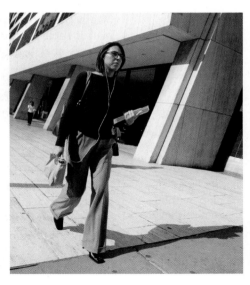

● Mobile technology is useful not only for entertainment, but can also be used for employees who travel and need to be in touch with the office. iPods and Personal Digital Assistants also give employees the ability to listen to and participate in training programs at their own leisure.

Capital One, a financial services company, provides iPods (portable audio players) for employees enrolled in training courses.[69] More than 2,000 iPods have been distributed as part of the Audio Learning program. The iPods can be used for business or personal reasons such as listening to music. Capital One decided that a new way to deliver training was needed based on employee surveys suggesting that employees did not have the time at work to attend classroom training. As a result, Capital One experimented with an audio channel for learning and found that employees liked learning on iPods and were able to gain access to programs that they would have been unable to attend in a classroom. Employees can access digitized audio, such as mp3 files, which are downloaded to their computers and can be transferred to their iPods. Approximately 30 training programs use the iPod. Employees can access a variety of programs, including leadership development and workshops on conflict management. Books and Harvard Business School cases are provided to employees on the iPod and have been used in executive-level programs to discuss leadership and new-hire programs to understand customer service. Besides using the iPod as a primary training content delivery mechanism, some programs use the iPod to provide books or articles for employees for pre-work before they attend a classroom program, and others use it to enhance transfer of training. For example, scenarios and role-plays discussed in classroom training are recorded and available for iPod upload. Employees can listen to the role-plays, which reinforces the use of the training content on the job and motivates them to think about using what they have learned. Capital One has determined that despite the costs related to purchasing and providing each employee with an iPod, if employees were listening to four to six hours of training content outside the classroom, the company was breaking even. Some of the benefits of the iPod programs include employees' increased enthusiasm for learning (attending courses that use the iPod), employees' willingness to take on new roles and broader job responsibilities, and time savings over traditional learning methods.

Some of the challenges of using mobile technology for learning include ensuring that employees know when and how to take advantage of the technology; encouraging communication, collaboration, and interaction with other employees in communities of practice; and ensuring that employees can connect to a variety of networks no matter their location or mobile device they are using.[70] However, simply digitizing lectures and distributing them to employees will not facilitate learning. Thus, for example, Capital One creates simulated radio shows with phone-in questions and answers given by the announcers to create an audio learning environment that is enjoyable and interesting. The best approach may be to use iPods as part of a blended learning approach involving face-to-face interaction between trainees as well as audio learning.

Hands-on Methods

Hands-on Methods
Training methods that actively involve the trainee in learning.

Hands-on methods are training methods that require the trainee to be actively involved in learning. Hands-on methods include on-the-job training, simulations, business games and case studies, behavior modeling, interactive video, and Web-based training. These methods are ideal for developing specific skills, understanding how skills and behaviors can be transferred to the job, experiencing all aspects of completing a task, and dealing with interpersonal issues that arise on the job.

On-the-Job Training (OJT)

On-the-Job Training (OJT)
Peers or managers training new or inexperienced employees who learn the job by observation, understanding, and imitation.

On-the-job training (OJT) refers to new or inexperienced employees learning through observing peers or managers performing the job and trying to imitate their behavior. OJT can be useful for training newly hired employees, upgrading experienced employees' skills when new technology is introduced, cross-training employees within a department or work unit, and orienting transferred or promoted employees to their new jobs.

OJT takes various forms, including apprenticeships and self-directed learning programs. (Both are discussed later in this section.) OJT is an attractive training method because, compared to other methods, it needs less investment in time or money for materials, trainer's salary, or instructional design. Managers or peers who are job knowledge experts are used as instructors. As a result, it may be tempting to let them conduct the training as they believe it should be done.

This unstructured approach to OJT has several disadvantages[71] Managers and peers may not use the same process to complete a task. They may pass on bad habits as well as useful skills. Also, they may not understand that demonstration, practice, and feedback are important conditions for effective on-the-job training. Unstructured OJT can result in poorly trained employees, employees who use ineffective or dangerous methods to produce a product or provide a service, and products or services that vary in quality.

OJT must be structured to be effective. Table 7.8 shows the principles of structured OJT. Because OJT involves learning by observing others, successful OJT is based on the principles emphasized by social learning theory. These include the use of a credible trainer, a manager or peer who models the behavior or skill, communication of specific key behaviors, practice, feedback, and reinforcement. Reliance Industries, one of India's largest businesses, uses on-the-job training in its Nagothane Manufacturing Division (a refinery that makes polymers and chemicals).[72] Because of rapid company growth and the need for experienced employees, the company needed to help new engineers contribute more quickly. The training staff identified mentors who would help accelerate learning for the new engineers. The mentors and new hires are carefully matched based on an assessment of the mentor's training style and

table 7.8

Principles of On-the-Job Training

PREPARING FOR INSTRUCTION

1. Break down the job into important steps.
2. Prepare the necessary equipment, materials, and supplies.
3. Decide how much time you will devote to OJT and when you expect the employees to be competent in skill areas.

ACTUAL INSTRUCTION

1. Tell the trainees the objective of the task and ask them to watch you demonstrate it.
2. Show the trainees how to do it without saying anything.
3. Explain the key points or behaviors. (Write out the key points for the trainees, if possible.)
4. Show the trainees how to do it again.
5. Have the trainees do one or more single parts of the task and praise them for correct reproduction (optional).
6. Have the trainees do the entire task and praise them for correct reproduction.
7. If mistakes are made, have the trainees practice until accurate reproduction is achieved.
8. Praise the trainees for their success in learning the task.

SOURCES: Based on W. J. Rothwell and H. C. Kazanas, "Planned OJT Is Productive OJT," *Training and Development Journal*, October 1990, pp. 53–55; P. J. Decker and B. R. Nathan, *Behavior Modeling Training* (New York: Praeger Scientific, 1985).

the new employee's learning style. Mentors are paired with up to three new employees each for nine months. The mentors and new employees work together on four learning modules, each module taking two months to complete. Each module includes predetermined lesson plans, and they track their progress using an online portal. The length of time it takes new engineers to contribute at work has decreased from 12 to 6 months.

Self-directed learning involves having employees take responsibility for all aspects of learning—when it is conducted and who will be involved. Self-directed learning for salespeople could involve reading newspapers or trade publications, talking to experts, or surfing the Internet to find new ideas related to the sales industry.[73] Also, self-directed learning could involve the company providing salespeople with information such as databases and training courses and seminars, but they are in charge of taking the initiative to learn. Because the effectiveness of self-directed learning is based on the employee's motivation to learn, companies may want to provide seminars on the self-directed learning process; self-management; and how to adapt to the environment, customers, and technology to better facilitate the process.

There are several advantages and disadvantages of self-directed learning.[74] It allows trainees to learn at their own pace and receive feedback about the learning performance. For the company, self-directed learning requires fewer trainers, reduces costs associated with travel and meeting rooms, and makes multiple-site training more realistic. Self-directed learning provides consistent training content that captures the knowledge of experts. Self-directed learning also makes it easier for shift employees to gain access to training materials. A major disadvantage of self-directed learning is that trainees must be willing and comfortable learning on their own; that is, trainees must be motivated to learn. From the company perspective, self-directed learning results in higher development costs, and development time is longer than with other types of

Self-Directed Learning
A program in which employees take responsibility for all aspects of learning.

training programs. Self-directed learning will likely be more common in the future as companies seek to train staff flexibly, to take advantage of technology, and to encourage employees to be proactive in their learning rather than driven by the employer.[75]

The Four Seasons Regent Hotel and Resorts is a luxury hotel operations and management group with 22,000 employees worldwide, including approximately 13,000 in international locations. The Four Seasons faced the challenge of opening a new hotel and resort at Jambaran Bay, Bali. To address training needs, the human resources staff created a self-directed learning center. The Self Access Learning Center emphasizes communication skills as well as English language skills. Its purpose is to teach skills and improve employees' confidence in their communications. The center includes video recorders, training modules, books, and magazines. Besides English, the center also teaches Japanese (the language of 20 percent of hotel visitors) and provides training for foreign managers in Bahasa Indonesian, the native language of Indonesia. The training process begins by administering an English test to potential employees to gauge the level of English training they need. As employees complete each level of the training, they receive a monetary incentive.

How has the training paid dividends? Travel experts rated the Four Seasons Bali as one of the top hotels in the world. Business has increased steadily since the hotel opened, with guests from North America, Europe, Asia, Australia, and South America. As a result of the training, the Four Seasons is prepared for expansion. As the hotel industry expands in Asia, the Four Seasons now has a trained and talented staff that can be used to meet human resource needs as new resorts are developed. Four Seasons learned that the company must combine the training needs of the local culture with the standards of the company's culture to create a successful international business.[76]

Apprenticeship
A work-study training method with both on-the-job and classroom training.

Apprenticeship is a work-study training method with both on-the-job training and classroom training.[77] To qualify as a registered apprenticeship program under state or federal guidelines, at least 144 hours of classroom instruction and 2,000 hours, or one year, of on-the-job experience are required.[78] Apprenticeships can be sponsored by individual companies or by groups of companies cooperating with a union. The majority of apprenticeship programs are in the skilled trades, such as plumbing, carpentry, electrical work, and bricklaying.

The hours and weeks that must be devoted to completing specific skill units are clearly defined. OJT involves assisting a certified tradesperson (a journeyman) at the work site. The on-the-job training portion of the apprenticeship follows the guidelines for effective on-the-job training.[79] Modeling, practice, feedback, and evaluation are involved. First, the employer verifies that the trainee has the required knowledge of the operation or process. Next, the trainer (who is usually a more experienced, licensed employee) demonstrates each step of the process, emphasizing safety issues and key steps. The senior employee provides the apprentice with the opportunity to perform the process until all are satisfied that the apprentice can perform it properly and safely.

A major advantage of apprenticeship programs is that learners can earn pay while they learn. This is important because programs can last several years. Learners' wages usually increase automatically as their skills improve. Also, apprenticeships are usually effective learning experiences because they involve learning why and how a task is performed in classroom instruction provided by local trade schools, high schools, or community colleges. Apprenticeships also usually result in full-time employment for trainees when the program is completed. From the company's perspective, apprenticeship programs meet specific business needs and help to attract talented employees.

At its manufacturing facility in Toledo, Ohio, Libbey Glass has apprenticeship programs in mold making, machine repair, millwrighting, and maintenance repair.[80] Each apprentice requires the support of a journeyman for each work assignment. The program also requires apprentices to be evaluated every 1,000 hours to meet Department of Labor standards. The reviews are conducted by a committee including representatives of management and department journeymen. The committee also develops tests and other evaluation materials. The committee members cannot perform their normal duties during the time they are reviewing apprentices so their workload has to be spread among other employees or rescheduled for some other time. The benefits of the program include the development of employees who are more receptive to change in the work environment, the ability to perform work at Libbey instead of having to outsource jobs to contract labor, and an edge for Libbey in attracting talented employees who like the idea that after completing an apprenticeship they are eligible for promotions to other positions in the company, including management positions. Also, the apprenticeship program helps Libbey tailor training and work experiences to meet specific needs in maintenance repair, which is necessary to create and repair production mold equipment used in making glass products.

Apprentice-type programs are also used to prepare new managers. The president and chief executive officer of Goldcorp Inc., a company in the mining industry, offers the chance for MBAs to apply for a nine-month apprenticeship.[81] The apprentice shadows Goldcorp's CEO, observing board meetings, negotiations, and the process of acquiring mines, and travels to learn important aspects of the mining industry. Goldcorp hopes the apprenticeships will attract more graduates to the mining industry, which many would not consider because of the mining industry's image as an unsafe, dirty business.

One disadvantage of many apprenticeship programs is limited access for minorities and women.[82] Another disadvantage is that there is no guarantee that jobs will be available when the program is completed. Finally, apprenticeship programs prepare trainees who are well trained in one craft or occupation. Due to the changing nature of jobs (thanks to new technology and use of cross-functional teams), many employers may be reluctant to employ workers from apprenticeship programs. Employers may believe that because apprentices are narrowly trained in one occupation or with one company, program graduates may have only company-specific skills and may be unable to acquire new skills or adapt their skills to changes in the workplace.

Simulations. A **simulation** is a training method that represents a real-life situation, with trainees' decisions resulting in outcomes that mirror what would happen if the trainee were on the job. Simulations, which allow trainees to see the impact of their decisions in an artificial, risk-free environment, are used to teach production and process skills as well as management and interpersonal skills.

At United Parcel Service (UPS), technology has made the drivers' job more complex.[83] They have to handle the truck safely, be proficient on the DIAD (handheld computer), and understand how to stay safe during a package delivery. As a result, UPS developed the Integrad training center in Maryland. Integrad includes a package car simulator designed to teach new hires how to load and unload packages from shelves, the floor, and the rear door—meeting company time standards for such activities while minimizing stress and strain that cause injuries. The average driver has to step off and on the truck at least 120 times on his or her route, which can strain ankles if done incorrectly. Trainees deliver packages with trainer and trainees serving as customers in a simulated town with stores, streets, and even a loading dock.

Simulation
A training method that represents a real-life situation, allowing trainees to see the outcomes of their decisions in an artificial environment.

Rogers Wireless Communications, a cell phone company, uses a simulation to train sales skills and product knowledge.[84] An online role-playing simulator that is used includes a variety of animated customers including a busy mother and a punk rocker, each providing a different customer service challenge. The simulation training has helped improve ratings of "mystery shoppers" at Rogers retail stores. Pitney Bowes, a mail-equipment and service company, uses an interactive spreadsheet program to simulate the company's product lines, key processes, and business culture. Executive teams are given a set of monthly revenue and product goals. They have to make a series of decisions including how many sales representatives to hire and how much time to invest in finding new clients. The decisions are plugged into the spreadsheet and both short- and long-term financial results are provided. The simulation has helped executives develop innovative ideas for transforming the sales organization with positive bottom-line dollar results.

Avatars

Computer depictions of humans that can be used as imaginary coaches, co-workers, and customers in simulations.

Avatars refer to computer depictions of humans that are being used as imaginary coaches, co-workers, and customers in simulations.[85] In second life (see www .secondlife.com), a virtual world built by its residents, avatars are used. Typically, trainees see the avatar who appears throughout the training course. For example, a sales training course at CDW Corporation, a technology products and service company, guides trainees through mock interviews with customers. The avatar introduces the customer situation, and the trainee hears the customer speaking in a simulated phone conversation. The trainee has to determine with help from the avatar what is happening in the sales process by reading the customer's voice. Loews Corporation's hotel chain uses "Virtual Leader," a program that helps participants learn how to be effective in meetings (e.g., how to build alliances, how to get a meeting agenda approved). As trainees attend the simulated meetings what they say (or don't say) results in scores that relate to their influence in the meeting.

Virtual Reality

Computer-based technology that provides trainees with a three-dimensional learning experience. Trainees operate in a simulated environment that responds to their behaviors and reactions.

A recent development in simulations is the use of virtual reality technology. **Virtual reality** is a computer-based technology that provides trainees with a three-dimensional learning experience. Using specialized equipment or viewing the virtual model on the computer screen, trainees move through the simulated environment and interact with its components.[86] Technology is used to stimulate multiple senses of the trainee.[87] Devices relay information from the environment to the senses. For example, audio interfaces, gloves that provide a sense of touch, treadmills, or motion platforms are used to create a realistic, artificial environment. Devices also communicate information about the trainee's movements to a computer. These devices allow the trainee to experience the perception of actually being in a particular environment. For example, Motorola's advanced manufacturing courses for employees learning to run the Pager Robotic Assembly facility use virtual reality. Employees are fitted with a head-mount display that allows them to view the virtual world, which includes the actual lab space, robots, tools, and the assembly operation. The trainees hear and see the actual sounds and sights as if they were using the real equipment. Also, the equipment responds to the employees' actions (such as turning on a switch or dial).

Second Life is a computer-based, simulated online virtual world, including a three-dimensional representation of the real world and a place to host learning programs or experiences. In Second Life, trainees use an avatar to interact with each other in classrooms, webinars, simulations, or role-play exercises. Second Life allows for employees to learn alone or with their peers or teams. Second Life can be used to create virtual classrooms, but its strength is the ability to create virtual reality simulations that actively involve the learner—such as putting the trainees' avatar in a realistic role-play where they have to deal with an upset customer. Stapoil, a Norwegian oil company, has an oil platform in Second Life that allows trainees to walk around it. Stapoil uses the oil platform for safety training. It catches fire, and employees have to find lifeboats to safely exit the platform.[88]

Employees at Silicon Image learn about making silicon chips by exploring a virtual world in Second Life that represents a corporate campus and by interacting with avatars.[89] Employees can visit the company's departments while watching videos and slide shows explaining what work is done within each unit. British Petroleum used Second Life to train new gas station employees in the safety features of gasoline storage tanks and piping systems.[90] BP builds three-dimensional replicas of the tank and pipe systems at a gas station. Trainees are able to see the underground storage tanks and piping systems and observe how safety devices control gasoline flow, which they could never do in real life.

As you can see from the example, simulations can be effective for several reasons.[91] First, trainees can use them on their desktop, eliminating the need to travel to a central training location. Second, simulations are meaningful, get trainees involved in learning, and are emotionally engaging (they can be fun!). This helps increase employees' willingness to practice, retain, and improve their skills. Third, simulators provide a consistent message of what needs to be learned; trainees can work at their own pace; and, compared to face-to-face instruction, simulators can incorporate more situations or problems that a trainee might encounter. Fourth, simulations can safely put employees in situations that would be dangerous in the real world. Fifth, simulations have been found to result in positive outcomes such as training being completed in a shorter time compared to traditional training courses, and providing a positive return on investment. The use of simulations has been limited by their development costs. As the development costs of simulations continue to decrease they will likely become a more popular training method. The costs of simulations varies. A customized simulation can cost between $200,000 and $300,000, while a simulation purchased from a supplier without any customization costs $100 to $200 per trainee.[92]

Business Games and Case Studies. Situations that trainees study and discuss (case studies) and business games in which trainees must gather information, analyze it, and make decisions are used primarily for management skill development. One organization that has effectively used case studies is the Central Intelligence Agency (CIA).[93] The cases are historically accurate and use actual data. For example, "The Libyan Attack" is used in management courses to teach leadership qualities. "The Stamp Case" is used to teach new employees about the agency's ethics structure. The CIA uses approximately 100 cases. One-third are focused on management; the rest focus on operations training, counterintelligence, and analysis. The cases are used in the training curriculum where the objectives include teaching students to analyze and resolve complex, ambiguous situations. The CIA found that for the cases used in training programs to be credible and meaningful to trainees, the material had to be as authentic as possible and stimulate students to make decisions similar to those they must make in their work environment. As a result, to ensure case accuracy, the CIA uses retired officers to research and write cases. The CIA has even developed a case writing workshop to prepare instructors to use the case method.

Games stimulate learning because participants are actively involved and they mimic the competitive nature of business. The types of decisions that participants make in games include all aspects of management practice, including labor relations (such as agreement in contract negotiations), marketing (the price to charge for a new product), and finance (financing the purchase of new technology). For example, at NetApp Inc., 25 managers participated in a game in which they played the role of top executives of an imaginary company modeled after their employer.[94] The managers worked in five-person teams to produce the strongest sales and operating profit, faced with challenges such as balancing long-term investments against short-term results. Managers received information including market analyses based on actual NetApp data and a menu of strategic initiatives such as improving college recruiting. The teams had to choose strategies and allocate employees and money. They had to respond to issues such as large customers seeking to add last-minute product features, considering whether to add the features and their related costs or refuse and risk angering an important client. The teams saw the consequences of their decisions. For example, one team declined to add the product features, which resulted in a decline in customer satisfaction and market share. At the end of the simulation, the sales and total profits of each team, as well as the effect of their strategies, were discussed.

Documentation on learning from games is anecdotal.[95] Games may give team members a quick start at developing a framework for information and help develop cohesive groups. For some groups (such as senior executives), games may be more meaningful training activities (because the game is realistic) than presentation techniques such as classroom instruction.

Cases may be especially appropriate for developing higher-order intellectual skills such as analysis, synthesis, and evaluation. These skills are often required by managers, physicians, and other professional employees. Cases also help trainees develop the willingness to take risks given uncertain outcomes, based on their analysis of the situation. To use cases effectively, the learning environment must let trainees prepare and discuss their case analyses. Also, face-to-face or electronic communication among trainees must be arranged. Because trainee involvement is critical for the effectiveness of the case method, learners must be willing and able to analyze the case and then communicate and defend their positions.

There are a number of available sources for preexisting cases (e.g., Harvard Business School). It is especially important to review preexisting cases to determine how meaningful they will be to the trainee.

Behavior Modeling.   Research suggests that behavior modeling is one of the most effective techniques for teaching interpersonal skills.[96] Each training session, which typically lasts four hours, focuses on one interpersonal skill, such as coaching or communicating ideas. Each session presents the rationale behind key behaviors, a videotape of a model performing key behaviors, practice opportunities using role-playing, evaluation of a model's performance in the videotape, and a planning session devoted to understanding how the key behaviors can be used on the job. In the practice sessions, trainees get feedback regarding how closely their behavior matches the key behaviors demonstrated by the model. The role-playing and modeled performance are based on actual incidents in the employment setting in which the trainee needs to demonstrate success.

Interactive Video.   Interactive video combines the advantages of video and computer-based instruction. Instruction is provided one-on-one to trainees via a personal computer. Trainees use the keyboard or touch the monitor to interact with the program. Interactive video is used to teach technical procedures and interpersonal skills. The training program may be stored on a compact disc (CD-ROM) or the company intranet. For example, the Shoney's and Captain D's restaurant chains have more than 350 restaurants in more than 20 states.[97] More than 8,000 employees each year must be trained on the basics of the operational parts of the business, including how to make french fries, hush puppies, and coleslaw. Also, each year 600 new managers must be trained in business issues and back-office operations of the restaurants. The biggest challenge that Shoney's faced was how to consistently train geographically dispersed employees. Shoney's solution was to implement OneTouch, a live integrated video and two-way voice and data application that combines synchronous video, voice, and data and live Web pages so that team members can interact with trainers. OneTouch can be delivered to desktop PCs as well as to warehouses and repair bays. Desktop systems can be positioned in any appropriate locations in the restaurant. Individuals or groups of employees can gather around the PC for training. The training modules include such topics as orientation, kitchen, and dining room. Each module is interactive. Topics are introduced and are followed up by quizzes to ensure that learning occurs. For example, the coleslaw program shows trainees what the coleslaw ingredients are and where they can be found in the restaurant. The coleslaw program includes a video that trainees can watch and practice with. After they practice, they have to complete a quiz, and their manager has to verify that they completed the topic before they move on to the next program. The training is consistent and is easy to update so as to ensure it is current. The program also allows kitchen and counter staff to learn each other's skills, which gives Shoney's flexibility in its staffing (e.g., counter employees who know how to cook). The main disadvantage of interactive video is the high cost of developing the courseware. This may be a particular problem for courses in which frequent updates are necessary.[98]

E-Learning. **E-learning** or online learning refers to instruction and delivery of training by computers through the Internet or company intranets.[99] E-learning includes Web-based training, distance learning, virtual classrooms, and use of CD-ROMs. E-learning can include task support, simulation training, distance learning, and learning portals. There are three important characteristics of e-learning. First, e-learning involves electronic networks that enable information and instruction to be delivered, shared, and updated instantly. Second, e-learning is delivered to the trainee via computers with Internet technology. Third, it focuses on learning solutions that go beyond traditional training to include information and tools that improve performance.

Figure 7.7 depicts the features of e-learning, which include collaboration and sharing, links to resources, learner control, delivery, and administration. As Figure 7.7 shows, e-learning not only provides training content but lets learners control what they learn, the speed at which they progress through the program, how much they practice, and even when they learn. E-learning also allows learners to collaborate or interact with other trainees and experts, and it provides links to other learning resources such as reference materials, company Web sites, and other training programs. Text, video, graphics, and sound can present course content. E-learning may also include various aspects of training administration such as course enrollment, testing and evaluating trainees, and monitoring learning progress. Various delivery methods can be incorporated into e-learning including distance learning, CD-ROM, and the Internet.

These features of e-learning give it advantages over other training methods. E-learning initiatives are designed to contribute to strategic business objectives.[100] E-learning supports company initiatives such as attracting customers, devising new ways to operate such as e-business, or quickly developing products or new services. E-learning may involve a larger audience than traditional training programs, which focused on employees; it may involve partners, suppliers, vendors, and potential customers.

LO6
Explain the potential advantages of e-learning for training.

E-Learning
Instruction and delivery of training by computers through the Internet or company intranet.

figure 7.7

Characteristics of E-Learning

For example, Ritz Camera Centers uses an e-learning program to help keep employees up-to-date on product information and enhance their selling skills.[101] E-learning was selected because the company needed a systematic way to reach all associates quickly, with easily managed and updated materials. Ritz Camera employees access short training courses online on a wide variety of technologies and brands. Each module provides insight into product features, competitive differences, and benefits. Training modules are created monthly and can stay live for up to a year based on product cycles. The modules feature training assessments in the form of a quiz that must be passed. In addition, Ritz can track employees' participation through a Web portal.

Learning is enhanced through e-learning because trainees are more engaged through the use of video, graphics, sound, and text, which appeal to multiple senses of the learner. Also, e-learning requires that learners actively participate in practice, questions, and interaction with other learners and experts.

Besides enhancing the training experience, e-learning can reduce training costs and time. E-learning brings training to geographically dispersed employees at their locations, reducing travel costs.

Effective e-learning is grounded on a thorough needs assessment and complete learning objectives. **Repurposing** refers to directly translating an instructor-led, face-to-face training program online. Online learning that merely repurposes an ineffective training program will remain ineffective. Unfortunately, in their haste to develop online learning, many companies are repurposing bad training! The best e-learning combines the advantages of the Internet with the principles of a good learning environment. Effective online learning takes advantage of the Web's dynamic nature and ability to use many positive learning features, including linking to other training sites and content through the use of hyperlinks, providing learner control, and allowing the trainee to collaborate with other learners. **Learner control** refers to the ability of trainees to actively learn through self-pacing, exercises, exploring links to other material, and conversations with other trainees and experts. That is, online learning allows activities typically led by the instructor (presentation, visuals, slides), trainees (discussion, questions), and group interaction (discussion of application of training content) to be incorporated into training without trainees or the instructor having to be physically present in a training room. Effective online learning gives trainees meaningful content, relevant examples, and the ability to apply content to work problems and issues. Also, trainees can practice and receive feedback through problems, exercises, assignments, and tests.

Blended Learning. Because of the limitations of online learning related to technology (e.g., insufficient bandwidth, lack of high-speed Web connections), because of trainee preference for face-to-face contact with instructors and other learners, and because of employees' inability to find unscheduled time during their workday to devote to learning from their desktops, many companies are moving to a hybrid, or blended, learning approach. *Blended learning* combines online learning, face-to-face instruction, and other methods for distributing learning content and instruction. The nearby "Competing through Technology" box shows how blended learning is benefiting several companies.

Learning Management System. A **learning management system** (LMS) refers to a technology platform that can be used to automate the administration, development, and delivery of all of a company's training programs. An LMS can provide employees, managers, and trainers with the ability to manage, deliver, and track learning activities.[102] LMSs are becoming more popular for several reasons. An LMS can help companies reduce travel and other costs related to training, reduce time for program completion, increase employees' accessibility to training across the business, and provide administrative capabilities to track program completion and course enrollments. An LMS allows companies to track all of the learning activity in the business. For example, both FedEx Kinkos and Turner Construction have LMSs.[103] FedEx Kinkos has document and shipping centers around the world and employs more than 20,000 people. The LMS at FedEx includes a software package that allows creation of individualized training for each employee, schedules classrooms, tracks employee progress, manages all aspects of the training curriculum, and delivers e-learning courses. Employees have access via personal computer to their personal learning plans based on their job, what their manager requires, and their own personal interests. Turner Construction has a competency model that divides jobs into nine job families and divides the families into job levels (senior management, administrative/clerical, and management). Employees receive an online performance evaluation of their skills based on their job family and level. The performance management system links to the company's LMS. The LMS analyzes the employees' skill weaknesses and recommends courses

Repurposing
Directly translating instructor-led training online.

Learner Control
Ability of trainees to actively learn through self-pacing, exercises, links to other materials, and conversations with other trainees and experts.

Learning Management System (LMS)
Technology platform that automates the administration, development, and delivery of a company's training program.

Many companies, recognizing the strengths and weaknesses of face-to-face instruction and technology-based training methods, are using both in a blended learning approach. Technology-based training can be used to provide consistent delivery of training content involving transfer of information (knowledge and skills) to geographically dispersed employees who can work at their own pace, practice, and collaborate with the trainer and trainee online. Then, trainees can be brought to a central location for face-to-face training (classroom, action learning, games, and role-plays), which can emphasize the application of knowledge and skills using cases and problems that require the application of training content. Face-to-face instruction is also more useful for facilitating interaction between trainees, collaboration, networking, and discussion.

Dunkin' Donuts training uses a blended learning approach involving online, classroom, and on-site work with follow-up and reinforcement. Franchisees attend an introductory course that focuses on the business as well as their roles and responsibilities (and those of the franchisor). This helps the franchisees learn from and build relationships with important individuals and teams at the corporation. Franchisees then complete 60 hours of online training on their own time in how donuts are made, equipment maintenance, food safety, and shift

management. A five-and-half-week instructor-led course and certification program runs at the same time as the online training. Both the online and instructor-led course are designed to simulate restaurant experiences with the goal of facilitating on-the-job practice that occurs in the restaurant. Practice sessions are supported with skills checklists to monitor progress and review training materials. Before opening the restaurant, franchisees train their new staffs, working side-by-side with regional market trainers or operations managers from Dunkin' Donuts. The goal is to have all employees working efficiently and effectively when the new restaurant opens. Extensive training also occurs after the restaurant opens. Market and network trainers and operations managers visit the store to evaluate them and provide ongoing training, support, and coaching. Based on the store evaluations, new training programs are developed to improve problem areas. The success of the training programs is measured in several different ways. Each of the training programs measures learning through the franchisee's ability to perform skills in restaurant operations. Dunkin' Donuts also asks franchisees for feedback on the training programs.

Cisco Systems offers 'Management 101,' a foundational program for management development. Cisco used to offer seven separate courses to

managers. The current program integrates the management development curriculum. In phase 1 of the program, a different topic that managers need to know is covered online each week for the first nine week of the course. The online learning includes testing (to ensure the managers have gained knowledge), multimedia exercises, case studies, and weekly facilitated online discussions. In phase 2, managers attend a four-day program in which they are together in a classroom to discuss and build on what they learned online. Phase 3 involves the manager learning along with his or her manager. At the conclusion of the program, each manager receives a 360-degree feedback evaluation. The 360 is used for tailoring each manager's development plan.

Gilbrane Inc., a building and development company, offers a change management course that includes an eight-hour face-to-face class combined with a two-hour online prerequisite module presenting change management principles. The face-to-face class allows trainees to apply the change management principles to possible project scenarios. Gilbrane also includes a performance support system that trainees can refer to when they return to their jobs.

SOURCES: Based on W. Webb, "Training = Franchise Success," *Training*, October 2008, pp. 54–55; M. Weinstein, "A Better Blend," *Training*, September 2008, pp. 30–39.

that can improve those skills. The LMS system allows Turner Construction to identify skill gaps for entire levels, job families, or business units. The results can be used to identify where to spend moneys allocated for training to develop new courses.

Group- or Team-Building Methods

Group- or team-building methods are training methods designed to improve team or group effectiveness. Training is directed at improving the trainees' skills as well as team effectiveness. In group-building methods, trainees share ideas and experiences, build group identity, understand the dynamics of interpersonal relationships, and get to know their own strengths and weaknesses and those of their co-workers. Group techniques focus on helping teams increase their skills for effective teamwork. A number of training techniques are available to improve work group or team performance, to establish a new team, or to improve interactions among different teams. They include trust falls (in which each trainee stands on a table and falls backward into the arms of fellow group members), paintball games, NASCAR pit crews, cooking, obstacle canes, and even drumming! All involve examination of feelings, perceptions, and beliefs about the functioning of the team; discussion; and development of plans to apply what was learned in training to the team's performance in the work setting. Group-building methods fall into three categories: adventure learning, team training, and action learning.

Group-building methods often involve experiential learning. *Experiential learning* training programs involve gaining conceptual knowledge and theory; taking part in a behavioral simulation; analyzing the activity; and connecting the theory and activity with on-the-job or real-life situations.[104]

For experiential training programs to be successful, several guidelines should be followed. The program needs to tie in to a specific business problem. The trainees need to be moved outside their personal comfort zones but within limits so as not to reduce trainee motivation or ability to understand the purpose of the program. Multiple learning modes should be used, including audio, visual, and kinesthetic. When preparing activities for an experiential training program, trainers should ask trainees for input on the program goals. Clear expectations about the purpose, expected outcomes, and trainees' role in the program are important. Finally, training programs that include experiential learning should be linked to changes in employee attitudes, behaviors, and other business results.

California-based Quantum Corporation developed a project to overhaul the company's online infrastructure across global operations.[105] The project included a diverse group of team members from the information technology, engineering, marketing, and graphic design departments. The team consisted of very talented employees who were not used to working with each other. Many of the team members were geographically dispersed, which increased the difficulties in working together. Quantum hired an actors' group to lead the team through a series of improvisational activities designed to get the team members to share personal stories. Using music, props, lighting, and costumes, the actors interpreted the stories told by team members. The actors portrayed team members who, for example, expressed isolation and frustration. Other times, team members would play the parts. The sessions allowed each team member to ask questions of the actors or each other. The team came away from the activity with more empathy and understanding for each other. Development of the personal relationships created positive interpersonal bonds that helped the team meet deadlines and complete projects.

Adventure Learning
Learning focused on the development of teamwork and leadership skills by using structured outdoor activities.

Adventure Learning. **Adventure learning** develops teamwork and leadership skills using structured outdoor activities.[106] Adventure learning appears to be best suited for developing skills related to group effectiveness, such as self-awareness, problem solving, conflict management, and risk taking. Adventure learning may involve strenuous, challenging physical activities such as dogsledding or mountain climbing. It can also use structured individual and group outdoor activities such as climbing walls, going through rope courses, making trust falls, climbing ladders, and traveling from one tower to another using a device attached to a wire that connects the two towers.

For example, a Chili's restaurant manager in adventure learning was required to scale a three-story-high wall.[107] About two-thirds away from the top of the wall the manager became very tired. She successfully reached the top of the wall using the advice and encouragement shouted from team members on the ground below. When asked to consider what she learned from the experience, she reported that the exercise made her realize that reaching personal success depends on other people. At her restaurant, everyone has to work together to make the customers happy.

Adventure learning can also include demanding activities that require coordination and place less of a physical strain on team members. For example, Cookin' Up Change is one of many team-building courses offered around the United States by chefs, caterers, hotels, and cooking schools.[108] These courses have been used by companies such as Honda and Microsoft. The underlying idea is that cooking classes help strengthen communications and networking skills by requiring team members to work together to create a full-course meal (a culinary feast!). Each team has to decide who does what kitchen tasks (e.g., cooking, cutting, cleaning) and prepares the main course, salads, or dessert. Often team members are required to switch assignments in midpreparation to see how the team reacts to change.

For adventure learning programs to succeed, the exercises should be related to the types of skills that participants are expected to develop. Also, after the exercises, a skilled facilitator should lead a discussion about what happened in the exercise, what was learned, how the exercise relates to the job situation, and how to set goals and apply what was learned on the job.[109]

Does adventure learning work? Rigorous evaluations of the impact of adventure learning on productivity and performance have not been conducted. However, participants often report that they gained a greater understanding of themselves and the ways they interact with their co-workers. One key to the success of an adventure learning program may be the insistence that whole work groups participate together so that group dynamics that inhibit effectiveness can emerge and be discussed.

The physically demanding nature of adventure learning and the requirement that trainees often have to touch each other in the exercises may increase the company's risk for negligence claims due to personal injury, intentional infliction of emotional distress, and invasion of privacy. Also, the Americans with Disabilities Act (discussed in Chapter 3) raises questions about requiring employees with disabilities to participate in physically demanding training experiences.[110]

Team Training. Team training coordinates the performance of individuals who work together to achieve a common goal. Such training is an important issue when information must be shared and individuals affect the overall performance of the group. For example, in the military as well as the private sector (think of nuclear power plants or commercial airlines), much work is performed by crews, groups, or teams. Success depends on coordination of individual activities to make decisions, team performance, and readiness to deal with potentially dangerous situations (like an overheating nuclear reactor).

Team training strategies include cross-training and coordination training.[111] In **cross-training** team members understand and practice each other's skills so that members are prepared to step in and take another member's place. **Coordination training** trains the team in how to share information and decisions to maximize team performance. Coordination training is especially important for commercial aviation and surgical teams, who monitor different aspects of equipment and the environment but must share information to make the most effective decisions regarding patient care or aircraft safety and performance. **Team leader training** refers to training the team manager or facilitator. This may involve training the manager how to resolve conflict within the team or help the team coordinate activities or other team skills.

United Airlines (UAL) is having its supervisors "lead" ramp employees in attending Pit Instruction & Training (Pit Crew U), which focuses on the preparation, practice, and teamwork of NASCAR pit crews. United is using the training to develop standardized methods to safely and efficiently unload, load, and send off its airplanes.[112] Pit Instruction & Training, located outside of Charlotte, North Carolina, has a quarter-mile race track and a pit road with places for six cars. The school offers programs to train new racing pit crews, but most of its business comes from companies interested in having their teams work as safely, efficiently, and effectively as NASCAR pit crews. The training is part of a multimillion-dollar investment that includes updating equipment and providing luggage scanners. The purpose of the training is to reinforce the need for ramp teams to be orderly and communicate, and to help standardize tasks of ramp team members, along with increasing morale. Training has been optional for ramp employees and they have survived layoffs and been asked to make wage concessions to help the company get out of bankruptcy. United already has started scheduling shorter ground times at some airports, anticipating the positive results of the program. Shorter ground times translate into more daily flights without having to buy more airplanes. United hopes to cut the average airplane ground time by eight minutes to make the airline more competitive.

The keys for safety, speed, and efficiency for NASCAR pit crews is that each member knows what tasks to do (change tires, use air gun, add gasoline, clean up spills) and, when the crew has finished servicing the race car, moves new equipment into position anticipating the next pit stop. The training involves the ramp workers actually working as pit crews. They learn how to handle jacks, change tires, and fill fuel tanks on race cars. They are videotaped and timed just like real pit crews. They receive feedback from professional pit crew members who work on NASCAR teams and trainers Also, the training requires them to deal with circumstances they might encounter on the job. For one pit stop, lug nuts had been sprinkled intentionally in the area where the car stops to see if the United employees would notice them and clean them up. On their jobs ramp employees are responsible for removing debris from the tarmac so it doesn't get sucked into jet engines or harm equipment. For another pit stop, teams had to work with fewer members, as sometimes occurs when ramp crews are understaffed due to absences.

Action Learning. In **action learning** teams or work groups get an actual business problem, work on solving it and commit to an action plan, and are accountable for carrying out the plan.[113] Typically, action learning involves between 6 and 30 employees; it may also include customers and vendors. There are several variations on the composition of the group. In one variation the group includes a single customer for the problem being dealt with. Sometimes the groups include cross-functional team members (members from different company departments) who all have a stake in the problem. Or the group may involve employees from multiple functions who all focus

Cross-Training
Team members understand and practice each other's skills.

Coordination Training
Trains the team in how to share information and decisions.

Team Leader Training
Training the team manager or facilitator.

Action Learning
Teams work on an actual business problem, commit to an action plan, and are accountable for carrying out the plan.

on their own functional problems, each contributing to helping solve the problems identified. For example, ATC, a public transportation services management company in Illinois, used action learning to help boost profitability by reducing operating costs.[114] Employees were divided into Action Workout Teams to identify ways of reducing costs and to brainstorm effective solutions. The process assumed that employees closest to where the work gets done have the best ideas about how to solve problems. Teams of five to seven employees met once a week for a couple of hours for 45 to 60 days. For example, a team working on parts inventory might have had a parts clerk, a couple of people from maintenance, a supervisor, and an operations employee. These teams studied problems and issues such as overtime, preventive maintenance, absenteeism, parts inventory, and inefficient safety inspection procedures. The teams brainstormed ideas, prioritized them according to their highest potential, developed action plans, installed them, tested them, and measured the outcomes. The solutions that the teams generated resulted in more than $1.8 million in savings for the company.

Six Sigma and black belt training programs involve principles of action learning. **Six Sigma training** provides employees with measurement and statistical tools to help reduce defects and to cut costs.[115] Six Sigma is a quality standard with a goal of only 3.4 defects per million processes. There are several levels of Six Sigma training, resulting in employees becoming certified as green belts, champions, or black belts.[116] To become black belts, trainees must participate in workshops and written assignments coached by expert instructors. The training involves four 4-day sessions over about 16 weeks. Between training sessions, candidates apply what they learn to assigned projects and then use them in the next training session. Trainees are also required to complete not only oral and written exams but also two or more projects that have a significant impact on the company's bottom line. After completing black belt training, employees are able to develop, coach, and lead Six Sigma teams; mentor and advise management on determining Six Sigma projects; and provide Six Sigma tools and statistical methods to team members. After black belts lead several project teams, they can take additional training and be certified as master black belts. Master black belts can teach other black belts and help senior managers integrate Six Sigma into the company's business goals.

McKesson Corporation trained 15 to 20 black belts and reassigned them to their original business units as their team's Six Sigma representatives.[117] When the two-year commitment ends, the black belts return to the business at higher positions, helping to spread the approach throughout the organization and ensuring that key leaders are committed to the Six Sigma philosophy. In most divisions of the company, Six Sigma training is mandated for senior vice presidents, who attend training that introduces Six Sigma and details how to identify a potential Six Sigma project. Across the company, every manager and director is expected to attend basic training. The Six Sigma effort has shown benefits every year since the program started.

Six Sigma Training
An action training program that provides employees with defect-reducing tools to cut costs and certifies employees as green belts, champions, or black belts.

Advice for Choosing a Training Method

LO7
Design a training session to maximize learning.

As a manager, you will likely be asked to choose a training method. Given the large number of training methods available to you, this task may seem difficult. One way to choose a training method is to compare methods. The first step in choosing a method is to identify the type of learning outcome that you want training to influence. These outcomes include verbal information, intellectual skills, cognitive strategies, attitudes, and motor skills. Training methods may influence one or several learning outcomes. Once you have identified a learning method, the next step is to consider the extent to which the method facilitates learning and transfer of training, the costs related to development and use of the method, and its effectiveness.

For learning to occur, trainees must understand the objectives of the training program, training content should be meaningful, and trainees should have the opportunity to practice and receive feedback. Also, a powerful way to learn is through observing and interacting with others. Transfer of training refers to the extent to which training will be used on the job. In general, the closer the training content and environment prepare trainees for use of learning outcomes on the job, the greater the likelihood that transfer will occur. Two types of costs are important: development costs and administrative costs. Development costs relate to design of the training program, including costs to buy or create the program. Administrative costs are incurred each time the training method is used. These include costs related to consultants, instructors, materials, and trainers.

Several trends are worth noting. First, there is considerable overlap between learning outcomes across the training methods. Group-building methods are unique because they focus on individual as well as team learning (e.g., improving group processes). If you are interested in improving the effectiveness of groups or teams, you should choose one of the group-building methods (e.g., action learning, team training, adventure learning). Second, comparing the presentation methods to the hands-on methods illustrates that most hands-on methods provide a better learning environment and transfer of training than do the presentation methods. The presentation methods are also less effective than the hands-on methods. E-learning or blended learning can be an effective training method for geographically dispersed trainees if it includes meaningful content, links to other resources, collaboration and sharing, and learner control. E-learning and other technology-driven training methods have higher development costs, but travel and housing cost savings will likely offset development costs over time. As the previous "Competing through Technology" box shows, many companies recognize the strengths and weaknesses of both technology-based training methods (such as iPods or e-learning) and face-to-face instruction. As a result, they are using both in a blended learning approach. The training budget for developing training methods can influence the method chosen. If you have a limited budget for developing new training methods, use structured on-the-job training—a relatively inexpensive yet effective hands-on method. If you have a larger budget, you might want to consider hands-on methods that facilitate transfer of training, such as simulators.

Evaluating Training Programs

Examining the outcomes of a program helps in evaluating its effectiveness. These outcomes should be related to the program objectives, which help trainees understand the purpose of the program. **Training outcomes** can be categorized as cognitive outcomes, skill-based outcomes, affective outcomes, results, and return on investment.[118] Table 7.9 shows the types of outcomes used in evaluating training programs and what is measured and how it is measured.

Which training outcomes measure is best? The answer depends on the training objectives. For example, if the instructional objectives identified business-related outcomes such as increased customer service or product quality, then results outcomes should be included in the evaluation. Both reaction and cognitive outcomes are usually collected before the trainees leave the training site. As a result, these measures do not help determine the extent to which trainees actually use the training content in

LO8
Choose an appropriate evaluation design based on training objectives and analysis of constraints.

Training Outcomes
A way to evaluate the effectiveness of a training program based on cognitive, skill-based, affective, and results outcomes.

table 7.9

Outcomes Used in Evaluating Training Programs

OUTCOME	WHAT IS MEASURED	HOW MEASURED	EXAMPLE
Cognitive outcomes	• Acquisition of knowledge	• Pencil-and-paper tests • Work sample	• Safety rules • Electrical principles • Steps in appraisal interview
Skill-based outcomes	• Behavior • Skills	• Observation • Work sample • Ratings	• Jigsaw use • Listening skills • Coaching skills • Airplane landings
Affective outcomes	• Motivation • Reaction to program • Attitudes	• Interviews • Focus groups • Attitude surveys	• Satisfaction with training • Beliefs regarding other cultures
Results	• Company payoff	• Observation • Data from information system or performance records	• Absenteeism • Accidents • Patents
Return on investment	• Economic value of training	• Identification and comparison of costs and benefits of the program	• Dollars

their jobs (transfer of training). Skill-based, affective, and results outcomes measured following training can be used to determine transfer of training—that is, the extent to which training has changed behavior, skills, or attitudes or directly influenced objective measures related to company effectiveness (such as sales).

For example, Ernst & Young's training function uses knowledge testing for all of the company's e-learning courses, which account for 50 percent of training.[119] New courses and programs use behavior transfer and business results. Regardless of the program, the company's leaders are interested in whether the trainees feel that it was a good use of their time and money and whether they would recommend it to other employees. The training function automatically tracks these outcomes because managers expect that training activities have a positive impact on business results (such as client satisfaction) and employee engagement (reduced turnover).

Reasons for Evaluating Training

Many companies are beginning to invest millions of dollars in training programs to gain a competitive advantage. Firms with high-leverage training practices not only invest large sums of money in developing and administering training programs but also evaluate training programs. Why should training programs be evaluated?

1. To identify the program's strengths and weaknesses. This includes determining whether the program is meeting the learning objectives, the quality of the learning environment, and whether transfer of training to the job is occurring.

2. To assess whether the content, organization, and administration of the program (including the schedule, accommodations, trainers, and materials) contribute to learning and the use of training content on the job.
3. To identify which trainees benefited most or least from the program.
4. To gather marketing data by asking participants whether they would recommend the program to others, why they attended the program, and their level of satisfaction with the program.
5. To determine the financial benefits and costs of the program.
6. To compare the costs and benefits of training to nontraining investments (such as work redesign or better employee selection).
7. To compare the costs and benefits of different training programs to choose the best program.

Walgreens is a good example of a company that has reconsidered the role of training based on evaluation data. A Walgreens training course for new technicians was developed to replace on-the-job training they received from the pharmacists who hired them. This course involved 20 hours of classroom training and 20 hours of supervision on the job. Because the company has several thousand stores, large amounts of money and time were invested in the training, so the company decided to evaluate the program.

The evaluation consisted of comparing technicians who had completed the program with some who had not. Surveys about new employees' performance were sent to the pharmacists who supervised the technicians. Some questions related to speed of entering patient and drug data into the store computer and how often the technician offered customers generic drug substitutes. The results showed that formally trained technicians were more efficient and wasted less of the pharmacist's time than those who received traditional on-the-job training. Sales in pharmacies with formally trained technicians exceeded sales in pharmacies with on-the-job–trained technicians by an average of $9,500 each year.[120]

Evaluation Designs

As shown in Table 7.10, a number of different evaluation designs can be applied to training programs. Table 7.10 compares each evaluation design on the basis of who is involved (trainees and/or a comparison group that does not receive training), when outcome measures are collected (pretraining, posttraining), the costs, the time needed to conduct the evaluation, and the strength of the design for ruling out alternative

table 7.10

Comparison of Evaluation Designs

DESIGN	GROUPS	MEASURES PRETRAINING	POSTTRAINING	COST	TIME	STRENGTH
Posttest only	Trainees	No	Yes	Low	Low	Low
Pretest/posttest	Trainees	Yes	Yes	Low	Low	Medium
Posttest only with comparison group	Trainees and comparison	No	Yes	Medium	Medium	Medium
Pretest/posttest with comparison group	Trainees and comparison	Yes	Yes	Medium	Medium	High
Time series	Trainees	Yes	Yes, several	Medium	Medium	Medium

explanations for the results (e.g., are improvements due to factors other than the training?). In general, designs that use pretraining and posttraining measures of outcomes and include a comparison group reduce the risk that factors other than training itself are responsible for the evaluation results. This builds confidence to use the results to make decisions. The trade-off is that evaluations using these designs are more costly and time-consuming to conduct than evaluations not using pretraining or posttraining measures or comparison groups.

There is no one appropriate evaluation design. Several factors need to be considered in choosing one:[121]

- Size of the training program.
- Purpose of training.
- Implications if a training program does not work.
- Company norms regarding evaluation.
- Costs of designing and conducting an evaluation.
- Need for speed in obtaining program effectiveness information.

For example, if a manager is interested in determining how much employees' communications skills have changed as a result of a behavior-modeling training program, a pretest/posttest comparison group design is necessary. Trainees should be randomly assigned to training and no-training conditions. These evaluation design features give the manager a high degree of confidence that any communication skill change is the result of participating in the training program.[122] This type of evaluation design is also necessary if the manager wants to compare the effectiveness of two training programs.

Consider the evaluation design that Mayo Clinic used to compare two methods for training new managers.[123] The Mayo Clinic, located in Rochester, Minnesota, is one of the world's leading centers of medical education and research. Recently, Mayo has undergone considerable growth, adding a new hospital and clinic in the Phoenix area. As a result, employees who were not fully prepared were moved into management positions. This resulted in increased employee dissatisfaction and employee turnover rates. After a needs assessment indicated that employees were leaving because of dissatisfaction with management, Mayo decided to initiate a new training program designed to help the new managers improve their skills. There was some debate whether the training would be best administered one-on-one with a coach or in a classroom. Because of the higher cost of using coaching instead of classroom training, Mayo decided to conduct an evaluation using a posttest comparison group design. Before training all managers, Mayo held three training sessions. No more than 75 managers were included in each session. Within each session managers were divided into three groups: a group that received four days of classroom training, a group that received one-on-one training from a coach, and a group that received no training (a comparison group). Mayo collected reaction (did the trainees like the program?), learning, transfer, and results outcomes. The evaluation found no statistically significant differences in the effects of the coaching compared to classroom training. As a result, Mayo decided to rely on classroom courses for new managers and consider coaching only for managers with critical and immediate job issues.

Cost–Benefit Analysis
The process of determining the economic benefits of a training program using accounting methods.

Determining Return on Investment

Cost–benefit analysis is the process of determining the economic benefits of a training program using accounting methods, which involves determining training costs and benefits. Training cost information is important for several reasons:

1. To understand total expenditures for training, including direct and indirect costs.
2. To compare the costs of alternative training programs.
3. To evaluate the proportion of money spent on training development, administration, and evaluation, as well as to compare moneys spent on training for different groups of employees (such as exempt versus nonexempt).
4. To control costs.[124]

Determining Costs. As we discussed earlier, training costs include direct and indirect costs.[125] One method for comparing costs of alternative training programs is the resource requirements model.[126] This model compares equipment, facilities, personnel, and materials costs across different stages of the training process (training design, implementation, needs assessment, development, and evaluation). The resource requirements model can help determine overall differences in costs between training programs. Also, costs incurred at different stages of the training process can be compared across programs.

Determining Benefits. To identify the potential benefits of training, the company must review the original reasons for the training. For example, training may have been conducted to reduce production costs or overtime costs or to increase repeat business. A number of methods may help identify the benefits of training:

1. Technical, academic, and practitioner literature summarizes the benefits that have been shown to relate to a specific training program.
2. Pilot training programs assess the benefits for a small group of trainees before a company commits more resources.
3. Observing successful job performers can help a company determine what they do differently than unsuccessful job performers.[127]
4. Trainees and their managers can provide estimates of training benefits.

Making the Analysis. To calculate return on investment, follow these steps:

1. Identify outcomes (e.g., quality, accidents).
2. Place a value on the outcomes.
3. Determine the change in performance after eliminating other potential influences on training results.
4. Obtain an annual amount of benefits (operational results) from training by comparing results after training to results before training (in dollars).
5. Determine the training costs (direct costs + indirect costs + development costs + overhead costs + compensation for trainees).
6. Calculate the total savings by subtracting the training costs from benefits (operational results).
7. Calculate the ROI by dividing benefits (operational results) by costs. The ROI gives an estimate of the dollar return expected from each dollar invested in training.

Recall our discussion earlier in the chapter on the evaluation of the new manager training program at Mayo Clinic.[128] To determine Mayo's return on investment, the human resource department calculated that one-third of the 84 employees retained (29 employees) would have left Mayo as a result of dissatisfaction. The department believed their retention was due to the impact of the training. The department calculated that the cost of a single employee turnover was 75 percent of average total compensation, or $42,000 per employee at Mayo. Multiplying $42,000 by 29 employees retained equals a savings of $609,000. However, the cost of the training program needs to be considered. If the annual cost of the training program ($125,000) was subtracted from the savings, the new savings were $484,000. These numbers were based on estimates but even if the net savings figure were cut in half, the ROI is still over 100 percent. Being able to quantify the benefits delivered by the program has given the human resource department greater credibility at Mayo.

EVIDENCE-BASED HR

A training and development consultant at Apple Computer was concerned with the quality and consistency of the training program used in assembly operations. She wanted to show that training was not only effective but also resulted in financial benefits. To do this, the consultant chose an evaluation design that involved two separately trained groups—each consisting of 27 employees—and two untrained groups (comparison groups). The consultant collected a pretraining history of what was happening on the production line in each outcome she was measuring (productivity, quality, and labor efficiency). She determined the effectiveness of training by comparing performance between the comparison and training groups for two months after training. The consultant was able to show that the untrained comparison group had 2,000 more minutes of downtime than the trained group did. This finding meant that the trained employees built and shipped more products to customers—showing definitively that training was contributing to Apple's business objectives.

To conduct a cost–benefit analysis, the consultant had each employee in the training group estimate the effect of behavior change on a specific business measure (e.g., breaking down tasks will improve productivity or efficiency). The trainees assigned a confidence percentage to the estimates. To get a cost–benefit estimate for each group of trainees, the consultant multiplied the monthly cost–benefit by the confidence level and divided by the number of trainees. For example, one group of 20 trainees estimated a total overall monthly cost benefit of $336,000 related to business improvements and showed an average 70 percent confidence level with that estimate. Seventy percent multiplied by $336,000 gave a cost benefit of $235,200. This number was divided by 20 ($235,200/20 trainees) to give an average estimated cost benefit for the 20 trainees ($11,760).

SOURCE: A. Purcell, "20/20 ROI," *Training and Development*, July 2000, pp. 28–33.

Special Training Issues

LO9
Design a cross-cultural
preparation program.

To meet the competitive challenges of sustainability, globalization, and technology discussed in Chapter 1, companies must successfully deal with several special training issues. The special training issues include preparing employees to work in different cultures abroad, managing workforce diversity, and socializing and orienting new employees.

Cross-Cultural Preparation

As we mentioned in Chapter 1, companies today are challenged to expand globally. Because of the increase in global operations, employees often work outside their country of origin or work with employees from other countries. An **expatriate** works in a country other than his or her country of origin. The most frequently selected location for expatriate assignments include the United States, China, United Kingdom, Singapore, Germany, and Japan.[129] Many U.S. companies are using international rotational assignments as a training tool. Microsoft has 14 divisions using international rotational programs. Companies are also increasing the movement of employees from one global location to another. These involve management or technical positions moving from one country, like India, to China or Vietnam. This type of relocation is less expensive than moving a U.S.-based manager (who would have to be paid wages comparable to what they would earn in the United States) to China. Unfortunately, only about 25 percent of companies make cultural training mandatory for international assignments.[130] This may be because of mistaken beliefs that employees who have already been on international assignments or traveled internationally will be able to adapt to a new culture.

Because of a growing pool of talented labor around the world, greater use of host-country nationals is occurring.[131] *Host-country nationals* are employees with citizenship in the country where a company is located. A key reason is that a host-country national can more easily understand the values and customs of the workforce than an expatriate can. Also, training and transporting U.S. employees and their families to a foreign assignment and housing them there tend to be more expensive than hiring a host-country national. We discuss international human resource management in detail in Chapter 15. Here the focus is on understanding how to prepare employees for expatriate assignments.

Cross-cultural preparation educates employees (expatriates) and their families who are to be sent to a foreign country. To successfully conduct business in the global marketplace, employees must understand the business practices and the cultural norms of different countries.

Steps in Cross-Cultural Preparation

To prepare employees for cross-cultural assignments, companies need to provide cross-cultural training. Most U.S. companies send employees overseas without any preparation. As a result, the number of employees who return home before completing their assignments is higher for U.S. companies than for European and Japanese companies.[132] U.S. companies lose more than $2 billion a year as a result of failed overseas assignments.

To succeed overseas, expatriates (employees on foreign assignments) need to be

1. Competent in their areas of expertise.
2. Able to communicate verbally and nonverbally in the host country.
3. Flexible, tolerant of ambiguity, and sensitive to cultural differences.
4. Motivated to succeed, able to enjoy the challenge of working in other countries, and willing to learn about the host country's culture, language, and customs.
5. Supported by their families.[133]

One reason for U.S. expatriates' high failure rate is that companies place more emphasis on developing employees' technical skills than on preparing them to work in other cultures. Research suggests that the comfort of an expatriate's spouse and family is the most important determinant of whether the employee will complete the assignment.[134] Studies have also found that personality characteristics are related to expatriates' desire to terminate the assignment and performance in the assignment.[135] Expatriates who were extroverted (outgoing), agreeable (cooperative and tolerant),

Expatriate
Employee sent by his or her company to manage operations in a different country.

Cross-Cultural Preparation
The process of educating employees (and their families) who are given an assignment in a foreign country.

and conscientious (dependable, achievement oriented) were more likely to want to stay on the assignment and perform well. This suggests that cross-cultural training may be effective only when expatriates' personalities predispose them to be successful in assignments in other cultures.

The key to a successful foreign assignment is a combination of training and career management for the employee and family. The "Competing through Globalization" box shows the importance of language and cultural training. Foreign assignments involve three phases: predeparture, on-site, and repatriation (preparing to return home). Training is necessary in all three phases.

Predeparture Phase

Before departure, employees need to receive language training and an orientation to the new country's culture and customs. It is critical that the family be included in orientation programs.[136] Expatriates and their families need information about housing, schools, recreation, shopping, and health care facilities in the areas where they will live. Expatriates also must discuss with their managers how the foreign assignment fits into their career plans and what types of positions they can expect upon return.

Cross-cultural training methods include presentational techniques, such as lectures that expatriates and their families attend on the customs and culture of the host country, immersion experiences, or actual experiences in the home country in culturally diverse communities.[137] Experiential exercises, such as miniculture experiences, allow expatriates to spend time with a family in the United States from the ethnic group of the host country. For example, an Indian trainer took 20 managers from Advanced Micro Devices on a two-week immersion trip during which the group traveled to New Delhi, Bangalore, and Mumbai, meeting with business persons and government officials.[138] The program required six months of planning, including providing the executives with information on foods to eat, potential security issues, how to interact in business meetings. For example, Indians prefer a relatively indirect way into business discussions, so the managers were advised to discuss current events and other subjects before talking business.

Research suggests that the degree of difference between the United States and the host country (cultural novelty), the amount of interaction with host country citizens and host nationals (interaction), and the familiarity with new job tasks and work environment (job novelty) all influence the "rigor" of the cross-cultural training method used.[139] Hands-on and group-building methods are most effective (and most needed) in assignments with a high level of cultural and job novelty that require a good deal of interpersonal interaction with host nationals.

On-Site Phase

On-site training involves continued orientation to the host country and its customs and cultures through formal programs or through a mentoring relationship. Expatriates and their families may be paired with an employee from the host country who helps them understand the new, unfamiliar work environment and community.[140] Companies are also using the Web to help employees on expatriate assignments get answers to questions.[141] Expatriates can use a Web site to get answers to questions such as How do I conduct a meeting here? or What religious philosophy might have influenced today's negotiation behavior? Knowledge management software allows employees to contribute, organize, and access knowledge specific to their expatriate assignment.

English is the common language at many multinational companies. But failing to speak the native language can cause employees to risk being misinterpreted or fail to understand informal conversations. Speaking and understanding the local language can help employees avoid misunderstandings and gain greater respect from business partners, subordinates, and customers. For example, a manager at ABB Ltd. oversees 7,000 employees in China and speaks basic Mandarin. Because Chinese employees are reluctant to say no to managers, conducting business is difficult. Because the manager isn't fluent in Chinese languages, he tries to read body language but often reaches the wrong conclusions.

At Intel, employees with a business need can take classes in Mandarin, Japanese, and Spanish at various offices throughout the United States, free of charge. The courses are not designed for expatriates destined for assignments abroad, but instead target employees who, through technology, are in direct contact with foreign clients or who work on cross-cultural teams within the company. With 78,000 employees in 294 offices in 48 countries, Intel has teams that are regularly made up of employees from different cultures working in different locations. The optional 12-week courses, taught at three levels by contracting companies, are designed to help minimize the culture gaps within these teams. The classes meet for two hours a week and cost the company approximately $300 per person. Employees are allowed to repeat courses.

Marcos Garciaacosta, a business alliance manager at Intel who is based in Arizona, has been taking Japanese classes since he joined the company seven years ago. He says that the "ease and flexibility of on-site classes" keep him motivated to continue to learn. And while he says he is far from fluent, he is now at a proficiency level that enables him to better communicate with business contacts and customers in Japan.

The in-house strategy is not new. Company spokeswoman Tracy Koon says that Intel offered its first language programs in Japanese in the 1980s. But despite its 20-year history, the program is still relatively small. Since January 2002, Intel has spent only $54,000 to train 180 employees in these three languages, a tiny fraction of its workforce, and one that does not include expatriates, who are compensated for language training outside these company classes. Without making a huge investment in the concept, Intel is receiving some positive results. Kathy Powell, the foundational development manager for Intel University, the division of the company that manages training, says the demand for foreign-language courses is increasing. Intel plans to expand the language-training program to overseas offices and to train 300 more employees by the end of this year.

The language classes are part of a larger in-house cultural-training curriculum for Intel employees. The company also offers optional one-day classes with titles such as "Working with Russia" and "Doing Business with the Japanese," which are designed to give employees basic information that they need to build relationships and do business cross-culturally. Class size is about 15 students, and subjects include culture, history and an overview of various countries and their business practices. Classes about other cultures are also becoming more popular. During the past 27 months, Intel has spent more than $762,000 on the program and has trained 2,495 employees. It plans to offer the classes to 2,300 more employees by the end of this year, at a cost of about $450,000.

"Our business is very global, and there are a large number of people here working across cultures," Koon says. "By having these language and cultural tools at your disposal when you work with employees from different countries, you can understand the do's and don'ts of the cultures. You're not going to be an effective team if you are constantly offending the other members without knowing it."

SOURCES: Based on G. Weber, "Intel's Internal Approach," *Workforce Management* 83 (2004), p. 49; K. Kranhold, D. Bileklan, M. Karnitschnig, and G. Parker, "Lost in Translation," *The Wall Street Journal*, May 18, 2004, pp. B1 and B6.

A major reason that employees refuse expatriate assignments is that they can't afford to lose their spouse's income or are concerned that their spouse's career could be derailed by being out of the workforce for a few years.[142] Some "trailing" spouses decide to use the time to pursue educational activities that could contribute to their long-term career goals. But it is difficult to find these opportunities in an unfamiliar place. Pfizer, the pharmaceutical firm, is taking action to help trailing spouses. It provides a $10,000 allowance that the spouse can use in many different ways. A person at the expatriate location is assigned to help the spouse with professional development and locating educational or other resources. In countries where spouses are allowed to work, Pfizer tries to find them jobs within the company. Pfizer also provides cross-cultural counseling and language assistance. The company tries to connect the family with the expatriate community. Several multinational companies including Hewlett-Packard, Axalto, and Group Danon have partnered to develop partnerjob.com, an online employment resource that tries to get expatriate spouses jobs posted by other member companies.[143] However, work permit restrictions requiring potential employers to demonstrate that the spouse has skills that are not locally available remains a major restriction to spouse employment.

Repatriation Phase

Repatriation
The preparation of expatriates for return to the parent company and country from a foreign assignment.

Repatriation prepares expatriates for return to the parent company and country from the foreign assignment. Expatriates and their families are likely to experience high levels of stress and anxiety when they return because of the changes that have occurred since their departure. Employees should be encouraged to self-manage the repatriation process.[144] Before they go on the assignment they need to consider what skills they want to develop and the types of jobs that might be available in the company for an employee with those skills. Because the company changes and colleagues, peers, and managers may leave while the expatriate is on assignment, they need to maintain contact with key company and industry contacts. Otherwise, on return the employees' reentry shock will be heightened when they have to deal with new colleagues, a new job, and a company culture that may have changed. This includes providing expatriates with company newsletters and community newspapers and ensuring that they receive personal and work-related mail from the United States while they are on foreign assignment. It is also not uncommon for employees and their families to have to readjust to a lower standard of living in the United States than they had in the foreign country, where they may have enjoyed maid service, a limousine, private schools, and clubs. Salary and other compensation arrangements should be worked out well before employees return from overseas assignments.

Aside from reentry shock, many expatriates decide to leave the company because the assignments they are given upon returning to the United States have less responsibility, challenge, and status than their foreign assignments.[145] As noted earlier, career planning discussions need to be held before the employees leave the United States to ensure that they understand the positions they will be eligible for upon repatriation.

Royal Dutch Shell, a joint Dutch and United Kingdom oil and gas company, has one of the world's largest expatriate work forces. To avoid expatriates who feel undervalued and leave the company, Royal Dutch gets involved with expatriates and their career. Resource planners track workers abroad, helping to identify their next assignment. Most expatriates know their next assignment three to six months before the move, and all begin the next assignment with a clear job description. Expatriates who have the potential to reach top-level management positions are placed in the home office every third assignment to increase their visibility to company executives. Expatriates are also assigned technical mentors who evaluate their skills and help them improve their skills through training at Royal Dutch's training center.

Because of family issues, poor economic times, and security issues, many companies are using virtual expatriates, relying more on short-time assignments, frequent business travel, and international commutes in which an employee lives in one country and works in another.[146] *Virtual expatriates* have an assignment to manage an operation abroad without being located permanently in that country. The employees periodically travel to the overseas location, return, and later use video conferencing and communications technology to manage the operation.[147] Virtual expatriates eliminate exposing the family to the culture shock of an overseas move. This setup also allows the employee to manage globally while keeping in close touch with the home office. Virtual expatriates are less expensive than traditional expatriates, who can cost companies over three times as much as a host national employee. One major disadvantage of virtual expatriates is that visiting a foreign operation on a sporadic basis may lengthen the time needed to build a local management team, so it will take longer to solve problems because of the lack of a strong personal relationship with local employees. One of the potential difficulties of short-term international assignments is that employees may be perceived as foreigners rather than colleagues because they haven't had the time to build relationships and develop trust among co-workers in their short-term location. Another is that traveling can take a physical and emotional toll on employees as they try to juggle business responsibilities with maintaining contact with family and friends. Procter & Gamble helps employees on short-term assignments by providing a trip fund that is based on the length of time an employee is on an extended business trip. For example, a U.S.-based employee working in western Europe for six months would get a fund containing the cost of five business-class round-trips. The employee can use money from the fund to take trips home or to cover family visits to the employee's location.

Managing Workforce Diversity

Diversity can be considered any dimension that differentiates a person from another.[148] For example at Verizon diversity means embracing differences and variety including age, ethnicity, education, sexual orientation, work style, race, gender, and more.

LO10
Develop a program for effectively managing diversity.

The goals of diversity training are (1) to eliminate values, stereotypes, and managerial practices that inhibit employees' personal development and therefore (2) to allow employees to contribute to organizational goals regardless of their race, sexual orientation, gender, family status, religious orientation, or cultural background.[149] Because of Equal Opportunity Employment laws, companies have been forced to ensure that women and minorities are adequately represented in their labor force. That is, companies have focused on ensuring equal access to jobs. As was discussed in Chapter 1, the impact of culture on the workplace, and specifically on training and development, has received heightened attention. Cultural factors that companies need to consider include the terrorist attacks of 9/11; employees' fear of discussing cultural differences; more work being conducted in teams whose members have many different characteristics; the realization that people from diverse cultures represent an important customer market; and, especially for professional and technical jobs, the availability of highly trained employees that has many companies seeking workers from overseas. These new immigrants need diversity training to help them understand such facets of American culture as obsession with time, individualistic attitudes, and capitalistic ideas.[150]

Managing Diversity
The process of creating an environment that allows all employees to contribute to organizational goals and experience personal growth.

Managing diversity involves creating an environment that allows all employees to contribute to organizational goals and experience personal growth. This environment includes access to jobs as well as fair and positive treatment of all employees. The company must develop employees who are comfortable working with people from a wide variety of ethnic, racial, and religious backgrounds. Managing diversity may require changing the company culture. It includes the company's standards and norms about how employees are treated, competitiveness, results orientation, innovation, and risk taking. The value placed on diversity is grounded in the company culture.

Managing Diversity through Adherence to Legislation

One approach to managing diversity is through affirmative action policies and by making sure that human resource management practices meet standards of equal employment opportunity laws.[151] This approach rarely changes employees' values, stereotypes, and behaviors that inhibit productivity and personal development. Figure 7.8 shows the cycle of disillusionment resulting from managing diversity by relying solely on adherence to employment laws. The cycle begins when the company realizes that it must change policies regarding women and minorities because of legal pressure or a discrepancy between the number or percentage of women and minorities in the company's workforce and the number available in the broader labor market. To address these concerns, a greater number of women and minorities are hired by the company. Managers see little need for additional action because women and minority employment rates reflect their availability in the labor market. However, as women and minorities gain experience in the company, they may become frustrated. Managers and co-workers may avoid providing coaching or performance feedback to women and minorities because they are uncomfortable interacting with individuals from different gender, ethnic, or racial backgrounds. Co-workers may express beliefs that women and minorities are employed only because they received special treatment (hiring standards were lowered).[152] As a result of their frustration, women and minorities may form support groups to voice their concerns to management. Because of the work atmosphere, women and minorities may fail to fully utilize their skills and leave the company.

Managing Diversity through Diversity Training Programs

The preceding discussion is not to suggest that companies should be reluctant to engage in affirmative action or pursue equal opportunity employment practices. However, affirmative action without additional supporting strategies does not deal with issues of assimilating women and minorities into the workforce. To successfully manage a diverse workforce, companies need to ensure that

Diversity Training
Training designed to change employee attitudes about diversity and/or develop skills needed to work with a diverse workforce.

- Employees understand how their values and stereotypes influence their behavior toward others of different gender, ethnic, racial, or religious backgrounds.
- Employees gain an appreciation of cultural differences among themselves.
- Behaviors that isolate or intimidate minority group members improve.

This can be accomplished through diversity training programs. **Diversity training** refers to training designed to change employee attitudes about diversity and/or develop skills needed to work with a diverse workforce. Diversity training programs differ according to whether attitude or behavior change is emphasized.[153]

figure 7.8
Cycle of
Disillusionment
Resulting from
Managing Diversity
through Adherence
to Legislation

SOURCE: From Cresencio Torres and Mary Bruxelles, *HR Magazine*, 1992. Copyright © 1992 by the Society for Human Resource Management. Reprinted with the permission of *HR Magazine* published by the Society for Human Resource Management, Alexandria, VA, via the Copyright Clearance Center.

Attitude Awareness and Change Programs

Attitude awareness and change programs focus on increasing employees' awareness of differences in cultural and ethnic backgrounds, physical characteristics (such as disabilities), and personal characteristics that influence behavior toward others. The assumption underlying these programs is that, by increasing their awareness of stereotypes and beliefs, employees will be able to avoid negative stereotypes when interacting with employees of different backgrounds. The programs help employees consider the similarities and differences between cultural groups, examine their attitudes toward affirmative action, or analyze their beliefs about why minority employees are successful or unsuccessful in their jobs. Many of these programs use videotapes and experiential exercises to increase employees' awareness of the negative emotional and performance effects of stereotypes, values, and behaviors on minority group members. Sodexho serves millions of customers each day in the cafeterias it operates in companies and universities.[154] As a result it is important that Sodexho understand the needs

Attitude Awareness and Change Program Program focusing on increasing employees' awareness of differences in cultural and ethnic backgrounds, physical characteristics, and personal characteristics that influence behavior toward others.

of a diverse customer base. As one part of how it manages diversity, the company has mandatory classes that provide managers with an overview of equal opportunity and affirmative action laws. The classes relate to other initiatives, including courses on generational differences and body language that can be offensive. The courses involve group dialogues and scenarios. One game requires participants to wear labels such as "Hearing impaired" and interact with others based on that description.

The attitude awareness and change approach has been criticized for several reasons.[155] First, by focusing on group differences, the program may communicate that certain stereotypes and attitudes are valid. For example, in diversity training a male manager may learn that women employees prefer to work by building consensus rather than by arguing until others agree with their point. He might conclude that the training has validated his stereotype. As a result, he will continue to fail to give women important job responsibilities that involve heated negotiations with customers or clients. Second, encouraging employees to share their attitudes, feelings, and stereotypes toward certain groups may cause employees to feel guilty, angry, and less likely to see the similarities among racial, ethnic, or gender groups and the advantages of working together. Third, if diversity training only covers issues such as race, gender, ethnicity, or sexual orientation, some employees may feel that their interests are not represented in the program.[156] Diversity programs purchased off-the-shelf or developed without taking into account the company's history, culture, and needs are not likely to be successful.

Behavior-Based Programs

Behavior-Based Program
A program focusing on changing the organizational policies and individual behaviors that inhibit employees' personal growth and productivity.

Behavior-based programs focus on changing the organizational policies and individual behaviors that inhibit employees' personal growth and productivity. These programs can take three approaches.

One approach of these programs is to identify incidents that discourage employees from working up to their potential. Groups of employees are asked to identify specific promotion opportunities, sponsorship, training opportunities, or performance management practices that they believe were handled unfairly. Their views regarding how well the work environment and management practices value employee differences and provide equal opportunity may also be collected. Specific training programs may be developed to address the issues presented in the focus groups.

Another approach is to teach managers and employees basic rules of behavior in the workplace.[157] For example, managers and employees should learn that it is inappropriate to use statements and engage in behaviors that have negative racial, sexual, or cultural content. Companies that have focused on teaching rules and behavior have found that employees react less negatively to this type of training than to other diversity training approaches.

Cultural Immersion
A behavior-based diversity program that sends employees into communities where they interact with persons from different cultures, races, and nationalities.

A third approach is **cultural immersion:** sending employees directly into communities where they have to interact with persons from different cultures, races, and nationalities. The degree of interaction varies but may involve talking with community members, working in community organizations, or learning about religious, cultural, or historically significant events. For example, the United Parcel Service Community Internship Program is designed to help UPS senior managers understand the needs of diverse customers and a diverse workforce through exposure to poverty and inequality.[158] UPS is the world's largest package delivery company and a leading global provider of transportation and logistic services. Since 1968, more then 1,200 senior managers have completed the program, an internship that typically lasts four weeks.

The internships take the managers to cities throughout the United States, where they work on the problems facing local populations. UPS managers may find themselves serving meals to the homeless, working in AIDS centers, helping migrant farm workers, building temporary housing and schools, and managing children in a Head Start program. These experiences take the managers outside their comfort zones, and the problems that they encounter—from transportation to housing to education to health care—help them better understand the issues that many UPS employees face daily. This enlightenment is a business necessity for UPS because three out of four managers are white whereas 35 percent of the employees are minorities. UPS has not formally evaluated the program, but the company continues to invest $10,000 per intern. The company has invested a total of more than $13.5 billion in the program since its start in 1968. Despite the lack of hard evaluation data, UPS managers report that the program helps them look for unconventional solutions to problems. One manager who spent a month working at a halfway house in New York was impressed by the creative ideas of uneducated addicts for keeping teens away from drugs. The manager realized that she had failed to capitalize on the creativity of the employees she supervised. As a result, when she returned to her job and faced problems, she started brainstorming with her entire staff, not just senior managers. Other managers report that the experience helped them empathize with employees facing crises at home.

Characteristics of Successful Diversity Efforts

Is a behavior-based or an attitude awareness and change program most effective? Increasing evidence shows that attitude awareness programs are ineffective and that one-time diversity training programs are unlikely to succeed. For example, R. R. Donnelley & Sons suspended its diversity awareness training program even though the company spent more than $3 million on it as a result of a racial discrimination lawsuit.[159]

At various training sessions participants were encouraged to voice their concerns. Many said that they were experiencing difficulty in working effectively due to abuse and harassment. The managers attending the training disputed the concerns. Also, after training, an employee who applied for an open position was rejected, because, she was told, she had been too honest in expressing her concerns during the diversity training session. Although R. R. Donnelley held many diversity training sessions, little progress was made in increasing the employment and promotion rates of women and minorities. Because of the low ratio of black employees to white employees, many black employees were asked to attend multiple training sessions to ensure diverse groups, which they resented. The company declined to release data requested by shareholders that it provided to the Equal Employment Opportunity Commission regarding female and minority representation in jobs throughout the company. The firm also failed to act on recommendations made by company-approved employee "diversity councils."

More generally, a survey of diversity training efforts found that[160]

- The most common area addressed through diversity efforts is the pervasiveness of stereotypes, assumptions, and biases.
- Fewer than one-third of companies do any kind of long-term evaluation or follow-up. The most common indicators of success were reduced grievances and lawsuits, increased diversity in promotions and hiring, increased self-awareness of biases, and increased consultation of HRM specialists on diversity-related issues.

- Most programs lasted only one day or less.
- Three-fourths of the survey respondents indicated that they believed the typical employee leaves diversity training with positive attitudes toward diversity. However, more than 50 percent reported that the programs have no effect over the long term.
- Twenty-nine percent of survey respondents reported that no tools were provided to reinforce diversity training, and 22 percent reported that no development or advancement issues were addressed.

Little research addresses the impact of diversity or diversity-management practices on financial success. Diversity may enhance performance when organizations have an environment that promotes learning from diversity. There is no evidence to support the direct relationship between diversity and business.[161] Rather, a company will see the success of its diversity efforts only if it makes a long-term commitment to managing diversity. Successful diversity requires that it be viewed as an opportunity for employees to (1) learn from each other how to better accomplish their work, (2) be provided with a supportive and cooperative organizational culture, and (3) be taught leadership and process skills that can facilitate effective team functioning. Diversity is a reality in labor and customer markets and is a social expectation and value. Managers should focus on building an organizational environment, on human resource practices, and on managerial and team skills that all capitalize on diversity. As you will see in the discussion that follows, managing diversity requires difficult cultural change, not just slogans on the wall!

Table 7.11 shows the characteristics associated with the long-term success of diversity programs. It is critical that a diversity program be tied to business objectives. For example, cultural differences affect the type of skin cream consumers believe they need or the fragrance they may be attracted to. Understanding cultural differences is part of understanding the consumer (which is critical to the success of companies such as Avon). Top management support can be demonstrated by creating a structure to support the initiative.

Pepsi's president believes that the full potential of diversity cannot be realized without employees being "comfortable being uncomfortable" so they are willing to share difficult issues in the workplace.[162] As a result, members of the senior management team were named sponsors for specific employee groups including African Americans, Latinos, Asians, women, women of color, white males, disabled, and gay, lesbian, and transgendered. The managers are expected to understand their group members' needs, identify talent, and mentor at least three employees in their group. Also, they are expected to provide updates to the president on their progress.

Consider Sodexo's diversity effort.[163] Sodexo is the leading food and facilities management company in the United States, Canada, and Mexico, daily serving 10 million customers. Diversity is seen as important for the company to meet business growth targets. As a result, diversity and inclusion are core elements of the business strategy. The objectives of the company's efforts to manage diversity are related to the business, employees, shareholders, and the community. For example, some of the objectives include understanding and living the business case for diversity and inclusion; increasing awareness of how diversity relates to business challenges; creating and fostering a diverse work environment by developing management practices that drive hiring, promotion, and retention of talent; engaging in relationship management and customer service to attract and retain diverse clients and customers; and partnering with women and minority businesses to deliver food and facility management services.

- Top management provides resources, personally intervenes, and publicly advocates diversity.
- The program is structured.
- Capitalizing on a diverse workforce is defined as a business objective.
- Capitalizing on a diverse workforce is seen as necessary to generate revenue and profits.
- The program is evaluated using metrics such as sales, retention, and promotion rates.
- Manager involvement is mandatory.
- The program is seen as a culture change, not a one-shot program.
- Managers and demographic groups are not blamed for problems.
- Behaviors and skills needed to successfully interact with others are taught.
- Managers are rewarded on progress toward meeting diversity goals.
- Management collects employee feedback and responds to it.
- Create a safe and open culture that all employees want to belong to, in which employees can discover and appreciate differences and where the benefits of diversity are recognized by all employees.

table 7.11

Characteristics Associated with Diversity Programs' Long-Term Success

SOURCES: M. Jayne and R. Dipboye, "Leveraging Diversity to Improve Business Performance: Research Findings and Recommendations for Organizations," *Human Resource Management* 43 (2004); pp. 409–24; S. Rynes and B. Rosen, "What Makes Diversity Programs Work?" *HR Magazine*, October 1994, pp. 67–73; S. Rynes and B. Rosen, "A Field Survey of Factors Affecting the Adoption and Perceived Success of Diversity Training," *Personnel Psychology* 48 (1995), pp. 247–70; J. Gordon, "Different from What? Diversity as a Performance Issue," *Training*, May 1995, pp. 25–33; Corporate Leadership Council, *The Evolution of Corporate Diversity* (Washington, DC: Corporate Executive Board, 2002); R. Anand and M. Winters, "A Retrospective View of Corporate Diversity Training from 1964 to the Present," *Academy of Management Learning & Education* 7 (2008), pp. 356–72; C. Chavez and J. Weisinger, "Beyond Diversity Training: A Social Infusion for Cultural Inclusion," *Human Resource Management* 47 (2008), pp. 331–50.

Sodexo separates Equal Employment Opportunity (EEO) and legal compliance training from diversity education. Every three years, employees are required to take EEO and affirmative action refresher courses. Top management is also involved in and committed to managing diversity. The senior executives program includes ongoing classroom training that is reinforced with community involvement, sponsoring employee groups, and mentoring diverse employees. Executives are engaged in learning the business case for diversity and are personally held accountable for the company's diversity agenda. Every manager takes an eight-hour introductory class (Spirit of Diversity). Other learning opportunities are available, including three- to four-hour learning labs that include topics such as cross-cultural communications, sexual orientation in the workplace, generations in the workplace, and gender in the workplace. The company's learning and development team develops customized learning solutions for different functions and work teams. For example, a course related to selling to a diverse client base was developed and offered to the sales force, and a cross-cultural communications program was provided for recruiters.

In addition to diversity training activities, Sodexo has six employee network groups—such as the African American Leadership Forum and People Respecting Individuality, Diversity, and Equality—that provide a forum for employee's professional development and sharing input and ideas to support the company's diversity efforts. Sodexo's "Champions of Diversity" program rewards and recognizes employees who advance diversity and inclusion.

table 7.12

Key Components of Effective Managing Diversity Programs

Top Management Support
- Make the business case for diversity.
- Include diversity as part of the business strategy and corporate goals.
- Participate in diversity programs, and encourage all managers to attend.
- Ensure that the composition of the executive management team mirrors the diversity of the workforce.

Recruitment and Hiring
- Ask search firms to identify wider arrays of candidates.
- Enhance the interviewing, selection, and hiring skills of managers.
- Expand college recruitment at historically minority colleges.

Identifying and Developing Talent
- Form a partnership with internship programs that target minority students for management careers.
- Establish a mentoring process.
- Refine the company's global succession planning system to improve identification of talent.
- Improve the selection and development of managers and leaders to help ensure that they are capable of maximizing team performance.
- Ensure that all employees, especially women and minorities, have access to management development and leadership programs.

Employee Support
- Form resource groups or employee network groups, including employees with common interests, and use them to help the company develop business goals and understand the issues they are concerned with (e.g., Asian Pacific employees, women, gays, lesbians, transgenders, Native Americans, veterans, Hispanics).
- Celebrate cultural traditions, festivities, and holidays.
- Make work/life balance initiatives (such as flextime, telecommuting, eldercare) available to all employees.

Ensuring Fair Treatment
- Conduct extensive diversity training.
- Implement an alternative dispute resolution process.
- Include women and minorities on all human resources committees throughout the company.

Holding Managers Accountable
- Link managers' compensation to their success in meeting diversity goals and creating openness and inclusion in the workplace.
- Use employee attitude or engagement surveys to track employees' attitudes such as inclusion, fairness, opportunities for development, work/life balance, and perceptions of the company culture.
- Implement 360-degree feedback for all managers and supervisors.

Improving Relationships with External Stakeholders
- Increase marketing to diverse communities.
- Provide customer service in different languages.
- Broaden the company's base of suppliers and vendors to include businesses owned by minorities and women.
- Provide scholarships and educational and neighborhood grants to diverse communities and their members.

SOURCES: Based on R. Anand and M. Winters, "A Retrospective View of Corporate Diversity Training from 1964 to the Present," *Academy of Management Learning & Education* 7 (2008), pp. 356–72; C. Chavez and J. Weisinger, "Beyond Diversity Training: A Social Infusion for Cultural Inclusion," *Human Resource Management* 47 (2008), pp. 331–50; V. Smith, "Texaco Outlines Comprehensive Initiatives," *Human Resource Executive*, February 1997, p. 13; Verizon's diversity program available at the company Web site, www.verizon.com.

To emphasize the importance of diversity for the company, at Sodexo each manager has a diversity scorecard that evaluates their success in recruitment, retention, promotion, and development of all employees. The scorecard includes both quantitative goals as well as evaluation of behaviors such as participating in training, mentoring, and doing community outreach. A proportion of their pay bonuses is determined by success in these areas.

Sodexo has found that its diversity training and efforts to manage diversity are having a positive impact on business results. Its mentoring program has led to increased productivity, engagement, and retention of women and people of color. There was an estimated return on investment of $19 for every dollar spent on the program. Sodexo also has been awarded several new business contracts and retained clients because of its involvement in managing diversity. Most effective programs to manage diversity, such as Sodexo's diversity program, include the key components shown in Table 7.12.

Other companies, such as Denny's (in response to a lawsuit) and Weyerhaeuser (in response to a retiring workforce survey and survey results suggesting the need for a more accepting workplace) have established diversity programs with the same features as Texaco's program (recruitment and hiring, identifying and developing talent, etc.).[164] As should be apparent from this discussion, successful diversity programs involve more than just an effective training program. They require an ongoing process of culture change that includes top management support as well as diversity policies and practices in the areas of recruitment and hiring, training and development, and administrative structures, such as conducting diversity surveys and evaluating managers' progress on diversity goals.[165]

Socialization and Orientation

Organizational socialization is the process by which new employees are transformed into effective members of the company. As Table 7.13 shows, effective socialization involves being prepared to perform the job effectively, learning about the organization, and establishing work relationships. Socialization involves three phases: antici-

Organizational Socialization
The process used to transform new employees into effective company members.

table 7.13

What Employees Should Learn and Develop through the Socialization Process

History	The company's traditions, customs, and myths; background of members
Company goals	Rules, values, or principles directing the company
Language	Slang and jargon unique to the company; professional technical language
Politics	How to gain information regarding the formal and informal work relationships and power structures in the company
People	Successful and satisfying work relationships with other employees
Performance proficiency	What needs to be learned; effectiveness in using and acquiring the knowledge, skills, and abilities needed for the job.

SOURCE: Based on G. T. Chao, A. M. O'Leary-Kelly, S. Wolf, H. Klein, and P. D. Gardner, "Organizational Socialization: Its Content and Consequences," *Journal of Applied Psychology* 79 (1994), pp. 730–43.

figure 7.9

Phases of Socialization and Necessary Company Actions

Anticipatory Socialization
• Provide a realistic job preview as well as accurate information about the positive and negative aspects of the job, including working conditions, company, and location.

Encounter
• Provide training, challenging work, and orientation, thus reducing shock and surprise. Manager can help new employees understand their roles, provide information about the company, and empathize with stress of new job.

Settling In
• Provide performance evaluation and information on career opportunities.

SOURCES: Based on D. T. Hall, *Careers In and Out of Organizations* (Thousand Oaks, CA: Sage Publications, 2002); J. D. Kammeyer-Mueller and C. R. Wanberg, "Unwrapping the Organizational Entry Process: Disentangling Multiple Antecedents and Their Pathway to Adjustment," *Journal of Applied Psychology* 88 (2003), pp. 779–94; G. M. McEnvoy and W. F. Cascio, "Strategies for Reducing Employee Turnover: A Meta-analysis," *Journal of Applied Psychology* 70 (1985), pp. 342–53; M. R. Louis, "Surprise and Sensemaking: What Newcomers Experience in Entering Unfamiliar Organizational Settings," *Administrative Science Quarterly* 25 (1980), pp. 226–51; R. F. Morrison and T. M. Brantner, "What Enhances or Inhibits Learning a New Job? A Basic Career Issue," *Journal of Applied Psychology* 77 (1992), pp. 926–40; D. A. Major, S. W. J. Kozlowski, G. T. Chao, and P. D. Gardner, "A Longitudinal Investigation of Newcomer Expectations, Early Socialization Outcomes, and the Moderating Effect of Role Development Factors," *Journal of Applied Psychology* 80 (1995), pp. 418–31.

Anticipatory Socialization
Process that helps individuals develop expectations about the company, job, working conditions, and interpersonal relationships.

Encounter Phase
Phase of socialization that occurs when an employee begins a new job.

patory socialization, encounter, and settling in.[166] Figure 7.9 shows the three phases and the actions that should be taken to help employees at each phase.

Anticipatory socialization occurs before the individual joins the company. Through **anticipatory socialization,** expectations about the company, job, working conditions, and interpersonal relationships are developed through interactions with representatives of the company (recruiters, prospective peers, and managers) during recruitment and selection. The expectations are also based on prior work experiences in similar jobs. The **encounter phase** occurs when the employee begins a new job. No matter how realistic the information provided during interviews and site visits, individuals beginning new jobs will experience shock and surprise.[167] In the **settling-in phase,** employees begin to feel comfortable with their job demands and social relationships. They begin to resolve work conflicts (like too much work or conflicting job demands) and conflicts between work and nonwork activities. Employees are interested in the company's evaluation of their performance and in learning about potential career opportunities within the company.

Employees need to complete all three socialization phases to fully contribute to the company. For example, employees who do not feel that they have established good working relationships with co-workers will likely spend time and energy worrying about those relationships rather than being concerned with product development or customer service. Employees who experience successful socialization are more motivated, more committed to the company, and more satisfied with their jobs.[168]

Settling-in Phase
Phase of socialization that occurs when employees are comfortable with job demands and social relationships.

Socialization, Orientation, and Onboarding Programs

Socialization and orientation programs play an important role in socializing employees. Orientation involves familiarizing new employees with company rules, policies, and procedures. Typically, a program includes information about the company, department in which the employees will be working, and the community they will live in. Onboarding refers to the orientation process for newly hired managers.

Although the content of orientation programs is important, the process of orientation cannot be ignored. Too often, orientation programs consist of completing payroll forms and reviewing personnel policies with managers or human resource representatives. Although these are important activities, the new employee has little opportunity to ask questions, interact with peers and managers, or become familiar with the company's culture, products, and service.

Effective orientation programs actively involve the new employee. Table 7.14 shows the characteristics of effective orientation. An important characteristic of effective orientation is that peers, managers, and senior co-workers are actively involved in helping new employees adjust to the work group.[169]

Several companies offer programs that include the characteristics shown in Table 7.14.[170] For example, through its "52 weeks" program, Qualcomm uses e-mail to distribute 52 short stories, written to share the company's history, factors that make it successful, and future business directions. Each new employee receives one story per week throughout his or her first year. Each story relates company history and demonstrates how the corporate culture was formed. The stories cover the first employee meeting in the company parking lot and the development of the chip division. The stories help employees understand that innovation, doing whatever it takes, and camaraderie are Qualcomm values.

Clarkston Consulting, a management and technology consulting company with approximately 300 employees, has an orientation program that includes learning about the company after accepting a job offer as well as during the first days on the job.[171] An onboarding team consisting of trainers, recruiters, human resource representatives, and current employees maintain contact with each new employee using a Wiki. The

Employees are encouraged to ask questions.
Program includes information on both technical and social aspects of the job.
Orientation is the responsibility of the new employee's manager.
Debasing or embarrassing new employees is avoided.
Formal and informal interactions with managers and peers occur.
Programs involve relocation assistance (such as house hunting or information sessions on the community for employees and their spouses).
Employees learn about the company's products, services, and customers.

table 7.14

Characteristics of Effective Orientation Programs

Wiki provides information about the company culture, and a discussion blog is also accessible. Once they join the company, employees have eight weeks of instructor-led and e-learning training, a book assignment with a discussion, and individual and team assignments simulating actual projects with clients. Biweekly conference calls are arranged for new employees so they can share their knowledge and experiences.

Farmers Insurance shows how orientation can reduce turnover and contribute to the business. Farmer's 2,000 new field employees are involved in an immersion program that provides industry and job knowledge, group discussion and peer interaction, job shadowing, and peer mentoring, along with live, supervised interaction with customers. As a result of the program, new-hire turnover decreased 4 percent in one year, saving the company $1.96 million. Also, employees' quality consistency scores, measuring accuracy, efficiency, and service, improved from 87 to 92 percent on their 90-day evaluations.

Many companies are using technology to make orientation more interactive and reduce travel costs. For example, Arrow Electronics—an electronics component and computer products company with 11,000 employees in more than 200 locations in 53 countries—used to have a five-day orientation that introduced the industry and Arrow's culture, values, and history to new employees.[172] However, the program was not cost-effective because it was limited to the company's North American employees, which meant all new employees had to travel to one location to attend the program. Arrow now delivers the same content through an interactive computer game. New employees can view modules on industry basics, corporate history, and culture. Each module is followed by a quiz-show-based game to assess what employees learned, and they receive immediate feedback. The program is self-paced, can be accessed around the world, and can be completed in several different languages. The program has saved Arrow money. Total costs for game development were approximately 10 percent of what was spent on the classroom orientation. IBM uses Second Life for new hires to learn about corporate culture and business processes by having their avatars attend meetings, watch presentations, and interact with other avatars in a virtual IBM community.

Onboarding gives new managers an introduction to the work they will be supervising and an understanding of the culture and operations of the entire company. For example, at Pella Corporation, an Iowa-based manufacturer of windows and doors, new managers are sent on a tour of production plants, meeting and observing employees and department heads. These tours ensure that the managers will get a better sense of the market and how the company's products are designed, built, and distributed.[173] At The Limited, the Columbus, Ohio, retail clothing company, new vice presidents and regional directors spend their days talking to customers, reading company history, working the floor of retail stores, investigating the competition, and studying the company's current and past operations. They spend a month with no responsibilities for the tasks related to their new positions. Limited's philosophy is that managers are better able to perform their job by first taking time to understand the people, customers, company, and operations they will be working with.

A LOOK BACK

As the chapter opener highlighted, Wegmans Food Markets uses training to support the company's business strategy. Wegmans provides extensive training focused on service and product knowledge.

Questions

1. Suppose a manager asked you to determine whether training was supporting a company's business strategy. How would you conduct this type of analysis? What kind of information would you look for?
2. Is there a difference between a company supporting learning and a company supporting training? Explain.

 Please see the Video Case that corresponds to this chapter online at www.mhhe.com/noe7e.

SUMMARY

Technological innovations, new product markets, and a diverse workforce have increased the need for companies to reexamine how their training practices contribute to learning. In this chapter we discussed a systematic approach to training, including needs assessment, design of the learning environment, consideration of employee readiness for training, and transfer-of-training issues. We reviewed numerous training methods and stressed that the key to successful training was to choose a method that would best accomplish the objectives of training. We also emphasized how training can contribute to effectiveness through establishing a link with the company's strategic direction and demonstrating through cost–benefit analysis how training contributes to profitability. Managing diversity and cross-cultural preparation are two training issues that are relevant given company needs to capitalize on a diverse workforce and global markets.

KEY TERMS

Training, 273
High-leverage training, 273
Continuous learning, 273
Training design process, 275
Needs assessment, 276
Organizational analysis, 277
Person analysis, 277
Task analysis, 277
Strategic training and development initiatives, 278
Request for proposal (RFP), 280
Person characteristics, 281
Input, 281
Output, 281
Consequences, 281
Feedback, 281
Motivation to learn, 285
Self-efficacy, 286
Basic skills, 287
Cognitive ability, 287
Readability, 288
Communities of practice, 291
Transfer of training, 291

Climate for transfer, 292
Action plan, 293
Support network, 293
Opportunity to perform, 293
Electronic performance support system (EPSS), 294
Knowledge management, 294
Presentation methods, 296
Teleconferencing, 296
Webcasting, 297
Hands-on methods, 300
On-the-job training (OJT), 300
Self-directed learning, 301
Apprenticeship, 302
Simulation, 303
Avatar, 304
Virtual reality, 304
E-learning, 307
Repurposing, 309
Learner control, 309
Learning management system (LMS), 309
Group- or team-building methods, 311

Adventure learning, 312
Cross-training, 313
Coordination training, 313
Team leader training, 313
Action learning, 313
Six Sigma training, 314
Training outcomes, 315
Cost–benefit analysis, 318
Expatriate, 320
Cross-cultural preparation, 321
Repatriation, 324
Managing diversity, 326
Diversity training, 326
Attitude awareness and change program, 327
Behavior-based program, 328
Cultural immersion, 328
Organizational socialization, 333
Anticipatory socialization, 334
Encounter phase, 334
Settling-in phase, 335

● DISCUSSION QUESTIONS

1. Noetron, a retail electronics store, recently invested a large amount of money to train sales staff to improve customer service. The skills emphasized in the program include how to greet customers, determine their needs, and demonstrate product convenience. The company wants to know whether the program is effective. What outcomes should it collect? What type of evaluation design should it use?

2. "Melinda," bellowed Toran, "I've got a problem and you've got to solve it. I can't get people in this plant to work together as a team. As if I don't have enough trouble with the competition and delinquent accounts, now I have to put up with running a zoo. It's your responsibility to see that the staff gets along with each other. I want a human relations training proposal on my desk by Monday." How would you determine the need for human relations training? How would you determine whether you actually had a training problem? What else could be responsible?

3. Assume you are general manager of a small seafood company. Most training is unstructured and occurs on the job. Currently, senior fish cleaners are responsible for teaching new employees how to perform the job. Your company has been profitable, but recently wholesale fish dealers that buy your product have been complaining about the poor quality of your fresh fish. For example, some fillets have not had all the scales removed and abdomen parts remain attached to the fillets. You have decided to change the on-the-job training received by the fish cleaners. How will you modify the training to improve the quality of the product delivered to the wholesalers?

4. A training needs analysis indicates that managers' productivity is inhibited because they are reluctant to delegate tasks to their subordinates. Suppose you had to decide between using adventure learning and interactive video for your training program. What are the strengths and weaknesses of each technique? Which would you choose? Why? What factors would influence your decision?

5. To improve product quality, a company is introducing a computer-assisted manufacturing process into one of its assembly plants. The new technology is likely to substantially modify jobs. Employees will also be required to learn statistical process control techniques. The new technology and push for quality will require employees to attend numerous training sessions. More than 50 percent of the employees who will be affected by the new technology completed their formal education more than 10 years ago. Only about 5 percent of the company's employees have used the tuition reimbursement benefit. How should management maximize employees' readiness for training?

6. A training course was offered for maintenance employees in which trainees were supposed to learn how to repair and operate a new, complex electronics system. On the job, maintenance employees were typically told about a symptom experienced by the machine operator and were asked to locate the trouble. During training, the trainer would pose various problems for the maintenance employees to solve. He would point out a component on an electrical diagram and ask, "What would happen if this component was faulty?" Trainees would then trace the circuitry on a blueprint to uncover the symptoms that would appear as a result of the problem. You are receiving complaints about poor troubleshooting from maintenance supervisors of employees who have completed the program. The trainees are highly motivated and have the necessary prerequisites. What is the problem with the training course? What recommendations do you have for fixing this course?

7. What factors contribute to the effectiveness of Web training programs?

8. Choose a job you are familiar with. Design a new employee orientation program for that job. Explain how your program contributes to effective socialization.

9. Why might employees prefer blended learning to training using iPods?

10. What learning condition do you think is most necessary for learning to occur? Which is least critical? Why?

● SELF-ASSESSMENT EXERCISE:

In the chapter we discussed the need for learners to be motivated so that training will be effective. What is your motivation to learn? Find out by answering the following questions. Read each statement and indicate how much you agree with it, using the following scale:

5 = Strongly Agree
4 = Somewhat Agree
3 = Neutral
2 = Somewhat Disagree
1 = Strongly Disagree

1. I try to learn as much as I can from the courses I take.	5	4	3	2	1
2. I believe I tend to learn more from my courses than other students do.	5	4	3	2	1
3. When I'm involved in courses and can't understand something, I get so frustrated I stop trying to learn.	5	4	3	2	1

EXERCISING STRATEGY

Zappos Knows How to Kick It

Zappos, based in Las Vegas, is an online retailer with the initial goal of trying to be the best Web site for buying shoes by offering a wide variety of brands, styles, colors, sizes, and widths. The zappos.com brand has grown to offer shoes, handbags, eyewear, watches and accessories for online purchase. Zappos' vision is that in the future, online sales will account for 30 percent of all retail sales in the United States and that Zappos will be the company with the best service and selection. As a result, Zappos believes it can become the online service leader, drawing customers and expanding into selling other products. Zappos CEO Tony Heish has shaped the company's culture, brand, and business strategy around 10 core values:

- Deliver WOW through service.
- Embrace and drive change.
- Create fun and a little weirdness.
- Be adventurous, creative, and open-minded.
- Pursue growth and learning.
- Build open and honest relationships with communication.
- Build a positive team and family spirit.
- Do more with less.
- Be passionate and determined.
- Be humble.

For example, "Deliver WOW through service" means that call center employees need to provide excellent customer service. Call center employees encourage callers to order more than one size or color because shipping and return shipping is free. They are also encouraged to use their imaginations to meet customer needs.

Most employees at Zappos are hourly. All new hires complete four weeks of training, including two weeks working the phones. New recruits are offered $2,000 to leave the company during training to weed out individuals who will not be happy working at the company. Due to a downturn in sales, Zappos was forced to cut costs, including laying off 124 employees. Heish handled the downsizing in a positive way. Laid-off employees with less than two years of service were paid through the end of the year. Everyone received six months of paid health coverage. Zappos also allowed laid-off employees to keep their 40 percent employee discount through Christmas.

Questions

1. How can training help Zappos meet the competitive challenges it is facing?
2. Which of Zappos' 10 core values do you believe that training can influence the most compared to selection, work design, or compensation. The least? Why?

SOURCES: Zappos Web site, www.zappos.com; J. O'Brien, "Zappos Knows How to Kick It," *Fortune*, Februray 2, 2009, pp. 55–66.

MANAGING PEOPLE: FROM THE PAGES OF *BUSINESSWEEK*

BusinessWeek ### On-the-Job Video Gaming

Interactive training tools are captivating employees and saving companies money Laura Holshouser's favorite video games include *Halo, Tetris,* and an online training game developed by her employer. A training game? That's right. The 24-year-old graduate student, who manages a Cold Stone Creamery ice-cream store in Riverside, Calif., stumbled across the game on the corporate Web site in October.

It teaches portion control and customer service in a cartoon-like simulation of a Cold Stone store. Players scoop cones against the clock and try to avoid serving too much ice cream. The company says more than 8,000 employees, or about 30 percent of the total, voluntarily downloaded the game in the first week. "It's so much fun," says Holshouser. "I e-mailed it to everyone at work."

The military has used video games as a training tool since the 1980s. Now the practice is catching on with companies, too, ranging from Cold Stone to Cisco Systems Inc. to Canon Inc. Corporate trainers are betting that games' interactivity and fun will hook young, media-savvy employees like Holshouser and help them grasp and retain sales, technical, and management skills. "Video games teach resource management, collaboration, critical thinking, and tolerance for failure," says Ben Sawyer, who runs Digitalmill Inc., a game consultancy in Portland, Me.

The market for corporate training games is small but it's growing fast. Sawyer estimates that such games make up 15 percent of the "serious," or nonentertainment market, which also includes educational and medical training products. Over the next five years, Sawyer sees the serious-games market more than doubling, to $100 million, with trainers accounting for nearly a third of that. It's numbers like those that prompted Cyberlore Studios Inc., maker of *Playboy: The Mansion*, to refocus on training games—albeit based on its Playboy title. And training games will be top of mind at the Game Developers Conference in San Jose, Calif., this month.

Companies like video games because they are cost-effective. Why pay for someone to fly to a central training campus when you can just plunk them down in front of a computer? Even better, employees often play the games at home on their own time. Besides, by industry standards, training games are cheap to make. A typical military game costs up to $10 million, while sophisticated entertainment games can cost twice that. Since the corporate variety don't require dramatic, warlike explosions or complex 3D graphics, they cost a lot less. BreakAway Games Ltd., which designs simulation games for the military, is finishing its first corporate product, V-bank, to train bank auditors. Its budget? Just $500,000.

Drag and Drop

Games are especially well-suited to training technicians. In one used by Canon, repairmen must drag and drop parts into the right spot on a copier. As in the board game *Operation*, a light flashes and a buzzer sounds if the repairman gets it wrong. Workers who played the game showed a 5 percent to 8 percent improvement in their training scores compared with older training techniques such as manuals, says Chuck Reinders, who trains technical support staff at Canon. This spring, the company will unveil 11 new training games.

Games are also being developed to help teach customer service workers to be more empathetic. Cyberlore, now rechristened Minerva Software Inc., is developing a training tool for a retailer by rejiggering its *Playboy Mansion* game. In the original, guests had to persuade models to pose topless. The new game requires players to use the art of persuasion to sell products, and simulates a store, down to the carpet and point-of-purchase display details.

Don Field, director of certifications at Cisco, says games won't entirely replace traditional training methods such as videos and classes. But he says they should be part of the toolbox. Last year, Cisco rolled out six new training games—some of them designed to teach technicians how to build a computer network. It's hard to imagine a drier subject. Not so in the virtual world. In one Cisco game, players must put the network together on Mars. In a sandstorm. "Our employees learn without realizing they are learning," says Field. Sounds suspiciously like fun.

Questions

1. Considering the features of a good learning environment discussed in this chapter, how can video games enhance learning?
2. How can video games enhance transfer of training?
3. What features do you believe are essential for a video game to be used for training? Why?
4. What types of skills are best trained using video games? Why?

SOURCE: Reena Jana, "On-the-Job Video Gaming," *BusinessWeek*, March 27, 2006.

NOTES

1. R. Hughes and K. Beatty, "Five Steps to Leading Strategically," *Training and Development,* July 2001, pp. 32–38; I. I. Goldstein and P. Gilliam, "Training Systems Issues in the Year 2000," *American Psychologist* 45 (1990), pp. 134–43; E. Salas and J. A. Cannon-Bowers, "The Science of Training: A Decade of Progress," *Annual Review of Psychology* 52 (2002), pp. 471–99.
2. J. B. Quinn, P. Anderson, and S. Finkelstein, "Leveraging Intellect," *Academy of Management Executive* 10 (1996), pp. 7–27; R. Brinkenhoff and A. Apking, *High Impact Learning* (Cambridge, MA: Perseus, 2001).
3. T. T. Baldwin, C. Danielson, and W. Wiggenhorn, "The Evolution of Learning Strategies in Organizations: From Employee Development to Business Redefinition," *Academy of Management Executive* 11 (1997), pp. 47–58; J. J. Martocchio and T. T. Baldwin, "The Evolution of Strategic Organizational Training," in *Research in Personnel and Human Resource Management* 15, ed. G. R. Ferris (Greenwich, CT: JAI Press, 1997), pp. 1–46.
4. A. P. Carnevale, "America and the New Economy," *Training and Development Journal,* November 1990, pp. 31–52.
5. J. M. Rosow and R. Zager, *Training: The Competitive Edge* (San Francisco: Jossey-Bass, 1988).
6. L. Thornburg, "Accounting for Knowledge," *HR Magazine,* October 1994, pp. 51–56; T. A. Stewart, "Mapping Corporate Brainpower," *Fortune,* October 30, 1995, p. 209.
7. D. Miller, "A Preliminary Typology of Organizational Learning: Synthesizing the Literature," *Strategic Management Journal* 22 (1996), pp. 484–505; ed. S. Jackson, M. Hitt, and A. DeNisi, *Managing Knowledge for Sustained Competitive Advantage* (San Francisco: Jossey-Bass, 2003).
8. D. Delong and L. Fahey, "Diagnosing Cultural Barriers to Knowledge Management," *Academy of Management Executive* 14 (2000), pp. 113–27; A. Rossett, "Knowledge Management Meets Analysis," *Training and Development,* May 1999, pp. 71–78.

9. I. Nonaka and H. Takeuchi, *The Knowledge Creating Company* (New York: Oxford University Press, 1995).

10. L. Freifeld, "PWC Does It Again," *Training*, February 2009, pp. 24–28.

11. R. Noe, *Employee Training and Development*, 4th ed. (New York: Irwin/McGraw-Hill, 2008).

12. Ibid.

13. Based on Steelcase company Web site, www.steelcase.com; G. Wolfe, "Steelcase: Demonstrating the Connection between Learning and Strategic Business Results," *TD*, April 2005, pp. 28–34; T. Bingham and P. Galagan, "At c-Level: James P. Hackett, President and CEO, Steelcase," *TD*, April 2005, pp. 22–26.

14. J. B. Tracey, S. I. Tannenbaum, and M. J. Kavanaugh, "Applying Trained Skills on the Job: The Importance of the Work Environment," *Journal of Applied Psychology* 80 (1995), pp. 239–52; E. Holton, R. Bates, and W. Ruona, "Development of a Generalized Learning Transfer System Inventory," *Human Resource Development Quarterly* 11(2001), pp. 333–60; E. Helton III and T. Baldwin, eds., *Improving Learning Transfer in Organizations* (San Francisco: Jossey-Bass, 2003); J. S. Russell, J. R. Terborg, and M. L. Powers, "Organizational Performance and Organizational Level Training and Support," *Personnel Psychology* 38 (1985), pp. 849–63.

15. S. Tannenbaum, "A Strategic View of Organizational Training and Learning," in *Creating, Implementing, and Managing Effective Training and Development*, ed. K. Kraiger (San Francisco: Jossey-Bass, 2002), pp. 10–52.

16. A. P. Carnevale, L. J. Gainer, and J. Villet, *Training in America* (San Francisco: Jossey-Bass, 1990).

17. H. Dolezalek, "It's a Small World," *Training*, January 2008, pp. 22–26.

18. H. Dolezalek, "EMC's Competitive Advantage," *Training*, February 2009, pp. 42–46.

19. K. Linebaugh, "Idle Workers Busy at Toyota," *The Wall Street Journal*, October 13, 2008, pp. B1, B3.

20. B. Chapman, "How to Create the Ideal RFP," *Training*, January 2004, pp. 20–23; B. Gerber, "How to Buy Training Programs," *Training*, June 1989, pp. 59–68.

21. C. Reinhart, "How to Leap over Barriers to Performance," *Training and Development*, January 2000, pp. 20–29; G. Rummler, "In Search of the Holy Performance Grail," *Training and Development*, April 1996, pp. 26–31; D. G. Langdon, "Selecting Interventions," *Performance Improvement* 36 (1997), pp. 11–15.

22. R. F. Mager and P. Pipe, *Analyzing Performance Problems: Or You Really Oughta Wanna*, 2nd ed. (Belmont, CA: Pittman Learning, 1984); A. P. Carnevale, L. J. Gainer, and A. S. Meltzer, *Workplace Basics Training Manual*, 1990 (San Francisco: Jossey-Bass, 1990); Rummler, "In Search of the Holy Performance Grail."

23. C. E. Schneier, J. P. Guthrie, and J. D. Olian, "A Practical Approach to Conducting and Using Training Needs Assessment," *Public Personnel Management*, Summer 1988, pp. 191–205.

24. I. Goldstein, "Training in Organizations," in *Handbook of Industrial/Organizational Psychology*, 2nd ed., ed. M. D. Dunnette and L. M. Hough (Palo Alto, CA: Consulting Psychologists Press, 1991), vol. 2, pp. 507–619.

25. E. F. Holton III and C. Bailey, "Top-to-Bottom Curriculum Redesign," *Training and Development*, March 1995, pp. 40–44.

26. R. A. Noe, "Trainees' Attributes and Attitudes: Neglected Influences on Training Effectiveness," *Academy of Management Review* 11 (1986), pp. 736–49.

27. T. T. Baldwin, R. T. Magjuka, and B. T. Loher, "The Perils of Participation: Effects of Choice on Trainee Motivation and Learning," *Personnel Psychology* 44 (1991), pp. 51–66; S. I. Tannenbaum, J. E. Mathieu, E. Salas, and J. A. Cannon-Bowers, "Meeting Trainees' Expectations: The Influence of Training Fulfillment on the Development of Commitment, Self-Efficacy, and Motivation," *Journal of Applied Psychology* 76 (1991), pp. 759–69.

28. M. E. Gist, C. Schwoerer, and B. Rosen, "Effects of Alternative Training Methods on Self-Efficacy and Performance in Computer Software Training," *Journal of Applied Psychology* 74 (1989), pp. 884–91; J. Martocchio and J. Dulebohn, "Performance Feedback Effects in Training: The Role of Perceived Controllability," *Personnel Psychology* 47 (1994), pp. 357–73; J. Martocchio, "Ability Conceptions and Learning," *Journal of Applied Psychology* 79 (1994), pp. 819–25.

29. W. D. Hicks and R. J. Klimoski, "Entry into Training Programs and Its Effects on Training Outcomes: A Field Experiment," *Academy of Management Journal* 30 (1987), pp. 542–52.

30. R. A. Noe and N. Schmitt, "The Influence of Trainee Attitudes on Training Effectiveness: Test of a Model," *Personnel Psychology* 39 (1986), pp. 497–523.

31. M. A. Quinones, "Pretraining Context Effects: Training Assignments as Feedback," *Journal of Applied Psychology* 80 (1995), pp. 226–38; Baldwin, Magjuka, and Loher, "The Perils of Participation."

32. L. H. Peters, E. J. O'Connor, and J. R. Eulberg, "Situational Constraints: Sources, Consequences, and Future Considerations," in *Research in Personnel and Human Resource Management*, ed. K. M. Rowland and G. R. Ferris (Greenwich, CT: JAI Press, 1985), vol. 3, pp. 79–114; E. J. O'Connor, L. H. Peters, A. Pooyan, J. Weekley, B. Frank, and B. Erenkranz, "Situational Constraints Effects on Performance, Affective Reactions, and Turnover: A Field Replication and Extension," *Journal of Applied Psychology* 69 (1984), pp. 663–72; D. J. Cohen, "What Motivates Trainees?" *Training and Development Journal*, November 1990, pp. 91–93; Russell, Terborg, and Powers, "Organizational Performance."

33. J. Casner-Lotto and L. Barrington, "Are They Ready to Work?" in *United States: The Conference Board, Corporate Voices for Working Families, Partnerships for 21st Century Skills and Society for Human Resource Management, 2006*; R. Davenport, "Eliminate the Skills Gap," *TD*, February 2006, pp. 26–34; M. Schoeff, "Amid Calls to Bolster U.S. Innovation, Experts Lament Paucity of Basic Math Skills," *Workforce Management*, March 2006, pp. 46–49.

34. J. Nunally, *Psychometric Theory* (New York: McGraw-Hill, 1978).

35. L. Gottsfredson, "The g Factor in Employment," *Journal of Vocational Behavior* 19 (1986), pp. 293–96.

36. M. J. Ree and J. A. Earles, "Predicting Training Success: Not Much More Than g," *Personnel Psychology* 44 (1991), pp. 321–32.

37. D. R. Torrence and J. A. Torrence, "Training in the Face of Illiteracy," *Training and Development Journal*, August 1987, pp. 44–49.

38. C. E. Schneier, "Training and Development Programs: What Learning Theory and Research Have to Offer," *Personnel Journal*, April 1974, pp. 288–93; M. Knowles, "Adult Learning," in *Training and Development Handbook*, 3rd ed., ed. R. L. Craig (New York: McGraw-Hill, 1987), pp. 168–79; R. Zemke and S. Zemke, "30 Things We Know for Sure about Adult Learning," *Training*, June 1981, pp. 45–52; B. J. Smith and B. L. Delahaye, *How to Be an Effective Trainer*, 2nd ed. (New York: John Wiley and Sons, 1987).

39. Unisys Corporation Web site www.unisys.com; J. Salopek, "Unisys Corporation 2004 Best Award Winner," *TD*, October 2004, p. 3; J. Salopek, "Colorado Springs Utilities 2005 Best Award Winner," *TD*, October 2005, pp. 38–40; J. Salopek, "Toshiba America Business Solutions 2005 Best Award Winner," *TD*, October 2005, p. 67; J. Schettler, "Exelon Energy Delivery," *Training,* March 2003, p. 64; S. Caudron, "Learners Speak Out," *Training and Development,* April 2000, pp. 52–57, M. Weinstein, "Wake-up Call," *Training,* June 2007, pp. 48–50.

40. D. Stamps, "Communities of Practice," *Training,* February 1997, pp. 35–42.

41. D. Goldwasser, "Me, a Trainer," *Training,* April 2001, pp. 61–66.

42. T. Davenport, L. Prusak, and B. Strong, "Putting Ideas to Work," *The Wall Street Journal,* March 10, 2008, p. R11.

43. S. Allen, "Water Cooler Wisdom," *Training,* August 2005, pp. 30–34.

44. E. Holton III and T. Baldwin, eds, *Improving Learning Transfer in Organizations* (San Francisco: Jossey-Bass, 2003); J. B. Tracey, S. I. Tannenbaum, and M. J. Kavanaugh, "Applying Trained Skills on the Job: The Importance of the Work Environment," *Journal of Applied Psychology* 80 (1995), pp. 239–52; P. E. Tesluk, J. L. Farr, J. E. Mathieu, and R. J. Vance, "Generalization of Employee Involvement Training to the Job Setting: Individual and Situational Effects," *Personnel Psychology* 48 (1995), pp. 607–32; J. K. Ford, M. A. Quinones, D. J. Sego, and J. S. Sorra, "Factors Affecting the Opportunity to Perform Trained Tasks on the Job," *Personnel Psychology* 45 (1992), pp. 511–27.

45. D. Goldwasser, "Me, a Trainer."

46. H. Martin, "Lessons Learned," *The Wall Street Journal,* December 15, 2008, R11.

47. R. Smith, "Aligning Learning with Business Strategy," *T + D* November 2008, pp. 40–43.

48. J. M. Cusimano, "Managers as Facilitators," *Training and Development* 50 (1996), pp. 31–33.

49. C. M. Petrini, ed., "Bringing It Back to Work," *Training and Development Journal,* December 1990, pp. 15–21.

50. Ford, Quinones, Sego, and Sorra, "Factors Affecting the Opportunity to Perform Trained Tasks on the Job."

51. Ibid.; M. A. Quinones, J. K. Ford, D. J. Sego, and E. M. Smith, "The Effects of Individual and Transfer Environment Characteristics on the Opportunity to Perform Trained Tasks," *Training Research Journal* 1 (1995/96), pp. 29–48.

52. G. Stevens and E. Stevens, "The Truth about EPSS," *Training and Development* 50 (1996), pp. 59–61.

53. M. Weinstein, "Wake-up call."

54. S. E. Jackson, M. A. Hitt, and A. S. Denisi, eds., *Managing Knowledge for Sustained Competitive Advantage: Designing Strategies for Effective Human Resource Management* (San Francisco: Jossey-Bass, 2003); A. Rossett, "Knowledge Management Meets Analysis," *Training and Development,* May 1999, pp. 63–68; R. Davenport, "Why Does Knowledge Management Still Matter?" *T + D* 59 (2005), pp. 19–23.

55. J. MacGregor, "The Office Chart That Really Counts," *BusinessWeek,* February 27, 2006, pp. 48–49.

56. V. Powers, "Virtual Communities at Caterpillar Foster Knowledge Sharing," *TD,* June 2004, pp. 40–45.

57. R. D. Marx, "Relapse Prevention for Managerial Training: A Model for Maintenance of Behavior Change," *Academy of Management Review* 7 (1982), pp. 433–41; G. P. Latham and C. A. Frayne, "Self-Management Training for Increasing Job Attendance: A Follow-up and Replication," *Journal of Applied Psychology* 74 (1989), pp. 411–16.

58. P. Keller, "Soaring to New Safety Heights," *TD,* January 2006, pp. 51–54. Also see "About Us" on the Vanderbilt University Medical Center Web site at www.mc.vanderbilt.edu.

59. "Putting the Distance into Distance Learning," *Training,* October 1995, pp. 111–18.

60. D. Picard, "The Future Is Distance Training," *Training,* November 1996, pp. s3–s10.

61. A. F. Maydas, "On-line Networks Build the Savings into Employee Education," *HR Magazine,* October 1997, pp. 31–35.

62. J. M. Rosow and R. Zager, *Training: The Competitive Edge* (San Francisco: Jossey-Bass, 1988).

63. M. Weinstein, "Satellite Success," *Training,* January 2007, pp. 36–38.

64. S. Alexander, "Reducing the Learning Burden," *Training,* September 2002, pp. 32–34.

65. T. Skylar, "When Training Collides with a 35-Ton Truck," *Training,* March 1996, pp. 32–38.

66. R. B. Cohn, "How to Choose a Video Producer," *Training,* July 1996, pp. 58–61.

67. E. Wagner and P. Wilson, "Disconnected," *TD,* December 2005, pp. 40–43; J. Bronstein and A. Newman, "IM Learning, " *TD,* February 2006, pp. 47–50.

68. M. Weinstein, "Mobility Movement," *Training,* September 6, 2007, pp. 14–16.

69. M. Weinstein, "Ready or Not, Here Comes Podcasting," *Training,* January 2006, pp. 22–23; D. Sussman, "Now Here This," *TD,* September 2005, pp. 53–54; J. Pont, "Employee Training on iPod Playlist," *Workforce Management,* August 2005, p. 18; S. Boehle, "iPod Corporation," *Training,* September 6, 2007, pp. 17–19

70. E. Wagner and P. Wilson, "Disconnected," *TD,* December 2005, pp. 40–43.

71. B. Filipczak, "Who Owns Your OJT?" *Training,* December 1996, pp. 44–49.

72. "Reliance Industries Limited, Nagothane Manufacturing Division," *T + D,* October 2008, p. 78.

73. S. Boyer and B. Lambert, "Take the Handcuffs Off Sales Team Development with Self-Directed Learning," November 2008, pp. 62–66.

74. G. M. Piskurich, "Self-Directed Learning," in *The ASTD Training and Development Handbook,* 4th ed., pp. 453–72; G. M. Piskurich, "Developing Self-Directed Learning," *Training and Development,* March 1994, pp. 31–36.

75. P. Warr and D. Bunce, "Trainee Characteristics and the Outcomes of Open Learning," *Personnel Psychology* 48 (1995), pp. 347–75.

76. C. M. Solomon, "When Training Doesn't Translate," *Workforce* 76, no. 3 (1997), pp. 40–44.

77. R. W. Glover, *Apprenticeship Lessons from Abroad* (Columbus, OH: National Center for Research in Vocational Education, 1986).

78. Commerce Clearing House, Inc., *Orientation–Training* (Chicago, IL: Personnel Practices Communications, Commerce Clearing House, 1981), pp. 501–905.

79. A. H. Howard III, "Apprenticeships," in *The ASTD Training and Development Handbook,* pp. 803–13.

80. M. Rowh, "The Rise of the Apprentice," *Human Resource Executive,* January 2006, pp. 38–43.

81. A. Ciaccio, "You're Hired: Goldcorp Stint Touts Opportunities in Mining," *The Wall Street Journal,* September 25, 2005, p. B6.

82. *Eldredge v. Carpenters JATC* (1981), 27 Fair Employment Practices (Bureau of National Affairs), p. 479.

83. M. Weinstein, "Virtually Integrated," *Training*, April 2007, p. 10; A. Hira, "The Making of a UPS Driver," *Fortune*, November 12, 2007, pp. 118–29; P. Ketter, "What Can Training Do for Brown," *T + D*, May 2008, pp. 30–36.

84. C. Cornell, "Better than the Real Thing?" *Human Resource Executive*, August 2005, pp. 34–37.

85. J. Borzo, "Almost Human," *The Wall Street Journal*, May 24, 2004, pp. R1, R10; J. Hoff, "My Virtual Life," *BusinessWeek*, May 1, 2006, pp. 72–78.

86. N. Adams, "Lessons from the Virtual World," *Training*, June 1995, pp. 45–48.

87. Ibid.

88. H. Dolezalek, "Virtual Vision," *Training*, October 2007, pp. 40–46.

89. R. Flandez, "Small Business Link: Chip Maker Trains in the Virtual World," *The Wall Street Journal* (April 3, 2008), B6.

90. P. Galagan, "Second That," *T+D*, February 2008, pp. 34–37.

91. Cornell, "Better than the Real Thing?"; E. Frauenheim, "Can Video Games Win Points as Teaching Tools?" *Workforce Management*, April 10, 2006, pp. 12–14; S. Boehle, "Simulations: The Next Generation of e-Learning," *Training*, January 2005, pp. 22–31; Borzo, "Almost Human."

92. L. Freifeld, "Solid Sims," *Training*, October 2007, p. 48.

93. T. W. Shreeve, "On the Case at the CIA," *Training and Development*, March 1997, pp. 53–54.

94. P. Dvorak, "Theory & Practice: Simulation Shows What It Is Like to Be the Boss; Middle Managers at NetApp Receive Useful Taste of Reality," *The Wall Street Journal*, March 31, 2008, p. B7.

95. M. Hequet, "Games That Teach," *Training*, July 1995, pp. 53–58.

96. G. P. Latham and L. M. Saari, "Application of Social Learning Theory to Training Supervisors through Behavior Modeling," *Journal of Applied Psychology* 64 (1979), pp. 239–46.

97. E. Hollis, "Shoney's: Workforce Development on the Side," *Chief Learning Officer*, March 2003, pp. 32–34.

98. Hannum, *Application of Emerging Training Technology*.

99. M. Rosenberg, *E-Learning: Strategies for Delivering Knowledge in the Digital Age* (New York: McGraw-Hill, 2001).

100. P. Galagan, "The E-Learning Revolution," *Training and Development*, December 2000, pp. 24–30; D. Khirallah, "A New Way to Learn," *Information Week Online* (May 22, 2000).

101. S. Murphy, "Ritz Camera Focuses on Web-Based Teaching Tools," in "Techtalk Tuesday" at www.chainstoreage.com, December 23, 2008.

102. "Learning Management Systems: An Executive Summary," *Training*, March 2002, p. 4.

103. D. Sussman, "The LMS Value," *TD*, July 2005, pp. 43–45.

104. D. Brown and D. Harvey, *An Experiential Approach to Organizational Development* (Englewood Cliffs, NJ: Prentice Hall, 2000); J. Schettler, "Learning by Doing," *Training*, April 2002, pp. 38–43.

105. Schettler, "Learning by Doing."

106. R. J. Wagner, T. T. Baldwin, and C. C. Rowland, "Outdoor Training: Revolution or Fad?" *Training and Development Journal*, March 1991, pp. 51–57; C. J. Cantoni, "Learning the Ropes of Teamwork," *The Wall Street Journal*, October 2, 1995, p. A14.

107. C. Steinfeld, "Challenge Courses Can Build Strong Teams," *Training and Development*, April 1997, pp. 12–13.

108. D. Mishev, "Cooking for the Company," *Cooking Light*, August 2004, pp. 142–47.

109. P. F. Buller, J. R. Cragun, and G. M. McEvoy, "Getting the Most out of Outdoor Training," *Training and Development Journal*, March 1991, pp. 58–61.

110. C. Clements, R. J. Wagner, C. C. Roland, "The Ins and Outs of Experiential Training," *Training and Development*, February 1995, pp. 52–56.

111. Ibid.

112. S. Carey, "Racing to Improve," *The Wall Street Journal*, March 24, 2006, pp. B1, B6.

113. P. Froiland, "Action Learning," *Training*, January 1994, pp. 27–34.

114. "A Team Effort," *Training*, September 2002, p. 18.

115. H. Lancaster, "This Kind of Black Belt Can Help You Score Some Points at Work," *The Wall Street Journal*, September 14, 1999, p. B1; S. Gale, "Building Frameworks for Six Sigma Success," *Workforce*, May 2003, pp. 64–66.

116. J. DeFeo, "An ROI Story," *Training and Development*, July 2000, pp. 25–27.

117. S. Gale, "Six Sigma Is a Way of Life," *Workforce*, May 2003, pp. 67–68.

118. K. Kraiger, J. K. Ford, and E. Salas, "Application of Cognitive, Skill-Based, and Affective Theories of Learning Outcomes to New Methods of Training Evaluation," *Journal of Applied Psychology* 78 (1993), pp. 311–28; J. J. Phillips, "ROI: The Search for Best Practices," *Training and Development*, February 1996, pp. 42–47; D. L. Kirkpatrick, "Evaluation of Training," in *Training and Development Handbook,* 2nd ed., ed. R. L. Craig (New York: McGraw-Hill, 1976), pp. 18-1 to 18–27.

119. J. Gordon, "Eye on ROI," *Training*, May 2007, p. 43–45.

120. B. Gerber, "Does Your Training Make a Difference? Prove It!" *Training*, March 1995, pp. 27–34.

121. A. P. Carnevale and E. R. Schulz, "Return on Investment: Accounting for Training," *Training and Development Journal*, July 1990, pp. S1–S32; P. R. Sackett and E. J. Mullen, "Beyond Formal Experimental Design: Toward an Expanded View of the Training Evaluation Process," *Personnel Psychology* 46 (1993), pp. 613–27; S. I. Tannenbaum and S. B. Woods, "Determining a Strategy for Evaluating Training: Operating within Organizational Constraints," *Human Resource Planning* 15 (1992), pp. 63–81; R. D. Arvey, S. E. Maxwell, and E. Salas, "The Relative Power of Training Evaluation Designs under Different Cost Configurations," *Journal of Applied Psychology* 77 (1992), pp. 155–60.

122. D. A. Grove and C. O. Ostroff, "Program Evaluation," in *Developing Human Resources*, ed. K. N. Wexley (Washington, DC: BNA Books, 1991), pp. 185–219.

123. D. Sussman, "Strong Medicine Required," *TD*, November 2005, pp. 34–38.

124. Carnevale and Schulz, "Return on Investment."

125. Ibid.; G. Kearsley, *Costs, Benefits, and Productivity in Training Systems* (Boston: Addison-Wesley, 1982).

126. Ibid.

127. D. G. Robinson and J. Robinson, "Training for Impact," *Training and Development Journal*, August 1989, pp. 30–42.

128. Sussman, "Strong Medicine Required."

129. I. Speizer, "Rolling through the Downturn," *Workforce Management*, August 11, 2008, pp. 31–37.

130. Ibid.

131. B. Ettorre, "Let's Hear It for Local Talent," *Management Review*, October 1994, p. 9; S. Franklin, "A New World Order for Business Strategy," *Chicago Tribune*, May 15, 1994, sec. 19, pp. 7–8.

132. R. L. Tung, "Selection and Training of Personnel for Overseas Assignments," *Columbia Journal of World Business* 16 (1981), pp. 18–78.

133. W. A. Arthur Jr. and W. Bennett Jr., "The International Assignee: The Relative Importance of Factors Perceived to Contribute

to Success," *Personnel Psychology* 48 (1995), pp. 99–114; G. M. Spreitzer, M. W. McCall Jr., and Joan D. Mahoney, "Early Identification of International Executive Potential," *Journal of Applied Psychology* 82 (1997), pp. 6–29.

134. J. S. Black and J. K. Stephens, "The Influence of the Spouse on American Expatriate Adjustment and Intent to Stay in Pacific Rim Overseas Assignments," *Journal of Management* 15 (1989), pp. 529–44; M. Shaffer and D. A. Harrison, "Forgotten Partners of International Assignments: Development and Test of a Model of Spouse Adjustment," *Journal of Applied Psychology* 86 (2001), pp. 238–54.

135. M. Shaffer, D. A. Harrison, H. Gregersen, J. S. Black, and L. A. Ferzandi, "You Can Take It with You: Individual Differences and Expatriate Effectiveness," *Journal of Applied Psychology* 91(2006), pp. 109–25; P. Caligiuri, "The Big Five Personality Characteristics as Predictors of Expatriate's Desire to Terminate the Assignment and Supervisor-Rated Performance," *Personnel Psychology* 53 (2000), pp. 67–88.

136. E. Dunbar and A. Katcher, "Preparing Managers for Foreign Assignments," *Training and Development Journal*, September 1990, pp. 45–47.

137. J. S. Black and M. Mendenhall, "A Practical but Theory-Based Framework for Selecting Cross-Cultural Training Methods," in *Readings and Cases in International Human Resource Management*, ed. M. Mendenhall and G. Oddou (Boston: PWS-Kent, 1991), pp. 177–204.

138. P. Tam, "Culture Course," *The Wall Street Journal*, May 25, 2004, pp. B1, B12.

139. S. Ronen, "Training the International Assignee," in *Training and Development in Organizations*, ed. I. L. Goldstein (San Francisco: Jossey-Bass, 1989), pp. 417–53.

140. P. R. Harris and R. T. Moran, *Managing Cultural Differences* (Houston: Gulf, 1991).

141. J. Carter, "Globe Trotters," *Training*, August 2005, pp. 22–28.

142. C. Solomon, "Unhappy Trails," *Workforce*, August 2000, pp. 36–41.

143. J. Ramirez, "Lost in the Shuffle," *Human Resource Executive*, January 2006, pp. 54–57.

144. H. Lancaster, "Before Going Overseas, Smart Managers Plan Their Homecoming," *The Wall Street Journal*, September 28, 1999, p. B1; A. Halcrow, "Expats: The Squandered Resource," *Workforce*, April 1999, pp. 42–48.

145. Harris and Moran, *Managing Cultural Differences*.

146. J. Cook, "Rethinking Relocation," *Human Resources Executive*, June 2, 2003, pp. 23–26.

147. J. Flynn, "E-Mail, Cellphones, and Frequent-Flier Miles Let 'Virtual' Expats Work Abroad but Live at Home," *The Wall Street Journal*, October 25, 1999, p. A26; J. Flynn, "Multinationals Help Career Couples Deal with Strains Affecting Expatriates," *The Wall Street Journal*, August 8, 2000, p. A19; C. Solomon, "The World Stops Shrinking," *Workforce*, January 2000, pp. 48–51.

148. H. Dolezalek, "The Path to Inclusion," *Training*, May 2008, pp. 52–54.

149. S. E. Jackson and Associates, *Diversity in the Workplace: Human Resource Initiatives* (New York: Guilford Press, 1992).

150. M. Lee, "Post-9/11 Training," *TD*, September 2002, pp. 33–35.

151. R. R. Thomas, "Managing Diversity: A Conceptual Framework," in *Diversity in the Workplace* (New York: Guilford Press), pp. 306–18.

152. M. E. Heilman, C. J. Block, and J. A. Lucas, "Presumed Incompetent? Stigmatization and Affirmative Action Efforts," *Journal of Applied Psychology* 77 (1992), pp. 536–44.

153. B. Gerber, "Managing Diversity," *Training*, July 1990, pp. 23–30; T. Diamante, C. L. Reid, and L. Ciylo, "Making the Right Training Moves," *HR Magazine*, March 1995, pp. 60–65.

154. L. Egodigwe, "Back to Class," *The Wall Street Journal*, November 14, 2005, p. R4.

155. S. M. Paskoff, "Ending the Workplace Diversity Wars," *Training*, August 1996, pp. 43–47; H. B. Karp and N. Sutton, "Where Diversity Training Goes Wrong," *Training*, July 1993, pp. 30–34.

156. A. Aparna, "Why Diversity Training Doesn't Work . . . Right Now," *T + D*, November 2008, pp. 52–57.

157. Paskoff, "Ending the Workplace Diversity Wars."

158. L. Lavelle, "For UPS Managers, a School of Hard Knocks," *BusinessWeek*, July 22, 2002, pp. 58–59; M. Berkley, "UPS Community Internship Program (CIP) Fact Sheet" (Atlanta, GA: United Parcel Service, 2003).

159. A. Markels, "Diversity Program Can Prove Divisive," *The Wall Street Journal*, January, 30, 1997, pp. B1–B2; "R. R. Donnelley Curtails Diversity Training Moves," *The Wall Street Journal*, February 13, 1997, p. B3.

160. S. Rynes and B. Rosen, "A Field Study of Factors Affecting the Adoption and Perceived Success of Diversity Training," *Personnel Psychology* 48 (1995), pp. 247–70; Aparna, "Why Diversity Training Doesn't Work . . . Right Now."

161. T. Kochan, K. Bezrukova, R. Ely, S. Jackson, A. Joshi, K. Jehn, J. Leonard, D. Levine, and D. Thomas, "The Effects of Diversity on Business Performance: Report of the Diversity Research Network," *Human Resource Management* 42 (2003), pp. 8–21; F. Hansen, "Diversity's Business Case Just Doesn't Add Up," *Workforce*, June 2003, pp. 29–32; M. J. Wesson and C. I. Gogus, "Shaking Hands with the Computer: An Examination of Two Methods of Newcomer Socialization," *Journal of Applied Psychology* 90 (2005), pp. 1018–26; H. J. Klein and N. A., Weaver, "The Effectiveness of an Organizational-Level Orientation Training Program in the Socialization of New Hires," *Personnel Psychology* 53 (2000), pp. 47–66.

162. C. Terhune, "Pepsi, Vowing Diversity Isn't Just Image Polish, Seeks Inclusive Culture," *The Wall Street Journal*, April 19, 2005, p. B1.

163. R. Anand and M. Winters, "A Retrospective View of Corporate Diversity Training from 1964 to the Present," *Academy of Management Learning & Education*, 7 (2008), pp. 356–72; Dolezalek, "The Path to Inclusion." Also, see www.sodexousa.com.

164. I. Speizer, "Diversity on the Menu," *Workforce Management*, November 2004, pp. 41–45; F. Jossi, "Cultivating Diversity," *Human Resource Executive*, December 2004, pp. 37–40.

165. C. T. Schreiber, K. F. Price, and A. Morrison, "Workforce Diversity and the Glass Ceiling: Practices, Barriers, Possibilities," *Human Resource Planning* 16 (1994), pp. 51–69.

166. D. C. Feldman, "A Contingency Theory of Socialization," *Administrative Science Quarterly* 21 (1976), pp. 433–52; D. C. Feldman, "A Socialization Process That Helps New Recruits Succeed," *Personnel* 57 (1980), pp. 11–23; J. P. Wanous, A. E. Reichers, and S. D. Malik, "Organizational Socialization and Group Development: Toward an Integrative Perspective," *Academy of Management Review* 9 (1984), pp. 670–83; C. L. Adkins, "Previous Work Experience and Organizational Socialization: A Longitudinal Examination," *Academy of Management Journal* 38 (1995), pp. 839–62; E. W. Morrison, "Longitudinal Study of the Effects of Information Seeking on Newcomer Socialization," *Journal of Applied Psychology* 78 (1993), pp. 173–83.

167. M. R. Louis, "Surprise and Sense Making: What Newcomers Experience in Entering Unfamiliar Organizational Settings," *Administrative Science Quarterly* 25 (1980), pp. 226–51.

168. For example see J. D. Kammeyer-Mueller and C. R. Wanberg, "Unwrapping the Organizational Entry Process: Disentangling Multiple Antecedents and Their Pathway to Adjustment," *Journal of Applied Psychology* 88 (2003), pp. 779–94; M. R. Buckley, D. B. Fedor, J. G. Veres, D. S. Wiese, and S. M. Carraher, "Investigating Newcomer Expectations and Job-Related Outcomes," *Journal of Applied Psychology* 83 (1998), pp. 452–61; G. W. Maier and J. C. Brunstein, "The Role of Personal Work Goals in Newcomers' Job Satisfaction and Organizational Commitment: A Longitudinal Analysis," *Journal of Applied Psychology* 86 (2001), pp. 1034–42.

169. D. C. Feldman, *Managing Careers in Organizations* (Glenview, IL: Scott Foresman, 1988); D. Reed-Mendenhall and C. W. Millard, "Orientation: A Training and Development Tool," *Personnel Administrator* 25, no. 8 (1980), pp. 42–44; M. R. Louis, B. Z. Posner, and G. H. Powell, "The Availability and Helpfulness of Socialization Practices," *Personnel Psychology* 36 (1983), pp. 857–66; C. Ostroff and S. W. J. Kozlowski Jr., "Organizational Socialization as a Learning Process: The Role of Information Acquisition," *Personnel Psychology* 45 (1992), pp. 849–74; D. R. France and R. L. Jarvis, "Quick Starts for New Employees," *Training and Development*, October 1996, pp. 47–50.

170. J. Schettler, "Welcome to ACME Inc." *Training*, August 2002, pp. 36–43; J. Salopek, "A Story to Tell," *TD*, October 2005, pp. 54–56; D. Sussman, "A Monstrous Welcome," *TD*, April 2005, pp. 401–41; D. Sussman, "Getting Up to Speed," *TD*, December 2005, pp. 49–51.

171. "Clarkston Consulting," *T + D*, October 2008, p. 73.

172. J. Arnold, "Gaming Technology Used to Orient New Hires," *SHRM 2009 HR Trendbook* (Alexandria, VA: Society for Human Resource Management), pp. 36–38.

173. K. Rhodes, "Breaking in the Top Dogs," *Training*, February 2000, pp. 67–71

PART 3

Assessment and Development of HRM

Performance Management

LEARNING OBJECTIVES

After reading this chapter, you should be able to:

Lions . . . Tigers . . . and Bears . . . and Performance Management

It is reasonable to conclude that no one looks forward to performance reviews! But most of us do like to use Facebook, Twitter, or MySpace to interact with other. As a result, companies are developing or purchasing technology such as Web sites and software to make performance management more of an ongoing social process. These tools allow performance evaluation to become a more ongoing and dynamic process. For example, Accenture has developed a Facebook-type program called Performance Multiplier that allows employees to update their performance and post weekly performance goals. Rypple has developed software that gives employees the opportunity to post short questions such as "What did you think about my speech?" or "How can I handle angry customers better?" about their performance. The questions are e-mailed to managers, peers, customers, and anyone else from whom the employee wants to receive feedback. The responses are gathered together so they are anonymous and sent back to the employee, thus providing a quick and timely performance review.

Consider how the Zoological Society of San Diego used the Internet to improve employees' use of performance appraisal information and increase their satisfaction with performance management.

The Zoological Society of San Diego, which operates the San Diego Zoo, the San Diego Zoo's Wild Animal Park, and the Conservation and Research for Endangered Species scientific center, employs 2,600 people and has revenues of more than $160 million per year. For many years, performance appraisals were not a high priority. Measurement metrics used to rate employees were inconsistent, and managers not completing appraisals faced no consequences. Different versions of the one-page appraisal form were used. Managers evaluated employees on how well they thought they were doing rather than specific goals. Managers received annual cost-of-living raises not linked to their performance.

As part of the Zoological Society's emphasis on accountability outlined in the strategic plan, a new performance management system for its 225 managerial employees was recently developed. The goals for the system were to establish employee goals related to the organization's goals, include both a midyear and end-of-year performance review, and require year-end-review ratings be used to determine performance-based pay increases. Employee teams were used to help design the system. One team evaluated vendors from which a new appraisal system could be purchased. The other team investigated skills characterizing an effective leader. Use of the teams led to performance appraisals based on two categories: goals and leadership competencies. Goals and leadership competencies each make up 50 percent of the overall employee appraisal. At the beginning of each year, managers choose five goals, with three linked to the organization's objectives, such as visitor satisfaction or revenue, and the other two targeted to the manager's specific work area. Employees are rated on six leadership competencies, each including five subfactors. For example, "professionalism" includes ratings on teamwork, communications, interpersonal relations, Zoological Society mission, and customer focus.

The Zoological Society chose a Web-based system that helps guide managers through the appraisal process. The system allows employees to record accomplishments in an online journal they can share with their manager. This helps ensure the accuracy of performance reviews. It is especially useful for employees of the Zoological Society who are involved with many different conservation and other projects that their manager may not know about. The system also includes tools such as a "comment helper," which provides phrases to use in giving feedback, and a "language sensitivity checker," which flags offensive words and suggests alternatives. Despite the use of the Web-based system, HR requires that the appraisal must be given in person, with the manager printing and reviewing it or discussing the results with the employee as they review it on the computer screen. The manager must certify that a personal meeting occurred.

HR believes that the Web-based appraisal process has helped the zoo attract talented employees. Employees are attracted to companies that have clearly defined performance goals and objectives, offer timely feedback, and determine salary based on performance. Long-time employees like the system because it helps encourage discussions with managers, goal setting, and raises based on performance. Michele Stancer, who has been working at the zoo for 28 years, says, "If you perform well, you will get more. I think people should be held accountable. I've been here a long time. You see people who are 'working in retirement,' and that's not good for anyone."

Sources: Based on T. Henneman, "Employee Performance Management: What's Gnu at the Zoo?" *Workforce Management Online* (September 2006); J. McGregor, "Performance Review Takes a Page from Facebook," *BusinessWeek*, March 12, 2009, p. 58.

Introduction

Companies that seek competitive advantage through employees must be able to manage the behavior and results of all employees. Traditionally, the formal performance appraisal system was viewed as the primary means for managing employee performance. Performance appraisal was an administrative duty performed by managers and was primarily the responsibility of the human resource function. Managers now view performance appraisal as an annual ritual—they quickly complete the form and use it to catalog all the negative information they have collected on an employee over the previous year. Because they may dislike confrontation and feel that they don't know how to give effective evaluations, some managers spend as little time as possible giving employees feedback. Not surprisingly, most managers and employees dislike performance appraisals. Some of the reasons include the lack of consistency of use of performance appraisals across the company; inability to differentiate among different performance levels; and the inability of the appraisal system to provide useful data for development, to help employees build their skills and competencies, or to build a high-performance culture.[1]

Some have argued that all performance appraisal systems are flawed to the point that they are manipulative, abusive, autocratic, and counterproductive. Table 8.1 shows some of the criticism of performance appraisals and how the problems can be fixed. It is important to realize that the deficiencies shown in Table 8.1 are not the result of evaluating employee performance. Rather, they result from how the appraisal system is developed and used. As the chapter opener illustrated, if done correctly, performance appraisal can provide several valuable benefits to both employees and the company. An important part of appraising performance is to establish employee goals, which should be tied to the company's strategic goals. The performance appraisal process tells top performers that they are valued by the company. It requires managers to at least annually communicate to employees their performance strengths and deficiencies. A good appraisal process ensures that all employees doing similar jobs are evaluated according to the same standards. The use of technology, such as the Web, can reduce the administrative burden of performance appraisal and improve

table 8.1

Problems and Possible Solutions in Performance Management

PROBLEM	SOLUTION
Discourages teamwork	Make collaboration a criterion on which employees will be evaluated.
Evaluators are inconsistent or use different criteria and standards	Provide training for managers; have the HR department look for patterns on appraisals that suggest bias or over- or underevaluation.
Only valuable for very good or very poor employees	Evaluate specific behaviors or results to show specifically what employees need to improve.
Encourages employees to achieve short-term goals	Include both long-term and short-term goals in the appraisal process.
Manager has complete power over the employee	Managers should be appraised for how they appraise their employees.
Too subjective	Evaluate specific behavior or results.
Produces emotional anguish	Focus on behavior; do not criticize employees; conduct appraisal on time.

SOURCES: Based on G. Latham, J. Almost, S. Mann, and C. Moore, "New Developments in Performance Management," *Organizational Dynamics* 34 (2005), pp. 77–87; J. A. Siegel, "86 Your Appraisal Process?" *HR Magazine*, October 2000, pp. 199–202.

the accuracy of performance reviews. Also, a properly conducted appraisal can help the company identify the strongest and weakest employees. It can help legally justify many HRM decisions such as promotions, salary increases, discipline, and layoffs. Annually, *Fortune* magazine ranks the most globally admired companies. The Hay Group, which produces the Global Most Admired report for *Fortune*, says the companies on the list have chief executive officers who understand that performance measurement is about learning how to motivate people and link performance to rewards.[2] Many of the executives report that performance measurement encourages collaboration and cooperation. They believe performance measures help companies focus on operational excellence, customer loyalty, and development of people.

We believe that performance appraisal is only one part of the broader process of performance management. We define **performance management** as the process through which managers ensure that employees' activities and outputs are congruent with the organization's goals. Performance management is central to gaining competitive advantage.

Our performance management system has three parts: defining performance, measuring performance, and feeding back performance information. First, a performance management system specifies which aspects of performance are relevant to the organization, primarily through job analysis (discussed in Chapter 4). Second, it measures those aspects of performance through **performance appraisal,** which is only one method for managing employee performance. Third, it provides feedback to employees through **performance feedback** sessions so they can adjust their performance to the organization's goals. Performance feedback is also fulfilled through tying rewards to performance via the compensation system (such as through merit increases or bonuses), a topic to be covered in Chapters 11 and 12.

In this chapter, we examine a variety of approaches to performance management. First we provide a brief summary of current performance management practices. Next,

Performance Management
The means through which managers ensure that employees' activities and outputs are congruent with the organization's goals.

Performance Appraisal
The process through which an organization gets information on how well an employee is doing his or her job.

Performance Feedback
The process of providing employees information regarding their performance effectiveness.

we present a model of performance that helps us examine the system's purposes. Then we discuss specific approaches to performance management and the strengths and weaknesses of each. We also look at various sources of performance information. The errors resulting from subjective assessments of performance are presented, as well as the means for reducing those errors. Then we discuss some effective components to performance feedback. Finally, we address components of a legally defensible performance management system.

The Practice of Performance Management

Several recent surveys of human resource professionals suggest that most companies' performance management practices require annual paper-driven reviews that include both behaviors and business goals.[3] Figure 8.1 shows performance management practices. While many companies use performance management to manage employee performance and make pay decision, less than 25 percent of the companies use performance management to help manage talent through identifying training needs and developing leadership talent. More than half of companies do provide managers with a suggested distribution for their ratings; that is, they suggest the percentage of a percentage of employees that should be rated in each rating category. This is critical for ensuring that companies are able to provide pay, rewards, and development activities that differentiate excellent, average, and poor performers. Sixty-six percent of companies used the same performance management system across all levels of the

figure 8.1

Performance Management Practices

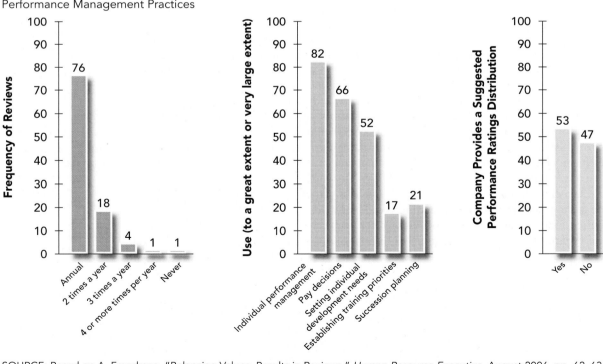

SOURCE: Based on A. Freedman, "Balancing Values, Results in Reviews," *Human Resource Executive*, August 2006, pp. 62–63.

organization. Three in four companies' systems included a second-level review, with managers reviewing evaluations with their own manager before sharing results with employees. Only 28 percent of companies have automated their performance management system.

Because companies are interested in continuous improvement and creating engaged employees—employees who know what to do and are motivated to do it—many companies are moving to more frequent, streamlined performance reviews. For example, Green Mountain Coffee Roasters, which roasts, imports, and retails coffee beans to businesses, is moving toward more frequent reviews to ensure that employees know what they did well and what needs to be immediately changed so performance can improve. Whirlpool now requires managers to meet with employees at least quarterly to give feedback on how they are doing, how the company is doing, and how the business unit is performing. The new appraisal process requires completing a one-page online form that can be printed out for the meeting, if necessary.

An Organizational Model of Performance Management

LO1
Identify the major determinants of individual performance.

For many years, researchers in the field of HRM and industrial–organizational psychology focused on performance appraisal as a measurement technique.[4] The goal of these performance appraisal systems was to measure individual employee performance reliably and validly. This perspective, however, tended to ignore some important influences on the performance management process. Thus, we begin this section by presenting the major purposes of performance management from an organizational rather than a measurement perspective. To do this, we need to understand the process of performance. Figure 8.2 depicts our process model of performance.

As the figure shows, individuals' attributes—their skills, abilities, and so on—are the raw materials of performance. For example, in a sales job, an organization wants someone who has good interpersonal skills and knowledge of the products. These raw materials are transformed into objective results through the employee's behavior. Employees can exhibit behaviors only if they have the necessary knowledge, skills, abilities, and other characteristics. Thus, employees with good product knowledge and interpersonal skills can talk about the advantages of various brands and can be friendly and helpful (not that they necessarily display those behaviors, only that they *can* display them). On the other hand, employees with little product knowledge or indifferent interpersonal skills cannot effectively display those behaviors. The objective results are the measurable, tangible outputs of the work, and they are a consequence of the employee's or the workgroup's behavior. In our example, a salesperson who displays the correct behaviors will likely make a number of sales.

Another important component in our organizational model of the performance management system is the organization's strategy. The link between performance management and the organization's strategies and goals is often neglected. Chapter 2 pointed out that most companies pursue some type of strategy to attain their revenue, profit, and market share goals. Divisions, departments, workgroups, and individuals within the company must align their activities with these strategies and goals. If they are not aligned, then the likelihood of achieving the goals becomes small. How is this link made in organizations? Primarily by specifying what needs to be accomplished and what behaviors must be exhibited for the company's strategy to be implemented. This

figure 8.2

Model of
Performance
Management in
Organizations

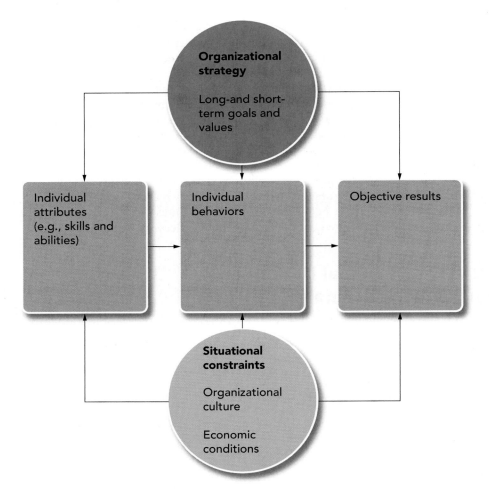

figure 8.2

Model of
Performance
Management in
Organizations

**Performance
Planning and
Evaluation (PPE)
System**
Any system that
seeks to tie the
formal performance
appraisal process to
the company's strat-
egies by specifying
at the beginning
of the evaluation
period the types and
level of performance
that must be accom-
plished in order to
achieve the strategy.

link is being recognized as necessary more and more often, through the increasing popularity of **performance planning and evaluation (PPE) systems.** PPE systems seek to
tie the formal performance appraisal process to the company's strategies by specifying
at the beginning of the evaluation period the types and level of performance that must
be accomplished to achieve the strategy. Then at the end of the evaluation period,
individuals and groups are evaluated based on how closely their actual performance
met the performance plan. In an ideal world, performance management systems would
ensure that all activities support the organization's strategic goals.

Finally, our model notes that situational constraints are always at work within the
performance management system. As discussed previously, an employee may have the
necessary skills and yet not exhibit the necessary behaviors. Sometimes the organizational culture discourages the employee from doing effective things. Workgroup norms
often dictate what the group's members do and the results they produce. On the other
hand, some people are simply not motivated to exhibit the right behaviors. This often
occurs if the employees do not believe their behaviors will be rewarded with pay raises,
promotions, and so forth. Finally, people may be performing effective behaviors, and
yet the right results do not follow. For example, an outstanding salesperson may not
have a large dollar volume because the economy is bad and people are not buying.

Thus, as you can see in Figure 8.2, employees must have certain attributes to perform a set of behaviors and achieve some results. To gain competitive advantage, the attributes, behaviors, and results must be tied to the company's strategy. Regardless of the job or company, effective performance management systems measure performance criteria (such as behaviors or sales) as precisely as possible. Effective performance management systems also serve a strategic function by linking performance criteria to internal and external customer requirements. Effective performance management systems include a process for changing the system based on situational constraints. Besides serving a strategic purpose, performance management systems also have administrative and developmental purposes. We next examine the various purposes of performance management systems.

Purposes of Performance Management

The purposes of performance management systems are of three kinds: strategic, administrative, and developmental.

LO2
Discuss the three general purposes of performance management.

Strategic Purpose

First and foremost, a performance management system should link employee activities with the organization's goals. One of the primary ways strategies are implemented is through defining the results, behaviors, and, to some extent, employee characteristics that are necessary for carrying out those strategies, and then developing measurement and feedback systems that will maximize the extent to which employees exhibit the characteristics, engage in the behaviors, and produce the results.

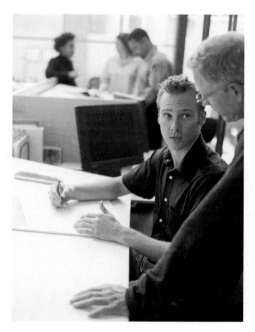

Performance management is critical for companies to execute their talent management strategy, that is, to identify employees' strengths and weaknesses, link employees to appropriate training and development activity, and reward good performance with pay and other incentives. As we mentioned in Chapter 1, talent management is critical for competitiveness. At Just Born, the company that makes Peeps and Mike and Ike candy, the performance management system is part of the company's broader People Development System (PDS), which is designed to ensure both that learning and development align with business strategy and drive business results and that employees have the skills to succeed in their current and future jobs.[5] The PDS includes the performance management process, learning and career development processes, and succession planning process. Information from each of these systems is shared to ensure that, through training and on-the-job experiences, employees are developing the skills needed for their current jobs as well as preparing for their future career interests. Just Born's system starts with a planning meeting between the employee and his or her manager. At this meeting the employee's role and strategic goals of the department are discussed. The manager and employee agree on up to four personal objectives that will help the department meet its objectives and the employee achieve the specific items described in the job description. Two competencies that the employee needs to deliver or improve on are identified. The manager and employee

● Performance management is critical for executing a talent management system and involves one-on-one contact with managers to ensure that proper training and development are taking place.

work together to develop a learning plan to help the employee gain the competencies. During the year, the employee and manager meet to discuss the progress in meeting the goals and improving the competencies. Pay decisions made at the end of each fiscal year are based on the achievement of performance objectives and learning goals.

Performance management systems can even help develop global business (see the "Competing through Globalization" box).

Administrative Purpose

Organizations use performance management information (performance appraisals, in particular) in many administrative decisions: salary administration (pay raises), promotions, retention–termination, layoffs, and recognition of individual performance.[6] Despite the importance of these decisions, however, many managers, who are the source of the information, see the performance appraisal process only as a necessary evil they must go through to fulfill their job requirements. They feel uncomfortable evaluating others and feeding those evaluations back to the employees. Thus, they tend to rate everyone high or at least rate them the same, making the performance appraisal information relatively useless. For example, one manager stated, "There is really no getting around the fact that whenever I evaluate one of my people, I stop and think about the impact—the ramifications of my decisions on my relationship with the guy and his future here. . . . Call it being politically minded, or using managerial discretion, or fine-tuning the guy's ratings, but in the end, I've got to live with him, and I'm not going to rate a guy without thinking about the fallout."[7]

Developmental Purpose

A third purpose of performance management is to develop employees who are effective at their jobs. When employees are not performing as well as they should, performance management seeks to improve their performance. The feedback given during a performance evaluation process often pinpoints the employee's weaknesses. Ideally, however, the performance management system identifies not only any deficient aspects of the employee's performance but also the causes of these deficiencies—for example, a skill deficiency, a motivational problem, or some obstacle holding the employee back.

Managers are often uncomfortable confronting employees with their performance weaknesses. Such confrontations, although necessary to the effectiveness of the work group, often strain everyday working relationships. Giving high ratings to all employees enables a manager to minimize such conflicts, but then the developmental purpose of the performance management system is not fully achieved.[8]

As you will see from this chapter there are many aspects to consider and a variety of choices for managers to make regarding performance management systems (e.g., source of performance information, approaches to measuring performance, and others). There is no one correct system that fits all companies. However, to make a performance management system that can best meet strategic, administrative, and developmental goals there are several things that should occur.[9] Table 8.2 provides recommendations for developing an effective performance management system that can meet strategic, administrative and developmental purposes. First, the system should ensure that values and beliefs are integrated into the system. For example, if employee involvement is an important value then self and/or peer appraisals should be part of the performance

Kimberly-Clark developed a new performance management system to help support the company's business plan shift from a consumer products company to a global health and hygiene company. The base for the new system was a multidimensional rating that allowed human resources to set expectations and evaluate performance for business objectives and on-the job behaviors. The system focuses on what was accomplished and how it was accomplished. Employees provide a list of co-workers they want to be part of their rater team. The new system also includes a calibration process that brings managers together to jointly review the raters' assessment of their team members and to ensure that ratings across the company are consistent. All white-collar employees are asked to establish individual objectives that are aligned with the business sector and company objectives. Performance management for managers includes an evaluation of six global leadership qualities: visionary, inspirational, innovative, decisive, collaborative, and able to build talent. The entire system is online. Employee objectives can be found in a secure area of the company's intranet. Employees and managers can go online and review performance achievements. The most recent performance information, including results and behavioral observations, is available for appraisal meetings. All users have been trained to use the system through classroom and online meetings.

The results of the new system have been impressive. The online performance management system is available in 14 languages, making a common performance management system available worldwide to all Kimberly-Clark employees. A new leadership development competency model was developed. A new compensation system linked to the performance management system was introduced, giving managers the ability to better differentiate the pay and rewards of excellent, average, and poor performers. Employee surveys and focus groups have been used to evaluate the new process. Employees feel the system has helped them get more regular feedback and coaching from their managers and report that their performance objectives are aligned with the business strategy and more meaningful to them.

SOURCE: S. Miller, "Kimberly-Clark Corp.," *HR Magazine*, November 2006, pp. 64–68.

measurement process. Second, visible CEO and senior management support for the system is necessary. Studies show that senior management plays an important role in the design and implementation of the performance management system in most companies. The stronger the role of senior management the more likely lower level managers will take responsibility for ensuring that appraisals are completed and the system is used consistently across the company.[10] Third, the critical company performance measures should be identified. These should provide the best barometer of how the company is doing in relation to achieving its strategy and business goals. Fourth, job descriptions should be linked to the performance management system. Employees need to be able to see the link between their job requirements, their job descriptions, and the goals and objectives included in their performance plans. Fifth, be sure that the performance management system assesses employees fairly and objectively based on clearly understood standards of performance or in terms of their contribution relative to other employees. The system needs to identify poor, good, and excellent performance. Sixth, managers need to be trained in how to use the performance measurement system and how to give performance feedback on a daily basis as well as during the formal performance appraisal interview. Seventh, effective performance management systems link appraisals to financial rewards. Also, to effectively motivate employee performance with rewards,

table 8.2

Recommendations for Developing an Effective Performance Management System

- Mirror the corporate culture and values.
- Have visible CEO and senior management support.
- Focus on the right company performance measures.
  Vital or "critical few"—relate to strategy, mission, and goals.
  Cascade company goals down the organization.
  Goals are linked to business drivers.
- Link job descriptions to the performance management system.
  Employees need to see the direct relationship between their job competencies, job description, and goals and objectives targeted in the performance plan.
  Establish accountabilities.
- Differentiate performance fairly and effectively.
- Train managers in performance management.
- Link compensation to the performance management system.
  Merit increases.
  Annual incentives.
  Long-term incentives.
  Discretionary incentives.
- Communicate the total rewards system.
- Require managers to actively search out, offer, and acquire performance feedback on a regular basis.
  Be involved in completing the performance cycle: planning, forecasting, progress review, end-of-year evaluation.
- Set clear expectations for employee development.
- Track effectiveness of the performance management system.
  Is it able to identify trends in performance differentiation, pay differentiation, performance gaps/developmental needs?
  Can data be shared with other applications (pay, training and development, workforce analysis, succession planning)?
- Adjust the system as required.

SOURCES: Based on H. Aguinis, *Performance Management* (Upper Saddle River, NJ: Pearson Prentice Hall, 2007); A. Walker, "Is Performance Management as Simple as ABC?" *T + D*, February 2007, pp. 54–57; K . Oakes, "Performance Management Lacks Consistency," *T + D*, April 2007, pp. 50–53; L. Weatherly, *Performance Management: Getting It Right from the Start* (Alexandria, VA: Society for Human Resource Management, 2004); H. J. Bernardin, C. M. Hagan, J. S. Kane, and P. Villanova, "Effective Performance Management: A Focus on Precision Customers, and Situational Constraints," in *Performance Appraisal: State of the Art in Practice*, ed. J. S. Smither (San Francisco: Jossey-Bass, 1998), pp. 3–48.

the program must be communicated and understood by employees. Eighth, employee training and development should be linked to the results of performance appraisals. Some companies establish a minimum number of training and development hours per year for each employee to set expectations. Finally, the effectiveness of the performance management system should be evaluated to make sure employee performance is linked to business goals and objectives and financial indicators such as return on investment. Based on the evaluation, the performance management system should be adjusted.

General Semiconductor has a workforce that is spread from North America to Asia and includes employees who speak five languages. Although General Semiconductor is headquartered on Long Island, New York, only 200 of its 5,600 employees are located in the United States. General Semiconductor makes power magnet components for the high-tech industry. These components power everything from automobiles to cell phones to dishwashers. It manufactures more than 17 million parts each day in facilities in Europe, Taiwan, Ireland, and China.

The company's interest in growth created the need to identify a core set of company values and make sure these values were adhered to at all of the worldwide facilities. The company has eight values that are referred to as "culture points": integrity; a passion for customer satisfaction; respect for, responsiveness to, and empowerment of, employees; technology and innovation; continual improvement; teamwork; job satisfaction; and a winning, competitive spirit. A leadership and problem-solving program developed by the company's HRM staff was used to spread these values throughout the company. The company also developed a program called People Plus that involves a 360-degree review of each employee, including an employee self-assessment matched with feedback from managers, peers, and subordinates chosen by the employee. Once the evaluations are completed, each employee meets with a psychologist to discuss the evaluations and make recommendations on how to improve the weaknesses identified.

Employees believe that the program brings the company together despite its global locations. The program focuses on identifying the unique talents and contributions of every employee. It also helps employees understand how others on the work team view them. The positive results of the program are measurable. Two years after the program was implemented, a survey of the senior management group showed that of 39 development areas, 36 showed improvement. The program has also contributed to a very stable workforce with a low turnover rate across all locations. This has helped General Semiconductor take pride in having the most knowledgeable and well-trained employees in its industry.[11]

An important step in performance management is to develop the measures by which performance will be evaluated. We next discuss the issues involved in developing and using different measures of performance.

Performance Measures Criteria

In Chapter 4 we discussed how, through job analysis, one can analyze a job to determine exactly what constitutes effective performance. Once the company has determined, through job analysis and design, what kind of performance it expects from its employees, it needs to develop ways to measure that performance. This section presents the criteria underlying job performance measures. Later sections discuss approaches to performance measurement, sources of information, and errors.

Although people differ about criteria to use to evaluate performance management systems, we believe that five stand out: strategic congruence, validity, reliability, acceptability, and specificity.

Strategic Congruence

Strategic congruence is the extent to which a performance management system elicits job performance that is congruent with the organization's strategy, goals, and culture. If a company emphasizes customer service, then its performance management system should assess how well its employees are serving the company's customers. Strategic congruence emphasizes the need for the performance management system to guide employees in contributing to the organization's success. This requires systems flexible enough to adapt to changes in the company's strategic posture.

LO3
Identify the five criteria for effective performance management systems.

Strategic Congruence
The extent to which the performance management system elicits job performance that is consistent with the organization's strategy, goals, and culture.

Many companies such as Hewlett-Packard, Federal Express, and Coca-Cola have introduced measures of critical success factors (CSFs) into their performance management systems.[12] CSFs are factors in a company's business strategy that give it a competitive edge. Companies measure employee behavior that relates to attainment of CSFs, which increases the importance of these behaviors for employees. Employees can be held accountable and rewarded for behaviors that directly relate to the company attaining the CSFs.

Take, for example, a drug company whose business strategy is to penetrate the North American market for dermatology compounds.[13] The company needs to shorten the drug development cycle, attract and retain research and development talent, and maximize the effectiveness of research teams. These are core competencies of the business; performance measures are linked directly to the core competencies. These include number of dermatology compound submissions to the Food and Drug Administration (FDA), number of compound approvals by the FDA, turnover of senior engineers, and team leadership and collaboration. The sources for information regarding these performance measures include FDA decisions, team member feedback on surveys, and turnover rates. Team and individual accountabilities are directly linked to the performance measures. For example, research teams' performance goals include FDA submission and approval of three compounds.

One challenge that companies face is how to measure customer loyalty, employee satisfaction, and other nonfinancial performance areas that affect profitability. To effectively use nonfinancial performance measures managers need to:[14]

- Develop a model of how nonfinancial performance measures link to the company's strategic goals. Identify the performance areas that are critical to success.
- Using already existing databases identify data that exists on key performance measures (e.g., customer satisfaction, employee satisfaction surveys). If data are not available, identify a performance area that affects the company's strategy and performance. Develop measures for those performance areas.
- Use statistical and qualitative methods for testing the relationship between the performance measures and financial outcomes. Regression and correlation analysis as well as focus groups and interviews can be used. For example, studies show that employees' involvement, satisfaction, and enthusiasm for work are significantly related to business performance including customer satisfaction, productivity, and profitability.[15]
- Revisit the model to ensure that the nonfinancial performance measures are appropriate and determine whether new measures should be added. This is important to understand the drivers of financial performance and to ensure that the model is appropriate as the business strategy and economic conditions change.
- Act on conclusions that the model demonstrates. For example, Sears found that employee attitudes about the supervision they received and the work environment had a significant impact on customer satisfaction and shareholder results. As a result, Sears invested in managerial training to help managers do a better job of holding employees accountable for their jobs while giving them autonomy to perform their roles.[16]
- Audit whether the actions taken and the investments made produced the desired result.

Most companies' appraisal systems remain constant over a long time and through a variety of strategic emphases. However, when a company's strategy changes, its employees' behavior needs to change too.[17] The fact that appraisal systems often do not change may account for why many managers see performance appraisal systems as having little impact on a firm's effectiveness.

Validity

Validity is the extent to which a performance measure assesses all the relevant—and only the relevant—aspects of performance. This is often referred to as "content validity." For a performance measure to be valid, it must not be deficient or contaminated. As you can see in Figure 8.3, one of the circles represents "true" job performance—all the aspects of performance relevant to success in the job. On the other hand, companies must use some measure of performance, such as a supervisory rating of performance on a set of dimensions or measures of the objective results on the job. Validity is concerned with maximizing the overlap between actual job performance and the measure of job performance (the green portion in the figure).

A performance measure is deficient if it does not measure all aspects of performance (the cranberry portion in the figure). An example is a system at a large university that assesses faculty members based more on research than teaching, thereby relatively ignoring a relevant aspect of performance.

A contaminated measure evaluates irrelevant aspects of performance or aspects that are not job related (the gold portion in the figure). The performance measure should seek to minimize contamination, but its complete elimination is seldom possible. An example of a contaminated measure is the use of actual sales figures for evaluating salespersons across very different regional territories. Often sales are highly dependent upon the territory (number of potential customers, number of competitors, economic conditions) rather than the actual performance of the salesperson. A salesperson who works harder and better than others might not have the highest sales totals because the territory simply does not have as much sales potential as others. Thus, these figures alone would be a measure that is strongly affected by things beyond the control of the individual employee.

Reliability

Reliability refers to the consistency of a performance measure. One important type of reliability is *interrater reliability*: the consistency among the individuals who evaluate the employee's performance. A performance measure has interrater reliability if two individuals give the same (or close to the same) evaluations of a person's job performance. Evidence seems to indicate that most subjective supervisory measures of job

Validity
The extent to which a performance measure assesses all the relevant—and only the relevant—aspects of job performance.

Reliability
The consistency of a performance measure; the degree to which a performance measure is free from random error.

figure 8.3
Contamination and Deficiency of a Job Performance Measure

Job performance measure

Actual, or "true," job performance

Contamination   Validity   Deficiency

performance exhibit low reliability.[18] With some measures, the extent to which all the items rated are internally consistent is important (*internal consistency reliability*).

In addition, the measure should be reliable over time (*test–retest reliability*). A measure that results in drastically different ratings depending on when the measures are taken lacks test–retest reliability. For example, if salespeople are evaluated based on their actual sales volume during a given month, it would be important to consider their consistency of monthly sales across time. What if an evaluator in a department store examined sales only during May? Employees in the lawn and garden department would have high sales volumes, but those in the men's clothing department would have somewhat low sales volumes. Clothing sales in May are traditionally lower than other months. One needs to measure performance consistently across time.

Acceptability

Acceptability
The extent to which a performance measure is deemed to be satisfactory or adequate by those who use it.

Acceptability refers to whether the people who use a performance measure accept it. Many elaborate performance measures are extremely valid and reliable, but they consume so much of managers' time that they refuse to use it. Alternatively, those being evaluated by a measure may not accept it.

Acceptability is affected by the extent to which employees believe the performance management system is fair. As Table 8.3 shows, there are three categories of perceived fairness: procedural, interpersonal, and outcome fairness. The table also shows specifically how the performance management system's development, use, and outcomes affect perceptions of fairness. In developing and using a performance management system, managers should take the steps shown in the column labeled "Implications"

table 8.3

Categories of Perceived Fairness and Implications for Performance Management Systems

FAIRNESS CATEGORY	IMPORTANCE FOR PERFORMANCE MANAGEMENT SYSTEM	IMPLICATIONS
Procedural fairness	Development	• Give managers and employees opportunity to participate in development of system. • Ensure consistent standards when evaluating different employees. • Minimize rating errors and biases.
Interpersonal fairness	Use	• Give timely and complete feedback. • Allow employees to challenge the evaluation. • Provide feedback in an atmosphere of respect and courtesy.
Outcome fairness	Outcomes	• Communicate expectations regarding performance evaluations and standards. • Communicate expectations regarding rewards.

SOURCE: Adapted from S. W. Gilliland and J. C. Langdon, "Creating Performance Management Systems That Promote Perceptions of Fairness," in *Performance Appraisal: State of the Art in Practice,* ed. J. W. Smither. Copyright © 1998 by Jossey-Bass, Inc. This material is used by permission of John Wiley & Sons, Inc.

in Table 8.3 to ensure that the system is perceived as fair. Research suggests that performance management systems that are perceived as unfair are likely to be legally challenged, be used incorrectly, and decrease employee motivation to improve.[19]

Specificity

Specificity is the extent to which a performance measure tells employees what is expected of them and how they can meet these expectations. Specificity is relevant to both the strategic and developmental purposes of performance management. If a measure does not specify what an employee must do to help the company achieve its strategic goals, it does not achieve its strategic purpose. Additionally, if the measure fails to point out employees' performance problems, it is almost impossible for the employees to correct their performance.

The "Competing through Sustainability" box shows how too much strategic emphasis on reaching short-term financial goals can hurt a company's sustainability.

Specificity
The extent to which a performance measure gives detailed guidance to employees about what is expected of them and how they can meet these expectations.

Approaches to Measuring Performance

The model of performance management presented in Figure 8.2 shows that we can manage performance by focusing on employee attributes, behaviors, or results. In addition, we can measure performance in a relative way, making overall comparisons among individuals' performance. Finally, we can develop a performance measurement system that incorporates some variety of the preceding measures, as evidenced by the quality approach to measuring performance. Various techniques combine these approaches. In this section we explore these approaches to measuring and managing performance, discussing the techniques that are associated with each approach and evaluating these approaches against the criteria of strategic congruence, validity, reliability, acceptability, and specificity.

LO4
Discuss the four approaches to performance management, the specific techniques used in each approach, and the way these approaches compare with the criteria for effective performance management systems.

The Comparative Approach

The comparative approach to performance measurement requires the rater to compare an individual's performance with that of others. This approach usually uses some overall assessment of an individual's performance or worth and seeks to develop some ranking of the individuals within a work group. At least three techniques fall under the comparative approach: ranking, forced distribution, and paired comparison.

Ranking

Simple ranking requires managers to rank employees within their departments from highest performer to poorest performer (or best to worst). *Alternation ranking,* on the other hand, consists of a manager looking at a list of employees, deciding who is the best employee, and crossing that person's name off the list. From the remaining names, the manager decides who the worst employee is and crosses that name off the list—and so forth.

Ranking has received specific attention in the courts. As discussed in Chapter 3, in the *Albermarle v. Moody* case the validation of the selection system was conducted using employee rankings as the measure of performance. The court actually stated,

Shareholders and company owners expect the company's managers and employees to work to increase the company's value typically measured by its stock price. Other financial goals include greater profits through greater sales or lower costs. But can too much of a focus on these goals actually hurt rather than increase sustainability?

Companies' fixation on hitting quarterly financial targets often works against their producing sustainable profit growth. One study of 31 corporations found that the highest financial returns were achieved at companies whose CEOs had challenging financial goals and communicated a vision of the company beyond making profits, such as creating an innovative product, providing great customer service, or improving the quality of life. Another study concluded that the main cause of employees' difficulties in improving profits and innovating was an excessive focus on short-term financial results. Of the approximately 40 percent of employees who said they worked in non-performing groups, one-third said their group had been high performing but began to fail when managers started raising their performance standards at the same time they were cutting budgets and staff.

The financial crisis exacerbated by the collapse of the private mortgage companies such as Countrywide Financial provides an important lesson of the power of financial objectives for motivating performance and the downside of focusing on narrow performance objectives. Loan officers, property assessors, employees in capital markets groups, and CEOs all received bonuses and generated future business if they met their objectives related to processing mortgages, valuing properties, or bundling and selling mortgages. Performance objectives related to the riskiness of the loans and the ability of the homeowner to afford the mortgage were either not included in performance evaluations or were ignored as a result of favorable market conditions that gave employees, managers, and executives of mortgage companies the opportunities to make record bonuses and profits. For example, consider the bottom level of the mortgage business: making mortgage loans for houses. Loan officers are evaluated on the number and size of loans they made. Typically, they are paid a commission for each loan sold. Mortgage brokers who match lenders and borrowers also receive commissions. Loan officers and brokers are likely to receive poor evaluations and lose their jobs if they are not processing loans. Performance evaluations were not adversely affected by making "bad" loans or forwarding loan applications that were rejected. In the short term, the goal was to get the mortgage through the approval process. The long-term consequences of homeowners defaulting on the loan would not be felt by either the loan officer or the mortgage company because mortgages were sold in bundles to other financial institutions and the loan officers could be at another bank.

The collapse of the private mortgage companies provides a strong reminder that managers recognize the powerful motivating influence of performance objectives, particularly those linked to individual financial incentives. Managers need to ensure that objectives encourage the kinds of behavior that the company wants to reward and that there are no unintended consequences. Also, it is important to consider not only "what" was achieved but "how" it was achieved. This includes evaluating behaviors and competencies and ensuring that results are obtained ethically and in a way that is congruent with company values.

SOURCES: Based on C. Hymowitz, "When Meeting Targets Becomes the Strategy, CEO Is on the Wrong Path," *The Wall Street Journal*, March 8, 2005, p. B1; W. Cascio and P. Cappelli, "Lessons from the Financial Services Crisis," *HR Magazine*, January 2009, pp. 47–49.

"There is no way of knowing precisely what criteria of job performance that supervisors were considering, whether each supervisor was considering the same criteria—or whether, indeed, any of the supervisors actually applied a focused and stable body of criteria of any kind."[20]

Forced Distribution

The *forced distribution* method also uses a ranking format, but employees are ranked in groups. This technique requires the manager to put certain percentages of employees into predetermined categories. Forced distribution was popularized by former General Electric CEO Jack Welch, who insisted that GE annually identify and remove the bottom 10 percent of the workforce. Such performance ranking takes several forms. Most commonly, employees are grouped into three, four, or five categories usually of unequal size indicating the best workers, the worst workers, and one or more categories in between. For example, at General Electric managers were to place employees into top (20 percent), middle (70 percent), and bottom (10 percent) categories. The bottom 10 percent usually receive no bonuses and can be terminated. The forced distribution method forces managers to categorize employees based on distribution rules, not on their performance. For example, Charles Schwab has three possible ratings for employees but the bottom rating is never assigned.[21] Forced distribution systems force managers to distinguish between employees, which avoids an entitlement mentality for pay, rewards, and development activities. Even if a manager's employees are all above average performers, the manager is forced to rate some employees as "Not Acceptable."

Advocates of these systems say that they are the best way to identify high-potential employees who should be given training, promotions, and financial rewards and to identify the poorest performers who should be helped or asked to leave. Top-level managers at many companies have observed that despite corporate performance and return to shareholders being flat or decreasing, compensation costs have continued to spiral upward and performance ratings continue to be high. They question how there can be such a disconnect between corporate performance and employees' evaluations and compensation. Forced distribution systems provide a mechanism to help align company performance and employee performance and compensation. Employees in the bottom 10 percent cause performance standards to be lowered, influence good employees to leave, and keep good employees from joining the company.

A forced distribution system helps managers tailor development activities to employees based on their performance. For example, as shown in Table 8.4, poor performers are given specific feedback about what they need to improve in their job and a timetable is set for their improvement. If they do not improve their performance, they are dismissed. Top performers are encouraged to participate in development activities such as job experiences, mentoring, and completion of leadership programs which will help prepare them for top management positions. The use of a forced distribution system is seen as a way for companies to increase performance, motivate employees, and open the door for new talent to join the company to replace poor performers.[22] Advocates say these systems force managers to make hard decisions about employee performance based on job-related criteria, rather than to be lenient in evaluating employees. Critics, on the other hand, say the systems in practice are arbitrary, may be illegal, and cause poor morale.[23] For example, one workgroup might have 20 percent poor performers while another might have only high performers, but the process mandates that 10 percent of employees be eliminated from both groups. Also, in many forced distribution systems an unintended consequence is the bottom category tends

table 8.4

Performance and Development Based on Forced Distribution and Ranking

RANKING OR DISTRIBUTION CATEGORY	PERFORMANCE AND DEVELOPMENT PLAN
A Above average exceptional A1 performer	• Accelerate development through challenging job assignments • Provide mentor from leadership team • Recognize and reward contributions • Praise employees for strengths • Consider leadership potential • Nominate for leadership development programs
B Average meets expectations steady performer	• Offer feedback on how B can become a high performer • Encourage development of strengths and improvement of weaknesses • Recognize and reward employee contributions • Consider enlarging job
C Below expectations poor performance	• Give feedback and agree upon what specific skills, behavior, and/or results need to be improved with timetable for accomplishment • Move to job that better matches skills • Ask to leave the company

SOURCES: Based on B. Axelrod, H. Handfield-Jones, and E. Michaels, "A New Game Plan for C Players," *HBR,* January 2002, pp. 80–88; A. Walker, "Is Performance Management as Simple as ABC?" *T + D,* February 2007, pp. 54–57; T. De Long and V. Vijayaraghavan, "Let's Hear It for B Players," *HBR,* June 2003, pp. 96–102.

to consist of minorities, women, and people over 40 years of age, causing discrimination lawsuits. Finally, it is difficult to rank employees into distinctive categories when criteria are subjective or when it is difficult to differentiate employees on the criteria (such as teamwork or communications skills). For example, in 2002, Ford Motors settled two class action lawsuits for $10.5 million.[24] Ford said it needed the forced ranking system because its culture discouraged candor in performance evaluations. Ford Motors Performance Management System involved grading 1,800 middle managers as A, B, or C. Managers who received a C for one year received no bonus; two years at the C level meant possible demotion and termination. Ten percent of the managers were to be graded as C. But some employees claimed the system had a negative impact on older, white workers because they received a larger proportion of C grades. Eventually, Ford eliminated the forced ranking system.

Although there are many opinions on the pros and cons of forced distribution performance systems, few studies have examined their effectiveness. Research simulating different features of a forced system and other factors that influence company performance (e.g., voluntary turnover rate, validity of selection methods) suggests that forced distribution rating systems can improve the potential performance of a company's workforce.[25] Companies that have clear goals and management criteria, train evaluators, use the rankings along with other HR metrics, and reward good performance may find them useful. The majority of improvement appears to occur during the first several years the system is used, mainly because of the large number of poorly performing employees who are identified and fired. Keep in mind that despite the potential advantages of forced choice systems for improving a company's workforce performance, the potential negative side effects on morale, teamwork, recruiting, and shareholder perceptions should be considered before adopting such as system. Forced ranking is ethical as long as the system is clearly communicated, the system is part of a positive dimension of the organization culture (innovation, continuous improvement), and the employees have the chance to appeal decisions.

Paired Comparison

The *paired comparison* method requires managers to compare every employee with every other employee in the work group, giving an employee a score of 1 every time he or she is considered the higher performer. Once all the pairs have been compared, the manager computes the number of times each employee received the favorable decision (i.e., counts up the points), and this becomes the employee's performance score.

The paired comparison method tends to be time-consuming for managers and will become more so as organizations become flatter with an increased span of control. For example, a manager with 10 employees must make 45 ($10 \times \frac{9}{2}$) comparisons. However, if the group increases to 15 employees, 105 comparisons must be made.

Evaluating the Comparative Approach

The comparative approach to performance measurement is an effective tool in differentiating employee performance; it virtually eliminates problems of leniency, central tendency, and strictness. This is especially valuable if the results of the measures are to be used in making administrative decisions such as pay raises and promotions. In addition, such systems are relatively easy to develop and in most cases easy to use; thus, they are often accepted by users.

One problem with these techniques, however, is their common failure to be linked to the strategic goals of the organization. Although raters can evaluate the extent to which individuals' performances support the strategy, this link is seldom made explicit. In addition, because of the subjective nature of the ratings, their actual validity and reliability depend on the raters themselves. Some firms use multiple evaluators to reduce the biases of any individual, but most do not. At best, we could conclude that their reliability and validity are modest.

These techniques lack specificity for feedback purposes. Based only on their relative rankings, individuals are completely unaware of what they must do differently to improve their ranking. This puts a heavy burden on the manager to provide specific feedback beyond that of the rating instrument itself. Finally, many employees and managers are less likely to accept evaluations based on comparative approaches. Evaluations depend on how employees' performance relates to other employees in a group, team, or department (normative standard) rather than on absolute standards of excellent, good, fair, and poor performance.

The Attribute Approach

The attribute approach to performance management focuses on the extent to which individuals have certain attributes (characteristics or traits) believed desirable for the company's success. The techniques that use this approach define a set of traits—such as initiative, leadership, and competitiveness—and evaluate individuals on them.

table 8.5

Example of a Graphic Rating Scale

The following areas of performance are significant to most positions. Indicate your assessment of performance on each dimension by circling the appropriate rating.

PERFORMANCE DIMENSION	RATING				
	DISTINGUISHED	EXCELLENT	COMMENDABLE	ADEQUATE	POOR
Knowledge	5	4	3	2	1
Communication	5	4	3	2	1
Judgment	5	4	3	2	1
Managerial skill	5	4	3	2	1
Quality performance	5	4	3	2	1
Teamwork	5	4	3	2	1
Interpersonal skills	5	4	3	2	1
Initiative	5	4	3	2	1
Creativity	5	4	3	2	1
Problem solving	5	4	3	2	1

Graphic Rating Scales

The most common form that the attribute approach to performance management takes is the *graphic rating scale*. Table 8.5 shows a graphic rating scale used in a manufacturing company. As you can see, a list of traits is evaluated by a five-point (or some other number of points) rating scale. The manager considers one employee at a time, circling the number that signifies how much of that trait the individual has. Graphic rating scales can provide a number of different points (a discrete scale) or a continuum along which the rater simply places a check mark (a continuous scale).

The legal defensibility of graphic rating scales was questioned in the *Brito v. Zia* (1973) case. In this case, Spanish-speaking employees had been terminated as a result of their performance appraisals. These appraisals consisted of supervisors' rating subordinates on a number of undefined dimensions such as volume of work, quantity of work, job knowledge, dependability, and cooperation. The court criticized the subjective appraisals and stated that the company should have presented empirical data demonstrating that the appraisal was significantly related to actual work behavior.

Mixed-Standard Scales

Mixed-standard scales were developed to get around some of the problems with graphic rating scales. To create a mixed-standard scale, we define the relevant performance dimensions and then develop statements representing good, average, and poor performance along each dimension. These statements are then mixed with the statements from other dimensions on the actual rating instrument. An example of a mixed-standard scale is presented in Table 8.6.

As we see in the table, the rater is asked to complete the rating instrument by indicating whether the employee's performance is above (+), at (0), or below (−) the statement. A special scoring key is then used to score the employee's performance

table 8.6

An Example of a
Mixed-Standard
Scale

Three traits being assessed:
   Initiative (INTV)
   Intelligence (INTG)
   Relations with others (RWO)

Levels of performance in statements:
   High (H)
   Medium (M)
   Low (L)

Instructions: Please indicate next to each statement whether the employee's performance is above (+), equal to (0), or below (−) the statement.

INTV	H	1.	This employee is a real self-starter. The employee always takes the initiative and his/her superior never has to prod this individual.	+
INTG	M	2.	While perhaps this employee is not a genius, s/he is a lot more intelligent than many people I know.	+
RWO	L	3.	This employee has a tendency to get into unnecessary conflicts with other people.	0
INTV	M	4.	While generally this employee shows initiative, occasionally his/her superior must prod him/her to complete work.	+
INTG	L	5.	Although this employee is slower than some in understanding things, and may take a bit longer in learning new things, s/he is of average intelligence.	+
RWO	H	6.	This employee is on good terms with everyone. S/he can get along with people even when s/he does not agree with them.	−
INTV	L	7.	This employee has a bit of a tendency to sit around and wait for directions.	+
INTG	H	8.	This employee is extremely intelligent, and s/he learns very rapidly.	−
RWO	M	9.	This employee gets along with most people. Only very occasionally does s/he have conflicts with others on the job, and these are likely to be minor.	−

Scoring Key:

STATEMENTS			SCORE
HIGH	**MEDIUM**	**LOW**	
+	+	+	7
0	+	+	6
−	+	+	5
−	0	+	4
−	−	+	3
−	−	0	2
−	−	−	1

Example score from preceding ratings:

	STATEMENTS			SCORE
	HIGH	**MEDIUM**	**LOW**	
Initiative	+	+	+	7
Intelligence	0	+	+	6
Relations with others	−	−	0	2

for each dimension. Thus, for example, an employee performing above all three statements receives a 7. If the employee is below the good statement, at the average statement, and above the poor statement, a score of 4 is assessed. An employee below all three statements is given a rating of 1. This scoring is applied to all the dimensions to determine an overall performance score.

Note that mixed-standard scales were originally developed as trait-oriented scales. However, this same technique has been applied to instruments using behavioral rather than trait-oriented statements as a means of reducing rating errors in performance appraisal.[26]

Evaluating the Attribute Approach

Attribute-based performance methods are the most popular methods in organizations. They are quite easy to develop and are generalizable across a variety of jobs, strategies, and organizations. In addition, if much attention is devoted to identifying those attributes relevant to job performance and carefully defining them on the rating instrument, they can be as reliable and valid as more elaborate measurement techniques.

However, these techniques fall short on several of the criteria for effective performance management. There is usually little congruence between the techniques and the company's strategy. These methods are used because of the ease in developing them and because the same method (list of traits, comparisons) is generalizable across any organization and any strategy. In addition, these methods usually have very vague performance standards that are open to different interpretations by different raters. Because of this, different raters often provide extremely different ratings and rankings. The result is that both the validity and reliability of these methods are usually low.

Virtually none of these techniques provides any specific guidance on how an employee can support the company's goals or correct performance deficiencies. In addition, when raters give feedback, these techniques tend to elicit defensiveness from employees. For example, how would you feel if you were told that on a five-point scale, you were rated a "2" in maturity? Certainly you might feel somewhat defensive and unwilling to accept that judgment, as well as any additional feedback. Also, being told you were rated a "2" in maturity doesn't tell you how to improve your rating.

The Behavioral Approach

The behavioral approach to performance management attempts to define the behaviors an employee must exhibit to be effective in the job. The various techniques define those behaviors and then require managers to assess the extent to which employees exhibit them. We discuss five techniques that rely on the behavioral approach.

Critical Incidents

The *critical incidents* approach requires managers to keep a record of specific examples of effective and ineffective performance on the part of each employee. Here's an example of an incident described in the performance evaluation of an appliance repair person:

> A customer called in about a refrigerator that was not cooling and was making a clicking noise every few minutes. The technician prediagnosed the cause of the problem and

checked his truck for the necessary parts. When he found he did not have them, he checked the parts out from inventory so that the customer's refrigerator would be repaired on his first visit and the customer would be satisfied promptly.

These incidents give specific feedback to employees about what they do well and what they do poorly, and they can be tied to the company's strategy by focusing on incidents that best support that strategy. However, many managers resist having to keep a daily or weekly log of their employees' behavior. It is also often difficult to compare employees because each incident is specific to that individual.

Behaviorally Anchored Rating Scales

A *behaviorally anchored rating scale (BARS)* builds on the critical incidents approach. It is designed to specifically define performance dimensions by developing behavioral anchors associated with different levels of performance.[27] An example of a BARS is presented in Figure 8.4. As you can see, the performance dimension has a number of examples of behaviors that indicate specific levels of performance along the dimension.

To develop a BARS, we first gather a large number of critical incidents that represent effective and ineffective performance on the job. These incidents are classified into performance dimensions, and the ones that experts agree clearly represent a particular level of performance are used as behavioral examples (or anchors) to guide the rater. The manager's task is to consider an employee's performance along each dimension and determine where on the dimension the employee's performance fits using the behavioral anchors as guides. This rating becomes the employee's score for that dimension.

Behavioral anchors have advantages and disadvantages. They can increase interrater reliability by providing a precise and complete definition of the performance dimension. A disadvantage is that they can bias information recall—that is, behavior that closely approximates the anchor is more easily recalled than other behavior.[28] Research has also demonstrated that managers and their subordinates do not make much of a distinction between BARS and trait scales.[29]

Behavioral Observation Scales

A *behavioral observation scale (BOS)* is a variation of a BARS. Like a BARS, a BOS is developed from critical incidents.[30] However, a BOS differs from a BARS in two basic ways. First, rather than discarding a large number of the behaviors that exemplify effective or ineffective performance, a BOS uses many of them to more specifically define all the behaviors that are necessary for effective performance (or that would be considered ineffective performance). Instead of using, say, 4 behaviors to define 4 levels of performance on a particular dimension, a BOS may use 15 behaviors. An example of a BOS is presented in Table 8.7.

A second difference is that rather than assessing which behavior best reflects an individual's performance, a BOS requires managers to rate the frequency with which the employee has exhibited each behavior during the rating period. These ratings are then averaged to compute an overall performance rating.

The major drawback of a BOS is that it may require more information than most managers can process or remember. A BOS can have 80 or more behaviors, and the manager must remember how frequently an employee exhibited each of

figure 8.4

Task-BARS Rating Dimension: Patrol Officer

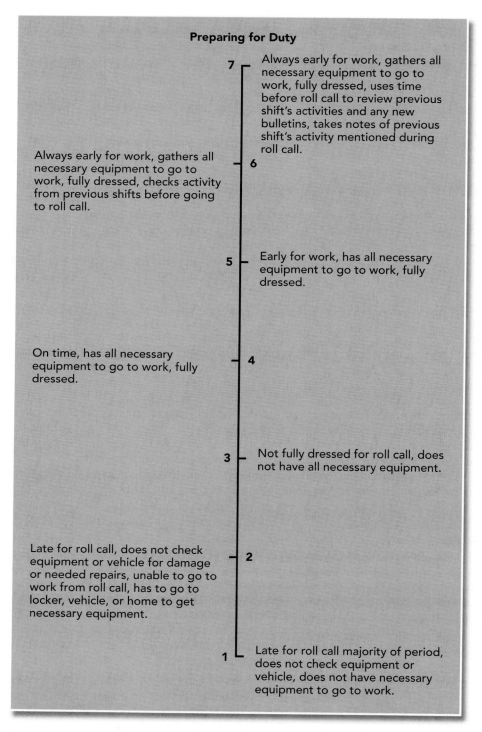

Preparing for Duty

7 — Always early for work, gathers all necessary equipment to go to work, fully dressed, uses time before roll call to review previous shift's activities and any new bulletins, takes notes of previous shift's activity mentioned during roll call.

Always early for work, gathers all necessary equipment to go to work, fully dressed, checks activity from previous shifts before going to roll call. — 6

5 — Early for work, has all necessary equipment to go to work, fully dressed.

On time, has all necessary equipment to go to work, fully dressed. — 4

3 — Not fully dressed for roll call, does not have all necessary equipment.

Late for roll call, does not check equipment or vehicle for damage or needed repairs, unable to go to work from roll call, has to go to locker, vehicle, or home to get necessary equipment. — 2

1 — Late for roll call majority of period, does not check equipment or vehicle, does not have necessary equipment to go to work.

SOURCE: Adapted from R. Harvey, "Job Analysis," in *Handbook of Industrial & Organizational Psychology,* 2nd ed., ed. M. Dunnette and L. Hough (Palo Alto, CA: Consulting Psychologists Press, 1991), p. 138.

Overcoming Resistance to Change						
(1) Describes the details of the change to subordinates.						
Almost Never	1	2	3	4	5	Almost Always
(2) Explains why the change is necessary.						
Almost Never	1	2	3	4	5	Almost Always
(3) Discusses how the change will affect the employee.						
Almost Never	1	2	3	4	5	Almost Always
(4) Listens to the employee's concerns.						
Almost Never	1	2	3	4	5	Almost Always
(5) Asks the employee for help in making the change work.						
Almost Never	1	2	3	4	5	Almost Always
(6) If necessary, specifies the date for a follow-up meeting to respond to the employee's concerns.						
Almost Never	1	2	3	4	5	Almost Always
Total = _____						
Below Adequate 6–10	Adequate 11–15	Full 16–20	Excellent 21–25	Superior 26–30		

table 8.7

An Example of a Behavioral Observation Scale (BOS) for Evaluating Job Performance

Scores are set by management.

SOURCE: From Gary Latham and Ken Wexley, *Increasing Productivity Through Performance Appraisal*, (Prentice Hall Series in Human Resources), 2nd edition, Copyright © 1994. Reproduced by permission of Pearson Education, Inc., Upper Saddle River, New Jersey.

these behaviors over a 6- or 12-month rating period. This is taxing enough for one employee, but managers often must rate 10 or more employees.

A direct comparison of BOS, BARS, and graphic rating scales found that both managers and employees prefer BOS for differentiating good from poor performers, maintaining objectivity, providing feedback, suggesting training needs, and being easy to use among managers and subordinates.[31]

Organizational Behavior Modification

Organizational behavior modification (OBM) entails managing the behavior of employees through a formal system of behavioral feedback and reinforcement. This system builds on the behaviorist view of motivation, which holds that individuals' future behavior is determined by past behaviors that have been positively reinforced. The techniques vary, but most have four components. First, they define a set of key behaviors necessary for job performance. Second, they use a measurement system to assess whether these behaviors are exhibited. Third, the manager or consultant informs employees of those behaviors, perhaps even setting goals for how often the employees should exhibit those behaviors. Finally, feedback and reinforcement are provided to employees.[32]

OBM techniques have been used in a variety of settings. For example, OBM was used to increase the rates and timeliness of critical job behaviors by showing the connection between job behaviors and the accomplishments of a community mental health agency.[33] Job behaviors were identified that related to administration, record keeping, and service provided to clients. Feedback and reinforcement improved staff performance. Figure 8.5 shows increases in staff performance in record keeping following the feedback and reinforcement intervention. "Baseline" refers to measures of record keeping prior to the intervention. "Interview" refers to record keeping when

figure 8.5

Increases in Record Keeping as a Result of OBM

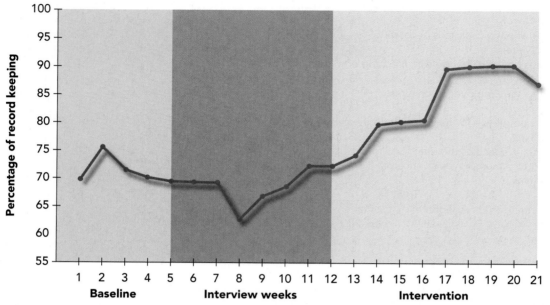

SOURCE: Based on K. L. Langeland, C. M. Johnson, and T. C. Mawhinney, "Improving Staff Performance in a Community Mental Health Setting: Job Analysis, Training, Goal Setting, Feedback, and Year of Data," *Journal of Organizational Behavior Management* 18 (1998), pp. 211–43.

interviews were being conducted with staff to better explain their jobs. Similar results have been observed with the frequency of safety behaviors in a processing plant.[34]

Assessment Centers

Assessment Centers
A process in which multiple raters evaluate employees' performance on a number of exercises.

Although assessment centers are usually used for selection and promotion decisions, they have also been used as a way of measuring managerial performance.[35] At an **assessment center,** individuals usually perform a number of simulated tasks, such as leaderless group discussions, in-basket management, and role-playing. Assessors observe the individuals' behavior and evaluate their skill or potential as managers. We discuss assessment centers more in Chapter 9.

The advantage of assessment centers is that they provide a somewhat objective measure of an individual's performance at managerial tasks. In addition, they allow specific performance feedback, and individualized developmental plans can be designed. For example, ARCO Oil & Gas Corporation sends its managers through assessment centers to identify their individual strengths and weaknesses and to create developmental action plans for each manager.

An interesting public sector application of assessment centers is in the state government of North Carolina. Managers there can be assessed to become "certified middle managers." This process includes an assessment center at the beginning of the certification program, from which an individualized developmental action plan is created. The developmental plan, implemented over approximately two years, consists of training and on-the-job developmental experiences. At the end of the two years, the manager attends the certification assessment center. Those who successfully meet the criteria set forth then become certified.

Evaluation of the Behavioral Approach

The behavioral approach can be very effective. It can link the company's strategy to the specific behavior necessary for implementing that strategy. It provides specific guidance and feedback for employees about the performance expected of them. Most of the techniques rely on in-depth job analysis, so the behaviors that are identified and measured are valid. Because those who will use the system develop the measures, the acceptability is also often high. Finally, with a substantial investment in training raters, the techniques are reasonably reliable.

The major weaknesses have to do with the organizational context of the system. Although the behavioral approach can be closely tied to a company's strategy, the behaviors and measures must be constantly monitored and revised to ensure that they are still linked to the strategic focus. This approach also assumes that there is "one best way" to do the job and that the behaviors that constitute this best way can be identified. One study found that managers seek to control behaviors when they perceive a clear relationship between behaviors and results. When this link is not clear, they tend to rely on managing results.[36] The behavioral approach might be best suited to less complex jobs (where the best way to achieve results is somewhat clear) and least suited to complex jobs (where there are multiple ways, or behaviors, to achieve success).

The Results Approach

The results approach focuses on managing the objective, measurable results of a job or work group. This approach assumes that subjectivity can be eliminated from the measurement process and that results are the closest indicator of one's contribution to organizational effectiveness.[37] We examine two performance management systems that use results: management by objectives and the productivity measurement and evaluation system.

Management by Objectives

Management by objectives (MBO) is popular in both private and public organizations.[38] The original concept came from the accounting firm of Booz, Allen, and Hamilton and was called a "manager's letter." The process consisted of having all the subordinate managers write a letter to their superiors, detailing what their performance goals were for the coming year and how they planned to achieve them. Harold Smiddy applied and expanded this idea at General Electric in the 1950s, and Douglas McGregor has since developed it into a philosophy of management.[39]

In an MBO system, the top management team first defines the company's strategic goals for the coming year. These goals are passed on to the next layer of management, and these managers define the goals they must achieve for the company to reach its goals. This goal-setting process cascades down the organization so that all managers set goals that help the company achieve its goals.[40] These goals are used as the standards by which an individual's performance is evaluated.[41]

MBO systems have three common components.[42] They require specific, difficult, objective goals. (An example of MBO-based goals used in a financial service firm is presented in Table 8.8.) The goals are not usually set unilaterally by management but with the managers' and subordinates' participation. And the manager gives objective feedback throughout the rating period to monitor progress toward the goals.

KEY RESULT AREA	OBJECTIVE	% COMPLETE	ACTUAL PERFORMANCE
Loan portfolio management	Increase portfolio value by 10% over the next 12 months	90	Increased portfolio value by 9% over the past 12 months
Sales	Generate fee income of $30,000 over the next 12 months	150	Generated fee income of $45,000 over the past 12 months

Research on MBO has revealed two important findings regarding its effectiveness.[43] Of 70 studies examined, 68 showed productivity gains, while only 2 showed productivity losses, suggesting that MBO usually increases productivity. Also, productivity gains tend to be highest when there is substantial commitment to the MBO program from top management: an average increase of 56 percent when commitment was high, 33 percent when commitment was moderate, and 6 percent when commitment was low.

Clearly, MBO can have a very positive effect on an organization's performance. Considering the process through which goals are set (involvement of staff in setting objectives), it is also likely that MBO systems effectively link individual employee performance with the firm's strategic goals. SecureWorks Inc., a small, 100-employee company providing Internet security services, bases employees' pay on their performance.[44] Pay is rewarded on the basis of results, not effort. When linking pay to performance, it is critical that employees understand the performance goals and how to meet them, see that pay is really based on performance (i.e., poor performers receive fewer pay and other rewards than good performers), and believe the performance management system used to determine pay is fair. At SecureWorks, company goals are set by the management team at the beginning of each year. The goals are displayed throughout the company so employees can see them. Department goals in support of the corporate goals are set by managers and their teams. Each employee has a set of goals which are discussed and agreed upon with their manager. The goals are realistic, measurable, achievable, and aligned with the company goals. Employees have several chances throughout the year to receive rewards for their performance. These rewards include cost-of-living salary increases and the opportunity to earn restricted stock and a bonus. Employees can receive no rewards or all available rewards depending on their performance. The CEO reviews each employee's pay recommendation, which is based on a self- and manager performance evaluation and reviewed by the vice president of human resources.

Productivity Measurement and Evaluation System (ProMES)

The main goal of ProMES is to motivate employees to higher levels of productivity.[45] It is a means of measuring and feeding back productivity information to personnel.

ProMES consists of four steps. First, people in an organization identify the products, or the set of activities or objectives, the organization expects to accomplish. The organization's productivity depends on how well it produces these products. At a repair shop, for example, a product might be something like "quality of repair." Second, the staff defines indicators of the products. Indicators are measures of how well the products are being generated by the organization. Quality of repair could be indicated by (1) return rate (percentage of items returned that did not function immediately after repair) and (2) percentage of quality-control inspections passed. Third, the staff establishes the contingencies between the amount of the indicators and the level of evaluation associated with that amount. Fourth, a feedback system is developed that provides employees and work groups with information about their specific level of performance on each of the indicators. An overall productivity score can be computed by summing the effectiveness scores across the various indicators.

Research thus far strongly suggests this technique is effective in increasing productivity. (Figure 8.6 illustrates the productivity gains in the repair shop described previously.) The research also suggests the system is an effective feedback mechanism. However, users found it time-consuming to develop the initial system.

Evaluation of the Results Approach
The results approach minimizes subjectivity, relying on objective, quantifiable indicators of performance. Thus, it is usually highly acceptable to both managers and employees. Another advantage is that it links an individual's results with the organization's strategies and goals.

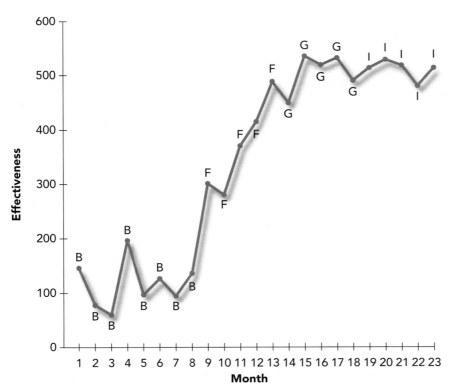

figure 8.6

Increases in Productivity for a Repair Shop Using ProMES Measures

SOURCE: P. Pritchard, S. Jones, P. Roth, K. Stuebing, and S. Ekeberg, "The Evaluation of an Integrated Approach to Measuring Organizational Productivity," *Personnel Psychology*, 42, (1989), pp. 69–115. Used by permission.

However, objective measurements can be both contaminated and deficient—contaminated because they are affected by things that are not under the employee's control, such as economic recessions, and deficient because not all the important aspects of job performance are amenable to objective measurement. Another disadvantage is that individuals may focus only on aspects of their performance that are measured, neglecting those that are not. For example, if the large majority of employees' goals relate to productivity, it is unlikely they will be concerned with customer service. One study found that objective performance goals led to higher performance but that they also led to helping co-workers less.[46] A final disadvantage is that, although results measures provide objective feedback, the feedback may not help employees learn how they need to change their behavior to increase their performance. If baseball players are in a hitting slump, simply telling them that their batting average is .190 may not motivate them to raise it. Feedback focusing on the exact behavior that needs to be changed (like taking one's eye off the ball or dropping one's shoulder) would be more helpful.[47]

John Deere takes specific actions to avoid these problems.[48] At the start of each fiscal year, manager and employees meet to discuss objectives for the year. A midyear review is then conducted to check on the employees' progress in meeting the goals. The year-end review meeting focuses on evaluating goal accomplishment. Goal achievement at the end of the year is linked to pay increases and other rewards. All company objectives are supported by division objectives that are available for employees to view online. Employees also have available a learning and activities courseware catalog they can use to help develop skills needed to achieve their performance objectives.

EVIDENCE-BASED HR

Children's Hospital in Boston wanted to improve cash flow and shorten the billing cycle (the time to receive payment of a bill). The hospital's accounts receivable department was taking more than 100 days to receive payment. To do this, the hospital decided to evaluate and reward team performance. Managers determine who will be rewarded and on what basis, and they have to communicate the plan and its benefits to employees. Team members have a set of three goals. In order of difficulty from least to greatest they are threshold, target, and optimal goals. These categories are defined in terms of how long a bill remains in accounts receivable. Teams receive a quarterly payment of $500 for meeting the threshold goal, $1,000 for meeting the target goal, or $1,500 for meeting the optimal goal. The payment is divided by team members according to the number of scheduled hours they worked. To reach the goals, team members must work together bill by bill, to process the paperwork faster.

To make sure employees understood the plan, the hospital held a series of meetings that presented information about the dollar value of each day a bill spends in accounts receivable and how the hospital is affected by poor cash flow. After employees understood how their work affects cash flow and how their efforts could improve it, they began working as a team. Employees started to take the initiative to follow up with patients, insurers, and medical records personnel. If any team members were not carrying their weight, peer pressure persuaded them to contribute more. Employees receive weekly progress reports so they can monitor their performance. The performance system has resulted in positive results. At the end of the first year, employees reduced the average number of days a bill spent in accounts receivable to just under 76. The plan also helped the hospital recruit and retain employees for its accounts payable team.

SOURCE: D. Cadrain, "Put Success in Sight," *HR Magazine*, May 2003, pp. 85–92.

The Quality Approach

Thus far we have examined the traditional approaches to measuring and evaluating employee performance. Two fundamental characteristics of the quality approach are a customer orientation and a prevention approach to errors. Improving customer satisfaction is the primary goal of the quality approach. Customers can be internal or external to the organization. A performance management system designed with a strong quality orientation can be expected to

- Emphasize an assessment of both person and system factors in the measurement system.
- Emphasize that managers and employees work together to solve performance problems.
- Involve both internal and external customers in setting standards and measuring performance.
- Use multiple sources to evaluate person and system factors.[49]

Based on this chapter's earlier discussion of the characteristics of an effective performance management system, it should be apparent to you that these characteristics are not just unique to the quality approach but are characteristics of an effective appraisal system!

Advocates of the quality approach believe that most U.S. companies' performance management systems are incompatible with the quality philosophy for a number of reasons:

1. Most existing systems measure performance in terms of quantity, not quality.
2. Employees are held accountable for good or bad results to which they contribute but do not completely control.
3. Companies do not share the financial rewards of successes with employees according to how much they have contributed to them.
4. Rewards are not connected to business results.[50]

Sales, profit margins, and behavioral ratings are often collected by managers to evaluate employees' performance. These are person-based outcomes. An assumption of using these types of outcomes is that the employee completely controls them. However, according to the quality approach, these types of outcomes should not be used to evaluate employees' performance because they do not have complete control over them (i.e., they are contaminated). For example, for salespersons, performance evaluations (and salary increases) are often based on attainment of a sales quota. Salespersons' abilities and motivation are assumed to be directly responsible for their performance. However, quality approach advocates argue that better determinants of whether a salesperson reaches the quota are "systems factors" (such as competitors' product price changes) and economic conditions (which are not under the salesperson's control).[51] Holding employees accountable for outcomes affected by systems factors is believed to result in dysfunctional behavior, such as falsifying sales reports, budgets, expense accounts, and other performance measures, as well as lowering employees' motivation for continuous improvement.

Quality advocates suggest that the major focus of performance evaluations should be to provide employees with feedback about areas in which they can improve. Two types of feedback are necessary: (1) subjective feedback from managers, peers, and customers about the personal qualities of the employee and (2) objective feedback based on the work process itself using statistical quality control methods.

Performance feedback from managers, peers, and customers should be based on such dimensions as cooperation, attitude, initiative, and communication skills. Performance evaluation should include a discussion of the employee's career plans. The quality approach also strongly emphasizes that performance appraisal systems should avoid providing overall evaluations of employees (like ratings such as excellent, good, poor). Categorizing employees is believed to encourage them to behave in ways that are expected based on their ratings. For example, "average" performers may not be motivated to improve their performance but rather may continue to perform at the expected level. Also, because employees do not have control over the quality of the system in which they work, employee performance evaluations should not be linked to compensation. Compensation rates should be based on prevailing market rates of pay, seniority, and business results, which are distributed equitably to all employees.

Statistical process control techniques are very important in the quality approach. These techniques provide employees with an objective tool to identify causes of problems and potential solutions. These techniques include process-flow analysis, cause-and-effect diagrams, Pareto charts, control charts, histograms, and scattergrams.

Process-flow analysis identifies each action and decision necessary to complete work, such as waiting on a customer or assembling a television set. Process-flow analysis is useful for identifying redundancy in processes that increase manufacturing or service time. For example, one business unit at Owens-Corning was able to confirm that customer orders were error-free only about 25 percent of the time (an unacceptable level of service). To improve the service level, the unit mapped out the process to identify bottlenecks and problem areas. As a result of this mapping, one simple change (installing an 800 number for the fax machine) increased overall accuracy of orders as well as transaction speed.[52]

In *cause-and-effect diagrams,* events or causes that result in undesirable outcomes are identified. Employees try to identify all possible causes of a problem. The feasibility of the causes is not evaluated, and as a result, cause-and-effect diagrams produce a large list of possible causes.

A *Pareto chart* highlights the most important cause of a problem. In a Pareto chart, causes are listed in decreasing order of importance, where *importance* is usually defined as the frequency with which that cause resulted in a problem. The assumption of Pareto analysis is that the majority of problems are the result of a small number of causes. Figure 8.7 shows a Pareto chart listing the reasons managers give for not selecting current employees for a job vacancy.

Control charts involve collecting data at multiple points in time. By collecting data at different times, employees can identify what factors contribute to an outcome and when they tend to occur. Figure 8.8 shows the percentage of employees hired internally for a company for each quarter between 1993 and 1995. Internal hiring increased dramatically during the third quarter of 1994. The use of control charts helps employees understand the number of internal candidates who can be expected to be hired each year. Also, the control chart shows that the amount of internal hiring conducted during the third quarter of 1994 was much larger than normal.

Histograms display distributions of large sets of data. Data are grouped into a smaller number of categories or classes. Histograms are useful for understanding the amount of variance between an outcome and the expected value or average outcome. Figure 8.9 is a histogram showing the number of days it took a company to fill nonexempt job

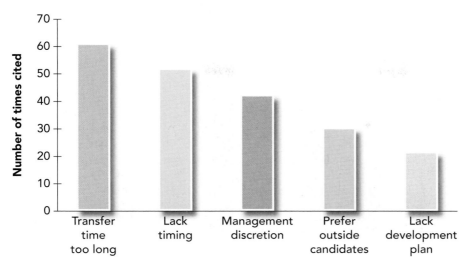

figure 8.7
Pareto Chart

SOURCE: From Clara Carter, *HR Magazine*, 1992. Copyright © 1992 by the Society for Human Resource Management. Reprinted with the permission of *HR Magazine* published by the Society for Human Resource Management, Alexandria, VA, via the Copyright Clearance Center.

figure 8.8
Control Chart

SOURCE: From Clara Carter, *HR Magazine*, 1992. Copyright © 1992 by the Society for Human Resource Management. Reprinted with the permission of *HR Magazine* published by the Society for Human Resource Management, Alexandria, VA, via the Copyright Clearance Center.

vacancies. The histogram shows that most nonexempt jobs took from 18 to 21 days to fill, and the amount of time to fill nonexempt jobs ranged from 1 to 33 days. If an HR manager relied simply on data from personnel files on the number of days it took to fill nonexempt positions, it would be extremely difficult to understand the variation and average tendency in the amount of time to fill the positions.

figure 8.9

Histogram

SOURCE: From Clara Carter, *HR Magazine*, 1992. Copyright © 1992 by the Society for Human Resource Management. Reprinted with the permission of *HR Magazine* published by the Society for Human Resource Management, Alexandria, VA, via the Copyright Clearance Center.

Scattergrams show the relationship between two variables, events, or different pieces of data. Scattergrams help employees determine whether the relationship between two variables or events is positive, negative, or zero.

Evaluation of the Quality Approach

LO5

Choose the most effective approach to performance measurement for a given situation.

The quality approach relies primarily on a combination of the attribute and results approaches to performance measurement. However, traditional performance appraisal systems focus more on individual employee performance, while the quality approach adopts a systems-oriented focus.[53] Many companies may be unwilling to completely abandon their traditional performance management system because it serves as the basis for personnel selection validation, identification of training needs, or compensation decisions. Also, the quality approach advocates evaluation of personal traits (such as cooperation), which are difficult to relate to job performance unless the company has been structured into work teams.

In summary, organizations can take five approaches to measuring performance: comparative, attribute, behavioral, results, and quality. Table 8.9 summarizes the various approaches to measuring performance based on the criteria we set forth earlier and illustrates that each approach has strengths and weaknesses. As the quality approach illustrates, the most effective way of measuring performance is to rely on a combination of two or more alternatives. For example, performance management systems in many companies evaluate the extent to which managers reach specific performance goals or results (what gets done) as well as evaluate their behavior (how the results are achieved). Figure 8.10 shows an example of a performance management system that evaluates behavior and results. The results (project development) are linked to the goals of the business. The performance standards include behaviors that the employee can demonstrate to reach the results. The system provides for feedback to the employee and holds both the employee and manager accountable for changing behavior.

table 8.9

Evaluation of Approaches to Performance Measurement

APPROACH	STRATEGIC CONGRUENCE	VALIDITY	RELIABILITY	ACCEPTABILITY	SPECIFICITY
Comparative	Poor, unless manager takes time to make link	Can be high if ratings are done carefully	Depends on rater, but usually no measure of agreement used	Moderate; easy to develop and use but resistant to normative standard	Very low
Attribute	Usually low; requires manager to make link	Usually low; can be fine if developed carefully	Usually low; can be improved by specific definitions of attributes	High; easy to develop and use	Very low
Behavioral	Can be quite high	Usually high; minimizes contamination and deficiency	Usually high	Moderate; difficult to develop, but accepted well for use	Very high
Results	Very high	Usually high; can be both contaminated and deficient	High; main problem can be test–retest— depends on timing of measure	High; usually developed with input from those to be evaluated	High regarding results, but low regarding behaviors necessary to achieve them
Quality	Very high	High, but can be both contaminated and deficient	High	High; usually developed with input from those to be evaluated	High regarding results, but low regarding behaviors necessary to achieve them

Choosing a Source for Performance Information

Whatever approach to performance management is used, it is necessary to decide whom to use as the source of the performance measures. Each source has specific strengths and weaknesses. We discuss five primary sources: managers, peers, subordinates, self, and customers.

LO6
Discuss the advantages and disadvantages of the different sources of performance information.

Managers

Managers are the most frequently used source of performance information. It is usually safe to assume that supervisors have extensive knowledge of the job requirements and that they have had adequate opportunity to observe their employees—in other words, that they have the ability to rate their employees. In addition, because supervisors have something to gain from the employees' high performance and something to lose from low performance, they are motivated to make accurate ratings.[54] Finally, feedback from supervisors is strongly related to performance and to employee perceptions of the accuracy of the appraisal if managers attempt to observe employee behavior or discuss performance issues in the feedback session.[55]

LO7
Choose the most effective source(s) for performance information for any situation.

figure 8.10

Example of a Performance Management System That Includes Behavior and Results

Accountabilities and Key Results	Performance Standards	Interim Feedback	Actual Results	Performance Rating	Areas for Development	Action
Key result areas that the employee will accomplish during the review period. Should align with company values, business goals, and job description.	How the key result area will be measured (quality, cost, quantity). Focus on work methods and accomplishments.	Employee and manager discuss performance on an ongoing basis.	Review actual performance for each key result.	Evaluate performance on each key result. 1 = Outstanding 2 = Highly effective 3 = Acceptable 4 = Unsatisfactory	Specific knowledge, skills, and behaviors to be developed that will help employee achieve key results.	What employee and manager will do to address development needs.
Project Development Manage the development of project scope, cost estimate studies, and schedules for approval.	Develop preliminary project material for approval within four weeks after receiving project scope. Eighty percent of new projects receive approval. Initial cost estimates are within 5% of final estimates.	Preliminary project materials are developed on time.	By end of year, approvals were at 75%, 5% less than standard.	3	Increase knowledge of project management software.	Read articles, research, and meet with software vendors.

Burlington Northern Santa Fe Corporation of Fort Worth, Texas, improved its performance management process by holding leaders accountable in setting annual goals, creating individual development plans, providing feedback and coaching to employees, and self-evaluation.[56] An online performance management system supports the process. The company's executive team creates the overall company objectives, which cascade down to each department and individual employees who can now see how they contribute to the company's success. The online system allows managers and employees to see how they and the department are progressing on the objectives. Required to be engaged in the performance management process, managers are more focused on the necessary communications, coaching, and giving feedback, and they are more inclined to seek out training to be sure that they have the necessary communications, feedback, and coaching skills. Managers' effectiveness is monitored by periodic employee surveys that ask questions about whether the manager discusses performance, whether the dialogue with the manager is two-way, and whether the employee receives ongoing feedback.

Problems with using supervisors as the source of performance information can occur in particular situations. In some jobs, for example, the supervisor does not have an adequate opportunity to observe the employee performing his job duties. For example, in outside sales jobs, the supervisor does not have the opportunity to see the salesperson at work most of the time. This usually requires that the manager occasionally spend a day accompanying the salesperson on sales calls. However, on those occasions the employee will be on best behavior, so there is no assurance that performance that day accurately reflects performance when the manager is not around.

Also, some supervisors may be so biased against a particular employee that to use the supervisor as the sole source of information would result in less-than-accurate measures for that individual. Favoritism is a fact of organizational life, but it is one that must be minimized as much as possible in performance management.[57] Thus, the performance evaluation system should seek to minimize the opportunities for favoritism to affect ratings. One way to do this is not to rely on only a supervisor's evaluation of an employee's performance.

Peers

Another source of performance information is the employee's co-workers. Peers are an excellent source of information in a job such as law enforcement, where the supervisor does not always observe the employee. Peers have expert knowledge of job requirements, and they often have the most opportunity to observe the employee in day-to-day activities. Peers also bring a different perspective to the evaluation process, which can be valuable in gaining an overall picture of the individual's performance. In fact, peers have been found to provide extremely valid assessments of performance in several different settings.[58]

One disadvantage of using peer ratings is the potential for friendship to bias ratings.[59] Little empirical evidence suggests that this is often a problem, however. Another disadvantage is that when the evaluations are made for administrative decisions, peers often find the situation of being both rater and ratee uncomfortable. When these ratings are used only for developmental purposes, however, peers react favorably.[60]

table 8.10

Example of Upward Feedback Survey Questions from "Tell Dell" Surveys

- Even if I were offered a comparable position with similar pay and benefits at another company, I would stay at Dell.
- I receive ongoing feedback that helps me to improve my performance.
- My manager/supervisor supports my efforts to balance my work and personal life.
- My manager/supervisor is effective at managing people.
- I can be successful at Dell and still retain my individuality.

SOURCE: Based on A. Pomeroy, "Agent of Change," *HR Magazine*, May 2005, pp. 52–56.

Subordinates

Upward Feedback
Managerial performance appraisal that involves subordinates' evaluations of the manager's behavior or skills.

Subordinates are an especially valuable source of performance information when managers are evaluated. Subordinates often have the best opportunity to evaluate how well a manager treats employees. **Upward feedback** refers to appraisals that involve collecting subordinates' evaluations of manager's behavior or skills. Dell Inc., the Texas-based computer company, recently took steps to focus not only on financial goals but also on making the company a great place to work to attract and keep talented employees.[61] To help develop what Dell calls a "winning culture," Dell added a people management component to its results-oriented performance management system. Managers are now rated by their employees on semiannual "Tell Dell" surveys. Managers who receive less than 50 percent favorable scores on five questions receive less favorable compensation, bonus, and promotion opportunities and are required to take additional training. Table 8.10 shows the five questions. Managers are expected to work continuously to improve their scores. Their goal is to receive at least 75 percent favorable ratings from employees on the five questions. One study found that managers viewed receiving upward feedback more positively when receiving feedback from subordinates who were identified, but subordinates preferred to provide anonymous feedback. When subordinates were identified, they inflated their ratings of the manager.[62]

One problem with subordinate evaluations is that they give subordinates power over their managers, thus putting the manager in a difficult situation.[63] This can lead to managers' emphasizing employee satisfaction over productivity. However, this happens only when administrative decisions are made from these evaluations. As with peer evaluations, it is a good idea to use subordinate evaluations only for developmental purposes. To assure subordinates that they need not fear retribution from their managers, it is necessary to use anonymous evaluations and at least three subordinates for each manager.

Self

Although self-ratings are not often used as the sole source of performance information, they can still be valuable.[64] Obviously, individuals have extensive opportunities to observe their own behavior, and they usually have access to information regarding their results on the job. For example, one of the most frequent criticisms the YMCA of Greater Rochester, New York, received about the performance appraisal process was that the process did not help employees develop and encourage performance discussions between managers and their employees. As a result, HR added a self-evaluation step to the appraisal process. Employees now feel they play an important role in the appraisal process. Self-evaluation gives employees the opportunity to explain to their manager what they have done well and to request training for areas they believe they need to improve. Managers find that the self-evaluation helps them make more appropriate performance ratings based on the discussion and feedback they receive from employees.[65]

One problem with self-ratings, however, is a tendency toward inflated assessments. Research has found that self-ratings for personal traits as well as overall performance ratings tend to be lenient compared to ratings from other sources.[66] This stems from two sources. If the ratings are going to be used for administrative decisions (like pay raises), it is in the employees' interests to inflate their ratings. And there is ample evidence in the social psychology literature that individuals attribute their poor performance to external causes, such as a co-worker who they think has not provided them with timely information. Although self-ratings are less inflated when supervisors provide frequent performance feedback, it is not advisable to use them for administrative purposes.[67] The best use of self-ratings is as a prelude to the performance feedback session to get employees thinking about their performance and to focus discussion on areas of disagreement.

Customers

As discussed in Chapter 1, service industries are expected to account for a major portion of job growth.[68] As a result, many companies are involving customers in their evaluation systems. One writer has defined *services* this way: "Services is something which can be bought and sold but which you cannot drop on your foot."[69] Because of the unique nature of services—the product is often produced and consumed on the spot—supervisors, peers, and subordinates often do not have the opportunity to observe employee behavior. Instead, the customer is often the only person present to observe the employee's performance and thus is the best source of performance information.

Many companies in service industries have moved toward customer evaluations of employee performance. Marriott Corporation provides a customer satisfaction card in every room and mails surveys to a random sample of customers after their stay in a Marriott hotel. Whirlpool's Consumer Services Division conducts both mail and telephone surveys of customers after factory service technicians have serviced their appliances. These surveys allow the company to evaluate an individual technician's customer-service behaviors while in the customer's home.

Using customer evaluations of employee performance is appropriate in two situations.[70] The first is when an employee's job requires direct service to the customer or linking the customer to other services within the company. Second, customer evaluations are appropriate when the company is interested in gathering information to determine what products and services the customer wants. That is, customer evaluations serve a strategic goal by integrating marketing strategies with human resource activities and policies. Customer evaluations collected for this purpose are useful for both evaluating the employee and helping to determine whether changes in other HRM activities (such as training or the compensation system) are needed to improve customer service.

The weakness of customer surveys is their expense. Printing, postage, telephone, and labor can add up to hundreds of dollars for the evaluation of one individual. Thus many companies conduct such evaluations only once a year for a short time.

In conclusion, the best source of performance information often depends on the particular job. One should choose the source or sources that provide the best opportunity to observe employee behavior and results. Table 8.11 summarizes this information for most jobs. Often, eliciting performance information from a variety of sources results in a performance management process that is accurate and effective. In fact, one recent popular trend in organizations is called **360-degree appraisals.**[71]

360-Degree Appraisal
A performance appraisal process for managers that includes evaluations from a wide range of persons who interact with the manager. The process includes self-evaluations as well as evaluations from the manager's boss, subordinates, peers, and customers.

table 8.11

Frequency of Observation for Various Sources of Performance Information

		SOURCE			
	SUPERVISOR	PEERS	SUBORDINATES	SELF	CUSTOMERS
Task					
Behaviors	Occasional	Frequent	Rare	Always	Frequent
Results	Frequent	Frequent	Occasional	Frequent	Frequent
Interpersonal					
Behaviors	Occasional	Frequent	Frequent	Always	Frequent
Results	Occasional	Frequent	Frequent	Frequent	Frequent

SOURCE: Adapted from K. Murphy and J. Cleveland, *Performance Appraisal: An Organizational Perspective* (Boston: Allyn & Bacon, 1991).

This technique consists of having multiple raters (boss, peers, subordinates, customers) provide input into a manager's evaluation. The major advantage of the technique is that it provides a means for minimizing bias in an otherwise subjective evaluation technique. It has been used primarily for strategic and developmental purposes and is discussed in greater detail in Chapter 9.[72]

The "Competing through Technology" box shows how several companies are using technology to increase access to performance information for employees and managers.

Rater Errors in Performance Measurement

Research consistently reveals that humans have tremendous limitations in processing information. Because we are so limited, we often use "heuristics," or simplifying mechanisms, to make judgments, whether about investments or about people.[73] These heuristics, which appear often in subjective measures of performance, can lead to rater errors. Performance evaluations may also be purposefully distorted to achieve personal or company goals (appraisal politics). We discuss rater errors and appraisal politics next.

Similar to Me

"Similar to me" is the error we make when we judge those who are similar to us more highly than those who are not. Research has demonstrated that this effect is strong, and when similarity is based on demographic characteristics such as race or sex, it can result in discriminatory decisions.[74] Most of us tend to think of ourselves as effective, and so if others are like us—in race, gender, background, attitudes, or beliefs—we assume that they too are effective.

Contrast

Contrast error occurs when we compare individuals with one another instead of against an objective standard. Consider a completely competent performer who works with a number of peers who are outstanding. If the competent employee receives lower-than-deserved ratings because of the outstanding colleagues, that is contrast error.

Many companies are moving to Web-based and online paperless performance management systems. These systems have several advantages including helping companies ensure that performance goals at all levels of the organizations are aligned, providing managers with greater access to employee performance information and tools for understanding and using the data, and improving the efficiency of appraisal systems. Serono, a biotechnology company, uses an online performance management system that allows all managers to see the performance of any employee that they are responsible for as well as the total distribution of ratings. Senior managers can see how managers rated their people and analyze the relationship between department productivity and the total average performance of employees in the department. If a lack of relationship is shown, this suggests that employees are being overrated. At Amcor Sunclipse, a nationwide distribution company headquartered in southern California, annual appraisals were consistently late, they were inconsistent, they had little connection to company objectives, and they weren't useful in assigning employees to training programs or filling open positions. The new online process allows e-mail notification to employees and their manager to complete performance evaluations and makes it easier

to weight the relative value of different performance goals. For example, all employees are measured on safety behaviors but safety is a more critical part of some jobs (such as manufacturing jobs) than others. The online system can be set up to automatically weight performance areas (safety, reduce waste, etc.) based on how important they are to the job. For example, for a manufacturing supervisor improving safety might count for 40 percent of the overall performance rating compared to 5 percent for an office worker.

Baxter Healthcare Corporation has an automated goal-alignment system that about half of its 55,000 employees participate in. At Baxter the process starts with the company's top strategic goals, known as the four B's (Best Team, Best Partner, Best Investments, Best Citizen). The executive team creates goals under each category. The top 150 executives then develop their goals, which are distributed to employees. The goals are collected in a performance management system. A Web site provides guidance on how to write goals, and achievement results are shared with the company's performance review and compensation systems. A manager of e-procurement of supplies at Baxter who reports to the VP of purchasing says, "The biggest value is the digitization and consistent fashion of performance information. Historically we'd put this information into

filing cabinets and pull it out once or twice a year. What this process is, really, is a tool that provides me with an opportunity to better understand Baxter's expectations of me and my team."

Automating the performance management system at New Balance Athletic Shoe Inc. in Boston allowed the human resources role to become more proactive and less administrative. HR can now stay better informed of performance issues as they occur throughout the year, rather than only hearing about them the first time when performance evaluations are completed. New Balance's system give employees (and HR) complete access to the system so they can track their progress against their goals and enter accomplishments. Managers can also enter performance-related data.

Regardless of advantages of the specific Web-based or online performance management system that is purchased, it still requires employees and managers to change how they use performance appraisal information—that is, to recognize and use performance information beyond once- or twice-a-year performance appraisals. To increase usage of any new system, it is important to train employees and managers and communicate how the system can be used. New Balance used a train-the-trainer approach in which HR staff members were first trained and then trained employees.

Monthly articles and reminders were posted on the Internet about how employees could use the system to track their performance.

SOURCES: K. Tyler, "Performance Art," *HR Magazine* August 2005, pp. 58–63;

M. Hayes, "Goals Oriented," *Information Week* (March 10, 2003), from *Information Week* Web site at www.informationweek.com; D. Silverstone, "Paperless Performance Reviews," *HR Professional* (February 2005), from *HR Professional* Web site at www.hrpao.org/HRPAO/KnowledgeCentre/

HRProfessional/newscluster/Paperless+Performance+Reviews.htm, retrieved February 19, 2005; M. Totty, "The Dreaded Performance Review," *The Wall Street Journal*, November 27, 2006, p. R7; D. Robb, "Appraising Appraisal Software," *HR Management*, October 2008, pp. 65–70.

Distributional Errors

Distributional errors are the result of a rater's tendency to use only one part of the rating scale. *Leniency* occurs when a rater assigns high (lenient) ratings to all employees. *Strictness* occurs when a manager gives low ratings to all employees—that is, holds all employees to unreasonably high standards. *Central tendency* reflects that a manager rates all employees in the middle of the scale. These errors pose two problems. First, they make it difficult to distinguish among employees rated by the same person. Second, they create problems in comparing the performance of individuals rated by different raters. If one rater is lenient and the other is strict, employees of the strict rater will receive significantly fewer rewards than those rated by the lenient rater.

Halo and Horns

These errors refer to a failure to distinguish among different aspects of performance. *Halo error* occurs when one positive performance aspect causes the rater to rate all other aspects of performance positively—for example, professors who are rated as outstanding researchers because they are known to be outstanding teachers. *Horns error* works in the opposite direction: one negative aspect results in the rater assigning low ratings to all the other aspects.

Halo and horns errors preclude making the necessary distinctions between strong and weak performance. Halo error leads to employees believing that no aspects of their performance need improvement. Horns error makes employees frustrated and defensive.

Appraisal Politics

Appraisal Politics
A situation in which evaluators purposefully distort ratings to achieve personal or company goals.

Appraisal politics refer to evaluators purposefully distorting a rating to achieve personal or company goals. Research suggests that several factors promote appraisal politics. These factors are inherent in the appraisal system and the company culture. Appraisal politics are most likely to occur when raters are accountable to the employee being rated, there are competing rating goals, and a direct link exists between performance appraisal and highly desirable rewards. Also, appraisal politics are likely to occur if top executives tolerate distortion or are complacent toward it, and if distortion strategies are part of "company folklore" and are passed down from senior employees to new employees. For example, employees at King Pharmaceutical resisted development of a centralized performance system.[75] King Pharmaceuticals is built from smaller acquired companies, each with a unique culture. Each department within the company had developed its own way of figuring out how to evaluate performance and link it to pay.

Reducing Rater Errors, Politics, and Increasing Reliability and Validity of Ratings

There are two training approaches to reducing rating errors.[76] *Rater error training* attempts to make managers aware of rating errors and helps them develop strategies for minimizing those errors.[77] These programs consist of having the participants view videotaped vignettes designed to elicit rating errors such as "contrast." They then make their ratings and discuss how the error influenced the rating. Finally, they get tips to avoid committing those errors. This approach has been shown to be effective for reducing errors, but there is evidence that reducing rating errors can also reduce accuracy.[78]

Rater accuracy training, also called *frame-of-reference training*, attempts to emphasize the multidimensional nature of performance and thoroughly familiarize raters with the actual content of various performance dimensions. This involves providing examples of performance for each dimension and then discussing the actual or "correct" level of performance that the example represents.[79] Accuracy training seems to increase accuracy, provided that in addition the raters are held accountable for ratings, job-related rating scales are used, and raters keep records of the behavior they observe.[80]

An important way to help ensure that performance is evaluated consistently across managers and to reduce the influence of rating errors and politics on appraisals is to hold calibration meetings.[81] **Calibration meetings** provide a way to discuss employees' performance with the goal of ensuring that similar standards are applied to their evaluations. These meeting include managers responsible for conducting performance appraisals and their managers and are facilitated by an internal HR representative or an external consultant. In the meetings, each employee's performance rating and the manager's reasons for the ratings are discussed. Managers have the opportunity to discuss the definition of each performance rating and ask questions. The calibration meetings help managers identify if their ratings are too positive or negative or tend to be based on employees' most recent performance. Managers are more likely to provide accurate evaluations that are well-documented when they know they may have to justify them in a calibration meeting. Calibration meetings can also help eliminate politics by discussing how performance ratings relate to business results. Also, in addition to rater training and calibration meetings, to minimize appraisal politics, managers should keep in mind the characteristics of a fair appraisal system, shown earlier in Table 8.3. Thus, managers should also:

Calibration Meetings
Meetings attended by managers in which employee performance ratings are discussed and evidence supporting the ratings is provided. The purpose of the meetings is to reduce the influence of rating errors and politics on performance appraisals.

- Build top management support for the appraisal system and actively discourage distortion.
- Give raters some latitude to customize performance objectives and criteria for their ratees.
- Recognize employee accomplishments that are not self-promoted.
- Provide employees with access to information regarding which behaviors are desired and acceptable at work.
- Encourage employees to actively seek and use feedback to improve performance.
- Make sure constraints such as budget do not drive the process.
- Make sure appraisal processes are consistent across the company.
- Foster a climate of openness to encourage employees to be honest about weaknesses.[82]

LO9
Conduct an effective
performance feedback
session.

Performance Feedback

Once the expected performance has been defined and employees' performances have been measured, it is necessary to feed that performance information back to the employees so they can correct any deficiencies. The performance feedback process is complex and provokes anxiety for both the manager and the employee. Table 8.12 provides examples of feedback that managers have given employees. You be the judge as to these statements' effectiveness in improving employees' performance!

Few of us feel comfortable sitting in judgment of others. The thought of confronting others with what we perceive to be their deficiencies causes most of us to shake in our shoes. If giving negative feedback is painful, receiving it can be excruciating—thus the importance of the performance feedback process.

The Manager's Role in an Effective Performance Feedback Process

If employees are not made aware of how their performance is not meeting expectations, their performance will almost certainly not improve. In fact, it may get worse. Effective managers provide specific performance feedback to employees in a way that elicits positive behavioral responses. To provide effective performance feedback managers should consider the following recommendations.[83]

Feedback Should Be Given Frequently, Not Once a Year. There are two reasons for this. First, managers have a responsibility to correct performance deficiencies immediately on becoming aware of them. If performance is subpar in January, waiting until December to appraise the performance could mean an 11-month productivity loss. Second, a major determinant of the effectiveness of a feedback session is the degree to which the subordinate is not surprised by the evaluation. An easy rule to follow is that employees should receive such frequent performance feedback that they already know almost exactly what their formal evaluation will be.

Surveys results from several companies suggest that many employees, especially those in Generation Y (employees born after 1980), want more frequent and candid performance feedback from managers beyond what is provided once or twice a year during their

table 8.12

Examples of
Performance
Feedback

Since my last report; this employee has reached rock bottom and has started to dig.
His men would follow him anywhere, but only out of morbid curiosity.
I would not allow this employee to breed.
This associate is really not so much of a "has-been," but more of a "definitely won't-be."
Works well when under constant supervision and cornered like a rat in a trap.
When she opens her mouth, it seems that this is only to change whichever foot was previously in there.
He would be out of his depth in a parking-lot puddle.
This young lady has delusions of adequacy.
He sets low personal standards, then consistently fails to achieve them.
This employee should go far—and the sooner he starts, the better.
This employee is depriving a village somewhere of an idiot.

SOURCE: Y. Harari, *The Daily Dose* (www.harari.org/index.html), July 22, 1997. Reprinted with permission.

formal performance review.[84] As a result, Ernst & Young LLC created an online "Feedback Zone" that prompts employees twice a year to request feedback but also allows them to request or submit feedback at any time. Other companies such as IBM and Accenture offer training for managers on how to provide effective performance feedback.

Create the Right Context for the Discussion. Managers should choose a neutral location for the feedback session. The manager's office may not be the best place for a constructive feedback session because the employee may associate the office with unpleasant conversations. Managers should describe the meeting as an opportunity to discuss the role of the employee, the role of the manager, and the relationship between them. Managers should also acknowledge that they would like the meeting to be an open dialogue.

Ask the Employee to Rate His or Her Performance before the Session. Having employees complete a self-assessment before the feedback session can be very productive. It requires employees to think about their performance over the past rating period, and it encourages them to think about their weaknesses. Although self-ratings used for administrative decisions are often inflated, there is evidence that they may actually be lower than supervisors' ratings when done for developmental purposes. Another reason a self-assessment can be productive is that it can make the session go more smoothly by focusing discussion on areas where disagreement exists, resulting in a more efficient session. Finally, employees who have thought about past performance are more able to participate fully in the feedback session.

Encourage the Subordinate to Participate in the Session. Managers can take one of three approaches in performance feedback sessions. In the "tell-and-sell" approach, managers tell the employees how they have rated them and then justify these ratings. In the "tell-and-listen" approach, managers tell employees how they have rated them and then let the employees explain their side of the story. In the "problem-solving" approach, managers and employees work together to solve performance problems in an atmosphere of respect and encouragement. In spite of the research demonstrating the superiority of the problem-solving approach, most managers still rely on the tell-and-sell approach.

When employees participate in the feedback session, they are consistently satisfied with the process. (Recall our discussion of fairness earlier in this chapter.) Participation includes allowing employees to voice their opinions of the evaluation, as well as discuss performance goals. One study found that, other than satisfaction with one's supervisor, participation was the single most important predictor of satisfaction with the feedback session.[85]

Recognize Effective Performance through Praise. One usually thinks of performance feedback sessions as focusing on the employee's performance problems. This should never be the case. The purpose of the session is to give accurate performance feedback, which entails recognizing effective performance as well as poor performance. Praising effective performance provides reinforcement for that behavior. It also adds credibility to the feedback by making it clear that the manager is not just identifying performance problems.

Focus on Solving Problems. A common mistake that managers make in providing performance feedback is to try to use the session as a chance to punish poorly performing employees by telling them how utterly lousy their performance is. This only reduces the employees' self-esteem and increases defensiveness, neither of which will improve performance.

To improve poor performance, a manager must attempt to solve the problems causing it. This entails working with the employee to determine the actual cause and then agreeing on how to solve it. For example, a salesperson's failure to meet a sales goal may be the result of lack of a proper sales pitch, lack of product knowledge, or stolen sales by another salesperson. Each of these causes requires a different solution. Without a problem-solving approach, however, the correct solution might never be identified.

Focus Feedback on Behavior or Results, Not on the Person. One of the most important things to do when giving negative feedback is to avoid questioning the employee's worth as a person. This is best accomplished by focusing the discussion on the employee's behaviors or results, not on the employee. Saying "You're screwing up! You're just not motivated!" will bring about more defensiveness and ill feelings than stating "You did not meet the deadline that you agreed to because you spent too much time on another project."

Minimize Criticism. Obviously, if an individual's performance is below standard, some criticism must take place. However, an effective manager should resist the temptation to reel off a litany of offenses. Having been confronted with the performance problem, an employee often agrees that a change is in order. However, if the manager continues to come up with more and more examples of low performance, the employee may get defensive.

Agree to Specific Goals and Set a Date to Review Progress. The importance of goal setting cannot be overemphasized. It is one of the most effective motivators of performance.[86] Research has demonstrated that it results in increased satisfaction, motivation to improve, and performance improvement.[87] Besides setting goals, the manager must also set a specific follow-up date to review the employee's performance toward the goal. This provides an added incentive for the employee to take the goal seriously and work toward achieving it.

What Managers Can Do to Diagnose Performance Problems and Manage Employees' Performance

LO10
Identify the cause of a
performance problem.

As we emphasized in the previous discussion, employees need performance feedback to improve their current job performance. As we discuss in Chapter 9, "Employee Development," performance feedback is also needed for employees to develop their knowledge and skills for the future. In addition to understanding how to effectively give employees performance feedback, managers need to be able to diagnose the causes of performance problems and take actions to improve and maintain employee performance. For example, giving performance feedback to marginal employees may not be sufficient for improving their performance.

Diagnosing the Causes of Poor Performance

Many different reasons can cause an employee's poor performance. For example, poor performance can be due to lack of employee ability, misunderstanding of performance expectations, lack of feedback, or the need for training an employee who does not have the knowledge and skills needed to meet the performance standards. When diagnosing the causes of poor performance it is important to consider whether the

Input

Does the employee recognize what he or she is supposed to do?

Are the job flow and procedures logical?

Do employees have the resources (tools, equipment, technology, time) needed for successful performance?

Are other job demands interfering with good performance in this area?

Employee Characteristics

Does the employee have the necessary skills and knowledge needed?

Does the employee know why the desired performance level is important?

Is the employee mentally, physically, and emotionally able to perform at the expected level?

Feedback

Has the employee been given information about his or her performance?

Is performance feedback relevant, timely, accurate, specific, and understandable?

Performance Standard/Goals

Do performance standards exist?

Does the employee know the desired level of expected performance?

Does the employee believe she or he can reach the performance standard?

Consequences

Are consequences (rewards, incentives) aligned with good performance?

Are the consequences of performance valuable to the employee?

Are performance consequences given in a timely manner?

Do work group or team norms encourage employees not to meet performance standards?

figure 8.11

Factors to Consider in Analyzing Poor Performance

SOURCES: Based on G. Rummler, "In Search of the Holy Performance Grail," *Training and Development,* April 1996, pp. 26–31; C. Reinhart, "How to Leap over Barriers to Performance," *Training and Development,* January 2000, pp. 20–24; F. Wilmouth, C. Prigmore, and M. Bray, "HPT Models: An Overview of the Major Models in the Field," *Performance Improvement* 41 (2002), pp. 14–21.

poor performance is detrimental to the business. That is, is poor performance critical to completing the job and does it affect business results? If it is detrimental, then the next step is to conduct a performance analysis to determine the cause of poor performance. The different factors that should be considered in analyzing poor performance are shown in Figure 8.11. For example, if an employee understands the expected level of performance, has been given sufficient feedback, understands the consequences, but lacks the knowledge and skills needed to meet the performance standard, this suggests that the manager may want to consider training the employee to improve performance, moving the employee to a different job that better fits that person's skills, or discharging the employee and making sure that selection methods to find a new employee measure the level of knowledge and skills needed to perform the job.

After conducting the performance analysis, managers should meet with the employee to discuss the results, agree to the next steps that the manager and employee will take to improve performance (e.g., training, providing resources, giving more feedback), discuss the consequences of failing to improve performance, and set a time line for improvement. This type of discussion is most beneficial if it occurs more frequently than the quarterly or yearly performance review, so performance issues can be quickly dealt with before they have adverse consequences for the company (and the employee). Below we discuss the actions that should be considered for different types of employees.

Marginal Employee
An employee performing at a barely acceptable level because of lack of ability and/or motivation to perform well, not poor work conditions.

Actions for Managing Employees' Performance

Marginal employees are those employees who are performing at a bare minimum level because of a lack of ability and/or motivation to perform well.[88] Table 8.13 shows actions for the manager to take with four different types of employees. As the table highlights, managers need to take into account whether employees lack ability,

table 8.13

Ways to Manage Employees' Performance

| | ABILITY | |
	HIGH	LOW
High	**Solid performers** • Reward good performance • Identify development opportunities • Provide honest, direct feedback	**Misdirected effort** • Coaching • Frequent performance feedback • Goal setting • Training or temporary assignment for skill development • Restructured job assignment
MOTIVATION **Low**	**Underutilizers** • Give honest, direct feedback • Provide counseling • Use team building and conflict resolution • Link rewards to performance outcomes • Offer training for needed knowledge or skills • Manage stress levels	**Deadwood** • Withholding pay increases • Demotion • Outplacement • Firing • Specific, direct feedback on performance problems

SOURCE: Based on M. London, *Job Feedback* (Mahwah, NJ: Lawrence Erlbaum Associates, 1997), pp. 96–97. Used by permission.

motivation, or both in considering ways to improve performance. To determine an employee's level of ability, a manager should consider if he or she has the knowledge, skills, and abilities needed to perform effectively. Lack of ability may be an issue if an employee is new or the job has recently changed. To determine employees' level of motivation, managers need to consider if employees are doing a job they want to do and if they feel they are being appropriately paid or rewarded. A sudden negative change in an employee's performance may indicate personal problems.

Employees with high ability and motivation are likely good performers (*solid performers*). Table 8.13 emphasizes that managers should not ignore employees with high ability and high motivation. Managers should provide development opportunities to keep them satisfied and effective. Poor performance resulting from lack of ability but not motivation (*misdirected effort*) may be improved by skill development activities such as training or temporary assignments. Managers with employees who have the ability but lack motivation (*underutilizers*) need to consider actions that focus on interpersonal problems or incentives. These actions include making sure that incentives or rewards that the employee values are linked to performance and making counseling available to help employees deal with personal problems or career or job dissatisfaction. Chronic poor performance by employees with low ability and motivation (*deadwood*) indicates that outplacement or firing may be the best solution.

Developing and Implementing a System That Follows Legal Guidelines

We now discuss the legal issues and constraints affecting performance management. Because performance measures play a central role in such administrative decisions as promotions, pay raises, and discipline, employees who sue an organization over these decisions ultimately attack the measurement systems on which the decisions were made. Two types of cases have dominated: discrimination and unjust dismissal.

In discrimination suits, the plaintiff often alleges that the performance measurement system unjustly discriminated against the plaintiff because of race or gender. Many performance measures are subjective, and we have seen that individual biases can affect them, especially when those doing the measuring harbor racial or gender stereotypes.

In *Brito v. Zia*, the Supreme Court essentially equated performance measures with selection tests.[89] It ruled that the *Uniform Guidelines on Employee Selection Procedures* apply to evaluating the adequacy of a performance appraisal instrument. This ruling presents a challenge to those involved in developing performance measures, because a substantial body of research on race discrimination in performance rating has demonstrated that both white and black raters give higher ratings to members of their own racial group, even after rater training.[90] There is also evidence that the discriminatory biases in performance rating are worse when one group makes up a small percentage of the workgroup. When the vast majority of the group is male, females receive lower ratings; when the minority is male, males receive lower ratings.[91]

In the second type of suit, an unjust dismissal suit, the plaintiff claims that the dismissal was for reasons other than those the employer claims. For example, an employee who works for a defense contractor might blow the whistle on the company for defrauding the government. If the company fires the employee, claiming poor performance, the employee may argue that the firing was, in fact, because of blowing the whistle on the employer—in other words, that the dismissal was unjust. The court case will likely focus on the performance measurement system used as the basis for claiming the employee's performance was poor. Unjust dismissal also can result from terminating for poor performance an employee who has a history of favorable reviews and raises. Rewarding poor performers or giving poor performers positive evaluations because of an unwillingness to confront a performance issue undermines the credibility of any performance management system. This makes it difficult to defend termination decisions based on a performance appraisal system.

Because of the potential costs of discrimination and unjust dismissal suits, an organization needs to determine exactly what the courts consider a legally defensible performance management system. Based on reviews of such court decisions, we offer the following characteristics of a system that will withstand legal scrutiny.[92]

1. The system should be developed by conducting a valid job analysis that ascertains the important aspects of job performance. The requirements for job success should be clearly communicated to employees.
2. The system should be based on either behaviors or results; evaluations of ambiguous traits should be avoided.
3. Raters should be trained in how to use the system rather than simply given the materials and left to interpret how to conduct the appraisal.
4. There should be some form of review by upper-level managers of all the performance ratings, and there should be a system for employees to appeal what they consider to be an unfair evaluation.
5. The organization should provide some form of performance counseling or corrective guidance to help poor performers improve their performance before being dismissed. Both short- and long-term performance goals should be included.
6. Multiple raters should be used, particularly if an employee's performance is unlikely to be seen by only one rating source such as manager or customer. At a minimum, employees should be asked to comment on their appraisals. There should be a dialogue between the manager and the employee.

Use of Technology for Performance Management: Electronic Monitoring

An increasing trend in companies is using sophisticated electronic tracking systems to ensure that employees are working when and how they should be. Electronic tracking systems include hand and fingerprint recognition systems, global positioning systems (GPSs), computer software, and systems that can track employees using handheld computers and cellphones. The systems are used on both blue-collar and white-collar employees.[93] For example, at the New York law firm Akin & Smith LLC, paralegals, receptionists, and clerks clock in by placing their finger on a sensor kept at a secretary's desk. The managing partners believe the system improves productivity and keeps everyone honest, holding them to their lunch times. At Mitsubishi Motors North American plant in Normal, Illinois, accounting managers can check from their desktop computers how many of the plant's 500 white-collar employees have shown up for work. The employees clock in using a Web-based system on their desk computers. The 2,600 assembly line workers are also tracked. They "clock in" for work with an identification badge instead of a paper time card.

Economic Advantages Corporation, a mortgage service company with offices in Vermont and New York, installed an attendance tracking system. The new system implies that the company's salaried workers, client services representatives, get paid by the hour. The company's president believes that most employees put in an honest day's work, but those employees who decide to take time off won't get paid for it. Illiana Financial Credit Union in Calumet City, Illinois, uses a fingerprint recognition system to track its tellers and loan officers. This has saved the company payroll costs by preventing employees from exaggerating their hours worked by staying late or starting early. Automated Waste Disposal, based in Danbury, Connecticut, was concerned with the amount of overtime hours of garbage collectors and sales staff. The operations manager installed a global positioning system (GPS) in garbage trucks and sales vehicles. The tracking technology has reduced the need for overtime hours to complete work, eliminating employees getting "lost" during the day and visiting friends or local restaurants during work hours.[94]

Meijer, a retail supercenter offering groceries and 40 other departments (including furniture, automotive, fashion, and health and beauty), is one of several retailers using software designed to improve the efficiency of cashiers.[95] The store's computer times how long it takes to complete each customer transaction, taking into account the kinds of merchandise being purchased as well as whether customers are paying with cash, credit, gift cards, or store credit. Each week the cashiers receive scores. If the cashier falls below the baseline score too many times, they may be carefully monitored by their manager, moved to a lower-paying job, or even lose their job!

The rationale behind the system is to maximize efficiency to improve customer service. Meijer suggests that the system has helped managers identify slow cashiers and work with them to improve their efficiency. It also allows the company to establish standards for identifying which newly hired cashiers in the 90-day probationary period should be transferred or fired. However, interviews with cashiers suggest that it has increased their stress and decreased other customer service behaviors not related to efficiency, such as making eye contact with customers, or rushing older or physically challenged customers who might need help unloading and paying for their merchandise. Some customers like the quicker checkout times, but others feel that the cashiers are not as friendly with them because they are rushed at checkout.

Despite the potential increased productivity and efficiency benefits that can result from these systems, they still present privacy concerns. Critics argue that these system threaten to reduce the workplace to an electronic sweatshop in which employees are treated as robots that are monitored to maximize productivity for every second they are at work. Also, electronic monitoring systems such as GPS threaten employees' rights and dignity to work without being monitored.

Some argue that electronic tracking systems are needlessly surveilling and tracking employees when there is no reason to believe that anything is wrong. Good managers know what their employees are doing, and electronic systems should not be a substitute for good management. Critics also argue that such systems result in less productivity and motivation, demoralize employees, and create unnecessary stress. A mentality is created that employees have to always be at their desks to be productive. Advocates, on the other hand, counter that these systems ensure that time is not abused, they improve scheduling, and they help managers identify lazy workers. To avoid the potential negative effects of electronic monitoring, managers must communicate why employees are being monitored. Monitoring can also be used as a way for more experienced employees to coach less experienced employees.

In addition to monitoring, other types of electronic systems are being used to track attendance. TriB Nursery Inc., an Oklahoma plant wholesaler, is testing a hand recognition system to replace a punch time clock to track employees who work across 300 acres during the company's busiest season. The hand readers make it easier for managers to figure out how many workers are on the job at any given time. The system allows the nursery to identify employees and to shift them to areas where they are most needed, increasing efficiency. The system also prevents friends' clocking in for each other.

A Look Back

The chapter opener on the Zoological Society discussed its Web-based appraisal system for managers.

Questions

1. Consider the five criteria for effective performance appraisals discussed in the chapter. Evaluate the new appraisal system on each criterion. That is, decide whether the new appraisal system met the criterion, fell short of the criterion, or exceeded the criterion. Provide evidence for each.
2. What are the strengths and weaknesses of Web-based appraisal systems such as the one used by the Zoological Society? What changes would you recommend for the Zoological Society's system to improve its weaknesses?

  Please see the Video Case and Case Study that correspond to this chapter online at www.mhhe.com/noe7e.

Summary

Measuring and managing performance is a challenging enterprise and one of the keys to gaining competitive advantage. Performance management systems serve strategic, administrative, and developmental purposes—their importance cannot be overestimated. A performance measurement system should be evaluated against the criteria of strategic congruence, validity, reliability, acceptability, and specificity. Measured against these criteria, the comparative, attribute, behavioral, results, and quality approaches have different strengths and weaknesses. Thus, deciding which approach and which source of performance information are best depends on the job in question. Effective managers need to be aware of the issues involved in determining the best method or combination of methods for their particular situations. In addition, once performance has been measured, a major component of a manager's job is to feed that performance information back to employees in a way that results in improved performance rather than defensiveness and decreased motivation. Managers should take action based on the causes for poor performance: ability, motivation, or both. Managers must be sure that their performance management system can meet legal scrutiny, especially if it is used to discipline or fire poor performers.

Key Terms

Performance management, 351
Performance appraisal, 351
Performance feedback, 351
Performance planning and evaluation (PPE) system, 354
Strategic congruence, 359

Validity, 361
Reliability, 361
Acceptability, 362
Specificity, 363
Assessment centers, 374
Upward feedback, 386

360-degree appraisal, 387
Appraisal politics, 390
Calibration meetings, 391
Marginal employee, 396

DISCUSSION QUESTIONS

1. What are examples of administrative decisions that might be made in managing the performance of professors? Developmental decisions?

2. What would you consider the strategy of your university (e.g., research, undergraduate teaching, graduate teaching, a combination)? How might the performance management system for faculty members fulfill its strategic purpose of eliciting the types of behaviors and results required by this strategy?

3. If you were developing a performance measurement system for faculty members, what types of attributes would you seek to measure? Behaviors? Results?

4. What sources of performance information would you use to evaluate faculty members' performance?

5. The performance of students is usually evaluated with an overall results measure of grade point average. How is this measure contaminated? How is it deficient? What other measures might you use to more adequately evaluate student performance?

6. Think of the last time you had a conflict with another person, either at work or at school. Using the guidelines for performance feedback, how would you provide effective performance feedback to that person?

7. Explain what fairness has to do with performance management.

8. Why might a manager intentionally distort appraisal results? What would you recommend to minimize this problem?

9. Can computer monitoring of performance ever be acceptable to employees? Explain.

10. A delivery driver contaminated a hospital's oxygen supply by refilling the hospital's main oxygen supply line with trichloroethane, a mild anesthetic. Following detection of the contamination, all patients were switched to oxygen tanks and no patients were injured. How would you diagnose the cause of this performance problem? Explain.

11. One of the weaknesses of using customer evaluations of employee performance is their expense (postage, phone interviews, etc.). Can you think of other weaknesses? Strengths?

SELF-ASSESSMENT EXERCISE

How do you like getting feedback? To test your attitudes toward feedback, take the following quiz. Read each statement, and write A next to each statement you agree with. If you disagree with the statement, write D.

_____ 1. I like being told how well I am doing on a project.

_____ 2. Even though I may think I have done a good job, I feel a lot more confident when someone else tells me so.

_____ 3. Even when I think I could have done something better, I feel good when other people think well of me for what I have done.

_____ 4. It is important for me to know what people think of my work.

_____ 5. I think my instructor would think worse of me if I asked him or her for feedback.

_____ 6. I would be nervous about asking my instructor how she or he evaluates my behavior in class.

_____ 7. It is not a good idea to ask my fellow students for feedback; they might think I am incompetent.

_____ 8. It is embarrassing to ask other students for their impression of how I am doing in class.

_____ 9. It would bother me to ask the instructor for feedback.

_____ 10. It is not a good idea to ask the instructor for feedback because he or she might think I am incompetent.

_____ 11. It is embarrassing to ask the instructor for feedback.

_____ 12. It is better to try to figure out how I am doing on my own, rather than to ask other students for feedback.

For statements 1–4, add the total number of As: _____

For statements 5–12, add the total number of As: _____

For statements 1–4, the greater the number of As, the greater your preference for and trust in feedback from others. For statements 5–12, the greater the number of As, the greater the risk you believe there is in asking for feedback.

How might this information be useful in understanding how you react to feedback in school or on the job?

SOURCES: Based on D. B. Fedor, R. B. Rensvold, and S. M. Adams, "An Investigation of Factors Expected to Affect Feedback Seeking: A Longitudinal Field Study," *Personnel Psychology* 45 (1992), pp. 779–805; S. J. Asford, "Feedback Seeking in Individual Adaptation: A Resource Perspective," *Academy of Management Journal* 29 (1986), pp. 465–87.

EXERCISING STRATEGY: A CUSTOMIZED APPRAISAL SYSTEM

Equifax provides information solutions to businesses and consumers regarding credit reporting, fraud protection, and debt recovery services. Equifax created a customized performance system to integrate organizational and individual performance, increase accountability, and improve follow-up. Managers are required to create annual objectives in four areas: strategy, operations, people, and finances. The objectives are weighted along with needed competencies for workplace tasks. A midyear evaluation is completed to ensure that objectives are being met, identify any objectives that need to be changed, and ensure that managers are discussing performance with their employees. Ratings are not given at the midyear review but are provided at the end of the year. As part of the performance management process, employees must include a learning objective, which states how and when the employee

intends to accomplish the objective and apply it in job or career development. The objective counts for 10 percent of the employee's overall evaluation.

Questions
1. How does this type of performance management system affect training and development?
2. Do you think it is more important for performance management systems such as this one to focus more, less, or about the same on what gets accomplished (objectives) or how it is accomplished (behaviors, competencies)? Explain your choice.
3. What recommendations would you give to Equifax to make this system even more effective?

SOURCE: Based on ASTD Best, "Equifax," *T + D*, October 2006, pp. 75–76.

MANAGING PEOPLE: FROM THE PAGES OF *BUSINESSWEEK*

BusinessWeek ### Sprint's Wake-Up Call

Reversing a miserable service reputation after the Nextel merger will be key to the company's turnaround When Daniel R. Hesse was named chief executive of Sprint Nextel in December, he figured that customer service was going to be one of his biggest challenges, given how poorly the wireless service provider had performed on that count in recent years. He quickly found out precisely how big. The lanky 54-year-old walked into his first operations meeting at Sprint headquarters in Overland Park, Kan., and found that customer service wasn't on the agenda at all. He changed course right away. Customer service is now the first item discussed at every one of the weekly meetings. "We weren't talking about the customer when I first joined," says Hesse. "Now this is the No. 1 priority of the company."

With good reason. Since Sprint and Nextel merged three years ago, the deal has turned into something of a fiasco, with the company's stock down 66% since the agreement was struck. Poor service is a central reason. After the merger, unhappy customers defected in droves, and profits evaporated. On Jan. 31, Sprint Nextel said it would take merger-related charges of as much as $31 billion, wiping out nearly all of the deal's value. In addition, two lawsuits have been filed against the company for allegedly extending customers' service contracts without their consent.

Employees like Paula Pryor saw the merger's impact firsthand. The 38-year-old, who worked in a call center in Temple, Tex., says the numbers-driven management

approach implemented after the combination led to poor morale and deteriorating customer service. Even bathroom trips were monitored. "They would micromanage us like children," says Pryor, who was fired last year after taking time off when her father died.

The toll on Sprint's reputation has been dear. The company has ranked last among the country's five major wireless carriers in customer service every year since the merger in 2005, according to annual surveys by J.D. Power & Associates.

Now, two months into his job, industry veteran Hesse is disclosing for the first time detailed plans for turning around customer service. He's increasing investments in customer care, adding service technicians in retail stores, and reversing many management practices in customer call centers. Hesse is convinced that restoring Sprint's reputation with customers is the key to its future. "You will see progress," he says. "We have the right people in place. We will get it done."

For the combined Sprint Nextel to be criticized for quality issues is a remarkable reversal. During the 1980s and '90s, when Sprint was the nation's third-largest long-distance company, it distinguished itself by advertising a fiber-optic network so high-quality you could "hear a pin drop." Nextel was known for its "push-to-talk" technology and the best rate of customer retention in the industry.

When the two unveiled plans to merge in December, 2004, there was a certain logic to the deal. Separately, they were much smaller than AT&T and Verizon Wireless, but together they would nearly rival the two wireless leaders in size. The theory was that, combined, they would have the bulk to get the latest phones, best prices on equipment, and most complete network for wireless customers. "The combination of Sprint and Nextel builds strength on strength," Gary D. Forsee, CEO of Sprint and later the combined companies, said then.

But as the two formally combined in August, 2005, it became clear this deal would be even more complex than the typical megamerger. At the same time Forsee and Executive Chairman Timothy M. Donahue were piecing the two companies together, they laid out an aggressive strategy for the combined entity to become a leader in wireless broadband services and content. That led to plans to spin off Sprint's local telephone business, form partnerships with the cable industry, and develop a wireless technology known as WiMAX. "There was so much going on after the merger that there was a lack of focus," says one former senior-level insider.

In September, 2005, the month after the merger closed, Forsee told Wall Street that the deal was going more smoothly than expected. He raised the projection for expected "synergies," or cost savings, to $14.5 billion, up from the original $12 billion estimate at the time of the merger announcement.

That boosted pressures to find cost savings throughout the company, say former employees and executives. An important component of the effort was importing the quantitative management approach of Sprint to Nextel. While some of the new metrics worked well, others had detrimental effects, former employees and executives say. In particular, call centers began to be measured and viewed primarily as cost centers, rather than opportunities for strategic advantage. Customer service ended up a secondary priority, say former executives. Forsee, now the president of the University of Missouri, declined to comment for this story.

In the fall of 2005, as board members gathered for their first meetings as a combined company, the directors from Nextel noticed another key change, according to the former senior-level insider. Before the merger, Nextel directors talked at every board meeting about "churn," the industry term for the percentage of existing customers who leave each month. The directors felt churn was a good shorthand way to understand the quality of customer service, and they prided themselves on Nextel having the lowest in the industry. But after the merger closed, the combined board paid little attention to churn, concentrating instead on the progress with synergies and strategic initiatives. "From the very beginning there was a philosophical difference on churn," says the former insider.

In the trenches, meanwhile, workers were dealing with fallout from the merger. Pryor remembers the conditions in her Texas call center, originally a Nextel facility, shifting

dramatically in the first months after the merger closed in late 2005. Managers began tracking what she was doing on her computer. Overtime pay became much harder to get. Most puzzling for her was the pressure to keep customer calls short. At Nextel, she was judged only on the number of customer problems she solved each month, however long they took, and she would occasionally spend 30 minutes to resolve a thorny issue. But after the merger, speed was the priority, she says. "They would say, 'Your calls need to be shortened,'" she says.

'Like Noah's Ark'

Other employees say they felt similar pressure. Gayle R. Romero, who worked in Sprint Nextel call centers for six years, says that at one team meeting after the merger, a manager said, "if you don't think you can handle this, I hear McDonald's is hiring." Says Romero: "Everyone was scared."

Customer service issues began to surface later that year. In January, 2006, Sprint unveiled plans to merge the two billing and customer care systems from the combined companies. But employees say there was little evidence of any progress in the following months. Service reps had to toggle back and forth between systems, and at times couldn't get access to billing or technical information for customers. "It was like Noah's Ark," says one former insider. "We had two of everything."

Churn rose quickly, hitting 2.4% in the third quarter of 2006. That was the highest among the country's major carriers and far above the 1.4% rate Nextel reported before the merger. At the same time, Sprint reported softer-than-expected earnings, punishing its stock.

As Sprint came under financial pressure in 2006, it began to ask call-center workers to engage more in sales. Whereas Nextel service reps had no sales quotas, workers at the combined companies were required to hit targets for renewing contracts or retaining customers who wanted to cancel accounts. One call-center employee says she was supposed to renew 600 to 900 contracts per month, and sometimes the target exceeded 1,000. In the customer retention unit, workers were given cash bonuses of $2,000 to $3,000 per month if they met monthly quotas. "They wanted those big bonuses," says Romero.

Allegations in the two lawsuits against Sprint raise questions about how far Sprint workers went in meeting those sales quotas. Selena L. Hayslett, a realtor from Apple Valley, Minn., says she called Sprint Nextel four times in late 2006 to dispute charges on her bill. Then she realized that each time she called, Sprint was extending her contract, without her consent, according to an affidavit filed in one of the suits. "I felt tricked," said Hayslett.

Her complaint is included in a lawsuit filed by the Minnesota attorney general, alleging that Sprint extended contracts when customers made small changes to their service. "It's kind of like the Hotel California," says Lori Swanson, the attorney general, "where you can check in and never leave." Sprint declined to comment in detail on the lawsuit. However, a spokesman says there are "discrepancies between our records and the lawsuit's portrayal of customer interactions."

Paula Appleby, a plaintiff in the other lawsuit, claims she tried to cancel her Sprint contract a number of times. But "each time she has attempted to cancel her service she has been told that her contract had been previously extended," according to the complaint, a federal lawsuit filed earlier this month seeking class action status. Sprint said it is still reviewing the Appleby lawsuit and declined to comment on specific claims.

In early 2007, as its financials deteriorated, Sprint cracked down on the freebies that call-center workers could give to keep customers happy, say current and former employees. One current manager in customer retention says that in the first half of 2007, Sprint cut back on virtually all the free minutes, service credits, and free phones that his workers used to be able to dole out. "One hundred minutes is it," says the manager, who asked for anonymity because he does not have authorization to speak to the press.

No Stopwatches

The new policies hurt Sprint's ability to build its customer base. In the third quarter of 2007, churn stayed high, and Sprint saw its subscriber numbers remain flat, at 54 million, while rivals AT&T and Verizon added millions. In October, Forsee stepped down as CEO under board pressure. Today, Hesse is reversing course on several fronts, hoping to salvage what he can from the troubled merger. He and his lieutenants aren't eliminating the quantitative approach entirely, but they're changing many of the old metrics to now emphasize service over efficiency.

Bob Johnson, Sprint's new chief service officer, has eliminated limits on the amount of time service reps spend on the phone with customers. Instead, he'll track how frequently reps resolve customers' problems on the first call.

Employees who don't solve a minimum percentage on the first call won't be eligible for sales bonuses. He'll also track how quickly customer calls are answered, to ensure they're getting prompt attention. "My incentives and policies are all driven around improving the experience," says Johnson. He says the long-delayed combined billing system will be done by May.

Hesse is also returning to the Nextel philosophy in a number of areas. Churn, for example, is once again a top priority, discussed at every operations meeting. The figure remained stubbornly high, at 2.3% in the fourth quarter of 2007.

As for the allegations in the two lawsuits, Johnson says Sprint has implemented a zero tolerance policy for shoddy customer service, which includes a new focus on extending contracts only with detailed approvals from customers. Among other things, Sprint sends a letter to customers outlining any changes to their account, and customers have 30 days to cancel the changes.

Hesse knows he has a long, hard road ahead of him. Still, he's convinced Sprint is at last moving in the right direction. "We're beginning to improve customer service already," he says. "There will be a lag between when it improves and when the world knows that Sprint's customer service has improved. There's always a perception lag."

Questions

1. Performance goals and objectives can have a powerful influence on employee behavior. What are the disadvantages of Sprint using only a numbers-driven approach (such as evaluating sales or amount of time spent on the phone with customers) to improve customer service?

2. What performance management approach (or combination of approaches) should Sprint use to improve customer service and customer retention? Justify your choice. What are the strengths and weaknesses of the approach you recommend?

SOURCE: Spencer E. Ante, "Sprint's Wake-Up Call," *BusinessWeek*, February 21, 2008.

○ NOTES

1. M. Laff, "Performance Management Gives a Shaky Performance," *T + D*, September 2007, p. 18; A. Fox, "Curing What Ails Performance Reviews," *HR Magazine*, January 2009, pp. 52–56.
2. "Measuring People Power," *Fortune*, October 2, 2000.
3. A. Freedman, "Balancing Values, Results in Reviews," *Human Resource Executive*, August 2006, pp. 62–63; G. Ruiz, "Performance Management Underperforms," *Workforce Management*, December 2006, pp. 47–49.
4. E. Pulakos, *Performance Management* (San Francisco: Wiley-Blackwell, 2009); K. Murphy and J. Cleveland, *Performance Appraisal: An Organizational Perspective* (Boston: Allyn & Bacon, 1991).
5. M. Sallie-Dosunmu, "Born to Grow," *TD*, May 2006, pp. 33–37.
6. J. Cleveland, K. Murphy, and R. Williams, "Multiple Uses of Performance Appraisal: Prevalence and Correlates," *Journal of Applied Psychology* 74 (1989), pp. 130–35.
7. C. Longenecker, "Behind the Mask: The Politics of Employee Appraisal," *Academy of Management Executive* 1 (1987), p. 183.
8. M. Beer, "Note on Performance Appraisal," in *Readings in Human Resource Management*, ed. M. Beer and B. Spector (New York: Free Press, 1985).
9. L. Weatherly, *Performance Management: Getting It Right from the Start* (Alexandria, VA: Society for Human Resource Management, 2004).

10. E. Lawler and M. McDermott, "Current Performance Management Practices," *World at Work Journal* 12, no. 2 (2003), pp. 49–60.

11. C. Cole, "Eight Values Bring Unity to a Worldwide Force," *Workforce*, March 2001, pp. 44–45; General Semiconductor Web site, www.generalsemiconductor.com, September 2, 2001.

12. C. G. Banks and K. E. May, "Performance Management: The Real Glue in Organizations," in *Evolving Practices in Human Resource Management*, ed. A. Kraut and A. Korman (San Francisco: Jossey-Bass, 1999), pp. 118–45.

13. C. E. Schneier, D. G. Shaw, and R. W. Beatty, "Performance Measurement and Management: A Tool for Strategic Execution," *Human Resource Management* 30 (1991), pp. 279–301.

14. C. D. Ittner and D. F. Larcker, "Coming Up Short on Nonfinancial Performance Measurement," *Harvard Business Review*, December 2003, pp. 88–95.

15. J. K. Harter, F. Schmidt, and T. L. Hayes, "Business-Unit Level Relationships between Employee Satisfaction, Employee Engagement, and Business Outcomes: A Meta-Analysis," *Journal of Applied Psychology* 87 (2002), pp. 268–79.

16. A. J. Rucci, S. P. Kim, and R. T. Quinn, "The Employee-Customer-Profit Chain at Sears," *Harvard Business Review*, January–February 1998, pp. 82–97.

17. R. Schuler and S. Jackson, "Linking Competitive Strategies with Human Resource Practices," *Academy of Management Executive* 1 (1987), pp. 207–19.

18. L. King, J. Hunter, and F. Schmidt, "Halo in a Multidimensional Forced-Choice Performance Evaluation Scale," *Journal of Applied Psychology* 65 (1980), pp. 507–16.

19. B. R. Nathan, A. M. Mohrman, and J. Millman, "Interpersonal Relations as a Context for the Effects of Appraisal Interviews on Performance and Satisfaction: A Longitudinal Study," *Academy of Management Journal* 34 (1991), pp. 352–69; M. S. Taylor, K. B. Tracy, M. K. Renard, J. K. Harrison, and S. J. Carroll, "Due Process in Performance Appraisal: A Quasi-experiment in Procedural Justice," *Administrative Science Quarterly* 40 (1995), pp. 495–523; J. M. Werner and M. C. Bolino, "Explaining U.S. Courts of Appeals Decisions Involving Performance Appraisal: Accuracy, Fairness, and Validation," *Personnel Psychology* 50 (1997), pp. 1–24.

20. *Albermarle Paper Company v. Moody*, 10 FEP 1181 (1975).

21. G. Ruiz, "Lessons from the Front Lines," *Workforce Management*, December 2006, pp. 50–52.

22. S. Bates, "Forced Ranking," *HR Magazine*, June 2003, pp. 63–68; A. Meisler, "Deadman's Curve," *Workforce Management*, July 2003, pp. 44–49; M. Lowery, "Forcing the Issue," *Human Resource Executive* (October 16, 2003), pp. 26–29.

23. Ibid.

24. Ibid.

25. S. Scullen, P. Bergey, and L. Aiman-Smith, "Forced Choice Distribution Systems and the Improvement of Workforce Potential: A Baseline Simulation," *Personnel Psychology* 58 (2005), pp. 1–32.

26. F. Blanz and E. Ghiselli, "The Mixed Standard Scale: A New Rating System," *Personnel Psychology* 25 (1973), pp. 185–99; K. Murphy and J. Constans, "Behavioral Anchors as a Source of Bias in Rating," *Journal of Applied Psychology* 72 (1987), pp. 573–77.

27. P. Smith and L. Kendall, "Retranslation of Expectations: An Approach to the Construction of Unambiguous Anchors for Rating Scales," *Journal of Applied Psychology* 47 (1963), pp. 149–55.

28. Murphy and Constans, "Behavioral Anchors"; M. Piotrowski, J. Barnes-Farrel, and F. Esrig, "Behaviorally Anchored Bias: A Replication and Extension of Murphy and Constans," *Journal of Applied Psychology* 74 (1989), pp. 823–26.

29. U. Wiersma and G. Latham, "The Practicality of Behavioral Observation Scales, Behavioral Expectation Scales, and Trait Scales," *Personnel Psychology* 39 (1986), pp. 619–28.

30. G. Latham and K. Wexley, *Increasing Productivity through Performance Appraisal* (Boston: Addison-Wesley, 1981).

31. Wiersma and Latham, "The Practicality of Behavioral Observation Scales, Behavioral Expectation Scales, and Trait Scales."

32. D. C. Anderson, C. Crowell, J. Sucec, K. Gilligan, and M. Wikoff, "Behavior Management of Client Contacts in a Real Estate Brokerage: Getting Agents to Sell More," *Journal of Organizational Behavior Management* 4 (1983), pp. 67–96; A. D. Stajkovic and F. Luthans, "Differential Effects of Incentive Motivation on Work Performance," *Academy of Management Journal* 4 (2001), pp. 580–90; F. Luthans and R. Kreitner, *Organizational Behavior Modification and Beyond* (Glenview, IL: Scott Foresman, 1975).

33. K. L. Langeland, C. M. Jones, and T. C. Mawhinney, "Improving Staff Performance in a Community Mental Health Setting: Job Analysis, Training, Goal Setting, Feedback, and Years of Data," *Journal of Organizational Behavior Management* 18 (1998), pp. 21–43.

34. J. Komaki, R. Collins, and P. Penn, "The Role of Performance Antecedents and Consequences in Work Motivation," *Journal of Applied Psychology* 67 (1982), pp. 334–40.

35. Latham and Wexley, *Increasing Productivity through Performance Appraisal*.

36. S. Snell, "Control Theory in Strategic Human Resource Management: The Mediating Effect of Administrative Information," *Academy of Management Journal* 35 (1992), pp. 292–327.

37. T. Patten Jr., *A Manager's Guide to Performance Appraisal* (New York: Free Press, 1982).

38. M. O'Donnell and R. O'Donnell, "MBO—Is It Passe?" *Hospital and Health Services Administration* 28, no. 5 (1983), pp. 46–58; T. Poister and G. Streib, "Management Tools in Government: Trends over the Past Decade," *Public Administration Review* 49 (1989), pp. 240–48.

39. D. McGregor, "An Uneasy Look at Performance Appraisal," *Harvard Business Review* 35, no. 3 (1957), pp. 89–94.

40. E. Locke and G. Latham, *A Theory of Goal Setting and Task Performance* (Englewood Cliffs, NJ: Prentice Hall, 1990).

41. S. Carroll and H. Tosi, *Management by Objectives* (New York: Macmillan, 1973).

42. G. Odiorne, *MBO II: A System of Managerial Leadership for the 80's* (Belmont, CA: Pitman, 1986).

43. R. Rodgers and J. Hunter, "Impact of Management by Objectives on Organizational Productivity," *Journal of Applied Psychology* 76 (1991), pp. 322–26.

44. S. Wells, "No Results, No Raise," *HR Magazine*, May 2005, pp. 77–79.

45. R. Pritchard, S. Jones, P. Roth, K. Stuebing, and S. Ekeberg, "The Evaluation of an Integrated Approach to Measuring Organizational Productivity," *Personnel Psychology* 42 (1989), pp. 69–115.

46. P. Wright, J. George, S. Farnsworth, and G. McMahan, "Productivity and Extra-Role Behavior: The Effects of Goals and Incentives on Spontaneous Helping," *Journal of Applied Psychology* 78, no. 3 (1993), pp. 374–81.

47. Latham and Wexley, *Increasing Productivity through Performance Appraisal*.

48. J. Liedman, "The Ongoing Conversation," *Human Resource Executive*, November 2006, pp. 71–74; R. Davenport, "John Deere Champions Workforce Development," *TD*, April 2006, pp. 41–43.

49. R. L. Cardy, "Performance Appraisal in a Quality Context: A New Look at an Old Problem," in *Performance Appraisal: State of the Art in Practice*, ed. J. W. Smither (San Francisco: Jossey-Bass, 1998), pp. 132–62.

50. E. C. Huge, *Total Quality: An Executive's Guide for the 1990s* (Homewood, IL: Richard D. Irwin, 1990): see Chapter 5, "Measuring and Rewarding Performance," pp. 70–88; W. E. Deming, *Out of Crisis* (Cambridge, MA: MIT Center for Advanced Engineering Study, 1986).

51. M. Caroselli, *Total Quality Transformations* (Amherst, MA: Human Resource Development Press, 1991); Huge, *Total Quality*.

52. J. D. Cryer and R. B. Miller, *Statistics for Business: Data Analysis and Modeling* (Boston: PWS-Kent, 1991); C. Carter, "Seven Basic Quality Tools," *HR Magazine,* January 1992, pp. 81–83; D. K. Denton, "Process Mapping Trims Cycle Time," *HR Magazine,* February 1995, pp. 56–61.

53. D. E. Bowen and E. E. Lawler III, "Total Quality-Oriented Human Resource Management," *Organizational Dynamics* 21 (1992), pp. 29–41.

54. R. Heneman, K. Wexley, and M. Moore, "Performance Rating Accuracy: A Critical Review," *Journal of Business Research* 15 (1987), pp. 431–48.

55. T. Becker and R. Klimoski, "A Field Study of the Relationship between the Organizational Feedback Environment and Performance," *Personnel Psychology* 42 (1989), pp. 343–58; H. M. Findley, W. F. Giles, and K. W. Mossholder, "Performance Appraisal and Systems Facets: Relationships with Contextual Performance," *Journal of Applied Psychology* 85 (2000), pp. 634–40.

56. K. Ellis, "Developing for Dollars," *Training,* May 2003, pp. 34–39.

57. L. Axline, "Performance Biased Evaluations," *Supervisory Management,* November 1991, p. 3.

58. K. Wexley and R. Klimoski, "Performance Appraisal: An Update," in *Research in Personnel and Human Resource Management* (vol. 2), ed. K. Rowland and G. Ferris (Greenwich, CT: JAI Press, 1984).

59. F. Landy and J. Farr, *The Measurement of Work Performance: Methods, Theory, and Applications* (New York: Academic Press, 1983).

60. G. McEvoy and P. Buller, "User Acceptance of Peer Appraisals in an Industrial Setting," *Personnel Psychology* 40 (1987), pp. 785–97.

61. A. Pomeroy, "Agent of Change," *HR Magazine,* May 2005, pp. 52–56.

62. D. Antonioni, "The Effects of Feedback Accountability on Upward Appraisal Ratings," *Personnel Psychology* 47 (1994), pp. 349–56.

63. Murphy and Cleveland, *Performance Appraisal: An Organizational Perspective*.

64. J. Bernardin and L. Klatt, "Managerial Appraisal Systems: Has Practice Caught Up with the State of the Art?" *Public Personnel Administrator,* November 1985, pp. 79–86.

65. Fox, "Curing What Ails Performance Reviews."

66. H. Heidemeier and K. Moser, "Self-Other Agreement in Job Performance Rating: A Meta-Analytic Test of a Process Model," *Journal of Applied Psychology* 94 (2008), pp. 353–70.

67. R. Steel and N. Ovalle, "Self-Appraisal Based on Supervisor Feedback," *Personnel Psychology* 37 (1984), pp. 667–85; L. E. Atwater, "The Advantages and Pitfalls of Self-Assessment in Organizations," in *Performance Appraisal: State of the Art in Practice,* pp. 331–65.

68. M. W. Horrigan, "Employment Projections to 2012: Concepts and Context," *Monthly Labor Review* 127 (2004), pp. 3–11.

69. E. Gummerson, "Lip Services—A Neglected Area of Service Marketing," *Journal of Services Marketing* 1 (1987), pp. 1–29.

70. J. Bernardin, B. Hagan, J. Kane, and P. Villanova, "Effective Performance Management: A Focus on Precision, Customers, and Situational Constraints," in *Performance Appraisal: State of the Art in Practice,* ed. J. W. Smither (San Francisco: Jossey-Bass, 1998), pp. 3–48.

71. R. Hoffman, "Ten Reasons You Should Be Using 360-Degree Feedback," *HR Magazine,* April 1995, pp. 82–84.

72. S. Sherman, "How Tomorrow's Best Leaders Are Learning Their Stuff," *Fortune,* November 27, 1995, pp. 90–104; W. W. Tornow, M. London, and Associates, *Maximizing the Value of 360-Degree Feedback* (San Francisco: Jossey-Bass, 1998); D. A. Waldman, L. E. Atwater, and D. Antonioni, "Has 360-Degree Feedback Gone Amok?" *Academy of Management Executive* 12 (1988), pp. 86–94.

73. A. Tversky and D. Kahneman, "Availability: A Heuristic for Judging Frequency and Probability," *Cognitive Psychology* 5 (1973), pp. 207–32.

74. K. Wexley and W. Nemeroff, "Effects of Racial Prejudice, Race of Applicant, and Biographical Similarity on Interviewer Evaluations of Job Applicants," *Journal of Social and Behavioral Sciences* 20 (1974), pp. 66–78.

75. G. Ruiz, "Lessons from the Front Lines," *Workforce Management,* December 2006, pp. 50–52.

76. D. Smith, "Training Programs for Performance Appraisal: A Review," *Academy of Management Review* 11 (1986), pp. 22–40.

77. G. Latham, K. Wexley, and E. Pursell, "Training Managers to Minimize Rating Errors in the Observation of Behavior," *Journal of Applied Psychology* 60 (1975), pp. 550–55.

78. J. Bernardin and E. Pence, "Effects of Rater Training: Creating New Response Sets and Decreasing Accuracy," *Journal of Applied Psychology* 65 (1980), pp. 60–66.

79. E. Pulakos, "A Comparison of Rater Training Programs: Error Training and Accuracy Training," *Journal of Applied Psychology* 69 (1984), pp. 581–88.

80. H. J. Bernardin, M. R. Buckley, C. L. Tyler, and D. S. Wiese, "A Reconsideration of Strategies in Rater Training," in *Research in Personnel and Human Resource Management,* vol. 18, ed. G. R. Ferris (Greenwich, CT: JAI Press, 2000), pp. 221–74.

81. J. Sammer, "Calibrating Consistency," *HR Magazine,* January 2008, pp. 73–75.

82. S. W. J. Kozlowski, G. T. Chao, and R. F. Morrison, "Games Raters Play: Politics, Strategies, and Impression Management in Performance Appraisal," in *Performance Appraisal: State of the Art in Practice,* pp. 163–205; C. Rosen, P. Levy, and R. Hall, "Placing Perceptions of Politics in the Context of the Feedback Environment, Employee Attitudes, and Job Performance," *Journal of Applied Psychology* 91 (2006), pp. 211–20.

83. K. Wexley, V. Singh, and G. Yukl, "Subordinate Participation in Three Types of Appraisal Interviews," *Journal of Applied Psychology* 58 (1973), pp. 54–57; K. Wexley, "Appraisal Interview," in *Performance Assessment,* ed. R. A. Berk (Baltimore: Johns Hopkins University Press, 1986), pp. 167–85; D. Cederblom, "The Performance Appraisal Interview: A Review, Implications, and Suggestions," *Academy of Management Review* 7 (1982), pp. 219–27; B. D. Cawley, L. M. Keeping, and P. E. Levy, "Participation in the Performance Appraisal Process and Employee Reactions: A Meta-analytic Review of Field Investigations," *Journal of Applied Psychology* 83, no. 3 (1998), pp. 615–63; H. Aguinis, *Performance Management* (Upper Saddle River, NJ: Pearson Prentice Hall, 2007); C. Lee, "Feedback, Not Appraisal," *HR Magazine,* November 2006, pp. 111–14.

84. B. Hite, "Employers Rethink How They Give Feedback," *Wall Street Journal,* October 13, 2008, p. B5.

85. W. Giles and K. Mossholder, "Employee Reactions to Contextual and Session Components of Performance Appraisal," *Journal of Applied Psychology* 75 (1990), pp. 371–77.

86. E. Locke and G. Latham, *A Theory of Goal Setting and Task Performance* (Englewood Cliffs, NJ: Prentice Hall, 1990).

87. H. Klein, S. Snell, and K. Wexley, "A Systems Model of the Performance Appraisal Interview Process," *Industrial Relations* 26 (1987), pp. 267–80.

88. M. London and E. M. Mone, "Managing Marginal Performance in Organizations Striving for Excellence," in *Human Resource Dilemmas in Work Organizations: Strategies for Resolution,* ed. A. K. Korman (New York: Guilford, 1993), pp. 95–124.

89. *Brito v. Zia Co.,* 478 F.2d 1200 (10th Cir 1973).

90. K. Kraiger and J. Ford, "A Meta-Analysis of Ratee Race Effects in Performance Rating," *Journal of Applied Psychology* 70 (1985), pp. 56–65.

91. P. Sackett, C. DuBois, and A. Noe, "Tokenism in Performance Evaluation: The Effects of Work Groups Representation on Male–Female and White–Black Differences in Performance Ratings," *Journal of Applied Psychology* 76 (1991), pp. 263–67.

92. G. Barrett and M. Kernan, "Performance Appraisal and Terminations: A Review of Court Decisions since *Brito v. Zia* with Implications for Personnel Practices," *Personnel Psychology* 40 (1987), pp. 489–503; H. Field and W. Holley, "The Relationship of Performance Appraisal System Characteristics to Verdicts in Selected Employment Discrimination Cases," *Academy of Management Journal* 25 (1982), pp. 392–406; J. M. Werner and M. C. Bolino, "Explaining U.S. Courts of Appeals Decisions Involving Performance Appraisal: Accuracy, Fairness, and Validation," *Personnel Psychology* 50 (1997), pp. 1–24; J. A. Segal, "86 Your Appraisal Process," *HR Magazine,* October 2000, pp. 199–202.

93. K. Maher, "Big Employer Is Watching," *The Wall Street Journal,* November 4, 2003, pp. B1 and B6.

94. D. Onley, "Technology Gives Big Brother Capability," *HR Magazine,* July 2005, pp. 99–102.

95. V. O'Connell, "Stores Count Seconds to Cut Labor Costs," *The Wall Street Journal,* November 17, 2008, pp. A1, A15.

Employee Development

 LEARNING OBJECTIVES

After reading this chapter, you should be able to:

LO1   Explain how employee development contributes to strategies related to employee retention, developing intellectual capital, and business growth. *page 410*

LO2   Discuss current trends in using formal education for development. *page 414*

LO3   Relate how assessment of personality type, work behaviors, and job performance can be used for employee development. *page 419*

LO4   Explain how job experiences can be used for skill development. *page 427*

LO5   Develop successful mentoring programs. *page 435*

LO6   Describe how to train managers to coach employees. *page 438*

LO7   Discuss the steps in the development planning process. *page 440*

LO8   Explain the employees' and company's responsibilities in planning development. *page 440*

LO9   Discuss what companies are doing for management development issues including succession planning, melting the glass ceiling, and helping dysfunctional managers. *page 444*

Helping Consultants Manage Their Own Development and Careers Leads to Retention at Accenture Consulting

Accenture Consulting has offices in 150 cities across the globe in countries such as Argentina, Botswana, South Korea, Poland, and the United States, but it encourages employees to spend time with clients—not in their offices. If employees want to spend time in one of the consulting firm's offices, they have to make a reservation for a desk! Accenture has a virtual management workforce of 178,000 employees who, at any one time, are working at different times and places around the world. Accenture's consultants analyze client's business needs and design and implement solutions. The consultants work in teams depending on the size of the client and the project. While the work and travel can be exciting, it also can take a heavy toll on the consultants—many at some point in their careers choose to take a stable job, often with one of the clients with whom they have worked. A consultant deciding to work for a client cannot be considered completely dysfunctional because it can help Accenture keep and maybe even add new business. However, a serious downside is that Accenture loses money when talented employees leave.

Accenture has taken several steps to reduce turnover by helping consultants manage their careers to recognize and take advantage of opportunities within the company. For example, after orientation every new hire is assigned a career counselor, a more senior Accenture employee in the same line of business who is available to meet face-to-face or electronically to discuss current work and potential career opportunities. Accenture's performance and compensation system encourages senior employees to make time in their schedules for career counseling. Every employee at Accenture is evaluated on people development skills as part of the annual performance review, which is tied to a percentage of their pay increase. To encourage career development, Accenture's human resources department is focusing on communicating the different available career paths to employees more effectively. Also, the company's career counselors attend mandatory one-day training on the different career paths at Accenture. Accenture has replaced the old "get promoted or leave" with a philosophy that emphasizes how its multiple workforces each contribute to the business in a different, but complementary, way. Accenture's business strategy depends on these different workforces blending together as an integrated whole, to help it and its clients achieve higher levels of performance. As a result, Accenture now has many different opportunities varying in both the type of work (consulting, technology, and outsourcing) and the type of client being served (for-profit and not-for-profit businesses).

A Web site known as Careers Marketplace was developed by Accenture to provide employees with information about changing careers within the company, and it provides links to unfilled positions. For example, one of the videos on the Web site explains how an employee has moved within the company from consulting to business operations work to human resources. The employee discusses how each move helped her develop her skills and experience. Accenture also recognizes the important role of nonwork life in a successful career. For example, Accenture has a leave program (Future Leave) through which employees can arrange for part of their paychecks to be set aside for up to three months of future time off. The company also asks employees to evaluate how well the company is doing in providing them with a high-quality life as well as to rank issues such as diversity, reputation, work, rewards, and career development in order of personal importance. This helps Accenture determine the work/life balance of employees. The surveys are also used by career counselors in their discussions with employees.

Sources: Based on J. Marquez, "Accentuating the Positive," *Workforce Management*, September 22, 2008, pp. 18–25. Also, see Accenture's Web site at www.accenture.com; S. Needleman, "New Career, Same Employer," *The Wall Street Journal*, April 21, 2008, p. B9.

Introduction

As the Accenture Consulting example illustrates, employee development and career management are key contributors to a company's competitive advantage by helping employees understand their strengths, weaknesses, and interests and by showing them how new jobs, expanded job responsibilities, and career paths are available to them to meet their personal growth needs. This helps retain valuable employees who might otherwise leave to join clients or competitors. Employee development is a necessary component of a company's efforts to compete in the new economy, to meet the challenges of global competition and social change, and to incorporate technological advances and changes in work design. Employee development is key to ensuring that employees have the competencies necessary to serve customers and create new products and customer solutions. Employee development is also important to ensure that companies have the managerial talent needed to successfully execute a growth strategy. Regardless of the business strategy, development is important for retaining talented employees. Also because companies (and their employees) must constantly learn and change to meet customer needs and compete in new markets, the emphasis placed on both training and development has increased. As we noted in Chapter 1, employee commitment and retention are directly related to how employees are treated by their managers.

This chapter begins by discussing the relationship between development, training, and careers. Second, we look at development approaches, including formal education, assessment, job experiences, and interpersonal relationships. The chapter emphasizes the types of skills, knowledge, and behaviors that are strengthened by each development method. Choosing an approach is one part of development planning. Before one or multiple developmental approaches are used, the employee and the company must have an idea of the employee's development needs and the purpose of development. Identifying the needs and purpose of development is part of its planning. The third section of the chapter describes the steps of the development planning process. Employee and company responsibilities at each step of the process are emphasized. The chapter concludes with a discussion of special issues in employee development, including succession planning, dealing with dysfunctional managers, and using development to help women and minorities move into upper-level management positions (referred to as "melting the glass ceiling").

Development
The acquisition of knowledge, skills, and behaviors that improve an employee's ability to meet changes in job requirements and in client and customer demands.

The Relationship among Development, Training, and Careers

LO1
Explain how employee development contributes to strategies related to employee retention, developing intellectual capital, and business growth.

Development and Training

Development refers to formal education, job experiences, relationships, and assessment of personality and abilities that help employees prepare for the future. The Accenture Consulting example illustrates that although development can occur

	TRAINING	DEVELOPMENT
Focus	Current	Future
Use of work experiences	Low	High
Goal	Preparation for current job	Preparation for changes
Participation	Required	Voluntary

table 9.1

Comparison between Training and Development

through participation in planned programs, it often results from performing different types of work or serving new clients. Because it is future-oriented, it involves learning that is not necessarily related to the employee's current job.[1] Table 9.1 shows the differences between training and development. Traditionally, training focuses on helping employees' performance in their current jobs. Development prepares them for other positions in the company and increases their ability to move into jobs that may not yet exist.[2] Development also helps employees prepare for changes in their current jobs that may result from new technology, work designs, new customers, or new product markets. Development is especially critical for talent management, particularly for senior managers and employees with leadership potential (recall our discussion of attracting and retaining talent in Chapter 1). Companies report that the most important talent management challenges they face include developing existing talent and attracting and retaining existing leadership talent.[3] Chapter 7 emphasized the strategic role of training. As training continues to become more strategic (that is, related to business goals), the distinction between training and development will blur. Both training and development will be required and will focus on current and future personal and company needs.

Development and Careers

Traditionally, careers have been described in various ways.[4] Careers have been described as a sequence of positions held within an occupation. For example, a university faculty member can hold assistant, associate, and full professor positions. A career has also been described in the context of mobility within an organization. For example, an engineer may begin her career as a staff engineer. As her expertise, experience, and performance increase, she may move through advisory engineering, senior engineering, and senior technical positions. Finally, a career has been described as a characteristic of the employee. Each employee's career consists of different jobs, positions, and experiences.

Today's careers are known as protean careers.[5] A **protean career** is based on self-direction with the goal of psychological success in one's work. Employees take major responsibility for managing their careers. For example, an engineer may decide to take a sabbatical from her position to work in management at the United Way Agency for a year. The purpose of this assignment could be to develop her managerial skills as well as help her personally evaluate if she likes managerial work more than engineering.

Changes in the psychological contract between employees and their companies have influenced the development of the protean career.[6] A **psychological contract** is the expectations that employers and employees have about each other. Today's psychological contract rarely provides employees with job security even if they perform well. Instead, companies can offer employees opportunities to attend training programs and participate in work experiences that can increase their employability

Protean Career
A career that is based on self-direction with the goal of psychological success in one's work.

Psychological Contract
The expectations that employers and employees have about each other.

with their current and future employers. For example, the term *blue-collar work* has always meant manufacturing work, but technology has transformed the meaning dramatically.[7] Traditional assembly-line jobs that required little skill and less education have been sent overseas. Today's blue-collar workers are more involved in customized manufacturing. At U.S. Steel employees make more than 700 different kinds of steel, requiring greater familiarity with additives and more understanding of customers and markets. Jobs once considered as lifetime employment are now more temporary, forcing employees to adapt by moving from one factory to another or by changing work shifts. Employees are taking classes to keep up with the latest developments in steelmaking, such as lathes and resins. Despite the lack of guaranteed lifetime employment, many blue-collar jobs are safer and better paying than they were 10 years ago.

Psychological Success
The feeling of pride and accomplishment that comes from achieving life goals.

The protean career has several implications for employee development. The goal of the new career is **psychological success:** the feeling of pride and accomplishment that comes from achieving life goals that are not limited to achievements at work (such as raising a family and having good physical health). Psychological success is more under the employee's control than the traditional career goals, which were not only influenced by employee effort but were controlled by the availability of positions in the company. Psychological success is self-determined rather than solely determined through signals the employee receives from the company (like salary increase and promotion). Psychological success appears to be especially important to the new generation of persons entering the workforce. For example, consider Jacqueline Strayer. Since graduating from college in 1976, she has held a series of positions with different companies including General Electric, GTE, United Technologies, and William Mercer.[8] At the same time, she earned a master's degree in professional studies in film and television and is currently working on a doctorate in management. Her motivation is finding interesting, challenging positions rather than trying to be promoted to a top management position. She is also passionate about running, so she wants to work with an employer that has a fitness center.

Employees need to develop new skills rather than rely on a static knowledge base. This has resulted from companies' need to be more responsive to customers' service and product demands. The types of knowledge an employee needs have changed.[9] In the traditional career, "knowing how" (having the appropriate skills and knowledge to provide a service or produce a product) was critical. Although knowing how remains important, employees also need to "know why" and "know whom." Knowing why refers to understanding the company's business and culture so the employee can develop and apply knowledge and skills that can contribute to the business. Knowing whom refers to relationships the employee may develop to contribute to company success. These relationships may include networking with vendors, suppliers, community members, customers, or industry experts. Learning to know whom and know why requires more than formal courses and training programs. Learning and development in the protean career are increasingly likely to involve relationships and job experiences rather than formal courses.

The emphasis on continuous learning and learning beyond knowing how as well as changes in the psychological contract are altering the direction and frequency of movement within careers (career pattern).[10] Traditional career patterns consisted of a series of steps arranged in a linear hierarchy, with higher steps related to increased authority, responsibility, and compensation. Expert career patterns involve a lifelong commitment to a field or specialization (such as law, medicine, or management). These types of career patterns will not disappear. Rather, career patterns involving movement across specializations or disciplines (a spiral career pattern) will become more prevalent. These new career patterns mean that developing employees (as well as employees taking control of their own careers) will require providing them with the opportunity to (a) determine their interests, skill strengths, and weaknesses and (b) based on this information, seek appropriate development experiences that will likely involve job experiences and relationships as well as formal courses.

The most appropriate view of today's careers are that they are "boundaryless and often change."[11] It may include movement across several employers or even different occupations. Statistics indicate that the average employment tenure for all American workers is only five years.[12] One study found that 60 percent of employees of all ages rate time and flexibility as very important reasons for staying with a company.[13] But Gen Xers (those in their mid-20s to late 40s) were more likely to leave a job than baby boomers (those in their mid-40s to late 50s). Some 51 percent of employees under age 40 reported they were looking for a new job within the next year, compared to only 25 percent of those 40 or older. For example, Craig Matison, 33 years old, took a job with Cincinnati Bell Information System, a unit of Cincinnati Bell Corporation that manages billing for phone and cable companies.[14] Although he had been on the job only six months, he was already looking to make his next career move. Not wanting to stay on the technical career path, he regularly explored company databases for job postings, looking for sales and marketing opportunities within the company.

"Boundaryless" means that careers may involve identifying more with a job or profession than with the present employer. A career can also be considered boundaryless in the sense that career plans or goals are influenced by personal or family demands and values. One way that employees cope with changes in their personal lives as well as in employment relationships is to rearrange and shift their roles and responsibilities. Employees can change their careers throughout their life based on awareness of strengths and weaknesses, perceived need to balance work and life, and the need to find stimulating and exciting work.[15] Career success may not be tied to promotions but to achieving goals that are personally meaningful to the employee rather than those set by parents, peers, or the company. As we discuss later in the chapter, careers are best managed through partnerships between employees and their company that create a positive relationship through which employees are committed to the organization but can take personal control for managing their own careers to benefit themselves and company.

As this discussion shows, to retain and motivate employees companies need to provide a system to identify and meet employees' development needs. This is especially important to retain good performers and employees who have potential for managerial positions. This system is often known as a **career management** or **development planning system**. We discuss these systems in detail later in the chapter.

Career Management System
A system to retain and motivate employees by identifying and meeting their development needs (also called *development planning systems*).

Approaches to Employee Development

Four approaches are used to develop employees: formal education, assessment, job experiences, and interpersonal relationships.[16] Many companies use a combination of these approaches. Figure 9.1 shows the frequency of use of different employee development practices. Larger companies are more likely to use leadership training and development planning more frequently than smaller companies. Children's Healthcare of Atlanta, a medical system specializing in pediatric care, has a Center for Leadership that includes assessment, workshops, action learning, and personal coaches.[17] High-performing employees with potential to become managers complete a full day of

figure 9.1

Frequency of
Use of Employee
Development
Practices

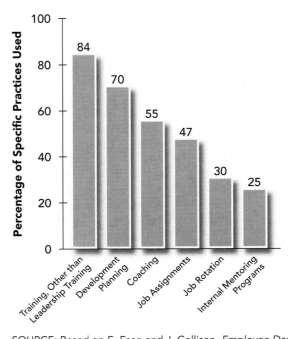

SOURCE: Based on E. Esen and J. Collison, *Employee Development* (Alexandria, VA: SHRM
Research, 2005).

assessment that includes participating in a business simulation requiring them to pretend they are managing a division of a major company. They also complete a personality inventory. Employees are given feedback about their behavior in the simulation and the results of the personality inventory. Employees attend five workshops each year that focus on helping employees work with the feedback they received during the assessment. The workshops cover topics such as leading change, developing a business strategy, and creating a personal vision. Action learning requires participants to work in teams on a topic that is of strategic importance to the medical system. Coaches work with the employees to identify long-term improvement goals.

Keep in mind that although much development activity is targeted at managers, all levels of employees may be involved in development. For example, most employees typically receive performance appraisal feedback (a development activity related to assessment) at least once per year. As we discussed in Chapter 8, as part of the appraisal process they are asked to complete individual development plans outlining (1) how they plan to change their weaknesses and (2) their future plans (including positions or locations desired and education or experience needed). Next we explore each type of development approach.

LO2
Discuss current trends in
using formal education for
development.

**Formal Education
Programs**
Employee
development
programs,
including short
courses offered by
consultants or
universities,
executive MBA
programs, and
university programs.

Formal Education

Formal education programs include off-site and on-site programs designed specifically for the company's employees, short courses offered by consultants or universities, executive MBA programs, and university programs in which participants actually live at the university while taking classes. These programs may involve lectures by business experts, business games and simulations, adventure learning, and meetings with customers.

Many companies such as Bank of Montreal and General Electric rely primarily on in-house development programs offered by training and development centers or corporate universities, rather than sending employees to programs offered by universities.[18] Companies rely on in-house programs because they can be tied directly to business needs, can be easily evaluated using company metrics, and can get senior-level management involved. The Bank of Montreal (BMO) has invested more than $400 million in training and development, including building the Institute for Learning, with high-tech classrooms, rooms to accommodate out-of-town employees, a presentation hall, restaurants, and a gym.[19] Each year 8,000 employees receive training at the Institute for Learning. A wide range of courses and programs are offered that are linked to the bank's business strategies. They include management leadership training, risk management training, project management programs, and a four-year MBA program in financial services offered through a partnership with the Dalhousie School of Management and the Institute for Canadian Bankers. BMO believes the programs provide immediate benefit to the company because they often require participants to provide solutions to issues the company is facing. Evaluation and feedback are used to determine the success of specific programs. BMO uses many different types of evaluation including skill tests and performance evaluations conducted by managers after the participant returns to the job to determine transfer of training. BMO also looks at the relationship between the bank's education spending and its performance. Employee surveys are used to determine the quality and relevance of programs.

General Electric (GE) has one of the oldest and most widely known management development centers in the world. GE invests approximately $1 billion each year for training and education programs for its employees.[20] Over the past 15 years, the 189 most senior executives in the company spent at least 12 months in training and professional development. GE develops managers at the John F. Welch Leadership Center at Crotonville, New York.[21] The facility has residence buildings where participants stay while attending programs as well as classrooms for courses, programs, and seminars. Each year GE employees chosen by their managers based on their performance and potential attend management development programs. The programs include professional skills development and specialized courses in areas such as risk analysis and loan structuring. All of the programs emphasize theory and practical application. Course time is spent discussing business issues facing GE. The programs are taught by in-house instructors, university faculty members, and even CEO Jeff Immelt. Examples of management development programs available at GE are shown in Table 9.2. As you can see, GE uses a combination of coursework and job experiences to develop entry-level and top levels of management. Other programs such as the Business Manager Course and the Executive Development Course involve action learning. As discussed in Chapter 7, action learning involves assigning a real problem that GE is facing to program participants who must present their recommendations to Jeff Immelt. Besides programs and courses for management development GE also holds seminars to better understand customer expectations and leadership conferences designed specifically for African-Americans, women, or Hispanic managers to discuss leading and learning.

Table 9.3 shows examples of institutions for executive education. There are several important trends in executive education. Leadership, entrepreneurship, and e-business are the most important topics in executive education programs. Programs directed at developing executives' understanding of global business issues and management of change are other important parts of executive development.[22] Many companies who compete in the global economy with a worldwide workforce are using

table 9.2

Examples of Leadership Development Programs at General Electric

PROGRAM	SUMMARY	QUALIFICATIONS TO ATTEND
Commercial Leadership Program: Commercial and Industrial	Formal courses, including Selling@GE, Marketing@GE, and negotiation skills. Challenging assignments in key sales and marketing roles within a business.	Bachelor's degree in engineering or industrial distribution; minimum 3.0 GPA; prior internship or co-op experience, willingness to relocate; demonstrated interest in sales career and results oriented.
Experienced Commercial Leadership Program (ECLP): Sales and Marketing	Four 6-month business rotations within a GE business; two rotations are marketing focused and two are sales focused. Every 3 months, review self-assessment and manager evaluations to identify accomplishments, development needs, and career interests. Strengthen commercial business and leadership skills by completing classroom and online training and in-residence symposiums at the John F. Welch Learning Center.	MBA; 4–6 years marketing or sales experience; demonstrated achievement and leadership in sales or marketing leadership, communications, and analytical skills; willingness to relocate; expertise aligned with a GE business; unrestricted U.S. work authorization.

SOURCE: Based on "Undergraduate Leadership Programs" and "Masters and MBA Leadership Programs at www.gecareers .com (April 6, 2009).

table 9.3

Examples of Institutions That Provide Executive Education

PROVIDER (LOCATION)	2004–05 REVENUE (MILLIONS)	NO. OF EXECUTIVE NONDEGREE PROGRAMS	NO. OF EXECUTIVES ATTENDING PROGRAMS	RANGE OF COSTS FOR PROGRAMS	CORPORATE CLIENTS
London Business School (London, England)	43.9	86	5,771	$5,570–33,245	Nokia Shell Michelin
University of Michigan (Ann Arbor)	17.2	77	3,893	2,000–31,300	TRW Ford Motor Pfizer
Stanford University (California)	21.2	44	2,070	5,500–45,900	Hewlett-Packard Cisco Systems Siemens AG
INSEAD (Fontainbleau, France)	85.1	136	7,000	3,300–42,000	IBM Royal Dutch Shell BASF
University of Virginia Darden School (Charlottesville)	17.2	68	3,151	3,700–29,400	U.S. Military State Farm Insurance Bacardi

SOURCE: Based on "2005 Executive Education Profile," *BusinessWeek Online*, October 24, 2005, www.businessweek.com.

a blended learning approach for management development (we discussed blended learning in Chapter 7). For example, Xerox Corporation's Emerging Leaders Program (ELP) is a five-month program that includes a two-hour program kickoff using Web-based conferencing, e-modules that employees complete at their own pace, face-to-face meetings, online assessment, coaching, and mentoring.[23] Employees from North America and Europe have participated in ELP. Each session in the European ELP includes high-potential managers from 14 countries who work in different functions and speak different languages. The most challenging part of ELP involves working as a cross-functional, cross-cultural, geographically dispersed team to identify, plan, and begin a business project based on the strategic initiatives. Each team presents their results to vice presidents and executives at the conclusion of the program. The "Competing through Technology" box shows how IBM is using technology for delivery and instruction of its management development programs.

There is another trend in executive education: business schools or other educational institutions have begun offering companies in-house, custom programs to help managers gain real-world skills and study problems in real-world environments—without requiring the managers to disrupt their work by requiring them to travel to campus. These programs supplement formal courses from consultants or university faculty with other types of development activities. For example, Duke Corporate Education conducts custom programs for ArcelorMittal, which was formed by the merger of two steel companies.[24] One of the challenges the company faces is how to get its managers to understand the global challenges facing the steel industry. As a result, the program involves middle managers visiting steel plants in both mature and emerging markets to gain an understanding of the technology and management processes of a more established steel plant compared with a growing steel plant. The managers are asked to develop proposals for improving the growing plant, such as how to identify environmental problems and expanding health and safety features. The Haas School of Business at the University of California, Berkeley, worked with StatoilHydro, the Norwegian oil and gas company that focuses on preparing employees to work in different cultures. The program includes challenges such as working with contractors who may not have the employees or equipment to complete a project on time or learning to deal with local government officials.

Managers who attend the Center for Creative Leadership development program take psychological tests; receive feedback from managers, peers, and direct reports; participate in group-building activities (like adventure learning, discussed in Chapter 7); receive counseling; and set improvement goals and write development plans.[25]

Enrollment in executive education programs or MBA programs may be limited to managers or employees identified to have management potential. As a result, many companies also provide tuition reimbursement as a benefit for all employees to encourage them to develop. **Tuition reimbursement** refers to the practice of reimbursing employees' costs for college and university courses and degree programs. Companies spend about $10 billion on tuition reimbursement for courses offered by nonprofit colleges and universities as well as for-profit universities like Capella University.[26] These courses include face-to-face classroom instruction, online learning, and blended learning. For example, United Technology's Employee Scholar Program allows employees to receive 100 percent tuition reimbursement of all educational costs including tuition, registration fees, and books. Courses do not have to be related to the employee's job. Employees receive three hours each week to study or attend class. Employees who earn a degree receive $10,000 of company stock. The company has paid more than $60 million for the program. About 15 percent of employees use the program.

Tuition Reimbursement The practice of reimbursing employees' costs for college and university courses and degree programs.

IBM is in the forefront of using technology to manage careers and build management talent. IBM's Blue Opportunities reinforces to employees that growing their careers is important to obtain challenging and interesting work and that they need to take responsibility, working with their managers, for identifying training and development activities that interest them. Blue Opportunities highlights the company's training and development opportunities such as short- and long-term job rotation, on-site job shadowing, and cross-functional projects on an employee-only Internet site that is accessible to employees in the United States and other global locations. The goals of Blue Opportunities are developing employees' skills and knowledge and offering them potential job or career

changes. Blue Opportunities provides a way for employees to develop skills across business units and explore career options that they would not have previously considered. For example, a Brazilian employee worked on a project with a manager in Ireland. As a result, he learned more about the opportunities available in another business unit. An employee in India completed a short-term assignment with customers in Italy and used the new skills to train less experienced engineers. Managers also benefit from Blue Opportunities. It helps managers assist their employees in developing competencies and careers and provides a way to share expertise across departments and multiple lines of business.

The Role of the Manager @ IBM is an expert system that provides a customized learning

portfolio for each manager based on their background, training, and management style. The expert system guides managers through prework that has to be completed prior to attending learning labs. Learning is reinforced through use of a knowledge management system that allows managers to post suggestions and store ideas. Managers who have completed the Role of the Manager @ IBM program have created action plans that have generated revenues of $184 million.

SOURCES: T. Barron, "IBM's New Fangled, Old-Fashioned Pep," *T + D*, April 2004, pp. 64–65; D. Robb, "Succeeding with Succession," *HR Magazine*, January 2006, pp. 89–92; N. Lewis and P. Orton, "The Five Attributes of Innovative E-Learning," *Training and Development*, June 2000, pp. 47–51; N. Davis, "One-on-One Training Crosses Continents," *HR Magazine*, November 2007, pp. 54–56.

EVIDENCE-BASED HR

Given the costs of executive education and tuition reimbursement programs, companies are asking for evaluation data that show the value of the program. As a result, many universities offering executive education programs are beginning to measure programs' return on investment. For example, Columbia Business School uses performance measures to track the success of program participants. Leadership skills, team building, and strategic thinking are measured using self-assessment, manager evaluations, and peer reviews collected before the participant attends the program as well as up to a year following program completion. The University of Virginia's Graduate School of Business Administration asks participants in executive education programs to complete surveys three months after attending programs to judge the program's practical value. Some of Darden's programs use action learning (recall our discussion of action learning in Chapter 7), which requires employees to make presentations to top-level managers showing how participating in the program helped them to successfully deal with work problems. This demonstrates how learning has benefited the company. Kum and Go, a large convenience store chain, has a tuition reimbursement program that allows employees to obtain their college degrees while working full-time.

The program reimburses students 100 percent of their tuition if they receive either an A or B, and 50 percent if they receive a C. Verizon Wireless has started on-site college degree programs at 14 corporate offices, each of which offers classes for associate's, bachelor's, and MBA degree programs. The program has an 18 percent participation rate. MBAs are not necessary for every position, but the degree provides employees with a broader understanding of business and business results and helps prepare potential future leaders of the business. Employees who earned their degrees were almost one and one-half times more likely than the overall workforce to receive a promotion or lateral move within the company.

SOURCES: A. Meisler, "A Matter of Degree," *Workforce Management*, May 2004, pp. 32–38; K. Merriman, "Employers Warm Up to Online Education," *HR Magazine*, January 2006, pp. 79–82; "Flexibility Fuels Employee Development," *TD*, April 2006, pp. 96–97. B. Yovovich, "Golden Opportunities," *Human Resource Executive*, August 2008, pp. 30–34.

Assessment

LO3
Relate how assessment of personality type, work behaviors, and job performance can be used for employee development.

Assessment involves collecting information and providing feedback to employees about their behavior, communication style, or skills.[27] The employees, their peers, managers, and customers may provide information. Assessments are used for several reasons. First, assessment is most frequently used to identify employees with managerial potential and to measure current managers' strengths and weaknesses. Assessment is also used to identify managers with the potential to move into higher-level executive positions, and it can be used with work teams to identify the strengths and weaknesses of individual team members and the decision processes or communication styles that inhibit the team's productivity. Assessments can help employees understand their tendencies, needs, the type of work environment they prefer, and the type of work they might prefer to do.[28] This information, along with the performance evaluations they receive from the company, can help employees decide what type of development goals might be most appropriate for them (e.g., leadership position, increase scope of their current position).

Assessment
Collecting information and providing feedback to employees about their behavior, communication style, or skills.

Companies vary in the methods and the sources of information they use in developmental assessment. Many companies use employee performance evaluations. Companies with sophisticated development systems use psychological tests to measure employees' skills, interests, personality types, and communication styles. Self, peer, and managers' ratings of employees' interpersonal styles and behaviors may also be collected. Popular assessment tools include personality tests, the Myers-Briggs Type Indicator®, assessment centers, benchmarks, performance appraisal, and 360-degree feedback.

Personality Tests

Tests are used to determine if employees have the personality characteristics necessary to be successful in specific managerial jobs or jobs involving international assignments. Personality tests typically measure five major dimensions: extroversion, adjustment, agreeableness, conscientiousness, and inquisitiveness (see Table 6.3 in Chapter 6). For example, Carmeuse North America uses personality tests in its leadership development program. The personality tests for employees who have been identified as having high potential for top management positions will be used to guide employees into development activities including coaching and formal courses.[29] Starwood Vacation Ownership, a subsidiary of Starwood Hotels and Resorts, uses several assessment tools to determine if the top managers value the commercial success of the business as well as tolerance for ambiguity, the ability to create and communicate a business strategy, the ability to build business partnerships, and the ability to develop staff. The assessment identifies managers who are ready for international assignments, may not fit their current position, or need coaching to better understand the company culture.[30] Edward Jones uses personality assessment to assess the leadership potential of financial advisers working outside its St. Louis, Missouri, headquarters.[31] The personality assessment is combined with 360-degree feedback from peers to provide the company with an idea of employees' leadership skills. Employees and their managers receive the results, which are used to determine if employees have the behaviors and personality needed to take a leadership role at headquarters.

Myers-Briggs Type Indicator® Personality Inventory

Myers-Briggs Type Indicator® Personality Inventory (MBTI)® is the most popular psychological assessment tool for employee development. As many as 2 million people take the MBTI® assessment tool in the United States each year. The personality assessment consists of more than 100 questions about how the person feels or prefers to behave in different situations (such as "Are you usually a good 'mixer' or rather quiet and reserved?"). The MBTI® assessment tool is based on the work of Carl Jung, a psychiatrist who believed that differences in individuals' behavior resulted from preferences in decision making, interpersonal communication, and information gathering. These concepts were further developed by the mother–daughter team of Katharine C. Briggs and Isabel Briggs Myers, who are credited with developing the MBTI® Inventory. The MBTI® is a self-scored forced-choice inventory through which one rates oneself along four different dimensions. The MBTI® assessment tool identifies individuals' preference for energy (introversion versus extroversion), information gathering (sensing versus intuition), decision making (thinking versus feeling), and lifestyle (judging versus perceiving).[32] The energy dimension determines where individuals gain interpersonal strength and vitality. Extroverts (E) gain energy through interpersonal relationships. Introverts (I) gain energy by focusing on personal thoughts and feelings. The information-gathering preference relates to the actions individuals take when making decisions. Individuals with a Sensing (S) preference tend to gather facts and details. Intuitives (I) tend to focus less on facts and more on possibilities and relationships between ideas. Decision-making preferences differ based on the amount of consideration the person gives to others' feelings in making a decision. Individuals with a Thinking (T) preference tend to be objective in making decisions. Individuals with a Feeling (F) preference tend to evaluate the impact of potential decisions on others and be more subjective in making a decision. The lifestyle preference reflects an individual's tendency to be flexible and adaptable. Individuals with a Judging (J) preference focus on goals, establish deadlines, and prefer to be conclusive. Individuals with a Perceiving (P) preference tend to enjoy surprises, like to change decisions, and dislike deadlines.

Sixteen unique personality types result from the combination of the four MBTI® assessment tool preferences. (See Table 9.4.) Each person has developed strengths and weaknesses as a result of using these preferences. For example, individuals who are Introverted, Sensing, Thinking, and Judging (known as ISTJs) tend to be serious, quiet, practical, orderly, and logical. These persons can organize tasks, be decisive, and follow through on plans and goals. ISTJs have several weaknesses because they have not used the opposite preferences: Extroversion, Intuition, Feeling, and Perceiving. Potential weaknesses for ISTJs include problems dealing with unexpected opportunities, appearing too task-oriented or impersonal to colleagues, and making overly quick decisions. Visit the Web site www.cpp.com for more information on the personality types.

The MBTI® assessment tool is used for understanding such things as communication, motivation, teamwork, work styles, and leadership. For example, it can be used by

table 9.4

The 16 Personality Types Used in the Myers-Briggs Type Indicator Assessment Tool

	SENSING TYPES (S)		INTUITIVE TYPES (N)	
	THINKING (T)	FEELING (F)	FEELING (F)	THINKING (T)
Introverts (I) Judging (J)	**ISTJ** Quiet, serious, earn success by thoroughness and dependability. Practical, matter-of-fact, realistic, and responsible. Decide logically what should be done and work toward it steadily, regardless of distractions. Take pleasure in making everything orderly and organized—their work, their home, their life. Value traditions and loyalty.	**ISFJ** Quiet, friendly, responsible, and conscientious. Committed and steady in meeting their obligations. Thorough, painstaking, and accurate. Loyal, considerate, notice and remember specifics about people who are important to them, concerned with how others feel. Strive to create an orderly and harmonious environment at work and at home.	**INFJ** Seek meaning and connection in ideas, relationships, and material possessions. Want to understand what motivates people and are insightful about others. Conscientious and committed to their firm values. Develop a clear vision about how best to serve the common good. Organized and decisive in implementing their vision.	**INTJ** Have original minds and great drive for implementing their ideas and achieving their goals. Quickly see patterns in external events and develop long-range explanatory perspectives. When committed, organize a job and carry it through. Skeptical and independent, have high standards of competence and performance—for themselves and others.
Perceiving (P)	**ISTP** Tolerant and flexible, quiet observers until a problem appears, then act quickly to find workable solutions. Analyze what makes things work and readily get through large amounts of data to isolate the core of practical problems. Interested in cause and effect, organize facts using logical principles, value efficiency.	**ISFP** Quiet, friendly, sensitive, and kind. Enjoy the present moment, what's going on around them. Like to have their own space and to work within their own time frame. Loyal and committed to their values and to people who are important to them. Dislike disagreements and conflicts, do not force their opinions or values on others.	**INFP** Idealistic, loyal to their values and to people who are important to them. Want an external life that is congruent with their values. Curious, quick to see possibilities, can be catalysts for implementing ideas. Seek to understand people and to help them fulfill their potential. Adaptable, flexible, and accepting unless a value is threatened.	**INTP** Seek to develop logical explanations for everything that interests them. Theoretical and abstract, interested more in ideas than in social interaction. Quiet, contained, flexible, and adaptable. Have unusual ability to focus in depth to solve problems in their area of interest. Skeptical, sometimes critical, always analytical.
Extroverts (E) Perceiving (P)	**ESTP** Flexible and tolerant, they take a pragmatic approach focused on immediate results. Theories and conceptual explanations bore them—they want to act energetically to solve the problem. Focus on the here-and-now, spontaneous, enjoy each moment that they can be active with others. Enjoy material comforts and style. Learn best through doing.	**ESFP** Outgoing, friendly, and accepting. Exuberant lovers of life, people, and material comforts. Enjoy working with others to make things happen. Bring common sense and a realistic approach to their work, and make work fun. Flexible and spontaneous, adapt readily to new people and environments. Learn best by trying a new skill with other people.	**ENFP** Warmly enthusiastic and imaginative. See life as full of possibilities. Make connections between events and information very quickly, and confidently proceed based on the patterns they see. Want a lot of affirmation from others, and readily give appreciation and support. Spontaneous and flexible, often rely on their ability to improvise and their verbal fluency.	**ENTP** Quick, ingenious, stimulating, alert, and outspoken. Resourceful in solving new and challenging problems. Adept at generating conceptual possibilities and then analyzing them strategically. Good at reading other people. Bored by routine, will seldom do the same thing the same way, apt to turn to one new interest after another.
Judging (J)	**ESTJ** Practical, realistic, matter-of-fact. Decisive, quickly move to implement decisions. Organize projects and people to get things done, focus on getting results in the most efficient way possible. Take care of routine details. Have a clear set of logical standards, systematically follow them and want others to also. Forceful in implementing their plans.	**ESFJ** Warmhearted, conscientious, and cooperative. Want harmony in their environment, work with determination to establish it. Like to work with others to complete tasks accurately and on time. Loyal, follow through even in small matters. Notice what others need in their day-by-day lives and try to provide it. Want to be appreciated for who they are and for what they contribute.	**ENFJ** Warm, empathetic, responsive, and responsible. Highly attuned to the emotions, needs, and motivations of others. Find potential in everyone, want to help others fulfill their potential. May act as catalysts for individual and group growth. Loyal, responsive to praise and criticism. Sociable, facilitate others in a group, and provide inspiring leadership.	**ENTJ** Frank, decisive, assume leadership readily. Quickly see illogical and inefficient procedures and policies, develop and implement comprehensive systems to solve organizational problems. Enjoy long-term planning and goal setting. Usually well informed, well read, enjoy expanding their knowledge and passing it on to others. Forceful in presenting their ideas.

salespeople or executives who want to become more effective at interpersonal communication by learning about their own personality styles and the way they are perceived by others. The MBTI® assessment tool can help develop teams by matching team members with assignments that allow them to capitalize on their preferences and helping employees understand how the different preferences of team members can lead to useful problem solving.[33] For example, employees with an Intuitive preference can be assigned brainstorming tasks. Employees with a Sensing preference can evaluate ideas.

Research on the validity, reliability, and effectiveness of the MBTI® assessment tool is inconclusive.[34] People who take the MBTI® assessment tool find it a positive experience and say it helps them change their behavior. MBTI® assessment tool scores appear to be related to one's occupation. Analysis of managers' MBTI® assessment tool scores in the United States, England, Latin America, and Japan suggests that a large majority of all managers have certain personality types (ISTJ, INTJ, ESTJ, or ENTJ). However, MBTI® assessment tool scores are not necessarily stable over time. Studies in which the MBTI® assessment tool was administered at two different times found that as few as 24 percent of those who took the test were classified as the same type the second time.

The MBTI® assessment tool is a valuable tool for understanding communication styles and the ways people prefer to interact with others. Because it does not measure how well employees perform their preferred functions, it should not be used to appraise performance or evaluate employees' promotion potential. Furthermore, MBTI® assessment tool types should not be viewed as unchangeable personality patterns.

Assessment Center

Assessment Center
A process in which multiple raters evaluate employees' performance on a number of exercises.

Leaderless Group Discussion
Process in which a team of five to seven employees solves an assigned problem together within a certain time period.

Interview
Employees are questioned about their work and personal experiences, skills, and career plans.

In-Basket
A simulation of the administrative tasks of a manager's job.

Role-Plays
A participant taking the part or role of a manager or other employee.

At an **assessment center** multiple raters or evaluators (assessors) evaluate employees' performance on a number of exercises.[35] An assessment center is usually an off-site location such as a conference center. From 6 to 12 employees usually participate at one time. Assessment centers are primarily used to identify if employees have the personality characteristics, administrative skills, and interpersonal skills needed for managerial jobs. They are also increasingly being used to determine if employees have the necessary skills to work in teams.

The types of exercises used in assessment centers include leaderless group discussions, interviews, in-baskets, and role-plays.[36] In a **leaderless group discussion**, a team of five to seven employees is assigned a problem and must work together to solve it within a certain time period. The problem may involve buying and selling supplies, nominating a subordinate for an award, or assembling a product. In the **interview**, employees answer questions about their work and personal experiences, skill strengths and weaknesses, and career plans. An **in-basket** is a simulation of the administrative tasks of the manager's job. The exercise includes a variety of documents that may appear in the in-basket on a manager's desk. The participants read the materials and decide how to respond to them. Responses might include delegating tasks, scheduling meetings, writing replies, or completely ignoring the memo! **Role-plays** refer to the participant taking the part or role of a manager or other employee. For example, an assessment center participant may be asked to take the role of a manager who has to give a negative performance review to a subordinate. The participant is told about the subordinate's performance and is asked to prepare for and actually hold a 45-minute meeting with the subordinate to discuss the performance problems. The role of the subordinate is played by a manager or other member of the assessment center design team or company. The assessment center might also include interest and aptitude tests to evaluate an employee's vocabulary, general mental ability, and reasoning skills. Personality tests may be used to determine if employees can get along with others, their tolerance for ambiguity, and other traits related to success as a manager.

table 9.5

Examples of Skills Measured by Assessment Center Exercises

		EXERCISES			
	IN-BASKET	SCHEDULING EXERCISE	LEADERLESS GROUP DISCUSSION	PERSONALITY TEST	ROLE-PLAY
SKILLS					
Leadership (Dominance, coaching, influence, resourcefulness)	X		X	X	X
Problem solving (Judgment)	X	X	X		X
Interpersonal (Sensitivity, conflict resolution, cooperation, oral communication)			X	X	X
Administrative (Organizing, planning, written communications)	X	X	X		
Personal (Stress tolerance, confidence)			X	X	X

X indicates skill measured by exercise.

Assessment center exercises are designed to measure employees' administrative and interpersonal skills. Skills typically measured include leadership, oral and written communication, judgment, organizational ability, and stress tolerance. Table 9.5 shows an example of the skills measured by the assessment center. As we see, each exercise gives participating employees the opportunity to demonstrate several different skills. For example, the exercise requiring scheduling to meet production demands evaluates employees' administrative and problem-solving ability. The leaderless group discussion measures interpersonal skills such as sensitivity toward others, stress tolerance, and oral communication skills.

Managers are usually used as assessors. The managers are trained to look for employee behaviors that are related to the skills that will be assessed. Typically, each assessor observes and records one or two employees' behaviors in each exercise. The assessors review their notes and rate each employee's level of skills (for example, 5 = high level of leadership skills, 1 = low level of leadership skills). After all employees have completed the exercises, the assessors discuss their observations of each employee. They compare their ratings and try to agree on each employee's rating for each of the skills.

As we mentioned in Chapter 6, research suggests that assessment center ratings are related to performance, salary level, and career advancement.[37] Assessment centers may also be useful for development because employees who participate in the process receive feedback regarding their attitudes, skill strengths, and weaknesses.[38] For example, Steelcase, the office furniture manufacturer based in Grand Rapids, Michigan, uses assessment centers for first-level managers.[39] The assessment center exercises include in-basket, interview simulation, and a timed scheduling exercise requiring participants to fill positions created by absences. Managers are also required to confront an employee on a performance issue, getting the employee to commit to improve. Because the exercises relate closely to what managers are required to do at work, feedback given to managers based on their performance in the assessment center can target specific skills or competencies that they need to be successful managers.

Benchmarks

Benchmarks©
An instrument designed to measure the factors that are important to managerial success.

Benchmarks© is an instrument designed to measure the factors that are important to being a successful manager. The items measured by Benchmarks are based on research that examines the lessons executives learn at critical events in their careers.[40] This includes items that measure managers' skills in dealing with subordinates, acquiring resources, and creating a productive work climate. Table 9.6 shows the 16 skills and perspectives believed to be important for becoming a successful manager. These skills and perspectives have been shown to be related to performance evaluations, bosses' ratings of promotability, and actual promotions received.[41] To get a complete picture of managers' skills, the managers' supervisors, their peers, and the managers themselves all complete the instrument. A summary report presenting the self-ratings and ratings by others is provided to the manager, along with information about how the ratings compare with those of other managers. A development guide with examples of experiences that enhance each skill and how successful managers use the skills is also available.

table 9.6

Skills Related to Managerial Success

Resourcefulness	Can think strategically, engage in flexible problem solving, and work effectively with higher management.
Doing whatever it takes	Has perseverance and focus in the face of obstacles.
Being a quick study	Quickly masters new technical and business knowledge.
Building and mending relationships	Knows how to build and maintain working relationships with co-workers and external parties.
Leading subordinates	Delegates to subordinates effectively, broadens their opportunities, and acts with fairness toward them.
Compassion and sensitivity	Shows genuine interest in others and sensitivity to subordinates' needs.
Straightforwardness and composure	Is honorable and steadfast.
Setting a developmental climate	Provides a challenging climate to encourage subordinates' development.
Confronting problem subordinates	Acts decisively and fairly when dealing with problem subordinates.
Team orientation	Accomplishes tasks through managing others.
Balance between personal life and work	Balances work priorities with personal life so that neither is neglected.
Decisiveness	Prefers quick and approximate actions to slow and precise ones in many management situations.
Self-awareness	Has an accurate picture of strengths and weaknesses and is willing to improve.
Hiring talented staff	Hires talented people for the team.
Putting people at ease	Displays warmth and a good sense of humor.
Acting with flexibility	Can behave in ways that are often seen as opposites.

SOURCE: Adapted with permission from C. D. McCauley, M. M. Lombardo, and C. J. Usher, "Diagnosing Management Development Needs: An Instrument Based on How Managers Develop," *Journal of Management* 15 (1989), pp. 389–403.

Performance Appraisals and 360-Degree Feedback Systems

As we mentioned in Chapter 8, **performance appraisal** is the process of measuring employees' performance. Performance appraisal information can be useful for employee development under certain conditions.[42] The appraisal system must tell employees specifically about their performance problems and how they can improve their performance. This includes providing a clear understanding of the differences between current performance and expected performance, identifying causes of the performance discrepancy, and developing action plans to improve performance. Managers must be trained in frequent performance feedback. Managers also need to monitor employees' progress in carrying out action plans.

Recall our discussion in Chapter 8 of how Just Born uses performance appraisals for evaluation and development.[43] The appraisal starts with a planning meeting between employee and manager. The strategic initiatives of the department are discussed along with the employee's role. The employee and manager agree on four personal objectives that will help the department reach its goals as well as key performance outcomes related to the employee's job description. Competencies the employee needs to reach the personal objectives are identified. The manager and employee jointly develop a plan for improving or learning the competencies. During the year, the manager and employee monitor the progress toward reaching the performance and personal objectives and achievement of the learning plan. Pay decisions made at the end of each year are based on the achievement of both performance and learning objectives. General Electric has a unique process for reviewing top managers known as "Session C."[44] Session C includes full-day reviews at all major business locations and follow-up sessions. The sessions focus on evaluating managers' strengths and weaknesses. They also include presentations of business results and reviews of accomplishments.

A recent trend in performance appraisals for management development is the use of upward feedback and 360-degree feedback. **Upward feedback** refers to appraisal that involves collecting subordinates' evaluations of managers' behaviors or skills. The 360-degree feedback process is a special case of upward feedback. In **360-degree feedback systems**, employees' behaviors or skills are evaluated not only by subordinates but by peers, customers, their bosses, and themselves. The raters complete a questionnaire asking them to rate the person on a number of different dimensions. Table 9.7 provides an example of the types of competencies that are rated in a 360-degree feedback questionnaire. This example evaluates the management competency of decision making. Each of the five items relates to a specific aspect of decision making (e.g., takes accountability for results of individual and team decisions). Typically, raters are asked to assess the manager's strength in a particular item or whether development is needed. Raters may also be asked to identify how frequently they observe a competency or skill (e.g., always, sometimes, seldom, never).

Performance Appraisal
The process through which an organization gets information on how well an employee is doing his or her job.

Upward Feedback
A performance appraisal process for managers that includes subordinates' evaluations.

360-Degree Feedback Systems
A performance appraisal system for managers that includes evaluations from a wide range of persons who interact with the manager. The process includes self-evaluations as well as evaluations from the manager's boss, subordinates, peers, and customers.

table 9.7
Sample Competency and Items from a 360-Degree Feedback Instrument

---

Decision Making

Identifies the key decisions that have the greatest impact on business goals.
Understands and integrates conflicting or contradictory information.
Balances business sense with data and logic to make effective decisions.
Takes accountability for results of individual and team decisions.
Makes appropriate trade-offs between complete analysis and speed when making decisions.

table 9.8

Activities in
Development
Planning

> 1. **Understand strengths and weaknesses.**
>   Review ratings for strengths and weaknesses.
>   Identify skills or behaviors where self and others' (manager, peer, customer) ratings agree and disagree.
> 2. **Identify a development goal.**
>   Choose a skill or behavior to develop.
>   Set a clear, specific goal with a specified outcome.
> 3. **Identify a process for recognizing goal accomplishment.**
> 4. **Identify strategies for reaching the development goal.**
>   Establish strategies such as reading, job experiences, courses, and relationships.
>   Establish strategies for receiving feedback on progress.
>   Establish strategies for reinforcing the new skill or behavior.

The results of a 360-degree feedback system show how the manager was rated on each item. The results also show how self-evaluations differ from evaluations from the other raters. Typically managers review their results, seek clarification from the raters, and set specific development goals based on the strengths and weaknesses identified.[45] Table 9.8 shows the type of activities involved in development planning using 360-degree feedback.[46]

The benefits of 360-degree feedback include collecting multiple perspectives of managers' performance, allowing employees to compare their own personal evaluations with the views of others, and formalizing communications about behaviors and skills ratings between employees and their internal and external customers. Several studies have shown that performance improves and behavior changes as a result of participating in upward feedback and 360-degree feedback systems.[47] The most change occurs in individuals who receive lower ratings from others than they gave themselves (overraters).

Potential limitations of 360-degree feedback include the time demands placed on the raters to complete the evaluations, managers seeking to identify and punish raters who provided negative information, the need to have a facilitator help interpret results, and companies' failure to provide ways that managers can act on the feedback they receive (development planning, meeting with raters, taking courses).

In effective 360-degree feedback systems, reliable or consistent ratings are provided, raters' confidentiality is maintained, the behaviors or skills assessed are job-related (valid), the system is easy to use, and managers receive and act on the feedback.[48]

Technology allows 360-degree questionnaires to be delivered to the raters via their personal computers. This increases the number of completed questionnaires returned, makes it easier to process the information, and speeds feedback reports to managers.

Regardless of the assessment method used, the information must be shared with the employee for development to occur. Along with assessment information, the employee needs suggestions for correcting skill weaknesses and using skills already learned. These suggestions might be to participate in training courses or develop skills through new job experiences. Based on the assessment information and available development opportunities, employees should develop action plans to guide their self-improvement efforts.

Capital One has developed effective 360-degree feedback systems.[49] Capitol One, a consumer credit company, has included a number of features in its 360-degree feedback system to minimize the chance that the ratings will be used as ways to get back at an employee or turned into popularity contests. The 360-degree assessments are based on the company's competency model, so raters are asked for specific feedback on a competency area. Rather than a lengthy form that places a large burden on raters to assess many different competencies, Capital One's assessment asks the raters to concentrate on three or four strengths or development opportunities. It also seeks comments rather than limiting raters to merely circling numbers corresponding to how much of each competency the employee has demonstrated. These comments often provide specific information about what aspect of a competency needs to be developed or identifies work situations in which a competency needs to be improved. This comment system helps tailor development activities to fit competency development. To increase the chances that the assessment will result in change, the feedback from the 360-degree assessment is linked to development plans, and the company offers coaching and training to help employees strengthen their competencies. Employees are encouraged to share feedback with their co-workers. This creates a work environment based on honest and open feedback that helps employees personally grow.

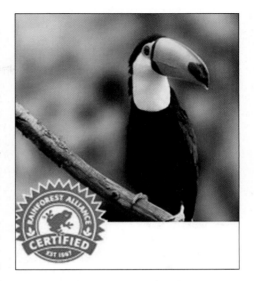

● The Rainforest Alliance seal of approval ensures that goods and services were produced in compliance with strict guidelines protecting the environment, wildlife, workers, and local communities.

Job Experiences

Most employee development occurs through **job experiences:**[50] relationships, problems, demands, tasks, or other features that employees face in their jobs. A major assumption of using job experiences for employee development is that development is most likely to occur when there is a mismatch between the employee's skills and past experiences and the skills required for the job. To succeed in their jobs, employees must stretch their skills—that is, they are forced to learn new skills, apply their skills and knowledge in a new way, and master new experiences.[51] New job assignments help take advantage of employees' existing skills, experiences, and contacts, while helping them develop new ones.[52] General Electric uses experienced managers to integrate newly acquired companies. The Rainforest Alliance, an international nonprofit organization with 265 employees that helps product makers employ sustainable land practices, is challenged by quick growth (it has doubled in size since 2003) and the need it created to identify and develop managerial staff.[53] The Rainforest Alliance gives many junior employees the chance to lead research and other initiatives and, if they are successful, promotes them to manage the initiatives. For example, one employee who is now the coordinator of a new climate initiative, started with the company as an administrative assistant, but she was asked to take on more responsibilities, including researching climate change. Junior employees also can take part in internship programs in foreign offices to learn more about the organization and work on the "front lines" in implementing sustainable land practices.

LO4
Explain how job experiences can be used for skill development.

Job Experiences
The relationships, problems, demands, tasks, and other features that employees face in their jobs.

Most of what we know about development through job experiences comes from a series of studies conducted by the Center for Creative Leadership.[54] Executives were asked to identify key career events that made a difference in their managerial styles and the lessons they learned from these experiences. The key events included those involving the job assignment (such as fixing a failing operation), those involving interpersonal relationships (getting along with supervisors), and the specific type of transition required (situations in which the executive did not have the necessary

table 9.9

Job Demands and the Lessons Employees Learn from Them

Making transitions	*Unfamiliar responsibilities:* The manager must handle responsibilities that are new, very different, or much broader than previous ones. *Proving yourself:* The manager has added pressure to show others she can handle the job.
Creating change	*Developing new directions:* The manager is responsible for starting something new in the organization, making strategic changes in the business, carrying out a reorganization, or responding to rapid changes in the business environment. *Inherited problems:* The manager has to fix problems created by a former incumbent or take over problem employees. *Reduction decisions:* Decisions about shutting down operations or staff reductions have to be made. *Problems with employees:* Employees lack adequate experience, are incompetent, or are resistant.
Having high level of responsibility	*High stakes:* Clear deadlines, pressure from senior managers, high visibility, and responsibility for key decisions make success or failure in this job clearly evident. *Managing business diversity:* The scope of the job is large with responsibilities for multiple functions, groups, products, customers, or markets. *Job overload:* The sheer size of the job requires a large investment of time and energy. *Handling external pressure:* External factors that affect the business (e.g., negotiating with unions or government agencies; working in a foreign culture; coping with serious community problems) must be dealt with.
Being involved in nonauthority relationships	*Influencing without authority:* Getting the job done requires influencing peers, higher management, external parties, or other key people over whom the manager has no direct authority.
Facing obstacles	*Adverse business conditions:* The business unit or product line faces financial problems or difficult economic conditions. *Lack of top management support:* Senior management is reluctant to provide direction, support, or resources for current work or new projects. *Lack of personal support:* The manager is excluded from key networks and gets little support and encouragement from others. *Difficult boss:* The manager's opinions or management style differs from those of the boss, or the boss has major shortcomings.

SOURCE: C. D. McCauley, L. J. Eastman, and J. Ohlott, "Linking Management Selection and Development through Stretch Assignments," *Human Resource Management* 84 (1995), pp. 93–115. Copyright © 1995 Wiley Periodicals, Inc., a Wiley Company.

background). The job demands and what employees can learn from them are shown in Table 9.9.

One concern in the use of demanding job experiences for employee development is whether they are viewed as positive or negative stressors. Job experiences that are seen as positive stressors challenge employees to stimulate learning. Job challenges viewed as negative stressors create high levels of harmful stress for employees exposed to them. Recent research findings suggest that all of the job demands, with the exception of obstacles, are related to learning.[55] Managers reported that obstacles and job demands related to creating change were more likely to lead to negative stress than the other job demands. This suggests that companies should carefully weigh the potential negative consequences before placing employees in development assignments involving obstacles or creating change.

Although the research on development through job experiences has focused on executives and managers, line employees can also learn from job experiences. As we noted earlier, for a work team to be successful, its members now need the kinds of skills that only managers were once thought to need (such as dealing directly with customers, analyzing data to determine product quality, and resolving conflict among team members). Besides the development that occurs when a team is formed, employees can further develop their skills by switching work roles within the team.

Figure 9.2 shows the various ways that job experiences can be used for employee development. These include enlarging the current job, job rotation, transfers, promotions, downward moves, and temporary assignments. For companies with global operations (multinationals), it is not uncommon for employee development to involve international assignments that require frequent travel or relocation.

Enlarging the Current Job

Job enlargement refers to adding challenges or new responsibilities to employees' current jobs. This could include special project assignments, switching roles within a work team, or researching new ways to serve clients and customers. For example, an engineering employee may join a task force developing new career paths for technical employees. Through this project work, the engineer may lead certain aspects of career path development (such as reviewing the company's career development process). As a result, the engineer not only learns about the company's career development system, but uses leadership and organizational skills to help the task force reach its goals. Some companies are enlarging jobs by giving two managers the same responsibilities and job title and allowing them to divide the work (two-in-a-box).[56] This helps managers learn from a more experienced employee; helps companies fill jobs

Job Enlargement
Adding challenges or new responsibilities to an employee's current job.

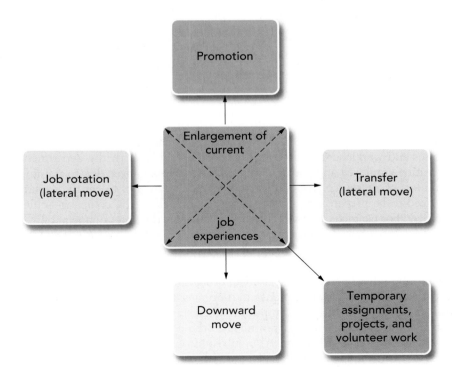

figure 9.2

How Job Experiences Are Used for Employee Development

that require multiple skills; and, for positions requiring extensive travel, ensures that one employee is always on site to deal with work-related issues. For example, at Cisco Systems, the head of the Cisco routing group, who was trained as an engineer but now works in business development, shared a job with an engineer. Each employee was exposed to the other's skills, which has helped both perform their jobs better.

Job Rotation

Job Rotation
The process of systematically moving a single individual from one job to another over the course of time. The job assignments may be in various functional areas of the company or movement may be between jobs in a single functional area or department.

Job rotation gives employees a series of job assignments in various functional areas of the company or movement among jobs in a single functional area or department. Arrow Electronics allows employees to take a 10-week sabbatical after seven years with the company.[57] While an employee is taking the sabbatical, the company uses the job vacancy as a job rotation for a different employee. Assignments to open positions are based on an employee's development needs. Employees who rotate to new positions are required to document their experiences and learning, especially emphasizing how the position helped them better understand the business. India-based Tata Consultancy Services job rotation program sends native employees to operation in China, Hungary, and South America.[58] The program helps the company have skilled employees who are prepared to work in any of the company's offices in 42 countries. Employees also gain an understanding of the culture of the country they work in. It also helps improve customer service because the company can draw on the strength of its entire workforce, rather than just relying on employees who are located close to the customer. The assignments typically last 18 to 24 months, involving learning from both the customers and the local employees based at the location. After the assignment is completed, the employee usually works on the same kinds of projects they worked on in the overseas assignment, which helps transfer the knowledge gained to their home operations.

Job rotation helps employees gain an overall appreciation of the company's goals, increases their understanding of different company functions, develops a network of contacts, and improves problem-solving and decision-making skills.[59] Job rotation has also been shown to be related to skill acquisition, salary growth, and promotion rates. But there are several potential problems with job rotation for both the employee and the work unit. The rotation may create a short-term perspective on problems and solutions in rotating employees and their peers. Employees' satisfaction and motivation may be adversely affected because they find it difficult to develop functional specialties and they don't spend enough time in one position to receive a challenging assignment. Productivity losses and workload increases may be experienced by both the department gaining a rotating employee and the department losing the employee due to training demands and loss of a resource. Top-level managers may rotate jobs to get the experiences they need to be prepared for the top management job in the company—chief executive officer. For example, two top Citigroup managers, the chief financial officer and head of strategy and the chairman and chief executive of the SmithBarney, Citigroup's stock-research and brokerage group, swapped jobs, so each could get the experiences needed to become a top leader in the company.[60] One manager needed financial experience and the other operations experience. Promotion of a chief financial officer to the company's top job requires experience in running a business unit.

The characteristics of effective job rotation systems are shown in Table 9.10. As we see, effective job rotation systems are linked to the company's training, development, and career management systems. Also, job rotation should be used for all types of employees, not just those with managerial potential.

1. Job rotation is used to develop skills as well as give employees experience needed for managerial positions.
2. Employees understand specific skills that will be developed by rotation.
3. Job rotation is used for all levels and types of employees.
4. Job rotation is linked with the career management process so employees know the development needs addressed by each job assignment.
5. Benefits of rotation are maximized and costs are minimized through managing timing of rotations to reduce workload costs and helping employees understand job rotation's role in their development plans.
6. All employees have equal opportunities for job rotation assignments regardless of their demographic group.

table 9.10

Characteristics of Effective Job Rotation Systems

SOURCES: Based on L. Cheraskin and M. Campion, "Study Clarifies Job Rotation Benefits," *Personnel Journal*, November 1996, pp. 31–38; M. Fiester, A. Collis, and N. Cossack, "Job Rotation, Total Rewards, Measuring Value," *HR Magazine*, August 2008, pp. 33–34.

Transfers, Promotions, and Downward Moves

Upward, lateral, and downward mobility is available for development purposes in most companies.[61] In a **transfer**, an employee is assigned a job in a different area of the company. Transfers do not necessarily increase job responsibilities or compensation. They are likely lateral moves (a move to a job with similar responsibilities). **Promotions** are advancements into positions with greater challenges, more responsibility, and more authority than in the previous job. Promotions usually include pay increases.

Transfers may involve relocation within the United States or to another country. This can be stressful not only because the employee's work role changes, but if the employee is in a two-career family, the spouse must find new employment. Also, the family has to join a new community. Transfers disrupt employees' daily lives, interpersonal relationships, and work habits.[62] People have to find new housing, shopping, health care, and leisure facilities, and they may be many miles from the emotional support of friends and family. They also have to learn a new set of work norms and procedures; they must develop interpersonal relationships with their new managers and peers; and they are expected to be as productive in their new jobs as they were in their old jobs even though they may know little about the products, services, processes, or employees for whom they are responsible.

Because transfers can provoke anxiety, many companies have difficulty getting employees to accept them. Research has identified the employee characteristics associated with a willingness to accept transfers:[63] high career ambitions, a belief that one's future with the company is promising, and a belief that accepting a transfer is necessary for success in the company. Employees who are not married and not active in the community are generally most willing to accept transfers. Among married employees, the spouse's willingness to move is the most important influence on whether an employee will accept a transfer.

A **downward move** occurs when an employee is given less responsibility and authority.[64] This may involve a move to another position at the same level (lateral demotion), a temporary cross-functional move, or a demotion because of poor performance. Temporary cross-functional moves to lower-level positions, which give employees experience working in different functional areas, are most frequently used for employee development. For example, engineers who want to move into management often take lower-level positions (like shift supervisor) to develop their management skills.

Transfer
The movement of an employee to a different job assignment in a different area of the company.

Promotions
Advancement into positions with greater challenge, more responsibility, and more authority than the employee's previous job.

Downward Move
A job change involving a reduction in an employee's level of responsibility and authority.

Because of the psychological and tangible rewards of promotions (such as increased feelings of self-worth, salary, and status in the company), employees are more willing to accept promotions than lateral or downward moves. Promotions are more readily available when a company is profitable and growing. When a company is restructuring or experiencing stable or declining profits—especially if numerous employees are interested in promotions and the company tends to rely on the external labor market to staff higher-level positions—promotion opportunities may be limited.[65]

Unfortunately, many employees have difficulty associating transfers and downward moves with development. They see them as punishments rather than as opportunities to develop skills that will help them achieve long-term success with the company. Many employees decide to leave a company rather than accept a transfer. Companies need to successfully manage transfers not only because of the costs of replacing employees but because of the costs directly associated with them. For example, GTE spends approximately $60 million a year on home purchases and other relocation costs such as temporary housing and relocation allowances.[66] One challenge companies face is learning how to use transfers and downward moves as development opportunities—convincing employees that accepting these opportunities will result in long-term benefits for them.

To ensure that employees accept transfers, promotions, and downward moves as development opportunities, companies can provide

- Information about the content, challenges, and potential benefits of the new job and location.
- Involvement in the transfer decision by sending the employees to preview the new location and giving them information about the community.
- Clear performance objectives and early feedback about their job performance.
- A host at the new location to help them adjust to the new community and workplace.
- Information about how the job opportunity will affect their income, taxes, mortgage payments, and other expenses.
- Reimbursement and assistance in selling and purchasing or renting a place to live.
- An orientation program for the new location and job.
- Information on how the new job experiences will support the employee's career plans.
- Assistance for dependent family members, including identifying schools and child care and elder care options.
- Help for the spouse in identifying and marketing skills and finding employment.[67]

Externship
When a company allows an employee to take a full-time operational role at another company.

Externship refers to a company allowing employees to take a full-time operational role at another company. Mercer Management, a consulting firm, uses externship to develop employees interested in gaining experience in a specific industry.[68] Mercer Management promises to employ the externs after their assignments end. For example, one employee who has been a Mercer consultant for five years is now vice president of Internet services for Binney & Smith, the maker of Crayola crayons. A year ago he was consulting on an Internet project for Binney & Smith. But he wanted to actually implement his recommendations rather than just give them to the client and move on to another project—so he started working at Binney & Smith. He remains on Mercer Management's payroll, though his salary comes from Binney & Smith. Mercer believes that employees who participate in the externship program will remain committed to the company because they have had the opportunity to learn and grow professionally and have not had to disrupt their personal and professional lives with a job search. Although externships give employees other employment options and some employees will leave, Mercer believes that it not only is a good development strategy but also helps in recruitment. The externship program signals to potential employees that Mercer is creative and flexible with its employees.

Temporary Assignments, Projects, Volunteer Work, and Sabbaticals

Employee exchange is one type of temporary assignment. Procter & Gamble (P&G) and Google have started to swap employees.[69] Employees from the two companies participate in each other's training programs and attend meetings where business plans are discussed. Both companies hope to benefit from the employee swap. Procter & Gamble is trying to increase its understanding of how to market laundry detergent, toilet paper, and skin cream products to a new generation of consumers who spend more time online than watching television. Google wants to gain more ad revenue by persuading companies to shift from showcasing their brands on television to video-sharing sites such as YouTube. The idea of the employee swap occurred when P&G recognized that a switch to a smaller Tide laundry soap bottle with a more concentrated formula did not include an online campaign, where buyers could find answers as to why the bottle decreased in size. Employees of both companies have benefited from the swap. Google employees have learned that Tide's bright orange packaging is a critical part of the brand and have adopted P&G's marketing language. P&G employees have recognized that online ad campaigns can increase brand awareness—even for products such as diapers that are not purchased online. P&G has invited mommy-bloggers to visit their baby division to better understand how their diapers can meet their needs.

Temporary assignments can include a **sabbatical** (a leave of absence from the company to renew or develop skills). Employees on sabbatical often receive full pay and benefits. Sabbaticals let employees get away from the day-to-day stresses of their jobs and acquire new skills and perspectives. Sabbaticals also allow employees more time for personal pursuits such as writing a book or spending more time with young children. Sabbaticals are common in a variety of industries ranging from consulting firms to the fast-food industry.[70] Fallon Worldwide, an advertising agency, offers a program called Dreamcatchers to staff members who want to work on a project or travel.[71] Dreamcatchers was developed to help the agency avoid having employees burn out and lose their creative edge. Employees have taken time off to write novels, kayak, and motorcycle through the Alps. Fallon Worldwide matches employee contributions of up to $1,000 annually for two years and offers up to two extra weeks of paid vacation. The agency partners believe that the program has helped in the retention of key employees and the recruiting of new ones. The partners also believe that the program helps recharge employees' creativity, which is key for employees to do their best work for customers.

Volunteer assignments can also be used for development. Volunteer assignments may give employees opportunities to manage change, teach, have a high level of responsibility, and be exposed to other job demands shown earlier in Table 9.9. For General Mills, volunteer assignments and involvement with community projects is one of the ways the company lives its corporate values.[72] Employees work in a wide variety of charities, with duties ranging from serving meals to the homeless, painting child care center rooms, or serving on corporate board members. Besides providing valuable services to community organizations, General Mills believes volunteer

Sabbatical
A leave of absence from the company to renew or develop skills.

PricewaterhouseCoopers (PwC) designed the Ulysses program in response to the interconnected global challenges that businesses face. The program's key objectives are to develop responsible leaders who are able to assume senior international leadership roles; who understand the role of business in influencing the economic, political, social, and environmental well-being of world communities and markets; and who can deliver responsible and sustainable business solutions. Ulysses participants are selected from around the world on the basis of their leadership skills and potential within the local firm. Typically they are in their first 10 years of partnership; they come from different regions and countries; and their expertise varies across accounting and finance, strategy, tax advisory, and management consultancy. The Ulysses program involves sending partners to developing areas of the world for eight weeks to use their business skills to benefit locals and learn how to overcome barriers, connect with clients from different cultures, and identify answers to very difficult problems. Partners are forced to take on projects outside their areas of expertise. The partners work on projects in multicultural teams in developing countries in collaboration with local social or governmental organizations, social entrepreneurs, and international institutions. The cost to PwC is $15,000 per participant for travel and expenses plus three months of salary. Each partner also spends two weeks in training to prepare for the trip and debriefing when they return. For example, one partner was sent to a village in Namibia, Africa, along with partners from Mexico and the Netherlands to help village leaders deal with the community's AIDS crisis. The partner helped the village leaders understand what was needed to get support from the community for AIDS prevention programs. Other projects have involved working with an ecotourism collective in Belize, small organic farmers in Zambia, and an organization in Ghana to alleviate the suffering of people with mental illnesses and promoting rural development through microfinancing and entrpreneurship in Paraguay. PwC has some evidence showing that the program is a success and is working on developing more measures such as impact on productivity rates.

Progress in meeting leadership goals set by program participants before they attend the program are evaluated. All 24 program participants are still working at PwC, half have been promoted, and most have new job responsibilities. The ability of program participants to win contracts with global clients appears to have improved. The partners who have participated believe that the experience has helped them better relate to their colleagues and clients. The partner who worked on the AIDS project has seen how slowly decisions are made in other places, which has helped him become more patient with his peers at work. Also, he now favors face-to-face conversations over e-mail because it is more valuable for building trust—a lesson learned in Namibia, where there was no electricity, e-mail, or Power-Point presentations.

SOURCES: Based on J. Hempel, "It Takes a Village—and a Consultant," *BusinessWeek*, September 6, 2004, pp. 76–77; J. Marquez, "Companies Send Employees on Volunteer Projects Abroad to Cultivate Leadership Skills," *Workforce Management*, November 2005, pp. 50–51. Also see "The Ulysses Project" and related links at www.pwc.com, the Web site for PricewaterhouseCoopers, April 6, 2009.

assignments help employees improve team relationships and develop leadership and strategic thinking skills.

The "Competing through Globalization" box shows how PricewaterhouseCoopers is using project work to help improve managers' ability to work with global clients and benefit local communities in need.

Interpersonal Relationships

Employees can also develop skills and increase their knowledge about the company and its customers by interacting with a more experienced organization member. Mentoring and coaching are two types of interpersonal relationships that are used to develop employees.

LO5
Develop successful mentoring programs.

Mentoring

A **mentor** is an experienced, productive senior employee who helps develop a less experienced employee (the protégé). Most mentoring relationships develop informally as a result of interests or values shared by the mentor and protégé. Research suggests that employees with certain personality characteristics (like emotional stability, the ability to adapt their behavior based on the situation, and high needs for power and achievement) are most likely to seek a mentor and be an attractive protégé for a mentor.[73] Mentoring relationships can also develop as part of a planned company effort to bring together successful senior employees with less experienced employees.

Mentor
An experienced, productive senior employee who helps develop a less experienced employee.

Developing Successful Mentoring Programs. Although many mentoring relationships develop informally, one major advantage of formalized mentoring programs is that they ensure access to mentors for all employees, regardless of gender or race. An additional advantage is that participants in the mentoring relationship know what is expected of them.[74] One limitation of formal mentoring programs is that mentors may not be able to provide counseling and coaching in a relationship that has been artificially created.[75] To overcome this limitation, it is important that mentors and protégés spend time discussing work styles, their personalities, and their backgrounds, which helps build the trust needed for both parties to be comfortable with their relationship.[76]

Table 9.11 presents the characteristics of a successful formal mentoring program. Mentors should be chosen based on interpersonal and technical skills. They also need to be trained.[77]

A key to successful mentoring programs is that the mentor and protégé are well-matched and can interact with each other face-to-face or virtually using video-conferencing.

Web-based matching systems are available to help match mentors and protégés. For example, both Dow Chemical and Intel have a Web system that allows protégés to input the qualities they want in a mentor. Then, similar to the results of a Google search, a list of names appears with the closest match to their qualities at the top.[78] Wyndham Hotels and Resorts found that a Web-based matching system has tripled the number of employees participating in mentoring. At Wyndham, once the list of names has been generated, the protégé selects the mentor who he or she believes is the best fit and has seven days to contact the mentor to arrange a meeting to decide if there is a good match. The mentor and protégé then sign a contract committing to meeting a certain amount of time each month. The system sends reminders of planned meetings to both the mentor and protégé. Software is also available to track mentor's and protégé's work, help build development plans, and schedule mentor and protégé meetings.[79] For example, at SAIC, a company specializing in technology solutions, a Web-based tool is used to provide online forms, make calendar appointments, set goals for mentoring relationships, and outline an action plan to ensure that protégé needs are discussed.

table 9.11

Characteristics of Successful Formal Mentoring Programs

1. Mentor and protégé participation is voluntary. Relationship can be ended at any time without fear of punishment.
2. The mentor–protégé matching process does not limit the ability of informal relationships to develop. For example, a mentor pool can be established to allow protégés to choose from a variety of qualified mentors.
3. Mentors are chosen on the basis of their past record in developing employees, willingness to serve as a mentor, and evidence of positive coaching, communication, and listening skills.
4. Mentor–protégé matching is based on how the mentor's skills can help meet the protégé's needs.
5. The purpose of the program is clearly understood. Projects and activities that the mentor and protégé are expected to complete are specified.
6. The length of the program is specified. Mentor and protégé are encouraged to pursue the relationship beyond the formal period.
7. A minimum level of contact between the mentor and protégé is specified.
8. Mentors and protégés need to determine the mechanics of the relationship: when they will meet, how often, and how they will communicate outside of the meetings.
9. Protégés are encouraged to contact one another to discuss problems and share successes.
10. The mentor program is evaluated. Interviews with mentors and protégés give immediate feedback regarding specific areas of dissatisfaction. Surveys gather more detailed information regarding benefits received from participating in the program.
11. Employee development is rewarded, which signals managers that mentoring and other development activities are worth their time and effort.

Career Support
Coaching, protection, sponsorship, and providing challenging assignments, exposure, and visibility.

Professional services firm Ernst & Young has mentoring programs pairing high-potential employees with executive mentors (Executive Mentoring Program) and minority employees with senior leaders (Learning Partnerships). Mentors are not forced to serve; they volunteer their time. The programs require mentors and protégés to meet in person four times a year to set goals, for a six-month review, at a year-end evaluation session, and at one other time.[80] Any topics can be discussed in the confidential conversations including career goals, work/life balance, performance issues, and problems with managers. The mentors also introduce their protégés to senior managers whom they otherwise would not meet. Protégés grade their mentors using the company's performance appraisal system. The company has adjusted salaries and denied promotions to managers who were poor mentors.

Benefits of Mentoring Relationships. Both mentors and protégés can benefit from a mentoring relationship. Research suggests that mentors provide career and psychosocial support to their protégés. **Career support** includes coaching, protection, sponsorship, and providing challenging assignments, exposure, and visibility. **Psychosocial support** includes serving as a friend and a role model, providing positive regard and acceptance, and creating an outlet for the protégé to talk about anxieties and fears. Additional benefits for the protégé include higher rates of promotion, higher salaries, and greater organizational influence.[81]

Psychosocial Support
Serving as a friend and role model, providing positive regard and acceptance, and creating an outlet for a protégé to talk about anxieties and fears.

Mentoring relationships provide opportunities for mentors to develop their interpersonal skills and increase their feelings of self-esteem and worth to the organization. For individuals in technical fields such as engineering or health services, the protégé may help them gain knowledge about important new scientific developments in their field (and therefore prevent them from becoming technically obsolete). For example, General Electric launched an initiative in e-business. However, many veteran managers faced the challenge of trying to understand how to effectively use the Internet. Jack Welch, former CEO of General Electric, created a mentoring program for his top 600 managers.[82] The program involved having younger employees who have more experience with the Internet serving as mentors for the top managers. Welch generated interest in the program by getting his own mentor, who was approximately half his age and has much less business experience than he does—but is a Web expert who runs the company's Web site. The purpose of the program was to help managers become familiar with competitors' Web sites, experience the difficulty of ordering products online, and understand what the best Web sites are doing right. Welch started the program because he believed that e-business knowledge is generally inversely related to age and position in the company hierarchy. GE managers met with their mentors for Web lessons, where they critique Web sites, discuss articles and books about e-commerce they had been given to read, and asked the mentors questions. The sessions benefitted both the mentors and the protégés. The protégés learned about the Web, and the mentoring sessions made the younger employees more comfortable talking to their bosses. The mentors also learned about the skills that a manager needs to run a large business operation (such as the ability to communicate with different people).

Mentoring can also occur between mentors and protégés from different organizations and can allow small business owners access to experienced mentors they might not otherwise meet.[83] Web sites such as MicroMentor are available to help small business owners find online mentors. For example, Sturdy McKee wanted to expand his physical therapy practice but needed help understanding financial statements so he could plan the growth of his business and seek outside funding. Using MicroMentor, he completed a personal profile, listed his goals, and then searched potential mentor profiles. Sturdy and his mentor had weekly phone conversations discussing the basics of balance sheets and financial vocabulary. As a result of his positive experience, Sturdy has mentored other entrepreneurs seeking help on how to start a physical therapy practice.

Purposes of Mentoring Programs. Mentor programs socialize new employees, increase the likelihood of skill transfer from training to the work setting, and provide opportunities for women and minorities to gain the exposure and skills needed to evolve into managerial positions. Consider the New York Hospital–Cornell Medical Center mentoring program.[84] The program is designed to help new employees more quickly learn housekeeping duties and understand the culture of the hospital. One benefit of the program is that new employees' performance deficiencies are more quickly corrected. Although the formal mentoring of new employees lasts only two weeks, mentors are available to provide support many months later.

At E. I. Du Pont de Nemours and Company's corporate headquarters, Steve Croft and Janet Graham have met at least once a month for the past seven years to share problems, information, and advice as part of Du Pont's mentoring program.[85] He is a planning manager in Du Pont's research division. She is an administrative assistant in the toxicology lab where Steve used to work. From a list of volunteers, protégés choose mentors (managers and executives) whose skills and experience they want to learn about. Croft, the mentor, has answered Graham's questions about corporate programs and given her the opportunity to meet scientists and managers in the company. Graham has also learned more about the role of other departments in the company and budgetary priorities. Croft too has benefited from the relationship. He has learned about how management decisions affect employees. For example, when the toxicology lab was forced to begin to charge departments for its services (rather than being supported from the company's general fund), Croft learned about employees' reactions and anxieties from Graham.

Because of the lack of potential mentors or a formal reward system supporting mentoring, and the belief that the quality of mentorships developed in a formal program is poorer than informal mentoring relationships, some companies have initiated group mentoring programs. In **group mentoring programs**, a successful senior employee is paired with a group of four to six less experienced protégés. One potential advantage of the mentoring group is that protégés can learn from each other as well as from a more experienced senior employee. Also, group mentoring acknowledges the reality that it is difficult for one mentor to provide an employee with all the guidance and support they need. Group mentoring provides a development network for employees: a small group an employee can use for mentoring support and also have an interest in their learning and development. The leader helps protégés understand the organization, guides them in analyzing their experiences, and helps them clarify career directions. Each member of the group may complete specific assignments, or the group may work together on a problem or issue.[86]

The "Competing through Sustainability" box shows how mentoring programs can lead to value for different company stakeholders.

Coaching

A **coach** is a peer or manager who works with an employee to motivate him, help him develop skills, and provide reinforcement and feedback. There are three roles that a coach can play.[87] The main reasons coaches are used include developing high-potential managers, acting as a sounding board for managers, or specifically trying to change behaviors that are making managers ineffective.[88] Part of coaching may be one-on-one with an employee (such as giving feedback). Another role is to help employees learn for themselves. This involves helping them find experts who can assist them with their concerns and teaching them how to obtain feedback from others. Third, coaching may involve providing resources such as mentors, courses, or job experiences that the employee may not be able to gain access to without the coach's help. Becton Dickinson uses peer coaching as part of its leadership development programs.[89] The topics discussed include job challenges as a development method, ambiguity as a change agent, and how to influence others. Evaluation of the peer coaching has found that coaches gain confidence in their abilities and participants learn about the topics discussed. Wachovia Corporation, a financial services company, has an executive coaching program that uses both internal and external coaches.[90] Participants in the executive leadership development program receive 360-degree assessments that they take to their internal coaches, who are from a different division in the company. Together the manager and coach review the assessment results and agree on an action plan. The coaches are trained how to coach and understand the positive and negative aspects of 360-degree feedback. Research suggests that coaching improves managers' use of 360-degree feedback by helping them set specific improvement goals and solicit ideas for improvement, which results in improved performance.[91]

The best coaches should be empathetic, supportive, practical, and self-confident but not appear as someone who knows all the answers or wants to tell others what to do.[92] Employees who are going to be coached need to be open-minded and interested, not defensive, closed-minded, or concerned with their reputation. Both the coach

Group Mentoring Program
A program pairing a successful senior employee with a group of four to six less experienced protégés.

Coach
A peer or manager who works with an employee to motivate her, help her develop skills, and provide reinforcement and feedback.

LO6
Describe how to train managers to coach employees.

COMPETING THROUGH SUSTAINABILITY
Mentoring Programs Have Potential to Pay Individual, Corporate, and Societal Dividends

A company's sustainability is determined by the extent to which it satisfies the needs of shareholders, customers, employees, community, and society. KLA-Tencor, the Woman's Alliance at Xerox, and General Electric are using mentoring programs to help employees learn new skills, encourage women and minorities to move into management positions, and develop management talent that can help sustain a business strategy.

KLA-Tencor, a supplier of process control solutions for the semiconductor industry, uses mentoring to improve senior managers' skills. The senior managers receive mentoring from company board members as well as retired company executives. The senior managers are expected to increase their functional expertise, identify specific performance goals and developmental activities to address job-related weaknesses, and increase their understanding of the company's culture, vision, and political

structure. KLA-Tencor also has an online mentoring program for managers identified as having high potential for upper-level positions. The program includes an automated relationship pairing function and a 360-degree assessment that is used in the mentoring relationship to improve skill weaknesses.

The Women's Alliance (TWA) at Xerox is using electronic self-service mentor matching software to help women overcome one of the problems they face in establishing a mentoring relationship: finding a suitable mentor. Mentors and mentees both complete online profiles, which include information on their background and interests, areas of expertise, development needs (mentees), and what they hope to gain by participating in the mentoring program. After completing the profile, a TWA mentee can use the search capability to locate a match from the pool of mentors. An e-mail is sent to the selected mentor, who reviews the mentee's profile and accepts

or declines the invitation. The TWA mentoring program started in July 2007. There are currently 60 active mentorships. The program continues to grow because Xerox has overcome the need for mentees to find mentors on their own.

Top females at General Electric are assigned leadership roles within GE's Women's Network (GEWN) local and regional groups so they can get leadership experience. The women also have the opportunity to meet and talk with members of GE's senior management team by attending speaker seminars, workshops, and networking dinners. The network opportunities help the women form an ongoing relationship with a senior leader, which can develop into a mentoring relationship.

SOURCES: Based on T. Galvin, "Best Practices: Mentoring, KLA-Tencor Corp.," *Training*, March 2003, p. 58; A. Poe, "Establishing Positive Mentoring Relationships," *HR Magazine*, February 2002, pp. 62–69; H. Dolezalek, "Got High Potentials?" *Training* 44 (2007), pp. 18–22; B. Carvin, "The Great Mentor Match," *T + D*, January 2009, pp. 46–50.

and the employee to be coached take risks in the relationship. Coaches use their expertise and experiences to help an employee. Employees are vulnerable by honestly communicating about their weaknesses.

To develop coaching skills, training programs need to focus on four issues related to managers' reluctance to provide coaching.[93] First, managers may be reluctant to discuss performance issues even with a competent employee because they want to avoid confrontation. This is especially an issue when the manager is less of an expert than the employee. Second, managers may be better able to identify performance problems than to help employees solve them. Third, managers may also feel that the employee interprets coaching as criticism. Fourth, as companies downsize and operate with fewer employees, managers may feel that there is not enough time for coaching.

Career Management and Development Planning Systems

LO7
Discuss the steps in the development planning process.

Companies' career management systems vary in the level of sophistication and the emphasis they place on different components of the process. Steps and responsibilities in the career management system are shown in Figure 9.3.

Self-Assessment

Self-assessment refers to the use of information by employees to determine their career interests, values, aptitudes, and behavioral tendencies. It often involves psychological tests such as the Myers-Briggs Type Indicator (described earlier in the chapter), the Strong-Campbell Interest Inventory, and the Self-Directed Search. The Strong-Campbell helps employees identify their occupational and job interests; the Self-Directed Search identifies employees' preferences for working in different types of environments (like sales, counseling, landscaping, and so on). Tests may also help employees identify the relative values they place on work and leisure activities. Self-assessment can involve exercises such as the one in Table 9.12. This type of exercise helps an employee consider where she is now in her career, identify future plans, and gauge how her career fits with her current situation and available resources. In some companies, counselors assist employees in the self-assessment process and interpret the results of psychological tests.

LO8
Explain the employees' and company's responsibilities in planning development.

Through the assessment, a development need can be identified. This need can result from gaps between current skills and/or interests and the type of work or position the employee wants. For example, Verizon Wireless provides an online tool that allows employees to assess their current skills and abilities in order to benchmark themselves against job openings throughout the company. The assessment allows employees to identify capabilities they are lacking and provides them with specific

figure 9.3

Steps and Responsibilities in the Career Management Process

	Self-assessment	Reality check	Goal setting	Action planning
Employee responsibility	Identify opportunities and needs to improve.	Identify what needs are realistic to develop.	Identify goal and method to determine goal progress.	Identify steps and timetable to reach goal.
Company responsibility	Provide assessment information to identify strengths, weaknesses, interests, and values.	Communicate performance evaluation, where employee fits in long-range plans of the company, changes in industry, profession, and workplace.	Ensure that goal is specific, challenging, and attainable; commit to help employee reach the goal.	Identify resources employee needs to reach goal, including courses, work experiences, relationships.

table 9.12

Example of a Self-Assessment Exercise

ACTIVITY	(PURPOSE)
Step 1: *Where am I?* (Examine current position of life and career.) Think about your life from past and present to the future. Draw a time line to represent important events.	
Step 2: *Who am I?* (Examine different roles.) Using 3 × 5 cards, write down one answer per card to the question "Who am I?"	
Step 3: *Where would I like to be and what would I like to happen?* *(This helps in future goal setting.)* Consider your life from present to future. Write an autobiography answering three questions: What do you want to have accomplished? What milestones do you want to achieve? What do you want to be remembered for?	
Step 4: *An ideal year in the future* (Identify resources needed.) Consider a one-year period in the future. If you had unlimited resources, what would you do? What would the ideal environment look like? Does the ideal environment match step 3?	
Step 5: *An ideal job* (Create current goal.) In the present, think about an ideal job for you with your available resources. Consider your role, resources, and type of training or education needed.	
Step 6: *Career by objective inventory* (Summarize current situation.) • What gets you excited each day? • What do you do well? What are you known for? • What do you need to achieve your goals? • What could interfere with reaching your goals? • What should you do now to move toward reaching your goals? • What is your long-term career objective?	

SOURCE: From J. E. McMahon and S. K. Merman, "Career Development," in *The ASTD Training and Development Handbook,* 4/e, edited by R. L. Craig, 1996. Copyright © 1996, The McGraw–Hill Companies.

information about what they can do to develop skills through training, job experience, or enrolling in an academic program.[94]

Reality Check

Reality check refers to the information employees receive about how the company evaluates their skills and knowledge and where they fit into the company's plans (potential promotion opportunities, lateral moves). Usually this information is provided by the employee's manager as part of performance appraisal. It is not uncommon in well-developed career management systems for the manager to hold separate performance appraisals and career development discussions.

For example, as part of Caterpillar's performance management process, career development is discussed between the employee and his or her manager.[95] To facilitate this discussion, employees complete a data sheet that serves as an internal résumé. The data sheet includes information about the employee's skills, education, academic degrees, languages spoken, and previous positions. Managers are expected to indicate an employee's readiness for a new job, whether the job will be a promotion or lateral move, and what education or training the employee needs to be ready for the move. Managers discuss with employees where they want to go next and what they have to do to prepare themselves for the next position. Managers also identify where they think the employee has the best opportunities in different functional areas and provide an overall rating of potential and promotability.

Goal Setting

Goal setting refers to the process of employees developing short- and long-term career objectives. These goals usually relate to desired positions (such as becoming sales manager within three years), level of skill application (use one's budgeting skills to improve the unit's cash flow problems), work setting (move to corporate marketing within two years), or skill acquisition (learn how to use the company's human resource information system). These goals are usually discussed with the manager and written into a development plan. A development plan for a product manager is shown in Figure 9.4. Development plans usually include descriptions of strengths and weaknesses, career goals, and development activities for reaching the career goal.

Consider Just Born's Career Development Process (CDP) used by high-performing employees to identify their career path within the company and ready themselves for their next position.[96] The career development plan involves identifying both short- and long-term career goals. Employees commit to two goals to help them progress in their career. Just Born provides a competency dictionary on the company's intranet that can be used for identifying development needs. The CDP gives both employees and their managers the opportunity to discuss future career plans and becomes a reality check by raising expectations and increasing performance standards. Employees initiate the career development program by first defining future job interests, identifying work experiences that help prepare for the future job, and establishing the long-term career goal. The CDP is discussed with the employee's manager. The manager can support the CDP or suggest changes. If employees' future job interests are outside their current department, the interests are communicated to the manager of that department.

Action Planning

During this phase, employees determine how they will achieve their short- and long-term career goals. Action plans may involve any one or combination of development approaches discussed in the chapter (such as enrolling in courses and seminars, getting additional assessment, obtaining new job experiences, or finding a mentor or coach).[97] The development approach used depends on the needs and developmental goal.

Examples of Career Management and Development Systems

Effective career management and development systems include several important design features (see Table 9.13). Sprint's individual development plan is based on five core competencies: act with integrity, focus on the customer, deliver results, build relationships, and develop leadership.[98] These competencies are used by each business unit to establish its strategy as well as by each manager and employee in creating development plans. The competencies are the foundations for development conversations between managers and employees. Among the resources available to support the development plan is a development activities guide, which includes audiotapes, books, and specific courses designed to improve each of the competencies, as well as a Web site where employees can learn about the process. General Mills' development

figure 9.4

Career Development Plan

Name: | **Title:** Project Manager | **Immediate Manager:**

Competencies

Please identify your three greatest strengths and areas for improvement.

Strengths

- Strategic thinking and execution (confidence, command skills, action orientation)
- Results orientation (competence, motivating others, perseverance)
- Spirit for winning (building team spirit, customer focus, respect colleagues)

Areas for Improvement

- Patience (tolerance of people or processes and sensitivity to pacing)
- Written communications (ability to write clearly and succinctly)
- Overly ambitious (too much focus on successful completion of projects rather than developing relationships with individuals involved in the projects)

Career Goals

Please describe your overall career goals.

- **Long-term:** Accept positions of increased responsibility to a level of general manager (or beyond). The areas of specific interest include but are not limited to product and brand management, technology and development, strategic planning, and marketing.
- **Short-term:** Continue to improve my skills in marketing and brand management while utilizing my skills in product management, strategic planning, and global relations.

Next Assignments

Identify potential next assignments (including timing) that would help you develop toward your career goals.

- Manager or director level in planning, development, product, or brand management. Timing estimated to be Spring 2010.

Training and Development Needs

List both training and development activities that will either help you develop in your current assignment or provide overall career development.

- Master's degree classes will allow me to practice and improve my written communications skills. The dynamics of my current position, teamwork, and reliance on other individuals allow me to practice patience and to focus on individual team members' needs along with the success of the projects.

Employee _____ **Date** _____
Immediate Manager _____ **Date** _____
Mentor _____ **Date** _____

---

plan follows the process shown in Figure 9.4. Each employee completes a development plan that asks employees to consider four areas:

- *Professional goals and motivation:* What professional goals do I have? What excites me to grow professionally?
- *Talents or strengths:* What are my talents and strengths?
- *Development opportunities:* What development needs are important to improve?

table 9.13

Design Factors of
Effective Career
Management and
Development
Systems

1. System is positioned as a response to a business need.
2. Employees and managers participate in development of the system.
3. Employees are encouraged to take an active role in career management and development.
4. Evaluation is ongoing and used to improve the system.
5. Business units can customize the system for their own purposes (with some constraints).
6. Employees have access to career information sources (including advisers and positions available).
7. Senior management supports the career system.
8. Career management is linked to other human resource practices such as performance management, training, and recruiting systems.
9. A large, diverse talent pool is created.
10. Career plan and talent evaluation information is available and accessible to all managers.

SOURCE: Based on B. Baumann, J. Duncan, S. E. Former, and Z. Leibowitz, "Amoco Primes the Talent Pump," *Personnel Journal*, February 1996, pp. 79–84; D. Hall, *Careers In and Out of Organizations* (Thousand Oaks, CA: Sage, 2002).

- *Development objectives and action steps:* What will be my objective for this plan? What steps can I take to meet the objectives?

Managers and employees are encouraged to discuss the development plan at least once a year. Speakers, online tools, and workshops to help employees complete the development plan and prepare for a development discussion with their manager increase the visibility and emphasize the importance of the development planning process.

John Deere, the consumer and residential equipment provider, has an online career development program that encourages employees to manage their careers.[99] The online system includes a "job-fit analysis" to help employees compare themselves with positions they would like to have in the future. This gives employees control and responsibility for identifying skill deficiencies and encourages them to have discussions with their managers to design a development plan to help them reach their career goals. Employees can access job competencies for each position. Employees can prepare an online internal résumé for the company's job posting system. The résumés give employees' credentials exposure to managers throughout the company. In the first three months the online system was available, employees made more than 10,000 hits on the job catalogue. More than 6,000 internal résumés are posted in the system.

Special Issues in Employee Development

Melting the Glass Ceiling

LO9

Discuss what companies are doing for management development issues, including succession planning, melting the glass ceiling, and helping dysfunctional managers.

A major development issue facing companies today is how to get women and minorities into upper-level management positions—how to break the **glass ceiling**. Although women represent half of all managers and professionals, they only hold approximately 10 to 15 percent of corporate officer positions.[100] Seventy-four of the top 500 companies had no female corporate officers. The glass ceiling is a barrier to advancement to the higher levels of the organization. This barrier may be due to stereotypes or company systems that adversely affect the development of women or minorities.[101] The glass ceiling is likely caused by lack of access to training programs, appropriate developmental job experiences, and developmental relationships (such as mentoring).[102] Research has found no gender differences in access to job experiences involving transitions or creating change.[103] However, male managers receive significantly more assignments involving high levels of responsibility (high stakes, managing business diversity, handling external pressure) than female managers of similar ability and managerial level. Also, female managers report experiencing more challenge due to lack of personal support (a type of job demand considered to be an obstacle that has been found to relate to harmful stress) than male managers. Career encouragement from peers and senior managers does help women advance to the higher management levels.[104] Managers making developmental assignments need to carefully consider whether gender biases or stereotypes are influencing the types of assignments given to women versus men.

Women and minorities often have trouble finding mentors because of their lack of access to the "old boy network," managers' preference to interact with other managers of similar status rather than with line employees, and intentional exclusion by managers who have negative stereotypes about women's and minorities' abilities, motivation, and job preferences.[105] Potential mentors may view minorities and women as a threat to their job security because they believe affirmative action plans give those groups preferential treatment.

Wal-Mart's strong corporate culture—emphasizing leadership, trust, willingness to relocate on short notice, and promotion from within—may have unintentionally created a glass ceiling.[106] In 2003, 86 percent of store manager positions are held by men. More than two-thirds of Wal-Mart managers started as hourly employees. Hourly job openings are posted at each store, but Wal-Mart never posted openings for management training positions that allowed hourly employees to move up into salaried, management positions. Part of the reason for this practice was that Wal-Mart values efficiency and never saw the need for job postings to fill open management positions. The other reason is that Wal-Mart trusts its managers to promote individuals who deserve promotion. However, women at Wal-Mart claimed that it is difficult to find out about manager jobs. Traditionally, managers at Wal-Mart had to be willing to move with short notice. At Wal-Mart, this relocation requirement results in more opportunities for management jobs for men than for women. Male employees had more access to information about management job openings because they spent more time socializing and talking with management employees (who are primarily male). Wal-Mart has taken steps to melt the glass ceiling.[107] Wal-Mart provided the Diversity Development Series to help all employees better understand their skills and talents and provide ideas for professional growth. The Women's Resource Council was one of several Associate Resource Groups created to build a sense of community among employees with similar backgrounds and interests. The councils focus on recruitment and retention, diversity best-practices insights, business support, employee development, and community involvement. As a result of Wal-Mart's efforts to melt the glass ceiling, in 2009 more than 40 percent of the company's officials and managers are women.

Consider Safeway's efforts to melt the glass ceiling.[108] Safeway has 1,775 grocery stores in the United States and Canada. To meet the challenges of specialty grocers and big-box, low-price competitors such as Wal-Mart and Target, and recognizing that 70 percent of its customers were women, Safeway took steps to help develop women

Glass Ceiling
A barrier to advancement to higher-level jobs in the company that adversely affects women and minorities. The barrier may be due to lack of access to training programs, development experiences, or relationships (e.g., mentoring).

for advancement into management. A women's initiative, Championing Change for Women: An Integrated Strategy, includes programs that focus on leadership development, mentoring, and work/life balance. Safeway typically promotes from within and has focused on the retail level as a source for potential managers through the company's Retail Leadership Development (RLD) program. Ninety percent of Safeway's 1,800 store managers moved up through the company's management ranks through the program, and all but 1 of the company's 10 division presidents began their careers working in one of the stores.

To help women and minorities achieve top-level management positions, the RLD was used to increase the number of women and minorities who complete the program. Those who complete the program are assigned to a store or an assistant manager position that can lead to corporate-level leadership positions. To help support women's efforts to gain leadership positions, Safeway ensures that women who work part-time and use flexible schedules have similar opportunities for coaching, advancement, and development as employees who are on traditional work schedules. The company also realized that frequent relocations did not work for some employees, especially women. As a result, rejecting a relocation to a different location is no longer considered a career-busting decision.

Safeway also provides a women's leadership network for women interested in advancing into management. The network sponsors events such as presentations at different company locations that highlight the success of Safeway women and provide learning opportunities. Executives who attend these presentations meet with women who have been identified as candidates for management positions and are targeted for development opportunities in stores. These discussion focus on the women's career interests, and the executives suggest job opportunities and encourage them to apply for positions that can help them advance to the next management level. Safeway's mentoring program emphasizes that a manager's first protégé should be a woman because of the lack of female mentors. Safeway's work/life balance program, which includes flextime, allows all women, regardless of their family status, to have a healthy balance between work and life. Safeway realizes that its managers are responsible for helping women reach management positions. As a result, all managers attend a Managing Diversity Workshop. Managers are evaluated on their success in meeting diversity goals. Managers who reach their targets can increase their pay bonus by 10 percent.

Safeway's women's initiative has been successful. Since 2000, the number of female store managers has increased by 42 percent. The number of women who have qualified for and completed the RLD program increased 31 percent over the past five years. A research report prepared by Lehman Brothers showed that the program increased the company's sales and earnings. Enhancing its reputation as an employer of choice for women and minorities, Safeway received the Catalyst Award, which is presented annually to outstanding companies that promote the career advancement of women and minorities. Table 9.14 provides recommendations for melting the glass ceiling and helping retain talented women.

Although most of LeasePlan USA's 450 employees were women, the majority of the company's top managers were men.[109] To help promote more women to management positions, LeasePlan USA hired a consultant to develop a program that focuses on skill assessment, career guidance, and tips on communications. The program also features networking events and a panel discussion with female executives from other companies. One in five women participating in the program has been promoted. Six of the company's top 14 managers are now women, an increase of 10 women from

Make sure senior management supports and is involved in the program.

Make a business case for change.

Make the change public.

Gather data on problems causing the glass ceiling using task forces, focus groups, and questionnaires.

Create awareness of how gender attitudes affect the work environment.

Force accountability through reviews of promotion rates and assignment decisions.

Promote development for all employees.

table 9.14

Recommendations for Melting the Glass Ceiling

SOURCE: Based on D. McCracken, "Winning the Talent War for Women," *Harvard Business Review,* November–December 2000, pp. 159–67.

two years ago. The program is also improving job satisfaction and engagement among women employees. Survey results showed that one year after the program was first implemented, there was a 12 percent increase in the number of women who felt that management supported their efforts to manage their careers and said they think that positions at LeasePlan are fairly awarded.

Succession Planning

Many companies are losing sizable numbers of upper-level managers due to retirement and company restructurings that reduced the number of potential upper-level managers. They are finding that their middle managers are not ready to move into upper management positions due to skill weaknesses or lack of needed experience. This creates the need for succession planning. Succession planning refers to the process of identifying and tracking high-potential employees. **Succession planning** helps organizations in several different ways.[110] It requires senior management to systematically review leadership talent in the company. It ensures that top-level managerial talent is available. It provides a set of development experiences that managers must complete to be considered for top management positions; this avoids premature promotion of managers who are not ready for upper management ranks. Succession planning systems also help attract and retain managerial employees by providing them with development opportunities that they can complete if upper management is a career goal for them. **High-potential employees** are those the company believes are capable of being successful in higher-level managerial positions such as general manager of a strategic business unit, functional director (such as director of marketing), or chief executive officer (CEO).[111] High-potential employees typically complete an individual development program that involves education, executive mentoring and coaching, and rotation through job assignments. Job assignments are based on the successful career paths of the managers whom the high-potential employees are being prepared to replace. High-potential employees may also receive special assignments, such as making presentations and serving on committees and task forces.

Research suggests that the development of high-potential employees involves three stages.[112] A large pool of employees may initially be identified as high-potential employees, but the numbers are reduced over time because of turnover, poor performance, or a personal choice not to strive for a higher position. In stage 1, high-potential employees are selected. Those who have completed elite academic programs (like an MBA at Stanford) or who have been outstanding performers are identified. Psychological tests such as assessment centers may also be used.

Succession Planning
The identification and tracking of high-potential employees capable of filling higher-level managerial positions.

High-Potential Employees
Employees the company believes are capable of being successful in high-level management positions.

In stage 2, high-potential employees receive development experiences. Those who succeed are the ones who continue to demonstrate good performance. A willingness to make sacrifices for the company is also necessary (such as accepting new assignments or relocating to a different region). Good oral and written communication skills, an ease in interpersonal relationships, and a talent for leadership are critical. In what is known as a "tournament model" of job transitions, high-potential employees who meet their senior managers' expectations in this stage advance into the next stage of the process.[113] Employees who do not meet the expectations are ineligible for higher-level managerial positions in the company.

To reach stage 3, high-potential employees usually have to be seen by top management as fitting into the company's culture and having the personality characteristics needed to successfully represent the company. These employees have the potential to occupy the company's top positions. In stage 3, the CEO becomes actively involved in developing the employees, who are exposed to the company's key personnel and are given a greater understanding of the company's culture. It is important to note that the development of high-potential employees is a slow process. Reaching stage 3 may take 15 to 20 years.

Table 9.15 shows the process used to develop a succession plan. The first step is to identify what positions are included in the succession plan, such as all management positions or only certain levels of management. The second step is to identify which employees are part of the succession planning system. For example, in some companies only high-potential employees are included in the succession plan. Third, the company needs to identify how positions will be evaluated. For example, will the emphasis be on competencies needed for each position or on the experiences an individual needs to have before moving into the position? Fourth, the company should identify how employee potential will be measured. That is, will employees' performance in their current jobs as well as ratings of potential be used? Will employees' position interests and career goals be considered? Fifth, the succession planning review process needs to be developed. Typically, succession planning reviews first involve employees' managers and human resources. A talent review could also include an overall assessment of leadership talent in the company, an identification of high-potential employees, and a discussion of plans to keep key managers from leaving the company.

table 9.15

The Process of Developing a Succession Plan

1. Identify what positions are included in the plan.
2. Identify the employees who are included in the plan.
3. Develop standards to evaluate positions (e.g., competencies, desired experiences, desired knowledge, developmental value).
4. Determine how employee potential will be measured (e.g., current performance and potential performance).
5. Develop the succession planning review.
6. Link the succession planning system with other human resource systems, including training and development, compensation, and staffing systems.
7. Determine what feedback is provided to employees.
8. Evaluate the succession plan.

SOURCES: Based on B. Dowell, "Succession Planning," in *Implementing Organizational Interventions*, ed. J. Hedge and E. Pulaskos (San Francisco: Jossey-Bass, 2002), pp. 78–109; R. Barnett and S. Davis, "Creating Greater Success in Succession Planning," *Advances in Developing Human Resources* 10 (2008), pp. 721–39.

Sixth, succession planning is dependent on other human resource systems, including compensation, training and development, and staffing. Incentives and bonuses may be linked to completion of development opportunities. Activities such as training courses, job experiences, mentors, and 360-degree feedback can be used to meet development needs. Companies need to make decisions such as will they fill an open management position internally with a less-experienced employee who will improve in the role over time, or will they hire a manager from outside the company who can immediately deliver results. Seventh, employees need to be provided with feedback on future moves, expected career paths, and development goals and experiences. Finally, the succession planning process needs to be evaluated. This includes identifying and measuring appropriate results outcomes (such as reduced time to fill manager positions, increased use of internal promotions) as well as collecting measures of satisfaction with the process (reaction outcomes) from employees and managers. Also, modifications that will be made to the succession planning process need to be identified, discussed, and implemented.

A good example of succession planning is the system at WellPoint, a health care company headquartered in Thousand Oaks, California.[114] WellPoint has a Web-based corporate database that identifies employees for management jobs throughout the company and tracks the development of employee talent. WellPoint has operations across the United States, including locations in California and Georgia. The succession planning system includes 600 managers and executives across five levels of the company. The Human Resource Planning System (HRPS) has detailed information on possible candidates, including performance evaluations, summaries of the candidates' accomplishments at the company, self-evaluations, information about career goals, and personal data such as the candidates' willingness to relocate to another part of the company. Part of the development of HRPS involved identifying the company's strength and weaknesses at each position. Senior management team members developed standards, or benchmarks, to use to identify the best candidates for promotion. The HRPS system allows managers and the human resource team to identify and evaluate candidates for every management position in the company. It helps identify and track the development of promising internal candidates and also identifies areas where internal candidates are weak, so that (1) external candidates can be recruited, (2) a special development program can be initiated to develop employee talent, and (3) the company can place more emphasis on developing the missing skills and competencies in internal candidates. For example, because WellPoint lacked candidates for two levels of management, the company created a special training program that used business case simulations for 24 managers and executives who had been identified as high-potential candidates for upper-level management positions.

WellPoint's process of succession planning includes several steps. First, each employee who is eligible for succession planning completes a self-evaluation that is sent to his or her manager. The manager adds a performance appraisal, a rating on the employee's core competencies, and a promotion assessment, that is, an assessment of the employee's potential for promotion. The promotion assessment includes the manager's opinion regarding what positions the employee might be ready for and when the employee should be moved. It also includes the manager's view on who could fill the open position if the employee is promoted. The information from the employee and the manager is used to create an online résumé for each eligible employee. The system has benefited the company's bottom line. WellPoint realized an 86 percent internal promotion rate, which exceeded its goal of filling 75 percent of management positions from within. By improving employees' opportunities for promotion, WellPoint has reduced its turnover rate by 6 percent since 1997 and has saved $21 million on recruitment and training expenses. The time to fill open management positions has been reduced from 60 days to 35 days.

Helping Managers with Dysfunctional Behaviors

A number of studies have identified managerial behavior that can cause an otherwise competent manager to be a "toxic" or ineffective manager. Such behavior includes insensitivity to others, inability to be a team player, arrogance, poor conflict management skills, inability to meet business objectives, and inability to change or adapt during a transition.[115] For example, a skilled manager who is interpersonally abrasive, aggressive, and an autocratic leader may find it difficult to motivate subordinates, may alienate internal and external customers, and may have trouble getting ideas accepted by superiors. These managers are in jeopardy of losing their jobs and have little chance of future advancement because of the dysfunctional behavior. Typically, a combination of assessment, training, and counseling is used to help managers change the dysfunctional behavior.

For example, a middle manager at PG&E, an energy company, was hurting her relationships with her associates, and her career, by her brash personality.[116] PG&E hired a coach to work with her. The coach videotaped her as she role-played an actual clash that she had had with another manager over a new information system. During the confrontation (and the role-play) she was aloof, abrasive, cold, and condescending. The coach helped her see the limitations of her approach. She apologized to colleagues and listened to their ideas. Coaching helped this manager learn how to maintain her composure and focus on what is being said rather than on the person. Wachovia hires external coaches for top executives who have been identified as high-potential leaders who are facing a specific job challenge or problem such as moving into a new position after a merger. The coaching involves nine months to a year and includes 360-degree assessments, interviews, and psychological tests.[117]

A LOOK BACK

The chapter opener described Accenture Consulting's career management and employee development efforts.

Questions

1. How might job experiences that provide consultants with different types of work or the opportunity to serve different clients help them develop?
2. What should be included in a development plan that a consultant at Accenture Consulting would complete with his or her career counselor?
3. Would the development activities for the highest performing consultants vary from the activities used for satisfactory performing consultants? Why? Explain the differences.

Please see the Video Case that corresponds to this chapter online at www.mhhe.com/noe7e.

● SUMMARY

This chapter emphasized the various development methods that companies use: formal education, assessment, job experiences, and interpersonal relationships. Most companies use one or more of these approaches to develop employees. Formal education involves enrolling employees in courses or seminars offered by the company or educational institutions. Assessment involves measuring the employee's performance, behavior, skills, or personality characteristics. Job experiences include job enlargement, rotating to a new job, promotions, or transfers. A more experienced, senior employee (a mentor) can help

employees better understand the company and gain exposure and visibility to key persons in the organization. Part of a manager's job responsibility may be to coach employees. Regardless of the development approaches used, employees should have a development plan to identify (1) the type of development needed, (2) development goals, (3) the best approach for development, and (4) whether development goals have been reached. For development plans to be effective, both the employee and the company have responsibilities that need to be completed.

● KEY TERMS

Development, 410
Protean career, 411
Psychological contract, 411
Psychological success, 412
Career management system, 413
Formal education programs, 414
Tuition reimbursement, 417
Assessment, 419
Myers-Briggs Type Indicator
    personality assessment
    (MBTI)®, 420
Assessment center, 422

Leaderless group discussion, 422
Interview, 422
In-basket, 422
Role-plays, 422
Benchmarks ©, 424
Performance appraisal, 425
Upward feedback, 425
360-degree feedback systems, 425
Job experiences, 427
Job enlargement, 429
Job rotation, 430
Transfer, 431

Promotions, 431
Downward move, 431
Externship, 432
Sabbatical, 433
Mentor, 435
Career support, 436
Psychosocial support, 436
Group mentoring programs, 438
Coach, 438
Glass ceiling, 445
Succession planning, 447
High-potential employees, 447

● DISCUSSION QUESTIONS

1. How could assessment be used to create a productive work team?
2. List and explain the characteristics of effective 360-degree feedback systems.
3. Why do companies develop formal mentoring programs? What are the potential benefits for the mentor? For the protégé?
4. Your boss is interested in hiring a consultant to help identify potential managers among current employees of a fast-food restaurant. The manager's job is to help wait on customers and prepare food during busy times, oversee all aspects of restaurant operations (including scheduling, maintenance, on-the-job training, and food purchase), and help motivate employees to provide high-quality service. The manager is also responsible for resolving disputes that might occur between employees. The position involves working under stress and coordinating several activities at one time. She asks you to outline the type of assessment program you believe

would do the best job of identifying employees who will be successful managers. What will you tell her?
5. Many employees are unwilling to relocate because they like their current community, and spouses and children prefer not to move. Yet employees need to develop new skills, strengthen skill weaknesses, and be exposed to new aspects of the business to prepare for management positions. How could an employee's current job be changed to develop management skills?
6. What is coaching? Is there one type of coaching? Explain.
7. Why are many managers reluctant to coach their employees?
8. Why should companies be interested in helping employees plan their careers? What benefits can companies gain? What are the risks?
9. What are the manager's roles in a career management system? Which role do you think is most difficult for the typical manager? Which is the easiest role? List

the reasons why managers might resist involvement in career management.

10. What are the characteristics of the most effective company development strategies? Which characteristic do you believe is most important? Why?

11. Nationwide Financial, a 5,000-employee life insurance company based in Columbus, Ohio, found that its management development program contained four types of managers. One type, unknown leaders, have the right skills but their talents are unknown to top managers in the company. Another group, arrogant leaders, believe they have all the skills they need. What types of development program would you recommend for these managers?

● SELF-ASSESSMENT EXERCISE

The Department of Labor's Occupational Information Network (O*NET) is designed to meet the goal of promoting the education, training, counseling, and employment needs of the American workforce. Go to http://online.onetcenter.org/. Click on Skills Search. Complete the skills search than click Go. What occupations match your skills? How might Skills Search be useful for career management?

● EXERCISING STRATEGY: RANDSTAD'S PARTNERING PROGRAM

Randstad USA is one of the largest recruiting agencies in the United States with more than 600 branch offices. Randstad USA encourages its younger employees to pair with older, more experienced employees. Every new sales agent is assigned a partner to work with until his or her business has grown to a specific size, then he or she serves as a partner for someone who has just joined the company. Randstad uses this approach to help 20-something employees identify with their jobs and reduce new employee turnover. Randstad managers believe that if Generation Y employees shared a job with someone whose own success depended on their success, they would get all of the support they needed. Randstad has been pairing people since the company was started nearly 40 years ago. Based on the company founder's motto that "Nobody should be left alone," the original goal was to increase productivity by having sales agents share one job and trade off responsibilities. Currently, the way the pairing works is that each week one person is out making sales calls and the other is in the office handling paperwork and interviewing potential workers. Then the partners switch responsibilities. One of the most important parts of the partnering program is that neither person is the boss and both are expected to teach each other. For example, one 61-year-old senior agent is paired with a 28-year-old partner who is working in her first office job. The senior partner is helping the new agent understand how to ask clients the right questions and not to be timid when giving job applicants advice (such as appropriate apparel for a job interview). The senior employee has gained a new perspective from the younger employee about how to relax at work. Working with a younger partner encouraged another senior partner to overcome hesitation of using the electronic payroll system that Randstad offers to save time and reduce paperwork. Randstad also encourages the partners to solve their own problems and dissolves them only when major problems are occurring, such as one person is sabotaging the other or productivity is suffering. In these cases, which occur infrequently, the uncooperative partner usually leaves the company.

Questions

1. Randstad's partnering program uses interpersonal relationships as a development strategy. What steps should Randstad take to ensure that this is a successful strategy? Are other development activities necessary? Why?

2. What data or outcomes should be collected to monitor the effectiveness of the partnering program? Explain the business reason for your choice(s) of outcomes or data.

● MANAGING PEOPLE: FROM THE PAGES OF *BUSINESSWEEK*

BusinessWeek   Two for the Cubicle

Sharing a job is always dicey. How one pair has made it work for 15 years   They share a title and a salary, a desk, a phone, and an e-mail account. Their résumés are nearly identical: For the past 15 years, Sharon Cercone, 48, and Linda Gladziszewski, 45, have been partners in seven human resources jobs at three different companies. They are now compensation consultants at PNC Financial Services Group Inc. in Pittsburgh, where one executive describes them in a way that might unnerve even the most collaborative among us: "I think of them as a single individual," says Valentine Przezdecki.

Successfully sharing a job is more demanding than pretty much any other flexible work arrangement. Partners have to trust each other with their careers. They receive the same recognition, and if one falters, both take the blame. They have to communicate the details of their days precisely and without fail. Theirs is an intricate pas de deux, requiring a certain familiarity and ease, and like most things in life, it can't be forced. "All of the stars have to be aligned. You have to be able to complete each other's sentences and have a manager who doesn't mind adding another level of complexity," says Kathleen C. D'Appolonia, a senior vice-president at PNC. "When it doesn't work, it is very disruptive, and it can not work for all kinds of reasons. It's sort of like marriage." She says that nearly half of PNC's 25,000 employees have some kind of flexible arrangement; a total of 12 share jobs.

The decision to share a job is usually the result of a cool appraisal of the workplace: that the arrangement confers more status than a part-time job does. "If the position is full-time, it's less likely that the contribution will be marginalized," says Pat Katepoo, the founder of WorkOptions.com.

No one has an estimate of how many workers share jobs nowadays. But as companies try to retain talented women (and men) with young families as well as those baby boomers who want more time to themselves, the number that offer job shares is rising. The 2005 National Study of Employers by the Families and Work Institute found that 44% of businesses allow some employees to share jobs; in 1998, 38% did.

Cementing the Bond

Sharon and Linda happened upon the idea at a time of transition in their home and work lives. In the late 1980s, Mellon Financial Corp., where they were full-time compensation consultants, was in turmoil. The bank had cut 20% of its workforce and was looking for ways to encourage its most talented employees to stay. After the birth of her first child, Sharon proposed sharing her job and was matched with another woman. When her partner left Mellon to teach, Sharon asked Linda, who had just returned from maternity leave and wanted more time with her son, to apply for the job. In October, 1991, they began to work together.

The practice of constant communication and intense organization that they developed then remains intact today, though made vastly easier by mobile phones and e-mail. Sharon works Mondays and Tuesdays, Linda Thursdays and Fridays; they alternate Wednesdays. They talk or exchange text messages several times a day, and more often on Wednesdays. They check in at night. They

keep project notes and a phone log, and even describe the body language of those with whom they meet. "We overcompensate so people understand that we don't let anything fall through the cracks," says Sharon. "We make references to our notes when talking to others." The back-and-forth can add up to three hours to their workweeks, but, says Linda, "We know the arrangement could end at any time, so whatever we can do, we do." They even schedule face time; colleagues tease them about planning lunches weeks ahead.

In the early days of their job share, co-workers weren't always supportive. "People would try to drive a wedge between us," says Sharon. They'd say, 'Yesterday, Linda told me this.' And I would know she hadn't. Or people would say, 'Wow, you're so lucky.' And I would say, 'You do realize we only get half pay.'"

Joined at the Hip

The pair moved from compensation to recruiting at Mellon in 1995, a job that proved far more demanding on their time than they'd expected, with a boss who was less comfortable with the arrangement than they'd hoped. "We were told that if we wanted to be on the A-team, we needed to work full-time," says Sharon. "So we decided to look elsewhere."

It didn't take them long to find another compensation consultant job to share. The financial-services industry in Pittsburgh is relatively small: Sandy Short, a colleague at Mellon who'd helped set up Sharon and Linda's job share, had moved to PNC and was hiring. But even Short needed some convincing. PNC was in the midst of a reorganization, and she wondered about having to manage two people instead of one. Sharon and Linda assured her that they would manage each other. In 2002, after five years on the job, they moved to another that was created for them but soon eliminated in a restructuring.

Following a two-year turn at Crown Castle International Corp., which leases cell tower space, they were rehired at PNC by Renee Rossi, a senior human resources manager who initially was unsure that two people could share the position. Sharon and Linda's work as compensation consultants didn't require daily interaction with colleagues outside their department. The role of a human resources generalist would be different, and the finance managers who Sharon and Linda would be advising worried that the job share would complicate their lives. As Rossi says: "They had to be reassured that if they had a conversation about an employee issue with Sharon on Tuesday that they wouldn't have to start over with Linda on Wednesday." After extensive interviews and reference checks, Rossi could tell the managers they wouldn't.

By then, Sharon and Linda were expert at one of the most important things anyone can do for their career: managing a boss's expectations. As Rossi recalls: "Sharon warned me, 'Remember that you didn't hire two people who are on call all the time.' And I did find myself excited that I had two people. I had to remind myself that they were really one person." Rossi also had to resist the tendency to divide assignments based on each one's strengths. Sharon is very organized, Linda less so. Sharon is a confident public speaker who likes leading group training sessions; Linda prefers one-on-one interactions.

A year and a half ago, Linda and Sharon's position was eliminated. They returned to dealing with compensation at PNC, their seventh job together. As is often the case with them, the move was lateral. As Linda says: "Would we be in the same place if we both worked full-time? No." But over the years they have rejected offers of full-time jobs. "There may be certain situations we don't like, but we're willing to do pretty much anything because we treasure working with each other," says Sharon.

This spring, Sharon began working at home on her days off on an independent project for PNC. Her department is short-staffed, and she is ready to work more now that her kids are older. But she's uneasy about the new situation. "I'm not used to it, and I don't really like it," she says. "Linda and I are not as connected."

Questions

1. How does the job-sharing arrangement help Sharon and Linda manage their careers?
2. How could job sharing be used to develop employees?
3. What difficulties does job-sharing arrangements cause for clients or customers? Managers? What advantages do job-sharing arrangements provide for clients or customers? Managers? Are certain types of jobs best suited for job sharing? Explain your answer.

SOURCE: Susan Berfield, "Two for the Cubicle," *BusinessWeek*, July 24, 2006.

● NOTES

1. D. Day, *Developing Leadership Talent* (Alexandria, VA: SHRM Foundation, 2007); M. London, *Managing the Training Enterprise* (San Francisco: Jossey-Bass, 1989); C. McCauley and S. Heslett, "Individual Development in the Workplace," in *Handbook of Industrial, Work, and Organizational Psychology*, Vol. 1, ed. N. Anderson, D. Ones, H. Sinangil, and C. Viswesveran (London: Sage Publications, 2001), pp. 313–35.

2. R. W. Pace, P. C. Smith, and G. E. Mills, *Human Resource Development* (Englewood Cliffs, NJ: Prentice Hall, 1991); W. Fitzgerald, "Training versus Development," *Training and Development Journal*, May 1992, pp. 81–84; R. A. Noe, S. L. Wilk, E. J. Mullen, and J. E. Wanek, "Employee Development: Issues in Construct Definition and Investigation of Antecedents," in *Improving Training Effectiveness in Work Organizations*, ed. J. K. Ford (Mahwah, NJ: Lawrence Erlbaum, 1997), pp. 153–89.

3. Towers Perrin HR Services, *Talent Management: The State of the Art* (Chicago, IL: Towers Perrin, 2005). Available at www.towersperrin.com.

4. J. H. Greenhaus and G. A. Callanan, *Career Management*, 2nd ed. (Fort Worth, TX: Dryden Press, 1994); D. C. Feldman, *Managing Careers in Organizations* (Glenview, IL: Scott Foresman, 1988); D. Hall, *Careers In and Out of Organizations* (Thousand Oaks, CA: Sage, 2002).

5. D. T. Hall, "Protean Careers of the 21st Century," *Academy of Management Executive* 11 (1996), pp. 8–16; Hall, *Careers In and Out of Organizations*.

6. D. M. Rousseau, "Changing the Deal while Keeping the People," *Academy of Management Executive* 11 (1996), pp. 50–61; D. M. Rousseau and J. M. Parks, "The Contracts of Individuals and Organizations," in *Research in Organizational Behavior* 15, ed. L. L. Cummings and B. M. Staw (Greenwich, CT: JAI Press, 1992), pp. 1–47.

7. C. Ansberry, "A New Blue-Collar World," *The Wall Street Journal*, June 30, 2003, p. B1.

8. K. Kathryn, "Three Generations, Three Perspectives," *The Wall Street Journal*, March 29, 2004, p. R8.

9. M. B. Arthur, P. H. Claman, and R. J. DeFillippi, "Intelligent Enterprise, Intelligent Careers," *Academy of Management Executive* 9 (1995), pp. 7–20.

10. K. R. Brousseau, M. J. Driver, K. Eneroth, and R. Larsson, "Career Pandemonium: Realigning Organizations and Individuals," *Academy of Management Executive* 11 (1996), pp. 52–66.

11. M. B. Arthur, "The Boundaryless Career: A New Perspective of Organizational Inquiry," *Journal of Organization Behavior* 15 (1994), pp. 295–309; P. H. Mirvis and D. T. Hall, "Psychological Success and the Boundaryless Career," *Journal of Organization Behavior* 15 (1994), pp. 365–80; M. Lazarova and S. Taylor, "Boundaryless Careers, Social Capital, and Knowledge Management: Implications for Organizational Performance," *Journal of Organizational Behavior* 30 (2009), pp. 119–39; D. Feldman and T. Ng, "Careers: Mobility, Embeddedness, and Success," *Journal of Management* 33 (2007), pp. 350–77.

12. B. P. Grossman and R. S. Blitzer, "Choreographing Careers," *Training and Development*, January 1992, pp. 67–69.

13. Harris Interactive, Emerging workforce study, (Ft. Lauderdale, FL: Spherion, 2005); Available at www.spherion.com/pressroom/ L. Chao, "What GenXers Need to Be Happy at Work," *The Wall Street Journal*, November 29, 2005, p. B6; E. Kaplan-Leiserson, "The Changing Workforce," *TD*, February 2005, pp. 10–11.

14. J. S. Lubin and J. B. White, "Throwing Off Angst, Workers Are Feeling in Control of Their Careers," *The Wall Street Journal*, September 11, 1997, pp. A1, A6.

15. L. Mainiero and S. Sullivan, "Kaleidoscope Careers: An Alternative Explanation for the "Opt-Out" Revolution," *Academy of Management Executive* 19 (2005), pp. 106–23; S. Sullivan and L. Mainiero, "Benchmarking Ideas for Fostering Family-Friendly Workplaces," *Organizational Dynamics* 36 (2007), pp. 45–62.

16. R. Noe, *Employee Training and Development*, 4th ed. (New York: McGraw-Hill, Irwin, 2008).

17. M. Weinstein, "Teaching the Top," *Training*, February 2005, pp. 30–33.

18. C. Waxer, "Course Review," *Human Resource Executive*, December 2005, pp. 46–48.

19. C. Waxer, "Bank of Montreal Opens Its Checkbook in the Name of Employee Development," *Workforce Management*, October 24, 2005, pp. 46–48.

20. www.ge.com/company/culture/leaderhip_learning.html, January 15, 2009.

21. R. Knight, "GE's Corporate Boot Camp cum Talent Spotting Venue," *Financial Times Business Education*, March 20, 2006, p. 2; J. Durett, "GE Hones Its Leaders at Crotonville," *Training*, May 2006, pp. 25–27.

22. J. Bolt, *Executive Development* (New York: Harper Business, 1989); M. A. Hitt, B. B. Tyler, C. Hardee, and D. Park, "Understanding Strategic Intent in the Global Marketplace," *Academy of Management Executive* 9 (1995), pp. 12–19.

23. Center for Creative Leadership, "Xerox Corporation" (2007), from Web site, www.ccl.org.

24. "Client Stories," www.dukece.com, Web site of Duke Corporate Education.

25. L. Bongiorno, "How'm I Doing," *BusinessWeek*, October 23, 1995, pp. 72, 74.

26. Waxer, "Course Review."

27. A. Howard and D. W. Bray, *Managerial Lives in Transition: Advancing Age and Changing Times* (New York: Guilford, 1988); Bolt, *Executive Development*; J. R. Hinrichs and G. P. Hollenbeck, "Leadership Development," in *Developing Human Resources*, ed. K. N. Wexley (Washington, DC: BNA Books, 1991), pp. 5-221 to 5-237; Day, *Developing Leadership Talent*.

28. M. Weinstein, "Personalities & Performance," *Training*, July/August 2008, pp. 36–40.

29. E. Krell, "Personality Counts," *HR Magazine*, November 2005, pp. 47–52.

30. C. Cornell, "The Value of Values," *Human Resource Executive*, November 2004, pp. 68–72.

31. Weinstein, "Personalities & Performance."

32. S. K. Hirsh, *MBTI Team Member's Guide* (Palo Alto, CA: Consulting Psychologists Press, 1992); A. L. Hammer, *Introduction to Type and Careers* (Palo Alto, CA: Consulting Psychologists Press, 1993).

33. A. Thorne and H. Gough, *Portraits of Type* (Palo Alto, CA: Consulting Psychologists Press, 1991).

34. D. Druckman and R. A. Bjork, eds., *In the Mind's Eye: Enhancing Human Performance* (Washington, DC: National Academy Press, 1991); M. H. McCaulley, "The Myers-Briggs Type Indicator and Leadership," in *Measures of Leadership*, ed. K. E. Clark and M. B. Clark (West Orange, NJ: Leadership Library of America, 1990), pp. 381–418.

35. G. C. Thornton III and W. C. Byham, *Assessment Centers and Managerial Performance* (New York: Academic Press, 1982); L. F. Schoenfeldt and J. A. Steger, "Identification and Development of Management Talent," in *Research in Personnel and Human Resource Management*, ed. K. N. Rowland and G. Ferris (Greenwich, CT: JAI Press, 1989), vol. 7, pp. 151–81.

36. Thornton and Byham, *Assessment Centers and Managerial Performance*.

37. B. B. Gaugler, D. B. Rosenthal, G. C. Thornton III, and C. Bentson, "Metaanalysis of Assessment Center Validity," *Journal of Applied Psychology* 72 (1987), pp. 493–511; D. W. Bray, R. J. Campbell, and D. L. Grant, *Formative Years in Business: A Long-Term AT&T Study of Managerial Lives* (New York: Wiley, 1974).

38. R. G. Jones and M. D. Whitmore, "Evaluating Developmental Assessment Centers as Interventions," *Personnel Psychology* 48 (1995), pp. 377–88.

39. J. Schettler, "Building Bench Strength," *Training*, June 2002, pp. 55–58.

40. C. D. McCauley and M. M. Lombardo, "Benchmarks: An Instrument for Diagnosing Managerial Strengths and Weaknesses," in *Measures of Leadership*, pp. 535–45; "Benchmarks©—Overview," at www.ccl.org, Web site for the Center for Creative Leadership, March 28, 2006.

41. C. D. McCauley, M. M. Lombardo, and C. J. Usher, "Diagnosing Management Development Needs: An Instrument Based on How Managers Develop," *Journal of Management* 15 (1989), pp. 389–403.

42. S. B. Silverman, "Individual Development through Performance Appraisal," in *Developing Human Resources*, pp. 5–120 to 5–151.

43. M. Sallie-Dosunmu, "Born to Grow," *TD*, May 2006, pp. 34–37.

44. "Master of HR at GE," *Human Resource Executive*, October 2004, pp. 16–24.

45. J. S. Lublin, "Turning the Tables: Underlings Evaluate Bosses," *The Wall Street Journal*, October 4, 1994, pp. B1, B14; O'Reilly, "360-Degree Feedback Can Change Your Life," *Fortune*, October 17, 1994, pp. 93–100; J. F. Milliman, R. A. Zawacki, C. Norman, L. Powell, and J. Kirksey, "Companies Evaluate Employees from All Perspectives," *Personnel Journal*, November 1994, pp. 99–103.

46. Center for Creative Leadership, *Skillscope for Managers: Development Planning Guide* (Greensboro, NC: Center for Creative Leadership, 1992); G. Yukl and R. Lepsinger, "360-Degree Feedback," *Training*, December 1995, pp. 45–50.

47. L. Atwater, P. Roush, and A. Fischthal, "The Influence of Upward Feedback on Self- and Follower Ratings of Leadership," *Personnel Psychology* 48 (1995), pp. 35–59; J. F. Hazucha, S. A. Hezlett, and R. J. Schneider, "The Impact of 360-Degree Feedback on Management Skill Development," *Human Resource Management* 32 (1993), pp. 325–51; J. W. Smither, M. London, N. Vasilopoulos, R. R. Reilly, R. E. Millsap, and N. Salvemini, "An Examination of the Effects of an Upward Feedback Program over Time," *Personnel Psychology* 48 (1995), pp. 1–34; J. Smither and A. Walker, "Are the Characteristics of Narrative Comments Related to Improvements in Multirater Feedback Ratings over Time?" *Journal of Applied Psychology* 89 (2004), pp. 575–81; J. Smither, M. London, and R. Reilly, "Does Performance Improve Following Multisource Feedback? A Theoretical Model, Meta-analysis, and Review of Empirical Findings," *Personnel Psychology* 58 (2005), pp. 33–66.

48. D. Bracken, "Straight Talk about Multirater Feedback," *Training and Development*, September 1994, pp. 44–51; K. Nowack, J. Hartley, and W. Bradley, "How to Evaluate Your 360-Feedback Efforts," *Training and Development*, April 1999, pp. 48–52.

49. A. Freedman, "The Evolution of 360s," *Human Resource Executive*, December 2002, pp. 47–51.

50. M. W. McCall Jr., M. M. Lombardo, and A. M. Morrison, *Lessons of Experience* (Lexington, MA: Lexington Books, 1988).

51. R. S. Snell, "Congenial Ways of Learning: So Near yet So Far," *Journal of Management Development* 9 (1990), pp. 17–23.

52. R. Morrison, T. Erickson, and K. Dychtwald, "Managing Middlescence," *Harvard Business Review*, March 2006, pp. 78–86.

53. *The Wall Street Journal*, October 13, 2008, p. R6.

54. McCall, Lombardo, and Morrison, *Lessons of Experience*; M. W. McCall, "Developing Executives through Work Experiences," *Human Resource Planning* 11 (1988), pp. 1–11; M. N. Ruderman, P. J. Ohlott, and C. D. McCauley, "Assessing Opportunities for Leadership Development," in *Measures of Leadership*, pp. 547–62; C. D. McCauley, L. J. Estman, and P. J. Ohlott, "Linking Management Selection and Development through Stretch Assignments," *Human Resource Management* 34 (1995), pp. 93–115.

55. C. D. McCauley, M. N. Ruderman, P. J. Ohlott, and J. E. Morrow, "Assessing the Developmental Components of Managerial Jobs," *Journal of Applied Psychology* 79 (1994), pp. 544–60.

56. S. Thurm, "Power-Sharing Prepares Managers," *The Wall Street Journal*, December 5, 2005, p. B4.

57. T. Galvin, "Best Practice: Job Rotation, Arrow Electronics," *Training*, March 2003, p. 59.

58. M. Weinstein, "Foreign but Familiar," *Training*, January 2009, pp. 20–23.

59. M. London, *Developing Managers* (San Francisco: Jossey-Bass, 1985); M. A. Campion, L. Cheraskin, and M. J. Stevens, "Career-Related Antecedents and Outcomes of Job Rotation," *Academy of Management Journal* 37 (1994), pp. 1518–42; M. London, *Managing the Training Enterprise* (San Francisco: Jossey-Bass, 1989).

60. M. Pacelle, "Job Swap Is Meant to Groom 'Next Generation,'" *The Wall Street Journal*, September 28, 2004, pp. C1, C4.

61. D. C. Feldman, *Managing Careers in Organizations* (Glenview, IL: Scott Foresman, 1988).

62. J. M. Brett, L. K. Stroh, and A. H. Reilly, "Job Transfer," in *International Review of Industrial and Organizational Psychology: 1992*, ed. C. L. Cooper and I. T. Robinson (Chichester, England: John Wiley and Sons, 1992); D. C. Feldman and J. M. Brett, "Coping with New Jobs: A Comparative Study of New Hires and Job Changers," *Academy of Management Journal* 26 (1983), pp. 258–72.

63. R. A. Noe, B. D. Steffy, and A. E. Barber, "An Investigation of the Factors Influencing Employees' Willingness to Accept Mobility Opportunities," *Personnel Psychology* 41 (1988), pp. 559–80; S. Gould and L. E. Penley, "A Study of the Correlates of Willingness to Relocate," *Academy of Management Journal* 28 (1984), pp. 472–78; J. Landau and T. H. Hammer, "Clerical Employees' Perceptions of Intraorganizational Career Opportunities," *Academy of Management Journal* 29 (1986), pp. 385–405; R. P. Duncan and C. C. Perruci, "Dual Occupation Families and Migration," *American Sociological Review* 41 (1976), pp. 252–61; J. M. Brett and A. H. Reilly, "On the Road Again: Predicting the Job Transfer Decision," *Journal of Applied Psychology* 73 (1988), pp. 614–620.

64. D. T. Hall and L. A. Isabella, "Downward Moves and Career Development," *Organizational Dynamics* 14 (1985), pp. 5–23.

65. H. D. Dewirst, "Career Patterns: Mobility, Specialization, and Related Career Issues," in *Contemporary Career Development Issues*, ed. R. F. Morrison and J. Adams (Hillsdale, NJ: Lawrence Erlbaum, 1991), pp. 73–108.

66. N. C. Tompkins, "GTE Managers on the Move," *Personnel Journal*, August 1992, pp. 86–91.

67. J. M. Brett, "Job Transfer and Well-Being," *Journal of Applied Psychology* 67 (1992), pp. 450–63; F. J. Minor, L. A. Slade, and R. A. Myers, "Career Transitions in Changing Times," in *Contemporary Career Development Issues*, pp. 109–20; C. C. Pinder and K. G. Schroeder, "Time to Proficiency Following Job Transfers," *Academy of Management Journal* 30 (1987), pp. 336–53; G. Flynn, "Heck No—We Won't Go!" *Personnel Journal*, March 1996, pp. 37–43.

68. R. E. Silverman, "Mercer Tries to Keep Employees Through Its 'Externship' Program," *The Wall Street Journal*, November 7, 2000, p. B18.

69. E. Byron, "A New Odd Couple: Google, P&G Swap Workers to Spur Innovation," *The Wall Street Journal*, November 19, 2008, pp. A1, A18.

70. C. J. Bachler, "Workers Take Leave of Job Stress," *Personnel Journal*, January 1995, pp. 38–48.

71. F. Jossi, "Taking Time Off from Advertising," *Workforce*, April 2002, p. 15.

72. M. Weinstein, "Charity Begins @ Work," *Training*, May 2008, pp. 56–58; K. Ellis, "Pass It On," *Training*, June 2005, pp. 14–19.

73. D. B. Turban and T. W. Dougherty, "Role of Protégé Personality in Receipt of Mentoring and Career Success," *Academy of Management Journal* 37 (1994), pp. 688–702; E. A. Fagenson, "Mentoring: Who Needs It? A Comparison of Protégés' and Nonprotégés' Needs for Power, Achievement, Affiliation, and Autonomy," *Journal of Vocational Behavior* 41 (1992), pp. 48–60.

74. A. H. Geiger, "Measures for Mentors," *Training and Development Journal*, February 1992, pp. 65–67.

75. K. E. Kram, *Mentoring at Work: Developmental Relationships in Organizational Life* (Glenview, IL: Scott Foresman, 1985); K. Kram, "Phases of the Mentoring Relationship," *Academy of Management Journal* 26 (1983), pp. 608–25; G. T. Chao, P. M. Walz, and P. D. Gardner, "Formal and Informal Mentorships: A Comparison of Mentoring Functions and Contrasts with Nonmentored Counterparts," *Personnel Psychology* 45 (1992), pp. 619–36; C. Wanberg, E. Welsh, and S. Hezlett, "Mentoring Research: A Review and Dynamic Process Model," in *Research in Personnel and Human Resources Management*, ed. J. Martocchio and G. Ferris (New York: Elsevier Science, 2003), pp. 39–124.

76. E. White, "Making Mentorships Work," *The Wall Street Journal*, October 23, 2007, p. B11; E. Holmes, "Career Mentors Today Seem Short on Advice but Give a Mean Tour," *The Wall Street Journal*, August 28, 2007, p. B1; J. Sandberg, "With Bad Mentors It's Better to Break Up than to Make Up," *The Wall Street Journal*, March 18, 2008, p. B1.

77. L. Eby, M. Butts, A. Lockwood, and A. Simon, "Protégés' Negative Mentoring Experiences: Construct Development and Nomological Validation," *Personnel Psychology* 57 (2004), pp. 411–47; M. Boyle, "Most Mentoring Programs Stink—but Yours Doesn't Have To," *Training*, August 2005, pp. 12–15.

78. E. Tahmincioglu, "Looking for a Mentor? Technology Can Help Make the Right Match," *Workforce Management*, December 2004, pp. 63–65; D. Owens, "Virtual Mentoring," *HR Magazine*, March 2006, pp. 105–7.

79. M. Weinstein, "Tech Connects," *Training*, September 2008, pp. 58–59.

80. Boyle, "Most Mentoring Programs Stink."

81. G. F. Dreher and R. A. Ash, "A Comparative Study of Mentoring among Men and Women in Managerial, Professional, and Technical Positions," *Journal of Applied Psychology* 75 (1990), pp. 539–46; T. D. Allen, L. T. Eby, M. L. Poteet, E. Lentz, and L. Lima, "Career Benefits Associated with Mentoring for Protégés: A Meta-Analysis," *Journal of Applied Psychology* 89 (2004), pp. 127–36; R. A. Noe, D. B. Greenberger, and S. Wang, "Mentoring: What We Know and Where We Might Go," in *Research in Personnel and Human Resources Management*, ed. G. Ferris and J. Martucchio (New York: Elsevier Science, 2002), pp. 129–74; R. A. Noe, "An Investigation of the Determinants of Successful Assigned Mentoring Relationships," *Personnel Psychology* 41 (1988), pp. 457–79; B. J. Tepper, "Upward Maintenance Tactics in Supervisory Mentoring and Nonmentoring Relationships," *Academy of Management Journal* 38 (1995), pp. 1191–205; B. R. Ragins and T. A. Scandura, "Gender Differences in Expected Outcomes of Mentoring Relationships," *Academy of Management Journal* 37 (1994), pp. 957–71.

82. M. Murray, "GE Mentoring Program Turns Underlings into Teachers of the Web," *The Wall Street Journal*, February 15, 2000, pp. B1, B16.

83. K. Spors, "Websites Offer Access to Mentors," *The Wall Street Journal*, June 3, 2008, p. B7.

84. C. M. Solomon, "Hotel Breathes Life Into Hospital's Customer Service," *Personnel Journal*, October 1995, p. 120.

85. F. Jossi, "Mentoring in Changing Times," *Training*, August 1997, pp. 50–54.

86. B. Kaye and B. Jackson, "Mentoring: A Group Guide," *Training and Development*, April 1995, pp. 23–27.

87. D. B. Peterson and M. D. Hicks, *Leader as Coach* (Minneapolis, MN: Personnel Decisions, 1996).

88. D. Coutu and C. Kauffman, "What Coaches Can Do for You," *Harvard Business Review,* January 2009, pp. 91–97.

89. J. Toto, "Untapped World of Peer Coaching," *TD,* April 2006, pp. 69–71.

90. H. Johnson, "The Ins and Outs of Executive Coaching," *Training,* May 2004, pp. 36–41.

91. J. Smither, M. London, R. Flautt, Y. Vargas, and L. Kucine, "Can Working with an Executive Coach Improve Multisource Ratings over Time? A Quasi-Experimental Field Study," *Personnel Psychology* 56 (2003), pp. 23–44.

92. Toto, "Untapped World of Peer Coaching."

93. R. Zemke, "The Corporate Coach," *Training,* December 1996, pp. 24–28.

94. B. Yovovich, "Golden Opportunities," *Human Resource Executive,* August 2008, pp. 30–34.

95. S. Needleman, "New Career, Same Employer," *The Wall Street Journal,* April 21, 2008, p. B9.

96. Sallie-Dosunmu, "Born to Grow."

97. D. T. Jaffe and C. D. Scott, "Career Development for Empowerment in a Changing Work World," in *New Directions in Career Planning and the Workplace,* ed. J. M. Kummerow (Palo Alto, CA: Consulting Psychologists Press, 1991), pp. 33–60; L. Summers, "A Logical Approach to Development Planning," *Training and Development* 48 (1994), pp. 22–31; D. B. Peterson and M. D. Hicks, *Development First* (Minneapolis, MN: Personnel Decisions, 1995).

98. K. Ellis, "Individual Development Plans: The Building Blocks of Development," *Training,* December 2004, pp. 20–25.

99. R. Davenport, "John Deere Champions Workforce Development," *TD,* April 2006, pp. 40–43.

100. *Women in U.S. Corporate Leadership: 2003* (New York: Catalyst, 2003); C. Hymowitz, "On Diversity, America Isn't Putting Its Money Where Its Mouth Is," *The Wall Street Journal,* February 25, 2008, p. B1.

101. U.S. Department of Labor, *A Report on the Glass Ceiling Initiative* (Washington, DC: U.S. Department of Labor, 1991).

102. P. J. Ohlott, M. N. Ruderman, and C. D. McCauley, "Gender Differences in Managers' Developmental Job Experiences," *Academy of Management Journal* 37 (1994), pp. 46–67; D. Mattioli, "Programs to Promote Female Managers Win Citations," *The Wall Street Journal,* January 30, 2007, p. B7.

103. L. A. Mainiero, "Getting Anointed for Advancement: The Case of Executive Women," *Academy of Management Executive* 8 (1994), pp. 53–67; J. S. Lublin, "Women at Top Still Are Distant from CEO Jobs," *The Wall Street Journal,* February 28, 1995,

pp. B1, B5; P. Tharenov, S. Latimer, and D. Conroy, "How Do You Make It to the Top? An Examination of Influences on Women's and Men's Managerial Advancement," *Academy of Management Journal* 37 (1994), pp. 899–931.

104. P. Tharenou, "Going Up? Do Traits and Informal Social Processes Predict Advancement in Management?" *Academy of Management Journal* 44 (2001), pp. 1005–17.

105. U.S. Department of Labor, *A Report on the Glass Ceiling Initiative*; R. A. Noe, "Women and Mentoring: A Review and Research Agenda," *Academy of Management Review* 13 (1988), pp. 65–78; B. R. Ragins and J. L. Cotton, "Easier Said Than Done: Gender Differences in Perceived Barriers to Gaining a Mentor," *Academy of Management Journal* 34 (1991), pp. 939–51.

106. C. Daniels, "Women vs. Wal-Mart," *Fortune,* July 21, 2003, pp. 78–82.

107. Advancement of Women Fact Sheet, "Wal-Mart's Diversity Commitment Translates into Support for Women at All Levels," "Working Mother Magazine Names Wal-Mart a 2007 Best Company for Multicultural Women," both from www.walmartstores.com, March 25, 2009.

108. A. Pomeroy, "Cultivating Female Leaders," *HR Magazine,* February 2007, pp. 44–50.

109. C. Tuna, "Initiative Moves Women up Corporate Ladder," *The Wall Street Journal,* October 20, 2008, p. B4.

110. W. J. Rothwell, *Effective Succession Planning,* 2nd ed. (New York: AMACOM, 2001).

111. C. B. Derr, C. Jones, and E. L. Toomey, "Managing High-Potential Employees: Current Practices in Thirty-Three U.S. Corporations," *Human Resource Management* 27 (1988), pp. 273–90.

112. Ibid.; K. M. Nowack, "The Secrets of Succession," *Training and Development* 48 (1994), pp. 49–54; J. S. Lublin, "An Overseas Stint Can Be a Ticket to the Top," *The Wall Street Journal,* January 29, 1996, pp. B1, B2.

113. Nowack, "The Secrets of Succession"; Lublin, "An Overseas Stint Can Be a Ticket to the Top."

114. P. Kiger, "Succession Planning Keeps WellPoint Competitive," *Workforce,* April 2002, pp. 50–54; E. Fravenheim, "Succession Progression," *Workforce Management,* January 2006, pp. 31–34.

115. M. W. McCall Jr., and M. M. Lombardo, "Off the Track: Why and How Successful Executives Get Derailed," *Technical Report no. 21* (Greensboro, NC: Center for Creative Leadership, 1983); E. V. Veslor and J. B. Leslie, "Why Executives Derail: Perspectives across Time and Cultures," *Academy of Management Executive* 9 (1995), pp. 62–72.

116. J. Lublin, "Did I Just Say That?! How You Can Recover from Foot-in-Mouth," *The Wall Street Journal,* June 18, 2002, p. B1.

117. Johnson, "The Ins and Outs of Executive Coaching."

Employee Separation and Retention

 LEARNING OBJECTIVES

After reading this chapter, you should be able to:

LO1 Distinguish between involuntary and voluntary turnover, and discuss how each of these forms of turnover can be leveraged for competitive advantage. *page 462*

LO2 List the major elements that contribute to perceptions of justice and how to apply these in organizational contexts involving discipline and dismissal. *page 465*

LO3 Specify the relationship between job satisfaction and various forms of job withdrawal, and identify the major sources of job satisfaction in work contexts. *page 477*

LO4 Design a survey feedback intervention program, and use this to promote retention of key organizational personnel. *page 485*

Boosting Morale at Home Depot

The business model at Home Depot is built around homes, and the hope that people will be buying homes, selling homes, and improving homes. Thus, when confronted with the worst housing market in three decades, it is not that surprising that the company and its employees were experiencing stress. In terms of financial stress, in May 2008, Home Depot reported a 66 percent drop in first-quarter profits, along with a 7 percent drop in sales. Expansion plans were scrapped, and 15 of its flagship stores were closed, affecting 1,300 employees. This created stress among the surviving workers and triggered higher rates of turnover among the most skilled and knowledgeable workers, who had the best alternative employment opportunities.

When CEO Robert Nardelli and his hand-picked vice president for human resources, Dennis Donovan, resigned in 2007, this created an opportunity for transformation, and new CEO Frank Blake and new vice president for human resources Tim Crow decided that restoring employee morale was the single most important change that had to be made at the retail chain. In Crow's words, "If people aren't happy, they aren't going to be happy to customers. That's why morale is so important in our business, and that's my focus." Crow's strategy for achieving this goal for enhanced morale had three basic components,

First, Crow wanted to reestablish a sense of employee ownership of the work. Many of Home Depot employees had already become disaffected because of a perception that Nardelli had so centralized all decision-making in the organization that people felt they had little say in how to do their own work. This stood in stark contrast to the philosophy of the Home Depots founders, Arthur Blank and Bernie Marcus, who empowered store managers and encouraged them to be entrepreneurial in orientation. To promote this new spirit, Crow eliminated the practice of having one HR professional in every store. Although a strategic HR team was made available to store managers on an "as-needed basis," the expectation was that store managers would be given more control over hiring and promotion decisions. The more transactional aspects of HR were then in-sourced to a 220-person HR call center.

Second, Crow was bent on increasing the skill level of the workers so that they are more confident about being able to do an effective job. During the Nardelli regime, Home Depot began hiring more part-time workers, with limited skill sets, and this resulted in customer service ratings that lagged far behind competitors like Lowe's. Training was often based on an e-learning model, where workers logged into a training site and slogged through material alone. Crow overturned this and replaced it with a model where workers interact face-to-face with one another on the store floor and share stories of specific successes and failures they have had with respect to customer service. Many of the best sales personnel who had left the store were re-recruited, and the ratio of part-time workers to full-time workers went from 20 percent to close to 80 percent.

Finally, Crow wanted to align the rewards and recognition programs at Home Depot to boost morale. In fact, even though sales and profits were down, the amount of money that Home Depot rewarded to managers who reached their sales goals actually doubled in the last two years. The company also introduced a systematic system that raises pay for each certified skill that an associate learns. Each department (e.g., plumbing) has a certification test, and the more tests the associate passes, the more he or she is paid. This level of skill is also recognized via a badge system that makes it clear to everyone on the floor who knows what. Although it is too early to tell how all of these changes will turn out, one immediate impact has been made with respect to employee turnover, which went down by 15 percent from 2007 to 2008.

Sources: J. Marquez, "Rallying the Home Team," *Workforce Management*, July 14, 2008, pp. 24–28; R. J. Grossman, "Remodeling HR at Home Depot," *HRMagazine*, November 1, 2008, pp. 3–13; G. Ruiz, "Home Depot's New HR Leader Faces Tall Order," *Workforce Management*, February 12, 2007, pp. 24–28.

Introduction

Every executive recognizes the need for satisfied, loyal customers. If the firm is publicly held, it is also safe to assume that every executive appreciates the need to have satisfied, loyal investors. Customers and investors provide the financial resources that allow the organization to survive. Unlike Home Depot's Tim Crow, however, not every executive understands the need to generate satisfaction and loyalty among employees. Yet, retention rates among employees are related to retention rates among customers.[1] In fact, research has established a direct link between employee retention rates and sales growth[2] and companies that are cited as one of the "100 Best Companies to Work For" routinely outperform their competition on many other financial indicators of performance.[3] For example Figure 10.1 shows the average annual returns for the "100 Best Companies to Work For" over various time periods ending in 2005. The figure reveals that sustained (10 years) competitive advantage in capital markets is directly attributable to successfully managing the workforce.[4] Job satisfaction and retention are also related to organizational performance.[5] This is especially the case in service industries, where disgruntled workers often create large numbers of dissatisfied customers.[6] Lack of experience and cohesiveness within work units destroys efficiency, and the costs associated with constantly replacing workers erodes a firm's competitive position.[7] For example, after bankruptcy proceedings in 2007 forced United Airlines to cut the pay of flight attendants to 1985 levels, the high level of dissatisfaction within the ranks of these workers on the front line immediately spilled

figure 10.1

Stock Performance: Average Annual Return Best Companies to Work For vs. S&P 500

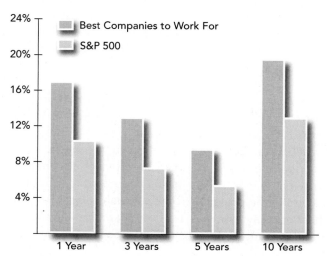

SOURCE: M. Boyle, "Happy People, Happy Returns," *BusinessWeek*, January 22, 2007, p. 100.

over into customer ratings of service. Thus, just at a time when United was finally putting its financial problems behind it, new problems related to customer service threatened to throw them back into bankruptcy court again. As Greg Davidowitch, president of the Associated United Flight Attendants noted, "You can't run a service business when you are at war with your employees."[8] Indeed, study after study has shown a direct causal connection between poor worker attitudes on the one hand, and poor customer service on the other.[9]

In addition to holding onto key personnel, another hallmark of successful firms is their ability and willingness to dismiss employees who are engaging in counter-productive behavior. Indeed, it is somewhat ironic that one of the keys to retaining productive employees is ensuring that these people are not being made miserable by supervisors or co-workers who are engaging in unproductive, disruptive, or dangerous behavior. Unfortunately, surveys indicate that many managers—indeed as many as 70 percent—struggle to give frank and honest feedback to poorly performing subordinates, and then wind up experiencing and tolerating poor performance for very long periods.[10] It is precisely for this reason that many organizations have resorted to forced distribution rating systems like those we discussed earlier in Chapter 8, which require some percentage of employees to be given "unsatisfactory" ratings. However, in the absence of honest, accurate, and diagnostic feedback, even these systems do little to spur improvement. For example, at Microsoft, employees felt that some managers who were poor at giving negative feedback just used the distribution system as a crutch. As one Microsoft worker noted, managers would just say, "I really wanted to give to you a 4, but I had the curve so I had to give you a 3."[11] Feedback like that does not give the employee any sense of justice—and does nothing to promote focused improvement.

Thus, to compete effectively, organizations must take steps to ensure that good performers are motivated to stay with the organization, whereas chronically low performers are allowed, encouraged, or, if necessary, forced to leave. Retaining top performers is not always easy, however. Competing organizations are constantly looking to steal top performers, and "poaching talent" is becoming an increasingly common way for organizations to build themselves up, while at the same time, tearing their competitors down.[12] It is also not nearly as easy to fire employees as many people think. The increased willingness of people to sue their employer, combined with an unprecedented level of violence in the workplace, has made discharging employees who lack talent legally complicated and personally dangerous.[13]

The purpose of this chapter (the last in Part 3 of this book) is to focus on employee separation and retention. The material presented in Part 3's previous two chapters ("Performance Management" and "Employee Development") can be used to help establish who are the current effective performers as well as who is likely to respond well to future developmental opportunities. This chapter completes Part 3 by discussing what can be done to retain high-performing employees who warrant further development as well as managing the separation process for low-performing employees who have not responded well to developmental opportunities.

Since much of what needs to be done to retain employees involves compensation and benefits, this chapter also serves as a bridge to Part 4, which addresses these issues in more detail. The chapter is divided into two sections. The first examines **involuntary turnover,** that is, turnover initiated by the organization (often among people who would prefer to stay). The second deals with **voluntary turnover,** that is, turnover initiated by employees (often whom the company would prefer to keep). Although both types of turnover reflect employee separation, they are clearly different phenomena that need to be examined separately.

Involuntary Turnover
Turnover initiated by the organization (often among people who would prefer to stay).

Voluntary Turnover
Turnover initiated by employees (often whom the company would prefer to keep).

Managing Involuntary Turnover

Despite a company's best efforts in the area of personnel selection, training, and design of compensation systems, some employees will occasionally fail to meet performance requirements or will violate company policies while on the job. When this happens, organizations need to invoke a discipline program that could ultimately lead to the individual's discharge. For a number of reasons, discharging employees can be a very difficult task that needs to be handled with the utmost care and attention to detail.

First, legal aspects to this decision can have important repercussions for the organization. Historically, in the absence of a specified contract, either the employer or the employee could sever the employment relationship at any time. The severing of this relationship could be for "good cause," "no cause," or even "bad cause." Over time, this policy has been referred to as the **employment-at-will doctrine.** This employment-at-will doctrine has eroded significantly over time, however. Today employees who are fired sometimes sue their employers for wrongful discharge. Some judges have been willing to consider employees who meet certain criteria regarding longevity, promotions, raises, and favorable past performance reviews as having an implied contract to dismissal only for good cause—even in the face of direct language in the company handbook that states an employment-at-will relationship.[14]

A wrongful discharge suit typically attempts to establish that the discharge either (1) violated an implied contract or covenant (that is, the employer acted unfairly) or (2) violated public policy (that is, the employee was terminated because he or she refused to do something illegal, unethical, or unsafe). Wrongful discharge suits can also be filed as a civil rights infringement if the person discharged is a member of a protected group. The number of such "protected groups" is large, however, and includes, racial minorities, women, older workers (over 40 years of age), homosexuals, disabled workers (including the obese), whistle-blowers, people who have filed workers compensation claims, and if one counts reverse discrimination claims—Caucasians. Indeed, as noted by Lisa Cassilly, a defense attorney for the firm Alston and Bird, "It's difficult to find someone who doesn't have some capacity to claim protected status."[15] This means that in almost any instance when someone is fired for poor performance, the alternative possibility that this person was a victim of discrimination can be raised.

Not surprisingly, this has led to an increase in litigation, such that while there were roughly 8,000 wrongful termination lawsuits filed in 1991, by 2006 the number of lawsuits filed annually was close to 15,000. Moreover, because the Civil Rights Act of 1991 allowed for jury trials and "punitive" damages, in some well-known cases, the size of the awards are attention-getting. For example, in a recent case at General Electric, an employee was awarded more than $11 million in a wrongful discharge suit.[16] The vividness of these highly publicized cases often distorts the perceptions of how infrequently plaintiffs actually win such cases, however. For example, Figure 10.2 shows the base rate probabilities for various outcomes in such cases. As you can see, a plaintiff rarely achieves a victory in this kind of case should it survive appeal (odds are roughly one-tenth of 1 percent). However, the high legal cost associated with winning the case is often enough to make some employers reluctant to fire workers. When this happens, the employer's short-term emphasis on staying out of court has come into conflict with the long-term need to develop a competitive workforce.

For example, one reaction to this dilemma is enduring long stretches of poor performance in order to create the extensive "paper trail" that would support a negative

Out of 10,000 Employment Suits	Stage of Lawsuit	Cumulative Cost for a Company to Defend a Single Lawsuit
	FILING	
7,000	Settle (most settlements are for nuisance value)	$10,000
	SUMMARY JUDGMENT	
2,400	Get resolved by summary judgment and other pretrial rulings	$100,000
	START OF TRIAL	
600	Go to trial	$175,000
	END OF TRIAL	
186	Trials are won by plaintiffs	$250,000*
	APPEAL	
13**	Plaintiff victories survive appeal	$300,000

figure 10.2

Probable Outcomes of Wrongful Discharge Suits

*Assumes a five-day trial
**Out of 22 trial losses typically appealed by companies
SOURCES: M. Orey, "Fear of Firing," *BusinessWeek,* April 23, 2007, p. 60; Cornell Law School; *Hofstra Labor & Employment Law Journal;* BW reporting.

action. While HR professionals often point the finger of blame at supervisors who have not done a diligent job documenting past performance problems, supervisors often turn around and accuse HR of being "nervous Nellies" who never seem satisfied with the amount of evidence provided by supervisors. Moreover, keeping poor performers in their roles does not directly affect HR professionals every day, like it does supervisors, who have to watch helplessly as the morale of the rest of the workforce erodes. Indeed, there is nothing more corrosive to team-based structures than wide variability in effort and performance between different members, and hence it is somewhat ironic that the key to prompting and sustaining a collaborative and productive culture is maintaining the firm's right to "at-will" employment. As one member of a research team in a pharmaceutical firm noted with respect to the idea of "carrying" a poor performer for fear of litigation, "As a female and also of a minority race, I am appalled and saddened by this scenario as I must bear the weight of this constant underperformer."[17]

Another questionable reaction is to initiate punitive actions short of termination, in an effort to get the employee to quit on his or her own. This reaction is often a result of frustrated supervisors, who, unable to fire someone because of HR, resort to punishing the employee in other ways. This might include giving the person a low-level work assignment, a downsized office, or some other form of undesirable treatment. The problem with this approach, however, is that it might be construed as "retaliation," and the employer could be sued for this, even if the original discrimination suit is dismissed. In 2005 and 2006, 30 percent of EEOC filings were this type of "retaliation lawsuits," which was three times the percentage just 10 years ago.[18] In fact, some attorneys advise any clients who are expecting a poor performance appraisal or some other adverse job event to file a discrimination suit as part of a preemptive attack that sets up the groundwork for a subsequent "retaliation" lawsuit.

Finally, a third unsustainable reaction is to pay off the employee with thousands of dollars in excess severance pay in return for waiving their right to sue for wrongful dismissal. That is, even if the employer feels the case is unwarranted, in order to avoid litigation itself, the employer may offer the terminated employee $20,000 or more to waive their right to sue. The problem with this strategy is that it sets the expectation that all poor performers are entitled to compensation on their way out the door, and this eventually increases the amount of potential future litigation by rewarding frivolous charges. As we have seen in this chapter, this strategy grossly overestimates the plaintiff's probability of winning such a case. A more effective and sustainable strategy for employers would be to develop a reputation that you will defend the firm' right to terminate low performers, rather than invite bullying by an overly aggressive attorney or employee. As defense attorney Mark Dichter notes, "I can design HR policies that can virtually eliminate your risk of facing employment claims, but you'll have a pretty lousy workforce. At the end of the day, you have to run your business."[19]

The costs associated with letting poor performers stay on within the organization cannot be discounted. Organizations that introduce forced distributions rating systems where low performers are systematically identified and, where necessary, eliminated from payrolls often experience quick improvement gains in the range of 40 percent.[20] Over time, research shows that the gains achieved by such programs get smaller and smaller, but the initial jump illustrates how many organizations drift into a situation where tolerating low performance has become an unsustainable business practice.[21] This fact is even being realized in many European countries where worker protections embody a critical cultural value. Recent legislation passed in both France and Germany have simplified the procedures that firms have to go through to eliminate poor performers and lowered the bar for the evidence that has to be provided in such cases.[22] Paradoxically, one of the countries they are trying to compete against, China, is actually moving in the opposite direction, trying to make it more difficult for employers to fire workers, in an effort to become more "worker-friendly."[23]

In addition to the financial risks associated with having to legally defend a dismissal, there are issues related to personal safety. Although the fact that some former employees use the court system to get back at their former employers may be distressing, even more problematic are employees who respond to a termination decision with violence directed at the employer.[24] Violence in the workplace has become a major organizational problem and workplace homicide is the fastest-growing form of murder in the United States.[25] Although any number of organizational actions or decisions may incite violence among employees, the "nothing else to lose" aspect of employee dismissal cases makes for a dangerous situation, especially in the presence of other risk factors associated with the nature of the work.[26]

Given the critical financial and personal risks associated with employee dismissal, it is easy to see why the development of a standardized, systematic approach to discipline and discharge is critical to all organizations. These decisions should not be left solely to the discretion of individual managers or supervisors. In the next section we explore aspects of an effective discipline and discharge policy.

Principles of Justice

In Chapter 8 ("Performance Management") we touched on the notion of justice, particularly as this relates to the notions of outcome justice, procedural justice, and interactional justice. There we noted that employees are more likely to respond positively to negative feedback regarding their performance if they perceive the appraisal process as being fair on these three dimensions. Obviously, if fairness is important with respect to ongoing feedback, this is even more critical in the context of a final termination decision. Therefore, we will explore the three types of fairness perceptions in greater detail here, with an emphasis on how these need to be operationalized in effective discipline and discharge policies that support the type of "psychological contracts" that tend to govern employer–employee relationships.[27]

As we noted earlier in Chapter 8, **outcome fairness** refers to the judgment that people make with respect to the *outcomes received* relative to the outcomes received by other people with whom they identify (referent others). Clearly, a situation where one person is losing his or her job while others are not is conducive to perceptions of outcome unfairness on the part of the discharged employee. The degree to which this potentially unfair act translates into the type of anger and resentment that might spawn retaliation in the form of violence or litigation, however, depends on perceptions of procedural and interactional justice.[28]

Whereas outcome justice focuses on the ends, procedural and interactional justice focus on means. If methods and procedures used to arrive at and implement decisions that impact the employee negatively are seen as fair, the reaction is likely to be much more positive than if this is not the case. **Procedural justice** focuses specifically on the *methods used to determine the outcomes received.* Table 10.1 details six key principles that determine whether people perceive procedures as being fair. Even given all the negative ramifications of being dismissed from one's job, the person being dismissed may accept the decision with minimum anger if the procedures used to arrive at the decision are consistent, unbiased, accurate, correctable, representative, and ethical. When the procedures for the decisions are perceived in this fashion, the individual does not feel unfairly singled out, and this helps maintain his or her faith in the system as a whole, even if he or she is unhappy with the specific decision that was triggered by the system.[29]

Whereas procedural justice deals with how a decision was made, **interactional justice** refers to the *interpersonal nature of how the outcomes were implemented.* For

LO2
List the major elements that contribute to perceptions of justice and how to apply these in organizational contexts involving discipline and dismissal.

Outcome Fairness
The judgment that people make with respect to the outcomes received relative to the outcomes received by other people with whom they identify.

Procedural Justice
A concept of justice focusing on the methods used to determine the outcomes received.

Interactional Justice
A concept of justice referring to the interpersonal nature of how the outcomes were implemented.

table 10.1
Six Determinants of Procedural Justice

(1) **Consistency.** The procedures are applied consistently across time and other persons.
(2) **Bias suppression.** The procedures are applied by a person who has no vested interest in the outcome and no prior prejudices regarding the individual.
(3) **Information accuracy.** The procedure is based on information that is perceived to be true.
(4) **Correctability.** The procedure has built-in safeguards that allow one to appeal mistakes or bad decisions.
(5) **Representativeness.** The procedure is informed by the concerns of all groups or stakeholders (co-workers, customers, owners) affected by the decision, including the individual being dismissed.
(6) **Ethicality.** The procedure is consistent with prevailing moral standards as they pertain to issues like invasion of privacy or deception.

table 10.2

Four Determinants
of Interactional
Justice

> (1) **Explanation.** Emphasize aspects of procedural fairness that justify the decision.
> (2) **Social sensitivity.** Treat the person with dignity and respect.
> (3) **Consideration.** Listen to the person's concerns.
> (4) **Empathy.** Identify with the person's feelings.

example, in many documented cases, after giving employees the news of their termination, employers immediately have security guards whisk them out of the building with their various personal items haphazardly thrown together in cardboard boxes. This strips the person of their dignity, as well as their job, and employees who witness this happen to a co-worker show a drastically lower level of organizational commitment from that day forward.[30] Table 10.2 lists the four key determinants of interactional justice. When the decision is explained well and implemented in a fashion that is socially sensitive, considerate, and empathetic, this helps defuse some of the resentment that might come about from a decision to discharge an employee. As one human research director noted, the key is to ensure that the affected individual "walks out with their dignity and self-respect intact."[31] Going through these steps is especially important if the individual who is being managed is already high in hostility, and hence a threat to respond in violent fashion.[32] Indeed, beyond the context of employee termination, the use of systems that promote procedural and interactive justice across the organization results in both more satisfied employees[33] and a more productive workforce[34] and a more collaborative and innovative organizational culture.[35]

Progressive Discipline and Alternative Dispute Resolution

Except in the most extreme cases, employees should generally not be terminated for a first offense. Rather, termination should come about at the end of a systematic discipline program. Effective discipline programs have two central components: documentation (which includes specific publication of work rules and job descriptions that should be in place prior to administering discipline) and progressive punitive measures. Thus, as shown in Table 10.3, punitive measures should be taken in steps of increasing magnitude, and only after having been clearly documented. This may start with an unofficial warning for the first offense, followed by a written reprimand for additional offenses. At some point, later offenses may lead to a temporary suspension. Before a company suspends an employee, it may even want to issue a "last chance notification," indicating that the next offense will result in termination. Such procedures may seem exasperatingly slow, and they may fail to meet one's emotional need for quick and satisfying retribution. In the end, however, when problem employees are discharged, the chance that they can prove they were discharged for poor cause has been minimized.

At various points in the discipline process, the individual or the organization might want to bring in outside parties to help resolve discrepancies or conflicts. As a last

OFFENSE FREQUENCY	ORGANIZATIONAL RESPONSE	DOCUMENTATION
First offense	Unofficial verbal warning	Witness present
Second offense	Official written warning	Document filed
Third offense	Second official warning, with threat of temporary suspension	Document filed
Fourth offense	Temporary suspension and "last chance notification"	Document filed
Fifth offense	Termination (with right to go to arbitration)	Document filed

table 10.3

An Example of a Progressive Discipline Program

resort, the individual might invoke the legal system to resolve these types of conflicts, but in order to avoid this, more and more companies are turning to **alternative dispute resolution (ADR)** techniques that show promise in resolving disputes in a timely, constructive, cost-effective manner. Alternative dispute resolution can take on many different forms, but in general, ADR proceeds through the four stages shown in Table 10.4. Each stage reflects a somewhat broader involvement of different people, and the hope is that the conflict will be resolved at earlier steps. However, the last step may include binding arbitration, where an agreed upon neutral party resolves the conflict unilaterally if necessary. The key word in this context is "neutral," and if there is one common complaint about ADR systems it is that, more often than not, arbitrators wishing to do more business lean in favor of the organizations that are paying their salaries, and not the workers. As Damon Silvers, the general counsel for the AFL-CIO noted, "There is a mountain of evidence that these kinds of things are captive of the industry," and this makes some workers reluctant to abide by their rulings.[36] This reluctance sometimes leads to lawsuits being filed anyway; hence, on the flip side, some employers find that ADR, rather than streamlining the process, just adds another layer to the problem.[37]

Whereas ADR is effective in dealing with problems related to performance and interpersonal differences in the workplace, many of the problems that lead an organization to want to terminate an individual's employment relate to drug or alcohol

Alternative Dispute Resolution (ADR)
A method of resolving disputes that does not rely on the legal system. Often proceeds through the four stages of open door policy, peer review, mediation, and arbitration.

Stage 1: Open-door policy
The two people in conflict (e.g., supervisor and subordinate) attempt to arrive at a settlement together. If none can be reached, they proceed to

Stage 2: Peer review
A panel composed of representatives from the organization that are at the same level of those people in the dispute hears the case and attempts to help the parties arrive at a settlement. If none can be reached, they proceed to

Stage 3: Mediation
A neutral third party from outside the organization hears the case and, via a nonbinding process, tries to help the disputants arrive at a settlement. If none can be reached, the parties proceed to

Stage 4: Arbitration
A professional arbitrator from outside the organization hears the case and resolves it unilaterally by rendering a specific decision or award. Most arbitrators are experienced employment attorneys or retired judges.

table 10.4

Stages in Alternative Dispute Resolution

abuse. In these cases, the organization's discipline and dismissal program should also incorporate an employee assistance program. Due to the increased prevalence of EAPs in organizations, we describe them in detail here.

Employee Assistance and Wellness Programs

Employee Assistance Programs (EAPs)
Employer programs that attempt to ameliorate problems encountered by workers who are drug dependent, alcoholic, or psychologically troubled.

An **employee assistance program (EAP)** is a referral service that supervisors or employees can use to seek professional treatment for various problems. EAPs began in the 1950s with a focus on treating alcoholism, but in the 1980s they expanded into drug treatment as well. EAPs continue to evolve, and many are now fully integrated into companies' overall health benefits plans, serving as gatekeepers for health care utilization.[38] EAPs vary widely, but most share some basic elements. First, the programs are usually identified in official documents published by the employer (such as employee handbooks). Supervisors (and union representatives, where relevant) are trained to use the referral service for employees whom they suspect of having health-related problems. Employees are also trained to use the system to make self-referrals when necessary. Finally, costs and benefits of the programs (as measured in positive employee outcomes such as return-to-work rates) are evaluated, typically annually.

Given EAPs' wide range of options and evolving nature, we need to constantly analyze their effectiveness. For example, there is a current debate about the short-term versus long-term costs with respect to the area of treating depression. In the past, hospitalization plus psychiatric care was the main way to treat employees who were clinically depressed. However, the advent of managed care and the widespread effectiveness of Prozac and other pharmaceutical interventions for depression have made it possible for regular physicians to treat depression with medication.[39] By eliminating hospitalization and psychiatric care, employers can save a great deal of money in treating this problem, but some have questioned its long-term effectiveness relative to more traditional treatments.[40]

The key to the effectiveness of an EAP is striking the right balance between collecting information that can be used to promote employee health on the one hand and the employee's right to privacy on the other. In particular, in an age of digitalization, organizations can do a great deal to help employees provide more detailed and accurate information to their health care providers. For example, most people who go to their physician fill out a form on their past history over and over again; in many cases, because they do not feel well or feel rushed, they wind up preparing inaccurate and unreliable histories. This can lead to treatment errors and complications that are bad for the patient and drive up the health care costs that companies have to pay. To help solve this problem, Wal-Mart provides employees with a digital tool that allows them to enter their health data once, very slowly and carefully, and then keeps this in digitalized form so that it can be accessed by health care providers whenever it is needed. This reduces errors and costs, but it also places a great deal of personal information that needs to be protected in the hands of the employer.[41]

Whereas EAPs deal with employees who have developed problems at work because of health-related issues, employee wellness programs take a proactive and preemptive focus on trying to prevent health-related problems in the first place. Some of these programs take a very positive approach and are not very controversial. For example, accounting firm Grant Thornton spent roughly $200,000 in 2008 to help more than 200 of their employees train for and run in marathons. Most of these employees reported that they would not have taken this step toward a more active lifestyle without this kind of support.[42]

EVIDENCE-BASED HR

For example, Microsoft's weight management employee benefit offers employees $6,000 to use toward a comprehensive, clinically managed program that includes a counselor, personal trainer, medical supervision, and a support group. The $6,000 benefit was chosen because internal analyses produced evidence to suggest this would be exactly what the company would save in expenditures with the employees who were most at risk. The companywide result of this program from 2002 to 2006 was that the organization's 2,000 employees lost more than 60,000 pounds. As Cecily Hall, Microsoft's HR director of benefits, notes, "These people are coming off prescription drugs, they're seeing their primary physician less, and not having as much hospitalization." Moreover, the positive, incentive-laden, and voluntary approach taken by Microsoft is perceived as much less intrusive and controversial relative to programs like Miracle Gro's.

SOURCE: M. Conlin, "More Micro, Less Soft," *BusinessWeek*, November 27, 2006, p 42.

Not all employees will necessarily respond to positive incentives like this, however, and hence some companies take a more punitive approach to wellness. Scott's Miracle Gro Company is at the forefront of firms that are taking extreme steps to curtail rising health care costs. Scott's has a "no-tobacco policy" that bars all employees from smoking or chewing tobacco (which was common in the company). In addition to this, employees being considered for employment are asked the following questions: Do you drink alcohol, and how much? Do you suffer from high cholesterol or high blood pressure? Are you depressed or burned-out? How stressful are your relationships with your spouse or children? What were the causes of death for your parents? All of this seems highly intrusive and an invasion of privacy on the part of the employer; however, the company only took this step when it became clear that its workforce was in such bad physical shape that the costs it was incurring for health care expenses was destroying its ability to compete effectively. Indeed, Miracle Gro's health care expenditures had essentially doubled from roughly $10 million in 1999 to $20 million in 2003—and were projected to go up another 20 percent the next year.[43]

Although perhaps on the edge of how far it is willing to go to reduce these costs, Miracle Gro is certainly not alone in terms of its concerns about such costs. For example, cell phone service provider Sprint realized in 2004 that its annual increase for health care expenditures was going up $50 million a year, and that it would take a 12 percent increase in sales revenue each year to simply cover that cost—an increase that was twice the industry average. Delta Airlines performed a similar analysis and discovered that it was paying more than $5,000 annually per employee for health care, and that this was going up close to 10 percent a year. More pointedly, Delta's analysis revealed that much of this cost was attributable to a small percentage of its workers. For example, as Lynn Zonakis, director of health strategy and resources noted, "We saw that 1/10 of 1 percent of our participants were responsible for 10 percent of our health care costs, and that 1 percent was responsible for 33 percent of our cost."[44]

Most employers that run the numbers come to similar conclusions that a small percentage of workers drive a big percentage of costs, and it is not difficult to predict which workers are in this group. Indeed, the very factors that Miracle Gro screens for reflect this list of valid predictors. Thus, although this may seem invasive from the employees' perspective because a lot of the troublesome behavior occurs outside of work, much of this becomes job-related when the costs are born by the employer.

Indeed, a recent survey of 135 executives at *Fortune* 500 firms indicated that more than 60 percent of them believed that employees who exhibit unhealthy behaviors such as smoking or failing to manage obesity should be required to pay a greater share of health insurance premiums.[45]

In the meantime, individual employers have to make their own decisions regarding how to balance privacy concerns with cost concerns and how much pressure to place on employees whose lifestyles put them at risk. They also have to decide how intrusive they are going to be into employees' lives, knowing that some will lie and falsify records in order to avoid more costly premiums or losing their jobs. For example, at the Whirlpool plant in Benton Harbor, Michigan, 40 workers who were caught on videotape smoking in the parking lot had to be fired because they claimed they were nonsmokers on their benefits enrollment form.[46]

Although financial costs are often the driving force behind these programs, one should not lose sight of the fact that the quality of life enjoyed by employees both on and off the job is also affected. For example, while some employees were suing Miracle Gro over its program, another employee, Joe Pellegrini, was celebrating the fact that the very same program saved his life. Although physically fit, Pellegrini's health assessment indicated a high level of cholesterol, and the company forced him to see a physician. That trip to the doctor revealed a 95 percent blockage in a heart valve that would have probably killed him within five days. Obviously, Pellegrini has a different perception of Miracle Gro's policies than most employees, noting that when it came to his own life, "It was that close."[47]

Outplacement Counseling

Outplacement Counseling
Counseling to help displaced employees manage the transition from one job to another.

The terminal nature of an employee discharge not only leaves the person angry, it also leads to confusion as to how to react and in a quandary regarding what happens next. If the person feels there is nothing to lose and nowhere else to turn, the potential for violence or litigation is higher than most organizations are willing to tolerate. Therefore, many organizations provide **outplacement counseling,** which tries to help dismissed employees manage the transition from one job to another. There is a great deal of variability in the services offered via outplacement programs, typically including career counseling, job search support, résumé critiques, job interviewing training, and provision of networking opportunities. The number of companies offering outplacement support has increased dramatically in recent years. This was most clearly evident in the recession of 2008, when the percentage of employers offering this service was 55 percent compared with just 39 percent during the 2001 recession. Although it may seem counterintuitive to help someone find a new job after just concluding they did not perform well in their last job, most outplacement services frame this as just a bad fit between the person and the job, and work to find jobs where the fit is better.[48]

Outplacement counseling is aimed at helping people realize that losing a job is not the end of the world and that other opportunities exist. Indeed, for many people, losing a job can be a critical learning experience that plants the seed for future success. For example, when John Morgridge was fired from his job as branch manager at Honeywell, it made him realize that his own assertiveness and need for independence were never going to cut it in a large, bureaucratic institution like Honeywell. Morgridge took his skills and went on to build computer network maker Cisco Systems, which is now worth more than $1 billion.[49] This is a success story for Morgridge, but the fact that a major corporation like Honeywell let his talent go certainly reflects a lost opportunity for the company. Retaining people who can make such contributions is a key to gaining and maintaining competitive advantage. The second half of this chapter is devoted to issues related to retention.

Managing Voluntary Turnover

In the first section of this chapter, our focus was on how to help employees who were not contributing to the organization's goal in a manner that protected the firm's ability to compete, and on how to support former employees' transition into alternative employment. In this second section, we focus on the other side of the separation equation—preventing employees who are highly valued by the organization from leaving (and perhaps even joining the competition). At the organizational level, turnover results in lowered work unit performance, which, in turn, harms the firm's financial performance.[50] This causal chain is especially strong when the organization is losing its top performers. Research suggests that some of the organization's top performers are up to 300 percent more productive than average employees, and retaining these workers is especially difficult.[51] Moreover, in organizations that rely on teams or long-term customer contacts, the loss of workers who are central to employee teams or customer networks can be especially disruptive.[52]

In 2007, Yahoo witnessed a mass exodus of engineers and vice presidents who left to either join small startups or even worse—Google, one of Yahoo's top competitors. The stream of attrition started with lower level workers, but as one former vice president notes, "Now it's the people who have institutional knowledge who are leaving." Google was the top destination spot for most of this talent because the firm was widely recognized as being a great place to work; in fact, it was rated number 1 on *Fortune* magazine's 2007 list of "100 Best Places to Work." Google is renowned for its outrageous employee benefits, which include 11 free gourmet cafeterias, five fully staffed on-site doctors' offices, on-site car washes and oil changes, free on-site washers and dryers, unlimited sick days, all-expense-paid ski trips, free shuttles with WiFi for commuters, lap pool, climbing wall, and volleyball courts.

Google's employees respond to all of this by working incredibly long hours and by putting all headhunter calls into their autoreject bin. Most employees are committed to the organization's general well-being not for annual raises but because they are heavily vested in stock options that will make them all millionaires if the company can maintain its current trajectory. Teamwork is demanded and salaries, while not high for the industry, tend to be uniform in order to promote collaboration and teamwork while discouraging "lone wolves." Individuals are given autonomy to run their own experimental projects (up to 20 percent of their time can be devoted to these), but collective decisions on most large-scale group projects are arrived at via open and spirited public debates that tend to unfold very quickly. In contrast, many workers who are leaving Yahoo complain that most large Yahoo projects have to be signed off by multiple division heads, which both slows the process and minimizes the sense of employee ownership. As noted by one former Yahoo employee, who now works for Google, "Hard core geeks are here because there's no place they'd rather be," which is pretty convincing evidence with respect to who is winning and losing the war for talent in this industry.[53]

In this section of the chapter, we examine the job withdrawal process that characterizes voluntary employee turnover, and we illustrate the central role that job satisfaction plays in this process. Replacing workers is an expensive undertaking, and recent estimates for 2008 place this cost at roughly $50,000 for a professional or managerial workers and $25,000 for clerical or manufacturing employees.[54] Replacement costs reflect just a tip of the iceberg, however, when it comes to the costs of job dissatisfaction and turnover. One recent study showed that firms in the top quartile in terms of employee job satisfaction had profit rates that were 4 percent higher than firms in the bottom quartile. There is also a demonstrable relationship between employee satisfaction and customer satisfaction at the individual level,[55] and turnover rates and customer satisfaction at the organizational level.[56] Indeed, the whole employee satisfaction–firm performance relationship can become part of a virtuous cycle, where firms with more highly satisfied employees perform better and increase their profits, which in turn they use to shore up employee pay and benefits—further adding to their competitive advantage.[57] We will discuss what aspects of job satisfaction seem most critical to retention and how to measure these facets and we show how survey–feedback interventions, designed around these measures, can be used to strategically manage the voluntary turnover process.

Process of Job Withdrawal

Job withdrawal is a set of behaviors that dissatisfied individuals enact to avoid the work situation. The right side of Figure 10.3 shows a model grouping the overall set of behaviors into three categories: behavior change, physical job withdrawal, and psychological job withdrawal.

Progression of Withdrawal
Theory that dissatisfied individuals enact a set of behaviors in succession to avoid their work situation.

We present the various forms of withdrawal in a progression, as if individuals try the next category only if the preceding is either unsuccessful or impossible to implement. This theory of **progression of withdrawal** has a long history and many adherents.[58] For example, someone who is dissatisfied with the job or organization might not be able to just jump to another job right away but will instead either disengage temporarily (through absenteeism or tardiness) or psychologically (through lower job involvement and organizational commitment) until the right opportunity comes along.[59] During an economic recession like the one experienced in 2008, for example, many employers bent on cutting costs engaged in practices that created dissatisfied employees. The poor job market did not really allow these employees to leave, but many were just biding their time. As Michael Kesner, a principal at Deloitte Consulting's Human Capital unit notes, "Companies that took advantage of employees in past downturns were rewarded with people bailing when things turned around."[60] Others have suggested that there is no tight progression in that any one of the categories can

figure 10.3
An Overall Model of the Job Dissatisfaction–Job Withdrawal Process

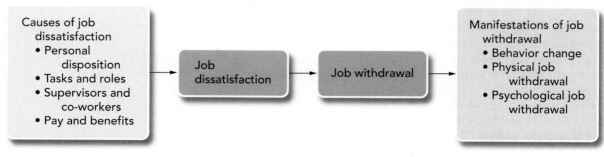

compensate for another, and people choose the category that is most likely to redress the specific source of dissatisfaction.[61] Still other theories maintain that turnover is set up by a general level of persistent dissatisfaction that then is triggered abruptly by some single disruptive event at work that either pushes the employee away (such as a dispute with supervisor or co-worker) or pulls the employee away (an alternative employment opportunity).[62] This model focuses on "the straw that breaks the camel's back" but shares with all the other theories an emphasis on job dissatisfaction as the necessary but insufficient cause of turnover.[63] Regardless of what specific theory one endorses, there is a general consensus that withdrawal behaviors are clearly related to one another, and they are all at least partially caused by job dissatisfaction.[64]

Behavior Change

One might expect that an employee's first response to dissatisfaction would be to try to change the conditions that generate the dissatisfaction. This can lead to supervisor–subordinate confrontation, perhaps even conflict, as dissatisfied workers try to bring about changes in policy or upper-level personnel. Indeed, as shown in the "Competing through Globalization" box there are many different ways people might "voice" their concerns, and different cultures approach this in different ways. Where employees are unionized, it can lead to an increased number of grievances being filed.[65] Although at first this type of conflict can feel threatening to the manager, on closer inspection, this is really an opportunity for the manager to learn about and perhaps solve an important problem. For example, Don McAdams, a manager at Johnsonville Foods, recalls an incident where one particular employee had been very critical of the company's incentive system. McAdams listened to the person's concerns and then asked him to head a committee charged with developing a better incentive system. At first the employee was taken aback, but he eventually accepted the challenge and became so enthusiastic about the project that he was the one who presented the new system to the general membership. Because this person was known to be highly critical of the old system, he had a high level of credibility with the other workers, who felt, "If this guy likes it, it must be pretty good." In the end, this critic-turned-champion was immensely successful in solving a specific organizational problem.[66]

Less constructively, employees can initiate change through **whistle-blowing** (making grievances public by going to the media).[67] Whistle-blowers are often dissatisfied individuals who cannot bring about internal change and, out of a sense of commitment or frustration, take their concerns to external constituencies. For example, Russell Tice was an employee of the U.S. National Security Agency (NSA) whose job was to electronically eavesdrop (i.e., spy) on our nation's enemies. He was devoted to his job and noted that "the mentality at NSA was we need to get these guys and we're going to do whatever it takes to get them." However, when his job was changed in the wake of 9/11 to focus on calls being made by U.S. citizens, he was concerned that without the proper warrants, this type of surveillance of his fellow Americans was illegal. No one at NSA would take Tice's concerns seriously, and so he took his concerns to the *New York Times,* which eventually published an article that accused the Bush administration of conducting widespread illegal wiretapping. The White House first denied the allegations, but when the evidence became too overwhelming to dispute, the administration admitted that the program was inappropriate and hence ended its existence. Tice eventually had his security clearance revoked, but he noted that it was worth it. "We need to clean up the intelligence community. We've had abuses and they need to be addressed."[68]

Whistle-blowing
Making grievances public by going to the media or government.

When heavy construction manufacturer Caterpillar announced that it was going to shed 733 jobs in plants in Grenoble, France, in April 2009, the workers at the site did what any reasonable and rationale Frenchman would do—they kidnapped their bosses and held them hostage. Although this may seem like an unreasonable act to many outside that country, in fact, the Caterpillar incident was the fourth kidnapping of bosses that had occurred in France in 2009. Earlier that year, managers at Sony and 3M were also held hostage by their workers at their plant, and the CEO of the firm that controls Gucci and Yves St. Laurent was surrounded and sequestered by workers while in his car. At Caterpillar, union representative Pierre Piccarreta stated that "At a time when the company is making a profit and distributing dividends to shareholders, we want to find a favorable outcome for all the workers and know as quickly as possible."

In terms of strict legal doctrine, kidnapping one's bosses is technically a crime in France. Yet despite this, kidnapping of bosses is tolerated by both police and organizational executives as a negotiating strategy for establishing the "social plan" that is also legally mandated by law in the case of company layoffs. The social plan is a document negotiated between union and management listing the amount of severance pay workers are to receive, as well as the support they are going to be provided in terms of finding new jobs or training. When the union does not like the terms they are being offered, some resort to kidnapping to have their voice heard by drawing media attention to their cause. This is often an effective strategy, and at Caterpillar, the company increased the amount of severance granted to workers from 37 million euros to 47 million euros in order to resolve the situation.

Although the practice of kidnapping one's boss may sound barbaric, in fact, there are strong cultural norms for how such a kidnapping works, and both sides of the negotiation play by a certain set of unspoken rules. The workers never engage in any outright violence against the bosses and treat them with as much respect and dignity as the basic nature of a kidnapping would allow. Kidnappings rarely last more than two or three days, and cots are often brought in so that people do not have to sleep on the floor. The kidnapped executives are allowed to contact their families as much as they would like, and in cases of health-related issues (such as hostages with heart problems), get any treatment that might be necessary. In return, the company never calls in the police and never presses for criminal charges against the workers.

Still, for most U.S. executives, the thought that they might be kidnapped by their workers is not one that would ever enter their minds, and this illustrates a big difference between the cultures of the United States and France. In the United States, people are much more likely to accept getting fired on the spot, without complaining, but in France they are more willing to pick a fight. French history is littered with revolutions of all kinds, and the idea of manning the barricades as a form of protest is ingrained in the minds of French people, both workers and management alike. Indeed, as one former kidnapped CEO, Maurice Levy, noted, "Protest is inscribed in the genes of French culture. In the past, peasants protested against their lords. Today, the difference is that the lords are chief executives."

SOURCES: D. Jolly, "Caterpillar Workers Detain Bosses in France," *The New York Times*, April 1, 2009, p. B1; L. Abboud and M. Colchester, "French Bosses Beseiged as Worker Anger Rises," *The Wall Street Journal*, April 1, 2009, p. A1; D. Gauthier-Villars and L. Abboud, "In France, the Bosses Can Become Hostages," *The Wall Street Journal*, April 3, 2009, pp. A1–A2.

Physical Job Withdrawal

If the job conditions cannot be changed, a dissatisfied worker may be able to solve the problem by leaving the job. This could take the form of an internal transfer if the dissatisfaction is job-specific (the result of an unfair supervisor or unpleasant working conditions). On the other hand, if the source of the dissatisfaction relates to organizationwide policies (lack of job security or below-market pay levels), organizational turnover is likely.

Many employees who would like to quit their jobs have to stay on if they have no other employment opportunities. In other cases, employees may want to leave because their firms are struggling, but they are stigmatized because other organizations are reluctant to hire individuals whose previous experience was all with an employer that was generally perceived to be uncompetitive. For example, one Midwest headhunter noted that "I get a call a week from someone at a high level at the Ford Motor Company saying they want to get out of the automotive world, but they are hard to place because people feel they are running away from something, not to something."[69] In these cases, another way of physically removing oneself from the dissatisfying work short of quitting altogether is to be absent. One recent survey indicated that, on average, companies spend 15 percent of their payroll costs to make up for absent or tardy workers.[70] Part of the reason that absenteeism is costly is that, like a virus, it often spreads from one worker to another, even if no one is really sick with any communicable health disorder. The evidence suggests that there are strong social norms associated with absenteeism, and that it "snowballs" in groups so that once it gets rolling it becomes more and more acceptable.[71] To get around the nonstandardized way various units treat the issue, some companies like Wal-Mart have centralized the process by which an employee requests a day off, taking it out of the hands of local managers. Wal-Mart employees seeking a day off need to call a 1-800 number and provide a standardized set of documentation supporting the reason underlying the request.[72]

Psychological Withdrawal

When dissatisfied employees are unable to change their situation or remove themselves physically from their jobs, they may psychologically disengage themselves from their jobs. Although they are physically on the job, their minds may be somewhere else.

This psychological disengagement can take several forms. First, if the primary dissatisfaction has to do with the job itself, the employee may display a very low level of job involvement. **Job involvement** is the degree to which people identify themselves with their jobs. People who are uninvolved with their jobs consider their work an unimportant aspect of their lives. A second form of psychological disengagement, which can occur when the dissatisfaction is with the employer as a whole, is a low level of organizational commitment. **Organizational commitment** is the degree to which an employee identifies with the organization and is willing to put forth effort on its behalf. Individuals who feel they have been unjustly treated by their employer often respond by reducing their level of commitment and are often looking for the first good chance to quit their jobs.[73] They may also respond to perceived unjust treatment by trying to get back at the employer via theft, fraud, or sabotage, and, as can be seen in the "Competing through Technology" box, companies are employing an expanded array of technological techniques to prevent this.

Job Involvement
The degree to which people identify themselves with their jobs.

Organizational Commitment
The degree to which an employee identifies with the organization and is willing to put forth effort on its behalf.

Although theft by employees is a constant concern among all employers, history reveals that during economic recessions, cases of fraud and malfeasance often rise as fast as the stock market falls. Part of the problem, of course, is that when people are struggling to make ends meet they are also subject to greater levels of temptation. This might especially be the case if they believe that they are about to be laid off and, hence, are angry and perceive an act of theft as a just, retaliatory behavior aimed at the organization. The other part of the problem, however, is that during hard times, organizations become more vigilant of bottom-line concerns and, in the hunt to reduce costs, often trip over irregularities that might not have been noticed during more flush periods. As security consultant Brian Mich notes, "It is often hard to tell which is the chicken or the egg in these cases, but the evidence that recessions cause a spike in documented employee theft is irrefutable."

For example, in the case of the most recent recession, one 2009 survey revealed that roughly 20 percent of managers polled were able to document an increase in theft of both financial and physical assets from 2006 to 2008. A separate study by PricewaterhouseCoopers found that companies lost an average of $2.4 million to fraud in 2007, up from $1.7 million in 2005. Ironically, the evidence from fraud cases suggests that it is often the most educated and trusted employees who do the most damage. For example, the average organizational tenure of employees convicted of fraud is roughly eight years, and most have graduate degrees. This is a group of smart employees who have earned trust and worked their way into the best position—and know exactly how to get away with various fraud schemes.

Instead of hoping to just trip over theft and fraud cases as part an overall cost cutting hunt, however, organizations are increasingly using electronic means of sleuthing to catch people in the act. For example, at Wendy's and Chili's restaurant franchises, managers have begun to install fingerprint scanners on cash registers to more definitively link each transaction to specific employees. This has cut down on theft and also reduced conflict within the chains that was formerly caused by employees who were constantly arguing about who rang up what transactions. At IBM, tracking technology installed into computers has allowed the organization to track down stolen laptops (or machines that employees falsely report being stolen) on the Internet.

Increasingly sophisticated software for tracking expenses has also been used to monitor fraud associated with business travel and entertainment. For example, a company called Concur Technology has developed expense reporting software that scours data files to uncover double expense recording (e.g., two executives claim the same bill at a restaurant), unauthorized travel upgrades (first-class airline tickets), or unusual trends or spikes in account activity. As Gunter Ollmann, security chief for IBM notes, "Every time someone sends a file, whether over e-mail or a Web site, or transfers data onto a cell phone or a thumb drive, it can be monitored, recorded, and then analyzed if anything suspicious appears."

SOURCES: S. E. Needleman, "Businesses Say Theft by Their Workers Is Up," The Wall Street Journal, December 11, 2008, pp. C1–C2; S. Covel, "Small Businesses Face More Fraud in Downturn," The Wall Street Journal, February 19, 2009, p. C2; M. Conlin, "To Catch a Corporate Thief," BusinessWeek, February 16, 2009, p. 52.

Job Satisfaction and Job Withdrawal

As we see in Figure 10.3, the key driving force behind all the different forms of job withdrawal is **job satisfaction,** which we will define as a pleasurable feeling that results from the perception that one's job fulfills or allows for the fulfillment of one's important job values.[74] This definition reflects three important aspects of job satisfaction. First, job satisfaction is a function of *values*, defined as "what a person consciously or unconsciously desires to obtain." Second, this definition emphasizes that different employees have different views of which values are important, and this is critical in determining the nature and degree of their job satisfaction. One person may value high pay above all else; another may value the opportunity to travel; another may value staying within a specific geographic region. The third important aspect of job satisfaction is perception. An individual's perceptions may not be a completely accurate reflection of reality, and different people may view the same situation differently.

In particular, people's perceptions are often strongly influenced by their frame of reference. A **frame of reference** is a standard point that serves as a comparison for other points and thus provides meaning. For example, an upper-level executive who offers a 6 percent salary increase to a lower-level manager might expect this to make the manager happy because inflation (the executive's frame of reference) is only 3 percent. The manager, on the other hand, might find the raise quite unsatisfactory because it is less than the 9 percent raise received by a colleague who does similar work (the manager's frame of reference).

Sources of Job Dissatisfaction

Many aspects of people and organizations can cause dissatisfaction among employees. Managers and HR professionals need to be aware of these because they are the levers which can raise job satisfaction and reduce employee withdrawal. This is an issue that is particularly salient in the current economy where pressures to raise productivity have pushed many workers to the limit.

Unsafe Working Conditions

Earlier in this chapter we discussed the employer's role in helping employees stay healthy via employee assistance programs for specific problems like drug addiction and alcohol dependency, as well as general wellness initiatives to promote health and reduce health care–related expenditures. Obviously, if employers care this much about the risk employees are exposed to off the job, there needs to be an even more important emphasis on risk exposure that occurs on the job.

Of course, each employee has a right to safe working conditions, and previously in this book (see Chapter 3) we reviewed the Occupational Safety and Health Act of 1970 (OSHA), which spells out those rights in a very detailed fashion. We also discussed in that chapter how to develop safety awareness programs that identify and communicate job hazards, as well as how to reinforce safe work practices that would allow one to pass an OSHA inspection. Although our emphasis in that chapter on safety was primarily directed at legal compliance, we need to revisit the topic in this chapter, because OSHA is not the only audience that is likely to evaluate the safety of jobs. The perception and reaction of the organization's own employees to working conditions has implications for satisfaction, retention, and competitive advantage that go well beyond merely meeting the legal requirements. That is, if applicants

LO3
Specify the relationship between job satisfaction and various forms of job withdrawal, and identify the major sources of job satisfaction in work contexts.

Job Satisfaction
A pleasurable feeling that results from the perception that one's job fulfills or allows for the fulfillment of one's important job values.

Frame of Reference
A standard point that serves as a comparison for other points and thus provides meaning.

The wars being waged in Iraq and Afghanistan are now the longest ever endured by an all-volunteer army in U.S. history. As with any war, casualties are to be expected; however, one surprising source of military deaths has been a series of suicides within the ranks of military recruiters. In 2008, the suicide rate for military recruiters was three times the rate for the next highest job category, making it one of the most dangerous positions in the Army. In the Houston Recruiting Battalion alone, four separate suicides were reported in a 12-month period, and Army Staff Sergeant Amanda Henderson lost both her supervisor and her husband to suicides in a five-week period. Those two most recent deaths finally caught the public's attention, and an investigation ordered by Texas Senator John Cornyn uncovered a number of issues related to working conditions within the recruiter's ranks that appeared to be direct causes of the suicides.

One of the most obvious problems with the Army recruiting jobs was that the goals required of recruiters were almost impossible to meet. Official policy, stated in a letter from Major General Thomas Bostick in 2006, was labeled "Must Do Two," and recruiters were told that "all of your training is geared toward prospecting and processing at least two enlistments monthly." This was converted at the Houston brigade into a set of work rules that seemed to require a 13-hour workday, bridged by conference calls that took place at 7 AM and 10 PM each day. Even working a 13-hour day was rarely enough to meet the required standards, however, and many recruiters were encouraged (or apparently in some cases, ordered directly) to break other rules just to make quota. For example, some recruiters were told to coach unqualified applicants on how to lie on their application forms or help applicants pass drug tests that otherwise would have disqualified them for service. As one recruiter noted, "There is one set of values for the Army, and when you go to the Recruiting Command, you're basically forced to do things outside of what would normally be considered moral or ethical."

Failure to make one's quota then resulted in very harsh punishment that included attending mandatory "low production training sessions" that were all-day affairs held on Saturdays. Recruiters at these sessions were told to write long essays detailing their specific failures over the course of the previous week, as well as the lessons they learned from these experiences that might help them during the next week. One of the suicide victims in Texas had just come out of one of these sessions, where he was publicly berated and humiliated by his commander. That particular recruiter was actually a decorated battlefield soldier who could take just about anything the enemy threw at him, but reached the limit of what he could take from those who were supposedly on the same side.

Although it might be easy for readers to just chalk all of this up to unique features associated with working in a military context, this would be a mistake. The exact same pattern of practices was found when an investigation was conducted at a Paris design center, operated by French automaker Renault. In an attempt to meet the goal of boosting sales by 800,000 cars in 2007, the CEO of Renault demanded that the design center double the number of models under development from 13 to 26. This led to 16-hour workdays, which were attributed as causal factors associated with the suicides of three engineers at the Paris facility. The suicide notes left by the engineers mirrored the conditions uncovered by Senator Cornyn's investigation in Texas, documenting the stress that the engineers experienced due to "unreasonable workloads, high-pressure management tactics, exhaustion, and humiliating criticism in front of colleagues during performance reviews." Working conditions such as these may promote a short-term jump in performance but are unsustainable. They create a recipe for disaster and constitute an indictment of the organization's leaders and human resource professionals.

SOURCES: M. Thompson, "Why Are Army Recruiters Killing Themselves?" *Time*, April 2, 2009, pp. 32–36; M. Roberts, "Army General to Investigate Recruiter Suicides," *USA Today*, November 7, 2008, pp. A1–A2; J. Goudreau, "Dispatches from the War on Stress," *BusinessWeek*, August 6, 2007, pp. 74–76.

or job incumbents conclude that their health or lives are at risk because of the job, attracting and retaining workers will be impossible.

Not all jobs pose safety risks, but the nature of the work in a whole host of jobs makes managing safety-related perceptions critical. This includes jobs such as fishing boat operators, timber cutters, airline pilot/flight attendants, structural metal workers, garbage collectors, and taxi drivers/chauffeurs, which all have been identified as jobs where people are most likely to be involved in fatal accidents. In fact, in these job categories alone, close to 1,000 people die annually. Other jobs that rate low in terms of fatal accidents rate higher in nonfatal accidents, and this includes many jobs in eating establishments, hospitals, nursing homes, convenience stores, and the long-haul trucking industry. Still other jobs pose risks in terms of contracting occupational diseases due to exposure to chemicals. Finally, as is evident in the "Competing through Sustainability" box, some jobs create health risks simply because of the long hours and high stress that are associated with them.[75] In industries like these, one of the foremost responsibilities of human resources is to ensure that workers and management both know and execute "best practices."

Although one would think that workers and managers would do this naturally, the fact is the longer one is exposed to a particular risk environment the more comfortable one gets in that environment and the less vigilant one becomes. Upper level management needs to continually emphasize and stress compliance with worker safety regulations and carefully monitor statistics related to workplace accidents. Many employers link financial bonuses to attaining specific safety-related goals, and this helps keep employees focused on doing the job the right way every day.[76] These programs more than pay for themselves over time. Research suggests that it is not unusual for a midsize company that reduces accidents by 10 percent to see a $50,000 reduction in premiums. Assuming that the firm has a profit margin of 5 percent, this is essentially the equivalent of bringing in another $1 million in sales. Based on these numbers, Jim Hatherley, a vice president at Liberty Mutual Group, notes that "the companies that have better profit-and-loss statements are the ones that take everything more seriously, including safety. When they look at safety as a business issue, they win."[77] Even beyond the straight financial characteristics, however, firms that emphasize safety send workers a clear signal that they care about them. This is an important aspect of organizational culture which strengthens the employee–employer relationship and promotes both attraction of new employees and retention of current employees.

Personal Dispositions

Because dissatisfaction is an emotion that ultimately resides within the person, it is not surprising that many who have studied these outcomes have focused on individual differences. For example, in Chapter 6, we described the Five Factor Model of Personality, and several of these traits have been linked to higher turnover intentions and actual turnover. In general, turnover is more likely to be an issue for employees who are low in emotional stability, low in conscientiousness, and low in agreeableness.[78]

Negative affectivity is a term used to describe a dispositional dimension that reflects pervasive individual differences in satisfaction with any and all aspects of life. Individuals who are high in negative affectivity report higher levels of aversive mood states, including anger, contempt, disgust, guilt, fear, and nervousness across all contexts (work and nonwork). People who are high in negative affectivity tend to focus extensively on the negative aspects of themselves and others.[79] They also tend to persist in their negative attitudes even in the face of organizational interventions, such as

Negative Affectivity
A dispositional dimension that reflects pervasive individual differences in satisfaction with any and all aspects of life.

increased pay levels, that generally increase the levels of satisfaction of other people.[80] Research has even shown that negative affectivity in early adolescence is predictive of overall job dissatisfaction in adulthood. There were also significant relationships between work attitudes measured over 5-year[81] and 10-year[82] periods, even for workers who changed employers and/or occupations. All of this implies that some individuals tend to bring low satisfaction with them to work. Thus these people may be relatively dissatisfied regardless of what steps the organization or the manager takes.

The evidence on the linkage between these kinds of traits and job satisfaction suggests the importance of personnel selection as a way of raising overall levels of employee satisfaction. If job satisfaction remains relatively stable across time and jobs because of characteristics like negative affectivity or core self-evaluations, this suggests that transient changes in job satisfaction will be difficult to sustain in these individuals, who will typically revert to their "dispositional" or adaptation level over time.[83] Thus, some employers actually try to screen for this when selecting job candidates. For example, at Zappo's, the online retailer of shoes and apparel, CEO Tony Hsei notes that "We do our best to hire positive people and put them where their positive thinking is reinforced."[84] Interviews should assess the degree to which any job applicant has a history of chronic dissatisfaction with employment. The logic is, if an applicant states that he was dissatisfied with his past six jobs, what makes Hsei think that person won't be dissatisfied with this one?

Tasks and Roles

As a predictor of job dissatisfaction, nothing surpasses the nature of the task itself.[85] Many aspects of a task have been linked to dissatisfaction. Several elaborate theories relating task characteristics to worker reactions have been formulated and extensively tested. We discussed several of these in Chapter 4. In this section we focus on three primary aspects of tasks that affect job satisfaction: the complexity of the task, the amount of flexibility in where and when the work is done, and, finally, the value the employee puts on the task.[86]

With a few exceptions, there is a strong positive relationship between task complexity and job satisfaction. That is, the boredom generated by simple, repetitive jobs that do not mentally challenge the worker leads to frustration and dissatisfaction.[87] One of the major interventions aimed at reducing job dissatisfaction by increasing job complexity is job enrichment. As the term suggests, this intervention is directed at jobs that are "impoverished" or boring because of their repetitive nature or low scope. Many job enrichment programs are based on the job characteristics theory discussed earlier in Chapter 4.

For example, many job enrichment programs provide increased opportunities for workers to have input into important organizational decisions that involve their work, and this has been routinely found to reduce role conflict and ambiguity. We saw this in our opening vignette on Home Depot, where a major effort was made to make employees feel more ownership for their work by decentralizing the decision-making process. Another example of this can be seen at Crouse Hospital in upstate New York, where turnover was reduced from 49 percent to 18 percent after initiating a program that promoted formal, small-group discussion about how to improve patient care at every level of the organization. In addition to the reduction in turnover, cost savings and increased customer service led to $11 million net gain in 2007 that compared very favorably to the $15 million net loss the hospital recorded prior to the program.[88]

In some cases, job enrichment programs may have to be complemented with training programs to ensure people have the skills to expand their jobs. This, too, was part of the program initiated by Home Depot in our opening vignette, but this is hardly an isolated case. For example, at University of Chicago Hospital, many technical employees struggled with interpersonal tasks associated with customers, resulting in conflict with clients and stress at work. Training programs in customer service, critical thinking, and situational judgment were provided, and the technicians were each encouraged to develop their own "Ideal Patient Encounter" associated for their specific job. Complaints from patients dropped precipitously, and the reduction in conflict led to less stress for the technicians, as well as a 33 percent reduction in turnover in those job categories. With this type of training, participants decide on their most important work values. They then learn how to pinpoint goals, identify roadblocks to successful goal accomplishment, and seek the collaboration of co-workers in achieving these goals. In general, skills training gives job incumbents the ability to better predict, understand, and control events occurring on the job, which in turn increases their ability to make their own decisions.[89]

Another task-based intervention is **job rotation.** This is a process of systematically moving a single individual from one job to another over the course of time. Although employees may not feel capable of putting up with the dissatisfying aspects of a particular job indefinitely, they often feel they can do so temporarily. Job rotation can do more than simply spread out the dissatisfying aspects of a particular job. It can increase work complexity for employees and provide valuable cross-training in jobs so that employees eventually understand many different jobs. This makes for a more flexible workforce and increases workers' appreciation of the other tasks that have to be accomplished for the organization to complete its mission.[90]

Because of the degree to which nonwork roles often spill over and affect work roles, and vice versa, a third critical aspect of work that affects satisfaction and retention is the degree to which scheduling is flexible. To help employees manage their multiple roles, companies have turned to a number of family-friendly policies to both recruit new talent and hold onto the talent they already have. These policies may include provisions for child care, elder care, flexible work schedules, job sharing, telecommuting, and extended maternal and paternal leaves.[91] Although these programs create some headaches for managers in terms of scheduling work and reporting requirements, they have a number of demonstrable benefits. First, the provision of these sorts of benefits is a recruitment aid that helps employers attract potential job applicants.[92] Second, once hired, flexible work arrangements result in reduced absenteeism.[93] This is particularly true for firms that employ large numbers of women with children. In fact, one nonprofit company that could not compete on wages, was able to reduce its turnover rate from 30 percent to 7 percent just by initiating a program that let mothers bring their babies to work.[94] Third, over the long term, these programs result in higher levels of employee commitment to the organization.[95] They have also been linked to increased organizational citizenship behaviors on the part of individual employees,[96] as well as enhanced organizational performance, especially in organizations that employ a large percentage of female employees.[97] Indeed, the benefits of these kinds of programs are so well documented that the mere announcement that an organization is initiating some sort of flexible work policy has a positive impact on the share price of the company's stock.[98]

By far, the most important aspect of work in terms of generating satisfaction is the degree to which it is meaningfully related to core values of the worker. The term **prosocial motivation** is often used explicitly to capture the degree to which people are

Job Rotation
The process of systematically moving a single individual from one job to another over the course of time. The job assignments may be in various functional areas of the company or movement may be between jobs in a single functional area or department.

Prosocial Motivation
The degree to which people are energized to do their jobs because it helps other people.

motivated to help other people. When people believe that their work has an important impact on other people, they are much more willing to work longer hours.[99] This prosocial motivation could be directed at co-workers and has been found to relate to helping behavior.[100] This form of motivation can also be triggered by recognizing that one's work has a positive impact on those who benefit from one's service, such as customer or clients.[101] In contrast, when one's social needs are thwarted, they often react negatively and in self-defeating ways that drive people further away from them.[102]

For example, Genentech is a small San Francisco–based biotech pharmaceutical company that competes directly with the largest and most well-funded pharmaceutical giants in the industry including Merck, Lilly, and Johnson & Johnson. From the outset, Genentech knew that the ultimate success of its venture depended on attracting and retaining the best minds within the field of bioscience, despite having less capital relative to the competition.

Genentech focused its mission on developing and testing "big ideas," particularly as this relates to life and death issues (e.g., drugs to fight cancer) in the field of health care. It then searched out scientists who had passionate feelings about work in this area, and surrounded them with a supportive corporate culture that was more like working in a small, close-knit research university than a large pharmaceutical company. Researchers were given the autonomy to pursue their own ideas in a context where every success was celebrated (often in a sophomoric fashion), and every failure was treated as a learning experience rather than a career-ending catastrophe. The strategy was a "swing for the fences" approach emphasizing hitting a few home runs, rather than trying to incrementally tinker with existing products. As CEO Art Levinson notes, "At the end of the day, we want to make drugs that really matter—that's the transcendent issue," and this is captured in the corporate motto: "In Business for Life."

This strategy was clearly a risky bet, since in this industry, up to $800 million may be spent to invent a new drug, only to have 90 percent of these drugs fail to reach the market, but so far this bet has paid off. According to Wall Street estimates, Genentech's year-end revenues for 2006 stood at $6.6 billion, three times what the company earned in 2002, and the stock price doubled from $47 to $95 a share between 2005 and 2006. The company has attracted many of the top graduating doctoral students, as well as many scientists who have left their larger, more conservative and hierarchical competitors. As one industry analyst noted, "From the day the company was founded, Genentech's culture has been its competitive advantage."[103]

Supervisors and Co-workers

The two primary sets of people in an organization who affect job satisfaction are co-workers and supervisors. A person may be satisfied with her supervisor and co-workers for one of two reasons. First, she may have many of the same values, attitudes, and philosophies that the co-workers and supervisors have. Research shows the diversity in values and beliefs can create a "misfit" between the person and the work group that increases the likelihood of turnover.[104] Over time, this creates an environment where groups can become increasingly homogeneous, and this "attraction–selection–attrition" cycle can be a powerful determinant of the organization's culture.[105] Indeed, even if one cannot generate a unifying culture throughout an entire organization, it is worth noting that increases in job satisfaction can be derived simply from congruence among supervisors and subordinates at one level.[106]

Second, people may be satisfied with their supervisor and co-workers because they provide support that helps them achieve their own goals. Social support means the degree to which the person is surrounded by other people who are sympathetic and caring. Considerable research indicates that social support is a strong predictor of job satisfaction and lower employee turnover.[107] In contrast, abusive supervision is a major cause of turnover, and some organizations find that they can reduce turnover in some units by 25 percent to 33 percent in a single year simply by removing a specific supervisor who lacks interpersonal skills.[108] This is especially the case when individuals are promoted from operational roles to managerial roles because of their technical, rather than interpersonal skills. The lack of leadership skills and interpersonal sensitivity that was not a large part of the person's prior role is often exposed in that person's first managerial experience.[109] Leaders and supervisors are not the only source of problems, however, and incivility and lack of interpersonal skills among co-workers or team members also had to be addressed in many contexts.[110]

Because of the powerful role played by supervisors and other more experienced workers in terms of supporting the organization's culture, some organizations are going to great lengths to develop the mentoring skills of their managers and other highly experienced workers.[111] In fact, recent statistics show that the number of *Fortune* 500 companies that provided formal mentoring programs jumped from 10 percent in 2002 to over 50 percent in 2007. Much of this is attributed to the fact that many organizations are facing a wave of retirements as baby boomers prepare to leave the workforce, and organizations are scrambling to develop systems that would promote critical knowledge transfer from older to younger workers. As William Arnone, a human capital consultant at Ernst & Young, notes, "Companies know there is a looming 'wisdom withdrawal' but they're putting off addressing it."[112]

This is not the case at the Tennessee Valley Authority, however, where the mentoring model provides a good generic example of how to transfer knowledge in a way that protects the organization's interests and helps to quickly develop the depth and breadth of younger workers' skills. The TVA provides nuclear-based electric power to much of the southern United States, but is faced with an aging workforce. The TVA program, based on interviews with the workforce, assigns workers a score from 1 to 5 that rates how impending their retirement might be (from 1, not within the next 6 years, to 5, within the next year). Then, based on interviews with senior managers, each person is rated on a 1 to 5 scale in terms of how much critical, irreplaceable knowledge he or she possesses.

If the resulting score for a unit or department indicates that there are three or four people with scores in the 20–25 range, this is a "red flag" that triggers a mentoring program where younger workers are assigned to shadow a longer term employee, in an effort to learn not just a role but the culture and norms of the organization as a whole.[113] Lockheed Martin has a very similar program in terms of transferring knowledge and culture, but its program places slightly more emphasis on the mentor's role in championing specific younger workers within the system. Turnover rates in jobs staffed primarily by younger workers dropped from 12 percent to 2.5 percent after the introduction of this program.[114]

Because a supportive environment reduces dissatisfaction, many organizations foster team building both on and off the job (such as via softball or bowling leagues). The idea is that group cohesiveness and support for individual group members will be increased through exposure and joint efforts. Although management certainly cannot ensure that each stressed employee develops friends, it can make it easier for employees to interact—a necessary condition for developing friendship and rapport. In fact, results of surveys indicate that endorsing the item "Most of my closest friendships are with people at work" is one of the most powerful tools for predicting turnover.[115]

Pay and Benefits

We should not discount the influence of the job incumbent, the job itself, and the surrounding people in terms of influencing job satisfaction, but for most people, work is their primary source of income and financial security. Pay is also seen as an indicator of status within the organization as well as in society at large. Thus, for many individuals, the standing of their pay relative to those within their organization, or the standing of their pay relative to others doing similar work for other employers, becomes even more important than the level of pay itself.[116] Thus, for some people, pay is a reflection of self-worth, so pay satisfaction takes on critical significance when it comes to retention.[117] Indeed, the role of pay and benefits is so large that we devote the entire next part of this book to these topics. Within this chapter we focus primarily on satisfaction with two aspects of pay (pay levels and benefits) and how these are assessed within the organization. Methods for addressing these issues are discussed in Part 4 of this book.

One of the main dimensions of satisfaction with pay deals with pay levels relative to market wages. Indeed, when it comes to retention, employees being recruited away from one organization by another are often lured with promises of higher pay levels. In fact, exit surveys of high-performing employees who have left their organization indicate "better pay" as the reason in over 70 percent of the cases compared to only 33 percent who indicate "better opportunity." Ironically, when the managers of those same workers are polled, 68 percent cite "better opportunity" versus 45 percent who indicate it was "better pay," suggesting quite a difference of opinion.[118] Satisfaction with benefits is another important dimension of overall pay satisfaction. Because many individuals have a difficult time ascertaining the true dollar value of their benefits package, however, this dimension may not always be as salient to people as pay itself. To derive competitive advantage from benefits' expenditures, it is critical not only to make them highly salient to employees, however, but also link them to the organization's strategic direction.

Measuring and Monitoring Job Satisfaction

Most attempts to measure job satisfaction rely on workers' self-reports. There is a vast amount of data on the reliability and validity of many existing scales as well as a wealth of data from companies that have used these scales, allowing for comparisons across firms. Established scales are excellent places to begin if employers wish to assess the satisfaction levels of their employees. An employer would be foolish to "reinvent the wheel" by generating its own versions of measures of these broad constructs. Of course, in some cases, organizations want to measure their employees' satisfaction with aspects of their work that are specific to that organization (such as satisfaction with one particular health plan versus another). In these situations the organization may need to create its own scales, but this will be the exception rather than the rule.

One standardized, widely used measure of job satisfaction is the Job Descriptive Index (JDI). The JDI emphasizes various facets of satisfaction: pay, the work itself, supervision, co-workers, and promotions. Table 10.5 presents several items from the JDI scale. Other scales exist for those who want to get even more specific about different facets of satisfaction. For example, although the JDI we just examined assesses satisfaction with pay, it does not break pay up into different dimensions.[119] The Pay Satisfaction Questionnaire (PSQ) focuses on these more specific dimensions (pay levels, benefits, pay structure, and pay raises); thus this measure gives a more detailed view of exactly what aspects of pay are most or least satisfying.[120]

Instructions: Think of your present work. What is it like most of the time? In the blank beside each word given below, write

<u>Y</u> for "Yes" if it describes your work

<u>N</u> for "No" if it does NOT describe your work

<u>?</u> if you cannot decide

Work Itself		**Pay**		**Promotion Opportunities**	
<u>?</u>	Routine	<u>?</u>	Less than I deserve	<u>?</u>	Dead-end job
<u>?</u>	Satisfying	<u>?</u>	Highly paid	<u>?</u>	Unfair policies
<u>?</u>	Good	<u>?</u>	Insecure	<u>?</u>	Based on ability
Supervision				**Co-workers**	
<u>?</u>	Impolite			<u>?</u>	Intelligent
<u>?</u>	Praises good work			<u>?</u>	Responsible
<u>?</u>	Doesn't supervise enough			<u>?</u>	Boring

table 10.5

Sample Items from a Standardized Job Satisfaction Scale (the JDI)

SOURCE: W. K. Balzar, D. C. Smith, D. E. Kravitz, S. E. Lovell, K. B. Paul, B. A. Reilly, and C. E. Reilly, *User's Manual for the Job Descriptive Index (JDI)* (Bowling Green, OH: Bowling Green State University, 1990).

Clearly there is no end to the number of satisfaction facets that we might want to measure, but the key in operational contexts, where the main concern is retention, is making sure that scores on whatever measures taken truly relate to voluntary turnover among valued people. For example, satisfaction with co-workers might be low, but if this aspect of satisfaction is not too central to employees, it may not translate into voluntary turnover. Similarly, in an organization that bases raises on performance, low performers might report being dissatisfied with raises, but this may not reflect any operational problem. Indeed, the whole strategic purpose of many pay-for-performance plans is to create this type of dissatisfaction among low performers to motivate them to higher levels of performance.

Survey-Feedback Interventions

Regardless of what measures are used or how many facets of satisfaction are assessed, a systematic, ongoing program of *employee survey research* should be a prominent part of any human resource strategy for a number of reasons. First, it allows the company to monitor trends over time and thus prevent problems in the area of voluntary turnover before they happen. For example, Figure 10.4 shows the average profile for different facets of satisfaction for a hypothetical company in 2005, 2007, and 2009. As the figure makes clear, the level of satisfaction with promotion opportunities in this company has eroded over time, whereas the satisfaction with co-workers has improved. If there was a strong relationship between satisfaction with promotion opportunities and voluntary turnover among high performers, this would constitute a threat that the organization might need to address via some of the techniques discussed in our previous chapter, "Employee Development." For example, Sun Healthcare Group found exactly this kind of trend in its survey of nurses, aides, and other caregivers. The company responded to this feedback by creating the Career Pathways Initiative that allowed the employees to develop new skills and grow professionally. The program provided time off and financial support—some of which was obtained from seeking a

LO4
Design a survey feedback intervention program and use this to promote retention of key organizational personnel.

figure 10.4

Average Profile for Different Facets of Satisfaction over Time

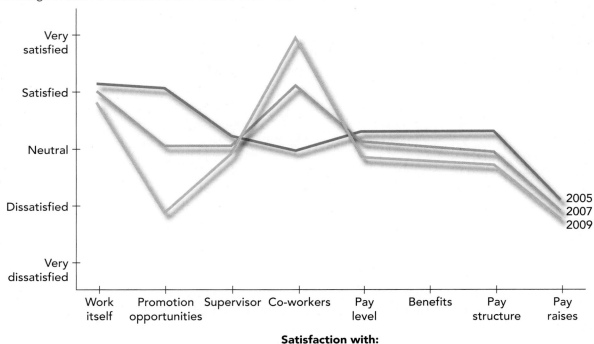

Satisfaction with:

federal grant—to workers who wanted to go back to school and obtain higher degrees. Many former nurses aides became fully certified nursing assistants, many nursing assistants became licensed practical nurses (LPNs) and registered nurses (RNs), and many LPNs and RNs became nurse practitioners and physician assistants. The organization not only wound up having a higher skilled staff, in addition, turnover was reduced by 20 percent after the initiation of the program.[121]

A second reason for engaging in an ongoing program of employee satisfaction surveys is that it provides a means of empirically assessing the impact of changes in policy (such as introduction of a new performance appraisal system) or personnel (e.g., introduction of a new CEO) on worker attitudes. Figure 10.5 shows the average profile for different satisfaction facets for a hypothetical organization one year before and one year after a merger. An examination of the profile makes it clear that since the merger, satisfaction with supervision and pay structure have gone down dramatically, and this has not been offset by any increase in satisfaction along other dimensions. Again, this might point to the need for training programs for supervisors (like those discussed in Chapter 7) or changes in the pay system (like those discussed in Chapter 11). This was the exact pattern of results that was found by HCL Technologies, an India-based technology services provider. More specifically, the company learned from its survey that its variable pay-for-performance program was creating too many wild swings in the workers' paychecks, and many were leaving to take jobs with more stable month-to-month paychecks. The company responded by reducing the variable component in pay from 30 percent to just 10 percent. The result was an increase in customer satisfaction, a 140 percent growth in revenue, and a 50 percent reduction in turnover.[122] We also saw this as part of our opening vignette featuring

figure 10.5

Average Profile for Different Facets of Satisfaction before and after a Major Event

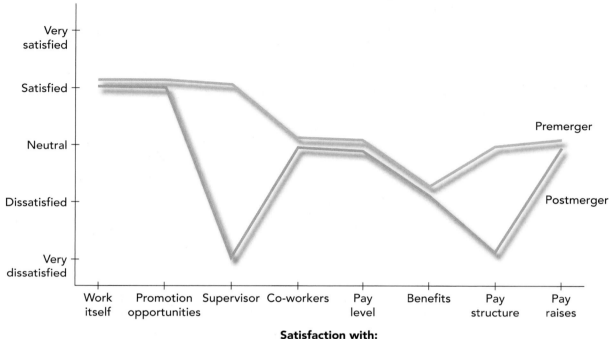

Home Depot, where the pay system was modified to recognize and reward associates for learning new skills and getting certified in additional departments.

Third, when these surveys incorporate standardized scales like the JDI, they often allow the company to compare itself with others in the same industry along these dimensions. For example, Figure 10.6 shows the average profile for different satisfaction facets for a hypothetical organization and compares this to the industry average. Again, if we detect major differences between one organization and the industry as a whole (on overall pay levels, for example), this might allow the company to react and change its policies before there is a mass exodus of people moving to the competition.

According to Figure 10.6, the satisfaction with pay levels is low relative to the industry, but this is offset by higher-than-industry-average satisfaction with benefits and the work itself. As we showed in Chapter 6 ("Selection and Placement"), the organization might want to use this information to systematically screen people. That is, the fit between the person and the organization would be best if the company selected applicants who reported being most interested in the nature of the work itself and benefits, and rejected those applicants whose sole concern was with pay levels.

Within the organization, a systematic survey program also allows the company to check for differences between units and hence benchmark "best practices" that might be generalized across units. For example, Figure 10.7 shows the average profile for five different regional divisions of a hypothetical company. The figure shows that satisfaction with pay raises is much higher in one of the regions relative to the others. If the overall amount of money allocated to raises was equal through the entire company, this implies that the manner in which raises are allocated or communicated in the Midwest region might be something that the other regions should look into.

figure 10.6

Average Profile for Different Facets of Satisfaction versus the Industry Average

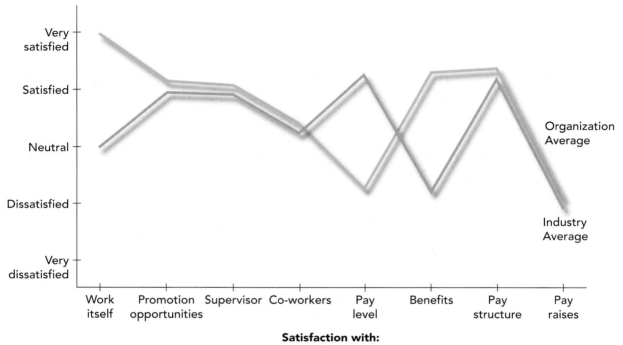

Satisfaction with:

figure 10.7

Average Profile for Different Facets of Satisfaction for Different Regional Divisions

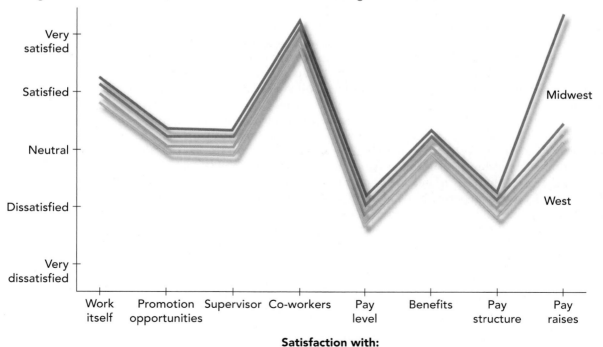

Satisfaction with:

Although findings such as these are leading more companies to do such surveys, conducting an organizational opinion survey is not something that should be taken lightly. Especially in the beginning, surveys such as this often raise expectations. If people fail to see any timely actions taken on matters identified as problems in the survey, satisfaction is likely to be even lower than it would be in the absence of a survey.

Finally, although the focus in this section has been on surveys of current employees, any strategic retention policy also has to consider surveying people who are about to become ex-employees. Exit interviews with departing workers can be a valuable tool for uncovering systematic concerns that are driving retention problems. If properly conducted, an exit interview can reveal the reasons why people are leaving, and perhaps even set the stage for their later return.[123] Indeed, in the new economy, it is now so common for people who once left their firm to return that they are given a special name—"boomerangs."[124] A good exit interview sets the stage for this phenomenon because if a recruiter is armed with information about what caused a specific person to leave (such as an abusive supervisor or a lack of family-friendly policies), when the situation changes, the person may be willing to come back.[125] Indeed, in the war for talent, the best way to manage retention is to engage in a battle for every valued employee, even in situations when it looks like the battle may have been lost.

A LOOK BACK

In the story that opened this chapter, we saw how Home Depot tried to raise the morale of their workforce. The belief at Home Depot was that if their workers weren't happy, their customers were probably not going to be happy either, and the company initiated many changes in order to change the organizational mood and culture.

Questions

1. What are some of the major causes of job dissatisfaction and turnover that were targeted by Home Depot, and why are those so central to address in service-oriented industries?
2. What were some of the sources of job satisfaction that were not addressed by Home Depot, and what might have been done along these other lines to change the culture?
3. Despite their documented value in comprehensively addressing sources of job dissatisfaction, employee attitude surveys did not seem to play a large role in the remake of Home Depot. Other than surveys, what are alternative methods for taking an organization's pulse, and how can these methods be used to complement surveys?

  Please see the Video Case and Case Study that correspond to this chapter online at www.mhhe.com/noe7e.

SUMMARY

This chapter examined issues related to employee separation and retention. Involuntary turnover reflects a separation initiated by the organization, often when the individual would prefer to stay a member of the organization. Voluntary turnover reflects a separation initiated by the individual, often when the organization would prefer that the person stay a member. Organizations can gain competitive advantage by strategically managing the separation process so that involuntary turnover is implemented in a fashion that does not invite retaliation, and voluntary turnover among high performers is kept to a minimum. Retaliatory reactions to organizational discipline and dismissal decisions can be minimized by implementing these decisions in a manner that promotes feelings of procedural and interactive justice. Voluntary turnover can be minimized by measuring and monitoring employee levels of satisfaction with critical facets of job and organization, and then addressing any problems identified by such surveys.

KEY TERMS

Involuntary turnover, 461
Voluntary turnover, 461
Employment-at-will
doctrine, 462
Outcome fairness, 465
Procedural justice, 465
Interactional justice, 465

Alternative dispute resolution
(ADR), 467
Employee assistance programs
(EAPs), 468
Outplacement counseling, 470
Progression of withdrawal, 472
Whistle-blowing, 473

Job involvement, 475
Organizational commitment, 475
Job satisfaction, 477
Frame of reference, 477
Negative affectivity, 479
Job rotation, 481
Prosocial motivation, 481

DISCUSSION QUESTIONS

1. The discipline and discharge procedures described in this chapter are systematic but rather slow. In your opinion, should some offenses lead to immediate dismissal? If so, how would you justify this to a court if you were sued for wrongful discharge?
2. Organizational turnover is generally considered a negative outcome, and many organizations spend a great deal of time and money trying to reduce it. What situations would indicate that an increase in turnover might be just what an organization needs? Given the difficulty of terminating employees, what organizational policies might promote the retention of high-performing workers but voluntary turnover among low performers?
3. Three popular interventions for enhancing worker satisfaction are job enrichment, job rotation, and role

analysis. What are the critical differences between these interventions, and under what conditions might one be preferable to the others?
4. If off-the-job stress and dissatisfaction begin to create on-the-job problems, what are the rights and responsibilities of the human resource manager in helping the employee to overcome these problems? Are intrusions into such areas an invasion of privacy, a benevolent and altruistic employer practice, or simply a prudent financial step taken to protect the firm's investment?
5. Discuss the advantages of using published, standardized measures in employee attitude surveys. Do employers ever need to develop their own measures for such surveys? Where would one turn to learn how to do this?

SELF-ASSESSMENT EXERCISE

The characteristics of your job influence your overall satisfaction with the job. One way to be satisfied at work is to find a job with the characteristics that you find desirable. The following assessment is a look at what kind of job is likely to satisfy you.

The following phrases describe different job characteristics. Read each phrase, then circle a number to indicate

how much of the job characteristic you would like. Use the following scale: 1 = very little; 2 = little; 3 = a moderate amount; 4 = much; 5 = very much.

1. The opportunity to perform a number
   of different activities each day   1 2 3 4 5
2. Contributing something significant
   to the company   1 2 3 4 5

3. The freedom to determine how to
   do my job   1 2 3 4 5
4. The ability to see projects or jobs
   through to completion, rather than
   performing only one piece of the job   1 2 3 4 5
5. Seeing the results of my work, so
   I can get an idea of how well I am
   doing the job   1 2 3 4 5
6. A feeling that the quality of my work
   is important to others in the company   1 2 3 4 5
7. The need to use a variety of complex
   skills   1 2 3 4 5
8. Responsibility to act and make
   decisions independently of managers
   or supervisors   1 2 3 4 5
9. Time and resources to do an entire
   piece of work from beginning to end   1 2 3 4 5
10. Getting feedback about my
    performance from the work itself   1 2 3 4 5

Add the scores for the pairs of items that measure each job characteristic. A higher score for a characteristic means that characteristic is more important to you.

Skill Variety: The degree to which a job requires you to use a variety of skills.

Item 1: ____ + Item 7: ____ = ____

Task Identity: The degree to which a job requires completion of a whole and identifiable piece of work.

Item 4: ____ + Item 9: ____ = ____

Task Significance: The degree to which a job has an impact on the lives or work of others.

Item 2: ____ + Item 6: ____ = ____

Autonomy: The degree to which a job provides freedom, empowerment, and discretion in scheduling the work and determining processes and procedures for completing the work.

Item 3: ____ + Item 8: ____ = ____

Feedback: The degree to which carrying out job-related tasks and activities provides you with direct and clear information about your effectiveness.

Item 5 ____ + Item 10: ____ = ____

SOURCE: Adapted from R. Daft and R. Noe, *Organizational Behavior* (New York: Harcourt, 2001).

EXERCISING STRATEGY: FEELING INSECURE ABOUT AIRLINE SECURITY

Becoming an expert in any field takes some degree of training and on-the-job experience. When working as part of a team, it also takes some time to learn about the strengths and weaknesses of one's team members so that a unit can operate like a well-oiled machine. For this reason, turnover in just one position can drastically reduce the effectiveness of work units. However, imagine the case where the entire work unit changes *every four months!*

Although it may seem hard to believe, this was the turnover rate at the security checkpoints at Logan International Airport in September 2001, when two planes were hijacked and used as guided missiles in the attacks on the World Trade Center. And Logan was not even the worst airport in this regard. The turnover rates at both St. Louis and Atlanta were over 400 percent—meaning that the entire crew turned over every three months. Given the lack of experience that workers in these positions had on the job, as well as their lack of experience working together, it is not at all surprising that performance of these work units was abysmal. In fact, as Max Cleland, chairman of the Senate Armed Services Subcommittee on Personnel, noted, "This was our front line, and what we found is we didn't have security, we had a sieve."

A number of factors explain the incredibly high turnover rates in these jobs. First, the job is low in pay. Most airport security personnel make less than $6 an hour, well below the rate of even those who work in the airport's fast-food restaurants. Second, these are dead-end jobs. There

is no career progression that would lead the incumbent to think that if he or she worked hard and stuck with it, he or she could climb into some managerial position. Third, the work itself is boring and monotonous. In addition, it is performed in a context of resentment, where hurried passengers look down on the security personnel who are perceived as being beneath those they are trying to serve. Finally, there is very little job security. A person can be fired for a single mistake, and the notion that a quality job is demanded is undermined by airline pressure to keep people moving during peak departure periods.

The airlines, which are currently responsible for security, blame this situation on the economics of the industry, where costs need to be kept low in order to maintain profitability. However, most airlines need to fill 65 percent of cabin capacity to clear a profit, and even two months after the terrorist attacks, fear of flying kept the capacity levels below 35 percent, putting even greater financial pressure on the carriers. As Cleland notes, as far as the industry is concerned, "Security is No. 1 in a series of confidence-building measures that will bring people back to fly."

Many of the security measures that are being considered will be imported from Europe and Israel, which have far better records than the United States in this area. There, airline security screening is treated as a police function, and the pay, training, and benefits are all much higher than what is seen in the United States. Moreover, a close emotional attachment between the security personnel and the airlines, many of which are nationalized, makes this work seem like a patriotic duty. This type of emotional attachment never develops in the revolving door that serves as the context for airline security work in the United States.

SOURCES: M. Fish, "Airport Security: A System Driven by the Minimum Wage," CNN.com (October 31, 2001), pp. 1–5; M. Fish, "Many Warnings over Security Preceded Terrorist Attacks," CNN.com (November 1, 2001), pp. 1–3; S. Candiotti, "FBI Arrests Man Who Tried to Board Flight Armed with Knives," CNN.com (November 5, 2001), pp. 1–2; M. Fish, "Outside the U.S., a Different Approach to Air Security," CNN.com (November 1, 2001), pp. 1–2.

Questions

1. Many now look back at the way airport security was selected and managed prior to the 9/11 attacks with disbelief. What was the relationship between the airlines, the airports, the government, and the security agents prior to the attacks? How did the nature of these relationships explain why airport security agents were managed so poorly?

2. How has the relationship between the airlines, airports, government, and security agents changed since 9/11, and in what ways has the new Transportation Safety Administration changed the nature of airport security work?

3. Much of the task in keeping air travel safe requires teamwork between the airlines, the airports, the government, and the security agents. In what way does high interdependence between people working together heighten the negative impact of employee turnover and performance?

● Managing People: From the Pages of *BusinessWeek*

BusinessWeek Hide the Doritos! Here Comes HR

With an eye on soaring health-care costs, companies are getting pushy about employees' eating habits The lawyers at the boutique law firm Littler Mendelson have always liked their carbs. For years the firm's sumptuous San Francisco headquarters overflowed with endless trays of Krispy Kremes, gooey sweet rolls, and gigantic muffins. Then one day the attorneys showed up for a firm breakfast and found . . . hard-boiled eggs, yogurt, mini quiches, cottage cheese, and fresh fruit. "Where's the donuts?" ranted the associates.

Littler Mendelson's human resources chief, Suzanne Perez, feared mass sugar withdrawal, but she yanked the junk anyway. And while she's not too popular at the office right now, she's in good company. Google, Yamaha Corp. of America, Caterpillar, and others are putting health food in corporate break rooms, cafeterias, and vending machines; dumping donuts in favor of organic fresh fruit deliveries; and slapping "calorie taxes" on fatty foods.

For several years the company wellness police—the folks obsessed with bringing down exploding health insurance costs—have confined themselves to targeting chunky cube dwellers with subsidized cholesterol drugs, free gym memberships, and New Age–spouting health coaches. But what good is all that if the office vending machine is filled with candy, cola, and chips—or cookies and cake are served at every meeting? "I didn't think we were being aggressive enough," says Carol Baker, the HR boss at Yamaha. But getting junkies to detox isn't easy. "People aren't ready to give up everything," she says.

Don't Let Them Eat Cake

Google, the company famously committed to doing no evil, is a case in point. Yes, the Googleplex swarms with svelte twentysomethings in snug tops and low-slung denim. But even these workers aren't immune to the so-called Google 15—the number of pounds Googlers say they typically gain after joining the company and partaking in its famous gratis grub. As one blogger put it, "I fully expect a Google Infarct Room to be opened within two years."

Google's "microkitchens"—the snack stations within 200 feet of every worker's desk—were like mini 7-Elevens. "We kept adding things and adding things and adding things," says Google's food services chief, John Dickman (who is leaving the company at the end of April [2008]). Like 20 kinds of sugared cereal. Or, in the cafeteria, the Luther Burger, a bacon-cheese number with Krispy Kreme donuts as bun. And it wasn't long before some Googlers were pondering the philosophical implications on the company's in-house message boards. Wretched excess with stock options was one thing. But wasn't free junk food kind of, ahem, evil?

Yet when Dickman ditched the M&M's, employees argued that the measure was about costs, not calories. (A hard case to make given Google's valet parking, free massages, and bidet-equipped restrooms.) "There were certain things they couldn't live without," Dickman says. So the M&M's returned. But the junk-healthy ratio is now 50–50, with agave-sweetened beverages, roasted nuts, sulfate-free dried fruit, and platters of organic crudités.

At Yamaha, Baker has done away with the "zillions" of pies in favor of regular shipments of organic fruit from San Francisco's Fruit Guys, whose business in providing workplaces across the U.S. with pesticide-free, locally grown fruit is exploding. (Turns out fruit is cheaper than the pies.) Lunchtime is another battle. Yamaha's Buena Park (Calif.) headquarters is situated near a thoroughfare chockablock with fast-food joints. So Baker brought in a catering company offering healthy salads and sandwiches. "We're trying to change people's behaviors," she says.

"Calorie Tax"

She soon found out that employees are not the only resisters. "The vending machine people were not very supportive," says Baker. At first, she says, they grudgingly tossed in some trail mix and stuck a little heart sticker next to those fluorescent orange crackers with peanut butter. But within weeks, Baker says, the potato chips and candy bars were back. Junk moves.

That's why some companies are getting to employees' stomachs through their wallets. After Caterpillar offered garden burgers in its cafeteria for a buck last year, sales soared fivefold, to 2,500 a month. At mortgage giant Freddie Mac, workers who order six healthy meals in the cafeteria get the seventh free. Florida Power & Light, Dow Corning, and Sprint Nextel all charge more for unhealthy food (the so-called calorie tax) and less for healthier fare. At Pitney Bowes, they moved the desserts away from the cash register to curb impulse buys.

Some companies feel like a re-education camp. Microsoft's food honcho, Mark Freeman, created a color-coded system of icons to help make the healthy stuff as recognizable as a Snickers bar. In each of Microsoft's 31 cafeterias, there are icons for vegan, gluten-free, organic, sustainable, sugar-free, carb control, and nondairy. Freeman has also made the company's metropolis-like headquarters a trans-fat-free zone. At first, "everybody was yelling and screaming about the healthy food," says Freeman. But the Microserfs are coming around.

For those who don't, there is always tough love. HR types swarmed the New York Marriott Marquis hotel in February to learn how to implement lean-worker campaigns, biggest-loser contests, and strategic-eating seminars. During breaks over yogurt and fruit, the attendees swapped war stories about how overweight workers eat up health-care dollars. As one executive from a major software company quipped: "We're waging a war on fat people." Junk food lovers, beware. These people are serious.

Questions

1. In what ways does the value of providing some of the nonfinancial perks like those discussed in this article provide a greater boost to employee morale relative to the cash equivalent of the perk that might instead be given as a raise in pay?

2. How do concerns regarding employee wellness change the way one views various nonfinancial perks like those discussed in this article?

3. In what way does the negative value of taking away an existing nonfinancial perk like those discussed in the article detract from morale more than the positive boost obtained by providing that same perk in the first place?

4. How much responsibility should managers assume for the eating habits of their employees, and how should HR professionals balance the need to make people happy with the need to make people do what's good for them, even if it makes them unhappy?

SOURCE: M. Conlin, "Hide the Doritos! Here Comes HR," *BusinessWeek*, April 17, 2008, pp. 94–96.

● NOTES

1. J. D. Shaw, M. K. Duffy, J. L. Johnson, and D. E. Lockhart, "Turnover, Social Capital Losses, and Performance," *Academy of Management Journal* 48 (2005), pp. 594–606.

2. R. Batt, "Managing Customer Services: Human Resource Practices, Quit Rates, and Sales Growth," *Academy of Management Journal* 45 (2002), pp. 587–97.

3. I. S. Fulmer, B. Gerhart, and K. S. Scott, "Are the 100 Best Better? An Empirical Investigation of the Relationship between Being a 'Great Place to Work' and Firm Performance," *Personnel Psychology* 56 (2003), pp. 965–93.

4. M. Boyle, "Happy People, Happy Returns," *Fortune*, January 22, 2007, p. 100.

5. J. P. Guthrie, "High-Involvement Work Practices, Turnover, and Productivity: Evidence from New Zealand," *Academy of Management Journal* 44 (2001), pp. 180–90.

6. S. S. Masterson, "A Trickle-Down Model of Organizational Justice: Relating Employees' and Customers' Perceptions of and Reactions to Fairness," *Journal of Applied Psychology* 86 (2001), pp. 594–604.

7. K. M. Kacmer, M. C. Andrews, D. L. Van Rooy, R. C. Steilberg, and S. Cerrone, "Sure Everyone Can Be Replaced . . . But at What Cost? Turnover as a Predictor of Unit-Level Performance," *Academy of Management Journal* 49 (2006), pp. 133–44.

8. D. Foust, "Why United Is Ready to Unite," *BusinessWeek*, December 3, 2007, pp. 22–23.

9. M. Riketta, "The Causal Relation between Job Attitudes and Performance: A Meta-analysis of Panel Studies," *Journal of Applied Psychology* 93 (2008), pp. 472–81.

10. K. Sulkowicz, "Straight Talk at Review Time," *BusinessWeek*, September 10, 2007, p. 16.

11. M. Conlin, and J. Greene, "How to Make a Microserf Smile," *BusinessWeek*, September 10, 2007, pp. 57–59.

12. F. Hanson, "'Poaching' Can Be Pricey, but Benefits May Outweigh Costs," *Workforce Management*, January 30, 2006, pp. 37–39.

13. S. A. Feeney, "The High Cost of Employee Violence," *Workforce*, August 2003, pp. 23–24.

14. M. Heller, "A Return to At-Will Employment," *Workforce*, May 2001, pp. 42–46.

15. M. Orey, "Fear of Firing," *BusinessWeek*, April 23, 2007, pp. 52–62.

16. M. Conlin, "Litigation Inoculation," *BusinessWeek*, May 28, 2007, p. 35.

17. G. Casellas, "Fired Up Over Firing," *BusinessWeek*, May 14, 2007, p. 76.

18. C. Holahan, "Virtually Addicted," *BusinessWeek*, December 14, 2006, p. 41.

19. Orey, "Fear of Firing."

20. D. Foust, "Tough Love at the Office," *BusinessWeek*, May 29, 2006, p. 106.

21. S. E. Scullen, P. K. Bergey, and L. Aimon-Smith, "Forced Distribution Rating Systems and the Improvement of Workforce Potential: A Baseline Simulation," *Personnel Psychology* 58 (2005), pp. 1–32.

22. J. Rossant and J. Ewing, "Every Little Reform Counts," *BusinessWeek*, March 7, 2005, pp. 54–55.

23. D. Roberts, "Rumbles Over Chinese Labor Reforms," *BusinessWeek*, March 12, 2007, p. 57.

24. M. Orey, "Attacks by Colleagues are Creeping Up," *BusinessWeek*, May 7, 2007, p. 14.

25. J. McGregor, "Sweet Revenge," *BusinessWeek*, January 22, 2007, pp. 65–70.

26. M. M. Le Blanc and K. Kelloway, "Predictors and Outcomes of Workplace Violence and Aggression," *Journal of Applied Psychology* 87 (2002), pp. 444–53.

27. A. G. Tekleab, R. Takeuchi, and M. S. Taylor, "Extending the Chain of Relationships among Organizational Justice, Social Exchange, and Employee Reactions: The Role of Contract Violations," *Academy of Management Journal* 48 (2005), pp. 146–57.

28. D. P. Skarlicki and R. Folger, "Retaliation in the Workplace: The Roles of Distributive, Procedural, and Interactional Justice," *Journal of Applied Psychology* 82 (1997), pp. 434–43.

29. C. M. Holmvall, and D. R. Bobocel, "What Fair Procedures Say About Me: Self-Construals and Reactions to Procedural Fairness" *Organizational Behavior and Human Decision Processes* 105 (2008), pp. 147–68.

30. H. Y. Li, J. B. Bingham, and E. E. Umphress, "Fairness from the Top: Perceived Procedural Justice and Collaborative Problem Solving in New Product Development," *Organization Science* 18 (2007), pp. 200–16.

31. P. Dvorak, "Firing Workers Who Are a Bad Fit," *The Wall Street Journal*, May 1, 2006, p. B5.

32. T. A. Judge, B. A. Scott, and R. Ilies, "Hostility, Job Attitudes and Workplace Deviance: A Test of a Multilevel Model," *Journal of Applied Psychology* 91 (2006), pp. 126–38.

33. B. J. Tepper, "Relationship among Supervisors' and Subordinates' Procedural Justice Perceptions and Organizational Citizenship Behaviors," *Academy of Management Journal* 46 (2003), pp. 97–105.

34. T. Simons and Q. Roberson, "Why Managers Should Care About Fairness: The Affects of Aggregate Justice Perceptions on Organizational Outcomes," *Journal of Applied Psychology* 88 (2003), pp. 432–43.

35. K. K. Spors, "If You Fire People, Don't Be a Jerk About It," *The Wall Street Journal*, December 22, 2008, pp. C1–C2.

36. M. Orey, "The Vanishing Trial," *BusinessWeek*, April 30, 2007, pp. 38–39.

37. M. Orey, "Arbitration Aggravation," *BusinessWeek*, April 30, 2007, pp. 38–39.

38. C. S. Spel and T. C. Blum, "Adoption of Workplace Substance Abuse Prevention Programs: Strategic Choice and Institutional Perspectives," *Academy of Management Journal* 48 (2005), pp. 1125–42.

39. A. Meisler, "Mind Field," *Workforce* (2003), pp. 57–60.

40. S. Sonnenberg and C. McEnerney, "Medical Leave: A Prescription," *Workforce*, April 2004, pp. 16–17.

41. R. Jana, "A Shot in the Arm for E-Health," *BusinessWeek*, December 8, 2008, pp. 58–59.

42. K. Doheny, "Going the Extra Mile," *Workforce Management*, January 19, 2009, pp. 27–28.

43. M. Colin, "Get Healthy—Or Else," *BusinessWeek*, February 26, 2007, pp. 58–69.

44. J. Marquez, "Being Healthy May Be Its Own Reward, but a Little Cash Can Also Help Keep Workers Fit," *Workforce Management*, September 2005, pp. 66–69.

45. D. Stevens, "Target: Fat Smokers," *Workforce Management*, December 10, 2007, p. 26.

46. J. Marquez, "Wellness: Bad Side Effects," *Workforce Management*, May 5, 2008, pp. 1–3.

47. V. Leo, "Wellness—Or Orwellness?" *BusinessWeek*, March 19, 2007, p. 82.

48. S. E. Needleman, "More Employers Help the Laid Off Find Jobs," *The Wall Street Journal*, April 1, 2009, pp. C1.

49. J. Jones, "How to Bounce Back if You're Bounced Out," *BusinessWeek*, January 27, 1998, pp. 22–23.

50. J. D. Shaw, N. Gupta, and J. E. Delery, "Alternative Conceptualizations of the Relationship between Voluntary Turnover and Organizational Performance," *Academy of Management Journal* 48 (2005), pp. 50–68.

51. J. Sullivan, "Not All Turnover Is Equal," *Workforce Management*, May 21, 2007, p. 42.

52. J. Lublin, "Keeping Clients by Keeping Workers," *The Wall Street Journal*, November 20, 2006, p. B1.

53. A. Lashinsky, "Search and Enjoy," *Fortune*, January 22, 2007, pp. 70–82.

54. J. Banks, "Turnover Costs," *Workforce Management*, June 23, 2008, p. 22.

55. S. C. Payne and S. S. Weber, "Effects of Service Provider Attitudes and Employment Status on Citizenship Behaviors and Customer's Attitudes and Loyalty Behavior," *Journal of Applied Psychology* 91 (2006), pp. 365–78.

56. G. A. Gelade and M. Ivery, "The Impact of Human Resource Management and Work Climate on Organizational Performance," *Personnel Psychology* 56 (2003), pp. 383–404.

57. B. Schneider, P. J. Hanges, D. B. Smith, and A. N. Salvaggio, "Which Come First, Employee Attitudes or Organizational Financial and Market Performance?" *Journal of Applied Psychology* 88 (2003), pp. 838–51.

58. D. W. Baruch, "Why They Terminate," *Journal of Consulting Psychology* 8 (1944), pp. 35–46; J. G. Rosse, "Relations among Lateness, Absence and Turnover: Is There a Progression of Withdrawal?" *Human Relations* 41 (1988), pp. 517–31.

59. E. R. Burris, J. R. Detert, and D. S. Chiaburu, "Quitting before Leaving: The Mediating Effects of Psychological Attachment and Detachment on Voice," *Journal of Applied Psychology* 93 (2008), pp. 912–22.

60. J. McGregor, "Keeping Talent in the Fold," *BusinessWeek*, November 3, 2008, pp. 51–52.

61. C. Hulin, "Adaptation, Persistence and Commitment in Organizations," in *Handbook of Industrial & Organizational Psychology* 2nd ed., ed. M. D. Dunnette and L. M. Hough (Palo Alto, CA: Consulting Psychologists Press, 1991), pp. 443–50.

62. C. Sablynski, T. Mitchell, T. Lee, J. Burton, and B. Holtom, "Turnover: An Integration of Lee and Mitchell's Unfolding Model and Job Embeddedness Construct and Hulin's Withdrawal Construct," in *The Psychology of Work*, ed. J. Brett and F. Drasgow (Mahwah, NJ: Lawrence Erlbaum Associates, 2002).

63. J. D. Kammeyer-Mueller, C. R. Wanberg, T. M. Glomb, and D. Ahlburg, "The Role of Temporal Shifts in Turnover Processes:

It's About Time," *Journal of Applied Psychology* 90 (2005), pp. 644–58.

64. D. A. Harrison, D. A. Newman, and P. L. Roth, "How Important Are Job Attitudes? Meta-analytic Comparisons of Integrative Behavioral Outcomes and Time Sequences," *Academy of Management Journal* 49 (2006), pp. 305–25.

65. C. E. Labig and I. B. Helburn, "Union and Management Policy Influences on Grievance Initiation," *Journal of Labor Research* 7 (1986), pp. 269–84.

66. J. Cook, "Positively Negative," *Human Resource Executive* (June 15, 2001), pp. 101–4.

67. M. P. Miceli and J. P. Near, "Characteristics of Organizational Climate and Perceived Wrongdoing Associated with Whistle-Blowing Decisions," *Personnel Psychology* 38 (1985), pp. 525–44.

68. V. Walter, and A. Patel, "NSA Whistleblower Alleges Illegal Spying," *ABCNews.com*, January 10, 2006, p. 1.

69. C. Jones, "As Ford Stumbles, More Managers See Leaving as the Way Forward," *The Wall Street Journal*, August 28, 2006, pp. B1, B2.

70. S. F. Gale, "Sickened by Costs of Absenteeism, Companies Look for Solutions," *Workforce*, September 2003, pp. 72–75.

71. P. Bamberger and M. Biron, "Group Norms and Excessive Absenteeism: The Role of Peer Referent Others," *Organizational Behavior and Human Decision Processes* 103 (2007), pp. 179–96.

72. M. Conlin, "Shirking Working: The War on Hooky," *BusinessWeek*, November 12, 2007, pp. 70–71.

73. M. L. Ambrose and M. Schminke, "The Role of Overall Justice Judgments in Organizational Research: A Test of Mediation," *Journal of Applied Psychology* 94 (2009), pp. 491–500.

74. E. A. Locke, "The Nature and Causes of Job Dissatisfaction," in *The Handbook of Industrial & Organizational Psychology*, ed. M. D. Dunnette (Chicago: Rand McNally, 1976), pp. 901–69.

75. F. Jones, D. B. O'Connor, M. Conner, B. McMillan, and E. Ferguson, "Impact of Daily Mood, Work Hours and Iso-strain Variables on Self-Reported Health Behaviors," *Journal of Applied Psychology* 92 (2007), pp. 1731–40.

76. L. Woellert, "Does Welding Make You Sick?" *BusinessWeek*, July 10, 2006, p. 32.

77. J. Bailey, "Improving Safety for Workers Also Improves Company Health," *The Wall Street Journal*, May 1, 2006, p. B3.

78. R. D. Zimmerman, "Understanding the Impact of Personality Traits on Individuals' Turnover Decisions: A Meta-analysis," *Personnel Psychology* 61 (2008), pp. 309–48.

79. T. A. Judge, E. A. Locke, C. C. Durham, and A. N. Kluger, "Dispositional Effects on Job and Life Satisfaction: The Role of Core Evaluations," *Journal of Applied Psychology* 83 (1998), pp. 17–34.

80. T. Begley and C. Lee, "The Role of Negative Affectivity in Pay-at-Risk Reactions: A Longitudinal Study," *Journal of Applied Psychology*, 2005, pp. 382–88; G. E. Hardy, D. Woods, and T. D. Wall, "The Impact of Psychological Distress on Absence from Work," *Journal of Applied Psychology* 88 (2003), pp. 306–14.

81. B. M. Staw, N. E. Bell, and J. A. Clausen, "The Dispositional Approach to Job Attitudes: A Lifetime Longitudinal Test," *Administrative Science Quarterly* 31 (1986), pp. 56–78; B. M. Staw and J. Ross, "Stability in the Midst of Change: A Dispositional Approach to Job Attitudes," *Journal of Applied Psychology* 70 (1985), pp. 469–80.

82. R. P. Steel and J. R. Rentsch, "The Dispositional Model of Job Attitudes Revisited: Findings of a 10-Year Study," *Journal of Applied Psychology* 82 (1997), pp. 873–79.

83. N. A. Bowling, T. A. Beehr, S. H. Wagner, and T. M. Libkuman, "Adaptation-Level Theory, Opponent Process Theory, and Dispositions: An Integrated Approach to the Stability of Job Satisfaction," *Journal of Applied Psychology* 90 (2005), pp. 1044–53.

84. J. M. O'Brian, "Zappos Knows How to Kick It," *Fortune*, January 2, 2009, pp. 55–60.

85. B. A. Gerhart, "How Important Are Dispositional Factors as Determinants of Job Satisfaction? Implications for Job Design and Other Personnel Programs," *Journal of Applied Psychology* 72 (1987), pp. 493–502.

86. E. F. Stone and H. G. Gueutal, "An Empirical Derivation of the Dimensions along Which Characteristics of Jobs Are Perceived," *Academy of Management Journal* 28 (1985), pp. 376–96.

87. L. W. Porter and R. M. Steers, "Organizational, Work and Personal Factors in Employee Absenteeism and Turnover," *Psychological Bulletin* 80 (1973), pp. 151–76.

88. P. J. Kiger, "Crouse Hospital," *Workforce Management*, October 20, 2008, p. 17.

89. D. Isen, "Reduce Employee Turnover, Build Customer Loyalty," *Workforce Management*, May 19, 2008, p. 34.

90. J. R. Hackman and G. R. Oldham, "Motivation through the Design of Work," *Organizational Behavior and Human Performance* 16 (1976), pp. 250–79.

91. E. C. Dierdorff and J. K. Ellington, "It's the Nature of the Work: Examining Behavior-based Sources of Work-Family Conflict," *Journal of Applied Psychology* 93 (2008), pp. 883–92.

92. B. L. Rau and M. M. Hyland, "Role Conflict and Flexible Work Arrangements: The Effects on Applicant Attraction," *Personnel Psychology* 55 (2002), pp. 111–36.

93. G. Weber, "Flexible Jobs Mean Fewer Absences," *Workforce*, November 2003, pp. 26–28.

94. M. Hammers, "Babies Deliver a Loyal Workforce," *Workforce*, April 2003, p. 52.

95. G. Flynn, "The Legalities of Flextime," *Workforce*, October 2001, pp. 62–66.

96. S. L. Lambert, "Added Benefits: The Link between Work–Life Benefits and Organizational Citizenship Behaviors," *Academy of Management Journal* 43 (2000), pp. 801–15.

97. J. E. Perry-Smith, "Work Family Human Resource Bundles and Perceived Organizational Performance," *Academy of Management Journal* 43 (2000), pp. 1107–17.

98. M. M. Arthur, "Share Price Reactions to Work-Family Initiatives: An Institutional Perspective," *Academy of Management Journal* 46 (2003), pp. 497–505.

99. A. M. Grant, "Relational Job Design and the Motivation to Make a Prosocial Difference," *Academy of Management Review* 32 (2007), pp. 393–417.

100. A. M. Grant, "Does Intrinsic Motivation Fuel the Prosocial Fire? Motivational Synergy in Predicting Persistence, Performance, and Productivity," *Journal of Applied Psychology* 93 (2007), pp. 48–58.

101. A. M. Grant, "The Significance of Task Significance," *Journal of Applied Psychology* 93 (2007), pp. 108–24.

102. A. M. Grant, E. M. Campbell, G. Chen, K. Cottone, D. Lapedia, and K. Lee, "Impact and Art of Motivation Maintenance: The Effects of Contact with Beneficiaries on Persistance Behavior," *Organizational Behavior and Human Decision Processes* 103 (2007), pp. 53–67.

103. B. Morris, "The Best Place to Work Now," *Fortune*, January 20, 2006, pp. 79–86.

104. J. M. Sacco and N. Schmitt, "A Dynamic Multi-level Model of Demographic Diversity and Misfit Effects," *Journal of Applied Psychology* 90 (2005), pp. 203–31.

105. R. E. Ployhart, J. A. Weekley, and K. Baughman, "The Structure and Function of Human Capital Emergence: A Multilevel Examination of the Attraction–Selection–Attrition Model," *Academy of Management Journal* 49 (2006), pp. 661–77.

106. B. M. Meglino, E. C. Ravlin, and C. L. Adkins, "A Work Values Approach to Corporate Culture: A Field Test of the Value Congruence Process and Its Relationship to Individual Outcomes," *Journal of Applied Psychology* 74 (1989), pp. 424–33.

107. R. Eisenberger, F. Stinghamber, C. Vandenberghe, I. L. Sucharski, and L. Rhoades, "Perceived Supervisor Support: Contributions to Perceived Organizational Support and Employee Retention," *Journal of Applied Psychology* 87 (2002), pp. 565–73.

108. P. Lattman, "Does Thank You Help Keep Associates?" *The Wall Street Journal*, January 24, 2007.

109. S. Aryee, Z. X. Chen, L. Y. Sun, and Y. A. Debrah, "Antecedents and Outcomes of Abusive Supervision: Test of a Trickle-Down Model," *Journal of Applied Psychology* 92 (2007), pp. 191–201.

110. S. Lim, L. M. Cortina, and V. J. Magley, "Personal and Workgroup Incivility: Impact on Work and Health Outcomes," *Journal of Applied Psychology* 93 (2008), pp. 95–107.

111. S. C. Payne and A. H. Huffman, "A Longitudinal Examination of the Influence of Mentoring on Organizational Commitment and Turnover," *Academy of Management Journal* 48 (2005), pp. 158–168.

112. S. Berfield, "Mentoring Can Be Messy," *BusinessWeek*, January 29, 2007, pp. 80–81.

113. A. Fisher, "Retain Your Brains," *Fortune*, July 24, 2006, pp. 49–50.

114. A. Fisher, "Have You Outgrown Your Job?" *Fortune*, August 21, 2006, pp. 46–54.

115. G. C. Ganster, M. R. Fusiler, and B. T. Mayes, "Role of Social Support in the Experience of Stress at Work," *Journal of Applied Psychology* 71 (1986), pp. 102–11.

116. C. O. Trevor and D. L. Wazeter, "Contingent View of Reactions to Objective Pay Conditions: Interdependence among Pay Structure Characteristics and Pay Relative to Internal and External Referents," *Journal of Applied Psychology* 91 (2006), pp. 1260–75.

117. S. C. Currall, A. J. Towler, T. A. Judge, and L. Kohn, "Pay Satisfaction and Organizational Outcomes," *Personnel Psychology* 58 (2005), pp. 613–40.

118. E. White, "Opportunity Knocks, and It Pays a Lot Better," *The Wall Street Journal*, November 13, 2006, p. B3.

119. H. G. Heneman and D. S. Schwab, "Pay Satisfaction: Its Multidimensional Nature and Measurement," *International Journal of Applied Psychology* 20 (1985), pp. 129–41.

120. T. Judge and T. Welbourne, "A Confirmatory Investigation of the Dimensionality of the Pay Satisfaction Questionnaire," *Journal of Applied Psychology* 79 (1994), pp. 461–66.

121. J. Smerd, "Healthcare Staffing Firm Tackles its Perennial Turnover Problem," *Workforce Management*, March 2007, p. 32.

122. E. Frauenheim, "Tech Services Provider Sees Reduced Turnover and Explosive Revenue Growth After Making Employee Satisfaction Its Top Priority," *Workforce Management*, October 20, 2008, p. 25.

123. J. Applegaste, "Plan an Exit Interview," CNNMoney.com (November 13, 2000), pp. 1–2.

124. M. Conlin, "Job Security, No. Tall Latte, Yes," *BusinessWeek*, April 2, 2001, pp. 62–63.

125. J. Lynn, "Many Happy Returns," CNNMoney.com (March 2, 2001), pp. 1–2.

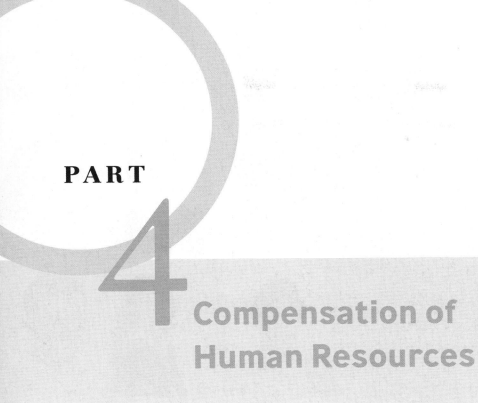

PART 4

Compensation of Human Resources

CHAPTER

11

Pay Structure Decisions

LO LEARNING OBJECTIVES

After reading this chapter, you should be able to:

Toyota Takes the Knife to U.S. Labor Costs

In Chapter 4, we saw how Toyota worked to restore profitability through restructuring organizational design and job design. In this opening vignette, we touch on how Toyota is weathering the economic storm by cutting U.S. labor costs.

Last summer, when Toyota temporarily shuttered three U.S. plants as part of a move to build more fuel-efficient vehicles and fewer large trucks, it won plaudits for not laying off employees. Instead, workers undertook extra training sessions, helped out at other plants, or even became involved in projects in the local community. Now, though, with the U.S. market showing few signs of recovery—Toyota's sales slumped 32% in January—and lossess mounting, the Japanese automaker has no choice but to cut labor costs in the U.S. While no layoffs are planned, Toyota is offering buyouts to some of its 30,000 American employees, slashing bonuses, and cutting executive pay.

According to a statement issued on February 12, 2009, Toyota will offer voluntary exit programs and work-sharing schemes at selected plants. Worker bonuses will be reduced, and there will be no wage increases "for the foreseeable future." Executives will have their pay cut and see their bonuses disappear. There will be additional nonproduction days in April, too. "We've taken responsible, step-by-step actions to address this issue in recent months, and we hope the new measures will help us adjust while protecting jobs," Jim Wiseman, vice-president for external affairs at Toyota Motor Engineering & Manufacturing North America, said in the statement.

Toyota says it is unsure how many workers will take up the offer of the buyouts and that it doesn't have a target in mind. Workers who sign up for the voluntary plan will get 10 weeks' salary, plus two weeks' salary for every year worked, and $20,000. The offer will be made to 18,000 U.S. Toyota workers.

REDUCED HOURS

Under the "work-sharing" scheme, affected workers will now work and be paid for 72 hours, rather than the usual 80, over a two-week period. A Toyota spokesman said the reduced hours will be in force for an unspecified period of time. He added that discussions were under way or planned to extend the work-sharing scheme to unionized workers, depending on the union involved.

While unwelcome, the moves are not unexpected. On Feb. 6, Toyota said it will lose $3.9 billion for the year through March, marking its first net loss since 1950.

Executive Vice-President Mitsuo Kinoshita told reporters that the poor results were largely due to the strong Japanese yen and plunging sales in the U.S.—traditionally where Toyota earns its biggest chunk of profits—and Europe. Kinoshita added that it was necessary to slash production to prevent a stockpile of unsold cars, but he said the company will try to avoid firing permanent staff. "We intend to make every possible effort to protect employees," he said.

In Japan, Toyota has already laid off temporary employees and is closing factories for an additional 11 days this month and next to cut production. On two of those days, workers are receiving 80 percent of their normal pay. Other days are taken from paid holiday allowances. Last fall the company formed an "Emergency Profit Improvement Committee," which it hopes will ferret out an extra $1.4 billion in savings this year—in addition to the $3.3 billion in new savings Toyota looks to make in normal years.

EXTRA SWEATERS

No cost-cutting, it seems, is too small. Workers are being encouraged to take the stairs rather than elevators, to save electricity. The heat in factories has been turned down, so workers are now wearing extra sweaters to stay warm. And on Jan. 19, Lexus engineer Takayuki Katsuda and two colleagues drove from headquarters in Toyota City to Tokyo for the Japan launch of the Lexus RX sport-utility vehicle. Though the trip took four hours, vs. 90 minutes on the Shinkansen bullet train, they saved about $300 in train fares. "We're facing a once-in-a-hundred-years crisis," Akio Toyoda, a scion of the founding family who will become president in June, told reporters on Jan. 20.

Analysts say Toyota is aiming to avoid cutting permanent employees in large numbers, which is about more than presenting a good image and strengthening employee relations. Tatsuo Yoshida, an analyst at UBS in Tokyo, says that despite grim headlines, Japanese automakers are wary of the cost of having to rehire and retrain new workers if the economic outlook improves. "Plant closures and huge layoffs aren't really happening," he says. "The Japanese manufacturers strongly believe that at some point in time the demand will come back."

Nissan, for example, said on Feb. 9 that it would reduce its head count by an eye-catching 20,000 to 215,000, but, a bit like Toyota, its cuts will mainly be through trimming temporary workers and putting a freeze on new hires while it is planning work-sharing schemes. "Investors might be disappointed that no radical measures are being taken, but [huge job cuts] are no good for solving the problem they are facing today," adds Yoshida.

Of course, if stimulus packages in key auto markets, such as the U.S. and China, fail to reignite auto demand, that could change. Indeed, while Japanese automakers are in better financial shape than Detroit rivals, losses are already mounting. With Toyota, Nissan, Mazda, Mitsubishi Motors, and Subaru parent Fuji Heavy Industries all predicting full-year losses, only Honda Motor, Suzuki, and Toyota's minicar maker Daihatsu expect to make a profit this financial year. And analysts say Toyota's latest labor cost-cutting measures in the U.S., combined with previous plans, are unlikely to be enough to get it back in the black.

As long as the Japanese yen, currently hovering around an unpalatable 90 yen to the dollar, stays high and auto demand remains weak, most company watchers expect Toyota to post an even bigger loss in the financial year that ends in March 2010. Yasuhiro Matsumoto, an analyst at Shinsei Securities in Tokyo, reckons Toyota's net loss could swell to $11 billion. "I don't think Toyota's proposed labor cut in the U.S. would be sufficient for the company to restore its profitability, but it is better than doing nothing," he says. "In 2009 there will be no winners in the global auto industry."

Source: Ian Rowley, "Toyota Takes the Knife to U.S. Labor Costs," *BusinessWeek*, February 13, 2009.

Introduction

LOI
List the main decision areas and concepts in employee compensation management.

From the employer's point of view, pay is a powerful tool for furthering the organization's strategic goals. First, pay has a large impact on employee attitudes and behaviors. It influences the kind of employees who are attracted to (and remain with) the organization, and it can be a powerful tool for aligning current employees' interests with those of the broader organization. Second, employee compensation is typically a significant organizational cost and thus requires close scrutiny. As Table 11.1 shows, total compensation (cash and benefits) averages 22 percent of revenues and varies

	PERCENTILE		
INDUSTRY	**25TH**	**50TH**	**75TH**
Hospitals/health care	43%	46%	49%
Manufacturing	22	27	34
Insurance/health care	6	8	11
All industries	13	22	32

table 11.1
Total Compensation as a Percentage of Revenues

SOURCES: Data from Saratoga Institute, *Human Capital Benchmarking Report 2000* and Saratoga/PricewaterhouseCoopers, *Key Trends in Human Capital: A Global Perspective, 2006.*

both within and across industries. In the chapter opener, Toyota's goal is to reduce its labor costs, without jeopardizing its relationship with its workforce. It also wants to have an efficient workforce in place and ready to go when the demand for its cars picks up again.

From the employees' point of view, policies having to do with wages, salaries, and other earnings affect their overall income and thus their standard of living. Both the level of pay and its seeming fairness compared with others' pay are important. Pay is also often considered a sign of status and success. Employees attach great importance to pay decisions when they evaluate their relationship with the organization. Therefore, pay decisions must be carefully managed and communicated.

Pay decisions can be broken into two areas: pay structure and individual pay. In this chapter we focus on **pay structure,** which in turn entails a consideration of pay level and job structure. **Pay level** is defined here as the average pay (including wages, salaries, and bonuses) of jobs in an organization. (Benefits could also be included, but these are discussed separately in Chapter 13.) **Job structure** refers to the relative pay of jobs in an organization. Consider the same two jobs in two different organizations. In Organization 1, jobs A and B are paid an annual average compensation of $40,000 and $60,000, respectively. In Organization 2, the pay rates are $45,000 and $55,000, respectively. Organizations 1 and 2 have the same pay level ($50,000), but the job structures (relative rates of pay) differ.

Both pay level and job structure are characteristics of organizations and reflect decisions about jobs rather than about individual employees. This chapter's focus is on why and how organizations attach pay policies to jobs. In the next chapter we look within jobs to discuss the different approaches that can determine the pay of individual employees as well as the advantages and disadvantages of these different approaches.

Why is the focus on jobs in developing a pay structure? As the number of employees in an organization increases, so too does the number of human resource management decisions. In determining compensation, for example, each employee must be assigned a rate of pay that is acceptable in terms of external, internal, and individual equity (defined later) and in terms of the employer's cost. Although each employee is unique and thus requires some degree of individualized treatment, standardizing the treatment of similar employees (those with similar jobs) can help greatly to make compensation administration and decision making more manageable and more equitable. Thus pay policies are often attached to particular jobs rather than tailored entirely to individual employees.

Pay Structure
The relative pay of different jobs (job structure) and how much they are paid (pay level).

Pay Level
The average pay, including wages, salaries, and bonuses, of jobs in an organization.

Job Structure
The relative pay of jobs in an organization.

Equity Theory and Fairness

In discussing the consequences of pay decisions, it is useful to keep in mind that employees often evaluate their pay relative to that of other employees. Equity theory suggests that people evaluate the fairness of their situations by comparing them with those of other people.[1] According to the theory, a person (P) compares her own ratio of perceived outcomes O (pay, benefits, working conditions) to perceived inputs I (effort, ability, experience) to the ratio of a comparison other (o).

$$O_P/I_P <, >, \text{ or } = O_o/I_o?$$

If P's ratio (O_P/I_P) is smaller than the comparison other's ratio (O_o/I_o), underreward inequity results. If P's ratio is larger, overreward inequity results, although evidence suggests that this type of inequity is less likely to occur and less likely to be sustained because P may rationalize the situation by reevaluating her outcomes less favorably or inputs (self-worth) more favorably.[2]

The consequences of P's comparisons depend on whether equity is perceived. If equity is perceived, no change is expected in P's attitudes or behavior. In contrast, perceived inequity may cause P to restore equity. Some ways of restoring equity are counterproductive, including (1) reducing one's own inputs (not working as hard), (2) increasing one's outcomes (such as by theft), (3) leaving the situation that generates perceived inequity (leaving the organization or refusing to work or cooperate with employees who are perceived as overrewarded).

Equity theory's main implication for managing employee compensation is that to an important extent, employees evaluate their pay by comparing it with what others get paid, and their work attitudes and behaviors are influenced by such comparisons. For example, consider the contract that shortstop Alex Rodriquez (now a New York Yankee) signed in 2000 with the Texas Rangers baseball team. One provision stated that during the 2001 to 2004 seasons, his base compensation must be at least $2 million higher than any other shortstop's in major league baseball. A second provision permitted Rodriquez to void seasons after 2008 unless his 2009 and 2010 base compensation was at least $1 million higher than any position player's in major league baseball. Otherwise, Rodriquez would be free to leave his current team. These provisions that pegged Rodriquez's pay to other players' pay is a compelling example of the importance of being paid well in *relative* terms. (We later learned that "A-Rod" felt compelled to break some rules in hopes of helping his on-field performance live up to his pay.)

Another implication is that employee perceptions are what determine their evaluation. The fact that management believes its employees are paid well compared with those of other companies does not necessarily translate into employees' beliefs. Employees may have different information or make different comparisons than management. For example, Toyota recently set a goal to move from using wages in the U.S. auto industry as the standard of comparison to using the (lower) prevailing wages in the state where each plant is located. To do so, however, Toyota recognizes its "challenge will be how to educate team members and managers . . . so they can understand and accept [this] change."

Two types of employee social comparisons of pay are especially relevant in making pay level and job structure decisions. (See Table 11.2.) First, *external equity* pay comparisons focus on what employees in other organizations are paid for doing the same general job. Such comparisons are likely to influence the decisions of applicants to accept job offers as well as the attitudes and decisions of employees about whether

table 11.2

Pay Structure Concepts and Consequences

PAY STRUCTURE DECISION AREA	ADMINISTRATIVE TOOL	FOCUS OF EMPLOYEE PAY COMPARISONS	CONSEQUENCES OF EQUITY PERCEPTIONS
Pay level	Market pay surveys	External equity	External employee movement (attraction and retention of quality employees); labor costs; employee attitudes
Job structure	Job evaluation	Internal equity	Internal employee movement (promotion, transfer, job rotation); cooperation among employees; employee attitudes

to stay with an organization or take a job elsewhere. (See Chapters 5 and 10.) The organization's choice of pay level influences its employees' external pay comparisons and their consequences. A market pay survey is the primary administrative tool organizations use in choosing a pay level.

Second, *internal equity* pay comparisons focus on what employees within the same organization, but in different jobs, are paid. Employees make comparisons with lower-level jobs, jobs at the same level (but perhaps in different skill areas or product divisions), and jobs at higher levels. These comparisons may influence general attitudes of employees; their willingness to transfer to other jobs within the organization; their willingness to accept promotions; their inclination to cooperate across jobs, functional areas, or product groups; and their commitment to the organization. The organization's choice of job structure influences its employees' internal comparisons and their consequences. Job evaluation is the administrative tool organizations use to design job structures.

In addition, employees make internal equity pay comparisons with others performing the same job. Such comparisons are most relevant to the following chapter, which focuses on using pay to recognize individual contributions and differences.

We now turn to ways to choose and develop pay levels and pay structures, the consequences of such choices, and the ways two administrative tools—market pay surveys and job evaluation—help in making pay decisions.

Developing Pay Levels

Market Pressures

Any organization faces two important competitive market challenges in deciding what to pay its employees: product market competition and labor market competition.

LO2
Describe the major administrative tools used to manage employee compensation.

Product Market Competition

First, organizations must compete effectively in the product market. In other words, they must be able to sell their goods and services at a quantity and price that will bring a sufficient return on their investment. Organizations compete on multiple dimensions (quality, service, and so on), and price is one of the most important dimensions. An important influence on price is the cost of production.

An organization that has higher labor costs than its product market competitors will have to charge higher average prices for products of similar quality. Thus, for example, if labor costs are 30 percent of revenues at Company A and Company B, but Company A has labor costs that are 20 percent higher than those of Company B, we would expect Company A to have product prices that are higher by $(0.30 \times 0.20) = 6$ percent. At some point, the higher price charged by Company A will contribute to a loss of its business to competing companies with lower prices (like Company B). In the automobile industry, labor-related expenses per vehicle (including retiree and active worker benefits such as health care) recently averaged $606 higher for the Big Three (General Motors, Ford, Chrysler) than for Japanese producers in the United States, Toyota, Nissan, and Honda. This labor cost advantage is a major factor in the pre-tax profit advantage per vehicle of $2,271 that these Japanese producers held over the Big Three.[3] Recently, however, U.S. producers have negotiated changes with their workers to improve competitiveness. For example, a new Ford agreement with the United Auto Workers (UAW) is expected to reduce hourly labor costs from $60 to $55 per hour immediately and perhaps down to $50 by 2011. Japanese and European producers in the United States are thought to be currently in the $48 to $49 range. GM has negotiated a similar deal with the UAW.[4]

Therefore, *product market competition* places an *upper bound* on labor costs and compensation. This upper bound is more constrictive when labor costs are a larger share of total costs and when demand for the product is affected by changes in price (i.e., when demand is *elastic*). Although costs are only one part of the competitive equation (productivity is just as important), higher costs may result in a loss of business. In the absence of clear evidence on productivity differences, costs need to be closely monitored.

What components make up labor costs? A major component is the average cost per employee. This is made up of both direct payments (such as wages, salaries, and bonuses) and indirect payments (such as health insurance, Social Security, and unemployment compensation). A second component of labor cost is the staffing level (number of employees). Not surprisingly, financially troubled organizations often seek to cut costs by focusing on one or both components. Staff reductions, hiring freezes, wage and salary freezes, and sharing benefits costs with employees are several ways of enhancing the organization's competitive position in the product market.

Labor Market Competition

A second important competitive market challenge is *labor market competition*. Essentially, labor market competition is the amount an organization must pay to compete against other companies that hire similar employees. These labor market competitors typically include not only companies that have similar products but also those in different product markets that hire similar types of employees. If an organization is not competitive in the labor market, it will fail to attract and retain employees of sufficient numbers and quality. For example, even if a computer manufacturer offers newly graduated electrical engineers the same pay as other computer manufacturers, if automobile manufacturers and other labor market competitors offer salaries $5,000 higher, the computer company may not be able to hire enough qualified electrical engineers. Labor market competition places a *lower bound* on pay levels.

Employees as a Resource

Because organizations have to compete in the labor market, they should consider their employees not just as a cost but as a resource in which the organization has invested and from which it expects valuable returns. Although controlling costs directly affects an organization's ability to compete in the product market, the organization's competitive position can be compromised if costs are kept low at the expense of employee productivity and quality. Having higher labor costs than your competitors is not necessarily bad if you also have the best and most effective workforce, one that produces more products of better quality.

Pay policies and programs are one of the most important human resource tools for encouraging desired employee behaviors and discouraging undesired behaviors. Therefore, they must be evaluated not just in terms of costs but in terms of the returns they generate—how they attract, retain, and motivate a high-quality workforce. For example, if the average revenue per employee in Company A is 20 percent higher than in Company B, it may not be important that the average pay in Company A is 10 percent higher than in Company B.

Deciding What to Pay

Although organizations face important external labor and product market pressures in setting their pay levels, a range of discretion remains.[5] How large the range is depends on the particular competitive environment the organization faces. Where the range is broad, an important strategic decision is whether to pay above, at, or below the market average. The advantage of paying above the market average is the ability to attract and retain the top talent available, which can translate into a highly effective and productive workforce. The disadvantage, however, is the added cost.[6]

Under what circumstances do the benefits of higher pay outweigh the higher costs? According to **efficiency wage theory,** one circumstance is when organizations have technologies or structures that depend on highly skilled employees. For example, organizations that emphasize decentralized decision making may need higher-caliber employees. Another circumstance where higher pay may be warranted is when an organization has difficulties observing and monitoring its employees' performance. It may therefore wish to provide an above-market pay rate to ensure the incentive to put forth maximum effort. The theory is that employees who are paid more than they would be paid elsewhere will be reluctant to shirk because they wish to retain their good jobs.[7]

Efficiency Wage Theory
A theory stating that wages influence worker productivity.

Market Pay Surveys

To compete for talent, organizations use **benchmarking,** a procedure in which an organization compares its own practices against those of the competition. In compensation management, benchmarking against product market and labor market competitors is typically accomplished through the use of one or more pay surveys, which provide information on going rates of pay among competing organizations.

The use of pay surveys requires answers to several important questions:[8]

1. Which employers should be included in the survey? Ideally, they would be the key labor market and product market competitors.
2. Which jobs are included in the survey? Because only a sample of jobs is ordinarily used, care must be taken that the jobs are representative in terms of level,

Benchmarking
Comparing an organization's practices against those of the competition.

functional area, and product market. Also, the job content must be sufficiently similar.

3. If multiple surveys are used, how are all the rates of pay weighted and combined? Organizations often have to weight and combine pay rates because different surveys are often tailored toward particular employee groups (labor markets) or product markets. The organization must decide how much relative weight to give to its labor market and product market competitors in setting pay.

Several factors affect decisions on how to combine surveys.[9] Product market comparisons that focus on labor costs are likely to deserve greater weight when (1) labor costs represent a large share of total costs, (2) product demand is elastic (it changes in response to product price changes), (3) the supply of labor is inelastic, and (4) employee skills are specific to the product market (and will remain so). In contrast, labor market comparisons may be more important when (1) attracting and retaining qualified employees is difficult and (2) the costs (administrative, disruption, and so on) of recruiting replacements are high.

As this discussion suggests, knowing what other organizations are paying is only one part of the story. It is also necessary to know what those organizations are getting in return for their investment in employees. To find that out, some organizations examine ratios such as revenues/employees and revenues/labor cost. The first ratio includes the staffing component of employee cost but not the average cost per employee. The second ratio, however, includes both. Note that comparing these ratios across organizations requires caution. For example, different industries rely on different labor and capital resources. So comparing the ratio of revenues to labor costs of a petroleum company (capital intensive, high ratio) to a hospital (labor intensive, low ratio) would be like comparing apples and oranges. But within industries, such comparisons can be useful. Besides revenues, other return-on-investment data might include product quality, customer satisfaction, and potential workforce quality (such as average education and skill levels).

Rate Ranges

As the preceding discussion suggests, obtaining a single "going rate" of market pay is a complex task that involves a number of subjective decisions; it is both an art and a science. Once a market rate has been chosen, how is it incorporated into the pay structure? Typically—especially for white-collar jobs—it is used for setting the midpoint of pay ranges for either jobs or pay grades (discussed next). Market survey data are also often collected on minimum and maximum rates of pay as well. The use of **rate ranges** permits a company to recognize differences in employee performance, seniority, training, and so forth in setting individual pay (discussed in the next chapter). For some blue-collar jobs, however, particularly those covered by collective bargaining contracts, there may be a single rate of pay for all employees within the job.

Rate Ranges
Different employees in the same job may have different pay rates.

Key Jobs and Nonkey Jobs

In using pay surveys, it is necessary to make a distinction between two general types of jobs: key jobs (or benchmark jobs) and nonkey jobs. **Key jobs** have relatively stable content and—perhaps most important—are common to many organizations. Therefore, it is possible to obtain market pay survey data on them. Note, however, that to avoid too much of an administrative burden, organizations may not gather market

Key Jobs
Benchmark jobs, used in pay surveys, that have relatively stable content and are common to many organizations.

pay data on all such jobs. In contrast to key jobs, **nonkey jobs** are, to an important extent, unique to organizations; thus, by definition, they cannot be directly valued or compared through the use of market surveys. Therefore, they are treated differently in the pay-setting process.

Developing a Job Structure

Although external comparisons of the sort we have been discussing are important, employees also evaluate their pay using internal comparisons. So, for example, a vice president of marketing may expect to be paid roughly the same amount as a vice president of information systems because they are at the same organizational level, with similar levels of responsibility and similar impacts on the organization's performance. A job structure can be defined as the relative worth of various jobs in the organization, based on these types of internal comparisons. We now discuss how such decisions are made.

Job Evaluation

One typical way of measuring internal job worth is to use an administrative procedure called **job evaluation.** A job evaluation system is composed of compensable factors and a weighting scheme based on the importance of each **compensable factor** to the organization. Simply stated, compensable factors are the characteristics of jobs that an organization values and chooses to pay for. These characteristics may include job complexity, working conditions, required education, required experience, and responsibility. Most job evaluation systems use several compensable factors. Job analysis (discussed in Chapter 4) provides basic descriptive information on job attributes, and the job evaluation process assigns values to these compensable factors.

Scores can be generated in a variety of ways, but they typically include input from a number of people. A job evaluation committee commonly generates ratings. Although there are numerous ways to evaluate jobs, the most widely used is the point-factor system, which yields job evaluation points for each compensable factor.[10]

The Point-Factor System

After generating scores for each compensable factor on each job, job evaluators often apply a weighting scheme to account for the differing importance of the compensable factors to the organization. Weights can be generated in two ways. First, *a priori* weights can be assigned, which means factors are weighted using expert judgments about the importance of each compensable factor. Second, weights can be derived empirically based on how important each factor seems in determining pay in the labor market. (Statistical methods such as multiple regression can be used for this purpose.) For the sake of simplicity, we assume in the following example that equal a priori weights are chosen, which means that the scores on the compensable factors can be simply summed.

Table 11.3 shows an example of a three-factor job evaluation system applied to three jobs. Note that the jobs differ in the levels of experience, education, and complexity required. Summing the scores on the three compensable factors provides an internally oriented assessment of relative job worth in the organization. In a sense, the computer programmer job is worth 41 percent (155/110 − 1) more than the computer operator

Nonkey Jobs
Jobs that are unique to organizations and that cannot be directly valued or compared through the use of market surveys.

Job Evaluation
An administrative procedure used to measure internal job worth.

Compensable Factors
The characteristics of jobs that an organization values and chooses to pay for.

table 11.3

Example of a
Three-Factor Job
Evaluation System

	COMPENSABLE FACTORS			
JOB TITLE	EXPERIENCE	EDUCATION	COMPLEXITY	TOTAL
Computer operator	40	30	40	110
Computer programmer	40	50	65	155
Systems analyst	65	60	85	210

job, and the systems analyst job is worth 91 percent (210/110 − 1) more than the computer operator job. Whatever pay level is chosen (based on benchmarking and competitive strategy), we would expect the pay differentials to be somewhat similar to these percentages. The internal job evaluation and external survey-based measures of worth can, however, diverge.

Developing a Pay Structure

In the example provided in Table 11.4, there are 15 jobs, 10 of which are key jobs. For these key jobs, both pay survey and job evaluation data are available. For the five nonkey jobs, by definition, no survey data are available, only job evaluation information. Note that, for simplicity's sake, we work with data from only two pay surveys and we use a weighted average that gives twice as much weight to survey 1. Also, our example works with a single structure. Many organizations have multiple structures

table 11.4

Job Evaluation and Pay Survey Data

JOB	KEY JOB?	JOB TITLE	JOB EVALUATION	SURVEY 1 (S1)	SURVEY 2 (S2)	SURVEY COMPOSITE (2/3*S1 + 1/3*S2)
A	y	Computer operator	110	$2,012	$1,731	$1,919
B	y	Engineering tech I	115	2,206	1,908	2,106
C	y	Computer programmer	155	2,916	2,589	2,807
D	n	Engineering tech II	165	—	—	—
E	n	Compensation analyst	170	—	—	—
F	y	Accountant	190	3,613	3,099	3,442
G	y	Systems analyst	210	4,275	3,854	4,134
H	n	Computer programmer—senior	225	—	—	—
I	y	Director of personnel	245	4,982	4,506	4,823
J	y	Accountant—senior	255	5,205	4,270	4,893
K	y	Systems analyst—senior	270	5,868	5,652	5,796
L	y	Industrial engineer	275	5,496	4,794	5,262
M	n	Chief accountant	315	—	—	—
N	y	Senior engineer	320	7,026	6,572	6,875
O	n	Senior scientist	330	—	—	—

SOURCE: Adapted from S. Rynes, B. Gerhart, G.T. Milkovich, and J. Boudreau, *Current Compensation Professional Institute* (Scottsdale, AZ: American Compensation Association, 1988). Reprinted with permission.

that correspond to different job families (like clerical, technical, and professional) or product divisions.

How are the data in Table 11.4 combined to develop a pay structure? First, it is important to note that both internal and external comparisons must be considered in making compensation decisions. However, because the pay structures suggested by internal and external comparisons do not necessarily converge, employers must carefully balance them. Studies suggest that employers may differ significantly in the degree to which they place priority on internal- or external-comparison data in developing pay structures.[11]

At least three pay-setting approaches, which differ according to their relative emphasis on external or internal comparisons, can be identified.[12]

Market Survey Data

The approach with the greatest emphasis on external comparisons (market survey data) is achieved by directly basing pay on market surveys that cover as many key jobs as possible. For example, the rate of pay for job A in Table 11.5 would be $1,919; for job B, $2,106; and for job C, $2,807. For nonkey jobs (jobs D, E, H, M, and O), however, pay survey information is not available, and we must proceed differently. Basically, we develop a market **pay policy line** based on the key jobs (for which there are both job evaluation and market pay survey data available). As Figure 11.1 shows, the data can be plotted with a line of best fit estimated. This line can be generated using a statistical procedure (regression analysis). Doing so yields the equation − $661 + $22.69 × job evaluation points. In other words, the predicted monthly salary (based on fitting a line to the key job data) is obtained by plugging the number

Pay Policy Line
A mathematical expression that describes the relationship between a job's pay and its job evaluation points.

table 11.5

Pay Midpoints under Different Approaches

JOB	KEY JOB?	JOB TITLE	JOB EVALUATION	(1) SURVEY + POLICY	(2) PAY MIDPOINTS POLICY	(3) GRADES
A	y	Computer operator	110	$1,919	$1,835	$2,175
B	y	Engineering tech I	115	2,106	1,948	2,175
C	y	Computer programmer	155	2,807	2,856	3,310
D	n	Engineering tech II	165	3,083	3,083	3,310
E	n	Compensation analyst	170	3,196	3,196	3,310
F	y	Accountant	190	3,442	3,650	3,310
G	y	Systems analyst	210	4,134	4,104	4,444
H	n	Computer programmer—senior	225	4,444	4,444	4,444
I	y	Director of personnel	245	4,823	4,898	4,444
J	y	Accountant—senior	255	4,893	5,125	5,579
K	y	Systems analyst—senior	270	5,796	5,465	5,579
L	y	Industrial engineer	275	5,262	5,579	5,579
M	n	Chief accountant	315	6,486	6,486	6,713
N	y	Senior engineer	320	6,875	6,600	6,713
O	n	Senior scientist	330	6,826	6,826	6,713

SOURCE: Adapted from S. Rynes, B. Gerhart, G. T. Milkovich, and J. Boudreau, *Current Compensation Professional Institute* (Scottsdale, AZ: American Compensation Association, 1988). Reprinted with permission.

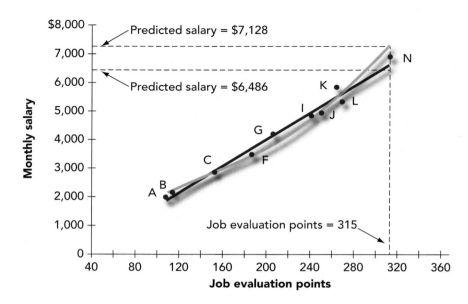

of job evaluation points into this equation. Thus, for example, job D, a nonkey job, would have a predicted monthly salary of −$661 + $22.69 × 165 = $3,083.

As Figure 11.1 also indicates, it is not necessary to fit a straight line to the job evaluation and pay survey data. In some cases, a pay structure that provides increasing monetary rewards to higher-level jobs may be more consistent with the organization's goals or with the external market. For example, nonlinearity may be more appropriate if higher-level jobs are especially valuable to organizations and the talent to perform such jobs is rare. The curvilinear function in Figure 11.1 is described by the equation

$$\text{Natural logarithm of pay} = \$6.98 + (0.006 \times \text{job evaluation points})$$

Pay Policy Line

A second pay-setting approach that combines information from external and internal comparisons is to use the pay policy line to derive pay rates for both key and nonkey jobs. This approach differs from the first approach in that actual market rates are no longer used for key jobs. This introduces a greater degree of internal consistency into the structure because the pay of all the jobs is directly linked to the number of job evaluation points.

Pay Grades

Pay Grades
Jobs of similar worth or content grouped together for pay administration purposes.

A third approach is to group jobs into a smaller number of pay classes or **pay grades.** Table 11.6 (see also Table 11.5, last column), for example, demonstrates one possibility: a five-grade structure. Each job within a grade would have the same rate range (i.e., would be assigned the same midpoint, minimum, and maximum). The advantage of this approach is that the administrative burden of setting separate rates of pay for hundreds (even thousands) of different jobs is reduced. It also permits greater flexibility in moving employees from job to job without raising concerns about, for

table 11.6

Sample Pay Grade Structure

	JOB EVALUATION POINTS RANGE		MONTHLY PAY RATE RANGE		
PAY GRADE	**MINIMUM**	**MAXIMUM**	**MINIMUM**	**MIDPOINT**	**MAXIMUM**
1	100	150	$1,740	$2,175	$2,610
2	150	200	2,648	3,310	3,971
3	200	250	3,555	4,444	5,333
4	250	300	4,463	5,579	6,694
5	300	350	5,370	6,713	8,056

example, going from a job having 230 job evaluation points to a job with 215 job evaluation points. What might look like a demotion in a completely job-based system is often a nonissue in a grade-based system. Note that the **range spread** (the distance between the minimum and maximum) is larger at higher levels, in recognition of the fact that performance differences are likely to have more impact on the organization at higher job levels. (See Figure 11.2.)

Range Spread
The distance between the minimum and maximum amounts in a pay grade.

The disadvantage of using grades is that some jobs will be underpaid and others overpaid. For example, job C and job F both fall within the same grade. The midpoint for job C under a grade system is $3,310 per month, or about $400 or so more than under the two alternative pay-setting approaches. Obviously, this will contribute to higher labor costs and potential difficulties in competing in the product market. Unless there is an expected return to this increased cost, the approach is questionable. Job F, on the other hand, is paid between $130 and $340 less per month under the grades system than it would be otherwise. Therefore, the company may find it more difficult to compete in the labor market.

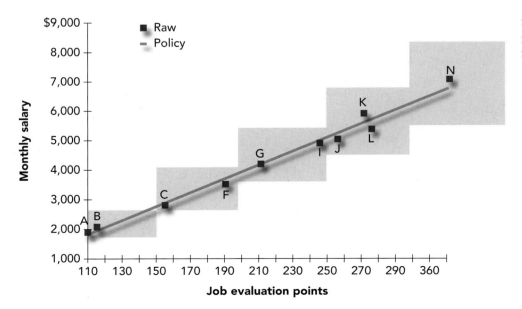

figure 11.2

Sample Pay Grade Structure

L03
Explain the importance of competitive labor market and product market forces in compensation decisions.

Conflicts between Market Pay Surveys and Job Evaluation

An examination of Table 11.5 suggests that the relative worth of jobs is quite similar overall, whether based on job evaluation or pay survey data. However, some inconsistencies typically arise, and these are usually indicated by jobs whose average survey pay is significantly below or above the pay policy line. The closest case in Table 11.5 is job L, for which the average pay falls significantly below the policy line. One possible explanation is that a relatively plentiful supply of people in the labor market are capable of performing this job, so the pay needed to attract and retain them is lower than would be expected given the job evaluation points. Another kind of inconsistency occurs when market surveys show that a job is paid higher than the policy line (like job K). Again, this may reflect relative supply and demand, in this case driving pay higher.

How are conflicts between external and internal equity resolved, and what are the consequences? The example of the vice presidents of marketing and information technology may help illustrate the type of choice faced. The marketing VP job may receive the same number of job evaluation points, but market survey data may indicate that it typically pays less than the information technology VP job, perhaps because of tighter supply for the latter. Does the organization pay based on the market survey (external comparison) or on the job evaluation points (internal comparison)?

Emphasizing the internal comparison would suggest paying the two VPs the same. In doing so, however, either the VP of marketing would be "overpaid" or the VP of information technology would be "underpaid." The former drives up labor costs (product market problems); the latter may make it difficult to attract and retain a quality VP of information technology (labor market problems).

Another consideration has to do with the strategy of the organization. In some organizations (like Pepsi and Nike) the marketing function is critical to success. Thus, even though the market for marketing VPs is lower than that for information technology VPs, an organization may choose to be a pay leader for the marketing position (pay at the 90th percentile, for example) but only meet the market for the information technology position (perhaps pay at the 50th percentile). In other words, designing a pay structure requires careful consideration of which positions are most central to dealing with critical environmental challenges and opportunities in reaching the organization's goals.[13]

What about emphasizing external comparisons? Two potential problems arise. First, the marketing VP may be dissatisfied because she expects a job of similar rank and responsibility to that of the information technology VP to be paid similarly. Second, it becomes difficult to rotate people through different VP positions (for training and development) because going to the marketing VP position might appear as a demotion to the VP of information technology.

There is no one right solution to such dilemmas. Each organization must decide which objectives are most essential and choose the appropriate strategy. However, there seems to be a growing sentiment that external comparisons deserve greater weight because organizations are finding it increasingly difficult to ignore market competitive pressures.

Monitoring Compensation Costs

Pay structure influences compensation costs in a number of ways. Most obviously, the pay level at which the structure is pegged influences these costs. However, this is only part of the story. The pay structure represents the organization's intended policy, but

EMPLOYEE	JOB	PAY	MIDPOINT	EMPLOYEE COMPA-RATIOS
	Grade 1			
1	Engineering tech I	$2,306	$2,175	1.06
2	Computer programmer	2,066	2,175	.95
3	Engineering tech I	2,523	2,175	1.16
4	Engineering tech I	2,414	2,175	1.11
				1.07
	Grade 2			
5	Computer programmer	3,906	3,310	1.18
6	Accountant	3,773	3,310	1.14
7	Accountant	3,674	3,310	1.11
				1.15

table 11.7

Compa-Ratios for Two Grades

actual practice may not coincide with it. Take, for example, the pay grade structure presented earlier. The midpoint for grade 1 is $2,175, and the midpoint for grade 2 is $3,310. Now, consider the data on a group of individual employees in Table 11.7. One frequently used index of the correspondence between actual and intended pay is the **compa-ratio,** computed as follows:

$$\text{Grade compa-ratio} = \text{Actual average pay for grade/Pay midpoint for grade}$$

The compa-ratio directly assesses the degree to which actual pay is consistent with the pay policy. A compa-ratio less than 1.00 suggests that actual pay is lagging behind the policy, whereas a compa-ratio greater than 1.00 indicates that pay (and costs) exceeds that of the policy. Although there may be good reasons for compa-ratios to differ from 1.00, managers should also consider whether the pay structure is allowing costs to get out of control.

Compa-Ratio
An index of the correspondence between actual and intended pay.

Globalization, Geographic Region, and Pay Structures

As Figure 11.3 shows, market pay structures can differ substantially across countries both in terms of their level and in terms of the relative worth of jobs. Compared with the labor markets in Germany and the United States, markets in Slovakia and Korea provide much lower levels of pay overall and much lower payoffs to skill, education, and advancement. These differences create a dilemma for global companies. For example, should a German engineer posted to Korea be paid according to the standard in Germany or Korea? If the Germany standard is used, a sense of inequity is likely to exist among peers in Korea. If the Korea market standard is used, it may be all but impossible to find a German engineer willing to accept an assignment in Korea. Typically, expatriate pay and benefits (like housing allowance and tax equalization) continue to be linked more closely to the home country. However, this link appears to be slowly weakening and now depends more on the nature and length of the assignment.[14]

Within the United States, Runzheimer International reports that 56 percent of companies have either a formal (30 percent) or informal (26 percent) policy that

● Geographic location is an important factor for Human Resources to consider when establishing a pay structure. Living in New York City is more expensive than other places, and employers need to factor in living costs when deciding upon salaries in order to hire a strong workforce.

provides for pay differentials based on geographic location.[15] These differentials are intended to prevent inequitable treatment of employees who work in more expensive parts of the country. For example, according to Salary.com the cost of living index for New York City is 68 percent higher than in Madison, Wisconsin. Therefore, an

figure 11.3

Earnings in Selected Occupations in Four Countries

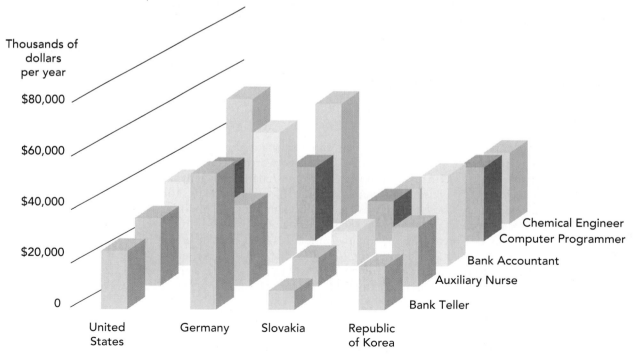

SOURCE: International Labor Organization Web site, at http://laborsta.ilo.org, accessed February 16, 2009. Earnings converted to U.S. dollars using 2008 year-end exchange rates.

employee receiving annual pay of $50,000 in Madison would require annual pay of more than $84,128 in New York City to retain the same purchasing power. The most common approach (74 percent of companies) is to move an employee higher in the pay structure to compensate for higher living costs. However, the drawback of this approach is that it may be difficult to adjust the salary downward if costs in that location fall or the employee moves to a lower-cost area. Thus, 22 percent of the companies choose to pay an ongoing supplement that changes or disappears in the event of such changes.

EVIDENCE-BASED HR

Wal-Mart's legendary obsession with cost containment shows up in countless ways, including aggressive control of employee benefits and wages. Managing labor costs isn't a crazy idea, of course. But stingy pay and benefits don't necessarily translate into lower costs in the long run.

Consider Costco and Wal-Mart's Sam's Club, which compete fiercely on low-price merchandise. Among warehouse retailers, Costco—with 338 stores and 67,600 full-time employees in the United States—is number one, accounting for about 50 percent of the market. Sam's Club—with 551 stores and 110,200 employees in the United States—is number two, with about 40 percent of the market.

Although the businesses are direct competitors and quite similar overall, a remarkable disparity shows up in their wage and benefits structures. The average wage at Costco is $17 an hour. Wal-Mart does not break out the pay of its Sam's Club workers, but a full-time worker at Wal-Mart makes $10.11 an hour on average, and a variety of sources suggest that Sam's Club's pay scale is similar to Wal-Mart's. A 2005 *New York Times* article by Steven Greenhouse reported that at $17 an hour, Costco's average pay is 42 percent higher than Sam's Club's ($9.86 an hour). Interviews that a colleague and I conducted with a dozen Sam's Club employees in San Francisco and Denver put the average hourly wage at about $10. And a 2004 *BusinessWeek* article by Stanley Holmes and Wendy Zellner estimated Sam's Club's average hourly wage at $11.52.

On the benefits side, 82 percent of Costco employees have health insurance coverage, compared with less than half at Wal-Mart. And Costco workers pay just 8 percent of their health premiums, whereas Wal-Mart workers pay 33 percent of theirs. Ninety-one percent of Costco's employees are covered by retirement plans, with the company contributing an annual average of $1,330 per employee, while 64 percent of employees at Sam's Club are covered, with the company contributing an annual average of $747 per employee.

Costco's practices are clearly more expensive, and Wall Street has been known to complain that Costco cares more about its employees (and customers) than it does about its shareholders. But they have an offsetting cost-containment effect: turnover is unusually low, at 17 percent overall and just 6 percent after one year's employment. In contrast, turnover at Wal-Mart is 44 percent a year—close to the industry average. In skilled and semiskilled jobs, the fully loaded cost of replacing a worker who leaves (excluding lost productivity) is typically 1.5 to 2.5 times the worker's annual salary. To be conservative, let's assume that the total cost of replacing an hourly employee at Costco or Sam's Club is only 60 percent of his or her annual salary. If a Costco employee quits, the cost of replacing him or her is therefore $21,216. If a Sam's Club employee leaves, the cost is $12,617. At first glance, it may seem that the low-wage approach at Sam's Club would result in lower turnover costs. But if its turnover rate is the same as Wal-Mart's, Sam's Club loses more than twice as many people as Costco does: 44 percent versus 17 percent. *By this calculation*, the total annual cost to Costco of employee churn is $244 million, whereas the total annual cost to Sam's Club is $612 million. That's $5,274 per Sam's Club employee, versus $3,628 per Costco employee.

In return for its generous wages and benefits, Costco gets one of the most loyal and productive workforces in all of retailing—and, probably not coincidentally, the lowest shrinkage (employee theft) figures in the industry. While Sam's Club and Costco generated $37 billion and $43 billion, respectively, in U.S. sales last year, Costco did it with 38 percent fewer employees—admittedly, in part by selling to higher-income shoppers and offering more high-end goods. As a result, Costco generated $21,805 in U.S. operating profit per hourly employee, compared with $11,615 at Sam's Club. Costco's stable, productive workforce more than offsets its higher costs.

These figures challenge the common assumption that labor rates equal labor costs. Costco's approach shows that when it comes to wages and benefits, a cost-leadership strategy need not be a race to the bottom.

SOURCES: W. F. Cascio, "The High Cost of Low Wages," *Harvard Business Review* 84 (December 2006), p. 23; J. Chu and K. Rockwood, "CEO Interview: Costco's Jim Sinegal, *Fast Company*, October 13, 2008.

The Importance of Process: Participation and Communication

LO4
Discuss the significance of process issues such as communication in compensation management.

Compensation management has been criticized for following the simplistic belief that "if the right technology can be developed, the right answers will be found."[16] In reality, however, any given pay decision is rarely obvious to the diverse groups that make up organizations, regardless of the decision's technical merit or basis in theory. Of course, it is important when changing pay practices to decide which program or combination of programs makes most sense, but how such decisions are made and how they are communicated also matter.[17]

Participation

Employee participation in compensation decision making can take many forms. For example, employees may serve on task forces charged with recommending and designing a pay program. They may also be asked to help communicate and explain its rationale. This is particularly true in the case of job evaluation as well as many of the programs discussed in the next chapter. To date, for what are perhaps obvious reasons, employee participation in pay level decisions remains fairly rare.

It is important to distinguish between participation by those affected by policies and those who must actually implement the policies. Managers are in the latter group (and often in the former group at the same time). As in other areas of human resource management, line managers are typically responsible for making policies work. Their intimate involvement in any change to existing pay practices is, of course, necessary.

Communication

A dramatic example of the importance of communication was found in a study of how an organization communicated pay cuts to its employees and the effects on theft rates and perceived equity.[18] Two organization units received 15 percent across-the-board pay cuts. A third unit received no pay cut and served as a control group. The reasons for the pay cuts were communicated in different ways to the two pay-cut groups. In the "adequate explanation" pay-cut group, management provided a significant amount of information to explain its reasons for the pay cut and also expressed significant remorse. In contrast, the "inadequate explanation" group received much less information and no indication of remorse. The control group received no pay cut (and thus no explanation).

The control group and the two pay-cut groups began with the same theft rates and equity perceptions. After the pay cut, the theft rate was 54 percent higher in the "adequate explanation" group than in the control group. But in the "inadequate explanation" condition, the theft rate was 141 percent higher than in the control group. In this case communication had a large, independent effect on employees' attitudes and behaviors.

Communication is likely to have other important effects. We know, for example, as emphasized by equity theory that not only actual pay but the comparison standard influences employee attitudes.[19] Under two-tier wage plans, employees doing the same jobs are paid two different rates, depending on when they were hired. Moreover, the lower-paid employees do not necessarily move into the higher-paying tier. Common sense might suggest that the lower-paid employees would be less satisfied, but this is not necessarily true. In fact, a study by Peter Cappelli and Peter Sherer found that the lower-paid employees were more satisfied on average.[20] Apparently, those in the lower tier used different (lower) comparison standards than those in the higher tier. The lower-tier employees compared their jobs with unemployment or lower-paying jobs they had managed to avoid. As a result, they were more satisfied, despite being paid less money for the same work. This finding does not mean that two-tier wage plans are likely to be embraced by an organization's workforce. It does, however, support equity theory through its focus on the way employees compare their pay with other jobs and the need for managers to take this into consideration. Employees increasingly have access to salary survey information, which is likely to result in more comparisons and thus a greater need for effective communication. See the "Competing through Technology" Box.

Managers play the most crucial communication role because of their day-to-day interactions with their employees. Therefore, they must be prepared to explain why the pay structure is designed as it is and to judge whether employee concerns about the structure need to be addressed with changes to the structure. One common issue is deciding when a job needs to be reclassified because of substantial changes in its content. If an employee takes on more responsibility, she will often ask the manager for assistance in making the case for increased pay for the job.

Current Challenges

Problems with Job-Based Pay Structures

LO5
Describe new developments in the design of pay structures.

The approach taken in this chapter, that of defining pay structures in terms of jobs and their associated responsibilities, remains the most widely used in practice. However, job-based pay structures have a number of potential limitations.[21] First, they may encourage bureaucracy. The job description sets out specific tasks and activities for which the incumbent is responsible and, by implication, those for which the incumbent is not responsible. Although this facilitates performance evaluation and control by the manager, it can also encourage a lack of flexibility and a lack of initiative on the

Popular real-estate Web site Zillow.com offers a glimpse of what your friends' and neighbors' homes may be worth. Now, Zillow founder Rich Barton plans to pull back the curtain on another cache of data that many people like to keep quiet: employee salaries.

He is launching a job-and-career site, Glassdoor.com, that includes compensation figures for jobs at specific companies, as well as reviews provided anonymously by employees. So far, the site has gathered about 2,000 salary reports and 1,300 employee-written reviews for more than 250 companies, many of them in the high-tech and financial industries.

Glassdoor, which opens with a test version of its service Wednesday, could provide a new window into the pay and other practices of big companies—and give employees leverage in salary negotiations, analysts and corporate executives say.

Though some company executives may wince at seeing Glassdoor's unfiltered, raw information, "it could be good for our company," said Ken Klein, chief executive of Alameda, Calif.,

software maker Wind River Systems Inc., which has about 1,500 employees and has been reviewed by two employees on Glassdoor. Mr. Klein said two job salaries posted on the site— $100,000 a year for a "systems administration architect" and $135,000 for a "senior member of the technical staff"—seemed accurate. He also said the accompanying reviews, which were generally positive, were "thoughtful."

Glassdoor includes information on jobs at some of the nation's most high-profile employers. The average salary of a product manager at Google Inc., for example, is

reported to be $129,400; software engineers earn just shy of $98,000. A Google spokeswoman declined to comment, except to say the company's salaries are competitive.

Glassdoor's information is only as good as the accuracy and quantity of employee submissions. So far, just 10 software engineers and two product managers have shared salary data for Google. Glassdoor's Mr. Barton, a former Microsoft Corp. executive who started online-travel company Expedia Inc. before founding Zillow, said the quality of the data will improve as more people contribute to the site.

The War for Software Engineering Talent

Zillow faced early criticism over the accuracy of its home-value estimates; the company has encouraged homeowners to help improve its estimates by offering updated information on their homes.

Reviews and salary figures submitted to Glassdoor are examined by a five-person research department that sometimes contacts employees seeking additional information. The company uses technology to flag suspicious submissions, such as multiple reviews sent in from the same computer. Still, Glassdoor largely relies on the honesty of submitters, and doesn't attempt to verify data directly with companies, at least not yet.

So far, data on the site come from employees the company sought out through phone and online surveys. Glassdoor said it expects more submissions to come directly from employees when the site becomes better known.

Glassdoor's service is free, but visitors have to first submit a company review or salary data in order to browse what others have written. As a teaser, Glassdoor is offering free access to salary data and company reviews for Google, Yahoo Inc., Microsoft and Cisco Systems Inc.

. . .

For now, Glassdoor expects to make money by selling online advertising. Glassdoor won't allow users to apply for particular jobs, though the company said it could work with recruiters in the future. The site may also aim to help employers conduct employee surveys.

The company enters a crowded field. Job-related Web sites such as Jobster Inc. and one run by Vault.com Inc., contain information about and reviews of companies. Others, such as Salary.com, offer some free compensation data, though information is generally for job descriptions in specific ZIP codes and not for specific companies.

Glassdoor differs from many of its competitors because "it's not a recruitment site," so a "company can't threaten to not list jobs there if they see bad things," says Henry Harteveldt, an e-business analyst with Forrester Research in San Francisco.

SOURCE: Rebecca Buckman, "What Do You Make? Job Site Promises Peek at Salaries," *The Wall Street Journal*, June 11, 2008, p. B6. Copyright © 2008 by Dow Jones & Co., Inc. Reproduced with permission of Dow Jones & Co., Inc. via Copyright Clearance Center.

part of employees: "Why should I do that? It's not in my job description." Second, the structure's hierarchical nature reinforces a top-down decision making and information flow as well as status differentials, which do not lend themselves to taking advantage of the skills and knowledge of those closest to production. Third, the bureaucracy required to generate and update job descriptions and job evaluations can become a barrier to change because wholesale changes to job descriptions can involve a tremendous amount of time and cost. Fourth, the job-based pay structure may not reward desired behaviors, particularly in a rapidly changing environment where the knowledge, skills, and abilities needed yesterday may not be very helpful today and tomorrow. Fifth, the emphasis on job levels and status differentials encourages promotion-seeking behavior but may discourage lateral employee movement because employees are reluctant to accept jobs that are not promotions or that appear to be steps down.

Responses to Problems with Job-Based Pay Structures

Delayering and Banding

In response to the problems caused by job-based pay structures, some organizations are **delayering,** or reducing the number of job levels to achieve more flexibility in job assignments and in assigning merit increases. Pratt and Whitney, for example,

Delayering
Reducing the number of job levels within an organization.

table 11.8

Example of Pay
Bands

TRADITIONAL STRUCTURE		BANDED STRUCTURE	
GRADE	TITLE	BAND	TITLE
14	Senior accountant	6	Senior accountant
12	Accountant III		
10	Accountant II	5	Accountant
8	Accountant I		

SOURCE: P. LeBlanc, *Perspectives in Total Compensation 2*, no. 3 (March 1992), pp. 1–6. Used with permission of the National Practice Director, Sibson & Company, Inc.

changed from 11 pay grades and 3,000 job descriptions for entry-level through middle-management positions to 6 pay grades and several hundred job descriptions.[22] These broader groupings of jobs are also known as *broad bands*. Table 11.8 shows how banding might work for a small sample of jobs. IBM's change to broad bands was accompanied by a change away from a point-factor job evaluation system to a more streamlined approach to evaluating jobs, as Figure 11.4 shows.

At the same time, IBM greatly reduced the bureaucratic nature of the system, going from 5,000 job titles and 24 salary grades to a simpler 1,200 jobs and 10 bands. Within their broad bands, managers were given more discretion to reward high performers and to choose pay levels that were competitive in the market for talent.

One possible disadvantage of delayering and banding is a reduced opportunity for promotion. Therefore, organizations need to consider what they will offer employees instead. In addition, to the extent that there are separate ranges within bands, the new structure may not represent as dramatic a change as it might appear. These distinctions can easily become just as entrenched as they were under the old system. Broad bands, with their greater spread between pay minimums and maximums, can also lead to weaker budgetary control and rising labor costs. Alternatively, the greater spread can permit managers to better recognize high performers with high pay. It can also permit the organization to reward employees for learning.

Paying the Person: Pay for Skill, Knowledge, and Competency

A second, related response to job-based pay structure problems has been to move away from linking pay to jobs and toward building structures based on individual characteristics such as skill or knowledge.[23] Competency-based pay is similar but usually refers to a plan that covers exempt employees (such as managers). The basic idea is that if you want employees to learn more skills and become more flexible in the jobs they perform, you should pay them to do it. (See Chapter 7 for a discussion of the implications of skill-based pay systems on training.) According to Gerald Ledford, however, it is "a fundamental departure" because employees are now "paid for the skills they are capable of using, not for the job they are performing at a particular point in time."[24]

Skill-Based Pay
Pay based on the skills employees acquire and are capable of using.

Skill-based pay systems seem to fit well with the increased breadth and depth of skill that changing technology continues to bring.[25] For example, in a production environment, workers might be expected not only to operate machines but also to take responsibility for maintenance and troubleshooting, quality control, even modifying computer programs.[26] Toyota concluded years ago that "none of the specialists

figure 11.4

IBM's New Job Evaluation Approach

Below is an abbreviated schematic illustration of the new—and simple—IBM job evaluation approach:

POSITION REFERENCE GUIDE

Band	Skills required	Leadership/Contribution	Scope/Impact
1			
2			
3			
4			
5			
6			
7			
8			
9			
10			

Factors: Leadership/Contribution

Band 06: Understand the mission of the professional group and vision in own area of competence.

Band 07: Understand the departmental mission and vision.

Band 08: Understand departmental/functional mission and vision.

Band 09: Has vision of functional or unit mission.

Band 10: Has vision of overall strategies.

Both the bands and the approach are global. In the U.S., bands 1–5 are nonexempt; bands 6–10 are exempt. Each cell in the table contains descriptive language about key job characteristics. Position descriptions are compared to the chart and assigned to bands on a "best fit" basis. There are no points or scoring mechanisms. Managers assign employees to bands by selecting a position description that most closely resembles the work being done by an employee using an online position description library.

That's it!

SOURCE: A. S. Richter, "Paying the People in Black at Big Blue," *Compensation and Benefits Review,* May–June 1998, pp. 51–59. Copyright © 1998 by Sage Publications, Inc. Reprinted with permission of Sage Publications, Inc.

[e.g., quality inspectors, many managers, and foremen] beyond the assembly worker was actually adding any value to the car. What's more . . . assembly workers could probably do most of the functions of specialists much better because of their direct acquaintance with conditions on the line."[27]

In other words, an important potential advantage of skill-based pay is its contribution to increased worker flexibility, which in turn facilitates the decentralization of decision making to those who are most knowledgeable. It also provides the opportunity for leaner staffing levels because employee turnover or absenteeism can now be covered by current employees who are multiskilled.[28] In addition, multiskilled employees are important in cases where different products require different manufacturing processes or where supply shortages or other problems call for adaptive or flexible responses—characteristics typical, for example, of many newer so-called advanced manufacturing environments (like flexible manufacturing and just-in-time systems).[29] More generally, it has been suggested that skill-based plans also contribute to a climate of learning and adaptability and give employees a broader view of how the organization functions. Both changes should contribute to better use of employees' know-how and ideas. Consistent with the advantages just noted, a field study found that a change to a skill-based plan led to better quality and lower labor costs in a manufacturing plant.[30]

Of course, skill-based and competency-based approaches also have potential disadvantages.[31] First, although the plan will likely enhance skill acquisition, the organization may find it a challenge to use the new skills effectively. Without careful planning, it may find itself with large new labor costs but little payoff. In other words, if skills change, work design must change as quickly to take full advantage. Second, if pay growth is based entirely on skills, problems may arise if employees "top out" by acquiring all the skills too quickly, leaving no room for further pay growth. (Of course, this problem can also afflict job-based systems.) Third, and somewhat ironically, skill-based plans may generate a large bureaucracy—usually a criticism of job-based systems. Training programs need to be developed. Skills must be described, measured, and assigned monetary values. Certification tests must be developed to determine whether an employee has acquired a certain skill. Finally, as if the challenges in obtaining market rates under a job-based system were not enough, there is almost no body of knowledge regarding how to price combinations of skills (versus jobs) in the marketplace. Obtaining comparison data from other organizations will be difficult until skill-based plans become more widely used.

Can the U.S. Labor Force Compete?

LO6
Explain where the United States stands from an international perspective on pay issues.

We often hear that U.S. labor costs are simply too high to allow U.S. companies to compete effectively with companies in other countries. The average hourly labor costs (cash and benefits) for manufacturing production workers in the United States and in other advanced industrialized and newly industrialized countries are given in the following table in U.S. dollars:[32]

	1985	1990	1995	2000	2005	2007
Industrialized						
United States	$13.01	$14.77	$17.19	$19.76	$23.65	$24.59
Canada	10.95	15.95	16.10	16.04	23.82	28.91
Czech Republic				2.83	6.11	8.20
Germany[a]	9.57	21.53	30.26	23.38	33.00	37.66
France	7.52	15.49	20.01	15.70	24.63	28.57
Japan	6.43	12.64	23.82	22.27	21.76	19.75
Newly industrialized						
Mexico	1.60	1.80	1.51	2.08	2.63	2.92
Hong Kong[b]	1.73	3.20	4.82	5.63	5.65	5.78
South Korea	1.25	3.82	7.29	8.19	13.56	16.02
China					0.62[c]	0.81

[a]West Germany for 1985 and 1990 data.
[b]Special Administrative Region of China.
[c]2006

Based solely on a cost approach, it would perhaps make sense to try to shift many types of production from a country like Germany to other countries, particularly the newly industrialized countries. Would this be a good idea? Not necessarily. There are several factors to consider.

Instability of Country Differences in Labor Costs

First, note that relative labor costs are very unstable over time. For example, in 1985, U.S. labor costs were (13.01/9.57) or 36 percent greater than those of (West) Germany. But by 1990, the situation was reversed, with (West) German labor costs exceeding those of the United States by (21.53/14.77), or 46 percent, and remaining higher. Did German employers suddenly become more generous while U.S. employers clamped down on pay growth? Not exactly. Because all our figures are expressed in U.S. dollars, currency exchange rates influence such comparisons, and these exchange rates often fluctuate significantly from year to year. For example, in 1985, when German labor costs were 74 percent of those in the United States, the U.S. dollar was worth 2.94 German marks. But in 1990 the U.S. dollar was worth 1.62 German marks. If the exchange rate in 1990 were still 1 to 2.94, the average German hourly wage in U.S. dollars would have been $11.80, or about 80 percent of the U.S. average. In any event, relative to countries like Germany, U.S. labor costs are now a bargain; this explains, in part, decisions by BMW and Mercedes-Benz to locate production facilities in South Carolina and Alabama, respectively, where labor costs are lower than Germany's by a substantial amount (30 percent). The euro, Germany's current currency, rose from €1 = US$.89 at the end of 2001 to €1 = US$1.47 by the end of 2007, reinforcing the rising labor cost in Germany relative to the United States (when expressed in U.S. dollars).

Skill Levels

Second, the quality and productivity of national labor forces can vary dramatically. This is an especially important consideration in comparisons between labor costs in industrialized countries like the United States and developing countries like Mexico. For example, the high school graduation rate in the United States is 88 percent versus 25 percent in Mexico.[33] Thus, lower labor costs may reflect the lower average skill level of the workforce; certain types of skilled labor may be less available in low–labor-cost countries. On the other hand, any given company needs only enough skilled employees for its own operations. Some companies have found that low labor costs do not necessarily preclude high quality.

Productivity

Third, and most directly relevant, are data on comparative productivity and unit labor costs, essentially meaning labor cost per hour divided by productivity per hour worked. One indicator of productivity is gross domestic product (or total output of the economy) per person, adjusted for differences in purchasing power. On this measure, the United States fares well. These figures (in U.S. dollars) for 2007 are represented in Figure 11.5. The combination of lower labor costs and higher productivity translates into lower unit labor costs in the United States than in Japan and western Europe.[34]

figure 11.5

Gross Domestic
Product per Person,
2007

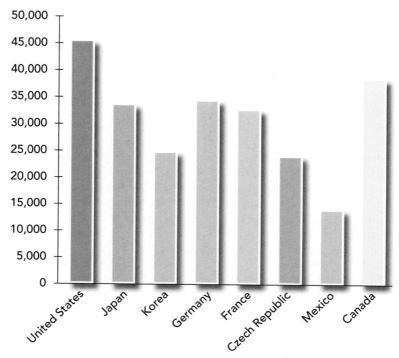

SOURCE: Annual National Accounts, www.oecd.org.

Nonlabor Considerations

Fourth, any consideration of where to locate production cannot be based on labor considerations alone. For example, although the average hourly labor cost in Country A may be $15 versus $10 in Country B, if labor costs are 30 percent of total operating costs and nonlabor operating costs are roughly the same, then the total operating costs might be $65 (50 + 15) in Country A and $60 (50 + 10) in Country B. Although labor costs in Country B are 33 percent less, total operating costs are only 7.7 percent less. This may not be enough to compensate for differences in skills and productivity, customer wait time, transportation costs, taxes, and so on. Further, the direct labor component of many products, particularly high-tech products (such as electronic components), may often be 5 percent or less. Thus the effect on product price-competitiveness may be insignificant.[35]

In fact, an increasing number of organizations have decided that it is more important to focus on nonlabor factors in deciding where to locate production. Product development speed may be greater when manufacturing is physically close to the design group. Quick response to customers (like making a custom replacement product) is difficult when production facilities are on the other side of the world. Inventory levels can be dramatically reduced through the use of manufacturing methods like just-in-time production, but suppliers need to be in close physical proximity.

On the other hand, as the "Competing through Globalization" box indicates, some firms are aggressively offshoring jobs (including professional or knowledge worker jobs) primarily to reduce labor costs.

On the top floor of a seven-story building in this dusty aspiring metropolis, Copal Partners churns out equity, fixed-income and trading research for big name analysts and banks. It is a long way from the well-cooled corridors of Wall Street, and quarters are tight; business is up about 40 percent this year alone.

. . .

The banks edit and add to what they get from Copal, a research provider, then repackage the information under their own names as research reports, pitch books and trading recommendations.

Wall Street's losses are fast becoming India's gain. After outsourcing much of their back-office work to India, banks are now exporting data-intensive jobs from higher up the food chain to cities that cost less than New York, London and Hong Kong, either at their own offices or to third parties.

Bank executives call this shift "knowledge process outsourcing," "offshoring" or "high-value outsourcing." It is affecting just about everyone, including Goldman Sachs, Morgan Stanley, JPMorgan, Credit Suisse, and Citibank—to name a few.

The jobs most affected so far are those with grueling hours, traditionally done by fresh-faced business school graduates—research associates and junior bankers on deal-making teams—paid in the low to mid six figures.

Cost-cutting in New York and London has already been brutal thus far this year, and there is more to come in the next few months. New York City financial firms expect to hand out some $18 billion less in pay and benefits this year than 2007, the largest one-year drop ever. Overall, United States banks will cut 200,000 employees by 2009, the banking consultancy Celent said in April.

The work these bankers were doing is not necessarily going away, though. Instead, jobs are popping up in places like India and Eastern Europe, often where healthier local markets exist.

In addition to moving some lower-level banking and research positions to support bankers and analysts in New York and London, firms are shipping some of their top bankers from those cities to faster-growing developing markets to handle clients there.

Owing in part to credit weaknesses and billion-dollar charges from the subprime crisis, "people who were off-shoring high value jobs are increasing the intensity of that, and people who were not are now in the planning stage," said Andrew Power, a financial services partner at Deloitte Consulting.

Wall Street banks started cautiously sending research jobs to India a few years ago, hiring employees by the handful and running pilot programs with firms like Copal, Office Tiger, Pipal Research and Tata Consultancy Services.

. . .

[The trickle is now a flood.] Third-party firms say they are seeing a 20 to 40 percent upswing in business this year alone.

Morgan Stanley has about 500 people employed in India doing research and statistical analysis. About 100 of Goldman Sachs' 3,000 employees in Bangalore are working on investment research.

JPMorgan has 200 analysts in Mumbai working for its investment banking operations around the world, doing industry analysis, and compiling data and charts for marketing materials. It has an additional 125 analysts in Mumbai supporting the bank's global research division.

Citigroup employs about 22,000 people in India, several hundred of whom work in investment research. Deutsche Bank has 6,000 employees in India, according to the bank's Web site. Deutsche started a pilot program to outsource some research in 2003, and would not provide any update.

Theoretically, as much as 40 percent of the research-related jobs on Wall Street, tens of thousands of jobs, could be sent off-shore, said Deloitte's Mr. Power, though the reality will be less than that.

The jobs off-shore are more likely to come from the investment bank and trading divisions of Wall Street firms, rather than the sales side, which produces analyst reports about companies and industries, said Andy Kessler, a former analyst who has written several books about Wall Street.

"There's a huge amount of grunt work that has been done by $250,000-a-year Wharton M.B.A.'s," Mr. Kessler said. "Some of that stuff, it's natural to outsource it."

He added, "These are middle of the office jobs, not back office, but they're not the people on the front line."

After research, the next wave may include more sophisticated jobs like the creation of derivative products, quantitative trading models and even sales jobs from the trading floors.

Proponents of the change say Wall Street's wary embrace of the activity may signal the beginning of a profound shift in the way investment banks are structured, with everyone but the top deal makers, client representatives and the bank management permanently relocated to cheaper locales like India, the Philippines and Eastern Europe.

In the future, executives in India like to joke, the only function for highly paid bankers in New York or London will be to greet clients and shake hands when the deals close.

"Wall Street has to look at the world differently," said Manoj Jain, the chairman of Pipal Research, a 400-person firm with offices in Chicago, Delhi and Gurgaon. Moving high-value jobs out of high-cost cities is "no longer a hypothesis," he said.

SOURCE: Heather Timmons, "Cost-Cutting in New York, but a Boom in India," *New York Times*, August 12, 2008, p. C1. Reprinted with permission of PARS International.

Executive Pay

LO7
Explain the reasons for the controversy over executive pay.

The issue of executive pay has been given widespread attention in the press. In a sense, the topic has received more coverage than it deserves because there are very few top executives and their compensation accounts for only a small share of an organization's total labor costs. On the other hand, top executives have a disproportionate ability to influence organization performance, so decisions about their compensation are critical. They can also be symbolic. During the recent financial crisis, the U.S. government, as part of the Troubled Asset Relief Program (TARP), decided it was appropriate to further regulate executive pay in firms receiving government "bailout" money." The "Computing through Sustainability" box shows how such regulatory (and labor market) factors influence executive pay. (The Managing People: From the Pages of *BusinessWeek* article at the end of Chapter 12 provides more on recent developments in the regulation of executive pay.) Top executives also help set the tone or culture of the organization. If, for example, the top executive's pay seems unrelated to the organization's performance, staying high even when business is poor, employees may not understand why some of their own pay should be at risk and depend on how the organization is performing.

How much do executives make? Table 11.9 provides some data. Long-term compensation, typically in the form of stock plans, is the major component of CEO pay, which means that CEO pay varies with the performance of the stock market (see the "change in S&P 500" column). Table 11.10 shows that some CEOs are paid well above the averages shown in Table 11.9.

As Table 11.11 shows, U.S. top executives are also the highest paid in the world. (These figures are lower than those from *BusinessWeek* and *Forbes* because the latter reports pertain to larger companies.) The fact that the differential between top-executive pay and that of an average manufacturing worker is so much higher in the United States than in some other countries has been described as creating a "trust gap"—that is, in employees' minds, a "frame of mind that mistrusts senior management's

President Barack Obama's new proposals on banker pay were a striking reminder of just how the balance of power is changing on Wall Street—away from the big banks reliant on federal aid and to foreign-based or boutique firms that haven't required any bailout money.

Wednesday, investment bankers across the industry were calling this week the most devastating to hit their industry since the collapse of Lehman Brothers in September. The new guidelines on executive pay—which technically would apply only to top officers at those firms requiring still more capital—were seen as an evisceration of a professional culture rooted at the likes of J.P. Morgan Chase & Co., Goldman Sachs Group Inc., Morgan Stanley, and Citigroup Inc.

For years bankers often vied to work for the firms with the biggest, most prestigious names. Now, investment bankers are wary of signing up for several more years of reduced bonuses, public shame by politicians, and the other perceived consequences of taking government money. They are sending out résumés and making calls to smaller investment banks—often called "boutiques" for their smaller size—and European banks that haven't taken government money, such as Credit Suisse Group AG and Deutsche Bank AG.

Many who left boutiques to seek their fortunes at larger firms are returning. Houlihan Lokey, for instance, has rehired four bankers in the past three months—all of whom left the 750-person firm to join bigger banks. "They're like salmon. They come home to spawn," quipped one boutique executive who has experienced the phenomenon.

There aren't nearly enough positions to satisfy all the seekers, however, and executives at several boutiques and European banks said they expect to be choosy in their hiring.

In 2008, one boutique bank, Greenhill & Co., hired 14 managing directors, each with two decades or more of experience. "Last year was a great recruiting year for us. It's clear that in the first few weeks of 2009 we're in an even better recruiting environment than we were last year. It's an absolute flood of inquiries," said Scott Bok, Greenhill's co-chief executive.

For two years, Deutsche Bank Securities had been on the hunt for a team of investment bankers to do deals in the financial services industry. But the bank's ambitions had been stymied by the unwillingness of many veteran investment bankers to join the German firm, which, by Wall Street prestige, is perceived as a rung below the likes of Goldman or Morgan or Merrill Lynch.

After Bank of America Corp. bought Merrill Lynch, however, the clouds parted for rivals. This week, Deutsche Bank hired 12 of the coveted financial institutions group bankers it had sought, including Merrill Lynch Treasurer Eric Heaton and his brothers David Heaton and Seth Heaton.

Perella Weinberg, a firm founded by bankers from Goldman Sachs and Morgan Stanley two years ago, receives 25 to 50 résumés a day. Moelis & Co. has received dozens in the past month. Greenhill, which has 48 managing directors, receives about one approach a day from senior bankers with more than 20 years' experience. "Everyone who reaches out to us says that they want to go to a boutique. Very few want to go to a big bank," said Pat Wieser, co-head of the financial-services practice at executive recruiting firm Rhodes Associates.

The prevalence of federal money on Wall Street has made investment bankers wary of entrusting their paychecks—and their futures—to the federal government. Citing the wave of negative coverage of plane trips and junkets, one executive of a boutique groused, "If you're taking government money, you can't have a conference. This is the way we get to know people. You may not be able to take a client to dinner. Who knows? Next week, we may have to shoot every third employee. I just look out my window and look for the guillotine."

Many boutique banks are using the dislocation and bonus disappointment to pitch their virtues to clients and potential hires alike, particularly in contrast to the perceived failures of trading systems and risk management at larger rivals.

"The prestige that was attached to a name brand has been tarnished and the coverage has eroded," said Marshall Sonenshine, a banker who survived several rounds of mergers at Salomon Brothers and Wolfensohn & Co., and who now runs advisory firm Sonenshine Partners.

SOURCE: Heidi N. Moore, "For Boutiques, Time to Shop as Bankers Flee Big Firms," *The Wall Street Journal*, February 5, 2009, p. C3. Copyright © 2009 by Dow Jones & Co., Inc. Reproduced with permission of Dow Jones & Co., Inc. via Copyright Clearance Center.

intentions, doubts its competence, and resents its self-congratulatory pay." The issue becomes more salient when many of the same companies with high executive pay simultaneously engage in layoffs or other forms of employment reduction. Employees might ask, "If the company needs to cut costs, why not cut executive pay rather than our jobs?"[36] The issue is one of perceived fairness. One study, in fact, reported that business units with higher pay differentials between executives and rank-and-file employees had lower customer satisfaction, which was speculated to result from employees' perceptions of inequity coming through in customer relations.[37] Perhaps

table 11.9

CEO Compensation

	CEO PAY							
YEAR	SALARY PLUS BONUS	STOCK GAINS	OTHER	TOTAL PAY	CHANGE IN CEO PAY	CHANGE IN S&P 500	WORKER PAY*	CEO PAY/ WORKER PAY**
2008	$3 million	$6 million	$3 million	$13 million	−18%	−38%	$31,617	405
2007	4 million	8 million	4 million	16 million	34	5	30,682	508
2006	4 million	6 million	2 million	12 million	3	16	29,529	393
2005	3 million	6 million	2 million	11 million	51	5	28,305	399
2004	3 million	3 million	2 million	8 million	6	11	27,513	273
2003	3 million	3 million	1 million	7 million	−37	29	26,939	264
2002	3 million	7 million	1 million	11 million	−9	−22	26,351	429
2001	3 million	8 million	2 million	12 million	−5	−12	25,677	483
2000	3 million	6 million	4 million	13 million	56	−9	25,013	524
1999	2 million	3 million	1 million	8 million	31	21	24,084	349
1995	2 million	1 million	1 million	3 million	25	38	20,804	144
1990	2 million	1 million	0.2 million	2 million	4	−3	18,187	132

SOURCES: CEO pay data from *Forbes* magazine Web site; Worker pay data from U.S. Bureau of Labor Statistics, Employment and Earnings.

Through the year 1999, *Forbes* data pertain to the 800 largest U.S. companies. Beginning with year 2000, data pertain to the 500 largest U.S. companies.

*Worker pay data pertain to production workers in mining and logging and manufacturing, construction workers in construction, and nonsupervisory workers in the service-providing industries.

**Ratio of CEO pay to hourly employee pay.

table 11.10
Highest-Paid CEOs

	TOTAL COMPENSATION
Lawrence J. Ellison, Oracle	$192.9 million
Frederic M. Poses, Trane	127.1 million
Aubrey K. McClendon, Chesapeake Energy	116.9 million

SOURCE: *Forbes* magazine Web site, accessed February 20, 2009.

more important than how much top executives are paid is how they are paid (i.e., whether performance-based). This is an issue we return to in the next chapter.

table 11.11

Total Remuneration of CEOs in Selected Countries (U.S. dollars)

COUNTRY	CEO TOTAL REMUNERATION	CEO/MANUFACTURING EMPLOYEE TOTAL REMUNERATION MULTIPLE
United States	$2,160,000	39
Canada	1,100,000	24
Mexico	1,000,000	60
Brazil	849,000	60
Argentina	431,000	45
France	1,200,000	23
Germany	1,180,000	20
China	211,000	36
India	291,000	51
Japan	543,000	11
Korea	584,000	23

Notes: Data based on a company with $500 million in sales; total remuneration includes salary, bonus, company contributions, perquisites, and long-term incentives. Table 11.11 values are based on much smaller companies than those in Table 11.9, thus explaining the table differences.
SOURCE: Towers Perrin, "2005–2006 Worldwide Total Remuneration," Stamford, CT, 2006.

Government Regulation of Employee Compensation

Equal Employment Opportunity

Equal employment opportunity (EEO) regulation (such as Title VII of the Civil Rights Act) prohibits sex- and race-based differences in employment outcomes such as pay, unless justified by business necessity (like pay differences stemming from differences in job performance). In addition to regulatory pressures, organizations must deal with changing labor market and demographic realities. At least two trends are directly relevant in discussing EEO. First, women have gone from 33 percent of all employees in 1960 to 47 percent in 2007. Second, between 1960 and 2007, whites have gone from 90 percent to 82 percent of all employees. The percentage of white males in organizations will probably continue to decline, making attention to EEO issues in compensation even more important.

LO8
Describe the regulatory framework for employee compensation.

Is there equality of treatment in pay determination? Typically, the popular press focuses on raw earnings ratios. For example, in 2007, among full-time workers, the ratio of female-to-male median earnings was 0.80, the ratio of black-to-white earnings was 0.79, and Hispanic–Latino-to-white earnings was 0.70.[38] These percentages have generally risen over the last two to three decades, but significant race and sex differences in pay clearly remain.[39] In contrast, Asian Americans earn 16 percent more than whites.

The usefulness of raw percentages is limited, however, because some portion of earnings differences arises from differences in legitimate factors: education, labor market experience, and occupation. Adjusting for such factors reduces earnings differences based on race and sex, but significant differences remain. With few exceptions, such adjustments rarely account for more than half of the earnings differential.[40]

What aspects of pay determination are responsible for such differences? In the case of women, it is suggested that their work is undervalued. Another explanation rests on the "crowding" hypothesis, which argues that women were historically restricted to entering a small number of occupations. As a result, the supply of workers far exceeded demand, resulting in lower pay for such occupations. If so, market surveys would only perpetuate the situation.

Comparable Worth
A public policy that advocates remedies for any undervaluation of women's jobs (also called *pay equity*).

Comparable worth (or pay equity) is a public policy that advocates remedies for any undervaluation of women's jobs. The idea is to obtain equal pay, not just for jobs of equal content (already mandated by the Equal Pay Act of 1963) but for jobs of equal value or worth, on the basis of Title VII of the Civil Rights Act. Typically, job evaluation is used to measure worth. Table 11.12, which is based on Washington State data from one of the first comparable worth cases, suggests that measures of worth based on internal comparisons (job evaluation) and external comparisons (market surveys) can be compared. In this case many disagreements between the two measures appear. Internal comparisons suggest that women's jobs are underpaid, whereas external comparisons are less supportive of this argument. For example, although the licensed practical nurse job receives 173 job evaluation points and the truck driver position receives 97 points, the market rate (and thus the state of Washington employer rate) for the truck driver position is $1,493 per month versus only $1,030 per month for the nurse. The truck driver is paid nearly 127 percent more than the pay policy line would predict, whereas the nurse is paid only 75 percent of the pay policy line prediction.

One potential problem with using job evaluation to establish worth independent of the market is that job evaluation procedures were never designed for this purpose.[41] Rather, as demonstrated earlier, their major use is in helping to capture the market pay policy and then applying that to nonkey jobs for which market data are not available. In other words, job evaluation has typically been used to help apply the market pay policy, quite the opposite of replacing the market in pay setting.

As with any regulation, there are also concerns that EEO regulation obstructs market forces, which, according to economic theory, provide the most efficient means of pricing and allocating people to jobs. In theory, moving away from a reliance on market forces would result in some jobs being paid too much and others too little, leading to an oversupply of workers for the former and an undersupply for the latter. In addition, some empirical evidence suggests that a comparable worth policy would not have much impact on the relative earnings of women in the private sector.[42] One limitation of such a policy is that it targets single employers, ignoring that men and women tend to work for different employers.[43] To the extent that segregation by employer contributes to pay differences between men and women, comparable worth would not be effective. In other words, to the extent that sex-based pay differences

table 11.12

Job Evaluation Points, Monthly Prevailing Market Pay Rates, and Proportion of Incumbents in Job Who Are Female

BENCHMARK TITLE	MONTHLY EVALUATION POINTS	PREVAILING RATES[a]	PREVAILING RATE AS PERCENTAGE OF PREDICTED[b]	PERCENTAGE OF FEMALE INCUMBENTS
Warehouse worker	97	$1,286	109.1%	15.4%
Truck driver	97	1,493	126.6	13.6
Laundry worker	105	884	73.2	80.3
Telephone operator	118	887	71.6	95.7
Retail sales clerk	121	921	74.3	100.0
Data entry operator	125	1,017	82.1	96.5
Intermediate clerk typist	129	968	76.3	96.7
Highway engineering tech	133	1,401	110.4	11.1
Word processing equipment operator	138	1,082	83.2	98.3
Correctional officer	173	1,436	105.0	9.3
Licensed practical nurse	173	1,030	75.3	89.5
Automotive mechanic	175	1,646	120.4	0.0
Maintenance carpenter	197	1,707	118.9	2.3
Secretary	197	1,122	78.1	98.5
Administrative assistant	226	1,334	90.6	95.1
Chemist	277	1,885	116.0	20.0
Civil engineer	287	1,885	116.0	0.0
Highway engineer 3	345	1,980	110.4	3.0
Registered nurse	348	1,368	76.3	92.2
Librarian 3	353	1,625	90.6	84.6
Senior architect	362	2,240	121.8	16.7
Senior computer systems analyst	384	2,080	113.1	17.8
Personnel representative	410	1,956	101.2	45.6
Physician	861	3,857	128.0	13.6

[a]Prevailing market rate as of July 1, 1980. Midpoint of job range set equal to this amount.

[b]Predicted salary is based on regression of prevailing market rate on job evaluation points $2.43 \times$ Job evaluation points $+ 936.19$, $r = 0.77$.

SOURCE: Reprinted with permission of *Public Personnel Management,* published by the International Personnel Management Association.

are the result of men and women working in different organizations with different pay levels, such policies will have little impact.

Perhaps most important, despite potential problems with market rates, the courts have consistently ruled that using the going market rates of pay is an acceptable defense in comparable worth litigation suits.[44] The rationale is that organizations face competitive labor and product markets. Paying less or more than the market rate will put the organization at a competitive disadvantage. Thus there is no comparable worth legal mandate in the U.S. private sector.

On the other hand, by the early 1990s, almost one-half of the states had begun or completed comparable worth adjustments to public-sector employees' pay. In addition, in 1988 the Canadian province of Ontario mandated comparable worth in both the private and public sectors. Further, although comparable worth is not mandated in the U.S. private sector, the Department of Labor (Office of Federal Contracts

Compliance) which enforces Executive Order 11246, put into place new enforcement standards and guidelines in 2006 that prohibit race or sex-based "systemic compensation discrimination," which it defines as a situation "where there are statistically significant compensation disparities (as established by a regression analysis) between similarly situated employees, after taking into account the legitimate factors which influence compensation, such as: education, prior work experience, performance, productivity, and time in the job."[45] Further, passage of the 2009 Lilly Ledbetter Fair Pay Act means that employers may face claims in situations where a discriminatory decision (e.g., too small of a pay raise) was made many years earlier, but the effect (lower pay) continues into the more current period.

Some work has focused on pinpointing where women's pay falls behind that of men. One finding is that the pay gap is wider where bonus and incentive payments (not just base salary) are examined. Other evidence indicates that women lose ground at the time they are hired and actually do better once they are employed for some time.[46] One interpretation is that when actual job performance (rather than the limited general qualification information available on applicants) is used in decisions, women may be less likely to encounter unequal treatment. If so, more attention needs to be devoted to ensuring fair treatment of applicants and new employees.[47] On the other hand, a "glass ceiling" is believed to exist in some organizations that allows women (and minorities) to come within sight of the top echelons of management, but not advance to them.

It is likely, however, that organizations will differ in terms of where women's earnings disadvantages arise. For example, advancement opportunities for women and other protected groups may be hindered by unequal access to the "old boy" or informal network. This, in turn, may be reflected in lower rates of pay. Mentoring programs have been suggested as one means of improving access. Indeed, one study found that mentoring was successful, having a significant positive effect on the pay of both men and women, with women receiving a greater payoff in percentage terms than men.[48]

Minimum Wage, Overtime, and Prevailing Wage Laws

Fair Labor Standards Act (FLSA)
The 1938 law that established the minimum wage and overtime pay.

Minimum Wage
The lowest amount that employers are legally allowed to pay; the 1990 amendment of the Fair Labor Standards Act permits a subminimum wage to workers under the age of 20 for a period of up to 90 days.

The 1938 **Fair Labor Standards Act (FLSA)** establishes a **minimum wage** for jobs that was $6.55 per hour as of July 2008, and $7.25 per hour as of July 24, 2009. State laws may specify higher minimum wages. The FLSA also permits a subminimum training wage that is approximately 85 percent of the minimum wage, which employers are permitted to pay most employees under the age of 20 for a period of up to 90 days.

The FLSA also requires that employees be paid at a rate of one and a half times their hourly rate for each hour of overtime worked beyond 40 hours in a week. The hourly rate includes not only the base wage but also other components such as bonuses and piece-rate payments. The FLSA requires overtime pay for any hours beyond 40 in a week that an employer "suffers or permits" the employee to perform, regardless of whether the work is done at the workplace or whether the employer explicitly asked or expected the employee to do it. If the employer knows the employee is working overtime but neither moves to stop it nor pays time and a half, a violation of the FLSA may have occurred. A department store was the target of a lawsuit that claimed employees were "encouraged" to, among other things, write thank-you notes to customers outside of scheduled work hours but were not compensated for this work. Although the company denied encouraging this off-the-clock work, it reached an out-of-court settlement to pay between $15 million and $30 million in back pay (plus legal fees of $7.5 million) to approximately 85,000 sales representatives it employed over a three-year period.[49]

Executive, professional, administrative, outside sales, and certain "computer employees" occupations are **exempt** from FLSA coverage. *Nonexempt* occupations are covered and include most hourly jobs. One estimate is that just over 20 percent of employees fall into the exempt category.[50] Exempt status depends on job responsibilities and salary. All exemptions (except for outside sales) require that an employee be paid no less than $455 per week. The job responsibility criteria vary. For example, the executive exemption is based on whether two or more people are supervised, whether there is authority to hire and fire (or whether particular weight is given to the employee's recommendations), and whether the employee's primary duty is managing the enterprise, recognized department, or subdivision of the enterprise. The Wage and Hour Division, Employment Standards Administration (www.dol.gov/esa), U.S. Department of Labor, and its local offices can provide further information on these definitions. (The exemptions do *not* apply to police, firefighters, paramedics, and first responders.)

Two pieces of legislation—the 1931 Davis-Bacon Act and the 1936 Walsh-Healy Public Contracts Act—require federal contractors to pay employees no less than the prevailing wages in the area. Davis-Bacon covers construction contractors receiving federal money of more than $2,000. Typically, prevailing wages have been based on relevant union contracts, partly because only 30 percent of the local labor force is required to be used in establishing the prevailing rate. Walsh-Healy covers all government contractors receiving $10,000 or more in federal funds.

Finally, employers must take care in deciding whether a person working on their premises is classified as an employee or independent contractor. We address this issue in Chapter 13.

> **Exempt**
> Employees who are not covered by the Fair Labor Standards Act. Exempt employees are not eligible for overtime pay.

A LOOK BACK

We began this chapter by showing how Toyota hopes to reduce its labor costs, while at the same time maintaining the quality and commitment of its workforce, which will position it to be ready to respond when customer demand for its cars picks up again. We also saw other strategies to control labor costs in these difficult times. For example, some financial services firms are shifting work to places like India. We have seen in this chapter that pay structure decisions influence the success of strategy execution by influencing not only labor costs, but also employee perceptions of equity, and the way that different structures provide flexibility and incentives for employees to learn and be productive.

Questions

1. What types of changes have the companies discussed in this chapter made to their pay structures to support execution of their business strategies?
2. Would other companies seeking to better align their pay structures with their business strategies benefit from imitating the changes made at these companies?

 Please see the Video Case that corresponds to this chapter online at www.mhhe.com/noe7e.

SUMMARY

In this chapter we have discussed the nature of the pay structure and its component parts, the pay level, and the job structure. Equity theory suggests that social comparisons are an important influence on how employees evaluate their pay. Employees make external comparisons between their pay and the pay they believe is received by employees in other organizations. Such comparisons may have consequences for employee attitudes and retention. Employees also make internal comparisons between what they receive and what they perceive others within the organization are paid. These types of comparisons may have consequences for internal movement, cooperation, and attitudes (like organization commitment). Such comparisons play an important role in the controversy over executive pay, as illustrated by the focus of critics on the ratio of executive pay to that of lower-paid workers.

Pay benchmarking surveys and job evaluation are two administrative tools widely used in managing the pay level and job structure components of the pay structure, which influence employee social comparisons. Pay surveys also permit organizations to benchmark their labor costs against other organizations. Globalization is increasing the need for organizations to be competitive in both their labor costs and productivity.

The nature of pay structures is undergoing a fundamental change in many organizations. One change is the move to fewer pay levels to reduce labor costs and bureaucracy. Second, some employers are shifting from paying employees for narrow jobs to giving them broader responsibilities and paying them to learn the necessary skills.

Finally, a theme that runs through this chapter and the next is the importance of process in managing employee compensation. How a new program is designed, decided on, implemented, and communicated is perhaps just as important as its core characteristics.

KEY TERMS

Pay structure, 501
Pay level, 501
Job structure, 501
Efficiency wage theory, 505
Benchmarking, 505
Rate ranges, 506
Key jobs, 506

Nonkey jobs, 507
Job evaluation, 507
Compensable factors, 507
Pay policy line, 509
Pay grades, 510
Range spread, 511
Compa-ratio, 513

Delayering, 519
Skill-based pay, 520
Comparable worth, 530
Fair Labor Standards
   Act (FLSA), 532
Minimum wage, 532
Exempt, 533

DISCUSSION QUESTIONS

1. You have been asked to evaluate whether your organization's current pay structure makes sense in view of what competing organizations are paying. How would you determine what organizations to compare your organization with? Why might your organization's pay structure differ from those in competing organizations? What are the potential consequences of having a pay structure that is out of line relative to those of your competitors?

2. Top management has decided that the organization is too bureaucratic and has too many layers of jobs to compete effectively. You have been asked to suggest innovative alternatives to the traditional "job-based" approach to employee compensation and to list the advantages and disadvantages of these new approaches.

3. If major changes of the type mentioned in question 2 are to be made, what types of so-called process issues need to be considered? Of what relevance is equity theory in helping to understand how employees might react to changes in the pay structure?

4. Are executive pay levels unreasonable? Why or why not?

5. Your company plans to build a new manufacturing plant but is undecided where to locate it. What factors would you consider in choosing in which country (or state) to build the plant?

6. You have been asked to evaluate whether a company's pay structure is fair to women and minorities. How would you go about answering this question?

● SELF-ASSESSMENT EXERCISE

Consider your current job or a job you had in the past. For each of the following pay characteristics, indicate your level of satisfaction by using the following scale: 1 = very dissatisfied; 2 = somewhat dissatisfied; 3 = neither satisfied nor dissatisfied; 4 = somewhat satisfied; 5 = very satisfied.

_____ 1. My take-home pay
_____ 2. My current pay
_____ 3. My overall level of pay
_____ 4. Size of my current salary
_____ 5. My benefit package
_____ 6. Amount the company pays toward my benefits
_____ 7. The value of my benefits
_____ 8. The number of benefits I receive
_____ 9. My most recent raise
_____10. Influence my manager has over my pay
_____11. The raises I have typically received in the past
_____12. The company's pay structure
_____13. Information the company gives about pay issues of concern to me
_____14. Pay of other jobs in the company

_____ 15. Consistency of the company's pay policies
_____ 16. How my raises are determined
_____ 17. Differences in pay among jobs in the company
_____ 18. The way the company administers pay

These 18 items measure four dimensions of pay satisfaction. Find your total score for each set of item numbers to measure your satisfaction with each dimension.

Pay Level
Total of items 1, 2, 3, 4, 9, 11: _____
Benefits
Total of items 5, 6, 7, 8: _____
Pay Structure and Administration
Total of items 12, 13, 14, 15, 17, 18: _____
Pay Raises
Total of items 10, 11, 16: _____

Considering the principles discussed in this chapter, how could your company improve (or how could it have improved) your satisfaction on each dimension?

SOURCE: Based on H. G. Heneman III and D. P. Schwab, "Pay Satisfaction: Its Multidimensional Nature and Measurement," *International Journal of Psychology* 20 (1985), pp. 129–41.

● EXERCISING STRATEGY: CHANGING COMPENSATION TO SUPPORT CHANGES IN CORPORATE STRATEGY

By realigning its strategy and compensation and benefits programs, Corning Inc., once a traditional economy company, hopes to compete successfully in the new economy. First, the company divested itself of several business units, including Corning Consumer Products. These divestitures reduced its annual revenues from $5 billion to $3 billion. Next Corning pursued a "high-octane" growth strategy in optical communications (optical fiber, cable systems, photo technologies, optical networking devices), environmental technologies, display technologies, and specialty materials. To support this shift in corporate strategy, Corning sought to support growth by creating an environment that bolstered innovation, risk taking, teaming, and speed. One major change was in its compensation system. The salary structure was streamlined from 11 grades to 5 broad bands for exempt employees and from 7 grades to 3 broad bands for nonexempt employees. In a new economy company, products have a short life cycle and change in markets is a way of life. This means that the nature of work also changes rapidly, so the detailed job descriptions and traditional promotion paths of the past may not fit

this fluid environment. By changing its salary structure, Corning hopes to increase its ability to move quickly in responding to and anticipating customer needs in rapidly changing markets by encouraging flexibility, teamwork, and learning among its employees. Decentralizing more pay decisions to managers contributes to this flexibility, and giving employees an increasing stake in the success of the company by making more employees eligible for stock options contributes to the increased focus on teamwork. Finally, employee compensation is increasingly tied to individual employee learning and performance as the broad bands allow managers more flexibility to recognize outstanding achievements.

SOURCE: B. Parus, "How an Old Economy Company Became a New Economy Enterprise," *Workspan* 44:6 (June 2001), pp. 34–41.

Questions
1. What are the pros and cons of Corning's new pay structure?
2. How did shifting product market conditions affect Corning's restructuring and its success?

BusinessWeek How to Cut Payroll Costs Without Layoffs

In tough times, you can't help scrutinizing your biggest expense. But it is possible to reduce wage costs without laying off employees Ask any entrepreneur about his worst business experiences, and laying people off is sure to top the list. After all, people who work together in an intimate setting often form personal connections that mirror family bonds. Craig Lindell, chief executive of 17-person wastewater treatment company Aquapoint, remembers having to lay off staff in the mid-'80s, when he was chief operating officer of a fashion accessories company. "I faced those people when they lost their jobs," says Lindell, who still gets choked up talking about it. Reka Mostella, area manager of the Small Business Development Center at the University of South Carolina Aiken, sympathizes. "Business management is not about running a company under ideal circumstances," she says. "It's knowing what to change when things change."

Aside from the personal toll, losing highly skilled workers can inflict long-term damage on a business, making it hard to bounce back and forcing managers to spend precious time and money recruiting and training when conditions improve.

But salaries and wages typically account for 60% to 80% of a small company's expenses, according to Jeff Cornwall, director of the Center for Entrepreneurship at Belmont University in Nashville. And with nearly 70% of small businesses suffering sales declines, their owners are doing "things that they hoped they would not have to do," says Alice Bredin, an adviser to American Express Open, AmEx' small business division. That often includes tightening payroll. In a survey fielded by Open late in January, one-quarter of small business owners said they were cutting staff hours or jobs, and 9 out of 10 said they were curtailing hiring plans. It adds up. In January, small businesses with fewer than 50 workers shed 175,000 jobs, according to payroll firm ADP.

Yet many entrepreneurs are trimming payroll costs without laying off hard-to-replace employees. Some, including Jim Strite, CEO of Strite Design & Remodeling, are working with staff to devise ways to save jobs and minimize the blow to workplace culture if cuts are unavoidable. Naturally, the first line of defense has been to shrink nonessential expenses such as travel and business meals, make do in smaller quarters, and postpone or cancel big-ticket investments. But some business owners are preserving jobs by reducing hours, encouraging employees to take unpaid leaves, and chopping pay (often their own).

If you're feeling the squeeze, it may be possible to squeak by without losing your company's best assets. Following are three strategies to help keep your prized employees on board.

Talk Straight, Get Employees Involved—*Jim Strite, Strite Design & Remodeling*

On Thursday, Mar. 20, 2008, Jim Strite gathered his staff around the oval table in his "education room," where charts illustrating the company's progress adorn the walls. The owner of Strite Design & Remodeling in Boise, and a former economics lecturer, Strite showed his 14 employees how the housing meltdown was affecting the company: Revenue was a third below target. Gross profit, off 40%, wasn't enough to cover overhead, putting the firm in the red. Quick improvement was unlikely. Spring usually yielded projects that lasted through the summer, but calls about kitchen remodels, bathroom makeovers, and dream additions weren't coming in nearly often enough, despite a stepped-up marketing effort.

Strite's employees were accustomed to straight talk, although they were surprised at the urgency of Strite's message. The firm is an "open-book" company, where employees see finances regularly, are schooled in the business, and are expected to drive its success. "Communication is important at all times. In tough times, it just becomes all that more important," says Rich Armstrong, president of Great Game of Business, a Springfield (Mo.) consulting company that promotes open-book principles. Armstrong says that candid dialogue eliminates distracting rumors and fears and fosters teamwork.

In Strite's case, staffers immediately volunteered cost-cutting ideas, including offers to cut their own hours and take unpaid vacation. Strite asked them to brainstorm over the weekend and bring ideas in writing on Monday.

Among the ideas Strite used: get rid of bottled water in the office, save on car washes by asking employees to hose down the company's seven trucks, and delay a planned office renovation. Those cuts didn't add up to big money—only about $1,900 a month—but they "demonstrated that we were all buying into cutting overhead and maintaining as many people as we could," he says. "We were a team that had the same objective in mind."

That left payroll as the only place Strite could trim enough to balance the budget. Twelve days later, office staff went to 32 hours a week from 40. Each week, one of the seven project managers also cut their hours to 32. Strite and two salaried managers cut their pay by a third, and one woman went on maternity leave. Still, Strite had to let three people go, choosing who would leave based on whether their work could be picked up by others. The cuts were accepted in peace. "Our employees know that they are highly valued," he says. "They understand the entity has to survive."

A few months later, several projects came through and, in July, Strite brought back two laid-off employees and restored normal hours, though the leadership's pay cut remains. But it's not over. Declines in the stock market and home equity loans hurt home improvement budgets further. By the end of 2008, the company posted $2.56 million in revenues, about 30% below 2007's $3.8 million, Strite says. He's hoping work will pick up—so he won't have to cut again.

Take One for the Team—*Craig Lindell, Aquapoint*

While other executives look to share the pain, those at Aquapoint in New Bedford, Mass., decided to shoulder the burden of reducing payroll costs themselves.

Troubles in the construction industry began to squeeze Aquapoint in February 2008, when delays for new housing developments held up orders for the company's eco-friendly wastewater treatment systems. Then a planned retirement community that had placed a $400,000 order lost its bank funding. "Our liquidity just disappeared," says Chief Executive Craig Lindell.

By June, something had to give. So Lindell and two other top executives, Stephen Sedgwick and Raymond Cullum, took 50% pay cuts and asked employees to take a 10% trim. In August, "we realized we probably wouldn't come out of the year with better than $5 million" in sales, compared to the $8 to $12 million they expected, Lindell says.

The trio considered licensing their technology, bringing in an investor, or reducing staff. But they were convinced that, after 16 years of straining to build a new market, the company was on the brink of taking off. The company is "full of engineers and marketing people and technical sellers, and you don't want to lose that base," Lindell says. "Memory and experience is so critical. . . . I wasn't about to jeopardize it."

So for the last quarter of the year, Lindell, Sedgwick, and Cullum took no pay. They asked two clerical staff to work three days a week rather than five. By January, Lindell and Sedgwick had restored 25% of their salaries, but Cullum continues to work for free. The company posted $4 million in sales in 2008. If business picks up soon, the trio will receive bonuses to make up for the lost salaries. Sedgwick and Cullum could receive larger ownership stakes, says Lindell, who owns 60% of the company.

Owners and managers see more rewards in good times, and so it's fair that they sacrifice more in the bad, says Lane Transou, a member of the Society for Human Resource Management's Total Rewards panel. "You do what you can at the top until you get the number you have to have," she says. "It sends a message to employees that you are doing what you can to keep the doors open and keep the company solvent."

Cut Hours, Take Unpaid Leave—*Gina Stern, d_parture spa*

For Gina Stern, a lot has changed since September 11, 2001. Back then, the founder of d_parture spa had one full-service airport spa, while today she operates three. Her Harrington Park (N.J.) firm had 15 employees and $457,000 in annual revenue in 2001, while today it has 45 people and brings in well over $1 million in annual sales.

But business in the airports now feels eerily similar to seven years ago, when travel fell off amid terrorism fears and a faltering economy, Stern says. Her numbers "are starting to drop" in Continental's domestic terminal at Newark International, where her business was born in 2000. By October, weekly sales were down 12% from a year earlier, a dramatic turnabout from the 36% growth pace she was clocking in July. She ended the year with $1.4 million in revenue, about $400,000 less than she had forecast.

Stern made the "easy" cuts first. In August she put full-time employees on a less expensive health-care plan with higher co-pays and deductibles.

But by the end of 2008 she was forced to implement the first phase of the 9/11 response plan that saved both her business and her employees' jobs eight years ago. As she did then, she's asked staff to take extended unpaid vacations. Next, she may once again ask people with more than one job to sacrifice hours, or encourage others to go back to school, promising them a job when they return. Back in 2001, the spa manager waived a raise and Stern was paid when there was money to spare—steps they may consider again.

"We go to the same mode because it worked. It was the only thing we could do to respond to the numbers, because my goal is to not let anyone go," Stern says. "My people are the backbone of my company, and they're like my family."

She's also looking for new customers who can keep her employees productive. Stern's spa outside security at Newark's international terminal is thriving, thanks to European travelers. So she has asked the airport's management company for more space near the gates, where people with long waits might be enticed to have a massage or manicure. Now if only Stern could relax, too.

Questions

1. In Chapter 5, we discussed the pros and cons of layoffs and their alternatives. Thinking of that discussion, do you feel these companies chose the right approaches to reducing compensation costs? What alternatives would you have suggested as better?
2. Have you or a friend or relative worked at a company that went through similar challenges? How was it done? Was it handled well? What could have been done better?

SOURCE: Riva Richmond, "How to Cut Payroll Costs Without Layoffs," *BusinessWeek*, April 3, 2009.

● NOTES

1. J. S. Adams, "Inequity in Social Exchange," in *Advances in Experimental Social Psychology*, ed. L. Berkowitz (New York: Academic Press, 1965); P. S. Goodman, "An Examination of Referents Used in the Evaluation of Pay," *Organizational Behavior and Human Performance* 12 (1974), pp. 170–95; C. O. Trevor and D. L. Wazeter, "A Contingent View of Reactions to Objective Pay Conditions: Interdependence among Pay Structure Characteristics and Pay Relative to Internal and External Referents," *Journal of Applied Psychology* 91 (2006), pp. 1260–1275; M. M. Harris, F. Anseel, and F. Lievens, "Keeping Up with the Joneses: A Field Study of the Relationships among Upward, Lateral, and Downward Comparisons and Pay Level Satisfaction," *Journal of Applied Psychology* 93, no. 3 (May 2008), pp. 665–73; Gordon D. A. Brown, Jonathan Gardner, Andrew J. Oswald, Jing Qian, "Does Wage Rank Affect Employees' Well-being?" *Industrial Relations* 47, no. 3 (July 2008), p. 355.

2. J. B. Miner, *Theories of Organizational Behavior* (Hinsdale, IL: Dryden Press, 1980); B. Gerhart and S. L. Rynes, *Compensation: Theory, Evidence, and Strategic Implications* (Thousand Oaks, CA: Sage, 2003).

3. The Harbour Report™ North America 2008, www.oliverwyman.com.

4. J. Green, "GM UAW Savings Said to Be Double Ford's $500 Million," www.bloombers.com, March 11, 2009, accessed March 16, 2009.

5. B. Gerhart and G. T. Milkovich, "Organizational Differences in Managerial Compensation and Financial Performance," *Academy of Management Journal* 33 (1990), pp. 663–91; E. L. Groshen, "Why Do Wages Vary among Employers?" *Economic Review* 24 (1988), pp. 19–38; Gerhart and Rynes, *Compensation*.

6. M. L. Williams, M. A. McDaniel, N. T. Nguyen, "A Meta-analysis of the Antecedents and Consequences of Pay Level Satisfaction," *Journal of Applied Psychology* 91 (2006), pp. 392–413; M. C. Sturman, C. O. Trevor, J. W. Boudreau, and B. Gerhart, "Is It Worth It to Win the Talent War? Evaluating the Utility of Performance-Based Pay," *Personnel Psychology* 56 (2003), pp. 997–1035; B. Klaas and J. A. McClendon, "To Lead, Lag or Match: Estimating the Financial Impact of Pay Level Policies," *Personnel Psychology* 49 (1996), pp. 121–41. S. C. Currall, A. J. Towler T. A. Judge, and L. Kohn, "Pay Satisfaction and Organizational Outcomes," *Personnel Psychology* 58 (2005), pp. 613–40; M. P. Brown, M. C. Sturman, and M. J. Simmering, "Compensation Policy and Organizational Performance: The Efficiency, Operational, and Financial Implications of Pay Levels and Pay Structures," *Academy of Management Journal* 46 (2003), pp. 752–62; Eric A. Verhoogen, Stephen V. Burks, and Jeffrey P. Carpenter, "Fairness and Freight-Handlers: Local Labor Market Conditions and Wage-Fairness Perceptions in a Trucking Firm," *Industrial & Labor Relations Review* 60, no. 4 (July 2007), p. 477.

7. G. A. Akerlof, "Gift Exchange and Efficiency-Wage Theory: Four Views," *American Economic Review* 74 (1984), pp. 79–83; J. L. Yellen, "Efficiency Wage Models of Unemployment," *American Economic Review* 74 (1984), pp. 200–5.

8. S. L. Rynes and G. T. Milkovich, "Wage Surveys: Dispelling Some Myths about the "Market Wage," *Personnel Psychology* 39 (1986), pp. 71–90.

9. B. Gerhart and G. T. Milkovich, "Employee Compensation: Research and Practice," in *Handbook of Industrial and Organizational Psychology*, 2nd ed., ed. M. D. Dunnette and L. M. Hough (Palo Alto, CA: Consulting Psychologists Press, 1992).

10. G. T. Milkovich, J. M. Newman, and B. Gerhart, *Compensation,* 10th ed. (New York: McGraw-Hill/Irwin, 2010).

11. B. Gerhart, G. T. Milkovich, and B. Murray, "Pay, Performance, and Participation," in *Research Frontiers in Industrial Relations and Human Resources*, ed. D. Lewin, O. S. Mitchell, and P. D. Sherer (Madison, WI: IRRA, 1992).

12. C. H. Fay, "External Pay Relationships," in *Compensation and Benefits*, ed. L. R. Gomez-Mejia (Washington, DC: Bureau of National Affairs, 1989).

13. J. P. Pfeffer and A. Davis-Blake, "Understanding Organizational Wage Structures: A Resource Dependence Approach," *Academy of Management Journal* 30 (1987), pp. 437–55; M. A. Carpenter and J. B. Wade, "Micro-Level Opportunity Structures as Determinants of Non-CEO Executive Pay," *Academy of Management Journal* 45 (2002), pp. 1085–1103.

14. C. M. Solomon, "Global Compensation: Learn the ABCs," *Personnel Journal*, July 1995, p. 70; R. A. Swaak, "Expatriate Management: The Search for Best Practices," *Compensation and Benefits Review*, March–April 1995, p. 21.

15. *1997–1998 Survey of Geographic Pay Differential Policies and Practices* (Rochester, WI: Runzeimer International). Actually, data from the American Chamber of Commerce Research Association (ACCRA) estimate the cost of living in New York City (in 2001) to be 239.2, compared to 100 for the average metropolitan area.

16. E. E. Lawler III, *Pay and Organizational Development* (Reading, MA: Addison-Wesley, 1981).

17. R. Folger and M. A. Konovsky, "Effects of Procedural and Distributive Justice on Reactions to Pay Raise Decisions," *Academy of Management Journal* 32 (1989), pp. 115–30; H. G. Heneman III and T. A. Judge, "Compensation Attitudes," in S. L. Rynes and B. Gerhart, eds., *Compensation in Organizations* (San Francisco: Jossey-Bass, 2002), pp. 61–103; J. Greenberg, "Determinants of Perceived Fairness of Performance Evaluations," *Journal of Applied Psychology* 71 (1986), pp. 340–42; H. G. Heneman III, "Pay Satisfaction," *Research in Personnel and Human Resource Management* 3 (1985), pp. 115–39.

18. J. Greenberg, "Employee Theft as a Reaction to Underpayment of Inequity: The Hidden Cost of Pay Cuts," *Journal of Applied Psychology* 75 (1990), pp. 561–68.

19. Adams, "Inequity in Social Exchange"; C. J. Berger, C. A. Olson, and J. W. Boudreau, "The Effect of Unionism on Job Satisfaction: The Role of Work-Related Values and Perceived Rewards," *Organizational Behavior and Human Performance* 32 (1983), pp. 284–324; P. Cappelli and P. D. Sherer, "Assessing Worker Attitudes under a Two-Tier Wage Plan," *Industrial and Labor Relations Review* 43 (1990), pp. 225–44; R. W. Rice, S. M. Phillips, and D. B. McFarlin, "Multiple Discrepancies and Pay Satisfaction," *Journal of Applied Psychology* 75 (1990), pp. 386–93.

20. Cappelli and Sherer, "Assessing Worker Attitudes."

21. R. M. Kanter, *When Giants Learn to Dance* (New York: Simon & Schuster, 1989); E. E. Lawler III, *Strategic Pay* (San Francisco: Jossey-Bass, 1990); "Farewell, Fast Track," *BusinessWeek*, December 10, 1990, pp. 192–200; R. L. Heneman, G. E. Ledford, Jr., and M. T. Gresham, "The Changing Nature of Work and Its Effects on Compensation Design and Delivery," in S. L. Rynes and B. Gerhart, eds., *Compensation in Organizations*.

22. P. R. Eyers, "Realignment Ties Pay to Performance," *Personnel Journal*, January 1993, p. 74.

23. Lawler, *Strategic Pay*; G. Ledford, "3 Cases on Skill-Based Pay: An Overview," *Compensation and Benefits Review*, March–April 1991, pp. 11–23; G. E. Ledford, "Paying for the Skills, Knowledge, Competencies of Knowledge Workers," *Compensation and Benefits Review*, July–August 1995, p. 55; Heneman et al., "The Changing Nature of Work." G. Ledford, "Factors Affecting the Long-term Success of Skill-based Pay," *WorldatWork Journal*, First Quarter (2008), pp. 6–18. J. Canavan, "Overcoming the Challenge of Aligning Skill-based Pay Levels to the External Market," *WorldatWork Journal*, First Quarter (2008), pp. 18–24. E. C. Dierdorff and E. A. Surface, "If You Pay for Skills, Will They Learn? Skill Change and Maintenance Under a Skill-Based Pay System," *Journal of Management* 34 (2008), pp. 721–743.

24. Ledford, "3 Cases."

25. Heneman et al., "The Changing Nature of Work."

26. T. D. Wall, J. M. Corbett, R. Martin, C. W. Clegg, and P. R. Jackson, "Advanced Manufacturing Technology, Work Design, and Performance: A Change Study," *Journal of Applied Psychology* 75 (1990), pp. 691–97.

27. Womack et al., *The Machine That Changed the World*, p. 56.

28. Lawler, *Strategic Pay*.

29. Ibid.; Gerhart and Milkovich, "Employee Compensation."

30. B. C. Murray and B. Gerhart, "An Empirical Analysis of a Skill-Based Pay Program and Plant Performance Outcomes," *Academy of Management Journal* 41, no. 1 (1998), pp. 68–78.

31. Ibid.; N. Gupta, D. Jenkins, and W. Curington, "Paying for Knowledge: Myths and Realities," *National Productivity Review*, Spring 1986, pp. 107–23; J. D. Shaw, N. Gupta, A. Mitra, and G. E. Ledford, "Success and Survival of Skill-Based Pay Plans," *Journal of Management* 31 (2005), pp. 28–49.

32. Data from U.S. Bureau of Labor Statistics Web site, www.bls.gov.

33. *Education at a Glance—OECD Indicators 2001* (Paris: OECD, 2001).

34. C. Sparks and M. Greiner, "U.S. and Foreign Productivity and Labor Costs," *Monthly Labor Review*, February 1997, pp. 26–35.

35. E. Faltermayer, "U.S. Companies Come Back Home," *Fortune*, December 30, 1991, pp. 106ff; M. Hayes, "Precious Connection: Companies Thinking about Using Offshore Outsourcing Need to Consider More than Just Cost Savings," *Information Week Online*, www.informationweek.com (October 20, 2003).

36. A. Farnham, "The Trust Gap," *Fortune*, December 4, 1989, pp. 56ff; Scott McCartney, "AMR Unions Express Fury," *The Wall Street Journal*, April 17, 2003.

37. D. M. Cowherd and D. I. Levine, "Product Quality and Pay Equity between Lower-Level Employees and Top Management: An Investigation of Distributive Justice Theory," *Administrative Science Quarterly* 37 (1992), pp. 302–20.

38. Bureau of Labor Statistics, *Current Population Surveys* (Web site).

39. Ibid.

40. B. Gerhart, "Gender Differences in Current and Starting Salaries: The Role of Performance, College Major, and Job Title," *Industrial and Labor Relations Review* 43 (1990), pp. 418–33; G. G. Cain, "The Economic Analysis of Labor-Market Discrimination: A Survey," in *Handbook of Labor Economics*, ed. O. Ashenfelter and R. Layard (New York: North-Holland, 1986), pp. 694–785. F. D. Blau and L. M. kahn, "The Gender Pay, Gap: Have Women Gone as Far as They Can?" *Academy of Management Perpectives*, February 2007, pp. 7–23.

41. D. P. Schwab, "Job Evaluation and Pay-Setting: Concepts and Practices," in *Comparable Worth: Issues and Alternatives*, ed. E. R. Livernash (Washington, DC: Equal Employment Advisory Council, 1980).

42. B. Gerhart and N. El Cheikh, "Earnings and Percentage Female: A Longitudinal Study," *Industrial Relations* 30 (1991), pp. 62–78; R. S. Smith, "Comparable Worth: Limited Coverage and the Exacerbation of Inequality," *Industrial and Labor Relations Review* 61 (1988), pp. 227–39.

43. W. T. Bielby and J. N. Baron, "Men and Women at Work: Sex Segregation and Statistical Discrimination," *American Journal of Sociology* 91 (1986), pp. 759–99.

44. Rynes and Milkovich, "Wage Surveys"; G. T. Milkovich, J. M. Newman, and B. Gerhart, *Compensation*, 10th ed. (New York: McGraw-Hill/Irwin, 2010).

45. U.S. Department of Labor Web site, at www.dol.gov/esa/regs/compliance/ofccp/faqs/comstrds.htm.

46. Gerhart, "Gender Differences in Current and Starting Salaries"; B. Gerhart and G. T. Milkovich, "Salaries, Salary Growth, and Promotions of Men and Women in a Large, Private Firm," in *Pay Equity: Empirical Inquiries*, ed. R. Michael, H. Hartmann, and B. O'Farrell (Washington, DC: National Academy Press, 1989); K. W. Chauvin and R. A. Ash, "Gender Earnings Differentials in Total Pay, Base Pay, and Contingent Pay," *Industrial and Labor Relations Review* 47 (1994), pp. 634–49; M. M. Elvira and M. E. Graham, "Not Just a Formality: Pay System Formalization and Sex-Related Earnings Effects," *Organization Science* 13 (2002), pp. 601–17.

47. Gerhart, "Gender Differences in Current and Starting Salaries"; B. Gerhart and S. Rynes, "Determinants and Consequences of Salary Negotiations by Graduating Male and Female MBAs," *Journal of Applied Psychology* 76 (1991), pp. 256–62.

48. G. F. Dreher and R. A. Ash, "A Comparative Study of Mentoring among Men and Women in Managerial, Professional, and Technical Positions," *Journal of Applied Psychology* 75 (1990), pp. 539–46.

49. G. A. Patterson, "Nordstrom Inc. Sets Back-Pay Accord on Suit Alleging 'Off-the-Clock' Work," *The Wall Street Journal*, January 12, 1993, p. A2; for additional information on overtime legal issues, see A. Weintraub and J. Kerstetter, "Revenge of the Overworked Nerds," *BusinessWeek Online*, www.businessweek.com (December 8, 2003).

50. R. I. Henderson, *Compensation Management in a Knowledge-Based World* (Upper Saddle River, NJ: Prentice Hall, 2003).

Recognizing Employee Contributions with Pay

LO **LEARNING OBJECTIVES**

After reading this chapter, you should be able to:

LO1 Discuss how pay influences individual employees, and describe three theories that explain the effect of compensation on individuals. *page 543*

LO2 Describe the fundamental pay programs for recognizing employees' contributions to the organization's success. *page 547*

LO3 List the advantages and disadvantages of the pay programs. *page 547*

LO4 Describe how organizations combine incentive plans in a balanced scorecard. *page 564*

LO5 Discuss issues related to performance-based pay for executives. *page 565*

LO6 Explain the importance of process issues such as communication in compensation management. *page 568*

LO7 List the major factors to consider in matching the pay strategy to the organization's strategy. *page 569*

Goldman Chiefs Give Up Bonuses (But Others Don't)

After months of internal debate at Goldman, the seven top executives at the firm, including Chief Executive Officer Lloyd Blankfein, asked the board's compensation committee to grant them no bonuses. The board approved the request.

The executives will only be eligible for their base salaries, $600,000 for each. A firm spokesman said the executives felt it was "the right thing" to do.

"While the firm has distinguished itself through many aspects of the crisis, we cannot ignore the fact that we are part of an industry that is directly associated with the ongoing economic distress," the firm spokesman said.

Just a year ago firms across Wall Street were still more or less untouched by the mortgage meltdown and were ringing up record profits. Blankfein took home $68.5 million in cash and stock in 2007, a record payday for the head of a publicly traded securities firm.

But over the past year, mortgage-related losses have slammed the firms, starting in March 2008 with the shotgun marriage of Bear Stearns Cos. to J.P. Morgan Chase & Co. Then, in September, Lehman Brothers Holdings Inc. filed for bankruptcy protection, and Merrill Lynch agreed to be bought by Bank of America Corp.

Goldman has fared better than other firms, but its stock is down more than 60 percent this year. Analysts are predicting it is on course to post its first quarterly loss as a public company in December 2008, when it reports its fourth-quarter earnings.

At many financial firms, about half of all revenue is allocated to compensation, and multi-million-dollar bonuses are routinely paid out to ensure the best talent stays put. Top traders and bankers on Wall Street typically make a base salary of about $250,000, with the rest coming as a bonus. Employees tend to get their bonus numbers in the first two weeks of December—with the cash coming early in the New Year.

Since the start of 2002, Goldman, Morgan Stanley, Merrill, Lehman, and Bear have paid a total of $312 billion in compensation and benefits to its employees. But this compensation model has come under pressure since the Treasury Department recently announced plans to inject capital into financial institutions. Goldman is among the initial nine companies getting a combined $125 billion in government capital, which has fueled worries that taxpayer funds will be used to essentially subsidize Wall Street bonuses.

Regulators, including New York Attorney General Andrew Cuomo, have asked firms for information about compensation plans. Cuomo said that Goldman Sachs "has taken an important step in the right direction," adding, "we strongly encourage other banks to follow Goldman Sach's step."

That advice, however, does not seem to have been followed. The January 28, 2009, report on Wall Street bonuses by New York State Comptroller Thomas DiNapoli found that overall, bonuses fell 44 percent in 2008—yet the size of the securities industry bonus pool, estimated at $18.4 billion, was the sixth-highest on record.

The report comes at a time when any report of Wall Street excess—whether it's the reported $1.2 million former Merrill Lynch CEO John Thain spent to redecorate his office last year or the $50 million business jet Citigroup had on order until this week—is being used by critics as an example of unfettered greed that the financial collapse has done little to curtail.

Thain resigned from Merrill acquirer Bank of America following reports that Merrill paid billions of dollars in bonuses late last year, even as it was about to report a $15 billion fourth-quarter loss and while Bank of America was seeking more federal funds because of the Merrill losses. New York's attorney general is probing the bonus payments as well as executive compensation practices at firms that received federal funds.

In brief but stern remarks in the Oval Office, President Barack Obama called the bonuses "shameful" and "the height of irresponsibility." Obama, sitting with Treasury Secretary Timothy Geithner, made clear that executive compensation—already expected to be a central focus of the new Congress—would be a key factor in his economic team's proposals to stabilize the financial system and improve regulation in the sector. But "part of what we're going to need is for folks on Wall Street who are asking for help to show some restraint, and show some discipline, and show some sense of responsibility," he said.

As Washington policymakers are struggling to come up with solutions to the financial crisis, the pay issue is moving to the forefront. Alice Rivlin, a former director of the Congressional Budget Office, told the National Economics Club in Washington that she was surprised by Citigroup's

efforts to go ahead with the jet purchase and by Thain's "tin ear for the right thing to do in the circumstances." Rivlin added: "We have created a culture of people at the top [of companies] who are disconnected from rest of world, people who don't talk to ordinary people. I know some of them; I'm on corporate boards with them. They've somehow got to get reconnected to the real world—and a lot of them will be, because they are losing their jobs."

Meanwhile, the idea of paying bonuses after many firms have collapsed or required bailouts unleashed a torrent of criticism on the Web. As one commenter wrote on the *New York Times* Web site, "This is hard to believe and impossible to read with equanimity. Wall Street should be hanging [its] head with shame. Instead, it plunges forward with mad self-enrichment at the expense of the rest of the country, even the rest of the world!"

Sources: Susanne Craig, "Goldman Chiefs Give Up Bonuses," *The Wall Street Journal*, November 17, 2008; Phil Mintz and Theo Francis, "Obama Blasts Wall Street Bonuses," *BusinessWeek*, January 29, 2009.

◉ Introduction

The opening story illustrates how firms in the securities industry have sought to use compensation in the form of bonuses to motivate performance, while at the same time controlling fixed compensation costs. The chapter opening also provides an example of how different firms in the industry followed different strategies in responding to a crisis of sharply declining performance. When shareholders are losing billions of dollars, should executives be receiving billions of dollars in bonuses? What about when these same firms are also receiving billions of dollars in taxpayer assistance? Is this pay-for-performance?

The preceding chapter discussed setting pay for jobs. In this chapter we focus on using pay to recognize and reward employees' contributions to the organization's success. Employees' pay does not depend solely on the jobs they hold. Instead, differences in performance (individual, group, or organization), seniority, skills, and so forth are used as a basis for differentiating pay among employees.[1] In some cases, as we saw in the chapter opening, large amounts of compensation can be at stake.

Several key questions arise in evaluating different pay programs for recognizing contributions. First, what are the costs of the program? Second, what is the expected return (in terms of influences on attitudes and behaviors) from such investments? Third, does the program fit with the organization's human resource strategy and its overall business strategy? Fourth, what might go wrong with the plan in terms of unintended consequences? For example, will the plan encourage managers and employees to pay more attention to some objectives (e.g., short-term sales) than to some others (e.g., customer service and long-term customer satisfaction)?

Organizations have a relatively large degree of discretion in deciding how to pay, especially compared with the pay level decisions discussed in the previous chapter. The same organizational pay level (or "compensation pie") can be distributed (shared) among employees in many ways. Whether each employee's share is based on individual performance, profits, seniority, or other factors, the size of the pie (and thus the cost to the organization) can remain the same.

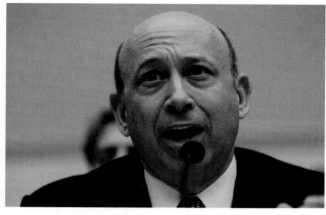

● CEO Lloyd Blankfein of Goldman Sachs requested to forego his bonus after profits fell in 2008.

Regardless of cost differences, different pay programs can have very different consequences for productivity and return on investment. Indeed, a study of how much 150 organizations paid found not only that the largest differences between organizations had to do with how they paid, but that these differences also resulted in different levels of profitability.[2]

How Does Pay Influence Individual Employees?

Pay plans are typically used to energize, direct, or control employee behavior. Equity theory, described in the previous chapter, is relevant here as well. Most employees compare their own pay with that of others, especially those in the same job. Perceptions of inequity may cause employees to take actions to restore equity. Unfortunately, some of these actions (like quitting or lack of cooperation) may not help the organization.

Three additional theories also help explain compensation's effects: reinforcement, expectancy, and agency theories.

LO1
Discuss how pay influences individual employees, and describe three theories that explain the effect of compensation on individuals.

Reinforcement Theory

E. L. Thorndike's Law of Effect states that a response followed by a reward is more likely to recur in the future. The implication for compensation management is that high employee performance followed by a monetary reward will make future high performance more likely. By the same token, high performance not followed by a reward will make it less likely in the future. The theory emphasizes the importance of a person's actual experience of a reward.

Expectancy Theory

Although **expectancy theory** also focuses on the link between rewards and behaviors, it emphasizes expected (rather than experienced) rewards. In other words, it focuses on the effects of incentives. Behaviors (job performance) can be described as a function of ability and motivation. In turn, motivation is hypothesized to be a function of expectancy, instrumentality, and valence perceptions. Compensation systems differ according to their impact on these motivational components. Generally speaking, the

Expectancy Theory
The theory that says motivation is a function of valence, instrumentality, and expectancy.

main factor is instrumentality: the perceived link between behaviors and pay. Valence of pay outcomes should remain the same under different pay systems. Expectancy perceptions (the perceived link between effort and performance) often have more to do with job design and training than pay systems. A possible exception would be skill-based pay, which directly influences employee training and thus expectancy perceptions.

Although expectancy theory implies that linking an increased amount of rewards to performance will increase motivation and performance, some authors have questioned this assumption, arguing that monetary rewards may increase extrinsic motivation but decrease intrinsic motivation. Extrinsic motivation depends on rewards (such as pay and benefits) controlled by an external source, whereas intrinsic motivation depends on rewards that flow naturally from work itself (like performing interesting work).[3] In other words, paying a child to read books may diminish the child's natural interest in reading, and the child may in the future be less likely to read books unless there are monetary incentives. Although monetary incentives may reduce intrinsic motivation in some settings (such as education), the evidence suggests that such effects are small and probably not very relevant to most settings.[4] Therefore, while it is important to keep in mind that money is not the only effective way to motivate behavior and that monetary rewards will not always be the answer to motivation problems, it does not appear that monetary rewards run much risk of compromising intrinsic motivation in most work settings.

Agency Theory

This theory focuses on the divergent interests and goals of the organization's stakeholders and the ways that employee compensation can be used to align these interests and goals. We cover agency theory in some depth because it provides especially relevant implications for compensation design.

An important characteristic of the modern corporation is the separation of ownership from management (or control). Unlike the early stages of capitalism, where owner and manager were often the same, today, with some exceptions (mostly smaller companies), most stockholders are far removed from the day-to-day operation of companies. Although this separation has important advantages (like mobility of financial capital and diversification of investment risk), it also creates agency costs—the interests of the **principals** (owners) and their **agents** (managers) may no longer converge. What is best for the agent, or manager, may not be best for the owner.

Agency costs can arise from two factors. First, principals and agents may have different goals (goal incongruence). Second, principals may have less than perfect information on the degree to which the agent is pursuing and achieving the principal's goals (information asymmetry).

Three examples of agency costs can occur in managerial compensation.[5] First, although shareholders seek to maximize their wealth, management may spend money on things such as perquisites (corporate jets, for example) or "empire building" (making acquisitions that do not add value to the company but may enhance the manager's prestige or pay). Second, managers and shareholders may differ in their attitudes toward risk. Shareholders can diversify their investments (and thus their risks) more easily than managers (whose only major source of income may be their jobs), so managers are typically more averse to risk. They may be less likely to pursue projects or acquisitions with high potential payoff. It also suggests a preference on the part of managers for

Principal
In agency theory, a person (e.g., an owner) who seeks to direct another person's behavior.

Agent
In agency theory, a person (e.g., a manager) who is expected to act on behalf of a principal (e.g., an owner).

relatively little risk in their pay (high emphasis on base salary, low emphasis on uncertain bonuses or incentives). Indeed, research shows that managerial compensation in manager-controlled firms is more often designed in this manner.[6] Third, decision-making horizons may differ. For example, if managers change companies more than owners change ownership, managers may be more likely to maximize short-run performance (and pay), perhaps at the expense of long-term success. In a country like China, these issues (and how they affect executive pay levels) have only recently begun to receive significant attention. (See the "Competing through Globalization" box.)

Agency theory is also of value in the analysis and design of nonmanagers' compensation. In this case, interests may diverge between managers (now in the role of principals) and their employees (who take on the role of agents).

In designing either managerial or nonmanagerial compensation, the key question is, How can such agency costs be minimized? Agency theory says that the principal must choose a contracting scheme that helps align the interests of the agent with the principal's own interests (that is, it reduces agency costs). These contracts can be classified as either behavior-oriented (such as merit pay) or outcome-oriented (stock options, profit sharing, commissions, and so on).[7]

At first blush, outcome-oriented contracts seem to be the obvious solution. If profits are high, compensation goes up. If profits drop, compensation goes down. The interests of "the company" and employees are aligned. An important drawback, however, is that such contracts increase the agent's risk. And because agents are averse to risk, they may require higher pay (a compensating wage differential) to make up for it.[8]

Behavior-based contracts, on the other hand, do not transfer risk to the agent and thus do not require a compensating wage differential. However, the principal must be able to overcome the information asymmetry issue noted previously and monitor with little cost what the agent has done. Otherwise, the principal must either invest in monitoring (e.g., add more supervisors) and information or structure the contract so that pay is linked at least partly to outcomes.[9]

Which type of contract should an organization use? It depends partly on the following factors:[10]

- *Risk aversion.* Risk aversion among agents makes outcome-oriented contracts less likely.
- *Outcome uncertainty.* Profit is an example of an outcome. Agents are less willing to have their pay linked to profits to the extent that there is a risk of low profits. They would therefore prefer a behavior-oriented contract.
- *Job programmability.* As jobs become less programmable (less routine), outcome-oriented contracts become more likely because monitoring becomes more difficult.[11]
- *Measurable job outcomes.* When outcomes are more measurable, outcome-oriented contracts are more likely.
- *Ability to pay.* Outcome-oriented contracts contribute to higher compensation costs because of the risk premium.
- *Tradition.* A tradition or custom of using (or not using) outcome-oriented contracts will make such contracts more (or less) likely.

In summary, the reinforcement, expectancy, and agency theories all focus on the fact that behavior–reward contingencies can shape behaviors. However, agency theory is of particular value in compensation management because of its emphasis on the risk–reward trade-off, an issue that needs close attention when companies consider variable pay plans, which can carry significant risk.

During my two-hour-long interview with a senior Chinese banker recently, we covered a lot of topics, from the credit crisis in the U.S. to the emergence of consumerism in China. He was unusually open for a Chinese executive. But when I asked about his multi-million yuan ($1 is about seven yuan) compensation last year, he fell silent.

If you think executive pay is a controversial topic in the U.S., or that the tension between highly-paid CEOs and shareholders is high here, you should see China. Publicly-traded Chinese companies didn't start disclosing executive-pay information until a couple of years ago, and it instantly became an explosive topic in proxy seasons. Many Chinese raised questions such as, "What do they base their pay on?" and "How could they make more than the state chairman?"

The senior banker said he would be more than happy if his name weren't associated with the topic. On the one hand, he explained, top executives at public companies do make a lot more than executives at state-owned enterprises and government officials, not to mention the majority of ordinary Chinese. On the other hand, he said, people like him make far less than their counterparts on Wall Street and in Hong Kong. To attract and retain talented people who are increasingly moving around globally, public Chinese companies need to offer comparable salaries and bonuses. So the pay of executives like him are more or less a compromise between China's reality and market competition.

"But how can I say this to those who make very little?" he asked. "They won't understand, and I don't expect them to understand."

I see his point. I can't imagine China going back to the egalitarian society that we escaped 30 years ago, in which everybody received a salary based on their educational background and seniority, instead of their capabilities and achievements. Few people will work hard unless they know they will be rewarded, whether that reward is a bonus for a banker, power for a politician, or a harvest for a farmer. That's simply human nature, and China's economic growth in the past three decades is the best evidence of it.

But I also understand why the unemployed, the middle class and lowly-paid government officials get angry at what they see as astronomical pay. The average annual income of urban workers in China last year was 24,932 yuan ($3,561), according to the National Bureau of State Statistics. Farmers and migrant workers make far less than that. Meanwhile, Shenzhen Development Bank Chairman and Chief Executive Frank Newman made roughly 23 million yuan ($3.3 million) in 2007, about 922 times the average urban pay, and Ping An Insurance Co. Chairman Ma Mingzhe made more than 66 million yuan ($9.3 million), or 2,647 times a regular worker's pay. (He donated 20 million yuan to a charity.)

The executive-compensation figures have triggered a public backlash. In an online vote on Sina.com, one of China's top portals, 93 percent of voters disapproved of the executive-pay practices at Ping An and Shenzhen Development Bank.

Mr. Ma of Ping An has also been made a villain in Internet chat rooms and on online forums since his pay information became public late last month. "Is the 66 Million Yuan Pay an April Fool's Joke?" demands a post on the popular online forum Tianya.cn. . . .

More importantly, some state-controlled public companies rely on monopolies and preferential government policies for their profits, so there's an understandable debate about whether these firms' government-appointed executives should get paid handsomely—and if their compensation should be linked to those "guaranteed" profits.

. . .

[These companies] need to answer the questions raised on online forums again and again: Do these officials deserve more than 10 times their government pay once they are appointed as CEOs of public companies? Do they have the managerial talent to be retained with shareholders' money? Is their loyalty to the government, or to their shareholders? If some of the bank's income comes from its monopoly position and preferential government policies, should the CEO be rewarded for that?

There are no easy answers to these questions: While the U.S. and other industrial countries have been debating executive

pay for many years, China has just started the discussion—and has to conduct it against the backdrop of a complex asset structure and political system. But it seems that the Chinese public is determined to ask these tough questions every

proxy season. And that in itself is encouraging.

SOURCE: Li Yuan, "Executive Pay Hits China's Radar," *The Wall Street Journal Online,* April 10, 2008. Copyright © 2008 by Dow Jones & Co., Inc. Reproduced with permission of Dow Jones & Co., Inc. via Copyright Clearance Center.

How Does Pay Influence Labor Force Composition?

Traditionally, using pay to recognize employee contributions has been thought of as a way to influence the behaviors and attitudes of current employees, whereas pay level and benefits have been seen as a way to influence so-called membership behaviors: decisions about whether to join or remain with the organization. However, there is increasing recognition that individual pay programs may also affect the nature and composition of an organization's workforce.[12] For example, it is possible that an organization that links pay to performance may attract more high performers than an organization that does not link the two. There may be a similar effect with respect to job retention.[13]

Continuing the analysis, different pay systems appear to attract people with different personality traits and values.[14] Organizations that link pay to individual performance may be more likely to attract individualistic employees, whereas organizations relying more heavily on team rewards are more likely to attract team-oriented employees. The implication is that the design of compensation programs needs to be carefully coordinated with the organization and human resource strategy. Increasingly, both in the United States and abroad, employers are seeking to establish stronger links between pay and performance.

Programs

In compensating employees, an organization does not have to choose one program over another. Instead, a combination of programs is often the best solution. For example, one program may foster teamwork and cooperation but not enough individual initiative. Another may do the opposite. Used in conjunction, a balance may be attained. Such balancing of objectives, combined with careful alignment with the organization and human resource strategy, may help increase the probability that a pay for performance program has its intended effects and reduce the probability of unintended consequences and problems.[15]

Table 12.1 provides an overview of the programs for recognizing employee contributions. Each program shares a focus on paying for performance. The programs differ according to three design features: (1) payment method, (2) frequency of payout, and (3) ways of measuring performance. In a perhaps more speculative vein, the table also suggests the potential consequences of such programs for (1) performance motivation of employees, (2) attraction of employees, (3) organization culture, and (4) costs.

LO2
Describe the fundamental pay programs for recognizing employees' contributions to the organization's success.

LO3
List the advantages and disadvantages of the pay programs.

table 12.1

Programs for Recognizing Employee Contributions

	MERIT PAY	INCENTIVE PAY	PROFIT SHARING	OWNERSHIP	GAIN SHARING	SKILL-BASED
Design features						
Payment method	Changes in base pay	Bonus	Bonus	Equity changes	Bonus	Change in base pay
Frequency of payout	Annually	Weekly	Semiannually or annually	When stock sold	Monthly or quarterly	When skill or competency acquired
Performance measures	Supervisor's appraisal of individual performance	Individual output, productivity, sales	Company profit	Company stock returns	Production or controllable costs of stand-alone work unit	Skill or competency acquisition of individuals
Consequences						
Performance motivation	Relationship between pay and performance varies	Clear performance–reward connection	Stronger in smaller firms	Stronger in smaller firms	Stronger in smaller units	Encourages learning
Attraction	Over time pays better performers more	Pays higher performers more	Helps with all employees if plan pays out	Can help lock in employees	Helps with all employees if plan pays out	Attracts learning-oriented employees
Culture	Individual competition	Individual competition	Knowledge of business and cooperation	Sense of ownership and cooperation	Supports cooperation, problem solving	Learning and flexible organization
Costs	Requires well-developed performance appraisal system	Setting and maintaining acceptable standards	Relates costs to ability to pay	Relates costs to ability to pay	Setting and maintaining acceptable standards	Training and certification
Contingencies						
Management style	Some participation desirable	Control	Fits participation	Fits participation	Fits participation	Fits participation
Type of work	Individual unless group appraisals done	Stable, individual, easily measurable	All types	All types	All types	Significant skill depth or breadth

SOURCE: Adapted and modified from E. E. Lawler III, "Pay for Performance: A Strategic Analysis," in *Compensation and Benefits*, ed. L. R. Gomez-Mejia (Washington, DC: Bureau of National Affairs, 1989).

Finally, there are two contingencies that may influence whether each pay program fits the situation: (1) management style and (2) type of work. We now discuss the different programs and some of their potential consequences in more depth.

figure 12.1

Performance Dimensions for Lower to Midlevel Managers, Arrow Electronics

1. Exercises good business judgment
2. Inspires enthusiasm, energy, understanding, loyalty for company goals
3. Attracts, grows, and retains outstanding talent
4. Shows initiative
5. Has position-specific knowledge
6. Delivers results
7. Builds internal good will

SOURCE: From "Compensation and Performance Evaluation at Arrow Electronics" (Boston: Harvard Business School), Case 9-800-290. Copyright © 2000 by the President and Fellows of Harvard College. Reprinted with permission.

Merit Pay

In merit pay programs, annual pay increases are usually linked to performance appraisal ratings. (See Chapter 8.) Some type of merit pay program exists in almost all organizations (although evidence on merit pay effectiveness is surprisingly scarce).[16] As the chapter opening demonstrated, some employers have moved toward a form of merit pay that relies on bonuses rather than increases to base pay. One reason for the widespread use of merit pay is its ability to define and reward a broad range of performance dimensions. (See Figure 12.1 for an example.) Indeed, given the pervasiveness of merit pay programs, we devote a good deal of attention to them here.

Basic Features

Many merit pay programs work off of a **merit increase grid.** As Table 12.2 indicates, the size and frequency of pay increases are determined by two factors. The first factor is the individual's performance rating (because better performers should receive higher pay). The second factor is position in range (that is, an individual's compa-ratio). So, for example, an employee with a performance rating of EX and a compa-ratio

Merit Increase Grid
A grid that combines an employee's performance rating with the employee's position in a pay range to determine the size and frequency of his or her pay increases.

table 12.2

Example of Merit Increase Grid from Merck & Co., Inc.

		SUGGESTED MERIT INCREASE PERCENTAGE			
PERFORMANCE RATING		COMPA-RATIO 80.00–95.00	COMPA-RATIO 95.01–110.00	COMPA-RATIO 110.01–120.00	COMPA-RATIO 120.01–125.00
EX	(Exceptional within Merck)	13–15%	12–14%	9–11%	To maximum of range
WD	(Merck Standard with Distinction)	9–11	8–10	7–9	—
HS	(High Merck Standard)	7–9	6–8	—	—
RI	(Merck Standard Room for Improvement)	5–7	—	—	—
NA	(Not Adequate for Merck)	—	—	—	—

SOURCE: From "Compensation and Performance Evaluation at Arrow Electronics" (Boston: Harvard Business School), Case 9-800-290. Copyright © 2000 by the President and Fellows of Harvard College. Reprinted with permission.

table 12.3

Performance Ratings and Compa-ratio Targets

PERFORMANCE RATING	COMPA-RATIO TARGET
EX (Exceptional within Merck)	115–125
WD (Merck Standard with Distinction)	100–120
HS (High Merck Standard)	90–110
RI (Merck Standard Room for Improvement)	80–95
NA (Not Adequate for Merck)	None

SOURCE: From "Compensation and Performance Evaluation at Arrow Electronics" (Boston: Harvard Business School), Case 9-800-290. Copyright © 2000 by the President and Fellows of Harvard College. Reprinted with permission.

of 120 would receive a pay increase of 9 to 11 percent. By comparison, an employee with a performance rating of EX and a compa-ratio of 85 would receive an increase of 13 to 15 percent. (Note that the general magnitude of increases in such a table is influenced by inflation rates. Thus the percentage increases in such a grid would have been considerably lower in recent years.) One reason for factoring in the compa-ratio is to control compensation costs and maintain the integrity of the pay structure. If a person with a compa-ratio of 120 received a merit increase of 13 to 15 percent, she would soon exceed the pay range maximum. Not factoring in the compa-ratio would also result in uncontrolled growth of compensation costs for employees who continue to perform the same job year after year. Instead, some organizations think in terms of assessing where the employee's pay is now and where it should be, given a particular performance level. Consider Table 12.3. An employee who consistently performs at the EX level should be paid at 115 to 125 percent of the market (that is, a compa-ratio of 115 to 125). To the extent that the employee is far from that pay level, larger and more frequent pay increases are necessary to move the employee to the correct position. On the other hand, if the employee is already at that pay level, smaller pay increases will be needed. The main objective in the latter case would be to provide pay increases that are sufficient to maintain the employee at the targeted compa-ratio.

In controlling compensation costs, another factor that requires close attention is the distribution of performance ratings. (See Chapter 8.) In many organizations, 60 to 70 percent of employees fall into the top two (out of four to five) performance rating categories.[17] This means tremendous growth in compensation costs because most employees will eventually be above the midpoint of the pay range, resulting in compa-ratios well over 100. To avoid this, some organizations provide guidelines regarding the percentage of employees who should fall into each performance category, usually limiting the percentage that can be placed in the top two categories. These guidelines are enforced differently, ranging from true guidelines to strict forced-distribution requirements.

In general, merit pay programs have the following characteristics. First, they identify individual differences in performance, which are assumed to reflect differences in ability or motivation. By implication, system constraints on performance are not seen as significant. Second, the majority of information on individual performance is collected from the immediate supervisor. Peer and subordinate ratings are rare, and where they exist, they tend to receive less weight than supervisory ratings.[18] Third, there is a policy of linking pay increases to performance appraisal results.[19] Fourth, the feedback under such systems tends to occur infrequently, often once per year at the formal performance review session. Fifth, the flow of feedback tends to be largely unidirectional, from supervisor to subordinate.

Criticisms of Traditional Merit Pay Programs

Criticisms of this process have been raised. For example, W. Edwards Deming, a leader of the total quality management movement, argued that it is unfair to rate individual performance because "apparent differences between people arise almost entirely from the system that they work in, not from the people themselves."[20] Examples of system factors include co-workers, the job, materials, equipment, customers, management, supervision, and environmental conditions. These are believed to be largely outside the worker's control, instead falling under management's responsibility. Deming argued that the performance rating is essentially "the result of a lottery."[21]

Deming also argued that the individual focus of merit pay discourages teamwork: "Everyone propels himself forward, or tries to, for his own good, on his own life preserver. The organization is the loser."[22] As an example, if people in the purchasing department are evaluated based on the number of contracts negotiated, they may have little interest in materials quality, even though manufacturing is having quality problems.

Deming's solution was to eliminate the link between individual performance and pay. This approach reflects a desire to move away from recognizing individual contributions. What are the consequences of such a move? It is possible that fewer employees with individual-achievement orientations would be attracted to and remain with the organization. One study of job retention found that the relationship between pay growth and individual performance over time was weaker at higher performance levels. As a consequence, the organization lost a disproportionate share of its top performers.[23] In other words, too little emphasis on individual performance may leave the organization with average and poor performers.[24]

Thus, although Deming's concerns about too much emphasis on individual performance are well taken, one must be careful not to replace one set of problems with another. Instead, there needs to be an appropriate balance between individual and group objectives. At the very least, ranking and forced-distribution performance-rating systems need to be considered with caution, lest they contribute to behavior that is too individualistic and competitive.

Another criticism of merit pay programs is the way they measure performance. If the performance measure is not perceived as being fair and accurate, the entire merit pay program can break down. One potential impediment to accuracy is the almost exclusive reliance on the supervisor for providing performance ratings, even though peers, subordinates, and customers (internal and external) often have information on a person's performance that is as good as or better than that of the supervisor. A 360-degree performance feedback approach (discussed in Chapter 9) gathers feedback from each of these sources. To date, however, organizations have mainly used such data for development purposes and have been reluctant to use these multisource data for making pay decisions.[25]

In general, process issues appear to be important in administering merit pay. In any situation where rewards are distributed, employees appear to assess fairness along two dimensions: distributive (based on how much they receive) and procedural (what process was used to decide how much).[26] Some of the most important aspects of procedural fairness, or justice, appear in Table 12.4. These items suggest that employees desire clear and consistent performance standards, as well as opportunities to provide input, discuss their performance, and appeal any decision they believe to be incorrect.

Perhaps the most basic criticism is that merit pay does not really exist. High performers are not paid significantly more than mediocre or even poor performers in most

table 12.4

Aspects of
Procedural Justice in
Pay Raise Decisions

Indicate the extent to which your supervisor did each of the following:
1. Was honest and ethical in dealing with you.
2. Gave you an opportunity to express your side.
3. Used consistent standards in evaluating your performance.
4. Considered your views regarding your performance.
5. Gave you feedback that helped you learn how well you were doing.
6. Was completely candid and frank with you.
7. Showed a real interest in trying to be fair.
8. Became thoroughly familiar with your performance.
9. Took into account factors beyond your control.
10. Got input from you before a recommendation.
11. Made clear what was expected of you.

Indicate how much of an opportunity existed, after the last raise decision, for you to do each of the following things:
12. Make an appeal about the size of a raise.
13. Express your feelings to your supervisor about the salary decision.
14. Discuss, with your supervisor, how your performance was evaluated.
15. Develop, with your supervisor, an action plan for future performance.

SOURCE: From R. Folger, and M.A. Konorsky, "Effects of Procedural and Distributive Justice on Reactions to Pay Raise Decisions," *Academy of Management Journal* 32 (1989), p. 115. Copyright © 1989 by Academy of Management (NY). Reproduced with permission of Academy of Management (NY) via Copyright Clearance Center.

cases.[27] For example, with a merit increase budget of 4 to 5 percent, suppose high performers receive 6 percent raises, versus 3.5 to 4 percent raises for average performers. On a salary of $40,000 per year, the difference in take-home pay would not be more than about $300 per year, or about $6 per week. Critics of merit pay point out that this difference is probably not significant enough to influence employee behaviors or attitudes. Indeed, as Figure 12.2 indicates, many employees do not believe there is any payoff to higher levels of performance.

figure 12.2

Percentage of
Employees Who
Agree That Better
Performance Leads
to Better Increases

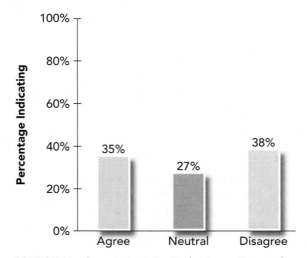

SOURCE: Hay Group, *Managing Performance: Survey of Employees in 335 Companies*, Philadelphia: Hay Group, 2002. Reprinted with permission.

Of course, small differences in pay can accumulate into large differences over time. The present value of the salary advantage would be $29,489 (based on a discount rate of 5 percent). For example, over a 30-year career, an initial annual salary difference of $740 with equal merit increases thereafter of 7 percent would accumulate into a career salary advantage of $75,738.[28] Whether employees think in these terms is open to question. But even if they do not, nothing prevents an organization from explaining to employees that what may appear to be small differences in pay can add up to large differences over time. It should also be kept in mind that merit ratings are often closely linked to promotions, which in turn are closely linked to salary. Thus, even in merit pay settings where performance differences are not recognized in the short run, high performers are likely to have significantly higher career earnings.

Finally, the accumulation effect just described can also be seen as a drawback if it contributes to an entitlement mentality. Here the concern is that a big merit increase given early in an employee's career remains part of base salary "forever." It does not have to be re-earned each year, and the cost to the organization grows over time, perhaps more than either the employee's performance or the organization's profitability would always warrant. Merit bonuses (payouts that do not become part of base salary), in lieu of traditional merit increases, are thus used by some organizations instead.

EVIDENCE-BASED HR

In a bid to reduce high turnover rates among restaurant employees, Applebee's, the United States's biggest casual-dining chain by number of restaurants, reviews and ranks its hourly employees, and then rewards managers for retaining their better workers. When it first started this program, Applebee's turnover rate was 146 percent, well above even the industrywide casual dining turnover rate of around 100 percent.

At Applebee's, Overland Park, Kansas, managers must now divide hourly workers into "A" players, the top 20 percent; B, the middle 60 percent; the C, the bottom 20 percent. The managers then are eligible for merit raises and bonuses based on how well they retain employees in the top 80 percent. The practice is unusual in the restaurant industry, where managers tend to worry more about staffing the next shift than career development and performance evaluation. "Among the hourly retail or service employees, there is certainly a tendency to say, 'Let's bring warm bodies in here,' and then to just try to hold down turnover in general," says Rick Beal, a senior compensation consultant at Watson Wyatt Worldwide, a human resources consulting firm in Washington, DC. Beal says rewarding managers for retaining the better workers is a great idea in theory, but will prove effective only if employers develop straightforward, and simple, ways to judge hourly workers. "Otherwise you're going to burn more time than it's worth," he says.

Applebee's says the system is time-consuming, but worth the effort. Before introducing the system, Applebee's measured overall turnover but didn't use the numbers to evaluate managers. Then, executives realized, "there is a different value if you lose a top-20 person than if you lose a bottom-20 person," says John Prutsman, who is in charge of human resources for the restaurants. In order to reward managers for keeping the best people, the company had to develop a system for reviewing hourly workers, including the grading criteria. Today, Applebee's evaluates all hourly employees twice a year on nine counts, including reliability, attitude, guest service, and teamwork. First, employees complete a self-evaluation. Then, managers grade employees.

Managers, in turn, get rewarded on how well they retain the top 80 percent, or their As and Bs. To win employees' loyalty, managers can give out small raises; award them "Applebucks," points toward prizes such as bicycles, radios, or DVD players; or distribute special pins for highly ranked employees. Workers generally aren't told their grades. Many managers also employ their own motivational tricks, such as displaying posters of employee photos or not scheduling employees to work on their birthdays and anniversaries. Applebee's credits the system with helping to reduce annual turnover among hourly employees at company-owned restaurants almost by half in four years, to 84 percent from 146 percent. Applebee's owns 485 restaurants; a further 1,301 are franchises, where Applebee's doesn't control the retention practices but shares its techniques with the franchisees.

Linda Saleeby, general manager at an Applebee's in Chester, Virginia, for several years, says the evaluation process takes her management team about six weeks from start to finish. But she says the benefits extend beyond reduced turnover. She says employees like knowing what is expected of them and generally where they stand. "They know what it is we're focusing on," she says. "I don't think any kind of time we spend on people is a waste of time or hassle, because it's such a huge portion of our business," she says.

Saleeby has benefited from the system, too, by earning raises and bonuses based partly on her high retention scores. This is important in an industry where manager turnover is also high (27 percent) and where evidence shows that retention of managers goes hand-in-hand with higher store sales. Some of her techniques include giving out ice-cream bars to employees who work on Saturdays, meeting with parents of newly hired teen workers, and holding "round-table meetings" with employees to give them a say in things like scheduling. She likes the focus on the top 80 percent. "There's a certain number of people, despite all the tools you use to hire them, that just don't work out," she says.

SOURCES: E. White, "Theory & Practice: How To Reduce Turnover; Restaurant Chain Retains Workers Using Rankings And Rewards," *The Wall Street Journal*, November 21, 2005, P. B5; D. Berta, "People Report: Worker Turnover Rate Continues to Climb," *Nation's Restaurant News*, November 20, 2006; D. Berta, "People Report: Reduced Turnover Helps Restaurants Fight Recession," *Nation's Restaurant News*, November 24, 2008.

Individual Incentives

Like merit pay, individual incentives reward individual performance, but with two important differences. First, payments are not rolled into base pay. They must be continuously earned and re-earned. Second, performance is usually measured as physical output (such as number of water faucets produced) rather than by subjective ratings. Individual incentives have the potential to significantly increase performance. Locke and his colleagues found that monetary incentives increased production output by a median of 30 percent—more than any other motivational device studied.[29]

Nevertheless, individual incentives are relatively rare for a variety of reasons.[30] Most jobs (like those of managers and professionals) have no physical output measure. Instead, they involve what might be described as "knowledge work." Also, many potential administrative problems (such as setting and maintaining acceptable

figure 12.3

How Incentives Sometimes "Work"

SOURCE: DILBERT © Scott Adams/Dist. by United Feature Syndicate, Inc.

standards) often prove intractable. Third, individual incentives may do such a good job of motivating employees that they do whatever they get paid for and nothing else. (See the Dilbert cartoon in Figure 12.3.) Fourth, as the name implies, individual incentives typically do not fit well with a team approach. Fifth, they may be inconsistent with the goals of acquiring multiple skills and proactive problem solving. Learning new skills often requires employees to slow or stop production. If the employees are paid based on production volume, they may not want to slow down or stop. Sixth, some incentive plans reward output volume at the expense of quality or customer service.

Therefore, although individual incentives carry potential advantages, they are not likely to contribute to a flexible, proactive, problem-solving workforce. In addition, such programs may not be particularly helpful in the pursuit of total quality management objectives. Consider the incentive plan described in the "Competing through Technology" box. Do you think the plan will be successful?

Profit Sharing and Ownership

Profit Sharing

At the other end of the individual–group continuum are profit sharing and stock ownership plans. Under **profit sharing,** payments are based on a measure of organization performance (profits), and the payments do not become part of the base salary. Profit sharing has two potential advantages. First, it may encourage employees to think more like owners, taking a broad view of what needs to be done to make the organization more effective. Thus, the sort of narrow self-interest encouraged by individual incentive plans (and perhaps also by merit pay) is presumably less of an issue. Instead, increased cooperation and citizenship are expected. Second, because payments do not become part of base pay, labor costs are automatically reduced during difficult economic times, and wealth is shared during good times. Consequently, organizations may not need to rely on layoffs as much to reduce costs during tough times.[31]

Does profit sharing contribute to better organization performance? The evidence is not clear. Although there is consistent support for a correlation between profit sharing

Profit Sharing
A compensation plan in which payments are based on a measure of organization performance (profits) and do not become part of the employees' base salary.

Retailers have a new tool to turn up the heat on their salespeople: computer programs that dictate which employees should work when, and for how long.

Ann Taylor Stores Corp. installed a system last year. When saleswoman Nyla Houser types her code number into a cash register at the Ann Taylor store at the Oxford Valley Mall in Langhorne, Pennsylvania, it displays her "performance metrics": average sales per hour, units sold, and dollars per transaction. The system schedules the most productive sellers to work the busiest hours.

"We are under the gun to be a much more efficiently running organization," said Scott Knaul, director of store operations at the women's apparel retailer, which said earlier this year that it is closing 117 underperforming stores over the next few years. There was an initial "ego hit" for some employees, he said at a gathering of retailers in May. But the system, he said, has helped turn more store browsers into buyers.

Such "workforce management" systems are sweeping the industry as retailers fight to improve productivity and cut payroll costs. Limited Brands Inc., Gap Inc., Williams-Sonoma Inc., and GameStop Corp. have all installed them recently. Some employees aren't happy about the trend. They say the systems leave them with shorter shifts, make it difficult to schedule their lives, and unleash Darwinian forces on the sales floor that damage morale.

"There was a lot of animosity" toward the system, says Kelly Engle, who worked at an Ann Taylor store in Beavercreek, Ohio, until late last year. "Computers aren't very forgiving when it comes to an individual's life."

The systems stand to have a broad impact on the work lives of Americans. Some 15 million people work in the U.S. retail industry, making it the nation's third-largest private-sector employer. The work isn't especially lucrative. Many jobs are part-time, the hourly pay is low, and most sales floors aren't unionized. At Ann Taylor, part-time sales clerks have no guaranteed weekly minimum pay.

The sluggish national economy has put pressure on many retailers to pinch pennies. "The single biggest controllable cost in retail is people," says Carl Steidtmann, chief economist at Deloitte LLP. Because few retail workers belong to unions, he says, it is easier for employers to "move people around."

Vendors of the systems claim they can boost productivity by 15 percent or more and can help cut labor costs by 5 percent or more. Wal-Mart Stores Inc. just completed a yearlong rollout of a computerized scheduling system for 1.3 million workers. It cited 12 percent labor-productivity gains as a key reason for improved results in its fiscal quarter ended January 31, 2009.

"There's been a natural resistance to thinking about human beings as pieces in a puzzle rather than individuals," says John M. Gibbons, a senior research adviser at the Conference Board and a former director of human resources at Gap. "When you have those clear methods of measurement, and just-in-time delivery for supply-chain management, it's a natural transition to apply it to human resources as well."

Ann Taylor, which targets fashion-conscious working women, operates 959 stores, including its namesake Ann Taylor stores, factory outlets, and LOFT casual apparel stores. Battered by slumping mall traffic, it is immersed in an overhaul that has included store closings, job cuts and senior management changes. Its shares have fallen about 15 percent over the past year.

Ann Taylor calls its system the Ann Taylor Labor Allocation System—Atlas for short. Before it installed the system, Ann Taylor spent a year studying labor efficiencies. It established standards for how long it should take for employees to complete certain tasks: three seconds to greet a shopper; two minutes to help someone trying on clothing; 32 seconds to fold a sweater; and most importantly, five minutes to clinch a sale. Its goal was to figure out how many employees it needed in a store at any given time, based on customer traffic.

"If we know that it takes five minutes to work with a client when they walk in the store, we won't go over five minutes" in time planning per store, Knaul explained to other retailers at the May gathering for RedPrairie software customers, which was attended by a *Wall Street Journal* reporter. "We don't need it. It's surplus." He added that the time standards can be modified for labor-budget purposes.

AnnTaylor decided that employees were taking too long to open stores. Workers who came in two hours before opening "got a coffee and sat down and caught up with what was on TV the night before," Knaul noted. The time was cut to one hour.

Because the system awards more-productive salespeople with favorable hours, it gives employees an incentive to persuade shoppers to buy things.

In May 2007, after Atlas was tested in some stores, James M. Smith, chief financial officer at the time, said those stores were seeing a "pickup" in comparable-store sales. Kay Krill, AnnTaylor's chief executive, reported a "very promising" increase in conversion, meaning that more browsers were becoming buyers. AnnTaylor declined to elaborate on the financial effect.

The system was rolled out that spring in nearly 350 Ann Taylor stores. Kristi Connell, an assistant manager at the time in the Langhorne, Pennsylvania, store, recalls that headquarters had high hopes for Atlas. "They were trying to have less staff on hand and see how the level of service was," she says.

It used to be up to store managers to come up with weekly schedules for employees, and to accommodate their personal preferences. The system automated that task. It created shorter shifts—part of its push to more closely align staffing levels with customer traffic. The system, for example, showed that many stores had too many people starting at 9 A.M. and not enough on hand at peak hours, such as 2 P.M. and later in the afternoon, Knaul said.

In the Langhorne store, after sales-per-hour figures became the determining factor in scheduling, the atmosphere changed dramatically, current and former employees say. When a customer entered the store, employees would angle to get credit for a sale, and thus boost their sales-per-hour numbers, says Abrams, who started as a cashier but was later moved to the sales floor, at $8.85 an hour. After one salesperson greeted a shopper, she explains, another would butt in to offer an opinion, then take over the transaction.

AnnTaylor began ranking its salespeople according to their average sales-per-hour, among other things. When Abrams's sales-per-hour dropped, so did her ranking, she says. Her schedule changed accordingly. "My hours started being less when the heavy traffic was in the store," she recalls. The slow shifts, in turn, made it harder to boost her ranking.

Her pay varied widely week to week, she says. Before the system was installed, she says, her weekly pay sometimes was nearly $300, for about 34 hours of work. Afterward, she says, "I remember some weeks when the most hours I was getting was just eight. It is hard to budget that way." She took on two other part-time jobs. In April, she quit Ann Taylor to take a job that guaranteed her 30 hours a week.

Many other Langhorne employees also saw their hours cut back, and a few of them left, according to several former and current employees.

"A lot of people would be really upset about the way [the system] would schedule," says Tim Fasnacht, who managed an Ann Taylor Factory store in Philadelphia. "Sometimes, people would get a three-hour shift—and you have people coming on public transportation from far away." Because the system didn't award seniority, he says, longtime employees would sometimes be scheduled for as little as 10 hours a week. "There was this huge battle between some of the longtime workers and the management over their schedules."

Pete Reilly, a senior vice president at RedPrairie, which developed the Ann Taylor system, says it's possible for retailers to get too aggressive about slicing and dicing work schedules to match customer traffic. "The system will allow you to push it too far," he says. "But at the end of the day, it is based on business principles and how I treat my employees. That is really up to the retailer."

At AnnTaylor headquarters, executives were braced for complaints about the scheduling system. "Store managers have to talk to [employees] and tell them, this is about the business needs and not about the associate needs," Knaul, the operations director, said to other retailers. "You anticipate the avalanche of complaints and that a lot of people will quit. But then people just go on ahead and change their availability." Overall, not as many people quit as AnnTaylor feared, he said.

Nearly a year after Atlas was rolled out, 76 percent of store managers said they believed the system was better than writing schedules by hand on spreadsheets, Knaul said. AnnTaylor's target was for 80 percent of store managers to view the system as an improvement, he said. Knaul said the new system exceeded the company's targets for converting more browsers into buyers. He said that AnnTaylor hopes to refine the system, possibly with features that rank employees based on skills other than their sales proficiency, such as how well they operate cash registers. Another option, Knaul added, was to begin using the system to more efficiently schedule managers.

SOURCE: Vanessa O'Connell, "Retailers Reprogram Workers in Efficiency Push," *The Wall Street Journal*, September 10, 2008. Copyright © 2008 by Dow Jones & Co., Inc. Reproduced with permission of Dow Jones & Co., Inc. via Copyright Clearance Center.

payments and profits, questions have been raised about the direction of causality.[32] For example, Ford, Chrysler, and GM all have profit sharing plans in their contracts with the United Auto Workers (UAW). (See Figure 12.4 for provisions of the GM–UAW plan.) The average profit sharing payment at Ford one year was $4,000 per worker versus an average of $550 per worker at GM and $8,000 at Chrysler. Given that the profit sharing plans are similar, it seems unlikely they caused Ford and Chrysler to be more profitable. Rather, it would appear that profits were higher at Ford for other reasons, resulting in higher profit sharing payments.

This example also helps illustrate the fundamental drawback of profit sharing. Why should automobile workers at GM receive profit sharing payments that are only 1/15 the size received by those doing the same type of work at Chrysler? Is it because Chrysler UAW members performed 15 times better than their counterparts at GM that year? Probably not. Rather, workers are likely to view top management decisions regarding products, engineering, pricing, and marketing as more important. As a result, with the exception of top (and perhaps some middle) managers, most employees are unlikely to see a strong connection between what they do and what they earn under profit sharing. This means that performance motivation is likely to change very little under profit sharing. Consistent with expectancy theory, motivation depends on a strong link between behaviors and valued consequences such as pay (instrumentality perceptions).

Another factor that reduces the motivational impact of profit sharing plans is that most plans are of the deferred type. Roughly 16 percent of full-time employees in medium-size and large private establishments participate in profit sharing plans, but only 1 percent of employees overall (about 6 percent of those in profit sharing plans) are in cash plans where profits are paid to employees during the current time period.[33]

Not only may profit sharing fail to increase performance motivation, but employees may also react very negatively when they learn that such plans do not pay out during business downturns.[34] First, they may not feel they are to blame because they have been performing their jobs well. Other factors are beyond their control, so why should they be penalized? Second, what seems like a small amount of risked pay for a manager earning $80,000 per year can be very painful to someone earning $15,000 or $20,000.

Consider the case of the Du Pont Fibers Division, which had a plan that linked a portion of employees' pay to division profits.[35] After the plan's implementation, employees' base salary was about 4 percent lower than similar employees in other

figure 12.4

Profit Sharing in the General Motors–UAW Contract

2.14 **"Profits"** . . . means income earned by U.S. operations before income taxes and "extraordinary" items. . . . Profits are before any profit sharing charges are deducted. Profits also are before incentive program charges for U.S. operations.

2.18 **"Total Profit Share"** . . . means an obligation of the corporation for any plan year in an amount equal to the sum of:

(a) 6 percent of the portion of profits . . . which exceeds 0.0 percent of sales and revenues . . . but does not exceed 1.8 percent . . .;

(b) 8 percent of the portion of profits . . . which exceeds 1.8 percent of sales and revenues . . . but does not exceed 2.3 percent . . .;

(c) 10 percent of the portion of profits . . . which exceeds 2.3 percent of sales and revenues . . . but does not exceed 4.6 percent . . .;

(d) 14 percent of the portion of profits . . . which exceeds 4.6 percent of sales and revenues . . . but does not exceed 6.9 percent . . .;

(e) 17 percent of the portion of profits . . . which exceeds 6.9 percent of sales and revenues.

4.02 **Allocation of Profit Sharing Amount to Participants**
The portion of the total profit share for the plan year allocated to this plan . . . will be allocated to each participant entitled to a distribution . . . in the proportion that (a) the participant's compensation hours for the plan year bears to (b) the total compensated hours for all participants in the plan entitled to a distribution for the plan year.

SOURCE: From J. A. Fossum, *Labor Relations: Development, Structure and Process,* 10th ed., 2009. Copyright © 2009 The McGraw-Hill Companies, Inc. Reprinted with permission.

divisions unless 100 percent of the profit goal (a 4 percent increase over the previous year's profits) was reached. Thus, there was what might be called downside risk. However, there was also considerable upside opportunity: if 100 percent of the profit goal was exceeded, employees would earn more than similar employees in other divisions. For example, if the division reached 150 percent of the profit goal (6 percent growth in profits), employees would receive 12 percent more than comparable employees in other divisions.

Initially, the plan worked fine. The profit goal was exceeded, and employees earned slightly more than employees in other divisions. In the following year, however, profits were down 26 percent, and the profit goal was not met. Employees received no profit sharing bonus; instead, they earned 4 percent less than comparable employees in other divisions. Profit sharing was no longer seen as a very good idea. Du Pont management responded to employee concerns by eliminating the plan and returning to a system of fixed base salaries with no variable (or risk) component. This outcome is perhaps not surprising from an agency theory perspective, which suggests that employees must somehow be compensated before they will be willing to assume increased risk.

One solution some organizations choose is to design plans that have upside but not downside risk. In such cases, when a profit sharing plan is introduced, base pay is not reduced. Thus, when profits are high, employees share in the gain, but when profits are low, they are not penalized. Such plans largely eliminate what is purported to be a major advantage of profit sharing: reducing labor costs during business downturns. During business upturns, labor costs will increase. Given that the performance benefits of such plans are not assured, an organization runs the risk under such plans of increasing its labor costs with little return on its investment.

In summary, although profit sharing may be useful as one component of a compensation system (to enhance identification with broad organizational goals), it may need to be complemented with other pay programs that more closely link pay to outcomes that individuals or teams can control (or "own"), particularly in larger companies. In addition, profit sharing runs the risk of contributing to employee dissatisfaction or higher labor costs, depending on how it is designed.

Ownership

Recent data show that 20 million Americans own stock in their company.[36] Employee ownership is similar to profit sharing in some key respects, such as encouraging employees to focus on the success of the organization as a whole. In fact, with ownership, this focus may be even stronger. Like profit sharing, ownership may be less motivational the larger the organization. And because employees may not realize any financial gain until they actually sell their stock (typically upon leaving the organization), the link between pay and performance may be even less obvious than under profit sharing. Thus, from a reinforcement theory standpoint (with its emphasis on actually experiencing rewards), the effect on performance motivation may be limited.

Stock Options
An employee ownership plan that gives employees the opportunity to buy the company's stock at a previously fixed price.

One way of achieving employee ownership is through **stock options,** which give employees the opportunity to buy stock at a fixed price. Say the employees receive options to purchase stock at $10 per share in 2009, and the stock price reaches $30 per share in 2014. They have the option of purchasing stock ("exercising" their stock options) at $10 per share in 2014, thus making a tidy return on investment if the shares are then sold. If the stock price goes down to $8 per share in the year 2014, however, there will be no financial gain. Therefore, employees are encouraged to act in ways that will benefit the organization.

For many years, stock options had typically been reserved for executives in larger, established companies. More recently, there was a trend toward pushing eligibility farther down in the organization.[37] In fact, many companies, including PepsiCo, Merck, McDonald's, Wal-Mart, and Procter & Gamble, began granting stock options to employees at all levels. Among start-up companies like these in the technology sector, these broad-based stock option programs have long been popular and companies like Microsoft and Cisco Systems attribute much of their growth and success to these option plans. Some studies suggest that organization performance is higher when a large percentage of top and midlevel managers are eligible for long-term incentives such as stock options, which is consistent with agency theory's focus on the problem of encouraging managers to think like owners.[38] However, it is not clear whether these findings would hold up for lower-level employees, particularly in larger companies, who may see much less opportunity to influence overall organization performance.

The Golden Age of stock options may be coming to an end. Investors have long questioned the historically favorable tax treatment of employee stock options. In 2004, the Financial Accounting Standards Board (FASB) issued SFAS 123R, a landmark change, requiring companies to expense options on their financial statements, which reduces reported net income, dramatically in some cases. Microsoft decided to eliminate stock options in favor of actual stock grants. This is partly in response to the new accounting standards and partly in recognition of the fact that Microsoft's stock price is not likely to grow as rapidly as it once did, making options less effective in recruiting, retaining, and motivating its employees. It appears that many companies are cutting back on stock options overall, and especially for nonexecutive employees.

Those companies that continue to use broad-based stock options have encountered difficulties in keeping employees motivated because of the steep decline in stock prices that most have experienced. The "Competing through Sustainability" box shows Google's response to this challenge.

Employee stock ownership plans (ESOPs), under which employers give employees stock in the company, are the most common form of employee ownership, with the number of employees in such plans increasing from 4 million in 1980 to over 11 million in 2007 in the United States.[39] In Japan, 91 percent of companies listed on Japanese stock markets have an ESOP, and these companies appear to have higher average productivity than non-ESOP companies.[40] ESOPs raise a number of unique issues. On the negative side, they can carry significant risk for employees. An ESOP must, by law, invest at least 51 percent of assets in its company's stock, resulting in less diversification of investment risk (in some cases, no diversification). Consequently, when employees buy out companies in poor financial condition to save their jobs, or when the ESOP is used to fund pensions, employees risk serious financial difficulties if the company does poorly.[41] This is not just a concern for employees, because, as agency theory suggests, employees may require higher pay to offset increased risks of this sort.

ESOPs can be attractive to organizations because they have tax and financing advantages and can serve as a takeover defense (under the assumption that employee owners will be "friendly" to management). ESOPs give employees the right to vote their securities (if registered on a national exchange).[42] As such, some degree of participation in a select number of decisions is mandatory, but overall participation in decision making appears to vary significantly across organizations with ESOPs. Some studies suggest that the positive effects of ownership are larger in cases where employees have greater participation,[43] perhaps because the "employee–owner comes to psychologically experience his/her ownership in the organization."[44]

Employee Stock Ownership Plan (ESOP)
An employee ownership plan that gives employers certain tax and financial advantages when stock is granted to employees.

Gainsharing, Group Incentives, and Team Awards

Gainsharing

Gainsharing programs offer a means of sharing productivity gains with employees. Although sometimes confused with profit sharing plans, gainsharing differs in two key respects. First, instead of using an organization-level performance measure (profits), the programs measure group or plant performance, which is likely to be seen as more controllable by employees. Second, payouts are distributed more frequently and not deferred. In a sense, gainsharing programs represent an effort to pull out the best features of organization-oriented plans like profit sharing and individual-oriented plans like merit pay and individual incentives. Like profit sharing, gainsharing encourages pursuit of broader goals than individual-oriented plans do. But, unlike profit sharing, gainsharing can motivate employees much as individual plans do because of the more controllable nature of the performance measure and the frequency of payouts. Indeed, studies indicate that gainsharing improves performance.[45]

One type of gainsharing, the Scanlon plan (developed in the 1930s by Joseph N. Scanlon, president of a local union at Empire Steel and Tin Plant in Mansfield, Ohio), provides a monetary bonus to employees (and the organization) if the ratio of labor

Gainsharing
A form of compensation based on group or plant performance (rather than organizationwide profits) that does not become part of the employee's base salary.

COMPETING THROUGH SUSTAINABILITY
Google's "One-to-One" Exchange Could Prompt Others to Follow

Google Inc.'s exchange offer for employees with worthless stock options is relatively generous and could prompt other companies to follow suit, shareholders and corporate-governance watchers say.

The Internet-search giant Thursday said it would exchange stock options whose exercise prices are higher than the current price of Google stock for new options, on a one-to-one basis. Google expects the new options to be priced at its closing price on March 2, 2009. Many Google options are worthless—or "underwater"—because its stock, which closed Thursday [January 22, 2009] at $306.50, is down more than 58 percent from its high of $741.79 in November 2007.

The offer makes Google the latest, and among the biggest, of a flood of companies looking to help employees whose compensation has suffered in the stock-market meltdown. Compensation-tracker Equilar says 50 companies completed such exchanges last year, more than three times as many as in 2007. Experts expect the number to rise this year.

Shareholders and corporate-governance watchers criticized the move, which Google said would prompt it to record a $460 million expense.

"Our funds are getting clobbered," said Edward Durkin, who oversees corporate-governance issues for the United Brotherhood of Carpenters and Joiners, whose pension funds own 160,000 Google shares. "We can't knock on the door at Google and say, 'How about $460 million for us?'"

Alexander Cwirko-Godycki, a research manager at Equilar, said more than 60 percent of companies who have exchanged options have given employees less than one new option for every old, worthless option they exchange.

Google's offer "is definitely not one of the most progressive exchange programs we have seen," said Patrick S. McGurn, special counsel for RiskMetrics Group Inc., a proxy-advisory firm.

McGurn and others predicted that Google's offer may prompt more companies to offer option exchanges. "Having a company this big doing it will predictably be a factor in other companies' decisions," suggested Bob Profusek, an attorney and executive-pay expert for Jones Day in New York.

But Profusek said Google needed to act because it uses options as a key recruitment and retention tool for employees and so many of its options were underwater. For a

company that's highly committed to stock options, "having underwater options is worse than no options," he said "It's demoralizing."

Google's three top officers, Chief Executive Eric Schmidt, and co-founders Larry Page and Sergey Brin, won't benefit from the exchange because they don't hold stock options. In an interview, Schmidt said the company's incorporation allowed it to implement the program without a shareholder vote.

Schmidt called the program appropriate. "Generosity is in the eye of the beholder," he said, noting that employees have to wait an additional year to exercise any new options they receive.

He said the option exchange is better for other shareholders than Google issuing new shares, which would dilute other shareholders' ownership stake. "In our local economics, a stock-swap is a very good option for shareholders and employees," he said.

table 12.5

Example of Gainsharing (Modified Scanlon Plan) Report

ITEMS	AVERAGE OF 1ST AND 2ND PERIODS	AVERAGE OF 2ND AND 3RD PERIODS
1. Sales in dollars	$1,000,000	$1,000,000
2. Inventory change and work in process	100,000	100,000
3. Sales value of production	1,100,000	1,100,000
4. Allowable costs (82.5% × 3 above)	907,500	907,500
5. Actual costs	850,000	917,500
6. Gain (4 – 5 above)	57,500	−10,000
7. Employee share (55% of 6 above)	31,625	−5,500
8. Monthly reserve (20% of 7 above)	6,325	−5,500
*If no bonus, 100% of 7 above		
9. Bonus to be distributed (7 – 8)	25,300	0
10. Company share (45% of 6 above)	25,875	−4,500
11. Participating payroll	132,000	132,000
12. Bonus percentage (9/11)	19.2%	0.0%
13. Monthly reserve (8 above)	6,325	−5,500
14. Reserve at the end of last period	0	6,325
15. Year-end reserve to date	6,325	825

SOURCE: From *Gainsharing and Goalsharing* by Kenneth Mericle. Copyright © 2004 by Praeger Publishers. Reproduced with permission by ABC -CLIO, LLC.

costs to the sales value of production is kept below a certain standard. Table 12.5 shows a modified (i.e., costs in addition to labor are included) Scanlon plan. Because actual costs ($850,000) were less than allowable costs ($907,500) in the first and second periods, there is a gain of $57,500. The organization receives 45 percent of the savings, and the employees receive the other 55 percent, although part of the employees' share is set aside in the event that actual costs exceed the standard in upcoming months (as Table 12.5 shows did occur).

Gainsharing plans like the Scanlon plan and pay-for-performance plans in general often encompass more than just a monetary component. As Table 12.6 indicates, there is often a strong emphasis on taking advantage of employee know-how to improve the production process through teams and suggestion systems. A number of recommendations have been made about the organization conditions that should be in place for gainsharing to succeed. Commonly mentioned factors include (1) management commitment, (2) a need to change or a strong commitment to continuous improvement, (3) management's acceptance and encouragement of employee input, (4) high levels of cooperation and interaction, (5) employment security, (6) information sharing on productivity and costs, (7) goal setting, (8) commitment of all involved parties to the process of change and improvement, and (9) agreement on a performance standard and calculation that is understandable, seen as fair, and closely related to managerial objectives.[46]

Group Incentives and Team Awards

Whereas gainsharing plans are often plantwide, group incentives and team awards typically pertain to a smaller work group.[47] Group incentives (like individual incentives) tend to measure performance in terms of physical output, whereas team award

table 12.6

Employee Involvement Plans for Nonmanagement Employees

TYPE OF EMPLOYEE INVOLVEMENT PROGRAM	PERCENTAGE USING PROGRAM	MEDIAN PERCENTAGE OF EMPLOYEES PARTICIPATING	MEDIAN NUMBER OF HOURS SPENT PER PARTICIPATING EMPLOYEE PER YEAR
Individual suggestion plans	42%	20%	5
Ad hoc problem solving groups	44	20	22
Team group suggestion plans	28	25	10
Employee–management teams	19	15	40
Quality circles	26	16	50
Percentage of all plans using any type of employee involvement program	66		

SOURCE: J. L. McAdams, "Design, Implementation, and Results: Employee Involvement and Performance Reward Plans," *Compensation and Benefits Review,* March–April 1995, pp. 45–55. Copyright © 1995 by Sage Publications, Inc. Reprinted with permission of Sage Publications, Inc.

plans may use a broader range of performance measures (like cost savings, successful completion of product design, or meeting deadlines). As with individual incentive plans, these plans have a number of potential drawbacks. Competition between individuals may be reduced, but it may be replaced by competition between groups or teams. Also, as with any incentive plan, a standard-setting process must be developed that is seen as fair by employees, and these standards must not exclude important dimensions such as quality.

LO4
Describe how organizations combine incentive plans in a balanced scorecard.

Balanced Scorecard

As the preceding discussion indicates, every pay program has advantages and disadvantages. Therefore, rather than choosing one program, some companies find it useful to design a mix of pay programs, one that has just the right chemistry for the situation at hand. Relying exclusively on merit pay or individual incentives may result in high levels of work motivation but unacceptable levels of individualistic and competitive behavior and too little concern for broader plant or organization goals. Relying too heavily on profit sharing and gainsharing plans may increase cooperation and concern for the welfare of the entire plant or organization, but it may reduce individual work motivation to unacceptable levels. However, a particular mix of merit pay, gainsharing, and profit sharing could contribute to acceptable performance on all these performance dimensions.

One approach that seeks to balance multiple objectives is the balanced scorecard (see Chapter 1), which Kaplan and Norton describe as a way for companies to "track financial results while simultaneously monitoring progress in building the capabilities and acquiring the intangible assets they would need for future growth."[48]

Table 12.7 shows how a mix of measures might be used by a manufacturing firm to motivate improvements in a balanced set of key business drivers.

table 12.7

Illustration of Balanced Scorecard Incentive Concept

PERFORMANCE MEASURE	INCENTIVE SCHEDULE				
	TARGET INCENTIVE	PERFORMANCE	% TARGET	ACTUAL PERFORMANCE	INCENTIVE EARNED
Financial • Return on capital employed	$100	20% + 16–20% 12–16% Below 12%	150% 100% 50% 0%	18%	$100
Customer • Product returns	$ 40	1 in: 1,000 + 900–999 800–899 Below 800	 150% 100% 50% 0%	1 in 876	$ 20
Internal • Cycle time reduction (%)	$ 30	9% + 6–9% 3–6% 0–3%	150% 100% 50% 0%	11%	$ 45
Learning and growth • Voluntary employee turnover	$ 30	Below 5% 5–8% 8–12%	150% 100% 50%	7%	$ 30
Total	$200				$195

SOURCE: F. C. McKenzie and M. P. Shilling, "Avoiding Performance Traps: Ensuring Effective Incentive Design and Implementation," *Compensation and Benefits Review,* July–August 1998, pp. 57–65. Copyright © 1998 by Sage Publications, Inc. Reprinted with permission of Sage Publications, Inc.

Managerial and Executive Pay

LO5
Discuss issues related to performance-based pay for executives.

Because of their significant ability to influence organization performance, top managers and executives are a strategically important group whose compensation warrants special attention. In the previous chapter we discussed how much this group is paid. Here we focus on the issue of how their pay is determined.

Business magazines such as *Forbes* and *BusinessWeek* often publish a lists of top executives who did the most for their pay and those who did the least. The latter group has been the impetus for much of the attention to executive pay. The problem seems to be that in some companies, top executive pay is high every year, regardless of profitability or stock market performance. One study, for example, found that CEO pay changes by $3.25 for every $1,000 change in shareholder wealth. Although this relationship was interpreted to mean that "the compensation of top executives is virtually independent of corporate performance, later work suggests this is not the case in most companies."[49]

How can executive pay be linked to organization performance? From an agency theory perspective, the goal of owners (shareholders) is to encourage the agents (managers and executives) to act in the best interests of the owners. This may mean less emphasis on noncontingent pay, such as base salary, and more emphasis on outcome-oriented "contracts" that make some portion of executive pay contingent on the organization's profitability or stock performance.[50] Among midlevel and top managers, it is common to

table 12.8

The Relationship between Managerial Pay and Organization Return on Assets

BONUS/BASE RATIO	PREDICTED RETURN ON ASSETS		
	LONG-TERM INCENTIVE ELIGIBILITY	%	$[a]
10%	28%	5.2%	$250 million
20	28	5.6	269 million
10	48	5.9	283 million
20	48	7.1	341 million

[a]Based on the assets of the average *Fortune* 500 company in 1990.

SOURCE: B. Gerhart and G. T. Milkovich, "Organizational Differences in Managerial Compensation and Financial Performance," *Academy of Management Journal* 33 (1990), pp. 663–91.

use both short-term bonus and long-term incentive plans to encourage the pursuit of both short- and long-term organization performance objectives. Indeed, the bulk of executive compensation comes from restricted stock, stock options, and other forms of long-term compensation. Putting pay "at risk" in this manner can be a strong incentive. However, agency theory suggests that while too little pay at risk may weaken the incentive effect, too much pay at risk can also be a problem if executives take too big of risks with firm assets.[51] The banking and mortgage industry problems of late provide an example.

To what extent do organizations use such pay-for-performance plans, and what are their consequences? Research suggests that organizations vary substantially in the extent to which they use both long-term and short-term incentive programs. Further, greater use of such plans among top and midlevel managers was associated with higher subsequent levels of profitability. As Table 12.8 indicates, greater reliance on short-term bonuses and long-term incentives (relative to base pay) resulted in substantial improvements in return on assets.[52]

Earlier, we saw how the balanced scorecard approach could be applied to paying manufacturing employees. It is also useful in designing executive pay. Table 12.9 shows how the choice of performance measures can be guided by a desire to balance shareholder, customer, and employee objectives. Sears sees financial results as a lagging indicator that tells the company how it has done in the past, whereas customer and employee metrics like those in Table 12.9 are leading indicators that tell the company how its financial results

table 12.9

Whirlpool's Three-Stakeholder Scorecard

STAKEHOLDER	MEASURES
Shareholder value	Economic value added Earnings per share Cash flow Total cost productivity
Customer value	Quality Market share Customer satisfaction
Employee value	High-performance culture index High-performance culture deployment Training and development diversity

SOURCE: From Edward Gubman, *The Talent Solution: Aligning Strategy and People to Achieve Extraordinary Results*, 1998. Copyright © 1998 The McGraw-Hill Companies, Inc.

table 12.10

Guidelines for Board of Directors Independence and Leadership

1. **Majority of independent directors:** At a minimum, a majority of the board consists of directors who are independent. Boards should strive to obtain board composition made up of a substantial majority of independent directors.
2. **Independent executive session:** Independent directors meet periodically (at least once a year) alone in an executive session, without the CEO. The independent board chair or lead (or presiding) independent director should preside over this meeting.
3. **Independent director definition:** Each company should disclose in its annual proxy statement the definition of "independence" relied upon by its board.
4. **Independent board chairperson:** The board should be chaired by an independent director. The CEO and chair roles should only be combined in very limited circumstances; in these situations, the board should provide a written statement in the proxy materials discussing why the combined role is in the best interest of shareowners, and it should name a lead independent director to fulfill duties that are consistent with those provided in other company material.
5. **Examine separate chair/CEO positions:** When selecting a new chief executive officer, boards should reexamine the traditional combination of the "chief executive" and "chair" positions.
6. **Board role of retiring CEO:** Generally, a company's retiring CEO should not continue to serve as a director on the board and at the very least be prohibited from sitting on any of the board committees.
7. **Board access to management:** The board should have a process in place by which all directors can have access to senior management.
8. **Independent board committees:** Committees who perform the audit, director nomination, and executive compensation functions should consist entirely of independent directors.
9. **Board oversight:** The full board is responsible for the oversight function on behalf of shareowners. Should the board decide to have other committees (e.g., executive committee) in addition to those required by law, the duties and membership of such committees should be fully disclosed.
10. **Board resources:** The board, through its committees, should have access to adequate resources to provide independent counsel advice, or other tools that allow the board to effectively perform its duties on behalf of shareowners.

SOURCE: "Global Principles of Accountable Corporate Governance," The California Public Employees' Retirement System, August 18, 2008.

will be in the future. Importantly, Sears conducted empirical research to validate these presumed linkages.[53] Thus, Sears ties its executive compensation to achievement of objectives to "(1) drive profitable growth, (2) become customer-centric, (3) foster the development of a diverse, high-performance culture, and (4) focus on productivity and returns."[54]

Finally, there is pressure from regulators and shareholders to better link pay and performance. The Securities and Exchange Commission (SEC) requires companies to report compensation levels for the five highest paid executives and the company's performance relative to that of competitors over a five-year period. In 2006, the SEC put additional rules into effect that require better disclosure of the value of executive perquisites and retirement benefits.

Large retirement fund investors such as TIAA-CREF and CalPERS have proposed guidelines to better ensure that boards of directors act in shareholders' best interests when making executive pay decisions, rather than being beholden to management. Some of the governance practices believed to be related to director independence from management are shown in Table 12.10. In addition, when a firm's future is at risk, the board may well need to demonstrate its independence from management by taking dramatic action, which may include removing the chief executive.

LO6

Explain the importance of process issues such as communication in compensation management.

 # Process and Context Issues

In Chapter 11 we discussed the importance of process issues such as communication and employee participation. Significant differences in how such issues are handled can be found both across and within organizations, suggesting that organizations have considerable discretion in this aspect of compensation management.[55] As such, it represents another strategic opportunity to distinguish one's organization from the competition.

Employee Participation in Decision Making

Consider employee participation in decision making and its potential consequences. Involvement in the design and implementation of pay policies has been linked to higher pay satisfaction and job satisfaction, presumably because employees have a better understanding of and greater commitment to the policy when they are involved.[56]

What about the effects on productivity? Agency theory provides some insight. The delegation of decision making by a principal to an agent creates agency costs because employees may not act in the best interests of top management. In addition, the more agents there are, the higher the monitoring costs.[57] Together, these suggest that delegation of decision making can be very costly.

On the other hand, agency theory suggests that monitoring would be less costly and more effective if performed by employees because they have knowledge about the workplace and behavior of fellow employees that managers do not have. As such, the right compensation system might encourage self-monitoring and peer monitoring.[58]

Researchers have suggested that two general factors are critical to encouraging such monitoring: monetary incentives (outcome-oriented contracts in agency theory) and an environment that fosters trust and cooperation. This environment, in turn, is a function of employment security, group cohesiveness, and individual rights for employees—in other words, respect for and commitment to employees.[59]

Communication

Another important process issue is communication. Earlier, we spoke of its importance in the administration of merit pay, both from the perspective of procedural fairness and as a means of obtaining the maximum impact from a merit pay program.[60] More generally, a change in any part of the compensation system is likely to give rise to employee concerns. Rumors and assumptions based on poor or incomplete information are always an issue in administering compensation, partly because of its importance to employee economic security and well-being. Therefore, in making any changes, it is crucial to determine how best to communicate reasons for the changes to employees. Some organizations now rely heavily on video messages from the chief executive officer to communicate the rationale for major changes. Brochures that include scenarios for typical employees are also used, as are focus group sessions where small groups of employees are interviewed to obtain feedback about concerns that can be addressed in later communication programs.

Pay and Process: Intertwined Effects

The preceding discussion treats process issues such as participation as factors that may facilitate the success of pay programs. At least one commentator, however, has described an even more important role for process factors in determining employee performance:

> Worker participation apparently helps make alternative compensation plans . . . work better—and also has beneficial effects of its own. . . . It appears that changing the way workers are treated may boost productivity more than changing the way they are paid.[61]

This suggestion raises a broader question: How important are pay decisions, per se, relative to other human resource practices? Although it may not be terribly useful to attempt to disentangle closely intertwined programs, it is important to reinforce the notion that human resource programs, even those as powerful as compensation systems, do not work alone.

Consider gainsharing programs. As described earlier, pay is often only one component of such programs. (See Table 12.6.) How important are the nonpay components?[62] There is ample evidence that gainsharing programs that rely almost exclusively on the monetary component can have substantial effects on productivity.[63] On the other hand, a study of an automotive parts plant found that adding a participation component (monthly meetings with management to discuss the gainsharing plan and ways to increase productivity) to a gainsharing pay incentive plan raised productivity. In a related study, employees were asked about the factors that motivated them to engage in active participation (such as suggestion systems). Employees reported that the desire to earn a monetary bonus was much less important than a number of nonpay factors, particularly the desire for influence and control in how their work was done.[64] A third study reported that productivity and profitability were both enhanced by the addition of employee participation in decisions, beyond the improvement derived from monetary incentives such as gainsharing.[65]

Organization Strategy and Compensation Strategy: A Question of Fit

LO7
List the major factors to consider in matching the pay strategy to the organization's strategy.

Although much of our focus has been on the general, or average, effects of different pay programs, it is also useful to think in terms of matching pay strategies to organization strategies. To take an example from medicine, using the same medical treatment regardless of the symptoms and diagnosis would be foolish. In choosing a pay strategy, one must consider how effectively it will further the organization's overall business strategy. Consider again the findings reported in Table 12.8. The average effect of moving from a pay strategy with below-average variability in pay to one with above-average variability is an increase in return on assets of almost two percentage points (from 5.2 percent to 7.1 percent). But in some organizations, the increase could be smaller. In fact, greater variability in pay could contribute to a lower return on assets in some organizations. In other organizations, greater variability in pay could contribute to increases in return on assets of greater than two percentage points. Obviously, being able to tell where variable pay works and where it does not could have substantial consequences.

In Chapter 2 we discussed directional business strategies, two of which were growth (internal or external) and concentration ("sticking to the knitting"). How should

table 12.11

Matching Pay
Strategy and
Organization
Strategy

PAY STRATEGY DIMENSIONS	ORGANIZATION STRATEGY	
	CONCENTRATION	GROWTH
Risk sharing (variable pay)	Low	High
Time orientation	Short-term	Long-term
Pay level (short run)	Above market	Below market
Pay level (long-run potential)	Below market	Above market
Benefits level	Above market	Below market
Centralization of pay decisions	Centralized	Decentralized
Pay unit of analysis	Job	Skills

SOURCE: Adapted from L. R. Gomez-Mejia and D. B. Balkin, *Compensation, Organizational Strategy, and Firm Performance* (Cincinnati: South-Western, 1992), Appendix 4b.

compensation strategies differ according to whether an organization follows a growth strategy or a concentration strategy? Table 12.11 provides some suggested matches. Basically, a growth strategy's emphasis on innovation, risk taking, and new markets is linked to a pay strategy that shares risk with employees but also gives them the opportunity for high future earnings by having them share in whatever success the organization has.[66] This means relatively low levels of fixed compensation in the short run but the use of bonuses and stock options, for example, that can pay off handsomely in the long run. Stock options have been described as the pay program "that built Silicon Valley," having been used by companies such as Apple, Microsoft, and others.[67] When such companies become successful, everyone from top managers to secretaries can become millionaires if they own stock. Growth organizations are also thought to benefit from a less bureaucratic orientation, in the sense of having more decentralization and flexibility in pay decisions and in recognizing individual skills, rather than being constrained by job or grade classification systems. On the other hand, concentration-oriented organizations are thought to require a very different set of pay practices by virtue of their lower rate of growth, more stable workforce, and greater need for consistency and standardization in pay decisions. As noted earlier, Microsoft has eliminated stock options in favor of stock grants to its employees, in part because it is not the growth company it once was.

A LOOK BACK

In this chapter, we discussed the potential advantages and disadvantages of different types of incentive or pay for performance plans. We also saw that these pay plans can have both intended and unintended consequences. Designing a pay for performance strategy typically seeks to balance the pros and cons of different plans and reduce the chance of unintended consequences. To an important degree, pay strategy will depend on the particular goals and strategy of the organization and its units. For example, Microsoft determined that its pay strategy needed to be revised (less emphasis on stock options, more on stock grants) to support a change in its business strategy and to recognize the slower-paced growth of its stock price. At the beginning of this chapter, we saw that many organizations are working to link pay to performance and reduce fixed labor costs, although sometimes executives appear slow to reduce what are supposed to be performance-based bonuses when firm performance declines.

Questions

1. Does money motivate? Use the theories and examples discussed in this chapter to address this question.
2. Think of a job that you have held. Design an incentive plan. What would be the potential advantages and disadvantages of your plan? If your money was invested in the company, would you adopt the plan?

 Please see the Video Case that corresponds to this chapter online at www.mhhe.com/noe7e.

SUMMARY

Our focus in this chapter has been on the design and administration of programs that recognize employee contributions to the organization's success. These programs vary as to whether they link pay to individual, group, or organization performance. Often, it is not so much a choice of one program or the other as it is a choice between different combinations of programs that seek to balance individual, group, and organization objectives.

Wages, bonuses, and other types of pay have an important influence on an employee's standard of living. This carries at least two important implications. First, pay can be a powerful motivator. An effective pay strategy can substantially promote an organization's success; conversely, a poorly conceived pay strategy can have detrimental effects.

Second, the importance of pay means that employees care a great deal about the fairness of the pay process. A recurring theme is that pay programs must be explained and administered in such a way that employees understand their underlying rationale and believe it is fair.

The fact that organizations differ in their business and human resource strategies suggests that the most effective compensation strategy may differ from one organization to another. Although benchmarking programs against the competition is informative, what succeeds in some organizations may not be a good idea for others. The balanced scorecard suggests the need for organizations to decide what their key objectives are and use pay to support them.

KEY TERMS

Expectancy theory, 543
Principal, 544
Agent, 544

Merit increase grid, 549
Profit sharing, 555
Stock options, 560

Employee stock ownership plan
  (ESOP), 561
Gainsharing, 561

DISCUSSION QUESTIONS

1. To compete more effectively, your organization is considering a profit sharing plan to increase employee effort and to encourage employees to think like owners. What are the potential advantages and disadvantages of such a plan? Would the profit sharing plan have the same impact on all types of employees? Is the size of your organization an important consideration? Why? What alternative pay programs should be considered?

2. Gainsharing plans have often been used in manufacturing settings but can also be applied in service organizations. How could performance standards be developed for gainsharing plans in hospitals, banks, insurance companies, and so forth?

3. Your organization has two business units. One unit is a long-established manufacturer of a product that competes on price and has not been subject to many

technological innovations. The other business unit is just being started. It has no products yet, but it is working on developing a new technology for testing the effects of drugs on people via simulation instead of through lengthy clinical trials. Would you recommend that the two business units have the same pay programs for recognizing individual contributions? Why?

4. Beginning with the opening vignette and continuing throughout the chapter, we have seen many examples of companies (e.g., Google, Applebee's, AnnTaylor) making changes to how they pay for performance. Do you believe the changes at these companies make sense? What are the potential payoffs and pitfalls of their new pay strategies?

● SELF-ASSESSMENT EXERCISE

Pay is only one type of incentive that can motivate you to perform well and contribute to your satisfaction at work. This survey will help you understand what motivates you at work. Consider each aspect of work and rate its importance to you, using the following scale: 5 = very important, 4 = somewhat important, 3 = neutral, 2 = somewhat unimportant, 1 = very unimportant.

Salary or wages	1	2	3	4	5
Cash bonuses	1	2	3	4	5
Boss's management style	1	2	3	4	5
Location of workplace	1	2	3	4	5
Commute	1	2	3	4	5
Job security	1	2	3	4	5
Opportunity for advancement	1	2	3	4	5

Work environment	1	2	3	4	5
Level of independence in job	1	2	3	4	5
Level of teamwork required for job	1	2	3	4	5
Other (enter your own):					
_____	1	2	3	4	5
_____	1	2	3	4	5
_____	1	2	3	4	5

Which aspects of work received a score of 5? A score of 4? These are the ones you believe motivate you to perform well and make you happy in your job. Which aspects of work received a score of 1 or 2? These are least likely to motivate you. Is pay the only way to motivate you?

SOURCE: Based on the "Job Assessor" found at www.salarymonster.com, accessed August 2002.

● EXERCISING STRATEGY: PAYING FOR GOOD EMPLOYEE RELATIONS

Organizations understand that reaching financial objectives, or satisfying shareholders, depends to a considerable degree on how well they manage relationships with other important stakeholders such as customers and employees. One suggestion has been to link compensation, in part, to customer satisfaction and employee satisfaction. Is this a good idea in the case of employee satisfaction? There is some disagreement on this issue. Eastman Kodak has, since 1995, used employee opinion survey results as one factor in deciding executive bonuses. Likewise, United Airlines, which is employee-owned, is moving to a system where executive bonuses will depend to some degree on employee-satisfaction surveys. Although the idea of rewarding managers for good employee relations has some intuitive appeal, there may be unintended consequences. Indeed, Gordon Bethune, CEO of Continental Airlines, described such an idea as "absolutely stupid." Bethune argues, "Being an effective leader and having a company where people enjoy coming to work is not a popularity contest. When you run popularity contests, you tend to do things that may get you more points. That may not be good for shareholders and may not be good for the company." This is not to say that Bethune and Continental do not see employee relations as an important part of their competitive advantage. Continental was named the

2001 airline of the year by *Air Transport World* and number 18 on *Fortune's* 2001 list of best companies to work for in America. And many companies use employee opinion survey results to adjust their employee relations policies as needed. Rather, the issue is whether an incentive plan that explicitly rewards employee satisfaction will produce only intended positive consequences or might also produce unintended, less desirable consequences. Eastman Kodak and United are two examples of companies that have decided some direct incentive makes sense, even if it is small relative to other factors (like financial performance) that determine executive pay. Other companies, even those that use strong employee relations as an important source of competitive advantage, have been too concerned about unintended consequences to use explicit incentives.

Questions

1. Should companies worry about employee attitudes? Why or why not?
2. If positive employee attitudes are an objective, should organizations directly link pay incentives to attitudes?

SOURCE: "Bottom-up Pay: Companies Regularly Survey How Employees Feel about Their Bosses, But They Rarely Use Ratings to Set Compensation," *The Wall Street Journal*, April 6, 2000, pp. R5+.

● MANAGING PEOPLE: FROM THE PAGES OF *BUSINESSWEEK*

BusinessWeek ## Executive Pay: Will the Big Bucks Stop Here?

The President fires a warning shot across executives' bow, but the history of government efforts to rein in CEO pay is not encouraging President Obama's new restrictions on the pay of bailed-out finance executives is likely to ripple across the broader U.S. economy, experts say. But if the history of executive pay is any guide, it's more likely to influence how the money is doled out, not how much of it makes its way into the pockets of top brass.

Obama's cutbacks will certainly reduce executive pay at the largest firms directly affected in the short term. According to Equilar, which tracks executive compensation, companies with $10 billion or more in assets that took taxpayer money from the Troubled Asset Relief Program (TARP) paid their CEO an average of $11 million last year, including an average cash bonus of $2.5 million. By contrast, Obama is capping pay at $500,000, with no short-term bonus.

Long term, though, bank executives could still make out quite well. Pearl Meyer, senior managing director at pay consultants Steven Hall & Partners, notes that the plan does allow for long-term grants of unrestricted stock. Considering the low stock prices these banks currently trade for, that could represent a lot of upside.

Nix on Lavish Perks

Like many pay observers, Meyer thinks even non-TARP companies will embrace certain restrictions in order to seem in step with the new frugality the public is demanding. Severance packages should come down, and luxury perks such as company cars and lavish office redos are certain to be out, she says. Companies are already reducing merit pay because of poor business performance. Meyer's clients typically are cutting merit pay for all staffers from 3% or 4% of pay to 2%.

That's being applied to the top brass as well as the rank and file, something that didn't always happen in the past. And two-thirds of the largest U.S. companies have already put in place the kind of "claw-back" provisions that Obama advocates, where companies reclaim bonuses that were paid out for performance that later turns out to be illusory.

But the potential for long-term payouts on stock grants provided for in Obama's plan—even though they won't come through until taxpayers are paid back—provides a significant escape hatch for executives. That's why Meyers doubts the rules set forth by Obama on Feb 4 [2009] will drop pay over the long haul.

Indeed, if anything, past government attempts at reining in pay have generally had the opposite effect. After Richard Nixon put in caps on raises for everyone, not just executives, during the inflationary 1970s, compensation went up across the board. One reason: A loophole let you get a raise if you were promoted, which led to a rise in promotions. Also, people demanded the maximum government-allowed raise, even if they would have settled for less without it.

Rules that Boomerang

A congressional $1 million cap on CEO salary tax deductibility in 1993 led to the current popularity of enormous stock option grants, mega-pension awards, huge severance payments, and perks galore. Special life-insurance arrangements arose that guaranteed executives substantially more income in future years, often subject to little or no taxes. Executive health-care benefits have grown richer as well, at times not only covering more services with less cost to the executives, but also extending for years—or even a lifetime—after departure. They were extended in many cases to cover spouses and children as well.

"Every single endeavor by the government through legislation or regulation to limit executive or employee compensation has had the exact opposite effect," says Meyer. "It has boomeranged."

Even if a pay cap works, not everyone thinks Obama's deal is fair. Alan Johnson, an executive pay consultant to the financial-services industry, believes the restrictions on the TARP companies are onerous.

"In a perverse way, the companies most on the edge of going under are the most hard-hit," he says. And if other companies don't embrace similar restrictions, managers at TARP companies will have incentives to move to their more healthy rival banks, or out to hedge funds or private equity where government restrictions are not an issue. Or, they may just stop working so hard.

More to Come?

Johnson says he's worried this is not the end of pay restrictions, either. "Mr. Obama has got to balance the political theater with not killing these firms," says Johnson. "This is a pound of flesh for political consumption. And if you're an executive, you can't be sure this is it."

David Wise, a pay consultant at Hay Group, who works with many boards, also thinks Obama's plan is flawed. "Salary caps are going to result in some of the top people on Wall Street finding other things to do," says Wise. "A good compensation program is all about balancing short- and long-term performance. The old banking model relied very heavily on annual performance. The President's puts too much reliance on long-term compensation. The right answer is somewhere in the middle."

But for companies that want more government aid, pay concessions were just the price of admission, says Representative Barney Frank (D-Mass.), chair of the House Financial Services Committee. Frank argues that without a show of pay contrition, and a better explanation of how they're spending the money already given, there's little chance that big financial institutions would be able to tap further into TARP funds. Otherwise "the chances of talking the American people out of this kind of anger is zero," Frank said at a Feb. 3 press conference,

Others point out that Wall Street's huge bonuses reflect a risk culture that contributed to the current crisis. Thus, a reordering of incentives might be welcome. In a hearing before the Senate Banking Committee, former Federal Reserve Chairman Paul Volcker said: "When you mix together those enormous compensation practices [and] enormous gains possible with obscure financial engineering, you had a recipe . . . that came back to haunt us." As for the creative talent that fueled the complexity, he said: "I wish more of it would go to building bridges instead of financial markets."

Penalty for Failure of Leadership

Investor activists, meanwhile, have little sympathy for the plight of the newly clipped. "This is the inevitable consequence of their failure of leadership," says Nell Minow, co-founder of The Corporate Library. "It would have been really smart for the business community to clean up their own act instead of waiting for this to happen." Minow sees the government's move not as one a regulator made, but as something any capitalist-minded investor would demand.

Better than most, Minow knows the frustration of watching compensation grow despite efforts to curb it. Her group has for years been fighting for corporate governance reform. She agrees with Obama's support for "Say on Pay" provisions that would allow shareholders to vote on executive pay, but says even more important is fixing board compensation committees, which ultimately design and dole out pay.

"The focus should not be on the symptom, excessive compensation, but on the disease, which is bad boards of directors," Minow says. She advocates giving shareholders the right to vote off board members who are not doing a good job, especially those sitting on the compensation committee.

"They deserve to be under the microscope," says Minow.

Questions

1. What role did the executive bonuses described in the chapter opening play in the executive pay restrictions announced by President Obama?
2. Are these restrictions a good idea? Explain the potential pros and cons.
3. Should the federal government regulate executive pay? Will these restrictions actually contain executive pay in affected companies? which companies will be affected?

SOURCE: Nanette Byrnes and Theo Francis, "Exective Pay: Will the Big Bucks Stop Here?" *BusinessWeek*, February 9, 2008.

NOTES

1. We draw freely in this chapter on several literature reviews: B. Gerhart and G. T. Milkovich, "Employee Compensation: Research and Practice," in *Handbook of Industrial and Organizational Psychology*, vol. 3, 2nd ed., ed. M. D. Dunnette and L. M. Hough (Palo Alto, CA: Consulting Psychologists Press, 1992); B. Gerhart and S. L. Rynes, *Compensation: Theory, Evidence, and Strategic Implications* (Thousand Oaks, CA: Sage, 2003); B. Gerhart, "Compensation Strategy and Organization Performance," in S. L. Rynes and B. Gerhart, eds., *Compensation in Organizations: Current Research and Practice* (San Francisco: Jossey-Bass, 2000), pp. 151–94; B. Gerhart, S. L. Rynes, and I. S. Fulmer, "Compensation," *Academy of Management Annals* 3 (2009).

2. B. Gerhart and G. T. Milkovich, "Organizational Differences in Managerial Compensation and Financial Performance," *Academy of Management Journal* 33 (1990), pp. 663–91.

3. E. Deci and R. Ryan, *Intrinsic Motivation and Self-Determination in Human Behavior* (New York: Plenum, 1985); A. Kohn, "Why Incentive Plans Cannot Work," *Harvard Business Review*, September–October 1993.

4. R. Eisenberger and J. Cameron, "Detrimental Effects of Reward: Reality or Myth?" *American Psychologist* 51, no. 11 (1996), pp. 1153–66; S. L. Rynes, B. Gerhart, and L. Parks, "Personnel Psychology: Performance Evaluation and Compensation," *Annual Review of Psychology* (2005).

5. D. R. Dalton, M. A. Hitt, S. T. Certo, and C. M. Dalton, "The Fundamental Agency Problem and Its Mitigation: Independence, Equity, and the Market for Corporate Control," *Academy of Management Annals* 1 (2007), pp. 1–64; R. A. Lambert and D. F. Larcker, "Executive Compensation, Corporate Decision Making, and Shareholder Wealth," in *Executive Compensation*, ed. F. Foulkes (Boston: Harvard Business School Press, 1989), pp. 287–309.

6. L. R. Gomez-Mejia, H. Tosi, and T. Hinkin, "Managerial Control, Performance, and Executive Compensation," *Academy of Management Journal* 30 (1987), pp. 51–70; H. L. Tosi Jr. and L. R. Gomez-Mejia, "The Decoupling of CEO Pay and Performance: An Agency Theory Perspective," *Administrative Science Quarterly* 34 (1989), pp. 169–89.

7. K. M. Eisenhardt, "Agency Theory: An Assessment and Review," *Academy of Management Review* 14 (1989), pp. 57–74.

8. R. E. Hoskisson, M. A. Hitt, and C. W. L. Hill, "Managerial Incentives and Investment in R&D in Large Multiproduct Firms," *Organizational Science* 4 (1993), pp. 325–41; M. Bloom and G. T. Milkovich, "Relationships among Risk, Incentive Pay, and Organizational Performance," *Academy of Management Journal* 41 (1998), pp. 283–97.

9. Eisenhardt, "Agency Theory."

10. Ibid.; E. J. Conlon and J. M. Parks, "Effects of Monitoring and Tradition on Compensation Arrangements: An Experiment

with Principal–Agent Dyads," *Academy of Management Journal* 33 (1990), pp. 603–22; K. M. Eisenhardt, "Agency- and Institutional-Theory Explanations: The Case of Retail Sales Compensation," *Academy of Management Journal* 31 (1988), pp. 488–511; Gerhart and Milkovich, "Employee Compensation."

11. G. T. Milkovich, J. Hannon, and B. Gerhart, "The Effects of Research and Development Intensity on Managerial Compensation in Large Organizations," *Journal of High Technology Management Research* 2 (1991), pp. 133–50.

12. G. T. Milkovich and A. K. Wigdor, *Pay for Performance* (Washington, DC: National Academy Press, 1991); Gerhart and Milkovich, "Employee Compensation"; Gerhart and Rynes, *Compensation: Theory, Evidence, and Strategic Implications*.

13. C. Trevor, B. Gerhart, and J. W. Boudreau, "Voluntary Turnover and Job Performance: Curvilinearity and the Moderating Influences of Salary Growth and Promotions," *Journal of Applied Psychology* 82 (1997), pp. 44–61; C. B. Cadsby, F. Song, and F. Tapon, "Sorting and Incentive Effects of Pay-for-Performance: An Experimental Investigation," *Academy of Management Journal* 50 (2007), pp. 387–405; A. Salamin and P. W. Hom, "In Search of the Elusive U-Shaped Performance-Turnover Relationship: Are High Performing Swiss Bankers More Liable to Quit?" *Journal of Applied Psychology* 90 (2005), pp. 1204–16; J. D. Shaw, and N. Gupta, "Pay System Characteristics and Quit Patterns of Good, Average, and Poor Performers," *Personnel Psychology* 60 (2007), pp. 903–28.

14. R. D. Bretz, R. A. Ash, and G. F. Dreher, "Do People Make the Place? An Examination of the Attraction–Selection–Attrition Hypothesis," *Personnel Psychology* 42 (1989), pp. 561–81; T. A. Judge and R. D. Bretz, "Effect of Values on Job Choice Decisions," *Journal of Applied Psychology* 77 (1992), pp. 261–71; D. M. Cable and T. A. Judge, "Pay Performances and Job Search Decisions: A Person–Organization Fit Perspective," *Personnel Psychology* 47 (1994), pp. 317–48.

15. E. E. Lawler III, *Strategic Pay* (San Francisco: Jossey-Bass, 1990); Gerhart and Milkovich, "Employee Compensation"; Gerhart and Rynes, *Compensation: Theory, Evidence, and Strategic Implications*; B. Gerhart, C. Trevor, and M. Graham, "New Directions in Employee Compensation Research" in G. R. Ferris (ed.), *Research in Personnel and Human Resources Management* (London: JAI Press, 1996), pp. 143–203; M. Beer and M. D. Cannon, "Promise and Peril in Implementing Pay-for-Performance," *Human Resource Management* 43 (2004), pp. 3–20.

16. R. D. Bretz, G. T. Milkovich, and W. Read, "The Current State of Performance Appraisal Research and Practice," *Journal of Management* 18 (1992), pp. 321–52; R. L. Heneman, "Merit Pay Research," *Research in Personnel and Human Resource Management* 8 (1990), pp. 203–63; Milkovich and Wigdor, *Pay for Performance*; Rynes, Gerhart, and Parks, "Personnel Psychology: Performance Evaluation and Compensation."

17. Bretz et al., "Current State of Performance Appraisal."

18. Ibid.

19. Ibid.

20. W. E. Deming, *Out of the Crisis* (Cambridge, MA: Center for Advanced Engineering Study, Massachusetts Institute of Technology, 1986), p. 110.

21. Ibid.

22. Ibid.

23. Trevor et al., "Voluntary Turnover."

24. Rynes and Gerhart, *Compensation: Theory, Evidence, and Strategic Implications.*

25. Rynes, Gerhart, and Parks, "Personnel Psychology: Performance Evaluation and Compensation."

26. R. Folger and M. A. Konovsky, "Effects of Procedural and Distributive Justice on Reactions to Pay Raise Decisions," *Academy of Management Journal* 32 (1989), pp. 115–30; J. Greenberg, "Determinants of Perceived Fairness of Performance Evaluations," *Journal of Applied Psychology* 71 (1986), pp. 340–42.

27. Rynes, Gerhart, and Parks, "Personnel Psychology: Performance Evaluation and Compensation."

28. B. Gerhart and S. Rynes, "Determinants and Consequences of Salary Negotiations by Graduating Male and Female MBAs," *Journal of Applied Psychology* (1991), pp. 256–62; Gerhart and Rynes, *Compensation: Theory, Evidence, and Strategic Implications.*

29. E. A. Locke, D. B. Feren, V. M. McCaleb, K. N. Shaw, and A. T. Denny, "The Relative Effectiveness of Four Methods of Motivating Employee Performance," in *Changes in Working Life,* ed. K. D. Duncan, M. M. Gruenberg, and D. Wallis (New York: Wiley, 1980), pp. 363–88; for a summary of additional evidence, see also Gerhart and Rynes, *Compensation: Theory, Evidence, and Strategic Implications.*

30. Gerhart and Milkovich, "Employee Compensation."

31. This idea has been referred to as the "share economy." See M. L. Weitzman, "The Simple Macroeconomics of Profit Sharing," *American Economic Review* 75 (1985), pp. 937–53. For supportive empirical evidence, see the following studies: J. Chelius and R. S. Smith, "Profit Sharing and Employment Stability," *Industrial and Labor Relations Review* 43 (1990), pp. 256S–73S; B. Gerhart and L. O. Trevor, "Employment Stability under Different Managerial Compensation Systems," working paper 1995 (Cornell University: Center for Advanced Human Resource Studies); D. L. Kruse, "Profit Sharing and Employment Variability: Microeconomic Evidence on the Weitzman Theory," *Industrial and Labor Relations Review* 44 (1991), pp. 437–53.

32. Gerhart and Milkovich, "Employee Compensation"; M. L. Weitzman and D. L. Kruse, "Profit Sharing and Productivity," in *Paying for Productivity,* ed. A. S. Blinder (Washington, DC: Brookings Institution, 1990); D. L. Kruse, *Profit Sharing: Does It Make a Difference?* (Kalamazoo, MI: Upjohn Institute, 1993); M. Magnan and S. St-Onge, "The Impact of Profit Sharing on the Performance of Financial Services Firms," *Journal of Management Studies* 42 (2005), pp. 761–91.

33. "GM/UAW: The Battle Goes On," *Ward's Auto World* (May 1995), p. 40; E. M. Coates III, "Profit Sharing Today: Plans and Provisions," *Monthly Labor Review* (April 1991), pp. 19–25.

34. Gerhart and Rynes, *Compensation: Theory, Evidence, and Strategic Implications.*

35. American Management Association, *CompFlash,* April 1991, p. 3.

36. "New Data Show Widespread Employee Ownership in U.S.," National Center for Employee Ownership, www.nceo.org/library/widespread.html.

37. "Executive Compensation: Taking Stock," *Personnel* 67 (December 1990), pp. 7–8; "Another Day, Another Dollar Needs Another Look," *Personnel* 68 (January 1991), pp. 9–13; J. Blasi, D. Kruse, and A. Bernstein, *In the Company of Owners* (New York: Basic Books, 2003).

38. Gerhart and Milkovich, "Organizational Differences in Managerial Compensation."

39. Corey Rosen, *EBRI Databook on Employee Benefits* (Washington, DC: Employee Benefit Research Institute, 1995) www.

nceo.org (National Center for Employee Ownership Web site), updated February 14, 2008.

40. D. Jones and T. Kato, "The Productivity Effects of Employee Stock Ownership Plans and Bonuses: Evidence from Japanese Panel Data," *American Economic Review* 185, no. 3 (June 1995), pp. 391–414.

41. "Employees Left Holding the Bag," *Fortune* (May 20, 1991), pp. 83–93; M. A. Conte and J. Svejnar, "The Performance Effects of Employee Ownership Plans," in *Paying for Productivity*, pp. 245–94.

42. Conte and Svejnar, "Performance Effects of Employee Ownership Plans."

43. Ibid.; T. H. Hammer, "New Developments in Profit Sharing, Gainsharing, and Employee Ownership," in *Productivity in Organizations*, ed. J. P. Campbell, R. J. Campbell and Associates (San Francisco: Jossey-Bass, 1988); K. J. Klein, "Employee Stock Ownership and Employee Attitudes: A Test of Three Models," *Journal of Applied Psychology* 72 (1987), pp. 319–32.

44. J. L. Pierce, S. Rubenfeld, and S. Morgan, "Employee Ownership: A Conceptual Model of Process and Effects," *Academy of Management Review* 16 (1991), pp. 121–44.

45. R. T. Kaufman, "The Effects of Improshare on Productivity," *Industrial and Labor Relations Review* 45 (1992), pp. 311–22; M. H. Schuster, "The Scanlon Plan: A Longitudinal Analysis," *Journal of Applied Behavioral Science* 20 (1984), pp. 23–28; M. M. Petty, B. Singleton, and D. W. Connell, "An Experimental Evaluation of an Organizational Incentive Plan in the Electric Utility Industry," *Journal of Applied Psychology* 77 (1992), pp. 427–36; W. N. Cooke, "Employee Participation Programs, Group-Based Incentives, and Company Performance: A Union–Nonunion Comparison," *Industrial and Labor Relations Review* 47 (1994), pp. 594–609; J. B. Arthur and L. Aiman-Smith, "Gainsharing and Organizational Learning: An Analysis of Employee Suggestions over Time," *Academy of Management Journal* 44 (2001), pp. 737–54; J. B. Arthur and G. S. Jelf, "The Effects of Gainsharing on Grievance Rates and Absenteeism over Time," *Journal of Labor Research* 20 (1999), pp. 133–45.

46. T. L. Ross and R. A. Ross, "Gainsharing: Sharing Improved Performance," in *The Compensation Handbook*, 3rd ed., ed. M. L. Rock and L. A. Berger (New York: McGraw-Hill, 1991).

47. T. M. Welbourne and L. R. Gomez-Mejia, "Team Incentives in the Workplace," in *The Compensation Handbook*, 3rd ed; E. Siemsen, S. Balasubramanian, and A. V. Roth, "Incentives That Induce Task-Related Effort, Helping, and Knowledge Sharing in Workgroups," *Management Science* 10 (2007), pp. 1533–50.

48. R. S. Kaplan and D. P. Norton "Using the Balanced Scorecard as a Strategic Management System," *Harvard Business Review*, January–February 1996, pp. 75–85.

49. M. C. Jensen and K. J. Murphy, "Performance Pay and Top-Management Incentives," *Journal of Political Economy* 98 (1990), pp. 225–64; A stronger relationship between CEO pay and performance was found by R. K. Aggarwal and A. A. Samwick, "The Other Side of the Trade-off: The Impact of Risk on Executive Compensation," *Journal of Political Economy* 107 (1999), pp. 65–105; A. J. Nyberg, I. S. Fulmer, B. Gerhart, and M. A. Carpenter, "The Future of Agency Theory in Executive Compensation Research: Separating Fact from Fiction." Unpublished working paper. Also, these observed relationships actually translate into significant changes in CEO pay in response to modest changes in financial performance of a company, as made clear by Gerhart and Rynes, *Compensation: Theory, Evidence, and Strategic Implications*.

50. M. C. Jensen and K. J. Murphy, "CEO Incentives—It's Not How Much You Pay, but How," *Harvard Business Review* 68 (May–June 1990), pp. 138–53. The definitive resource on executive pay is B. R. Ellig, *The Complete Guide to Executive Compensation*, 2nd ed. (New York: McGraw-Hill).

51. C. E. Devers, A. A. Cannella, G. P. Reilly, and M. E. Yoder, "Executive Compensation: A Multidisciplinary Review of Recent Developments," *Journal of Management* 33 (2007), pp. 1016–72; W. G. Sanders and D. C. Hambrick, "Swinging for the Fences: The Effects of CEO Stock Options on Company Risk Taking and Performance, *Academy of Management Journal* 50 (2007), pp. 1055–78.

52. Gerhart and Milkovich, "Organizational Differences in Managerial Compensation."

53. See Anthony J. Rucci, Steven P. Kirn, and Richard T. Quinn, "The Employee-Customer-Profit Chain at Sears," *Harvard Business Review*, January-February 1998; pp. 82–97; Christopher D. Ittner and David F. Larcker, "Coming Up Short on Nonfinancial Performance Measurement," *Harvard Business Review*, November 2003, pp. 88–95.

54. Sears, Roebuck proxy statement to shareholders, March 22, 2004. Available at www.sec.gov.

55. J. Cutcher-Gershenfeld, "The Impact on Economic Performance of a Transformation in Workplace Relations," *Industrial and Labor Relations Review* 44 (1991), pp. 241–60; Irene Goll, "Environment, Corporate Ideology, and Involvement Programs," *Industrial Relations* 30 (1991), pp. 138–49.

56. L. R. Gomez-Mejia and D. B. Balkin, *Compensation, Organizational Strategy, and Firm Performance* (Cincinnati: South-Western, 1992); G. D. Jenkins and E. E. Lawler III, "Impact of Employee Participation in Pay Plan Development," *Organizational Behavior and Human Performance* 28 (1981), pp. 111–28.

57. D. I. Levine and L. D. Tyson, "Participation, Productivity, and the Firm's Environment," in *Paying for Productivity*.

58. T. Welbourne, D. Balkin, and L. Gomez-Mejia, "Gainsharing and Mutual Monitoring: A Combined Agency–Organizational Justice Interpretation," *Academy of Management Journal* 38 (1995), pp. 881–99.

59. Ibid.

60. A. Colella, R. L. Paetzold, A. Zardkoohi, and M. J. Wesson, "Exposing Pay Secrecy," *Academy of Management Review* 32 (2007), pp. 55–71; J. Schaubroeck et al., "An Under-Met and Over-Met Expectations Model of Employee Reactions to Merit Raises," *Journal of Applied Psychology* 93, no. 2 (March 2008), pp. 424–434.

61. Blinder, *Paying for Productivity*.

62. Hammer, "New Developments in Profit Sharing"; Milkovich and Wigdor, *Pay for Performance*; D. J. B. Mitchell, D. Lewin, and E. E. Lawler III, "Alternative Pay Systems, Firm Performance and Productivity," in *Paying for Productivity*.

63. Kaufman, "The Effects of Improshare on Productivity"; M. H. Schuster, "The Scanlon Plan: A Longitudinal Analysis," *Journal of Applied Behavioral Science* 20 (1984), pp. 23–28; J. A. Wagner III, P. Rubin, and T. J. Callahan, "Incentive Payment and Nonmanagerial Productivity: An Interrupted Time Series Analysis of Magnitude and Trend," *Organizational Behavior and Human Decision Processes* 42 (1988), pp. 47–74.

64. C. R. Gowen III and S. A. Jennings, "The Effects of Changes in Participation and Group Size on Gainsharing Success: A Case Study," *Journal of Organizational Behavior Management* 11 (1991), pp. 147–69.

65. L. Hatcher, T. L. Ross, and D. Collins, "Attributions for Participation and Nonparticipation in Gainsharing-Plan Involvement Systems," *Group and Organization Studies* 16 (1991), pp. 25–43; Mitchell et al., "Alternative Pay Systems."

66. B. R. Ellig, "Compensation Elements: Market Phase Determines the Mix," *Compensation and Benefits Review* 13 (3) (1981), pp. 30–38; L. R. Gomez-Mejia and D. B. Balkin, *Compensation, Organizational Strategy, and Firm Performance* (Cincinnati, Ohio: South-Western Publishing, 1992); M. K. Kroumova and J. C. Sesis, "Intellectual Capital, Monitoring, and Risk: What Predicts the Adoption of Employee Stock Options?" *Industrial Relations* 45 (2006), pp. 734–52; Y. Yanadori and J. H. Marler, "Compensation Strategy: Does Business Strategy Influence Compensation in High-Technology Firms?" *Strategic Management Journal* 27 (2006), pp. 559–70; B. Gerhart, "Compensation Strategy and Organizational Performance" in S. L. Rynes and B. Gerhart (eds.), *Compensation in Organizations* (San Francisco: Jossey-Bass, 2000).

67. A. J. Baker, "Stock Options—a Perk That Built Silicon Valley," *The Wall Street Journal*, June 23, 1993, p. A20.

Employee Benefits

LO LEARNING OBJECTIVES

After reading this chapter, you should be able to:

'We Are All in a Daze,' Says One Employee; Life Savings Wiped Out

The bagpipes from New York's famed St. Patrick's Day parade a block away provided a funereal soundtrack as workers at Bear Stearns headquarters mourned their company and the loss of billions in personal savings.

J.P. Morgan Chase & Co.'s deal to buy Bear Stearns for $2 a share wiped out the life savings of many of Bear's 14,000 employees, who owned one-third of the firm's shares. Most employees at Bear, known for its loyalty and a strong merit-driven culture, expected to lose their jobs.

"It's devastating," said Stephen Raphael, 62 years old, a semiretired Bear broker who joined the firm in 1974. "I have a lot of good friends here, from mail clerks to senior people. I've spent more time at Bear Stearns than I have with my own family."

Raphael, a Bear Stearns board member until recently, said he spent the weekend telling clients their money was safe and added that all Wall Street brokers were vulnerable. "I blame the system, I blame greed," he said. "Wall Street is really predicated on greed. This could happen to any firm."

Bear Stearns' shares were worth $160 each a year ago and $87 fewer than three weeks ago, which left employees gaping at the $2-a-share deal price. At its peak, the employees' stake in Bear was valued at $6.3 billion. At the deal price, it was worth $79 million. (At Bear's price of $4.81 in 4 p.m. New York Stock Exchange composite trading yesterday, the stake had jumped to about $190 million.) Recently, employees were unable to sell shares because of a blackout period before Bear's earnings release.

One trader said that when he first saw the $2 price, he thought it was a typo. "Two dollars a share?" he said. "I thought it had to be $20."

Two employees who service the mortgage-trading desk have been with Bear Stearns for nine years and seven years, respectively. One, a resident of Staten Island, says he has lost $600,000 in Bear Stearns stock, virtually his entire life savings. The other, from Port Washington, New York, her lip quivering, said she has lost $400,000.

"I am very, very upset—heartbroken, actually. I figure I will probably be laid off," said Carol Guenther, 38, an executive administrative assistant who has worked at Bear Stearns for 13 years. "I love the people I work with. And Bear is very good to employees. So, we have a great sense of teamwork. Now, we are all in a daze," she said.

The obvious parallel is with the collapse of Enron, the energy trading giant that entered bankruptcy proceedings in December 2001 with accounting problems and billions of dollars in debt. In addition to thousands of jobs, more than $2 billion in pensions were wiped out.

"It's Enron all over again," said Don Delves, president of the Delves Group, a Chicago-based executive compensation consulting firm. "Enron had the same problem; everyone was locked up in their stock."

Now employees all over Wall Street are wondering about the wisdom of owning large chunks of their own companies' stock.

One Citigroup Inc. executive who receives deferred stock as part of his bonus, said, "I've heard people saying they have nothing but Citi in their 401(k). That is the classic mistake."

And a veteran Citi broker said, "Don't limit your investments to your company stock. That's standard advice to our clients," and now "the same advice we give to ourselves."

Time and again, company collapses show the perils of employee ownership of huge chunks of company stock. At Lucent, the telecom giant matched employee contributions to its 401(k) plan with company stock, and employees often invested in the stock in their 401(k) plan. They suffered in the telecom crash; the company later merged, becoming Alcatel-Lucent.

Of course, employee stock ownership goes much broader than Wall Street. Last year, 11.2 million Americans held $928 billion in employee stock ownership plans, stock bonus plans, and profit-sharing plans that primarily invest in company stock. That was up from 2006 when 10.5 million plan participants held $675 billion in similar plans, according to the National Center for Employee Ownership in Oakland, California.

According to Hewitt Associates, a third of workers don't have company stock in their 401(k) plans, but almost 40 percent have at least 20 percent, and 16 percent have more than a 50 percent balance in company stock.

Sources: Peter Lattman and Jenny Strasburg, " 'We Are All in a Daze,' Says One Employee; Life Savings Wiped Out," *The Wall Street Journal,* March 18, 2008; Daisy Maxey, Jaime Levey Pessin, and Ian Salisbury, "The Job/Stock Double Whammy: Bear Saga Shows Perils of Loading Up On Employer Equity," The *Wall Street Journal,* March 18, 2008.

Introduction

If we think of benefits as a part of total employee compensation, many of the concepts discussed in the two previous chapters on employee compensation apply here as well. This means, for example, that both cost and behavioral objectives are important. The cost of benefits adds an average of 37 percent to every dollar of payroll, thus accounting for about 27 percent of the total employee compensation package. Controlling labor costs is not possible without controlling benefits costs. On the behavioral side, benefits seem to influence whether potential employees come to work for a company, whether they stay, when they retire—perhaps even how they perform (although the empirical evidence, especially on the latter point, is surprisingly limited).[1] Different employees look for different types of benefits. Employers need to regularly reexamine their benefits to see whether they fit the needs of today rather than yesterday. The chapter-opening story captures an important trend in retirement benefits. Employees must increasingly take responsibility for investing their own retirement funds (under defined contribution plans). Making a mistake, like putting "all of one's eggs in one basket," can spell disaster, especially if it is the same company where your job may by at risk.

Although it makes sense to think of benefits as part of total compensation, benefits have unique aspects. First, there is the question of legal compliance. Although direct compensation is subject to government regulation, the scope and impact of regulation on benefits is far greater. Some benefits, such as Social Security, are mandated by law. Others, although not mandated, are subject to significant regulation or must meet certain criteria to achieve the most favorable tax treatment; these include pensions and savings plans. The heavy involvement of government in benefits decisions reflects the central role benefits play in maintaining economic security.

A second unique aspect of benefits is that organizations so typically offer them that they have come to be institutionalized. Providing medical and retirement benefits of some sort remains almost obligatory for many (e.g., large) employers. A large employer that did not offer such benefits to its full-time employees would be highly unusual, and the employer might well have trouble attracting and retaining a quality workforce.

A third unique aspect of benefits, compared with other forms of compensation, is their complexity. It is relatively easy to understand the value of a dollar as part of a salary, but not as part of a benefits package. The advantages and disadvantages of different types of medical coverage, pension provisions, disability insurance, and investment options for retirement funds are often difficult to grasp, and their value (beyond a general sense that they are good to have) is rarely as clear as the value of one's salary. Most fundamentally, employees may not even be aware of the benefits available to them; and if they are aware, they may not understand how to use them. When employers spend large sums of money on benefits but employees do not understand the benefits or attach much value to them, the return on employers' benefits investment will be fairly dismal.[2] Thus, one reason for giving more responsibility to employees for retirement planning and other benefits is to increase their understanding of the value of such benefits. As the chapter opening indicates, however, there is a risk to this approach.

Reasons for Benefits Growth

In thinking about benefits as part of total compensation, a basic question arises: why do employers choose to channel a significant portion of the compensation dollar away from cash (wages and salaries) into benefits? Economic theory tells us that people prefer a dollar in cash over a dollar's worth of any specific commodity because the cash can be used to purchase the commodity or something else.[3] Thus, cash is less restrictive. Several factors, however, have contributed to less emphasis on cash and more on benefits in compensation. To understand these factors, it is useful to examine the growth in benefits over time and the underlying reasons for that growth.

LOI
Discuss the growth in benefits costs and the underlying reasons for that growth.

Figure 13.1 gives an indication of the overall growth in benefits. Note that in 1929, on the eve of the Great Depression, benefits added an average of only 3 percent to every dollar of payroll. By 1955 this figure had grown to 17 percent, and it has continued to grow, now accounting for about 43 cents on top of every payroll dollar.

Many factors contributed to this tremendous growth.[4] First, during the 1930s several laws were passed as part of Franklin Roosevelt's New Deal, a legislative program aimed at buffering people from the devastating effects of the Great Depression. The Social Security Act and other legislation established legally required benefits (such as the Social Security retirement system) and modified the tax structure in such a way as to effectively make other benefits—such as workers' compensation (for work-related injuries) and unemployment insurance—mandatory. Second, wage and price controls instituted during World War II, combined with labor market shortages, forced employers to think of new ways to attract and retain employees. Because benefits were not covered by wage controls, employers channeled more resources in this direction. Once institutionalized, such benefits tended to remain even after wage and price controls were lifted.

Third, the tax treatment of benefits programs is often more favorable for employees than the tax treatment of wages and salaries, meaning that a dollar spent on benefits has the potential to generate more value for the employees than the same dollar spent on wages and salaries. The **marginal tax rate** is the percentage of additional earnings that goes to taxes. Consider the hypothetical employee in Table 13.1 and the effect on take-home pay of a $1,000 increase in salary. The total effective marginal tax rate is higher for higher-paid employees and also varies according to state and city. (New York State and New York City are among the highest.) A $1,000 annual raise for the employee earning $50,000 per year would increase net pay $594.50 ($1,000 × [1 − 0.4055]). In contrast, an extra $1,000 put into benefits would lead to an increase of $1,000 in "take-home benefits."

Marginal Tax Rate
The percentage of an additional dollar of earnings that goes to taxes.

figure 13.1

Growth of Employee Benefits, Percentage of Wages and Salaries and of Total Compensation, 1929–2008

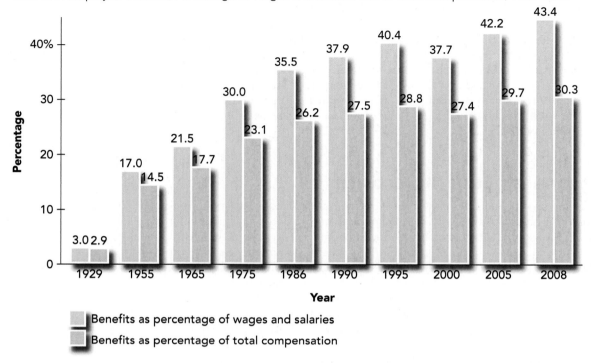

SOURCES: Data through 1990, U.S. Chamber of Commerce Research Center, *Employee Benefits 1990, Employee Benefits 1997, Employee Benefits 2000* (Washington, DC: U.S. Chamber of Commerce, 1991, 1997, and 2000). Data from 1995 onward, "Employer Cost for Employee Compensation," www.bls.gov.

table 13.1

Example of Marginal Tax Rates for an Employee Salary of $50,000

	NOMINAL TAX RATE	EFFECTIVE TAX RATE
Federal	25.0%	25.0%
State (New York)	6.8	5.1
City (New York)	3.7	2.8
Social Security	6.2	6.2
Medicare	1.45	1.45
Total tax rate		40.55

NOTE: State and city taxes are deductible on the federal tax return, reducing their effective tax rate.

Employers, too, realize tax advantages from certain types of benefits. Although both cash compensation and most benefits are deductible as operating expenses, employers (like employees) pay Social Security tax on salaries below a certain amount ($106,800 in 2009) and Medicare tax on the entire salary, as well as other taxes like workers' compensation and unemployment compensation. However, no such taxes are paid on most employee benefits. The bottom line is that the employer may be able to provide more value to employees by spending the extra $1,000 on benefits instead of salary.

The tax advantage of benefits also takes another form. Deferring compensation until retirement allows the employee to receive cash, but at a time (retirement) when the employee's tax rate is sometimes lower because of a lower income level. More important, perhaps, is that investment returns on the deferred money typically accumulate tax free, resulting in much faster growth of the investment.

A fourth factor that has influenced benefits growth is the cost advantage that groups typically realize over individuals. Organizations that represent large groups of employees can purchase insurance (or self-insure) at a lower rate because of economies of scale, which spread fixed costs over more employees to reduce the cost per person. Insurance risks can be more easily pooled in large groups, and large groups can also achieve greater bargaining power in dealing with insurance carriers or medical providers.

A fifth factor influencing the growth of benefits was the growth of organized labor from the 1930s through the 1950s. This growth was partly a result of another piece of New Deal legislation, the National Labor Relations Act, which greatly enhanced trade unions' ability to organize workers and negotiate contracts with employers. Benefits were often a key negotiation objective. (Indeed, they still are. Benefits issues continue to be a common reason for work stoppages.) Unions were able to successfully pursue their members' interests in benefits, particularly when tax advantages provided an incentive for employers to shift money from cash to benefits. For unions, a new benefit such as medical coverage was a tangible success that could have more impact on prospective union members than a wage increase of equivalent value, which might have amounted to only a cent or two per hour. Also, many nonunion employers responded to the threat of unionization by implementing the same benefits for their own employees, thus contributing to benefits growth.

Finally, employers may also provide unique benefits as a means of differentiating themselves in the eyes of current or prospective employees. In this way, employers communicate key aspects of their culture that set them apart from the rest of the pack. Table 13.2 shows some examples.

20 days of free backup care for 3- to 6-month-olds	Goldman Sachs
Paid week off for new grandparents	MBNA
Pregnant employees can take a paid month off before their due date	Eli Lilly
Use of the company plane for family emergencies	BE&K
Dinner with the president and CEO after 10 years	Cerner
A free stay at any company-run hotel	Four Seasons
Pet Insurance	Timberland
$4 on-site haircuts	Worthington Industries
$10,000 total benefit for infertility treatments and adoption aid	CMP Media
10 paid hours a month for volunteer work	Fannie Mae
35 extra vacation days on 10th year and every fifth year after	Moog
1,200-acre camping and recreational area for employee use	Steelcase
Life Cycle account of $10,000 to help employees cross major thresholds such as buying first house or paying tuition	Xerox

table 13.2

Differentiating via Benefits

SOURCE: Brian Ballou and Norman H. Goodwin, "Quality of Work Life," *Strategic Finance*, October 2007, pp. 40–48.

LO2
Explain the major provisions of employee benefits programs.

Benefits Programs

Most benefits fall into one of the following categories: social insurance, private group insurance, retirement, pay for time not worked, and family-friendly policies.[5] Table 13.3, based on Bureau of Labor Statistics (BLS) data, provides an overview of the prevalence of specific benefits programs. As Table 13.3 shows, the percentage of employees covered by these benefits programs increases with establishment size. Among the largest employers, these percentages would be higher still. Likewise, as shown in Table 13.4, benefits (and total compensation) costs also increase with establishment size.

Social Insurance (Legally Required)

Social Security

Among the most important provisions of the Social Security Act of 1935 was the establishment of old-age insurance and unemployment insurance. The act was later amended to add survivor's insurance (1939), disability insurance (1956), hospital

table 13.3

Percentage of Full-Time Workers in U.S. Private Sector with Access to Selected Benefits Programs, 2008, by Establishment Size

	ESTABLISHMENTS HAVING 100 WORKERS OR MORE	ESTABLISHMENTS HAVING LESS THAN 100 WORKERS
Medical care	84%	60%
Dental care	50[a]	24[a]
Short-term disability insurance	52[a]	25[a]
Long-term disability insurance	42[a]	18[a]
All retirement	79	45
Defined benefit pension	35	9
Defined contribution plan	71	42
Life insurance	77	43
Paid leave		
Holidays	86	69
Vacation	86	71
Personal	50	26

[a]2006.
SOURCE: http://stats.bls.gov/ebs/home.htm.

table 13.4

Total Hourly Compensation and Benefits Costs, U.S. Private Sector, by Establishment Size

	ESTABLISHMENT SIZE		
	ALL	1–99 EMPLOYEES	100 OR MORE EMPLOYEES
Total compensation	$26.78	$22.47	$32.01
Wages and salaries	18.92	16.58	21.89
Benefits	7.86	5.88	10.12

SOURCE: "Employer Cost for Employee Compensation," September 2008, www.bls.gov.

insurance (Medicare Part A, 1965), and supplementary medical insurance (Medicare Part B, 1965) for the elderly. Together these provisions constitute the federal Old Age, Survivors, Disability, and Health Insurance (OASDHI) program. More than 90 percent of U.S. employees are covered by the program, the main exceptions being railroad and federal, state, and local government employees, who often have their own plans. Note, however, that an individual employee must meet certain eligibility requirements to receive benefits. To be fully insured typically requires 40 quarters of covered employment and minimum earnings of $1,090 per quarter in 2009. However, the eligibility rules for survivors' and disability benefits are somewhat different.

Social Security retirement (old-age insurance) benefits for fully insured workers begin at age 65 years and 6 months (full benefits) or age 62 (at a permanent reduction in benefits) for those born in 1940. The full retirement age now rises with birth year, reaching age 67 for those born in 1960 or later. Although the amount of the benefit depends on one's earnings history, benefits go up very little after a certain level (the maximum monthly benefit in 2009 was $2,323); thus high earners help subsidize benefit payments to low earners. Cost-of-living increases are provided each year that the consumer price index increases.

An important attribute of the Social Security retirement benefit is that it is free from state tax in about half of the states and entirely free from federal tax. However, the federal tax code has an earnings test for those who are still earning wages (and not yet at full retirement age). In 2009, beneficiaries between age 62 and the full retirement age were allowed to make $14,160; in the year an individual reaches full retirement age, the earnings test is $37,680. If these amounts are exceeded, the Social Security benefit is reduced $1 for every $2 in excess earnings for those under the full retirement age and $1 for every $3 in the year a worker reaches the full retirement age. These provisions are important because of their effects on the work decisions of those between 62 and full retirement age. The earnings test increases a person's incentive to retire (otherwise full Social Security benefits are not received), and if she continues to work, the incentive to work part-time rather than full-time increases.

A major change made in January 2000 is that there is no earnings test once full retirement age is reached. Therefore, these workers no longer incur any earnings penalty (and thus have no tax-related work disincentive).

How are retirement and other benefits financed? Both employers and employees are assessed a payroll tax. In 2009, each paid a tax of 7.65 percent (a total of 15.3 percent) on the first $106,800 of the employee's earnings. Of the 7.65 percent, 6.2 percent funds OASDHI, and 1.45 percent funds Medicare (Part A). In addition, the 1.45 percent Medicare tax is assessed on all earnings.

What are the behavioral consequences of Social Security benefits? Because they are legally mandated, employers do not have discretion in designing this aspect of their benefits programs. However, Social Security does affect employees' retirement decisions. The eligibility age for benefits and any tax penalty for earnings influence retirement decisions. The elimination of the tax penalty on earnings for those at full retirement age should mean a larger pool of older workers in the labor force for employers to tap into.

Unemployment Insurance

Established by the 1935 Social Security Act, this program has four major objectives: (1) to offset lost income during involuntary unemployment, (2) to help unemployed workers find new jobs, (3) to provide an incentive for employers to stabilize employment, and (4) to preserve investments in worker skills by providing income during short-term layoffs (which allows workers to return to their employer rather than start over with another employer).

The unemployment insurance program is financed largely through federal and state taxes on employers. Although, strictly speaking, the decision to establish the program is left to each state, the Social Security Act created a tax incentive structure that quickly led every state to establish a program. The federal tax rate is currently 0.8 percent on the first $7,000 of wages. The state tax rate varies, the minimum being 5.4 percent on the first $7,000 of wages. Many states have a higher rate or impose the tax on a greater share of earnings. As a percent of total wages, the average tax rate paid by employers ranges from 0.1 percent in Virginia to 1.5 percent in Arkansas.[6]

A very important feature of the unemployment insurance program is that no state imposes the same tax on every employer. Instead, the size of the tax depends on the employer's experience rating. Employers that have a history of laying off a large share of their workforces pay higher taxes than those who do not. In some states, an employer that has had very few layoffs may pay no state tax. In contrast, an employer with a poor experience rating could pay a tax as high as 5 to 10 percent, depending on the state.[7]

Unemployed workers are eligible for benefits if they (1) have a prior attachment to the workforce (often 52 weeks or four quarters of work at a minimum level of pay); (2) are available for work; (3) are actively seeking work (including registering at the local unemployment office); and (4) were not discharged for cause (such as willful misconduct), did not quit voluntarily, and are not out of work because of a labor dispute.

Benefits also vary by state, but they are typically about 50 percent of a person's earnings and last for 26 weeks. Extended benefits for up to 13 weeks are also available in states with a sustained unemployment rate above 6.5 percent. Emergency extended benefits are also sometimes funded by Congress. All states have minimum and maximum weekly benefit levels. In contrast to Social Security retirement benefits, unemployment benefits are taxed as ordinary income.

Because unemployment insurance is, in effect, legally required, management's discretion is limited here, too. Management's main task is to keep its experience rating low by avoiding unnecessary workforce reductions (e.g., by relying, on the sorts of actions described in Chapter 5).

Workers' Compensation

Workers' compensation laws cover job-related injuries and death.[8] Prior to enactment of these laws, workers suffering work-related injuries or diseases could receive compensation only by suing for damages. Moreover, the common-law defenses available to employers meant that such lawsuits were not usually successful. In contrast, these laws operate under a principle of no-fault liability, meaning that an employee does not need to establish gross negligence by the employer. In return, employers receive immunity from lawsuits. (One exception is the employer who intentionally contributes to a dangerous workplace.) Employees are not covered when injuries are self-inflicted or stem from intoxication or "willful disregard of safety rules."[9] Approximately 90 percent of all U.S. workers are covered by state workers' compensation laws, although again there are differences among states, with coverage ranging from 70 percent to more than 95 percent.

Workers' compensation benefits fall into four major categories: (1) disability income, (2) medical care, (3) death benefits, and (4) rehabilitative services.

Disability income is typically two-thirds of predisability earnings, although each state has its own minimum and maximum. In contrast to unemployment insurance benefits, disability benefits are tax free. The system is financed differently by different states, some having a single state fund, most allowing employers to purchase coverage from private insurance companies. Self-funding by employers is also permitted in most states. The cost to the employer is based on three factors. The first factor is the nature of the occupations and the risk attached to each. Premiums for low-risk occupations may be less than 1 percent of payroll; the cost for some of the most hazardous occupations may be as high as 100 percent of payroll. The second factor is the state where work is located. For example, the loss of a leg may be worth $264,040 in Pennsylvania versus $67,860 in Colorado.[10] The third factor is the employer's experience rating.

The experience rating system again provides an incentive for employers to make their workplaces safer. Dramatic injuries (like losing a finger or hand) are less prevalent than minor ones, such as sprains and strains. Back strain is the most expensive benign health condition in developed countries. Each year in the United States, 3 to 4 percent of the population is temporarily disabled and 1 percent is permanently and totally disabled.[11] Many actions can be taken to reduce workplace injuries, such as work redesign and training; and to speed the return to health, and thus to work (e.g., exercise).[12] Some changes can be fairly simple (such as permitting workers to sit instead of having them bend over). It is also important to hold managers accountable (in their performance evaluations) for making workplaces safer and getting employees back to work promptly following an injury. With the passage of the Americans with Disabilities Act, employers came under even greater pressure to deal effectively and fairly with workplace injuries. See the discussion in Chapter 3 on safety awareness programs for some of the ways employers and employees are striving to make the workplace safer.

Private Group Insurance

As we noted earlier, group insurance rates are typically lower than individual rates because of economies of scale, the ability to pool risks, and the greater bargaining power of a group. This cost advantage, together with tax considerations and a concern for employee security, helps explain the prevalence of employer-sponsored insurance plans. We discuss two major types: medical insurance and disability insurance. Note that these programs are not legally required; rather, they are offered at the discretion of employers.

Medical Insurance

Not surprisingly, public opinion surveys indicate that medical benefits are by far the most important benefit to the average person.[13] As Table 13.3 indicates, most full-time employees in medium-size and large companies get such benefits. Three basic types of medical expenses are typically covered: hospital expenses, surgical expenses, and physicians' visits. Other benefits that employers may offer include dental care, vision care, birthing centers, and prescription drug programs. Perhaps the most important issue in benefits management is the challenge of providing quality medical benefits while controlling costs, a subject we return to in a later section.

For now, take a look at the "Competing through Technology" box for some ideas on reform and the role of digital records.

The **Consolidated Omnibus Budget Reconciliation Act (COBRA)** of 1985 requires employers to permit employees to extend their health insurance coverage

Consolidated Omnibus Budget Reconciliation Act (COBRA)
The 1985 act that requires employers to permit employees to extend their health insurance coverage at group rates for up to 36 months following a qualifying event, such as a layoff.

Health care reform is crucial to most U.S. corporations as they recalibrate for an Obama administration. The reason is obvious: about 60 percent of Americans receive health insurance through their employer. "We absolutely think it needs to be at the top of the agenda," says Maria Ghazal, director of health public policy for the Business Roundtable.

But for business, extending coverage to the 45.7 million uninsured is secondary to bringing down the cost of care, which adds up to 16 percent of U.S. gross domestic product and rising. "Our situation is simply not sustainable," says Dr. Robert S. Galvin, director of global health care for General Electric. "After 15 year's of cost increases, this is not a "let it ride' situation."

The cost of insuring employees will increase by almost 7 percent this year, with no relief in sight. Yet business executives emphatically do not want reforms that would uncouple insurance from employment. In a 2007 survey of members by the HR Policy Association 84 percent said their company favors maintaining the existing employer-based system, with improvements—just what Barack Obama is proposing. "Companies know they are going to end up paying the bill some how or other, so they want to have an influence on how those benefits are designed," says James A. Klein, president of the American Benefits Council, a trade association for employer-based benefit plans.

Obama's health reform proposal does indeed expect business to shoulder the bill, either by covering employees or paying into a new Medicare-like plan that offers affordable coverage to the uninsured. His plan is modeled after Massachusetts' new universal care plan, which was designed with considerable input from the business community. The reality is "that the majority of Americans receive their health insurance benefits from their employer," says WellPoint CEO Angela F. Braly. "We need to focus on [fixing] what is broken, without breaking what works."

Corporate America's own health care reform efforts have been modest. But in 2007 the coalition Divided We Fail was formed by the AARP, the Business Roundtable, the National Federation of Independent Business, and the Service Employees International Union expressly to push for universal health care. Since then, Divided We Fail has focused on pushing the woefully behind-the-times health sector to embrace information technology.

That would be no small feat. If the new administration moved toward electronic medical records "it would improve outcomes and further reduce redundancies and inefficiencies in patient care," says Dr. Steve Sayfer, CEO of Montefiore Medical Center in the Bronx. In fact, it is almost impossible to institute cost-saving measures without computers.

Digital records would yield data to pinpoint cost-effective treatments. Price and quality comparisons between hospitals would be possible. Most important, electronic records could reduce the errors and unnecessary treatments that chew up an estimated one-third of U.S. health care spending.

Executives fear, however, that health care reform will fall victim to the financial crisis because little money will be available for big new policy initiatives. As Bristol-Myers Squibb CEO James M. Cornelius says, covering the uninsured is "one more thing that has to be considered in a budget that's already too big. That's why I'm not a politician."

Budget crisis or not, Obama has named health care reform as one of his top domestic priorities, and the electorate agrees. In a national poll conducted by Marist College in October 2008, 78 percent of voters said the next president should reform the health care system even if it means a larger national debt.

Because Obama has proposed an incremental approach that extends the employer-based system, he is likely to enjoy far more support than President Clinton's more ambitious effort. Still, independent groups estimate that Obama's plan will cost anywhere from $1.2 trillion to $1.6 trillion over 10 years, making it a tough sell in the current economy. But health care policy experts think the odds are good that Obama will get Congress and the public to back at least one of his proposals: a $50 billion federal investment in health information technology.

SOURCE: Catherine Arnst, "Health Care: Turning to Info Tech for a Remedy," *BusinessWeek*, November 5, 2008.

at group rates for up to 36 months following a "qualifying event" such as termination (except for gross misconduct), a reduction in hours that leads to the loss of health insurance, death, and other events. The beneficiary (whether the employee, spouse, or dependent) must have access to the same services as employees who have not lost their health insurance. Note that the beneficiaries do not get free coverage. Rather, they receive the advantage of purchasing coverage at the employer rather than the individual rate. However, an important program applies to workers involuntarily terminated (currently, between September 1, 2008, and December 31, 2009), who may be eligible to receive a federal subsidy to pay for 65 percent of COBRA coverage premiums. Given that annual family coverage averages about $13,000, this represents a substantial savings.[14]

EVIDENCE-BASED HR

Even as employers push a greater share of rising medical costs on to workers, a growing number of companies also are providing services like free check-ups, screening exams, and prescription drugs that potentially can save employees hundreds of dollars a year. Companies say the programs also will save them money in the long run. Although a few employers have long offered on-site clinics, the trend is gathering steam as more companies expect to reduce their overall health care spending by focusing more attention on preventing illness, including complications from such conditions as hypertension and diabetes. Companies also expect employees will be more productive if they don't have to leave the workplace to seek medical treatment.

Some employers, such as Intel Corp., Walt Disney Co., and Toyota Motor Corp., are opening fully equipped on-site medical centers staffed by physicians and nurses that offer primary-care-type services. At these centers, employees often don't have to pay any fee for annual physicals or blood-pressure and cholesterol screenings. Getting treated for, say, a cold or stomachache might cost you $5 or $10, well below the typical co-payment for a doctor's office visit.

To make sure people take their medications, other companies, such as Marriott International Inc., provide insured employees with free genetic prescription drugs for controlling chronic conditions like diabetes or asthma. SmartHealth Inc., a health care products company, does on-site melanoma screenings at its headquarters. "Phoenix, Arizona, has a bit too much UVA and UVB" radiation, says Curtis P. Hamann, the company's president and chief executive.

Some companies' on-site services are sophisticated enough that some workers are using them as primary-care centers. Olivia Skiffington, a marketing specialist at Pitney Bowes Inc.'s offices in Stamford, Connecticut, says she uses the company's workplace clinic for most of her ailments. The 27-year-old figures she has saved $200 to $300 in co-payments since she was hired in 2006.

Most recently, Ms. Skiffington visited her company's clinic for a sore throat that had lasted five days. "They tested me for strep throat and gave me the proper medication to get rid of it. It is all free, I don't have to make a doctor's appointment, I don't have co-pays, and I don't have to miss any work," she says.

Such comprehensive care is still found at only a small number of companies. More generally, employers are forcing a growing share of medical costs on workers to help pay for company health plans. Workers this year are paying on average $1,806 toward the premium for their employer-sponsored insurance, up 9.8 percent from last year, according to consulting firm Hewitt Associates. The figure represents 22 percent of the total premium. And out-of-pocket expenses, such as co-payments, are up 10.1

percent to an average $1,707 this year. Both types of employee contributions have doubled since 2002, Hewitt says.

Some companies say the workplace clinics cut overall medical expenses, and thus help contain employee premiums. "We've passed our health care savings on to team members with lower premiums, co-pays, deductibles, co-insurance, and out of pocket maximums," says a spokeswoman for Toyota, which has a primary care clinic at its San Antonio facility.

Pitney Bowes says that for every $1 it spends on its clinics, it saves $1 in health-care costs and gains an additional $1 in increased productivity. "We believe this will keep you healthier and contain costs. It is a long-term investment in employees," says Andrew Gold, Pitney Bowes's executive director, benefits planning.

Doctors' groups are concerned about the proliferation of alternative treatment centers, including clinics being set up in supermarkets and drug stores. The groups caution that such clinics should augment primary care physicians, not replace them.

"I don't blame employers for looking at what might be most cost-effective for them to help their employees and keep health costs down. But they must take the extra step" to inform the physician who cares for the patient on a continuing basis, says Ted Epperly, president of the American Academy of Family Physicians.

The academy says its suggested guidelines for retail clinics also should apply to workplace centers. These include a request that the scope of services the clinic is meant to provide be posted along with a description of the qualifications and training of the staff.

Companies say the clinics generally aren't designed to replace family doctors. However, most on-site centers leave it to patients to notify their primary care physicians about test results and treatments they might have had at the workplace.

About 29 percent of big employers had or were planning to install on-site health clinics in 2008, according to a survey by consulting firm Watson Wyatt and the nonprofit National Business Group on Health. The clinics are generally operated by outside providers, including Take Care Health Systems, a Walgreen Co. subsidiary that runs 366 on-site clinics for various employers, including 40 facilities offering a wide range of primary care services. CVS Caremark Corp. and CareHere LLC also manage clinics for major employers, including some smaller facilities mainly meant to handle routine coughs and sniffles.

"The hugest impact for a company is that by getting people into wellness programs, and making the case for convenience and preventive care, you are increasing productivity and saving time" because people don't need to leave the work site, says Sue Adams, Intel's global health and well-being manager.

Intel last month opened two large medical centers, one at each of its two facilities in Chandler, Arizona. The centers, each of which has a full-time doctor and registered nurses, provide, among other things, primary and urgent care, lab services, and physical therapy. Intel also has less-comprehensive clinics in 11 other locations.

SOURCE: M. P. McQueen, "Workers Get Health Care at the Office," *The Wall Street Journal*, November 18, 2008. Copyright © 2008 by Dow Jones & Co., Inc. Reproduced with permission of Dow Jones & Co., Inc. via Copyright Clearance Center.

Disability Insurance

Two basic types of disability coverage exist.[15] As Table 13.3 indicates, 25 to 52 percent of employees are covered by short-term disability plans and 18 to 42 percent are covered by long-term disability plans. Short-term plans typically provide benefits for six months or less, at which point long-term plans take over, potentially covering the person for life. The salary replacement rate is typically between 50 and 70 percent, although short-term plans are sometimes higher. There are often caps on the amount that can be paid each month. Federal income taxation of disability benefits depends on the funding method. Where employee contributions completely fund the plan, there is no federal tax. Benefits based on employer contributions are taxed. Finally, disability benefits, especially long-term ones, need to be coordinated with other programs, such as Social Security disability benefits.

Retirement

Earlier we discussed the old-age insurance part of Social Security, a legally required source of retirement income. Although this remains the largest single component of the elderly's overall retirement income (39 percent), the combination of private pensions (18 percent) and earnings from assets (savings and other investments like stock) account for an even larger share (16 percent). The remainder of the elderly's income comes from earnings (24 percent) and other sources (3 percent).[16]

Employers have no legal obligation to offer private retirement plans, but many do. As we note later, if a private retirement plan is provided, it must meet certain standards set forth by the Employee Retirement Income Security Act.

Defined Benefit

A *defined benefit plan* guarantees ("defines") a specified retirement benefit level to employees based typically on a combination of years of service and age as well as on the employee's earnings level (usually the five highest earnings years). For instance, an organization might guarantee a monthly pension payment of $1,500 to an employee retiring at age 65 with 30 years of service and an average salary over the final 5 years of $40,000. As Table 13.3 indicates, full-time employees in 35 percent of larger companies and 9 percent in smaller companies are covered by such plans. (As recently as the mid-1990s 50 percent of larger companies and 15 percent of smaller companies had such plans.) The replacement ratio (pension payment/final salary) ranges from about 21 percent for a worker aged 55 with 30 years of service who earned $35,000 in her last year to about 36 percent for a 65-year-old worker with 40 years of service who earned the same amount. With Social Security added in, the ratio for the 65-year-old worker increases to about 77 percent.[17]

Defined benefit plans insulate employees from investment risk, which is borne by the company. In the event of severe financial difficulties that force the company to terminate or reduce employee pension benefits, the **Pension Benefit Guaranty Corporation (PBGC)** provides some protection of benefits. Established by the **Employee Retirement Income Security Act (ERISA)** of 1974, the PBGC guarantees a basic benefit, not necessarily complete pension benefit replacement, for employees who were eligible for pensions at the time of termination. It insures the retirement benefits of 44 million workers in more than 30,000 plans. The maximum annual benefit is limited to the lesser of an employee's annual gross income during a PBGC-defined period or $54,000 for plans terminated in 2009. This amount is not adjusted for cost-of-living changes. The PBGC is funded by an annual contribution of $34 per plan participant, plus an additional variable rate premium for underfunded plans.[18] Note that the PBGC does not guarantee health care benefits.

Pension Benefit Guaranty Corporation (PBGC)
The agency that guarantees to pay employees a basic retirement benefit in the event that financial difficulties force a company to terminate or reduce employee pension benefits.

Employee Retirement Income Security Act (ERISA)
The 1974 act that increased the fiduciary responsibilities of pension plan trustees, established vesting rights and portability provisions, and established the Pension Benefit Guaranty Corporation (PBGC).

Defined Contribution

Unlike defined benefit plans, *defined contribution plans* do not promise a specific benefit level for employees upon retirement. Rather, an individual account is set up for each employee with a guaranteed size of contribution. The advantage of such plans for employers is that they shift investment risk to employees and present fewer administrative challenges because there is no need to calculate payments based on age and service and no need to make payments to the PBGC. As Table 13.3 indicates, defined contribution plans are especially preferred in smaller companies, perhaps because of small employers' desire to avoid long-term obligations or perhaps because small companies tend to be younger, often being founded since the trend toward defined contribution plans. Some companies have both defined benefit and defined contribution plans.

There is a wide variety of defined contribution plans, a few of which are briefly described here. One of the simplest is a money purchase plan, under which an employer specifies a level of annual contribution (such as 10 percent of salary). At retirement age, the employee is entitled to the contributions plus the investment returns. The term "money purchase" stems from the fact that employees often use the money to purchase an annuity rather than taking it as a lump sum. Profit sharing plans and employee stock ownership plans are also often used as retirement vehicles. Both permit contributions (cash and stock, respectively) to vary from year to year, thus allowing employers to avoid fixed obligations that may be burdensome in difficult financial times. Section 401(k) plans (named after the tax code section) permit employees to defer compensation on a pretax basis. Annual contributions in 2009 are limited to $16,500, increasing by up to $500 annually thereafter through 2010, depending on inflation.[19] For those age 50 or over, an additional $5,500 par year in catch-up contributions are also permitted. Additionally, many employers match some portion of employee contributions. A final incentive is tax based. For example, based on our earlier Table 13.1, $10,000 contributed to a 401(k) plan would only be worth $(1 - 0.4055) \times \$10,000 = \$5,945$ if taken in salary.

Defined contribution plans continue to grow in importance, while, as we saw earlier, defined benefit plans have become less common. An important implication is that defined contribution plans put the responsibility for wise investing squarely on the shoulders of the employee. These investment decisions will become more critical because 401(k) plans continue to grow rapidly, covering 64 million people in 2003, up from 16 million in 1978.[20] Several factors affect the amount of income that will be available to an employee upon retirement. First, the earlier the age at which investments are made, the longer returns can accumulate. As Figure 13.2 shows, an annual investment of $3,000 made between ages 21 and 29 will be worth much more at age 65 than a similar investment made between ages 31 and 39. Second, different investments have different historical rates of return. Between 1946 and 1990, the average annual return was 11.4 percent for stocks, 5.1 percent for bonds, and 5.3 percent for cash (bank savings accounts).[21] As Figure 13.2 shows, if historical rates of return were to continue, an investment in a mix of 60 percent stock, 30 percent bonds, and 10 percent cash between the ages of 21 and 29 would be worth almost four times as much at age 65 as would the same amount invested in a bank savings account. A third consideration is the need to counteract investment risk by diversification because stock and bond prices can be volatile in the short run. Although stocks have the greatest historical rate of return, that is no guarantee of future performance, particularly over shorter time periods. (This fact has become painfully obvious to many during the recent dramatic drop in stock market values around the world.) Thus some investment advisers recommend a mix of stock, bonds, and cash, as shown in Figure 13.2, to

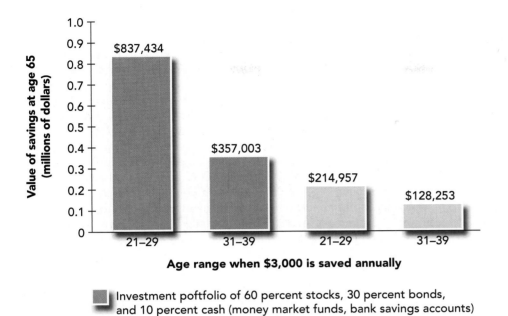

figure 13.2

The Relationship of Retirement Savings to Age When Savings Begins and Type of Investment Portfolio

reduce investment risk. Younger investors may wish to have more stock, while those closer to retirement age typically have less stock in their portfolios. It's also important not to invest too heavily in any single stock. Some Enron employees had 100 percent of their 401(k) assets in Enron stock. When the price dropped from $90 to less than $1 in 2001, their retirement money was gone. As the chapter opening shows, risk is further compounded by risk of job loss when one's employer struggles financially.

The Pension Protection Act of 2006 requires defined contribution plans holding publicly traded securities to provide employees with (1) the opportunity to divest employer securities and (2) at least three investment options other than employer securities.

Cash Balance Plans

One way to combine the advantages of defined benefit plans and defined contribution plans is to use a **cash balance plan**. This type of retirement plan consists of individual accounts, as in a 401(k) plan. But in contrast to a 401(k), all the contributions come from the employer. Usually, the employer contributes a percentage of the employee's salary, say, 4 or 5 percent. The money in the cash balance plan earns interest according to a predetermined rate, such as the rate paid on U.S. Treasury bills. Employers guarantee this rate as in a defined benefit plan. This arrangement helps employers plan their contributions and helps employees predict their retirement benefits. If employees change jobs, they generally can roll over the balance into an individual retirement account.

Many organizations have switched from traditional defined benefit plans to cash balance plans. The change, like any major change, requires employers to consider the effects on employees as well as on the organization's bottom line. Defined benefit plans are most generous to older employees with many years of service, and cash

Cash Balance Plan
Retirement plan in which the employer sets up an individual account for each employee and contributes a percentage of the employee's salary; the account earns interest at a predefined rate.

balance plans are most generous to young employees who will have many years ahead in which to earn interest. For an organization with many experienced employees, switching from a defined benefit plan can produce great savings in pension benefits. In that case, the older workers are the greatest losers, unless the organization adjusts the program to retain their benefits.

In recent years, however, few if any companies converted their defined benefit plans to cash balance plans because of legal uncertainties. In a closely watched case, IBM was sued for age discrimination after converting its plan in 1999. A district court ruled in 2003 that IBM had discriminated, but this was overturned in 2006 by the Seventh Circuit Court of Appeals. Also, the Pension Protection Act of 2006 seeks to clarify the legal requirements of such plans. As of 2008, all five appelate courts that had reviewed age discrimination–based cases against companies using cash balance plans had rejected the claims. Thus, renewed movement to cash balance plans may occur. IBM, however, announced in 2006 that it would freeze its pension and cash balance plan benefits and instead place greater emphasis on its 401(k) plan.

Funding, Communication, and Vesting Requirements

ERISA does not require organizations to have pension plans, but those that are set up must meet certain requirements. In addition to the termination provisions discussed earlier, plans must meet certain guidelines on management and funding. For example, employers are required to make yearly contributions that are sufficient to cover future obligations. (As noted previously, underfunded plans require higher premiums.) ERISA also specifies a number of reporting and disclosure requirements involving the IRS, the Department of Labor, and employees.[22] Employees, for example, must receive within 90 days after entering a plan a **summary plan description (SPD)** that describes the plan's funding, eligibility requirements, risks, and so forth. Upon request, an employer must also make available to an employee an individual benefit statement, which describes the employee's vested and unvested benefits. Obviously, employers may wish to provide such information on a regular basis anyway as a means of increasing the understanding and value employees attach to their benefits.

ERISA guarantees employees that when they become participants in a pension plan and work a specified minimum number of years, they earn a right to a pension upon retirement. These are referred to as *vesting rights*.[23] Vested employees have the right to their pension at retirement age, regardless of whether they remain with the employer until that time. Employee contributions to their own plans are always completely vested. The vesting of employer-funded pension benefits must take place under one of two schedules. Employers may choose to vest employees after five years; until that time, employers can provide zero vesting if they choose. Alternatively, employers may vest employees over a three- to seven-year period, with at least 20 percent vesting in the third year and each year thereafter. These two schedules represent minimum requirements; employers are free to vest employees more quickly. These are the two choices relevant to the majority of employers. However, so-called top-heavy plans, where pension benefits for "key" employees (like highly paid top managers) exceed a certain share of total pension benefits, require faster vesting for nonkey employees. On the other hand, multiemployer pension plans need not provide vesting until after 10 years of employment.

These requirements were put in place to prevent companies from terminating employees before they reach retirement age or before they reach their length-of-service requirements in order to avoid paying pension benefits. It should also be noted

Summary Plan Description (SPD)
A reporting requirement of the Employee Retirement Income Security Act (ERISA) that obligates employers to describe the plan's funding, eligibility requirements, risks, and so forth within 90 days after an employee has entered the plan.

that transferring employees or laying them off as a means of avoiding pension obligations is not legal either, even if such actions are motivated partly by business necessity.[24] On the other hand, employers are free to choose whichever of the two vesting schedules is most advantageous. For example, an employer that experiences high quit rates during the fourth and fifth years of employment may choose five-year vesting to minimize pension costs.

The traditional defined benefit pension plan discourages employee turnover or delays it until the employer can recoup the training investment in employees.[25] Even if an employee's pension benefit is vested, it is usually smaller if the employee changes employers, mainly because the size of the benefit depends on earnings in the final years with an employer. Consider an employee who earns $30,000 after 20 years and $60,000 after 40 years.[26] The employer pays an annual retirement benefit equal to 1.5 percent of final earnings times the number of years of service. If the employee stays with the employer for 40 years, the annual benefit level upon retirement would be $36,000 (0.015 × $60,000 × 40). If, instead, the employee changes employers after 20 years (and has the same earnings progression), the retirement benefit from the first employer would be $9,000 (0.015 × $30,000 × 20). The annual benefit from the second employer would be $18,000 (0.015 × $60,000 × 20). Therefore, staying with one employer for 40 years would yield an annual retirement benefit of $36,000, versus a combined annual retirement benefit of $27,000 ($9,000 + $18,000) if the employee changes employers once. It has also been suggested that pensions are designed to encourage long-service employees, whose earnings growth may eventually exceed their productivity growth, to retire. This is consistent with the fact that retirement benefits reach their maximum at retirement age.[27]

The fact that in recent years many employers have sought to reduce their workforces through early retirement programs is also consistent with the notion that pensions are used to retain certain employees while encouraging others to leave. One early retirement program approach is to adjust years-of-service credit upward for employees willing to retire, resulting in a higher retirement benefit for them (and less monetary incentive to work). These workforce reductions may also be one indication of a broader trend toward employees becoming less likely to spend their entire careers with a single employer.[28] On one hand, if more mobility across employers becomes necessary or desirable, the current pension system's incentives against (or penalties for) mobility may require modification. On the other hand, perhaps increased employee mobility will reinforce the continued trend toward defined contribution plans [like 401(k)s], which have greater portability (ease of transfer of funds) across employers.[29]

Pay for Time Not Worked

At first blush, paid vacation, holidays, sick leave, and so forth may not seem to make economic sense. The employer pays the employee for time not spent working, receiving no tangible production value in return. Therefore, some employers may see little direct advantage. Perhaps for this reason, a minimum number of vacation days (20) is mandated by law in the European Community. As many as 30 days of vacation is not uncommon for relatively new employees in Europe. By contrast, there is no legal minimum in the United States, but 10 days is typical for large companies. U.S. workers must typically be with an employer for 20 to 25 years before they receive as much paid vacation as their western European counterparts.[30]

LO3
Discuss how employee benefits in the United States compare with those in other countries.

Sick leave programs often provide full salary replacement for a limited period of time, usually not exceeding 26 weeks. The amount of sick leave is often based on length of service, accumulating with service (one day per month, for example). Sick leave policies need to be carefully structured to avoid providing employees with the wrong incentives. For example, if sick leave days disappear at the end of the year (rather than accumulate), a "use it or lose it" mentality may develop among employees, contributing to greater absenteeism. Organizations have developed a number of measures to counter this.[31] Some allow sick days to accumulate, then pay employees for the number of sick days when they retire or resign. Employers may also attempt to communicate to their employees that accumulated sick leave is better saved to use as a bridge to long-term disability, because the replacement rate (the ratio of sick leave or disability payments to normal salary) for the former is typically higher. Sick leave payments may equal 100 percent of usual salary, whereas the replacement ratio for long-term disability might be 50 percent, so the more sick leave accumulated, the longer an employee can avoid dropping to 50 percent of usual pay when unable to work.

Although vacation and other paid leave programs help attract and retain employees, there is a cost to providing time off with pay, especially in a global economy. The fact that vacation and other paid leave practices differ across countries contributes to the differences in labor costs described in Chapter 11. Consider that, on average, in manufacturing, German workers work 368 fewer hours per year than their U.S. counterparts, who work 1,804 hours per year, and over 500 fewer hours than workers in the Czech Republic, in central Europe. (See Figure 13.3.) In other words, German workers are at work approximately 9 fewer weeks per year than their U.S. counterparts and 12 to 13 fewer weeks than workers in the Czech Republic next door (and as of 2004, a member of the European Community). It is perhaps not surprising then that German manufacturers have looked outside Germany in many cases for alternative production sites.

figure 13.3

Normal Annual Hours Worked Relative to United States

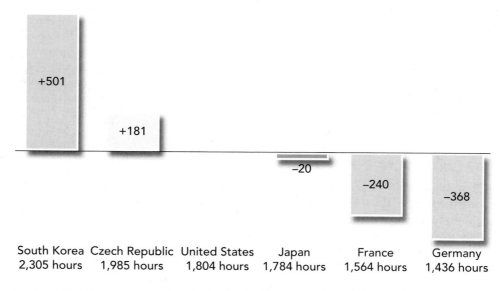

SOURCE: U.S. Department of Labor, *A Chartbook of International Labor Comparisons, January 2008.* Original data from Organization for Economic Cooperation and Development.

Family-Friendly Policies

To ease employees' conflicts between work and nonwork, organizations may use *family-friendly policies* such as family leave policies and child care. Although the programs discussed here would seem to be targeted to a particular group of employees, these programs often have "spillover effects" on other employees, who see them as symbolizing a general corporate concern for human resources, thus promoting loyalty even among employee groups that do not use the programs possibly resulting in improved organizational performance.[32]

Since 1993 the **Family and Medical Leave Act** requires organizations with 50 or more employees within a 75-mile radius to provide as much as 12 weeks of unpaid leave after childbirth or adoption; to care for a seriously ill child, spouse, or parent; or for an employee's own serious illness. Employees are guaranteed the same or a comparable job on their return to work. Employees with less than one year of service or who work under 25 hours per week or who are among the 10 percent highest paid are not covered.

Many employers had already taken steps to deal with this issue, partly to help attract and retain key employees. Less than 10 percent of American families fit the image of a husband working outside the home and a wife who stays home to take care of the children.[33]

The United States still offers significantly less unpaid leave than most western European countries and Japan. Moreover, paid family leave remains rare in the United States (fewer than 5 percent are eligible for paid leave, despite some state laws), in even sharper contrast to western Europe and Japan, where it is typically mandated by law.[34] Until the passage of the Americans with Disabilities Act, the only applicable law was the Pregnancy Discrimination Act of 1978, which requires employers that offer disability plans to treat pregnancy as they would any other disability.

Experience with the Family and Medical Leave Act suggests that a majority of those opting for this benefit fail to take the full allotment of time. This is especially the case among female executives. Many of these executives find they do not enjoy maternity leave as much as they expected they would and miss the challenges associated with their careers. Others fear that their careers would be damaged in the long run by missing out on opportunities that might arise while they are out on leave.[35]

> **Family and Medical Leave Act**
> The 1993 act that requires employers with 50 or more employees to provide up to 12 weeks of unpaid leave after childbirth or adoption; to care for a seriously ill child, spouse, or parent; or for an employee's own serious illness.

Child Care

U.S. companies increasingly provide some form of child care support to their employees. This support comes in several forms that vary in their degree of organizational involvement.[36] The lowest level of involvement, offered by 36 percent of companies, is when an organization supplies and helps employees collect information about the cost and quality of available child care. At the next level, organizations provide vouchers or discounts for employees to use at existing child care facilities (5 percent of companies). At the highest level, firms provide child care at or near their worksites (9 percent of companies). Toyota's Child Development Program provides 24-hours-a-day care for children of workers at its Georgetown, Kentucky, plant. This facility is designed to meet the needs of employees working evening and night shifts who want their children to be on the same schedule. In this facility, the children are kept awake all night. At the end of the night shift, the parents pick up their children and the whole family goes home to bed.[37]

An organization's decision to staff its own child care facility should not be taken lightly. It is typically a costly venture with important liability concerns. Moreover, the results, in terms of reducing absenteeism and enhancing productivity, are often mixed.[38] One reason for this is that many organizations are "jumping on the day care bandwagon" without giving much thought to the best form of assistance for their specific employees.

As an alternative example, Memphis-based First Tennessee Bank, which was losing 1,500 days of productivity a year because of child care problems, considered creating its own on-site day care center. Before acting, however, the company surveyed its employees. This survey indicated that the only real problem with day care occurred when the parents' regular day care provisions fell through because of sickness on the part of the child or provider. Based on these findings, the bank opted to establish a sick-child care center, which was less costly and smaller in scope than a full-time center and yet still solved the employees' major problem. As a result, absenteeism dropped so dramatically that the program paid for itself in the first nine months of operation.[39]

Managing Benefits: Employer Objectives and Strategies

LO4
Describe the effects of benefits management on cost and workforce quality.

Although the regulatory environment places some important constraints on benefits decisions, employers retain significant discretion and need to evaluate the payoff of such decisions.[40] As discussed earlier, however, this evaluation needs to recognize that employees have come to expect certain things from employers. Employers who do not meet these expectations run the risk of violating what has been called an "implicit contract" between the employer and its workers. If employees believe their employers feel little commitment to their welfare, they can hardly be expected to commit themselves to the company's success.

Clearly, there is much room for progress in the evaluation of benefits decisions.[41] Despite some of the obvious reasons for benefits—group discounts, regulation, and minimizing compensation-related taxes—organizations do not do as well as they could in spelling out what they want their benefits package to achieve and evaluating how well they are succeeding. Research suggests that most organizations do not have written benefits objectives.[42] Obviously, without clear objectives to measure progress, evaluation is difficult (and less likely to occur). Table 13.5 provides an example of one organization's written benefits objectives.

Surveys and Benchmarking

As with cash compensation, an important element of benefits management is knowing what the competition is doing. Survey information on benefits packages is available from private consultants, the U.S. Chamber of Commerce, and the Bureau of Labor Statistics (BLS).[43] BLS data of the sort in Table 13.3 and the more detailed information on programs and provisions available from consultants are useful in designing competitive benefits packages. To compete effectively in the product market, cost information is also necessary. A good source is again the BLS, which provides information on benefits costs for specific categories as well as breakdowns by industry, occupation, union status, and organization size. Figure 13.4 shows some of these data for 2008.

- To establish and maintain an employee benefit program that is based primarily on the employees' needs for leisure time and on protection against the risks of old age, loss of health, and loss of life.
- To establish and maintain an employee benefit program that complements the efforts of employees on their own behalf.
- To evaluate the employee benefit plan annually for its effect on employee morale and productivity, giving consideration to turnover, unfilled positions, attendance, employees' complaints, and employees' opinions.
- To compare the employee benefit plan annually with that of other leading companies in the same field and to maintain a benefit plan with an overall level of benefits based on cost per employee that falls within the second quintile of these companies.
- To maintain a level of benefits for nonunion employees that represents the same level of expenditures per employee as for union employees.
- To determine annually the costs of new, changed, and existing programs as percentages of salaries and wages and to maintain these percentages as much as possible.
- To self-fund benefits to the extent that a long-run cost savings can be expected for the firm and catastrophic losses can be avoided.
- To coordinate all benefits with social insurance programs to which the company makes payments.
- To provide benefits on a noncontributory basis except for dependent coverage, for which employees should pay a portion of the cost.
- To maintain continual communications with all employees concerning benefit programs.

table 13.5

One Company's Written Benefits Objectives

SOURCE: *Employee Benefits,* 3rd ed., Burton T. Beam Jr. and John J. McFadden. © 1992 by Dearborn Financial Publishing, Inc. Published by Dearborn Financial Publishing, Inc., Chicago. All rights reserved.

Portion of Benefits Compensation

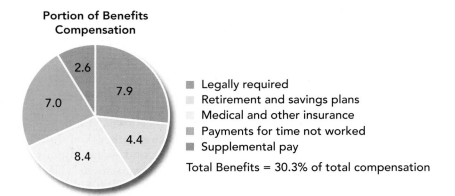

- Legally required
- Retirement and savings plans
- Medical and other insurance
- Payments for time not worked
- Supplemental pay

Total Benefits = 30.3% of total compensation

figure 13.4

Employee Benefits Cost by Category, 2008

SOURCE: "Employer Cost for Employee Compensation," December 2008, www.bls.gov.

Cost Control

In thinking about cost control strategies, it is useful to consider several factors. First, the larger the cost of a benefit category, the greater the opportunity for savings. Second, the growth trajectory of the benefit category is also important: even if costs are currently acceptable, the rate of growth may result in serious costs in the future.

Third, cost containment efforts can only work to the extent that the employer has significant discretion in choosing how much to spend in a benefit category. Much of the cost of legally required benefits (like Social Security) is relatively fixed, which constrains cost reduction efforts. Even with legally required benefits, however, employers can take actions to limit costs because of "experience ratings," which impose higher taxes on employers with high rates of unemployment or workers' compensation claims.

One benefit—medical and other insurance—stands out as a target for cost control for two reasons. Its costs are substantial; they have, except for the 1994 to 1999 period, grown at a significant pace, and this growth is expected to continue. Second, employers have many options for attacking costs and improving quality.

Health Care: Controlling Costs and Improving Quality

As Table 13.6 indicates, the United States spends more on health care than any other country in the world. U.S. health care expenditures have gone from 5.3 percent of the gross national product ($27 billion) in 1960 to 15.3 percent (approximately $2.1 trillion) today. Yet the percentage of full-time workers receiving job-related health benefits has declined, with more than 46 million Americans uninsured as of 2007.[44] The United States also trails Japan and western Europe on measures of life expectancy and infant mortality.

Unlike workers in most western European countries, who have nationalized health systems, the majority of Americans receiving health insurance get it through their (or a family member's) employers.[45] Consequently, health insurance, like pensions, discourages employee turnover because not all employers provide health insurance benefits.[46] Not surprisingly, the fact that many Americans receive coverage through their employers has meant that many efforts at controlling costs and increasing quality and coverage have been undertaken by employers. These efforts, broadly referred to as managed care, fall into six major categories: (1) plan design, (2) use of alternative providers, (3) use of alternative funding methods, (4) claims review, (5) education and prevention, and (6) external cost control systems.[47] Examples appear in Table 13.7. As the "Competing through Globalization" box on page 602 shows, some individuals now even travel overseas to obtain more affordable health care. Some employers have implemented such programs as well.

One trend in plan design has been to shift costs to employees through the use of deductibles, coinsurance, exclusions and limitations, and maximum benefits.[48] These costs can be structured such that employees act on incentives to shift to less expensive plans.[49] Another trend has been to focus on reducing, rather than shifting, costs through such activities as preadmission testing and second surgical opinions. The use of alternative providers like **health maintenance organizations (HMOs)** and **preferred provider organizations (PPOs)** has also increased. HMOs differ from more traditional providers by focusing on preventive care and outpatient treatment, requiring employees to use only HMO services, and providing benefits on a prepaid basis. Many HMOs pay physicians and other health care workers a flat salary instead of using the traditional fee-for-service system, under which a physician's pay may depend on the number of patients seen. Paying on a salary basis is intended to reduce incentives for physicians to schedule more patient visits or medical procedures than might be necessary. (Of course, there is the risk that incentives will be reduced too much, resulting in inadequate access to medical procedures and specialists.) PPOs are

Health Maintenance Organization (HMO)
A health care plan that provides benefits on a prepaid basis for employees who are required to use only HMO medical service providers.

Preferred Provider Organization (PPO)
A group of health care providers who contract with employers, insurance companies, and so forth to provide health care at a reduced fee.

	LIFE EXPECTANCY AT BIRTH, FEMALE	INFANT MORTALITY RATE (PER 1,000)	HEALTH EXPENDITURES AS A PERCENTAGE OF GDP
Japan	86	3	8%
Korea	82	5	6
Canada	83	5	10
United Kingdom	81	6	8
France	84	4	11
Germany	82	4	11
Mexico	77	18	7
United States	81	7	15

table 13.6

Health Care Costs and Outcomes in Various Countries

SOURCES: Organization for Economic Cooperation and Development, *OECD Health*. Data 2008, www.OECD.org and World Bank, *World Development Report 2009*, www.worldbank.org.

table 13.7

Ways Employers Use Managed Care to Control Health Care Costs

Plan design
Cost shifting to employees
    Deductibles
    Coinsurance
    Exclusions and limitations
    Maximum benefits
Cost reduction
    Preadmission testing
    Second surgical opinions
    Coordination of benefits
    Alternatives to hospital stays (such as home health care)
Alternative providers
Health maintenance organizations (HMOs)
Preferred provider organizations (PPOs)
Alternative funding methods
Self-funding
Claims review
Health education and preventive care
Wellness programs
Employee assistance programs (EAPs)
Encouragement of external control systems
National Council on Health Planning and Development
Employer coalitions

SOURCE: Adapted from B. T. Beam Jr. and J. J. McFadden, *Employee Benefits,* 3rd ed. (Chicago: Dearborn Financial Publishing, 1992).

essentially groups of health care providers that contract with employers, insurance companies, and so forth to provide health care at a reduced fee. They differ from HMOs in that they do not provide benefits on a prepaid basis and employees often are not required to use the preferred providers. Instead, employers may provide incentives

While laying down for a relaxing nap on a Sunday afternoon last summer, David Jones never suspected that his life was about to change. In his sleep, Jones, a self-employed housing contractor and independent insurance adjuster, had a heart attack. In an instant, he went from healthy to ailing.

At the hospital, the 46-year-old Katy, Texas, resident found out he needed a triple bypass, but without medical insurance, Jones's greatest challenge would be paying for the procedure, not surviving it. Because he was uninsured, the doctors could only stabilize him. "They put me in the ICU for four days, medicated me, and sent me home," says Jones.

A week later, his heart gave out again. This time, thankfully, it was just a mild attack. He soon found out that he had three arteries that were fully or mostly blocked and a triple bypass was now imperative.

The clock was ticking. He needed surgery immediately. "The bottom half of my heart wasn't even working anymore," he says. "It wasn't functioning."

Jones, once again in the ICU, found himself faced with some tough choices: pay $80,000 up front, then finance another $170,000 to pay for the surgery, or risk death or serious complications. "The surgeon came in and said, 'David, I can keep you alive on pills for one to five years, so see what you can do,'" he says.

Although his Southern Baptist church group helped him raise money, there was no way he could get close to the amount he needed. He couldn't even qualify for any financial-aid services from the government because his wife still held her part-time job working for the church for modest pay.

With his back against the wall, Jones found out about a third option from a friend—having his surgery in India, where procedures are far less expensive.

"It wasn't an option for me when I first heard it. I said, 'There ain't no way.' I mean, that's crazy. [India is] 7,000 miles away," says Jones, who recently spoke about his experience at the World Medical Tourism & Global Health Congress, held in mid-September 2008 in San Francisco.

But then he started doing the math: The surgery would cost $11,000. Adding in round-trip airfare along with food and accommodations at the hospital for himself and his brother brought the grand total to $16,000—easily more manageable than $250,000 in the United States.

Just like Jones, employers facing increasing health care costs have been exploring the option of medical tourism—the act of sending patients abroad for medical procedures. While the option proved a good fit for an uninsured individual such as Jones, could it be a solution for employers faced with ever-increasing health care costs?

On August 11, 2007, Jones landed in an airport in New Delhi.

More than a year later, he is healthy and back to his contracting work. Yes, the New Delhi hospital looked a bit older than the American hospitals he's accustomed to, but the constant nursing care, affordable price and—perhaps most importantly—qualified surgeon made it all worthwhile, Jones says.

So far, employers have not made medical tourism a common practice. In a survey of 400 companies of varying sizes and industries by the International Foundation of Employee Benefit Plans, 11 percent offer a medical tourism benefit. However, while the bulk of large employers are not yet offering the overseas option, 9 percent are either interested or very interested in the practice, according to another survey of 3,000 employers released in April 2008 by New York-based Mercer.

Employers with large populations of foreign-born workers—such as companies in California with large numbers of Hispanic employees—have also benefited from medical tourism, says Piper.

"They don't have an aversion to travel. They grew up in another country, so they are open to it," he says, noting that almost every *Fortune* 500 company has operations in more than one country, and that at least some of those employees would undoubtedly feel comfortable with medical tourism.

One company that has implemented medical tourism

is Hannaford Bros. Co., a Portland, Maine-based supermarket chain with stores across the northeastern United States. Hannaford started with medical tourism after assessing its rising health care costs and calculating the potential savings without sacrificing quality, says Peter Hayes, the company's director of associate health and wellness, who also spoke at the conference.

So far, the company only offers a medical tourism option for knee or hip replacements at one specific hospital in Singapore.

A hip replacement, for example, costs $50,000 in the United States, but only $10,000 to $15,000 outside the country, says Hayes. When you take an employee's deductible under a conventional domestic network into account, a hip replacement in the United States would cost about $2,000 to $3,000 out of pocket. If a Hannaford employee or family member elects to have the surgery in Singapore, however, they won't have to pay anything.

"We will pay 100 percent," says Hayes. In fact, the Singapore hospital offers the company such a cost break, he adds, that "we will waive that $3,000 you otherwise would have had to pay in deductibles and out of pocket. We'll pay for travel and we'll pay for travel for a significant other."

Hannaford settled on the hospital in Singapore because it knows that many employees speak English there and that the hospital has passed rigorous tests and has been recognized as a quality facility by the

company's insurance provider, Aetna.

When Hayes announced the program to the company's 26,000 employees—it took effect on January 1, 2008—the response was overwhelmingly positive. A big reason employees accepted medical tourism as an option, he says, was because Hannaford did not take any benefits out of its existing package—it just added the medical-tourism option.

"It was really embraced; it was really well-accepted," says Hayes.

While the employees enjoyed the idea of a price break without losing quality, many also liked the program because it meant the chance to see a different culture, which they might not otherwise get the opportunity to do.

"If they had the chance to get really good health care and see a different part of the world and experience a different culture, that would be intriguing," says Hayes, noting that many of the workers figured they would never leave their home state, let alone go on a trip abroad—even if for medical reasons.

Another reason for offering medical tourism is because area hospitals seemed to have no intention of lowering prices.

"We had hospitals in our system, in our networks, in our footprint say, 'We really don't have to worry about what prices or values are in Boston or across the country, because we don't think a single patient's going to move out of our hospital service area,'" Hayes says.

So far, Hayes doesn't know of any employees that have taken

the company's medical tourism offer; however, it has already had a positive effect on the company's relations with medical centers here at home. After newspaper articles surfaced about the plan, Hayes says, hospitals called Hannaford Bros ready to offer better deals.

Officials from other companies were not quite as sold on medical tourism and planned to take a wait-and-see approach before offering the benefit to their workers.

Sandra Morris, senior manager of health care benefits at Cincinnati-based Procter & Gamble, said her company understands the role that medical tourism plays, but it's just not right for P&G, a large company that already gets good coverage for a good price.

"There is absolutely no question there is a need for cost-efficient care in the United States for the uninsured and the underinsured," she said during a panel discussion at the conference, "but our employees and family members have very rich coverage."

Before Procter & Gamble would consider adding a medical-tourism component, the quality and safety of overseas procedures would need to be addressed, she said, noting the need for accreditation, FDA approval, and hospitals being recognized as "centers of excellence."

Other questions have "gone unaddressed" so far, she said. Can a patient sue for malpractice? If there are complications and the patient needs to stay abroad longer, should an employer pay for that? Who pays for travel costs for a companion? If the patient dies, is the employer responsible for paying to transfer the body back to the United States?

"It only takes one key person to have complications develop . . . for this whole concept to go right down the drain in terms of people's perceptions of it," Morris warned. "If one person has a disastrous result, the outcome of that result can be communicated on a worldwide basis.

"P&G has made a choice to step back," she said, noting that the company will keep its eye on the development of the industry. "Other large employers are choosing to do the same thing."

The company would consider changing its mind if some quality and legal questions were answered or if health care here became much more expensive, said Morris.

Colleen DePadua, manager of insurance programs for Towson, Maryland-based Black & Decker, said in an interview after her formal remarks that the idea is interesting, but the company doesn't plan to pursue it anytime soon. One reason, she said, is that the numbers often don't add up.

"You can talk about the differential between the $10,000 procedure in India and the supposed $100,000 procedure

here, but the $100,000 procedure is . . . really retail," she said, noting that large companies such as Black & Decker are able to negotiate better prices, thanks to their size. She estimates that a $100,000 procedure would probably cost Black & Decker around $50,000 or $60,000.

She added that the $10,000 price tag for the procedure in India may not include travel expenses. "Give me an all-in cost," said DePadua.

One concern she did not mention was quality of care. "I do think that the quality is extremely good [at hospitals overseas]," she said, adding that many countries abroad have electronic medical records, something the United States still does not have.

For now, Black & Decker, much like Procter & Gamble, is staying out of the medical tourism game, preferring to let other, perhaps smaller employers, test the waters first. "We'll seriously start to consider it when . . . the large insurance carriers start to get into this business," she said.

While employers may still have questions, recovered patients seem convinced. Fremont, California, resident Vicky Marlow, who also spoke at the conference as part of a panel with other medical tourism

patients, can now cross her legs, sit on the floor "Indian style," and bend down to pick things off the floor. Just three years ago, she couldn't imagine doing any of those things because her hip was so damaged that she needed a cane to walk.

Doctors in the United States told her she needed a full hip replacement, something that can limit mobility and is prone to dislocations. Searching online, Marlow found out about "bone conserving" hip resurfacing surgery, whereby surgeons cover a hip's ball and socket with smooth metal, rather than cutting away and replacing damaged bone.

Instead of having the surgery in Los Angeles, which would have cost her $24,000, she chose to go to India, where the entire process—including flight, surgery, and accommodations—cost less than $12,000.

"[Americans] have a complete misconception of reality, because I know the normal American would think, 'Oh my God, India, the care is nowhere near as good as the U.S.,'" says Marlow. "When it's exactly the opposite."

Now, a few years later, her mobility is excellent. "There's no limitation at all," she says.

SOURCE: Jared Shelly, "Transformation Vacation," *Human Resource Executive*, November 1, 2008. Reprinted with permission.

for employees to choose, for example, a physician who participates in the plan. In general, PPOs seem to be less expensive than traditional delivery systems but more expensive than HMOs.[50] Another trend in employers' attempts to control costs has been to vary required employee contributions based on the employee's health and risk factors rather than charging each employee the same premium.

Employee Wellness Programs. Employee wellness programs (EWPs) focus on changing behaviors both on and off work time that could eventually lead to future health problems. EWPs are preventive in nature; they attempt to manage health care costs by decreasing employees' needs for services. Typically, these programs aim at specific health risks such as high blood pressure, high cholesterol levels, smoking, and obesity. They also try to promote positive health influences such as physical exercise and good nutrition.[51] The "Competing through Sustainability" box on page 606 provides some examples.

EWPs are either passive or active. Passive programs use little or no outreach to individuals, nor do they provide ongoing support to motivate them to use the resources. Active wellness centers assume that behavior change requires not only awareness and opportunity but support and reinforcement.

One example of a passive wellness program is a health education program. Health education programs have two central goals: raising awareness levels of health-related issues and informing people on health-related topics. In these kinds of programs, a health educator usually conducts classes or lunchtime lectures (or co-ordinates outside speakers). The program may also have various promotions (like an annual mile run or a "smoke-out") and include a newsletter that reports on current health issues.

Another kind of passive employee wellness program is a fitness facility. In this kind of program, the company sets up a center for physical fitness equipped with aerobic and muscle-building exercise machines and staffed with certified athletic trainers. The facility is publicized within the organization, and employees are free to use it on their own time. Aetna, for example, has created five state-of-the-art health clubs that serve more than 7,500 workers.[52] Northwestern Mutual Life's fitness facilities are open 24 hours a day to its 3,300 employees.[53] Health education classes related to smoking cessation and weight loss may be offered in addition to the facilities.

Although fitness facility programs are usually more expensive than health education programs, both are classified as passive because they rely on individual employees to identify their problems and take corrective action. In contrast, active wellness centers assume that behavior change also requires encouragement and assistance. One kind of active wellness center is the outreach and follow-up model. This type of wellness center contains all the features of a passive model, but it also has counselors who handle one-on-one outreach and provide tailored, individualized programs for employees. Typically, tailored programs obtain baseline measures on various indicators (weight, blood pressure, lung capacity, and so on) and measure individuals' progress relative to these indicators over time. The programs set goals and provide small, symbolic rewards to individuals who meet their goals.

This encouragement needs to be particularly targeted to employees in high-risk categories (like those who smoke, are overweight, or have high blood pressure) for two reasons. First, a small percentage of employees create a disproportionate amount of health care costs; therefore, targeted interventions are more efficient. Second, research shows that those in high-risk categories are the most likely to perceive barriers (like family problems or work overload)[54] to participating in company-sponsored fitness programs. Thus untargeted interventions are likely to miss the people that most need to be included.

Research on these different types of wellness centers leads to several conclusions.[55] First, the costs of health education programs are significantly less than those associated with either fitness facility programs or the follow-up model. Second, as indicated

To Bill Pratt, two things seemed to grow out of proportion at Wesley Willows Corp. retirement community in recent years: employees' health insurance premiums, and their waistlines.

Pratt, the chief executive, could see there was a connection. Each time he walked around his nonprofit's leafy campus, he noticed that the "employee base could stand to lose a few pounds," he says. Meanwhile, like many companies around the country, the organization had seen its health care costs soar for several years running, due in part to claims from its less-than-healthy-looking workforce.

But a little over a year later, employees on the 290-person staff at Wesley Willows have lost a cumulative 750 pounds—and health insurance claims by the staff have dropped dramatically. When the company renewed its health insurance for 2008, premiums edged up just over 3 percent—the lowest increase in at least a decade, company executives say.

How did it happen? Wesley Willows, in Rockford, Illinois, embarked on a companywide wellness contest that pitted groups of employees against one another in friendly competition. In effect, it paid workers to lose weight.

Inspired by TV shows like *The Biggest Loser* and plagued by rising health care costs, a growing number of small companies are using contest-style incentive programs to spur employees to

get healthy. The format is a natural fit for small companies, where executives say the natural camaraderie lends itself to teamwork and competitive spirit.

Developing such contests can be time-consuming—and expensive. But these small companies say it pays off with healthier employees and lower health care costs.

Wesley Willows got help from Tangerine Wellness Inc., a Boston firm that designs incentive-based weight-loss programs. The retirement community now spends $20,000 to $30,000 a year on the program, Pratt says, including Tangerine's fees and cash rewards for workers. Employees earn $3 for every 1 percent of body weight they lose. In addition, at the end of a quarter, each member of the winning team receives as much as $50, and second-place-team members a little less. Health insurance claims at the company, meanwhile, for the 12 months ended in August 2007—a period that includes the first six months of the program—dropped 19 percent to less than $640,000. And for the 12 months ended in March 2008, turnover plunged 30 percent—a benefit Pratt attributes to a more collegial environment.

To get started, a Tangerine representative took height and weight information—on a voluntary basis—from workers who wished to participate. Employees also decided whether they'd like to be part of a team. Some teams, Mr. Pratt says, will try to coax a potential big loser

over to their group to bolster their results for the next quarter.

Through a customized Web site, employees can track their own weights to see how much they're losing—and earning—and follow their team's results. Individual results aren't released.

Tangerine Chairman and Chief Executive Aaron Day notes that the company is careful not to encourage weight loss when it's not needed; those within a healthy weight range are rewarded for staying in the range, and those underweight are rewarded for gaining.

About half of Wesley Willows employees participate, Pratt says. "I see anywhere from 15 to 20 people out walking in groups on company grounds on a regular basis," he says—something that almost never happened before the contest.

Confluence, a Pittsburgh-based software company, designed its own wellness contest. Executives at the company have long encouraged healthy living, for instance, by installing bike racks and workplace showers for employees to use after midday jogs. The 170-person company started its Live for Life Challenge—known internally as "The Biggest Loser-meets-NASCAR." The grand prize: $1,500 toward exercise equipment or a gym membership, in addition to a $1,500 spa package and $500 cash.

So far, 35 employees are participating in the nine-month contest. They earn points by completing health-and-fitness challenges: playing on a company dodge ball team, for instance, is worth 250 points per game; a $5 weekly purchase of fruits and vegetables is worth 25 points.

"We went in with the attitude that prizes and rewards have to be substantial," says Dennis Farkos, chief financial officer and a senior vice president. Second prize is $1,500 toward exercise equipment or a health club membership, and $500 cash. Third prize is $500 and a $500 gift card for a sporting goods vendor.

Aside from the prizes, Farkos estimates that the program will cost the company about $2,000, for time spent tracking points and for perks like fresh fruit delivered to the office for everyone. Meanwhile, the company says that its insurance provider already has reduced its premiums 4 percent, or $28,000, and that another decrease is likely next year after the program ends. Executives say they're likely to hold the competition again, depending on this year's results.

Some companies make participation mandatory. Starting 10 years ago, workers at Lincoln Industries, a 580-employee metal-finishing company in Lincoln, Nebraska, have competed in an annual Wellness Olympics, with events like trash-can basketball. Then, in 2003, the company began requiring them to participate in a year-round, points-based wellness contest called Go! Platinum.

Points are awarded for, among other things, reducing tobacco use and body fat and attending wellness seminars. The goal is to amass enough points to earn platinum status, and a company-paid trip to Colorado for a one-

day hike up a mountain. Last year, 77 employees made the climb, the company says.

The program "encourages people to have fun at work and to view wellness as less of a burden," says Tonya Vyhlidal, wellness and life enhancement director at Lincoln.

The cost is significant: more than $400,000, including the salaries of Vyhlidal, a wellness specialist and a nurse. But Vyhlidal says wellness initiatives more than pay for themselves. Workers' compensation costs at the company have plummeted to less than $140,000 last year from more than $500,000 in 2000, says Vyhlidal. And tobacco use declined to 21 percent of employees this year from 31 percent in 2003.

Occasionally, job applicants are turned off by the company's heavy-handed approach, Vyhlidal says. Workers stretch together before shifts, the campus is tobacco-free, and mandatory physicals are given each quarter. But "we are a wellness company," Vyhlidal says. The focus is on hiring workers who fit the company culture.

Wellness competitions can get out of hand. When 95-employee insurance firm PMSLIC Insurance Co. issued pedometers in 2005, executives

encouraged employees to get in shape by walking at least 10,000 steps per day, or four to five miles. The company tracked the results on a big map depicting the Appalachian Trail. The program took off, largely because "we were kind of like one big team," says Julie Burns, vice president of human resources at the Mechanicsburg, Pennsylvania company.

But some people fixated on their number of steps, push-

● Lincoln employees stretching at the office

ing as high as 40,000 daily. The same people were winning the weekly contest over and over again. So after a few weeks, the company switched to random drawings for rewards, so employees wouldn't get discouraged and quit.

"It was too much for some people," says Burns. "We had some people who were crazy competitive."

SOURCE: Simona Covell, "Companies Win as Workers Lose Pounds," *The Wall Street Journal*, July 10, 2008, p. B6. Copyright © 2008 by Dow Jones & Co., Inc. Reproduced with permission of Dow Jones & Co., Inc. via Copyright Clearance Center.

in Figure 13.5, all three models are effective in reducing the risk factors associated with cardiovascular disease (obesity, high blood pressure, smoking, and lack of exercise). However, the follow-up model is significantly better than the other two in reducing the risk factors.

Whether the added cost of follow-up programs compared with health education programs is warranted is a judgment that only employers, employees, and unions can make. However, employers like Sony and Quaker Oats believe that incentives are worth the extra cost, and their employees can receive up to several hundred dollars for reducing their risk factors. There appears to be no such ambiguity associated with the fitness facility model, however. This type of wellness center costs as much or more than the follow-up model but is only as effective as the health education model. Providing a fitness facility that does not include systematic outreach and routine long-term follow-up to assist people with risk factors is not cost-effective in reducing health risks. "Attendants may sit in the fitness center like the 'Maytag repairman' waiting for people to come."[56]

Health Care Costs and Quality: Ongoing Challenges. In 2008, the average annual premium for family coverage was $12,680, with employers paying $9,325 (74 percent) and employees paying $3,354 (26 percent) on average.[57] (These numbers pertain only to employers that provide health care benefits.) Although premiums for employer-sponsored health care (family coverage) grew by a modest 2.2 percent in 2008, since 2000, health care premium costs have more than doubled. Thus, control of health care costs is an ongoing challenge.

figure 13.5

The Cost and Effectiveness of Three Different Types of Employee Wellness Designs

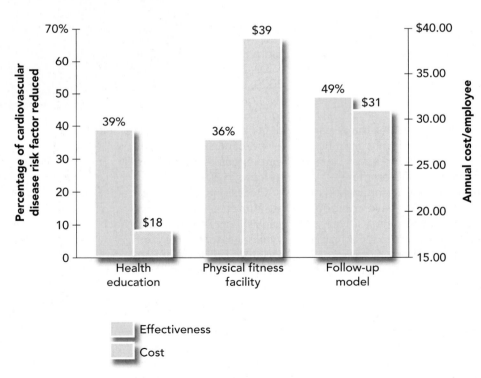

SOURCE: J. C. Erfurt, A. Foote, and M. A. Heirich, "The Cost Effectiveness of Worksite Wellness Programs for Hypertension Control, Weight Loss, Smoking Cessation and Exercise," *Personnel Psychology* 45 (1992), pp. 5–27. Used with permission.

Two important phenomena are often encountered in cost control efforts. First, piecemeal programs may not work well because steps to control one aspect (such as medical cost shifting) may lead employees to "migrate" to other programs that provide medical treatment at no cost to them (like workers' compensation). Second, there is often a so-called Pareto group, which refers to a small percentage (perhaps 20 percent) of employees being responsible for generating the majority (often 60 to 80 percent) of health care costs. Obviously, cost control efforts will be more successful to the extent that the costs generated by the Pareto group can be identified and managed effectively.[58]

Although cost control will continue to require a good deal of attention, there is a growing emphasis on monitoring health care quality, which has been described as "the next battlefield." A major focus is on identifying best medical practices by measuring and monitoring the relative success of alternative treatment strategies using large-scale databases and research.[59] In addition, employers increasingly cooperate with one another to develop "report cards" on health care provider organizations to facilitate better choices by their employers and to receive improved health care. General Motors, Ford, and Chrysler, for example, have developed this type of system and made it Web-accessible.[60]

In addition, several companies, including Intel, Wal-Mart, and British Petroleum, have announced a plan to provide digital health records to their employees. By doing so, they hope that costs will be reduced and better care delivered by providing consumers, hospitals, doctors, and pharmacies accurate and accessible data.[61]

Staffing Responses to Control Benefits Cost Growth

Employers may change staffing practices to control benefits costs. First, because benefits costs are fixed (in that they do not usually go up with hours worked), the benefits cost per hour can be reduced by having employees work more hours. However, there are drawbacks to having employees work more hours. The Fair Labor Standards Act (FLSA), introduced in Chapter 11, requires that nonexempt employees be paid time-and-a-half for hours in excess of 40 per week. Yet the decline in U.S. work hours tapered off in the late 1940s; work hours have actually gone up since then. It is estimated that Americans were working the equivalent of one month longer in 1987 than they were in 1969, and these higher levels have continued.[62] Increased benefits were identified as one of the major reasons for this.

A second possible effect of FLSA regulations (although this is more speculative) is that organizations will try to have their employees classified as exempt whenever possible (although such attempts may run afoul of FLSA law). The growth in the number of salaried workers (many of whom are exempt) may also reflect an effort by organizations to limit the benefits cost per hour without having to pay overtime. A third potential effect is the growth in part-time employment and the use of temporary workers, which may be a response to rising benefits costs. Part-time workers are less likely to receive benefits than full-time workers although labor market shortages in recent years have reduced this difference.[63] Benefits for temporary workers are also usually quite limited.

Third, employers may be more likely to classify workers as independent contractors rather than employees, which eliminates the employer's obligation to provide legally required employee benefits. However, the Internal Revenue Service (IRS) scrutinizes such decisions carefully, as Microsoft and other companies have discovered. Microsoft was compelled to reclassify a group of workers as employees (rather than as independent contractors) and to grant them retroactive benefits. The IRS looks at several factors, including the permanency of the relationship between employer and worker, how much control the employer exercises in directing the worker, and whether the worker offers services to only that employer. Permanency, control, and dealing with a single employer are viewed by the IRS as suggestive of an employment relationship.

Nature of the Workforce

Although general considerations such as cost control and "protection against the risks of old age and loss of health and life" (see Table 13.5) are important, employers must also consider the specific demographic composition and preferences of their current workforces in designing their benefits packages.

At a broad level, basic demographic factors such as age and sex can have important consequences for the types of benefits employees want. For example, an older workforce is more likely to be concerned about (and use) medical coverage, life insurance, and pensions. A workforce with a high percentage of women of childbearing age may care more about disability leave. Young, unmarried men and women often have less interest in benefits generally, preferring higher wages and salaries.

Although some general conclusions about employee preferences can be drawn based on demographics, more finely tuned assessments of employee benefit preferences need to be done. One approach is to use marketing research methods to assess employees' preferences the same way consumers' demands for products and services are assessed.[64] Methods include personal interviews, focus groups, and questionnaires. Relevant questions might include

- What benefits are most important to you?
- If you could choose one new benefit, what would it be?
- If you were given *x* dollars for benefits, how would you spend it?

As with surveys generally, care must be taken not to raise employee expectations regarding future changes. If the employer is not prepared to act on the employees' input, surveying may do more harm than good.

The preceding discussion may imply that the current makeup of the workforce is a given, but this is not the case. As discussed earlier, the benefits package may influence the composition of the workforce. For example, a benefits package that has strong medical benefits and pensions may be particularly attractive to older people or those with families. An attractive pension plan may be a way to attract workers who wish to make a long-term commitment to an organization. Where turnover costs are high, this type of strategy may have some appeal. On the other hand, a company that has very lucrative health care benefits may attract and retain people with high health care costs. Sick leave provisions may also affect the composition of the workforce. Organizations need to think about the signals their benefits packages send and the implications of these signals for workforce composition. In this vein, Table 13.8 shows the benefits used by Google, the number 1 ranked company on *Fortune*'s list of "100 Best Companies to Work For in 2007 and 2008," to attract and retain its desired workforce.

Communicating with Employees

LO5
Explain the importance of effectively communicating the nature and value of benefits to employees.

Effective communication of benefits information to employees is critical if employers are to realize sufficient returns on their benefits investments. Research makes it clear that current employees and job applicants often have a very poor idea of what benefits provisions are already in place and the cost or market value of those benefits. One study asked employees to estimate both the amount contributed by the employer to their medical insurance and what it would cost the employees to provide their

- Up to $8,000/year in tuition reimbursement
- On-site perks include medical and dental facilities; oil change and bike repair; valet parking; free washers and dryers; and free breakfast, lunch, and dinner on a daily basis at 11 gourmet restaurants
- Unlimited sick leave
- 27 days of paid time off after one year of employment
- Global Education Leave program enables employees to take a leave of absence to pursue further education for up to 5 years and $150,000 in reimbursement.
- Free shuttles equipped with WiFi from locations around the Bay Area to headquarter offices.
- Classes on a variety of subjects from estate planning and home purchasing to foreign-language lessons in French, Spanish, Japanese, and Mandarin.

table 13.8

Employee Benefits at Google

SOURCE: The Great Place to Work® Institute, 2007, www.greatplacetowork.com.

own health insurance. Table 13.9 shows that employees significantly underestimated both the cost and market value of their medical benefits. In the case of family coverage, employees estimated that the employer contributed $24, only 38 percent of the employer's actual contribution. This employer was receiving a very poor return on its benefits investment: $0.38 for every $1.00 spent.[65] As we saw earlier, the average employer today providing health care benefits spends $9,325 per year for family coverage. One wonders whether today's employees are any more aware of this fact.

The situation with job applicants is no better. One study of MBAs found that 46 percent believed that benefits added 15 percent or less on top of direct payroll. Not surprisingly, perhaps, benefits were dead last on the applicants' priority lists in making job choices.[66] A study of undergraduate business majors found similar results, with benefits ranked 15th (out of 18) in importance in evaluating jobs. These results must be interpreted with caution, however. Some research suggests that job attributes can be ranked low in importance, not because they are unimportant per se, but because all employers are perceived to be about the same on that attribute. If some employers offered noticeably poorer benefits, the importance of benefits could become much greater.

Organizations can help remedy the problem of applicants' and employees' lack of knowledge about benefits. One study found that employees' awareness of benefits information was significantly increased through several media, including memoranda, question-and-answer meetings, and detailed brochures. The increased awareness, in turn, contributed to significant increases in benefits satisfaction. Another study

	EMPLOYER CONTRIBUTION			MARKET VALUE[a]		
COVERAGE	ACTUAL	EMPLOYEE PERCEPTION	RATIO	ACTUAL	EMPLOYEE PERCEPTION	RATIO
Individual	$34	$23	68%	$ 61	$37	61%
Family	64	24	38	138	43	31

table 13.9

Employee Perceptions versus Actual Cost and Market Value of Employer Contributions to Employee Medical Insurance

Note: Dollar values in table represent means across three different insurance carriers for individual coverage and three different carriers for family coverage.

[a]Defined as the amount a nonemployee would have to pay to obtain the same level of coverage.

SOURCE: Adapted from M. Wilson, G. B. Northcraft, and M. A. Neale, "The Perceived Value of Fringe Benefits," *Personnel Psychology* 38 (1985), pp. 309–20. Used with permission.

suggests, however, that increased employee knowledge of benefits can have a positive or negative effect, depending on the nature of the benefits package. For example, there was a negative, or inverse, correlation between cost to the employee and benefits satisfaction overall, but the correlation was more strongly negative among employees with greater knowledge of their benefits.[67] The implication is that employees will be least satisfied with their benefits if their cost is high and they are well informed.

One thing an employer should consider with respect to written benefits communication is that more than 27 million employees in the United States may be functionally illiterate. Of course, there are many alternative ways to communicate benefits information. (See Table 13.10.) Nevertheless, most organizations spend little to communicate information about benefits, and much of this is spent on general written communications. Considering that Bureau of Labor Statistics data cited earlier indicate that private-sector organizations spend an average of more than $16,000 per worker per year on benefits, together with the complex nature of many benefits and the poor understanding of most employees, the typical communication effort may be inadequate.[68] On a more positive note, organizations are increasingly using Web-based tools to personalize and tailor communications to individual employees. In addition, effective use of traditional approaches (e.g., booklets) can have a large effect on employee awareness.[69]

Rather than a single standard benefits package for all employees, flexible benefit plans (flex-plans or cafeteria-style plans) permit employees to choose the types and amounts of benefits they want for themselves. The plans vary according to such things as whether minimum levels of certain benefits (such as health care coverage) are prescribed and whether employees can receive money for having chosen a "light" benefits package (or have to pay extra for more benefits). One example is vacation, where some plans permit employees to give up vacation days for more salary or, alternatively, purchase extra vacation days through a salary reduction.

What are the potential advantages of such plans?[70] In the best case, almost all of the objectives discussed previously can be positively influenced. First, employees can gain a greater awareness and appreciation of what the employer provides them, particularly with plans that give employees a lump sum to allocate to benefits. Second, by permitting employee choice, there should be a better match between the benefits

table 13.10

Benefits Communication Media Examples for Different Audiences and Purposes

MEDIA	AUDIENCE	PURPOSE
Enrollment package	All employees (English and Spanish)	Announce changes or new hire enrollment only by deadline
Meetings	Local employees	Provide information on benefits and changes
Teleconference messaging	Remote employees	Provide information on benefits and changes
Intranet	All employees (personalized)	Provide information on benefits, training, and employment policies
E-mail alerts	Supervisors	Provide employees with information
Summary plan descriptions	All employees	Make available compliance information
Paycheck attachments	All employees	Provide information on benefits
Webcasts	Regional managers	Share context for changes and their roles and responsibilities

SOURCE: A. Parsons and K. Groh, "The New Road Effective Communications," *Compensation Benefits Review* 38 (2006), p. 57.

package and the employees' preferences. This, in turn, should improve employee attitudes and retention.[71] Third, employers may achieve overall cost reductions in their benefits programs. Cafeteria plans can be thought of as similar to defined contribution plans, whereas traditional plans are more like defined benefit plans. The employer can control the size of the contribution under the former, but not under the latter, because the cost and utilization of benefits is beyond the employer's control. Costs can also be controlled by designing the choices so that employees have an incentive to choose more efficient options. For example, in the case of a medical flex-plan, employees who do not wish to take advantage of the (presumably more cost-effective) HMO have to pay significant deductibles and other costs under the alternative plans.

One drawback of cafeteria-style plans is their administrative cost, especially in the initial design and start-up stages. However, software packages and standardized flex-plans developed by consultants offer some help in this regard. Another possible drawback to these plans is adverse selection. Employees are most likely to choose benefits that they expect to need the most. Someone in need of dental work would choose as much dental coverage as possible. As a result, employer costs can increase significantly as each employee chooses benefits based on their personal value. Another result of adverse selection is the difficulty in estimating benefits costs under such a plan, especially in small companies. Adverse selection can be controlled, however, by limiting coverage amounts, pricing benefits that are subject to adverse selection higher, or using a limited set of packaged options, which prevents employees from choosing too many benefits options that would be susceptible to adverse selection.

Flexible Spending Accounts

A flexible spending account permits pretax contributions to an employee account that can be drawn on to pay for uncovered health care expenses (like deductibles or copayments). A separate account of up to $5,000 per year is permitted for pretax contributions to cover dependent care expenses. The federal tax code requires that funds in the health care and dependent care accounts be earmarked in advance and spent during the plan year. Remaining funds revert to the employer. Therefore, the accounts work best to the extent that employees have predictable expenses. The major advantage of such plans is the increase in take-home pay that results from pretax payment of health and dependent care expenses. Consider again the hypothetical employee with annual earnings of $50,000 and an effective total marginal tax rate of 41 percent from Table 13.1. The take-home pay from an additional $10,000 in salary with and without a flexible dependent care account is as follows:

	NO FLEXIBLE SPENDING CARE ACCOUNT	FLEXIBLE SPENDING CARE ACCOUNT
Salary portion	$10,000	$10,000
Pretax dependent care contribution	0	−5,000
Taxable salary	10,000	5,000
Tax (41 percent)	−4,100	−2,050
Aftertax cost of dependent care	−5,000	0
Take-home Pay	$ 900	$ 2,950

Therefore, the use of a flexible spending account saves the employee $2,050 ($2,950 − $900) per year.

LO6
Describe the regulatory constraints that affect the way employee benefits are designed and administered.

General Regulatory Issues

Although we have already discussed a number of regulatory issues, some additional ones require attention.

Nondiscrimination Rules and Qualified Plans

As a general rule, all benefits packages must meet certain rules to be classified as qualified plans. What are the advantages of a qualified plan? Basically, it receives more favorable tax treatment than a nonqualified plan. In the case of a qualified retirement plan, for example, these tax advantages include (1) an immediate tax deduction for employers for their contributions to retirement funds, (2) no tax liability for the employee at the time of the employer deduction, and (3) tax-free investment returns (from stocks, bonds, money markets, or the like) on the retirement funds.[72]

What rules must be satisfied for a plan to obtain qualified status? Each benefit area has different rules. It would be impossible to describe the various rules here, but some general observations are possible. Taking pensions as an example again, vesting requirements must be met. More generally, qualified plans must meet so-called nondiscrimination rules. Basically, this means that a benefit cannot discriminate in favor of "highly compensated employees." One rationale behind such rules is that the tax benefits of qualified benefits plans (and the corresponding loss of tax revenues for the U.S. government) should not go disproportionately to the wealthy.[73] Rather, the favorable tax treatment is designed to encourage employers to provide important benefits to a broad spectrum of employees. The nondiscrimination rules discourage owners or top managers from adopting plans that benefit them exclusively.

Sex, Age, and Disability

Beyond the Pregnancy Discrimination Act's requirements that were discussed earlier in the chapter, a second area of concern for employers in ensuring legal treatment of men and women in the benefits area has to do with pension benefits. Women tend to live longer than men, meaning that pension benefits for women are more costly, all else being equal. However, in its 1978 *Manhart* ruling, the Supreme Court declared it illegal for employers to require women to contribute more to a defined benefit plan than men: Title VII protects individuals, and not all women outlive all men.[74]

Two major age-related issues have received attention under the Age Discrimination in Employment Act (ADEA) and later amendments such as the Older Workers Benefit Protection Act (OWBPA). First, employers must take care not to discriminate against workers over age 40 in the provision of pay or benefits. As one example, employers cannot generally cease accrual (stop the growth) of retirement benefits at some age (like 65) as a way of pressuring older employees to retire.[75] Second, early retirement incentive programs need to meet the following standards to avoid legal liability: (1) the employee is not coerced to accept the incentive and retire, (2) accurate information is provided regarding options, and (3) the employee is given adequate time (is not pressured) to make a decision.

Employers also have to comply with the Americans with Disabilities Act (ADA), which went into effect in 1992. The ADA specifies that employees with disabilities must have "equal access to whatever health insurance coverage the employer provides other employees." However, the act also notes that the terms and conditions of health insurance can be based on risk factors as long as this is not a subterfuge for denying the benefit to those with disabilities. Employers with risk-based programs in place would be in a stronger position, however, than employers who make changes after hiring employees with disabilities.[76]

Monitoring Future Benefits Obligations

Financial Accounting Statement (FAS) 106, issued by the Financial Accounting Standards Board, became effective in 1993. This rule requires that any benefits (excluding pensions) provided after retirement (the major one being health care) can no longer be funded on a pay-as-you-go basis. Rather, they must be paid on an accrual basis, and companies must enter these future cost obligations on their financial statements. The effect on financial statements can be substantial. Between the end of 2007 and 2008, for example, General Motors (GM) saw its U.S. pension assets drop from $104 billion to $84 billion.

Increasing retiree health care costs (and the change in accounting standards) have also led some companies to require white-collar employees and retirees to pay insurance premiums for the first time in history and to increase copayments and deductibles. Survey data indicate that some companies are ending retiree health care benefits altogether. GM, for example, recently eliminated retiree health care benefits for white-collar workers. Union contracts prevent GM from eliminating the blue-collar plan, but it is working to set up a trust fund (which could cost it $20 billion) as part of its bankruptcy proceeding so as to remove the obligation from its books. Other companies have reduced benefits or increased retiree contributions. Obviously, such changes hit the elderly hard, especially those with relatively fixed incomes. Not surprisingly, legal challenges have arisen. The need to balance the interests of shareholders, current employees, and retirees in this area will be one of the most difficult challenges facing managers in the future.

Financial Accounting Statement (FAS) 106
The rule issued by the Financial Accounting Standards Board in 1993 requiring companies to fund benefits provided after retirement on an accrual rather than a pay-as-you-go basis and to enter these future cost obligations on their financial statements.

A LOOK BACK

We have seen that many organizations have become less paternalistic in their employee benefits strategies. Employees now have more responsibility, and sometimes more risk, regarding their benefits choices. One change has been in the area of retirement income plans, where employers have moved toward greater reliance on defined contribution plans. Such plans require employees to understand investing; otherwise, their retirement years may not be so happy, as we saw in the chapter opener. The risk to employees is especially great when defined contribution plans invest a substantial portion of their assets in company stock. One reason companies do this is because they wish to move away from an entitlement mentality and instead link benefits to company performance. However, if the company has financial problems, employees risk losing not only their jobs, but also their retirement money. As we saw in the beginning of the chapter, another change has been in the area of health care benefits, where companies have reduced or sometimes eliminated such benefits. Again, the responsibility for anticipating this possibility increasingly falls with employees. In the health care area, employees are being asked to increase the proportion of costs that they pay and also to use data on health care quality to make better choices about health care.

Questions

1. Why do employers offer benefits? Is it because the law requires it, because it makes good business sense, or because it is the right thing to do? How much responsibility should employers have for the health and well-being of their employees? Take the perspective of both a shareholder and an employee in answering this question.
2. If you were advising a new company on how to design its health care plan, what would you recommend?

Please see the Video Case that corresponds to this chapter online at www.mhhe.com/noe7e.

SUMMARY

Effective management of employee benefits is an important means by which organizations successfully compete. Benefits costs are substantial and continue to grow rapidly in some areas, most notably health care. Control of such costs is necessary to compete in the product market. At the same time, employers must offer a benefits package that permits them to compete in the labor market. Beyond investing more money in benefits, this attraction and retention of quality employees can be helped by better communication of the value of the benefits package and by allowing employees to tailor benefits to their own needs through flexible benefits plans.

Employers continue to be a major source of economic security for employees, often providing health insurance, retirement benefits, and so forth. Changes to benefits can have a tremendous impact on employees and retirees. Therefore, employers carry a significant social responsibility in making benefits decisions. At the same time, employees need to be aware that they will increasingly become responsible for their own economic security. Health care benefit design is changing to encourage employees to be more informed consumers, and retirement benefits will depend more and more on the financial investment decisions employees make on their own behalf.

KEY TERMS

Marginal tax rate, 581
Consolidated Omnibus Budget
    Reconciliation Act
    (COBRA), 587
Pension Benefit Guaranty
    Corporation (PBGC), 591

Employee Retirement Income
    Security Act (ERISA), 591
Cash balance plan, 593
Summary plan description
    (SPD), 594
Family and Medical Leave Act, 597

Health maintenance organization
    (HMO), 600
Preferred provider organization
    (PPO), 600
Financial Accounting Statement
    (FAS) 106, 615

DISCUSSION QUESTIONS

1. The chapter-opening story described how relationships between employers and employees are changing with employees needing to take more responsibility for their own futures. What are the likely consequences of this change? Where does the social responsibility of employers end, and where does the need to operate more efficiently begin?
2. Your company, like many others, is experiencing double-digit percentage increases in health care costs.

What suggestions can you offer that may reduce the rate of cost increases?
3. Why is communication so important in the employee benefits area? What sorts of programs can a company use to communicate more effectively? What are the potential positive consequences of more effective benefits communication?
4. What are the potential advantages of flexible benefits and flexible spending accounts? Are there any potential drawbacks?

5. Although benefits account for a large share of employee compensation, many feel there is little evidence on whether an employer receives an adequate return on the benefits investment. One suggestion has been to link benefits to individual, group, or organization performance. Explain why you would or would not recommend this strategy to an organization.

SELF-ASSESSMENT EXERCISE

One way companies determine which types of benefits to provide is to use a survey asking employees which types of benefits are important to them. Read the following list of employee benefits. For each benefit, mark an X in the column that indicates whether it is important to you or not.

Benefit	Important to Have	Not Important to Have	% Employers Offering
Dependent-care flexible spending account			70%
Flextime			64
Ability to bring child to work in case of emergency			30
Elder-care referral services			21
Adoption assistance			21
On-site child care center			6
Gym subsidy			28
Vaccinations on site (e.g., flu shots)			61
On-site fitness center			26
Casual dress days (every day)			53
Organization-sponsored sports teams			39
Food services/subsidized cafeteria			29
Travel-planning services			27
Dry-cleaning services			15
Massage therapy services at work			12
Self-defense training			6
Concierge services			4

Compare your importance ratings for each benefit to the corresponding number in the right-hand column that indicates the percentage of employers that offer the benefit. Are you likely to find jobs that provide the benefits you want? Explain.

SOURCE: Based on Figure 2, "Percent of Employers Offering Work/Life Benefits (by Year)," in *Workplace Visions* 4 (2002), p. 3, published by the Society for Human Resource Management.

EXERCISING STRATEGY: COMPANIES LEARN THAT IT PAYS TO KEEP EMPLOYEES FIT

Physical fitness—or at least wellness—does matter, as more and more companies and their insurers are learning. A healthy workforce means better productivity and fewer workdays lost, not to mention reduced medical costs by keeping injuries and illnesses to a minimum. A study published by the Presidents' Council on Physical Fitness and Sports found that fitness programs provided by companies saved from $1.15 to $5.52 for every dollar spent.

At 3Com, the network communications company, employees spend their lunch hours at the WellCom Center, a 13,500-square-foot fitness facility right on site. There they can cycle, walk a treadmill, lift weights, take a fitness class, or relax in the sauna. Or they can play a game of basketball or beach volleyball outside. Afterward, they can cool off at the juice bar with a fruit smoothie. The center is open 24 hours a day, seven days a week, to meet the needs of employees who work at all hours. More than 40 percent of the 4,200 workers at 3Com are WellCom members, and 70 percent take advantage of the center's seminars on wellness, smoking cessation, or weight loss.

"A healthy workforce is good for employees and good for 3Com," says Peter Sandman, a manager of strategic planning at the company. "It helps recruiting and it helps retention, especially in a competitive environment like Silicon Valley [California]."

Applied Materials Inc. of Santa Clara, California, conducted its own study that showed that for fitness center participants, medical payments were reduced by 20 percent, hospital admissions were 70 percent lower, costs for accident-related disability claims were 30 percent less, and workers' compensation claims were 79 percent less than those of employees who didn't use the company's fitness center. Even a five-minute stretch break has been shown to reduce strains and sprains by as much as 65 percent. "Just moving and getting away from their PC makes them feel better," says Judy Webster, director of corporate wellness for the company.

Boeing's health care package also includes access to its fitness centers as part of its overall recreation program.

"When you're happy and healthy, you're able to perform at your best," explains the aircraft manufacturer's Web site. The recreation program includes indoor and outdoor facilities as well as discount packages for sports and cultural events. These companies have embraced the wisdom of the old adage, "an ounce of prevention is worth a pound of cure," and it has literally paid off.

Questions
1. Why don't more companies emphasize employee wellness? Does it work better for some companies than for others?
2. The companies here have on-site facilities. Is that the right model for all companies?

SOURCES: Boeing Web site, www.boeing.com, accessed October 30, 2001; D. Beck, "Your Company Needs Its Own Best Practices," *Career Journal* from *The Wall Street Journal* (July 30–August 5, 2001), www.careerjournal.com; M. Chase, "Healthy Assets," *The Wall Street Journal* (May 1. 2000), http://interactive.wsj.

● MANAGING PEOPLE: FROM THE PAGES OF *BUSINESSWEEK*

BusinessWeek | 401(k)s: Employer Contributions Get the Ax

Desperate to cut costs, more and more companies are eliminating their matching contributions to employee 401(k) plans When times are tough, companies find cost savings wherever they can. Now some employers are doing away with the 401(k) match, a benefit once considered almost sacred.

The list of companies that have suspended or cut back corporate matching in their defined-contribution retirement plans this year is not trivial. It includes General Motors, Frontier Airlines, car-rental company Dollar Thrifty Automotive, broadcaster Entercom Communications, newspaper chain Lee Enterprises, and real estate brokerage Cushman & Wakefield. A recent study by benefits consultant Watson Wyatt of 248 U.S. companies found that 2% had already reduced or eliminated the match and another 4% expected to do so within the next 12 months. The national number could creep higher, however, if the economy continues to worsen. "It depends how long this goes on," says Pamela Hess, director of retirement research at benefits consultant Hewitt Associates. "In another year, you could have another 3% to 5% [cutting back on matches], or you could have 10%."

Lesser of Two Evils
The psychological impact of these cuts may be almost as damaging as the financial harm. Coming at a time when many Americans are struggling to save for retirement and face shrunken stock portfolios, the cutbacks make the goal of a secure retirement even more elusive. Yet for all the unhappiness over slashed 401(k)s, employees understand the alternative of increased layoffs may be worse, says Robyn Credico, Watson Wyatt's national director of defined-contribution plans. In general, they "would rather have their jobs and a reduced match."

Workers who have survived earlier downturns may have a sense of déjà vu. From 2001 to 2003, for example, GM, Charles Schwab, Ford Motor, CMS Energy, Great Northern Paper, and at least 10 others reduced or eliminated the match, according to a study by the Center for Retirement Research at Boston College. And even though most companies reinstated the benefit a few years later as business improved, the match continues to be an easy target. It typically amounts to 50% of employees' contributions on up to 6% of their annual salaries. That means the average company spends nearly 2% of employee pay on this one benefit, according to research by fund company Vanguard. The vast majority of companies that offer 401(k)s include the benefit, and "they can save millions by cutting [it]," says Hewitt's Hess. "It's usually one of a company's biggest expenditures after wages and health care."

Even if the benefit eventually is restored, that won't be enough to ease retirement woes for many employees. Goodyear Tire & Rubber cut its match in 2003; it now plans to reinstate it in January 2009. In the intervening years, the company froze its pension, so the return of the match will not bring retirement benefits back to the earlier level. "The company is moving away from a pension plan and we are enhancing our 401(k) plan," explains spokesman Scott Baughman.

New-Employee Enrollment Could Drop

The trend away from pensions—many of which are now underfunded—leaves retiring employees increasingly reliant on their 401(k)s. In the Watson Wyatt study, for example, 11% of companies said they had frozen or closed their pension plans this year, and another 4% said they expected to do so in the next 12 months. That throws even greater weight on matching plans as part of the nest egg.

What does this trend signify for employee savings behavior? Academic studies show that the existence of a 401(k) match increases contribution rates among employees, but the research doesn't address what happens when a match is cut. Brigitte Madrian, a professor of public policy and corporate management at Harvard University, has studied 401(k) design and behavior. She thinks the end result will be a "small fall" in 401(k) participation as fewer new employees sign up and existing employees stick with the status quo, neither pulling money out of the plan nor adding to contributions. Says Madrian: "You will find the biggest effect on new employees walking in the door. Employees who were already signed on for the plan aren't going to drop out because there's not a match."

Questions

1. For employers that need to cut employment-related costs, what other cuts could be made? What are the pros and cons of cutting 401(k) matches versus making these other types of cuts?
2. Are 401(k) plans more or less important today than they were in the past? Why? Does this increase or reduce your concern with 401(k) match cuts?
3. How does the recent performance of the stock market affect the role of 401(k) plans?

SOURCE: Amy Feldman, "401(k)s: Employer Contributions Get the Ax," *BusinessWeek*, November 12, 2008.

● NOTES

1. James H. Dulebohn, Janice C. Molloy, Shaun M. Pichler, Brian Murray, "Employee Benefits: Literature Review and Emerging Issues," *Human Resource Management Review* 19 (2009), pp. 86–103. Joseph J. Martocchio, *Employee Benefits*, 2nd ed. (New York: McGraw-Hill, 2006).
2. H. W. Hennessey, "Using Employee Benefits to Gain a Competitive Advantage," *Benefits Quarterly* 5, no. 1 (1989), pp. 51–57; B. Gerhart and G.T. Milkovich, "Employee Compensation: Research and Practice," in *Handbook of Industrial and Organizational Psychology*, vol. 3, 2nd ed., ed. M. D. Dunnette and L. M. Hough (Palo Alto, CA: Consulting Psychologists Press, 1992); J. Swist, "Benefits Communications: Measuring Impact and Value," *Employee Benefit Plan Review*, September 2002, pp. 24–26.
3. R. Ehrenberg and R. S. Smith, *Modern Labor Economics: Theory and Public Policy*, 7th ed. (Upper Saddle River, NJ: Addison Wesley Longman, 2000).
4. B. T. Beam Jr. and J. J. McFadden, *Employee Benefits*, 6th ed. (Chicago: Dearborn Financial Publishing, 2000).
5. The organization and description in this section draws heavily on Beam and McFadden, *Employee Benefits*.
6. See www.doleta.gov for further information.
7. J. A. Penczak, "Unemployment Benefit Plans," in *Employee Benefits Handbook*, 3rd ed., ed. J. D. Mamorsky (Boston: Warren, Gorham & Lamont, 1992).
8. J. V. Nackley, *Primer on Workers' Compensation* (Washington, DC: Bureau of National Affairs, 1989).
9. Beam and McFadden, *Employee Benefits*, p. 81.
10. www.dol.gov/esa.
11. A. H. Wheeler, "Pathophysiology of Chronic Back Pain," www.emedicine.com (2002).
12. J. R. Hollenbeck, D. R. Ilgen, and S. M. Crampton, "Lower Back Disability in Occupational Settings: A Review of the Literature from a Human Resource Management View," *Personnel Psychology* 45 (1992), pp. 247–78; J. J. Martocchio, D. A. Harrison, and H. Berkson, "Connections between Lower Back Pain, Interventions, and Absence from Work: A Time-Based Meta-Analysis," *Personnel Psychology* (2000), p. 595.
13. Employee Benefit Research Institute, "Value of Employee Benefits Constant in a Changing World," www.ebri.org (March 28, 2002).
14. M.P. McQueen, "Stimulus Makes COBRA Coverage a Better Bet," *The Wall Street Journal,* February 19, 2009.
15. Beam and McFadden, *Employee Benefits*, 6th ed.
16. Social Security Administration, "Fast Facts and Figures about Social Security." Data for 2001, published 2003, www.ssa.gov.
17. K. A. Bender, "Pension Integration and Retirement Benefits," *Monthly Labor Review*, February 2001, pp. 49–58, http://stats.bls.gov/opub/mlr.
18. www.pbgc.gov.
19. www.irs.gov. Those age 50 and over have higher contribution limits.
20. R. A. Ippolito, "Toward Explaining the Growth of Defined Contribution Plans," *Industrial Relations* 34 (1995), pp. 1–20; Employee Benefit Research Institute, "Historical Statistics," EBRI May 2004 Policy Forum, www.ebri.org.
21. J. Fierman, "How Secure Is Your Nest Egg?" *Fortune,* August 12, 1991, pp. 50–54.
22. Beam and McFadden, *Employee Benefits*.
23. B. J. Coleman, *Primer on Employee Retirement Income Security Act*, 3rd ed. (Washington, DC: Bureau of National Affairs, 1989).
24. *Continental Can Company v. Gavalik*, summary in *Daily Labor Report* (December 8, 1987): "Supreme Court Lets Stand Third Circuit Ruling That Pension Avoidance Scheme Is ERISA Violation," No. 234, p. A-14.
25. A. L. Gustman, O. S. Mitchell, and T. L. Steinmeier, "The Role of Pensions in the Labor Market: A Survey of the Literature," *Industrial and Labor Relations* 47 (1994), pp. 417–38.
26. D. A. DeCenzo and S. J. Holoviak, *Employee Benefits* (Englewood Cliffs, NJ: Prentice-Hall, 1990).
27. E. P. Lazear, "Why Is There Early Retirement?" *Journal of Political Economy* 87 (1979), pp. 1261–84; Gustman et al., "The Role of Pensions."

28. P. Cappelli, *The New Deal at Work: Managing the Market-Driven Workforce* (Boston: Harvard Business School Press, 1999).

29. S. Dorsey, "Pension Portability and Labor Market Efficiency," *Industrial and Labor Relations* 48, no. 5 (1995), pp. 276–92.

30. Commission of the European Communities, European Community Directive 93/104/EC, issued November 23, 1993 and amended June 22, 2000, by Directive 2000/34/EC, http://europa.eu.int/comm/index_en.htm.

31. DeCenzo and Holoviak, *Employee Benefits*, 6th ed.

32. S. L. Grover and K. J. Crooker, "Who Appreciates Family Responsive Human Resource Policies: The Impact of Family-Friendly Policies on the Organizational Attachment of Parents and Non-parents," *Personnel Psychology* 48 (1995), pp. 271–88; T. J. Rothausen, J. A. Gonzalez, N. E. Clarke, and L. L. O'Dell, "Family-Friendly Backlash: Fact or Fiction? The Case of Organizations' On-Site Child Care Centers," *Personnel Psychology* 51 (1998), p. 685; M. A. Arthur, "Share Price Reactions to Work-Family Initiatives: An Institutional Perspective," *Academy of Management Journal* 46 (2003), p. 497; J. E. Perry-Smith and T. Blum, "Work-Family Human Resource Bundles and Perceived Organizational Performance," *Academy of Management Journal* 43 (2000), pp. 1107–17.

33. "The Employer's Role in Helping Working Families." For examples of child care arrangements in some well-known companies (e.g., AT&T, Apple, Exxon, IBM, Merck), see "A Look at Child-Care Benefits," *USA Today*, March 14, 1989, p. 4B; U.S. Census Bureau, "America's Families and Living Arrangements," June 2001, www.census.gov.

34. J. Waldfogel, "International Policies toward Parental Leave and Child Care," *Future of Children* 11, no. 1 (2001), pp. 99–111.

35. P. Hardin, "Women Execs Should Feel at Ease about Taking Full Maternity Leave," *Personnel Journal*, September 1995, p. 19.

36. "The Families and Work Institute's 1998 Business Work–Life Study," www.familiesandwork.org. Results based on a nationally representative survey of employers having 100 or more employees.

37. J. Fierman, "It's 2 A.M.: Let's Go to Work," *Fortune*, August 21, 1995, pp. 82–88.

38. E. E. Kossek, "Diversity in Child Care Assistance Needs: Employee Problems, Preferences, and Work-Related Outcomes," *Personnel Psychology* 43 (1990), pp. 769–91.

39. "A Bank Profits from Its Work/Life Program," *Workforce*, February 1997, p. 49.

40. R. Broderick and B. Gerhart, "Nonwage Compensation," in *The Human Resource Management Handbook*, ed. D. Lewin, D. J. B. Mitchell, and M. A. Zadi (San Francisco: JAI Press, 1996).

41. Dulabohn et al., "Employee Benefits."

42. Hennessey, "Using Employee Benefits to Gain a Competitive Advantage."

43. U.S. Bureau of Labor Statistics, "Employer Cost for Employee Compensation," www.bls.gov; U.S. Chamber of Commerce Research Center, Employee Benefits Study, annual (Washington, D.C.: U.S. Chamber of Commerce).

44. www.census.gov.

45. Employee Benefit Research Institute, *EBRI's Fundamentals of Employee Benefit Programs*, ebri.org, 6th ed., 2009.

46. A. C. Monheit and P. F. Cooper, "Health Insurance and Job Mobility: The Effects of Public Policy on Job-Lock," *Industrial and Labor Relations Review* 48 (1994), pp. 86–102.

47. Beam and McFadden, *Employee Benefits*.

48. R. Lieber, "New Way to Curb Medical Costs: Make Employees Feel the Sting," *The Wall Street Journal*, June 23, 2004, p. A1.

49. M. Barringer and O. S. Mitchell, "Workers' Preferences among Company-Provided Health Insurance Plans," *Industrial and Labor Relations Review* 48 (1994), pp. 141–52.

50. Beam and McFadden, *Employee Benefits*.

51. Wellness Councils of America, "101 Ways to Wellness," www.welcoa.org, 2001; Wellness Councils of America, "A Guide to Developing Your Worksite Wellness Program," www.welcoa.org, 1997.

52. S. Tully, "America's Healthiest Companies," *Fortune*, June 12, 1995, pp. 98–106.

53. G. Flynn, "Companies Make Wellness Work," *Personnel Journal*, February 1995, pp. 63–66.

54. D. A. Harrison and L. Z. Liska, "Promoting Regular Exercise in Organizational Fitness Programs: Health-Related Differences in Motivational Building Blocks," *Personnel Psychology* 47 (1994), pp. 47–71.

55. J. C. Erfurt, A. Foote, and M. A. Heirich, "The Cost-Effectiveness of Worksite Wellness Programs for Hypertension Control, Weight Loss, Smoking Cessation and Exercise," *Personnel Psychology* 45 (1992), pp. 5–27.

56. Ibid.

57. The Henry J. Kaiser Family Foundation and Health Research and Educational Trust, *Survey of Employer Health Benefits 2008*, www.kff.org.

58. H. Gardner, unpublished manuscript (Cheyenne, WY: Options & Choices, 1995).

59. H. B. Noble, "Quality Is Focus for Health Plans," *The New York Times*, July 3, 1995, p. A1; J. D. Klinke, "Medicine's Industrial Revolution," *The Wall Street Journal*, August 21, 1995, p. A8.

60. J. B. White, "Business Plan," *The Wall Street Journal*, October 19, 1998, p. R18.

61. G. McWilliams, "Big Employers Plan Electronic Health Records," *The Wall Street Journal*, November 29, 2006, p. B1.

62. J. Schor, *The Overworked American: The Unexpected Decline of Leisure* (New York: Basic Books, 1991); U.S. Bureau of Labor Statistics, "Workers Are on the Job More Hours over the Course of a Year," *Issues in Labor Statistics*, February 1997.

63. Hewitt Associates. http://www.hewitt.com.

64. Beam and McFadden, *Employee Benefits*.

65. M. Wilson, G. B. Northcraft, and M. A. Neale, "The Perceived Value of Fringe Benefits," *Personnel Psychology* 38 (1985), pp. 309–20. Similar results were found in other studies reviewed by H. W. Hennessey, P. L. Perrewe, and W. A. Hochwarter, "Impact of Benefit Awareness on Employee and Organizational Outcomes: A Longitudinal Field Experiment," *Benefits Quarterly* 8, no. 2 (1992), pp. 90–96; MetLife, Employee Benefits Benchmarking Report, www.metlife.com. Accessed June 24, 2007.

66. R. Huseman, J. Hatfield, and R. Robinson, "The MBA and Fringe Benefits," *Personnel Administrator* 23, no. 7 (1978), pp. 57–60. See summary in H. W. Hennessey Jr., "Using Employee Benefits to Gain a Competitive Advantage," *Benefits Quarterly* 5, no. 1 (1989), pp. 51–57.

67. Hennessey et al., "Impact of Benefit Awareness"; the same study found no impact of the increased awareness and benefits satisfaction on overall job satisfaction. G. F. Dreher, R. A. Ash, and R. D. Bretz, "Benefit Coverage and Employee Cost: Critical Factors in Explaining Compensation Satisfaction," *Personnel Psychology* 41 (1988), pp. 237–54.

68. M. C. Giallourakis and G. S. Taylor, "An Evaluation of Benefit Communication Strategy," *Employee Benefits Journal* 15, no. 4 (1991), pp. 14–18; Employee Benefits Research Institute, "How Readable Are Summary Plan Descriptions for Health Care Plans," *EBRI Notes*, October 2006, ebri.org.

69. J. Abraham, R. Feldman, and C. Carlin, "Understanding Employee Awareness of Health Care Quality Information: How Can Employers Benefit?" *Health Services Research* 39 (2004), pp. 1799–1816.

70. Beam and McFadden, *Employee Benefits*; M. W. Barringer and G. T. Milkovich, "A Theoretical Explanation of the Adoption and Design of Flexible Benefit Plans: A Case of Human Resource Innovation," *Academy of Management Review* 23 (1998), pp. 305–24.

71. For supportive evidence, see A. E. Barber, R. B. Dunham, and R. A. Formisano, "The Impact of Flexible Benefits on Employee Satisfaction: A Field Study," *Personnel Psychology* 45 (1992), pp. 55–75; E. E. Lawler, *Pay and Organizational Development* (Reading, MA: Addison-Wesley, 1981).

72. Beam and McFadden, *Employee Benefits*.

73. Ibid.

74. *Los Angeles Dept. of Water & Power v. Manhart*, 435 US SCt 702 (1978), 16 EPD, 8250.

75. S. K. Hoffman, "Discrimination Litigation Relating to Employee Benefits," *Labor Law Journal*, June 1992, pp. 362–81.

76. Ibid., p. 375.

PART

5

Special Topics in Human Resource Management

Collective Bargaining and Labor Relations

LEARNING OBJECTIVES

After reading this chapter, you should be able to:

"It's a Question of Survival"

With its highly educated hourly workers, flexible structure and—perhaps most remarkable—blessing from the UAW, the Global Engine Manufacturing Alliance's plant in Dundee, Michigan, could be the workforce model for the future of U.S. automaking. "It's a question of survival" according to Bruce Baumhower, president of UAW Local 12 in Toledo, Ohio.

The plant seems to be doing its part. The 2008 Harbour Report™ found the Dundee plant to be the most efficient engine plant in North America, taking only 1.84 hours to assemble an engine. Whatever happens to the U.S. auto companies, the Dundee plant seems well positioned to survive to make engines for someone. It is too efficient not to.

On a Thursday morning, the Global Engine Manufacturing Alliance plant in Dundee, Michigan, is open as it always is, 21 hours a day, six days a week, 294 days a year. But a visitor to the plant might wonder where all the workers are.

True, for an auto engine plant, GEMA is more automated and thus leaner than most. The facility's total headcount is 275, significantly less than a typical engine plant, which has 600 to 2,000 workers. But that's not why the assembly lines seem empty, GEMA president Bruce Coventry says. "Since we're ahead of schedule, a lot of our people are in training," he says. Sure enough, down the hall are three rooms filled with employees being taught a wide array of subjects, ranging from how to assemble and engine to the study of mathematical formulas designed to teach problem-solving skills. Over the next several months, these employees will receive up to 1,160 hours of such training in class and on the assembly floor. "The fact that we are ahead of our production schedule allows us to focus our people on problem solving and continuous improvement," Coventry says. "That's luxury that most organizations don't usually have."

And that's why automakers from around the world, including GEMA's three owners—DaimlerChrysler, Mitsubishi, and Hyundai—are keeping close track of this facility, located 60 miles outside of Detroit. As General Motors and Ford seek to shed thousands of their union-represented employees, they are looking ahead to what kind of workforce they will need to compete in the increasingly global market. "They need a new business model for labor agreements and new kinds of workers," says Sean McAlinden, chief economist and vice president of research at the Center for Automotive Research in Ann Arbor, Michigan. Many are thinking that GEMA may prove to be that model, he says.

The Dundee facility, which opened in October, stands out from other auto plants in every aspect of how it manages its workforce. Its hourly employees are highly educated and rotate jobs and shifts to provide for greater flexibility. That's an unheard of concept in the traditional auto plant, where each worker is usually assigned to one and only one job.

Another unique aspect of GEMA's workforce model is that contractors, whom the plant refers to as "partners," work alongside assembly workers and engineers, sporting the same black-and-white uniforms. "We want everyone to feel like they are part of a team," Coventry says.

But the most unheard of thing for the auto industry is that the United Auto Workers has agreed to the concept. "This is an agreement that every automaker is looking at with laser eyes," McAlinden says.

The initial investment for the two plants was $804 million, 50 percent less than DaimlerChrysler had ever invested in an engine plant, Coventry says.

The automakers' joint venture also has two non-GEMA plants in South Korea and one in Japan that produce engines for Hyundai and Mitsubishi, respectively. When all of the plants are operational by year's end, the venture will have the capacity to produce 1.8 million engines annually.

Coventry, who had been an engine plant manager for Chrysler since 1995, wanted to find a way to get rid of the waste and inefficiencies he had seen in traditional plants. "My pet peeves are bureaucracy, structure and management," he says.

Over the next several months, Coventry and a team of executives from the three automakers brainstormed over meetings in Korea and the United States. During these discussions, the group came up with a list of companies within and outside of the industry, such as Dell, Wal-Mart and Toyota, to serve as benchmarks for the business model they wanted.

Like its Japanese peers, the alliance wanted to focus on kaizen, the Japanese term for continuous improvement. But Coventry says that GEMA doesn't want to just replicate Toyota, which he concedes is "the rabbit" all automakers are trying to catch. "We are doing many things that a Toyota employee would recognize, but the big differentiator is that our workforce has a much higher level of technical skill," he says.

GEMA's nonexempt workers, who start at $21 an hour and work up to $30 within five years, must have either a two-year technical degree, a skilled journeyman's card or five years' experience in advanced machining. This level of education is key to GEMA being more flexible, and thus faster than its competitors, Dunning says.

The other guiding principles of the plant's culture are problem solving and "the four A's": anyone can do anything anytime, anywhere. This means that workers rotate jobs—a model that is designed to give the plant more flexibility. Everyone on the floor has a similar title: They are "team members" and "team leaders."

By rotating jobs, the plant hopes to keep workers engaged and reduce the potential for injury,

Coventry says. The chance of workers developing ergonomic injuries is lower if they aren't repeating the exact same motions all day long, he says. So far there have been no ergonomical injuries at the plant.

There are also no foremen overseeing the workers at GEMA. In their place are the team leaders. In contrast to foremen, the team leaders don't stand on the sidelines observing how the teams work. They work alongside six-person groups, each one including an engineer. Coventry bristles if he sees engineers at their desks while he's walking through the plant. "Having engineers on the floor enables us to solve problems right away when they happen," he says.

Bringing a new concept to the table is never easy in labor relations, but GEMA's management was ready to spend as much time as needed explaining the benefits of the workforce model. The UAW initially was concerned about the "four A's" concept, says Bruce Baumbach, the GEMA plant manager who helped oversee the negotiations. "Their concern was that it would give management the ability to pull out anybody, anytime," he says. Baumbach explained to the union leaders that the idea was to have a flexible model and that it would encompass all positions, including managers.

GEMA management also had to spend a lot of time making union leaders comfortable with the shift structure. "The UAW leadership understands the competitive situation that we are in," Coventry says. "None of us are happy about it, but they are realistic. The only reason they support this is because they believe it will allow us to be here in 40 years."

The question remains whether GEMA's workforce model is replicable. It's one thing to build a plant from scratch, but it's a completely different challenge to apply this model to an existing plant, where workers are already accustomed to doing things a certain way, analysts say.

The biggest hurdle for GEMA, though, may be persuading the local UAW chapters throughout the country to accept this new way of doing things. DaimlerChrysler, for one, is convinced this is the way to go, and it is implementing the GEMA model in new and existing plants as contracts come up for renewal, says Ed Saenz, a DaimlerChrysler spokesman.

The automaker was able sign agreements to use the GEMA model at plants in Kenosha, Wisconsin, and Trenton, Michigan. As noted earlier, "It's a question of survival," says Bruce

Baumhower, president of UAW Local 12 in Toledo, Ohio. He has negotiated for a job classification structure and team approach similar to GEMA's at a DaimlerChrysler Jeep plant. "To compete, we need to be creative, or we lose our jobs."

Sources: J. Marquez, "Streamlined Model: Engine of Change," *Workforce Management*, July 17, 2006, pp. 1, 20–30; B. Visnic, "Harbour—Topping Chrysler JV Engine Plant Attracting Foreign Attention," *Edmunds Auto Observer*, July 20, 2008, www.autoobserver.com.

Introduction

The events at GEMA illustrate both the important role of labor relations in running a business and the influence of competitive challenges on the nature of labor relations. Global competition has forced a rethinking of core strategies. To be more competitive, automakers must reduce cost but also improve quality. To do so, GEMA needed to convince UAW workers to cooperate in developing a new model of labor relations. Their employment depends on their efficiency. This common goal is what binds management and labor together in a search for improved competitiveness.

The Labor Relations Framework

John Dunlop, former secretary of labor and a leading industrial relations scholar, suggested in the book *Industrial Relations Systems* (1958) that a successful industrial relations system consists of four elements: (1) an environmental context (technology, market pressures, and the legal framework, especially as it affects bargaining power); (2) participants, including employees and their unions, management, and the government; (3) a "web of rules" (rules of the game) that describe the process by which labor and management interact and resolve disagreements (such as the steps followed in settling contract grievances); and (4) ideology.[1] For the industrial relations system to operate properly, the three participants must, to some degree, have a common ideology (like acceptance of the capitalist system) and must accept the roles of the other participants. Acceptance does not translate into convergence of interests, however. To the contrary, some degree of worker–management conflict is inevitable because, although the interests of the two parties overlap, they also diverge in key respects (such as how to divide the economic profits).[2]

Therefore, according to Dunlop and other U.S. scholars of like mind, an effective industrial relations system does not eliminate conflict. Rather, it provides institutions (and a "web of rules") that resolve conflict in a way that minimizes its costs to management, employees, and society. The collective bargaining system is one such institution, as are related mechanisms such as mediation, arbitration, and participation in decision making. These ideas formed the basis for the development in the 1940s of schools and departments of industrial and labor relations to train labor relations professionals who, working in both union and management positions, would have the skills to minimize costly forms of conflict such as strikes (which were reaching record levels at the time) and maximize integrative (win–win) solutions to such disagreements.

LO1
Describe what is meant by collective bargaining and labor relations.

A more recent industrial relations model, developed by Harry Katz and Thomas Kochan, is particularly helpful in laying out the types of decisions management and unions make in their interactions and the consequences of such decisions for attainment of goals in areas such as wages and benefits, job security, and the rights and responsibilities of unions and managements.[3] According to Katz and Kochan, these choices occur at three levels.

First, at the strategic level, management makes basic choices such as whether to work with its union(s) or to devote its efforts to developing nonunion operations. Environmental factors (or competitive challenges) offer both constraints and opportunities in implementing strategies. For example, if public opinion toward labor unions becomes negative during a particular time period, some employers may see that as an opportunity to rid themselves of unions, whereas other employers may seek a better working relationship with their unions. Similarly, increased competition may dictate the need to increase productivity or reduce labor costs, but whether this is accomplished by shifting work to nonunion facilities or by working with unions to become more competitive is a strategic choice that management faces.

Although management has often been the initiator of change in recent years, unions face a similar choice between fighting changes to the status quo and being open to new labor–management relationships (like less adversarial forms of participation in decision making, such as labor–management teams).

Katz and Kochan suggest that labor and management choices at the strategic level in turn affect the labor–management interaction at a second level, the functional level, where contract negotiations and union organizing occur, and at the final workplace level, the arena in which the contract is administered. In the opening story, GEMA's strategic-level choice was to work toward its labor unions being not part of the problem, but part of the solution. By doing so, they hope to have labor peace (functional level) and an effective day-to-day working relationship (workplace level). Although the relationships between labor and management at each of the three levels are somewhat interdependent, the relationship at the three levels may also differ. For example, while management may have a strategy of building an effective relationship with its unions at the strategic level, there may be significant day-to-day conflicts over work rules, grievances, and so forth at any given facility or bargaining unit (workplace level).

The labor relations framework depicted in Figure 14.1 incorporates many of the ideas discussed so far, including the important role of the environment (the competitive challenges); union, management, and societal goals; and a separation of union–management interactions into categories (union organizing, contract negotiation, contract administration) that can have important influences on one another but may also be analyzed somewhat independently. The model also highlights the important role that relative bargaining power plays in influencing goals, union–management interactions, and the degree to which each party achieves its goals. Relative bargaining power, in turn, is significantly influenced by the competitive environment (legal, social, quality, high-performance work systems, and globalization competitive challenges) and the size and depth of union membership.[4]

We now describe the components of this model in greater depth. The remainder of the chapter is organized into the following sections: the goals and strategies of society, management, and unions; union structure (including union administration and membership); the legal framework, perhaps the key aspect of the competitive environment for labor relations; union and management interactions (organizing,

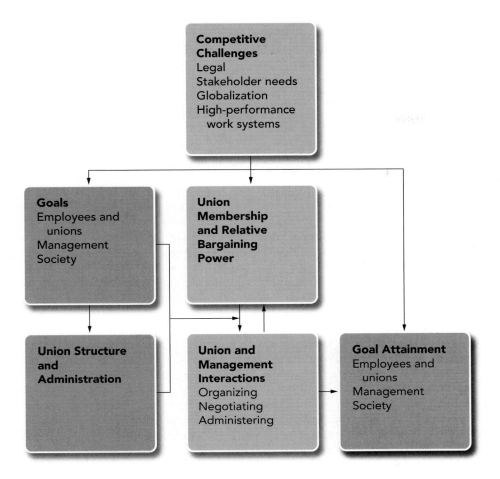

figure 14.1

A Labor Relations Framework

contract negotiation, contract administration); and goal attainment. Environmental factors (other than legal) and bargaining power are discussed in the context of these sections. In addition, two special topics, international comparisons and public sector labor relations, are discussed.

EVIDENCE-BASED HR
Seven Myths about Detroit Automakers

The debate over aid to the Detroit-based automakers is awash with half-truths and misrepresentations that are endlessly repeated by everyone from members of Congress to journalists. Here are seven myths about the companies and their vehicles, and the reality in each case.

Myth No. I: Nobody Buys Their Vehicles
Reality: General Motors Corp., Ford Motor Co., and Chrysler LLC sold 8.5 million vehicles in the United States last year and millions more around the world. GM outsold Toyota by about 1.2 million vehicles in the United States last year and holds

a U.S. lead over Toyota of nearly 700,000 so far this year. Globally, GM in 2007 remained the world's largest automaker, selling 9,369,524 vehicles worldwide—about 3,000 more than Toyota.

Ford outsold Honda by about 850,000 and Nissan by more than 1.3 million vehicles in the United States last year.

Chrysler sold more vehicles here than Nissan and Hyundai combined in 2007 and so far this year.

Myth No. 2: They Build Unreliable Junk

Reality: The creaky, leaky vehicles of the 1980s and 1990s are long gone. *Consumer Reports* recently found that "Ford's reliability is now on par with good Japanese automakers."

The independent J.D. Power Initial Quality Study scored Buick, Cadillac, Chevrolet, Ford, GMC, Mercury, Pontiac, and Lincoln brands' overall quality as high as or higher than that of Acura, Audi, BMW, Honda, Nissan, Scion, Volkswagen, and Volvo.

J.D. Power rated the Chevrolet Malibu the highest-quality midsize sedan. Both the Malibu and Ford Fusion scored better than the Honda Accord and Toyota Camry.

Myth No. 3: They Build Gas-Guzzlers

Reality: All of the Detroit Three build midsize sedans that the Environmental Protection Agency rates at 29 to 33 miles per gallon on the highway.

The most fuel-efficient Chevrolet Malibu gets 33 mpg on the highway, 2 mpg better than the best Honda Accord. The most fuel-efficient Ford Focus has the same highway fuel economy ratings as the most efficient Toyota Corolla. The most fuel-efficient Chevrolet Cobalt has the same city fuel economy and better highway fuel economy than the most efficient nonhybrid Honda Civic.

A recent study by Edmunds.com found that the Chevrolet Aveo subcompact is the least expensive car to buy and operate.

Myth No. 4: They Already Got a $25 Billion Bailout

Reality: None of that money has been lent out and may not be for more than a year. In addition, it can, by law, be used only to invest in future vehicles and technology, so it has no effect on the shortage of operating cash the companies face because of the economic slowdown that's killing them now.

Myth No. 5: GM, Ford, and Chrysler Are Idiots for Investing in Pickups and SUVs

Reality: The domestics' lineup has been truck-heavy, but Toyota, Nissan, Mercedes-Benz, and BMW have spent billions of dollars on pickups and SUVs because trucks are a large and historically profitable part of the auto industry.

The most fuel-efficient full-size pickups from GM, Ford, and Chrysler all have higher EPA fuel-economy ratings than Toyota and Nissan's full-size pickups.

Myth No. 6: They Don't Build Hybrids

Reality: The Detroit Three got into the hybrid business late, but Ford and GM each now offer more hybrid models than Honda or Nissan, with several more due to hit the road in early 2009.

Myth No. 7: Their Union Workers Are Lazy and Overpaid

Reality: Chrysler tied Toyota as the most productive automaker in North America this year, according to the Harbour Report on manufacturing, which measures the amount of work done per employee. Eight of the 10 most productive vehicle assembly plants in North America belong to Chrysler, Ford, or GM.

The oft-cited $70-an-hour wage and benefit figure for UAW workers inaccurately adds benefits that millions of retirees get to the pay of current workers, but divides the total only by current employees. That's like assuming you get your parents' retirement and Social Security benefits in addition to your own income.

Hourly pay for assembly line workers tops out around $28; benefits add about $14. New hires at the Detroit Three get $14 an hour. There's no pension or health care when they retire, but benefits raise their total hourly compensation to $29 while they're working. UAW wages are now comparable with Toyota workers, according to a *Free Press* analysis.

SOURCE: Mark Phelan, "7 Myths about Detroit Automakers," *Free Press*, December 5, 2008.

Goals and Strategies

Society

In one sense, labor unions, with their emphasis on group action, do not fit well with the individualistic orientation of U.S. capitalism. However, industrial relations scholars such as Beatrice and Sidney Webb and John R. Commons argued in the late 1800s and early 1900s that individual workers' bargaining power was far smaller than that of employers, who were likely to have more financial resources and the ability to easily replace workers.[5] Effective institutions for worker representation (like labor unions) were therefore seen as a way to make bargaining power more equal.

Labor unions' major benefit to society is the institutionalization of industrial conflict, which is therefore resolved in the least costly way. Thus, although disagreements between management and labor continue, it is better to resolve disputes through discussion (collective bargaining) than by battling in the streets. As an influential group of industrial relations scholars put it in describing the future of advanced industrial relations around the world, "Class warfare will be forgotten. The battles will be in the corridors instead of the streets, and memos will flow instead of blood."[6] In this sense, collective bargaining not only has the potential to reduce economic losses caused by strikes but may also contribute to societal stability. For this reason, industrial relations scholars have often viewed labor unions as an essential component of a democratic society.[7] These were some of the beliefs that contributed to the enactment of the National Labor Relations Act (NLRA) in 1935, which sought to provide an environment conducive to collective bargaining and has since regulated labor and management activities and interactions.

Even Senator Orrin Hatch, described by *BusinessWeek* as "labor's archrival on Capitol Hill," has spoken of the need for unions:

> There are always going to be people who take advantage of workers. Unions even that out, to their credit. We need them to level the field between labor and management. If you didn't have unions, it would be very difficult for even enlightened employers not to take advantage of workers on wages and working conditions, because of [competition from] rivals. I'm among the first to say I believe in unions.[8]

LO2
Identify the labor relations goals of management, labor unions, and society.

Although an industrial relations system based on collective bargaining has drawbacks, so too do the alternatives. Unilateral control by management sacrifices workers' rights. Extensive involvement of government and the courts can result in conflict resolution that is expensive, slow, and imposed by someone (a judge) with much less firsthand knowledge of the circumstances than either labor or management.

Management

One of management's most basic decisions is whether to encourage or discourage the unionization of its employees. It may discourage unions because it fears higher wage and benefit costs, the disruptions caused by strikes, and an adversarial relationship with its employees or, more generally, greater constraints placed on its decision-making flexibility and discretion. Historically, management has used two basic strategies to avoid unionization.[9] It may seek to provide employment terms and conditions that employees will perceive as sufficiently attractive and equitable so that they see little gain from union representation. Or it may aggressively oppose union representation, even where there is significant employee interest. Use of the latter strategy has increased significantly during the last 20 to 30 years.

If management voluntarily recognizes a union or if employees are already represented by a union, the focus is shifted from dealing with employees as individuals to employees as a group. Still, certain basic management objectives remain: controlling labor costs and increasing productivity (by keeping wages and benefits in check) and maintaining management prerogatives in important areas such as staffing levels and work rules. Of course, management always has the option of trying to decertify a union (that is, encouraging employees to vote out the union in a decertification election) if it believes that the majority of employees no longer wish to be represented by the union.

Labor Unions

Labor unions seek, through collective action, to give workers a formal and independent voice in setting the terms and conditions of their work. Table 14.1 shows typical provisions negotiated by unions in collective bargaining contracts. Labor unions attempt to represent their members' interests in these decisions.

A major goal of labor unions is bargaining effectiveness, because with it comes the power and influence to make the employees' voices heard and to effect changes in the workplace.[10] The right to strike is one important component of bargaining power. In turn, the success of a strike (actual or threatened) depends on the relative magnitude of the costs imposed on management versus those imposed on the union. A critical factor is the size of union membership. More members translate into a greater ability to halt or disrupt production and also into greater financial resources for continuing a strike in the face of lost wages.

Union Structure, Administration, and Membership

A necessary step in discussing labor–management interactions is a basic knowledge of how labor and management are organized and how they function. Management has been described throughout this book. We now focus on labor unions.

table 14.1

Typical Provisions in Collective Bargaining Contracts

Establishment and administration of the agreement	Wage determination and administration	Plant operations
Bargaining unit and plant supplements	General provisions	Work and shop rules
Contract duration and reopening and renegotiation provisions	Rate structure and wage differentials	Rest periods and other in-plant time allowances
Union security and the checkoff	Allowances	Safety and health
Special bargaining committees	Incentive systems and production bonus plans	Plant committees
Grievance procedures	Production standards and time studies	Hours of work and premium pay practices
Arbitration and mediation	Job classification and job evaluation	Shift operations
Strikes and lockouts	Individual wage adjustments	Hazardous work
Contract enforcement	General wage adjustments during the contract period	Discipline and discharge
Functions, rights, and responsibilities	**Job or income security**	**Paid and unpaid leave**
Management rights clauses	Hiring and transfer arrangements	Vacations and holidays
Plant removal	Employment and income guarantees	Sick leave
Subcontracting	Reporting and call-in pay	Funeral and personal leave
Union activities on company time and premises	Supplemental unemployment benefit plans	Military leave and jury duty
Union–management cooperation	Regulation of overtime, shift work, etc.	**Employee benefit plans**
Regulation of technological change	Reduction of hours to forestall layoffs	Health and insurance plans
Advance notice and consultation	Layoff procedures; seniority; recall	Pension plans
	Worksharing in lieu of layoff	Profit-sharing, stock purchase, and thrift plans
	Attrition arrangements	Bonus plans
	Promotion practices	**Special groups**
	Training and retraining	Apprentices and learners
	Relocation allowances	Workers with disabilities and older workers
	Severance pay and layoff benefit plans	Women
	Special funds and study committees	Veterans
		Union representatives
		Nondiscrimination clauses

SOURCE: From Harry Katz, Thomas Kochan, and Alexander Colvin, *An Introduction to Collective Bargaining and Industrial Relations* 4E, 2008. Copyright © 2008. The McGraw-Hill Companies.

National and International Unions

Most union members belong to a national or international union. In turn, most national unions are composed of multiple local units, and most are affiliated with the American Federation of Labor and Congress of Industrial Organizations (AFL-CIO).

The largest national unions are listed in Table 14.2. (The National Education Association, with 2.5 million members, is not affiliated with the AFL-CIO.) An important characteristic of a union is whether it is a craft or industrial union.

The electrical workers' and carpenters' unions are craft unions, meaning that the members all have a particular skill or occupation. Craft unions often are responsible for training their members (through apprenticeships) and for supplying craft workers to employers. Requests for carpenters, for example, would come to the union hiring hall, which would decide which carpenters to send out. Thus craft workers may work

table 14.2

Largest Labor Unions in the United States

ORGANIZATION	NUMBER OF MEMBERS
National Education Association	3,167,612
Service Employees International Union	1,575,485
American Federation of State, County, and Municipal Employees	1,470,095
International Brotherhood of Teamsters	1,398,573
United Food and Commercial Workers International Union	1,304,061
American Federation of Teachers	832,058
United Steel, Paper and Forestry, Rubber, Manufacturing, Energy, Allied Industrial, and Service Workers International Union	730,936
International Brotherhood of Electrical Workers	697,863
Laborers' International Union of North America	657,197
International Association of Machinists and Aerospace Workers	646,933
Communications Workers of America	559,083
United Automobile, Aerospace, and Agricultural Implement Workers of America	538,448
United Brotherhood of Carpenters and Joiners of America	523,126
UNITE HERE	458,901
International Union of Operating Engineers	397,348
United Association of Journeymen and Apprentices of the Plumbing and Pipe Fitting Industry of the United States and Canada	332,205
National Association of Letter Carriers	287,036
International Association of Fire Fighters	283,932
American Postal Workers Union	283,279
National Postal Mail Handlers Union	249,509
American Federation of Government Employees	229,248
Amalgamated Transit Union	182,109
Screen Actors Guild	176,455
United American Nurses	157,055
Sheet Metal Workers International Association	149,149
International Association of Bridge, Structural, Ornamental, and Reinforcing Iron Workers	134,134
International Union of Painters and Allied Trades	129,499
Transport Workers Union of America	115,145
National Rural Letter Carriers' Association	111,893
International Alliance of Theatrical Stage Employes, Moving Picture Technicians, Artists, and Allied Crafts of the United States and Canada	108,386
Office and Professional Employees International Union	104,596

SOURCE: Reprinted with permission from Directory of U.S. Labor Organizations, 2008 edition by D. Gifford. Copyright © 2008 by the Bureau of National Affairs, Washington, DC 20037. For copies of BNA Books publications call toll free 1-800-960-1220.

for many employers over time, their constant link being to the union. A craft union's bargaining power depends greatly on the control it can exercise over the supply of its workers.

In contrast, industrial unions are made up of members who are linked by their work in a particular industry (such as steelworkers and autoworkers). Typically they represent many different occupations. Membership in the union is a result of working for a particular employer in the industry. Changing employers is less common than it is among craft workers, and employees who change employers remain members of the same union only if they happen to move to other employers covered by that union. Whereas a craft union may restrict the number of, say, carpenters to maintain higher wages, industrial unions try to organize as many employees in as wide a range of skills as possible.

Local Unions

Even when a national union plays the most critical role in negotiating terms of a collective bargaining contract, negotiation occurs at the local level as well as over work rules and other issues that are locally determined. In addition, administration of the contract is largely carried out at the local union level. Consequently, the bulk of day-to-day interaction between labor and management takes place at the local union level.

The local of an industrial-based union may correspond to a single large facility or to a number of small facilities. In a craft-oriented union, the local may cover a city or a region. The local union typically elects officers (like president, vice president, treasurer). Responsibility for contract negotiation may rest with the officers, or a bargaining committee may be formed for this purpose. Typically the national union provides assistance, ranging from background data about other settlements and technical advice to sending a representative to lead the negotiations.

Individual members' participation in local union meetings includes the election of union officials and strike votes. However, most union contact is with the shop steward, who is responsible for ensuring that the terms of the collective bargaining contract are enforced. The shop steward represents employees in contract grievances. Another union position, the business representative, performs some of the same functions, especially where the union deals with multiple employers, as is often the case with craft unions.

American Federation of Labor and Congress of Industrial Organizations (AFL-CIO)

The AFL-CIO is not a labor union but rather an association that seeks to advance the shared interests of its member unions at the national level, much as the Chamber of Commerce and the National Association of Manufacturers do for their member employers. As Figure 14.2 indicates, there are 54 affiliated national and international unions and thousands of locals. An important responsibility of the AFL-CIO is to represent labor's interests in public policy issues such as civil rights, economic policy, safety, and occupational health. It also provides information and analysis that member unions can use in their activities: organizing new members, negotiating new contracts, and administering contracts.

figure 14.2

AFL-CIO Organization Chart

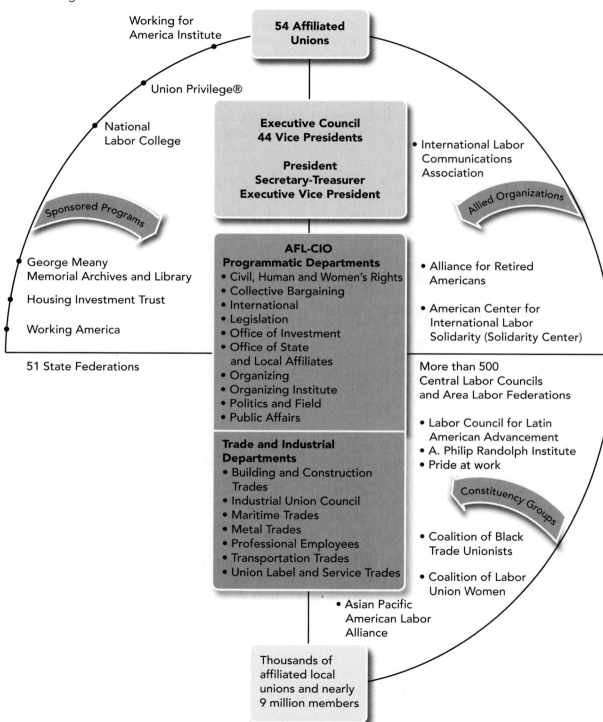

SOURCE: AFL-CIO, www.aflcio.org, accessed March 18, 2007.

Union Security

The survival and security of a union depends on its ability to ensure a regular flow of new members and member dues to support the services it provides. Therefore, unions typically place high priority on negotiating two contract provisions with an employer that are critical to a union's security or viability: checkoff provisions and union membership or contribution. First, under a **checkoff provision**, the employer, on behalf of the union, automatically deducts union dues from employees' paychecks.

A second union security provision focuses on the flow of new members (and their dues). The strongest union security arrangement is a **closed shop**, under which a person must be a union member (and thus pay dues) before being hired. A closed shop is, however, illegal under the NLRA. A **union shop** requires a person to join the union within a certain amount of time (30 days) after beginning employment. An **agency shop** is similar to a union shop but does not require union membership, only that dues be paid. **Maintenance of membership** rules do not require union membership but do require that employees who choose to join must remain members for a certain period of time (such as the length of the contract).

Under the 1947 Taft–Hartley Act (an amendment to the NLRA), states may pass so-called **right-to-work laws**, which make union shops, maintenance of membership, and agency shops illegal. The idea behind such laws is that compulsory union membership (or making employees pay union dues) infringes on the employee's right to freedom of association. From the union perspective, a big concern is "free riders," employees who benefit from union activities without belonging to a union. By law, all members of a bargaining unit, whether union members or not, must be represented by the union. If the union is required to offer service to all bargaining unit members, even those who are not union members, it may lose its financial viability.

Union Membership and Bargaining Power

At the strategic level, management and unions meet head-on over the issue of union organizing. Increasingly, employers are actively resisting unionization in an attempt to control costs and maintain their flexibility. Unions, on the other hand, must organize new members and hold on to their current members to have the kind of bargaining power and financial resources needed to achieve their goals in future organizing and to negotiate and administer contracts with management. For this reason we now discuss trends in union membership and possible explanations for those trends.

Since the 1950s, when union membership rose to 35 percent of employment, membership has consistently declined as a percentage of employment. It now stands at 12.4 percent of all employment and 7.6 percent of private-sector employment.[11] As Figure 14.3 indicates, this decline shows no indication of reversing.[12]

What factors explain the decline in union membership? Several have been identified.[13]

Structural Changes in the Economy

At the risk of oversimplifying, we might say that unions have traditionally been strongest in urban workplaces (especially those outside the South) that employ middle-aged men in blue-collar jobs. However, much recent job growth has occurred among women and youth in the service sector of the economy. Although unionizing such groups is possible, unions have so far not had much success organizing these groups

---

Checkoff Provision
A union contract provision that requires an employer to deduct union dues from employees' paychecks.

Closed Shop
A union security provision requiring a person to be a union member before being hired. Illegal under NLRA.

Union Shop
A union security provision that requires a person to join the union within a certain amount of time after being hired.

Agency Shop
A union security provision that requires an employee to pay union membership dues but not to join the union.

Maintenance of Membership
Union rules requiring members to remain members for a certain period of time (such as the length of the union contract).

Right-to-Work Laws
State laws that make union shops, maintenance of membership, and agency shops illegal.

figure 14.3

Union Membership Density among U.S. Wage and Salary Workers, 1973–2008

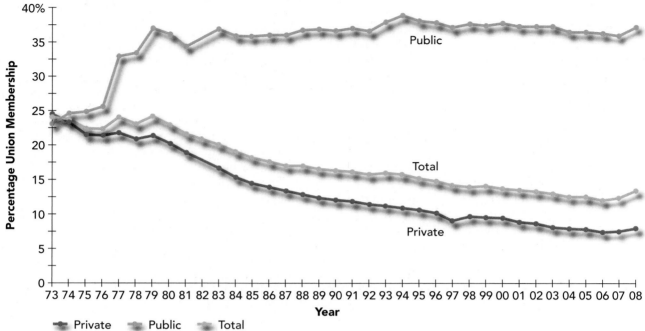

SOURCE: From B. T. Hirsch and D. A. MacPherson, *Union Membership and Earnings Data Book 2001* (Washington, DC: The Bureau of National Affairs, Inc., 2001). Reprinted with permission. Data for 2001 to 2008 obtained from U.S. Bureau of Labor Statistics, www.bls.gov.

in the private sector. Despite the importance of structural changes in the economy, studies show that they account for no more than one-quarter of the overall union membership decline.[14] Also, Canada, which has been undergoing similar structural changes, has experienced growth in union membership since the early 1960s. Union membership in Canada now stands at over 30 percent of employment, compared with roughly 12 percent in the United States.

Increased Employer Resistance

Almost one-half of large employers in a survey reported that their most important labor goal was to be union-free. This contrasts sharply with 50 years ago, when Jack Barbash wrote that "many tough bargainers [among employers] prefer the union to a situation where there is no union. Most of the employers in rubber, basic steel and the automobile industry fall in this category." The idea then was that an effective union could help assess and communicate the interests of employees to management, thus helping management make better decisions. But product-market pressures, such as foreign competition and deregulation (e.g., trucking, airlines, telecommunications), have contributed to increasing employer resistance to unions.[15] These changes in the competitive environment have contributed to a change in management's perspective and goals.[16]

In the absence of significant competition from foreign producers, unions were often able to organize entire industries. For example, the UAW organized all four major producers in the automobile industry (GM, Ford, Chrysler, and American Motors). The UAW usually sought and achieved the same union–management contract at each company. As a consequence, a negotiated wage increase in the industry could be passed on to the consumer in the form of higher prices. No company was undercut by its competitors because the labor cost of all major producers in the industry was determined by the same union–management contract, and the U.S. public had little option but to buy U.S.-made cars. However, the onset of foreign competition in the automobile market changed the competitive situation as well as the UAW's ability to organize the industry.[17] U.S. automakers were slow to recognize and respond to the competitive threat from foreign producers, resulting in a loss of market share and employment.

Competitive threats have contributed to increased employer resistance to union organizing and, in some cases, to an increased emphasis on ridding themselves of existing unions. Unionized workers receive, on average, 10 to 15 percent higher wages than their nonunion counterparts and this advantage is still larger if benefits are also included. Many employers have decided that they can no longer compete with these higher labor costs, and union membership has suffered as a result.[18] One measure of increased employer resistance is the dramatic increase in the late 1960s in the number of unfair employer labor practices (violations of sections of the NLRA such as section 8(a)(3), which prohibits firing employees for union organizing, as we discuss later) even though the number of elections held did not change much. (See Figure 14.4.) The use of remedies such as back pay for workers also grew, but the costs to employers of such penalties does not appear to have been sufficient to prevent the growth in employer unfair labor practices. Not surprisingly, the union victory rate in representation elections decreased from almost 59 percent in 1960 to below 50 percent by 1975. Although the union victory rate in recent years has been over 50 percent, the number of elections has declined by more than 50 percent since the 1960s and 1970s. Moreover, decertification elections have gone from about 4 percent of elections in 1960 to about 17 percent of elections in 2007.[19] Given the significant decline in both elections and union membership percentage, the increases in the number of unfair labor practice charges and back pay awards is all the more notable.

Finally, even if a union wins the right to represent employees, its ability to successfully negotiate a contract with the employer is not guaranteed. Indeed, refusal to bargain by the employer is the unfair labor practice most frequently filed (over half of all charges) against employers. As a result, only one in seven union representation election petitions with the National Labor Relations Board (NLRB) results in both a union victory *and* successful negotiation of a first contract. Further, where an unfair labor practice charge was filed against an employer during the organizing campaign, the chance of union success was substantially lower.[20]

At a personal level, some managers may face serious consequences if a union successfully organizes a new set of workers or mounts a serious organizing drive. One study indicated that 8 percent of the plant managers in companies with organizing drives were fired, and 10 percent of those in companies where the union was successful were fired (compared with 2 percent in a control group).[21] Furthermore, only 3 percent of the plant managers facing an organizing drive were promoted, and none of those ending up with a union contract were promoted (compared with 21 percent of the managers in the control group). Therefore, managers are often under intense pressure to oppose unionization attempts.

figure 14.4

Employer Resistance to Union Organizing, 1950–2007

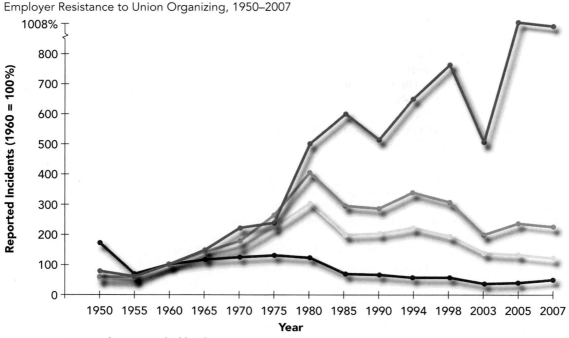

NOTE: 8(a)(3) charges refer to the section of the NLRA that makes it an unfair employer labor practice to discriminate against (e.g., fire) employees who engage in union activities such as union organizing.

SOURCE: Adapted and updated from R. B. Freeman and J. L. Medoff, *What Do Unions Do?* (New York: Basic Books, 1984). Data for 1985, 1989, 1990, 1994, 1998, 2003, 2005, and 2007 from National Labor Relations Board annual reports.

Substitution with HRM

A major study of the human resource management strategies and practices among large, nonunion employers found that union avoidance was often an important employee relations objective.[22] Top management's values in such companies drive specific policies such as promotion from within, an influential personnel–human resource department, and above-average pay and benefits. These policies, in turn, contribute to a number of desirable outcomes such as flexibility, positive employee attitudes, and responsive and committed employees, which ultimately lead to higher productivity and better employee relations. In other words, employers attempt to remain nonunion by offering most of the things a union can offer, and then some, while still maintaining a productivity advantage over their competitors. Of course, one aspect of union representation that employers cannot duplicate is the independent employee voice that a union provides.

Substitution by Government Regulation

Since the 1960s, regulation of many employment areas has increased, including equal employment opportunity, pensions, and worker displacement. Combined with existing regulations, this increase may result in fewer areas in which unions can provide worker rights or protection beyond those specified by law. Yet western European countries generally have more regulations and higher levels of union membership than the United States.[23]

Worker Views

Industrial relations scholars have long argued that the absence in the United States of a history of feudalism and of strong class distinctions found in western Europe have contributed to a more pragmatic, business-oriented (versus class-conscious) unionism. Although this may help explain the somewhat lower level of union membership in the United States, its relevance in explaining the downward trend is not clear.

Union Actions

In some ways, unions have hurt their own cause. First, corruption in unions such as the Teamsters may have had a detrimental effect. Second, questions have been raised about how well unions have adapted to recent changes in the economic structure. Employee groups and economic sectors with the fastest growth rates tend to have the lowest rates of unionization.[24] Women are less likely to be in unions than men (11 percent versus 14 percent), and nonmanufacturing industries such as finance, insurance, and real estate have a lower union representation (2 percent) than does manufacturing (14 percent). The South is also less heavily organized than the rest of the country, with, for example, South Carolina having a unionization rate of 4 percent, compared with 25 percent in New York State.[25] For example, none of the foreign-owned automobile assembly plants (e.g., BMW, Mercedes-Benz, Toyota), most of which are located in the South, are unionized (although they would be in their home countries). One reason for the smaller union presence in southern states is the existence of right-to-work laws (see our earlier discussion) in such states.

Legal Framework

Although competitive challenges have a major impact on labor relations, the legal framework of collective bargaining is an especially critical determinant of union membership and relative bargaining power and, therefore, of the degree to which employers, employees, and society are successful in achieving their goals. The legal framework also constrains union structure and administration and the manner in which unions and employers interact. Perhaps the most dramatic example of labor laws' influence is the 1935 passage of the Wagner Act (also known as the National Labor Relations Act or NLRA), which actively supported collective bargaining rather than impeding it. As a result, union membership nearly tripled, from 3 million in 1933 (7.7 percent of all employment) to 8.8 million (19.2 percent of employment) by 1939.[26] With increased membership came greater union bargaining power and, consequently, more success in achieving union goals.

Before the 1930s, the legal system was generally hostile to unions. The courts generally viewed unions as coercive organizations that hindered free trade. Unions' focus on collective voice and collective action (strikes, boycotts) did not fit well with the U.S. emphasis on capitalism, individualism, freedom of contract, and property rights.[27]

LO3
Explain the legal environment's impact on labor relations.

The Great Depression of the 1930s, however, shifted public attitudes toward business and the free-enterprise system. Unemployment rates as high as 25 percent and a 30 percent drop in the gross national product between 1929 and 1933 focused attention on employee rights and on the shortcomings of the system as it existed then. The nation was in a crisis, and President Franklin Roosevelt responded with dramatic action, the New Deal. On the labor front, the 1935 NLRA ushered in a new era of public policy for labor unions, enshrining collective bargaining as the preferred mechanism for settling labor–management disputes.

The introduction to the NLRA states:

> It is in the national interest of the United States to maintain full production in its economy. Industrial strife among employees, employers, and labor organizations interferes with full production and is contrary to our national interest. Experience has shown that labor disputes can be lessened if the parties involved recognize the legitimate rights of each in their relations with one another. To establish these rights under the law, Congress enacted the National Labor Relations Act. Its purpose is to define and protect the rights of employees and employers, to encourage collective bargaining, and to eliminate certain practices on the part of labor and management that are harmful to the general welfare.[28]

The rights of employees are set out in Section 7 of the act, including the "right to self-organization, to form, join, or assist labor organizations, to bargain collectively through representatives of their own choosing, and to engage in other concerted activities for the purpose of collective bargaining. The act also gives employees the right to refrain from any or all of such activities except [in cases] requiring membership in a labor organization as a condition of employment."[29] Examples of protected activities include

- Union organizing.
- Joining a union, whether it is recognized by the employer or not.
- Going out on strike to secure better working conditions.
- Refraining from activity on behalf of the union.[30]

Although the NLRA has broad coverage in the private sector, Table 14.3 shows that there are some notable exclusions.

Unfair Labor Practices—Employers

The NLRA prohibits certain activities by both employers and labor unions. Unfair labor practices by employers are listed in Section 8(a) of the NLRA. Section 8(a) (1) prohibits employers from interfering with, restraining, or coercing employees in

table 14.3

Are You Excluded from the NLRA's Coverage?

The NLRA specifically excludes from its coverage individuals who are
- Employed as a supervisor.
- Employed by a parent or spouse.
- Employed as an independent contractor.
- Employed in the domestic service of any person or family in a home.
- Employed as agricultural laborers.
- Employed by an employer subject to the Railway Labor Act.
- Employed by a federal, state, or local government.
- Employed by any other person who is not an employer as defined in the NLRA.

SOURCE: www.nlrb.gov/publications/engulp.html.

table 14.4

Examples of Employer Unfair Labor Practices

- Threatening employees with loss of their jobs or benefits if they join or vote for a union.
- Threatening to close down a plant if organized by a union.
- Questioning employees about their union membership or activities in a manner that restrains or coerces them.
- Spying or pretending to spy on union meetings.
- Granting wage increases that are timed to discourage employees from forming or joining a union.
- Taking an active part in organizing a union or committee to represent employees.
- Providing preferential treatment or aid to one of several unions trying to organize employees.
- Discharging employees for urging other employees to join a union or refusing to hire applicants because they are union members.
- Refusing to reinstate workers when job openings occur because the workers participated in a lawful strike.
- Ending operation at one plant and opening the same operation at another plant with new employees because employees at the first plant joined a union.
- Demoting or firing employees for filing an unfair labor practice or for testifying at an NLRB hearing.
- Refusing to meet with employees' representatives because the employees are on strike.
- Refusing to supply the employees' representative with cost and other data concerning a group insurance plan covering employees.
- Announcing a wage increase without consulting the employees' representative.
- Failing to bargain about the effects of a decision to close one of employer's plants.

SOURCE: National Labor Relations Board, *Basic Guide to the National Labor Relations Act* (Washington, DC: U.S. Government Printing Office, 1997). Available at www.nlrb.gov.

exercising their rights to join or assist a labor organization or to refrain from such activities. Section 8(a)(2) prohibits employer domination of or interference with the formation or activities of a labor union. Section 8(a)(3) prohibits discrimination in any aspect of employment that attempts to encourage or discourage union-related activity. Section 8(a)(4) prohibits discrimination against employees for providing testimony relevant to enforcement of the NLRA. Section 8(a)(5) prohibits employers from refusing to bargain collectively with a labor organization that has standing under the act. Examples of employer unfair labor practices are listed in Table 14.4.

Unfair Labor Practices—Labor Unions

Originally the NLRA did not list any union unfair labor practices. These were added through the 1947 **Taft-Hartley Act**. The 1959 *Landrum-Griffin Act* further regulated unions' actions and their internal affairs (like financial disclosure and conduct of elections). Section 8(b)(1)(a) of the NLRA states that a labor organization is not to "restrain or coerce employees in the exercise of the rights guaranteed in section 7" (described earlier). Table 14.5 provides examples of union unfair labor practices.

Taft-Hartley Act, 1947
The 1947 act that outlawed unfair union labor practices.

Enforcement

Enforcement of the NLRA rests with the National Labor Relations Board, which is composed of a five-member board, the general counsel, and 33 regional offices. The basis for the NLRA is the commerce clause of the U.S. Constitution. Therefore, the NLRB's jurisdiction is limited to employers whose operations affect commerce

table 14.5

Examples of Union Unfair Labor Practices

- Mass picketing in such numbers that nonstriking employees are physically barred from entering the plant.
- Acts of force or violence on the picket line or in connection with a strike.
- Threats to employees of bodily injury or that they will lose their jobs unless they support the union's activities.
- Fining or expelling members for crossing a picket line that is unlawful.
- Fining or expelling members for filing unfair labor practice charges or testifying before the NLRB.
- Insisting during contract negotiations that the employer agree to accept working conditions that will be determined by a group to which it does not belong.
- Fining or expelling union members for the way they apply the bargaining contract while carrying out their supervisory responsibilities.
- Causing an employer to discharge employees because they spoke out against a contract proposed by the union.
- Making a contract that requires an employer to hire only members of the union or employees "satisfactory" to the union.
- Insisting on the inclusion of illegal provisions in a contract.
- Terminating an existing contract and striking for a new one without notifying the employer, the Federal Mediation and Conciliation Service, and the state mediation service (where one exists).
- Attempting to compel a beer distributor to recognize a union (the union prevents the distributor from obtaining beer at a brewery by inducing the brewery's employees to refuse to fill the distributor's orders).
- Picketing an employer to force it to stop doing business with another employer who has refused to recognize the union (a "secondary boycott").

SOURCE: National Labor Relations Board, *A Guide to Basic Law and Procedures under the National Labor Relations Act* (Washington, DC: U.S. Government Printing Office, 1997). Available at www.nlrb.gov.

generally and interstate commerce in particular. In practice, only purely local firms are likely to fall outside the NLRB's jurisdiction. Specific jurisdictional standards (nearly 20) that vary by industry are applied. Two examples of businesses that are covered (and the standards) are retail businesses that had more than $500,000 in annual business and newspapers that had more than $200,000 in annual business.

The NLRB's two major functions are to conduct and certify representation elections and prevent unfair labor practices. In both realms, it does not initiate action. Rather, it responds to requests for action. The NLRB's role in representation elections is discussed in the next section. Here we discuss unfair labor practices.

Unfair labor practice cases begin with the filing of a charge, which is investigated by a regional office. A charge must be filed within six months of the alleged unfair practice, and copies must be served on all parties. (Registered mail is recommended.) If the NLRB finds the charge to have merit and issues a complaint, there are two possible actions. It may defer to a grievance procedure agreed on by the employer and union. Otherwise, a hearing is held before an administrative law judge. The judge makes a recommendation, which can be appealed by either party. The NLRB has the authority to issue cease-and-desist orders to halt unfair labor practices. It can also order reinstatement of employees, with or without back pay. In 2007, for example, $117.3 million in back pay was awarded and 1,771 workers were offered reinstatement (of whom 72 percent accepted). Note, however, that the NLRA is not a criminal statute, and punitive damages are not available. If an employer or union refuses to comply with an NLRB order, the board has the authority to petition the U.S. Court

Hollywood studios reached a tentative labour agreement yesterday with the Directors Guild of America (DGA), a development that they hope will build momentum to restart talks with striking writers and actors.

The three-year collective bargaining agreement will give DGA members jurisdiction over all but the lowest-budget programming produced for the Internet.

It will also award them a greater share of revenue from content that is downloaded or streamed online, addressing one of the talent community's chief complaints. However, the deal also calls for both sides to adjust the financial terms governing new media depending on how those nascent markets develop.

That flexibility was praised by studio executives, who have argued that the new businesses remained too uncertain for them to commit to rigid, long-term agreements.

"It's less about ground gained than ground established," one studio executive said of the deal, arguing that the two sides had succeeded in defining key aspects of an emerging media landscape.

Michael Apted, president of the DGA, called the negotiations "difficult" but said the guild had succeeded in enshrining key principles.

"The Internet is not free," Mr. Apted said. "We must receive fair compensation for the use and reuse of our work on the Internet, whether it was originally created for other media platforms or expressly for online distribution."

In a joint statement, the chiefs of Hollywood's largest film and television studios expressed hope that the agreement would "signal the beginning of the end of this extremely difficult period for our industry." They also invited striking writers at least to resume informal

discussions, with the hope that these might set the stage for formal negotiations.

The Writers Guild of America, which has taken a harder line against the studios, did not immediately respond.

The cumulative cost of the strike, which has dragged on for nearly three months, has exceeded $1.4 billion, according to the Los Angeles County Economic Development Corporation.

Television studios and networks prepared for the work stoppage by stockpiling scripts and reality programs, and say that they have so far weathered the storm.

However, the strike wreaked havoc on the Golden Globe Awards, which actors and writers picketed.

SOURCE: Joshua Chaffin, "Studios Reach Deal with Directors," USA 2nd Edition *Financial Times*, January 18, 2008, p. 17. Reprinted with permission of *Financial Times*.

of Appeals. The court can choose to enforce the order, remand it to the NLRB for modification, change it, or set it aside altogether.

Union and Management Interactions: Organizing

To this point we have discussed macro trends in union membership. Here we shift our focus to the more micro questions of why individual employees join unions and how the organizing process works at the workplace level.

LO4
Describe the major labor–management interactions: organizing, contract negotiations, and contract administration.

Why Do Employees Join Unions?

Virtually every model of the decision to join a union focuses on two questions.[31] First, is there a gap between the pay, benefits, and other conditions of employment that employees actually receive versus what they believe they should receive? Second, if such a gap exists and is sufficiently large to motivate employees to try to remedy the situation, is union membership seen as the most effective or instrumental means of change? The outcome of an election campaign hinges on how the majority of employees answer these two questions.

The Process and Legal Framework of Organizing

The NLRB is responsible for ensuring that the organizing process follows certain steps. At the most general level, the NLRB holds a union representation election if at least 30 percent of employees in the bargaining unit sign authorization cards (see Figure 14.5). If more than 50 percent of the employees sign authorization cards, the union may request that the employer voluntarily recognize it. If 50 percent or fewer of the employees sign, or if the employer refuses to recognize the union voluntarily, the NLRB conducts a secret-ballot election. The union is certified by the NLRB as the exclusive representative of employees if more than 50 percent of employees vote for the union. If more than one union appears on the ballot and neither gains a simple majority, a runoff election is held. Once a union has been certified as the exclusive representative of a group of employees, no additional elections are permitted for one year. After the negotiation of a contract, an election cannot be held for the contract's duration or for three years, whichever comes first. The parties to the contract may agree not to hold an election for longer than three years, but an outside party cannot be barred for more than three years.

The Employee Free Choice Act, which President Barack Obama supports, would make major changes to the organizing process. One change would be to eliminate the secret-ballot election and instead simply require that a majority of employees sign authorization cards. A second change would have the Federal Mediation and

figure 14.5
Authorization Card

YES, I WANT THE IAM

I, the undersigned employee of

(Company) _____

authorize the International Association of Machinists and Aerospace Workers (IAM) to act as my collective bargaining agent for wages, hours and working conditions. I agree that this card may be used either to support a demand for recognition or an NLRB election, at the discretion of the union.

Name (print)_____ Date _____

Home Address_____ Phone_____

City_____ State_____ Zip_____

Job Title_____ Dept. _____ Shift _____

Sign Here X_____

Note: This authorization to be SIGNED and DATED in employee's own handwriting. YOUR RIGHT TO SIGN THIS CARD IS PROTECTED BY FEDERAL LAW.

RECEIVED BY (Initial) _____

SOURCE: From John Fossum, *Labor Relations: Development, Structure and Process*, 2002. Copyright © 2002 The McGraw-Hill Companies.

Conciliation Service (FMCS) ensure that a first contract agreement is reached. If it is not, the FMCS would have the authority to impose a contract. The act includes other provisions, including stronger protections for union organizers. The act is strongly supported by unions and just as strongly opposed by most employers. It was passed by the United States House of Representatives in 2007, but died in the Senate. We will soon see whether the act or related legislation passes this time.

As mentioned previously, union members' right to be represented by leaders of their own choosing was expanded under the Taft–Hartley Act to include the right to vote an existing union out—that is, to decertify it. The process follows the same steps as a representation election. A decertification election is not permitted when a contract is in effect. Research indicates that when decertification elections are held, unions typically do not fare well, losing about 65 percent of the time during 2007. Moreover, the number of such elections increased from roughly 5 percent of all elections in the 1950s and 1960s to about 17 percent in 2007.[32]

The NLRB also is responsible for determining the appropriate bargaining unit and the employees who are eligible to participate in organizing activities. A unit may cover employees in one facility or multiple facilities within a single employer, or the unit may cover multiple employers. In general, employees on the payroll just prior to the ordering of an election are eligible to vote, although this rule is modified in some cases where, for example, employment in the industry is irregular. Most employees who are on strike and who have been replaced by other employees are eligible to vote in an election (such as a decertification election) that occurs within 12 months of the onset of the strike.

As shown in Table 14.3, the following types of employees cannot be included in bargaining units: agricultural laborers, independent contractors, supervisors, and managers. Beyond this, the NLRB attempts to group together employees who have a community of interest in their wages, hours, and working conditions. In many cases this grouping will be sharply contested, with management and the union jockeying to include or exclude certain employee subgroups in the hope of influencing the outcome of the election.

Organizing Campaigns: Management and Union Strategies and Tactics

Tables 14.6 and 14.7 list common issues that arise during most campaigns.[33] Unions attempt to persuade employees that their wages, benefits, treatment by employers, and opportunity to influence workplace decisions are not sufficient and that the union will be effective in obtaining improvements. Management emphasizes that it has provided a good package of wages, benefits, and so on. It also argues that, whereas a union is unlikely to provide improvements in such areas, it will likely lead to certain costs for employees, such as union dues and the income loss resulting from strikes.

As Table 14.8 indicates, employers use a variety of methods to oppose unions in organizing campaigns, some of which may go beyond what the law permits, especially in the eyes of union organizers. This perception is supported by our earlier discussion, which noted a significant increase in employer unfair labor practices since the late 1960s. (See Figure 14.4.)

Why would employers increasingly break the law? Fossum suggests that the consequences (like back pay and reinstatement of workers) of doing so are "slight."[34] His

table 14.6

Prevalence of Certain Union Issues in Campaigns

UNION ISSUES	PERCENTAGE OF CAMPAIGNS
Union will prevent unfairness and will set up a grievance procedure and seniority system.	82%
Union will improve unsatisfactory wages.	79
Union strength will give employees voice in wages, working conditions.	79
Union, not outsider, bargains for what employees want.	73
Union has obtained gains elsewhere.	70
Union will improve unsatisfactory sick leave and insurance.	64
Dues and initiation fees are reasonable.	64
Union will improve unsatisfactory vacations and holidays.	61
Union will improve unsatisfactory pensions.	61
Employer promises and good treatment may not be continued without union.	61
Employees choose union leaders.	55
Employer will seek to persuade or frighten employees to vote against union.	55
No strike without vote.	55
Union will improve unsatisfactory working conditions.	52
Employees have legal right to engage in union activity.	52

SOURCE: From John Fossum, *Labor Relations: Development, Structure and Process*, 1992. Copyright © 1992 The McGraw-Hill Companies.

table 14.7

Prevalence of Certain Management Issues in Campaigns

MANAGEMENT ISSUES	PERCENTAGE OF CAMPAIGNS
Improvements not dependent on unionization.	85%
Wages good, equal to, or better than under union contract.	82
Financial costs of union dues outweigh gains.	79
Union is outsider.	79
Get facts before deciding; employer will provide facts and accept employee decision.	76
If union wins, strike may follow.	70
Loss of benefits may follow union win.	67
Strikers will lose wages; lose more than gain.	67
Unions not concerned with employee welfare.	67
Strike may lead to loss of jobs.	64
Employer has treated employees fairly and/or well.	60
Employees should be certain to vote.	54

SOURCE: From John Fossum, *Labor Relations: Development, Structure and Process*, 1992. Copyright © 1992 The McGraw-Hill Companies.

review of various studies suggests that discrimination against employees involved in union organizing decreases union organizing success significantly and that the cost of back pay to union activists reinstated in their jobs is far smaller than the costs that

Survey of employers	
Consultants used	41%
Unfair labor practice charges filed against employer	24
Survey of union organizers	
Consultants and/or lawyers used	70
Unfair labor practices by employer	
Charges filed	36
Discharges or discriminatory layoffs	42[a]
Company leaflets	80
Company letters	91
Captive audience speech	91[b]
Supervisor meetings with small groups of employees	92
Supervisor intensity in opposing union	
Low	14
Moderate	34
High	51

table 14.8

Percentage of Firms Using Various Methods to Oppose Union Organizing Campaigns

[a]This percentage is larger than the figure for charges filed because it includes cases in which no unfair labor practice charge was actually filed against the employer.

[b]Refers to management's requiring employees to attend a session on company time at which the disadvantages of union membership are emphasized.

SOURCE: R. B. Freeman and M. M. Kleiner, "Employer Behavior in the Face of Union Organizing Drives," *Industrial and Labor Relations Review* 43, no. 4 (April 1990), pp. 351–65. © Cornell University.

would be incurred if the union managed to organize and gain better wages, benefits, and so forth.

Still, the NLRB attempts to maintain a noncoercive atmosphere under which employees feel they can exercise free choice. It will set aside an election if it believes that either the union or the employer has created "an atmosphere of confusion or fear of reprisals."[35] Examples of conduct that may lead to an election result being set aside include

- Threats of loss of jobs or benefits by an employer or union to influence votes or organizing activities.
- A grant of benefits or a promise of benefits as a means of influencing votes or organizing activities.
- An employer or union making campaign speeches to assembled groups of employees on company time less than 24 hours before an election.
- The actual use or threat of physical force or violence to influence votes or organizing activities.[36]

Supervisors have the most direct contact with employees. Thus, as Table 14.9 indicates, it is critical that they be proactive in establishing good relationships with employees if the company wishes to avoid union organizing attempts. It is also important for supervisors to know what not to do should a drive take place.

In response to organizing difficulties, the union movement has tried alternative approaches. **Associate union membership** is not linked to an employee's workplace and does not provide representation in collective bargaining. Instead the union provides other services, such as discounts on health and life insurance or credit cards.[37] In return, the union receives membership dues and a broader base of support for its

Associate Union Membership
A form of union membership by which the union receives dues in exchange for services (e.g., health insurance, credit cards) but does not provide representation in collective bargaining.

table 14.9

What Supervisors Should and Should Not Do to Stay Union-Free

WHAT TO DO:

Report any direct or indirect signs of union activity to a core management group.

Deal with employees by carefully stating the company's response to pro-union arguments. These responses should be coordinated by the company to maintain consistency and to avoid threats or promises.

Take away union issues by following effective management practice all the time:
Deliver recognition and appreciation.
Solve employee problems.
Protect employees from harassment or humiliation.
Provide business-related information.
Be consistent in treatment of different employees.
Accommodate special circumstances where appropriate.
Ensure due process in performance management.
Treat all employees with dignity and respect.

WHAT TO AVOID:

Threatening employees with harsher terms and conditions of employment or employment loss if they engage in union activity.

Interrogating employees about pro-union or anti-union sentiments that they or others may have or reviewing union authorization cards or pro-union petitions.

Promising employees that they will receive favorable terms or conditions of employment if they forgo union activity.

Spying on employees known to be, or suspected of being, engaged in pro-union activities.

SOURCE: From J. A. Segal, *HR Magazine,* 1998 Copyright © 1998 by the Society for Human Resource Management. Reprinted with the permission of *HR Magazine,* published by the Society for Human Resource Management, Alexandria, VA, via the Copyright Clearance Center.

activities. Associate membership may be attractive to employees who wish to join a union but cannot because their workplace is not organized by a union.

Corporate Campaigns
Union activities designed to exert public, financial, or political pressure on employers during the union-organizing process.

Corporate campaigns seek to bring public, financial, or political pressure on employers during the organizing (and negotiating) process.[38] For example, the Building and Construction Trades Department of the AFL-CIO successfully lobbied Congress to eliminate $100 million in tax breaks for a Toyota truck plant in Kentucky until Toyota agreed to use union construction workers and pay union wages.[39] The Amalgamated Clothing and Textile Workers Union (ACTWU) corporate campaign against J. P. Stevens during the late 1970s was one of the first and best known. The ACTWU organized a boycott of J. P. Stevens products and threatened to withdraw its pension funds from financial institutions where J. P. Stevens officers acted as directors. J. P. Stevens subsequently agreed to a contract with the ACTWU.[40]

Unions also hope to use their financial assets to influence companies. Recent estimates suggest that unions directly control roughly $250 billion in pension funds and share control with employers over another $1.04 trillion.[41] In addition, public sector pension funds control another $2.0 trillion. The AFL-CIO and the United Steelworkers have also set up a separate fund, the Heartland Labor Capital Network, which invests in worker-friendly companies.[42]

In some success stories unions have eschewed elections in favor of strikes and negative publicity to pressure corporations to accept a union. The Hotel Employees and Restaurant Employees (HERE) organized 9,000 workers in 2001, with 80 percent of these memberships resulting from pressure on employers rather than a vote. The Union of Needletrade, Industrial, and Textile Employees (UNITE), which organized 15,000 workers in 2001, has also succeeded with this approach. After losing an election by just two votes among employees of Up-to-Date Laundry, which cleans linens for Baltimore hotels and hospitals, UNITE decided to try other tactics, including a corporate campaign. It called a strike to demand that Up-to-Date recognize the union. It also persuaded several major customers of the laundry to threaten to stop using the laundry's services, shared claims of racial and sexual harassment with state agencies and the National Association for the Advancement of Colored People (NAACP), and convinced the Baltimore city council to require testimony from Up-to-Date. Eventually, the company gave in, recognized the union, and negotiated a contract that raised the workers' $6-an-hour wages and gave them better benefits.

Another winning union organizing strategy is to negotiate employer neutrality and card-check provisions into a contract. Under a *neutrality provision*, the employer pledges not to oppose organizing attempts elsewhere in the company. A *card-check provision* is an agreement that if a certain percentage—by law, at least a majority—of employees sign an authorization card, the employer will recognize their union representation. An impartial outside agency, such as the American Arbitration Association, counts the cards. The Communication Workers of America negotiated these provisions in its dispute with Verizon. Evidence suggests that this strategy can be very effective for unions.

Union and Management Interactions: Contract Negotiation

The majority of contract negotiations take place between unions and employers that have been through the process before. The "Competing through Technology" box on page 645 provides an example of a contract agreement between Hollywood studios and directors, which included the thorny issue of royalties for online content. In most cases, management has come to accept the union as an organization that it must work with. But when the union has just been certified and is negotiating its first contract, the situation can be very different. In fact, unions are unable to negotiate a first contract in 27 to 37 percent of the cases.[43] As noted previously, more than half of all unfair labor practice charges filed against employers pertain to the refusal to negotiate.

Labor–management contracts differ in their bargaining structures—that is, the range of employees and employers that are covered. As Table 14.10 indicates, the contracts differ, first, according to whether narrow (craft) or broad (industrial) employee interests are covered. Second, they differ according to whether they cover multiple employers or multiple plants within a single employer. (A single employer may have multiple plants, some union and some nonunion.) Different structures have different implications for bargaining power and the number of interests that must be incorporated in reaching an agreement.

table 14.10

Types and Examples of Bargaining Structures

EMPLOYER INTERESTS COVERED	EMPLOYEE INTERESTS COVERED		
	MULTIEMPLOYER (CENTRALIZED)	SINGLE-EMPLOYER— MULTIPLANT	SINGLE-EMPLOYER— SINGLE PLANT (DECENTRALIZED)
Craft (Narrow)	Construction trades Interstate trucking Longshoring Hospital association	Airline Teacher Police Firefighters Railroad	Craft union in small manufacturing plant Hospital
Industrial or Multiskill (Broad)	Coal mining (underground) Basic steel (pre-1986) Hotel association	Automobiles Steel (post-1986) Farm equipment State government Textile	Industrial union in small manufacturing plant

SOURCE: From Harry Katz, Thomas Kochan, and Alexander Colvin, *An Introduction to Collective Bargaining & Industrial Relations* 4E, 2008. Copyright © 2008. The McGraw-Hill Companies.

Distributive Bargaining
The part of the labor–management negotiation process that focuses on dividing a fixed economic "pie."

Integrative Bargaining
The part of the labor–management negotiation process that seeks solutions beneficial to both sides.

Attitudinal Structuring
The aspect of the labor–management negotiation process that refers to the relationship and level of trust between the negotiators.

The Negotiation Process

Richard Walton and Robert McKersie suggested that labor–management negotiations could be broken into four subprocesses: distributive bargaining, integrative bargaining, attitudinal structuring, and intraorganizational bargaining.[44] **Distributive bargaining** focuses on dividing a fixed economic "pie" between the two sides. A wage increase, for example, means that the union gets a larger share of the pie, management a smaller share. It is a win–lose situation. **Integrative bargaining** has a win–win focus; it seeks solutions beneficial to both sides. So if management needs to reduce labor costs, it could reach an agreement with the union to avoid layoffs in return for the union agreeing to changes in work rules that might enhance productivity.

Attitudinal structuring refers to the relationship and trust between labor and management negotiators. Where the relationship is poor, it may be difficult for the two sides to engage in integrative bargaining because each side hesitates to trust the other side to carry out its part of the deal. For example, the union may be reluctant to agree to productivity-enhancing work-rule changes to enhance job security if, in the past, it has made similar concessions but believes that management did not stick to its assurance of greater job security. Thus the long-term relationship between the two parties can have a very important impact on negotiations and their outcomes.

Intraorganizational bargaining reminds us that labor–management negotiations involve more than just two parties. Within management, and to an even greater extent within the union, different factions can have conflicting objectives. High-seniority workers, who are least likely to be laid off, may be more willing to accept a contract that has layoffs (especially if it also offers a significant pay increase for those whose jobs are not at risk). Less senior workers would likely feel very differently. Thus negotiators and union leaders must simultaneously satisfy both the management side and their own internal constituencies. If they do not, they risk the union membership's rejecting the contract, or they risk being voted out of office in the next election. Management, too, is unlikely to be of one mind about how to approach negotiations. Some will focus more on long-term employee relations, others will focus on cost control, and still others will focus on what effect the contract will have on stockholders.

Management's Preparation for Negotiations

Clearly, the outcome of contract negotiations can have important consequences for labor costs and labor productivity and, therefore, for the company's ability to compete in the product market. Adapting Fossum's discussion, we can divide management preparation into the following seven areas, most of which have counterparts on the union side.[45]

1. *Establishing interdepartmental contract objectives:* The employer's industrial relations department needs to meet with the accounting, finance, production, marketing, and other departments and set contract goals that will permit each department to meet its responsibilities. As an example, finance may suggest a cost figure above which a contract settlement would seriously damage the company's financial health. The bargaining team needs to be constructed to take these various interests into account.

2. *Reviewing the old contract:* This step focuses on identifying provisions of the contract that might cause difficulties by hindering the company's productivity or flexibility or by leading to significant disagreements between management and the union.

3. *Preparing and analyzing data:* Information on labor costs and the productivity of competitors, as well as data the union may emphasize, needs to be prepared and analyzed. The union data might include cost-of-living changes and agreements reached by other unions that could serve as a target. Data on employee demographics and seniority are relevant for establishing the costs of such benefits as pensions, health insurance, and paid vacations. Finally, management needs to know how much it would be hurt by a strike. How long will its inventory allow it to keep meeting customer orders? To what extent are other companies positioned to step in and offer replacement products? How difficult would it be to find replacement workers if the company decided to continue operations during a strike?

4. *Anticipating union demands:* Recalling grievances over the previous contract, having ongoing discussions with union leaders, and becoming aware of settlements at other companies are ways of anticipating likely union demands and developing potential counterproposals.

5. *Establishing the cost of possible contract provisions:* Wages have not only a direct influence on labor costs but often an indirect effect on benefit costs (such as Social Security and paid vacation). Recall that benefits add 35 to 40 cents to every dollar's worth of wages. Also, wage or benefit increases that seem manageable in the first year of a contract can accumulate to less manageable levels over time.

6. *Preparing for a strike:* If management intends to operate during a strike, it may need to line up replacement workers, increase its security, and figure out how to deal with incidents on the picket line and elsewhere. If management does not intend to operate during a strike (or if the company will not be operating at normal levels), it needs to alert suppliers and customers and consider possible ways to

Intraorganizational Bargaining
The part of the labor–management negotiation process that focuses on the conflicting objectives of factions within labor and management.

avoid the loss of their business. This could even entail purchasing a competitor's product in order to have something to sell to customers.

7. *Determining strategy and logistics:* Decisions must be made about the amount of authority the negotiating team will have. What concessions can it make on its own, and which ones require it to check with top management? On which issues can it compromise, and on which can it not? Decisions regarding meeting places and times must also be made.

Negotiation Stages and Tactics

Negotiations go through various stages.[46] In the early stages, many more people are often present than in later stages. On the union side, this may give all the various internal interest groups a chance to participate and voice their goals. This, in turn, helps send a message to management about what the union feels it must do to satisfy its members, and it may also help the union achieve greater solidarity. Union negotiators often present an extensive list of proposals at this stage, partly to satisfy their constituents and partly to provide themselves with issues on which they can show flexibility later in the process. Management may or may not present proposals of its own; sometimes it prefers to react to the union's proposals.

During the middle stages, each side must make a series of decisions, even though the outcome is uncertain. How important is each issue to the other side? How likely is it that disagreement on particular issues will result in a strike? When and to what extent should one side signal its willingness to compromise on its position?

In the final stage, pressure for an agreement increases as the deadline for a strike approaches. Public negotiations may be only part of the process. Negotiators from each side may have one-on-one meetings or small-group meetings where public relations pressures are reduced. In addition, a neutral third party may become involved, someone who can act as a go-between or facilitator. In some cases, the only way for the parties to convince each other of their resolve (or to convince their own constituents of the other party's resolve) is to allow an impasse to occur.

Various books suggest how to avoid impasses by using mutual gains or integrative bargaining tactics. For example, *Getting to Yes* (New York: Penguin Books, 1991), by Roger Fisher and William Ury, describes four basic principles:

1. Separate the people from the problem.
2. Focus on interests, not positions.
3. Generate a variety of possibilities before deciding what to do.
4. Insist that the results be based on some objective standard.

Bargaining Power, Impasses, and Impasse Resolution

Employers' and unions' conflicting goals are resolved through the negotiation process just described. An important determinant of the outcome of this process is the relative bargaining power of each party, which can be defined as the "ability of one party to achieve its goals when faced with opposition from some other party to the bargaining process."[47] In collective bargaining, an important element of power is the relative ability of each party to withstand a strike. Although strikes are rare, the threat of a strike often looms large in labor–management negotiations. The relative ability to take a strike, whether one occurs or not, is an important determinant of bargaining power and, therefore, of bargaining outcomes.

Management's Willingness to Take a Strike

Management's willingness to take a strike comes down to two questions:

1. *Can the company remain profitable over the long run if it agrees to the union's demands?* The answer is more likely to be yes to the extent that higher labor costs can be passed on to consumers without losing business. This, in turn, is most likely when (1) the price increase is small because labor costs are a small fraction of total costs or (2) there is little price competition in the industry. Low price competition can result from regulated prices, from competition based on quality (rather than price), or from the union's organizing all or most of the employers in the industry, which eliminates labor costs as a price factor.

   Unions share part of management's concern with long-term competitiveness because a decline in competitiveness can translate into a decline in employment levels. On the other hand, the majority of union members may prefer to have higher wages, despite employment declines, particularly if a minority of the members (those with low seniority) suffer more employment loss and the majority keep their employment with higher wages.

2. *Can the company continue to operate in the short run despite a strike?* Although "hanging tough" on its bargaining goals may pay off for management in the long run, the short-run concern is the loss of revenues and profits from production being disrupted. The cost to strikers is a loss of wages and possibly a permanent loss of jobs.

Under what conditions is management most able to take a strike? The following factors are important:[48]

1. *Product demand:* Management is less able to afford a strike when the demand for its product is strong because that is when more revenue and profits are lost.
2. *Product perishability:* A strike by certain kinds of employees (farm workers at harvest time, truckers transporting perishable food, airline employees at peak travel periods) will result in permanent losses of revenue, thus increasing the cost of the strike to management.
3. *Technology:* An organization that is capital intensive (versus labor intensive) is less dependent on its employees and more likely to be able to use supervisors or others as replacements. Telephone companies are typically able to operate through strikes, even though installing new equipment or services and repair work may take significantly longer than usual.
4. *Availability of replacement workers:* When jobs are scarce, replacement workers are more available and perhaps more willing to cross picket lines. Using replacement workers to operate during a strike raises the stakes considerably for strikers who may be permanently replaced. Most strikers are not entitled to reinstatement until there are job openings for which they qualify. If replacements were hired, such openings may not occur for some time (if at all).
5. *Multiple production sites and staggered contracts:* Multiple sites and staggered contracts permit employers to shift production from the struck facility to facilities that, even if unionized, have contracts that expire at different times (so they are not able to strike at the same time).

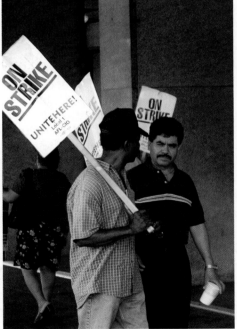

● Management has several factors to consider before taking a strike. Most negotiations do not result in a strike since it is often not in the best interest of either party.

6. *Integrated facilities:* When one facility produces something that other facilities need for their products, the employer is less able to take a strike because the disruption to production goes beyond that single facility. The just-in-time production system, which provides very little stockpiling of parts, further weakens management's ability to take a strike.

7. *Lack of substitutes for the product:* A strike is more costly to the employer if customers have a readily available alternative source from which to purchase the goods or services the company provides.

Bargaining outcomes also depend on the nature of the bargaining process and relationship, which includes the types of tactics used and the history of labor relations. The vast majority of labor–management negotiations do not result in a strike because a strike is typically not in the best interests of either party. Furthermore, both the union and management usually realize that if they wish to interact effectively in the future, the experience of a strike can be difficult to overcome. When strikes do occur, the conduct of each party during the strike can also have a lasting effect on labor–management relations. Violence by either side or threats of job loss by hiring replacements can make future relations difficult.

Impasse Resolution Procedures: Alternatives to Strikes

Mediation
A procedure for resolving collective bargaining impasses by which a mediator with no formal authority acts as a facilitator and go-between in the negotiations.

Fact Finder
A person who reports on the reasons for the labor–management dispute, the views and arguments of both sides, and a nonbinding recommendation for settling the dispute.

Arbitration
A procedure for resolving collective bargaining impasses by which an arbitrator chooses a solution to the dispute.

Given the substantial costs of strikes to both parties, procedures that resolve conflicts without strikes have arisen in both the private and public sectors. Because many public sector employees do not have the right to strike, alternatives are particularly important in that arena.

Three often-used impasse resolution procedures are mediation, fact finding, and arbitration. All of them rely on the intervention of a neutral third party, most typically provided by the Federal Mediation and Conciliation Service, which must be notified 60 days prior to contract expiration and 30 days prior to a planned change in contract terms (including a strike). **Mediation** is the least formal but most widely used of the procedures (in both the public and private sectors). One survey found it was used by nearly 40 percent of all large private sector bargaining units.[49] A mediator has no formal authority but, rather, acts as a facilitator and go-between in negotiations.

A **fact finder**, most commonly used in the public sector, typically reports on the reasons for the dispute, the views and arguments of both sides, and (in some cases) a recommended settlement, which the parties are free to decline. That these recommendations are made public may give rise to public pressure for a settlement. Even if a fact finder's settlement is not accepted, the hope is that he or she will identify or frame issues in such a way as to facilitate an agreement. Sometimes, for the simple reason that fact finding takes time, the parties reach a settlement during the interim.

The most formal type of outside intervention is **arbitration**, under which a solution is actually chosen by an arbitrator (or arbitration board). In some instances the arbitrator can fashion a solution (conventional arbitration). In other cases the arbitrator must choose either the management's or union's final offer (final offer arbitration) on either the contract as a whole or on an issue-by-issue basis. Traditionally, arbitrating the enforcement or interpretation of contract terms (rights arbitration) has been widely accepted, whereas arbitrating the actual writing or setting of contract terms (interest arbitration, our focus here) has been reserved for special circumstances. These include some public sector negotiations, where strikes may be especially costly (such as those by police or firefighters) and a very few private sector situations, where strikes have been especially debilitating to both sides (the steel industry in the 1970s).[50] One reason for avoiding greater use of interest arbitration is a strong belief that the parties closest to the situation (unions and management, not an arbitrator) are in the best position to effectively resolve their conflicts.

Union and Management Interactions: Contract Administration

Grievance Procedure

Although the negotiation process (and the occasional resulting strike) receive the most publicity, the negotiation process typically occurs only about every three years, whereas contract administration goes on day after day, year after year. The two processes—negotiation and administration—are linked, of course. Vague or incomplete contract language developed in the negotiation process can make administration of the contract difficult. Such difficulties can, in turn, create conflict that can spill over into the next negotiation process.[51] Furthermore, events during the negotiation process—strikes, the use of replacement workers, or violence by either side—can lead to management and labor difficulties in working successfully under a contract.

A key influence on successful contract administration is the grievance procedure for resolving labor–management disputes over the interpretation and execution of the contract. During World War II, the War Labor Board helped institutionalize the use of arbitration as an alternative to strikes to settle disputes that arose during the term of the contract. The soon-to-follow Taft–Hartley Act further reinforced this preference. Today the great majority of grievance procedures have binding arbitration as a final step, and only a minority of strikes occur during the term of a contract. (Most occur during the negotiation stage.) Strikes during the term of a contract can be especially disruptive because they are more unpredictable than strikes during the negotiation phase, which occur only at regular intervals.

Beyond its ability to reduce strikes, a grievance procedure can be judged using three criteria.[52] First, how well are day-to-day contract questions resolved? Time delays and heavy use of the procedure may indicate problems. Second, how well does the grievance procedure adapt to changing circumstances? For example, if the company's business turns downward and the company needs to cut costs, how clear are the provisions relating to subcontracting of work, layoffs, and so forth? Third, in multiunit contracts, how well does the grievance procedure permit local contract issues (like work rules) to be included and resolved?[53]

From the employees' perspective, the grievance procedure is the key to fair treatment in the workplace, and its effectiveness rests both on the degree to which employees feel they can use it without fear of recrimination and whether they believe their case will be carried forward strongly enough by their union representative. The **duty of fair representation** is mandated by the NLRA and requires that all bargaining unit members, whether union members or not, have equal access to and representation by the union in the grievance procedure. Too many grievances may indicate a problem, but so may too few. A very low grievance rate may suggest a fear of filing a grievance, a belief that the system is not effective, or a belief that representation is not adequate.

Duty of Fair Representation
The National Labor Relations Act requirement that all bargaining unit members have equal access to and representation by the union.

Companies that rushed into China during the boom years may find it difficult amid the global downturn to extract themselves, labor law attorneys say.

"It wasn't too long ago when the burning issue was hiring, recruiting and retention," said Joseph Deng, a labor contract attorney with Baker & McKenzie in China. "Now it seems the No. 1 issue for many companies in China is cost cutting, termination and redundancies."

Landmark labor laws enacted in China this year have strengthened protections for workers, including wage standards and Social Security benefits. But worker protections against employers looking to downsize their workforce may be among the most stringent, China law experts say.

Chinese labor law prohibits "at will" firing practices common in the United States, which means employers must have a legal basis for firing any employee. "The first thing you have to keep in mind is that employees have contracts," Deng said. "You cannot unilaterally terminate a contract."

Before making any layoffs, employers need to present their plans to employee-represented work councils at each company—called employee representative congresses, which are union organizations elected by employees. For employers whose workers have not organized into unions, any indication that the company intends to lay employees off could incite workers to organize.

Deng recommends that employers file a report of a strategic plan with local labor bureaus. "They don't approve a plan, but they play an important role in providing guidance," he said.

Firing workers remains something of a taboo in China, as it is in much of Asia. Employers should present layoffs as part of a strategic plan rather than a cost-cutting measure, said Baker & McKenzie attorney Guenther Heckelmann; otherwise, employers open themselves up to challenges from workers regarding how companies calculate their costs.

Employers are unlikely to be able to lay off groups of workers using criteria usually reserved for firing individuals, like showing a worker is incompetent or has behaved improperly. Employers must show a change in the company's circumstances. For example, a company's decision to idle a plant could qualify. Employers must then attempt to find new work for the employee before giving that person 30 days' notice of his termination.

Dan Harris, a Seattle lawyer with the firm Harris & Moure, wrote in his China Law Blog that restrictions against at-will terminations may be the most stringently enforced requirements in China's new labor law, which took effect January 1, 2008, and was preceded by a backlash among workers to worsening working conditions in China.

Harris wrote of a client who was told by a Chinese government official in Shangdong, a coastal province southeast of Beijing, that "so long as this company did not lay off any of its approximately 250 Chinese employees, the government would look the other way regarding other labor law violations."

The popularity of the new law has tripled the number of disputes brought by workers against their employers, said Andreas Lauffs, the Hong Kong-based head of the employment law group at Baker & McKenzie. "There's not a single worker that doesn't know this law inside out," Lauffs said.

Earlier this year, a large multinational corporation represented by Baker & McKenzie negotiated severance packages with employee-established labor unions as a precondition for laying off the workers, Lauffs said.

All unions in China are organized under the nationalized All-China Federation of Trade Unions. While striking is illegal in China, workers have been known to engage in work stoppages and slowdowns. China legal experts are watching to see whether the economic slowdown will loosen the new contract laws in China.

The Chinese economy has been growing at around 12 percent a year. Officials have worried that a lower growth rate of 8 percent is the minimum needed to forestall public unrest. For now, though, the new labor laws remain intact.

"For multinationals, if they want to downsize as a result of the current economy, they'll have to tread very, very cautiously," Lauffs said. "China is no longer the place where you can go and set up shop with cheap labor and no labor laws."

SOURCE: From Jeremy Smerd, "Employers in China Have Issues Shedding Workers," *Workforce Management*, December 29, 2008, http://www.workforce.com/section/00/article/26/05/57 printer.php. Reprinted with permission of Crain Communications.

As Table 14.11 suggests, most grievance procedures have several steps prior to arbitration. Moreover, the majority of grievances are settled during the earlier steps of the process, which is desirable both to reduce time delays and to avoid the costs of arbitration. If the grievance does reach arbitration, the arbitrator makes the final ruling in the matter. A series of Supreme Court decisions in 1960, commonly known as the Steelworkers' Trilogy, established that the courts should essentially refrain from

table 14.11

Steps in a Typical Grievance Procedure

Employee-initiated grievance

Step 1

a. Employee discusses grievance or problem orally with supervisor.
b. Union steward and employee may discuss problem orally with supervisor.
c. Union steward and employee decide (1) whether problem has been resolved or (2) if not resolved, whether a contract violation has occurred.

Step 2

a. Grievance is put in writing and submitted to production superintendent or other designated line manager.
b. Steward and management representative meet and discuss grievance. Management's response is put in writing. A member of the industrial relations staff may be consulted at this stage.

Step 3

a. Grievance is appealed to top line management and industrial relations staff representatives. Additional local or international union officers may become involved in discussions. Decision is put in writing.

Step 4

a. Union decides on whether to appeal unresolved grievance to arbitration according to procedures specified in its constitution and/or bylaws.
b. Grievance is appealed to arbitration for binding decision.

Discharge grievance

a. Procedure may begin at step 2 or step 3.
b. Time limits between steps may be shorter to expedite the process.

Union or group grievance

a. Union representative initiates grievance at step 1 or step 2 on behalf of affected class of workers or union representatives.

SOURCE: Harry Katz, Thomas Kochan, and Alexander Colvin, *An Introduction to Collective Bargaining and Industrial Relations,* 2008. Copyright © 2008 The McGraw-Hill Companies.

reviewing the merits of arbitrators' decisions and, instead, limit judicial review to the question of whether the issue was subject to arbitration under the contract.[54] Furthermore, unless the contract explicitly states that an issue is not subject to arbitration, it will be assumed that arbitration is an appropriate means of deciding the issue. Giving further strength to the role of arbitration is the NLRB's general policy of deferring to arbitration.

What types of issues most commonly reach arbitration? Data from the FMCS on a total of 2,473 grievances show that discharge and disciplinary issues topped the list with 913 cases.[55] Other frequent issues include the use of seniority in promotion, layoffs, transfers, work assignments, and scheduling (309 cases); wages (178); and benefits (127).

What criteria do arbitrators use to reach a decision? In the most common case—discharge or discipline—the following due process questions are important:[56]

1. *Did the employee know what the rule or expectation was and what the consequences of not adhering to it were?*
2. *Was the rule applied in a consistent and predictable way?* In other words, are all employees treated the same?
3. *Are facts collected in a fair and systematic manner?* An important element of this principle is detailed record keeping. Both employee actions (such as tardiness) and management's response (verbal or written warnings) should be carefully documented.
4. *Does the employee have the right to question the facts and present a defense?* An example in a union setting is a hearing with a shop steward present.
5. *Does the employee have the right to appeal a decision?* An example is recourse to an impartial third party, such as an arbitrator.
6. *Is there progressive discipline?* Except perhaps for severe cases, an arbitrator will typically look for evidence that an employee was alerted as early as possible that behavior was inappropriate and the employee was given a chance to change prior to some form of severe discipline, such as discharge.
7. *Are there unique mitigating circumstances?* Although discipline must be consistent, individuals differ in terms of their prior service, performance, and discipline record. All of these factors may need to be considered.

New Labor–Management Strategies

LO5
Describe new, less adversarial approaches to labor–management relations.

Jack Barbash described the nature of the traditional relationship between labor and management (during both the negotiation and administration phases) as follows:

> Bargaining is a love–hate, cooperation–conflict relationship. The parties have a common interest in maximizing the total revenue which finances their respective returns. But they take on adversarial postures in debating how the revenue shall be divided as between wages and profits. It is the adversarial posture which has historically set the tone of the relationship.[57]

Although there have always been exceptions to the adversarial approach, there are signs of a more general transformation to less adversarial workplace relations (at least where the union's role is accepted by management).[58] This transformation has two basic objectives: (1) to increase the involvement of individuals and work groups in overcoming adversarial relations and increasing employee commitment, motivation, and problem solving and (2) to reorganize work so that work rules are minimized and flexibility in managing people is maximized. These objectives are especially important for companies that need to be able to shift production quickly in response to changes in markets and customer demands. The specific programs aimed at achieving these objectives include employee involvement in decision making, self-managing employee teams, labor–management problem-solving teams, broadly defined jobs, and sharing of financial gains and business information with employees.[59] Examples include the chapter opening story on GEMA and the UAW, as well as the labor-management relationships at Ford and Harley-Davidson.[60]

Union resistance to such programs has often been substantial, precisely because the programs seek to change workplace relations and the role that unions play. Without the union's support, these programs are less likely to survive and less likely to be effective if they do survive.[61] Union leaders have often feared that such programs will weaken unions' role as an independent representative of employee interests. Indeed, according to the NLRA, to "dominate or interfere with the formation or administration of any labor organization or contribute financial or other support to it" is an unfair labor practice. An example of a prohibited practice is "taking an active part in organizing a union or committee to represent employees."[62]

One case that has received much attention is that of Electromation, a small electrical parts manufacturer. In 1992 the NLRB ruled that the company had violated Section 8(a)(2) of the NLRA by setting up worker–management committees (typically about six workers and one or two managers) to solve problems having to do with absenteeism and pay scales.[63] The original complaint was filed by the Teamsters union, which was trying to organize the (nonunion) company and felt that the committees were, in effect, illegally competing with them to be workers' representatives. Similarly, Polaroid dissolved an employee committee that had been in existence for over 40 years in response to the U.S. Department of Labor's claim that it violated the NLRA. The primary functions of the employee committee had been to represent employees in grievances and to advise senior management on issues such as pay and company rules and regulations. In a third case, the NLRB ruled in 1993 that seven worker–management safety committees at DuPont were illegal under the NLRB because they were dominated by management. The committee members were chosen by management and their decisions were subject to the approval of the management members of the committees. Finally, the committees made decisions about issues that were mandatory subjects of bargaining with the employees' elected representative— the chemical workers' union.[64] The impact of such cases will be felt both in nonunion companies, as union organizers move to fill the worker representation vacuum, and in unionized companies, as managers find they must deal more directly and effectively with their unions.

In 1994 the Commission on the Future of Worker–Management Relations (also referred to as the Dunlop Commission, after its chair, former Secretary of Labor John Dunlop) recommended that Congress clarify Section 8(a)(2) and give employers more freedom to use employee involvement programs without risking legal challenges. In 1996 the U.S. Congress passed the Teamwork for Employees and Managers Act, which supporters said would remove legal roadblocks to greater employee involvement. Critics claimed the act went too far and would bring back employer-dominated labor organizations, which existed prior to the passage of the NLRA in 1935. The Clinton administration vetoed the bill, meaning that employers will continue to face some uncertainty about legal issues. Table 14.12 provides some guidance on when the use of teams might be illegal.

table 14.12

When Teams May Be Illegal

Primary factors to look for that could mean a team violates national labor law:	
Representation	Does the team address issues affecting nonteam employees? (Does it represent other workers?)
Subject matter	Do these issues involve matters such as wages, grievances, hours of work, and working conditions?
Management involvement	Does the team deal with any supervisors, managers, or executives on any issue?
Employer domination	Did the company create the team or decide what it would do and how it would function?

SOURCE: From *BusinessWeek*, January 25, 1993. Reprinted with permission.

Employers must take care that employee involvement meets the legal test, but the NLRB has clearly supported the legality of involvement in important cases. For example, in a 2001 ruling, the NLRB found that the use of seven employee participation committees at a Crown Cork & Seal aluminum can manufacturing plant did not violate federal labor law. The committees in question make and implement decisions regarding a wide range of issues, including production, quality, training, safety, and certain types of worker discipline. The NLRB determined that these committees were not employer-dominated labor organizations, which would have violated federal labor law. Instead of "dealing with" management in a bilateral manner where proposals are made that are either rejected or accepted by management, the teams and committees exercise authority, delegated by management, to operate the plant within certain parameters. Indeed, the NLRB noted that rather than "dealing with management," the evidence indicated that within delegated areas of authority, the teams and committees "are management." This authority was found to be similar to that delegated to a first-line supervisor. Thus the charge that the teams and committees did not have final decision-making authority (and so were not acting in a management capacity) did not weigh heavily with the NLRB, which noted, "Few, if any, supervisors in a conventional plant have authority that is final and absolute." Instead, it was noted that managers typically make recommendations that move up through "the chain of command."[65]

Although there are legal concerns to address, some evidence suggests that these new approaches to labor relations—incorporating greater employee participation in decisions, using employee teams, multiskilling, rotating jobs, and sharing financial gains—can contribute significantly to an organization's effectiveness,[66] as well as to workers' wages and job satisfaction.[67] One study, for example, compared the features of traditional and transformational approaches to labor relations at Xerox.[68] As Table 14.13 indicates, the transformational approach was characterized by better conflict resolution, more shop-floor cooperation, and greater worker autonomy and feedback in decision making. Furthermore, compared with the traditional approach, transformational labor relations were found to be associated with lower costs, better product quality, and higher productivity. The Commission on the Future of Worker–Management Relations concluded that the evidence is "overwhelming that employee participation and labor–management partnerships are good for workers, firms, and the national economy." National survey data also indicate that most employees want

	PATTERN	
DIMENSION	**TRADITIONAL**	**TRANSFORMATIONAL**
Conflict resolution		
Frequency of conflicts	High	Low
Speed of conflict resolution	Slow	Fast
Informal resolution of grievances	Low	High
Third- and fourth-step grievances	High	Low
Shop-floor cooperation		
Formal problem-solving groups (such as quality, reducing scrap, employment security)	Low	High
Informal problem-solving activity	Low	High
Worker autonomy and feedback		
Formal autonomous work groups	Low	High
Informal worker autonomous activity	Low	High
Worker-initiated changes in work design	Low	High
Feedback on cost, quality, and schedule	Low	High

table 14.13

Patterns in Labor–Management Relations Using Traditional and Transformational Approaches

SOURCE: Adapted from J. Cutcher-Gershenfeld, "The Impact of Economic Performance of a Transformation in Workplace Relations," *Industrial and Labor Relations Review* 44 (1991), pp. 241–60. Reprinted with permission.

more influence in workplace decisions and believe that such influence leads to more effective organizations.[69]

Labor Relations Outcomes

The effectiveness of labor relations can be evaluated from management, labor, and societal perspectives. Management seeks to control costs and enhance productivity and quality. Labor unions seek to raise wages and benefits and exercise control over how employees spend their time at work (such as through work rules). Each of the three parties typically seeks to avoid forms of conflict (like strikes) that impose significant costs on everyone. In this section we examine several outcomes.

Strikes

Table 14.14 presents data on strikes in the United States that involved 1,000 or more employees. Because strikes are more likely in large units, the lack of data on smaller units is probably not a major concern, although such data would, of course, raise the figure on the estimated time lost to strikes. For example, for the 1960s, this estimate is 0.12 percent using data on strikes involving 1,000 or more employees versus 0.17 percent for all strikes. Although strikes impose significant costs on union members, employers, and society, it is clear from Table 14.14 that strikes are the exception rather than the rule. Very little working time is lost to strikes in the United States

table 14.14

Work Stoppages
Involving 1,000 or
More Workers

YEAR	STOPPAGES	NUMBER OF WORKERS (THOUSANDS)	PERCENTAGE OF TOTAL WORKING TIME
1950	424	1,698	0.26%
1955	363	2,055	0.16
1960	222	896	0.09
1965	268	999	0.10
1970	381	2,468	0.29
1975	235	965	0.09
1980	187	795	0.09
1985	54	324	0.03
1990	44	185	0.02
1995	31	192	0.02
2000	39	394	0.06
2002	19	46	0.005
2004	17	171	0.01
2006	20	70	0.01
2008	15	72	0.03

SOURCE: http://stats.bls.gov.

(with annual work hours of 1,800, about 27 minutes per union member in 2008), and their frequency in recent years is generally low by historical standards. Does this mean that the industrial relations system is working well? Not necessarily. Some would view the low number of strikes as another sign of labor's weakness.

Wages and Benefits

In 2008, private-sector unionized workers received, on average, wages 21 percent higher than their nonunion counterparts.[70] Total compensation was 40 percent higher for union-covered employees because of an even larger effect of unions on benefits.[71] However, these are raw differences. To assess the net effect of unions on wages more accurately, adjustments must be made.[72] We now briefly highlight a few of these.

The union wage effect is likely to be overestimated to the extent that unions can more easily organize workers who are already highly paid or who are more productive. The gap is likely to be underestimated to the extent that nonunion employers raise wages and benefits in response to the perceived "union threat" in the hope that their employees will then have less interest in union representation. When these and other factors are taken into account, the net union advantage in wages, though still substantial, is reduced to 10 to 15 percent. The union benefits advantage is also reduced, but it remains larger than the union wage effect, and the union effect on total compensation is therefore larger than the wage effect alone.[73]

Beyond differences in pay and benefits, unions typically influence the way pay and promotions are determined. Whereas management often seeks to deal with employees as individuals, emphasizing performance differences in pay and promotion decisions, unions seek to build group solidarity and avoid the possibly arbitrary treatment of employees. To do so, unions focus on equal pay for equal work. Any differences among employees in pay or promotions, they say, should be based on seniority (an objective measure) rather than on performance (a subjective measure susceptible to favoritism). It is very common in union settings for there to be a single rate of pay for all employees in a particular job classification.

Productivity

There has been much debate regarding the effects of unions on productivity.[74] Unions are believed to decrease productivity in at least three ways: (1) the union pay advantage causes employers to use less labor and more capital per worker than they would otherwise, which reduces efficiency across society; (2) union contract provisions may limit permissible workloads, restrict the tasks that particular workers are allowed to perform, and require employers to use more employees for certain jobs than they otherwise would; and (3) strikes, slowdowns, and working-to-rule (slowing down production by following every workplace rule to an extreme) result in lost production.[75] The "Competing through Sustainability" box provides a look at a change in the U.S. automobile industry agreement with the UAW that is expected to improve productivity.

On the other hand, unions can have positive effects on productivity.[76] Employees, whether members of a union or not, communicate to management regarding how good a job it is doing by either the "exit" or "voice" mechanisms. "Exit" refers to simply leaving the company to work for a better employer. "Voice" refers to communicating one's concerns to management without necessarily leaving the employer. Unions are believed to increase the operation and effectiveness of the voice mechanism.[77] This, in turn, is likely to reduce employee turnover and its associated costs. More broadly, voice can be seen as including the union's contribution to the success of labor–management cooperation programs that make use of employee suggestions and increased involvement in decisions. A second way that unions can increase productivity is (perhaps ironically) through their emphasis on the use of seniority in pay, promotion, and layoff decisions. Although management typically prefers to rely more heavily on performance in such decisions, using seniority has a potentially important advantage—namely, it reduces competition among workers. As a result, workers may be less reluctant to share their knowledge with less senior workers because they do not have to worry about less senior workers taking their jobs. Finally, the introduction of a union may have a "shock effect" on management, pressuring it into tightening standards and accountability and paying greater heed to employee input in the design and management of production.[78]

Although there is evidence that unions have both positive and negative effects on productivity, most studies have found that union workers are more productive than nonunion workers. Nevertheless, it is generally recognized that most of the findings on this issue are open to a number of alternative explanations, making any clear conclusions difficult. For example, if unions raise productivity, why has union representation of employees declined over time, even within industries?[79] A related concern is that unionized establishments are more likely to survive where there is some inherent productivity advantage unrelated to unionism that actually offsets a negative impact of unionism. If so, these establishments would be overrepresented, whereas establishments that did not survive the negative impact of unions would be underrepresented. Consequently, any negative impact of unions on productivity would be underestimated.

On the eve of Detroit's latest date with fate in Washington, the United Auto Workers have surrendered the union's version of corporate jets.

The union is suspending its most ridiculed perk, called the JOBS bank. That program, set up as part of a contract agreement reached between Detroit's Big Three and the union decades ago, pays auto workers 85 percent of their pay while furloughed. Some workers reported for years to meeting rooms where they would sit and wait for an assignment or be sent to clean public parks. All the while, they would get paid most of their wages.

The union also agreed to defer payments that the Big Three will make to a union-led health care trust that is to take responsibility to pay medical benefits to auto workers starting in 2010.

The JOBS bank was costly in more ways than one for General Motors, Ford, and Chrysler. By making labor a fixed cost, it altered their manufacturing strategy. For most of the past 10 years, the car companies preferred to discount models with big rebates rather than cut production, because they had to pay workers no matter what.

The provision also became an emblem of union abuse and what industry outsiders call Detroit's entitlement culture. "The JOBS bank became a sound bite that people used to beat us up," said UAW President Ron Gettelfinger. "It became a lightning rod." The

JOBS bank has become less of a financial burden since the union has accepted tens of thousands of job cuts over the past two years, though. In 2006, GM had as many as 7,000 workers in the bank. Today, the three carmakers combined have just half that number awaiting a new assignment.

On December 4, 2008, the CEOs of Detroit's Big Three and Gettelfinger will take another stab at convincing Congress that the government should lend the automakers big bucks to stay afloat. Their request has climbed to $34 billion from $25 billion since last month's hearings, when the CEOs were turned away after being lambasted for not adequately explaining how the money would make their companies competitive with Japanese rivals. They didn't help their case by flying in on company planes. Members of Congress derided the auto execs for failing to display proper willingness to sacrifice. The UAW came in for criticism of its own, some of it focused on the JOBS bank.

Getting rid of the program will be painful for the union. The UAW will have to work out a way for laid-off workers to get buyouts or severance from their companies. Otherwise, they will simply be cut loose. Right now, laid-off workers still get most of their pay during the first 48 weeks of furlough from a combination of state unemployment benefits and company-funded supplemental unemployment benefits, or

SUB pay. After those 48 weeks, they go to the JOBS bank and get most of their pay from the automakers.

"These are painful sacrifices," says Harley Shaiken, labor economist at the University of California at Berkeley. "It symbolizes job security that has been built up over decades."

Now, workers may still get SUB pay. But the JOBS bank is suspended. The union will have to deal with more than 3,500 workers who are now in the JOBS bank at Ford, GM, and Chrysler. That's about the same number of people who are employed at a large car plant. One GM source said they may get buyouts. Gettelfinger wasn't specific, either. "We will work out the mechanics of it," Gettelfinger said. "We're going to think outside the box."

All of the automakers have set aside cash to seed the UAW health care fund, which will pay unionized worker and retiree health care benefits at all three companies. But they still have to put more cash in. GM, for example, has to give the UAW $32 billion to start a fund that will be invested to cover a long-term health care liability of $47 billion. The automaker has to put $7 billion by early 2010, a sum that company president and chief operations officer Frederick A. "Fritz" Henderson said will be difficult to pay.

Ford and Chrysler also owe future payments. Gettelfinger said the union will let the companies defer them, but he didn't say by how much. The union has hired investment bank Lazard to figure that out.

The union also said it will make adjustments to its current labor contract. Gettelfinger said he doesn't know what those changes will entail, since they will have to be negotiated with the companies. But the moves are aimed at helping GM attain parity with Toyota's labor costs by 2012. UAW workers make $29 an hour; most are older and have reached the top of the wage scale. Toyota workers average about $25 an hour. Including benefits and retiree costs, UAW workers cost $76 an hour, about $18 more than Toyota staffers.

Those contract changes could include cutting wages or making UAW members pay more for health care benefits. But that would require a vote of members. The union may also agree to cut staffing levels, which GM signaled as well in its proposal to Congress. Whatever GM gets, Ford and Chrysler will probably receive from the UAW, too.

Gettelfinger conceded that increasing pressure from global automakers and the nation's economic crisis have hurt the unions' ability to bargain. "Because of the environment we're in, we face difficult challenges," Gettelfinger said. "I use to cringe from the word 'concessions.' But that's what we did. The important thing is to secure these jobs."

The union hopes that its latest concessions—along with some financial help from Washington— will do just that. But it's all in the hands of Congress now.

Profits and Stock Performance

Even if unions do raise productivity, a company's profits and stock performance may still suffer if unions raise costs (such as wages) or decrease investment by a greater amount. Evidence shows that unions have a large negative effect on profits and that union coverage tends to decline more quickly in firms experiencing lower shareholder returns, suggesting that some firms become more competitive partly by reducing union strength.[80] Similarly, one study finds that each dollar of unexpected increase in collectively bargained labor costs results in a dollar reduction in shareholder wealth. Other research suggests that investment in research and development is lower in unionized firms.[81] Strikes, although infrequent, lower shareholder returns in both the struck companies and firms (like suppliers) linked to those companies.[82] These research findings describe the average effects of unions. The consequences of more innovative union–management relationships for profits and stock performance are less clear.

The International Context

Except for China, Russia, and Ukraine, the United States has more union members than any other country. Yet, as Table 14.15 indicates, aside from France and Korea, the United States has the lowest unionization rate (union density) of any country in the table. Even more striking are differences in union coverage, the percentage of employees whose terms and conditions of employment are governed by a union contract. (See Table 14.15.) In parts of western Europe, it is not uncommon to have coverage rates of 80 to 90 percent, meaning that the influence of labor unions far outstrips what would be implied by their membership levels.[83] Why are the unionization rate and coverage comparatively low? One explanation is that the United States does not have as strong a history of deep class-based divisions in society as other countries do. For example, labor and social democratic

LO6
Explain how changes in competitive challenges (e.g., product market competition and globalization) are influencing labor–management interactions.

table 14.15

Union Membership and Union Coverage, Selected Countries

| | MEMBERSHIP | | COVERAGE |
COUNTRY	NUMBER (THOUSANDS)	PERCENTAGE OF EMPLOYMENT (DENSITY)	PERCENTAGE OF EMPLOYMENT
United States	15,776	12	14
Canada	4,037	30	32
Japan	10,531	20	24
Korea	1,606	11	—
Australia	1,867	23	50
Netherlands	1,575	25	82
France	1,830	8	95
United Kingdom	6,524	29	35

SOURCE: J. Visser, "Union Membership Statistics in 24 Countries," *Monthly Labor Review,* January 2006, pp. 38–49.

political parties are commonplace in western Europe, and they are major players in the political process. Furthermore, the labor movement in western Europe is broader than that in the United States. It extends not just to the workplace but—through its own or closely related political parties—directly into the national political process.

What is the trend in union membership rates and coverage? In the United States, we saw earlier that the trend is clearly downward, at least in the private sector. Although there have also been declines in membership rates in many other countries, coverage rates have stayed high in many of these countries. In the United States, deregulation and competition from foreign-owned companies have forced companies to become more efficient. Combined with the fact that the union wage premium in the United States is substantially larger than in other advanced industrialized countries, it is not surprising that management opposition would be higher in the United States than elsewhere.[84] This, in turn, may help explain why the decline in union influence has been especially steep in the United States.

It seems likely that—with the growing globalization of markets—labor costs and productivity will continue to be key challenges. The European Union (EU) added 10 new member countries in 2004, and 2 more in 2007 bringing its total to 27 countries and 490 million people, or about 60 percent larger than the United States. The newer EU countries (e.g., Bulgaria, the Czech Republic, Poland, Romania, Slovakia) have much lower wages than the existing EU countries. Closer to home, we have the North American Free Trade Agreement among the United States, Canada, and Mexico. These common market agreements mean that goods, services, and production will continue to move more freely across international borders. Where substantial differences in wages, benefits, and other costs of doing business (such as regulation) exist, there will be a tendency to move to areas that are less costly, unless skills are unavailable or productivity is significantly lower there. Unless labor unions can increase their productivity sufficiently or organize new production facilities, union influence is likely to decline.

In addition to membership and coverage, the United States differs from western Europe in the degree of formal worker participation in decision making. Works' councils (joint labor–management decision-making institutions at the enterprise level) and worker representation on supervisory boards of directors (codetermination) are mandated by law in countries such as Germany. The Scandinavian countries, Austria, and Luxembourg have similar legislation. German works' councils make decisions about changes in work or the work environment, discipline, pay systems, safety, and other human resource issues. The degree of codetermination on supervisory boards depends on the size and industry of the company. For example, in German organizations having more than 2,000 employees, half of the board members must be worker representatives. (However, the chairman of the board, a management representative, can cast a tie-breaking vote.) In contrast, worker representation on boards of directors in the United States is still rare.[85]

The works' councils exist in part because collective bargaining agreements in countries such as Germany tend to be oriented toward industrywide or regional issues, with less emphasis on local issues. However, competitive forces have led employers to increasingly opt out of centralized bargaining, even in the countries best known for centralized bargaining, like Sweden and Germany.[86]

The "Competing through Globalization box" on page 658 shows that works' councils also play an important role in other countries, in this example, China.

The Public Sector

Unlike the private sector, union membership in the public sector grew in the 1960s and 1970s and remained fairly stable through the 1980s. As we saw earlier, in Figure 14.3 in 2008 some 36.8 percent of government employees were union members. Like the NLRA in the private sector, changes in the legal framework contributed significantly to union growth in the public sector. One early step was the enactment in Wisconsin of collective bargaining legislation in 1959 for its state employees.[87] Executive Order 10988 provided collective bargaining rights for federal employees in 1962. By the end of the 1960s, most states had passed similar laws. The Civil Service Reform Act of 1978, Title VII, later established the Federal Labor Relations Authority (modeled after the NLRB). Many states have similar administrative agencies to administer their own laws.

LO7
Explain how labor relations in the public sector differ from labor relations in the private sector.

An interesting aspect of public sector union growth is that much of it has occurred in the service industry and among white-collar employees—groups that have traditionally been viewed as difficult to organize. The American Federation of State, County, and Municipal Employees (AFSCME) with more than 1.4 million members, has about 325,000 members in health care, 325,000 in clerical jobs, and more than 400,000 in all white-collar occupations.[88]

In contrast to the private sector, strikes are illegal at the federal level of the public sector and in most states. At the local level, all states prohibit strikes by police (Hawaii being a partial exception) and firefighters (Idaho being the exception). Teachers and state employees are somewhat more likely to have the right to strike, depending on the state. Legal or not, strikes nonetheless do occur in the public sector. In 2006, for example, of the 20 work stoppages involving 1,000 or more workers, 8 were in state and local government. In 2008, 3 of the 15 major work stoppages were in the public sector.

A Look Back

The membership rate, and thus influence, of labor unions in the United States and in many other countries has been on the decline in the private sector. In the meantime, however, as we saw in the opening to this chapter, there continue to be companies where labor unions represent a large share of employees and thus play a major role in the operation and success of those companies. In such companies, whatever the national trend, effective labor relations are crucial for both companies and workers.

Questions

1. Many people picture labor union members as being men in blue-collar jobs in manufacturing plants. Is that accurate? Are there certain types of jobs where an employer can be fairly certain that employees will not join a union? Give examples.
2. Why do people join labor unions? Would you be interested in joining a labor union if given the opportunity? Why or why not? As a manager, would you prefer to work with a union or would you prefer that employees be unrepresented by a union? Explain.
3. What led to a change in labor relations at the Global Engine Manufacturing Alliance? What was the nature of the change and do you think it is an important and sustainable change?

  Please see the Video Case and Case Study that correspond to this chapter online at www.mhhe.com/noe7e.

SUMMARY

Labor unions seek to represent the interests of their members in the workplace. Although this may further the cause of industrial democracy, management often finds that unions increase labor costs while setting limits on the company's flexibility and discretion in decision making. As a result, the company may witness a diminished ability to compete effectively in a global economy. Not surprisingly, management in nonunion companies often feels compelled to actively resist the unionization of its employees. This, together with a host of economic, legal, and other factors, has contributed to union losses in membership and bargaining power in the private sector. There are some indications, however, that managements and unions are seeking new, more effective ways of working together to enhance competitiveness while giving employees a voice in how workplace decisions are made.

KEY TERMS

Checkoff provision, 637
Closed shop, 637
Union shop, 637
Agency shop, 637
Maintenance of membership, 637
Right-to-work laws, 637

Taft-Hartley Act, 1947, 643
Associate union membership, 649
Corporate campaigns, 650
Distributive bargaining, 652
Integrative bargaining, 652
Attitudinal structuring, 652

Intraorganizational bargaining, 652
Mediation, 656
Fact finder, 656
Arbitration, 656
Duty of fair representation, 657

DISCUSSION QUESTIONS

1. Why do employees join unions?
2. What has been the trend in union membership in the United States, and what are the underlying reasons for the trend?
3. What are the consequences for management and owners of having a union represent employees?
4. What are the general provisions of the National Labor Relations Act, and how does it affect labor–management interactions?

5. What are the features of traditional and nontraditional labor relations? What are the potential advantages of the "new" nontraditional approaches to labor relations?
6. How does the U.S. industrial and labor relations system compare with systems in other countries, such as those in western Europe?

SELF-ASSESSMENT EXERCISE

Would you join a union? Each of the following phrases expresses an opinion about the effects of a union on employees' jobs. For each phrase, circle a number on the scale to indicate whether you agree that a union would affect your job as described by the phrase.

Having a union would result in . . .	Strongly Disagree				Strongly Agree
1. Increased wages	1	2	3	4	5
2. Improved benefits	1	2	3	4	5
3. Protection from being fired	1	2	3	4	5
4. More promotions	1	2	3	4	5
5. Better work hours	1	2	3	4	5
6. Improved productivity	1	2	3	4	5
7. Better working conditions	1	2	3	4	5
8. Fewer accidents at work	1	2	3	4	5
9. More interesting work	1	2	3	4	5
10. Easier handling of employee problems	1	2	3	4	5
11. Increased work disruptions	5	4	3	2	1
12. More disagreements between employees and management	5	4	3	2	1
13. Work stoppages	5	4	3	2	1

Add up your total score. The highest score possible is 65, the lowest 13. The higher your score, the more you see value in unions, and the more likely you would be to join a union.

SOURCE: Based on S. A. Youngblood, A. S. DeNisi, J. L. Molleston, and W. H. Mobley, "The Impact of Work Environment, Instrumentality Beliefs, Perceived Union Image, and Subjective Norms on Union Voting Intentions," *Academy of Management Journal* 27 (1984), pp. 576–90.

EXERCISING STRATEGY: HOW NISSAN LAPS DETROIT

Jonathan Gates slaps a wide slab of tan-colored, hard foam rubber on his workbench. He fastens a numbered tag in one corner and some black foam insulation at the edges. As soon as he puts a number on the piece of foam, which will become the top of a dashboard for a Nissan Quest minivan, the vehicle has an identity. All of the parts for a big chunk of the minivan's interior, decked out with the customer's choice of colors, fabrics, and options, will come together in the next 42 minutes.

Gates and his co-workers fill a crucial role at Nissan Motor Co.'s new Canton, Mississippi, assembly plant: Almost everything a driver touches inside a new Quest, Titan pickup, or Armada sport-utility vehicle is put together in a single module, starting at Gates's workbench. "This is the most important job," he says. And yet, amazingly, Gates doesn't even work for Nissan. He works

for Lextron/Visteon Automotive Systems, a parts supplier that also builds the center console between the front seats and a subassembly of the car's front end. The finished modules pass over a wall to be bolted into a car or truck body rolling down the assembly line. Lextron/Visteon does the work faster than Nissan could and pays $3 an hour less than the carmaker pays assembly workers. Nissan is using a similar strategy for its vehicle frames, seats, electrical systems, and completed doors.

It's a level of efficiency that Detroit auto makers are only beginning to attempt. Along with other features in Nissan's eight-month-old, $1.4 billion factory, the wholesale integration of outside suppliers is another reason why General Motors, Ford, and Chrysler are still playing catch-up with Japanese car manufacturers. The Big Three have made great strides in productivity in recent years: General Motors Corp.'s best plants now actually beat Toyota's factories. But overall, every time Detroit gets close, the competition seems to get a little better.

Nissan's secret? Sure, its plants use cheaper, nonunion labor. Besides lower wages, its Smyrna, Tennessee, workers get about $3 an hour less in benefits than Big Three assemblers represented by the United Auto Workers. But there's more to it. Outsourcing offers huge savings, whereas the Big Three must negotiate the outsourcing of subassembly work with the union. And Nissan's plants are far more flexible in adjusting to market twists and turns. Nissan's Canton plant can send a minivan, pickup truck, and sport-utility vehicle down the same assembly line, one after the other, without interruption. At first glance, a Nissan factory does not look much different than one you would see in Detroit or St. Louis. But talk to the workers, and it soon becomes clear how relentlessly the company squeezes mere seconds out of the assembly process.

The United Auto Workers is slowly allowing more outsourcing. But the UAW wants to outsource work only to union-friendly suppliers. And even then it has to be negotiated. Nissan, meanwhile, has free rein to outsource jobs. Two of Smyrna's vehicles—the Maxima and Altima sedans—were engineered to be built using modules built by suppliers. Every vehicle built in Canton was designed that way. All together, buying modules saves 15 percent to 30 percent on the total cost of that section of the car, according to the Center for Automotive Research (CAR) in Ann Arbor, Michigan. And the Big Three? GM is the most "modular" of the domestic manufacturers, but only a few of its plants have been designed to build cars using many big modules.

Detroit is slowly making headway. Prudential says half of GM's 35 North American assembly lines can make multiple vehicles. GM's two-year-old Cadillac plant in Lansing, Michigan, will make three luxury vehicles: the CTS and STS sedans and SRX SUV. It has also been designed to get some large, preassembled modules from suppliers. GM is using the Cadillac plant as a model for upgrading other plants. "We're getting much more flexible," says Gary L. Cowger, president of GM North America.

But it's much easier to design a new factory to be flexible from the ground up than to refurbish those built 30 or more years ago. And with so much excess capacity, the Big Three have no room to build new plants. Even if they could match the Japanese in productivity, they would have to account for the costs of laid-off workers, whose contracts entitle them to 75 percent of their pay.

By contrast, Nissan runs a tight ship and works its employees harder. During the UAW's failed attempt to organize Smyrna in 2001, workers told the union that line speeds were too fast and people were getting injured, says Bob King, the UAW's vice president of organizing. The union says that in 2001, Nissan reported 31 injuries per 1,000 workers—twice the average at Big Three plants—according to logs reported to the Occupational Safety and Health Administration.

Nissan does not dispute the OSHA figures, but it denies its assembly lines are any less safe than Detroit's. Although the company won't release current numbers, executives do say that they have taken steps to reduce injuries. For instance, the company has workers do four different jobs during a typical eight-hour shift, to try to cut down on repetitive-motion injuries. Nissan claims that injury rates have fallen 60 percent in the past two years.

Questions

1. Can unionized plants compete with Nissan's nonunion plants?
2. Why isn't there a union at Nissan? Would a union be a good thing or a bad thing for Nissan workers? Nissan shareholders?

SOURCE: From "How Nissan Laps Detroit," *BusinessWeek*, December 22, 2003. Reprinted with permission.

● MANAGING PEOPLE: FROM THE PAGES OF *BusinessWeek*

BusinessWeek ### Auto Bailout: Southern Workers Watch and Worry

Workers at Honda's Lincoln, Ala., plant support a Detroit rescue more than politicians do. They fear cuts, too The tiny town of Lincoln, Ala., is 706 miles from Detroit. But as the U.S. recession deepens, the distance between this Southern enclave of the American auto industry and the Big Three's headquarters to the North seems to be shrinking.

At the edge of the 4,500-resident town looms a massive Honda plant, marked only by two tall towers bearing the Japanese automaker's name and by the sounds of industry that drift into Lincoln on otherwise sleepy afternoons. The plant, which opened in 2001, makes Honda Odyssey minivans and Honda Pilot SUVs.

Like other "transplant" factories set up by Japanese, Korean, and European companies in the South, the Lincoln Honda plant has no union, reflecting a wariness in the region about a typically Northern institution. Many in the South feel that General Motors, Ford Motor, and Chrysler—and their unionized workers—have no one but themselves to blame for their difficulties. That opinion came through loud and clear during the debate that left Congress killing a legislative bailout of the Detroit car companies. Sen. Richard Shelby (R-Ala.) blasted the Detroit companies as "dinosaurs" and the bailout legislation as "a bridge loan to nowhere."

Yet it was also clear in a visit to Lincoln on Friday, Dec. 19—the day that President George W. Bush announced he was extending a $17.4 billion lifeline to GM and Chrysler—that some workers and residents here think the woes of the auto industry are not entirely due to mismanagement or the high costs of pensions and health care for Detroit's retirees.

Stalled Foreign Automakers

The souring U.S. economy is hurting the Japanese companies to which Detroit automakers are so frequently and unfavorably compared. Honda has been cutting production to match its plummeting U.S. sales, and its leaders in Japan are sending ominous signals that things are expected to get worse in 2009. On Dec. 17, Honda CEO Takeo Fukui said the company probably will earn 62% less this fiscal year than what it had projected just six weeks earlier. That sense of alarm was reflected in the latest November results, which showed Honda's U.S. sales were down 32%, roughly in line with declines at other companies.

The transplant factories have responded by chopping work hours and production. In October, Mercedes-Benz offered buyouts at its Vance, Ala., plant, which makes SUVs and crossovers. Earlier this year, Nissan offered buyouts to white collar workers at its Tennessee headquarters, as well as to line workers. On Dec. 15, Toyota announced it would delay the opening of a factory in Blue Springs, Miss., where it was to start U.S. production of the Prius hybrid gas-electric car. Toyota workers at the company's brand-new San Antonio pickup truck plant were idle from August to November.

Honda says it will sharply cut the number of vehicles it produces in the U.S. and Canada in the coming year. While no layoffs have yet been announced in Lincoln, Honda has pulled back on production several times: In January it plans to reduce the number of vehicles built there, from 1,300 a day to 1,150. The plant was closed for two days in August and in the fall a second Friday shift of workers was eliminated.

Just a Northern Problem?

For many workers in Lincoln, the drama of the last-minute rescue of Detroit seemed distant.

"Really, [they] don't feel that the bailout has anything to do with them," says Debra Cochrum, 63, a former Honda employee who is now treasurer of the UAW's Alabama branch, which keeps an organizing operation just down 1–20 from the plant. "They think that the Northern people created this mess and that's their problem."

Still, some workers and residents interviewed in Lincoln say they're pleased with Friday's $17.4 billion bailout.

"It doesn't do anyone no good if those boys go under," says Donald Snow, 39, who has worked on the assembly line at the Lincoln plant for seven years. "What a lot of these guys at the plant don't realize is that it's all connected. If Detroit goes down, the suppliers get hurt. If the suppliers get hurt, we get hurt."

Southern Benefits Are Far Lower

According to CSM Worldwide, 58% of GM's suppliers—and 65% of Ford's—also provision the Asian transplant factories. A GM, Ford, or Chrysler bankruptcy could send hundreds of supplier companies into bankruptcy or liquidation, jeopardizing production at Honda, Toyota, Nissan, Hyundai, Mercedes, and BMW plants for months.

The fate of the Detroit companies could ripple through the South in other ways. One of the goals of the restructuring envisioned in the bailout is to close the gap in wages—and other costs—between GM, Ford, and Chrysler and the transplant factories. Southern autoworkers make less than their northern counterparts: UAW workers make an average of $29 an hour, vs. about $25 for a Toyota worker in the U.S., according to the Center for Automotive Research in Ann Arbor, Mich. However, if you factor in the expense of health-care and other benefits for active workers, plus pension and health-care costs for retirees, a UAW worker costs about $76 an hour, vs. $58 for a Toyota worker.

Why? The automakers have been in business for a century in the U.S. Many autoworkers go to the assembly line after high school and then put in 30 years. At age 48, they're seventeen years from qualifying for Social Security or Medicare, and they count on the hard-won pension and health-care benefits the UAW has negotiated over the decades.

Yet experts agree that the pay of Southern auto workers is benchmarked to the wages of UAW workers in the North. If the UAW were to make concessions and Northern wages dropped drastically. Southern workers' salaries might be held down as well.

Issue No. 1: Jobs

"Southern workers should take no glee in Detroit's problems because their pay is absolutely dependent on what the UAW gets paid," says George Hoffer, an economics professor at Virginia Commonwealth University who has studied the auto industry for 40 years.

The issue that most heavily weighs on the minds of the Lincoln plant's workers is preserving their jobs. In the wake of recent production cutbacks, rumors have spread that some part-time workers—who make up a sizable share of the plant's 4,000 employees—could be laid off if the economy continues to worsen.

After a hard day of physical labor, several of the plant's workers are unwinding at a local bar. As they sip beer and shoot pool, opinion seems split between those who feel that the best way to maintain job stability is to unionize and others who fear unionization would price Honda out of Lincoln, forcing the plant to shut its doors permanently.

Elvis Cox, 41, worked in the steel industry and was a member of the United Steel Workers Union before he took a job seven years ago at Honda's Lincoln plant. Cox says he lost his job when his steel factory closed because it couldn't meet the union's financial demands. He is content with his post—which, after all, pays more than most in the area—and doesn't want to make any waves that could endanger the income that supports his family.

Could the Union Secure Pensions?

Cox has pointed advice for those seeking to unionize: "If you don't like the job, then quit," he says. "What's the purpose for a union? What's the purpose?"

Snow doesn't want a union to bring his pay up to the level of the UAW workers; he simply wants to know that his job will be there and that his pension will be strong. "All I want is long-term security," he says shaking his head. "I can't do this job for too long. It's just so hard—physically."

When companies like Honda, Hyundai, and Mercedes-Benz opened plants in Alabama over the past 15 years, they did so in a state whose blue-collar employees had been decimated by the exodus of textile work to Mexico, China, and other parts of Asia in the 1980s. It was not uncommon to hear stories that those who signed on at Honda's Lincoln plant had previously worked simultaneous jobs with no benefits. Many workers fear that rocking the boat will chase the automakers to Mexico, or to some other state.

In the South, Employers Come First

Thus, historians agree that unionizing southern plants would require a dramatic cultural shift.

"In the North you work for the UAW first and the company second," says Hoffer at Virginia Commonwealth University. "It's just never been that way in the South. You work for the company first."

That attitude certainly is reflected in previous failed attempts to organize the transplant factories. Two decades of work by the UAW to force a vote at a Toyota factory in Georgetown, Ky., have yielded no results; votes at a Nissan plant in Smyrna, Tenn., were rejected out of hand by workers in 1989 and 2001.

"There is considerable tension between the union and Southern autoworkers," says John Heitmann, a history professor at the University of Dayton in Dayton, Ohio, who has studied the auto industry for a decade. "It's in part due to the strong strain of individualism that's a part of the South. There's no real compassion for union brothers down there."

Questions

1. Why have "transplant" plants avoided unions?
2. What employer actions might make them more susceptible to union organizing?
3. Is it in the best interests of workers in these plants to stay nonunion? Why or why not?
4. Thinking of the UAW and, more broadly, labor unions in the private sector, what might unions do in the future to maintain (or increase) their influence?
5. Is the decline of the UAW and private sector unionism, should it continue, a good thing or a bad thing for workers, companies, and society? Explain.
6. Should nonunion workers care about what happens to the UAW and other unions? Why or why not?

SOURCE: Brian Burnsed, "Auto Bailout: Southern Workers Watch and Worry," *BusinessWeek*, December 21, 2008.

NOTES

1. J. T. Dunlop, *Industrial Relations Systems* (New York: Holt, 1958).
2. C. Kerr, "Industrial Conflict and Its Mediation," *American Journal of Sociology* 60 (1954), pp. 230–45.
3. T. A. Kochan, *Collective Bargaining and Industrial Relations* (Homewood, IL: Richard D. Irwin, 1980), p. 25; H. C. Katz and T. A. Kochan, *An Introduction to Collective Bargaining and Industrial Relations*, 3rd ed. (New York: McGraw-Hill, 2004).
4. Katz and Kochan, *An Introduction to Collective Bargaining*.
5. S. Webb and B. Webb, *Industrial Democracy* (London: Longmans, Green, 1897); J. R. Commons, *Institutional Economics* (New York: Macmillan, 1934).
6. C. Kerr, J. T. Dunlop, F. Harbison, and C. Myers, "Industrialism and World Society," *Harvard Business Review*, February 1961, pp. 113–26.
7. T. A. Kochan and K. R. Wever, "American Unions and the Future of Worker Representation," in *The State of the Unions*, ed. G. Strauss et al. (Madison, WI: Industrial Relations Research Association, 1991).
8. "Why America Needs Unions, but Not the Kind It Has Now," *BusinessWeek*, May 23, 1994, p. 70.
9. Katz and Kochan, *An Introduction to Collective Bargaining*.
10. J. Barbash, *The Elements of Industrial Relations* (Madison, WI: University of Wisconsin Press, 1984).
11. U.S. Bureau of Labor Statistics, www.bls.gov.
12. J. T. Bennett and B. E. Kaufman, *The Future of Private Sector Unionism in the United States* (Armonk, NY: M. E. Sharpe, 2002).
13. Katz and Kochan, *An Introduction to Collective Bargaining*. Katz and Kochan in turn build on work by J. Fiorito and

C. L. Maranto, "The Contemporary Decline of Union Strength," *Contemporary Policy Issues* 3 (1987), pp. 12–27.

14. G. N. Chaison and J. Rose, "The Macrodeterminants of Union Growth and Decline," in *The State of the Unions*, George Strauss et al. (eds.) (Madison, WI: Industrial Relations Research Association, 1991).

15. D. L. Belman and K. A. Monaco, "The Effects of Deregulation, Deunionization, Technology, and Human Capital on the Work and Work Lives of Truck Drivers," *Industrial and Labor Relations Review* 54 (2001), pp. 502–24.

16. T. A. Kochan, R. B. McKersie, and J. Chalykoff, "The Effects of Corporate Strategy and Workplace Innovations in Union Representation," *Industrial and Labor Relations Review* 39 (1986), pp. 487–501; Chaison and Rose, "The Macrodeterminants of Union Growth"; J. Barbash, *Practice of Unionism* (New York: Harper, 1956), p. 210; W. N. Cooke and D. G. Meyer, "Structural and Market Predictors of Corporate Labor Relations Strategies," *Industrial and Labor Relations Review* 43 (1990), pp. 280–93; T. A. Kochan and P. Cappelli, "The Transformation of the Industrial Relations and Personnel Function," in *Internal Labor Markets*, ed. P. Osterman (Cambridge, MA: MIT Press, 1984); J. Logan, "The Union Avoidance Industry in the United States," *British Journal of Industrial Relations* 44 (2006), pp. 651–75.

17. Kochan and Cappelli, "The Transformation of the Industrial Relations and Personnel Function."

18. S. B. Jarrell and T. D. Stanley, "A Meta-Analysis of the Union–Nonunion Wage Gap," *Industrial and Labor Relations Review* 44 (1990), pp. 54–67; P. D. Lineneman, M. L. Wachter, and W. H. Carter, "Evaluating the Evidence on Union Employment and Wages," *Industrial and Labor Relations Review* 44 (1990), pp. 34–53; L. Mischel and M. Walters, "How Unions Help All Workers," Economic Policy Institute Briefing Paper (2003).

19. National Labor Relations Board annual reports.

20. John-Paul Ferguson, "The Eyes of the Needles: A Sequential Model of Union Organizing Drives, 1999–2004," *Industrial & Labor Relations Review* 62, no. 1 (October 2008), p. 3.

21. R. B. Freeman and M. M. Kleiner, "Employer Behavior in the Face of Union Organizing Drives," *Industrial and Labor Relations Review* 43 (1990), pp. 351–65.

22. F. K. Foulkes, "Large Nonunionized Employers," in *U.S. Industrial Relations 1950–1980: A Critical Assessment*, eds. J. Steiber et al. (Madison, WI: Industrial Relations Research Association, 1981).

23. Katz and Kochan, *An Introduction to Collective Bargaining*.

24. E. E. Herman, J. L. Schwarz, and A. Kuhn, *Collective Bargaining and Labor Relations* (Englewood Cliffs, NJ: Prentice Hall, 1992), p. 32.

25. BLS Web site; AFL-CIO Web site.

26. Herman et al., *Collective Bargaining*, p. 33.

27. Kochan, *Collective Bargaining and Industrial Relations*, p. 61.

28. National Labor Relations Board, *A Guide to Basic Law and Procedures under the National Labor Relations Act* (Washington, DC: U.S. Government Printing Office, 1991).

29. Ibid.

30. Ibid.

31. H. N. Wheeler and J. A. McClendon, "The Individual Decision to Unionize," in *The State of the Unions*.

32. National Labor Relations Board annual reports, www.nlrb.gov.

33. J. G. Getman, S. B. Goldberg, and J. B. Herman, *Union Representation Elections: Law and Reality* (New York: Russell Sage Foundation, 1976).

34. J. A. Fossum, *Labor Relations*, 8th ed. (New York: McGraw-Hill, 2002), p. 149.

35. National Labor Relations Board, *A Guide to Basic Law*, p. 17.

36. Ibid.

37. Herman et al., *Collective Bargaining*; P. Jarley and J. Fiorito, "Associate Membership: Unionism or Consumerism?" *Industrial and Labor Relations Review* 43 (1990), pp. 209–24.

38. Katz and Kochan, *An Introduction to Collective Bargaining*, R. L. Rose, "Unions Hit Corporate Campaign Trail," *The Wall Street Journal*, March 8, 1993, p. B1.

39. P. Jarley and C. L. Maranto, "Union Corporate Campaigns: An Assessment," *Industrial and Labor Relations Review* 44 (1990), pp. 505–24.

40. Katz and Kochan, *An Introduction to Collective Bargaining*.

41. A. Fung, T. Hebb, and J. Rogers (eds.), *Working Capital: The Power of Labor's Pensions* (Ithaca, NY: Cornell University Press, 2001).

42. A. Bernstein, "Working Capital: Labor's New Weapon?" *BusinessWeek*, September 27, 1997; A. Michaud, "Investments with the Union Label," *BusinessWeek*, August 22, 2001.

43. Chaison and Rose, "The Macrodeterminants of Union Growth."

44. R. E. Walton and R. B. McKersie, *A Behavioral Theory of Negotiations* (New York: McGraw-Hill, 1965).

45. Fossum, *Labor Relations*. See also C. S. Loughran, *Negotiating a Labor Contract: A Management Handbook*, 2nd ed. (Washington, DC: Bureau of National Affairs, 1990).

46. C. M. Steven, *Strategy and Collective Bargaining Negotiations* (New York: McGraw-Hill, 1963); Katz and Kochan, *An Introduction to Collective Bargaining*.

47. Kochan, *Collective Bargaining and Industrial Relations*.

48. Fossum, *Labor Relations*.

49. Kochan, *Collective Bargaining and Industrial Relations*, p. 272.

50. Herman et al., *Collective Bargaining*.

51. Katz and Kochan, *An Introduction to Collective Bargaining*.

52. Kochan, *Collective Bargaining and Industrial Relations*, p. 386.

53. Alternative criteria would be efficiency, equity, and worker voice. John W. Budd and Alexander J. S. Colvin, "Improved Metrics for Workplace Dispute Resolution Procedures: Efficiency, Equity, and Voice," *Industrial Relations* 47, no. 3 (July 2008), p. 460.

54. *United Steelworkers v. American Manufacturing Co.*, 363 U.S. 564 (1960); *United Steelworkers v. Warrior Gulf and Navigation Co.*, 363 U.S. 574 (1960); *United Steelworkers v. Enterprise Wheel and Car Corp.*, 363 U.S. 593 (1960).

55. Original data from U.S. Federal Mediation and Conciliation Service, *Fiftieth Annual Report, Fiscal Year 2006* (Washington, DC: U.S. Government Printing Office, 2006); www.fmcs.gov.

56. J. R. Redecker, *Employee Discipline: Policies and Practices* (Washington, DC: Bureau of National Affairs, 1989).

57. Barbash, *The Elements of Industrial Relations*, p. 6.

58. T. A. Kochan, H. C. Katz, and R. B. McKersie, *The Transformation of American Industrial Relations* (New York: Basic Books, 1986), chap. 6.

59. J. B. Arthur, "The Link between Business Strategy and Industrial Relations Systems in American Steel Minimills," *Industrial and Labor Relations Review* 45 (1992), pp. 488–506; M. Schuster, "Union Management Cooperation," in *Employee and Labor Relations*, ed. J. A. Fossum (Washington, DC: Bureau of National Affairs, 1990); E. Cohen-Rosenthal and C. Burton, *Mutual Gains: A Guide to Union–Management Cooperation*, 2nd ed. (Ithaca, NY: ILR Press, 1993); T. A. Kochan and P. Osterman, *The Mutual Gains Enterprise* (Boston: Harvard Business School Press, 1994); E. Applebaum and R. Batt, *The New American Workplace* (Ithaca, NY: ILR Press, 1994).

60. J. McCracken, "Desperate to Cut Costs, Ford Gets Union's Help," *The Wall Street Journal*, March 2, 2007, p. A1; M. Oneal, "Model Partnership: Automakers, Labor Could Learn from Harley-Davidson's Kansas City Operation," *Columbus Dispatch*, May 27, 2006 (original article in *Chicago Tribune*).

61. A. E. Eaton, "Factors Contributing to the Survival of Employee Participation Programs in Unionized Settings," *Industrial and Labor Relations Review* 47, no. 3 (1994), pp. 371–89.

62. National Labor Relations Board, *A Guide to Basic Law*.

63. A. Bernstein, "Putting a Damper on That Old Team Spirit," *BusinessWeek*, May 4, 1992, p. 60.

64. Bureau of National Affairs, "Polaroid Dissolves Employee Committee in Response to Labor Department Ruling," *Daily Labor Report*, June 23, 1992, p. A3; K. G. Salwen, "DuPont Is Told It Must Disband Nonunion Panels," *The Wall Street Journal*, June 7, 1993, p. A2.

65. "NLRB 4-0 Approves Crown Cork & Seal's Use of Seven Employee Participation Committees," *HR News*, September 3, 2001.

66. Kochan and Osterman, *Mutual Gains*; J. P. MacDuffie, "Human Resource Bundles and Manufacturing Performance: Organizational Logic and Flexible Production Systems in the World Auto Industry," *Industrial and Labor Relations Review* 48, no. 2 (1995), pp. 197–221; W. N. Cooke, "Employee Participation Programs, Group-Based Incentives, and Company Performance: A Union–Nonunion Comparison," *Industrial and Labor Relations Review* 47, no. 4 (1994), pp. 594–609; C. Doucouliagos, "Worker Participation and Productivity in Labor-Managed and Participatory Capitalist Firms: A Meta-Analysis," *Industrial and Labor Relations Review* 49, no. 1 (1995), pp. 58–77; L. W. Hunter, J. P. MacDuffie, and L. Doucet, "What Makes Teams Take? Employee Reactions to Work Reforms," *Industrial and Labor Relations Review* 55 (2002), pp. 448–72; S. J. Deery and R. D. Iverson, "Labor-Management Cooperation: Antecedents and Impact on Organizational Performance," *Industrial and Labor Relations Review* 58 (2005), pp. 588–609; James Combs, Yongmei Liu, Angela Hall, and David Ketchen, "How Much Do High-Performance Work Practices Matter? A Meta-Analysis of Their Effects on Organizational Performance," *Personnel Psychology* 59, no. 3 (2006), pp. 501–28.

67. Robert D. Mohr and Cindy Zoghi, "High-Involvement Work Design and Job Satisfaction," *Industrial & Labor Relations Review* 61, no. 3 (April 2008), pp. 275–296; Paul Osterman, "The Wage Effects of High Performance Work Organization in Manufacturing," *Industrial and Labor Relations Review* 59 (2006), pp. 187–204.

68. J. Cutcher-Gershenfeld, "The Impact of Economic Performance of a Transformation in Workplace Relations," *Industrial and Labor Relations Review* 44 (1991), pp. 241–60.

69. R. B. Freeman and J. Rogers, *Proceedings of the Industrial Relations Research Association*, 1995. A survey of workers represented by the United Autoworkers at six Chrysler manufacturing plants found generally positive worker reactions to the implementation of work teams, streamlined job classifications, and skill-based pay. See L. W. Hunter, J. P. Macduffie, and L. Doucet, "What Makes Teams Take? Employee Reactions to Work Reforms," *Industrial and Labor Relations Review* 55 (2002), p. 448. A study of the airline industry, moreover, concludes that relational factors, such as conflict and workplace culture, also play an important role in firm performance. See J. H. Gittell, A. vonNordenflycht, and T. A. Kochan, "Mutual Gains or Zero Sum? Labor Relations and Firm Performance in the Airline Industry," *Industrial and Labor Relations Review* 57 (2004), p. 163.

70. http://stats.bls.gov, Employer Costs for Employee Compensation (ECEC).

71. Ibid.

72. Mckinley L. Blackburn, "Are Union Wage Differentials in the United States Falling?" *Industrial Relations* 47, no. 3 (July 2008), p. 390.

73. Jarrell and Stanley, "A Meta-Analysis"; R. B. Freeman and J. Medoff, *What Do Unions Do?* (New York: Basic Books, 1984); L. Mishel and M. Walters, "How Unions Help All Workers," *Economic Policy Institute Briefing Paper*, August 2003, www.epinet.org.

74. J. T. Addison and B. T. Hirsch, "Union Effects on Productivity, Profits, and Growth: Has the Long Run Arrived?" *Journal of Labor Economics* 7 (1989), pp. 72–105.

75. R. B. Freeman and J. L. Medoff, "The Two Faces of Unionism," *Public Interest* 57 (Fall 1979), pp. 69–93.

76. Ibid.; L. Mishel and P. Voos, *Unions and Economic Competitiveness* (Armonk, NY: M. E. Sharpe, 1991); M. Ash and J. A. Seago, "The Effect of Registered Nurses' Unions on Heart-Attack Mortality," *Industrial and Labor Relations Review* 57 (2004), p. 422; C. Doucouliagos and P. Laroche, "What Do Unions Do to Productivity? A Meta-Analysis," *Industrial Relations* 42 (2003), pp. 650–91.

77. Freeman and Medoff, "Two Faces."

78. S. Slichter, J. Healy, and E. R. Livernash, *The Impact of Collective Bargaining on Management* (Washington, DC: Brookings Institution, 1960); Freeman and Medoff, "Two Faces."

79. Freeman and Medoff, *What Do Unions Do?*; Herman et al., *Collective Bargaining*; Addison and Hirsch, "Union Effects on Productivity"; Katz and Kochan, *An Introduction to Collective Bargaining*; Lineneman et al., "Evaluating the Evidence."

80. B. E. Becker and C. A. Olson, "Unions and Firm Profits," *Industrial Relations* 31, no. 3 (1992), pp. 395–415; B. T. Hirsch and B. A. Morgan, "Shareholder Risks and Returns in Union and Nonunion Firms," *Industrial and Labor Relations Review* 47, no. 2 (1994), pp. 302–18. Hristos Doucouliagos and Partice Laroche, "Unions and Profits: A Meta-Regression Analysis," *Industrial Relations*. 48, no. 1 (January 2008), p. 146.

81. Addison and Hirsch, "Union Effects on Productivity." See also B. T. Hirsch, *Labor Unions and the Economic Performance of Firms* (Kalamazoo, MI: W. E. Upjohn Institute, 1991); J. M. Abowd, "The Effect of Wage Bargains on the Stock Market Value of the Firm," *American Economic Review* 79 (1989), pp. 774–800; Hirsch, *Labor Unions*.

82. B. E. Becker, and C. A. Olson, "The Impact of Strikes on Shareholder Equity," *Industrial and Labor Relations Review* 39, no. 3 (1986), pp. 425–38; O. Persons, "The Effects of Automobile Strikes on the Stock Value of Steel Suppliers," *Industrial and Labor Relations Review* 49, no. 1 (1995), pp. 78–87.

83. C. Brewster, "Levels of Analysis in Strategic HRM: Questions Raised by Comparative Research," Conference on Research and Theory in HRM, Cornell University, October 1997.

84. C. Chang and C. Sorrentino, "Union Membership in 12 Countries," *Monthly Labor Review* 114, no. 12 (1991), pp. 46–53; D. G. Blanchflower and R. B. Freeman, "Going Different Ways: Unionism in the U.S. and Other Advanced O.E.C.D. Countries" (Symposium on the Future Role of Unions, Industry, and Government in Industrial Relations. University of Minnesota), cited in Chaison and Rose, "The Macrodeterminants of Union Growth," p. 23.

85. J. P. Begin and E. F. Beal, *The Practice of Collective Bargaining* (Homewood, IL: Richard D. Irwin, 1989); T. H. Hammer, S. C. Currall, and R. N. Stern, "Worker Representation on Boards of

Directors: A Study of Competing Roles," *Industrial and Labor Relations Review* 44 (1991), pp. 661–80; Katz and Kochan, *An Introduction to Collective Bargaining*; H. Gunter and G. Leminsky, "The Federal Republic of Germany," in *Labor in the Twentieth Century,* ed. J. T. Dunlop and W. Galenson (New York: Academic Press, 1978), pp. 149–96.

86. "Adapt or Die," *The Economist,* July 1, 1995, p. 54; G. Steinmetz, "German Firms Sour on Stem That Keeps Peace with Workers: Centralized Bargaining, a Key to Postwar Gains, Inflates Costs, Companies Fear," *The Wall Street Journal,* October 17, 1995, p. A1; H. C. Katz, W. Lee, and J. Lee, *The New Structure of Labor Relations: Tripartism and Decentralization* (Ithaca, NY: ILR Press/Cornell University, 2004).

87. J. F. Burton and T. Thomason, "The Extent of Collective Bargaining in the Public Sector," in *Public Sector Bargaining,* ed. B. Aaron, J. M. Najita, and J. L. Stern (Washington, DC: Bureau of National Affairs, 1988).

88. www.afscme.org.

15

Managing Human Resources Globally

LO LEARNING OBJECTIVES

After reading this chapter, you should be able to:

LO1   Identify the recent changes that have caused companies to expand into international markets. *page 681*

LO2   Discuss the four factors that most strongly influence HRM in international markets. *page 683*

LO3   List the different categories of international employees. *page 691*

LO4   Identify the four levels of global participation and the HRM issues faced within each level. *page 693*

LO5   Discuss the ways companies attempt to select, train, compensate, and reintegrate expatriate managers. *page 697*

ENTER THE WORLD OF BUSINESS

Starbucks Seeks Global Growth during Tough Times

The opening case in Chapter 1 discussed Starbucks efforts to cope with the economic downturn in the United States. Starbucks is also looking to other areas of the globe for ways to keep afloat during these uncertain times.

Starbucks kicked off a global coffee craze when it was founded in 1971 to the point that it has become ubiquitous in the United States. You can't walk more than a few blocks in most large cities without bumping into a Starbucks store. However, as the economy has soured and its competition increased, Starbucks has begun to retrench its North American operations, looking for more areas of potential greater growth, such as China or central Europe.

In particular, in mid-April 2009, Starbucks will open its first store in Poland. Usually this would be greeted with ecstatic responses, but a slew of problems have made this grand opening not so grand. First, repeated delays of the opening have frustrated potential customers. In addition, because they delayed their expansion into Poland (not jumping in as soon as Poland had acceded into the European Union), competitors such as Coffee Heaven, Tchibo, Mercer's, or Nescafé were able to obtain prime real estate locations. So, now Starbucks will find it difficult to access prestigious locations, and in these economic times, it will not be easy to tempt the customers with the prices.

Increasingly U.S. companies find that their capital and know-how are no longer guarantees of success in developing markets. Local businesses now have the money, knowledge, and experience—and if they establish a foothold before the U.S. company comes in, the entry barriers may be insurmountable. In addition, it seems that Americans never developed the ability to adapt to other cultures, and they often tend to be overconfident. This results in products, prices, and marketing that are often unattractive to local customers.

● Above, the first Starbucks in Poland located near the university in Warsaw.

How successful will Starbucks be in Poland? The jury is still out. However, launching a premium-priced product in a country with existing competitors at a time of economic uncertainty may not prove to be the most effective global strategy.

Sources: "Twilight of the American Myth; U.S. Capitalism Icons Have Ceased to Epitomize Business Success in Poland" *Polish News Bulletin*, April 14, 2009; Wendy Stueck, "High-End Coffee King Retrenches Breaking News," globeandmail.com, April 15, 2009.

Introduction

The environment in which business competes is rapidly becoming globalized. More and more companies are entering international markets by exporting their products overseas, building plants in other countries, and entering into alliances with foreign companies. Back in the middle of the 1980s, 61 of the top 100 organizations had their headquarters in the United States. By 2004, that number had dropped to 35, and, as you can see in Table 15.1, of the world's largest 25 organizations, only 9 are headquartered in the United States, with 13 in Europe and 3 in Asia. Of *Fortune* magazine's Global 500 (the 500 largest companies), 170 are headquartered in the United States, 70 in Japan, 38 in the United Kingdom, 38 in France, 35 in Germany, 20 in China, 14 in the Netherlands, and 12 in South Korea. In addition, for the first time in history, an automaker from outside the United States (Toyota) became the largest in worldwide sales, surpassing General Motors in the first quarter of 2007.

A survey of 12,000 managers from 25 different countries indicates how common international expansion has become, both in the United States and in other countries.[1] Of the U.S. managers surveyed, 26 percent indicated that their companies had recently expanded internationally. Among the larger companies (10,000 or more employees), 45 percent had expanded internationally during the previous two years. Currently, exports account for 11 percent of the gross domestic product

table 15.1

Fortune Global 500—25 Largest Organizations Ranked by Revenues

RANK	COMPANY	REVENUES ($ MILLIONS)	PROFITS ($ MILLIONS)
1	ExxonMobil	$442,851.0	$45,220.0
2	Wal-Mart Stores	405,607.0	13,400.0
3	Chevron	263,159.0	23,931.0
4	ConocoPhillips	230,764.0	-16,998.0
5	General Electric	183,207.0	17,410.0
6	General Motors	148,979.0	-30,860.0
7	Ford Motor	146,277.0	-14,672.0
8	AT&T	124,028.0	12,867.0
9	Hewlett-Packard	118,364.0	8,329.0
10	Valero Energy	118,298.0	-1,131.0
11	Bank of America Corp.	113,106.0	4,008.0
12	Citigroup	112,372.0	-27,684.0
13	Berkshire Hathaway	107,786.0	4,994.0
14	International Business Machines	103,630.0	12,334.0
15	McKesson	101,703.0	990.0
16	JPMorgan Chase & Co.	101,491.0	5,605.0
17	Verizon Communications	97,354.0	6,428.0
18	Cardinal Health	91,091.4	1,300.6
19	CVS Caremark	87,471.9	3,212.1
20	Procter & Gamble	83,503.0	12,075.0
21	UnitedHealth Group	81,186.0	2,977.0
22	Kroger	76,000.0	1,249.4
23	Marathon Oil	73,504.0	3,528.0
24	Costco Wholesale	72,483.0	1,282.7
25	Home Depot	71,288.0	2,260.0

in the United States, and they have been growing at a rate of 12 percent a year since 1987.[2]

Indeed, most organizations now function in the global economy. Thus U.S. businesses are entering international markets at the same time foreign companies are entering the U.S. market.

What is behind the trend toward expansion into global markets? Companies are attempting to gain a competitive advantage, which can be provided by international expansion in a number of ways. First, these countries are new markets with large numbers of potential customers. For companies that are producing below their capacity, they provide a means of increasing sales and profits. Second, many companies are building production facilities in other countries as a means of capitalizing on those countries' lower labor costs for relatively unskilled jobs. For example, many of the *maquiladora* plants (foreign-owned plants located in Mexico that employ Mexican laborers) provide low-skilled labor at considerably lower cost than in the United States. In 2007, the average manufacturing hourly wage in Mexico was $2.92, versus more than $24.00 in the United States.[3] Third, the rapid increase in telecommunications and information technology enables work to be done more rapidly, efficiently, and effectively around the globe. With the best college graduates available for $2.00 an hour in India versus $12–$18 an hour in the United States, companies can hire the best talent (resulting in better work) at a lower cost. And because their day is our night, work done in the United States can be handed off to those in India for a 24/7 work process.[4]

According to a survey of almost 3,000 line executives and HR executives from 12 countries, international competition is the number one factor affecting HRM. The globalization of business structures and globalization of the economy ranked fourth and fifth, respectively.[5] Deciding whether to enter foreign markets and whether to develop plants or other facilities in other countries, however, is no simple matter, and many human resource issues surface.

This chapter discusses the human resource issues that must be addressed to gain competitive advantage in a world of global competition. This is not a chapter on international human resource management (the specific HRM policies and programs companies use to manage human resources across international boundaries).[6] The chapter focuses instead on the key factors that must be addressed to strategically manage human resources in an international context. We discuss some of the important events that have increased the global nature of business over the past few years. We then identify some of the factors that are most important to HRM in global environments. Finally, we examine particular issues related to managing expatriate managers. These issues present unique opportunities for firms to gain competitive advantage.

Current Global Changes

LOI
Identify the recent changes that have caused companies to expand into international markets.

Several recent social and political changes have accelerated the movement toward international competition. The effects of these changes have been profound and far-reaching. Many are still evolving. In this section we discuss the major developments that have accentuated the need for organizations to gain a competitive advantage through effectively managing human resources in a global economy.

European Economic Community

European countries have managed their economies individually for years. Because of the countries' close geographic proximity, their economies have become intertwined. This created a number of problems for international businesses; for example, the regulations of one country, such as France, might be completely different from those of another country, such as Germany. In response, most of the European countries agreed to participate in the European Economic Community, which began in 1992. The EEC is a confederation of most of the European nations that agree to engage in free trade with one another, with commerce regulated by an overseeing body called the European Commission (EC). Under the EEC, legal regulation in the participating countries has become more, although not completely, uniform. Assuming the EEC's trend toward free trade among members continues, Europe has become one of the largest free markets in the world. In addition, as of 1999, all of the members of the European Economic Community share a common currency, the euro. This ties the members' economic fates even more closely with one another. In addition to the previous 15 EU states, as of May 1, 2004, 12 EU accession states—Bulgaria, Cyprus, the Czech Republic, Estonia, Hungary, Latvia, Lithuania, Malta, Poland, Romania, Slovakia, and Slovenia—were added to the EU, expanding the economic zone covered by the European Union.

North American Free Trade Agreement

The North American Free Trade Agreement (NAFTA) is an agreement among Canada, the United States, and Mexico that has created a free market even larger than the European Economic Community. The United States and Canada already had a free trade agreement since 1989, but NAFTA brought Mexico into the consortium. The agreement was prompted by Mexico's increasing willingness to open its markets and facilities in an effort to promote economic growth.[7] As previously discussed, the *maquiladora* plants exemplify this trend. In addition, some efforts have been made to expand the membership of NAFTA to other Latin American countries, such as Chile.

NAFTA has increased U.S. investment in Mexico because of Mexico's substantially lower labor costs for low-skilled employees. This has had two effects on employment in the United States. First, many low-skilled jobs went south, decreasing employment opportunities for U.S. citizens who lack higher-level skills. Second, it has increased employment opportunities for Americans with higher-level skills beyond those already being observed.[8]

The Growth of Asia

An additional global market that is of economic consequence to many firms lies in Asia. Whereas Japan has been a dominant economic force for over 20 years, recently countries such as Singapore, Hong Kong, and Malaysia have become significant economic forces. In addition, China, with its population of more than 1 billion and trend toward opening its markets to foreign investors, presents a tremendous potential market for goods. In fact, a consortium of Singaporean companies and governmental agencies has jointly developed with China a huge industrial township in eastern China's Suzhou City that will consist of ready-made factories for sale to foreign companies.[9] While Asia has been affected by the recent recession, the main impact has only been to slow its rate of growth.

General Agreement on Tariffs and Trade

The General Agreement on Tariffs and Trade (GATT) is an international framework of rules and principles for reducing trade barriers across countries around the world. It currently consists of more than 100 member-nations. The most recent round of

GATT negotiations resulted in an agreement to cut tariffs (taxes on imports) by 40 percent, reduce government subsidies to businesses, expand protection of intellectual property such as copyrights and patents, and establish rules for investing and trading in services. It also established the World Trade Organization (WTO) to resolve disputes among GATT members.

These changes—the European Economic Community, NAFTA, the growth of Asia, and GATT—all exemplify events that are pushing companies to compete in a global economy. These developments are opening new markets and new sources of technology and labor in a way that has never been seen in history. However, this era of increasing international competition accentuates the need to manage human resources effectively to gain competitive advantage in a global marketplace. This requires understanding some of the factors that can determine the effectiveness of various HRM practices and approaches.

Factors Affecting HRM in Global Markets

Companies that enter global markets must recognize that these markets are not simply mirror images of their home country. Countries differ along a number of dimensions that influence the attractiveness of direct foreign investment in each country. These differences determine the economic viability of building an operation in a foreign location, and they have a particularly strong impact on HRM in that operation. Researchers in international management have identified a number of factors that can affect HRM in global markets, and we focus on four factors, as depicted in Figure 15.1: culture, education–human capital, the political–legal system, and the economic system.[10]

LO2
Discuss the four factors that most strongly influence HRM in international markets.

Culture

By far the most important factor influencing international HRM is the culture of the country in which a facility is located. Culture is defined as "the set of important assumptions (often unstated) that members of a community share."[11] These

figure 15.1

Factors Affecting Human Resource Management in International Markets assumptions consist of beliefs about the world and how it works and the ideals that are worth striving for.[12]

Culture is important to HRM for two reasons. First, it often determines the other three factors affecting HRM in global markets. Culture can greatly affect a country's laws, in that laws are often the codification of right and wrong as defined by the culture. Culture also affects human capital, because if education is greatly valued by the culture, then members of the community try to increase their human capital. Finally, as we discuss later, cultures and economic systems are closely intertwined.[13]

However, the most important reason that culture is important to HRM is that it often determines the effectiveness of various HRM practices. Practices found to be effective in the United States may not be effective in a culture that has different beliefs and values.[14] For example, U.S. companies rely heavily on individual performance appraisal, and rewards are tied to individual performance. In Japan, however, individuals are expected to subordinate their wishes and desires to those of the larger group. Thus, individual-based evaluation and incentives are not nearly as effective there and, in fact, are seldom observed among Japanese organizations.[15]

In this section we examine a model that attempts to characterize different cultures. This model illustrates why culture can have a profound influence on HRM.

Individualism–Collectivism
One of Hofstede's cultural dimensions; describes the strength of the relation between an individual and other individuals in a society.

Hofstede's Cultural Dimensions

In a classic study of culture, Geert Hofstede identified four dimensions on which various cultures could be classified.[16] In a later study he added a fifth dimension that aids in characterizing cultures.[17] The relative scores for 10 major countries are provided in Table 15.2. **Individualism–collectivism** describes the strength of the relation between an individual and other individuals in the society—that is, the degree to which people act as individuals rather than as members of a group. In individualist cultures, such as the United States, Great Britain, and the Netherlands, people are expected to look

table 15.2

Cultural Dimension Scores for 10 Countries

	PD[a]	ID	MA	UA	LT
United States	40 L[b]	91 H	62 H	46 L	29 L
Germany	35 L	67 H	66 H	65 M	31 M
Japan	54 M	45 M	95 H	92 H	80 H
France	68 H	71 H	43 M	86 H	30[c] L
Netherlands	38 L	80 H	14 L	53 M	44 M
Hong Kong	68 H	25 L	57 H	29 L	96 H
Indonesia	78 H	14 L	46 M	48 L	25[c] L
West Africa	77 H	20 L	46 M	54 M	16 L
Russia	95[c] H	50[c] M	40[c] L	90[c] H	10[c] L
China	80[c] H	20[c] L	50[c] M	60[c] M	118 H

[a]PD = power distance; ID = individualism; MA = masculinity; UA = uncertainty avoidance; LT = long-term orientation.

[b]H = top third; M = medium third; L = bottom third (among 53 countries and regions for the first four dimensions; among 23 countries for the fifth).

[c]Estimated.

SOURCE: From Geert Hofstede, "Cultural Constraints in Management Theories," *Academy of Management Executive*, February 1993, Volume 7, number 1, p. 91. Copyright © 1993 by the Academy of Management (NY). Reproduced with permission of the Academy of Management (NY), via the Copyright Clearance Center.

after their own interests and the interests of their immediate families. The individual is expected to stand on her own two feet rather than be protected by the group. In collectivist cultures, such as Colombia, Pakistan, and Taiwan, people are expected to look after the interest of the larger community, which is expected to protect people when they are in trouble.

The second dimension, **power distance,** concerns how a culture deals with hierarchical power relationships—particularly the unequal distribution of power. It describes the degree of inequality among people that is considered to be normal. Cultures with small power distance, such as those of Denmark and Israel, seek to eliminate inequalities in power and wealth as much as possible, whereas countries with large power distances, such as India and the Philippines, seek to maintain those differences.

Differences in power distance often result in miscommunication and conflicts between people from different cultures. For example, in Mexico and Japan individuals are always addressed by their titles (Señor Smith or Smith-san, respectively). Individuals from the United States, however, often believe in minimizing power distances by using first names. Although this is perfectly normal, and possibly even advisable in the United States, it can be offensive and a sign of disrespect in other cultures.

The third dimension, **uncertainty avoidance,** describes how cultures seek to deal with the fact that the future is not perfectly predictable. It is defined as the degree to which people in a culture prefer structured over unstructured situations. Some cultures, such as those of Singapore and Jamaica, have weak uncertainty avoidance. They socialize individuals to accept this uncertainty and take each day as it comes. People from these cultures tend to be rather easygoing and flexible regarding different views. Other cultures, such as those of Greece and Portugal, socialize their people to seek security through technology, law, and religion. Thus these cultures provide clear rules as to how one should behave.

The **masculinity–femininity dimension** describes the division of roles between the sexes within a society. In "masculine" cultures, such as those of Germany and Japan, what are considered traditionally masculine values—showing off, achieving something visible, and making money—permeate the society. These societies stress assertiveness, performance, success, and competition. "Feminine" cultures, such as those of Sweden and Norway, promote values that have been traditionally regarded as feminine, such as putting relationships before money, helping others, and preserving the environment. These cultures stress service, care for the weak, and solidarity.

Finally, the fifth dimension comes from the philosophy of the Far East and is referred to as the **long-term–short-term orientation.** Cultures high on the long-term orientation focus on the future and hold values in the present that will not necessarily provide an immediate benefit, such as thrift (saving) and persistence. Hofstede found that many Far Eastern countries such as Japan and China have a long-term orientation. Short-term orientations, on the other hand, are found in the United States, Russia, and West Africa. These cultures are oriented toward the past and present and promote respect for tradition and for fulfilling social obligations.

The current Japanese criticism of management practices in the United States illustrates the differences in long-term–short-term orientation. Japanese managers, traditionally exhibiting a long-term orientation, engage in 5- to 10-year planning. This leads them to criticize U.S. managers, who are traditionally much more short-term in orientation because their planning often consists of quarterly to yearly time horizons.

These five dimensions help us understand the potential problems of managing employees from different cultures. Later in this chapter we will explore how these

Power Distance
One of Hofstede's cultural dimensions; describes how a culture deals with hierarchical power relationships.

Uncertainty Avoidance
One of Hofstede's cultural dimensions; describes how cultures seek to deal with an unpredictable future.

Masculinity–Femininity Dimension
One of Hofstede's cultural dimensions; describes the division of roles between the sexes within a society.

Long-Term–Short-Term Orientation
One of Hofstede's cultural dimensions; describes how a culture balances immediate benefits with future rewards.

cultural dimensions affect the acceptability and utility of various HRM practices. However, it is important to note that these differences can have a profound influence on whether a company chooses to enter a given country. One interesting finding of Hofstede's research was the impact of culture on a country's economic health. He found that countries with individualist cultures were more wealthy. Collectivist cultures with high power distance were all poor.[18] Cultures seem to affect a country's economy through their promotion of individual work ethics and incentives for individuals to increase their human capital. Figure 15.2 maps the countries Hofstede studied on the two characteristics of individualism–collectivism and economic success.

Implications of Culture for HRM

Cultures have an important impact on approaches to managing people. As we discuss later, the culture can strongly affect the education–human capital of a country, the political–legal system, and the economic system. As Hofstede found, culture also has a profound impact on a country's economic health by promoting certain values that either aid or inhibit economic growth.

More important to this discussion, however, is that cultural characteristics influence the ways managers behave in relation to subordinates, as well as the perceptions of the appropriateness of various HRM practices. First, cultures differ strongly on such things as how subordinates expect leaders to lead, how decisions are handled within the hierarchy, and (most important) what motivates individuals. For example, in Germany, managers achieve their status by demonstrating technical skills, so employees look to them to assign their tasks and resolve technical problems. In the Netherlands, on the other hand, managers focus on seeking consensus among all parties and must engage in an open-ended exchange of views and balancing of interests.[19] Clearly, these methods have different implications for selecting and training managers in the different countries.

Second, cultures may influence the appropriateness of HRM practices. For example, as previously discussed, the extent to which a culture promotes an individualistic versus a collectivist orientation will impact the effectiveness of individually oriented human resource management systems. In the United States, companies often focus selection systems on assessing an individual's technical skill and, to a lesser extent, social skills. In collectivist cultures, on the other hand, companies focus more on assessing how well an individual will perform as a member of the work group.

Similarly, cultures can influence compensation systems. Individualistic cultures such as those found in the United States often exhibit great differences between the highest- and lowest-paid individuals in an organization, with the highest-paid individual often receiving 200 times the salary of the lowest. Collectivist cultures, on the other hand, tend to have much flatter salary structures, with the top-paid individual receiving only about 20 times the overall pay of the lowest-paid one.

Cultural differences can affect the communication and coordination processes in organizations. Collectivist cultures, as well as those with less of an authoritarian orientation, value group decision making and participative management practices more highly than do individualistic cultures. When a person raised in an individualistic culture must work closely with those from a collectivist culture, communication problems and conflicts often appear. Much of the emphasis on "cultural diversity" programs in organizations focuses on understanding the cultures of others in order to better communicate with them.

figure 15.2

The Position of the Studied Countries on Their Individualism Index (IDV) versus Their 1970 National Wealth

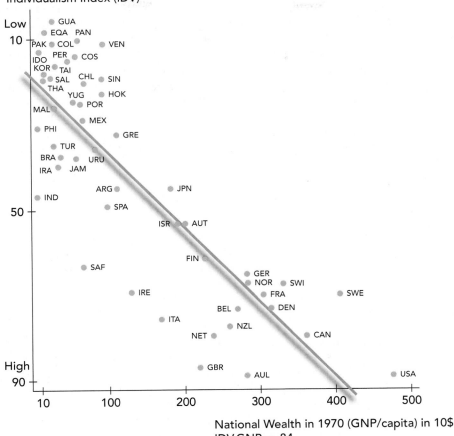

ARG	Argentina	FIN	Finland	KOR	South Korea	SWE	Sweden
AUL	Australia	FRA	France	MAL	Malaysia	SWI	Switzerland
AUT	Austria	GBR	Great Britain	MEX	Mexico	TAI	Taiwan
BEL	Belgium	GER	Germany	NET	Netherlands	THA	Thailand
BRA	Brazil	GRE	Greece	NOR	Norway	TUR	Turkey
CAN	Canada	GUA	Guatemala	NZL	New Zealand	URU	Uruguay
CHL	Chile	HOK	Hong Kong	PAK	Pakistan	USA	United States
COL	Colombia	IDO	Indonesia	PAN	Panama	VEN	Venezuela
COS	Costa Rica	IND	India	PER	Peru	WAF	West Africa
DEN	Denmark	IRA	Iran	PHI	Philippines		(Nigeria,
EAF	East Africa	IRE	Ireland	POR	Portugal		Ghana,
	(Kenya,	ISR	Israel	SAF	South Africa		Sierra Leone)
	Ethiopia,	ITA	Italy	SAL	El Salvador	YUG	Yugoslavia
	Zambia)	JAM	Jamaica	SIN	Singapore		
EQA	Equador	JPN	Japan	SPA	Spain		

SOURCE: G. Hofstede, "The Cultural Relativity of Organizational Practices and Theories," *Journal of International Business Studies* 14, no. 2 (Fall 1982), p. 89. Reprinted with permission of the author.

EVIDENCE-BASED HR

While national culture is important, recent research also suggests that its importance may be overstated. Researchers reexamining Hofstede's original work found that while differences existed across nations, significant cultural differences also existed within nations. They further found that the differences in cultures across organizations within countries was larger than the differences across countries. Their results imply that while one cannot ignore national culture, one must not think that certain HR practices may not be effective simply based on a regard for national culture. People of varying cultural backgrounds within a nation will be drawn to organizations whose cultures better match their individual, as opposed to national, value systems.

SOURCE: B. Gerhart and M. Fang, "National Culture and Human Resource Management: Assumptions and Evidence," *International Journal of Human Resource Management* 16, no. 6 (June 2005), pp. 971–86.

Education–Human Capital

A company's potential to find and maintain a qualified workforce is an important consideration in any decision to expand into a foreign market. Thus a country's human capital resources can be an important HRM issue. *Human capital* refers to the productive capabilities of individuals—that is, the knowledge, skills, and experience that have economic value.[20]

Countries differ in their levels of human capital. For example, as discussed in Chapter 1, the United States suffers from a human capital shortage because the jobs being created require skills beyond those of most new entrants into the workforce.[21] In former East Germany, there is an excess of human capital in terms of technical knowledge and skill because of that country's large investment in education. However, East Germany's business schools did not teach management development, so there is a human capital shortage for managerial jobs.[22] Similarly, companies in what used to be West Germany have shifted toward types of production and service that require high-skilled workers; this is creating a human capital shortage for high-skill jobs, yet the unemployment rate remains high because of a large number of low-skilled workers.[23] However, the high skills and low wages of workers in many countries make their labor forces quite attractive.

A country's human capital is determined by a number of variables. A major variable is the educational opportunities available to the labor force. In the Netherlands, for instance, government funding of school systems allows students to go all the way through graduate school without paying.[24] Similarly, the free education provided to citizens in the former Soviet bloc resulted in high levels of human capital, in spite of the poor infrastructure and economy that resulted from the socialist economic systems. In contrast, some Third World countries, such as Nicaragua and Haiti, have relatively low levels of human capital because of a lack of investment in education.

A country's human capital may profoundly affect a foreign company's desire to locate there or enter that country's market. Countries with low human capital attract facilities that require low skills and low wage levels. This explains why U.S. companies desire to move their currently unionized low-skill–high-wage manufacturing and assembly jobs to Mexico, where they can obtain low-skilled workers for substantially lower wages. Similarly, Japan ships its messy, low-skill work to neighboring countries while maintaining its high-skill work at home.[25] Countries like Mexico, with relatively low levels of human capital, might not be as attractive for operations that consist of more high-skill jobs.

Countries with high human capital are attractive sites for direct foreign investment that creates high-skill jobs. In Ireland, for example, more than 25 percent of 18-year-olds attend college, a rate much higher than other European countries. In addition, Ireland's economy supports only 1.1 million jobs for a population of 3.5 million. The combination of high education levels, a strong work ethic, and high unemployment makes the country attractive for foreign firms because of the resulting high productivity and low turnover. The Met Life insurance company set up a facility for Irish workers to analyze medical insurance claims. It has found the high levels of human capital and the high work ethic provide such a competitive advantage that the company is currently looking for other work performed in the United States to be shipped to Ireland. Similarly, as already discussed, the skills of newly graduated technology workers in India are as high or higher than those found among their counterparts in the United States. In addition, because jobs are not as plentiful in India, the worker attitudes are better in many of these locations.[26]

Political–Legal System

The regulations imposed by a country's legal system can strongly affect HRM. The political–legal system often dictates the requirements for certain HRM practices, such as training, compensation, hiring, firing, and layoffs. In large part, the legal system is an outgrowth of the culture in which it exists. Thus the laws of a particular country often reflect societal norms about what constitutes legitimate behavior.[27]

For example, the United States has led the world in eliminating discrimination in the workplace. Because of the importance this has in our culture, we also have legal safeguards such as equal employment opportunity laws (discussed in Chapter 3) that strongly affect the hiring and firing practices of firms. As a society, we also have strong beliefs regarding the equity of pay systems; thus the Fair Labor Standards Act (discussed in Chapter 11), among other laws and regulations, sets the minimum wage for a variety of jobs. We have regulations that dictate much of the process for negotiation between unions and management. These regulations profoundly affect the ways human resources are managed in the United States.

Similarly, the legal regulations regarding HRM in other countries reflect their societal norms. For example, in Germany employees have a legal right to "codetermination" at the company, plant, and individual levels. At the company level, a firm's employees have direct influence on the important decisions that affect them, such as large investments or new strategies. This is brought about through having employee representatives on the supervisory council (*Aufsichtsrat*). At the plant level, codetermination exists through works councils. These councils have no rights in the economic management of the company, but they can influence HRM policies on such issues as working hours, payment methods, hirings, and transfers. Finally, at the individual level, employees have contractual rights, such as the right to read their personnel files and the right to be informed about how their pay is calculated.[28]

The EEC provides another example of the effects of the political–legal system on HRM. The EEC's Community Charter of December 9, 1989, provides for the fundamental social rights of workers. These rights include freedom of movement, freedom to choose one's occupation and be fairly compensated, guarantee of social protection via Social Security benefits, freedom of association and collective bargaining, equal treatment for men and women, and a safe and healthful work environment, among others.

Economic System

A country's economic system influences HRM in a number of ways. As previously discussed, a country's culture is integrally tied to its economic system, and these systems provide many of the incentives for developing human capital. In socialist economic systems there are ample opportunities for developing human capital because the education system is free. However, under these systems, there is little economic incentive to develop human capital because there are no monetary rewards for increasing human capital. In addition, in former Soviet bloc countries, an individual's investment in human capital did not always result in a promotion. Rather, it was investment in the Communist Party that led to career advancements.

In capitalist systems the opposite situation exists. There is less opportunity to develop human capital without higher costs. (You have probably observed tuition increases at U.S. universities.) However, those who do invest in their individual human capital, particularly through education, are more able to reap monetary rewards, thus providing more incentive for such investment. In the United States, individuals' salaries usually reflect differences in human capital (high-skill workers receive higher compensation than low-skill workers). In fact, research estimates that an individual's wages increase by between 10 and 16 percent for each additional year of schooling.[29]

In addition to the effects of an economic system on HRM, the health of the system can have an important impact. For example, we referred earlier to lower labor costs in India. In developed countries with a high level of wealth, labor costs tend to be quite high relative to those in developing countries. While labor costs are related to the human capital of a country, they are not perfectly related, as shown by Figure 15.3. This chart provides a good example of the different hourly labor costs for manufacturing jobs in various countries.

An economic system also affects HRM directly through its taxes on compensation packages. Thus, the differential labor costs shown in Figure 15.3 do not always reflect the actual take-home pay of employees. Socialist systems are characterized by tax systems that redistribute wealth by taking a higher percentage of a person's income as she moves up the economic ladder. Capitalist systems attempt to reward individuals for their efforts by allowing them to keep more of their earnings. Companies that do business in other countries have to present compensation packages to expatriate managers that are competitive in take-home, rather than gross, pay. HRM responses to these issues affecting expatriate managers will be discussed in more detail later in this chapter.

These differences in economies can have a profound impact on pay systems, particularly among global companies seeking to develop an international compensation and reward system that maintains cost controls while enabling local operations to compete in the war for talent. One recent study examining how compensation managers design these systems indicates that they look at a number of factors including the global firm strategy, the local regulatory/political context, institutions and stakeholders, local markets, and national culture. While they try to learn from the best practices that exist globally, they balance these approaches with the constraints imposed by the local environment.[30] However, not just the hourly labor costs, but

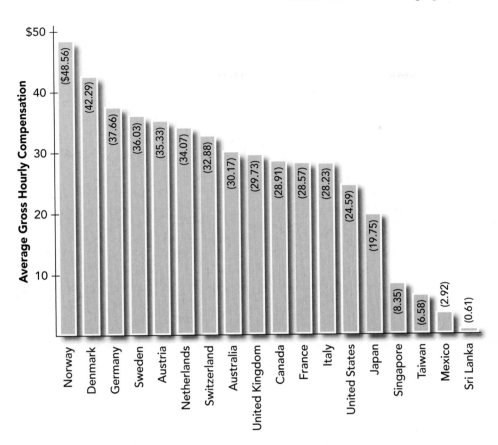

figure 15.3

Average Gross Hourly Compensation for Production Workers in Several Countries

SOURCE: U.S. Bureau of Labor Statistics, www.bls.gov/news.release/pdf/ichcc.pdf.

also the total cost of employees, affect decisions about where to locate workers. The "Competing through Globalization" box describes how and why cost-cutting strategies in India differ from those in the West.

In conclusion, every country varies in terms of its culture, human capital, legal system, and economic systems. These variations directly influence the types of HRM systems that must be developed to accommodate the particular situation. The extent to which these differences affect a company depends on how involved the company is in global markets. In the next sections we discuss important concepts of global business and various levels of global participation, particularly noting how these factors come into play.

Managing Employees in a Global Context

Types of International Employees

Before discussing the levels of global participation, we need to distinguish between parent countries, host countries, and third countries. A **parent country** is the country in which the company's corporate headquarters are located. For example, the United States is the parent country of General Motors. A **host country** is the country

Parent Country
The country in which a company's corporate headquarters is located.

Host Country
The country in which the parent country organization seeks to locate or has already located a facility.

LO3
List the different categories of international employees.

COMPETING THROUGH GLOBALIZATION
Managing the Economic Downturn: The Indian Way

As the global recession expands, one often sees different strategies for dealing with it across different countries. For instance, in the United States, companies quickly resort to laying off workers as a way of reducing labor costs and keeping headcount in line with production and demand. However, in India, companies by no means default to layoffs.

According to Vasanthi Srinivasan, a professor of organizational behavior and human resource management at the Indian Institute of Management, Bangalore (IIMB), "There is this paternalistic culture in our organizations, and therefore a sense of a moral obligation on the part of most managers to care for their employees. Organizations in India prefer to hold on to their people as much as possible. The feeling is that the employees have been with us in good times and contributed to the growth of the organization, so how can we let them go in tough times?"

Research suggests that Western and Indian companies have different approaches to managing the crisis. A survey by Watson Wyatt, revealed that 26 percent of U.S. employers expect to make layoffs in the next 12 months, while 25 percent will institute hiring freezes, 23 percent companywide restructurings, 12 percent salary freezes, and 4 percent salary reductions.

In contrast, Pothen Jacob, head of the human capital group, Watson Wyatt India, notes that "Watson Wyatt's Strategic Rewards Survey reveals that the most common approach in India is a combination of restructuring (67 percent), slower rates of salary increase (51 percent), and a hiring freeze (62 percent). Only a small percentage of companies have considered options like reduced workweek (10 percent), broad-based base pay reduction (3 percent), and early retirement (15 percent)." Pay cuts and job cuts do not make as much sense in India because

of the lack of a social safety net—which are not even on the radar in most places. Jacob suggests, "In the absence of a structured social net, the implications of a workforce reduction are both economic and emotional."

The implications are emotional because of the social stigma attached to losing a job. "In India, losing a job has more than just financial implications," says Srinivasan. "Because people work long hours at the workplace and are paid very well, their families tend to believe that they play a crucial role within the organization. If they were to suddenly lose their jobs, it is perceived as a reflection on their competence. The social environment does not understand that one can be asked to leave a job because there is an economic downturn."

SOURCE: "Job Cuts vs. Pay Cuts: In a Slowing Economy What's Better for India?" http://knowledge.wharton.upenn.edu/india/article.cfm?articleid=4333, accessed April 21, 2009.

Third Country
A country other than a host or parent country.

Expatriate
An employee sent by his or her company in one country to manage operations in a different country.

in which the parent country organization seeks to locate (or has already located) a facility. Thus Great Britain is a host country for General Motors because GM has operations there. A **third country** is a country other than the host country or parent country, and a company may or may not have a facility there.

There are also different categories of employees. **Expatriate** is the term generally used for employees sent by a company in one country to manage operations in a different country. With the increasing globalization of business, it is now important to distinguish among different types of expatriates. **Parent-country nationals (PCNs)** are employees who were born and live in the parent country. **Host-country nationals (HCNs)** are those employees who were born and raised in the host, as opposed to the parent, country. Finally, **third-country nationals (TCNs)** are employees born in a country other than the parent country and host country but who work in the host country. Thus, a manager born and raised in Brazil employed by an organization located in the United States and assigned to manage an operation in Thailand would be considered a TCN.

Research shows that countries differ in their use of various types of international employees. One study revealed that Japanese multinational firms have more ethnocentric HRM policies and practices (they tend to use Japanese expatriate managers more than local host-country nationals) than either European or U.S. firms. This study also found that the use of ethnocentric HRM practices is associated with more HRM problems.[31]

Levels of Global Participation

We often hear companies referred to as "multinational" or "international." However, it is important to understand the different levels of participation in international markets. This is especially important because as a company becomes more involved in international trade, different types of HRM problems arise. In this section we examine Nancy Adler's categorization of the various levels of international participation from which a company may choose.[32] Figure 15.4 depicts these levels of involvement.

Domestic

Most companies begin by operating within a domestic marketplace. For example, an entrepreneur may have an idea for a product that meets a need in the U.S. marketplace. This individual then obtains capital to build a facility that produces the product or service in a quantity that meets the needs of a small market niche. This requires recruiting, hiring, training, and compensating a number of individuals who will be involved in the production process, and these individuals are usually drawn from the local labor market. The focus of the selection and training programs is often on the employees' technical competence to perform job-related duties and to some extent on interpersonal skills. In addition, because the company is usually involved in only one labor market, determining the market rate of pay for various jobs is relatively easy.

Parent-Country Nationals (PCNs) Employees who were born and live in a parent country.

Host-Country Nationals (HCNs) Employees who were born and raised in the host, not the parent, country.

Third-Country Nationals (TCNs) Employees born in a country other than the parent or host country.

LO4
Identify the four levels of global participation and the HRM issues faced within each level.

figure 15.4
Levels of Global Participation

As the product grows in popularity, the owner might choose to build additional facilities in different parts of the country to reduce the costs of transporting the product over large distances. In deciding where to locate these facilities, the owner must consider the attractiveness of the local labor markets. Various parts of the country may have different cultures that make those areas more or less attractive according to the work ethics of the potential employees. Similarly, the human capital in the different areas may vary greatly because of differences in educational systems. Finally, local pay rates may differ. It is for these reasons that the U.S. economy in the past 10 years has experienced a movement of jobs from northern states, which are characterized by strong unions and high labor costs, to the Sunbelt states, which have lower labor costs and are less unionized.

Incidentally, even domestic companies face problems with cultural diversity. In the United States, for example, the representation of women and minorities is increasing within the workforce. These groups come to the workplace with worldviews that differ from those of the traditional white male. Thus, we are seeing more and more emphasis on developing systems for managing cultural diversity within single-country organizations, even though the diversity might be on a somewhat smaller scale than the diversity of cultures across national boundaries.[33]

It is important to note that companies functioning at the domestic level face an environment with very similar cultural, human capital, political–legal, and economic situations, although some variation might be observed across states and geographic areas.

International

As more competitors enter the domestic market, companies face the possibility of losing market share; thus they often seek other markets for their products. This usually requires entering international markets, initially by exporting products but ultimately by building production facilities in other countries. The decision to participate in international competition raises a host of human resource issues. All the problems regarding locating facilities are magnified. One must consider whether a particular location provides an environment where human resources can be successfully acquired and managed.

Now the company faces an entirely different situation with regard to culture, human capital, the political–legal system, and the economic system. For example, the availability of human capital is of utmost importance, and there is a substantially greater variability in human capital between the United States and other countries than there is among the various states in the United States.

A country's legal system may also present HRM problems. For example, France has a relatively high minimum wage, which drives labor costs up. In addition, regulations make it extremely difficult to fire or lay off an employee. In Germany companies are legally required to offer employees influence in the management of the firm. Companies that develop facilities in other countries have to adapt their HRM practices to conform to the host country's laws. This requires the company to gain expertise in the country's HRM legal requirements and knowledge about how to deal with the country's legal system, and it often requires the company to hire one or more HCNs. In fact, some countries legally require companies to hire a certain percentage of HCNs for any foreign-owned subsidiary.

Finally, cultures have to be considered. To the extent that the country's culture is vastly different from that of the parent organization, conflicts, communication problems, and morale problems may occur. Expatriate managers must be trained to identify these cultural differences, and they must be flexible enough to adapt their styles to those of their host country. This requires an extensive selection effort to identify individuals who are capable of adapting to new environments and an extensive training program to ensure that the culture shock is not devastating.

Multinational

Whereas international companies build one or a few facilities in another country, they become multinational when they build facilities in a number of different countries, attempting to capitalize on lower production and distribution costs in different locations. The lower production costs are gained by shifting production from higher-cost locations to lower-cost locations. For example, some of the major U.S. automakers have plants all over the world. They continue to shift their production from the United States, where labor unions have gained high wages for their members, to *maquiladora* facilities in Mexico, where the wages are substantially lower. Similarly, these companies minimize distribution and labor costs by locating facilities in central and eastern European countries such as Poland, Hungary, and the Slovak Republic for manufacturing and assembling automobiles to sell in the European market.

The HRM problems multinational companies face are similar to those international companies face, only magnified. Instead of having to consider only one or two countries' cultural, human capital, legal, and economic systems, the multinational company must address these differences for a large number of countries. This accentuates the need to select managers capable of functioning in a variety of settings, give them necessary training, and provide flexible compensation systems that take into account the different market pay rates, tax systems, and costs of living.

Multinational companies now employ many "inpatriates"—managers from different countries who become part of the corporate headquarters staff. This creates a need to integrate managers from different cultures into the culture of the parent company. In addition, multinational companies now take more expatriates from countries other than the parent country and place them in facilities of other countries. For example, a manager from Scotland, working for a U.S. company, might be assigned to run an operation in South Africa. This practice accentuates the need for cross-cultural training to provide managerial skills for interaction with individuals from different cultures.

Global

Many researchers now propose a fourth level of integration: global organizations. Global organizations compete on state-of-the-art, top-quality products and services and do so with the lowest costs possible. Whereas multinational companies attempt to develop identical products distributed worldwide, global companies increasingly emphasize flexibility and mass customization of products to meet the needs of particular clients. Multinational companies are usually driven to locate facilities in a country as a means of reaching that country's market or lowering production costs, and the company must deal with the differences across the countries. Global firms, on the other hand, choose to locate a facility based on the ability to effectively, efficiently, and flexibly produce a product or service and attempt to create synergy through the cultural differences.

This creates the need for HRM systems that encourage flexible production (thus presenting a host of HRM issues). These companies proactively consider the cultures,

Sustainable development usually consists of a focus in three areas: the environmental, economic, and social performance. Dow Chemical Company recently announced an effort that exemplifies how strategically thinking about sustainability can simultaneously promote all three aspects. Recycling of paper and plastic is a key component of Dow's 2015 Sustainability Goals, according to Jim Hummel, human resources director for Michigan Operations and the WeCycle team leader. While some materials are easy to recycle, others present great problems. "We've had recycling programs in the past, but we could not recycle sticky notes or envelopes with windows."

Enter a partnership with the Arnold Center, a group that for 40 years has focused on providing people with disabilities with work skills and income from performing that work. Arnold employees perform all types of jobs, from shipping and sorting recyclables to caring for flower beds. Dow will use Arnold employees to help sort through their recycled goods, employing 15 new workers initially, with the expectation to grow that to 26 later on.

In addition to creating jobs for disabled people, Dow projects tremendous environmental and economic impact. The recycling effort can save 3 million gallons of water, 1,800 barrels of oil, and 1 million kilowatt-hours and can keep pollutants out of the air. They will also recycle three-ring binders for local schools to use. Hummel says, "We are projecting savings in tens of thousands of dollars, and reducing the refuse that goes to landfills by 30 percent."

SOURCE: C. Heng, "Dow Partners with Recycling Initiative," *Saginaw News (Michigan)*, July 8, 2008.

Transnational Scope
A company's ability to make HRM decisions from an international perspective.

Transnational Representation
Reflects the multinational composition of a company's managers.

Transnational Process
The extent to which a company's planning and decision-making processes include representatives and ideas from a variety of cultures.

human capital, political–legal systems, and economic systems to determine where production facilities can be located to provide a competitive advantage. Global companies have multiple headquarters spread across the globe, resulting in less hierarchically structured organizations that emphasize decentralized decision making. This results in the need for human resource systems that recruit, develop, retain, and use managers and executives who are competent transnationally.

A transnational HRM system is characterized by three attributes.[34] **Transnational scope** refers to the fact that HRM decisions must be made from a global rather than a national or regional perspective. This creates the need to make decisions that balance the need for uniformity (to ensure fair treatment of all employees) with the need for flexibility (to meet the needs of employees in different countries). **Transnational representation** reflects the multinational composition of a company's managers. Global participation does not necessarily ensure that each country is providing managers to the company's ranks. This is a prerequisite if the company is to achieve the next attribute. **Transnational process** refers to the extent to which the company's planning and decision-making processes include representatives and ideas from a variety of cultures. This attribute allows for diverse viewpoints and knowledge associated with different cultures, increasing the quality of decision making.

These three characteristics are necessary for global companies to achieve cultural synergy. Rather than simply integrating foreigners into the domestic organization, a successful transnational company needs managers who will treat managers from other cultures as equals. This synergy can be accomplished only by combining selection, training, appraisal, and compensation systems in such a way that managers have a transnational rather than a parochial orientation. However, a survey of 50 companies in the United States and Canada found that global companies' HRM systems are far less transnational in scope, representation, and process than the companies' strategic planning systems and organizational structures.[35]

In conclusion, entry into international markets creates a host of HRM issues that must be addressed if a company is to gain competitive advantage. Once the choice has been made to compete in a global arena, companies must seek to manage employees who are sent to foreign countries (expatriates and third-country nationals). This causes the need to shift from focusing only on the culture, human capital, political–legal, and economic influences of the host country to examining ways to manage the expatriate managers who must be located there. Selection systems must be developed that allow the company to identify managers capable of functioning in a new culture. These managers must be trained to identify the important aspects of the new culture in which they will live as well as the relevant legal–political and economic systems. Finally, these managers must be compensated to offset the costs of uprooting themselves and their families to move to a new situation vastly different from their previous lives. In the next section we address issues regarding management of expatriates.

Managing Expatriates in Global Markets

We have outlined the major macro-level factors that influence HRM in global markets. These factors can affect a company's decision whether to build facilities in a given country. In addition, if a company does develop such facilities, these factors strongly affect the HRM practices used. However, one important issue that has been recognized over the past few years is the set of problems inherent in selecting, training, compensating, and reintegrating expatriate managers.

According to a recent study by the National Foreign Trade Council (NFTC), there were 250,000 Americans on assignments overseas and that number was expected to increase. In addition, the NFTC estimates that the average one-time cost for relocating an expatriate is $60,000.[36] The importance to the company's profitability of making the right expatriate assignments should not be underestimated. Expatriate managers' average compensation package is approximately $250,000,[37] and the cost of an unsuccessful expatriate assignment (that is, a manager returning early) is approximately $100,000.[38] The failure rate for expatriate assignments among U.S. firms had been estimated at between 15 and 40 percent. However, more recent research suggests that the current figure is much lower. Some recent studies of European multinationals put the rate at 5 percent for most firms. While the failure rate is generally recognized as higher among U.S. multinationals, it is doubtful that the number reaches the 15–40 percent range.[39]

In the final section of the chapter, we discuss the major issues relevant to the management of expatriate managers. These issues cover the selection, training, compensation, and reacculturation of expatriates.

Selection of Expatriate Managers

One of the major problems in managing expatriate managers is determining which individuals in the organization are most capable of handling an assignment in a different culture. Expatriate managers must have technical competence in the area of operations; otherwise they will be unable to earn the respect of subordinates. However, technical competence has been almost the sole variable used in deciding whom

LO5
Discuss the ways companies attempt to select, train, compensate, and reintegrate expatriate managers.

to send on overseas assignments, despite the fact that multiple skills are necessary for successful performance in these assignments.[40]

A successful expatriate manager must be sensitive to the country's cultural norms, flexible enough to adapt to those norms, and strong enough to make it through the inevitable culture shock. In addition, the manager's family must be similarly capable of adapting to the new culture. These adaptive skills have been categorized into three dimensions:[41] (1) the self dimension (the skills that enable a manager to maintain a positive self-image and psychological well-being), (2) the relationship dimension (the skills required to foster relationships with the host-country nationals), and (3) the perception dimension (those skills that enable a manager to accurately perceive and evaluate the host environment). One study of international assignees found that they considered the following five factors to be important in descending order of importance: family situation, flexibility and adaptability, job knowledge and motivation, relational skills, and extracultural openness.[42] Table 15.3 presents a series of considerations and questions to ask potential expatriate managers to assess their ability to adapt to a new cultural environment.

Little evidence suggests that U.S. companies have invested much effort in attempting to make correct expatriate selections. One researcher found that only 5 percent of the firms surveyed administered any tests to determine the degree to which expatriate candidates possessed cross-cultural skills.[43] More recent research reveals that only 35 percent of firms choose expatriates from multiple candidates and that those firms emphasize only technical job-related experience and skills in making these decisions.[44] These findings glaringly demonstrate that U.S. organizations need to improve their success rate in overseas assignments. As discussed in Chapter 6, the technology for assessing individuals' knowledge, skills, and abilities has advanced. The potential for selection testing to decrease the failure rate and productivity problems of U.S. expatriate managers seems promising. For instance, recent research has examined the "Big Five" personality dimensions as predictors of expatriate success (remember these from Chapter 6). For instance, one study distinguished between expatriate success as measured by not terminating the assignment and success as measured by supervisory evaluations of the expatriate. The researcher found that agreeableness, emotional stability, and extraversion were negatively related to the desire to terminate the assignment (i.e., they wanted to stay on the assignment longer), and conscientiousness was positively related to supervisory evaluations of the expatriate.[45]

A final issue with regard to expatriate selection is the use of women in expatriate assignments. For a long time U.S. firms believed that women would not be successful managers in countries where women have not traditionally been promoted to management positions (such as in Japan and other Asian countries). However, recent evidence indicates that this is not true. Robin Abrams, an expatriate manager for Apple Computer's Hong Kong office, states that nobody cares whether "you are wearing trousers or a skirt if you have demonstrated core competencies." In fact, some women believe that the novelty of their presence among a group of men increases their credibility with locals. In fact, some research suggests that male and female expatriates can perform equally well in international assignments, regardless of the country's cultural predispositions toward women in management. However, female expatriates self-rate their adjustment lower in countries that have few women in the workforce.[46] Also research has shown that female expatriates were perceived as being effective regardless of the cultural toughness of the host country.[47] And the fact is that female expatriates feel more strongly than their supervisors that prejudice does

table 15.3

Interview Worksheet for International Candidates

Motivation
- Investigate reasons and degree of interest in wanting to be considered.
- Determine desire to work abroad, verified by previous concerns such as personal travel, language training, reading, and association with foreign employees or students.
- Determine whether the candidate has a realistic understanding of what working and living abroad requires.
- Determine the basic attitudes of the spouse toward an overseas assignment.

Health
- Determine whether any medical problems of the candidate or his or her family might be critical to the success of the assignment.
- Determine whether he or she is in good physical and mental health, without any foreseeable change.

Language ability
- Determine potential for learning a new language.
- Determine any previous language(s) studied or oral ability (judge against language needed on the overseas assignment).
- Determine the ability of the spouse to meet the language requirements.

Family considerations
- How many moves has the family made in the past among different cities or parts of the United States?
- What problems were encountered?
- How recent was the last move?
- What is the spouse's goal in this move?
- What are the number of children and the ages of each?
- Has divorce or its potential, or death of a family member, weakened family solidarity?
- Will all the children move? Why or why not?
- What are the location, health, and living arrangements of grandparents and the number of trips normally made to their home each year?
- Are there any special adjustment problems that you would expect?
- How is each member of the family reacting to this possible move?
- Do special educational problems exist within the family?

Resourcefulness and initiative
- Is the candidate independent; can he make and stand by his decisions and judgments?
- Does she have the intellectual capacity to deal with several dimensions simultaneously?
- Is he able to reach objectives and produce results with whatever personnel and facilities are available, regardless of the limitations and barriers that might arise?
- Can the candidate operate without a clear definition of responsibility and authority on a foreign assignment?
- Will the candidate be able to explain the aims and company philosophy to the local managers and workers?
- Does she possess sufficient self-discipline and self-confidence to overcome difficulties or handle complex problems?
- Can the candidate work without supervision?
- Can the candidate operate effectively in a foreign environment without normal communications and supporting services?

Adaptability
- Is the candidate sensitive to others, open to the opinions of others, cooperative, and able to compromise?
- What are his reactions to new situations, and efforts to understand and appreciate differences?
- Is she culturally sensitive, aware, and able to relate across the culture?
- Does the candidate understand his own culturally derived values?
- How does the candidate react to criticism?
- What is her understanding of the U.S. government system?
- Will he be able to make and develop contacts with peers in the foreign country?
- Does she have patience when dealing with problems?
- Is he resilient; can he bounce back after setbacks?

(continues)

table 15.3

Interview Worksheet for International Candidates (*concluded*)

Career planning
- Does the candidate consider the assignment anything other than a temporary overseas trip?
- Is the move consistent with her progression and that planned by the company?
- Is his career planning realistic?
- What is the candidate's basic attitude toward the company?
- Is there any history or indication of interpersonal problems with this employee?

Financial
- Are there any current financial and/or legal considerations that might affect the assignment, such as house purchase, children and college expenses, car purchases?
- Are financial considerations negative factors? Will undue pressures be brought to bear on the employee or her family as a result of the assignment?

SOURCE: Reprinted with permission from *Multinational People Management*, pp. 55–57, by D. M. Noer. Copyright © 1989 by the Bureau of National Affairs, Inc., Washington, DC 20037.

not limit women's ability to be successful.[48] The "Competing through Technology" box describes how companies utilize computerized scheduling systems to help with labor costs, especially in retail settings.

Training and Development of Expatriates

Once an expatriate manager has been selected, it is necessary to prepare that manager for the upcoming assignment. Because these individuals already have job-related skills, some firms have focused development efforts on cross-cultural training. A review of the cross-cultural training literature found support for the belief that cross-cultural training has an impact on effectiveness.[49] However, in spite of this, cross-cultural training is hardly universal. According to one 1995 survey, nearly 40 percent of the respondents offered no cross-cultural preparation to expatriates.[50]

What exactly is emphasized in cross-cultural training programs? The details regarding these programs were discussed in Chapter 7. However, for now, it is important to know that most attempt to create an appreciation of the host country's culture so that expatriates can behave appropriately.[51] This entails emphasizing a few aspects of cultural sensitivity. First, expatriates must be clear about their own cultural background, particularly as it is perceived by the host nationals. With an accurate cultural self-awareness, managers can modify their behavior to accentuate the effective characteristics while minimizing those that are dysfunctional.[52]

Second, expatriates must understand the particular aspects of culture in the new work environment. Although culture is an elusive, almost invisible phenomenon, astute expatriate managers must perceive the culture and adapt their behavior to it. This entails identifying the types of behaviors and interpersonal styles that are considered acceptable in both business meetings and social gatherings. For example, Germans value promptness for meetings to a much greater extent than do Latin Americans. Table 15.4 displays some ways body language conveys different messages in different countries.

Finally, expatriates must learn to communicate accurately in the new culture. Some firms attempt to use expatriates who speak the language of the host country, and a few

```
1001 0100 0110
1100
100
1011    WWW
```

COMPETING THROUGH TECHNOLOGY
The Perils of Technology-Based Scheduling

One of the boxes in Chapter 2 discussed the ways that computerized scheduling systems can help manage labor costs, particularly with retail stores. While companies such as Wal-Mart and Payless Shoes are using these systems as means of scheduling the right number of people given the predicted customer volume, one should be cautious before heading full-bore in such a direction—because sometimes the systems have unintended consequences.

First, some of the scheduling systems, such as that used by Ann Taylor, include sales performance as one of the variables considered when designing the human resource plan for the week. High performers get the best schedules and the most hours, while low performers are scheduled for fewer hours and at less-than-optimum times.

Certainly this rewards the high performers (and, thus, encourages them to stay) and punishes the low performers (and encourages them to leave), both of which are positive outcomes. However, it can also have detrimental effects on the workforce. For instance, the new hire who has great motivation to sell, and will, with experience and the right opportunities, end up being effective, may not get scheduled in a way that gives them the experience and opportunities they need, causing them to leave for a competitor.

In addition, in the retail industry success often derives less from great corporate tower strategies and more from skilled, committed employees who constantly face customers. Erin Armendinger, managing director of Wharton's Jay H.

Baker Retailing, notes, "To your customer, your store's people are your brand," she says. Those "in the corporate office sometimes forget that people on the front line mean more than any strategy you come up with at the corporate office. To treat them as if they are numbers is a little bit disturbing."

While information systems can provide value to organizations, one must never lose sight of the "humans" in human resource management. Stores may have regular fluctuations in customer volumes, but employees have mortgages, car payments, and family responsibilities that don't lend themselves to fluctuating schedules.

SOURCE: "On the Clock: Are Retail Sales People Getting the Wrong End of the Stick?" http://knowledge.wharton. upenn.edu/article.cfm?articleid=2066, accessed April 21, 2009.

provide language training. However, most companies simply assume that the host-country nationals all speak the parent-country's language. Although this assumption might be true, seldom do these nationals speak the parent-country language fluently. Thus, expatriate managers must be trained to communicate with others when language barriers exist. Table 15.5 offers some tips for communicating across language barriers.

Effective cross-cultural training helps ease an expatriate's transition to the new work environment. It can also help avoid costly mistakes, such as the expatriate who attempted to bring two bottles of brandy into the Muslim country of Qatar. The brandy was discovered by customs; not only was the expatriate deported, the company was also "disinvited" from the country.[53]

Compensation of Expatriates

One of the more troublesome aspects of managing expatriates is determining the compensation package. As previously discussed, these packages average $250,000, but it is necessary to examine the exact breakdown of these packages. Most use a

table 15.4

International Body Language

COUNTRY	NONVERBAL MESSAGES
Argentina	If the waiter approaches pointing to the side of his head and making a spinning gesture with their finger, don't think they've lost it—they're trying to say you have a phone call.
Bangladesh	Bursting to go to the toilet? Hold it. It is considered very rude to excuse yourself from the table to use the bathroom.
Bolivia	Don't make "the sign of the fig" (thumb protruding between index and middle finger), historically a sign that you couldn't care less—it is very insulting.
Bulgaria	Bulgarians nod the head up and down to mean no, not yes. To say yes, a Bulgarian nods the head back and forth.
China	In Eastern culture, silence really can be golden. So don't panic if long periods of silence form part of your meeting with Chinese clients. It simply means they are considering your proposal carefully.
Egypt	As across the Arab world the left hand is unclean, use your right to accept business cards and to greet someone. Use only your right hand for eating.
Fiji	To show respect to your Fijian hosts when addressing them, stand with your arms folded behind your back.
France	The French don't like strong handshakes, preferring a short, light grip or air kissing. If your French colleague is seen to be playing an imaginary flute, however, it means he thinks you are not being truthful.
Germany	When Germans meet across a large conference table and it is awkward to reach over and shake hands, they will instead rap their knuckles lightly on the table by way of a greeting.
Greece	Beware of making the okay sign to Greek colleagues as it signifies bodily orifices. A safer bet is the thumbs-up sign. The thumbs-down, however, is the kind of gesture reserved for when a Greek motorist cuts you off on the highway.
Hong Kong	When trying to attract someone's attention, don't use your index finger with palm extended upward. This is how the Cantonese call their dogs.
India	Beware of whistling in public—it is the height of rudeness here.
Japan	Japan is a real minefield for Western businesspeople, but one that always gets to them is the way the Japanese heartily slurp their noodles at lunch. Far from being rude, it actually shows appreciation of the food in Japanese culture.
Jordan	No matter how hungry you are, it is customary to refuse seconds from your host twice before finally accepting a third time.
Lebanon	Itchy eyebrow? Don't scratch it. Licking your little finger and brushing it across your eyebrow is provocative.
Malaysia	If you find a Malaysian standing with hands on hips before you, you've clearly said something wrong. It means he's livid.
Mexico	Mexicans are very tactile and often perform a bizarre handshake whereby, after pressing together the palms, they will slide their hands upward to grasp each other's thumbs.
Netherlands	The Dutch may seem open-minded, but if Dutch people tap the underside of their elbow, it means they think you're unreliable.
Pakistan	The overt display of a closed fist is an incitement to war.
Philippines	The "Roger Moore" is a common greeting here—a quick flash of the eyebrows supersedes the need for handshakes.
Russia	The Russians are highly tactile meet and greeters, with bear hugs and kisses direct on the lips commonplace. Don't take this habit to nearby Uzbekistan, however. They'd probably shoot you.
Saudi Arabia	If a Saudi man takes another's hand on the street, it's a sign of mutual respect.
Samoa	When your new Samoan host offers you a cup of the traditional drink, kava, make sure to deliberately spill a few drops on the ground before taking your first sip.
Turkey	Be careful not to lean back on your chair and point the sole of your foot at anyone in a meeting in Istanbul. Pointing with the underside of the foot is highly insulting.

SOURCES: http://www.businesstravelerusa.com/articles.php?articleID=490 Business Traveler Center; R. Axtell, *Gestures: The Dos and Taboos of Body Language Around the World,* (New York: John Wiley and Sons, 1991); P. Harris and R. Moran, *Managing Cultural Differences,* 3rd ed. (Houston, TX: Gulf Publishing Company, 1991); R. Linowes, "The Japanese Manager's Traumatic Entry into the United States: Understanding the American-Japanese Cultural Divide," *Academy of Management Executive* 7, no. 4 (1993), p. 26; D. Doke, "Perfect Strangers," *HR Magazine,* December 2004, pp. 62–68.

table 15.5

Communicating across Language Barriers

Verbal behavior

- *Clear, slow speech.* Enunciate each word. Do not use colloquial expressions.
- *Repetition.* Repeat each important idea using different words to explain the same concept.
- *Simple sentences.* Avoid compound, long sentences.
- *Active verbs.* Avoid passive verbs.

Nonverbal behavior

- *Visual restatements.* Use as many visual restatements as possible, such as pictures, graphs, tables, and slides.
- *Gestures.* Use more facial and hand gestures to emphasize the meaning of words.
- *Demonstration.* Act out as many themes as possible.
- *Pauses.* Pause more frequently.
- *Summaries.* Hand out written summaries of your verbal presentation.

Attribution

- *Silence.* When there is a silence, wait. Do not jump in to fill the silence. The other person is probably just thinking more slowly in the nonnative language or translating.
- *Intelligence.* Do not equate poor grammar and mispronunciation with lack of intelligence; it is usually a sign of second-language use.
- *Differences.* If unsure, assume difference, not similarity.

Comprehension

- *Understanding.* Do not just assume that they understand; assume that they do not understand.
- *Checking comprehension.* Have colleagues repeat their understanding of the material back to you. Do not simply ask whether they understand or not. Let them explain what they understand to you.

Design

- *Breaks.* Take more frequent breaks. Second-language comprehension is exhausting.
- *Small modules.* Divide the material into smaller modules.
- *Longer time frame.* Allocate more time for each module than usual in a monolingual program.

Motivation

- *Encouragement.* Verbally and nonverbally encourage and reinforce speaking by nonnative language participants.
- *Drawing out.* Explicitly draw out marginal and passive participants.
- *Reinforcement.* Do not embarrass novice speakers.

SOURCE: From Nancy Adler, *International Dimensions of Organizational Behavior,* 2nd ed., pp. 84–85. Copyright © 1991. South-Western, a part of Cengage Learning, Inc. Reproduced by permission. www.cengage.com/permissions.

balance sheet approach to determine the total package level. This approach entails developing a total compensation package that equalizes the purchasing power of the expatriate manager with that of employees in similar positions in the home country and provides incentives to offset the inconveniences incurred in the location. Purchasing power includes all of the expenses associated with the expatriate assignment. Expenses include goods and services (food, personal care, clothing, recreation, and transportation), housing (for a principal residence), income taxes (paid to federal and

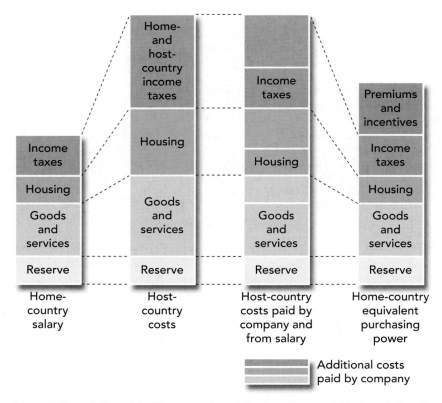

figure 15.5

The Balance Sheet for Determining Expatriate Compensation

SOURCE: From C. Reynolds, "Compensation of Overseas Personnel," in Joseph Famularo, ed., *Handbook of Human Resource Administration*, 2nd ed., 1986. Copyright © 1986 The McGraw-Hill Companies.

local governments), reserve (savings, payments for benefits, pension contributions), and shipment and storage (costs associated with moving and/or storing personal belongings). A typical balance sheet is shown in Figure 15.5.

As you can see from this figure, the employee starts with a set of costs for taxes, housing, goods and services, and reserve. However, in the host country, these costs are significantly higher. Thus the company must make up the difference between costs in the home and those in the host country, and then provide a premium and/or incentive for the employee to go through the trouble of living in a different environment. Table 15.6 provides an idea of just how much these add-ons can cost for an

table 15.6

Average Amount of Allowance as a Percentage of Base Pay

Housing (purchase)	38%
Goods and services (cost of living)	24
Education	22
Position	17
Hardship	13

SOURCE: From B. Fitzgerald-Turner, *HR Magazine*, 1997. Copyright © 1997 by the Society for Human Resource Management. Reprinted with permission of *HR Magazine*, published by the Society for Human Resource Management, Alexandria, VA, via the Copyright Clearance Center.

expatriate. As we see, these combined benefits amount to a 114 percent increase in compensation cost above the base pay.

Total pay packages have four components. First, there is the base salary. Determining the base salary is not a simple matter, however. Fluctuating exchange rates between countries may make an offered salary a raise some of the time, a pay cut at other times. In addition, the base salary may be based on comparable pay in the parent country, or it may be based on the prevailing market rates for the job in the host country. Expatriates are often offered a salary premium beyond that of their present salary as an inducement to accept the expatriate assignment.

Tax equalization allowances are a second component. They are necessary because of countries' different taxation systems in high-tax countries. For example, a senior executive earning $100,000 in Belgium (with a maximum marginal tax rate of 70.8 percent) could cost a company almost $1 million in taxes over five to seven years.[54] Under most tax equalization plans, the company withholds the amount of tax to be paid in the home country, then pays all of the taxes accrued in the host country.

A third component, benefits, presents additional compensation problems. Most of the problems have to do with the transportability of the benefits. For example, if an expatriate contributing to a pension plan in the United States is moved to a different country, does the individual have a new pension in the host country, or should the individual be allowed to contribute to the existing pension in her home country? What about health care systems located in the United States? How does the company ensure that expatriate employees have equal health care coverage? For example, in one company, the different health care plans available resulted in situations where it might cost significantly less to have the employee fly to the United States to have a procedure performed rather than to have it done in the host country. However, the health plans did not allow this alternative.

Finally, allowances are often offered to make the expatriate assignment less unattractive. Cost-of-living allowances are payments that offset the differences in expenditures on day-to-day necessities between the host country and the parent country. For instance, Table 15.7 shows the differences in cost of living among some of the larger international cities. Housing allowances ensure that the expatriate can maintain the same home-country living standard. Education allowances reimburse expatriates for

CITY	INDEX
1 Tokyo, Japan	134.7
2 London	120.3
9 Hong Kong	109.5
13 New York City	100.0
14 Dublin	100.0
20 Sydney	95.2
30 Shanghai	90.4
34 Singapore	88.0
40 Glasgow	87.5
47 Birmingham	85.8

table 15.7
Global Cost of Living Survey: Ranking of Selected Cities among the Top 50 International Cities, 2005

Note: Base city New York = 100.
SOURCE: Mercer Human Resource Consulting, "Worldwide Cost of Living—City Rankings, 2005," *Global Cost of Living Survey*, 2005.

figure 15.6

International
Assignment
Allowance Form

John H. Doe		1 October 2004	
Name		**Effective date**	
Singapore		Manager, SLS./Serv. AP/ME	
Location of assignment		**Title**	

Houston, Texas	1234	202	202
Home base	**Emp. no.**	**LCA code**	**Tax code**

Reason for Change: _____ International Assignment _____

	Old	New
Monthly base salary	_____	$5,000.00
Living cost allowance	_____	$1,291.00
Foreign service premium	_____	$ 750.00
Area allowance	_____	-0-
Gross monthly salary	_____	$7,041.00
Housing deduction	_____	$ 500.00
Hypothetical tax	_____	$ 570.00
Other	_____	_____
Net monthly salary	_____	$5,971.00

_____	_____
Prepared by	**Date**
_____	_____
Vice President, Human Resources	**Date**

the expense of placing their children in private English-speaking schools. Relocation allowances cover all the expenses of making the actual move to a new country,
including transportation to and from the new location, temporary living expenses,
and shipping and/or storage of personal possessions. Figure 15.6 illustrates a typical
summary sheet for an expatriate manager's compensation package.

The cost of a U.S. expatriate working in another country is approximately three
to four times that of a comparable U.S. employee.[55] In addition, "about 38 percent
of multinational companies surveyed by KPMG LLP for its 2006 Global Assignment
Policies and Practices say overseas assignment programs are 'more generous than they

need to be.'"[56] These two facts combined have put pressure on global organizations to rethink their tax equalization strategy and expatriate packages.

Reacculturation of Expatriates

A final issue of importance to managing expatriates is dealing with the reacculturation process when the managers reenter their home country. Reentry is no simple feat. Culture shock takes place in reverse. The individual has changed, the company has changed, and the culture has changed while the expatriate was overseas. According to one source, 60 to 70 percent of expatriates did not know what their position would be upon their return, and 46 percent ended up with jobs that gave them reduced autonomy and authority.[57] Twenty percent of workers want to leave the company when they return from an overseas assignment, and this presents potentially serious morale and productivity problems.[58] In fact, the most recent estimates are that 25 percent of expatriate managers leave the company within one year of returning from their expatriate assignments.[59] If these repatriates leave, the company has virtually no way to recoup its substantial investment in human capital.[60]

Companies are increasingly making efforts to help expatriates through reacculturation. Two characteristics help in this transition process: communication and validation.[61] *Communication* refers to the extent to which the expatriate receives information and recognizes changes while abroad. The closer the contact with the home organization while abroad, the more proactive, effective, and satisfied the expatriate will be upon reentry. *Validation* refers to the amount of recognition received by the expatriate upon return home. Expatriates who receive recognition from their peers and their bosses for their foreign work and their future potential contribution to the company have fewer troubles with reentry compared with those who are treated as if they were "out of the loop." Given the tremendous investment that firms make in expatriate employees, usually aimed at providing global experience that will help the company, firms certainly do not want to lose expatriates after their assignments have concluded.

Finally, one research study noted the role of an expatriate manager's expectations about the expatriate assignment in determining repatriation adjustment and job performance. This study found that managers whose job expectations (constraints and demands in terms of volume and performance standards) and nonwork expectations (living and housing conditions) were met exhibited a greater degree of repatriation adjustment and higher levels of job performance.[62] Monsanto has an extensive repatriation program that begins long before the expatriate returns. The program entails providing extensive information regarding the potential culture shock of repatriation and information on how family members, friends, and the office environment might have changed. Then, a few months after returning, expatriate managers hold "debriefing" sessions with several colleagues to help work through difficulties. Monsanto believes that this program provides them with a source of competitive advantage in international assignments.[63]

In sum, a variety of HR practices can support effective expatriation. In general, the selection system must rigorously assess potential expatriates' skills and personalities and even focus on the candidate's spouse. Training should be conducted prior to and during the expatriate assignment, and the assignment itself should be viewed as a career development experience. Effective reward systems must go beyond salary and benefits, and while keeping the employee "whole" and even offering a monetary premium, should also provide access to career development and learning opportunities. Finally, serious efforts should be made to manage the repatriation process.[64] A summary of the key points is provided in Table 15.8.

table 15.8

Human Resource Practices That Support Effective Expatriation

Staffing and Selection
- Communicate the value of international assignments for the company's global mission.
- Ensure that those with the highest potential move internationally.
- Provide short-term assignments to increase the pool of employees with international experience.
- Recruit employees who have lived or who were educated abroad.

Training and Career Development
- Make international assignment planning a part of the career development process.
- Encourage early international experience.
- Create learning opportunities during the assignment.
- Use international assignments as a leadership development tool.

Performance Appraisal and Compensation
- Differentiate performance management based on expatriate roles.
- Align incentives with expatriation objectives.
- Tailor benefits to the expatriate's needs.
- Focus on equality of opportunities, not cash.
- Emphasize rewarding careers rather than short-term outcomes.

Expatriation and Repatriation Activities
- Involve the family in the orientation program at the beginning and the end of the assignment.
- Establish mentor relationships between expatriates and executives from the home location.
- Provide support for dual careers.
- Secure opportunities for the returning manager to use knowledge and skills learned while on the international assignment.

SOURCE: From Paul Evans, and Vladimir Pucik, *The Global Challenge: Framework for International Human Resource Management*, 2002. Copyright © 2002 The McGraw-Hill Companies.

A LOOK BACK

Starbucks built its brand in the United States not just on the quality of the coffee, but on its reputation as the "third place" between work and home, where one could enjoy a relaxing atmosphere with friendly employees. As they grew, the business became more complex, and the company faced difficulty in expanding its workforce fast enough, particularly being able to hire enough employees who bought into the Starbucks experience. When growing internationally, one also has to think about how the differences in human capital and culture might affect Starbucks' ability to attract and retain the kinds of people that can provide that "third place" experience.

Leaders at Starbucks have often repeated the mantra that "It's not about the coffee." For instance, Howard Behar, a senior executive (now retired), developed a saying that has spread throughout the Starbucks culture: "We're in the people business serving coffee, not in the coffee business serving people." With the increasing competition on price and coffee quality, Starbucks' future success may lie in its ability to effectively instill that belief in its people.

Questions:

1. Do you think Starbucks will be able to attract and retain the right kinds of people they need to deliver the "third place" experience in Poland? How about in other countries? Why or why not?
2. How might Starbucks use expatriate employees as part of its international expansion? What will be the challenges in selecting the right kinds of expatriates?

SOURCE: Howard Behar, *It's Not about the Coffee: Lessons for Putting People First from a Life at Starbucks* (New York: Penguin Group, 2007).

 Please see the Video Case that corresponds to this chapter online at www.mhhe.com/noe7e.

SUMMARY

Today's organizations are more involved in international commerce than ever before, and the trend will continue. Recent historic events such as the development of the EEC, NAFTA, the economic growth of Asia, and GATT have accelerated the movement toward a global market. Companies competing in the global marketplace require top-quality people to compete successfully. This requires that managers be aware of the many factors that significantly affect HRM in a global environment, such as culture, human capital, and the political–legal and economic systems, and that they understand how these factors come into play in the various levels of global participation. Finally, it requires that they be adept at developing HRM systems that maximize the effectiveness of all human resources, particularly with regard to expatriate managers. Managers cannot overestimate the importance of effectively managing human resources to gain competitive advantage in today's global marketplace.

KEY TERMS

Individualism–collectivism, 684
Power distance, 685
Uncertainty avoidance, 685
Masculinity–femininity dimension, 685
Long-term–short-term orientation, 685
Parent country, 691

Host country, 691
Third country, 692
Expatriate, 692
Parent-country nationals (PCNs), 692
Host-country nationals (HCNs), 692

Third-country nationals (TCNs), 692
Transnational scope, 696
Transnational representation, 696
Transnational process, 696

DISCUSSION QUESTIONS

1. What current trends and/or events (besides those mentioned at the outset of the chapter) are responsible for the increased internationalization of the marketplace?
2. According to Hofstede (in Table 15.2), the United States is low on power distance, high on individuality, high on masculinity, low on uncertainty avoidance, and low on long-term orientation. Russia, on the other hand, is high on power distance, moderate on individuality, low on masculinity, high on uncertainty avoidance, and low on long-term orientation. Many U.S. managers are transplanting their own HRM practices into Russia while companies seek to develop operations there. How acceptable

and effective do you think the following practices will be and why? (a) Extensive assessments of individual abilities for selection? (b) Individually based appraisal systems? (c) Suggestion systems? (d) Self-managing work teams?

3. The chapter notes that political–legal and economic systems can reflect a country's culture. The former Eastern bloc countries seem to be changing their political–legal and economic systems. Is this change brought on by their cultures, or will culture have an impact on the ability to change these systems? Why?

4. Think of the different levels of global participation. What companies that you are familiar with exhibit the different levels of participation?

5. Think of a time when you had to function in another culture (on a vacation or job). What were the major obstacles you faced, and how did you deal with them? Was this a stressful experience? Why? How can companies help expatriate employees deal with stress?

6. What types of skills do you need to be able to manage in today's global marketplace? Where do you expect to get those skills? What classes and/or experiences will you need?

● SELF-ASSESSMENT EXERCISE

The following list includes a number of qualities that have been identified as being associated with success in an expatriate assignment. Rate the degree to which you possess each quality, using the following scale:

1 = very low
2 = low
3 = moderate
4 = high
5 = very high

____ Resourcefulness/resilience
____ Adaptability/flexibility
____ Emotional stability
____ Ability to deal with ambiguity/uncertainty/differences
____ Desire to work with people who are different
____ Cultural empathy/sensitivity

____ Tolerance of others' views, especially when they differ from your own
____ Sensitivity to feelings and attitudes of others
____ Good health and wellness

Add up your total score for the items. The higher your score, the greater your likelihood of success. Qualities that you rated low would be considered weaknesses for an expatriate assignment. Keep in mind that you will also need to be technically competent for the assignment, and your spouse and family (if applicable) must be adaptable and willing to live abroad.

SOURCE: Based on "Rating Scale on Successful Expatriate Qualities," from P. R. Harris and R. T. Moran, *Managing Cultural Differences*, 3rd ed. (Houston: Gulf, 1991), p. 569.

● EXERCISING STRATEGY: TERRORISM AND GLOBAL HUMAN RESOURCE MANAGEMENT

Globalization has continued to increase as companies expand their operations in a number of countries, employing an increasingly global workforce. Although this process has resulted in a number of positive outcomes, it has also occasionally presented new types of problems for firms to face.

On September 11, 2001, terrorists with Middle Eastern roots (alleged to be part of Osama bin Laden's al Qaeda network) hijacked four U.S. planes, crashing two of them into the World Trade Center's twin towers and one into the Pentagon (a fourth was crashed in Pennsylvania in a scuffle with passengers). President Bush and U.K. Prime Minister Tony Blair, after their demands that the Taliban government in Afghanistan turn over bin Laden and his leaders were ignored, began military action against that country on October 7, 2001. Both the terrorist acts and the subsequent war on terrorism have created a host of issues for multinational companies.

First, companies doing business overseas, particularly in Muslim-dominated countries such as the Arab states and Indonesia, must manage their expatriate workforce (particularly U.S. and British citizens) in what has the potential to become hostile territory. These employees fear for their security, and some have asked to return to their home countries.

Second, companies with global workforces must manage across what have become increasingly nationalistic boundaries. Those of us in the United States may view the terrorist attacks as an act of war and our response as being entirely justified. However, those in the Arab world, while not justifying the terrorist attacks, may similarly feel that the military response toward Afghanistan (and later Iraq) is hostile aggression. One executive at a global oil company noted the difficulty in managing a workforce that is approximately 25 percent Arab. He stated that many of the Arab executives have said, "While we know that you are concerned about the events of September 11, you should know that we are equally concerned about the events of October 7 and since."

Questions

1. How can a global company manage the inevitable conflicts that will arise among individuals from different religious, racial, ethnic, and national groups who must work together within firms? How can these conflicts be overcome to create a productive work environment?
2. What will firms have to do differently in managing expatriates, particularly U.S. or British citizens who are asked to take assignments in predominantly Muslim countries?

● MANAGING PEOPLE: FROM THE PAGES OF *BUSINESSWEEK*

BusinessWeek The Toyota Way to No. I

Toyota's top U.S. executive on how it managed to become the world's No. 1 carmaker and why the company can hang on to the top spot It happened. Toyota passed General Motors in worldwide sales globally in the first quarter. We knew it was coming. It's likely that the trend will continue and hold up for the entire year, and for years to come.

As the baton gets passed this year, there's a mix of opinions and perspectives in the auto industry about whether Toyota is succeeding fairly. Does its lack of health-care and pension responsibilities, which hobble GM, Ford, and DaimlerChrysler's Chrysler division, allow Toyota an advantage on an unlevel playing field? Does Japan's insular economy, which has made it so difficult for U.S. auto makers to achieve sales in Japan, offer an unfair advantage? Do charges that the Japanese government weakens the yen against the dollar to keep prices down and profit up abroad hold water?

Toyota isn't accepting the No. 1 position comfortably. It makes some of its executives nervous to be the chased, rather than the chaser. Yuki Funo is the chairman and CEO of Toyota Motor Sales USA—the top Japanese executive for Toyota in North America. He recently sat down with *BusinessWeek* Senior Correspondent David Kiley to discuss some of the issues confronting Toyota as it achieves top-dog status. Edited excerpts form their conversation follow:

Have you been talking among yourselves about protecting your culture, which could be vulnerable to change as you become the world's largest automaker?

As far as Toyota culture goes . . . we regard ourselves as Japanese, but more important than the Japanese nature of our company is the "Toyota Way," which is embodied in our concepts and systems.

Toyota Way is more than just a Japanese Way. It's about constant improvement. If it was a Japanese Way only, then we wouldn't have Japanese companies that perform poorly or go into bankruptcy. Toyota doesn't monopolize this idea. And it has to translate beyond Japanese culture to be successful. We employ close to 400,000 worldwide, excluding dealers. If we include dealers, it might be about 1 million.

Of that, a significant number are Japanese. But there are people from every culture working for Toyota that share the concept and this way of doing business. From that viewpoint, growing larger doesn't suggest that we're stepping out of anything that's part of our culture.

Someone I know says Toyota really believes and nurtures the idea that the company should be able to build a car with no problems or flaws. When this person does business with Ford and GM, it's different, they tell me. Those companies strive to be better, but you don't get the idea they think a perfect car is possible.

With the Toyota Way . . . one of the key elements is *kaizen*: continuous improvement. There's no end to it. It's a never-ending journey. Respect for people is another important element. Employees. Customers. Suppliers. When it comes to consumers, they demand changes from time to time. We have to always keep watching what the consumer wants. If we base our business on what the customer wants, there's no end to the improvement we can achieve.

I remember a story related to me by a supplier company: They entered into a contract to supply axles for pickup trucks. It was the first contract his company had with Toyota. He said he was awarded the contract with no discussion of price. It was all based on whether his company's processes and quality were acceptable to Toyota. He was flabbergasted. Is that a common way Toyota does business?

Toyota's thinking based on the Toyota Way is teamwork with suppliers. This teamwork is going to be a long-lasting relationship. Price is only one element. Trust is a more important element. The relationship is a sharing concept, and should always be win-win. Price is important, too. But trust is perhaps more so. This is an idea that American business schools have come to preach. IBM, General Electric, and other companies talk about how important the mission of the company is. Toyota is only doing intelligently what the business schools are teaching.

In the church when you get married, the priest or minister doesn't ask each partner how much each will get from the other in terms of money. You're asked about how well you get along. What is your commitment to one another? Now, in real-life situations, some companies practice this, and some don't. Some practice this in the United States. Some don't. It's the same in Japan. So there are fantastic achievements in both countries, and there are bankruptcies in both countries. So, it isn't a Japanese issue or an American issue. It's a company-culture issue.

Growth comes from both new products and boosting volume of existing products. Will your sales growth come more from new products or from existing products in new geographic markets?

I think 15 percent global market share isn't low, but it's not that high either. There are a lot of opportunities for our product lineup as it is. But now that we have gone into full-size pickups with the new product, we fill in a significant segment.

I think we need to pursue more niches in the future. We had a car at the Detroit Auto Show that could be a replacement for the former Supra sports car. But what's more important is to keep improving the products we have. Like Camry—what consumers want out of Camry is always changing. That's my understanding of how to keep a product strong for the future. We will look after Camry customers by looking after Camry as a product. Same goes with RAV4 and others.

From time to time, a GM or Ford exec will complain about an uneven playing field: a health-care advantage for Toyota, or monetary policy that favors Japanese products. Do you and your colleagues read that and pay attention?

We always read the stuff in the newspapers. We know health care is very difficult situation for the Big Three. It's a fact of life that they incur more costs. That's the political and economic history of the United States. A decision was made some years back on what they would give to workers. To some degree, the problem is of their own creation.

Not all the workers in every industry receive as high a medical benefit as in the auto industry. Who decided that? It's their management. They complain sometimes about the currency valuation. It's very difficult. For example, the biggest economy in the world is the United States. Bigger than Japan. It's the Big Three who have an advantage in operating in the biggest economy in the world. For myself, I invested in my English education. If you're born here, there's no need to invest in that. So, that's not a level playing field. It's very difficult to define what a level playing field is.

You would think that GM and Ford execs, given the fact they all grew up here, should have a better idea of how to design and package a family sedan and minivan, yet

these are two product segments where you and Honda have done especially well against the Big Three.

Increasingly, we're doing the development of our vehicles in the States. The Camry chief engineer is a Japanese man. Why the heck does he develop the most favorite car in the United States? That Camry car doesn't sell in Japan. It's a failure. Why? He applies himself to understanding what the customer wants. He visits here and learns things.

If we talk about the level playing field, what is it? He had to overcome such a big handicap being Japanese to create a car that's the top seller in America. It's very difficult to talk about what the level playing field is.

U.S. companies are saying that while they're improving manufacturing processes, costs, etc. they will never out-Toyota Toyota. They have decided the best way to outdo you as they close the gap on those things is by out designing you. Do you feel a greater pressure to compete on expressive design than you once did?

Toyota, if you look at the history, our design hasn't been very expressive. If we aren't careful, design could fall into the dull category. Our designers have been seeing design as a critical challenge. If you look at the last 5 to 10 years, designers have done a great job of advancing here.

Look at the FJ Cruiser. People look at that and say, "Who designed that? Toyota? I can't believe it." Every organization has strengths and weaknesses. Twenty years ago, Toyota had no confidence in how we would operate manufacturing in the United States. That's why we regard the NUMMI joint-venture plant [where Toyota builds the Matrix and Corolla alongside the Pontiac Vibe] with GM as very beneficial. GM helped us a great deal.

The corporate advertising you have been running seems to be quite effective. Some of your Detroit rivals resent the fact that you're acting and talking like an American company.

We have a lot of dialogue about what should be the corporate message. That advertising is what we wanted to accomplish. We knew that many people didn't know what we have been doing in the United States for 50 years. In San Antonio, Texas, for example, we gave a lot of money to the local family-literacy program. We have been giving money to this organization nationally for 20 years. But we had never advertised it. People need to have a clearer and more correct image of Toyota.

Is your decision to advertise more aggressively a response to those kinds of remarks by people like Ford President of the Americas Mark Fields or GM Vice-Chairman Bob Lutz?

More important than the political consideration, Toyota is known as a product. No one knows what Toyota is. Toyota is a faceless organization. It doesn't have a human element in the eyes of the consumer. Toyota is just a car.

Toyota is bigger than that though. It's people. We have some 40,000 people working for us in the United States. We need to have more of a face. That we are people. That's the most critical thing we have been trying to achieve. **Perhaps you would like to star in some ads yourself? DaimlerChrysler Chairman Dieter Zetsche did that last year as "Dr. Z." Do you want to be known as "Dr. T"?** No. We want to show everybody in the company. The heroes. Not one single person.

Questions

1. As you look at how Toyota has surpassed GM and the other U.S. automakers, in what ways do you think its workforce has provided a competitive advantage?
2. What do you think are the major HR issues that Toyota will face in the future?

SOURCE: D. Kiley, "The Toyota Way to No.1," *BusinessWeek*, April 26, 2007.

● Notes

1. R. M. Kanter, "Transcending Business Boundaries: 12,000 World Managers View Change," *Harvard Business Review*, May–June 1991, pp. 151–64.
2. R. Norton, "Will a Global Slump Hurt the U.S.?" *Fortune*, February 22, 1993, pp. 63–64.
3. U.S. Department of Labor, "International Comparisons of Hourly Compensation Costs for Production Workers in Manufacturing, 1975–2007," Bureau of Labor Statistics news release, www.bls.gov.
4. D. Kirkpatrick, "The Net Makes It All Easier—Including Exporting U.S. Jobs," http://www.fortune.com/fortune/print/0,15935,450755,00.html (May 2003).
5. Towers Perrin, *Priorities for Competitive Advantage: A Worldwide Human Resource Study* (Valhalla, NY: Towers Perrin, 1991).
6. R. Schuler, "An Integrative Framework of Strategic International Human Resource Management," *Journal of Management* (1993), pp. 419–60.
7. L. Rubio, "The Rationale for NAFTA: Mexico's New 'Outward Looking' Strategy," *Business Economics* (1991), pp. 12–16.
8. H. Cooper, "Economic Impact of NAFTA: It's a Wash, Experts Say," *The Wall Street Journal*, interactive edition (June 17, 1997).
9. J. Mark, "Suzhou Factories Are Nearly Ready," *Asian Wall Street Journal*, August 14, 1995, p. 8.
10. R. Peiper, *Human Resource Management: An International Comparison* (Berlin: Walter de Gruyter, 1990).
11. V. Sathe, *Culture and Related Corporate Realities* (Homewood, IL: Richard D. Irwin, 1985).
12. M. Rokeach, *Beliefs, Attitudes, and Values* (San Francisco: Jossey-Bass, 1968).
13. L. Harrison, *Who Prospers? How Cultural Values Shape Economic and Political Success* (New York: Free Press, 1992).
14. N. Adler, *International Dimensions of Organizational Behavior*, 2nd ed. (Boston: PWS-Kent, 1991).
15. R. Yates, "Japanese Managers Say They're Adopting Some U.S. Ways," *Chicago Tribune*, February 29, 1992, p. B1.
16. G. Hofstede, "Dimensions of National Cultures in Fifty Countries and Three Regions," in *Expectations in Cross-Cultural Psychology*, eds. J. Deregowski, S. Dziurawiec, and R. C. Annis (Lisse, Netherlands: Swets and Zeitlinger, 1983).
17. G. Hofstede, "Cultural Constraints in Management Theories," *Academy of Management Executive* 7 (1993), pp. 81–90.
18. G. Hofstede, "The Cultural Relativity of Organizational Theories," *Journal of International Business Studies* 14 (1983), pp. 75–90.
19. G. Hofstede, "Cultural Constraints in Management Theories."
20. S. Snell and J. Dean, "Integrated Manufacturing and Human Resource Management: A Human Capital Perspective," *Academy of Management Journal* 35 (1992), pp. 467–504.
21. W. Johnston and A. Packer, *Workforce 2000: Work and Workers for the Twenty-first Century* (Indianapolis, IN: Hudson Institute, 1988).
22. H. Meyer, "Human Resource Management in the German Democratic Republic: Problems of Availability and the Use of Manpower Potential in the Sphere of the High-Qualification Spectrum in a Retrospective View," in *Human Resource Management: An International Comparison*, ed. R. Peiper (Berlin: Walter de Gruyter, 1990).
23. P. Conrad and R. Peiper, "Human Resource Management in the Federal Republic of Germany," in ibid.
24. N. Adler and S. Bartholomew, "Managing Globally Competent People," *The Executive* 6 (1992), pp. 52–65.
25. B. O'Reilly, "Your New Global Workforce," *Fortune*, December 14, 1992, pp. 52–66.
26. A. Hoffman, "Are Technology Jobs Headed Offshore?" Monster. com, http://technology.monster.com/articles/offshore.
27. J. Ledvinka and V. Scardello, *Federal Employment Regulation in Human Resource Management* (Boston: PWS-Kent, 1991).
28. Conrad and Peiper, "Human Resource Management in the Federal Republic of Germany."
29. R. Solow, "Growth with Equity through Investment in Human Capital," The George Seltzer Distinguished Lecture, University of Minnesota.
30. M. Bloom, G. Milkovich, and A. Mitra, "Toward a Model of International Compensation and Rewards: Learning from How Managers Respond to Variations in Local Host Contexts," working paper 00-14 (Center for Advance Human Resource Studies, Cornell University: 2000).
31. R. Kopp, "International Human Resource Policies and Practices in Japanese, European, and United States Multinationals," *Human Resource Management* 33 (1994), pp. 581–99.
32. Adler, *International Dimensions of Organizational Behavior*.
33. S. Jackson and Associates, *Diversity in the Workplace: Human Resource Initiatives* (New York: Guilford Press, 1991).
34. Adler and Bartholomew, "Managing Globally Competent People."
35. Ibid.
36. S. Dolianski, "Are Expats Getting Lost in the Translation?" *Workforce*, February 1997.
37. L. Copeland and L. Griggs, *Going International* (New York: Random House, 1985).
38. K. F. Misa and J. M. Fabriacatore, "Return on Investments of Overseas Personnel," *Financial Executive* 47 (April 1979), pp. 42–46.
39. N. Forster, "The Persistent Myth of High Expatriate Failure Rates: A Reappraisal," *International Journal of Human Resource Management* 8, no. 4 (1997), pp. 414–34.

40. M. Mendenhall, E. Dunbar, and G. R. Oddou, "Expatriate Selection, Training, and Career-Pathing: A Review and Critique," *Human Resource Management* 26 (1987), pp. 331–45.

41. M. Mendenhall and G. Oddou, "The Dimensions of Expatriate Acculturation," *Academy of Management Review* 10 (1985), pp. 39–47.

42. W. Arthur and W. Bennett, "The International Assignee: The Relative Importance of Factors Perceived to Contribute to Success," *Personnel Psychology* 48 (1995), pp. 99–114.

43. R. Tung, "Selecting and Training of Personnel for Overseas Assignments," *Columbia Journal of World Business* 16, no. 2 (1981), pp. 68–78.

44. Moran, Stahl, and Boyer, Inc., *International Human Resource Management* (Boulder, CO: Moran, Stahl, & Boyer, 1987).

45. P. Caligiuri, "The Big Five Personality Characteristics as Predictors of Expatriates' Desire to Terminate the Assignment and Supervisor Rated Performance," *Personnel Psychology* 53 (2000), pp. 67–88.

46. P. Caligiuri and R. Tung, "Comparing the Success of Male and Female Expatriates from a U.S.-based Multinational Company," *International Journal of Human Resource Management* 10, no. 5 (1999), pp. 763–82.

47. L. Stroh, A. Varma, and S. Valy-Durbin, "Why Are Women Left at Home? Are They Unwilling to Go on International Assignments?" *Journal of World Business* 35, no. 3 (2000), pp. 241–55.

48. A. Harzing, *Managing the Multinationals: An International Study of Control Mechanisms* (Cheltenham: Edward Elgar, 1999).

49. J. S. Black and M. Mendenhall, "Cross-Cultural Training Effectiveness: A Review and Theoretical Framework for Future Research," *Academy of Management Review* 15 (1990), pp. 113–36.

50. B. Fitzgerald-Turner, "Myths of Expatriate Life," *HRMagazine* 42, no. 6 (June 1997), pp. 65–74.

51. P. Dowling and R. Schuler, *International Dimensions of Human Resource Management* (Boston: PWS-Kent, 1990).

52. Adler, *International Dimensions of Organizational Behavior.*

53. Dowling and Schuler, *International Dimensions of Human Resource Management.*

54. R. Schuler and P. Dowling, *Survey of ASPA/I Members* (New York: Stern School of Business, New York University, 1988).

55. C. Joinson, "No Returns: Localizing Expats Saves Companies Big Money and Can Be a Smooth Transition with a Little Due Diligence by HR," *HRMagazine* 11, no. 47 (2002), p. 70.

56. J. J. Smith, "Firms Say Expats Getting Too Costly, but Few Willing to Act" (2006), *SHRM Online*, retrieved March 9, 2007, www.shrm.org/global/library_published/subject/nonIC/CMS_018300.asp.

57. C. Solomon, "Repatriation: Up, Down, or Out?" *Personnel Journal* (1995), pp. 28–37.

58. "Workers Sent Overseas Have Adjustment Problems, a New Study Shows," *The Wall Street Journal,* June 19, 1984, p. 1.

59. J. S. Black, "Repatriation: A Comparison of Japanese and American Practices and Results," *Proceedings of the Eastern Academy of Management Bi-annual International Conference* (Hong Kong, 1989), pp. 45–49.

60. J. S. Black, "Coming Home: The Relationship of Expatriate Expectations with Repatriation Adjustment and Job Performance," *Human Relations* 45 (1992), pp. 177–92.

61. Adler, *International Dimensions of Organizational Behavior.*

62. Black, "Coming Home."

63. C. Solomon, "Repatriation: Up, Down, or Out?"

64. P. Evans, V. Pucik, and J. Barsoux, *The Global Challenge: International Human Resource Management* (New York: McGraw-Hill, 2002), p. 137.

CHAPTER
16

Strategically Managing the HRM Function

 LEARNING OBJECTIVES

After reading this chapter, you should be able to:

LO1 Describe the roles that HRM plays in firms today and the categories of HRM activities. *page 718*

LO2 Discuss how the HRM function can define its mission and market. *page 721*

LO3 Explain the approaches to evaluating the effectiveness of HRM practices. *page 725*

LO4 Describe the new structures for the HRM function. *page 730*

LO5 Describe how outsourcing HRM activities can improve service delivery efficiency and effectiveness. *page 733*

LO6 Relate how process reengineering is used to review and redesign HRM practices. *page 734*

LO7 Discuss the types of new technologies that can improve the efficiency and effectiveness of HRM. *page 736*

LO8 List the competencies the HRM executive needs to become a strategic partner in the company. *page 747*

HR Drives Success at IBM

In the technology world, change is constant, fast, and difficult to manage, so running the human resource function in a company such as IBM presents a tremendous set of challenges. However, for the past 11 years, J. Randall MacDonald has taken on this challenge, driving change in the business and change in HR.

Since joining IBM, the company has moved from a predominantly computer manufacturer to a software and services company. Such a strategic shift requires an entirely new set of organizational capabilities and, consequently, different kinds of people with different skills. In addition, the company has consistently increased its global footprint with decreasing employment in the United States and vast increases in areas such as central Europe, China, and India. This "global transformation," cannot work by having seemingly unconnected operations in 170 countries, each practically working in a vacuum. Rather, the company needs to be nimble, ready to meet and exceed client expectations around the world quickly and effectively. In his role as chief human resource officer (CHRO), MacDonald has overseen a function that has added value through this transformation.

For instance, IBM has tied its bonus plans and performance-management programs more closely to business results, focused its benefit programs more on prevention and healthy living, and developed new learning and career-development programs. For example, MacDonald personally suggested a "children's health rebate," introduced in October 2007, that rewards good nutrition and physical activity for the entire family.

MacDonald co-led a technology project aimed at creating a single, integrated approach to hiring, managing, developing, and deploying IBM's global workforce. The result, called the "Workforce Management Initiative (WMI)," provided a more efficient, effective way to find and deploy skilled IBMers to help solve clients' problems or respond to their requests. WMI provides a consistent taxonomy to describe skills; the ability to measure talent supply and demand; and a built-in, integrated approach to sharing talent data across each of the applications within the WMI application suite. Over the past three years, WMI has saved the company more than $276 million.

MacDonald also led a process at IBM called the Integration and Values Team (I&VT). The company identified senior leaders and charged them with working to better align IBM's workforce with customer needs and to serve as role models for the company's values-based leadership. Teams of leaders were assigned business topics identified as some of IBM's toughest customer integration challenges. This required the leaders to dig into issues outside their core jobs, developing their leadership skills while solving real company problems. "If you know how to cut benefits and lay off people, HR can get a so-called seat at the table," MacDonald says. "My idea is to be a catalyst, a provocateur for change that drives business necessity. You need to talk business first, HR second. I&VT is about talking business first."

Source: Tom Starner, "A Passion at the Helm," October 16, 2008, http://www.hreonline.com/HRE/story.jsp?storyId=136568343&query=IBM.

Introduction

Throughout this book we have emphasized how human resource management practices can help companies gain a competitive advantage. We identified specific practices related to managing the internal and external environment; designing work and measuring work outcomes; and acquiring, developing, and compensating human resources. We have also discussed the best of current research and practice to show how they may contribute to a company's competitive advantage.

As we said in Chapter 1, the role of the HRM function has been evolving over time. As we see in this chapter's opening story, it has now reached a crossroads. Although it began as a purely administrative function, most HR executives now see the function's major role as being much more strategic. However, this evolution has resulted in a misalignment between the skills and capabilities of members of the function and the new requirements placed on it. Virtually every HRM function in top companies is going through a transformation process to create a function that can play this new strategic role while successfully fulfilling its other roles. This transformation process is also going on globally. Managing this process is the subject of this chapter. First we discuss the various activities of the HRM function. Then we examine how to develop a market- or customer-oriented HRM function. We then describe the current structure of most HRM functions. Finally, we explore measurement approaches for assessing the effectiveness of the function.

Activities of HRM

LO1
Describe the roles that HRM plays in firms today and the categories of HRM activities.

To understand the transformation going on in HRM, one must understand HRM activities in terms of their strategic value. One way of classifying these activities is depicted in Figure 16.1. Transactional activities (the day-to-day transactions such as benefits administration, record keeping, and employee services) are low in their strategic value. Traditional activities such as performance management, training, recruiting, selection, compensation, and employee relations are the nuts and bolts of HRM. These activities have moderate strategic value because they often form the practices and systems to ensure strategy execution. Transformational activities create long-term capability and adaptablity for the firm. These activities include knowledge management, management development, cultural change, and strategic redirection and renewal. Obviously, these activities comprise the greatest strategic value for the firm.

As we see in the figure, most HRM functions spend the vast majority of their time on transactional activities, with substantially less on traditional and very little on transformational activities. However, virtually all HRM functions, in order to add value to the firm, must increase their efforts in the traditional and transformational activities. To do this, however, requires that HR executives (1) develop a strategy for the HRM function, (2) assess the current effectiveness of the HRM function, and (3) redesign, reengineer, or outsource HRM processes to improve efficiency and effectiveness. These issues will be discussed in the following sections.

Strategic Management of the HRM Function

In light of the various roles and activities of the HRM function, we can easily see that it is highly unlikely that any function can (or should) effectively deliver on all roles and all activities. Although this is a laudable goal, resource constraints in terms of

figure 16.1

Categories of HRM Activities and Percentages of Time Spent on Them

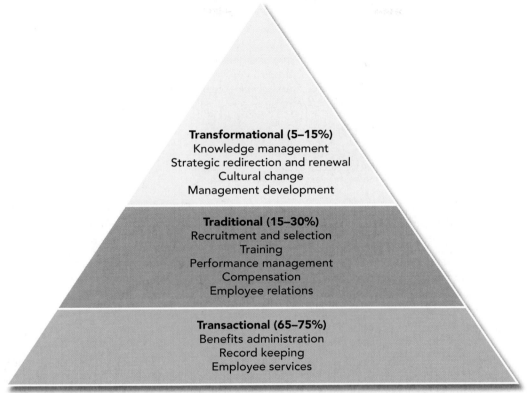

Transformational (5–15%)
Knowledge management
Strategic redirection and renewal
Cultural change
Management development

Traditional (15–30%)
Recruitment and selection
Training
Performance management
Compensation
Employee relations

Transactional (65–75%)
Benefits administration
Record keeping
Employee services

SOURCE: P. Wright, G. McMahan, S. Snell, and B. Gerhart, *Strategic Human Resource Management: Building Human Capital and Organizational Capability.* Technical report. Cornell University, 1998.

time, money, and head count require that the HR executive make strategic choices about where and how to allocate these resources for maximum value to the firm.

Chapter 2 explained the strategic management process that takes place at the organization level and discussed the role of HRM in this process. HRM has been seen as a strategic partner that has input into the formulation of the company's strategy and develops and aligns HRM programs to help implement the strategy. However, for the HRM function to become truly strategic in its orientation, it must view itself as a separate business entity and engage in strategic management in an effort to effectively serve the various internal customers.

In this respect, one recent trend within the field of HRM, consistent with the total quality management philosophy, is for the HR executive to take a customer-oriented approach to implementing the function. In other words, the strategic planning process that takes place at the level of the business can also be performed with the HRM function. HR executives in more progressive U.S. companies have begun to view the HRM function as a strategic business unit and have tried to define that business in terms of their customer base, their customers' needs, and the technologies required to satisfy customers' needs (Figure 16.2). For example, Weyerhaeuser Corporation's human resources department identified 11 characteristics

figure 16.2

Customer-Oriented
Perspective of the
HRM Function

that would describe a quality human resource organization; these are presented in Table 16.1.

A customer orientation is one of the most important changes in the HRM function's attempts to become strategic. It entails first identifying customers. The most obvious example of HRM customers are the line managers who require HRM services. In addition, the strategic planning team is a customer in the sense that it requires the identification, analysis, and recommendations regarding people-oriented business problems. Employees are also HRM customers because the rewards they receive from the employment relationship are determined and/or administered by the HRM department.

table 16.1

Characteristics
of HRM Quality
at Weyerhaeuser
Corporation

- Human resources products and service are linked to customer requirements.
- Customer requirements are translated into internal service applications.
- Processes for producing products and services are documented with cost/value relationships understood.
- Reliable methods and standardized processes are in place.
- Waste and inefficiency are eliminated.
- Problem solving and decision making are based on facts and data.
- Critical success variables are tracked, displayed, and maintained.
- Human resources employees are trained and educated in total quality tools and principles.
- Human resource systems have been aligned to total quality implementation strategies.
- Human resource managers provide leadership and support to organizations on large-scale organizational change.
- Human resource professionals function as "strategic partners" in managing the business and implementing total quality principles.

In addition, the products of the HRM department must be identified. Line managers want to have high-quality employees committed to the organization. The strategic planning team requires information and recommendations for the planning process as well as programs that support the strategic plan once it has been identified. Employees want compensation and benefit programs that are consistent, adequate, and equitable, and they want fair promotion decisions. At Southwest Airlines, the "People" department administers customer surveys to all clients as they leave the department to measure how well their needs have been satisfied.

Finally, the technologies through which HRM meets customer needs vary depending on the need being satisfied. Selection systems ensure that applicants selected for employment have the necessary knowledge, skills, and abilities to provide value to the organization. Training and development systems meet the needs of both line managers and employees by giving employees development opportunities to ensure they are constantly increasing their human capital and, thus, providing increased value to the company. Performance management systems make clear to employees what is expected of them and assure line managers and strategic planners that employee behavior will be in line with the company's goals. Finally, reward systems similarly benefit all customers (line managers, strategic planners, and employees). These systems assure line managers that employees will use their skills for organizational benefit, and they provide strategic planners with ways to ensure that all employees are acting in ways that will support the strategic plan. Obviously, reward systems provide employees with an equitable return for their investment of skills and effort.

For example, Whirlpool Corporation's HR managers go through a formalized process of identifying their customer, the need/value they satisfy, and the technology used to satisfy the customer. As Whirlpool planned for start-up of a centralized service supercenter, the plan called for hiring between 100 and 150 employees to serve as call takers who receive service requests from Whirlpool appliance owners and set up service appointments from these calls. The HR manager in charge of developing a selection system for hiring these call takers identified the operations manager in charge of phone service as the HRM department's customer, the delivery of qualified phone call takers as the need satisfied, and the use of a structured interview and paper-and-pencil tests as the technologies employed. This customer service orientation may be the trend of the future. It provides a means for the HRM function to specifically identify who its customers are, what customers' needs are being met, and how well those needs are being met.

Building an HR Strategy

The Basic Process

How do HR functions build their HR strategies? Recent research has examined how HR functions go about the process of building their HR strategies that should support the business strategies. Conducting case studies on 20 different companies, Wright and colleagues describe the generic approach as somewhat consistent with the process for developing a business strategy.[1]

As depicted in Figure 16.3, the function first scans the environment to determine the trends or events that might have an impact on the organization (e.g., future talent shortage, increasing immigrant population, aging of the workforce). It then examines the strategic business issues or needs (e.g., is the company growing, expanding internationally, needing to develop new technologies?). For instance, Figure 16.4 displays

LO2
Discuss how the HRM function can define its mission and market.

figure 16.3

Basic Process for HR Strategy

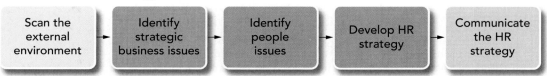

figure 16.4

IBM Priorities and
the On-Demand Era

IBM Strategic Priorities on Demand

1. Delivering business value
2. Offering world class open infrastructure
3. Developing innovative leadership technology
4. Exploiting new profitable growth opportunities
5. Creating brand leadership and a superior customer experience
6. ***Attracting, motivating, and retaining the best talent in our industry***

"An enterprise whose business processes—integrated end-to-end across the company and with key partners, suppliers, and customers—can respond with speed to any customer demand, market opportunity or external threat."

—Sam Palmisano, *IBM Chairman and CEO*

IBM's major business strategy priorities. As can be seen in this example, a clear strategic priority is the attraction, motivation, and retention of talent.

From these issues, the HR strategy team needs to identify the specific people issues that will be critical to address in order for the business to succeed (a potential leadership vacuum, lack of technological expertise, lack of diversity, etc.). All of this information is used in designing the HR strategy, which provides a detailed plan regarding the major priorities and the programs, policies, and processes that must be developed or executed. Finally, this HR strategy is communicated to the relevant parties, both internal and external to the function. Again, IBM's HR strategy, depicted in Figure 16.5,

figure 16.5

IBM HR Strategy

shows how IBM seeks to differentiate itself in the labor market as well as the major priority areas that the HR strategy seeks to address.

Involving Line Executives

This generic process provides for the potential to involve line executives in a number of ways. Because the HR strategy seeks to address business issues, involving those in charge of running the business can increase the quality of information from which the HR strategy is created. This involvement can occur in a few ways. First, line executives could simply provide input, by either surveying or interviewing them regarding the business challenges and strategy. Second, they could be members of the team that actually develops the HR strategy. Third, once the strategy is developed, they could receive communications with the HR strategy information. Finally, they could have to formally approve the strategy, in essence "signing off" that the HR strategy fully supports the business strategy. The most progressive organizations use all four forms of involvement, asking a large group of executives for input, having one or two executives on the team, communicating the HR strategy broadly to executives, and having the senior executive team formally approve it.

Characterizing HR Strategies

As you can see in Figure 16.6, the variety of ways that HR strategies can be generated results in various levels of linkage with the business. In general, four categories of this relationship can be identified.

First, at the most elementary level, "HR-focused" HR functions' articulation of people outcomes stems more from an analysis of what their functions currently do

figure 16.6

Approaches to Developing an HR Strategy

The Obama administration has begun floating a proposal to tax offshore profits that may drive further globalization of U.S. companies. The current law allows companies to defer taxation of profits from overseas operations until they "repatriate" those profits back to the United States. The Obama administration would like to change the law and has already included such tax receipts in its 2011 budget figures.

On the one hand, such a proposal could generate significant receipts to the U.S. Treasury. Just the top 10 companies had $58 billion in such earnings in 2008, which would represent close to $20 billion in tax revenue. For instance, General Electric generated $13 billion in overseas earnings in 2008 and had a cumulative total of $75 billion as of the end of 2008. The deferral of profits from overseas activity and favorable tax treatment of exports lowered GE's tax rate by 26.9 percentage points during 2008, driving the company's effective

tax rate down to 5.5 percent. A spokeswoman from the Treasury Department said the administration "is committed to reforming deferral to improve the overall efficiency and equity of the tax code by reducing incentives to divert investment from the U.S. in order to avoid taxation."

On the other hand, some tax experts fear that changing the current law will cause companies to move more and more of their jobs overseas. In 2004, Congress granted a one-time amnesty where companies could bring home the overseas earnings at a 5.25 percent rate. While it generated tax receipts for the government, its effect on creating new jobs was mixed.

Some propose that the United States government only tax earnings generated within the United States. That would be similar to the systems of other countries, a so-called territorial approach. However, that might encourage companies to manipulate their books to aggressively shift taxable income to low-tax countries

overseas, such as Ireland and Singapore.

While such a debate seems like a theoretical/financial concern, how it is resolved will have tremendous impact on the makeup and location of the workforce. As one chief human resource officer said, "With 70 percent of our revenues coming from outside of the U.S., we're asking ourselves what it means to be a global company. We are a global company that happens to have its headquarters in the U.S., and we wonder why that has to be the case. Why can't we shift our headquarters to somewhere else in the world?" If companies can save a billion dollars or more each year by being based in a lower tax country, we may see moves not just of jobs, but also of companies.

SOURCES: J. Drucker, "Titans Vow Overseas Tax Fight," April 22, 2009, http://online.wsj.com/article/SB124035794000941117.html#mod=testMod; confidential personal communication at Cornell University's "Understanding the Top Seat" Executive Education Program, October 2008.

than from an understanding of how those people outcomes relate to the larger business. Second, "people-linked" functions have clearly identified, articulated, and aligned their HR activities around people issues and outcomes, but not business issues and outcomes. Third, "business-linked" HR functions begin with an assessment of what HR is doing, then identify the major people outcomes they should focus on, and, in a few cases, how those might translate into positive business outcomes. Finally, "business-driven" functions have fully developed HR strategies which begin by identifying the major business needs and issues, consider how people fit in and what people outcomes are necessary, and then build HR systems focused on meeting those needs.

The HR strategy must help address the issues that the business faces which will determine its success. As finding, attracting, and retaining talent has become a critical issue, virtually every HR function is addressing this as part of the HR strategy (as can be seen in IBM's HR strategy). The "Competing through Globalization" box discusses how the tax system of a country can make it more or less attractive for businesses to operate there.

Measuring HRM Effectiveness

The strategic decision-making process for the HRM function requires that decision makers have a good sense of the effectiveness of the current HRM function. This information provides the foundation for decisions regarding which processes, systems, and skills of HR employees need improvement. Often HRM functions that have been heavily involved in transactional activities for a long time tend to lack systems, processes, and skills for delivering state-of-the-art traditional activities and are thoroughly unable to contribute in the transformational arena. Thus diagnosis of the effectiveness of the HRM function provides critical information for its strategic management.

In addition, having good measures of the function's effectiveness provides the following benefits:[2]

- *Marketing the function:* Evaluation is a sign to other managers that the HRM function really cares about the organization as a whole and is trying to support operations, production, marketing, and other functions of the company. Information regarding cost savings and benefits is useful to prove to internal customers that HRM practices contribute to the bottom line. Such information is also useful for gaining additional business for the HRM function.
- *Providing accountability:* Evaluation helps determine whether the HRM function is meeting its objectives and effectively using its budget.

Approaches for Evaluating Effectiveness

Two approaches are commonly used to evaluate the effectiveness of HRM practices: the audit approach and the analytic approach.

Audit Approach

The **audit approach** focuses on reviewing the various outcomes of the HRM functional areas. Both key indicators and customer satisfaction measures are typically collected. Table 16.2 lists examples of key indicators and customer satisfaction measures for staffing, equal employment opportunity, compensation, benefits, training, performance management, safety, labor relations, and succession planning. The development of electronic employee databases and information systems has made it much easier to collect, store, and analyze the functional key indicators (more on this later in the chapter) than in the past, when information was kept in file folders.

We previously discussed how HRM functions can become much more customer-oriented as part of the strategic management process. If, in fact, the function desires to be more customer-focused, then one important source of effectiveness data can be the customers. Just as firms often survey their customers to determine how effectively the customers feel they are being served, the HRM function can survey its internal customers.

One important internal customer is the employees of the firm. Employees often have both direct contact with the HRM function (through activities such as benefits

LO3
Explain the approaches to evaluating the effectiveness of HRM practices.

Audit Approach
Type of assessment of HRM effectiveness that involves review of customer satisfaction or key indicators (like turnover rate or average days to fill a position) related to an HRM functional area (such as recruiting or training).

table 16.2

Examples of Key Indicators and Customer Satisfaction Measures for HRM Functions

KEY INDICATORS	CUSTOMER SATISFACTION MEASURES
Staffing Average days taken to fill open requisitions Ratio of acceptances to offers made Ratio of minority/women applicants to representation in local labor market Per capita requirement costs Average years of experience/education of hires per job family	Anticipation of personnel needs Timeliness of referring qualified workers to line supervisors Treatment of applicants Skill in handling terminations Adaptability to changing labor market conditions
Equal employment opportunity Ratio of EEO grievances to employee population Minority representation by EEO categories Minority turnover rate	Resolution of EEO grievances Day-to-day assistance provided by personnel department in implementing affirmative action plan Aggressive recruitment to identify qualified women and minority applicants
Compensation Per capita (average) merit increases Ratio of recommendations for reclassification to number of employees Percentage of overtime hours to straight time Ratio of average salary offers to average salary in community	Fairness of existing job evaluation system in assigning grades and salaries Competitiveness in local labor market Relationship between pay and performance Employee satisfaction with pay
Benefits Average unemployment compensation payment (UCP) Average workers' compensation payment (WCP) Benefit cost per payroll dollar Percentage of sick leave to total pay	Promptness in handling claims Fairness and consistency in the application of benefit policies Communication of benefits to employees Assistance provided to line managers in reducing potential for unnecessary claims
Training Percentage of employees participating in training programs per job family Percentage of employees receiving tuition refunds Training dollars per employee	Extent to which training programs meet the needs of employees and the company Communication to employees about available training opportunities Quality of introduction/orientation programs
Employee appraisal and development Distribution of performance appraisal ratings Appropriate psychometric properties of appraisal forms	Assistance in identifying management potential Organizational development activities provided by HRM department
Succession planning Ratio of promotions to number of employees Ratio of open requisitions filled internally to those filled externally	Extent to which promotions are made from within Assistance/counseling provided to employees in career planning
Safety Frequency/severity ratio of accidents Safety-related expenses per $1,000 of payroll Plant security losses per square foot (e.g., fires, burglaries)	Assistance to line managers in organizing safety programs Assistance to line managers in identifying potential safety hazards Assistance to line managers in providing a good working environment (lighting, cleanliness, heating, etc.)

(continues)

table 16.2

Examples of Key Indicators and Customer Satisfaction Measures for HRM Functions *(concluded)*

KEY INDICATORS	CUSTOMER SATISFACTION MEASURES
Labor relations	
Ratio of grievances by pay plan to number of employees	Assistance provided to line managers in handling grievances
Frequency and duration of work stoppages	Efforts to promote a spirit of cooperation in plant
Percentage of grievances settled	Efforts to monitor the employee relations climate in plant
Overall effectiveness	
Ratio of personnel staff to employee population	Accuracy and clarity of information provided to managers and employees
Turnover rate	Competence and expertise of staff
Absenteeism rate	Working relationship between organizations and HRM department
Ratio of per capita revenues to per capita cost	
Net income per employee	

SOURCE: Reprinted with permission. Excerpts from Chapter 1.5, "Evaluating Human Resource Effectiveness," pp. 187–222, by Anne S. Tsui and Luis R. Gomez-Mejia, from *Human Resource Management: Evolving Roles and Responsibilities;* edited by Lee Dyer. Copyright © 1988 by The Bureau of National Affairs, Inc., Washington, DC 20037. To order BNA publications call toll free 1-800-960-1220.

administration and payroll) and indirect contact with the function through their involvement in activities such as receiving performance appraisals, pay raises, and training programs. Many organizations such as AT&T, Motorola, and General Electric use their regular employee attitude survey as a way to assess the employees as users/customers of the HRM programs and practices.[3] However, the problem with assessing effectiveness only from the employees' perspective is that often they are responding not from the standpoint of the good of the firm, but, rather, from their own individual perspective. For example, employees notoriously and consistently express dissatisfaction with pay level (who doesn't want more money?), but to simply ratchet up pay across the board would put the firm at a serious labor cost disadvantage.

Thus, many firms have gone to surveys of top line executives as a better means of assessing the effectiveness of the HRM function. The top-level line executives can see how the systems and practices are impacting both employees and the overall effectiveness of the firm from a strategic standpoint. This can also be useful for determining how well HR employees' perceptions of their function's effectiveness align with the views of their line colleagues. For example, a study of 14 firms revealed that HR executives and line executives agreed on the relative effectiveness of HR's delivery of services such as staffing and training systems (that is, which were most and least effectively delivered) but not on the absolute level of effectiveness. As Figure 16.7 shows, HR executives' ratings of their effectiveness in different roles also diverged significantly from line executives'. In addition, line executives viewed HRM as being significantly less effective with regard to HRM's actual contributions to the firm's overall effectiveness, as we see in Figure 16.8.[4]

The Analytic Approach

The **analytic approach** focuses on either (1) determining whether the introduction of a program or practice (like a training program or a new compensation

Analytic Approach
Type of assessment of HRM effectiveness that involves determining the impact of, or the financial cost and benefits of, a program or practice.

figure 16.7

Comparing HR and Line Executives' Evaluations of the Effectiveness of HRM Roles

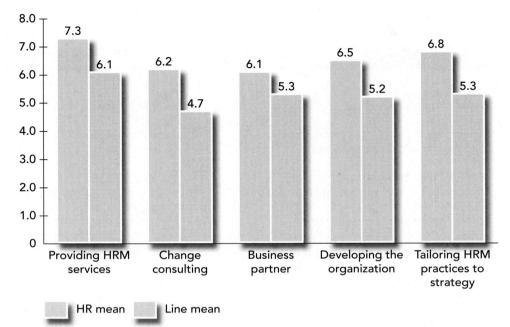

SOURCE: P. Wright, G. McMahan, S. Snell, and B. Gerhart, "Comparing Line and HR Executives' Perceptions of HR Effectiveness: Services, Roles, and Contributions," CAHRS (Center for Advanced Human Resource Studies) working paper 98-29, School of ILR, Cornell University, Ithaca, NY.

figure 16.8

Comparing HR and Line Executives' Evaluations of the Effectiveness of HRM Contributions

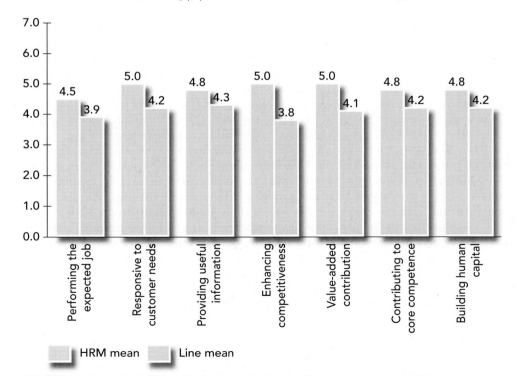

SOURCE: P. Wright, G. McMahan, S. Snell, and B. Gerhart, "Comparing Line and HR Executives' Perceptions of HR Effectiveness: Services, Roles, and Contributions," CAHRS (Center for Advanced Human Resource Studies) working paper 98-29, School of ILR, Cornell University, Ithaca, NY.

table 16.3

Types of
Cost–Benefit
Analysis

Human resource accounting
- Capitalization of salary
- Net present value of expected wage payments
- Returns on human assets and human investments

Utility analysis
- Turnover costs
- Absenteeism and sick leave costs
- Gains from selection programs
- Impact of positive employee attitudes
- Financial gains of training programs

SOURCE: Based on A. S. Tsui and L. R. Gomez-Mejia, "Evaluating HR Effectiveness," in *Human Resource Management: Evolving Roles and Responsibilities*, ed. L. Dyer (Washington, DC: Bureau of National Affairs, 1988), pp. 1–196.

system) has the intended effect or (2) estimating the financial costs and benefits resulting from an HRM practice. For example, in Chapter 7 we discussed how companies can determine a training program's impact on learning, behavior, and results. Evaluating a training program is one strategy for determining whether the program works. Typically, in an overall evaluation of effectiveness, we are interested in determining the degree of change associated with the program.

The second strategy involves determining the dollar value of the training program, taking into account all the costs associated with the program. Using this strategy, we are not concerned with how much change occurred but rather with the dollar value (costs versus benefits) of the program. Table 16.3 lists the various types of cost–benefit analyses that are done. The human resource accounting approach attempts to place a dollar value on human resources as if they were physical resources (like plant and equipment) or financial resources (like cash). Utility analysis attempts to estimate the financial impact of employee behaviors (such as absenteeism, turnover, job performance, and substance abuse).

For example, wellness programs are a popular HRM program for reducing health care costs through reducing employees' risk of heart disease and cancer. One study evaluated four different types of wellness programs. Part of the evaluation involved determining the costs and benefits associated with the four programs over a three-year period.[5] A different type of wellness program was implemented at each site. Site A instituted a program involving raising employees' awareness of health risks (distributing news articles, blood pressure testing, health education classes). Site B set up a physical fitness facility for employees. Site C raised awareness of health risks and followed up with employees who had identified health risks. Site D provided health education and follow-up counseling and promoted physical competition and health-related events. Table 16.4 shows the effectiveness and cost-effectiveness of the Site C and Site D wellness models.

The analytic approach is more demanding than the audit approach because it requires the detailed use of statistics and finance. A good example of the level of sophistication that can be required for cost–benefit analysis is shown in Table 16.5. This table shows the types of information needed to determine the dollar value of a new selection test for entry-level computer programmers.

table 16.4

Effectiveness and Cost-Effectiveness of Two Wellness Programs for Four Cardiovascular Disease Risk Factors

	SITE C	SITE D
Annual direct program costs, per employee per year	$30.96	$38.57
Percentage of cardiovascular disease risks[a] for which risk was moderately reduced or relapse prevented	48%	51%
Percentage of preceding entry per annual $1 spent per employee	1.55%	1.32%
Amount spent per 1% of risks reduced or relapse prevented	$.65	$.76

[a]High blood pressure, overweight, smoking, and lack of exercise.

SOURCE: J. C. Erfurt, A. Foote, and M. A. Heirich, "The Cost-Effectiveness of Worksite Wellness Programs," *Personnel Psychology* 45 (1992), p. 22.

table 16.5

Example of Analysis Needed to Determine the Dollar Value of a Selection Test

Cost–benefit information

Current employment	4,404
Number separating	618
Number selected	618
Average tenure	9.69 years

Test information

Number of applicants	1,236
Testing cost per applicant	$10
Total test cost	$12,360
Average test score	0.80 SD
Test validity	0.76
SD_y (per year)[a]	$10,413

Computation

Quantity = Average tenure × Applicants selected
  = 9.69 years × 618 applicants
  = 5,988 person-years

Quality = Average test score × Test validity × SD_y
  = 0.80 × 0.76 × $10,413
  = $6,331 per year

Utility = (Quantity × Quality) − Costs
  = (5,988 person-year × $6,331 per year) − $12,360
  = $37.9 million

[a]SD_y = Dollar value of one standard difference in job performance. Approximately 40% of average salary.

SOURCES: From J. W. Boudreau, "Utility Analysis," in *Human Resource Management: Evolving Roles and Responsibilities,* ed. L. Dyer (Washington, DC: Bureau of National Affairs, 1988), p. 150; F. L. Schmidt, J. E. Hunter, R. C. McKenzie, and T. W. Muldrow, "Impact of Valid Selection Procedures on Work-Force Productivity," *Journal of Applied Psychology* 64 (1979), pp. 609–26.

Improving HRM Effectiveness

LO4
Describe the new structures for the HRM function.

Once a strategic direction has been established and HRM's effectiveness evaluated, leaders of the HRM function can explore how to improve its effectiveness in contributing to the firm's competitiveness. Returning briefly to Figure 16.1, which depicted the different activities of the HRM function, often the improvement focuses on two

figure 16.9

Improving HRM Effectiveness

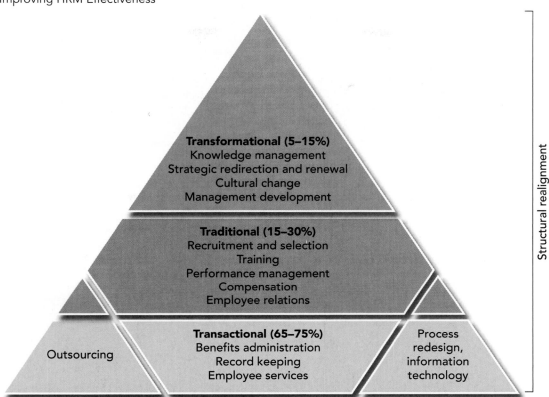

aspects of the pyramid. First, within each activity, HRM needs to improve both the efficiency and effectiveness in performing each of the activities. Second, often there is a push to eliminate as much of the transactional work as possible (and some of the traditional work) to free up time and resources to focus more on the higher-value-added transformational work. Redesign of the structure (reporting relationships) and processes (through outsourcing and information technology) enables the function to achieve these goals simultaneously. Figure 16.9 depicts this process.

Restructuring to Improve HRM Effectiveness

Traditional HRM functions were structured around the basic HRM subfunctions such as staffing, training, compensation, appraisal, and labor relations. Each of these areas had a director who reported to the VP of HRM, who often reported to a VP of finance and administration. However, for the HRM function to truly contribute strategically to firm effectiveness, the senior HR person must be part of the top management team (reporting directly to the chief executive officer), and there must be a different structural arrangement within the function itself.

A recent generic structure for the HRM function is depicted in Figure 16.10. As we see, the HRM function effectively is divided into three divisions: the centers for expertise, the field generalists, and the service center.[6] The centers for expertise usually

figure 16.10

Old and New
Structures for the
HRM Organization

Historical HRM organization structure

SOURCE: P. Wright, G. McMahan, S. Snell, and B. Gerhart, *Strategic Human Resource Management: Building Human Capital and Organizational Capability.* Technical report. Cornell University, 1998.

consist of the functional specialists in the traditional areas of HRM such as recruitment, selection, training, and compensation. These individuals ideally act as consultants in the development of state-of-the-art systems and processes for use in the organization. The field generalists consist of the HRM generalists who are assigned to a business unit within the firm. These individuals usually have dual reporting relationships to both the head of the line business and the head of HRM (although the line business tends to take priority). They ideally take responsibility for helping the line executives in their business strategically address people issues, and they ensure that the HRM systems enable the business to execute its strategy. Finally, the service center consists of individuals who ensure that the transactional activities are delivered throughout the organization. These service centers often leverage information technology to efficiently deliver employee services. For example, organizations such as Chevron have created call-in service centers where employees can dial a central number where service center employees are available to answer their questions and process their requests and transactions.

Such structural arrangements improve service delivery through specialization. Center for expertise employees can develop current functional skills without being distracted by transactional activities, and generalists can focus on learning the business environment without having to maintain expertise in functional specializations. Finally, service center employees can focus on efficient delivery of basic services across business units.

Outsourcing to Improve HRM Effectiveness

LO5
Describe how outsourcing HRM activities can improve service delivery efficiency and effectiveness.

Restructuring the internal HRM function and redesigning the processes represent internal approaches to improving HRM effectiveness. However, increasingly HR executives are seeking to improve the effectiveness of the systems, processes, and services the function delivers through outsourcing. **Outsourcing** entails contracting with an outside vendor to provide a product or service to the firm, as opposed to producing the product using employees within the firm.

Outsourcing
An organization's use of an outside organization for a broad set of services.

Why would a firm outsource an HRM activity or service? Usually this is done for one of two reasons: either the outsourcing partner can provide the service more cheaply than it would cost to do it internally, or the partner can provide it more effectively than it can be performed internally. Early on, firms resorted to outsourcing for efficiency reasons. Why would using an outsourced provider be more efficient than having internal employees provide a service? Usually it is because outsourced providers are specialists who are able to develop extensive expertise that can be leveraged across a number of companies.

For example, consider a relatively small firm that seeks to develop a pension system for employees. To provide this service to employees, the HRM function would need to learn all of the basics of pension law. Then it would need to hire a person with specific expertise in administering a pension system in terms of making sure that employee contributions are withheld and that the correct payouts are made to retired employees. Then the company would have to hire someone with expertise in investing pension funds. If the firm is small, requirements of the pension fund might not fill the time (80 hours per week) of these two new hires. Assume that it takes only 20 total hours a week for these people to do their jobs. The firm would be wasting 60 hours of employee time each week. However, a firm that specializes in providing pension administration services to multiple firms could provide the 20 hours of required time to that firm and three other firms for the same cost as had the firm performed this activity internally. Thus the specialist firm could charge the focal firm 50 percent of what it would cost the small firm to do the pensions internally. Of that 50 percent, 25 percent (20 hours) would go to paying direct salaries and the other 25 percent would be profit. Here the focal firm would save 50 percent of its expenses while the provider would make money.

Now consider the aspect of effectiveness. Because the outsourced provider works for a number of firms and specializes in pensions, its employees develop state-of-the-art knowledge of running pension plans. They can learn unique innovations from one company and transfer that learning to a new company. In addition, employees can be more easily and efficiently trained because all of them will be trained in the same processes and procedures. Finally, with experience in providing constant pension services, the firm is able to develop a capability to perform these services that could never be developed by two individuals working 25 percent of the time on these services.

What kind of services are being outsourced? Firms primarily outsource transactional activities and services of HRM such as pension and benefits administration as well as payroll. However, a number of traditional and some transformational activities have been outsourced as well. The "Competing through Technology" box describes how technology is making it extremely difficult for employers and employees to define privacy in the workplace.

Most employees are well aware that any information they access or post from their company computers can be obtained by the company, so few ever use company computers if sensitive information is involved. However, most would think that if they were on a private site, on their own computers, and using personal e-mail accounts, their companies would have no right to that information. However, recent developments may give employees pause.

Houston's restaurant bartender Brian Pietrylo and waitress Doreen Marino of Hackensack, New Jersey, created and managed a MySpace site devoted to their workplace. The goal was to create a safe place where employees could vent about things that bothered them. Employees had to log in using a personal e-mail addresses and passwords.

Pietrylo and Marino made fun of Houston's patrons and décor, made sexual jokes, and posted negative comments about their supervisors. However, a hostess at the restaurant logged into her account at an after-hours gathering and showed a Houston's manager the site. While they all had a laugh at the time, later a different supervisor called the hostess into his office and asked her to give him her e-mail and password. The information made its way up the supervisory chain of command until all the restaurant managers had seen it. A week later, Pietrylo and Marino were fired because the company claimed that their online posts violated the company's policies with regard to professionalism and a positive attitude.

The fired employees argue that the managers illegally accessed their online communications and also violated their privacy rights under New Jersey law. However, some questions arise as to whether or not online communications can be viewed as private. Lewis Maltby, president of the National Workrights Institute in Princeton, New Jersey, states, "You can't post something on the Internet and claim breach of privacy when someone sees it."

The case illustrates the intersection of technology with the rights of both employers and employees. The courts will ultimately have to decide who is in the right in this particular case. However, in the meantime, you would be wise to be careful what you post, regardless of whether or not you think your employer will ever see it.

SOURCE: CNN Student News Transcript: May 5, 2009, CNN.Com. May 4, 2009 Monday 10:28 PM EST. Copyright 2009 Cable News Network. All Rights Reserved. http://www.cnn.com cnn.com May 4, 2009 Monday 10:28 PM EST SECTION: STUDENTNEWS LENGTH: 1797 words HEADLINE: CNN Student News Transcript: May 5, 2009.

Improving HRM Effectiveness through Process Redesign

LO6
Relate how process reengineering is used to review and redesign HRM practices.

Reengineering
Review and redesign of work processes to make them more efficient and improve the quality of the end product or service.

In addition to structural arrangements, process redesign enables the HRM function to more efficiently and effectively deliver HRM services. Process redesign often uses information technology, but information technology applications are not a requirement. Thus we will discuss the general issue of process reengineering and then explore information technology applications that have aided HRM in process redesign.

Reengineering is a complete review of critical work processes and redesign to make them more efficient and able to deliver higher quality. Reengineering is especially critical to ensuring that the benefits of new technology can be realized. Applying new technology to an inefficient process will not improve efficiency or effectiveness. Instead, it will increase product or service costs related to the introduction of the new technology.

Reengineering can be used to review the HRM department functions and processes, or it can be used to review specific HRM practices such as work design or the performance management system. The reengineering process involves the four steps shown in Figure 16.11: identify the process to be reengineered, understand the process, redesign the process, and implement the new process.[7]

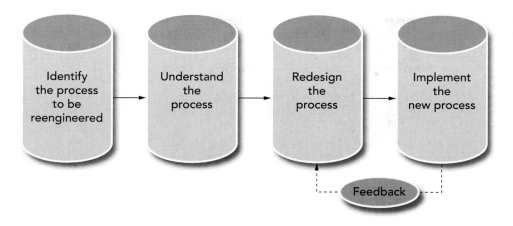

figure 16.11

The Reengineering
Process

Identifying the Process

Managers who control the process or are responsible for functions within the process (sometimes called "process owners") should be identified and asked to be part of the reengineering team. Team members should include employees involved in the process (to provide expertise) and those outside the process, as well as internal or external customers who see the outcome of the process.

Understanding the Process

Several things need to be considered when evaluating a process:

- Can jobs be combined?
- Can employees be given more autonomy? Can decision making and control be built into the process through streamlining it?
- Are all the steps in the process necessary?
- Are data redundancy, unnecessary checks, and controls built into the process?
- How many special cases and exceptions have to be dealt with?
- Are the steps in the process arranged in their natural order?
- What is the desired outcome? Are all of the tasks necessary? What is the value of the process?

Various techniques are used to understand processes. Data-flow diagrams are useful to show the flow of data among departments. Figure 16.12 shows a data-flow diagram for payroll data and the steps in producing a paycheck. Information about the employee and department are sent to the general account. The payroll check is issued based on a payment voucher that is generated from the general accounting ledger. Data-entity relationship diagrams show the types of data used within a business function and the relationship among the different types of data. In scenario analysis, simulations of real-world issues are presented to data end users. The end users are asked to indicate how an information system could help address their particular situations and what data should be maintained to deal with those situations. Surveys and focus groups collect information about the data collected, used, and stored in a functional area, as well as information about time and information-processing requirements. Users may be asked to evaluate the importance, frequency, and criticality of automating specific tasks within a functional area. For example, how critical is it to have an applicant tracking system that maintains data on applicants' previous work experience? Cost–benefit analyses compare the costs of completing tasks with and without

figure 16.12

A Data-Flow
Diagram for Payroll
Data

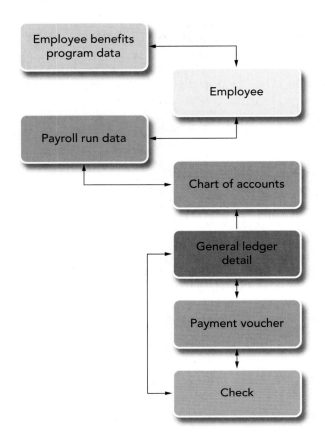

an automated system or software application. For example, the analysis should include the costs in terms of people, time, materials, and dollars; the anticipated costs of software and hardware; and labor, time, and material expenses.[8]

Redesigning the Process

During the redesign phase, the team develops models, tests them, chooses a prototype, and determines how to integrate the prototype into the organization.

Implementing the Process

LO7
Discuss the types of new technologies that can improve the efficiency and effectiveness of HRM.

The company tries out the process by testing it in a limited, controlled setting before expanding companywide. For example, J. M. Huber Corporation, a New Jersey–based conglomerate that has several operating divisions scattered throughout the United States, used reengineering to avoid installing new software onto inefficient processes.[9] HR staff began by documenting and studying the existing work flow and creating a strategy for improving efficiency. Top management, midlevel managers, and human resources staff worked together to identify the processes that they most wanted to improve. They determined that the most critical issue was to develop a client–server system that could access data more easily than the mainframe computer they were currently using. Also, the client–server system could eliminate many of the requisitions needed to get access to data, which slowed down work. The HRM department's efforts have streamlined record-keeping functions, eliminated redundant steps, and automated manual processes. The fully automated client–server system allows employees to sign up and change benefits information using an interactive voice-response system that is connected to the company's database. In addition, managers have easier access to employees' salary history, job descriptions, and other data. If an employee is eligible for a salary increase and the manager requests a change and it is approved, the system will process it (without entry by a clerical worker), and the changes will be seen on the employee's paycheck. Results of the reengineering effort are impressive. The redesigned processes have reduced the number of problems that HRM has to give to other departments by 42 percent, cut work steps by 26 percent, and eliminated 20 percent of the original work. Although the company is spending more than $1 million to make the technology work, it estimates that the investment should pay for itself in five years.

Improving HRM Effectiveness through Using New Technologies—HRM Information Systems

Several new and emerging technologies can help improve the effectiveness of the HRM function. **New technologies** are current applications of knowledge, procedures, and equipment that have not been used previously. New technology usually involves automation—that is, replacing human labor with equipment, information processing, or some combination of the two.

In HRM, technology has already been used for three broad functions: transaction processing, reporting, and tracking; decision support systems; and expert systems.[10] **Transaction processing** refers to computations and calculations used to review and document HRM decisions and practices. This includes documenting relocation, training expenses, and course enrollments and filling out government reporting requirements (such as EEO-1 reports, which require companies to report information to the government regarding employees' race and gender by job category). **Decision support systems** are designed to help managers solve problems. They usually include a "what if" feature that allows users to see how outcomes change when assumptions or data change. These systems are useful, for example, for helping companies determine the number of new hires needed based on different turnover rates or the availability of employees with a certain skill in the labor market. **Expert systems** are computer systems incorporating the decision rules of people deemed to have expertise in a certain area. The system recommends actions that the user can take based on the information provided by the user. The recommended actions are those that a human expert would take in a similar situation (such as a manager interviewing a job candidate). We discuss expert systems in more detail later in this chapter.

The newest technologies being applied to HRM include interactive voice technology, client–server architecture, relational databases, imaging, and development of specialized software. These technologies improve effectiveness through increasing access to information, improving communications, improving the speed with which HRM transactions and information can be gathered, and reducing the costs and facilitating the administration of HRM functions such as recruiting, training, and performance management. Technology enables

- Employees to gain complete control over their training and benefits enrollments (more self-service).
- The creation of a paperless employment office.
- Streamlining the HRM department's work.

New Technologies Current applications of knowledge, procedures, and equipment that have not been previously used. Usually involves replacing human labor with equipment, information processing, or some combination of the two.

Transaction Processing Computations and calculations used to review and document HRM decisions and practices.

Decision Support Systems Problem-solving systems which usually include a "what-if" feature that allows users to see how outcomes change when assumptions or data change.

Expert Systems Computer systems incorporating the decision rules of people recognized as experts in a certain area.

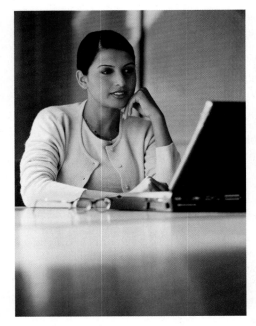

Technology has helped employers find leaner, more flexible ways of working. Human Resource professionals are increasingly using new technology to streamline HR functions.

- Knowledge-based decision support technology, which allows employees and managers to access knowledge as needed.
- Employees and managers to select the type of media they want to use to send and receive information.
- Work to be completed at any time and place.
- Closer monitoring of employees' work.[11]

There is evidence that new technology is related to improvements in productivity. Improvements in productivity have been credited largely to downsizing, restructuring, and reengineering. But technology is also responsible because new technology has allowed companies to find leaner, more flexible ways of operating.[12] A study of companies in a variety of industries found that investments in computers provided a better return than investments in other kinds of capital.[13] Technology requires companies to have appropriately skilled and motivated people and streamlined work processes. In some cases technology is replacing human capital.[14] For example, Statewide, the regional telephone unit of Pacific Telesis Group, used to dispatch about 20,000 trucks a day to fix customers' lines. New technology has enabled the company to find broken lines using computer signals. As a result, fewer truck dispatches (and fewer drivers) are necessary.

Interactive Voice Technology

Interactive voice technology uses a conventional personal computer to create an automated phone-response system. This technology is especially useful for benefits administration. For example, at Hannaford Brothers, a supermarket chain spread through the northeastern United States, the HRM department installed an interactive voice-response system that allows employees to get information on their retirement accounts, stock purchases, and benefits plans by using the touchtone buttons on their phone.[15] Employees can also directly enroll in programs and speak to an HRM representative if they have questions. As a result of the technology, the company was able to reduce the size of the HRM staff and more quickly serve employees' benefits needs.

Networks and Client–Server Architecture

Network
A combination of desktop computers, computer terminals, and mainframes or minicomputers that share access to databases and a method to transmit information throughout the system.

Traditionally, different computer systems (with separate databases) are used for payroll, recruiting, and other human resource management functions. A **network** is a combination of desktop computers, computer terminals, and mainframes or minicomputers that share access to databases and a means to transmit information throughout the system. A common form of network involves client–server architecture. **Client–server architecture** provides the means of consolidating data and applications into a single system (the client).[16] The data can be accessed by multiple users. Also, software applications can be stored on the server and "borrowed" by other users. Client–server architecture allows easier access to data, faster response time, and maximum use of the computing power of the personal computer.

For example, a pharmaceutical company with 50,000 employees worldwide uses client–server technology to create an employee information system that integrates data from six databases.[17] The available data include financial, operational, and human resource information. A manager at a European location can compare her plant's human resource costs with those for the entire company or a plant in Ohio, and at the same time senior management can use the same data to compare the productivity of the Ohio plant with a plant in Maine.

Relational Databases

Databases contain several data files (topics), which are made up of employee information (records) containing data fields. A data field is an element or type of information such as employee name, Social Security number, or job classification.

In a **relational database** information is stored in separate files, which look like tables. These files can be linked by common elements (fields) such as name, identification number, or location. This contrasts with the traditional file structure, in which all data associated with an employee was kept in one file. In the relational database shown in Figure 16.13, employees' personal information is located in one file and salary information in another, but both topics of information can be accessed via the employees' Social Security numbers.

Users of relational databases can file and retrieve information according to any field or multiple fields across different tables or databases. They provide an easy way to organize data. Also, the number of data fields that can be kept for any employee using a relational database is limitless. The ability to join or merge data from several different tables or to view only a subset of data is especially useful in human resource management. Databases that have been developed to track employee benefit costs, training courses, and compensation, for example, contain separate pieces of employee information that can be accessed and merged as desired by the user. Relational

Client–Server Architecture
Computer design that provides a method to consolidate data and applications into a single host system (the client).

Relational Database
A database structure that stores information in separate files that can be linked by common elements.

figure 16.13

Example of a Relational Database

technology also allows databases to be established in several different locations. Users in one plant or division location can access data from any other company location. Consider an oil company. Human resources data—such as the names, salaries, and skills of employees working on an oil rig in the Gulf of Mexico—can be stored at company headquarters. Databases at the oil rig site itself might contain employee name, safety equipment issued, and appropriate skill certification. Headquarters and oil rig managers can access information on each database as needed.

Imaging

Imaging
A process for scanning documents, storing them electronically, and retrieving them.

Imaging refers to scanning documents, storing them electronically, and retrieving them.[18] Imaging is particularly useful because paper files take a large volume of space and are difficult to access. Imaging has been used in applicant tracking and in benefits management. Applicants' résumés can be scanned and stored in a database so they will be available for access at a later date. Some software applications (such as Resumix) allow the user to scan the résumé based on key items such as job history, education, or experience. At Warner-Lambert, the compensation and benefits department provides HR-related services for over 15,000 retirees.[19] Eight employees retire or die each month; approximately 100 employees terminate each month. This "exit" activity created a tremendous volume of paper for each employee, as well as requests for data from analysts in the department. Locating and refiling the data was very time-consuming and inefficient. Using imaging, the compensation and benefits department was able to better serve its customers by reducing the time needed to locate a file or handle a phone inquiry from a retiree, providing the ability for sharing files among analysts simultaneously, eliminating the need to refile, and reducing the physical space needed to store the files.

Expert Systems

As we discussed earlier, expert systems are technologies that mimic a human expert. Expert systems have three elements:

- A knowledge base that contains facts, figures, and rules about a specific subject.
- A decision-making capability that draws conclusions from those facts and figures to solve problems and answer questions.
- A user interface that gathers and gives information to the person using the system.

The use of expert systems in HRM is relatively new. Some companies use expert systems to help employees decide how to allocate their money for benefits, help managers schedule the labor requirements for projects, and assist managers in conducting selection interviews. Pic 'n Pay stores (a chain of shoe stores) uses an expert system for the initial job interview. Candidates call a toll-free phone number. The candidates then respond to 100 questions, and the computer records the responses and scores them. At headquarters, a team of trained interviewers evaluates the responses and designs a list of follow-up questions, which are administered by the hiring manager. The expert system reduced employee turnover by 50 percent and reduced losses due to theft by 39 percent. Also, hiring of minorities has risen 8 percent, implying that decision biases may be less significant using the expert system.[20]

A large international food processor uses an expert system called Performer, designed to provide training and support to its plant operators. One of the problems the company was facing was determining why potato chips were being scorched in the fryer operation. An operator solved the problem using Performer. He selected the "troubleshooting" menu, then "product texture/flavor," then "off oil flavor." The program listed probable causes, beginning with high oxidation during frying. The operator chose that cause, and the system recommended adjusting the cooking line's oil flush, providing detailed steps for that procedure. Following those steps resolved the problem.[21]

Expert systems can deliver both high quality and lower costs. By using the decision processes of experts, the system enables many people to arrive at decisions that reflect the expert's knowledge. An expert system helps avoid the errors that can result from fatigue and decision biases. The efficiencies of an expert system can be realized if it can be operated by fewer employees or less skilled (and likely less costly) employees than the company would otherwise require.

Groupware

Groupware (electronic meeting software) is a software application that enables multiple users to track, share, and organize information and to work on the same document simultaneously.[22] Companies have been using groupware to improve business processes such as sales and account management, to improve meeting effectiveness, and to identify and share knowledge in the organization. (See our earlier discussion of creating a learning organization in Chapter 7.) Monsanto uses Lotus Notes to link salespeople, account managers, and competitor-intelligence analysts.[23] The database contains updated news on competitors and customers, information from public news sources, salespeople's reports, an in-house directory of experts, and attendees' notes from conventions and conferences. Many companies are also creating their own "intranet," a private company network that competes with groupware programs such as Lotus Notes. Intranets are cheaper and simpler to use than groupware programs but pose potential security problems because of the difficulty of keeping people out of the network.[24]

Groupware
Software that enables multiple users to track, share, and organize information and to work on the same database or document simultaneously.

Software Applications for HRM

Improving HRM Effectiveness through New Technologies—E-HRM

Since the mid-1990s, as HRM functions sought to play a more strategic role in their organizations, the first task was to eliminate transactional tasks in order to free up time to focus on traditional and transformational activities. Part of building a strategic HR function requires moving much of the transactional work away from being done by people so that the people can have time available to work on strategic activities. Consequently, the use of technology can both make HR more strategic and by doing so increase the value that HR adds to the business.[25] As indicated in Figure 16.9, outsourcing of many of these activities provided one mechanism for reducing this burden. However, more relevant today is the focus on the use of information technology to handle these tasks. Early on this was achieved by the development and implementation of information systems that were run by the HRM function but more recently have evolved into systems that allow employees to serve themselves. Thus,

figure 16.14
Change in Delivery

E-Enabled Delivery of HRM

Traditional face-to-face delivery

Electronic delivery

Tranformational (25–35%)
Knowledge management
Strategic redirection and renewal
Cultural change
Management development

Traditional (25–35%)
Recruitment and selection
Training
Performance management
Compensation
Employee relations

Transactional (15–25%)
Benefits administration
Record keeping
Employee services

Outsourcing

Process redesign, information technology

for example, employees can access the system and make their benefit enrollment, changes, or claims online. Clearly, technology has freed HRM functions from transactional activities to focus on more strategic actions.

However, the speed requirements of e-business force HRM functions to explore how to leverage technology for the delivery of traditional and transformational HRM activities. This does not imply that over time all of HRM will be executed over the Web, but that a number of HRM activities currently delivered via paper or face-to-face communications can be moved to the Web with no loss (and even gains) in effectiveness and efficiency. This is illustrated by Figure 16.14. We explore some examples next.

Recruitment and Selection

Traditional recruitment and selection processes have required considerable face-to-face communications with recruitment firms and potential employees, labor-intensive assessment devices, and significant monitoring of managerial decisions to ensure that hiring patterns and decisions do not run afoul of regulatory requirements. However, technology has transformed these processes.

For example, online recruiting accounted for one of every eight hires last year, according to k-force.com's poll of 300 U.S. companies. IBM employees now fill out forms on the Web to identify contract help they need, and that information is immediately sent to 14 temp agencies. Within an hour agencies respond with résumés for review, allowing IBM to cut hiring time from 10 days to 3 and save $3 million per year.

In addition, firms such as Q-Hire in Austin, Texas, provide online testing services. Applicants for positions at a firm are directed to a Web site where they complete an assessment device. Their scores are immediately compared to an ideal profile, and this profile comparison is communicated to the company screening manager. Firms can gather considerable amounts of relevant information about potential employees long before they ever need to set foot on company premises.

Finally, technology has enabled firms to monitor hiring processes to minimize the potential for discriminatory hiring decisions. For example, Home Depot was accused of forcing female applicants into cashier jobs while reserving the customer service jobs for males. While not admitting guilt, as part of their consent decree Home Depot uses technology to identify people who have skills for jobs they are not applying for based on key words in their résumés. In addition, the technology forces managers to interview diverse candidate sets before making decisions.

Compensation and Rewards

Compensation systems in organizations probably reflect the most pervasive form of bureaucracy within HRM. In spite of the critical role they play in attracting, motivating, and retaining employees, most systems consist of rigid, time-consuming, and ineffective processes. Managers fill out what they believe to be useless forms, ignore guidelines, and display a general disdain for the entire process.

Leveraging technology may allow firms to better achieve their compensation goals with considerably less effort. For example, one problem many merit or bonus pay plans face is that managers refuse to differentiate among performers, giving everyone similar pay increases. This allows them to spend less time thinking about how to manage (rate and review) performance as well as minimizes the potential conflict they might face. Thus, employees do not see linkages between performance and pay, resulting in lower motivation among all employees and higher turnover among top performers (and possibly lower turnover among bottom performers). To minimize this, Cypress Semiconductors requires managers to distinguish between equity and merit and forces distributions with regard to both concepts.[26] For example, equity means that the top-ranked performer in any group of peers should make 50 percent more than the lowest-ranked performer, and people with comparable performance should receive comparable salaries. With regard to merit, there must be at least a 7 percent spread between the lowest and highest pay raises (if the lowest raise is 3 percent, then the highest must be at least 10 percent). If ratings and raises are input into a system, the firm can monitor and control the rating process to ensure that adequate differentiations are made consistent with the policy.

Training and Development

Exploring different vehicles for delivering training (PC, video, and the like) certainly is not a new concept. In addition, a number of firms have begun delivering training via the Web. Their experience suggests that some types of training can be done effectively via the Internet or an intranet, whereas others might not. For example, companies such as IBM and Dell both boast that they have developed Internet-based training for some parts of their workforce.

Interestingly, the challenge of speedy delivery of HRM services brings the concept of Internet-based training to the forefront. In today's competitive environment, firms compete to attract and retain both customers and talented employees. How well a firm develops and treats existing employees largely determines how well it achieves these outcomes. Yet the challenges of speed, project focus, and changing technology create environments that discourage managers from managing their people, resulting in a situation where employees may not feel respected or valued.

This presents a challenge to firms to provide both the incentive and the skills for managers to treat employees as assets rather than commodities. Consider how Internet-based training might facilitate this. Assume that you work for Widget.com, a fast-growing, fast-paced e-business. You arrive at work Monday morning, and your e-mail contains a high-priority message with either an attachment or a link to a URL. It is your Monday morning challenge from the CEO, and you know that the system will track whether you link and complete this challenge. When you link to it, you see a digital video of your CEO telling you how people are Widget.com's competitive advantage, and that when they don't feel valued, they leave. Thus his challenge to you is to make your employees feel valued today. To do so, you will in the next 10 minutes learn how to express appreciation to an employee. You receive six learning points; you observe a digitized video model performing the learning points; you review the learning points again and take a quiz. You then see the CEO giving you the final challenge: that in the next 15 minutes you are to take one of your employees aside and express your appreciation using the skill you just developed.

Notice the advantages of this process. First, it was not time-consuming like most three-day or one-week training programs. The entire process (training and demonstration with a real employee) took less than 30 minutes; you have developed a skill; and an employee now probably feels better about the organization. It communicated a real organizational value or necessary competency. It didn't require any travel expenses to a training facility. It did not overwhelm you with so much information that you would be lucky to remember 10 percent of what you were exposed to. Finally, it was a push, rather than pull, approach to training. The firm did not wait for you to realize you had a deficiency and then go search and sign up for training. It pushed the training to you.

Thus technology allows firms to deliver training and development for at least some skills or knowledge faster, more efficiently, and probably more effectively. It can quickly merge training, communication, and immediate response to strategic contingencies.

Creating and nurturing a committed workforce presents a tremendous challenge to firms today. According to a recent survey conducted by Monster.com, 61 percent of Americans consider themselves overworked and 86 percent are not satisfied with their jobs.[27] Such findings suggest that firms need to find ways to monitor commitment levels, identify potential obstacles to commitment, and respond quickly to eliminate those obstacles. In large part, attitude surveys have constituted the platform from which these activities were managed in the past.

Consider the traditional attitude survey. Surveys are administered to employees over a period of four to six weeks. The data are entered and analyzed, requiring another six to eight weeks. A group interprets the results to identify the major problem areas, and task forces are formed to develop recommendations; this process easily takes another four to six months. Finally, decisions must be made about implementing the task force recommendations. In the end, at best employees might see responses to their concerns 12 to 18 months after the survey—and then the survey administrators cannot understand why employees think that completing the survey is a waste of time.

Now consider how technology can shorten that cycle. E-pulse represents one attempt to create a platform for almost real-time attitude surveys. Developed by Theresa Welbourne at the University of Michigan, E-pulse is a scalable survey device administered online. Normally three questions are asked regarding how employees feel about work, but more questions can be added to get feedback on any specific issue. The survey goes out online, and when employees complete it, the data are immediately entered and analyzed. In essence, the part of the process that took four months in the past has been reduced to a day.

Next the firm can decide how it wants to use the information. For example, it could be broken down by business, site, or work unit, with the relevant information going to the leader of the chosen unit of analysis. In essence, a supervisor could receive almost immediate feedback about the attitudes of his or her work group, or a general manager about his or her business unit. The supervisor or manager can respond immediately, even if only to communicate that she or he realizes a problem exists and will take action soon.

One must recognize that although the technology provides for faster HRM, only a more systemic approach will ensure better and smarter HRM. For example, disseminating the information to the supervisors and managers may be faster, but unless those individuals possess good problem-solving and communication skills, they may either ignore the information or, worse yet, exacerbate the problem with inappropriate responses. As we noted with regard to training, this systemic approach requires knocking down traditional functional walls to deliver organizational solutions rather than functional programs. Thus the challenge is to get beyond viewing the technology as a panacea or even as a functional tool, but rather as a catalyst for transforming the HRM organization. The "Competing through Sustainability" box describes how companies can manage downsizing processes while maintaining a sustainable employment relationship.

The Future for HR Professionals

The future for careers in the human resource profession seems brighter than ever. An increasing number of successful companies such as Microsoft have made the top HR job a member of the senior management team, reporting directly to the chief executive officer. CEOs recognize the importance of their workforce in driving competitive success. Firms need to seek the balance between attracting, motivating, and retaining the very best talent and keeping labor and administrative costs as low as possible. Finding such a balance requires HR leaders who have a deep knowledge of the business combined with a deep knowledge of HR issues, tools, processes, and technologies.

For a reader who is just getting a first glimpse of the HRM function, to portray what a vastly different role HRM must play today compared to 20 or even 10 years ago is impossible. As noted earlier, HRM has traditionally played a largely administrative role—simply processing paperwork plus developing and administering hiring, training, appraisal, compensation, and benefits systems—and all of this has been unrelated to the strategic direction of the firm. In the early 1980s HRM took on more of a one-way linkage role, helping to implement strategy. Now strategic decision makers are realizing the importance of people issues and so are calling for HRM to become the "source of people expertise" in the firm.[28] This requires that HR managers possess and use knowledge of how people can and do play a role in competitive advantage as

As the U.S. economy has tumbled, more and more companies have engaged in layoffs as a necessary component of reducing costs. However, the economic downturn will transform to economic growth at some point, thus requiring firms to think about how to manage their employees under challenging circumstances in ways that will enable them to manage well under munificent conditions.

As one would expect, employees feel tremendous uncertainty as they observe their companies' downsizings. Sirota Survey Intelligence's surveys show that the percentage of employees who felt valued fell to 44 percent in 2002 from 67 percent prior to the layoffs resulting from 9/11. The research reveals that employees miss co-workers and friends, experience higher levels of stress, and see less teamwork. However, central to employee morale is trust in management.

Sirota suggests the following strategies for building sustainable relationships with the workforce:

1. Communicate—quickly, openly, honestly. It is important to answer the most pressing questions right away, such as whether or not the company will be downsizing further.
2. Allow for their emotional response. Survivors naturally feel emotions such as anger, concern, insecurity, depression, and guilt, and managers need to reassure employees that these feelings are natural.
3. Address work frustrations due to the cutbacks. Cutbacks usually result in increased workloads for survivors, and this can damage teamwork at a time when teamwork is even more important. Managers need to engage employees in rethinking how work can be done differently.
4. Demonstrate continuing long-term interest in the careers of the survivors. People want to know that they have a future and that the company still wants to invest in them. In the absence of training budgets, "stretch" assignments can challenge people to gain new skills that will make them even more promotable when the company begins to grow again.
5. Assess whether it's working—don't guess. Use facts and data to gauge how employees are reacting and performing. Employee surveys, focus groups, and one-on-one discussion can provide important data while also communicating that employees views are still valued.

SOURCE: Douglas Klein, "Five Strategies for Managing after Layoffs," January 1, 2009. http://www.hreonline.com/HRE/story.jsp?storyId=156838048&query=sustainability.

well as the policies, programs, and practices that can leverage the firm's people as a source of competitive advantage. This leads to an entirely new set of competencies for today's strategic HR executive.[29]

In the future, HR professionals will need four basic competencies to become partners in the strategic management process (see Figure 2.7).[30] First, they will need "business competence"—knowing the company's business and understanding its economic financial capabilities. This calls for making logical decisions that support the company's strategic plan based on the most accurate information possible. Because in almost all companies the effectiveness of decisions must be evaluated in terms of dollar values, the HR executive must be able to calculate the costs and benefits of each alternative in terms of its dollar impact.[31] In addition, it requires that the nonmonetary impact be considered. The HR executive must be fully capable of identifying the social and ethical issues attached to HRM practices.

Second, HR professionals will need "professional–technical knowledge" of state-of-the-art HRM practices in areas such as staffing, development, rewards, organizational design, and communication. New selection techniques, performance appraisal methods, training programs, and incentive plans are constantly being developed. Some of these programs can provide value whereas others may be no more than the products of today's HRM equivalent of snake oil. HR executives must be able to critically evaluate the new techniques offered as state-of-the-art HRM programs and use only those that will benefit the company.

Third, they must be skilled in the "management of change processes," such as diagnosing problems, implementing organizational changes, and evaluating results. Every time a company changes its strategy in even a minor way, the entire company has to change. These changes result in conflict, resistance, and confusion among the people who must implement the new plans or programs. The HR executive must have the skills to oversee the change in a way that ensures its success. In fact, one survey of *Fortune* 500 companies found that 87 percent of the companies had their organization development/change function as part of the HR department.[32]

Finally, these professionals must also have "integration competence," meaning the ability to integrate the three other competencies to increase the company's value. This requires that, although specialist knowledge is necessary, a generalist perspective must be taken in making decisions. This entails seeing how all the functions within the HRM area fit together to be effective and recognizing that changes in any one part of the HRM package are likely to require changes in other parts of the package. For example, a health care company in central Texas was attempting to fill a position in the X-ray department. It was able to identify qualified candidates for the position, but none of the candidates accepted the offer. It was not until the company examined its total package (pay, benefits, promotion opportunities, and so on) and changed the composition of the package that it was able to fill the position.

The Role of the Chief Human Resource Officer

Having discussed the increasing importance of HR and the new strategic role of HR professionals, in closing we examine the role of the leader of the HR function. These chief human resource officers (CHROs) bear the responsibility for leading the HR function as well as ensuring that HR systems and processes deliver value to the company. Only recently have researchers attempted to examine what these HR leaders do and how they affect the business.

A recent survey identified seven roles that CHROs have to play to one degree or another, and then asked *Fortune* 150 CHROs to identify how they spend their time across those roles. As can be seen in Figure 16.15 CHROs reported spending the second most time (21 percent) as a **strategic advisor** to the executive team. This role entails sharing the people expertise as part of the decision-making process, as well as shaping how the human capital of the firm fits into its strategy. This also was the role that was most frequently cited as having the greatest impact on the firm. One CHRO described the importance of the strategic advisor role as:

> HR is critical, but it's a tool in the firm's portfolio. First to truly impact the success of the firm, the CHRO needs to have a broad credibility that only comes from understanding every facet of the business at a level deep enough to be able to add business value in discussions with every leader. That means understanding the firm's economics, customer behavior, products, technology, etc. at a level deep enough to steer and shape decisions in these areas. From that flows the trust and credibility to counter the "conventional wisdom" on how best to manage people and shape the firm's talent agenda. Without this broader

LO8
List the competencies the HRM executive needs to become a strategic partner in the company.

Strategic Advisor
A role of the CHRO that focuses on the formulation and implementation of the firm's strategy.

credibility, the CHRO can talk about talent, but risks not having sufficient context to make the right decisions. Second, from the CEO's perspective, the most useful thing is the integration of the people strategy with every other part of the firm's operations. The only way to truly integrate these areas is to be actively involved in the broader discussions as well.[33]

Talent Architect
A role of the CHRO that focuses on building and identifying the human capital critical to the present and future of the firm.

The role of **talent architect** also sees a significant portion of time spent (17 percent) and was also frequently cited as the role in which the CHRO has the greatest impact on the business. Playing the role of talent architect requires that CHROs help the executive team see the importance of talent, identify present and future talent gaps, and come to own the talent agenda. One CHRO described the importance of this role this way:

> Keeping the senior team focused on the strategic talent needs of the business allows proper identification of talent gaps and future needs, thus allowing time to develop best talent and design appropriate experiential assignments.[34]

**Counselor/
Confidante/Coach**
A role of the CHRO that focuses on counseling or coaching team members or resolving interpersonal or political conflicts among team members.

CHROs report spending as much time in the role of **counselor/confidante/coach** as they do in the talent architect role (17 percent), and a number of CHROs listed this role as one of the roles with the greatest impact. This role seemingly is a broad one, and it can entail anything from behavioral or performance counseling to being the personal sounding board for the CHRO. Perhaps as pressure mounts on CEOs from investors and analysts, the CHRO is the most trusted advisor that can be counted on to give personal advice or simply to listen to the CEO's problems. One poignant comment regarding this role was:

> If I do my job right, I am the copper wire that connects all the outlets of the firm together effectively. This includes OD work (which some might put in the strategic advisor category), performance counseling and relationship building, business consulting and the strategic elements of talent acquisition and planning.[35]

Leader of the HR Function
A role of the CHRO that focuses on working with HR team members regarding the development, design, and delivery of HR services.

The **leader of the HR function** is the role in which CHROs spent the most time, but it is not seen as one that has the greatest impact. This role deals with ensuring that the HR function is aligning its activities and priorities toward the needs of the business, and it usually entails meeting with direct reports to provide guidance and check on progress. However, CHROs increasingly rely on their direct reports to

table 16.6
Roles of the CHRO

Strategic advisor to the executive team—activities focused specifically on the formulation and implementation of the firm's strategy.
Counselor/confidante/coach to the executive team—activities focused on counseling or coaching team members or resolving interpersonal or political conflicts among team members.
Liaison to the board of directors—preparation for board meetings, phone calls with board members, attendance at board meetings.
Talent architect—activities focused on building and identifying the human capital critical to the present and future of the firm.
Leader of the HR function—working with HR team members regarding the development, design, and delivery of HR services.
Workforce sensor—activities focused on identifying workforce morale issues or concerns.
Representative of the firm—activities with external stakeholders, such as lobbying, speaking to outside groups, etc.

What percent of your time would you say you spend in each of the following roles?

Firm representative 5%
Other 0%
Workforce sensor 8%
Strategic advisor 21%
Functional leader 22%
Executive coach 17%
Talent architect 17%
Board liaison 10%

figure 16.15

Percentage of Time CHROs Spend in Each Role

design and deliver HR services while they shift their attention to advising and counseling the top executive team.

Liaison to the board entails all of the activities in which CHROs engage with the board of directors, including discussions of executive compensation, CEO performance, CEO succession, and performance of other members of the executive leadership team. This role is increasing in importance, although it has a long way to go before equaling the strategic advisor, talent architect, and counselor/confidante/coach roles.

The role of **workforce sensors** entails taking the pulse of the employee population to identify any morale or motivation issues. This is a role in which CHROs do not spent much time, and few viewed it as having the greatest impact on the business.

Finally, CHROs to some extent become the face of the organization to outside constituents such as labor unions, nongovernmental organizations, and the press. They spend the least amount of time in the **representative of the firm** role (see Table 16.6).

The new strategic role for HRM presents both opportunities and challenges. HRM has the chance to profoundly impact the way organizations compete through people. On the other hand, with this opportunity come serious responsibility and accountability.[36] HRM functions of the future must consist of individuals who view themselves as businesspeople who happen to work in an HRM function, rather than HRM people who happen to work in a business.

Liaison to the Board
A role of the CHRO that focuses on preparation for board meetings, phone calls with board members, and attendance at board meetings.

Workforce Sensor
A role of the CHRO that focuses on identifying workforce morale issues or concerns.

Representative of the Firm
A role of the CHRO that focuses on activities with external stakeholders, such as lobbying, speaking to outside groups, etc.

A LOOK BACK

IBM'S GLOBAL TRANSFORMATION CONTINUES

IBM's HR function has certainly been proactive in shaping the strategy of the business as well as aiding in its execution. Randy MacDonald exemplifies the true business-driven CHRO.

However, IBM also illustrates how the transformation is a journey, not a destination. Even as IBM has successfully transformed its capabilities and seems to continue to succeed financially, it continues to change. In fact, the company reported strong quarterly profits in January 2009, yet the next day announced that more than 1,400 of IBM's sales and distribution employee in the United States, would be laid off. MacDonald said it was routine for the company to lay off some employees while hiring elsewhere. "This business is in a constant state of transformation," he said. "I think of this as business as usual for us."

Questions:

1. What do you think of IBM's decision to lay off employees when they are making strong profits?
2. If you were sitting in MacDonald's chair, what do you think you would have done differently?

SOURCE: Steve Lohr, "Quiet Layoffs Sting Workers without Notice," *The New York Times*, March 6, 2009, p. A-1.

  Please see the Video Case and Case Study that correspond to this chapter online at www.mhhe.com/noe7e.

SUMMARY

The roles required of the HRM function have changed as people have become recognized as a true source of competitive advantage. This has required a transformation of the HRM function from focusing solely on transactional activities to an increasing involvement in strategic activities. In fact, according to a recent study, 64 percent of HR executives said that their HRM function is in a process of transformation.[37] The strategic management of the HRM function will determine whether HRM will transform itself to a true strategic partner or simply be blown up.

In this chapter we have explored the various changing roles of the HRM function. HRM today must play roles as an administrative expert, employee advocate, change agent, and strategic partner. The function must also deliver transactional, traditional, and transformational services and activities to the firm, and it must be both efficient and effective. HR executives must strategically manage the HRM function just as the firm must be strategically managed. This requires that HRM develop measures of the function's performance through customer surveys and analytical methods. These measures can form the basis for planning ways to improve performance. HRM performance can increase through new structures for the function, through using reengineering and information technology, and through outsourcing.

KEY TERMS

Audit approach, 725
Analytic approach, 727
Outsourcing, 733
Reengineering, 734
New technologies, 737
Transaction processing, 737
Decision support systems, 737

Expert systems, 737
Network, 738
Client–server architecture, 739
Relational database, 739
Imaging, 740
Groupware, 741
Strategic advisor, 747

Talent architect, 748
Counselor/confidante/coach, 748
Leader of the HR function, 748
Liaison to the board, 749
Workforce sensor, 749
Representative of the firm, 749

DISCUSSION QUESTIONS

1. Why have the roles and activities of the HRM function changed over the past 20 to 30 years? What has been driving this change? How effectively do you think HRM has responded?
2. How can the processes for strategic management discussed in Chapter 2 be transplanted to manage the HRM function?
3. Why do you think that few companies take the time to determine the effectiveness of HRM practices? Should a company be concerned about evaluating HRM practices? Why? What might people working in the HRM function gain by evaluating the function?
4. How might imaging technology be useful for recruitment? For training? For benefits administration? For performance management?
5. Employees in your company currently choose and enroll in benefits programs after reading communications brochures, completing enrollment forms, and sending them to their HR rep. A temporary staff has to be hired to process the large amount of paperwork that is generated. Enrollment forms need to be checked, sorted, batched, sent to data entry, keypunched, returned, and filed. The process is slow and prone to errors. How could you use process reengineering to make benefits enrollment more efficient and effective?
6. Some argue that outsourcing an activity is bad because the activity is no longer a means of distinguishing the firm from competitors. (All competitors can buy the same service from the same provider, so it cannot be a source of competitive advantage.) Is this true? If so, why would a firm outsource any activity?

SELF-ASSESSMENT EXERCISE

How ethical are you? Read each of the following descriptions. For each, circle whether you believe the behavior described is ethical or unethical.

1. A company president found that a competitor had made an important scientific discovery that would sharply reduce the profits of his own company. The president hired a key employee of the competitor in an attempt to learn the details of the discovery.   Ethical   Unethical
2. To increase profits, a general manager used a production process that exceeded legal limits for environmental pollution.   Ethical   Unethical
3. Because of pressure from her brokerage firm, a stockbroker recommended a type of bond that she did not consider to be a good investment.   Ethical   Unethical
4. A small business received one-fourth of its revenues in the form of cash. On the company's income tax forms, the owner reported only one-half of the cash receipts.   Ethical   Unethical
5. A corporate executive promoted a loyal friend and competent manager to the position of divisional vice president in preference to a better qualified manager with whom she had no close ties.   Ethical   Unethical
6. An employer received applications for a supervisor's position from two equally qualified applicants. The employer hired the male applicant because he thought some employees might resent being supervised by a female.   Ethical   Unethical
7. An engineer discovered what he perceived to be a product design flaw that constituted a safety hazard. His company declined to correct the flaw. The engineer decided to keep quiet, rather than taking his complaint outside the company.   Ethical   Unethical
8. A comptroller selected a legal method of financial reporting that concealed some embarrassing financial facts. Otherwise, those facts would have been public knowledge.   Ethical   Unethical
9. A company paid a $350,000 "consulting" fee to an official of a foreign country. In return, the official promised to help the company obtain a contract that should produce a $10 million profit for the company.   Ethical   Unethical
10. A member of a corporation's board of directors learned that his company intended to announce a stock split and increase its dividend. On the basis of this favorable information, the director bought additional shares of the company's stock. Following the announcement of the information, he sold the stock at a gain.   Ethical   Unethical

Now score your results. How many actions did you judge to be unethical?

All of these actions are unethical. The more of the actions you judged to be unethical, the better your understanding of ethical business behavior.

SOURCE: Based on S. Morris et al., "A Test of Environmental, Situational, and Personal Influences on the Ethical Intentions of CEOs," *Business and Society* 34 (1995), pp. 119–47.

EXERCISING STRATEGY: TRANSFORMING THE BUSINESS AND HR AT XEROX

In 1958, Xerox launched the Xerox 914, the first automatic, plain-paper office copier. This product went on to become the top-selling industrial product of all time. Xerox's successful xerography technology gave it a sustainable competitive advantage that endured for years. However, all good things must come to an end, and in Xerox's case, that end was the late 1990s. By 2000, Xerox experienced its biggest slide in history, and the consensus among analysts within the industry was that Xerox was working with "an unsustainable business model," meaning unless things changed drastically, Xerox would soon cease to exist. In 2000 Xerox had $17.1 billion in debt, with only $154 million in cash on hand. By 2001, Xerox's stock, which had peaked at $63, fell to about $4—a loss of 90 percent of its market capitalization. And as if that was not enough, it also faced an accounting investigation by the Securities and Exchange Commission for how it accounted for its customer leases on copiers.

Enter new VP of HR Pat Nazemetz in 1999 and new CEO Anne Mulcahy in 2000 to try to right a sinking ship. Mulcahy put the company on a starvation diet. This entailed selling major operations in China and Hong Kong, reducing global headcount to 61,100 from 91,500 through selloffs, early retirements, and layoffs, and implementing drastic cost controls. While Mulcahy's strategy has brought Xerox back to life (2003 saw Xerox triple its net income to $360 million) as an organization, the HR function had to drive the change in the business while simultaneously transforming the function.

While many HR functions look to outsource, Xerox transformed its HR function largely internally. According to Nazemetz, outsourcing providers say "'Let us in, let us take over your HR function and we can take 10 percent to 30 percent out of your cost base.' We began trimming down, finding synergies and opportunities to get more efficient. We found the savings ourselves."

The largest single savings came from consolidating and expanding the HR Service Center. The Center began with purely transactional work (e.g., address changes), then added Web-based processes to handle routine work. The Center now conducts research and analysis to HR operations and handles employee-relations issues. This has enabled HR to reduce headcount without reducing levels of service.

Also, as with any organization that has shed 30 percent of its workforce, employee morale was and continues to be an issue. Even before the fall, HR had been taking the pulse of employees through their "hearts and minds" surveys. This intranet-based survey taps into a number of employee attitudes and seeks to identify the problem areas for HR and line executives to focus on. Employees have noted concerns with items like "Company supports risk-taking," "Company considers impact on employees," "Senior-management behavior is consistent with words," and "Trust level is high."

"People often ask me how Xerox has found success" says Mulcahy. "My answer is that you have to have a strategy and a plan, but [more importantly], what you really need is excellence of execution, and that starts and ends with a talented, motivated group of people aligned around a common set of goals. Our HR people came through with a series of alignment workshops and retention incentives just when we needed them [to] make Xerox the stronger, better company it is today."

Questions

1. After having gone through the massive downsizing, morale obviously has presented challenges. While Xerox employees seem to understand the need for change (minds), they may not emotionally embrace it (hearts). How can Xerox gain both "hearts" and "minds"?

2. Xerox's HR function focuses on three initiatives: (a) employee value proposition (what can employees expect from the company, and what can the company expect from employees?), (b) performance culture (how can the company develop a culture that encourages continuous improvement and high performance from all employees?), and (c) "three exceptional candidates" (how can HR deliver a pipeline of three-deep bench talent for every position within the organization?). From everything you have learned, how might Xerox address each of these issues?

BusinessWeek   ## Saving Starbucks' Soul

Chairman Howard Schultz is on a mission to take his company back to its roots. Oh, yeah—he also wants to triple sales in five years.   *"A heady aroma of coffee reached out and drew me in. I stepped inside and saw what looked like a temple for the worship of coffee . . . it was my Mecca. I had arrived."—Howard Schultz on his first visit to Starbucks in 1981.*

On April 3, Starbucks launches a pair of confections called Dulce de Leche Latte and Dulce de Leche Frappuccino. A 16-oz. Grande latte has a robust 440 calories (about the same as two packages of M&M's) and costs about $4.50 in New York City—or about three times as much as McDonald's most expensive premium coffee. Starbucks Corp. describes its latest concoctions, which took 18 months to perfect, this way: "Topped with whipped cream and a dusting of toffee sprinkles, Starbucks' version of this traditional delicacy is a luxurious tasty treat."

If you find yourself at Starbucks in the next few weeks, letting a Dulce de Leche Latte slide over your taste buds, you might wonder how this drink came to be. It's a tale worth hearing. On the surface it's a story about how the Starbucks marketing machine conjures and sells café romance to millions of people around the world. On a deeper level it's a story about how a company, along with its messianic leader, is struggling to hold on to its soul.

Ask Schultz for the key to Starbucks and he'll tell you it's all about storytelling. Starbucks is centered on two oft-repeated tales: Schultz' trip to Seattle in 1981, where he first enjoyed gourmet coffee, and a 1983 trip to Milan, where he discovered espresso bar culture. Not only are these journeys useful touchstones for recruits, they also provide the original marketing story for a company that prides itself on giving customers an authentic experience. "The one common thread to the success of these stories and the company itself," says Schultz, "is that they have to be true—and they have to be authentic."

True Believers

Stories alone aren't enough, though, to fuel Starbucks' other obsession: to grow really, really big. By 2012, Schultz aims to nearly triple annual sales, to $23.3 billion. The company also plans to have 40,000 stores worldwide, up from 13,500 today, not long after that, to hit its profit targets. Starbucks has become expert at something that's decidedly unromantic—streamlining operations. Over the past 10 years the company has redesigned the space behind the counter to boost barista efficiency. Automatic espresso machines speed the time it takes to serve up a shot. Coffee is vacuum-sealed, making it easier to ship over long distances. To boost sales, the company sells everything from breath mints to CDs to notebooks. Add it up and you have an experience that's nothing like the worn wooden counters of the first store in Pike Place Market or an Italian espresso bar.

Somewhere along the way that disconnect began to gnaw at Schultz. Most recently it manifested itself in a note he wrote to his senior team. The Valentine's Day memo, which leaked to the Web, cut to the heart of what he sees as the company's dilemma. "We have had to make a series of decisions," Schultz wrote, "that, in retrospect, have led to the watering down of the Starbucks experience, and what some might call the commoditization of our brand."

Now, Schultz is asking his lieutenants to redouble their efforts to return to their roots. "We're constantly—I don't want to say battling—but we don't want to be that big company that's corporate and slick," says Michelle Gass, senior vice-president and chief merchant for global products. "We don't. We still think about ourselves as a small entrepreneurial company." That's a tricky business when you have 150,000 employees in 39 countries. But keeping that coffee joie de vivre alive inside Starbucks is crucial to Schultz' entire philosophy. Who better to sell something than a true believer?

In 2004, Starbucks introduced something called the Coffee Master program for its employees. It's a kind of extra-credit course that teaches the staff how to discern the subtleties of regional flavor. Graduates (there are now 25,000) earn a special black apron and an insignia on their business cards. The highlight is the "cupping ceremony," a tasting ritual traditionally used by coffee traders. After the grounds have steeped in boiling water, tasters "crest" the mixture, penetrating the crust on top with a spoon and inhaling the aroma. As employees slurp the brew, a Starbucks Coffee Educator encourages them to taste a Kenyan coffee's "citrusy" notes or the "mushroomy" flavor of a Sumatran blend.

If the ritual reminds you of a wine tasting, that's intentional. Schultz has long wanted to emulate the wine business. Winemakers, after all, command a premium by focusing on provenance: the region of origin, the vineyard, and, of course, the grape that gives the wine its particular notes—a story, in other words. Bringing wine's cachet to coffee would help take the brand upmarket and allow Starbucks to sell premium beans.

The product and marketing people call the strategy "Geography is a Flavor." And in 2005 they began selling this new story with whole-bean coffee. The company reorganized the menu behind the counter, grouping coffees by geography instead of by "smooth" or "bold." It replaced the colorful Starbucks coffee bags with clean white packages emblazoned with colored bands representing the region of origin. Later, for those connoisseurs willing to pay $28 a pound, Starbucks introduced single-origin beans called "Black Apron Exclusives."

The next step was to reach the masses who buy drinks in the stores. The team decided to launch a series of in-store promotions, each with a new set of drinks, that would communicate regional idiosyncrasies to customers. The first promotion, the team decided, would highlight Central and South America, where Starbucks buys more than 70 percent of its beans.

The sort of authenticity Schultz loves to talk about is hard to pull off when you're the size of Starbucks. Telling a story to a mass audience sometimes requires smoothing over inconvenient cultural nuances. Plus, the marketing folks have to work quickly to stay abreast of beverage trends, not to mention ahead of such rivals as Dunkin' Donuts and McDonald's. Diving deep is not an option.

A year ago, 10 Starbucks marketers and designers got on a plane and went looking for inspiration in Costa Rica. "It's being able to say: This is how and why this [drink] is made," says Angie McKenzie, who runs new product design. "Not because someone told us or we read it somewhere." The Starbucks team spent five days in Costa Rica, traveling on a minivan owned by TAM Tours. Later, a smaller group toured Mexico City and Oaxaca as well.

Made in China

The mission was to find products that would evoke an authentic vibe in the United States. That's harder than it sounds. Philip Clark, a merchandising executive, wanted to sell traditional Costa Rican mugs. But the ones typically used to drink coffee were drab and brown; they wouldn't pop on store shelves. Plus, they broke easily. Then he found Cecilia de Figueres, who handpaints ceramic mugs in a mountainside studio an hour from the capital, San Jose. The artist favors bright floral patterns; they would pop nicely. Starbucks paid de Figueres a flat fee for her designs. Each mug will have a tag bearing her name and likeness; on the bottom it will say "Made in China."

Starbucks will weave artisans and other Costa Ricans into the in-store promotional campaign. Painter Eloy Zuñiga Guevara will appear on a poster with a decidedly homespun Latin aesthetic. (And if customers want some authenticity to take home with them, they can buy one of five paintings of Costa Rican farmers that Guevara produced for Starbucks. They will sell for $25 apiece.) A second poster will feature Costa Rican coffee farmers from whom Starbucks buys beans. A third will show a grandmotherly figure cooking up dulce de leche on a gas stove. (She's a paid model from Seattle.) Each poster will feature the tagline "I am Starbucks."

Having devised a story, Starbucks needed a drink that would say "Latin America." Beverage brainstorming takes place in the Liquid Lab, an airy space painted in Starbucks' familiar blue, green, and orange hues. The room features huge bulletin boards plastered with the latest beverage trends. In this case it didn't take an anthropologist to figure out which drink Starbucks should use to promote its Latin American theme.

Dulce de leche is a caramel-and-milk dessert enjoyed throughout much of the region. What's more, Häagen-Dazs introduced dulce de leche ice cream in 1998, and Starbucks followed suit with its own ice cream in 1999. So Americans are familiar with the flavor, says McKenzie, but "it still has a nice exotic edge to it." Besides, she adds, caramel and milk go great with coffee.

Even so, concocting a drink is never simple at Starbucks. The research-and-development department routinely tackles 70 beverage projects a year, with 8 of them leading to new drinks. A drink must not only appeal to a broad swath of coffee drinkers but also be easy for a barista to make quickly so as to maximize sales per store (hello, Wall Street). "The store . . . is a little manufacturing plant," says Gass, and yet it must seem as though the drink is being handcrafted specially for the customer (hello, Howard Schultz).

Creating the Dulce de Leche Latte and Frappuccino fell to Debbie Ismon, a 26-year-old beverage developer who holds a degree in food science and has worked at Starbucks for 2 1/2 years. In late June 2006, the design team brought her a small sample they'd whipped up that they felt embodied the right tastes, plus a written description of the characteristics they hoped to see. For the next four months, Ismon fiddled with various ratios of caramel, cooked milk, and sweetness "notes." After the design group decided which version tasted most "in-concept," Ismon mixed up three different flavors for the big taste test. One hundred or so random Starbucks employees filed in, sampled the drinks, and rated them on computer screens. The process was repeated two more times for each drink. Finally, 18 months after starting the process, Starbucks had its two latest premium beverages.

If previous drinks, such as Caramel Macchiato, are any guide, Starbucks' Dulce de Leche drinks will sell briskly. That should please Wall Street and perhaps even help perk up the stock, which is down 20 percent from its May 2006 high on worries that operating margins are falling and that Starbucks could miss its ambitious growth targets.

And as you wait in line for your Dulce de Leche Latte, you might ask yourself: Are you paying $4.50 for a caffeine jolt and caramel topping? Or have you simply been dazzled by Howard Schultz' storytelling magic?

Questions

1. What are some of the HRM issues inherent in Howard Schultz's concerns?

2. How would an effective strategic HRM function contribute to keeping Starbucks on track?

SOURCE: B. Helm, "Saving Starbucks' Soul," *BusinessWeek*, April 9, 2007, pp. 56–61.

NOTES

1. P. Wright, S. Snell, and P. Jacobsen, "Current Approaches to HR Strategies: Inside-Out vs. Outside-In," *Human Resource Planning* (in press).

2. A. S. Tsui and L. R. Gomez-Mejia, "Evaluating HR Effectiveness," in *Human Resource Management: Evolving Roles and Responsibilities*, ed. L. Dyer (Washington, DC: Bureau of National Affairs, 1988), pp. 1-187–1-227.

3. D. Ulrich, "Measuring Human Resources: An Overview of Practice and a Prescription for Results," *Human Resource Management* 36, no. 3 (1997), pp. 303–20.

4. P. Wright, G. McMahan, S. Snell, and B. Gerhart, "Comparing Line and HR Executives' Perceptions of HR Effectiveness: Services, Roles, and Contributions," CAHRS (Center for Advanced Human Resource Studies) working paper 98-29, School of ILR, Cornell University, Ithaca, NY.

5. J. C. Erfurt, A. Foote, and M. A. Heirich, "The Cost-Effectiveness of Worksite Wellness Programs," *Personnel Psychology* 15 (1992), p. 22.

6. P. Wright, G. McMahan, S. Snell, and B. Gerhart, *Strategic HRM: Building Human Capital and Organizational Capability*, Technical report. Cornell University, Ithaca, NY, 1998.

7. T. B. Kinni, "A Reengineering Primer," *Quality Digest*, January 1994, pp. 26–30; "Reengineering Is Helping Health of Hospitals and Its Patients," *Total Quality Newsletter*, February 1994, p. 5; R. Recardo, "Process Reengineering in a Finance Division," *Journal for Quality and Participation*, June 1994, pp. 70–73.

8. L. Quillen, "Human Resource Computerization: A Dollar and Cents Approach," *Personnel Journal*, July 1989, pp. 74–77.

9. S. Greengard, "New Technology Is HR's Route to Reengineering," *Personnel Journal*, July 1994, pp. 32c–32o.

10. R. Broderick and J. W. Boudreau, "Human Resource Management, Information Technology, and the Competitive Edge," *Academy of Management Executive* 6 (1992), pp. 7–17.

11. S. E. O'Connell, "New Technologies Bring New Tools, New Rules," *HRMagazine*, December 1995, pp. 43–48; S. F. O'Connell, "The Virtual Workplace Moves at Warp Speed," *HRMagazine*, March 1996, pp. 51–57.

12. E. Brynjolfsson and L. Hitt, "The Productivity Paradox of Information Technology," *Communications of the ACM*, December 1993, pp. 66–77.

13. "Seven Critical Success Factors for Using Information Technology," *Total Quality Newsletter*, February 1994, p. 6.

14. J. E. Rigdon, "Technological Gains Are Cutting Costs in Jobs and Services," *The Wall Street Journal*, February 24, 1995, pp. A1, A5, A6.

15. S. Greengard, "How Technology Is Advancing HR," *Personnel Journal*, September 1993, pp. 80–90.

16. T. L. Hunter, "How Client/Server Is Reshaping the HRIS," *Personnel Journal*, July 1992, pp. 38–46; B. Busbin, "The Hidden Costs of Client/Server," *The Review*, August–September 1995, pp. 21–24.

17. D. Drechsel, "Principles for Client/Server Success," *The Review*, August–September 1995, pp. 26–29.

18. A. L. Lederer, "Emerging Technology and the Buy–Wait Dilemma: Sorting Fact from Fantasy," *The Review*, June–July 1993, pp. 16–19.

19. D. L. Fowler, "Imaging in HR: A Case Study," *The Review*, October–November 1994, pp. 29–33.

20. "Dial a Job Interview," *Chain Store Age Executive*, July 1994, pp. 35–36.

21. P. A. Galagan, "Think Performance: A Conversation with Gloria Gery," *Training and Development*, March 1994, pp. 47–51.

22. J. Clark and R. Koonce, "Meetings Go High-Tech," *Training and Development*, November 1995, pp. 32–38; A. M. Townsend, M. E. Whitman, and A. R. Hendrickson, "Computer Support Adds Power to Group Processes," *HRMagazine*, September 1995, pp. 87–91.

23. T. A. Stewart, "Getting Real about Brainpower," *Fortune*, November 27, 1994, pp. 201–3.

24. B. Ziegler, "Internet Software Poses Big Threat to Notes, IBM's Stake in Lotus," *The Wall Street Journal*, November 7, 1995, pp. A1, A8.

25. S. Shrivastava and J. Shaw, "Liberating HR through Technology," *Human Resource Management* 42, no. 3 (2003), pp. 201–17.

26. C. O'Reilly and P. Caldwell, *Cypress Semiconductor (A): Vision, Values, and Killer Software* (Stanford University Case Study, HR-8A, 1998).

27. "61 Percent of Americans Consider Themselves Overworked and 86 Percent Are Not Satisfied with Their Job, According to Monster's 2004 Work/Life Balance Survey," *Business Wire*, August 3, 2004.

28. G. McMahan and R. Woodman, "The Current Practice of Organization Development within the Firm: A Survey of Large Industrial Corporations," *Group and Organization Studies* 17 (1992), pp. 117–34.

29. B. Becker, M. Huselid, and D. Ulrich, *The HR Scorecard: Linking People, Strategy, and Performance* (Cambridge, MA: HBS Press, 2001).

30. D. Ulrich and A. Yeung, "A Shared Mindset," *Personnel Administrator*, March 1989, pp. 38–45.

31. G. Jones and P. Wright, "An Economic Approach to Conceptualizing the Utility of Human Resource Management Practices," *Research in Personnel/Human Resources* 10 (1992), pp. 271–99.

32. R. Schuler and J. Walker, "Human Resources Strategy: Focusing on Issues and Actions," *Organizational Dynamics*, Summer 1990, pp. 5–19.

33. P. Wright, "Strategies and Challenges of the Chief Human Resource Officer: Results of the First Annual Cornell/CAHRS Survey of CHROs" Technical report, 2009.

34. Ibid.

35. Ibid.

36. J. Paauwe, *Human Resource Management and Performance: Unique Approaches for Achieving Long-Term Viability* (Oxford: Oxford University Press, 2004).

37. S. Csoka and B. Hackett, *Transforming the HR Function for Global Business Success* (New York: Conference Board, 1998), Report 1209-19RR.

APPENDIX

Human Resource Certification Institute PHR/SPHR Test Specifications

HRCI conducts two levels of certification testing, the Professional in Human Resources (PHR) and the Senior Professional in Human Resources (SPHR). Following is the body of knowledge that HRCI recommends studying in preparing to take the certification exam. This body of knowledge is divided into six categories or functional areas within HR: Strategic Management, Workforce Planning and Employment, Human Resource Development, Total Rewards, and Risk Management. After the heading for each functional area, the PHR and SPHR weighted percentages are given. The PHR exam deals more heavily with questions on an operational level, whereas the SPHR exam focuses more on strategy. Additionally, within each functional area, the information is split under the headings Responsibilities and Knowledge.

Your text is a helpful resource in mastering many of the concepts that are tested in the PHR/SPHR exam. Visit the text Web site at www.mhhe.com/noe7e for a complete listing of page references for each of the knowledge requirements in the HRCI body of knowledge.

01 STRATEGIC MANAGEMENT (12%, 29%)

Developing, contributing to, and supporting the organization's mission, vision, values, strategic goals, and objectives; formulating policies; guiding and leading the change process; and evaluating HR's contributions to organizational effectiveness.

Responsibilities:

01 Interpret information related to the organization's operations from internal sources, including financial/accounting, business development, marketing, sales, operations, and information technology, in order to contribute to the development of the organization's strategic plan.

02 Interpret information from external sources related to the general business environment, industry practices and developments, technological developments, economic environment, labor pool, and legal and regulatory environment, in order to contribute to the development of the organization's strategic plan.

03 Participate as a contributing partner in the organization's strategic planning process.

04 Establish strategic relationships with key individuals in the organization to influence organizational decision-making.

05 Establish relationships/alliances with key individuals and organizations in the community to assist in achieving the organization's strategic goals and objectives.

06 Develop and utilize metrics to evaluate HR's contributions to the achievement of the organization's strategic goals and objectives.

07 Develop and execute strategies for managing organizational change that balance the expectations and needs of the organization, its employees, and all other stakeholders.

08 Develop and align the organization's human capital management plan with its strategic plan.

09 Facilitate the development and communication of the organization's core values and ethical behaviors.

10 Reinforce the organization's core values and behavioral expectations through modeling, communication, and coaching.

11 Develop and manage the HR budget in a manner consistent with the organization's strategic goals, objectives, and values.

12 Provide information for the development and monitoring of the organization's overall budget.

SOURCE: The PHR/SPHR test specifications are defined and updated by the Human Resource Certification Institute (HRCI) every three to five years to reflect actual HR practice.

13 Monitor the legislative and regulatory environment for proposed changes and their potential impact to the organization, taking appropriate proactive steps to support, modify, or oppose the proposed changes.

14 Develop policies and procedures to support corporate governance initiatives (e.g., board of directors training, whistleblower protection, code of conduct).

15 Participate in enterprise risk management by examining HR policies to evaluate their potential risks to the organization.

16 Identify and evaluate alternatives and recommend strategies for vendor selection and/or outsourcing (e.g., HRIS, benefits, payroll).

17 Participate in strategic decision-making and due diligence activities related to organizational structure and design (e.g., corporate restructuring, mergers and acquisitions [M&A], offshoring, divestitures). **SPHR ONLY**

18 Determine strategic application of integrated technical tools and systems (e.g., HRIS, performance management tools, applicant tracking, compensation tools, employee self-service technologies).

Knowledge of:

01 The organization's mission, vision, values, business goals, objectives, plans, and processes.

02 Legislative and regulatory processes.

03 Strategic planning process and implementation.

04 Management functions, including planning, organizing, directing, and controlling.

05 Techniques to promote creativity and innovation.

06 Corporate governance procedures and compliance (e.g., Sarbanes-Oxley Act).

07 Transition techniques for corporate restructuring, M&A, offshoring, and divestitures. **SPHR ONLY**

02 WORKFORCE PLANNING AND EMPLOYMENT (26%, 17%)

Developing, implementing, and evaluating sourcing, recruitment, hiring, orientation, succession planning, retention, and organizational exit programs necessary to ensure the workforce's ability to achieve the organization's goals and objectives.

Responsibilities:

01 Ensure that workforce planning and employment activities are compliant with applicable federal, state, and local laws and regulations.

02 Identify workforce requirements to achieve the organization's short- and long-term goals and objectives (e.g., corporate restructuring, M&A activity, workforce expansion or reduction).

03 Conduct job analyses to create job descriptions and identify job competencies.

04 Identify and document essential job functions for positions.

05 Establish hiring criteria based on job descriptions and required competencies.

06 Analyze labor market for trends that impact the ability to meet workforce requirements (e.g., SWOT analysis, environmental scan, demographic scan). **SPHR ONLY**

07 Assess skill sets of internal workforce and external labor market to determine the availability of qualified candidates, utilizing third party vendors or agencies as appropriate.

08 Identify internal and external recruitment sources (e.g., employee referrals, online job boards, résumé banks) and implement selected recruitment methods.

09 Evaluate recruitment methods and sources for effectiveness (e.g., return on investment [ROI], cost per hire, time to fill).

10 Develop strategies to brand/market the organization to potential qualified applicants.

11 Develop and implement selection procedures, including applicant tracking, interviewing, testing, reference and background checking, and drug screening.

12 Develop and extend employment offers and conduct negotiations as necessary.

13 Administer post-offer employment activities (e.g., execute employment agreements, complete I-9 verification forms, coordinate relocations, schedule physical exams).

14 Implement and/or administer the process for non-U.S. citizens to legally work in the United States.

15 Develop, implement, and evaluate orientation processes for new hires, rehires, and transfers.

16 Develop, implement, and evaluate retention strategies and practices.

17 Develop, implement, and evaluate succession planning process.

18 Develop and implement the organizational exit process for both voluntary and involuntary terminations, including planning for reductions in force (RIF).

19 Develop, implement, and evaluate an AAP, as required.

Knowledge of:

08 Federal/state/local employment-related laws and regulations related to workforce planning and employment (e.g., Title VII, ADA, ADEA, USERRA, EEOC Uniform Guidelines on Employee Selection Procedures, Immigration Reform and Control Act, Internal Revenue Code).

09 Quantitative analyses required to assess past and future staffing effectiveness (e.g., cost–benefit analysis, costs per hire, selection ratios, adverse impact).

10 Recruitment sources (e.g., Internet, agencies, employee referral) for targeting passive, semi-active and active candidates.

11 Recruitment strategies.

12 Staffing alternatives (e.g., temporary and contract, outsourcing, job sharing, part-time).

13 Planning techniques (e.g., succession planning, forecasting).

14 Reliability and validity of selection tests/tools/ methods.

15 Use and interpretation of selection tests (e.g., psychological/personality, cognitive, motor/physical assessments, performance, assessment center).

16 Interviewing techniques (e.g., behavioral, situational, panel).

17 Relocation practices.

18 Impact of total rewards on recruitment and retention.

19 International HR and implications of global workforce for workforce planning and employment. **SPHR ONLY**

20 Voluntary and involuntary terminations, downsizing, restructuring, and outplacement strategies and practices.

21 Internal workforce assessment techniques (e.g., skills testing, skills inventory, workforce demographic analysis) and employment policies, practices, and procedures (e.g., orientation and retention).

22 Employer marketing and branding techniques.

23 Negotiation skills and techniques.

03 HUMAN RESOURCE DEVELOPMENT (17%, 17%)

Developing, implementing, and evaluating activities and programs that address employee training and development, performance appraisal, talent and performance management, and the unique needs of employees, to ensure that the knowledge, skills, abilities, and performance of the workforce meet current and future organizational and individual needs.

Responsibilities:

01 Ensure that human resource development programs are compliant with all applicable federal, state, and local laws and regulations.

02 Conduct a needs assessment to identify and establish priorities regarding human resource development activities. **SPHR ONLY**

03 Develop/select and implement employee training programs (e.g., leadership skills, harassment prevention, computer skills) to increase individual and organizational effectiveness. Note that this includes training design and methods for obtaining feedback from training (e.g., surveys, pre- and post-testing).

04 Evaluate effectiveness of employee training programs through the use of metrics (e.g., participant surveys, pre- and post-testing). **SPHR ONLY**

05 Develop, implement, and evaluate talent management programs that include assessing talent, developing talent, and placing high-potential employees. **SPHR ONLY**

06 Develop/select and evaluate performance appraisal process (e.g., instruments, ranking and rating scales, relationship to compensation, frequency).

07 Implement training programs for performance evaluators. **PHR ONLY**

08 Develop, implement, and evaluate performance management programs and procedures (e.g., goal setting, job rotations, promotions).

09 Develop/select, implement, and evaluate programs (e.g., flexible work arrangements, diversity initiatives, repatriation) to meet the unique needs of employees. **SPHR ONLY**

Knowledge of:

24 Applicable federal, state, and local laws and regulations related to human resources development activities (e.g., Title VII, ADA, ADEA, USERRA, EEOC Uniform Guidelines on Employee Selection Procedures).

25 Career development and leadership development theories and applications.

26 OD theories and applications.

27 Training program development techniques to create general and specialized training programs.

28 Training methods, facilitation techniques, instructional methods, and program delivery mechanisms.

29 Task/process analysis.

30 Performance appraisal methods (e.g., instruments, ranking and rating scales).

31 Performance management methods (e.g., goal setting, job rotations, promotions).

32 Applicable global issues (e.g., international law, culture, local management approaches/practices, societal norms). **SPHR ONLY**

33 Techniques to assess training program effectiveness, including use of applicable metrics (e.g., participant surveys, pre- and post-testing).

34 E-learning.

35 Mentoring and executive coaching.

04 TOTAL REWARDS (16%, 12%)

Developing/selecting, implementing/administering, and evaluating compensation and benefits programs for all employee groups that support the organization's strategic goals, objectives, and values.

Responsibilities:

01 Ensure that compensation and benefits programs are compliant with applicable federal, state, and local laws and regulations.
02 Develop, implement, and evaluate compensation policies/programs and pay structures based upon internal equity and external market conditions that support the organization's strategic goals, objectives, and values.
03 Administer payroll functions (e.g., new hires, deductions, adjustments, terminations).
04 Conduct benefits programs needs assessments (e.g., benchmarking, employee survey).
05 Develop/select, implement/administer, and evaluate benefit programs that support the organization's strategic goals, objectives, and values (e.g., health and welfare, retirement, stock purchase, wellness, employee assistance programs [EAP], time-off).
06 Communicate and train the workforce in the compensation and benefits programs and policies (e.g., self-service technologies).
07 Develop/select, implement/administer, and evaluate executive compensation programs (e.g., stock purchase, stock options, incentive, bonus, supplemental retirement plans). **SPHR ONLY**
08 Develop, implement/administer, and evaluate expatriate and foreign national compensation and benefits programs. **SPHR ONLY**

Knowledge of:

36 Federal, state, and local compensation, benefits, and tax laws (e.g., FLSA, ERISA, COBRA, HIPAA, FMLA, FICA).
37 Total rewards strategies (e.g., compensation, benefits, wellness, rewards, recognition, employee assistance).
38 Budgeting and accounting practices related to compensation and benefits.
39 Job evaluation methods.
40 Job pricing and pay structures.
41 External labor markets and/or economic factors.
42 Pay programs (e.g., incentive, variable, merit).
43 Executive compensation methods. **SPHR ONLY**
44 Noncash compensation methods (e.g., stock options, ESOPs). **SPHR ONLY**
45 Benefits programs (e.g., health and welfare, retirement, wellness, EAP, time-off).
46 International compensation laws and practices (e.g., expatriate compensation, entitlements, choice of law codes). **SPHR ONLY**
47 Fiduciary responsibility related to total rewards management. **SPHR ONLY**

05 EMPLOYEE AND LABOR RELATIONS (22%, 18%)

Analyzing, developing, implementing/administering, and evaluating the workplace relationship between employer and employee, in order to maintain relationships and working conditions that balance employer and employee needs and rights in support of the organization's strategic goals, objectives, and values.

Responsibilities:

01 Ensure that employee and labor relations activities are compliant with applicable federal, state, and local laws and regulations.
02 Assess organizational climate by obtaining employee input (e.g., focus groups, employee surveys, staff meetings).
03 Implement organizational change activities as appropriate in response to employee feedback.
04 Develop employee relations programs (e.g., awards, recognition, discounts, special events) that promote a positive organizational culture.
05 Implement employee relations programs that promote a positive organizational culture.
06 Evaluate effectiveness of employee relations programs through the use of metrics (e.g., exit interviews, employee surveys).
07 Establish workplace policies and procedures (e.g., dress code, attendance, computer use) and monitor their application and enforcement to ensure consistency.
08 Develop, administer, and evaluate grievance/dispute resolution and performance improvement policies and procedures.
09 Resolve employee complaints filed with federal, state, and local agencies involving employment practices, utilizing professional resources as necessary (e.g., legal counsel, mediation/arbitration specialists, and investigators).
10 Develop and direct proactive employee relations strategies for remaining union-free in nonorganized locations.
11 Participate in collective bargaining activities, including contract negotiation and administration. **SPHR ONLY**

Knowledge of:

48 Applicable federal, state and local laws affecting employment in union and nonunion environments, such as antidiscrimination laws, sexual harassment, labor relations, and privacy (e.g., WARN Act, Title VII, NLRA).
49 Techniques for facilitating positive employee relations (e.g., employee surveys, focus groups, dispute resolution, labor/management cooperative strategies and programs).
50 Employee involvement strategies (e.g., employee management committees, self-directed work teams, staff meetings).
51 Individual employment rights issues and practices (e.g., employment-at-will, negligent hiring, defamation, employees rights to bargain collectively).

52 Workplace behavior issues/practices (e.g., absenteeism and performance improvement).

53 Unfair labor practices (e.g., employee communication strategies and management training).

54 The collective bargaining process, strategies, and concepts (e.g., contract negotiation and administration). **SPHR ONLY**

55 Positive employee relations strategies and nonmonetary rewards.

06 RISK MANAGEMENT (7%, 7%)

Developing, implementing/administering, and evaluating programs, plans, and policies which provide a safe and secure working environment and to protect the organization from liability.

Responsibilities:

01 Ensure that workplace health, safety, security, and privacy activities are compliant with applicable federal, state, and local laws and regulations.

02 Identify the organization's safety program needs.

03 Develop/select and implement/administer occupational injury and illness prevention, safety incentives, and training programs. **PHR ONLY**

04 Develop/select, implement, and evaluate plans and policies to protect employees and other individuals, and to minimize the organization's loss and liability (e.g., emergency response, evacuation, workplace violence, substance abuse, return-to-work policies).

05 Communicate and train the workforce on the plans and policies to protect employees and other individuals, and to minimize the organization's loss and liability.

06 Develop and monitor business continuity and disaster recovery plans.

07 Communicate and train the workforce on the business continuity and disaster recovery plans.

08 Develop internal and external privacy policies (e.g., identity theft, data protection, HIPAA compliance, workplace monitoring).

09 Administer internal and external privacy policies.

Knowledge of:

56 Federal, state, and local workplace health, safety, security, and privacy laws and regulations (e.g., OSHA, Drug-Free Workplace Act, ADA, HIPAA, Sarbanes-Oxley).

57 Occupational injury and illness compensation and programs.

58 Occupational injury and illness prevention programs.

59 Investigation procedures of workplace safety, health and security enforcement agencies (e.g., OSHA, National Institute for Occupational Safety and Health [NIOSH]).

60 Workplace safety risks.

61 Workplace security risks (e.g., theft, corporate espionage, asset and data protection, sabotage).

62 Potential violent behavior and workplace violence conditions.

63 General health and safety practices (e.g., evacuation, hazard communication, ergonomic evaluations).

64 Incident and emergency response plans.

65 Internal investigation, monitoring, and surveillance techniques.

66 Issues related to substance abuse and dependency (e.g., identification of symptoms, substance-abuse testing, discipline).

67 Business continuity and disaster recovery plans (e.g., data storage and backup, alternative work locations and procedures).

68 Data integrity techniques and technology (e.g., data sharing, firewalls).

CORE KNOWLEDGE REQUIRED BY HR PROFESSIONALS

69 Needs assessment and analysis.

70 Third-party contract negotiation and management, including development of requests for proposals (RFPs).

71 Communication skills and strategies (e.g., presentation, collaboration, influencing, diplomacy, sensitivity).

72 Organizational documentation requirements to meet federal and state requirements.

73 Adult learning processes.

74 Motivation concepts and applications.

75 Training techniques (e.g., computer-based, classroom, on-the-job).

76 Leadership concepts and applications.

77 Project management concepts and applications.

78 Diversity concepts and applications.

79 Human relations concepts and applications (e.g., interpersonal and organizational behavior).

80 HR ethics and professional standards.

81 Technology to support HR activities (e.g., HRIS, employee self-service, e-learning, ATS).

82 Qualitative and quantitative methods and tools for analysis, interpretation, and decision-making purposes (e.g., metrics and measurements, cost–benefit analysis, financial statement analysis).

83 Change management methods.

84 Job analysis and job description methods.

85 Employee records management (e.g., electronic/paper, retention, disposal).
86 The interrelationships among HR activities and programs across functional areas.
87 Types of organizational structures (e.g., matrix, hierarchy).
88 Environmental scanning concepts and applications.
89 Methods for assessing employee attitudes, opinions, and satisfaction (e.g., opinion surveys, attitude surveys, focus groups/panels).
90 Basic budgeting and accounting concepts.
91 Risk management techniques.

GLOSSARY

Acceptability The extent to which a performance measure is deemed to be satisfactory or adequate by those who use it.

Action learning Teams work on an actual business problem, commit to an action plan, and are accountable for carrying out the plan.

Action plan Document summarizing what the trainee and manager will do to ensure that training transfers to the job.

Action steps The part of a written affirmative plan that specifies what an employer plans to do to reduce underutilization of protected groups.

Adventure learning Learning focused on the development of teamwork and leadership skills by using structured outdoor activities.

Agency shop A union security provision that requires an employee to pay union membership dues but not to join the union.

Agent In agency theory, a person (e.g., a manager) who is expected to act on behalf of a principal (e.g., an owner).

Alternative dispute resolution (ADR) A method of resolving disputes that does not rely on the legal system. Often proceeds through the four stages of open door policy, peer review, mediation, and arbitration.

Alternative work arrangements Independent contractors, on-call workers, temporary workers, and contract company workers who are not employed full-time by the company.

Americans with Disabilities Act (ADA) A 1990 act prohibiting individuals with disabilities from being discriminated against in the workplace.

Analytic approach Type of assessment of HRM effectiveness that involves determining the impact of, or the financial costs and benefits of, a program or practice.

Anticipatory socialization Process that helps individuals develop expectations about the company, job, working conditions, and interpersonal relationships.

Appraisal politics A situation in which evaluators purposefully distort a rating to achieve personal or company goals.

Apprenticeship A work-study training method with both on-the-job and classroom training.

Arbitration A procedure for resolving collective bargaining impasses by which an arbitrator chooses a solution to the dispute.

Assessment Collecting information and providing feedback to employees about their behavior, communication style, or skills.

Assessment center A process in which multiple raters evaluate employees' performance on a number of exercises.

Associate union membership A form of union membership by which the union receives dues in exchange for services (e.g., health insurance, credit cards) but does not provide representation in collective bargaining.

Attitude awareness and change program Program focusing on increasing employees' awareness of differences in cultural and ethnic backgrounds, physical characteristics, and personal characteristics that influence behavior toward others.

Attitudinal structuring The aspect of the labor–management negotiation process that refers to the relationship and level of trust between the negotiators.

Audiovisual instruction Includes overheads, slides, and video.

Audit approach Type of assessment of HRM effectiveness that involves review of customer satisfaction or key indicators (e.g., turnover rate, average days to fill a position) related to an HRM functional area (e.g., recruiting, training).

Avatars Computer depictions of humans that can be used as imaginary coaches, co-workers, and customers in simulations.

Balanced scorecard A means of performance measurement that gives managers a chance to look at their company from the perspectives of internal and external customers, employees, and shareholders.

Basic skills Reading, writing, and communication skills needed to understand the content of a training program.

Behavior-based program A program focusing on changing the organizational policies and individual behaviors that inhibit employees' personal growth and productivity.

Benchmarking Comparing an organization's practices against those of the competition.

Benchmarks© An instrument designed to measure the factors that are important to managerial success.

Bona fide occupational qualification (BFOQ) A job qualification based on race, sex, religion, and so on that an employer asserts is a necessary qualification for the job.

Calibration meetings A way to discuss employees' performance with the goal of ensuring that similar standards are applied to their evaluations.

Career management system A system to retain and motivate employees by identifying and meeting their development needs (also called *development planning system*).

Career support Coaching, protection, sponsorship, and providing challenging assignments, exposure, and visibility.

Cash balance plan Retirement plan in which the employer sets up an individual account for each employee and contributes a percentage of the employee's salary; the account earns interest at a predetermined rate.

Centralization Degree to which decision-making authority resides at the top of the organizational chart.

Checkoff provision A union contract provision that requires an employer to deduct union dues from employees' paychecks.

Client–server architecture Computer design that provides a method to consolidate data and applications into a single host system (the client).

Climate for transfer Trainees' perceptions of characteristics of the work environment (social support and situational constraints) that can either facilitate or inhibit use of trained skills or behavior.

Closed shop A union security provision requiring a person to be a union member before being hired. Illegal under NLRA.

Coach A peer or manager who works with an employee to motivate her, help her develop skills, and provide reinforcement and feedback.

Cognitive ability Includes three dimensions: verbal comprehension, quantitative ability, and reasoning ability.

Cognitive ability tests Tests that include three dimensions: verbal comprehension, quantitative ability, and reasoning ability.

Communities of practice Groups of employees who work together, learn from each other, and develop a common understanding of how to get work accomplished.

Comparable worth A public policy that advocates remedies for any undervaluation of women's jobs (also called *pay equity*).

Compa-ratio An index of the correspondence between actual and intended pay.

Compensable factors The characteristics of jobs that an organization values and chooses to pay for.

Competitiveness A company's ability to maintain and gain market share in its industry.

Concentration strategy A strategy focusing on increasing market share, reducing costs, or creating and maintaining a market niche for products and services.

Concurrent validation A criterion-related validity study in which a test is administered to all the people currently in a job and then incumbents' scores are correlated with existing measures of their performance on the job.

Consequences The incentives that employees receive for performing well.

Consolidated Omnibus Budget Reconciliation Act (COBRA) The 1985 act that requires employers to permit employees to extend their health insurance coverage at group rates for up to 36 months following a qualifying event, such as a layoff.

Content validation A test validation strategy performed by demonstrating that the items, questions, or problems posed by a test are a representative sample of the kinds of situations or problems that occur on the job.

Continuous learning A learning system that requires employees to understand the entire work process and expects them to acquire new skills, apply them on the job, and share what they have learned with other employees.

Coordination training Training a team in how to share information and decision-making responsibilities to maximize team performance.

Corporate campaigns Union activities designed to exert public, financial, or political pressure on employers during the union-organizing process.

Cost–benefit analysis The process of determining the economic benefits of a training program using accounting methods.

Counselor/confidante/coach to the executive team A role of the CHRO that focuses on counseling or coaching team members or resolving interpersonal or political conflicts among team members.

Criterion-related validity A method of establishing the validity of a personnel selection method by showing a substantial correlation between test scores and job performance scores.

Cross-cultural preparation The process of educating employees (and their families) who are given an assignment in a foreign country.

Cross-training Training in which team members understand and practice each other's skills so that members are prepared to step in and take another member's place should he or she temporarily or permanently leave the team.

Cultural immersion A behavior-based diversity program that sends employees into communities where they interact with persons from different cultures, races, and nationalities.

Decision support systems Problem-solving systems that usually include a "what-if" feature that allows users to see how outcomes change when assumptions or data change.

Delayering Reducing the number of job levels within an organization.

Departmentalization Degree to which work units are grouped based on functional similarity or similarity of workflow.

Development The acquisition of knowledge, skills, and behaviors that improve an employee's ability to meet changes in job requirements and in client and customer demands.

Direct applicants People who apply for a job vacancy without prompting from the organization.

Disparate impact A theory of discrimination based on facially neutral employment practices that disproportionately exclude a protected group from employment opportunities.

Disparate treatment A theory of discrimination based on different treatment given to individuals because of their race, color, religion, sex, national origin, age, or disability status.

Distributive bargaining The part of the labor–management negotiation process that focuses on dividing a fixed economic "pie."

Diversity training Training designed to change employee attitudes about diversity and/or develop skills needed to work with a diverse workforce.

Downsizing The planned elimination of large numbers of personnel, designed to enhance organizational effectiveness.

Downward move A job change involving a reduction in an employee's level of responsibility and authority.

Due process policies Policies by which a company formally lays out the steps an employee can take to appeal a termination decision.

Duty of fair representation The National Labor Relations Act requirement that all bargaining unit members have equal access to and representation by the union.

Efficiency wage theory A theory stating that wage influences worker productivity.

E-learning Instruction and delivery of training by computers through the Internet or company intranet.

Electronic business (e-business) Any business that a company conducts electronically.

Electronic human resource management (e-HRM) The processing and transmission of digitized information used in HRM.

Electronic performance support systems (EPSS) Computer applications that can provide (as requested) skills training, information access, and expert advice.

Employee assistance programs (EAPs) Employer programs that attempt to ameliorate problems encountered by workers who are drug dependent, alcoholic, or psychologically troubled.

Employee engagement The degree to which employees are fully involved in their work and the strength of their job and company commitment.

Employee Retirement Income Security Act (ERISA) The 1974 act that increased the fiduciary responsibilities of pension plan trustees, established vesting rights and portability provisions, and established the Pension Benefit Guaranty Corporation (PBGC).

Employee stock ownership plan (ESOP) An employee ownership plan that provides employers certain tax and financial advantages when stock is granted to employees.

Employment-at-will doctrine The doctrine that, in the absence of a specific contract, either an employer or employee could sever the employment relationship at any time.

Employment-at-will policies Policies which state that either an employer or employee can terminate the employment relationship at any time, regardless of cause.

Empowering Giving employees the responsibility and authority to make decisions.

Encounter phase Phase of socialization that occurs when an employee begins a new job.

Equal employment opportunity (EEO) The government's attempt to ensure that all individuals have an equal opportunity for employment, regardless of race, color, religion, sex, age, disability, or national origin.

Equal Employment Opportunity Commission (EEOC) The government commission established to ensure that all individuals have an equal opportunity for employment, regardless of race, color, religion, sex, age, disability, or national origin.

Ergonomics The interface between individuals' physiological characteristics and the physical work environment.

Exempt Employees who are not covered by the Fair Labor Standards Act. Exempt employees are not eligible for overtime pay.

Expatriate Employee sent by his or her company to manage operations in a different country.

Expectancy theory The theory that says motivation is a function of valence, instrumentality, and expectancy.

Expert systems Computer systems incorporating the decision rules of people recognized as experts in a certain area.

External analysis Examining the organization's operating environment to identify strategic opportunities and threats.

External growth strategy An emphasis on acquiring vendors and suppliers or buying businesses that allow a company to expand into new markets.

External labor market Persons outside the firm who are actively seeking employment.

Externship When a company allows an employee to take a full-time operational role at another company.

Evidence-based HR Demonstrating that human resource practices have a positive influence on the company's bottom line or key stakeholders (employees, customers, community, shareholders).

Fact finder A person who reports on the reasons for a labor–management dispute, the views and arguments of both sides, and a nonbinding recommendation for settling the dispute.

Fair Labor Standards Act (FLSA) The 1938 law that established the minimum wage and overtime pay.

Family and Medical Leave Act The 1993 act that requires employers with 50 or more employees to provide up to 12 weeks of unpaid leave after childbirth or adoption; to care for a seriously ill child, spouse, or parent; or for an employee's own serious illness.

Feedback Information that employees receive while they are performing concerning how well they are meeting objectives.

Financial Accounting Statement (FAS) 106 The rule issued by the Financial Accounting Standards Board in 1993 requiring companies to fund benefits provided after retirement on an accrual rather than a pay-as-you-go basis and to enter these future cost obligations on their financial statements.

Forecasting The attempts to determine the supply of and demand for various types of human resources to predict areas within the organization where there will be future labor shortages or surpluses.

Formal education programs Employee development programs, including short courses offered by consultants or universities, executive MBA programs, and university programs.

Four-fifths rule A rule that states that an employment test has disparate impact if the hiring rate for a minority group is less than four-fifths, or 80 percent, of the hiring rate for the majority group.

Frame of reference A standard point that serves as a comparison for other points and thus provides meaning.

Gainsharing A form of group compensation based on group or plant performance (rather than organizationwide profits) that does not become part of the employee's base salary.

General duty clause The provision of the Occupational Safety and Health Act that states an employer has an overall obligation to furnish employees with a place of employment free from recognized hazards.

Generalizability The degree to which the validity of a selection method established in one context extends to other contexts.

Glass ceiling A barrier to advancement to higher-level jobs in the company that adversely affects women and minorities. The barrier may be due to lack of access to training programs, development experiences, or relationships (e.g., mentoring).

Goals What an organization hopes to achieve in the medium- to long-term future.

Goals and timetables The part of a written affirmative action plan that specifies the percentage of women and minorities that an employer seeks to have in each job group and the date by which that percentage is to be attained.

Group mentoring program A program pairing a successful senior employee with a group of four to six less experienced protégés.

Group- or team-building methods Training methods that help trainees share ideas and experiences, build group identity, understand the dynamics of interpersonal relationships, and get to know their own strengths and weaknesses and those of their co-workers.

Groupware Software application that enables multiple users to track, share, and organize information and to work on the same database or document simultaneously.

Hands-on methods Training methods that require the trainee to be actively involved in learning.

Health maintenance organization (HMO) A health care plan that provides benefits on a prepaid basis for employees who are required to use only HMO medical service providers.

High-leverage training Training practice that links training to strategic business goals, has top management support, relies on an instructional design model, and is benchmarked to programs in other organizations.

High-performance work systems Work systems that maximize the fit between employees and technology.

High-potential employees Employees the company believes are capable of being successful in high-level management positions.

Host country The country in which the parent-country organization seeks to locate or has already located a facility.

Host-country nationals (HCNs) Employees born and raised in a host, not parent, country.

HR dashboard HR metrics (such as productivity and absenteeism) that are accessible by employees and managers through the company intranet or human resource information system.

Human resource information system (HRIS) A system used to acquire, store, manipulate, analyze, retrieve, and distribute information related to human resources.

Human resource management (HRM) The policies, practices, and systems that influence employees' behavior, attitudes, and performances.

Human resource recruitment The practice or activity carried on by the organization with the primary purpose of identifying and attracting potential employees.

Imaging A process for scanning documents, storing them electronically, and retrieving them.

In-basket A simulation of the administrative tasks of a manager's job.

Individualism–collectivism One of Hofstede's cultural dimensions; describes the strength of the relation between an individual and other individuals in a society.

Input Instructions that tell the employee what, how, and when to perform; also the support they are given to help them perform.

Intangible assets A type of company asset including human capital, customer capital, social capital, and intellectual capital.

Integrative bargaining The part of the labor–management negotiation process that seeks solutions beneficial to both sides.

Intellectual capital Creativity, productivity, and service provided by employees.

Interactional justice A concept of justice referring to the interpersonal nature of how the outcomes were implemented.

Internal analysis The process of examining an organization's strengths and weaknesses.

Internal growth strategy A focus on new market and product development, innovation, and joint ventures.

Internal labor force Labor force of current employees.

Interview Employees are questioned about their work and personal experiences, skills, and career plans.

Intraorganizational bargaining The part of the labor–management negotiation process that focuses on the conflicting objectives of factions within labor and management.

Involuntary turnover Turnover initiated by the organization (often among people who would prefer to stay).

ISO 9000:2000 A series of quality assurance standards developed by the International Organization for Standardization in Switzerland and adopted worldwide.

Job analysis The process of getting detailed information about jobs.

Job description A list of the tasks, duties, and responsibilities that a job entails.

Job design The process of defining the way work will be performed and the tasks that will be required in a given job.

Job enlargement Adding challenges or new responsibilities to an employee's current job.

Job enrichment Ways to add complexity and meaningfulness to a person's work.

Job evaluation An administrative procedure used to measure internal job worth.

Job experience The relationships, problems, demands, tasks, and other features that employees face in their jobs.

Job hazard analysis technique A breakdown of each job into basic elements, each of which is rated for its potential for harm or injury.

Job involvement The degree to which people identify themselves with their jobs.

Job redesign The process of changing the tasks or the way work is performed in an existing job.

Job rotation The process of systematically moving a single individual from one job to another over the course of time. The job assignments may be in various functional areas of the company or movement may be between jobs in a single functional area or department.

Job satisfaction A pleasurable feeling that results from the perception that one's job fulfills or allows for the fulfillment of one's important job values.

Job specification A list of the knowledge, skills, abilities, and other characteristics (KSAOs) that an individual must have to perform a job.

Job structure The relative pay of jobs in an organization.

Key jobs Benchmark jobs, used in pay surveys, that have relatively stable content and are common to many organizations.

Knowledge management Process of enhancing company performance by designing and using tools, systems, and cultures to improve creation, sharing, and use of knowledge.

Knowledge workers Employees who own the intellectual means of producing a product or service.

Leader of the HR function A role of the CHRO that focuses on working with HR team members regarding the development, design, and delivery of HR services.

Leaderless group discussion Process in which a team of five to seven employees solves an assigned problem within a certain time period.

Leading indicator An objective measure that accurately predicts future labor demand.

Lean thinking A way to do more with less effort, equipment, space, and time, but providing customers with what they need and want.

Learner control Ability of trainees to actively learn through self-pacing, exercises, links to other materials, and conversations with other trainees and experts.

Learning management system (LMS) Technology platform that automates the administration, development, and delivery of a company's training program.

Learning organization An organization whose employees are continuously attempting to learn new things and apply what they have learned to improve product or service quality.

Liaison to the board of directors A role of the CHRO that focuses on preparation for board meetings, phone calls with board members, and attendance at board meetings.

Long-term–short-term orientation One of Hofstede's cultural dimensions; describes how a culture balances immediate benefits with future rewards.

Maintenance of membership Union rules requiring members to remain members for a certain period of time (e.g., the length of the union contract).

Malcolm Baldrige National Quality Award An award established in 1987 to promote quality awareness, to recognize quality achievements of U.S. companies, and to publicize successful quality strategies.

Managing diversity The process of creating an environment that allows all employees to contribute to organizational goals and experience personal growth.

Marginal employee An employee performing at a barely acceptable level because of lack of ability and/or motivation to perform well, not poor work conditions.

Marginal tax rate The percentage of an additional dollar of earnings that goes to taxes.

Masculinity–femininity dimension One of Hofstede's cultural dimensions; describes the division of roles between the sexes within a society.

Mediation A procedure for resolving collective bargaining impasses by which a mediator with no formal authority acts as a facilitator and go-between in the negotiations.

Mentor An experienced, productive senior employee who helps develop a less experienced employee.

Merit increase grid A grid that combines an employee's performance rating with his or her position in a pay range to determine the size and frequency of his or her pay increases.

Minimum wage The lowest amount that employers are legally allowed to pay; the 1990 amendment of the Fair Labor Standards Act permits a subminimum wage to workers under the age of 20 for a period of up to 90 days.

Motivation to learn The desire of the trainee to learn the content of a training program.

Myers-Briggs Type Indicator (MBTI)® A psychological test used for team building and leadership development that identifies employees' preferences for energy, information gathering, decision making, and lifestyle.

Needs assessment The process used to determine if training is necessary.

Negative affectivity A dispositional dimension that reflects pervasive individual differences in satisfaction with any and all aspects of life.

Network A combination of desktop computers, computer terminals, and mainframes or minicomputers that share access to databases and a method to transmit information throughout the system.

New technologies Current applications of knowledge, procedures, and equipment that have not been previously used. Usually involves replacing human labor with equipment, information processing, or some combination of the two.

Nonkey jobs Jobs that are unique to organizations and that cannot be directly valued or compared through the use of market surveys.

Objective The purpose and expected outcome of training activities.

Occupational Safety and Health Act (OSHA) The 1970 law that authorizes the federal government to establish and enforce occupational safety and health standards for all places of employment engaging in interstate commerce.

Offshoring A special case of outsourcing where the jobs that move actually leave one country and go to another.

Onshoring Exporting jobs to rural parts of the United States.

On-the-job training (OJT) Peers or managers training new or inexperienced employees who learn the job by observation, understanding, and imitation.

Opportunity to perform The trainee is provided with or actively seeks experience using newly learned knowledge, skills, or behavior.

Organizational analysis A process for determining the business appropriateness of training.

Organizational commitment The degree to which an employee identifies with the organization and is willing to put forth effort on its behalf.

Organizational socialization The process by which new employees are transformed into effective members of a company.

Outcome fairness The judgment that people make with respect to the outcomes received relative to the outcomes received by other people with whom they identify.

Outplacement counseling Counseling to help displaced employees manage the transition from one job to another.

Output A job's performance standards.

Outsourcing An organization's use of an outside organization for a broad set of services.

Parent country The country in which a company's corporate headquarters is located.

Parent-country nationals (PCNs) Employees who were born and live in a parent country.

Pay grades Jobs of similar worth or content grouped together for pay administration purposes.

Pay level The average pay, including wages, salaries, and bonuses, of jobs in an organization.

Pay policy line A mathematical expression that describes the relationship between a job's pay and its job evaluation points.

Pay structure The relative pay of different jobs (job structure) and how much they are paid (pay level).

Pension Benefit Guaranty Corporation (PBGC) The agency that guarantees to pay employees a basic retirement benefit in the event that financial difficulties force a company to terminate or reduce employee pension benefits.

Performance appraisal The process through which an organization gets information on how well an employee is doing his or her job.

Performance feedback The process of providing employees information regarding their performance effectiveness.

Performance management The means through which managers ensure that employees' activities and outputs are congruent with the organization's goals.

Performance planning and evaluation (PPE) system Any system that seeks to tie the formal performance appraisal process to the company's strategies by specifying at the beginning of the evaluation period the types and level of performance that must be accomplished in order to achieve the strategy.

Person analysis A process for determining whether employees need training, who needs training, and whether employees are ready for training.

Person characteristics An employee's knowledge, skills, abilities, and attitudes.

Power distance One of Hofstede's cultural dimensions; concerns how a culture deals with hierarchical power relationships—particularly the unequal distribution of power.

Predictive validation A criterion-related validity study that seeks to establish an empirical relationship between applicants' test scores and their eventual performance on the job.

Preferred provider organization (PPO) A group of health care providers who contract with employers, insurance companies, and so forth to provide health care at a reduced fee.

Presentation methods Training methods in which trainees are passive recipients of information.

Principal In agency theory, a person (e.g., the owner) who seeks to direct another person's behavior.

Procedural justice A concept of justice focusing on the methods used to determine the outcomes received.

Profit sharing A compensation plan in which payments are based on a measure of organization performance (profits) and do not become part of the employees' base salary.

Progression of withdrawal Theory that dissatisfied individuals enact a set of behaviors to avoid the work situation.

Promotions Advances into positions with greater challenge, more responsibility, and more authority than the employee's previous job.

Prosocial motivation The degree to which people are motivated to help other people.

Protean career A career that is frequently changing due to both changes in the person's interests, abilities, and values and changes in the work environment.

Psychological contract Expectations of employee contributions and what the company will provide in return.

Psychological success The feeling of pride and accomplishment that comes from achieving life goals.

Psychosocial support Serving as a friend and role model, providing positive regard and acceptance, and creating an outlet for a protégé to talk about anxieties and fears.

Quantitative ability Concerns the speed and accuracy with which one can solve arithmetic problems of all kinds.

Range spread The distance between the minimum and maximum amounts in a pay grade.

Rate ranges Different employees in the same job may have different pay rates.

Readability The difficulty level of written materials.

Realistic job preview Provides accurate information about the attractive and unattractive aspects of a job, working conditions, company, and location to ensure that potential employees develop appropriate expectations.

Reasonable accommodation Making facilities readily accessible to and usable by individuals with disabilities.

Reasoning ability Refers to a person's capacity to invent solutions to many diverse problems.

Recruitment The process of seeking applicants for potential employment.

Reengineering Review and redesign of work processes to make them more efficient and improve the quality of the end product or service.

Referrals People who are prompted to apply for a job by someone within the organization.

Relational database A database structure that stores information in separate files that can be linked by common elements.

Reliability The consistency of a performance measure; the degree to which a performance measure is free from random error.

Repatriation The preparation of expatriates for return to the parent company and country from a foreign assignment.

Representative of the firm A role of the CHRO that focuses on activities with external stakeholders, such as lobbying, speaking to outside groups, etc.

Repurposing Directly translating instructor-led training online.

Request for proposal (RFP) A document that outlines for potential vendors and consultants the type of service the company is seeking, references needed, number of employees who should be trained, project funding, the follow-up process, expected completion date, and the date when proposals must be received by the company.

Right-to-work laws State laws that make union shops, maintenance of membership, and agency shops illegal.

Role behaviors Behaviors that are required of an individual in his or her role as a job holder in a social work environment.

Role play A participant taking the part or role of a manager or other employee.

Sabbatical A leave of absence from the company to renew or develop skills.

Safety awareness programs Employer programs that attempt to instill symbolic and substantive changes in the organization's emphasis on safety.

Sarbanes-Oxley Act of 2002 A congressional act passed in response to illegal and unethical behavior by managers and executives. The Act sets stricter rules for business, especially accounting practices including requiring more open and consistent disclosure of financial data, CEOs' assurance that data are completely accurate, and provisions that affect the employee–employer relationship (e.g., development of a code of conduct for senior financial officers).

Selection The process by which an organization attempts to identify applicants with the necessary knowledge, skills, abilities, and other characteristics that will help it achieve its goals.

Self-directed learning A program in which employees take responsibility for all aspects of learning.

Self-efficacy The employees' belief that they can successfully learn the content of a training program.

Self-service Giving employees online access to human resources information.

Settling-in phase Phase of socialization that occurs when employees are comfortable with job demands and social relationships.

Simulation A training method that represents a real-life situation, allowing trainees to see the outcomes of their decisions in an artificial environment.

Situational interview An interview procedure where applicants are confronted with specific issues, questions, or problems that are likely to arise on the job.

Six Sigma process System of measuring, analyzing, improving, and controlling processes once they meet quality standards.

Six Sigma Training An action training program that provides employees with defect-reducing tools to cut costs and certifies employees as green belts, champions, or black belts.

Skill-based pay Pay based on the skills employees acquire and are capable of using.

Specificity The extent to which a performance measure gives detailed guidance to employees about what is expected of them and how they can meet these expectations.

Stakeholders The various interest groups who have relationships with and, consequently, whose interests are tied to the organization (e.g., employees, suppliers, customers, shareholders, community).

Standard deviation rule A rule used to analyze employment tests to determine disparate impact; it uses the difference between the expected representation for minority groups and the actual representation to determine whether the difference between the two is greater than would occur by chance.

Stock options An employee ownership plan that gives employees the opportunity to buy the company's stock at a previously fixed price.

Strategic advisor to the executive team A role of the CHRO that focuses on the formulation and implementation of the firm's strategy.

Strategic choice The organization's strategy; the ways an organization will attempt to fulfill its mission and achieve its long-term goals.

Strategic congruence The extent to which the performance management system elicits job performance that is consistent with the organization's strategy, goals, and culture.

Strategic human resource management (SHRM) A pattern of planned human resource deployments and activities intended to enable an organization to achieve its goals.

Strategic training and development initiatives Learning-related actions that a company takes to achieve its business strategy.

Strategy formulation The process of deciding on a strategic direction by defining a company's mission and goals, its external opportunities and threats, and its internal strengths and weaknesses.

Strategy implementation The process of devising structures and allocating resources to enact the strategy a company has chosen.

Succession planning The identification and tracking of high-potential employees capable of filling higher-level managerial positions.

Summary plan description (SPD) A reporting requirement of the Employee Retirement Income Security Act (ERISA) that obligates employers to describe the plan's funding, eligibility requirements, risks, and so forth within 90 days after an employee has entered the plan.

Support network Trainees who meet to discuss their progress in using learned capabilities on the job.

Sustainability The ability of a company to make a profit without sacrificing the resources of its employees, the community, or the environment. Based on an approach to organizational decision making that considers the long term impact of strategies on stakeholders (e.g., employees, shareholders, suppliers, community).

Taft-Hartley Act The 1947 act that outlawed unfair union labor practices.

Talent architect A role of the CHRO that focuses on building and identifying the human capital critical to the present and future of the firm.

Talent management Attracting, retaining, developing, and motivating highly skilled employees and managers.

Task analysis The process of identifying the tasks, knowledge, skills, and behaviors that need to be emphasized in training.

Team leader training Training of the team manager or facilitator.

Technic of operations review (TOR) Method of determining safety problems via an analysis of past accidents.

Teleconferencing Synchronous exchange of audio, video, or text between individuals or groups at two or more locations.

Third country A country other than a host or parent country.

Third-country nationals (TCNs) Employees born in a country other than a parent or host country.

360-degree appraisal (feedback systems) A performance appraisal process for managers that includes evaluations from a wide range of persons who interact with the manager. The process includes self-evaluations as well as evaluations from the manager's boss, subordinates, peers, and customers.

Total quality management (TQM) A cooperative form of doing business that relies on the talents and capabilities of both labor and management to continually improve quality and productivity.

Training A planned effort to facilitate the learning of job-related knowledge, skills, and behavior by employees.

Training design process A systematic approach for developing training programs.

Training outcomes A way to evaluate the effectiveness of a training program based on cognitive, skill-based, affective, and results outcomes.

Transaction processing Computations and calculations used to review and document HRM decisions and practices.

Transfer The movement of an employee to a different job assignment in a different area of the company.

Transfer of training The use of knowledge, skills, and behaviors learned in training on the job.

Transitional matrix Matrix showing the proportion or number of employees in different job categories at different times.

Transnational process The extent to which a company's planning and decision-making processes include representatives and ideas from a variety of cultures.

Transnational representation Reflects the multinational composition of a company's managers.

Transnational scope A company's ability to make HRM decisions from an international perspective.

Tuition reimbursement The practice of reimbursing employees' costs for college and university courses and degree programs.

Uncertainty avoidance One of Hofstede's cultural dimensions; describes how cultures seek to deal with an unpredictable future.

Union shop A union security provision that requires a person to join the union within a certain amount of time after being hired.

Upward feedback A performance appraisal process for managers that includes subordinates' evaluations.

Utility The degree to which the information provided by selection methods enhances the effectiveness of selecting personnel in real organizations.

Utilization analysis A comparison of the race, sex, and ethnic composition of an employer's workforce with that of the available labor supply.

Validity The extent to which a performance measure assesses all the relevant—and only the relevant—aspects of job performance.

Verbal comprehension Refers to a person's capacity to understand and use written and spoken language.

Virtual reality Computer-based technology that provides trainees with a three-dimensional learning experience. Trainees operate in a simulated environment that responds to their behaviors and reactions.

Virtual teams Teams that are separated by time, geographic distance, culture and/or organizational boundaries and rely exclusively on technology for interaction between team members.

Voluntary turnover Turnover initiated by employees (often whom the company would prefer to keep).

Webcasting Classroom instruction provided online via live broadcasts.

Whistle-blowing Making grievances public by going to the media or government.

Workforce sensor A role of the CHRO that focuses on identifying workforce morale issues or concerns.

Workforce utilization review A comparison of the proportion of workers in protected subgroups with the proportion that each subgroup represents in the relevant labor market.

Photo Credits

Name and Company Index

SUBJECT INDEX

COMPETING THROUGH GLOBALIZATION